Business Data
Communications

SIXTH EDITION

BUSINESS DATA COMMUNICATIONS

David A. Stamper

Thomas L. Case

Pearson Education International

AVP/Executive Editor: David Alexander
Project Manager (Editorial): Kyle Hannon
Editorial Assistant: Maat Van Uitert
VP/Publisher: Natalie Anderson
Marketing Manager: Sharon K. Turkovich
Marketing Assistant: Scott Patterson
Media Project Manager: Joan Waxman
Managing Editor (Production): John Roberts
Production Editor: Maureen Wilson
Permissions Coordinator: Suzanne Grappi
Associate Director, Manufacturing: Vincent Scelta
Production Manager: Arnold Vila
Manufacturing Buyer: Michelle Klein
Cover Design: Patricia Kelly
Cover Illustration/Photo: Getty Images
Full-Service Project Management and Composition: BookMasters, Inc.
Project Manager: Jennifer Welsch, BookMasters, Inc.
Printer/Binder: Courier–Westford

Pearson Education LTD.
Pearson Education Australia PTY, Limited
Pearson Education Singapore, Pte. Ltd
Pearson Education North Asia Ltd
Pearson Education, Canada, Ltd
Pearson Educación de Mexico, S.A. de C.V.
Pearson Education–Japan
Pearson Education Malaysia, Pte. Ltd
Pearson Education, Upper Saddle River, New Jersey

10 9 8 7 6 5 4 3 2 1
ISBN 0-13-120204-9

Brief Contents

Contents

Preface

Business Data Communications, Sixth Edition, is designed for an introductory course in data communications and networking, a required course in the information system curriculum. It addresses the requirements for the IS'02.6 (Networks and Telecommunications) course in the IS 2002 Information Systems Model Curriculum. It also addresses the topical coverage and objectives of the MSIS2000.3 Data Communications and Networking course in the MSIS 2000 Model Curriculum. Previous editions have been used at over 200 universities, colleges, and community colleges. The text provides a balanced treatment of the subject matter, emphasizing both the technical aspects of data communication and related managerial issues.

Data communication continues to be one of the most dynamic segments of the computer industry. One need only look at the high-flying (and sometimes crash-and-burn) technology companies on the stock exchanges to verify this. Many of these companies are involved in the communication segment of the market. In the 1990s the focus was on network interconnection and Internet-related services. Widespread use of the Internet by both businesses and individuals has spurred communication providers to expand their offerings. The industry continues to provide increased speeds for both switched and dedicated communication links. Wireless data communications continues to evolve and is positioned for explosive growth over the next decade. Business reliance on networks has enhanced management concerns about network security. These changes are the focal point of the new material in this edition.

Intended Audience

This book is intended for students pursuing degrees in the areas of information systems or information technology as well as in other disciplines geared toward preparing graduates for careers in business telecommunications, e-business, and information services. It is also intended for professionals who work in data communications and those in technical, management, or sales positions who need to gain a richer understanding of the business and managerial issues and trade-offs associated with data communication technologies. The book is designed to help both students and professionals gain a *practical* understanding of business data communications.

For students, this text is designed as an introductory textbook that provides an overview and summarizes fundamental data communication concepts and applications. It does not assume a prior background in networking or data communications, but does assume a basic knowledge of computers and data processing. Although networking and data communications are characterized by rapid changes in technologies and applications, the fundamental concepts providing the foundation for new technologies and applications evolve at a much slower pace. Stressing fundamental concepts ensures that this book will continue to have a useful life as an explanatory reference for many years to come.

Networking professionals, information technology managers, and staff personnel in a wide range of business functions need to have a basic understanding of business telecommunications in order to perform their jobs effectively. The strategic importance of data communications and networking has been recognized in both the private and public sectors. This book helps to position professionals in a wide range of organizations to understand and evaluate data communication technologies and to contribute to the evolution of their organizations' network infrastructures.

NEW AND EXPANDED IN THIS EDITION

The sixth edition includes new or expanded coverage of numerous data communication technologies and applications. Among the most notable additions to the text are sections devoted to home networks, personal area networks, storage area networks, wavelength division multiplexing, network operating system services, network operating products (including Linux, Windows 2000 Server, and NetWare 6), videoconferencing, e-business applications, network tuning, and Web-based network management systems. The Internet, network security, wireless data communication technologies (both LAN and WAN), routing protocols, internetworking technologies, and virtual LANs are among the topics receiving significantly expanded coverage in the sixth edition.

Emphasis on the Internet

In 1990 there were several hundred thousand Internet nodes and the Internet was still a vehicle for the exchange of scholarly and scientific information, usually in text-based form. Today, this "network of networks" is comprised of approximately 40 million networks and reaches virtually every corner of the world. The Internet and World Wide Web continue to expand. New networks and users are added daily and on a typical day, millions of new pages are added to the Web. By the middle of 2002, approximately half a billion people worldwide were Internet users and by 2004, the online population is expected to be somewhere between 700 million and 950 million. The Internet is now a place of business, recreation, communication, and other personal and commercial pursuits. It has become such a ubiquitous part of the societies of developed nations and deserves considerable attention in a data communication book. In this edition, three chapters are devoted to the Internet in their entirety: one on business use of the Internet use and e-business and two on Internet technologies. Coverage of the Internet in the sixth edition is not limited to these chapters. Internet technologies, applications, and impacts are also addressed in all of the other chapters in the text. The Internet serves as the backdrop for the sixth edition's coverage of traditional data communication technologies.

Emphasis on Wireless Communications

Industry experts predict that more than half of the U.S. domestic workforce (more than 65 million workers) will be mobile by 2006. Market researchers also predict that the commercial user base of wireless data/internet (WDI) solutions will nearly double every year between now and 2006 and will be more than 26 million in 2006.

Several factors are driving the growth of wireless data communications including aggressive deployment of next-generation wireless network technologies, aggressive service price plans, burgeoning interest and increased reliance on wireless local area networks (WLANs), and the refinement of an increasing variety of mobile applications, especially mobile commerce (m-commerce) applications. In response to this growth, coverage of wireless technologies and applications has been included in all parts of the sixth edition.

Emphasis on Network Security

Network security has emerged as a front-burner issue in most business organizations and, as a result, is the subject of greater attention in the sixth edition. Both new and expanded coverage of network threats, vulnerabilities, risks, and security architectures is included in this edition. Coverage of biometric authentication, access controls, intruder detection systems, encryption, security frameworks, and security standards has been expanded in response to increased emphasis on network security among business organizations. Special attention is devoted to Internet security technologies (including firewalls, proxy servers, virtual private networks [VPNs] and IPSec [IP Security Architecture]) and secure e-commerce protocols (including SSL [Secure Sockets Layer] and SET [Secure Electronic Transactions]).

Emphasis on Broadband Communication

An increasing number of businesses and consumers are leveraging broadband technologies to access Internet resources. At the end of 2001, approximately 9 percent of the approximately 150 million Internet users in the United States and Canada accessed the Internet via cable modem, DSL, ISDN, or wireless broadband channels; industry experts expected the total number of broadband subscriptions to increase by 40 percent during 2002. The percentage of citizens with broadband access to the Internet is *higher* in most countries with significant online populations than it is in the United States. In response to these changes, the sixth edition includes expanded coverage of cable modems, DSL, ISDN, T-n services, and other broadband communication technologies.

Emphasis on Local Area Networks

LANs are mainstream data communication systems and fundamental building blocks for today's enterprise-wide networks. Since the last edition, the speed of communication over Ethernet LANs has jumped two orders of magnitude; we have progressed from 10-Mbps through 100-Mbps to 1-Gbps speeds. LAN switches have become the predominant wiring center option thereby increasing the effective throughput of LANs and enabling the maturation of virtual LANs. Network attached storage (NAS), storage area networks (SANs), upgrades to network operating systems, and increased used of wireless local area networks (WLANs) have required continued attention to LANs in the sixth edition. New developments have been added to the LAN section while maintaining the coverage of basic technologies found in previous editions.

All in all, the sixth edition is a significant makeover from the previous editions. As the scope of data communication expands, we need to address the new technologies; meanwhile, traditional data communication and networking technologies continue to be used and merit attention as well. Hence, this edition of *Business Data Communications* combines coverage of new and traditional data communication technologies and applications. In order to provide the reader with a practical understanding of these technologies and applications, they are discussed from both a technical and managerial perspective.

ORGANIZATION

Overall Organization

The structure and organization of previous editions have been modified in this addition to reflect the permanent changes that the Internet and World Wide Web have had on the business world and business data communications. Coverage of Internet and World Wide Web technologies has been significantly expanded and brought forward to the first part of the text. This reorganization is designed to reflect the authors' belief that traditional data communication technologies addressed subsequently in the text are best understood in the context of Internet. Today, the Internet is the centerpiece of business data communications and students are most likely to appreciate the importance of traditional data communication technologies by emphasizing their interfaces with the Internet as well as among each other.

Previous editions used the seven-layer Open Systems Interconnection reference model to organize the order of the topics covered in the text. Over the last decade, the TCP/IP (Transmission Control Protocol/Internet Protocol) suite has taken its place alongside the OSI reference model as a framework for organizing and understanding data communication technologies. Although most data communication hardware is typically best understood in the context of the OSI reference model, networking software and communication protocols are often more appropriately mapped to both the OSI and TCP/IP frameworks. Both models are introduced in the early part of the text and play prominent roles in each of the other parts.

The sixth edition is organized into four parts. As just noted, this edition begins with an overview of data communications as a field and the fundamentals of communication systems and networks. It then turns to the Internet and World Wide Web, how businesses are leveraging the Internet for commercial purposes, and the nuts and bolts of Internet addressing and operations. In Part 2, the focus shifts to the technologies used by most consumers and business users to access the Internet and its vast store of resources: telephone networks and services, modems, and local area networks. Part 3 of the sixth edition addresses traditional wide area network technologies, architectures, and services. Internetworking technologies, the data communication equipment and software used to create enterprise-wide networks, are also discussed in Part 3. The last part of the text focuses on network management and network security. The ongoing development of network infrastructure, another important aspect of network management, is addressed in an appendix available on the Web. The rapidly growing importance of wireless data communication technologies and mobile commerce is evident in all parts of the book. The enhanced importance of network security has also influenced the content of all parts of the book, but its impacts are most pronounced in Part 4.

Chapter Organization

Each chapter opens with an introduction and learning objectives and closes with a summary of key points and a list of key terms. Each chapter also contains two sets of end-of-chapter questions. Review questions stimulate discussion and reflection on key points in the chapter. Problems and exercises provide specific research topics or situational problem solving to augment chapter material. A case can also be found at the end of each chapter to provide more detailed focus on topics covered in the chapter and/or part. A second case for each chapter is available on the Website. Over 500 key terms are found across the chapters. These are indicated in bold throughout each chapter and most are defined in the margins for easy reference.

Pedagogy and Learning Aids

Chapter introductions, summaries, review questions, problems and exercises, key terms, cases, and key term definitions found in page margins are the major pedagogical features associated with each chapter in the sixth edition. Student learning is also likely to be enhanced by the information on the OSI reference model, asynchronous transmission, synchronous transmission, and network development found in Appendices A, B, C, and D. Students will also appreciate the Acronym Glossary and Key Terms Glossary found on the Website.

SUPPLEMENTS

Instructor's Resource CD-ROM (0-13-009433-1)

The Instructor's Resource CD-ROM includes the Instructor's Manual, Test Item File, Test Manager, Microsoft PowerPoint slides, and Image Library.

Instructor's Manual

The Instructor's Manual, by the text's co-author Thomas L. Case, features teaching suggestions and answers to review questions, problems and exercises, and the chapter cases. This supplement is available on the Instructor's Resource CD-ROM and for download from the password-protected instructor's section of the book's Website at *www.prenhall.com/stamper*.

Test Item File and Test Manager

The Test Item File, by Richard V. McCarthy of Quinnipiac University, contains multiple choice, true-false, and essay questions. The questions are rated by the level of difficulty and answers are referenced by page number. For the instructor's convenience, the Test Item File and Prentice Hall Test Manager are included on the Instructor's Resource CD-ROM.

PowerPoint Presentations

The slides, by the text's co-author Thomas L. Case, illuminate and build upon key concepts in the text. They are available for both students and instructors for download at *www.prenhall.com/stamper*. They are also found on the Instructor's Resource CD-ROM.

Image Library

The Image Library is found on the Instructor's Resource CD-ROM and helps to enhance lecture presentations. Almost every figure in the text is provided and organized by chapter for convenience. These images can be imported easily into PowerPoint to create new presentations or to add to existing ones.

Companion Website (*www.prenhall.com/stamper*)

There is a dedicated Website for the text, located at *www.prenhall.com/stamper*. The site includes PowerPoint slides, four appendices, an acronym glossary, a key terms glossary, a second case study for each chapter, and cases from the previous editions of *Business Data Communications*. Access to the instructor's section of the Website, which houses the Instructor's Manual, requires a valid user ID and password. You simply need to register yourself as the instructor of the course by going to the Website and completing the initial instructor registration process. Upon completion of the process, your registration request will be forwarded to your sales representative for validation. If you have any problem with your authorization, please contact your Prentice Hall sales representative.

For more information about the sixth edition of *Business Data Communications* and its supplements, or to request the software described, please contact your Prentice Hall sales representative, or call Prentice Hall's Faculty & Field Services Department at 1-800-526-0485.

ACKNOWLEDGMENTS

We are indebted to a number of people who made significant contributions to the development of this book.

Special thanks are due to Omar Riera and Rita Barrantes for researching and writing 25 of the 32 end-of-chapter cases for the sixth edition.

We'd also like to thank the following professionals at Pearson Education/ Prentice Hall for their collaborative efforts in transforming a rough manuscript into a professionally polished book: Executive Editors David Alexander and Robert Horan; Editorial Project Manager Kyle Hannon; Senior Marketing Manager Sharon K. Turkovich; Production Editor Maureen Wilson; and Project Director Jennifer Welsch of BookMasters, Inc.

REVIEWERS

We are especially grateful for the feedback and recommendations for improvement from the following manuscript reviewers. The format and content of the book has been significantly shaped and improved as the result of their input.

Tom Caviani, Boise State University
Markus Geissler, Consumnes River College
Joseph Harder, Indiana State University
Mark J. Indelicato, Rochester Institute of Technology
Virginia Franke Kleist, West Virginia University
Joyce M. Koerfer, College of DuPage
Richard McCarthy, Quinnepiac University
Keith Morneau, Northern Virginia Community College
Craig J. Peterson, Utah State University
Nolan Taylor, Indiana University
Gary Turnquist, Eastern Michigan University
Chuck West, Bradley University
Michael Whitman, Kennesaw State University
Richard Ye, Cal State University Northridge

Another round of thanks goes out to the reviewers of the previous editions of *Business Data Communications* for providing the solid foundation that supports the sixth edition's enhancements.

David A. Stamper
Thomas L. Case

Introduction to Data Communications

After studying this chapter, you should be able to:

- Differentiate between data communications and telecommunications.
- Identify the essential elements of communication.
- Identify the essential features of networks.
- Discuss network requirements.
- List the seven layers of the OSI reference model.
- List the five layers of the TCP/IP protocol stack.
- Discuss several significant events in the history of data communications.
- Identify and briefly describe several business data communications applications.
- Discuss several business data communications issues.
- Identify business data communications occupation and career options.

The information technology infrastructures found in today's organizations may be viewed as an integration of subsystems that aid in solving business or scientific problems. Common subsystems include operating systems, database management systems, programming languages, applications, and data communication networks and services. Each subsystem is implemented as a combination of software and hardware. This text focuses on one part of information technology infrastructure: the data communication subsystem and its interfaces with the other subsystems.

WHAT IS DATA COMMUNICATIONS?

In some circles, the terms *telecommunications* and *data communications* have become almost synonymous. James Martin, a widely respected and published information technology (IT) professional, provides this following broad definition of telecommunications:

> Any process that permits the passage from sender to one or more receivers of information of any nature delivered in an easy to use form (printed copy, fixed or moving pictures, visible or audio signals, etc.) by

any electromagnetic system (electrical transmission by wire, radio, optical transmission, guided waves, etc.). Includes telegraphy, telephony, video-telephony, data transmission, etc.

data communications The transmission of data to and from computers and components of computer systems. The subset of business telecommunications that addresses the processes, equipment, facilities, and services used to transport data from devices at one location to devices at other locations.

In this book, the term *data communications* is *not* viewed as being interchangeable with the term *telecommunications*. We define **data communications** as the subset of telecommunications that involves the transmission of data to and from computers and components of computer systems. More specifically, data communications is the transmission of data through *conducted communication media* such as wires, coaxial cables, or fiber optic cables, or *radiated communication media* such as spread spectrum radio signals, infrared light, and microwaves. We limit our discussion of other facets of telecommunications, such as telephone systems and wireless communication systems, to those aspects that pertain to the transmission of data between business computer systems.

As you read this book, it is important for you to be aware that the field of data communications is so extensive that entire books are devoted to many of the chapter topics presented here. This field is also very dynamic with significant advancements in data communication technologies, applications, and capabilities occurring each year.

This text is intended to provide an overview of the field of data communications and to familiarize you with the terminology, fundamental concepts, and capabilities of today's data communications systems. Your mastery of this material is essential for understanding today's computing environment. It will also enable you to contribute to decisions about how to configure data communication components to address business needs.

THE INTERNET'S ROLE IN BUSINESS DATA COMMUNICATIONS

You have probably heard the phrase "the Internet is changing everything." The phrase definitely applies to business data communications. The Internet has dramatically affected many businesses, especially after being opened to commercial endeavors during the early 1990s and the explosive expansion of the World Wide Web (WWW). Throughout the last decade, an increasing number of business applications traditionally deployed on private, proprietary networks have been moved to the Internet. Businesses have created *extranets* to establish Web-based electronic links with suppliers, customers, and business partners. Many organizations have also created *intranets* that enable employees to exchange data and information with one another via easy-to-use Web browser interfaces. Most significantly, businesses have found that the Internet is a highly effective sales channel as well as a cost-effective medium for conducting business transactions (the actual buying and selling of goods and services).

The Internet's impacts on business data communications have earned it a prominent place in this text. One of the purposes of this text is to provide a clearer understanding of the Internet, how it works, and its interfaces with other data communication networks found in today's businesses. Such understanding necessarily begins with mastering several fundamental concepts, such as the essential features of communication and networks.

ESSENTIAL FEATURES OF COMMUNICATION

Data communication has several important features. Communication of any kind requires a message, a sender, a receiver, and a medium. In addition, the receiver should be able to understand the message. In data communication systems, some

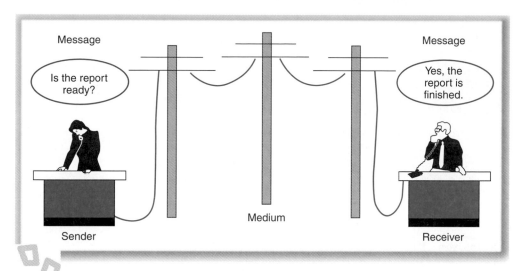

Figure 1-1   Essential Features of Communication

means of error detection are typically included in order to ensure that the content of the message received is the same as what was sent. Figure 1-1 illustrates the sender, receiver, medium, and message in a telephone connection.

Message

For two entities to communicate, there must be a message to be exchanged between them. Messages can assume several forms (such as text, audio, video, or image) and be of varying lengths. In business data communications, messages include files, requests for data/information, responses to requests, network status information, network control messages, and correspondence. Each of these major types of messages is briefly described here.

File   In any computing environment that performs data processing, including today's data communication systems, a file is often described as a meaningful collection of records. In business networks that connect multiple computers, it is not unusual for complete or partial files to be transferred between them. In **remote job entry (RJE)** applications, one of the first major business data communications applications, the messages transmitted to a central computer from users in remote locations were often complete files. As illustrated in Figure 1-2, complete files may be transmitted from servers in response to user requests.

Request   During real-time transaction processing, a user working at one computer may request another computer in the network to perform a specific computing task. Examples of requested tasks include database queries, accessing a Web page, accessing a customer's account information, or allowing the user to log on or log off the network.

Response   A user who has sent a request typically receives a return message or response from the computer to which the request was sent. For an information inquiry, the response is either the requested information or an error message saying why the

remote job entry (RJE) An application of data communication. Batches of data are collected at a remote site and transmitted to a host for processing. In early implementations the input was card format and the output was printer format.

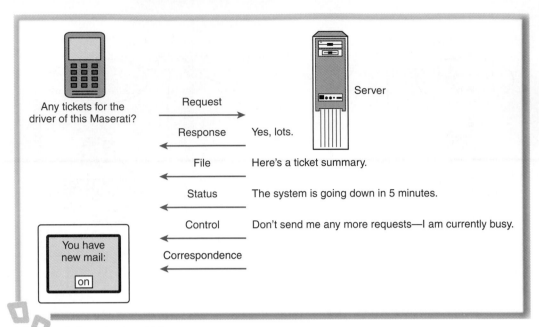

Figure 1-2 Kinds of Messages

requested information cannot be returned (such as "security violation," "Web server not found," "page cannot be displayed," "bad command or filename," or "hardware failure"). For database updates, the response can be an explicit message that the action was performed, an error message, or an implicit acknowledgement that the transaction has been performed successfully, such as "progressing to next transaction."

Status   A status message reveals the functional status of the network. It may be sent to all users or only to selected users. If a frequently accessed processor must be halted for scheduled or corrective maintenance, a status message is often broadcast to all network users so that they can bring their work to an orderly halt.

Control   Control messages are frequently transmitted among components in a data communications network. For example, an automated teller machine (ATM) might send a control message to a central processor that it is out of cash; a network printer might send a message to a print server that its buffer (data/information storage area) is full and that it cannot receive additional print jobs; a network server might notify the computers in the network that a new computer has been added to the network and is available to send and receive messages.

Correspondence   Correspondence refers to messages sent from one network user to another. Such messages include electronic mail messages, instant messages, bulletin board postings, messages exchanged by chat room users, automatic routing of document images by document management systems, and desktop-to-desktop video-conferences.

Sender

In a communication system, the sender is the transmitter of the message. A sender can be either a person or a machine. In today's networks, the sender is typically a computer; however, in some business networks, the sender may be a terminal with enough intelligence to originate a message or response without human intervention. Sensors, scanners, and other input devices may also be senders in today's networks.

Receiver

Receivers can include computers, terminals, network printers, display devices, people, and computer-controllable devices such as drill presses, lighting systems, and air conditioners. Even though a message and a sender can exist without a receiver, communication cannot take place unless there is a receiver. For example, radio signals have been beamed into space in an attempt to contact other life forms, but until these signals are received, communication has not occurred. In a computer network, a server may transmit a status message to all attached personal computers (PCs) informing them that the server will be shut down in 30 minutes to perform maintenance, but if all the PCs are turned off at that moment, no communication has occurred.

Medium

Messages are carried from sender to receiver through some medium of communication. In oral communications, sound waves are transmitted through air (the medium). In data communications, the term **medium** refers to the actual carrier of data signals between senders and receivers. Business data communication networks often use a variety of media to transmit data, including wires, radio waves, and light pulses. Media are discussed at numerous points throughout this book.

medium In data communication, the carrier of data signals. Twisted-pair wires, coaxial cables, and fiber optic cables are the most widely used cable-based media. Spread spectrum radio and infrared light are the most common wireless media.

Understandability

Even if there is a message, a sender, a receiver, and a medium, communication does not take place unless the receiver understands the message. In human communication, language differences are the most obvious obstacle to understandability, and translators or interpreters are sometimes necessary. Computer networks have similar communication obstacles. For example, the content of text-based messages and numeric data can be represented by any of several data encoding schemes; the three most common codes in use today are the American Standard Code for Information Interchange (ASCII), the Extended Binary Coded Decimal Interchange Code (EBCDIC), and Unicode. If a receiver attempts to use EBCDIC to decode a message sent in Unicode, the message will not be understood or will be incorrectly understood by the receiver.

Error Detection

In human communication, receivers can often detect and subsequently correct errors because humans have the ability to reason and interpret. Human receivers can often see past grammatical errors, misspellings, and misstatements and correctly understand what the sender was trying to communicate. (For example, if a teacher mistakenly states that the distance between the earth and the sun is 93 million light-years rather than 93 million miles, most students would probably realize the teacher's error and correct it.) Because computer networks do not reason, they are unable to detect or correct errors without the help of error detection and correction schemes. These are used to determine whether an original message has been distorted or changed during transmission. All error detection and correction schemes involve the transmission of both the data and additional information (about the data itself) that helps the receiver determine whether the message has been received correctly or changed en route to the receiver across the network. Message acknowledgments are sent by receivers to senders to indicate whether the messages came through error-free (see Figure 1-3). When changes (errors) are detected, the receiver's acknowledgment often includes a request for the sender to retransmit the message.

ESSENTIAL FEATURES OF NETWORKS

All data communication networks are, first and foremost, communication systems that include senders, messages, media, and receivers. However, data communication networks also have several other essential features. These include session, network, node, link, path, circuit, packetizing, routing, and store-and-forward systems. It is important for you to gain a basic understanding of these features because you will encounter these terms and concepts repeatedly throughout the text.

Session

The exchange of messages between two users over a computer network is called a **session**. The user may be a person (whose computer is attached to the network), an application or software program, or any other originator of messages. In some networks, sessions are quite formal, with well-defined conventions for establishing, continuing, and terminating the communication dialogue between users. The session layer of the Open Systems Interconnection (OSI) framework (introduced later in this chapter) is responsible for establishing, maintaining, and terminating sessions between two network users.

Network and Node

In most sections of this text, the term **network** refers to a group or set of computers and their attached communication devices (such as modems and multiplexors). Each computer is called a network **node**. Generally, you should think of a node as the

session The dialogue between two system users. A connection between two nodes that enables them to communicate.

network Two or more computers connected by a communication medium, together with all communication, hardware, and software components. Alternatively, a host processor together with its attached terminals, workstations, and communication equipment, such as transmission media and modems.

node A network junction or connection point. A personal computer in a LAN is a node; terminals connected to mainframes or midrange systems are also nodes.

Figure 1-3   Essential Features of Data Communication

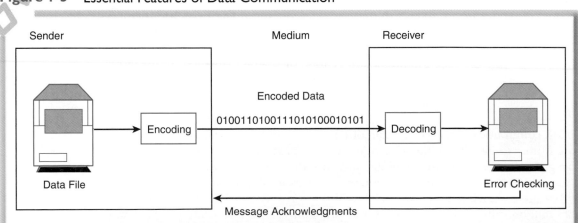

Sender · Medium · Receiver · Encoded Data · 01001101001110101000010101 · Encoding · Decoding · Data File · Error Checking · Message Acknowledgments

processor(s) within a computer that serve(s) as a termination point of a communication medium.

Link, Path, and Circuit

Although often used interchangeably, important differences exist among the terms *link, path,* and *circuit.* A **path** represents end-to-end routing within a network, whereas a **link** connects one node to an adjacent node. A link is also known as a **circuit**, the actual conduit over which data travels. It is important to note that by using techniques such as multiplexing, a circuit may be the conduit for multiple concurrent sessions

Four links are illustrated in Figure 1-4. These are the circuits connecting adjacent nodes. Figure 1-4 also illustrates that there are two possible paths available for a communication session between node A and node C. In path (A → B, B → C), node B serves as an intermediate node. In the other (A → D, D → C), node D is an intermediate node.

Today, large networks enable participants in a communication session to exchange messages over virtual circuits. A **virtual circuit** is established at the beginning of a communication session and, once established, all messages follow the same path across the network between sender and receiver throughout the duration of the session.

path The route between any two nodes in a network. The set of links, lines, channels, or circuits that allows a message to move from its point of origin to its destination.

link A line, channel, circuit, or transmission path over which data is transmitted.

circuit Either the medium connecting two communicating devices or a path between a sender and a receiver that may include one or more intermediary nodes. The exact meaning depends on the context.

virtual circuit A connection, established in setting up a communication session, between a sender and a receiver in which all messages are sent over the same path. A temporary communications path created between two nodes in a switched communication network.

Figure 1-4   Links and Paths in a Network

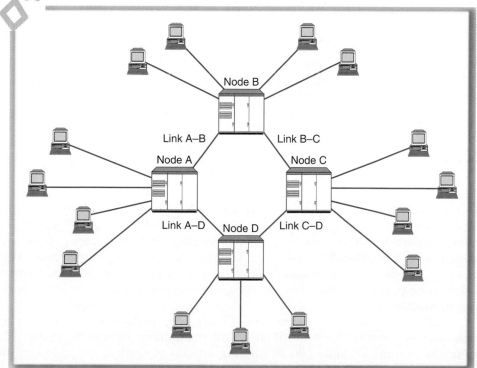

Packetizing

packetizing Dividing a message into packets prior to transmitting the message over a communication medium. Each packet contains a fixed sequence of data and control information that is transmitted and switched as a whole.

Packetizing refers to dividing a message into fixed-length packets prior to transmitting the message over a communication medium. The packets that are created include the data to be transmitted as well as additional information such as the receiver's network address, the sender's network address, and error-checking information that can be used by the receiver to ensure that the message has not been altered during transmission.

Routing

routing The process of selecting a circuit path for a message; an algorithm used to determine how to move a message from its source to its destination. Multiple routing algorithms exist.

Routing refers to how the path from sending node to receiving node is determined. In wide area networks (WANs) and other large networks, message routing is determined at the network layer of the OSI reference model. In some cases, the packets that make up a message all follow the same path (such as a virtual circuit) from sender to receiver. In other cases, each packet associated with a particular message may follow a different path from sender to receiver. In local area networks (LANs), routing is quite simple and often involves broadcasting the message to all nodes.

Store-and-Forward Systems

store-and-forward system A network system that enables the temporary storage of a message for transmission to its destination at a later time. Store-and-forward techniques allow messages to be routed over networks that are not accessible at all times. When transmitting data between two nodes in a store-and-forward system, messages are logged at intermediate nodes, which subsequently forward them to the next node in the network until they reach their destinations.

In a **store-and-forward system**, messages may be stored at intermediate nodes along the transmission path between source and destination. There are several reasons why this is desirable for large networks, including the Internet. First, there is the responsibility for being able to resend the message (for example, when the receiver detects a transmission error). If node A is transmitting a message to node Z, the path between the two may pass through multiple intermediate nodes. To ensure delivery, either node A must keep the message until it is delivered (to node Z) or an intermediate node that has received the message must assume this responsibility. In a store-and-forward system, a node that receives the message, including an intermediate node, will write it to disk or store it in memory and then send an acknowledgment to the sender indicating that the message has been received. When this happens, the responsibility for being able to resend the message shifts from the original sender to the intermediate node. Store-and-forward is especially attractive for financial transactions because it provides a trace (audit trail) of the progress of the transaction.

Second, store-and-forward algorithms are used for time-staged delivery systems. These systems allow users not only to send messages but also to specify a required delivery time, thereby providing several benefits. Corporations with offices in various time zones can assign a delivery time for their e-mail messages. If the delivery time is not immediate, the e-mail system can process a message during a period of low activity. Suppose that an e-mail message is posted at 2:00 P.M. for delivery to a time zone that is 4 hours later, where it is 6:00 P.M. If the delivery time is set at 9:00 A.M. the next day, the message can be stored locally and sent at midnight, when both the sending and receiving nodes are less busy. Time-staged delivery of large files can also allow their transmission to be paced over time, making the communication links more available for other transmissions.

Third, store-and-forward systems are valuable when paths to the destination are temporarily unavailable due to a circuit or link malfunction or a node "crash." If a link or the destination node fails during the process of sending the message, the node that has the message at the time of the failure can store the message. When the link is restored or the node recovers, the transmission process for the stored message can be completed.

Finally, store-and-forward techniques can be used in networks that assign priorities to different messages. Low priority messages may be stored for later delivery in order to give higher priority messages better access to the link during times of network congestion.

Network Topology and Architecture

The physical layout of a network, the way that nodes are attached to the communication medium, is called the **network topology**. For example, in Figure 1-4, nodes A, B, C, and D may be described as having a ring topology. **Network architecture** is a more comprehensive term than network topology and refers to the way in which media, hardware, and software are integrated to form a network. Common topologies and architectures for both LANs and WANs are discussed in later chapters.

Network Complexity

Data communication architectures may be simple or complex. A simple network might be composed of a midrange computer and a handful of personal computers or terminals, all located within a single room or building. Figure 1-5 illustrates how a midrange system (such as an IBM AS/400) might be implemented within a department or a small to medium-size business. Its main components include the midrange computer itself, the personal computers and/or terminals connected to it, and the wiring needed to interconnect them. Figure 1-6 illustrates a small LAN consisting of a server and six workstations. The server allows the microcomputers to share resources

network topology
The physical and logical arrangement of links and nodes within a network. Physical network topologies include bus, ring, and star.

network architecture The way in which media, hardware, software, access methods, and protocols are integrated to form a network.

Figure 1-5 Simple Data Communication System

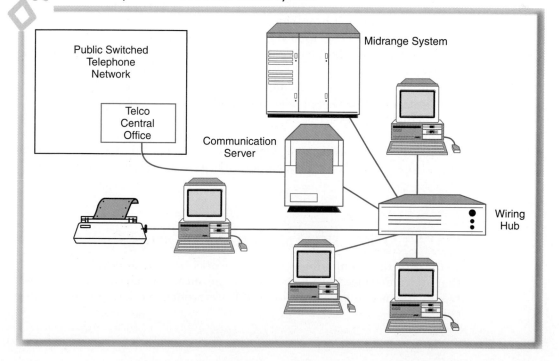

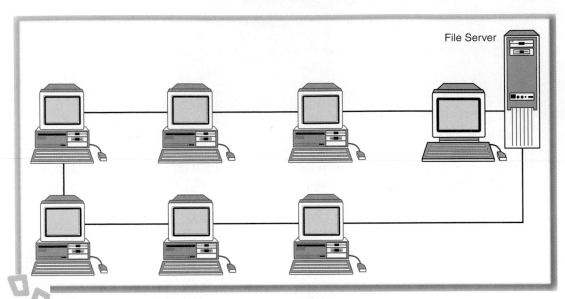

Figure 1-6   LAN with File Server and Six Workstations

such as data, programs, and printers; in this example, the server is the focal point of all shared resources.

A more elaborate network might consist of several LANs, each of which is interconnected with a mainframe or midrange computer, which in turn is connected in a WAN. Terminals that rely on the larger computers to perform processing requests may be distributed both locally and remotely. A network of this type may be called an *enterprise network* if it provides interconnections among the networks located at the organization's geographically distributed operating locations. Figure 1-7 depicts a data communication network that fits this description. The computers depicted in this figure may be dispersed over a large geographic area and be connected via an assortment of private wires, communication lines leased from common carriers (such telephone companies), and microwave and satellite transmission media.

Figures 1-4, 1-5, 1-6, and 1-7 provide a general picture of the variety and complexity of the business data communication networks found in today's organizations. As you read this book, you will gain a deeper understanding and appreciation of the complexity of today's networks and the variety of components that they include.

DATA COMMUNICATION FRAMEWORKS

Two major data communication frameworks have been developed to help ensure that networks meet business and communication requirements. These are the Open Systems Interconnection (OSI) reference model and the TCP/IP protocol stack.

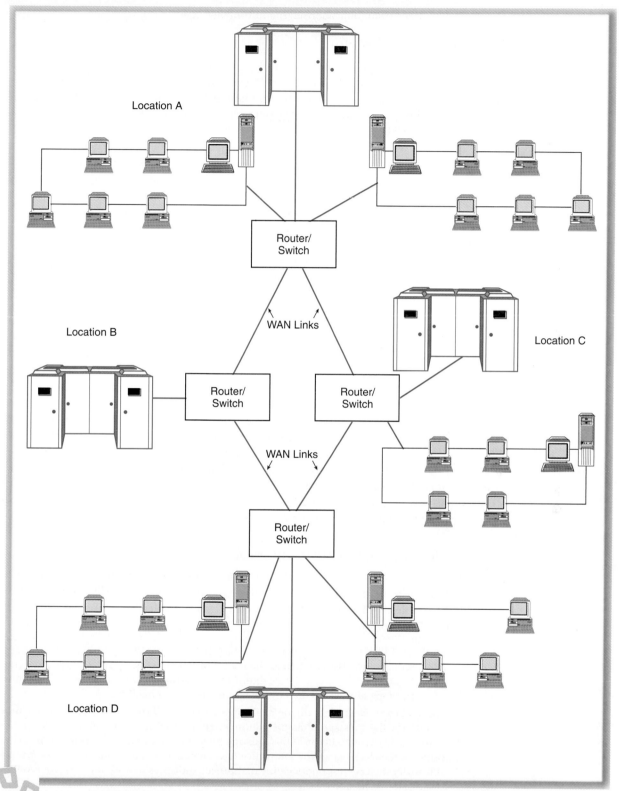

Figure 1-7 An Example of an Enterprise Network

OSI Reference Model

Regardless of the scope of a network and the equipment and media used, all networks share common functions. To contend with the proliferation of computer networks and their interconnections, the **International Standards Organization (ISO)** has identified and stratified the functions that every network must fulfill. This model makes it easier to develop interfaces among these diverse networks and networking technologies.

The ISO recommendation is called the **Open Systems Interconnection (OSI) reference model**. The reference model does more than describe network interconnections; it also defines a network architecture. Many ISO standards relating to the reference model have been established, and more are being formulated. Details and examples of this reference model are found in many of the following chapters. A brief description is provided here because the OSI reference model and standards arising from it play an important role in the development and evolution of networks and the technologies on which they are built.

The basic objective of a computer network is for an application on one node to communicate with an application or device on another node. Although this may sound simple, considerable complexities may be involved. In this chapter, you have already seen that many different WAN and LAN implementations are possible, and so are many different types of interfaces. As you progress through this book, you will learn that network developers have to be concerned with hardware-to-hardware interfaces, software-to-software interfaces, and software-to-hardware interfaces. This may mean that you need one kind of hardware and software to connect to one kind of LAN and a different set of hardware and software to connect to a different kind of LAN or to a particular WAN. Because of the variety of network types available and the need to interconnect them, a thriving business has been created for system integration firms and other organizations that specialize in establishing connections among networks. Building network interfaces is much more simple if the network is designed around an open architecture. An **open architecture** is one in which the network specifications are available to any company. This allows a variety of companies to design hardware and software components that can easily be integrated into new and existing networks based on the open architecture.

The Functions of Communication

To help us understand the OSI reference model, consider how a worker might send a message from his or her office to a colleague in another location. This simple act can closely resemble sending a message in a network. A possible scenario for this transmission might be as follows:

1. The worker writes a message on a tablet and delivers it to her or his administrative assistant.

2. The administrative assistant makes the memo presentable by typing it, correcting grammatical mistakes, and so on. The administrative assistant places the memo in an interoffice envelope and places the envelope in the outgoing mailbox.

3. The mail room clerk picks up the mail, takes it to the mail room, sorts it, and determines a route for the message. Possible routings are internal mail, postal mail, and private express mail carriers. Because this message must go to a distant office and no priority is assigned, the clerk places the interoffice envelope in an external mailing envelope, possibly with other correspondence for that office, addresses it, and deposits the envelope in the external mailbox.

4. The mail carrier picks up the mail, including the worker's message, and takes it to the post office, where it is sorted and placed on an outgoing mail truck.

5. The post office physically delivers the mail to the mail room of the destination office. That mail room clerk opens the outer envelope and sorts its contents.

International Standards Organization (ISO) An organization that is active in setting electronics, electrical, and data communication standards.

Open Systems Interconnection (OSI) reference model A seven-layered set of functions for transmitting data from one user to another. Specified by the ISO for the design of open systems networks.

open architecture An architecture whose network specifications are available to any company. This allows a variety of companies to design hardware and software components that can be easily integrated into new and existing networks.

6. The mail room clerk delivers the memo in its interoffice envelope to the recipient's administrative assistant.

7. The recipient's administrative assistant takes the memo out of the envelope and prepares the memo for the recipient. The administrative assistant may time-stamp the memo, summarize it, make comments, set a priority for the recipient's reading it, and so on.

8. The recipient receives the memo, reads it, and reacts to the worker's message.

The preceding scenario describes a variety of different functions necessary to move a message from the sender's desk to the recipient's desk. The functions consist of message composition, presentation services, address determination, enveloping, selecting transmission routes, physical transmission, and so on. In general, these same functions must be performed when transmitting a message between computers in a network. The OSI reference model explicitly identifies seven layers of functions that must be performed in network interconnections: application, presentation, session, transport, network, data link, and physical. Figure 1-8 represents the OSI layers in two network nodes: a sending and a receiving node.

In the letter-routing example, each functional layer on the sending side performed a specific set of functions, and a mirror image of each function was performed by a corresponding (peer) layer on the receiving side. For example, placing the message in the interoffice envelope was done by the sending administrative assistant and undone by the receiving administrative assistant. Likewise, in the OSI reference model, each layer in the sending network node is designed to perform a particular set of functions for its corresponding (peer) layer in the receiving network node. The application layer in the sending node prepares the data for the application layer in the receiving node. The application layer then passes the message to the presentation layer. The presentation layer formats the message properly for the presentation layer on the receiving node, passes the data to the session layer, and so on. In Figure 1-8, the solid lines show the physical route of the message, and the dotted lines show the logical route, from peer layer to peer layer. Also notice that each layer has a well-defined interface through which it communicates with adjacent layers.

Table 1-1 summarizes the major functions performed at each layer of the OSI reference model. An example of the activities that occur at each layer of the reference model as a bank customer uses an ATM machine attached to a bank network is provided in Appendix A (www.prenhall.com/stamper).

The OSI Reference Model in Practice

Network analysts, administrators, and technical support staff use the OSI reference model in a variety of ways. These include the following:

➤ When troubleshooting network problems, network professionals start at the physical layer and assure that the protocols and interfaces at each layer are working properly before moving up to the next layer.

➤ The OSI model provides a common terminology and framework that data communications technology developers can use to discuss the interconnection of two networks or computers.

➤ The OSI model facilitates the development of connectivity standards needed for flexible open architectures.

➤ The OSI model enables network professionals to develop a "protocol stack" for each network node by listing each of the node's protocols in its proper OSI layer. The resulting protocol profile provides insight into what is necessary to enable the node to communicate successfully with other network nodes.

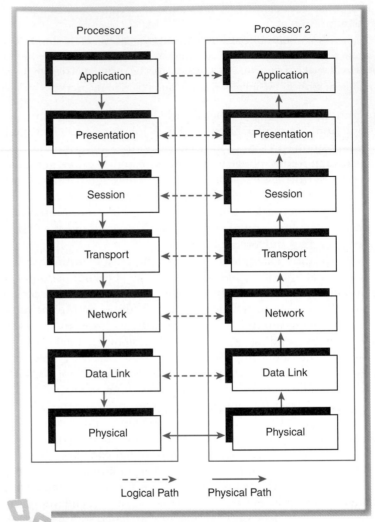

Figure 1-8   OSI Peer Layer Communication

Transmission Control Protocol/ Internet Protocol (TCP/IP) suite A set of layered protocols developed by the U.S. Department of Defense for Internet work file transfers, e-mail transfer, remote log ons, and terminal services. TCP/IP is the de facto communication protocol of the Internet and a global standard for communications.

As you read subsequent chapters of this text, the importance of the OSI reference model to network design, operations, and development will become more clear. Because this model will be used throughout the remainder of the text as a central reference point in numerous explanations of data communication technologies, it is important for you to understand what it is and the role it plays in understanding today's data communication networks.

The TCP/IP Protocol Suite

Although the OSI reference model is arguably the most important data communications framework, the **Transmission Control Protocol/Internet Protocol (TCP/IP) suite** has emerged as a second model that data communications students must master in order to understand the inner workings of the Internet. TCP/IP is the Internet's primary communications protocol, and the TCP/IP protocol suite,

Table 1-1   OSI Reference Model Layer Functions

Application Layer The application layer is functionally defined by the user. It is the layer at which users, running the applications they need to perform their jobs, interface with the network. Sometimes application programs must communicate with each other. For example, communication between sender and receiver e-mail applications is necessary when senders require message receipt confirmation from receivers. The content and format of the data being exchanged are dictated by the needs of the organization. The application in use determines which data is to be transmitted, the message format for the data, and any special codes that are needed to identify the data to the receiver. Suppose an order entry transaction started on a sales node needs to pass product shipping information to a warehouse node. In this application, the message contains the ship-to address, part identifiers, quantities to be shipped, and a message code showing the action to be taken by the receiving application.

Presentation Layer The presentation layer formats the data it receives from the application layer. If certain data preparation functions are common to several applications, they may be resolved by the presentation services rather than being embedded in each application. The types of functions performed at the presentation level are encoding (e.g., converting word processing text and/or formatting into ASCII or Unicode), encryption, compression, terminal screen formatting, and conversion from one encoding scheme to another (such as ASCII to EBCDIC).

Session Layer The session layer establishes the connection between applications, enforces the rules for carrying on the dialogue between them, and tries to reestablish the connection if a failure occurs. The dialogue rules specify both the order in which the applications are allowed to communicate and the pacing of information so as not to overload the recipient. For example, if an application is sending data to a printer with a limited buffer size, the agreed-upon dialogue may be to send a buffer-size block to the printer, wait for the printer to signal that its buffer has been emptied, and then send the next block of data. The session layer must control this flow to avoid buffer overflow at the printer.

Transport Layer The transport layer is the first layer concerned with the world external to the sending computer. It performs end-to-end delivery; that is, it ensures that all blocks or packets of data have been received by the destination computer, that there are no duplicate blocks, and that blocks are ordered in the proper sequence. It does this by affixing sequence numbers to packets being transmitted.

Network Layer The network layer is responsible for message routing across networks with multiple nodes. It relieves the upper layers from being responsible for having to know the data transmission and switching technologies that are used to interconnect the nodes and networks through which the messages must travel and provides transparent transfer of data between transport entities.

Data Link Layer The data link layer must establish and control the physical path of communication to the next node. This includes error detection and correction, defining the beginning and end of the data field, resolving competing requests for a shared communication link (deciding who can use the circuit and when), and ensuring that all forms of data can be sent across the circuit. The conventions used to accomplish these data link functions are known as protocols. With fully functional data link protocols, the network layer may assume virtually error-free transmission over the physical link.

Physical Layer The physical layer specifies the electrical connections between the transmission medium and the computer system. It describes how many wires are used to carry the signals, which wires carry specific signals, the size and shape of the connectors or adapters between the transmission medium and the communication circuit, the speed at which data is transmitted, and whether data (represented by voltages on a line, modification of radio waves, or light pulses) is allowed to flow in both directions and, if so, whether the flow can be in both directions simultaneously.

which is depicted in part in Figure 1-9, has become the de facto standard for open systems Internetworking. As you can see in Figure 1-9, this suite gets its name from TCP and IP, the primary protocols found at the transport and Internet layers of the five-layer TCP/IP model.

Like those for the OSI model, the protocols found at each layer of the TCP/IP model can operate independently from those found at the other layers. This means that a protocol for a given layer can be modified without having to change the protocols in the other layers. In the 30-plus years since its introduction, TCP/IP has evolved with the Internet. A major modification that is currently underway involves the

Figure 1-9   TCP/IP Layers and Protocols and How They Relate to the OSI Reference Model

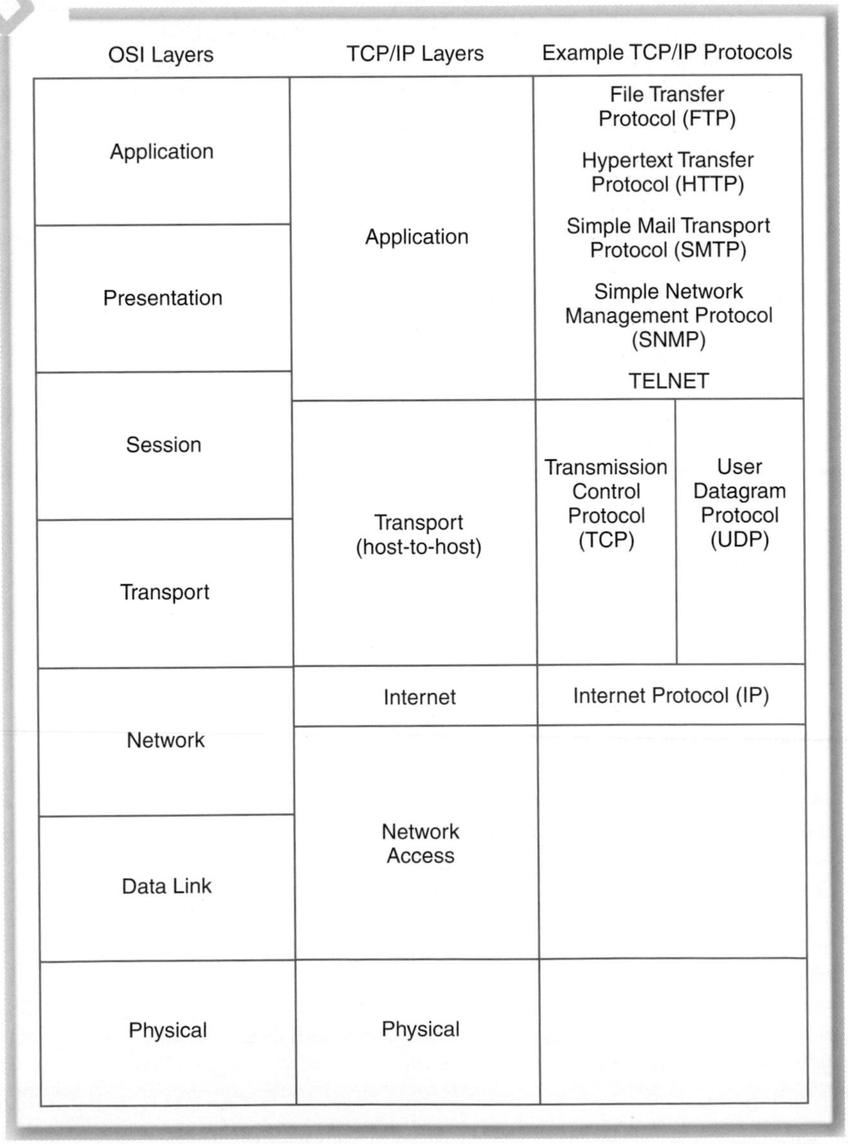

OSI Layers	TCP/IP Layers	Example TCP/IP Protocols	
Application	Application	File Transfer Protocol (FTP) Hypertext Transfer Protocol (HTTP) Simple Mail Transport Protocol (SMTP) Simple Network Management Protocol (SNMP) TELNET	
Presentation			
Session	Transport (host-to-host)	Transmission Control Protocol (TCP)	User Datagram Protocol (UDP)
Transport			
Network	Internet	Internet Protocol (IP)	
	Network Access		
Data Link			
Physical	Physical		

changeover to a new version of IP called IPng (IP next generation) or IPv6 (IP version 6). A pending shortage of IP addresses is driving this changeover.

Figure 1-9 compares the OSI and TCP/IP models. It also lists some of the major protocols found at the application, transport, and Internet layers of the TCP/IP model. These and other important protocols that make up the TCP/IP protocol suite will be explored more fully in Chapter 2.

DATA COMMUNICATIONS HISTORY

The need for creation of frameworks like the OSI and TCP/IP models grew from the evolution of data communications. To better understand why these models are important, an abbreviated history of data communications is provided here.

History of the Telecommunication Industry

The history of data communication differs significantly from that of other computer technologies, such as languages, hardware, database management, and applications. Data communication development has been stimulated by both independent and collaborative accomplishments of the communication and computer industries.

The modern telecommunication industry began in 1837 with the invention of the telegraph by Samuel Morse. This invention led to building a telecommunication infrastructure of poles and wires and further development of communication hardware and protocols. The invention of the telegraph was followed by the invention of the telephone by Alexander Graham Bell in 1876 and the development of wireless communication technology by Guglielmo Marconi in the 1890s. These pioneering efforts set the stage for today's communication industry. Because telephone companies have been the primary source of long-distance communication circuits, this abbreviated data communications history begins with the state of telephone companies at the start of the computer era.

By the early 1950s, at the beginning of the computer era, the communication industry was already well established. Telephone and telegraph companies had developed a network of communication facilities throughout the industrialized world. In the United States and many other countries, telephone companies had been given exclusive rights to install lines and provide services in specific geographical areas, with government agencies [such as the Federal Communications Commission (FCC) and state-level public service commissions (PSCs)] exercising control over tariffs and the services provided. This situation appeared to benefit both the telephone companies and consumers. The goal of the system was to provide affordable service. However, some users paid less than the actual cost of service whereas others paid more, because of the following pricing structure.

Every person was to have access to telephone service at a reasonable cost. Service was to be provided to all geographical areas, regardless of remoteness or population density. Small remote towns were to have the same kind of service as large metropolitan communities, at about the same rates. If the total cost of installing lines and switching equipment in a small town had been borne entirely by users in that town, the cost of service would have been prohibitive to most residents. Therefore, losses incurred in such towns were offset by profits from other, more populated geographical areas. The three major sources of profit in the United States were the major metropolitan areas, businesses, and long-distance service. The large metropolitan areas were profitable because of economies of scale and density of installations. Business rates were much higher than rates for individuals because the value received was ostensibly greater (because the telephone was being used to generate income) and because businesses could afford to pay more. Long-distance tariffs were set high to subsidize the portions of the system operating at a loss. Thus, the service provided was generally good, and prices were reasonable for each class of user. (Note that two of these profitable segments—business and long distance—also pertain to data communication.)

In addition to having exclusive rights to transmission facilities, the telephone companies in the United States and numerous other countries had exclusive rights to attach equipment to the telephone networks. This gave them a monopoly on the equipment needed to transmit and receive data, such as modems. (A modem changes a computer signal from digital to analog format for transmission along a medium such as telephone lines; another modem converts the signal back to digital format at the receiving end. Modems are discussed further in Chapter 10.) These exclusive rights allowed telephone companies to turn the sale or lease of such equipment to profit, which is what U.S. telephone companies did.

In the United States, telephone companies were viewed as "natural" monopolies, meaning that it was considered wasteful to have two or more telephone companies servicing the same location. The price attached to the monopoly was that telephone companies such as American Telephone & Telegraph (AT&T) were prohibited from involvement in certain business segments, such as the computer industry. Partly because of this monopoly on equipment, as well as the special status given providers of data transmission facilities, the growth of data communication was somewhat slower than that of other computer-related technologies. The development of databases, languages, operating systems, and hardware components was strong from the 1950s through the early 1970s, but large-scale expansion of data communication systems really did not occur until the 1970s. The growth experienced then was primarily the result of the following three developments:

➤ Large-scale integration of circuits reduced the cost and size of terminals and communication equipment.
➤ Development of software systems made the establishment of data communication networks easy.
➤ Competition among providers of transmission facilities reduced the cost of data circuits.

Without these developments, data communication systems would not have been affordable for many computer users. Consider the transmission costs in 1968 and 1973, just before and just after competition appeared. In 1968, AT&T charged an average of $315 for 100 miles of leased telephone line. In 1973, the average cost of the same line was as low as $85. A simple teletypewriter (TTY) terminal that sold for $2,595 in 1971 could be replaced in 1975 for $750, and the 1975 terminal had more features than the older model.

History of Data Communication

Significant data communication events are shown on the time line in Table 1-2. The most significant of these are discussed in this section.

The Transistor

The invention of the transistor by Walter H. Brattain, John Bardeen, and William Shockley at Bell Laboratories in 1947 was fundamental to the electronics we use in computers and communication equipment. The transistor replaced vacuum tubes, which were large and produced significant amounts of heat; in contrast, the transistor is small and produces little heat, characteristics that are essential to the electronic equipment that forms the basis of our computer and communication industry.

Table 1-2   Some Major Events in Data Communication History

1837:	Invention of the telegraph.
1876:	Invention of the telephone.
1890s:	Development of wireless technology.
1939:	ABC computer operational.
1940:	Data communication performed using COMPLEX computer.
1944:	MARK I computer operational.
1946:	ENIAC computer operational.
1947:	Invention of the transistor.
1948:	First commercial computer installed, the UNIVAC I.
1953:	First private commercial computer installed, UNIVAC at General Electric Corporation.
1954:	IBM introduces remote job entry (RJE).
1956:	Hush-a-Phone decision in favor of Hush-a-Phone Company.
1958:	First U.S. communications satellite sent into orbit; start of SAGE radar early warning system.
1959:	FCC approves private microwave communication networks.
1963:	First geosynchronous orbiting satellite, SYNCOM II. MCI files with FCC to provide communication services.
1964:	SABRE airline reservation system completed. Packet switching network concept proposed by the Rand Corporation.
1966:	IBM's binary synchronous (BISYNC or BSC) protocol announced.
1968:	Carterphone case concludes in favor of Carter Electronics.
1969:	ARPANET, first packet switching network (later to become the Internet), begins operation.
1972:	Ethernet LAN specifications formulated IBM's synchronous data link control (SDLC) protocol announced.
1974:	IBM announces its system network architecture (SNA).
1975:	General Telephone and Electronics' Telenet public packet distribution network (PDN) becomes operational. Personal computers introduced, the Altaire 8800.
1981:	IBM PC introduced.
1982:	Microcomputer LANs appear.
1984:	AT&T divestiture.
1985:	Cellular radio telephones are introduced.
1990:	A prototype of the Internet World Wide Web (WWW) is introduced.
1992:	The Internet grows to 1 million host computers and the World Wide Web opens to commerce.
1993:	The Internet grows to 2 million host computers.
1995:	The Internet grows to over 4 million host computers.
1996:	The Telecommunications Reform Act of 1996 is passed.
1997:	*A Framework for Global Electronic Commerce* is released by the Clinton administration.
1999:	The number of U.S. and Canadian households with Internet access surpasses 100 million. U.S. Department of Commerce begins quarterly reports on e-commerce volume in United States. M-commerce applications begin to proliferate.
2000:	The World Wide Web exceeds 2 billion unique Web pages and grows at more than 7 million new pages each day. E-commerce volume is more than double that in 1999. Electronic Signatures Act is signed into law.
2001:	Number of Internet users worldwide exceeds 375 million. M-commerce applications become mainstream.
2002:	Wireless Internet access expands along with B2B and B2C e-commerce.

The Hush-a-Phone Case

A 1948 court case not specifically related to data communication eventually had a significant impact on that industry: the Hush-a-Phone case. Recall that U.S. telephone companies had a legal monopoly over all equipment attached to their networks, to keep anyone from attaching devices that might interfere with or destroy signals and equipment in the network. The Hush-a-Phone Company developed and marketed a passive device (no electrical or magnetic components) that could be installed over the transmitting telephone handset to block background noise and provide more privacy; AT&T threatened to suspend service for users and distributors of the device. Hush-a-Phone appealed to the Federal Communications Commission. After several hearings, the FCC decided in favor of AT&T. In 1956, however, an appeals court overturned the FCC ruling and decided in favor of the Hush-a-Phone Company, holding that no harm to the AT&T network would result from use of such a device. This precedent opened the door for other companies to attach equipment to the telephone networks. The telephone regulations as modified by this decision stated that the telephone company could not prohibit a customer from using a device for his or her convenience as long as the device did not damage the telephone system, involve direct electrical connection to the system, provide a recording device on the line, or connect the telephone company line with any other communication device.

Competition for Long-Distance Transmission

In 1963, Microwave Communications Incorporated (MCI) filed with the FCC to provide microwave communication services between Chicago and St. Louis, their goal being to sell data transmission circuits to private industry. AT&T objected to MCI's petition because MCI could operate at much lower overhead than AT&T; MCI, unlike AT&T, would not have to serve lower-volume markets such as rural areas in Montana, Wyoming, Idaho, Texas, and Kansas. Despite AT&T's objections, MCI received approval for the communication link in 1970. This ruling opened the door for other carriers to compete with AT&T for long-distance services. This has resulted in heavy competition for data transmission circuits in the United States and has led to lower rates for data communication users.

The Carterphone Case

In 1968, another court case helped open data communication to competition: the Carterphone case. Carter Electronics Company had been marketing a radio telephone system that allowed communication between a moving vehicle and a base station via radio-wave transmission. Because the original Carterphone was unable to forward a mobile call to another location, the company introduced a device that could pass the radio transmission through a telephone network. AT&T objected to attaching the Carterphone to its network on the grounds of potential harm to the network and violation of the FCC prohibition against connecting an outsider's communication device to AT&T's telephone line. The 1968 ruling was in favor of Carter Electronics. As an outgrowth of the decision, it became legal for any device to be attached to the telephone network provided the telephone companies were allowed to install a protective device between the "foreign" equipment and the network. This provision later was changed to allow connection of FCC–approved equipment without any protective devices, which made it legal to attach other manufacturers' communication equipment to the network and led to improved products at lower prices. As another side effect of the Carterphone decision, individuals were allowed to purchase and install their own telephones.

Data Link Protocols

As noted in our discussion of the OSI reference model, the primary role of a data link protocol is to govern the flow of data between sending and receiving computers in a network. The original data communication protocols were borrowed from the telegraph and telephone industries. In 1967, IBM introduced the binary synchronous (BISYNC or BSC) protocol for use in remote job entry applications, and it was later expanded for use in other applications. In 1972, IBM introduced the synchronous data link control (SDLC) protocol, which has become the prototype for many current data link protocols.

Microcomputers

Microcomputers were introduced in 1975 with the Altaire 8800. Microcomputer technology began to proliferate business organizations in the 1980s and is continuing to do so today. A wide variety of microcomputer software and hardware, coupled with increased processing and storage capacity and low costs, have made microcomputers a key element in today's data communication networks both as servers and clients.

Local Area Networks (LANs), like the example shown in Figure 1-6, is a communication network whose components, unlike those in WANs, are all located within relatively close proximity to one another. The original specifications for Ethernet (now the dominant LAN architecture) were published by the Xerox Corporation in 1972. Later, Digital Equipment Corporation (DEC) and Intel joined Xerox in developing Ethernet further. In the early 1980s, microcomputer and LAN technologies were merged, and since that time, LANs are predominantly microcomputer-based networks. LANs have also emerged as fundamental building blocks in today's enterprise-wide and global networks. Today, microcomputer-based LANs form a significant portion of government, academic, and corporate computing power.

The Internet

The Internet of today is vastly different from what it was originally intended to be. The Internet began in 1969 as the ARPAnet, a network funded by the U.S. Defense Department's Advanced Research Projects Agency (ARPA). The ARPAnet linked leading universities and research organizations, and its primary use was to provide communication among scientists and researchers. By the mid-1980s, there were over 500 host nodes on the Internet, and additional communication tools and protocols had been developed to make communication easier. In the 1990s, the character of the Internet changed extensively. Thousands of new nodes were added, and more sophisticated tools such as Web browsers were developed to allow easier access to data. Most significantly, the Internet became a communication facility for businesses and individuals as well as for scientists. In the early days, using the Internet for commercial purposes was discouraged; in fact, it was not until the early 1990s that businesses were allowed to use the Internet for commercial purposes. Today, the Internet's primary use is for business and personal activities. A wealth of data—good and bad, accurate and inaccurate—is easily available to anyone with a computer, modem, or similar connection device and an Internet service provider. Because the Internet has emerged as a primary data communications context, it is the first major topic addressed by the text in Chapters 2, 3, and 4.

The Telecommunications Reform Act of 1996

The Telecommunications Reform Act of 1996 was passed to encourage competition in all aspects and markets of telecommunications services and carriers. The legislation directs the Federal Communications Commission to develop the rules for allowing local exchange carriers (LECs) and interexchange carriers (IXCs) to compete in each other's markets. It also opened the door for companies to provide local access service in competition with regional Bell operating companies (RBOCs); such companies are known as competitive access providers (CAPs) or competitive local exchange carriers (CLECs).

The Telecommunications Reform Act of 1996 enables some segments of the communications industry to offer new services once they have allowed competition in their own segment. For example, RBOCs will be allowed to provide long-distance services to their own in-region customers when they have demonstrated that they have adequately opened their local markets to competition (this process requires the successful completion of a 14-point checklist, and approval by state regulators, the U.S. Department of Justice, and ultimately, the FCC). Also, this act enables cable and telephone companies to enter each other's markets. Hence, although this act represents an important step toward deregulation, it creates new regulatory issues.

Since its passage, a number of important decisions have emerged via FCC policymaking, state public utility commission decisions, and court cases. To date, the FCC has adhered to a rigorous interpretation of its checklist provisions and has rejected RBOC proposals to provide long-distance services in many states. As a result, incumbent providers still control more than 99 percent of their local markets, suggesting that competition has made few inroads.

In 1998, the FCC began considering a proposal to deregulate high-speed data services. This would allow RBOCs to offer high-speed data transmission services without tariffs, so long as they do not use their regional advantage to drive out rivals. In addition, CLECs are marketing their services in most states and have signed hundreds of local interconnection agreements with incumbent local providers. In spite of these developments, a number of experts are concerned that the Telecommunications Reform Act of 1996 is not fostering competition quickly enough.

A Framework for Global Electronic Commerce

A Framework for Global Electronic Commerce was released by the Clinton Administration in July 1997. Its importance in data communications history rests in the fact that it squarely recognizes the role that Internet-based commerce has come to play in the global economy, outlines several overall guiding principles for e-commerce planners and strategists, and identifies key issues that must be addressed for e-commerce to flourish.

The report includes several guiding principles that are summarized in Table 1-3. Key issues related to e-commerce policymakers are in Table 1-4. Table 1-3 conveys the belief that governments around the world should generally take a "hands-off" approach to electronic commerce in order for it to gain a solid foothold from which it can grow and expand. Related issues that governments should address to facilitate the evolution of e-commerce are summarized in Table 1-4.

Table 1-3   Guiding Principles for E-Commerce from *A Framework for Global Electronic Commerce*

The private sector should lead.
Governments should avoid undue restrictions on electronic commerce.
Where government involvement is needed, its aim should be to support and enforce a predictable, minimalist, consistent, and simple legal environment for commerce.
Governments should recognize the unique qualities of the Internet.
Electronic commerce over the Internet should be facilitated on a global basis.

SOURCE: www.ecommerce.gov/framewrk.htm

Table 1-4   Key Issues for E-Commerce from *A Framework for Global Electronic Commerce*

Customs and taxation	Electronic payment systems
"Universal commercial code" for e-commerce	Intellectual property protection
Privacy	Security
Telecommunications infrastructure and IT	Content
Technical standards	

SOURCE: www.ecommerce.gov/framewrk.htm

This federal report recognizes the profound effect that the Internet is having on global trade and its ability to revolutionize business-to-business and business-to-consumer commerce across a vast array of industries. It also recognizes that to facilitate the realization of its potential, governments must adopt a nonregulatory, market-oriented approach to electronic commerce. This stance should

> ➤ Respect the unique nature of the medium (the Internet)
> ➤ Enable widespread competition and increased consumer choice as the defining features of the new digital marketplace
> ➤ Facilitate the emergence of a transparent and predictable legal environment to support global business and commerce
> ➤ Encourage governmental recognition, acceptance, and facilitation of electronic communications (i.e., contracts, notarized documents)
> ➤ Encourage consistent international rules to support the acceptance of electronic signatures and other authentication procedures
> ➤ Encourage private sector investment in appropriate telecommunication infrastructures
> ➤ Promote and preserve competition by introducing competition to monopoly phone markets, ensuring interconnection at fair prices, opening markets to foreign investment, and enforcing antitrust safeguards
> ➤ Guarantee open access to networks on a nondiscriminatory basis, so that *all* users have access to the broadest range of information and services
> ➤ Implement an independent regulatory agency charged with developing procompetitive and flexible regulation that keeps pace with technological development

To date, *A Framework for Global Electronic Commerce* has provided guidelines that have shaped the evolution of electronic commerce, which is the primary focus of Chapter 3. As such, it has played an important role in the evolution of the Internet itself.

There are many other significant events in the history of telecommunications and data communications that arguably could be included in the set that we have chosen to highlight in this section. Our purpose is not to provide an exhaustive treatment of the history of data communications, but rather to provide you with a general sense of why and how the area has evolved to where it is today. In fact, many of the applications discussed next would not be as advanced as they are if data communication history had been different.

NETWORK APPLICATIONS

The Application Environment

The history of data communications has played a key role in the evolution of business data communications applications. Before beginning our discussion of these applications, a general explanation of how business applications fit into the network environment is worthwhile. Let us take a brief look at the application environment of a data communication system. Within each major network node (such as a server, mainframe, or minicomputer) resides an operating system, together with data communication and application software. Nodes that provide network users with access to databases also include a database management system. This is illustrated in Figure 1-10. These major software subsystems perform the following functions.

Application Programs

Application programs are the heart of the system. They are the sole reason for having computers and networks and their associated software and hardware in business organizations. Business application software may be purchased from software vendors or a third party or developed as a customized application locally. There are many varieties

Figure 1-10 Application Environment

Terminals and Other Data Communication Devices

I/O Drivers

Data Communication Access Methods

Operating System

Transaction Control Process

Application Programs

Application 1 Application 2 Application 3 Application N

Messages

Database Management System

File Access Methods

I/O Drivers

Disk Drives

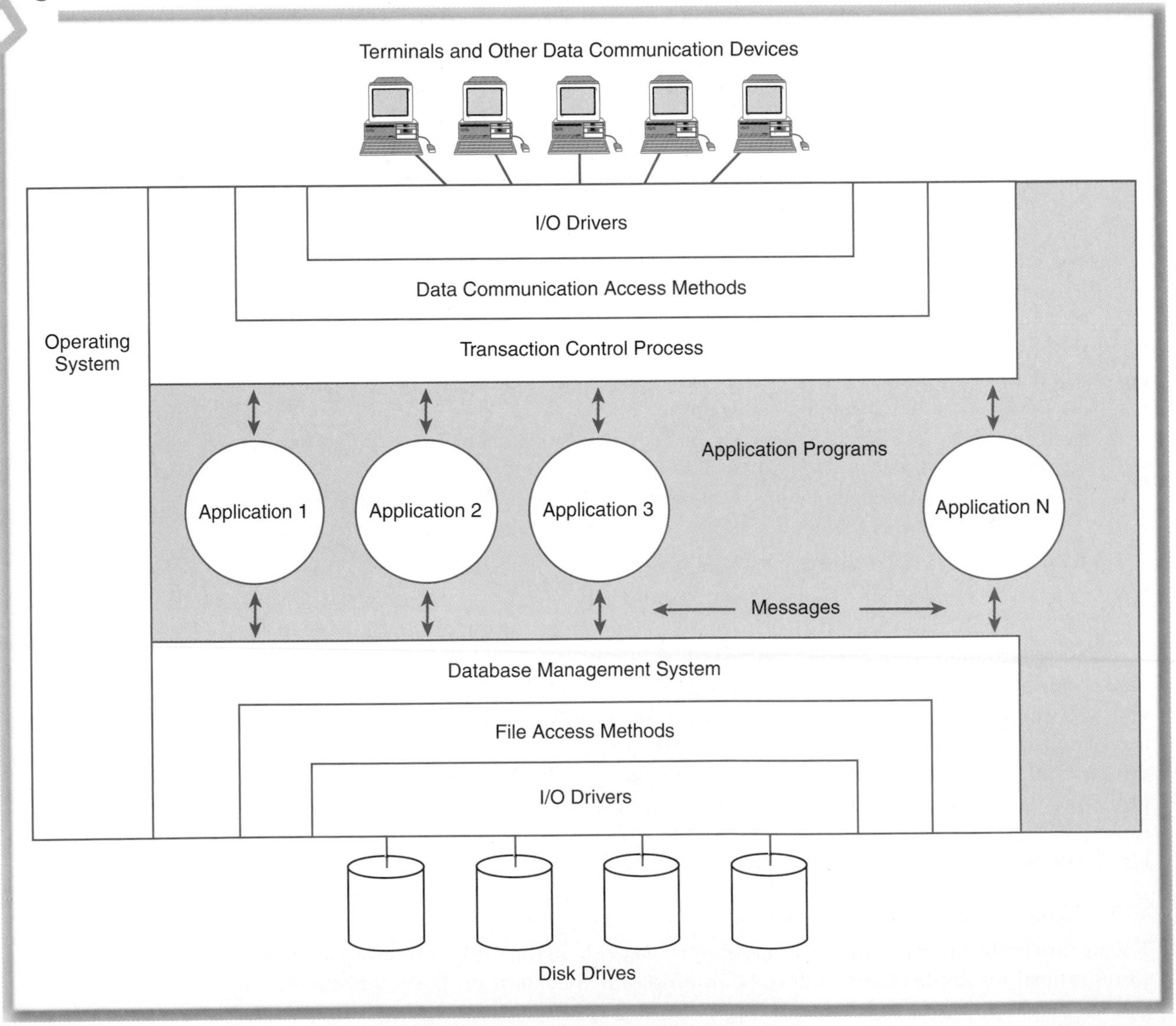

of business application programs. For example, an inventory system has many programs, each of which performs one or more inventory functions, such as inventory update, inventory listings, and printing packing lists. A banking system consists of many programs that provide functions such as creating new accounts, deleting accounts, updating accounts, and reporting account statuses.

To make the application development process efficient, business programmers should not have to concern themselves with the intricacies of data communication and storage. This is why application support software, such as the operating system, data communication system, and database system, play an important role in today's networks. The purpose of these systems is to allow application developers to concentrate on solving business problems rather than on the specifics of devices such as terminals and disk drives. By isolating applications from this level of detail, a company can also introduce devices into a system with minimal or no impact on existing application programs.

Operating System

The node's operating system manages the resources of the computer. It manages memory, controls access to the processor(s), and provides interfaces to users, the input/output (I/O) subsystems, and the file system. A variety of operating systems may be found in today's networks. MVS, UNIX, and VMS are widely used on mainframes and many minicomputers. Servers in LANs typically run the same operating systems as client workstations, namely Windows 98/2000, Windows NT/XP, Linux, Solaris, or Mac OS.

Data Communication

The data communication subsystem is responsible for interfacing nodes and other data communication devices within the network. These devices are distinguished from locally attached peripherals such as disk drives, printers, and tape drives, which are under the control of the node's operating system. In addition to the functions defined earlier, the data communication system provides a software bridge between applications and the devices with which they must communicate. In this capacity, it switches messages between nodes and applications and becomes involved in recovery in the event of a system failure. In mainframe-centric networks consisting of mainframes (or minicomputers) and the terminals that are attached to them, the data communication component that provides this service is called a *transaction control process*. In most of today's networks, these functions are carried out by a network operating system such as UNIX, Windows 2000 Server, Windows NT, Novell NetWare, Solaris, or Linux.

Database Management System

On nodes that provide shared access to databases, a database management system (DBMS) serves as an interface between the application programs and the data that network users need to resolve business problems. The functions provided by the DBMS include data definition, data manipulation, and data management and control. Data definition provides the ability to define fields, combine fields into records, and define files, data access methods, and associations. Data manipulation allows users to retrieve, insert, delete, and modify data in the database. Data management and control allow the database administrator and operations personnel to start, stop, monitor, and reorganize the database.

In order to better understand the role of each of these software systems, focus on how they work together to enable an employee to access records from a LAN server. The process begins when the employee, working on a workstation in a LAN, requests a database program located on the file server by clicking on a shortcut on the Windows 2000 desktop. The database program is transferred over the LAN medium into the workstation's memory. Once launched, from the user's perspective the file server appears to be another disk drive because each time the application issues a read or write request for a record, the request is handled by the file server. The database processing logic, however, is actually carried out by the workstation's processor. When the database application running on the employee's workstation needs access to records stored in a shared database on the file server, a request is sent from the workstation to the file server, asking the file server to access the desired record. The file server accepts the request, accesses the records from its disks, and transmits the records to the requesting workstation. In this example, the file server responds to requests by simply providing the workstation with the requested records. The file server does not participate in processing database records; this is handled by the processor in the employee's workstation. In a slightly different LAN scenario, we may find a database server that cooperates with the workstation in carrying out database requests. With this alternative, the workstation sends the database server a request for database processing rather than a request for individual records. The request might be something like "Give me the total sales for the Northwest Region." The database server acts on the request and returns the single figure answer rather than the set of records essential to deriving the answer. In this scenario, the database server cooperates with the workstation in processing the data.

There is a common thread in each of the previous examples: A user or program made a request that was acted on by one or more other processes at another node. In both LAN examples, the software needed to satisfy the request for specific data was located in two different processors (nodes). This is consistent with an important networking trend: distributing the processing for a single application over two or more network nodes. An application at one node makes requests that software on other nodes processes. The requester is called a *client process,* and the processes that act on those requests are called *server processes.* This general concept is called client/server computing. With client/server computing, the network is called upon to solve application problems rather than having a single node responsible for all application requirements. In essence, with client/server computing, the network becomes the computer!

Business Data Communication Applications

An understanding of how application programs interface with other major types of software in the network environment is an important step in understanding how networks work. In this section, however, we turn our attention to some of the major applications that businesses use to put networks to work.

Electronic Mail (E-Mail)   One of the most common business data communications applications is electronic mail (e-mail). An e-mail system has many of the capabilities of a conventional postal system, such as collecting and distributing correspondence of various sizes and types and routing the correspondence to recipients in a timely manner. However, over time, we have come to expect many more capabilities from an e-mail system than from a conventional postal system. Today's e-mail systems allow correspondents to exchange communication containing text, graphics, audio, image, and video in batch or real-time mode. The ability to exchange e-mail via wireless handheld devices such as Internet-ready wireless phones is also having a major impact on businesses. For many companies, e-mail has become a primary mode of communication, and because of its importance, we discuss its characteristics in some detail in this text.

Voice Applications   Historically, voice communications and data communication systems were treated as separate technologies in business organizations with distinct networks for both. Over time, however, many businesses have begun to integrate their voice and data communication networks. In many organizations, a digital private branch exchange (PBX) enables both voice and data communication messages to be transmitted simultaneously over telephone wires, thus minimizing the need for separate voice and data communication networks. Other organizations have implemented computer-telephony integration (CTI) in order to expedite the processing of orders by callers through the integration of their telephone networks and database processing systems. Other key voice applications that are impacting companies' business practices include personal communications services (PCS), Integrated Services Digital Network (ISDN), and voice-over IP (which enables voice messages to be transmitted over IP networks such as the Internet).

Groupware   Networks have expanded the potential of the microcomputer from individual productivity to work-group productivity; however, work-group software is not exclusively a microcomputer technology. Work-group productivity tools, collectively called groupware, have their roots in WANs. **Groupware** allows a group of users to communicate and coordinate activities. Basic groupware capabilities such as e-mail and project management systems were common WAN applications before the introduction of microcomputers. Some of the other work-group productivity tools are as follows:

> *Group calendar systems*. Group calendar systems are extensions of individual calendar applications that are used by a wide variety of workers via desktop or notebook microcomputers and/or personal digital assistants (PDAs) or other handheld computing devices with personal information management (PIM) capabilities. Group calendar systems enable work-group meetings to be automatically scheduled by simultaneously accessing the calendars of each of the individual group members online. If only two members of a work group need to meet to coordinate their activities, one of them can consult the other's appointment calendar online to identify a common time when both are available for a meeting. The electronic calendar system can then schedule the meeting for each participant. Today, these systems also send electronic messages to group members, notifying them of changes that have been made to their appointment calendars.

> *Electronic filing cabinets*. E-mail and other machine-readable documents can be stored in disk folders that are equivalent to file folders in conventional filing cabinets. Messages and documents in the folder can later be retrieved, modified, or deleted. Most filing systems maintain an index of the folders and their contents.

> *Project management software*. Project management software assists in planning projects and allocating resources. Microsoft Project is a widely used example. Such software helps project managers and team members agree on task parameters, updates the progress of individual team members, and monitors the progress of the entire project. As a result, project management software can play an important role in helping project teams complete their work on time and within budget.

> *Group support systems*. Group support systems (GSSs) assist individuals and groups in the decision-making process and help them set objectives. GSSs vary in complexity and sophistication. A low-end GSS essentially serves as a bulletin board for the exchange and development of ideas. Higher-level GSSs include a variety of decision support tools to assist the group in consensus building and decision making. Web-based GSSs have also emerged to facilitate the collaboration of group members, even when they are scattered across the globe.

> *Electronic meeting systems and videoconferencing*. The evolution of networking and telecommunication systems has made it possible for groups to meet electronically as

groupware Work-group productivity tools that allow a group of users to communicate and to coordinate activities; software that supports multiple users working on related tasks.

well as face-to-face. One of the first electronic conferencing systems was audio conferencing—better known as a "conference call"—which enabled three or more individuals to simultaneously participate in a telephone conversation. Computer conferencing systems and electronic meeting systems enable two or more participants to exchange machine-readable information in the form of graphics, text, audio, and full-motion video in real time. Videoconferencing systems, which enable meeting participants to see and hear each other in real time, have emerged as one of the most important types of electronic meeting systems found in today's organizations. Desktop-to-desktop videoconferencing systems are expected to become increasingly common in business organizations in the years ahead; they are also expected to play an increasingly important role in supporting telecommuters.

➤ *Document management systems.* Electronic document management systems (sometimes called image processing systems) help an organization manage and control its documents. Capabilities include indexing documents, finding documents based on keywords contained in the document, document routing, controlling document changes, and allowing several users to collaborate on document editing. Organizations that are interested in significantly reducing paper processing and moving toward "paperless offices" have implemented document management systems.

Knowledge Management   Many organizations have realized that one of the keys to sustainable competitive advantage in today's global marketplace lies in their ability to acquire, disseminate, and retain expertise and knowledge, especially knowledge related to customers, products, and services. In many organizations, intranets and groupware have played an important role in quickly disseminating newly acquired information and knowledge; hence, these networking technologies are often cornerstones in the information infrastructure that organizations have created to support knowledge management and organizational learning systems.

Electronic Commerce and Electronic Business   Since the opening of the Internet to commercial purposes during the early 1990s, businesses have moved rapidly to build the infrastructures needed to support Internet-based commerce. For most large business organizations, a Web strategy has become a competitive necessity. Industry experts predict that the total amount of commerce conducted over the Internet may exceed $8 trillion by 2005 and that business-to-business (B2B) e-commerce will account for at least 75 percent of the total. Interorganizational systems, which are built on electronic links between two or more companies, and extranets (Web-based interorganizational links) are the foundation of B2B e-commerce. To date, electronic data interchange (EDI) has been the most widely practiced form of B2B e-commerce, but other forms of e-business such as electronic marketplaces are rapidly emerging. Businesses have also developed the capabilities needed to allow consumers to order products and services and conduct other business transactions over the Internet. These applications are known as business-to-consumer (B2C) e-commerce and, like B2B e-commerce, the total dollar volume of these transactions is growing rapidly because of the dramatic increases in the number of households with Internet access in developed countries around the world. Because of the importance of electronic commerce and electronic business, Internet-based business is the primary focus of Chapter 3.

Wireless Applications   Wireless data communication applications are the wave of the future. Companies are already developing mobile commerce (m-commerce) applications to enable employees and consumers to conduct business transactions via handheld computing devices and Internet-ready digital cellular phones. Programmers with wireless application protocol (WAP) skills are in hot demand; WAP enables the content of an organization's Web site to be displayed on the small screen of a PDA or Internet-ready cell phone. Wireless applications are expected to explode in the United States during the first decade of the new century. They already have a strong foothold in northern Europe and Australia.

Other Data Communication Applications   There are several other broad classes of data communication applications: batch, data entry, distributed, inquiry/response, interactive, and sensor based. Note that the classes are not mutually exclusive; some business transactions may fall into more than one class.

➤ *Batch applications.* Batch applications, including remote job entry, are characterized by large data transfers in two directions. For example, information from a batch of inventory cards might be transferred from a warehouse to a remote computer center, and in return the warehouse would receive an updated inventory list. In some batch applications, large amounts of data flow in one direction only. When a sales representative records sales on a portable microcomputer but waits until the end of the workday to transmit the entire day's orders, a large amount of data flows in one direction, and little or no data flows in the other direction.

➤ *Data entry applications.* Data entry applications consist of lengthy inputs with short responses. In a credit authorization system in Australia, input for a batch of receipts consists of a credit card number, merchant number, and charge amount, plus the batch total. The system then calculates its own batch total and compares it with the input total; if the figures agree, the only response is a prompt to continue entering the next batch.

➤ *Distributed applications.* Distributed applications are characterized not so much by input and output size as by whether data or processing or both are distributed among several network nodes. Thus, requests as well as data flow between several network components, with possibly some parallelism in data access and processing. Order entry is an example of this type of processing. When an order for an item is entered, the system tries to determine whether the item is in stock in any of its several regionally located warehouses. Because each warehouse has a computer system and maintains its local inventory, the system inquires into these remote databases to find a location with enough stock to fill the order. The system then updates the inventory at the location(s) from which the order is to be filled, updates the invoicing and accounts receivable at the accounting location, and supplies the ordering location with a shipment date and other relevant data. Client/server computing is an example of a distributed processing application architecture.

➤ *Inquiry/response applications.* In inquiry/response applications, inputs generally have only a few characters, and output responses have many. Inquiry/response applications involve requests to display information. For example, a police inquiry might consist of a driver's license number, and the response could be several thousand characters of information detailing the driver's name, address, driving record, and so on. In a hospital application, a nurse might enter the nurse's station number (a few characters), and the output would probably consist of several thousand characters giving each patient's name, status, medical requirements, and so on.

➤ *Interactive applications.* An interactive application is characterized by short inputs and outputs. The computer system prompts the user for an input, eliciting a short response. Because the sender and receiver are essentially conversing with each other, this application is sometimes called conversational. Interactive applications are often used for online transaction processing with terminals that cannot locally store an entire screen full of information. Applications in which the user's response dictates the next prompt, such as certain computerized games, are also interactive.

➤ *Sensor-based applications.* Sensor-based applications involve special data collection devices for such uses as controlling temperature in buildings, monitoring and maintaining patient condition in hospitals, and controlling manufacturing processes. The processor receives data from the sensors and, if necessary, takes control action.

➤ *Combined applications.* A server in a network may support more than one type of activity. For example, it might support batch-processing applications as well as one or more types of online applications.

Application Service Providers   Many business organizations are turning to third-party services for some or all of their business and data communications applications. Today, many business managers feel that outsourcing services provides the best opportunity to gain access to scarce expertise and state-of-the-art applications that would be difficult or impossible to develop within their own firms. **Application service providers (ASPs)** are third-party organizations that manage and distribute software and services to other companies over the Web. Oracle Corporation, for example, rents many of its applications through its Business OnLine hosting service as well as through ASP partners. Many ASPs specialize in integrated e-commerce and e-business applications such as customer relationship management systems (CRMs) and enterprise resources planning systems (ERPs). By utilizing ASPs to gain access to such applications, businesses avoid the expense and implementation challenges associated with adding these applications to their own internal networking and computing infrastructures. Industry experts expect ASPs to become increasingly common in the years ahead.

> **application service provider (ASP)** An organization that hosts software applications on its own servers; customers rent the use of the application and access it over the Internet or via private line connections. An ASP may also be called a "commercial service provider."

BUSINESS DATA COMMUNICATIONS ISSUES

It should be clear from the foregoing discussion that businesses and other organizations are using their computer networks to support an increasing number and variety of applications. One result of this trend is the need for businesses to monitor and address a number of business data communications issues. Some of the major ones are introduced here.

Cost-Effectiveness

The primary business reason for implementing and developing a network is cost-effectiveness. The ability to share resources has a direct impact on an organization's expenses. If users can share hardware, less hardware is needed. If a network is only used for resource sharing, it is more cost-effective than a non-networked computing environment only when the cost of installing and operating the network is less expensive than the hardware, software, data preparation, and support costs for the non-networked environment. Less obviously, cost-effectiveness may derive from the ability of users to communicate and thus improve their productivity. One direct benefit is the reduction of paperwork. Electronic data exchange is one of the applications that is helping to convert paper-based offices to electronic offices.

The Internet

A commonly voiced sentiment in business circles is "The Internet is changing everything." The Internet is rapidly becoming the network of choice for conducting electronic commerce, communicating with customers, and coordinating business activities with suppliers. Designing, maintaining, and developing the organization's Web site and the networking infrastructure needed to support it has become a dominant information services responsibility in most business organizations. The Internet has resulted in the emergence of new business models as well as fundamental changes in how organizations conduct business.

CHAPTER 1 Introduction to Data Communications **31**

Bandwidth

Bandwidth refers to the capacity of the links and circuits connecting network nodes. Bandwidth usually plays an important role in network performance, including response times and throughput. It is also an important determinant of how rapidly large files and messages (such as those needed to send video, audio, images, and multimedia) can be transmitted among network nodes. Several of the business data communication applications described previously are often classified as "bandwidth-hungry" applications. These include electronic meeting and videoconferencing applications, document management systems, and Web-based group support systems. Bandwidth is also an important electronic commerce issue. A number of industry experts contend that B2C e-commerce would be increasing more rapidly if more consumers were not constrained by slow Internet connection speeds resulting from the limited bandwidth of numerous "last-mile" connections.

Evolving Technologies

Networking and data communication technologies are evolving rapidly. Data communication hardware and software manufacturers continue to pump out new and improved products. Common carriers, CAPs, and CLECs are also racing to roll out new data communication services for businesses and consumers. The upshot of this is that many organizations are continually faced with the challenges associated with monitoring and evaluating new technologies, services, and applications in order to determine if they should be incorporated into their network and computing architectures. Assimilation challenges must be addressed for the new technologies that organizations choose to pursue.

Convergence

In the area of data communications, **convergence** usually refers to the blending of communications and computing technologies. Internet-ready digital cell phones and personal digital assistants that have wireless e-mail and facsimile capabilities are among the best examples of convergence. Other examples of convergence identified previously in this chapter include computer-telephony integration (CTI), desktop-to-desktop videoconferencing, and group support systems (GSSs). WebTV and DirectPC are other examples of the convergence of computing and telecommunications technologies.

Standards

Standards play a key role in data communications. Without standards, data communication would be nearly impossible and end-to-end transmissions might only be possible over customized, single-vendor networks. The development of internationally recognized data communication standards facilitates the manufacture and implementation of interoperable network technologies. Such standards generally work to the advantage of data communication consumers because they stimulate competition among data communication technology manufacturers to develop competing products that should interoperate with existing networking technologies.

There are numerous standard-setting organizations whose activities and decisions impact data communication vendors and consumers. Some of the most widely known and officially sanctioned data communications standard-setting organizations are listed in Table 1-5. It is important to note, however, that there are a variety of other groups that are involved in developing standards for specific parts of the data communications industry. These include task forces, user groups, interest groups, forums, consortiums, institutes, and vendor alliances. For example, the Internet Engineering Task Force (IETF) is responsible for establishing standards and approving new protocols for the

bandwidth
Bandwidth is a measure of the amount of data that can be transmitted per unit of time. The greater the bandwidth is, the higher the possible data transmission rate is. On analog circuits, bandwidth is the difference between the minimum and the maximum frequencies allowed. On digital circuits, bandwidth is measured in bits per second (bps).

convergence In data communications, convergence refers to the blending of communications and computing technologies.

Table 1-5   Examples of Data Communications Standard-Setting Organizations

Abbreviation	Full Name	Types/Examples of Standards
ISO	International Standards Organization	Open system interconnection (OSI) reference model; OSI protocols.
CCITT	Comite Consultif International Telegraphique and Telephonique	Facsimile and modem standards (V.xx standards).
ITU	International Telecommunications Union	Modem, facsimile, and videoconferencing standards. The ITU is now the parent organization to the CCITT.
IEEE	Institute of Electrical and Electronics Engineers	802.x local area network standards, including those for Ethernet and token ring LANs.
EIA	Electronics Industries Association	Electrical signaling (e.g., RS232) and wiring standards.
NIST	National Institute of Standards and Technology	Encryption standards.

Internet. Similarly, the ATM Forum plays a key role in developing standards for asynchronous transfer mode (ATM) technologies.

We will be mentioning many standards throughout this book because these are an important aspect of numerous networking technologies and the context in which they are used. In many instances, it will be important for you to master the major distinctions among relevant standards.

Privacy and Security

The proliferation of networks in today's organizations presents a wide range of privacy and security concerns. Although networks facilitate access to business data and thus contribute to increases in employee productivity, they also open the door to hackers and unauthorized users who might want to use the data for their own purposes. Though a number of laws have been passed to dissuade unauthorized individuals from attempting to steal, change, or delete sensitive data, these are not enough. As a result, businesses are going to great lengths to protect the privacy of their data and to ensure the integrity of their networks. An increasing number of organizations are utilizing firewalls to inhibit unauthorized users from gaining access to data and other computing resources via the Internet. Encryption is widely used in today's networks to protect the integrity of transmitted data. Digital signatures are also being required in an increasing number of applications to authenticate user identity. Because of its importance, network security is a primary focus of Chapter 16.

BUSINESS DATA COMMUNICATIONS CAREERS

Given the importance of networks and data communications in today's business organizations, it should come as no surprise that there are numerous job opportunities for individuals who are interested in this field. Organizations often recruit university students majoring in computer science, computer information systems, and computer engineering for their networking and data communications positions. They also recruit technical college or institute graduates who have acquired the networking and data communications technical skills that they are seeking. As is the case for most IT professions, the demand for appropriately skilled networking and data communication professionals exceeds the supply, and there is nothing to indicate that this will change anytime in the near future.

Table 1-6 summarizes some of the major occupational titles associated with networking and data communications. Although the list of job opportunities is much broader than this, Table 1-6 should help you appreciate just how extensive this field is.

Network professionals and individuals who aspire to be network professionals often turn to certification programs as a means to authenticate and validate the technical skills they possess or to obtain the skills needed for a specific networking job. A wide range of networking and data communication certifications exists. Most certifications are sponsored by data communication and networking product vendors; others are sponsored by networking professional associations. A few, like the certified network professional (CNP), can only be pursued by individuals who already hold one or more

Table 1-6   Examples of Data Communication Job Titles and Niche Expertise Areas

Data Communication Job Titles (Examples)	Niche Expertise Areas (Examples)
Network Administrator/Manager	E-mail/communications analyst
Network Analyst	WAP developer/consultant
Call Center/Help Desk Manager/Technician	Disaster recovery consultant
LAN Manager	Cisco router specialist
Voice Communications Manager	ASP application engineer
Data Communications Systems Engineer	Computer telephony integration consultant
Java Developer	Storage area network designer/engineer
Network Engineer	SS7 voice engineer
Network Operations Technician/Engineer	RF engineer
WAN Systems Architect	Capacity planning analyst
Network Technical Support Specialist	Technical implementation consultant
WAN Engineer	Webcasting/streaming media developer
Client Systems Specialist	Telecommunications business consultant
EDI Applications Developer	Voice response system developer
Network Security Specialist/Engineer	Lotus Notes/domino developer
Infrastructure Manager	Network integrator
LAN Support Specialist	Network validation tester
Network Designer	CGI/Perl/Javascript developer
Webmaster	NT systems engineer
Web Site Designer	PBX consultant
Web Site Engineer/Developer	Network security consultant
Network Security Engineer	Solaris administrator/engineer
Telecommunications Systems Designer	Switch technician/engineer
E-Business/Internet Security Manager	WAN network design consultant
Telephony Analyst	IP network engineer
Desktop/PC Support Specialist	Optical networks engineer
UNIX Systems Administrator	VPN specialist

Table 1-7   Examples of Networking Certifications

Abbreviation	Certification Title	Vendor/Sponsor
MCSE	Microsoft Certified Systems Engineer	Microsoft
CNE	Certified Novell Engineer	Novell
ASE	Accredited System Engineer	Compaq
CCIE	Cisco Certified Internetwork Expert	Cisco
CWD	Certified Web Designer	Association of Web Professionals
Network+	Network+	CompTIA
CTE	Computer Telephony Engineer	Computer Telephony Institute, Inc.
CNX	Certified Network Expert	CNX Consortium
CNP	Certified Network Professional	Network Professional Association

vendor-specific certifications and require continuing education after the certification is earned. Table 1-7 provides a sampling of the networking-oriented certifications that individuals may pursue.

SUMMARY

Data communication is the electronic transmission of computer-readable data including text, graphics, image, sound, and video. The Internet has underscored the need to master data communication and networking concepts. For two networked devices to communicate, four essential elements must be present: a message, a sender, a receiver, and a communication medium. Received messages should be understandable, and communication systems should include mechanisms for ensuring that messages have not been altered during the transmission process.

Essential features of data communication networks include nodes, links and circuits, packetizing, routing, store-and-forward capabilities, and topology and architecture. Networks vary in complexity; some are small and relatively simple, although others, such as the Internet, are very complex because of the number of components they include and the variety of applications that they support.

Two important data communication frameworks have been developed: the OSI reference model and the TCP/IP protocol suite. The OSI reference model describes seven functional layers: application, presentation, session, transport, network, data link, and physical for moving data from an application in one network node to an application in another node. Many standards have been developed based on the OSI reference model. The key to the model is that the interfaces and protocols are open to all, and networks designed around the model and standards can be more easily interconnected. The TCP/IP protocol suite is a five-layer model that is focused on Internet protocols and operations. The emergence of the Internet as a vehicle for commerce has made the TCP/IP protocol suite the second important data communication framework for understanding today's business networks.

The data communication industry has experienced tremendous expansion over the last 3 decades. Several court cases and laws increased competition within this industry, and as a result, businesses have benefited from lower prices for both equipment and transmission media.

Some of the major applications supported on today's business networks and data communication systems are electronic mail, voice applications, groupware, videoconferencing, document management systems, knowledge management, and Internet-based electronic commerce/business applications. The proliferation of networks in business organizations demands that they address a number of issues including network cost-effectiveness, the impact of the Internet, bandwidth, convergence, the assimilation of evolving technologies, data communication standards, data privacy, and network security. The proliferation of networks has also increased employment and professional certification options for individuals who are interested in careers in data communications.

KEY TERMS

- application service provider (ASP)
- bandwidth
- circuit
- convergence
- data communications
- groupware
- International Standards Organization (ISO)
- link
- medium
- network
- network architecture
- network topology
- node
- open architecture
- Open Systems Interconnection (OSI) reference model
- packetizing
- path
- remote job entry (RJE)
- routing
- session
- store-and-forward system
- Transmission Control Protocol/Internet Protocol (TCP/IP) suite
- virtual circuit

REVIEW QUESTIONS

1. What is the distinction between telecommunication and data communications?
2. How has the Internet affected business data communications?
3. Identify and briefly describe each of the essential features of communications.
4. Briefly describe the distinctions among the following types of messages: file, request, response, status, control, and correspondence.
5. Identify and briefly describe each of the essential features of networks.
6. What is meant by network complexity?
7. What are the distinctions between network topology and network architecture?
8. List the seven layers of the OSI reference model.
9. List two functions of each layer in the OSI reference model.
10. List the five layers of the TCP/IP protocol suite.
11. List key protocols found at each of the following TCP/IP layers: application, transport, and Internet.
12. Explain the significance of each of the following in the history of business data communications:
   a. the Hush-a-Phone decision
   b. the Carterphone decision
   c. MCI
   d. the Internet and World Wide Web
   e. the Telecommunications Reform Act of 1996
   f. *A Framework for Global Electronic Commerce*
13. Briefly describe each of the following kinds of business data communications applications: e-mail, voice applications, knowledge management, e-commerce, e-business, and wireless applications.
14. Identify and briefly describe each of the major kinds of groupware applications.

15. Characterize each of the following kinds of network applications:
    a. interactive
    b. inquiry/response
    c. batch
    d. data entry
    e. distributed
    f. sensor based
16. Identify and briefly describe each of the major data communications issues.
17. Why are standards important in business data communications? Identify several standard-setting organizations and the kinds of standards developed by each.
18. Identify several examples of data communication job titles. Identify several niche expertise areas within data communications.
19. Why do some networking professionals obtain network certifications? What kinds of certifications can networking professionals pursue?

PROBLEMS AND EXERCISES

1. How does the history of data communication differ from that of database development?
2. Use online sources to investigate two data communication applications. Specifically note hardware requirements. Determine the categories of data communication into which each of the applications falls.
3. Select a specific data communication application, and identify the functions that would be required in the application, presentation, and session layers of the OSI reference model.
4. Discuss the history of telephone companies in the United States (or your home country) as that history relates to the data communication industry.
5. How do U.S. telephone companies differ from their counterparts in Great Britain, France, Germany, Japan, and Australia? In what respects are they the same?
6. How might data communication systems be used in the home?
7. Visit the main Web site for federal documents on electronic commerce (www. ecommerce.gov). Identify two of the most recently posted documents. Read and briefly summarize the executive summary/overview of each.
8. Visit the Web sites of three of the standard-setting organizations listed in Table 1-5. Identify the major standards approved by each during the last 12 months.
9. Identify what is required to obtain the MCSE certification as well as one other certification listed in Table 1-7. (*Hint:* Identify and peruse appropriate Web sites for this information.)

Chapter Cases
Networks and Productivity

During the last decade, we heard about the importance of information technology (IT) in a company's performance. We all know that IT, when properly applied, can be used to increase productivity, reduce costs, and increase sales. We might have been using this argument to convince management to increase IT budgets. However, senior management is becoming more skeptical about the real benefits of IT investments and is demanding tangible proof of how investments increase productivity. Some firms like McKinsey & Co., Forrester Research, NOP World Technology, and *InternetWeek* have been conducting studies aimed at finding the relationship between IT and productivity.

According to a report prepared by the consulting firm McKinsey, IT investment does not affect productivity. Even more, IT and productivity are unrelated. To evaluate the relationship between IT and productivity, McKinsey analyzed 59 economic sectors. From all these 59 sectors, 53 showed that IT investments had no impact on the company's productivity.

However, some industry analysts affirm that the McKinsey report should not be used as the definitive answer to questions about the effects of IT on productivity. In fact, many industry analysts assert that a positive IT–productivity relationship exists. Although the effects of IT on productivity may not be evident across an entire economic sector, as found by the McKinsey study, IT applications are often associated with specific productivity gains observed within companies.

Forrester Research, a technology research company, made a study about productivity gains associated with Internet-based applications. According to this study, e-business will produce a 15-percent productivity increase to the economy beginning in 2004. The research also identifies some specific cases in which IT is improving productivity; for example, business-to-business (B2B) standards are increasing and simplifying access to global partners, which is generating more competition and bringing new efficiencies into markets.

NOP World Technology, a Cisco-sponsored firm, performed a study to assess the impact of wireless LANs on productivity. The information revealed an increment in employee productivity, cost savings, and other gains achieved by users and IT network administrators in their sample of more than 300 U.S. organizations that have implemented wireless LANs. Wireless LANs allowed users to stay connected 15 to 45 minutes more each day and get accurate information when needed, thereby increasing their productivity by as much as 22 percent. Moreover, the study found that wireless networking had a measurable impact on return on investment (ROI), with organizations saving an average of $164,000 annually on cabling costs and labor.

InternetWeek conducted a survey of 1,000 IT and corporate managers in order to examine the returns on e-business. The respondents said their companies' Internet investments have improved worker productivity, increased revenue, and lowered costs. Managers also realized that the level of IT success depends on the kinds of projects it was applied to. For example, almost half of the respondents said intranets have produced tangible returns, and a third said investments in selling online to consumers are also generating returns. Other benefits that IT managers consider valuable are the strengthening of communication with partners, superior customer service, awareness of customers' preferences, and greater market share. However, less than one-fifth of the managers said extranets, electronic supply chains, electronic payment systems, and electronic marketplaces, among others, have produced financial returns. Furthermore, few say their company is seeing improvements in project development, teamwork procedures, organization structure, or timely project completion.

On core business processes, the Internet's impact also varies. For example, 82 percent of the IT managers say the Internet has improved their marketing process; 74 percent say the Internet has improved their customer service; 66 percent see an improvement in purchasing and procurement, and 65 percent see an increase in sales.

Finally, *InternetWeek*'s survey also shows that only one-third of the managers surveyed have a formal ROI model for Internet investments. Some IT managers are unwilling to quantify e-business ROI because they believe related revenue is difficult to predict. Costs are also hard to quantify because many of the infrastructure investments are also used by other non-Internet projects.

Despite all the differences among the reports from McKinsey, Forrester, NOP World, and *Internet-Week,* one thing is true: There is mounting evidence that Internet-based technologies are starting to deliver on promises to improve a company's productivity, efficiency, and tangible financial returns. Whether such returns will translate into productivity gains across entire economic sectors, however, is still open to debate.

CASE QUESTIONS

1. How are advocates for and against increased IT and networking budgets within a company likely to use the conflicting research data on IT and productivity to support their positions?
2. Why may it be easier to assess the impacts of internal IT applications (such as intranets) on productivity than it is to assess the impacts of interorganizational systems (such as extranets and electronic supply chains) on productivity?
3. Some industry experts assert that networking professionals must be able to justify proposed capital investments in IT and networking infrastructure by using terms and language understood by business managers rather than relying on the technical merits of proposed systems. How is this illustrated in the case?
4. It is typically more difficult for network managers to assess the productivity impacts of new data communication technologies (such as Internet-ready cell phones) than those of more mature technologies (such as enhanced e-mail systems)? Does this mean that organizations should avoid investing in new data communication technologies until there is proof that they can improve productivity? Why or why not?

SOURCES

Halligan, Tom. "Productivity Gains." *Internet World* (January 2002, Vol. 8, Issue 1, p. 4).

Keen, Peter G. W. "Wireless Productivity." *Computerworld* (November 13, 2000, p. 60).

Strassmann, Paul. "Fighting McKinsey." *Computerworld* (December 3, 2001, p. 27).

Violino, Bob. "The Search for E-Business Returns." *InternetWeek* (October 15, 2001, pp. 9–13).

Note: For more information on data communications, see an additional case on the Web site, www.prenhall.com/stamper, "Instant Messaging: The Next Global Communications Network?"

Introduction to the Internet

After studying this chapter, you should be able to:

- ■ Distinguish between an internet, the Internet, and an intranet.
- ■ Trace the history of the Internet.
- ■ Identify and briefly describe important Internet technologies.
- ■ Describe the distinctions between the Internet and the World Wide Web.
- ■ Identify and briefly describe key World Wide Web technologies.
- ■ Identify and briefly describe key TCP/IP protocols.
- ■ Identify and briefly describe the major text-based Internet services.
- ■ Describe different ways of gaining access to the Internet.
- ■ Discuss the role of ISPs in Internet access.

WHAT IS THE INTERNET?

If you read articles relating to Internet technology, three terms will probably surface: an internet, the Internet, and an intranet. Let us begin by defining these terms, beginning with the word internet. The term *internet* is used in two contexts. As you progress through this book, you will learn that there are different kinds of data communication networks, two of which are LANs and WANs; furthermore, a single company may have several LANs and a WAN. When this is the case, it is typical that the various networks are combined or interconnected to form a single company-wide network or internet. In this context, an **internet** is the interconnection of two or more networks. Within a company, an internet is a group of networks that are interconnected in a manner that makes them appear to users as one continuous large network. Sometimes a company's internet is called an enterprise network. The nodes in an internet can be addressed seamlessly at the Network layer of the OSI model through routers.

The **Internet** (with a capital I) is a specific collection of interconnected networks reaching all but a handful of countries throughout the world. The evolution

internet A large network made up of a number of smaller networks in a manner that makes them appear to be one continuous network.

Internet A "network of networks" linking commercial, academic, and government computers in more than 100 countries.

39

of Internet-ready wireless phones and PDAs will soon enable all countries to have Internet access. The Internet, or simply the Net, is a public network in the sense that private individuals are able to gain access to it and use its resources in a variety of ways. With today's technology, users typically "surf" the Internet using a software tool called a browser. A **browser** is a program that allows you to contact a location on the Internet, access data there, and follow hypertext links to other information. The most common browsers in use today are Netscape's *Navigator* and Microsoft's *Internet Explorer*. Figure 2-1 shows a browser screen. However, other software interfaces can also be used. Some of these are yesterday's technologies that are still viable, and others are emerging technologies such as the browsers for Internet-ready wireless telephones and PDAs. Today, these other interfaces would be used primarily by Internet nodes that do not have the processing power to support a browser; on nodes for which a browser has not yet been implemented; or, in the case of the newer wireless Internet access technologies, by users wanting to take advantage of new capabilities.

Hypertext is data that contains a link to other data. For example, suppose this were a hypertext document. When you read the term WAN in the previous paragraph, you might have wondered what a WAN was or wanted more information about it. Further information might be in this text or in another document, which could be located anywhere. In this book, you would probably consult the index, find the pages, go to those pages, and read the information. Then, you might want to follow another link there or return to this paragraph. In this case, you would have had to remember where you were before you followed the link. In a hypertext document, the presence of a link is indicated by some kind of formatting, and with a browser you could simply use a pointing device such as a mouse to point to the link and click. Immediately, you are transferred to the reference, which on the Internet could be on the node you are

browser A program that allows a user to navigate the Internet using hypertext links. A browser supports one or more Internet protocols, such as HTML.

hypertext Text in a document that contains links to other documents or text.

Figure 2-1   An Example of a Browser Screen

accessing or on another node that is halfway around the world. Later, you could click on a button and go back to previous pages or to the original page.

Browsers are powerful yet simple to use. They are largely responsible for the large-scale use of the Internet by nontechnical users (some of the older tools have interfaces with the Internet that are more easily mastered by computer professionals). Recognizing the ease with which information can be developed and accessed using Internet browsers and protocols, some businesses have begun using Internet technologies on their private networks. A private network that uses Internet technologies such as browsers and hypertext is called an **intranet**. Using an intranet, a company can make corporate information such as employee handbooks, price lists, and product information readily available to all users. Moreover, this information can be disseminated without large amounts of paper, and the information can be kept current by updating it in only one location. Many companies developed sophisticated intranets and use them to facilitate communication among work team members, for knowledge management, and for various e-commerce applications including customer relationship management systems.

Now that you know the similarities and differences among internets, the Internet, and intranets, let us assist you in furthering your understanding of the Internet by reviewing its history.

intranet A private network that uses Internet technology such as hypertext documents and Internet protocols to store and retrieve data. Usually located within an organization's firewalls, an intranet is not accessible by the general public.

INTERNET HISTORY

The Internet began as a concept in 1964 when the Rand Corporation introduced the idea of a **packet-switching network (PSN)**. A PSN divides a message into variable- or fixed-size packets and routes them to the destination. Because each packet contains overhead information about its intended destination, the individual packets that constitute a complete message may take different routes through the network as they make their way from sender to receiver. This means that they may arrive at their intended destination out of order. The receiving node is responsible for placing the packets in the proper order and for ensuring that all packets have been received (see X.25 networks in Chapter 8).

The physical implementation of the Internet began in 1969 as a 4-node network called the ARPAnet. The **ARPAnet** was named for and sponsored by the U.S. Defense Department's Advanced Research Projects Agency (ARPA). ARPA's goal was to build a network that (1) would allow researchers at different locations to share files and collaborate on military and scientific projects and (2) would continue to function even if parts of it were disabled or destroyed by warfare or a natural disaster. That is, if a portion of the network was lost because of a bomb or sabotage, other parts could continue to operate, and packets would be rerouted around the inaccessible portions of the network. Because a PSN has these characteristics, packet-switching concepts have played a significant role in the evolution of the Internet.

The original ARPAnet was a WAN connecting four main computers, one each at UCLA, University of California–Santa Barbara, the University of Utah, and the Stanford Research Institute. Researchers and others soon realized the benefits of using ARPAnet to share files and exchange electronic mail. As a result, the network continued to grow, and by 1984 over 1,000 host computers were connected.

During the Internet's early years, it was used as a communication medium for the military as well as for researchers, many of whom were involved in defense-related projects. The early Internet nodes were located in military organizations, research organizations, and colleges and universities, most of which were in North America and

packet-switching network (PSN) A networking technology used in WANs that breaks a message into smaller packets for transmission and that uses switches to get them to their required destination.

ARPAnet A packet-switching network implemented by the U.S. Defense Department's Advanced Research Projects Agency. The ARPAnet evolved into the Internet.

MILNET Military network. A U.S. Defense Department network that was once a key subnet on the Internet. MILNET is no longer an Internet subnet.

NSFnet National Science Foundation's network of supercomputer centers.

backbone A high-speed network that other networks can connect to.

Europe. The military portion of the Internet was named **MILNET**; however, in 1983 MILNET was taken off the Internet.

Other significant events in the history of the Internet occurred in 1983. On January 1, 1983, TCP/IP was officially deployed as the standard host protocol for ARPAnet. As of that day, all hosts were required to use TCP/IP to transfer data over ARPAnet.

In 1984, ARPAnet was shut down, but the remaining nodes and subnets continued to function. During the 1980s, several regional networks, such as BITNET and CSNET, joined the Internet. In 1986, the National Science Foundation (NSF) connected its huge network of five supercomputer centers, called **NSFnet**, to the network; once this happened, the resulting configuration of complex networks and hosts came to be known as the Internet. In 1987, the National Science Foundation assumed the responsibility for managing the backbone network and for administration of addresses and policy. NSF formed the NSFnet Network Service Center (NNSC) to carry out Internet management, and the NNSC became the single point of contact for Internet information.

Because of its advanced technology, NSFnet served as the major backbone network on the Internet until 1995. A **backbone** is a high-speed network that other networks can connect to. As the Internet's backbone, NSFnet handled the bulk of the communications activity between the networks that were attached to it. By 1989, over 80,000 hosts were interconnected via the Internet backbone. Figure 2-2 illustrates some of the major segments of the Internet backbone within the United States.

In 1993, the NSF replaced the NNSC with the InterNIC (Internet Network Information Center) and distributed the management functions among several companies. Network Solutions, Inc., was given the responsibility for registration services. Registration services are responsible for controlling Internet addresses and domain names. The AT&T Corporation assumed management of the directory and database services. Directory and database services are responsible for maintaining

Figure 2-2   Internet High-Speed Backbone Network

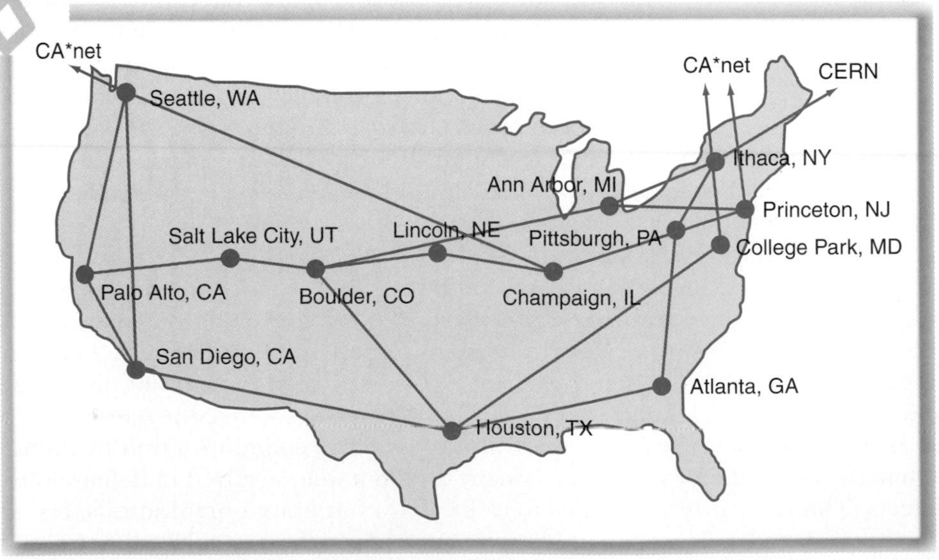

databases of Internet sites, information, and users. In 1995, the NSF quit all direct support of the Internet backbone to return to its original status as a research network. Since that time, a variety of corporations, commercial firms, and other companies have run the Internet's backbone networks and have provided access to networks that want to connect to the Internet. Telephone companies, cable and satellite companies, and the government all contribute to the development of the Internet's internal structure. Many donate resources, such as servers, communication lines, and the technical specialists needed for both the day-to-day operations and future growth of the Internet.

Until the 1990s, business was not conducted on the Internet, and any form of advertising or commercial use was discouraged. Only a few businesses, including America Online and CompuServe, were allowed to use the Internet to enable subscribers to access some of the services they offered; such use of the Internet did not begin until 1989. The U.S. Congress passed legislation in 1990 that opened the Internet to commercial endeavors. In 1991, NSFnet lifted its restrictions on using NSFnet for commercial purposes. In 1992, the first e-commerce applications were available. Needless to say, business use of the Net has grown rapidly.

Since its 4-node inception, the Internet has continued to grow, somewhat slowly at first and then very rapidly in the 1990s. On average, it has more than doubled in size each year since its inception. For example, in 1983 there were fewer than 500 hosts, but a year later, there were more than 1,000. By 1989, there were approximately 80,000, and by 1997 there were approximately 16 million Internet hosts representing all but a few of the countries in the world. By 2000, there were more than 70 million Internet hosts, and the number of Internet hosts eclipsed 100 million in 2001.

In spite of this phenomenal growth, the Internet remains a public, cooperative, and independent network. No single person, government, institution, or company owns the Internet. Several organizations, however, play a key role in the evolution of the Internet by developing recommendations and standards and addressing other issues. Some of these organizations are summarized in Table 2-1.

Much of the rapid growth in the 1990s can be attributed to three factors. First was the creation of the World Wide Web (WWW) in 1989 and browser products that made the Web easily accessible so that many new users could be accommodated. Second, microcomputer technology at low costs resulted in computers becoming a home appliance; this created a much larger market for the services provided by the Internet. Finally, the Internet became a tool for conducting business.

IMPORTANT INTERNET TECHNOLOGIES

To understand how the Internet works, it is important for you to have a fundamental understanding of three key Internet technologies. These are hosts, subnets, and routers.

Hosts

In the early days, all computers attached to the Internet were called hosts. As we discussed in Chapter 1, there was a time when the term *host* referred to a large computer, typically a mainframe or minicomputer that served multiple terminal users. In the early days of the Internet, only hosts with terminals had the power needed to attach to the Internet. During the 1980s and 1990s when microcomputers gained sufficient power to connect directly to the Internet, they too were included in the host category. The term *host* is still used to refer to the Internet's large computers and servers, especially those that function as major repositories of files or applications. Microcomputers

Table 2-1 Key Internet Advisory Groups and Governance Organizations

Abbreviation	Full Name	Role/Function
W3C	World Wide Web Consortium	The W3C is an international industry consortium founded in 1994 to develop common standards for the World Wide Web. Its Web site (www.w3.org) is hosted in the United States by the Laboratory for Computer Science at MIT.
IAB	Internet Architecture Board	The IAB (www.iab.org) is a predominantly volunteer organization that provides architectural guidance to and adjudicates conflicts for the Internet Engineering Task Force (IETF). The IAB is responsible for appointing the IETF chair and all other Internet Engineering Steering Group (IESG) candidates. It also advises the Internet Society (ISOC) on technical and procedural matters.
ICANN	Internet Corporation for Assigned Names and Numbers	ICANN (www.icann.org) is a nonprofit, international association founded in 1998. As the successor to IANA (Internet Assigned Numbers Authority), ICANN manages Internet addresses, domain names, and the huge number of parameters associated with Internet protocols (port numbers, router protocols, and multicast addresses). ICANN also provides a list of accredited registrars that accept domain registrations.
IESG	Internet Engineering Steering Group	The IESG (www.iesg.org) is responsible for the Internet standards-setting process and approves Internet standards specifications. It provides guidance to the IETF.
IETF	Internet Engineering Task Force	The IETF (www.ietf.org) has been in existence since 1986. It is primarily a volunteer organization whose working groups are dedicated to identifying problems and proposing technical solutions for the Internet. With the support of the Internet Society (ISOC), the IETF facilitates transfer of ideas from the Internet Research Task Force (IRTF) to the Internet community. The Internet Architecture Board (IAB) provides architectural guidelines for the IETF, and the Internet Engineering Steering Group (IESG) provides overall direction.
IANA	Internet Assigned Numbers Authority	The IANA (www.iana.org) used to be responsible for managing Internet addresses, domain names, and protocol parameters. It has been superseded by ICANN (Internet Corporation for Assigned Names and Numbers), which was formed in 1998. The IANA was chartered by the Internet Society (ISOC) and Federal Network Council (FNC). Since inception, it has been located at and operated by the Information Sciences Institute at the University of Southern California.
ISOC	Internet Society	The ISOC (www.isoc.org) is an international organization dedicated to extending and enhancing the Internet. Founded in 1992, the ISOC supports Internet bodies such as the IETF and works with governments, organizations, and the general public to promote Internet research, information, and education.

found in business LANs and residences, however, are often called *nodes* instead of hosts in order to differentiate them from servers and other machines that function as repositories for publicly available Web pages, files, and applications. Although some writers continue to use traditional Internet terminology and refer to any computer connected to the Internet as a "host", it has become common for "host" to refer to Internet servers and for microcomputers attached to the Internet to be called *nodes.*

To transmit a message, the sender only has to know the Internet address of the destination host or node (the receiver). The destination's official address is its *IP address,* which consists of four numbers separated by dots (e.g., 128.191.17.15). Every host and node on the Internet must have an IP address, including the microcomputer in your residence. Internet hosts may also have an optional *host name.* This consists of several text labels separated by dots. In Figure 2-3, for example, there is a host name that corresponds to each host; although it is not labeled as such in the figure, the host name for the computer whose IP address is 128.19.17.15 (Host C) is *gsaix2.cc.gasou. edu.* Host names are easier for people to remember than IP addresses.

Figure 2-3 illustrates some other important Internet fundamentals.

➤ First, each network attached to the Internet must contain at least one host.

➤ Second, a network attached to the Internet may be subdivided into smaller segments called *subnets.*

➤ Third, routers are used to send packets across the Internet from one network to another.

Figure 2-3   Key Internet Technologies: Networks, Subnets, Hosts, and Routers

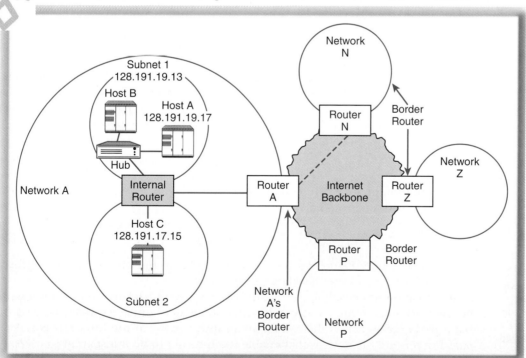

➤ Fourth, an organization may use internal routers to send packets from one subnet to another.

➤ Fifth, there may be multiple additional "hops" within the Internet backbone as messages make their way from one network to another. This is illustrated by the dotted line between Router A and Router N.

Subnets

When a packet arrives at a network, it must be routed to the correct host or node. Organizations with multiple hosts and nodes often choose to subdivide their network into groups of hosts called **subnets**. For example, all of the computers that make up a single LAN are typically included in the same subnet. When an organization's network consists of two or more subnets, there is a 2-step process involved in delivering packets from external senders. The packets must first be routed to the correct subnet; then they can be sent to the destination host or node.

The 2-step delivery process is not as complicated as it may seem because of the way in which IP addresses are composed. Reading from left to right, the first two parts of an IP address identify a host or node's network address; the last two parts uniquely identify the destination host or node's address within the subnet. For example, in Figure 2-3, the IP addresses for all the hosts and nodes in Network A begin with 128.191. Hence, all packets destined for a host or node with an IP address beginning with 128.191 will be delivered to Network A. As illustrated in Figure 2-3, Networks A's two subnets are identified by the third part of the IP address. For example, the router would know that a packet is intended for Subnet 1 if the first three parts of the IP address are 128.191.19; if the first three parts of the destination host's IP address are 128.191.17, the packet would be delivered to Subnet 2. In this example, the fourth part of the IP address uniquely identifies the host or node within the subnet.

It is important to note that in many instances, IP addressing is more complicated than what we have described in this relatively simple example. Because of this, IP addressing is the subject of further explanation in Chapter 4.

Also note that Figure 2-3 best illustrates routing among networks, such as those at many universities, that are directly connected to the Internet. As a result, although it serves as a vehicle for illustrating some important Internet fundamentals, it is not an accurate depiction of all Internet access scenarios. For example, almost all home and business users gain access to the Internet by connecting to an **Internet service provider (ISP)**. Such users generally establish dial-up connections to modems located at the ISP; they are then able to gain access to the Internet through the ISP's routers. This is illustrated in Figure 2-4. When accessing the Internet through an ISP, the computer you are working on is often assigned an IP address by the ISP that is only good for the duration of your connection. Your computer may be assigned a different IP address the next time you dial into the ISP.

Routers

As illustrated in both Figure 2-3 and 2-4, routers play an important role in transferring packets across the Internet backbone from one network to another. **Routers** are data communication devices that are capable of forwarding packets from a computer on one network to computers attached to any other interconnected network. The path that a packet takes across the routers in an internet (or in the Internet) is called its *route*. Routers are the devices that enable the Internet to be transparent to users; that is, they make the Internet look like a single network rather than like the set of interconnected networks that it really is.

subnet A portion of a network. A large network is often subdivided into multiple interconnected but independent segments or domains in order to improve network performance or security.

Internet service provider (ISP) A company that provides Internet connections and services.

router A network interconnection device and associated software that link two or more networks. The networks being linked can be different, but they must use a common routing protocol.

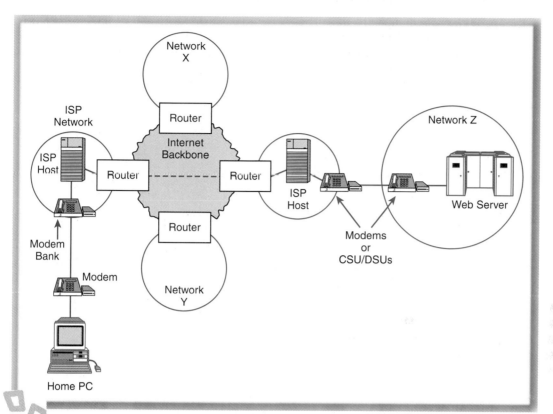

Figure 2-4   The Role of ISPs in Establishing Connections Between Consumers and Business over the Internet

When a user sends large messages (such as large data files) over the Internet, the message is divided into pieces called *packets*. In addition to data, each packet contains the recipient's (destination's) IP address, the sender's IP address, and a sequence number, sequence numbers enable the receiver to rearrange the packets into their appropriate sequence should they arrive at the destination out of order.

Routers read each of the packets they receive and identify the IP address of the destination host or node. The destination address plays the key role in what the router does next. If the destination address is in one of the subnets that it serves, the router delivers the packet to the appropriate subnet. If the destination address is in another network, the router forwards the packet directly to the router that serves that network or to a router located on the network backbone between it and the router that serves the destination network.

Because of their importance, you will be learning more about routers and how they work in several places in this book. The most extensive coverage of routers is found in the chapter on internetworking technologies.

THE WORLD WIDE WEB

Although many people treat the terms *World Wide Web* and *Internet* as interchangeable, it is important to note that the World Wide Web (WWW) is one of many services available on the Internet. As such, it may be described as a subset of the Internet. Although it has only been around for a short time, the World Wide Web (or Web) has grown phenomenally and is now the most widely used Internet service.

A formal definition of the Web, obtained from the *Internet Users' Glossary* compiled by G. Malkin of Xylogics, is as follows:

> A hypertext-based, distributed information system created by researchers at CERN in Switzerland.

In 1989, while working at CERN, the site of the European Laboratory for Particle Physics, Tim Berners-Lee proposed the idea of using distributed hypermedia technology to facilitate the exchange of research findings over the Internet. A prototype of what was to become the World Wide Web was developed at CERN in 1991, along with a command line–oriented browser. By 1992, there were about 200 Web servers in operation. Two years later, *Mosaic*, the first graphically oriented browser, was developed by Marc Andreesen and colleagues at the University of Illinois's National Center for Supercomputing Applications (NCSA). In 1994, Andreesen and James Baker formed Mosaic Communications, which later became Netscape Communications Corporation. By 1995, university students were using *Mosaic* and *Netscape Navigator* daily to surf the Web, and both large and small businesses were beginning to operate Web servers and to engage in commerce over the Web. In 1996, Microsoft demonstrated its desire to have a stake in Web-based commerce with the release of its *Internet Explorer* browser. The combination of these events laid the foundation for the explosive growth of the WWW that has taken place since 1995.

The Web is a superior integration of hardware, software, communication, and information technologies. From the hardware perspective, individuals and businesses can afford platforms necessary for Web access. The significant software capabilities are hypertext linkages and browsers that allow users to access locations and follow the links. The significant communication aspect is that large numbers of businesses, consumers, and users are connected to the Web. The hardware, software, and communication integration gives access to the wealth of text, graphics, video, and audio images that are stored on Web sites.

The Web consists of a worldwide collection of electronic documents that have built-in hyperlinks to other related documents. These hyperlinks allow users to move quickly from one document to another regardless of whether the documents are located on the same host or on hosts in different networks. An electronic document on the Web is called a *Web page,* and each Web page may contain text, graphics, sound, and video in addition to hyperlinks to related Web pages. A collection of related Web pages that can be accessed from the same starting location is often called a *Web site.* Most Web sites have a starting point called a *homepage* that is the Web site's central reference point.

uniform resource locator (URL) A string representation of an Internet address. A URL is the standard address of a Web page on the World Wide Web.

Each Web page at each Web site has a unique address called a **uniform resource locator (URL)**. The URL for the Web page shown in Figure 2-5 is *http://eshop.msn.com/category.asp?catId=584*. Like all URLs, the one in Figure 2-5 consists of a protocol, a domain name, and, if necessary, a path to the specific Web page. The protocol, domain name, and path for the Web page in Figure 2-5 are as follows:

➤ *Protocol:* http:// (Hypertext transfer protocol [HTTP] is the communication protocol used to transfer pages on the Web.)

➤ *Domain name:* eshop.msn.com

➤ *Path:* category.asp?catId=584

Users are able to access a specific Web page when they click on a hyperlink or key in a URL because HTTP translates the URL into the IP address of the host on which

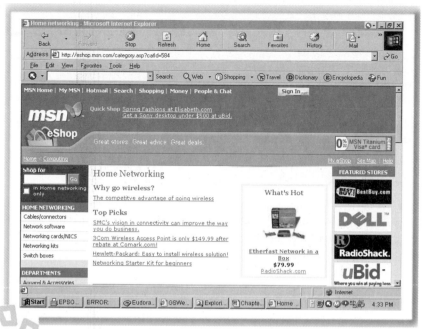

Figure 2-5   Each Web Page Has a Unique Address or
URL (Uniform Resource Locator)

the requested Web page is stored. This information is carried in the domain name. Once the host is contacted, HTTP is able to use the path to access the particular page at that host and transfer it to the user's computer.

The Web has become pervasive. In 2000, the Web was estimated to include at least 2 billion unique Web pages and to be growing at the rate of more than 7 million pages each day. The Web is largely responsible for the dramatic increase that occurred in the 1990s in the number of homes with Internet access in the United States and around the world. It is now commonplace to hear about the World Wide Web (also the Web, WWW, or W3) from television, radio, newspapers, magazines, and so on.

There are a variety of reasons for using the Web, but, for now, we will limit ourselves to four primary reasons.

➤ *Research.* We used to spend extensive time in libraries and had to conform to their hours. Now, we can get the same information and perhaps more current information on the Web whenever we want. However, you should be aware that just because things are published on the Web does not mean that they are true or accurate.

➤ *Communication.* We routinely use e-mail to correspond with associates in distant places and for work-related matters. It is often easier to send e-mail to members of committees than to attempt to contact them individually via telephone or regular mail.

➤ *Business.* We can find low-cost airfares; make airline, car, and hotel reservations; and order merchandise over the Web.

➤ *Downloading files.* We can access a wealth of software and data and download them to our computers, getting instant access to items we think we need. Some of these files are free or available for a nominal cost; some are for examination for a limited time; and some must be purchased. (If the files must be purchased, we must agree to pay by credit card before downloading.)

Other reasons why people use the Web include

➤ Entertainment and news (especially now that streaming audio and video technologies are maturing)

➤ Chatting socially with other Web users

➤ Business (selling rather than buying)

➤ Browsing (just seeing what is out there)

Because the Web has emerged as an important vehicle for commerce, business use of the Internet is the focus of Chapter 3.

KEY WORLD WIDE WEB TECHNOLOGIES

As you progress through this book, you will learn that there are a large number of important Internet and World Wide Web technologies. At this point, we want to briefly highlight three of these: Web servers, browsers, and firewalls.

Web Servers

The Web pages that comprise a Web site are stored on one or more servers called *Web servers*. In some instances, multiple Web sites may be stored on the same server. In the case of large Web sites, one Web server may contain the Web site's homepage while many of the individual pages are stored on other Web servers.

Like any Internet server, a Web server must have the following four components:

➤ An IP address that uniquely identifies the server among all servers attached to the Internet

➤ Hardware that is capable of being connected to the Internet and handling visitor (client) requests

➤ An appropriately sized communications link to the Internet to ensure acceptable performance and responsiveness to Internet user requests for Web pages

➤ Web server software that will run on the server's hardware and operating system

Technically, a Web server is not a hardware platform; it is a software program whose primary purpose is to service HTTP (Hypertext Transfer Protocol) requests. Web servers also perform the following functions:

➤ Determining which users can access particular directories or files stored on the Web server. This is often accomplished through passwords and other user authentication mechanisms.

➤ The execution of scripts (such as CGI scripts) or external programs (such as browser plug-ins) that provide real-time access to databases or add functionality to the Web pages stored on the Web server.

➤ Monitoring and management of Web server functions and Web site content.

➤ Logging user transactions. This information can be valuable in determining which pages at the Web site are most frequently accessed or the kinds of browsers visitors to the Web site are using.

Web server software varies in several ways, including the platform it is designed to run on (such as Linux, NetWare, UNIX, Windows NT, or Windows XP), the number of simultaneous requests it can handle, the sophistication of the access control mechanisms, and whether it is capable of supporting online selling and buying (e-commerce). The most widely used Web server software is listed in Table 2-2. Although this table focuses on the four most widely used Web server software products (Apache, Microsoft, iPlanet, and Zeus), more than 75 different products exist. The pervasive-

Table 2-2   Widely Used Web Server Software

Product Name	Market Share (December 2001) $n = 36,276,252$	Platform(s)
Apache	63.34%	UNIX, Linux
Microsoft	26.62%	Primarily Windows NT, Windows 2000 Server
iPlanet (includes Netscape products)	2.83%	UNIX, Windows NT
Zeus	1.27%	UNIX, Linux, Windows NT

SOURCE: www.netcraft.com

ness of UNIX as the platform of choice on the Internet is underscored by Apache's large market share. Apache can only be installed on hosts running UNIX or Linux.

Server Hardware   In order to ensure an acceptable response time for users that request Web pages stored on the Web server, organizations forecast the amount of traffic the server is expected to handle and choose an appropriately matched hardware configuration. Today, this often translates into the following:

➤ A 1 GHz (or faster) Pentium III, Intel Xeon, DEC Alpha, or MIPS processor.

➤ Multiple high-capacity (20 GB+) hard drives. RAID is often desirable for ensuring fault tolerance. SCSI controllers are often desirable because of their high data transfer rates.

➤ A PCI bus to ensure fast internal transfers among server components.

➤ 256 to 1024 MB of RAM.

➤ Multiple high-speed network interface cards (100 mbps or higher) in order to provide the capability of handling multiple simultaneous requests for Web pages.

Browsers

As noted earlier, the Web is essentially an international collection of multimedia files stored on Web servers. Through the use of URLs, the files are addressed in a consistent manner across Web servers. Internet users are able to access and view these multimedia files by using browsers such as *Netscape Navigator* and Microsoft's *Internet Explorer.* Although a variety of other browsers (such as *Opera*) exist, these two are the most widely used. Some Web sites attempt to capture data on browser use. For example, TheCounter.com and StatMarket.com provide data on Web browser use for their subscribers.

Most browsers have a graphical display and support multimedia—audio, image, and video—in addition to text. Internet users are able to move from file to file by using point-and-click devices (such as a mouse, trackball, or touchpad) to select specially highlighted text (hypertext) or image elements on the browser display. The transfer from one file to another is called a *hyperlink.*

The layout of the browser display is controlled by the **Hypertext Markup Language (HTML)** standard. This standard defines embedded commands in text files

Hypertext Markup Language (HTML) A language used to create documents with hypertext links. HTML was derived from SGML (Standard Generalized Markup Language) and is used to establish links between documents on the World Wide Web.

that specify how the file is displayed by the browser. The embedded commands specify text fonts and colors and their placement on the display. They also specify browser display locations of hyperlinks and their target files. Figure 2-6b shows the HTML code for the HTML document in Figure 2-6a.

Browser plug-ins and helper applications may be needed to display some of the multimedia elements in some Web files. Browser *plug-in* programs enable the browser to display/run a file's multimedia elements within the same browser window. Browser *helper applications* run Web file multimedia elements in a separate browser window. Plug-ins and helper applications can often be downloaded free of charge from Web sites. Examples of popular plug-ins and helper applications are included in Table 2-3.

Some of the multimedia elements found on Web pages are developed in **Java**, a popular programming language originated by Sun Microsystems. Web page developers use Java to create small programs called *applets* that can be downloaded and run in a browser window. ActiveX controls, championed by Microsoft, are similar to applets.

Java A platform-independent programming language used extensively to create World Wide Web applications (sometimes called applets).

Firewalls

Firewalls have emerged as another key World Wide Web application for businesses because of the dangers that are inherent in connecting a corporate network to the Internet. Connecting any network to the Internet increases the network's vulnerability to hackers and other unauthorized users who may wish to access the organization's internal computers for malicious purposes. They may perpetrate *denial of service attacks* that make it virtually impossible for legitimate users to access the organization's Web server by overloading it with simultaneous requests, filling storage to overcapacity, and causing server crashes. Hackers may also leverage the Internet to create accounts

Figure 2-6a   HTML Document

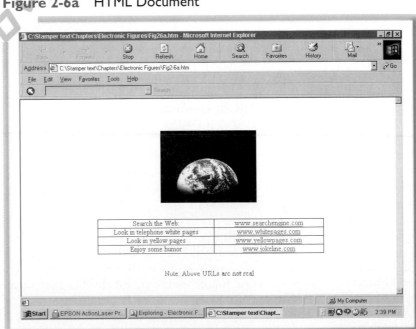

```
<HEAD>
<META HTTP-EQUIV="Content-Type" CONTENT="text/html;
charset=windows-1252">
<META NAME="Generator" CONTENT="Microsoft Word 97">
<META NAME="Template" CONTENT="C:\PROGRAM FILES\MICROSOFT
  OFFICE\OFFICE\html.dot">
</HEAD>

<IMG SRC="Image3.gif" WIDTH=299 HEIGHT=131>
<CENTER><TABLE BORDER CELLSPACING=1 CELLPADDING=7 WIDTH=408>
<TR><TD WIDTH="52%" VALIGN="TOP">
Search the web:&#9;&#9;</TD>
<TD WIDTH="48%" VALIGN="TOP">
<www.searchengine.com</TD>
</TR>
<TR><TD WIDTH="52%" VALIGN="TOP">
Look in telephone white pages:&#9;</TD>
<TD WIDTH="48%" VALIGN="TOP">
www.whitepages.com</TD>
</TR>
<TR><TD WIDTH="52%" VALIGN="TOP">
Look in yellow pages:&#9;&#9;</TD>
<TD WIDTH="48%" VALIGN="TOP">
www.yellopages.com</TD>
</TR>
<TR><TD WIDTH="52%" VALIGN="TOP">
Enjoy some humor:&#9;&#9;</TD>
<TD WIDTH="48%" VALIGN="TOP">
www.jokeline.com</TD>
</TR>
</TABLE>
</CENTER>

<h4 align="center">Note: above URLs are not real</h4>
```

Figure 2-6b   HTML Code for the HTML Document in Figure 2-6a.

Table 2-3   Examples of Web Browser Plug-Ins

Multimedia	Graphics	Sound	Document	Productivity	Virtual Reality
AVI	PNG	MIDI	Acrobat	Map viewers	VRML and
Flash	CMX	RealAudio	Envoy	Spell checkers	QD3D
Quick Time	DWG	TrueSpeech	MS Word		such as
Shock Wave		RealJukebox	Stamps.com		Quick
RealPlayer					Time
					Virtual
					Reality

recognized as those of authorized users. Subsequently, they use these accounts to log onto the organization's internal computers, view/destroy data, release viruses, or carry out other malicious activities.

Most companies want Internet access without exposing all of their systems to public access. This is accomplished by erecting a barrier called a firewall. A **firewall** is software (or a hardware/software combination) that sits between the Internet and the protected enterprise network and controls and monitors traffic between them.

Firewalls operate in a variety of ways. The essential idea is to restrict the data that flows between the Internet and the protected systems, which is done in two basic ways: defining the traffic (such as users or addresses) that is allowed and disallowing all other communication, or defining what is prohibited and allowing all other transmissions.

The primary purpose of a firewall is to intercept each packet transmitted over the Internet that is addressed to the network and to decide whether to pass it on to the destination host. Packets originating from unknown or unauthorized IP addresses are carefully scrutinized, and if there are sufficient red flags, these packets are blocked (not sent to the destination host). Firewall software can be implemented in routers, dedicated hosts, or both (see Figure 2-7). It is also possible to implement firewalls in other network technologies, including LAN hubs/switches and network adapter cards.

There are several major kinds of firewalls:

> *Packet filter firewalls* that are an acceptable first line of defense but are the least sophisticated and, therefore, the easiest for serious hackers to get around.

> *Application firewalls* that are capable of filtering out viruses and potentially malicious content such as Java applet and ActiveX controls. However, because of the more thorough checks that these perform, they have the potential to degrade network performance, especially when network traffic is high.

> *Proxy firewalls* that prevent outsiders from seeing the IP addresses of the network's hosts. Only the IP address of the firewall is visible to outsiders. These will even thwart hackers' attempts to pick up internal IP addresses by observing Internet traffic originating from the network, because the proxy firewalls substitute their IP addresses for originating hosts' IP addresses in outgoing packets. Any external response to an outgoing packet will come first to the proxy server; the proxy server will then deliver it to the appropriate internal host.

All three kinds of firewalls require the development of filtering rules. These are essentially if-then-else rules that dictate packet acceptance or rejection.

Because of the important role that firewalls have come to play in enhancing network security, they are discussed more fully in Chapter 16.

TCP/IP: THE INTERNET PROTOCOL

Recall from Chapter 1 that the TCP/IP protocol suite consists of five relatively independent layers. From top to bottom, these are as follows:

> Application layer
> Transport (host-to-host) layer
> Internet layer
> Network access layer
> Physical layer

Like that of the 7-layer OSI reference model, the physical layer of the TCP/IP protocol suite addresses the physical interfaces between network hosts (computers)

---

firewall Software (or a hardware/software combination) that sits between the Internet and the protected enterprise network and controls and monitors traffic between them.

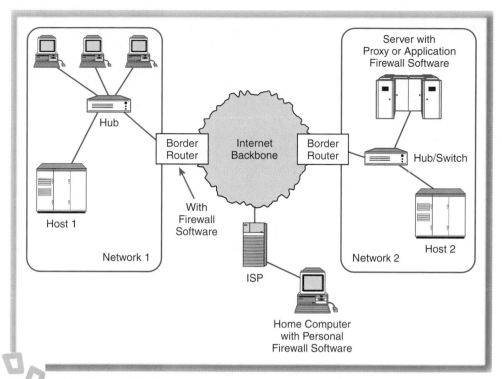

Figure 2-7   Firewall Alternatives

and the communication medium. As such, this layer specifies the characteristics of the communication medium, the characteristics of the signals that are transmitted, the transmission speed, and so on.

The network access layer is concerned with data exchanges between a specific computer and the network to which it is attached. At a minimum, the sending host (computer) must specify the destination address of the intended receiver. This is necessary for the network to be able to route the data from sender to receiver across the network. The software used to accomplish this depends on the kind of network to which the sender is attached. For example, when we focus on LAN architectures later in the text, you will learn that the *media access method* used in Ethernet LANs differs from that used in token ring LANs. Similarly, users who gain access to the Internet through individual dial-in connections to an ISP typically utilize different network access protocols than used in LANs. By segregating network access functions in a single layer, the higher layers of the TCP/IP protocol suite do not have to address the specifics relating to how a particular computer is attached to the network. This enables the higher layers in the protocol stack to carry out their functions regardless of the specific media access method used in the network to which the computer is attached.

Internet Protocol (IP)

Media access methods address communication between two or more computers attached to the same network. However, different procedures are needed to enable two computers to communicate when they are attached to different networks. In the

TCP/IP protocol stack, these procedures are carried out at the Internet layer, and the **Internet protocol (IP)** is used to provide the routing of data packets across multiple networks. For this to work, IP must be implemented in all network hosts as well as in routers.

Transmission Control Protocol (TCP)

The **Transmission Control Protocol (TCP)** is the key communications protocol at the transport or host-to-host layer of the TCP/IP protocol stack. It is responsible for ensuring that the data is exchanged reliably across hosts located in different networks. This involves ensuring that all the data packets transmitted by the sending host arrive at the destination host and are delivered to the destination host in the order in which they were sent. Unlike IP, which must be implemented in network hosts and routers, TCP only needs to be implemented in network hosts.

The application layer of the TCP/IP protocol suite consists of a number of data communication applications available to Internet users such as FTP, SMTP, Telnet, and HTTP. We will address some of these more fully after we take a closer at how TCP/IP operates.

TCP/IP Operation

Figure 2-8 illustrates how the layers of the TCP/IP protocol stack are configured for communication between two hosts in distinct networks. A network access protocol is needed within each network to enable a computer to transmit data to another host in the same network or to a router when the destination host is in another network. In order to enable communication between the two networks depicted in Figure 2-8, both TCP and IP must be implemented in each host in each network, and IP must be implemented in each of the routers used to interconnect the networks.

To enable peer-to-peer communication between an application in a host in one network and the corresponding application in another network, every computer in each network must have a unique IP address. Furthermore, each application within each host must have a unique address (within that host) to ensure that the data is delivered to the correct application within the host. The computer's IP address ensures delivery to the right host within the network. The unique addresses of applications within each host are called *ports*.

Let's trace a simple exchange between the hosts illustrated in Figure 2-8. Suppose Application 2 on each host is SMTP (simple mail transport protocol—the TCP/IP application layer protocol that is used to exchange e-mail messages among hosts in different networks). In order for Host 1 in Network A to do this, its SMTP application (Application 2) must hand the message down to the TCP layer through port 25 (the ICANN–designated port number for SMTP mail servers) along with the instruction to deliver the message to the SMTP application port (port 25) in Host 2 in Network B.

TCP attaches a TCP header to the message that includes the following:

➤ *Source port.* The application port address of the originating host. In this example, the source port would be the SMTP application (port 25) of Host 1. This is 16 bits (2 octets) in length.

➤ *Destination port.* The application port address of the destination host, in this case the port address of the SMTP application (port 25) of Host 2. Like the source port, this is 16 bits in length.

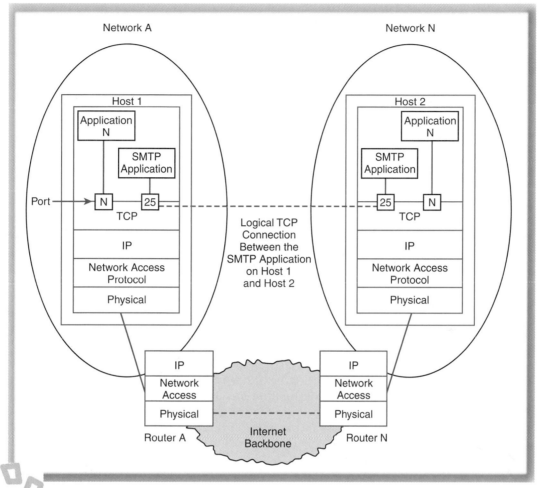

Figure 2-8   An Example of Host-to-Host Communication Across the Internet Backbone

➤ *Sequence number.* If the message is too large to fit in a single packet, TCP numbers the packets comprising the total message sequentially. This way, if the packets arrive out of order, the TCP function at the destination host can rearrange them into the proper sequence.

➤ *Acknowledgment number.* This contains the sequence number of the next packet that the host expects to receive. Both the sequence and acknowledge fields are 32 bits (4 octets) in length.

➤ *Header length.* This contains the number of 32-bit words in the TCP header. It is 4 bits long.

➤ *Reserved.* Not used; this 6-bit-long field is reserved for future use.

➤ *Flags.* This consists of six subfields, each 1 bit in length, that are related to controlling the flow of data between the two hosts.

➤ *Window.* This 16-bit field indicates the amount of data (in octets) that the sender is placing in the packet.

➤ *Checksum.* This 16-bit field is used by the destination host to determine whether the information in the sender's TCP header has been altered during transmission.

The role of checksums and other error-detection schemes is discussed more fully in Chapter 6.

➤ *Urgent pointer.* This points to the last octet in a sequence of urgent data in order to allow the receiver to know how much urgent data to accept. It is 2 octets (16 bits) long.

➤ *Options and padding.* Options include additional information such as the maximum total size (in octets) of the TCP packets being transmitted by the host during this session. This is a variable-length field. Padding is used to ensure that the TCP header size has a minimum length of 20 octets.

Figure 2-9 illustrates the change that takes place in the data packet after the host's TCP function has added the TCP header.

TCP then hands the packet down to the IP layer, along with instructions to deliver it to Host 2 in Network N. The IP function adds an IP header to the packet that contains the IP address of the destination host. The contents of an IP header of the version of IP that is currently used most widely (IPv4) is illustrated in Table 2-4.

As shown in Figure 2-9, the data packet is next handed down to the network access layer. A network header is appended to the packet at this point, creating the final packet. The appended network access layer header contains the *destination network address,* which is the IP address of the destination network; in this case the IP address of router N (see Figure 2-8). The appended network access layer header also contains the *network facilities request(s).* These specify the use of specific network facilities, such as priority message. Once this information is appended, the network access protocol delivers the packet to the router (router A) that sends it on its way across the Internet backbone to router N.

When the packet is delivered to router N, the process works in reverse. The packet is passed to the destination host via the network access protocol. Within the destination host, the network access, IP, and TCP headers are removed as the packet is passed up the TCP/IP layers and delivered to the SMTP application through the appropriate port (port 25 on Host 2).

Figure 2-9   Header Fields are Appended to User Data by Each Layer of the TCP/IP Suite

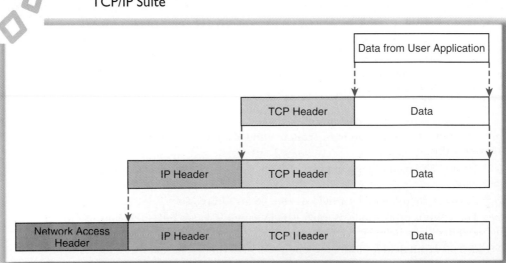

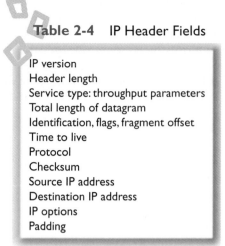

Table 2-4   IP Header Fields

IP version
Header length
Service type: throughput parameters
Total length of datagram
Identification, flags, fragment offset
Time to live
Protocol
Checksum
Source IP address
Destination IP address
IP options
Padding

Other Important TCP/IP Protocols

Thus far, we have focused on protocols in the TCP/IP protocol stack that are below the application layer. Several commonly used protocols found at the application layer are briefly described here.

File Transfer Protocol (FTP)

The **File Transfer Protocol (FTP)** provides a mechanism to transfer files between TCP/IP nodes. A user initiates the FTP from his computer system (host) and, because the user is usually trying to transfer a file from a target system to his machine, the processing is called *downloading*. The FTP requires the user to identify a target system from which the files are to be transferred. For example, if using a command-line interface, the user may enter *ftp archivedir.somesystem.edu* to establish a connection to the directory (archivedir) on the target system (somesystem.edu). Naturally, the FTP user cannot access any file on any target system; the user must have the proper privileges to transfer files. Therefore, the FTP connection requires a user log-on. One common use of FTP is anonymous FTP. Anonymous FTP allows access to a user without a log-on ID on the target system access. The user ID is "anonymous," and the usual practice is to enter a mail address as the password. Once properly logged on, the user can change directories, use directory commands to look at the available files, and transfer files to the host system. FTP capabilities are available through operating-system command languages or via browsers.

When a user wishes to transfer a file from the target system to his computer, FTP sets up a TCP connection to the target system so that control messages can be exchanged between the two hosts. This connection, for example, enables the user to transmit a user ID and password to the target system and to specify the file to download. When the file transfer request is accepted by the target system, a second TCP connection is established, and the actual file transfer occurs over this second connection. The first TCP connection is used to signal the completion of the file transfer and to carry any new file transfer commands from the user to the target system. Port 21 has been assigned by ICANN for initial FTP connections (those that control FTP transfers). Port 20 is used to actually transfer the data.

File Transfer Protocol (FTP) A protocol found at the application layer of the TCP/IP protocol stack that allows files to be transferred from one node to another over the network.

Simple Mail Transfer Protocol (SMTP)

The **Simple Mail Transfer Protocol (SMTP)** provides a standard for transferring electronic mail messages among TCP/IP hosts. SMTP supports forwarding, mailing lists, and return receipt. Because this protocol does not specify the way in which messages are created, any SMTP–compliant e-mail application can be used, including text-based systems (such as PINE and UNIX mail), e-mail applications with graphical user interfaces (such as Eudora), and Web-based systems such as Hotmail or Yahoo! mail. Interoperability of the various interfaces is assured if all adhere to the SMTP standard. SMTP describes the format of mail messages and describes how a mail message is to be handled by the recipient's software.

Once a message is created by an SMTP–compliant e-mail application, it is accepted by SMTP. SMTP then establishes a TCP connection to send the message to the SMTP application on the destination host. As noted previously, port 25 is the ICANN–assigned port number for SMTP mail servers. The target system's SMTP application will store the message in the appropriate recipient's electronic mailbox.

The **Multipurpose Internet Mail Extension (MIME)** works in conjunction with SMTP to enable e-mail users to exchange a wide range of file formats as attachments to e-mail messages. MIME, for example, allows e-mail users to send audio, video, text, and image files as e-mail message attachments.

Simple Network Management Protocol (SNMP)

The **Simple Network Management Protocol (SNMP)** assists in collecting and reporting on data traffic within a network. As such, it plays a key role in monitoring network performance and alerting network managers of existing or pending problems. SNMP is discussed in Chapter 15, along with other protocols that are commonly associated with network management systems. Two ports have been assigned by ICANN for SNMP. Port 161 is used for SNMP agents (the software that monitors the performance of data communication devices), and port 160 is used to deliver agent messages to network manager consoles.

Telnet

Telnet is a program that allows a user to connect to a host in another network. The computer from which the connection is made is called the *local computer;* the other is called the *remote computer.* Telnet enables users to log onto the remote computer and use it in the same way they would if they were directly connected to it. When a Telnet connection is set up, keyboard data is transmitted to the remote computer, and responses from the remote computer are displayed on the monitor of the local computer. This enables the user to run application programs stored on the remote computer. Commands and responses are carried between the local and remote computers via a TCP connection. Port 23 is the ICANN–assigned port number for Telnet.

Hypertext Transport Protocol (HTTP)

Hypertext Transport Protocol (HTTP) is the communication protocol used in TCP/IP networks that enables users to fetch Web page files from Web servers via hyperlinks and to display the Web pages in browser windows. When the user clicks on a hyperlink, the user's browser sends a request to the Web server, requesting a particular Web page file. In most instances, the Web server's response includes the requested Web page. The actual request and response messages are text-based and are exchanged over a TCP connection. Internet user requests for Web pages are delivered to HTTP Web servers via port 80.

Simple Mail Transfer Protocol (SMTP) A protocol within the TCP/IP protocol suite. SMTP is an application layer protocol used to implement mail services and message transfer. It is the standard e-mail protocol for the Internet.

Multipurpose Internet Mail Extension (MIME) Works in conjunction with SMTP to enable e-mail users to exchange a wide range of file formats (such as binary, audio, and video) as attachments to e-mail messages.

Simple Network Management Protocol (SNMP) A widely used network monitoring and control protocol that uses TCP/IP to send status messages from network devices (such as servers, bridges, routers, and hubs) to the workstation console used to oversee the network.

Telnet A TCP/IP terminal emulation protocol that allows entry from a keyboard to be passed from a local system to a remote system. Through this protocol, an application on the remote node believes it is communicating with a locally attached device.

Hypertext Transport Protocol (HTTP) A TCP/IP protocol used on the World Wide Web to transfer HTML documents.

You may have noticed that Web page files are often sent in pieces rather than as a single file. This is why you may see a sequence of "reading" and "done" text messages displayed on your browser screen before the entire Web page file is loaded. Generally, the more multimedia features the Web page file includes, the longer it takes to load, especially with slower Internet connection speeds. This is because a Web page typically consists of several files that the browser combines into a single on-screen image. The order in which the files making up a Web page are downloaded is as follows:

➤ *The Web page's HTML file.* This contains the Web page's text and references to the other files that the browser needs to combine into a single screen image.

➤ *The Web page's other files.* After the Web page's HTML file is downloaded, other files included on the Web page are downloaded, one at a time. If a Web page is complex, it may take dozens of HTTP request-response cycles to download the graphics, audio, image, and Java applet files that it contains.

Wireless Application Protocol (WAP)

Wireless Application Protocol (WAP) enables Internet-ready cell phones, pagers, PDAs, and other wireless communication devices to receive and display Web pages on their small screens. To be displayed, the Web page must be formatted in **Wireless Markup Language (WML)** rather than HTML. A *microbrowser* is used to display the Web pages on the small screens of these devices. The process used to download WML files is similar to how HTTP handles regular Web pages. WAP and WML are covered more fully in Chapter 5.

IPv6 (IPng)

The expansion of the Internet relative to the number of users, nodes, and kinds of uses has led to the need to extend the existing version of the IP. The new versions are IPng and **IPv6.**

The number of Internet nodes has grown exponentially, approximately doubling every year since its inception. Continued expansion is likely because more individuals and companies will connect to the Net, companies will expand their Net usage, and new technologies such as wireless connections coupled with handheld wireless communicators will allow people to connect to the Net from almost anywhere. Think about the number of people that you see using cellular telephones; each of these is a potential Internet user, and the number of cellular customers increases daily. Finally, the way in which the Internet is used will continue to change. One of the major changes is in the kind of bits being transferred. The trend has been from text-only data to graphics and then to audio and video. Audio and video transmissions have needs not found in text and graphics; they must be timely. If a person is listening to a live radio transmission over the Internet, delays in sending the data will distort the sound. The same is true of video transmission in real time. Couple this with the likely growth of the Internet in areas of low use, and the Internet as we know it today will need upgrading.

Key Upgrades in IPv6

Expanded Address Space   Currently, Internet addresses are 32 bits long. This limits the number of unique addresses to approximately 4 billion. The actual number of addresses available is less than that because some addresses are reserved (such as broadcast addresses) and some addresses in a class may not be used. IPv6 increases the size of the address field to 128 bits; this will allow up to 3×10^{38} addresses. The actual number of addresses will be smaller, of course.

Wireless Application Protocol (WAP) Enables Internet-ready cell phones, pagers, PDAs, and other wireless communication devices to receive and display Web pages on their small screens.

Wireless Markup Language (WML) A language used to format Web pages for display on the small screens of wireless communications devices.

IPv6 Version 6 of the Internet Protocol. IPv6 supersedes and provides significant improvements to IPv4. One major improvement is the expansion of the Internet address space from 32 bits to 128 bits.

Quality of Service (QoS)   To accommodate time-sensitive transmissions such as audio and video, IPv6 will institute service categories to prioritize the flow of data. Real-time transmissions will be provided with improved performance. Priority designations include classifications such as uncharacterized traffic; filler traffic, such as Net news; unattended data transfer, such as e-mail; bulk transfer, such as file transfers; interactive transfers; and real-time transfers

IP Header Changes   The format of the IP header will change. Changes will be necessary to provide for the larger address space and *quality of service*. Header fields that are currently not used will be dropped. Header extensions are allowed, in essence providing variable-length headers. Extension headers can provide functions such as security and integrity, destination-specific information, and routing control. The new header format is given in Table 2-5.

Security and Privacy   To better accommodate secure transmissions, IPv6 will allow extensions to the header to provide security capabilities. The extensions will allow a variety of authentication algorithms and allow detection or elimination of known techniques by which one node can impersonate another node for sending or receiving packets.

Interoperability with IPv4   Naturally, it will be impossible for all Internet nodes to make the conversion to IPv6 at the same instant. Therefore, the new version will be backward compatible with the current version. Implementation of IPv6 may be accomplished in an incremental fashion, allowing nodes to be upgraded to the new version in piecemeal fashion.

INTERNET SERVICES

We would be remiss in introducing the Internet if we failed to mention some of the other services commonly used on the Internet. In this section, search engines, text-based applications, and Internet chat applications are briefly discussed.

Search Engines

A variety of browser-oriented search engines have been developed that allow users to find resources on the Internet by supplying keywords. Through search engines, a user can find links to almost any Internet location. Several commonly used search engines

Table 2-5   IPv6 Header Format

Field	Size (bits)	Comments
Version	4	Contains protocol version 6 for IPv6
Priority	4	Message priority
Flow control	24	Quality of service identifier
Payload length	16	Size in octets of packet following the header
Next header	8	Type of header extension, if any
Hop limit	8	Number of hops allowed before datagram is discarded
Source address	128	Sender's IP address
Destination address	128	Recipient's IP address

Table 2-6   Popular World Wide Web Search Engines

Name	URL
Yahoo!	www.yahoo.com
Google	www.goggle.com
Lycos	www.lycos.com
Excite	www.excite.com
Hotbot	www.hotbot.com
Infoseek	www.infoseek.com
Metacrawler	www.metacrawler.com
Alta Vista	www.altavista.com
Bigbook	www.bigbook.com
Switchboard	www.switchboard.com

are listed in Table 2-6. Search engines are also common features on browser home-pages, such as *Netscape* and *Internet Explorer,* and on the homepages of online service providers such as America Online.

Search engines are made up of three major parts: a spider, an index, and a search engine utility (see Figure 2-10). The *spider* is a program that continuously searches the Internet for new Web pages. The spider is sometimes called a *crawler, robot,* or *bot.* When the spider finds a new page, it scans it to find out what the page is about and then creates an entry for the Web site in its database. Some spiders only read the first 100 words on a Web page. Knowing this, savvy Web site developers are careful to include important information about the Web page among the first 100 words. Developers put keywords that summarize Web page content within HTML tags called *meta tags.* Spiders also periodically recheck the Web pages in the database to make sure that they exist. If a Web page no longer exists, it is deleted from the database by the spider.

Data about Web pages is kept in a database that is often called the *index.* There is an entry in the index for every Web page found by the spider. The meta tags included

Figure 2-10   Search Engine Components

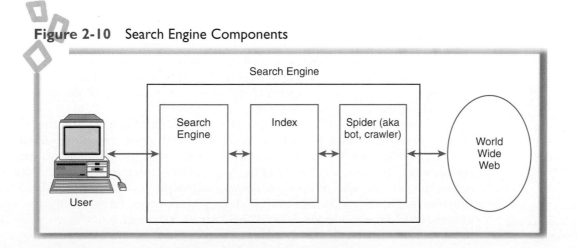

on the new Web pages are used to index the page within the database. Even though the spider is constantly searching the Web for new pages or pages that have been deleted, updating the index takes time, and as a result, it is usually somewhat out of date. An out-of-date index can cause the search engine to display links to Web pages that no longer exist or to miss (fail to display) relevant Web pages that have not yet been added to the index. Constant updating of the index also explains why the same search performed at two different points typically results in nonidentical results.

The third major search engine component is the actual *search engine* itself. This is the program installed on the search engine's Web site that searches the index to find links to Web pages that match search criteria specified by the user. Search engines typically rely on Boolean logic to filter the contents of the index to identify Web pages matching search criteria. Many search engines support basic and advanced search capabilities. Advanced search capabilities enable users to use more restrictive search criteria. Some search engines function as *meta search engines.* Meta search engines do not maintain their own database; instead they search the indices at other search engine sites.

Archie

Although we have grown accustomed to using a Web browser with a graphically oriented user (GUI) interface, before browsers and search engines, Internet users had a way to search for files, a system called **Archie**. Archie is a derivation of "archive." The Archie system consists of Archie servers and associated software. The servers house databases containing references to anonymous FTP documents stored on the Internet.

Gopher, Veronica, Jughead, and WAIS

Gopher is a menu-based system that allows you to access a variety of resources on a system. In many ways, it is the predecessor of today's browser software. Gopher client software installed on a user's computer enables the computer to interact with Gopher servers. Gopher servers are essentially text-based search engines that search multiple Internet hosts for user-requested information and deliver that information to the client computer that made the request. **Veronica** and **Jughead** are Gopher add-ons that allow a user to search Gopher servers for menu items that contain specific terms in the menu titles. **Wide Area Information Server (WAIS)** is a text-based search engine that allows users to look for documents located in indexes on multiple Internet servers by specifying keywords or text strings.

Usenet

Usenet servers, which are sometimes called *newsgroup servers,* share text-based news items over the Internet. There are more than 10,000 newsgroups included in Usenet that address a wide range of general and special-purpose topics. Usenet servers update each other on a regular basis with news items for supported newsgroups via *NNTP (network news transfer protocol),* a specialized transfer protocol. NNTP client software is needed to access Usenet servers and their newsgroups.

Usenet is essentially a worldwide bulletin board on which any Internet user can post or read information. Usenet is organized into interest-group categories, a few of which are computers (comp), business (biz), social issues (soc), recreation (rec), and teachers and students (K12). One of the largest of the interest categories is the alternative (alt) group. The alt group contains subgroupings that cover a wide range of subjects. In the alt category, you can find fan club postings, humor, language, music, politics, religion, sex, and television. Usenet access is through a news server that hosts the data and supports the Network News Transfer Protocol (NNTP).

Archie An Internet utility used to search for file names. Archie servers maintain catalogs of files available for downloading from various FTP sites.

Gopher A program that searches for file names and resources on the Internet.

Veronica An Internet search capability similar to Jughead that is capable of searching the Internet for specific resources using descriptions in addition to file names.

Jughead A Gopher add-on utility that allows a user to search Gopher servers for menu items containing specific words in their titles.

Wide Area Information Server (WAIS) An Internet document search system allowing natural language searches based on keywords.

Usenet A Public access network on the Internet that provides user news and group e-mail. USENET is organized into hundreds of interest groups in a variety of categories such as computers, social issues, business, and recreation.

Chatting, IRC, and Talk

The Internet has spawned a unique activity: chatting. The fundamentals of online chatting can be traced to newsgroups. Through newsgroups, people carry on conversations that are focused on a specific topic of mutual interest. **Chatting** moves the conversation to a different level. A group of users can gather at a virtual location and exchange ideas and comments on any subject. A variety of chat rooms are available on the Internet. The visitor can sit on the sidelines and listen to the conversations (recommended for first-time visitors) or participate. A different kind of chatting is available through **Internet Relay Chat (IRC)** servers. These chat forums are conducted in languages other than English. For example, a Spanish language student could use a Spanish IRC chat channel to improve language skills.

Talk is a UNIX utility that allows one user to communicate instantly with another user. Through the Talk utility, characters keyed at one host are immediately displayed on the other participant's monitor. IRC essentially extends Talk capability by allowing multiple users to communicate simultaneously.

In some instances, Internet chatting has evolved to personal chatting, meetings, and, in a few instances, marriage. Unfortunately, we must also issue a word of warning about chatting and personal contacts. Sometimes chatters are playing a role rather than representing their true persona. Some personal meetings arising out of chatroom contacts have resulted in one of the parties being victimized.

Instant Messaging

Instant messaging (IM) services such as America Online's Instant Messenger have attracted multitudes of users because of their ability to create and monitor lists of IM users that an individual wants to include in group chat sessions. When an IM user adds another to his or her "buddies' list," the IM service alerts the user when their buddy has logged onto the service. As noted in the case at the end of Chapter 1, IM services are growing dramatically and are expected to evolve and take their place alongside e-mail and the telephone network as a global communication system.

Miscellaneous Uses

The Internet has uses other than those previously described and business. Some of these include meeting people, exchanging ideas, obtaining advice on a variety of subjects, getting help with schoolwork, teaching classes, and listening to radio broadcasts unavailable in the user's locale.

Some people have become acquainted on the Internet and have subsequently been married. The Internet has also been used in bad ways. Law enforcement agencies are concerned that criminals and terrorist organizations are using the Net to plan and coordinate activities. The Net has been used to disseminate pornography and as a mechanism for child molesters to find victims. Consequently, legislative bodies have made several attempts to make certain activities illegal. A 1997 U.S. Supreme Court decision struck down one such law because it was considered to be a violation of free speech.

Two other negative aspects of Internet usage are practices known as flaming and spamming. **Flaming** is an e-mail or newsgroup posting, sometimes insulting or even obscene, that publicly chastises a user for a breach of Internet etiquette or for posting something that displeases the flamer. **Spamming** consists of flooding e-mail with advertising or sending high volumes of mail to an individual. In the latter case, the objective is to disrupt the user; this technique has been used as an electronic revenge mechanism. In both instances, the anonymity of the participants precipitates actions that would probably not occur between people who have met face-to-face.

chatting Using the Internet to send and receive messages to other Internet users in real-time conversations. The Internet supports chatting protocols, and various sites provide "chat rooms," virtual rooms wherein users can meet and converse.

Internet Relay Chat (IRC) A UNIX utility that allows two or more users to communicate interactively. IRC is used on the Internet for chatting and computer-conferencing.

Talk A UNIX utility that allows one user to communicate instantaneously with another user.

instant messaging (IM) The ability to communicate with other Internet users in real time by typing and sending messages.

flaming Severe criticism or condemnation of a user via e-mail or newsgroup posting.

spamming The indiscriminate distribution of annoying e-mail messages that often have commercial content.

GAINING ACCESS TO THE INTERNET

Individuals gain access to the Internet in a variety of ways, some of which are work, school, public services (such as libraries), freenets, and paid subscriptions.

When accessing the Internet from work, school, public services, and freenets, there is usually a policy regulating how you use the Net and consequences of misuse. At work, the policy usually requires that access be work related; the consequences might be as severe as being fired. At school, access is often restricted to course-related work, and students may be restricted from printing large volumes of Internet documents or be charged for such printing. Students misusing the Internet may lose their Internet privileges or receive grade reductions. Before accessing the Internet from any source, you should first understand the policies covering Internet use and the consequences of not adhering to those policies.

Work

Many companies are connected to the Internet, and employees of those companies may be able to access the Internet through their employers' connections. Ordinarily, this use of the Internet is intended to be work-related access; however, some studies indicate that employees use corporate Internet access for personal reasons such as planning vacations, reading magazines, and playing games. Before using your employer's Internet access for personal use, you should understand the corporate policy for such use and abide by that policy. The consequence of violating those policies may be disciplinary action, perhaps even resulting in your being fired.

School

Almost all colleges and universities have Internet access, and many public and private schools have access as well; thus, students may be able to gain Internet access through their school. In some schools, particularly those below the college level, Internet access is sometimes restricted to specific classes, and the access is structured around the school's curriculum. Some colleges and universities also provide access only for students enrolled in specific courses; other institutions provide all interested students with Internet accounts, often for a nominal fee. Providing all students with Internet accounts is beneficial because the Internet is an outstanding research tool.

Public Services

A variety of public or government agencies provide Internet services. For example, many public libraries have Internet stations available for their patrons. Also, some government agencies allow people to access the Internet through their connection. In some instances, access may be restricted to nonworking hours.

Freenets

freenet A community-based organization that provides free access to the Internet or to a bulletin board system.

Freenets are private, educational, or nonprofit organizations that provide Internet access for free. Some examples include Cleveland Free-Net, Dayton Free-Net, Erlangen Free-Net (Germany), Buffalo Free-Net, and Tallahassee Free-Net. Be aware that some freenets do not include the word *free* in their name. Some free access providers allow limited usage, such as Internet e-mail only.

Individual Paid Subscription

Finally, an individual may subscribe to Internet services. Let us look at how one goes about securing an individual subscription and the hardware and software necessary for making a connection.

Internet Hardware and Software

Before you obtain your Internet subscription, you need to have the correct hardware and software in place to make the connection. You have many options from which to choose. The most typical home connection is a personal computer (PC) equipped with a modem; however, there are lower-cost and higher-cost alternatives.

One of the lower-cost alternatives is a **network computer (NC)**. The concept behind the NC is simple: (1) a large number of companies and private individuals access the Internet; (2) economical access is desirable for some of these users; and (3) a hardware platform designed specifically to access the Internet is more economical than a standard PC.

In the mid-1990s, several companies, most notably Oracle, Microsoft, IBM, and Sun Microsystems, began to promote the idea of an NC and to develop such a product. An NC could conceivably be produced for approximately $500. Essentially, it might be a diskless PC or have small disk capacity. An NC might use a standard television or graphics display device as the monitor. The NC would support Java applications and provide high-resolution graphics and multimedia. Java is a platform-independent programming language that is used extensively to create Web applications. Many of these applications are small in size and are called *applets*. Applets may be quickly transferred to a user's computer to assist in processing the transaction. The NC would have an operating system optimized for Internet access and would not support standard PC applications and environments such as Windows. The target markets for NCs are businesses, schools, and individuals who want Internet access but are not interested in other personal computer technologies. The low cost of the system provides considerable savings for organizations such as schools that buy large numbers of computers to provide Internet services. Demand for NCs has been unsteady and to date, businesses have shown the greatest interest in them. Because they compete for consumer interest with PCs costing less than $1,000, set-top boxes, and WebTV, the future of NCs among household Internet users is uncertain.

Individuals who are willing to pay higher monthly fees in exchange for higher Internet access speeds may choose ISDN, cable modem, or xDSL connections. In the future, the monthly fees for these services is likely to decrease as a consequence of competition. ISDN, cable modem, and xDSL technologies are discussed more fully in Chapter 5.

network computer (NC) A low-cost computer designed to provide efficient access to the Internet and support Internet protocols and software. It is often designed as a "thin client" that downloads applications and data from network servers and stores data changes and files on network servers because it lacks floppy or hard disk storage.

Choosing a Service Provider

An individual who obtains a personal Internet connection does so through an Internet service provider (ISP). ISPs provide access to the Internet at three basic levels: national, regional, and local. National providers are commercial entities that sell access to the Internet in various cities. On a national scale you can access Internet services through providers such as America Online (AOL), UUnet, and regional or long-distance telephone providers. Regional providers sell access in a region. In the United States, a region might consist of several contiguous states, and an ISP would possibly provide toll-free access numbers within the region. Examples of regional providers in the United States are the local and regional telephone providers and regional network companies. Local providers are proprietors of networks attached to the Internet, and they provide individual access to the network. Examples include companies such as the one the author subscribes to, Hometown Computing (www.htcomp.net). Hometown Computing provides Internet connections in several small towns in Central Texas. Most countries that are large Internet users also have ISPs. A representative list of U.S. ISPs is given in Table 2-7, and Table 2-8 lists some ISPs outside the United States.

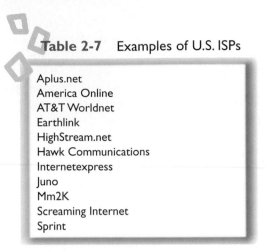

Table 2-7   Examples of U.S. ISPs

Aplus.net
America Online
AT&T Worldnet
Earthlink
HighStream.net
Hawk Communications
Internetexpress
Juno
Mm2K
Screaming Internet
Sprint

SOURCE: www.thelist.com

ISPs vary considerably in the rates they charge and the services they provide. Some guidelines you should follow when selecting an ISP are given in Table 2-9 and are discussed in the following sections.

Connection Type   Your Internet computer must be compatible with the equipment used by your ISP. The most common connection today is an analog, high-speed modem. We are currently reaching the upper speed limit for this class of connection. Typically, when new technologies extend modem speeds, several competing technologies emerge. This was the case in 1996, when the first 56-kbps modems were introduced. Two incompatible protocols were developed. If you purchased one of these modems and wanted to use it at its highest speeds, you would need to choose an ISP that had modems compatible with the model you chose. If you are using ISDN, DSL, or have a cable modem, you need to ensure that your ISP supports those kinds of connections and that the ISP's hardware is compatible with yours.

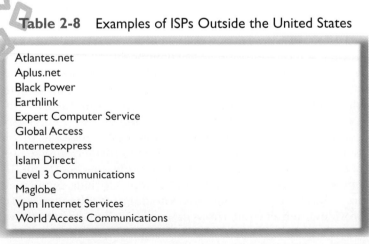

Table 2-8   Examples of ISPs Outside the United States

Atlantes.net
Aplus.net
Black Power
Earthlink
Expert Computer Service
Global Access
Internetexpress
Islam Direct
Level 3 Communications
Maglobe
Vpm Internet Services
World Access Communications

SOURCE: www.thelist.com

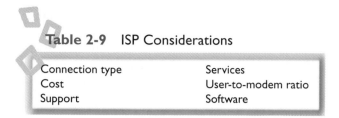

Table 2-9   ISP Considerations

Connection type	Services
Cost	User-to-modem ratio
Support	Software

The connection protocol you use is another consideration. You may connect to an Internet host using terminal emulation. With this kind of connection, the host is providing the Internet access and processing, and your computer is acting like a simple terminal, relaying keyboard and monitor information. Your computer is not "on" the Internet and does not have an Internet address. The host is the computer that is "on" the Net. Although this is the simplest kind of connection to manage, it requires you to do extra work when transferring data to your computer or printer. By default, all data is stored on the host, and you need to use file transfer protocols to download files to your computer. This kind of connection is more typical of company connections than personal connections.

The two protocols most commonly used by individual subscribers using dial-up facilities to connect to their ISPs are the **Serial Line Internet Protocal (SLIP)** and the **Point-to-Point Protocol (PPP)**. The SLIP protocol is older and less desirable than the PPP protocol. A third potential protocol is the AppleTalk Remote Access (ARA) for Macintosh computers. With each of these protocols, your computer has an Internet address and is a node on the Internet. In the next chapter, we will discuss Internet addressing and how an ISP subscriber obtains an address. SLIP and PPP allow the use of the IP protocol over serial lines. However, SLIP was not based on established data link protocols. In contrast, PPP was developed by the Internet Engineering Task Force (IETF) with the intention of improving the ability to connect to the Internet via switched, serial lines. The PPP protocol is based on the HDLC data link protocol and is more robust than the more simplistic SLIP.

PPP establishes the communication session between the user's computer and the ISP using the Link Control Protocol (LCP), which also handles authentication (such as PAP and CHAP—discussed in Chapter 16), compression, and encryption. PPP encapsulates packets used by other data communication protocols in specialized network control protocol packets. PPP can run on any full-duplex link from switched dial-up circuits to ISDN to high-speed lines such as T-1 and T-3.

Services   All ISPs provide Internet access; beyond that, there are differences in the additional services that may be available. Some ISPs provide each user with disk space on the ISP's Internet gateway node for a homepage. Because individual users are not permanently connected, homepages should be on the Internet gateway computer, where they will be continuously available. Some ISPs go beyond simple Web hosting by assisting their clients with Web page design and content.

ISPs also vary with respect to the speed of connection to the Internet. There are two speeds to consider: the speed of the user connection to the ISP and the speed of the ISP host's connection to the Internet. Subscriber-to-ISP speeds are based on the kind of line used, line interface (digital or analog), and the speed of the interface device. An ISP-to-Internet link should be at least T-1 speed (1.544 mbps) unless the ISP has only a few concurrent users. For example, suppose that there are 100 concurrent users all connected at 56 kbps. If all users are downloading files at the same time,

Serial Line Internet Protocol (SLIP) A protocol used for Internet access over serial lines, such as dial-up telephone access. SLIP has been generally replaced by the newer Point-to-Point Protocol.

Point-to-Point Protocol (PPP) A protocol used to provide serial transmission to the Internet over serial point-to-point links such as switched telephone connections. PPP encapsulates data communication frames/packets in Network Control Protocol (NCP) packets.

the aggregate data rate could be as high as 56 kbps $\times$ 100 = 5.6 mbps. As you can see, a single T-1 connection is not adequate for this task.

Another service the ISP should provide is continuity of operation. Although occasional short outages are to be expected, long periods of unavailability should not occur. One way they can be prevented is to have backup Internet servers. If one Internet host fails, another should be available to handle the network traffic. When choosing an ISP, particularly a smaller one, you should check to see whether backup systems are available to provide continuous operation (perhaps at lower performance levels) in the event of hardware or software failures.

Cost   Sometimes Internet access is free, but when it is not, you need to investigate the cost of the connection because costs can vary considerably. Many ISPs have adopted a flat rate for unlimited access, such as $15 per month. In some locations, the monthly fee for unlimited access is $5 or less. Some provide several pricing options, with the cost tied to the amount of connect time. Users who intend to be connected for long periods of time should find an ISP offering flat rate, unlimited access. If you live in a rural area, you may not have an ISP in your local calling area. If this is the case, and you intend to use your Internet connection extensively, you should look for an ISP that offers toll-free connections to avoid large long-distance bills.

Some ISPs provide users with free software essential to making the Internet connection, but others do not. Other costs you may incur include connection charges if you intend to use digital connections, such as ISDN or DSL, and upgrades to your equipment, such as a faster modem. If you intend to be connected to the Internet for long periods of time, you may want to install a separate telephone line. Having an extra line allows you to receive telephone calls while you are online, and the Internet line can be used for a fax machine or separate telephone line when you are not connected to the Internet.

User-to-Modem Ratio   The essential service provided by an ISP is connectivity. Figure 2-11 illustrates the configuration for a local ISP that only offers dial-in connections. The ISP installs a bank of modems for the subscribers and a high-speed connection to another node (in this case a T-1 line to a regional ISP) for the Internet connection. An ISP makes money from the number of subscribers it attracts. ISPs operate much like the telephone companies with respect to subscribers. That is, the system is not configured to provide one connection per subscriber. Some ISPs may have a user-to-modem ratio of 20 to 1 or more; others have a smaller ratio such as 5, 8, or 10 to 1. The user-to-modem ratio affects your ability to access the network. The lower the ratio, the more likely you are to get an Internet connection. You may have read articles regarding a national Internet provider whose subscriber base grew much faster than its modem pool. Consequently, many users were unable to connect to the service because all the available lines were busy. When selecting your ISP, it is wise to inquire about the user-to-modem ratio. Over time, the ratio will fluctuate as new subscribers enroll and new equipment is installed. However, the ISP should be willing and able to upgrade their system to maintain the ratio within a range that is likely to provide acceptable access to subscribers.

As illustrated in Figure 2-11, subscribers access the ISP via the local telephone company's central office. One or more modem banks (each of which is typically capable of supporting 16, 32, or 64 incoming telephone lines) are located at the ISP's operating location. The modem bank(s) may connect to the ISP's LAN via a terminal server. The terminal server supports a connection for each modem in the modem bank; its job is to consolidate the links to the modems into a single line connecting the

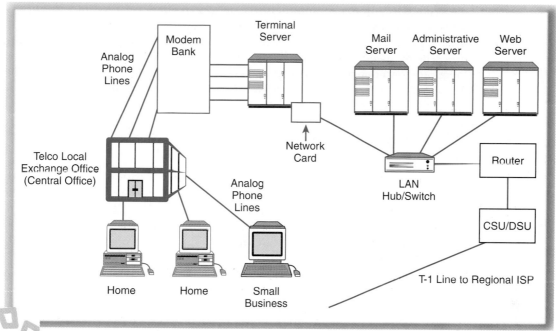

Figure 2-11   An Example Configuration for a Local ISP That Only Supports Dial-In Services

terminal server to the local area network by way of a network adapter card. The local network also includes servers and a router. In this example, traffic to/from the ISP router goes through a CSU/DSU (customer service unit/data service unit) and over a T-1 line to a regional ISP.

Support   The quantity and quality of support available can be the key to a user's ability to access the Internet effectively. New users particularly may depend on the ISP for support in setting up their hardware and software to make the Internet connection. Some of these users may benefit from elementary training by an instructor or a computer-based tutorial. The times at which the ISP's help desk is in operation are also important. Many individual users access the Net during the evenings and weekends when they are off work. A help desk that is available only from 9:00 A.M. to 5:00 P.M. Monday through Friday is of little benefit to them. Users who anticipate needing support should investigate the support hours, quality, and added cost (if any) when selecting an ISP.

Software and Hardware

In addition to a computer, you will need a modem or line adapter and Internet software to access the Net. The most common individual communication connection is an analog modem for use on standard telephone lines, although digital line connections are becoming more common. Speed and compatibility are the items to look for. Speed is important because it decreases your wait time while downloading files or Web pages. For example, downloading a 1-MB file over a 56-kbps link requires approximately

$$\frac{1,000,000 \text{ bytes} \times 10 \text{ bits } / \text{ byte}}{56,000 \text{ bits } / \text{ second} \times .75} = 238 \text{ seconds} = 3.97 \text{ minutes}$$

The 0.75 in the denominator is an approximation of the actual line use. It is unrealistic to expect 100 percent use of any communication link, and the 75 percent figure used is optimistic. In contrast, a 28.8-kbps modem requires at least twice the time. ISDN speeds for a typical home connection are twice as fast as the 56-kbps connection. For a digital subscriber line (DSL) connection, compatible transceivers must be installed at the subscriber's premises and at the telephone carrier's home office. Some DSL downstream speeds may be 6 mbps or higher. At that speed, the time to download the 1-MB file is approximately 3 seconds, or 107 times faster than that for the 56-kbps connection. At that speed, the delaying factor will probably be on the Internet itself, not between your premises and the ISP.

Software   The usual software interface is a Web browser. Some of these are free, but others are not. Naturally, today's pricing may change. The largest share of the browser market is divided between Microsoft and Netscape. Each company periodically releases new versions of the software with new features in an attempt to maintain technology leadership.

If you intend to design a Web page, you may want to invest in software that provides the proper formatting automatically. Originally, these products were self-contained; however, some word processing software now contains the capability to format a document as a hypertext markup language (HTML) document. For example, Microsoft Word 2000 allows you to edit a document and then save it as an HTML document. When you save the document in this format, Word provides the necessary format for links, text highlighting, and graphic images. Microsoft's Front Page, Netscape Composer, Macromedia, and Dream Weaver provide easy-to-use visual environments for Web page creation. An example of an HTML document is shown earlier in the chapter in Figure 2-6a.

Communication Line/Service Options   Consumers and businesses are increasingly choosing to connect to their ISPs via higher-speed services such as ISDN, DSL, and cable modems. Some businesses desire a direct T-1 connection to their ISP. Many local and regional ISPs have responded to customer preferences by supporting a wider range of connection options for consumers and business subscribers.

Figure 2-12 depicts an ISP that supports multiple subscriber connection options, including traditional dial-up analog phone line connections, DSL services, cable modem connections, and T-1 connections. Figure 2-13 provides an example of a regional ISP that supports multiple connection options for its subscribers, including smaller ISPs that gain access to the Internet through it.

Regional ISPs gain access to the Internet through one of several nodes that have been officially designated as network access points (NAPs) or as metropolitan area exchanges (MAEs). NAPs in the United States are illustrated in Figure 2-14. Smaller ISPs operating in or near the major metropolitan areas in which MAEs and NAPs are found often gain access to the Internet via direct connections to NAPs. Because huge volumes of Internet traffic to and from ISPs flow through network access points, they are key nodes on the Internet backbone.

Once ISP subscribers have connected to the Internet, a variety of services and capabilities are at their fingertips. Since the early 1990s, an increasing number of the available services are business and commerce oriented. We take a closer look at business use of the Internet in the next chapter.

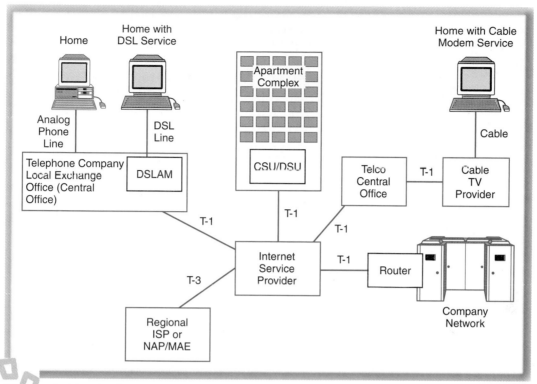

Figure 2-12   An Example of an ISP with Multiple Connection Options

SUMMARY

The Internet started in 1969 as a U.S. government military project called ARPAnet. Since that time, it has grown exponentially, and the Internet has become an important communication, research, and business tool. Businesses and individuals use the Internet in a variety of ways for work and recreation.

Key Internet technologies include hosts, subnets, and routers. All computers attached to the Internet are called hosts. Organizations whose networks include multiple hosts often choose to subdivide their networks into groups of hosts called subnets. Routers are data communication devices that are capable of forwarding packets from a computer on one network to any other computer on any other interconnected network.

The World Wide Web (WWW) is a hypertext-based, distributed information system created by researchers at CERN in Switzerland. The creation and evolution of browser technologies, especially those with graphical user interfaces, have resulted in the rapid growth of the Web. It is the most widely used aspect of the Internet and continues to increase in size and scope. Key WWW technologies include Web servers, browsers, and firewalls. Web servers store and control Internet user access to Web pages. Browsers enable Internet users to move from one Web page to another by following hyperlinks.

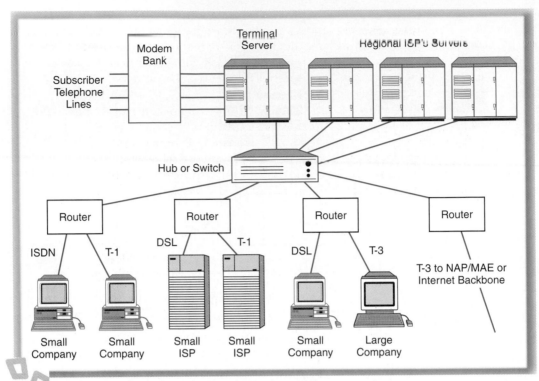

Figure 2-13   An Example of a Regional ISP Configuration

Figure 2-14   Network Access Point Map

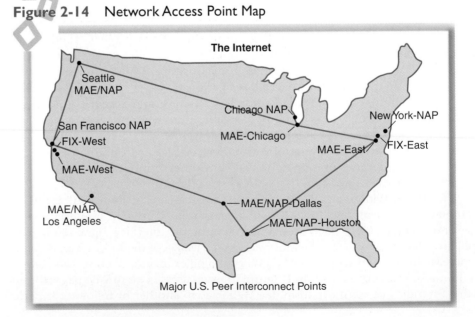

Search engines enable browser users to locate links to Web pages that contain specific kinds of information. Firewalls are software or software/hardware combinations that sit between organization networks and the Internet and help ensure that other authorized users are able to access the organization networks that they are designed to protect.

TCP/IP (Transmission Control Protocol/Internet Protocol) is the primary communication protocol used on the Internet. It is a 5-layer protocol stack; IP is found at the Internet layer, and TCP is found at the Transport layer. Other important protocols included in the TCP/IP protocol stack include File Transport Protocol (FTP), Hypertext Transport protocol (HTTP), Simple Mail Transport Protocol (SMTP), Simple Network Management Protocol (SNMP), and Telnet. Due to the evolution of the Internet applications and the need to accommodate the IP addresses of a growing number of Internet-attached devices, IPv6 (Internet Protocol Version 6) is being phased into use.

In addition to the World Wide Web, Internet users can take advantage of a wide range of services, including Archie, Gopher, WAIS, Usenet, Talk and IRC (Internet relay chat), and instant messaging services. Internet users can access the Internet through numerous avenues, including computer networks at work, schools, public services, freenets, or individual paid subscriptions.

Most consumers and businesses gain access to the Internet through an Internet service provider (ISP). Factors that should be considered when choosing an ISP include the kind/variety of connections that the ISP supports, services, installation, recurring costs (such as monthly charges), and technical support. Smaller ISPs gain access to the Internet backbone via regional ISPs, metropolitan area exchanges (MAEs), or network access points (NAPs).

KEY TERMS

- Archie
- ARPAnet
- backbone
- browser
- chatting
- File Transfer Protocol (FTP)
- firewall
- flaming
- freenet
- Gopher
- hypertext
- Hypertext Markup Language (HTML)
- Hypertext Transport Protocol (HTTP)
- instant messaging (IM)
- internet
- Internet
- Internet Protocol (IP)
- Internet Relay Chat (IRC)
- Internet service provider (ISP)
- intranet
- IPv6
- Java
- Jughead

- MILNET
- Multipurpose Internet Mail Extension (MIME)
- network computer (NC)
- NSFnet
- packet-switching network (PSN)
- Point-to-Point Protocol (PPP)
- router
- Serial Line Internet Protocol (SLIP)
- Simple Mail Transfer Protocol (SMTP)
- Simple Network Management Protocol (SNMP)
- spamming
- subnet
- Talk
- Telnet
- Transmission Control Protocol (TCP)
- uniform resource locator (URL)
- Usenet
- Veronica
- Wide Area Information Server (WAIS)
- Wireless Application Protocol (WAP)
- Wireless Markup Language (WML)

REVIEW QUESTIONS

1. Distinguish among an intranet, an internet, and the Internet.
2. Trace the history of the Internet.
3. Identify and briefly describe several organizations that play a key role in the evolution of the Internet by developing recommendations or standards and addressing major issues.
4. Briefly describe each of the following Internet technologies: hosts, subnets, and routers.
5. What are the differences among host names, URLs, and host IP addresses?
6. Trace the history of the World Wide Web.
7. Briefly describe the functions performed by Web servers.
8. Describe the differences among browsers, browser plug-ins, and browser helper applications.
9. What is a firewall? Briefly describe the differences between packet filter and proxy firewalls.
10. What are the five layers of the TCP/IP protocol stack? Identify examples of protocols found at the Internet, transport, and application layers.
11. How does TCP/IP operate? What happens to user application data as it is passed down the TCP/IP protocol stack?
12. Briefly describe each of the following protocols: FTP, HTTP, SMTP, SNMP, Telnet, and WAP.
13. What is IPv6? Why is it important? How does it differ from previous versions of IP?
14. Briefly describe each of the following Internet services: Archie, Gopher, Veronica, Jughead, WAIS, search engines, Usenet, Talk, and IRC.
15. What are flaming and spamming?
16. List and briefly describe five ways in which an individual might gain access to the Internet.
17. Describe the hardware and software used to make an Internet connection.
18. What is an ISP? What services are provided by ISPs?
19. List and briefly describe six guidelines an individual should consider when selecting an ISP.
20. Identify at least three different kinds of communication lines/services that consumers or businesses may use to connect to ISPs.
21. How do ISPs connect to the Internet? What kinds of communication lines/services do ISPs typically use to connect to the Internet?
22. What services are provided by regional ISPs?
23. What are network access points (NAPs) and metropolitan area exchanges (MAEs)?

PROBLEMS AND EXERCISES

1. Compare the pricing policies of two ISPs in your area.
2. Identify the kinds of user connections and services supported by ISPs in your area.
3. Take a poll of 10 Internet users to determine
   a. how much time they spend accessing the Internet
   b. what Internet services they use most frequently
   c. what Internet providers they use
   d. what they like most about using the Internet
   e. what they like least about using the Internet
   f. if they use the Internet to shop or make online purchases
4. In some instances, chatting has led to personal meetings. Investigate the literature and find two positive and two negative consequences of chatting.

5. Use Web sources to identify major firewall vendors. Briefly summarize the capabilities of the major products sold by each.
6. Use the Web to compare the major features of three browser plug-ins for each of two of the categories in Table 2-3.
7. Use the Web to identify major Web server hardware vendors. Compare the configurations recommended by each.
8. Use the Web to learn more about the Internet Engineering Task Force (IETF). Summarize its major responsibilities. Develop a table that lists and briefly summarizes several major standards it has adopted in the last 5 years. Develop a second table that lists and briefly summarizes several major standards it is currently considering.
9. Use the Internet to find out more about community access centers. Summarize the reasons why these are being implemented in communities across the United States.

Teledesic's "Internet-in-the-Sky™"

Teledesic hopes to respond to increasing global demand for bandwidth-hungry applications by building a global, broadband, "Internet-in-the-Sky™" satellite communications system. It represents the first satellite-based communication system designed with computer networking in mind. When fully operational in 2005, the Teledesic Network will consist of a constellation of low earth orbit (LEO) satellites capable of reaching 100 percent of the world's population. As such, it will be capable of providing millions of simultaneous users with access to wireless, broadband telecommunications services.

Teledesic's development is supported by deep pockets. Major backers include Craig McCaw (former owner of McCaw Cellular, which was purchased by AT&T in 1994), Bill Gates, Prince Alwaleed Bin Talal of Saudi Arabia, Lockheed Martin, and the Boeing Company. Motorola was also a major backer through the middle of 2000. As the network moves closer to implementation Teledesic hopes to partner with other companies to market and deliver its services worldwide.

Unlike Teledesic, most satellite communication systems consist of geostationary satellites (GEOs) that are positioned close to the equator at an altitude of 22,300 miles. In this position, GEO satellites orbit the earth at the same rate that the earth rotates on its access. The result is that the GEO is always in the same position in the sky. However, because GEOs are so far above the earth, round-trip communications through a GEO have a minimum end-to-end delay of approximately one-half second. The transmission delay (latency) is especially noticeable in international phone and video calls; generally, GEOs are best used for broadcast-type applications such as television programming.

Teledesic's low earth orbit (LEO) satellites will be 25 times closer to the earth than GEO satellites. Only 850 miles above the earth, Teledesic's satellites overcome the latency problems associated with GEOs. They also have the potential to provide broadband Internet access as well as interactive video and multimedia applications at speeds thousands of times faster than today's standard microcomputer modems. In addition, the same quality and capacity of service will be available to all parts of the globe whereas today, broadband services are spotty and typically limited to major urban centers in developed countries. Without Teledesic, many developing countries would be unlikely to have broadband telecommunications services because of the expense associated with implementing fiber optic cabling in these underserved areas.

Teledesic's satellites will be able to serve as the access link between a user and the terrestrial-based Internet backbone. They will also provide a means to link networks together in much the same way that the Internet backbone functions today. Technologies at the edge of the Teledesic Network will provide the interface between the satellite network and terrestrial end users and networks, including the Internet. These technologies will perform the translation between the Teledesic Network's internal protocols, TCP/IP, and other standard protocols used in terrestrial-based networks, including ISDN and ATM.

Most Teledesic users will have two-way communications with 64-mbps downlink (download) speeds and 2-mbps uplink (upload) speeds. These speeds are approximately 2,000 times faster than the microcomputer modems utilized by most Internet users to access the Internet. The Teledesic network will be flexible enough to support a wide range of applications, including the Internet services, corporate intranets, multimedia communication, and LAN interconnections.

Like the Internet, Teledesic's space-based network will rely on packet-switching technologies. Similar to TCP/IP packets, each packet in the Teledesic Network will contain a header that includes destination address and sequence information, an error-control section used to verify the integrity of the header, and a payload section that carries the digitally encoded user data (voice, video, data, and image). Conversion to and from the packet format used within the network will take place using technologies located at the edge of the network.

Because of the speed needed to keep Teledesic's LEO satellites in orbit, the network's topology can only be described as dynamic. As a result, the network will be required to continually adapt to changing conditions in order to achieve the optimal (least-delay) connections between the gateway technologies at the edge of the network. The Teledesic

Network will use a combination of destination-based packet addressing and a distributed, adaptive packet-routing algorithm to achieve low latency rates. Each packet carries the network address of the destination gateway device, and each node (satellite) independently selects the least-delay route to that destination. Because of constantly changing conditions, packets containing segments of the same file or message may follow different paths through the satellites in the network in order to reach the destination gateway.

As noted earlier, one of the primary advantages of the Teledesic Network is its potential to bring broadband communication services and high-speed Internet access to developing nations. Thus, it has the potential to enable citizens in such countries to participate in the information economy much sooner than they could have otherwise. As a result, economic development initiatives in developing countries may undergo dramatic changes as the result of the implementation of Teledesic's Internet-in-the-Sky™.

In spite of its potential, some industry experts are skeptical about Teledesic's implementation. In addition, Teledesic's proposed merger with ICO Global Limited was called off in late 2001. Skeptics argue that Teledesic's planned use of LEO satellites may have to be reevaluated and that a combination of LEO and GEO satellites is more likely. Despite the skepticism, Teledesic's partners and financial backers were forging ahead with plans to roll out the Internet-in-the-Sky™ in 2005.

CASE QUESTIONS

1. Identify and briefly describe several ways in which the Teledesic satellite network is similar to the Internet.
2. Could Teledesic's Internet-in-the-Sky™ be used to support internets and intranets? Why or why not?
3. Some industry experts have called Teledesic's LEO satellites "orbital routers." Is this claim defensible? Why or why not?
4. In what ways is Teledesic well positioned to capitalize on the explosion in wireless communications that is expected to take place during the next 5 years?
5. Visit Teledesic's Web site (www.teledesic.com), access recent press releases, and provide an update/summary of the progress being made toward the implement of the Teledesic network.

SOURCES

Bermont, Charles. "Internet Top Guns Talk About Haves, Have-Nots." *TechWeb News* (October 17, 2000). Available online at content.techweb.com/wire/story/TWB20001017S0014.

Flash, Cynthia. "Will Teledesic's Space-Based Internet Ever Fly?" *TechWeb News* (February 12, 2001). Available online at content.techweb.com/wire/story/TWB20010209S0011.

Glasscock, Stuart. "Teledesic Still Eyes 'Internet in the Sky.'" *TechWeb News* (October 17, 2000). Available online at content.techweb.com/wire/story/TWB20001017S0011.

Teledesic Newsroom Press Releases. Accessed March 4, 2002. Available online at teledesic.com/newsroom/nRele.htm.

Note: For more information on the Internet, see an additional case on the Web site, www.prenhall.com/stamper, "Getting Started as an ISP."

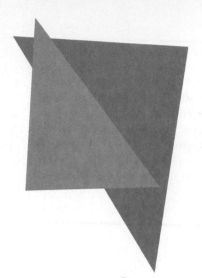

Business and the Internet

After studying this chapter, you should be able to:

- List the major Internet services used by businesses.
- List and briefly describe several major types of Internet businesses.
- Identify and briefly describe the different categories of electronic commerce.
- Identify and briefly describe Internet transaction requirements.
- Briefly describe major e-commerce and e-business applications.
- Discuss the consequences of e-commerce and e-business.
- Describe the characteristics of business communities and electronic marketplaces.
- Describe the efforts that are under way to build the information superhighway.

INTERNET SERVICES USED BY BUSINESSES

Businesses take advantage of many of the Internet services and TCP/IP protocols that were discussed in Chapter 2 including SMTP for e-mail; FTP for file transfer; HTTP for accessing/transferring Web pages; USENET for the distribution of news to newsgroups and special-interest groups; Telnet for remote log on to Internet hosts; and Talk, IRC, instant messaging, and chatting to support online dialogue among employers, suppliers, and customers

Business organizations are also using the Internet for marketing, business transactions, and delivering a variety of products and services including electronic magazines/catalogs and business services. Billions of dollars in sales transactions are currently taking place on the Internet, and continued increases in online sales will cause the volume to soar to trillion-dollar ranges in the next few years. The Internet is reshaping traditional business models and has led to the emergence of new business models.

From a strategic perspective, many businesses are in the process of developing a substantial presence on the Internet for a variety of reasons. These include the following:

➤ The number of existing or potential customers who use the Internet is rapidly increasing. Today, there are more than 150 million households in the United States and Canada with Internet access. The percentage of European consumers with Internet access is also steadily rising, and dramatic increases are anticipated in China, India, and other heavily populated countries around the world.

➤ The number of business partners, including vendors and suppliers, connected to the Internet is increasing. Online business-to-business transactions are helping companies reduce costs. Consumers are often the ultimate beneficiaries of this in the form of reduced prices and improved service.

➤ The maturation of electronic commerce Web server software has alleviated numerous security concerns and has made it easier to develop electronic commerce applications.

➤ There is great potential for lowering telecommunication costs by conducting business over the Internet.

➤ The Internet has the potential to improve a company's image, expedite access to information, improve direct or personalized marketing, reduce paper-based transactions, and improve worker productivity.

As you read this chapter, you will learn that these are just some of the reasons why business interest in the Internet continues to increase. In the remainder of this section, however, we will focus on business interest in particular applications.

Internet E-Mail

E-mail is the most widely used Internet application. By the end of 2000, there were more than 600 million e-mail accounts worldwide. Prognosticators maintain that by the end of 2002, there will be more than a billion.

Internet e-mail offers a cost-effective mechanism for the exchange of inter-company e-mail. It also provides an important communication link to millions of consumers worldwide. It represents an important marketing channel for the business's goods and services as well as an increasingly important customer service channel. Some companies periodically send e-mail messages announcing new products or pricing to customers willing to receive such notices. This use of e-mail is similar to bulk business mail except that delivery is almost instantaneous, and postage is not required. Internet auction sites often use e-mail to notify bidders that they have been outbid or have won the bid, and to advise them of upcoming auction items.

Users with e-mail accounts do not need to be online for their mail to be accepted. Each e-mail user designates a mail server that accepts the user's mail when they are not online. For many consumers, the mail server is a host at the ISP that they use to gain access to the Internet, but another computer may be designated (such as the mail servers at Yahoo! or America Online). When e-mail messages arrive at the mail server, they are stored in a file. When the user logs on, mail messages may be read and processed. Processing consists of a number of activities, such as replying, forwarding, saving, and deleting.

An Internet e-mail address has the general format of *User-name@computer/ company-name.domain-type*. The user name is made up by the user and typically is a form of the user's name. For example, one of the authors' e-mail user names is *dstamper*. It could also have been *stamperd* or *daves*. The authors' computer/company name is *htcomp,* and the domain type is *net.* Thus, the author's e-mail address is *dstamper@ htcomp.net.*

A mail interface is essential for sending and receiving mail. There are some text-oriented interfaces, such as Pine (a text-based interface found on many UNIX mail servers) and Eudora (which provides a graphical user interface [GUI] to the contents of the user's e-mail account). Internet users can also use the mail facility that is integrated with their browser software or take advantage of other free Web-based interfaces such as those available through Yahoo! or Hotmail.

File Transfer

Recall that the File Transfer Protocol (FTP) is included in the TCP/IP protocol suite and supports the ability to transfer files from one Internet host to another. Because of this, FTP can be used to electronically transfer business files between or within companies. It also enables companies to electronically deliver digitized products and services (such as music, photo images, and video clips) to consumers, thereby reducing or eliminating costs, such as shipping or postage, associated with traditional product distribution mechanisms.

World Wide Web

As noted in the previous chapter, the World Wide Web is the most widely used Internet service. It is also responsible for the explosive increases that have taken place in the number of Internet users and growth of Internet-based commerce. The ability to use HTTP to access Web pages for display in browser windows has changed the way that consumers "shop." Internet users are taking advantage of the Web for a wide range of business-related reasons, including the following:

➤ *Research on business products and services.* The Internet has made it possible for consumers to locate information about products and services quickly and conveniently. Whether they intend to purchase online or in a local business, shoppers can ensure that they are armed with up-to-date pricing information before they make a purchase. Increasingly, shoppers are using intelligent agents or shopping bots to search the Web for comparative product information or for the lowest prices being charged for a particular product. Add this to the convenience of being able to find such information on the shopper's preferred timetable, 24 hours a day, and the result is shoppers who are more knowledgeable and empowered.

➤ *Communication.* Internet users are making increasing use of the Internet to communicate directly with businesses. After a purchase, they may use e-mail or the Web for customer or technical service. Business partners also use Internet-based communication to coordinate activities.

➤ *Electronic transactions.* The variety of consumer products that can be purchased over the Internet continues to increase. Consumers and business employees use the Internet to find low-cost airfares; make airline, car, and hotel reservations; and order merchandise over the Web. Consumers are also using the Web to sell products to one another through auction sites such as eBay.

➤ *Downloading files.* Some business Web sites enable customers to access and download software, data, or digitized products (such as music). This means that the Internet has become another key distribution channel for some businesses, one that can provide customers with instant access to products and services. Over time, the Internet is expected to become the primary distribution channel for products and services that can be digitized.

USENET or Newsgroups

As noted in Chapter 2, USENET is a public access network on the Internet that provides user news and group e-mail. USENET is organized into interest group categories, a few of which are computers (comp), business (biz), social issues (soc), recreation (rec), and teachers and students (K12). One of the largest of the interest categories is the alternative (alt) group, which includes special-interest newsgroups such as those for celebrity fan clubs, humor, music, politics, religion, sex, and television shows. USENET users access posted information through a news server that hosts the data and supports the Network News Transfer Protocol (NNTP).

Online Commercial Services

Businesses often partner with online commercial service providers and portals such as America Online, CompuServe, and Prodigy in order to market their products/services to their subscribers. Business organizations also subscribe to business-oriented online information services such as LEXIS/NEXIS and Dow Jones News Retrieval Services.

Electronic Journals

You can find a wide collection of electronic journals on the Internet. Included among these are newspapers, magazines, and research papers. Versions of most major newspapers and periodicals can be found online. Often, publishers are able to supplement print versions of a newspaper or periodical with additional coverage, links to additional information services, reader reactions to published stories, and stories that are only published online between print editions. In order to maintain interest among readers, some publishers utilize global e-mail or ListServs to notify subscribers about new stories/information that are available on the publication's Web site. Some periodicals, called *e-zines,* are only published online.

Electronic Governance Services

Many consumers and business organizations are taking advantage of the increasing variety of electronic governance (e-governance) services that are available online. Many government agencies now enable businesses to place online bids to perform services or provide products needed by the agency. Others enable businesses to renew business and professional licenses online or to purchase surplus products.

INTERNET BUSINESSES

What began as a means of communication among military personnel and scientists has evolved to a mechanism for conducting business and personal communication. The Internet has become a marketplace, with millions of customers from around the world able to enter an electronic store and make purchases at any hour of the day. The kind of commerce that can be conducted is extensive and demands new technologies to make transactions easier to conduct and to prevent electronic crime.

Electronic commerce has grown tremendously since the early 1990s and is anticipated to continue to grow explosively during the first decade of the new millennium. This means that large amounts of money will be exchanged via bits being transmitted over the Net. This digital representation of money will pass from the client's computer through several Internet nodes on its journey to the recipient. When large amounts of money are involved, there are individuals and groups interested in taking a share illegally, in this case by diverting the funds or identifying cash equivalents such as credit card numbers. Consequently, the security of online transactions will be an important issue for some time to come, and Internet users need to be cautious when transferring cash equivalents over the network or when processing orders. Furthermore, there are legal issues regarding conducting business on the Internet, such as collection of sales taxes and international issues. Let's start looking at these issues by looking at how a company can provide an electronic store, security capabilities that should be used, and the coining of digital money.

In this section, we will look at how the Internet is used to conduct business with the public. In a later section, we will discuss the special features that need to be added to allow people to conduct Internet business safely.

Conducting business on the Internet is essentially the same as conducting business in a traditional store: The customer enters the premises, selects products or services, exchanges money, and receives goods. When a business transaction takes place in person, several activities occur. A cash transaction is the easiest to conduct because no verification is required to ensure the payment, and the transaction may be conducted anonymously; that is, identifying information about the purchaser is not divulged to the merchant (with the exception of transactions such as the purchase of weapons that require identification). The same basic rules apply to Internet commerce, but the mechanisms for conducting a transaction differ.

Let us begin by looking at some of the business capabilities from the perspective of both merchants and consumers.

Commercial Uses of the Internet

Virtually all classes of businesses can use the Internet in some way. The major uses are communicating via e-mail, transferring documents via electronic data interchange, advertising via Web pages and e-mail, selling goods and services, selling stocks or other financial instruments, providing travel services, and providing reference materials.

Intracompany Correspondence   A company can use Internet e-mail capabilities for intracompany correspondence as well as for external communication with suppliers, business partners, customers, or prospects. An increasing number of companies are implementing intranets to facilitate intracompany communications and knowledge sharing. An intranet is a private network that uses Internet technology such as hypertext documents and Internet protocols to store and retrieve data. An intranet is not accessible by the general public because it is located within the company's firewalls.

electronic data interchange (EDI) The electronic transmission of business documents from one company to another using a set of standard forms, data elements, and messages. EDI documents include purchase orders, invoices, shipping notifications, and remittance notices.

Intercompany Business Transactions   **Electronic data interchange (EDI)** is used to transfer business documents within a company and between a company and its suppliers or customers. Examples of documents that may be transferred are orders, product information, and invoices. EDI provides rapid exchange of such information and is easier to process than hard-copy equivalents. Because it continues to play a significant role in business-to-business electronic commerce, it is described more fully later in the chapter.

Advertising   Web pages, like that shown in Figure 3-1, are used by businesses of all sizes to advertise their goods and services. Web pages are easy to set up; have the potential to reach millions of customers; are available 24 hours a day, 7 days a week; are flexible enough to change so new products, services, and pricing can be kept current; and

Figure 3-1   Commercial Web Page

are inexpensive to maintain. The key to this form of advertising is attracting customers to the Web page. In a physical mall, large stores attract customers, who then may visit smaller stores in the mall. The Internet equivalent of this is having highly accessed locations on the Internet display links to other locations. To this end, some Internet services, such as search providers, sell reference services. For example, when an Internet user visits a search engine site, they will see one or more links to a merchant's Web site. Thus, the search provider receives revenues for advertising a merchant's Web site.

Selling Goods and Services   An extension to Internet advertising and product promotion is selling goods and services over the Internet. This application is similar to mail order with the exception that the entire transaction (except physical delivery of products) is conducted electronically. One term used to describe this capability is the *electronic store*. A merchant can establish an electronic store via a Web page. Sometimes the company maintains its own store; an alternative is to house the Web page (electronic store) with a third party that sets up a virtual shopping mall housing multiple stores—a close counterpart to a shopping mall. Selling and buying on the Internet require special capabilities and protocols to ensure that customers and merchants are not defrauded. We will look at some of these later in this chapter.

Selling Stocks or Other Financial Instruments   One of the business activities conducted on the Internet is the sale of stocks, bonds, mutual funds, and other investment instruments. This kind of activity is a special case of selling of goods and services. Another use of the Internet is selling stocks to raise capital for a company. Numerous online brokerage firms are available. Some such as E*Trade and Ameritrade are online-only brokerages with low per-trade transaction costs. Others, like ESchwab, provide online trading capabilities for traditional stockbrokers (in this case, for Charles Schwab & Co.). Industry experts predict that there will be more than 20 million online investment accounts by 2003.

Travel Services   An Internet user has many of the same capabilities as a travel agent. The user can book airline, hotel, and car reservations. Some of the systems look for best fares and alternative routes. Most airlines have Web pages through which a user can book flights directly; alternatively, a user could use the services of a travel agent's Web pages to look at flights, hotels, and car rentals from a variety of airlines, hotels, and car rental agencies.

Providing Reference Materials   Providing reference materials is another special service, and some applications of this service deserve special mention. Currently, there are many Internet sites that you can visit for free; however, this may not be true in the future. For example, when you visit the site for a newspaper or magazine, you can read articles without charge. Other than advertising, there is no profit for the business. In the future, some merchants may begin charging for site visits. Thus, if you download a page from a newspaper or magazine, you might incur a small charge for that activity—perhaps even a fraction of a cent. Furthermore, you might be able to set up a profile that will result in a virtual magazine or newspaper being created for you. For example, it may contain only articles you are interested in, such as business, world news, and sports. If you are in the market for a new car, you might add advertisements for cars and automotive news until you purchase one (which also can be done via the Internet). Later in this chapter, we discuss how small charges are collected.

Advantages and Disadvantages of Internet Use for Business

The Internet is good technology, and many benefits may result from using it intelligently; however, good technologies sometimes are used in bad ways, so the user must beware. In addition to the potential problems arising out of personal Internet activities, there are potential problems in using the Internet for business.

When we engage in commercial transactions, money and goods are exchanged. Transmitting money and machine-readable goods over any network can result in loss. Our Internet money may be redirected to the wrong location. Machine-readable goods such as programs may be corrupted (damaged) during transmission, and the potential for fraud is great because we do not necessarily know with whom we are dealing and where they are located. Furthermore, when a business connects its computers to the Internet, there is a potential for outsiders to access the company's private network. It is important to understand how money and goods are exchanged over the Internet and some of the safeguards that can be used to protect the buyer, seller, and resources of computers and networks attached to the Internet.

INTERNET TRANSACTION REQUIREMENTS

A business transaction requires the exchange of goods for equivalent value. The equivalent value is usually money or a representation thereof, such as a credit card number. Therefore, Internet transactions must provide a mechanism for such transfers. The following are desirable characteristics of Internet transactions: payment, security and verification, anonymity, and accountability/taxability.

Payment System

At the start of the Internet business era, access to information was mostly free. Information that was not free was usually made available through subscription and was protected by an access code. Goods that were sold were high-dollar items, typically costing $10 or more. Payment for these goods and services could be accomplished online by using a credit card.

Internet information proprietors have begun to realize that giving away valuable information is not profitable. For example, a user who accesses a magazine article online could be charged for reading that article; however, the charge would probably be quite low, say $10 or less. Some pieces of information, such as a single stock quote, might cost less, perhaps even a fraction of a cent. Other services, such as downloading a movie, might cost about $4. With low-cost transactions, payment by credit card is not feasible because the cost of processing the charge sometimes exceeds the charge itself. Therefore, new mechanisms are being developed to enable low-value online payments including *micropayments*—payments that are less than a $1. *Microcommerce* is often used to refer to low-value electronic commerce transactions for services that are too small to be feasibly paid by a single credit card transaction. The two primary technologies being proposed are smart cards and various forms of digital or electronic cash.

Smart Cards   **Smart cards** are similar to credit cards, but there is a major distinction between the two: Smart cards have an embedded computer chip that is capable of storing and updating data. Using a smart card for Internet-based transactions requires a card reader/writer attached to the computer. With the cost of these technologies dropping rapidly, the use of smart cards is expected to increase dramatically during the next decade. Internet Mondex (MasterCard) has been one of the leading developers of smart card technology for the Internet.

Smart card users obtain the cards by opening an account with an institution that provides smart cards, such as a bank, a financial services company (such as American Express), or perhaps an ISP. The smart card would be encoded with the user's identifying information and a dollar amount. The user then can use the smart card to pay for an Internet transaction by passing the card through the reader. A PIN (personal information number) is required to access the information stored on many smart cards. To gain access to the information stored on the smart card at merchant locations, the cardholder is required to enter a pin number on a PIN pad. Once the stored information is unlocked, the amount needed to complete the transaction is subtracted from the card's stored dollar total and "transferred" to the merchant's bank account. Payment is thus made directly between the cardholder and the merchant; it could also be used to transfer money directly between cardholders. Merchants that accept smart cards receive immediate, verified payment directly from the cardholder in a manner that is similar to receiving a direct cash payment. They do not have to rely on online authorization to make a transaction as they do for credit card transactions.

When the stored dollar amounts begin to run low, smart card holders are able to "load" the card with additional cash value at ATMs and by using other authorized load technologies. This is illustrated in Figure 3-2, along with the general transfer process between smart card holders and merchants.

Smart cards are widely used in Europe as an alternative to credit cards or other forms of payment. They are catching on in the United States, but not as fast as many industry experts predicted. An Internet smart card can also be used for transactions other than Internet transactions. For example, American Express's Blue Card can be

smart card A credit card with a built-in microprocessor and memory used for identification or financial transactions. When inserted into a smart card reader, it transfers data to and from a central computer. It is more secure than a traditional credit card and can be loaded with digital money that can be spent in variable amounts until the balance is zero.

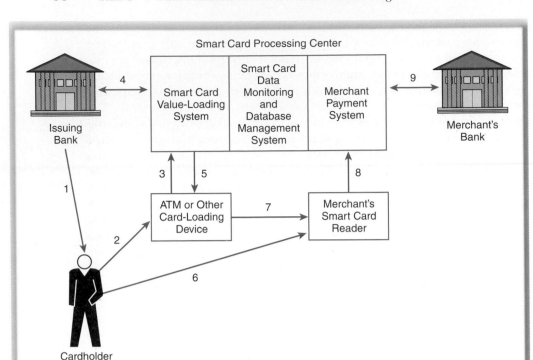

Steps:

1. Issuing bank approves and issues smart card.
2. Cardholder uses ATM or other smart card value-loading device to increase the card's total stored value.
3. ATM requests authorization from smart card processing center to increase the card's stored value.
4. Smart card processing center requests cardholder's issuing bank to transfer the amount by which the card's stored value is to be increased. Customer's account is debited for the amount transferred to the card.
5. Smart card processing center authorizes the stored value increase for the cardholder's smart card.
6. Cardholder uses smart card reader at merchant location.
7. Transaction amount is transferred to the merchant in real time; card's total stored value is decreased by transaction amount.
8. Batched smart card transactions are uploaded to merchant payment system at smart card processing center.
9. Merchant account is credited with batched transaction total.

Figure 3-2   An Example of the Smart Card Stored Value-Loading and Cash Transfer Processes

used for both smart card transactions as well as traditional credit card transactions. As is true for most current generation smart cards, Blue Card holders can obtain a smart card reader for their home computer to ensure secure transactions over the Internet.

biometric technology Technology that enables the biological identification of a person, which includes voiceprints, handprints, fingerprints, and handwritten signatures.

Biometric technologies promise to play a key role in verifying the identity of smart cardholders. Digitized images of the cardholder's fingerprints, retina, facial structure, or other physical features can be encoded on the card along with the information that is typically included. Digital images of the cardholder's physical feature(s), captured by digital readers at the point of sale, could be electronically compared with the images stored on the card to verify the cardholder's identity. Needless to say, widespread use of these biometric technologies would go a long way toward eliminating fraudulent smart card use.

Digital Cash   Another potential Internet payment mechanism suitable for micropayments is **digital cash (d-cash)** or **electronic cash (e-cash)**. For many years, we have represented and transferred money electronically. Banks transfer money from one place to another using electronic messages. With online shopping, people are able to initiate electronic transfers of cash. Several possibilities exist for doing this.

One alternative is to write what is essentially an electronic check. This requires at least three parties to the transaction: the customer, merchant, and customer's bank or financial agent. With this technology, the business is not privy to customer information such as credit card number, and the customer's account number is not transmitted over the network. The transfer of money from the customer to the merchant is accomplished by the customer's bank or authorized financial agent. In some instances, the customer is required to have a digital signature to ensure the security of the money transfer (digital signatures are discussed more fully in Chapter 16). Unlike paper checks, the merchant receives the payment instantly, and there are no insufficient fund or bad check losses.

Another form of e-cash is a money certificate that is obtained from a bank or other authorized distribution source. A customer can purchase such a certificate from a bank, and money will be transferred from the customer's account. The digital cash certificate bears a unique serial number, just like regular cash. Like cash, the certificate is anonymous. That is, when a customer pays for goods with a credit card or check, she gives the merchant identifying information such as a credit card or checking account number. If she pays in cash, no such identifying information is given. When a customer makes a purchase using e-cash, she transfers the digital cash certificate to the merchant. As with currency, the merchant may use the digital cash certificate or deposit it in the bank. If a merchant believes the e-cash is counterfeit, he can contact the issuing bank and verify its accuracy.

A third form of cash that may come into existence represents money in very small denominations, as little as a fraction of a cent. Clearly, this type of currency is not distributed to the general public by banks and other financial institutions, so why is it necessary on the Internet? Between the extremes of free and expensive, some Internet nodes charge visitors for access to information they provide. For example, a newspaper or magazine might charge a user one-half cent to access a page of their publication or a few pennies for access to an entire article stored in their archives. In addition, an online encyclopedia or dictionary could charge a penny or less to access a single entry or word. Micropayments enable Internet nodes to provide such pay-per-view services to their visitors. Micropayment systems are also common in Web-based advertising. Web sites that allow businesses to place banner ads on their Web pages often charge advertisers a micropayment for each page view (each visitor to the Web site) and a higher micropayment each time a visitor clicks on the ad to find out more about the product or service it promotes. Microcommerce is thriving on the Internet, and micropayment systems such as those devised by Digital and Carnegie Mellon University (CMU) play an important role.

Millicent   Digital has named its approach to small denomination currency *Millicent*. The term stands for one-thousandth of a cent. Millicent is similar to digital check technology. The monetary units are called *scrip* and may be used for transactions whose value is less than one cent. The scrip is identified by a serial number and a value. A consumer purchases scrip from a bank or financial provider. The user also receives a

digital cash (d-cash) Electronic money used on the Internet. Digital cash may take various forms, including credit/debit card or smart card transfers, and electronic scrip issued by an electronic cash agent.

electronic cash (e-cash) See *digital cash.*

key that is used to validate ownership of the scrip. The use of the key allows the user to conduct the transaction anonymously; that is, there is no (easy) way to attribute the scrip to a person. The recipient of scrip returns it to the provider for cash credit.

CMU's NetBill NetBill is CMU's small-denomination system. The customer obtains a book of chits that can be exchanged for services. The chits are available from a NetBill provider and can be redeemed by a vendor through the same provider. Like Millicent, NetBill provides anonymous payments. More information about the NetBill project can be found at www.ini.cmu.edu/NETBILL/.

Other Potential E-Cash Providers Other developers of e-cash systems are given in Table 3-1.

Why digital cash? Because we already are conducting business using credit cards, why is there a movement toward e-cash? As we progress, more business activities will be conducted online. E-cash provides a simple way to pay for these goods. It eliminates sending credit card numbers and sending bills and payments via postal mail. Merchants receive their money immediately, and (with the exception of electronic fraud) there will be no bad checks. Through the Internet, small merchants may be able to compete with large, traditional merchants because they might be able to attract as many customers without the large overhead of buildings and staff. With e-cash, Internet customers can shop 24 hours a day, 7 days a week and will not need to leave their home or place of business to do so. Digital money is less prone to theft than hard currency. If you carry cash with you, you may lose it or have it stolen. E-cash can be backed up so it can be replaced if it is accidentally erased or destroyed. An e-cash thief will need to access your computer to steal your digital money and will also need to know your access key to make it available. If the e-cash is stolen, the serial numbers of the cash can be deactivated, much like a stop-payment on a check. With e-cash, your employer can pay you digitally, and you will be able to monitor your expenses because they can be easily tracked.

Internet transactions require the transfer of monetary items over the network. The Department of Commerce estimates that there were $600 billion in Internet sales for the year 2000; this means that $1.64 billion was exchanged daily over the Internet. Today, daily Internet sales are much higher. The amount of money associated with online transactions is more than enough to entice some people to attempt to divert it illegally. Consequently, security measures must be in place to protect against fraud and theft. Let us now look at some of these security measures.

Table 3-1 Digital Cash Providers

Company	Product	Comments	Minimum Payment
Newshare	Clickshare	Oriented toward newspapers and magazines	10¢
CyberCash	CyberCoin	Netscape has adopted	25¢
DigiCash	E-cash	Tested in smart cards and on Internet	1¢
First Virtual Holdings	VirtualPIN	E-mail–based credit system	$1

Security and Verification

A transaction will be secure if the user gets the goods ordered, the merchant gets the money for the goods, and no uninvolved parties have access to any of the transaction data.

We will look at these aspects of security from the perspective of credit card, smart card, and e-cash transactions. Then we will see how a person's identity can be verified. We begin by looking at credit card transactions.

Credit Card Security

When a buyer uses a credit card, the credit card number must be transferred from the buyer to the seller and then to the credit card authorization center. An Internet credit card transaction essentially mirrors the activity of a credit card transaction in a store. Several protocols have been developed to ensure the security of electronic transactions. All these protocols involve the use of encryption to protect the credit card number and transaction data while they are being transmitted across the Internet backbone. This means that the software on the buyer's end and the software on the merchant's end must agree on the protocol and kind of encryption to be used. Commonly used encryption approaches are discussed in Chapter 16.

Secure Sockets Layer Protocol   Two of the most commonly used protocols for securing electronic transactions are **Secure Sockets Layer (SSL)** protocol and **Secure HTTP (S-HTTP)**. SSL is supported by Netscape and Microsoft browsers. S-HTTP was developed by Enterprise Integration Technologies and is used by Spyglass, Open Market, and several other software companies. It is possible to use both SSL and S-HTTP. The functional difference between the two is slight, so we shall discuss SSL as the example.

SSL is implemented at the presentation layer of the OSI reference model. It encrypts the uniform resource locator (URL) and the message, including the credit card number. The SSL protocol is implemented in Web browsers and business software. Information exchanged between the customer and business is automatically encrypted before being transmitted and unencrypted by the recipient.

SSL also provides authentication, which allows both parties to the transaction to verify the identity of the other. Authentication is accomplished via public keys or digital signatures. Several mechanisms—hashing, the U.S. government's Digital Signature Standard (required for some government transactions), and public key encryption—are used to exchange digital signatures. Although the algorithms differ somewhat, the basic idea is the same. We use the public key encryption algorithm as an example. Public key encryption requires two keys: a public key and a private key. When someone wants to send me a secure message, they can use my public key to encrypt it. If they do so, only my private key will decrypt the message. Because I am the only person (presumably) who knows the private key, only I can decrypt the message. On the other hand, if I want to secure a message containing my name with a digital signature, I can encrypt the message with my private key, and the recipient will be able to decrypt it with my public key. When the merchant decrypts the message with my public key, it will yield my name only if it was encrypted with my private key. As an adjunct to this, we may add a certification to our signature. This is accomplished by receiving a digital certificate of authenticity from a clearinghouse such as VeriSign. When this approach is used, the message is encrypted using my private key, and my digital certificate is attached to the message to assist the recipient in verifying that I am the sender of the message. The digital certificate contains information about my public key. The vendor

Secure Sockets Layer (SSL) The leading security protocol on the Internet for online transactions. SSL uses a combination of public and private key encryption to secure online transactions. When an SSL session is started, the server sends its public key to the browser. The browser uses the public key to send a randomly generated private key back to the server to use to encrypt subsequent transmissions between the server and the browser for the duration of that session.

Secure HTTP (S-HTTP) A protocol used for securing electronic transactions over the Internet. S-HTTP was developed by Enterprise Integration Technologies and is used by Spyglass, Open Market, and several other software companies.

who receives my message can then check with the clearinghouse to ensure that the certificate is valid and obtain the public key needed to decrypt the message.

SSL uses a combination of public and private (secret) key encryption to secure an online transaction between a server and an Internet user's browser. When an SSL session is started, the server sends its public key to the browser. The browser uses the public key to send a randomly generated secret key back to the server. The secret key is used to encrypt subsequent message transmissions between the server and the browser for the duration of that session. The SSL protocol is discussed more fully in Chapter 16.

Secure Electronic Transaction (SET)
A standard protocol developed by credit card companies for securing online credit card transactions over the Internet.

Secure Electronic Transaction (SET)   Another protocol, **Secure Electronic Transaction (SET)**, has been jointly developed by Visa, MasterCard, Netscape, Microsoft, IBM, and other companies to secure online transactions using credit cards. Like SSL, SET uses encryption to provide secure credit card transactions over the Internet. It includes features that ensure

➤ Integrity (The packets being transmitted cannot be modified en route.)
➤ Confidentiality (Only the transaction participants have knowledge of the transaction details.)
➤ Authenticity (A party to the transaction is assured of the identity of the other party.)
➤ Nonrepudiation (Neither party can deny that the transaction took place.)

In a SET transaction, the merchant does not have access to the credit card number because it is encrypted. The merchant forwards the encrypted credit card number to an authorization center, where it is decrypted and the purchase is authorized. This differs from the SSL approach, in which the merchant has access to the credit card number. The SET protocol is discussed more fully in Chapter 16.

Digital Cash Transactions

E-cash transactions differ from credit card transactions in that the merchant is paid directly by the purchaser with a digital equivalent of money. The merchant is able to redeem the e-cash for hard currency. In this section, we look at how a consumer can get e-cash, how it is stored and safeguarded, and how it is exchanged and redeemed.

E-cash is in circulation today. Digicash provides this capability in Europe, the United States, and Australia through several authorized banks. No doubt there will eventually be a variety of sources for e-cash and a variety of ways to obtain it. In general, the following will probably occur.

➤ The customer opens an account with the issuing authority, such as a bank.
➤ The bank issues e-cash certificates to the customer.
➤ Encryption is used to transfer e-cash from the e-cash holder to a merchant or another recipient.
➤ The recipient of e-cash sends notification of its receipt to the issuer, where the digital cash certificates are authenticated.
➤ The recipient is credited with the funds.

As with the other security issues, encryption is essential to protect the integrity of the transaction as messages are exchanged between purchaser, merchant, and e-cash issuer.

Anonymity

There is a possible drawback to becoming a world of Internet traders: Governments and organizations can monitor our spending habits. This possibility already exists when we use credit cards; the identity of the cardholder and the services or goods purchased become a matter of record with the credit card company. With Internet transactions, we can be tracked by our digital signatures and the serial numbers associated with our e-cash. This adds a new dimension to commerce. Today, if we pay for merchandise with cash, our transaction can be anonymous because there is no link between our identity and the serial numbers on the currency we use. This linkage exists with e-cash. However, techniques have been developed that allow anonymity when using e-cash. The algorithms allow the consumer to obtain digital cash certificates in such a way that when the bank receives the certificates from a merchant, it is impossible to identify the certificates with an individual. Details of this algorithm are complex and are beyond the scope of this book; however, in simple terms, it involves both bank and consumer encryption keys applied to random serial numbers generated by the consumer.

Accountability and Taxability

There are other issues surrounding electronic commerce besides transaction security. These issues include who has an opportunity to participate, calculation and collection of sales taxes, and crime detection and prevention.

Opportunity to Use   Access to the Internet marketplace gives one a large, competitive merchant base from which to purchase. The competition may result in an Internet buyer being able to obtain lower prices for goods than someone without access to this resource. Those who are less affluent will probably end up paying more for goods and services because they lack the resources to establish Internet connections.

Sales Taxes   Most of the states in the United States use sales taxes as a major source of revenue. Even without the Internet, there is concern among some states regarding mail-order sales. If a Texas resident makes a mail-order purchase from a company doing business in another state, the company may not charge a sales tax for the purchase. Many Internet transactions may also avoid being taxed. Consequently, we may see some changes in state taxes.

Crime and Fraud   Despite the best efforts of merchants and Internet software and hardware developers, the amount of money at stake will be a temptation for some. We must anticipate attempts to defraud consumers and merchants, which will necessitate new legislation and policing authorities. The fingerprints of the Internet criminal will be on his keyboard, not at the crime scene, which will be somewhere in cyberspace. The police will need new skills and tools to track down and apprehend cybercrooks.

In the previous sections, we have discussed several issues relating to Internet commerce. We now look at how they fit together in an Internet business transaction.

The Internet Store

Before Internet commerce begins, a business must establish an Internet presence and a way to conduct business. The first step is to establish a Web site that contains company information and product or service descriptions. There are several alternatives available for making transactions.

The simplest method is to use the Web as an advertisement medium only. For transactions, the customer would use conventional methods such as a personal visit or a telephone or fax message to place the order. The electronic commerce in this instance is advertising only. From an Internet purchaser's perspective, this is probably less satisfying than having the option to place the order and complete the transaction online. Some users prefer this method because they perceive that it allows them to avoid having their credit card information intercepted.

A second alternative is to have the entire transaction completed over the Internet. A company could implement the system to do this or could subscribe to the services of an Internet shopping service bureau. If the company handles the entire transaction, it must develop the necessary software and associated database to provide the Web page, an online catalog, and order taking and verification. Many Web hosting companies will provide these services for a fee. The trade-off between these two is the cost of setting up a server and software internally versus the costs of having a hosting service provide a Web presence. Hosting services of this type provide what is called an *electronic store* and establish stores for their clients in the mall. There is typically a setup charge to establish a store and a monthly fee for processing orders. The monthly fees can be a flat rate, a rate based on transactions processed, a rate based on a percentage of the dollar amount processed, or a combination of these alternatives. In the following discussion, we will focus on the issues of processing the order on the Net; we will assume that the business is providing the system for conducting business.

Today's Internet Transaction

Once the customer connects to the Net and accesses the business's Web page, the transaction can begin. Today, credit cards are used for payment in most business transactions. In the future, e-cash will become more common. Security should be inherent in all business transactions. An overview of the major ingredients in a secure Internet electronic commerce architecture is provided in Figure 3-3.

There are several components of Internet electronic commerce systems that must interoperate securely and reliably. For buyers, the principle components are a Web browser and an Internet connection.

For sellers, the major components include

➤ A merchant/storefront system that provides/presents buyers with the seller's product catalog and marketing materials, a mechanism for ordering/buying the seller's products, and access to customer service.

➤ Back-office systems that accept, process, and record sales transactions that originate with the merchant/storefront system. (The back-office systems include software for order processing, inventory management, accounting, tax calculation, electronic payment processing, shipping logistics, and customer account management.)

➤ A payment gateway for processing credit card transactions and/or other types of electronic payments.

To ensure efficiency and rapid order processing, there must be high levels of integration among the merchant/storefront, back office, and electronic payment system(s).

Merchant/storefront software is available from a number of vendors (see Table 3-2). Product offerings vary in the extent to which they are oriented toward consumer or business transactions and the extent to which they provide ready-made solutions ("out-of-the-box" solutions that simplify the creation of the seller's storefront or

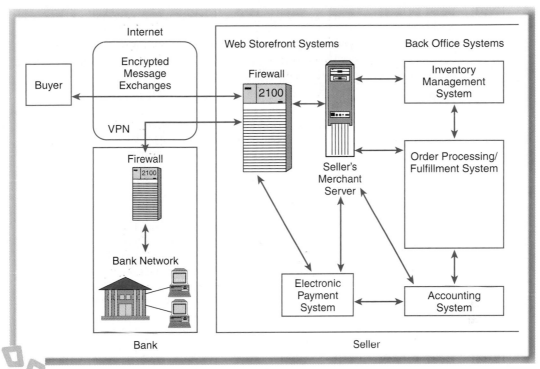

Figure 3-3   Elements of Secure Internet Electronic Commerce Architectures

e-catalog using wizards or design templates). They also vary in the underlying technologies that they employ. In spite of their differences, commerce servers address a common set of business functions. These are summarized in Table 3-3.

Now that you have a better understanding of how electronic commerce servers function, let's take a closer look at how an electronic cash transaction would be handled.

The general steps for making an electronic cash transaction are obtaining e-cash, selecting items to purchase, making payment, and receiving notification.

Table 3-2   Examples of Electronic Commerce Server Products

Product	Vendor
Domino Merchant	IBM/Lotus
Electronic Commerce Site	iCat
Internet Commerce Server	Oracle
Merchant Server	Netscape
Net.Commerce	IBM
OM-Transact	Open Market
Site Server Commerce Edition	Microsoft
Viaweb Store	Viaweb

Table 3-3   Business Functions Included in Merchant/Storefront Software

Business Function	Description
Product information	This function presents buyers with information about the seller's products/services. The commerce server must be able to query a database containing detailed product information and present the requested information to potential buyers.
Shopping cart	This function provides a dynamically generated HTML form that allows shoppers to accumulate products they want to buy. Using shopping carts, buyers can continue to add items from the seller's site; delete or change items; and place a single order after making all selections.
Merchant information	This function provides information about the seller's policies on sales returns, refunds, and basic ordering information.
Shopper information	This function gathers information about the buyer and data needed to personalize the Web pages displayed to the shopper. This enables the merchant server to personalize product information and pricing for particular customers.
Order initialization and inventory check	This function enables the merchant server to interact with the product inventory database to determine if a buyer's order can be processed. If an item is currently out of stock, the merchant server will tell the buyer before completing the transaction.
Order price adjustment	This function enables the merchant server to adjust prices on the basis of volume discounts, specials, or coupon redemption.
Shipping	This function presents buyers with shipping options and costs and calculates a total shipping charge based on the options selected by buyers.
Tax	This function determines applicable local and national taxes and adds these amounts to the total calculated for the contents of the shopping cart.
Payment	This function handles electronic payment details, including credit card processing.
Receipt	This function lets the buyer know that the electronic transaction is complete and presents the buyer with a printable order confirmation or an e-mail confirmation.

Obtain Digital Cash   If the consumer plans to use e-cash rather than a credit card to pay for the online transaction, she must first obtain the digital currency. The consumer withdraws e-cash from the bank and stores the e-cash on her computer. In obtaining the e-cash, the consumer provides the bank with her public encryption key. The public key is embedded in the certificate so the recipient can decrypt it. Once stored on disk, the e-cash can be backed up to avoid loss; however, the e-cash can be used only once because it is validated when exchanged. Because each e-cash certificate has a unique serial number, once the e-cash has been spent, the serial numbers are invalidated. The e-cash can be used in any Internet store that has made arrangements to accept it. The e-cash is controlled by the consumer's software. For example, the amount of available cash can be displayed so the consumer knows how much is available for spending, and the exchange of the e-cash is handled automatically.

Item Selection   The customer browses the seller's online catalog and selects products or services. How this is accomplished depends on the design of the Web pages. Companies with large product lines typically provide indexes and links to subcategories or to the products themselves. The product display may consist of a photograph (perhaps with several perspectives), description, size, weight, colors, and so on. After viewing the product information, the consumer can select it for purchase (add it to the shopping cart) or move on and continue browsing or exit from the merchant's page.

Payment   Once the buyer has added all desired items to the shopping cart and indicates that e-cash will be used to pay for them, the electronic commerce server typically presents the buyer with two options: The e-cash can be immediately transmitted, or the buyer may be prompted to authorize the payment. Regardless, the e-cash certificates are transferred to the merchant. The merchant then sends the digital cash certificate to the issuing bank or a certification authority to check its authenticity. If the certificate is verified, the transaction continues.

Notification   The buyer is notified of the order status. If the order has been accepted, the customer usually receives a confirmation number and shipping information; if the order is not accepted, the customer is provided with a reason and, perhaps, additional steps to take.

If the transaction is a credit card or smart card transaction, the payment step will differ somewhat. Credit card transactions require customer identification and authentication. When a customer connects to a merchant's Web site, the seller's electronic commerce server begins by identifying the buyer or gathering information during the buyer's first visit or transaction. Subsequent transactions with the merchant may be easier for the buyer to conduct because the merchant already has the buyer's relevant customer information on file (unless the buyer refuses to allow the merchant to save the information gathered during the first visit to the merchant's Web site). The customer information is usually protected by a password. Information collected about the customer may include the data given in Table 3-4.

When the credit card order is placed, the customer must provide credit card information, credit card number, kind of credit card, and expiration date. This is typed into an entry screen and sent to the merchant. Alternatively, a repeat customer can use a credit card number on file with the merchant. Secure transactions use the SSL protocol to encrypt the data. If SSL is not used, some browsers notify the user that the transaction is not secure. When the merchant receives the credit card information, the transaction must be authorized. The merchant sends the credit card information together with the transaction amount to the authorization center's node. The authorization center transmits an acceptance number or a rejection number. If accepted, the order information is processed by the merchant's order entry software, which causes goods to be shipped, inventory records to be updated, accounting files to be updated, and so on.

One other payment option may soon become available: electronic checks. With electronic checks, a consumer essentially writes a check using a digital signature. The check is sent to the merchant, who forwards it to the customer's bank for validation. If

Table 3-4   Customer Information

Name	Address	Ship-to address
Telephone numbers (home, work)	Fax number	E-mail address
	Credit card number and type	Purchase history
Mother's maiden name		

the digital signature is correct, the purchase amount is transferred from the customer's account to the merchant's account.

E-COMMERCE AND E-BUSINESS

Now that you have a general understanding of how transactions are conducted over the Internet, you are ready to take a look at the major kinds of commerce taking place on the Internet. We will begin by defining electronic commerce.

What Is E-Commerce?

electronic commerce (e-commerce) Doing business online, typically via the Web. E-commerce involves the use of computer applications communicating over networks that enable buyers and sellers to complete transactions (or significant parts of transactions) including the buying, selling, or exchanging of products, services, and information.

electronic business (e-business) Business activities on the Internet that include but go beyond buying and selling. E-business includes using the Internet to enhance customer service, coordinate activities with business partners, facilitate communication and knowledge management within organizations, and create electronic marketplaces to better serve the collective needs of entire industries.

Electronic commerce (e-commerce) is broadly defined as the use of computer networks to complete business transactions. The networks involved may be the Internet, intranets, extranets, and private networks. E-commerce is thus the use of computer applications communicating over networks that enable buyers and sellers to complete transactions (or significant parts of transactions). These transactions include the buying, selling, or exchanging of products, services, and information.

Today, many industry experts consider e-commerce to be a subset of e-business. **Electronic business (e-business)** refers to business activities beyond buying and selling, such as using the Internet to enhance customer service, coordinate activities with business partners, facilitate communication and knowledge management within organizations, and create electronic marketplaces to better serve the collective needs of entire industries.

Drivers of E-Commerce Expansion

E-commerce and e-business are growing rapidly worldwide. Among the major drivers of this expansion are (1) declining prices for computing and communications technologies, (2) increased business investment in information technologies, (3) the emergence of electronic business-to-business marketplaces, (4) rapid increases in the number of consumers with Internet access, and (5) continued expansion of the size and content of the World Wide Web. Each of these topics is briefly discussed here.

IT Price Declines and IT Investments   Rapid increases in e-commerce have coincided with dramatic cost reductions for computers, computer components, and communications equipment during the past 10 years. These price declines, combined with sustained economic growth in most developed nations including the United States, have encouraged massive business investments in computer and communications equipment and in new software to leverage the productive capacity of that equipment. Such investments have enabled organizations to build the hardware and software infrastructure needed for e-business and e-commerce.

Emergence of Electronic Markets   An increasing number of firms are investing in applications that will enable them to move supply networks and sales channels online and participate in new online marketplaces. Internally, firms are leveraging their investments in computer networks to improve a wide range of business processes—to coordinate product design, manage inventory, improve customer service, and reduce administrative and managerial costs.

The Internet is helping to level the playing field among large and small firms in business-to-business e-commerce. In the past, companies relied heavily on private networks and value-added services to carry out business-to-business electronic commerce. The high cost of such networks and services dissuaded most small businesses from pursuing business-to-business e-commerce. The Internet, however, has changed this by making it easier and cheaper for *all* businesses to transact business and exchange information.

Growing Customer Base   The growing number of consumers with Internet access cannot be overlooked as a driver of e-commerce expansion. As illustrated in Table 3-5, as of August 2001, there were more than 513 million Internet users worldwide, up from 171 million worldwide Internet users in March 1999 (see www.nua.ie/surveys/ how_many_online/index.html). Industry experts estimate that by the end of 2002, there will be nearly 675 million people around the world with Internet access; by 2005, there are expected to be more than a billion Internet users worldwide. Table 3-6 summarizes the 15 countries with the greatest number of Internet users at the end of 2000.

Increasing Size and Importance of the World Wide Web   The amount of information available online to people with Internet access has also grown very rapidly. Although estimates vary on the exact size of the Web and its growth rate, there is no question that it is huge and rapidly growing. For example, a study conducted by Cyveillance indicated that as of July 2000, there were more than 2 billion unique, publicly available pages on the Web. This study also concluded that the Web was growing at the rate of 7 million pages *per day,* meaning that it more than doubled in size between July 2000 and January 2003.

Types of E-Commerce

Electronic commerce transactions have been traditionally categorized in accord with the buyers and sellers involved in the transaction. These categories include

➤ **Business-to-business (B2B) e-commerce,** which includes transactions between businesses (such as between suppliers and manufacturers or between wholesalers and retailers) over the Internet or proprietary networks.

➤ **Business-to-consumer (B2C) e-commerce,** which includes Internet-based transactions between online merchants (*e-tailers*) and individual consumers.

➤ **Consumer-to-consumer (C2C) e-commerce,** which includes Internet-based selling and buying between consumers. This includes the use of online auction sites (such as eBay) and online classified ad sales (such as classified2000.com).

➤ **Intrabusiness/intracompany e-commerce,** which includes the internal exchange of goods, services, and information within a company over the company's intranet.

business-to-business (B2B) e-commerce One business selling to another business via the Web.

business-to-consumer (B2C) e-commerce Web-based sales transactions between businesses and consumers.

consumer-to-consumer (C2C) e-commerce Includes Internet-based selling and buying between consumers typically via online auction Web sites.

intrabusiness/ intracompany e-commerce Includes the exchange of goods, services, and information internally within a company typically via the company's intranet.

Table 3-5   Breakdown of Worldwide Internet Users as of August 2001

Location	August 2001
Africa	4.15 million
Asia/Pacific	143.99 million
Europe	154.63 million
Middle East	4.65 million
Canada and United States	180.68 million
Latin America	25.33 million
World Total	513.41 million

Table 3-6   Top 15 Nations in Internet Use at Year-End 2000

Rank	Country	Internet Users (Millions)	Share (percent) of Global Total
1	United States	135.7	36.20
2	Japan	26.9	7.18
3	Germany	19.1	5.10
4	United Kingdom	17.9	4.77
5	China	15.8	4.20
6	Canada	15.2	4.05
7	South Korea	14.8	3.95
8	Italy	11.6	3.08
9	Brazil	10.6	2.84
10	France	9.0	2.39
11	Australia	8.1	2.16
12	Russia	6.6	1.77
13	Taiwan	6.5	1.73
14	Netherlands	5.4	1.45
15	Spain	5.2	1.39
	Worldwide Total	**374.9**	**100.00%**

SOURCE: eTForecasts

These are illustrated in Figure 3-4. Their characteristics are summarized in Table 3-7.

Other forms of electronic commerce include *consumer-to-business (C2B)* e-commerce, electronic-governance (e-governance) applications, and electronic commerce transactions developed by nonprofit organizations. C2B e-commerce includes individual product/service sales to business organizations and individuals who solicit bids from business organizations for the products or services that they need. E-governance applications enable individuals and businesses to engage in Internet-based transactions with government agencies. This may include applying for or renewing business/professional licenses, paying fines, bidding on government contracts, and purchasing government surplus items. A number of nonprofit organizations such as social organizations, charities, and religious organizations have also embraced Internet-based e-commerce applications in order to cut costs, streamline operations, and improve customer service. However, because B2B, B2C, C2C, and intrabusiness e-commerce command the most attention of the media, each of these is described more fully here.

Business-to-Business (B2B) Electronic Commerce

Transactions between businesses account for the lion's share of commercial activity (online and offline) both domestically and in the global marketplace. E-commerce technologies have the potential to make these transactions less expensive and more efficient. Companies are also using these technologies to increase the efficiency of their internal operations.

Most B2B e-commerce involves the creation of **interorganizational information systems (IOS)** that enable the exchange of information between two or more organizations. IOS creation is often an offshoot of establishing business partnerships with an organization's suppliers or customers. By agreeing to exchange information (such as

interorganizational information system (IOS) An IOS enables business transactions or the exchange of information between two or more organizations. IOS creation is often an offshoot of establishing business partnerships with suppliers and/or customers.

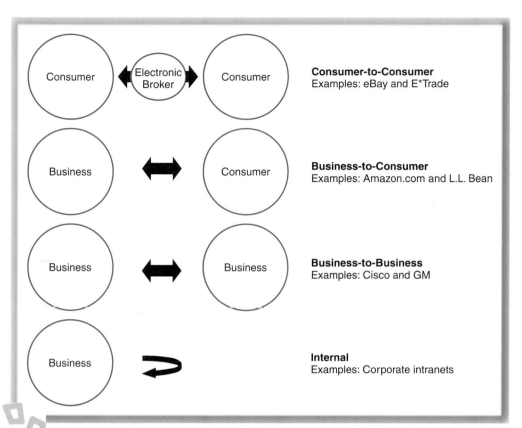

Figure 3-4   Types of E-Commerce

Table 3-7   Characteristics of the Four Major Categories of Electronic Commerce

Category	Major Characteristics
Business-to-business	➤ Extranet based ➤ Restricted to business partners ➤ Firewall, encryption, and authorization levels ➤ Payments by predetermined credit terms
Business-to-consumer	➤ Internet based ➤ Unrestricted access ➤ Verified credit card payments
Consumer-to-consumer	➤ Internet based ➤ Unrestricted access ➤ Credit card or cash equivalent payments ➤ Facilitated by electronic broker
Internal	➤ Intranet based ➤ Restricted to employees and customers ➤ Firewall security, passwords, and authorization ➤ Intracompany charge payments

orders, bills, and payments) over communications networks using prearranged formats, business partners are able to better coordinate their activities. In the past, most IOSs involved the use of proprietary communication links. Today, however, the trend is toward Internet-based communication links among business partners, such as extranets.

IOS systems encompass a wide range of business-to-business activities, including electronic data interchange (EDI); extranets; electronic funds transfers from one organization's bank account to that of a business partner; electronic forms transfers among business partners; integrated messaging—the ability to exchange EDI documents and data, e-mail, and fax documents over a single communication channel; shared databases—providing business partners with online access to the organization's databases so that they can better coordinate their activities with your needs; and supply chain management—cooperative arrangements among business partners that enable them to reduce inventories, facilitate order fulfillment, and support just-in-time and "pull" manufacturing.

IOSs are the foundation for virtually all forms of B2B e-commerce. Although there are many kinds of B2B electronic commerce, most fall into one of three categories: (1) electronic data interchange (EDI); (2) "buy-side" procurement applications that automate corporate purchasing processes; and (3) "sell-side" catalog-based applications that enable customers to configure and price orders.

Prior to conducting transactions, B2B buyers and sellers typically establish a contractual relationship with each other. This usually results in the seller extending credit to the buyer and the creation of an electronic linkage between the companies' computer systems. Most B2B transactions start with a purchase order (either paper or electronic) and involve processing the order, delivery and receipt of ordered products, invoicing, payment, and financial recording.

Electronic Data Interchange (EDI)   Prior to the widespread deployment of Internet-based technologies during the 1990s, companies that engaged in B2B electronic commerce did so using a secure form of computer-to-computer communication known as EDI. In fact, prior to 1990, EDI *was* electronic commerce.

Electronic data interchange (EDI) is the electronic transmission of business documents from one company to another using a set of standard forms, data elements, and messages. EDI documents include purchase orders, invoices, shipping notifications, acknowledgments, and remittance notices. EDI documents and data can be exchanged between businesses in several ways, including point-to-point connections over leased telephone lines; private, proprietary networks; value-added networks (VANs); and the Internet. By exchanging EDI documents and data, companies are able to reduce B2B transaction costs, reduce errors, and provide business partners with increased access to information.

Traditional EDI is characterized by

➤ Direct application-to-application exchange of information (e.g., automatic submittal of an invoice generated by the seller's computer system to the buyer's accounts payable system).

➤ Well-defined formats for EDI documents and data that conform to industry standards.

➤ Store-and-forward messaging to ensure security, authentication, delivery confirmation, and a transaction audit trail.

➤ Batch-oriented rather than interactive operation. Although documents and data are exchanged automatically, most exchanges involve multiple rather than single documents.

EDI Standards   Two groups have been involved in the establishment and evolution of the two most widely recognized and used EDI standards. The American National Standards Institute (ANSI) developed the *X.12* standard. The United Nations Economic Commission for Europe (UN/ECE) developed the other major EDI standard, *EDIFACT* (Electronic Data Interchange for Administration, Commerce, and Transport).

Both EDIFACT and X.12 define a common set of business forms, data elements, and data communication protocols that allow business applications in different organizations to exchange information automatically and securely.

Web-Based EDI   In the past, the cost of proprietary networks needed to support EDI transactions, along with the technical complexity of EDI itself, typically meant that EDI was feasible only for large organizations and their large suppliers. Now, however, the Internet has enabled more small and midsize businesses to economically use EDI because Web-based EDI requires only a PC, an Internet connection, and a Web browser to link to existing EDI infrastructures in other firms. The trend is toward Web-based EDI and away from proprietary EDI systems. The growth in Web-based EDI is one of the major reasons why significant increases in B2B e-commerce are expected over the next decade.

Web-based EDI is an example of an **extranet**. Extranets leverage TCP/IP protocols and applications, especially the Web. Today's extranet typically enables business partners (suppliers and customers) to access a company's computing resources. By using Internet technologies to enable information sharing between business partners, extranets have the potential to benefit companies in many ways, including the following:

> ➤ *Reduced costs and enhanced profits for suppliers.* Extranet links between suppliers and customers reduce the need for paper-based order fulfillment processing; they also enable suppliers to be more responsive to customer needs, even when these change quickly.

> ➤ *Reduced inventories in the supply chain.* Extranets can be used to support just-in-time manufacturing and quick-response retailing. A goal of each of these is to reduce the amount of inventory in the supply chain and, as a result, reduce supply-chain members' inventory costs.

> ➤ *Reduced product prices for the ultimate customer.* Order fulfillment and inventory cost reductions often translate into lower prices for the ultimate consumer. If everyone in the supply chain saves money because of the extranet, prices charged to the ultimate customer can be reduced.

> ➤ *Enhanced customer service.* Extranets can be used to respond quickly to customer complaints; they can also be used to track customer orders and identify needed corrections very quickly.

extranet Extranets leverage TCP/IP protocols and applications, especially the Web, to enable business partners (suppliers and customers) to access a company's computing resources. Extranets are also widely used for B2B e-commerce.

Buy-Side B2B E-Commerce Applications   **Buy-side B2B e-commerce** applications automate and facilitate business procurement and purchasing processes. In most organizations, there are many individuals involved in these business processes, including those requesting or approving expenditures, negotiating the purchase with suppliers/vendors, recording receipt of goods, approving the invoice, processing check or electronic funds transfer (EFT) payments, and handling the accounting and financial reporting associated with purchase transactions.

Procurement software systems available from vendors like Ariba, Commerce One, Fisher, and Harbinger are helping organizations reduce procurement order processing costs, expedite requisition approval, provide enterprise access to corporate procurement processes, and integrate procurement and back-office systems. These systems automate the selection and purchase of goods by moving these processes to

buy-side B2B e-commerce Applications that automate and facilitate business procurement and purchasing processes.

desktop systems; lower the administrative overhead associated with purchasing processes enterprise-wide; electronically exchange a full range of procurement documents between requests and buyers, including purchase orders/requisitions, invoices, shipping notices, and acknowledgments; facilitate the creation of reports summarizing organization-wide purchasing patterns; and strengthen procurement process controls.

sell-side B2B e-commerce These applications include software systems to make it easier for companies to sell their products to other businesses.

Sell-Side B2B E-Commerce Applications   **Sell-side B2B e-commerce** applications include software systems to make it easier for companies to sell their products to other businesses. These include systems that help the organization build and maintain online catalogs of product descriptions and pricing, maintain buyer information (such as payment history), track inventory and product warehousing, process and fulfill orders, record payments, and generate financial reports. Sell-side products, such as those available from FastParts, iCat, Netscape, and Open Market, include catalogs, order transaction processing mechanisms, inventory verification systems, credit verification systems, payment systems, order tracking systems, and supply chain management tools that enable seamless integration of supplier and buyer computer networks.

The evolution of B2B sell-side applications is enabling companies to move beyond traditional buyer-supplier business models (such as EDI) toward online trading communities. In an online trading community, the content of many suppliers' product catalogs is aggregated into one megacatalog located within a secure online trading "community" of buyers and suppliers. Buyers can access the aggregated catalog to comparison shop for the best prices. Suppliers benefit by having their products brought to the attention of a larger set of buyers; they also benefit by avoiding the costs associated with establishing and operating multiple point-to-point links with buyers.

The emergence of standards for Internet-based B2B transactions is also fueling the rapid growth of B2B e-commerce. One of the most important standards is Open Buying on the Internet (OBI).

The Future of B2B E-Commerce   During the late 1990s, B2B e-commerce accounted for more than 75 percent of the total volume of e-commerce. Prognosticators expect B2B's percentage of total e-commerce to rise to more than 85 percent by 2005 in spite of the dramatic increases that are expected in the other major categories of e-commerce (such as B2C and C2C). The explosion in e-commerce that we are witnessing is being driven by the tremendous growth of Internet-based B2B e-commerce. It goes without saying that businesses have recognized B2B e-commerce's potential to cut costs and increase efficiency by streamlining their purchasing, sales, and other core business processes.

Just how rapidly is B2B e-commerce growing? Table 3-8 summarizes the B2B growth estimates by several respected market research organizations. Industry researchers maintain that by 2004, B2B e-commerce will represent more than 5 percent of all business-to-business transactions worldwide. According to eMarketer, by 2005, online B2B transactions will represent more than 40 percent of the total number of business-to-business transactions among U.S. manufacturers and their suppliers and customers. In 2000, only 3 percent of such transactions were performed online (see cyberatlas.internet.com/markets/b2b/article/0,,10091_986661,00.html).

The Emergence of Electronic Marketplaces   The Internet is opening the doors to new business models such as net markets and coalition markets. Today, the vast majority of B2B e-commerce still conforms to a direct channel model (in a direct channel model, one seller has many buyers). The emergence of net markets, in which

Table 3-8   Forecasts of Worldwide and U.S. B2B E-Commerce (EC) by Several Internet Research Organizations

Focus	Organization	2000	2001	2002	2003	2004	2005
Worldwide B2B EC	Gartner/ Dataquest	$403 billion	$953 billion	$2.18 trillion	$3.95 trillion	$7.29 trillion	
Worldwide B2B EC	Emarketer	$185 billion	$336.2 billion	$684.3 billion	$1.26 trillion		
B2B EC in United States	Forrester Research	$400 billion	$700 billion	$1.2 trillion	$1.8 trillion	$2.7 trillion	
Industrial B2B EC in United States	Jupiter Communications	$336 billion	$700 billion	$1.51 trillion	$2.94 trillion	$4.59 trillion	$6.34 trillion

there are many buyers and many sellers, is occurring very rapidly and is expected to account for more than a third of B2B nonservice e-commerce in the United States by 2005. Some industry experts expect more than half a million enterprises will be participating in e-markets as either buyers or sellers worldwide by the end of 2005.

These important B2B intermediaries have emerged rapidly in virtually all industries, providing new places for buyers and sellers to meet, allowing a variety of pricing schemes to flourish, and enabling complex transactions. Net and coalition markets (the latter consist of a consortium of buyers and sellers) are altering the roles of traditional business-to-business intermediaries (such as distributors and wholesalers) and, by virtue of making vast amounts of information available at very low costs, shifting the balance of power among market participants. These online market spaces have expanded the reach of both buyers and sellers; they enable buyers to solicit bids from a broader range of suppliers and, in turn, allow suppliers to develop relationships with additional buyers.

By the end of 2002, more than 2,200 online B2B marketplaces had been established worldwide. Some networked marketplaces offer a broad array of functions for targeted client groups. Onvia, for example, is one of many sites serving as a small business portal for goods and services. Other sites leverage existing relationships within specific industries on a global basis. For example, Ford, General Motors, and DaimlerChrysler are working together to build Covisint, an online marketplace for the automobile industry. It is expected to eventually handle the more than $250 billion in parts and supplies needed by these companies each year. This online marketplace is also expected to reduce these companies' purchasing costs by 10 percent and the average cost of manufacturing an automobile by $1,000.

B2B online marketplaces are also being developed for nonmanufacturing industries. For example, Sears, Roebuck and Company, the second largest U.S. retailer, has joined with Carrefour SA, a Paris–based retailer, to create GlobalNetXchange, an online marketplace for the retail industry. These two companies buy more than $80 billion in goods and services each year from 50,000 different suppliers and are encouraging other retailers to join them in this endeavor.

Business-to-Consumer (B2C) E-Commerce

Like B2B e-commerce, business-to-consumer (B2C) e-commerce is growing rapidly. According to a report issued by the U.S. Department of Commerce, total business-to-consumer e-commerce (excluding travel services) grew more than 20 percent during 2001 to more than $32 billion. Research by Forrester Research estimates that B2C e-commerce in the United States exceeded $75 billion in 2002 and will increase to over $100 billion in 2003. Further growth is expected in the years ahead. The percentage of Internet users purchasing online is also increasing. For example, according to research by International Data Corporation (IDC), by the end of 2000, 29 percent of people who went online purchased a good or service. According to eMarketer estimates, more than half of the Internet users in the United States over 13 years of age (more than 60 million) made at least one online purchase in 2002 (see cyberatlas. internet.com/markets/retailing/article/0,,6061_1011911,00.html). Similar increases in the percentage of Internet users making online purchases is being observed worldwide.

Not only is the number of Web purchasers increasing, but so is the size of the average transaction per consumer. Steady annual increases can be observed in the average transaction size calculations reported monthly by the NRF/Forester Online Retail Index (see, for example, cyberatlas.internet.com/markets/retailing/article/0,,6061_961291,00.html#table).

Consumer Online Buying Patterns   According to Greenfield Online, consumers have traditionally been most likely to use the Internet to purchase books, music, and computer software from online retailers (e-tailers). This is illustrated in Table 3-9. However, consumers often go online to make airline, hotel, and rental car reservations. In addition, more and more consumers are taking advantage of the Internet to buy automobiles, buy/sell stocks, buy insurance, and use Internet banking services. Sustained increases in all these areas are expected in the years ahead.

Other Impacts of the Internet on Consumers   Online sales do not reflect the full impact that the Internet is having on consumer sales. The Web is also changing the way that consumers shop off-line. A large number of studies have shown that many consumers research products online before purchasing in traditional bricks-and-mortar outlets. In fact, shopping online and buying off-line continues to be more prevalent than consummating online shopping with an online purchase.

Internet-based e-commerce is benefiting *all* consumers in a variety of ways, even those that never shop or buy online. Among the benefits are price pressure on con-

Table 3-9   Top Five Items Purchased from E-Tailers

Item	April 1999 (%)	April 2000 (%)
Books	26	26
CDs	24	24
Computer software	21	18
Health/fitness/beauty	5	14
Clothing	11	14

SOURCE: Greenfield Online

sumer products, the availability of product and service information, the ability to research products prior to purchase, and the ability to engage in a variety of transactions with government agencies.

Pricing Impacts   For consumers, one of the most significant impacts of Internet-based commerce may be the effect that it is having on the pricing of goods and services. Potential buyers can check the price and availability of products from a variety of sites in far less time than it would take to conduct store-to-store comparisons in the traditional world of bricks-and-mortar. Because this can be done "24/7/365" (24 hours a day, 7 days a week, and 365 days a year), consumers are not limited to comparison shopping during "business hours." In addition, online shopping has been facilitated by software specialized to operate as digital shopping agents. Such digital agents, known as "bots" (derived from "robots"), cruise through large numbers of Internet sites almost instantaneously, searching for the most favorable price and feature combinations.

Shopping for bargains online has become more interesting through the emergence of online auctions. Because the Internet provides a relatively low-cost and convenient way of bringing buyers and sellers together, online auction Web sites such as eBay have grown rapidly. Reverse auction sites such as PriceLine.com have also flourished; at these sites, the consumer names the price, and the seller decides whether or not to accept it. At Mercata.com, consumers are able to band together to get lower prices; through this site, a product or service price is determined by the number of people who want to buy a product—the greater the number of buyers, the lower the price is.

The Internet also enables sellers to alert buyers quickly to "last minute deals." Airlines, cruise lines, travel, and ticket services take advantage of the Internet's ability to inform consumers of such bargains. Both buyers and sellers benefit from this.

Product and Service Information   Consumers with access to the Internet have a vast array of product and service price, quality, and availability information at their fingertips. Manufacturers, retailers, and online magazines offer detailed product, warranty, and repair information, along with head-to-head comparisons of competing products. Via the Web, consumers can now conveniently assemble comparison shopping information that was nearly impossible to assemble previously.

Those in the market for a new or used car are now able to do their homework online and subsequently approach dealers with a wealth of information that can strengthen their bargaining position and reduce some of the stress of car buying. According to J.D. Power and Associates, more than 60 percent of consumers who want to purchase an automobile use the Internet to help them shop. After the purchase, car buyers can find a wide range of additional information online, including authorized repair locations, warranty information, recalls, and information needed to troubleshoot problems.

Health Care   Thousands of health-care Web sites exist on the Internet. Industry researchers estimate that more than 100 million U.S. adults visited these sites in 2002 (see cyberatlas.internet.com/markets/healthcare/article/0,,10101_755471,00.html). An increasing number of patients arrive for their doctors' appointments with possible diagnoses for their symptoms; these diagnoses have been downloaded from sites such as WebMD or the America Online Health Channel. Patients with Internet access can also obtain information about their health-care plans, find doctors, and in some cases submit claims for fee reimbursement. Doctors, too, are increasing their use of the Internet as a source of information on the latest news in medical research.

Employment   The Internet is increasingly being used as a source of employment information. Many organizations post job openings on their company's Web site as well as on other employment-oriented Web sites. Some organizations also accept online applications. In their 2000 survey, recruitsoft.com and iLogos Research found that 79 percent of the global 500 companies used their Web sites for recruitment, up from 29 percent in 1998. Approximately 91 percent of the global 500 companies recruited online in 2002 (see www.ilogos.com/iLogosReport2002/).

A growing number of Web sites offer online employment classifieds, grouping the job postings of multiple employers. Some sites are maintained by newspapers, the traditional providers of employment classifieds. Others specialize in specific types of employment areas. For example, the U.S. government maintains www.usajobs.opm.gov, a site containing a listing of current federal job openings. Dice.com specializes in contract and full-time positions for computer programmers and other IT professionals.

Consumer-Oriented E-Governance   Citizens are benefiting from federal, state, and local government initiatives to use the Internet to communicate with clients and to provide public services to businesses and individuals. For example, the Internal Revenue Service Web site, www.irs.gov, enables taxpayers to download tax forms and instructions.

Many state and local governments are also moving services online. Individuals and businesses can find information on a wide variety of topics, including registration (voter, business, property, pets, or vehicle), parks, and trash removal schedules. In some locations, people can pay their local property taxes and parking tickets via third-party sites such as www.ezgov.com.

Business Impacts of B2C E-Commerce   Businesses have begun to realize that B2C e-commerce can dramatically lower the costs of traditional retail operations. They are also realizing that new business models are needed to fit the requirements of Net-savvy consumers. For example, there is a shift from mass marketing to personalized marketing. Specialized forms of businesses (such as product aggregators, auction sites, and service providers) are emerging in response to the needs of targeted customers.

The advent of the Internet and Web has enabled retailers to take catalog businesses online, thereby reducing the costs of presenting products and supporting around-the-clock shopping. The challenges they face now include developing and maintaining Web sites that are capable of attracting and retaining customers and sustained B2C e-commerce revenue increases.

Consumer-to-Consumer (C2C) E-Commerce

Because the Internet provides a relatively low-cost and convenient way of bringing buyers and sellers together, online auction Web sites such as eBay have grown rapidly. Although such sites are relative newcomers to the Internet, billions of dollars of goods/services are exchanged between consumers each year through online auction sites.

Online auction sites are able to stay in business by extracting small sales commissions from both the seller and buyer for each transaction that takes place. Sellers are typically obligated to accept the highest bid placed for the product/service they post online as long as it does not fall short of the seller's preset minimum acceptable bid level. Buyers using the site are also obligated to complete the transaction with the seller if they submit the highest bids for the products/services being offered for sale. Arrangements for the actual exchange of goods/services between consumers may take place off-line, although most sites provide online mechanisms for facilitating these.

Many auction sites, including eBay, have added B2C and B2B e-commerce features to their Web sites and have thus evolved toward being full-service online marketplaces. The success of eBay has spawned a number of competitors, including sites that specialize in particular types of products (such as used luxury automobiles, aircraft, baseball cards, and competition sailboats).

Intrabusiness/Intracompany E-Commerce

As noted previously, intrabusiness (intraorganizational) e-commerce includes the online exchange of goods, services, and information within an organization. Such exchanges often take place over an intranet. An **intranet** is a company-wide network (LAN or WAN) that uses Internet technologies to facilitate information exchange among employees. An intranet may also be used to support the internal exchange of goods/services. Firewalls are typically employed to protect intranets from unauthorized outside access.

Intranet building blocks include Web servers, Web publishing tools, browsers, databases, and TCP/IP networks. Various forms of groupware (see Chapter 1) are also commonly found in intranets. With these, intranet designers and developers are able to provide

> ➤ Web-enabled access to corporate databases
> ➤ Up-to-date corporate and subunit Web pages
> ➤ Web-enabled interactive communication (such as videoconferencing and chatting)
> ➤ Web-based document workflow and routing
> ➤ Web-based groupware and collaborative computing
> ➤ Computer/Web-based telephony and computer-integrated telephony
> ➤ Web-based interfaces to B2B e-commerce applications such as purchasing
> ➤ Integration with extranets

Organizations are leveraging intranets to

> ➤ Facilitate the internal exchange of goods and services
> ➤ Enhance customer service
> ➤ Enhance product development processes
> ➤ Facilitate knowledge sharing and the development of sophisticated knowledge management (KM) systems
> ➤ Facilitate the collaborative work of work teams
> ➤ Empower workers by increasing the volume, quality, and timeliness of the information they need to make decisions
> ➤ Enhance project management
> ➤ Reduce the need for paper-based information delivery within the organization
> ➤ Create and deliver Web-based training and development programs for new and existing employees

When compared to traditional corporate client/server networks, intranets offer a number of other potential benefits to businesses, including the following:

> ➤ Intranets allow businesses to quickly develop and deploy new applications (after the intranet infrastructure is in place).
> ➤ Virtually all organizational computing platforms can be used to support the intranet with minimal interoperability challenges.
> ➤ Legacy applications and information sources (back-office systems, databases, and groupware) can be integrated with the intranet.

intranet A private network that uses Internet technology such as hypertext documents and Internet protocols to store and retrieve data. Usually located within an organization's firewalls, an intranet is not accessible by the general public.

➤ Intranets allow scalability: Little investment in software and infrastructure is needed to get started, and because the intranet can be supported on most existing computing platforms, little investment is needed to grow the intranet.

➤ Like the Internet, intranets have open architectures; this means that the availability of new add-on applications from third-party vendors is increasing.

➤ A wide range of file types can be transferred across the intranet, including audio, video, and interactive multimedia files.

➤ Employees who are experienced browser users typically need little training on intranet use.

More and more companies are realizing the potential benefits of intranets. As a result, these are expected to grow tremendously in the years ahead and to become a standard component of the internal computing environment within businesses.

Other Types of E-Commerce

As noted previously, other major types of e-commerce include consumer-to-business (C2B) e-commerce and nonbusiness e-commerce. In C2B e-commerce, it is the consumer that initiates the business transaction by

➤ *Using the Internet to sell products and services to businesses or other organizations.* What distinguishes this from business-to-business e-commerce is that in the instance of C2B, the supplier is typically a self-employed individual rather than a business organization. Products sold to businesses are seasonal or specialty items (such as handicrafts) that may be resold by the businesses to consumers.

➤ *Soliciting potential sellers to make offers/bids to sell a particular product or service to the individual consumer.* This approach is similar to that used on a reverse auction site, except that the consumer is using the Internet to make direct contact with potential providers rather than going through an intermediary.

Nonbusiness e-commerce includes the use of the Internet and e-commerce transactions to reduce the expenses of nonbusiness entities such as charitable organizations, not-for-profit organizations, religious organizations, academic institutions, and government agencies. For example, an increasing number of charitable organizations enable individuals to make pledges or contributions via the Web (often as Web-based credit card transactions). Not-for-profit organizations, including National Public Radio, also encourage making contributions by credit card over the Internet, because these are much less expensive for them to process than paper-based transactions that are sent in by mail. Many churches and religious organizations are following suit. Other examples of nonbusiness e-commerce applications include the following:

➤ Publicly supported colleges and universities that use Web-based registration for classes and Web-based tuition and fee payment. (Some of these also deliver courses or entire degree programs online.)

➤ E-governance applications that enable consumers to file and pay their taxes, renew motor vehicle or professional licenses, and pay traffic fines online.

All forms of e-commerce are growing rapidly and will continue to do so in the foreseeable future. Such growth demonstrates that we have truly entered the information economy.

MAJOR E-BUSINESS AND E-COMMERCE APPLICATIONS

In the previous sections, several important e-commerce and e-business applications have been mentioned in passing, including supply chain management, e-procurement, Internet marketing, customer relationship management, and Internet banking and financial services. In this section, we will consider each of these more fully.

Supply Chain Management

A *supply chain* encompasses all the business processes involved in creating and delivering products to customers. This often involves a complex network of relationships among all the business partners involved in the manufacturing and delivering of products to customers. Figure 3-5 is a simplistic example of a supply chain. As Figure 3-5 illustrates, a supply chain includes the facilities and transportation links that business partners use to acquire and transform raw materials, store finished goods, and distribute/sell products to the ultimate customer.

Supply chain management (SCM) involves the coordination of material (such as raw materials and finished goods), information (orders, order tracking, and delivery notices), and financial flows (such as credit authorization and electronic funds transfers) between and among the business partners involved in the supply chain. The goal of SCM is to enable all the business partners to function as if they were a single company. In order to achieve this goal, the computer networks of the business partners must be integrated. There can be significant challenges to achieving such integration when business partners use a variety of computing platforms and applications. However, when appropriate integration is achieved, the total cost of the

supply chain management (SCM) Cooperative arrangements among business partners that enable them to reduce inventories, facilitate order fulfillment, and support just-in-time and "pull" manufacturing. SCM involves the coordination of material, information, and financial flows among the business partners in a supply chain.

Figure 3-5   An Example of a Supply Chain

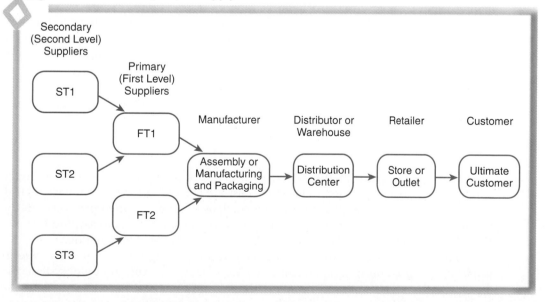

order-to-delivery process can be reduced to the benefit of all the business partners in the supply chain.

In the past, supply chains often consisted of several point-to-point EDI interfaces between suppliers and customers rather than end-to-end integration. Today, the trend is toward Internet-enabled and -coordinated supply chain management. Internet technologies are being used to enable information sharing and enhance communication among supply chain business partners. They are also being used to support collaborative planning processes in order to make the supply chain more efficient. Within some supply chains, efforts are underway to redesign the products that flow through them so that they can be handled more easily as they make their way from suppliers to customers.

Within many industries, SCM is necessary to remain competitive. As integration of business partner networks continues to improve, sophisticated coordination mechanisms such as *efficient customer response (ECR),* continuous replenishment, and *quick response (QR)* systems have been introduced in some industries. Advances in supply chain management are also facilitating the development of sophisticated build-to-order and mass customization capabilities.

E-Procurement

Internet-enhanced procurement processes often play a key role in supply chain management. Procurement management is concerned with obtaining the supplies that an organization needs to carry out its work. Some of these supplies include the raw materials used within the organization's manufacturing or service processes. Purchasing departments are also responsible for the cost-effective acquisition of back-office supplies (copier/printer paper and other office supplies) and computing hardware/software from vendors.

Many electronic procurement (e-procurement) applications are buy-side or sell-side applications described previously in the chapter. These typically include the ability to peruse integrated supplier catalogs to select products; electronic ordering via EDI, fax, or e-mail; facilitation of online approval for purchase orders that require management sign-off; connectivity with suppliers/vendors; order status tracking; and the ability to identify opportunities for further cost savings through the assessment of company-wide purchasing patterns. Because these capabilities are supported in the electronic marketplaces that have emerged in many industries, it should not be surprising to learn that electronic marketplaces are playing an increasingly important role in organizational procurement processes. With e-procurement processes at work throughout the supply chain, each company is positioned to reduce total procurement costs and to be more profitable.

Internet Marketing

The hardware/software platform that an organization uses to support e-commerce applications can also be used to enhance customer demand for the company's products or services. Sell-side B2B applications, such as those mentioned previously in the chapter, are used to facilitate sales to business partners. Needless to say, the Internet also plays a significant marketing role in B2C applications such as e-tailing.

The Internet is used by many manufacturers, including Dell Computer, as a *direct marketing channel.* Consumers can visit Dell's Web site, specify the computer system configuration that they want, and complete the sales transaction. Other manufacturers/vendors work with *infomediaries* or *online aggregators* to bring their products/services to the attention of customers. Infomediaries and online aggregators may create *electronic shopping malls* (*e-malls* or *cybermalls*) to showcase the products/services of multiple manu-facturers or vendors. The two major types of e-malls are

> ➤ *Electronic distributors.* Electronic distributors advertise products/services for business partners, conduct the online transaction, and take responsibility for order fulfill-ment.

> ➤ *Electronic brokers.* Electronic brokers help customers find products and services but hand off the sales transaction and responsibility for order fulfillment directly to the manufacturer or vendor.

Both electronic distributors and electronic brokers are examples of using the Internet as an indirect marketing channel.

Of course, Web sites are also being used as advertising vehicles. Many popular Web sites sell space on their homepage (and other pages) to advertisers. The cost to advertise on a given Web page is typically determined by the average number of daily visitors to the page. A Web site such as Yahoo.com that has exceptionally large num-bers of daily visitors is able to command premium prices for advertising on its home-page as well as hefty advertising charges for space on the other pages on its site that have high daily visitor counts.

E-Mail Marketing   Both business and not-for-profit organizations use e-mail as a mar-keting channel. Although such marketing often verges on being unsolicited spam, it is, nonetheless, an effective marketing approach. Typically, businesses only use e-mail to market to customers with existing accounts or individuals that have indicated that they are interested in being informed of sales or special offers via e-mail. For example, individuals that create an account with Travelocity.com can signify in a check box that they are interested in receiving information about last-minute travel deals via e-mail. Businesses that distribute browser plug-ins or helper programs (such as RealAudio or Adobe Acrobat Reader) over the Web also ask individuals if they want to be notified of new versions or upgrades via e-mail. Not-for-profit organizations often market upcom-ing conferences and other special events to Listservs and newsgroups whose sub-scribers are likely to be interested in attending.

An e-mail marketing trend is toward the distribution of marketing messages that look like Web pages. The ability of an increasing number of SMTP–compliant e-mail programs to support stylized text and colorful backgrounds with hyperlinks to busi-ness Web sites has stimulated organizations to move in this direction.

Customer Relationship Management Systems

Customer relationship management (CRM) systems are being incorporated into the e-business infrastructures of a growing number of firms. The primary goal of CRM is to increase an organization's ability to retain its most profitable customers by enabling the organization to provide them with outstanding customer service. Business interest in CRM applications is driven by mounting evidence that (1) it costs more to sell a product or service to a new customer than to an existing one; (2) increased customer retention is likely to translate into increased profitability; and (3) companies that are able to respond quickly to customers who have complaints are less likely to lose them to competitors.

CRM systems are designed to instill customer loyalty through facilitating out-standing customer service. They do so by integrating all channels that customers may use to contact the company: telephone, fax, e-mail, or the Web. By aggregating cus-tomer contact information acquired through each of these channels, the organization is better positioned to know a customer's preferences as well as their transaction

customer relation-ship management (CRM) system An integrated information system that is used to plan, schedule, and control customer sales and customer service activities.

history and order status. If the customer contacts the organization and reports a problem, the aggregated information enables the company to quickly identify the cause and resolve the problem, thereby reducing the likelihood of losing the customer to a competitor. All other contacts made by the customer can be treated as cross-selling and up-selling opportunities because employees will know immediately what products/services the customer has as well as others that should be brought to their attention.

Loyalty programs often play a major role in the customer retention aspects of CRM. Programs like Hilton Hotels' Hhonors program award loyalty points toward free room nights to frequent guests. Through business partnerships with other companies, Hhonors members can also earn frequent flyer miles for each hotel room they book, receive additional points for renting a car from specific car rental agencies in order to get to the hotel, and receive points toward free room nights by using a Hilton Honors credit card, such as that offered by American Express.

In order to achieve CRM goals using software systems available from Seibel, Oracle, and other major CRM vendors, organizations often employ computer-integrated telephony (CTI), data warehousing, and customer-oriented decision support system technologies. These enable superior customer service by putting knowledge about each customer at the fingertips of employees, no matter what contact channel is used by the customer.

CRM recognizes that outstanding customer service involves more than providing online technical support and a customer service hotline. In the past, businesses viewed customer service as something that took place after the sale. Now with CRM, customer service extends the sales transaction itself. For example, an increasing number of e-tailers now include hyperlinks on the Web pages used by customers to make online purchases. If a customer encounters a problem or has a question while attempting to complete the online transaction, they can click on the hyperlink. By doing so, the customer will instantly receive a phone call from a customer service representative or begin an online chat. In sum, customer service is just a click away, 24/7.

Many organizations are making significant investments in CRM systems, and the systems themselves are maturing rapidly. CRM is causing numerous organizations to rethink their traditional separation of sales and customer service and to blend these processes in new customer friendly ways. CRM is becoming one of the foundation e-business applications in today's networking infrastructure, and its importance is expected to increase in the years ahead.

Internet Banking and Financial Services

The Internet is reshaping the banking and financial services industries. Traditional banks, credit unions, and financial services companies are being challenged by Internet-only competitors. They are also being pushed by customers who are interested in 24/7 access to account information and who would prefer to do their banking and make investment decisions in the privacy of their homes. Having a Web strategy has become a competitive necessity within both of these industries.

electronic funds transfer (EFT) The transfer of money from one account to another by computer.

Internet Banking   Banks are not strangers to electronic commerce. **Electronic funds transfer (EFT)** is a popular electronic payment method for transferring money from one bank account to another in the same or a different bank. Banks have been using EFT for interbank funds transfers through automated clearinghouses (ACHs) since the 1970s. ACH EFT transactions are popular among bank and credit union customers for the payment of recurring bills, such as those for telephone service, ISP service, utilities (water and electricity), and cable service. Many bank customers prefer the convenience of automatic EFT "bank draft" payments for monthly bills. The EFT process is illustrated in Figure 3-6.

Another common "electronic" bank service is "banking by phone," which enables customers to call an 800 number and utilize touch-tone phone keys to carry out a variety of transactions, including checking account balances and transferring funds from one account to another. Automated teller machine (ATM) networks and debit/check cards are other examples of electronic banking services.

The trend today is to supplement these traditional electronic bank services with Internet banking services. Customers who sign up for Internet banking services are provided with a homepage from which they can access current account status information (account balances); review recent transactions (deposits, withdrawals, or loan payments); apply for loans and sometimes receive instant approvals; pay bills by activating ACH transactions; download account data directly into Quicken or Excel; and take advantage of other bank services such as car buying/leasing services, or financial planning and investment services. Customers who engage in Internet banking are able to print out their "bank statement" at the end of each month rather than having to wait for it to arrive in the mail. Some banks and credit unions also give their customers the option of receiving their bank statements by e-mail.

Many banks realize that Internet banking can play an important role in customer relationship management. Through Internet banking, a bank or credit union is able to retain account holders even if they move to a location without a local branch, even to locations in other countries.

Figure 3-6   The Electronic Funds Transfer (EFT) Process

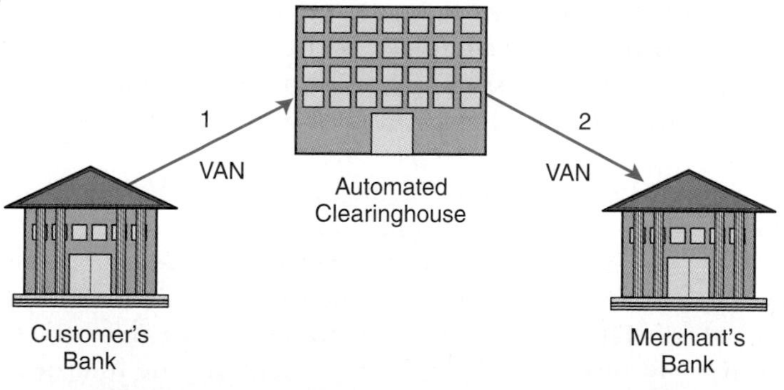

Customer's
Bank

Automated
Clearinghouse

Merchant's
Bank

Steps in ACH Processing:

1. EFT transfer is initiated by customer's (payer's) bank. Customer's account is debited for the transfer amount. Transfer amount is transferred over the ACH value-added Network (VAN) to the automated clearinghouse.

2. Automated clearinghouse initiates EFT transfer to merchant's (payee's) bank. Transfer amount is transferred from automated clearinghouse to merchant's bank. Merchant's account is credited for transfer amount.

Traditional banks offering Internet banking services compete with online-only banks such as First Virtual.com. Although online-only banks can provide a wide range of banking services (such as checking, savings, loans, and debit cards), they lack the ability to provide other services such as safety deposit boxes, which require a local presence.

Internet-Based Financial Services   Like banks and credit unions, traditional financial services companies have had to compete with Internet-only competitors. Companies such as Merrill Lynch and American Express have been forced to combat the potential loss of accounts to online competitors such as E*Trade and Ameritrade with very low per-trade fees by enabling their customers to buy/sell stocks, bonds, and mutual fund shares online.

Most online financial service Web sites provide access to current stock prices and stock market performance data. They also provide investors with a wide range of data and information (such as stock price tracking and recent financial reports) that is useful in making investment decisions. Push technologies enable account holders to instantly receive customized stock information (such as the current prices of a preselected set of stocks), which enables investors to stay on top of their investments and initiate online trades that are in their best interests.

The number of individuals with online investment accounts is skyrocketing. Industry experts expect the number of Americans with online investment accounts to surpass 20 million by 2003. In response, Wall Street and other major stock markets are considering extended trading hours for online investors.

CONSEQUENCES OF E-COMMERCE AND E-BUSINESS

It is apparent that e-commerce and e-business are having dramatic impacts on a wide range of industries and organizations. The Internet is spawning new business models such as electronic business-to-business marketplaces, infomediaries, and online aggregators. Online-only competitors are challenging traditional bricks-and-mortar businesses in many industries, including banking, financial services, insurance, and retailing. Some of these businesses are being transformed from bricks-and-mortar to clicks-and-mortar in order to take advantage of the Internet as another sales channel. The Internet is being used extensively as an electronic shopping mall for both businesses and consumers, and experts predict that this use will grow rapidly over the next several years.

The Internet is also having a major impact on existing businesses. Many businesses exist to provide services to users. Take, for example, the travel services industry. The travel industry serves as a broker between airlines, cruise companies, hotels, and car rental agencies and travelers. Essentially, their job is to find accommodations suitable for clients' needs. The travel agent is able to fulfill those needs via computer connections to a variety of reservation systems. Now, consider the Internet travel alternative. From an Internet connection, a traveler has access to almost all the resources of the travel agent, and online travel agent software is available to assist in making reservations. Moreover, the traveler can view pictures of points of interest at their destination and contact local chambers of commerce and city homepages to find things to do at places on the itinerary. Through e-mail, the traveler can solicit information from people living in the region being visited.

What impact is the Internet having on existing travel agencies? Some will probably make their services available on the Internet and serve travelers throughout the world. Others will continue with business as usual by serving clients who do not have Internet connections or do not want to do their own research. If a significant number

of Internet users make their own travel arrangements because they can find comparable airfares, hotel room rates, and tour package prices, some travel agencies will probably not survive. On the other hand, those travel agencies that adapt to new forms of
Internet-based competition and are capable of differentiating their products/services
on the basis of price or overall quality will continue to survive. The bottom line is that
the Internet is transforming the travel services industry.

The travel business is just one business that may need to adapt to the Internet.
Others include newspapers, book publishers, magazines, stock brokerage firms, and
retail stores. The laws of evolution may apply to some of these companies: Those that
adapt will survive and those that cannot will become extinct. Jobs may be lost in many
businesses because the customer and network software enable the customer to complete the sales transaction without the direct involvement of merchant employees. The
trend toward 24/7 self-service applications is expected to increase in the years ahead
and to impact a wider range of industries.

The impact of the Internet on businesses will be profound. Smaller businesses
that do not have an Internet presence may see an impact similar to that of large
department or discount stores on small retail shops: Some small businesses cannot
compete and will eventually go out of business. On the other hand, a small business
with an Internet presence has a worldwide customer base. Such businesses can compete with large businesses that have large capital investments and unwieldy corporate
structures. Such large companies, even those having an Internet presence, may not be
able to react as quickly to the changing global marketplace as their smaller competitors. In a very real sense, the Internet is leveling the playing field for small businesses
in both the business-to-consumer and business-to-business arenas.

THE INFORMATION SUPERHIGHWAY

Although former Vice President Al Gore did *not* invent the Internet, he did coin the
phrase "information superhighway." The role of the Clinton Administration in the
Internet's evolution within the United States follows a long history of involvement with
the development of the nation's economic infrastructure.

When the United States was primarily an industrial society, the federal government funded the building of a national highway system. This system, augmented by
state and local roads, provided transportation for people, raw materials, and finished
goods. The national highway system helped establish the strength of the U.S. economy. Today, the United States is primarily an information society, with well more than
half the workforce engaged in the business of information. We now envision a new
national information highway system geared to moving the raw materials (data) and
finished goods (information and ideas) of information to their needed locations. This
new highway system is formally called the *National Information Infrastructure (NII)*, but it
is commonly called the "information superhighway." If built and used correctly, the
information superhighway will help maintain and extend the economic strength of
the United States.

Building the Information Superhighway

Although the federal government was instrumental in funding and building the interstate highway system, the private business sector is the primary builder of the information superhighway. The federal government is providing guidance, legislation, procedures, and prototype systems, and is funding research and development efforts for
new Internet technologies. Both the federal government and state governments are

subsidizing connections to public entities such as libraries, schools, and hospitals. In the areas of procedures and legislation, it has already been recognized that privacy and security issues must be addressed. Federal regulations will undoubtedly be required to help control access and set penalties for abuses, just as the Interstate Commerce Commission regulates commercial use of the interstate highways and roads. To provide this guidance, the federal government has established an Information Infrastructure Task Force (IITF) to oversee information superhighway development.

Like the interstate highway system, the information superhighway will evolve over time. Many technologies needed for building the information superhighway are currently in place; still needed is the investment to integrate and install the technologies so they can be made available throughout the country. Different companies or consortiums may form regional segments of the information superhighway, and then the regional infrastructures will be integrated into a national or perhaps global supernetwork. This evolution will probably be similar to that of the Internet itself. The information superhighway will eventually extend across national borders and become a global information superhighway.

The building of the information superhighway is proceeding at a rapid pace. The following are among the key events that have occurred thus far:

➤ The information superhighway is envisioned as an integration of communication networks, information and service providers, and computer hardware and software. To provide these components, mergers and alliances are being formed among common carriers, computer hardware and software companies, cable TV companies, and the entertainment industry.

➤ A cross-industry working team is guiding the design of the information superhighway. The members represent communication, computer, banking, publishing, and cable TV companies. The cross-industry working team has formed subgroups including those overseeing applications, services, architecture, and portability. The role of the first three is apparent from their names. The portability subgroup will address the needs of mobile communication.

The architecture of the information superhighway will resemble that of the Internet. A high-speed backbone network of fiber optic and satellite links will speed data from one region to another. Local access and service delivery will be provided by regional providers over fiber optic cable, coaxial cable, and copper media. Businesses that make heavy use of the information superhighway will probably have the data delivered to their premises by fiber optic cable. Local distribution within the company will be over fiber optic cable, coaxial cable, twisted-pair wires, and wireless media.

For personal use, it is unlikely that fiber optic cable will be widely brought into homes in the near future. High-speed Internet access for consumers will most likely involve broadband services such as digital subscriber lines (DSLs), cable modems, digital satellite television services (such as DirectPC), and wireless services such as LMDS. Fiber optic cable will, however, bring the data to a local distribution point from which coaxial cable, twisted-pair wires, and high-speed wireless media will distribute the data to individual homes. There are several reasons why copper-based delivery to individual subscribers is likely to continue. In many locations, cable TV companies have already installed this kind of delivery mechanism, and thus it readily lends itself for use as a "last-mile" delivery system. Also, because data speeds required for effective home use are likely to remain lower than those required for business connections, the higher speed of fiber optic cable will not be necessary. Finally, the current cost of fiber optic cable and the difficulty of splicing and making new connections favor the use of copper-based end delivery. Figure 3-7 illustrates a potential information superhighway implementation.

Information Superhighway Uses

Several potential information superhighway uses include:

➤ A business might use the information superhighway to conduct a conference among employees in different locations.

➤ A software company might use the information superhighway to distribute software directly to customers.

➤ A publishing company might distribute books or magazines directly to readers or perhaps to a local outlet for on-demand printing.

➤ Companies and individuals could subscribe to information utilities such as stock market and financial news and congressional records.

➤ Companies and individuals will be able to shop for merchandise via online catalogs and make airline, car, hotel, and entertainment reservations.

➤ Movies and games may be available on demand.

Figure 3-7   Potential Information Superhighway Implementation

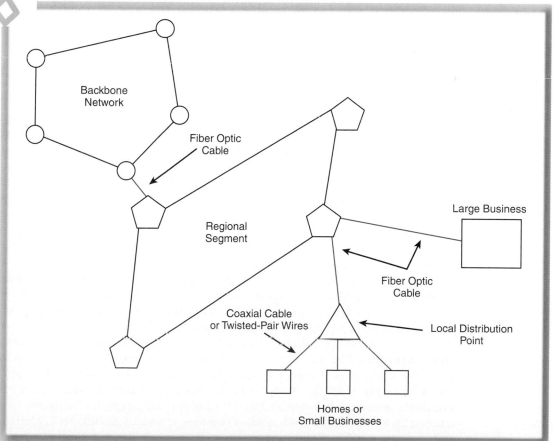

➤ Education classes at all levels may be available and allow people to learn new skills at their home or office.

➤ Some kinds of health care may be delivered remotely. A physician may be able to view patients at remote locations, coach paramedical personnel on procedures, and recommend treatment.

➤ E-mail and video images may be exchanged. Interactive use of such technologies may give rise to online discussion groups and conferencing.

From these few suggestions, it is apparent that possible information superhighway uses are varied. The information superhighway will deliver far more that just data; it can deliver information in a variety of formats including data, voice, and video. At issue is how individuals and companies will gain access to these resources and how much it will cost to use them. For some services, costs of more than $200 per connect hour are likely. Access to the information superhighway also will require the media connections and equipment necessary to send and receive the signals.

Social Implications

The information superhighway is likely to bring a profound change in the way businesses operate and in individuals' private lives. The costs required for information superhighway connection and services may also lead to new social issues. People who cannot afford these services will have fewer opportunities than those who have the services, which may create a *digital divide* between technological haves and have-nots. Consequently, publicly funded access through schools, libraries, and civic centers may be needed to ensure that all members of society have access to the opportunities the information superhighway will provide.

Internet2

During his administration, President Clinton initiated the *next generation Internet (NGI)* project, which is dedicated to researching high-speed network technologies for use by federal agencies. The University Corporation for Advanced Internet Development (UCAID) has worked closely with NGI researchers to design **Internet2**. In essence, Internet2 is a high-speed network for government, academic, and research use. It is administered by UCAID and is being developed by more than 100 universities, private companies, and the U.S. government. Internet2 is not intended for commercial use; however, the technological advancements that are being tested on Internet2 are likely to be leveraged commercially on the Internet eventually.

Internet2 A high-speed network for government, academic, and research use. It is administered by UCAID and is being developed by more than 100 universities, private companies, and the U.S. government.

Internet2 is being developed to enable real-time, high-speed, multimedia exchanges among nodes. Today's Internet, which was primarily designed to exchange text data, does not do a good job of handling the kinds of transfers that Internet2 will be doing. High-bandwidth applications such as full-motion video and 3-D animations are being developed and tested on Internet2 to determine the transport designs necessary to carry them in real time. The identification of such transport designs is likely to be used to reshape multimedia applications for the Internet.

Internet2 leverages existing networks such as the National Science Foundation's vBNS backbone. With the assistance of MCI, the NSF initially developed vBNS (**very high-speed Backbone Network Service**) to interconnect several supercomputer centers at 622 mbps (OC-12). vBNS has been expanded to provide backbone services for Internet2. *Abilene,* developed by UCAID with the assistance of equipment donations totaling more than $500 million from companies such as 3Com, MCI, Nortel, Cisco, and Qwest, is another high-speed backbone network on which Internet2 is being built.

Initially operating at 2.4 gbps (OC-48), links in the Abilene network are being upgraded to 9.6 gbps (OC-192).

Universities are developing high-speed switching points for Internet2. Such switching points are called *GigaPOPs* (for gigabit point of presence). The first GigaPOP was deployed in late 1997 in North Carolina's Research Triangle.

Additional information about Internet2 and the NGI project is available at a variety of Web sites. These include www.ucaid.org, www.ngi.gov, www.vbns.net, and www.ccic.gov.

SUMMARY

Businesses have traditionally taken advantage of a wide range of TCP/IP protocols, including SMTP, FTP, HTTP, USENET, Telnet, IRC, and chat. Today, they are leveraging these to develop Internet-based and Web-based e-commerce and e-business applications such as e-mail marketing, electronic data interchange (EDI), providing reference materials, and completing sales transactions.

Several requirements must be met for Internet and Web-based sales transactions, including online payment mechanisms and transaction security. A variety of online payment options are available, including smart card transactions, the use of digital cash (e-cash), and credit card transactions, which are most common. Protocols such as Secure Socket Layer (SSL) and Secure Electronic Transaction (SET) are widely used for secure online credit card transactions.

E-commerce is the use of computer networks to complete business transactions. It is one of the major categories of e-business. Beyond e-commerce, e-business involves using the Internet to enhance customer service, coordinate activities with business partners, facilitate communication and knowledge management within organizations, and create electronic marketplaces to better serve the collective needs of entire industries.

E-commerce and e-business are growing rapidly for a number of reasons, including declining prices for computing and communications technologies, increased business investment in information technologies needed to support e-commerce, the emergence of electronic business-to-business marketplaces, rapid increases in the number of consumers around the world with Internet access, and continued expansion of the size and content of the World Wide Web.

There are many forms of e-commerce. The four most common categories are business-to-business (B2B) e-commerce, business-to-consumer (B2C) e-commerce, consumer-to-consumer (C2C) e-commerce, and intrabusiness e-commerce. B2B e-commerce represents more than 80 percent of all e-commerce; most B2B e-commerce involves the creation of interorganizational systems (IOS). EDI has traditionally been the most common IOS application. Other important B2B e-commerce applications include buy-side and sell-side applications and electronic marketplaces.

Like B2B e-commerce, B2C e-commerce is rapidly increasing. The number of consumers with Internet access is growing, and they are making more online purchases from businesses that are providing an increasingly wider range of products and services for sale over the Web. Traditional off-line sales are being affected as more and more consumers use the Internet to research product information and to receive customer service. Consumers are also using the Internet for health-care information and job opportunities, and to access e-governance applications.

Online auctions are the most common form of C2C e-commerce. Intranets are the most common form of intrabusiness e-commerce. Intranets are becoming more common in businesses because they enable employees to share information through the use of Web technologies such as Web servers and browsers.

Major e-commerce and e-business applications include supply chain management, electronic procurement, Internet marketing, customer relationship management, and Internet banking and financial services. Supply chain management (SCM) leverages IOS links to enable business partners involved in the end-to-end delivery of products to customers to function as a single entity. E-procurement applications enable organizations to save money through enhanced integration and control of purchasing processes. Internet marketing applications are using the Internet as new customer sales channels through Internet stores, infomediaries, and online aggregators (cybermalls). Customer relationship management (CRM) systems are enabling businesses to retain their most profitable customers through the integration of customer contact channels (mail, phone, fax, e-mail, and Web). Internet banking and financial services are enabling financial institutions to make their products and services available 24/7 and to capitalize on growing customer demand for self-service options.

The growth of e-commerce and e-business is transforming numerous industries and the organizations within them. This has been especially apparent in the travel services industry. Traditional bricks-and-mortar businesses are being challenged by online-only competitors; some small businesses are unlikely to survive unless they adapt to the new competitive environment by developing Web strategies of their own. The Internet is making all businesses, both small and large, aware of the importance of secure online transactions. As a result, the use of virtual private networks (VPNs) is increasing.

The United States and developed nations around the world have recognized the economic power of e-commerce and e-business and are taking an active role in building the information superhighway. Careful planning is needed to avoid creating digital divides between individuals/countries with high-speed Internet access and those without that access. Internet2 is leveraging high-speed network backbones such as the Abilene network and vBNS to create a high-speed network for government, academic, and research applications. Internet2 is being used to design and test high-bandwidth applications such as full-motion video and multimedia data transfers among network nodes. Resulting technological advancements should eventually migrate to and reshape the Internet.

KEY TERMS

- biometric technology
- business-to-business (B2B) e-commerce
- business-to-consumer (B2C) e-commerce
- buy-side B2B e-commerce
- consumer-to-consumer (C2C) e-commerce
- customer relationship management (CRM) system
- digital cash (d-cash)
- electronic business (e-business)
- electronic cash (e-cash)
- electronic commerce (e-commerce)
- electronic data interchange (EDI)
- electronic funds transfer (EFT)

- extranet
- Internet2
- interorganizational information system (IOS)
- intrabusiness/intracompany e-commerce
- intranet
- Secure Electronic Transaction (SET)
- Secure HTTP (S-HTTP)
- Secure Sockets Layer (SSL)
- sell-side B2B e-commerce
- smart card
- supply chain management (SCM)

REVIEW QUESTIONS

1. List and briefly describe the strategic reasons why business presence on the Internet is increasing.
2. Briefly describe business use of each of the following: Internet e-mail, FTP, the Web, USENET, online commercial services, electronic journals, and e-governance services.
3. What are the advantages and disadvantages of using the Internet for business purposes?
4. What are the requirements for an Internet transaction, and how can each requirement be satisfied?
5. What are smart cards? Why are smart cards being more widely used for online transactions? What role can biometrics play in smart card transactions?
6. What is digital cash? What are the different forms of digital cash?
7. What is microcommerce? What are micropayments? Provide examples of micro-payment systems.
8. Briefly explain
   a. Secure Sockets Layer (SSL)
   b. Secure Electronic Transaction (SET)
9. What are the components of merchant e-commerce systems?
10. Describe the steps in an Internet transaction.
11. How can a person obtain e-cash? How is e-cash used in transactions?
12. What is e-commerce? What is e-business?
13. Identify and briefly describe each of the major drivers of e-commerce and e-business expansion.
14. Identify and briefly describe each of the major categories of e-commerce.
15. What is an interorganizational system (IOS)? What are some of the major forms of IOSs?
16. What are the characteristics of traditional EDI? What are the major EDI standards? Why is Web-based EDI becoming more common?
17. Identify examples of buy-side and sell-side B2B applications.
18. What are the characteristics of electronic marketplaces? Identify several examples.
19. Identify and briefly describe the trends in consumer buying patterns.
20. Identify and briefly describe the Internet's impacts on each of the following: prices for consumer items, health care, employment, and consumer access to government services.
21. Identify and briefly describe the major forms of consumer-to-consumer e-commerce.
22. What is intrabusiness e-commerce? What are the characteristics and business advantages/benefits of intranets?
23. Describe the characteristics of each of the following e-business applications: SCM, e-procurement, Internet marketing, CRM, and Internet banking and financial services.
24. What are the differences between infomediaries and online aggregators?
25. Briefly describe the consequences of e-commerce and e-business.
26. What is the information superhighway? What role is the federal government playing in its development?
27. What kinds of services are likely to be available on the information superhighway?
28. What are the social implications of the information superhighway?

PROBLEMS AND EXERCISES

1. Use the Internet to find current information and research on the "digital divide." How is "digital divide" defined? What are the social implications of the digital divide? What steps are being taken to close the gaps between technological "haves" and "have-nots"?

2. Use the Internet to identify and describe the different categories/kinds of smart cards being used today. Also identify and describe common smart card applications and how they are likely to be used in the years ahead.

3. Use the Internet to find information on the descriptions of Web portals. What are the major characteristics/features of Web portals? How do they generate revenue? Identify several examples of Web portals.

4. Use the Internet to find information that describes the characteristics of "push" technologies. What are the major characteristics/features of push technologies? How are they being used in Internet marketing and customer relationship management?

5. Use the Internet to find information concerning the differences between infomediaries and electronic brokers. Identify and briefly describe examples of each.

6. Use the Internet to identify the major vendors of customer relationship management (CRM) systems. Identify the vendors' major products, and describe the capabilities and functionality of these major products.

7. Use the Internet to find information about recent developments in biometric technologies. Identify the major trends in biometric technologies and how they are being used in e-commerce.

8. Use the Internet to research and describe WebTrust and Trust-e. Discuss what is signified when the WebTrust or Trust-e seal is displayed on an e-commerce Web site.

9. Use the Internet to find out more about Internet2, the Abilene network, and the NSF's vBNS network. Summarize your findings in a paper or PowerPoint presentation.

Internet-Based EDI Systems

During the past 20 years, electronic data interchange (EDI) has been widely used to exchange business documents, such as purchase orders, invoices, confirmation notices, or shipping notices, among more than 300,000 organizations. Traditional EDI is highly integrated into core business processes, typically relying on value-added networks (VANs) to provide direct connections to vendors' databases and systems. The Internet is expected to give EDI a boost, not by using private networks and the traditional EDI data formats, but by combining XML and EDI to connect trading partners.

VAN (or traditional) EDI provides the document tracking, security, reliability, and open standards required to share key documents among organizations. As recently as 1998, VANs carried about 95 percent of the volume of all EDI traffic. However, technologies that let companies send business documents over secure Internet links will supplant VANs as the primary transport of EDI in the future. Some analysts believe by 2005, less than 50 percent of all EDI transactions will be transported over VANs. A critical issue is the development of managed IP network services to guarantee the delivery of EDI transactions, which is not possible over the global Internet.

One reason companies are looking toward Internet EDI is the rapid increase of small businesses in business supply chains. Large companies are relying more heavily on small and specialized companies, but small companies often do not have the resources to set up traditional EDI services. The Internet offers an inexpensive alternative for medium- and small-sized companies to do business electronically without needing a lot of technical knowledge.

An Internet-based EDI can use either the Web browser (Web EDI) or an internal system to transfer EDI documents over the Internet. Web EDI consists of form-based orders that are converted online to EDI formats. They also include XML applications that allow EDI formats to be displayed in Web browsers. Widespread adoption of XML technology will allow the development of new EDI formats and will expand the ways that companies can transact business. Some of the XML–based dialects currently in use are xCBL, cXML, ebXML, BizTalk, and RosettaNet PIPs.

XML is based on text files that are both machine and human readable; EDI files are only machine readable. All that a company needs to use and view an XML file is a Web browser. Because most of the small companies do not have the technical and financial resources for EDI, the XML model is their best solution. In addition, EDI is ideal for handling high volumes of data between trading partners; XML is best used for small and frequent communications, which allows fast information sharing among partners.

Some companies are already planning to replace EDI with XML standards. For example, Intel will replace EDI with RosettaNet standards by 2006. Intel believes RosettaNet's error-checking features, not available in EDI, will make its transactions three times more accurate than those with EDI. Intel could save millions of dollars because customers and suppliers would enter their own data into Intel systems, which would eliminate the need for people to enter data manually and for specialized networks to transfer the data.

Another example is the new Internet EDI service developed by Dal-Tile. Lowe's approached Dal-Tile to discuss the possibility of transferring documents such as purchase orders and invoices over the Internet. Because Lowe's is a major seller of Dal-Tile's flooring products, Dal-Tile considered outsourcing a new system to improve collaboration and information sharing. Dal-Tile selected IBM Global Services to host all the hardware, software, and staff required to communicate via Internet EDI. The result: Dal-Tile will be able to gather online up-to-date demand information from Lowe's point of sales, which can be used to help meet Lowe's requirements.

VAN EDI is proven and reliable, and its pricing and billing models are lowering costs. As a result, new applications that provide the benefits of both the Internet and VANs are being introduced. XML will grow in usage, but the processing and exchange of data will still rely on EDI. A combination of EDI and XML formats is needed to enable organizations to take advantage of the newer benefits of XML. In addition, this will ensure that the more than 300,000 firms that have implemented EDI systems over the past 20 years can continue using these systems, most of which are integrated into complex business processes. XML will not replace EDI standards such as ANSI X.12 or EDIFACT in the near future. Instead, organizations will implement EDI/ XML translation software to allow the conversion of any X.12 or EDIFACT EDI document into XML–based dialects, and vice versa.

CASE QUESTIONS

1. Use the Internet and other sources to find out more about the costs of implementation and ongoing costs associated with VAN EDI. Why did these costs dissuade many small to moderate-size businesses from establishing EDI links with customers?
2. What are the advantages of having more small and moderate-size businesses in today's supply chains? How has Internet-based EDI leveled the playing field among small, moderate, and large suppliers?
3. Although some companies, such as Intel, are planning to migrate from EDI to other Web-based supply chain services, overall EDI revenues are projected to increase over the next few years. Why is this so?
4. Use the Internet to find out more about the future of EDI. How is EDI likely to be affected by the evolution of XML and the emergence of alternative B2B exchanges such as electronic marketplaces?

SOURCES

Adhikari, Richard. "Electronic Commerce: EDI Heads for the Net." *InformationWeek* (May 6, 1996). Available online at www.informationweek. com/578/78mtedi.htm.

Greenmaier, Larry. "Tile Manufacturer Turns to Internet-Based EDI System." *InformationWeek* (November 12, 2001). Available online at www.informationweek.com/story/IWK2001110 8S0022.

Levitt, Jason. "From EDI to XML and UDDI: A Brief History of Web Services." *InformationWeek* (October 12, 2001). Available online at www. informationweek.com/story/IWK20010928S0 006.

Wagner, Jason. "Intel Readies EDI Retirement." *InternetWeek* (December 12, 2001). Available online at www.internetwk.com/story/INW200 11217S0001.

Note: For more information on business and the Internet, see an additional case on the Web site, www. prenhall.com/stamper, "Online Learning: Is This the Classroom of the Future?"

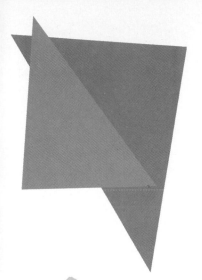

Chapter 4

Internet Addressing and Operation

After studying this chapter, you should be able to:

- Discuss Internet addressing.
- Describe subnets and how they are used.
- Describe the role of subnet masks in IP addressing.
- Discuss IP routing algorithms and protocols.
- Identify and briefly describe Internet tools used by network managers.
- Discuss Web page design tools.
- Briefly describe the importance of appropriate Web server configurations.
- Describe the roles of IPSEC and network address translation (NAT) in IP network security.

INTERNET ADDRESSES

As noted in Chapter 2, most communication over the Internet is based on the Transmission Control Protocol and Internet Protocol (TCP/IP). TCP provides services at the OSI transport layer, and IP is an OSI network layer protocol. Internet addresses are represented in a variety of formats; however, all the formats are ultimately resolved to a 32-bit number known as an IP address. Figure 4-1 illustrates an IPv4 header. Note that the header contains two addresses—the source address and the destination address. In Internet Protocol version 4 (IPv4), both of these addresses are 32 bits in length. In **Internet Protocol version 6 (IPv6)**, which is being used on Internet2 and will be widely used on the global Internet in the future), both source and destination addresses are 128 bits long. The shift from IPv4 to IPv6 is under way because Internet addresses must be unique, and the total number of available 32-bit addresses is limited. The use of 32-bit addresses means that a total of 2,294,967,294 distinct addressable devices could be attached to the Internet. When TCP/IP was developed, this number exceeded the world's population! Today, we are close to running out of assignable

Internet Protocol Version 6 (IPv6) Version 6 of the Internet Protocol. IPv6 supersedes and provides significant improvements to IPv4. One major improvement is the expansion of the IP address from 32 bits to 128 bits.

```
IP version
Header length
Service type: throughput parameters
Total length of datagram
Identification, flags, fragment offset
Time to live
Protocol
Checksum
Source IP address
Destination IP address
IP options
Padding
```

Figure 4-1   IPv4 Header

32-bit IP addresses, and the need to migrate to IPv6 and its 128-bit addresses is growing more acute. The longer address translates into significantly more unique Internet addresses and the capability of connecting a much larger number of communication devices to the Internet. IPv6 is also known as IPng (IP next generation).

Request for Comment 760 (RFC 760) RFCs contain documentation for the Internet; they describe Internet protocols and standards as well as proposed standards and protocols. RFC 760 describes IP addressing.

IP addressing was formally described in **Request for Comment 760 (RFC 760)**, which was published in early 1980. RFCs contain documentation for the Internet; they describe Internet protocols and standards as well as proposed standards and protocols. A catalog of RFCs is available at the University of Southern California's Information Sciences Institute (www.isi.edu). They may all be viewed at the IETF Web site (www.ietf.org/rfc). There is an RFC for IPv6.

IP addressing is primarily concerned with establishing a unique identity for networked computers. By doing so, IP addressing provides the mechanism that enables packets to be routed between networks as well as to be delivered to an appropriate host or node on a destination network.

IPv4 Addressing Basics

In Chapter 2, we mentioned that IP addresses are usually written as four separate numbers delineated by a period. It is important to note, however, that Internet hosts can also be represented as a URL or domain name (such as www.cnn.com or www.gsu.edu). Using the first convention, a host's address might be written as 101.209.33.17. Each number in the group represents an 8-bit octet, that is, representing decimal equivalents that range from 0 to 255 ($2^8 - 1$). This way of representing an IP address is called the **dotted-quad notation**. Although the use of URLs or domain names prevents Internet users from having to memorize host or node "dotted-quad" IP addresses, URLs and domain names must be resolved into 32-bit IP addresses to enable packet routing across the Internet backbone.

dotted-quad notation IPv4's four-octet address representation on the Internet. For example, a server whose IP address is 101.209.33.17 in dotted quad notation would have that IP address represented in an IPv4 header as 01100101 11010001 00100001 00010001.

When TCP/IP was developed, it was recognized that internetworking two or more networks required a unique address for each network in order to differentiate it from other networks. In addition, TCP/IP developers recognized that each host or node connected to a network must have a distinct address in order to differentiate it from other hosts or nodes attached to the same network. In order to satisfy these requirements, a two-level IP addressing hierarchy was developed. This is illustrated in Figure 4-2.

The network portion of an IPv4 address can be 1, 2, or 3 bytes in length. The length of the network portion of the address is designated in the composition of the

Network Portion	Host/Node Portion

In IPv4, each 32-bit IP address is subdivided into network and host portions. The composition of the first 4 bits of the IP address specifies whether the network portion is 1, 2, or 3 bytes in length. The length of the network portion determines whether the length of the host/node portion is 3, 2, or 1 byte in length.

Figure 4-2   IPv4's 2-Level IP Addressing Hierarchy

first 4 bits in the binary representation of the IP address (that is, the first 4 binary digits in the left-most byte of the IP address). As we shall see in a moment, the first 4 bits determine the network's class. The network's class, in turn, determines if the network portion of the IP address is 1, 2, or 3 bytes in length. If the network portion is 1 byte long, the host/node portion is 3 bytes in length. If the network portion is 2 bytes long, the host/node portion is also 2 bytes in length. If the first 3 bytes of the IP address are used to uniquely identify the network, then host/node addresses are identified in the last byte.

For example, a server whose IP address is 101.209.33.17 would have that IP address represented in an IPv4 header as 01100101 11010001 00100001 00010001 (spaces are added to help you visualize the 4 bytes that make up the IP address).

Currently there are four address classes, A through D; class E has been defined but reserved for future use. With the exception of class D, classes are based on the number of hosts in the subnet. As the number of hosts in the subnet increases, more bits of the address are needed to distinguish each host.

➤ **Class A** addresses are used for networks with more than 2^{16} hosts/nodes. The first bit of the 32-bit address is 0, to distinguish this class from the others, all of which start with 1. The next 7 bits represent the network portion of the IP address. Hence, for class A networks, the network portion of the IP address is 1 byte in length. This can be designated as follows:

network number.host number.host number.host number

There can be no more than 2^7 or 128 distinct class A networks, but because the first bit is fixed, the total number of class A networks cannot exceed 127. The remaining 24 bits are used to distinguish among the hosts/nodes within each network; the 24 bits can provide up to 16 million distinct host addresses within each class A network. Network addresses for class A networks can range from 1.0.0.0 (where the network portion [first byte] of the IP address is 00000001) to 127.0.0.0 (where the network portion of the IP address is 01111111).

➤ **Class B** addresses use the first 2 bytes of the 32-bit IP address for the network identifier. The first 2 bits of networks with class B addresses are always 1 and 0. The last 16 bits of class B network addresses are used to identify the hosts/nodes within the networks. This can be designated as follows:

network number.network number.host number.host number

class A address An IPv4 network address class that allows 127 networks and 16 million nodes per subnet. The first bit in the 4-octet binary (32 bit) address for a Class A address is 0 to differentiate it from other address classes. The network portion of a Class A network address is seven bits in length while the host portion is 24 bits long.

class B address An IPv4 network address class that allows 16,000 networks and 65,000 nodes per subnet. The first two bits in the 4-octet binary address for a Class B address are 1 and 0 to differentiate it from other address classes. The network portion of a Class B network address is 14 bits in length while the host portion is 16 bits long.

It is possible to have a total of 16,536 (2^{14}) class B networks, and each network could have 65,536 (2^{16}) hosts/nodes. Class B networks range from 128 to 191 in the first portion of the dotted-quad notation for the IP address, because the composition of the first byte of the 32-bit class B address is always 10xxxxxx (where x is any binary value).

➤ **Class C** addresses are identified by the assignment of the first 3 bits in the 32-bit address to 110. A total of 2^{21} (2,097,152) distinct class C network addresses are possible because the first 3 bytes of the IP address are used to identify the network. This can be designated as follows:

network number.network number.network number.host number

Because class C networks use the last 8 bits of the IP address to identify attached hosts/nodes, 256 (2^8) hosts/nodes can be uniquely identified. Decimal values of the first byte in class C dotted-quad representations range from 192 to 233; this is because the composition of the first byte always has the composition of 110xxxxx (where x represents any binary value).

➤ **Class D** addresses always begin with 1110 in the first 4 bit positions of the 32-bit IP address. The remaining 28 bits in the address are used to uniquely define 2^{38} (approximately 268 million) multicast addresses. Multicasting is an addressing technique that enables a source to send a single copy of a packet to a specific set of recipients through the use of multicast addresses. Unlike class A, B, and C addresses, which were created to designate specific hosts on specific networks, class D addressing is used to send the same packet to all hosts/nodes in a multicast group. Only the hosts/nodes in the multicast group will read the packet; other nodes need only read the first 4 bits of the destination IP address, determine that it is intended for a class D multicast group, and ignore the rest of the information in the packet. When a host/node puts another host's class A, B, or C address in an IP packet, the packet will go only to that host (this is called *unicasting*). However, when a host begins the destination IP address with 1110, the packet will be sent to all the hosts in the specified class D multicast group (this is called *broadcasting*). Because the first 4 bits of a class D multicast group address always have the composition 1110xxxx (where x is any binary value), the decimal values for class D addresses in dotted-quad form range from 224 to 239.

➤ **Class E** addresses always begin with the assignment of 1111 to the first 4 bits in the 32-bit IPv4 address. This address class is reserved for experimental uses. Because the composition of the first byte in the class E address is 1111xxxx (where x is any binary value), the decimal values for class E addresses in dotted-quad form range from 240 to 254.

In conclusion, class A uses 1 octet to represent the network portion of the IP address; class B uses 2 octets; and class C uses 3 octets to represent the network address portion of the IP address. As indicated in Table 4-1, the first bit in the 32-bit address

---

class C address An IPv4 network address class that allows 2 million networks and 254,000 nodes per subnet. The first three bits in the 4-octet binary address for a Class C address are 110 to differentiate it from other address classes. The network portion of a Class C network address is 21 bits in length while the host portion is 8 bits long.

class D address An IPv4 network address class that is used by nodes willing to accept multicast messages. Class D addresses always begin with 1110 in the first 4 bit positions of the 32-bit IP address. The remaining 28 bits in the address are used to uniquely define 2^{38} (approximately 268 million) multicast addresses.

class E address IPv4 addresses that always begin with the assignment of 1111 to the first 4 bits in the 32-bit IPv4 address. This address class is reserved for experimental uses.

Table 4-1   Internet Address Class Summary

Class	Networks	Hosts/Nodes per Network	Comments
A	$2^7 - 1 = 127$	$2^{24} = 16$ million	Address begins with a 0 bit
B	$2^{14} = 16,536$	$2^{16} = 65,536$	Address begins with bits 10
C	$2^{21} = 2$ million	$2^8 = 256$	Address begins with bits 110
D			Address begins with 1110
E			Address begins with 1110

Table 4-2   Characteristics of IPv4 Classes

IPv4	Length of Network Address Portion of IP Address in Bits	Decimal Value Range for First Byte of Dotted-Quad Notation
A	8	0–127
B	16	128–191
C	24	192–223
D	n/a	224–239
E	n/a	240–254

for class A networks is always 0; class B addresses always begin with 10; and class C addresses always begin with 110. Network addresses are assigned by the Internet Network Information Center (InterNIC) to ensure that address duplication is not a problem. Table 4-2 summarizes the length of the network address portion of IPv4 classes along with the decimal value ranges of the first bytes of the dotted-quad notation for networks in each class.

Reserved Addresses

The developers of the IPv4 addressing scheme reserved three blocks of addresses for networks that would not be connected to the Internet. These are identified and defined in *RFC 1918 (Address Allocation for Private Internets)*. Table 4-3 summarizes the address blocks that have been set aside for private internets.

When organizations create private internets, it is possible for them to use identical private addressing schemes. If the organizations were to subsequently attach their private internets to the Internet, addressing conflicts could result. In order to avoid such conflicts, organizations can use **routers** with Network Address Translation (NAT) capabilities or proxy firewalls to ensure that incoming messages are appropriately delivered to private internet addresses.

Internet Naming Conventions

For most Internet users, the 4-octet address (dotted quad) representation is too cumbersome. Therefore, most users substitute a naming convention called a **Uniform Resource Locator (URL)**. A URL uses names and abbreviations that are easier to use and remember than the dotted-quad representation. An example of a URL is http://www.cnn.com. A URL formally consists of two parts: the protocol used to access a resource (in this case *http*) followed by the resource name (in this case *cnn.com*). In this example, the *www* indicates that the resource is located on the World Wide Web.

router A network interconnection device and associated software that link two or more networks. The networks being linked can be different, but they must use a common routing protocol.

Uniform Resource Locator (URL) A string representation of an Internet address. A URL is the address used to access pages on the World Wide Web; it defines the route to a file on the Web or any other Internet facility. URLs are typed into the browser to access Web pages, and URLs are embedded within Web pages to provide the hypertext links to other Web pages.

Table 4-3   Reserved IPv4 Addresses for Private Internets

Reserved IP Address Blocks for Private Internets
10.0.0.0 to 10.255.255.255
172.16.0.0 to 172.31.255.255
192.168.0.0 to 192.168.255.255

As Web browsers have evolved, users have had to do less work when identifying URLs. Early browsers required users to enter the complete URL (*http://www.cnn.com*). Later versions enabled users to leave out the *http://* and only enter *www.cnn.com*. Today's browser versions only require users to enter the resource name *cnn.com*.

It is important to note that a URL is simply a different representation of IPv4's 32-bit Internet address, and before a message is transmitted, the URL must be translated into the appropriate 32-bit IP address. We will see how this happens later.

The protocol in the URL is used to define how the resource will be accessed. It may be the Hypertext Transfer Protocol (HTTP), the File Transfer Protocol (FTP), Gopher text reader, or another method such as mail or news readers. The resource may be a single article or file, a newsgroup, or a Web page located on an Internet host computer. In this case, the resource field may contain the name of a computer, an organization, and possibly a country designator, all of which make up what is called a **domain name**. Domain names are a hierarchical word-oriented representation of an Internet address. The hierarchy is similar to the notation used to address a letter. If you want to mail a letter to someone, you use the address hierarchy of recipient name, street address, city, state, zip code, and country (if the letter is international).

The combination of the address elements, which are ordered from the most specific (the recipient's name) to the most general (the country), uniquely identifies the recipient. Let us examine the sample domain name *frodo.mycompany.com.us* and explain its parts.

Like postal addresses, the domain naming hierarchy starts with the most specific part of the name and proceeds to the most general part. In the sample name, *frodo* (probably) represents the name of an Internet host computer owned by the company *mycompany*. The *com* term identifies the *mycompany* entity as a company. The set of Internet entity types that were initially recognized are summarized in Table 4-4. The combination of these three terms nearly maps to an IP address. The *mycompany.com* portion is a close approximation of the network identifier and host/node identifier within the network or one of the network's subnets. The *us* term identifies the country in which the network and host are located, the United States in this example. Examples of other country designators are given in Table 4-5. Designators such as .com and .us are called root-level or top-level domains. It is conceivable that a resource called *frodo.mycompany.com.uk* also exists, so that is why we used the term *nearly* when saying that *frodo.mycompany.com* nearly represented an IP address.

The Internet Corporation for Assigned Names and Numbers (ICANN) is the entity that is responsible for approving domain names, including the abbreviations used in URLs. Specifically, ICANN coordinates the assignment of the following identifiers, each of which must be unique for the global Internet to function: Internet

domain name An organization's unique name on the Internet. Internet domain names may be registered via dozens of designated registrars. At the beginning of 2002, there were more than 20 million registered domain names on the Internet.

Table 4-4 Initially Approved Root- (Top-) Level Domain Names

Initial Top-Level Domain Abbreviations	Description
com	For-profit company
edu	Educational institution
gov	U.S. government institution/agency
mil	U.S. military branch
net	Network service provider
org	Nonprofit organization

Table 4-5   Country Codes Found in Root-Level Domain Names

Country Code Abbreviations	Country
at	Austria
au	Australia
be	Belgium
ca	Canada
de	Denmark
es	Spain
fi	Finland
fr	France
il	Israel
it	Italy
jp	Japan
no	Norway
uk	United Kingdom
us	United States

domain names, IP address numbers, and protocol parameter and port numbers. ICANN also coordinates the operation of the Internet's root server system. More information about ICANN and its role in Internet operations is available at www.icann.org.

Several new suffixes have been approved by ICANN in order to more clearly delineate an organization's kind or classification for Internet users. As shown in Table 4-6, many of these help to further differentiate organizations that engage in e-commerce from one another. In the past, organizations with .aero, .biz, or .coop would all have been classified under .com. As of November 2000, more than 20 million entities were classified as .com (dot-com organizations). The start date for the new suffixes is 2002.

Table 4-6   New Root-Level Domain Names

New Top-Level Domain Abbreviations	Description
arts	Arts and cultural organizations
firm	Business firms
info	Information services
nom	Family or individual last names
rec	Recreation and entertainment organizations
store	Merchants/businesses offering goods for purchase
web	World Wide Web/Web organizations
aero	Airlines, airports, and aerospace organizations
biz	Business organizations
coop	Cooperative organizations, credit unions, electrical cooperatives
name	Second-level names (e.g., jane.doe.name)
pro	Professionals with recognized professional status

When a business obtains an Internet address from the Internet Network Information Center (InterNIC), it also registers a unique domain name. The domain name is associated with the IP addresses assigned to that business. When a domain name is used as part of a URL, it must be resolved to the IP address. This is done automatically by the Internet **Domain Name System (DNS)**. Domain names and their IP addresses are stored in databases on a number of Internet hosts called **domain name system (DNS) servers**. Domain names are organized hierarchically from the most general to the specific, as illustrated in Figure 4-3. When a domain name must be resolved, the local host first looks to see whether it has the URL and associated IP address already available. If not, the host sends a message to a domain name server and obtains the necessary information. The host then places the IP address in the network layer IP header and transmits the message. To resolve the domain name *frodo.mycompany.com.us,* the search would start at a local domain name server. If the domain name is not found there, the search would expand to the nearest available name server that contains all U.S. domain/IP address pairs.

Some of the possible URL protocols are listed in Table 4-7, and sample URLs are given in Table 4-8.

When sending e-mail to a user on the Internet, we use a slight variation of the domain name. In addition to identifying a host and subnet, we must also designate a user or recipient. The format of this kind of address is *user@domain.* The @ symbol is used to separate the user name from the domain name. In this naming convention, the domain represents the mail server for that individual, and the user represents an e-mail post office box (user or function name) to whom the mail will be delivered. The @ symbol was used in the very first e-mail software implemented on ARPAnet and has been part of e-mail addressing conventions ever since.

Domain Name System (DNS)
Name resolution software that lets users locate computers on the Internet and other TCP/IP networks by domain name.

domain name system (DNS) server
A server that resolves domain names to network addresses. A DNS server has DNS software that is used to locate computers on the Internet and other TCP/IP networks by domain name. DNS servers maintain a database of domain names (host names) and their corresponding IP addresses.

Figure 4-3   Domain Name Hierarchy

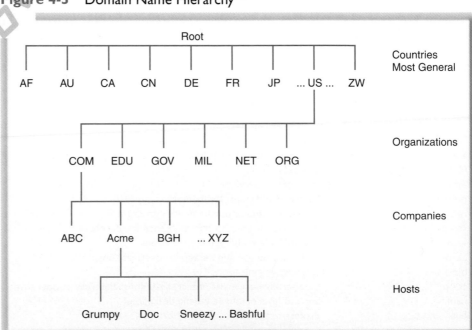

Table 4-7   Some URL protocols

Protocol	Explanation
http	Hypertext transfer protocol
ftp	File transfer protocol
file	File access
mailto	Send mail to a recipient
news	Access a newsgroup or news article
Gopher	Use the Gopher text-oriented access
finger	Use utility to access information about a user

Subnet Addressing

As noted previously, classes A, B, and C addresses are composed of two basic parts: a network address and a host/node address. The class type identifier is included in the network address. We have also noted that there are a limited number of IP addresses. IPv4 developers recognized the limited number of IP addresses available for use and provided a mechanism for sharing a single network address among two or more networks. These mechanisms are described in *RFC 950*. RFC 950 enables class A, B, and C networks to be subdivided. Subnetting is essentially a scheme that enables network managers to split a network into smaller networks using the same network assignment number. It has the following advantages:

➤ Subnetting allows simplified network administration: Each network segment can be maintained independently and efficiently.

➤ Intranets can be restructured without affecting the overall network's interfaces with the Internet and other external networks.

➤ Intranet subnetting is not visible to external networks; this helps to enhance the overall security of the organization's networks.

Subnetting enables network managers to extend the network portion of IP addresses by taking away some of the host portion of the IP address. This is illustrated

Table 4-8   Sample URLs

URL	Explanation
http://www.mycompany.com	HTTP protocol accessing the Web page of a company using the domain name *mycompany.com*
ftp://ftp.mycompany.com/pubs/usermanual.txt	Transfer a file called *usermanual.txt* in the pubs directory on the *mycompany.com* node
finger:jdoe@mycompany.com	Invoke the finger utility to get information on jdoe
gopher://frodo.abc.edu	Access the Gopher menu on node *frodo* at ABC University
mailto:jdoe@mycompany.com	Send mail to jdoe at *mycompany*
news:comp.newusers.announce	Access the newsgroup for announcements for new computer users

in Figure 4-4. In essence, an extended network address is created by subdividing the host/node portion of the address into two parts: a subnet address and a host/node address. In its most basic sense, a **subnet** is a subdivision of the network address that is created by taking some of the host/node identifier bits and using them as a subnet identifier.

Subnet Masking

As noted previously, class C addresses use the first 24 of the 32-bit IP address to identify the network and the last 8 to identify the host or node. When a class C network is divided into subnets, however, a subset of the host/node identifier bits is used to identify a particular host/node's subnet. The number of bits that identify a subnet as well as the number of bits that identify a host/node within a subnet are indicated by the network's **subnet mask**. The subnet mask is a binary pattern that is stored in network host/nodes and routers and is matched up with an incoming packet's destination IP addresses to determine whether to accept or reject the packet.

Every TCP/IP network host/node or router has a subnet mask along with its IP address. The subnet mask informs a host/node or data communications device (such as a router) as to which bits in an IP address should be treated as an extended network address. The rest of the bits indicate the host/node portion of the extended network address. Default subnet masks exist for class A, B, and C networks. These are summarized in Table 4-9. The binary form of the subnet mask conforms to the following rules: A binary one (1) in the subnet mask corresponds to the extended network address (the network identifier + subnet number), and all zeros (0) in the subnet mask correspond to the position of the host/node portion of the 3-level IP address.

In order to illustrate this, let's consider class C addresses. The local part of the address consists of 8 bits. This means that we could have 1 subnet with 256 host addresses.

subnet A portion of a network. Large networks can be subdivided into interconnected, but independent, segments, or domains, in order to improve performance and security. Each of these domains is a subnet.

subnet mask The number of bits that identify a subnet as well as the number of bits that identify a host/node within a subnet are indicated by the network's subnet mask. The subnet mask is a binary pattern that is stored in network nodes and is matched up with an incoming packet's destination IP addresses to determine whether to accept or reject the packet.

Figure 4-4   IPv4's 3-Level IP Addressing

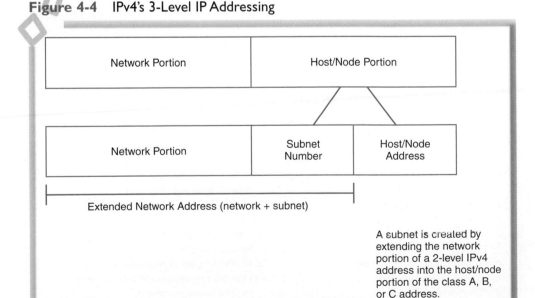

A subnet is created by extending the network portion of a 2-level IPv4 address into the host/node portion of the class A, B, or C address.

Table 4-9   Default IPv4 Subnet Masks

IPv4 Class	Subnet Mask (Decimal Form)	Subnet Mask (Binary Form)
A	255.0.0.0	11111111 00000000 00000000 00000000
B	255.255.0.0	11111111 11111111 00000000 00000000
C	255.255.255.0	11111111 11111111 11111111 00000000
D and E	n/a	n/a

However, as illustrated in Table 4-10, it is also possible for us to subdivide the class C network into as many as 62 subnets. This is accomplished by modifying the default subnet mask (255.255.255.0) for the class C network. If we have four LANs and want to place each in its own subnet, we could use the addressing scheme illustrated in Table 4-11.

In order to accomplish a local decomposition of this type, a subnet mask is applied to the address. In the mask, a 1 bit designates the portion of the address that is to be interpreted as the network/subnet number. Therefore, the local segment just described would have a subnet mask of 11000000 for the last octet. The actual subnet mask is a 32-bit entity; we have just shown the right-most portion of the mask. Bits in the mask set to a 1 bit are to be interpreted as the subnet portion of the address, and bits set to 0 are to be interpreted as host addresses within the subnet. In the mask, all 1 bits are on the left and all 0 bits are on the right. The complete binary subnet mask for our example in Table 4-11 is, therefore,

$$11111111\ 11111111\ 11111111\ 11000000$$

In decimal form, the subnet mask for this example is 255.255.255.192. Let's consider another example. In this instance, the IP address is 205.165.231.67, and the subnet mask for the network is 255.255.255.224. As Figure 4-5 illustrates, when we decompose the IP address, we can see that it is a class C address that uses the first 3 bits of the last octet to identify the subnet and the last 5 bits to identify the host or node. In the example provided in Figure 4-5, we find that the network identifier for this class C network is 205.165.231; the host/node associated with this IP address, 205.165.231.67, is part of subnet 2 for this network; and this host/node has the value of 3 within subnet 2.

Table 4-10   Subnet Masks, Subnets, and Hosts/Nodes for a Class C IPv4 Address

Subnet Mask (Decimal Form)	Subnet Mask (Binary Form)	Number of Subnets	Number of Hosts/Nodes
255.255.255.192	11111111 11111111 11111111 11000000	2	62
255.255.255.224	11111111 11111111 11111111 11100000	6	30
255.255.255.240	11111111 11111111 11111111 11110000	14	14
255.255.255.248	11111111 11111111 11111111 11111000	30	6
255.255.255.252	11111111 11111111 11111111 11111100	62	2

Table 4-11   Four Subnet Addresses for Class C Address

Bit Range	Subnet Address First Two Bits	Node Address Range Bits 3 Through 8
00000000–00111111	00	000000–111111
01000000–01111111	01	000000–111111
10000000–10111111	10	000000–111111
11000000–11111111	11	000000–111111

Workstation/Server TCP/IP Configuration

Most operating systems require the entry of at least three IP addresses and an optional subnet mask when configuring a workstation or server to work on a TCP/IP network. The three IP addresses are

➤ The IP address that serves as the workstation/server's unique identifier

➤ The IP address of the "gateway" responsible for relaying packets with destination addresses that are different from those on the local network

➤ The IP address of the domain name server (DNS server) used to identify the IP addresses of the registered domain names

Figure 4-5   Using a Subnet Mask to Decompose an IPv4 Address into Its Subnet and Host Values

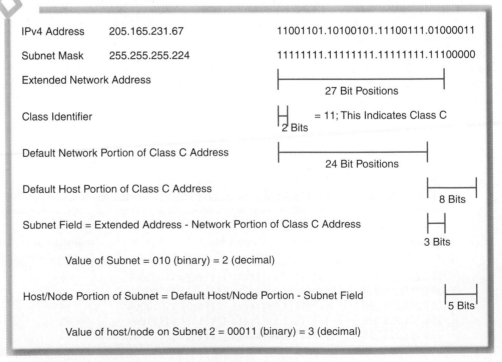

IPv4 Address	205.165.231.67	11001101.10100101.11100111.01000011
Subnet Mask	255.255.255.224	11111111.11111111.11111111.11100000

Extended Network Address — 27 Bit Positions

Class Identifier — 2 Bits = 11; This Indicates Class C

Default Network Portion of Class C Address — 24 Bit Positions

Default Host Portion of Class C Address — 8 Bits

Subnet Field = Extended Address - Network Portion of Class C Address — 3 Bits

Value of Subnet = 010 (binary) = 2 (decimal)

Host/Node Portion of Subnet = Default Host/Node Portion - Subnet Field — 5 Bits

Value of host/node on Subnet 2 = 00011 (binary) = 3 (decimal)

In Windows, these IP addresses are entered in TCP/IP properties screens (see Figures 4-6, 4-7, and 4-8). These are accessed via the network options on the control panel.

If the workstation with the IP address illustrated in Figure 4-6 wanted to send a packet to a host/node that was not part of the local network, the packet would be sent to a router (gateway) with the IP address identified in Figure 4-7. If workstations in other networks knew the host/node's name and DNS domain (tcase.bus.gasou.edu) and needed to obtain the host/node's IP address from a DNS server in order to request access, this can be accomplished when the information in Figure 4-8 is entered. The entries in Figure 4-8 inform the indicated domain servers that requests to access host/node tcase.bus.gasou.edu should be routed to the IP address specified in Figure 4-6. In an IP network such as the Internet, addresses are unique. Let us now look at how a host obtains an Internet address.

INTERNET HOST/NODE ADDRESSES

After obtaining a set of Internet addresses, say a class C address space, an organization must allocate its addresses to the hosts/nodes within the network. Host/node addresses can be allocated in one of two ways: They can be statically assigned or dynamically assigned.

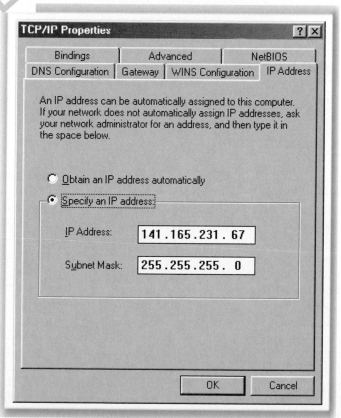

Figure 4-6   Windows TCP/IP Properties Screen Showing a Workstation's Host/Node Address and the Network's Subnet Mask

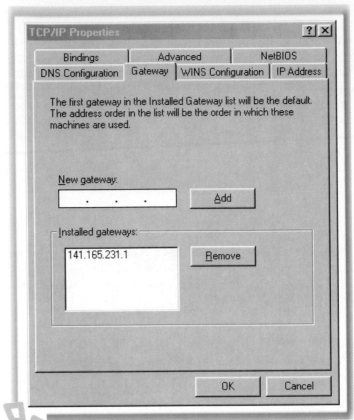

Figure 4-7   Windows TCP/IP Properties Screen Showing the IP Address of the Router Designated to Service Packets Addressed to Different Networks by the Workstation Illustrated in Figure 4-6

Static IP Addresses

static IP address
IP addresses that are permanently assigned to an organization's hosts and nodes. Servers and routers are usually assigned static IP addresses. Users connected to the Internet via cable modems and DSL either in the office or at home may also be assigned static IP addresses by their ISPs.

If a company has a class C address space and only 200 hosts/nodes that will be connecting to the Internet, it is possible to permanently assign each host/node one of the addresses. IP addresses that are permanently assigned to an organization's hosts and nodes are called **static IP addresses**. Data communication devices within a network, including routers, are typically assigned permanent IP addresses. Publicly accessible servers, such as Web servers, are also likely to have static IP addresses. Workstations, however, may have either static or dynamic IP addresses.

There are two primary ways that can be used by network managers to assign static IP addresses. The first involves the manual configuration of each host/node on the network by going from machine to machine and entering a unique IP address for each. This typically involves entering the information illustrated in Figures 4-6, 4-7, and 4-8 for each host/node in the network. The second approach is to have a server automatically assign an IP address to a host/node each time that it comes onto the network. How this is accomplished depends somewhat on the system's software, but essentially the address is located in a file on a network server. When the host/node is started (booted), it obtains its IP address from the server's file. If the

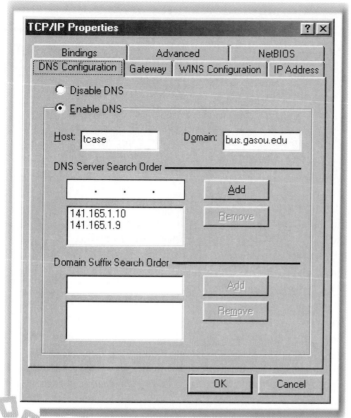

Figure 4-8   This Windows TCP/IP Properties Screen Enables a Host/Node to Be Identified by Its Host and Domain Names as Well as by Its IP Address

host/node is always assigned the same IP address by the server, the host/node has a static IP address.

Dynamic IP Addresses

In **dynamic IP addressing**, a host/node is assigned an Internet address when one is needed. When a workstation is assigned an IP address for the duration of the current communication session, it has a **dynamic IP address**. When the communication session is terminated, the IP address is returned to the server's list of available addresses. Because not all workstations are online at all times, fewer IP addresses than the total number of workstations in the network can satisfy the needs of the network when dynamic addressing is used. For example, consider the allocation of IP addresses by an Internet service provider (ISP). As mentioned in Chapter 2, ISPs may have modem-to-user ratios of 10 to 1 or more. Thus, an ISP that can allocate a total of 200 IP addresses could serve a total customer population of 2,000. When a customer connects to the ISP's host, their computer is dynamically assigned an IP address that is not currently in use. When a workstation is dynamically assigned an IP address, it is said that the workstation is "leasing" the IP address.

dynamic IP addressing The assignment of an IP address to a node that does not have a static address. When dynamic IP addressing is used, client stations are assigned dynamic IP addresses from a DHCP server each time they come online.

dynamic IP address An IP address that is automatically assigned to a client station in a TCP/IP network, typically by a DHCP server.

Dynamic Host Configuration Protocol (DHCP)

The most common mechanism for dynamically assigning Internet addresses is the **Dynamic Host Configuration Protocol (DHCP)**. (*Note:* An earlier protocol called BOOTP also provided dynamic addressing, but it was developed for diskless workstations. DHCP is more comprehensive.) Servers that manage the dynamic assignment of IP addresses are called *DHCP servers,* and the workstations that are dynamically assigned IP addresses by DHCP servers are called *DHCP clients.* DHCP servers may be computers attached to the network; alternatively, a router with DHCP software or firmware may function as the DHCP server for a network. DHCP software resides on both clients and servers in order to manage the dynamic assignment of IP addresses. Windows NT, Windows 9x, Windows 2000, and Windows XP include DHCP client software.

When DHCP servers are configured, the range of IP addresses that can be assigned to clients is specified. Suppose a router with DHCP software embedded as firmware is used as a DHCP server. Suppose further that the router's IP address, 141.165.231.1, is capable of allocating 100 IP addresses. If the starting IP address that can be assigned is 141.165.231.100, the range of IP addresses that this DHCP server can assign extends from 141.165.231.100 to 141.165.231.199.

DHCP servers maintain a list of currently leased (assigned) IP addresses from its assignable IP address range. When dynamic addressing is used in local area networks (LANs), such lists typically depict the client host/node's name (such as *dstamper* or *tcase*), the IP address that has been assigned to the client, and the client's media access control (MAC) addresses. MAC addresses uniquely identify the network adapter card installed in the client. Network adapter cards enable computers to be attached to LANs. MAC addresses are assigned to network adapter cards when they are manufactured. When dynamic addressing is used, a client can be allocated any IP address from its range of assignable addresses that are not currently in use.

A DHCP server can assign an IP address in one of three ways: automatic allocation, dynamic allocation, or manual allocation. With automatic allocation, the server attempts to always assign the same address to a given host/node. This is useful for hosts, such as servers, that provide services to users, such as mail servers. This kind of host needs the same address each time it boots because other hosts that use its services are likely to have its Internet address saved. Manual allocation means that a network administrator has assigned the address to a particular host/node. For example, a network manager may manually assign an IP address to an e-commerce server. This effectively removes the manually assigned IP address from the list of dynamically assignable IP addresses. The ISP mentioned earlier will assign a static IP address to its DHCP server and dynamically assign IP addresses to most of its customers. With dynamic addressing, a host is given any address that is not currently in use.

When an ISP customer wants to connect to the Internet, the process starts when the client sends a broadcast message to locate a DHCP server. (Larger ISPs often use several such servers to allow faster and more reliable Internet access to customers as well as to provide a level of fault tolerance. However, we will consider only the simple case in which there is only one DHCP server. For information about multiple DHCP servers, consult the Network Working Group's *RFC 2131* standard document.) This broadcast message contains the client's ID, a request for an IP address, and desired options such as subnet mask, DNS server, domain name, and static route. The broadcast message that is sent is called a DHCPDISCOVER message. Each DHCP server that receives the client's DHCPDISCOVER message can send a DHCPOFFER message to the client, offering an IP address that is not currently in use. Typically, the least

Dynamic Host Configuration Protocol (DHCP)
Software that automatically assigns IP addresses to client stations logging onto a TCP/IP network. DHCP clients obtain dynamic IP addresses from DHCP servers when logging onto the TCP/IP network. In many networks, DHCP servers dynamically update DNS servers after assigning dynamic IP addresses to clients.

recently used address in the server's assignable address pool is selected. The client indicates its acceptance of the IP address by broadcasting a DHCPREQUEST message. The server acknowledges the client's acceptance of the IP address in a DHCPACK message; this message also delivers additional configuration information to the client. The DHCP address allocation process is illustrated in Figure 4-9.

When dynamic addressing is used by ISPs, the ISP customer's request for an IP address may also specify a time frame for use of the address. If this is the case, the DHCP server may allocate the address to another user when the requested time plus a margin-of-error interval has elapsed. A customer's DHCP client can also re-negotiate its allowed time. When the customer is finished with the address, their computer notifies the DHCP server that it is releasing the address. Once released, the address is returned to the DHCP server's assignable address pool; this makes it eligible to be assigned to another ISP customer's computer that requests an IP address.

As the sole allocator of IP addresses, the DHCP server knows which addresses in its assignable range are in use and which are available. As an additional measure, DHCP servers are capable of transmitting an echo request message using the *Internet Control Message Protocol (ICMP)* to determine whether the address is currently being used. If the address is in use, the server receives an echo reply response from the host or node using the address.

Another dynamic address assignment algorithm is used by some software systems. In this approach, a host or node that needs an address chooses one from the set of assignable IP addresses and broadcasts a message to determine whether the address is in use. If another host or node responds to the message, the sender chooses another address, and the process repeats. If no response is received, the host assumes the address is not in use and adopts that address.

Internet Addressing in LANs

Sometimes, the host that needs to connect to the Internet is also a LAN node. In this instance, an additional addressing consideration must be made. In the LAN, a message is delivered to a node based on its physical address, that is, the media access control (MAC) address of its network interface card. Therefore, if a LAN node also has an IP address, an IP message can be delivered only if the IP address is first translated into

Figure 4-9   Dynamic IP Address Assignment with DHCP

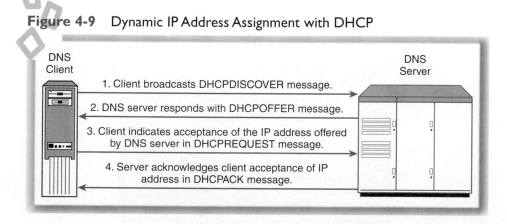

address resolution protocol (ARP) A TCP/IP protocol used to obtain a node's physical (hardware) address. When ARP is used, a network node broadcasts an ARP request onto the network with the IP address of the target node it wishes to communicate with, and the node with that address responds by sending back its physical address. Once the physical address is known, packets can be transmitted from the node that issued the ARP request to the target node.

reverse address resolution protocol (RARP) Works by broadcasting the node's hardware address and receiving an IP address in return from a RARP server. RARP was originally developed in networks with diskless workstations incapable of storing their TCP/IP configuration information.

a MAC address. The protocol that performs this function is called the **address resolution protocol (ARP)**.

The ARP assumes that the LAN node's IP address is known. For example, a LAN server may receive an IP message intended for a LAN node. The node's IP address is contained in the destination field of the IP header. The server will probably have an ARP table that contains IP addresses and the corresponding MAC addresses, as illustrated in Table 4-12. The first entry in the table is the ARP entry for the server itself; the second is a broadcast address used to search for an unknown address; and the remaining addresses are known IP/MAC addresses.

If the destination node's IP address is in the ARP table, the server extracts the corresponding MAC address, builds the MAC header, and sends the message to the node. If the destination node's IP address is not in the ARP table, its address must be discovered. The server broadcasts an ARP request packet on the network, and any node that knows the IP/MAC address pair responds. When the server receives the proper entry, it stores the address in its ARP table and forwards the message to the node.

Reverse address resolution protocol (RARP) does the opposite of ARP. Whereas ARP converts IP addresses into MAC (data link layer hardware) addresses, RARP works by broadcasting the node's hardware address and receiving an IP address in return from a RARP server. RARP was originally developed in networks with diskless workstations incapable of storing their TCP/IP configuration information. Because a RARP server can supply IP addresses to all computers on a network segment, it is often viewed as one of the precursors of DHCP. The bootstrap protocol (BOOTP) is another precursor of DHCP and is still used today in routers made by Cisco and other manufacturers. Unlike RARP, BOOTP is capable of delivering more than IP addresses to clients; TCP/IP configuration parameters can also be exchanged among clients and servers via BOOTP.

ARP is outlined in *RFC 826*. RARP is described in *RFC 903*. As illustrated in Figure 4-10, ARP and RARP are typically depicted as being found at the Internet layer of the TCP/IP protocol stack. It is important to note, however, that they might also be described as overlapping the Internet layer and network access layers because of their role in translating IP addresses to MAC (hardware) addresses and vice versa.

The Domain Name System (DNS)

The Domain Name System (DNS) maps host/node address to host/node domain names. Such mapping is provided by DNS servers. Essentially, DNS servers enable Internet users to reach another host/node without having to provide an explicit IP address. This enables Web browser users to type in a URL or click on a hyperlink and

Table 4-12   ARP Table

MAC Address	IP Address
03-A1-22-70-44-02	201.1.1.1
FF-FF-FF-FF-FF-FF	143.7.255.255
FF-FF-FF-FF-FF-FF	255.255.255.255
03-A1-22-70-44-07	201.1.1.8
03-A1-22-70-44-25	201.1.1.17
03-A1-22-70-44-B2	201.1.1.4

Application Layer	HTTP, FTP, SMTP, and SNMP
Transport/Host to Host Layer	TCP
Internet Layer	IP / UDP ARP RARP
Network Access Layer	
Physical Layer	

Figure 4-10   ARP in Relation to the TCP/IP Protocol Stack

instantly be taken to a particular Web page; it is not necessary for them to know the IP address of the Web server on which the Web page is stored.

The DNS is built around a database that contains domain names and their associated IP addresses for Internet-attached networks. Domain names are used as indexes in the DNS database. The DNS database has an entry for each domain name that identifies the DNS server that has the most detailed information about the host/node (such as its IP address and routing information). DNS servers communicate with one another in order to keep the database current. If a DNS server does not know the address of a particular host/node specified in a URL, it queries other DNS servers for this information. Once the information is found, the DNS server that initiated the request forwards the information to the Internet user's computer. Once the user's computer knows the destination host or node's IP address, it can build the TCP/IP packet needed to send a message or request to the destination host/node.

Obtaining a host/node's IP address is the first part of sending a message from one host/node to another across a TCP/IP network such as the Internet. The second part is moving the message from source host to destination host, a process called *routing*. Let us look at how the IP protocol does this.

IP ROUTING

When an Internet node sends a message to another Internet node, it must know the destination node's IP address. The address may be resolved from a URL supplied by the user or obtained from a hypertext link or similar mechanism. At the heart of the routing algorithm is a **routing table** that contains network information essential to making intelligent routing decisions. In discussing how IP routing works, let us consider the network illustrated in Figure 4-11. In the figure, the clouds represent networks, and the network addresses are shown within the clouds. Devices called routers (see Chapter 9) are the predominant data communication devices responsible for message routing in

routing table An information source containing node or network addresses and the identification of the path to be used in transmitting data to those nodes or networks.

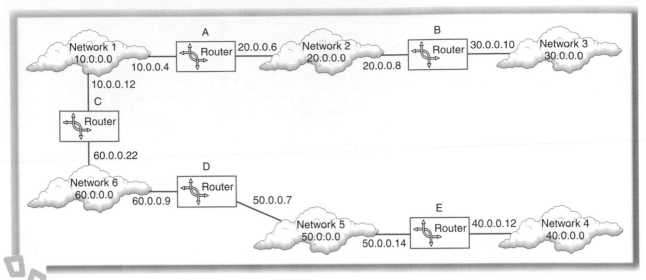

Figure 4-11   IP Network Routing

internets and the Internet. Each router is connected to two (or more) networks (some routers have more than two ports), and each router port has an address on the attached subnet. Therefore, router A is connected to subnet 1 and has the address of 10.0.0.4 on that subnet and address 20.0.0.6 for the attachment to subnet 2.

Each router maintains a routing table. Some of the information contained in those tables is given in Table 4-13, and the routing table for router A (based on the data in Table 4-13 and Figure 4-11) is given in Table 4-14. The next router column in Table 4-14 identifies the router that should receive a packet destined to the different network addresses. The number of hops to the network is a measure of the distance to the destination network from the current router. The hop count is the number of routers or gateways that must process the packet on its path to the destination network. The hop count does not consider the speed of the networks through which the packet will travel. It may be faster to cover four hops through fast networks such as fast Ethernet LANs than to pass through two WANs using slower communication links. Other routing implementations use an additional distance measure called *ticks*, which represent the speed of transmission over a route. The port address identifies the router's port through which the router will transmit the message to get it to the next router or to the subnet.

Table 4-13   Some IP Routing Table Data

Network address	Next router
Hops to network	Port address

Table 4-14   Router A's Routing Table

Net Address	Next Router	Hops	Port
10	None	Directly connected	10.0.0.4
20	None	Directly connected	20.0.0.6
30	B	1	20.0.0.6
40	C	3	10.0.0.4
50	C	2	10.0.0.4
60	C	1	10.0.0.4

IP Routing Algorithm

The algorithm that the IP uses to route a message from source node to destination node is essentially as follows:

1. The source host/node obtains the destination host/node's IP address. DNS may play a role in this.
2. The IP protocol builds the IP header and affixes it to the packet.
3. The source host/node sends the packet to its gateway router.
4. The router reads the network address of the destination host/node.
5. If the network address is this network, a local delivery method is used and the remaining steps are skipped. For example, use the ARP if the destination network is this LAN and transmit using MAC address.
6. The router consults the routing table to determine the best path to the destination network across the TCP/IP backbone.
7. The router transmits the packet addressed to the next router out the appropriate port.
8. The receiving router decrements the time-to-live field. The time-to-live field is a field in the IP header that indicates how long a packet will last before being discarded. The value of the time-to-live field is the number of hops remaining. The time-to-live field is decremented by each router and the router setting the field to 0 discards the packet.
9. If the time-to-live field is 0, the packet is discarded.
10. Return to step 4.

Note that in step 9, a packet may be discarded. The sending router sets the time-to-live counter to its initial value, and each time the packet passes through a router, the counter is decremented. The router that sets the counter to 0 will not attempt to forward the packet. This keeps packets from circulating endlessly through the network, an event that could occur if routing tables were not consistent. If a packet is discarded, it is the responsibility of the TCP module on the destination host/node to recognize the problem and request that the packet be resent. A flowchart of the routing process is shown in Figure 4-12.

PORTS AND SOCKETS

IP addresses make it possible to route network traffic across the Internet backbone. However, once they are received by the destination host/node and begin progressing up the TCP/IP protocol stack, they still must be directed to the appropriate application.

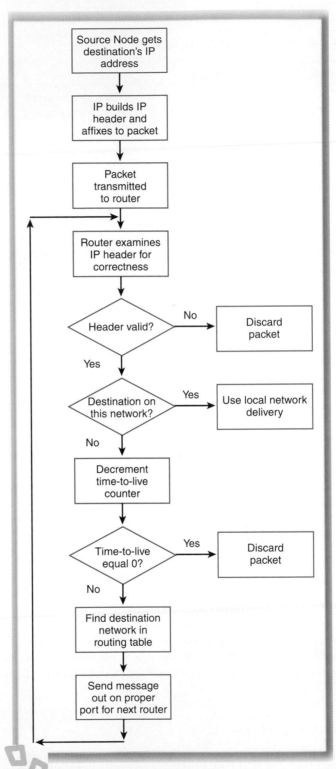

Figure 4-12   Routing Process

This is the job of either TCP or UDP. TCP and UDP use port numbers, which are included in every TCP or UDP header. Typically, the port number identifies the application layer protocol that generated the data carried in the packet.

Some port numbers are permanently assigned to specific services/applications. These are called *well-known ports* and are identified in IANA's *RFC 1700*. Every network attached to the Internet maintains a services file that lists the well-known port numbers and services that are available in the network. For example, if a network includes a DNS server and a Web (HTTP) server, its services file will include well-known ports 53 (for DNS) and 80 (for HTTP). The IP header of a DNS query message will contain the IP address of the network's DNS server in its destination address field. Once the packet has arrived at the server, the receiving computer will see that the destination port file contains well-known port value 53 and will pass the query to the DNS application. Examples of well-known ports are summarized in Table 4-15.

The combination of an IP address and a port number is called a **socket**. For example, a request for a Web page stored on a Web server whose IP address is 141.165.231.193 in socket notation would be 141.165.231.193:80.

socket A socket consists of a combination of a TCP port number and an IP address. Sockets are used in TCP/IP networks to direct data to appropriate applications on hosts.

INTERNET TOOLS FOR NETWORK MANAGERS

A number of tools are available to assist network managers to ensure that the Internet (on a TCP/IP enterprise-wide internet) is being used effectively. In reality, these tools are not just available to network managers. Internet users can access and utilize these tools as well.

Finger

Finger is a utility that allows a user to gather information about other network users. Depending on the finger syntax, a user can find out who is logged onto a given network host or get detailed information about a selected network user, such as telephone number, whether they are currently logged on, or the last time they logged onto the network. To be "fingered," a user's profile must exist on the system. Fingering requires entering a user's full *user@domain* address. For security reasons, some systems

Finger An Internet utility that is widely used to find out information about a particular user, such as telephone number, whether currently logged on, or the last time logged on.

Table 4-15   Examples of Well-Known Ports and Services

Port	Service	Service Description
7	Ping	Verify communication between two computers
20	FTP	File transfer data
21	FTP	File transfer control information
23	TELNET	Remote login
25	SMTP	E-mail transfer
53	DNS	Domain name service
79	Finger	Obtain information about users and their accounts
80	HTTP	Web page access/transfers
161	SNMP	Simple network management protocol; used to monitor and manage network traffic

Table 4-16   Output of Finger Request

Login	Name	TTY	Date	Time
johnd	John Doe	4	Sep 5	12:12
alicet	Alice Trask	9	Sep 5	15:30
maryb	Mary Boggs	11	Sep 5	14:20

ping An Internet utility used to determine whether a given system is active on the network (is online). It is often used to test and debug a network by sending out a packet and waiting for a response. Ping is an acronym for Packet Internet Gopher.

Tracert An Internet utility that describes the real-time path from a user's node to another node on the network. It reports the IP addresses of all the routers in between the user's node and the destination node.

WHOIS database A repository of data about domains and users. A WHOIS database is essentially a white pages directory for the organization.

do not allow the use of this utility. An edited output of a finger request for logged on users is given in Table 4-16.

Ping

Ping allows a user to determine whether a given system is active on the network. Some versions of ping also give performance information such as number of hops to the system and speed of the links if the system is available. The output from a ping command is shown in Figure 4-13.

Tracert

Tracert allows a user to trace the round trip between the user's computer and another host on the network. The output of a Tracert command is given in Figure 4-14.

WHOIS Database

The **WHOIS database** is a repository of data about domains and users. An Internet utility is used to query a host and find out if a certain user is registered on that system. Originally developed by the military, other organizations followed by creating their own WHOIS databases. A WHOIS database is essentially a white pages directory for the organization.

WEB PAGE DESIGN TOOLS

The explosive growth of the World Wide Web (WWW) and Web-based electronic commerce has made it important for network professionals to be familiar with the basic mechanics of Web page design and implementation. Some of the fundamental tools

Figure 4-13   Output of Ping Request

```
C:\WINDOWS>ping -a www.htcomp.net
Pinging www.htcomp.net [207.17.188.94] with 32 bytes of
data:
Reply from 207.17.188.94: bytes=32 time=251ms TTL=125
Reply from 207.17.188.94: bytes=32 time=240ms TTL=125
Reply from 207.17.188.94: bytes=32 time=235ms TTL=125
Reply from 207.17.188.94: bytes=32 time=193ms TTL=125
```

```
C:\WINDOWS>tracert 137.39.136.166
Tracing route to ms4-gw.customer.Alter.net [137.39.136.166] over a
maximum of 30 hops:
1     188 ms 182 ms 176 ms ppph101-110.htcomp.net [207.17.189.40]
2     175 ms 182 ms 177 ms 207.17.189.2
3     204 ms 205 ms 198 ms hmltn-clb-T1.htcomp.net [207.17.189.1]
4     212 ms 206 ms 206 ms Loopback0.GW1.DFW1.Alter.net [137.39.2.52]
5     254 ms 278 ms 217 ms 421.ATM11-0.CR2.DFW1.Alter.net
[137.39.21.10]
6     356 ms 349 ms 358 ms 108.Hssi4-0.CR2.SEA1.Alter.net
[137.39.58.129]
7     624 ms   *      627 ms Fddi1-0.GW2.SEA1.Alter.net [137.39.42.194]
8     304 ms 334 ms 317 ms ms4-gw.customer.Alter.net [137.39.136.166]
Trace complete.
C:\WINDOWS>
```

Figure 4-14   Output of Tracert Command

that today's network professionals need include a working knowledge of HTML, Dynamic HTML (DHTML), Extensible Markup Language (XML), and markup languages for Internet graphics formats.

Hypertext Markup Language (HTML)

Web pages were originally designed by using a text editor to insert the Hypertext Markup Language (HTML) control codes in a document. For example, the title of a page containing the text "My Home Page" is denoted as <TITLE>My Home Page</TITLE>. Similar control codes are used to provide effects such as bolding and font size, borders, and links. Today, specialized Web page design tools abound, including Dreamweaver, Microsoft's Front Page, and Netscape's Composer. In addition, most word processor programs now include modules for automatically inserting HTML tags in a document so that the document can be saved as a Web page. Because of its widespread use and importance to network professionals, it is important to take a closer look at HTML.

HTML can be traced back to Standard Generalized Markup Language (SGML), developed by IBM during the 1970s. In 1986, SGML received official recognition by the International Standards Organization (ISO). As illustrated in Figure 4-15, HTML is just one of the major offshoots of SGML.

HTML is a document description language that consists of text and fixed tags. *Tags* describe the attributes of the text (and other document content) to Web browsers. Like most languages, HTML has evolved over time, and with each new version, additional tags have been defined. Web browsers have evolved parallel to HTML's evolution to be able to keep up with new HTML tags. A tag is enclosed in "<" and ">" symbols such as <head> to indicate that the text that follows is a document header and </head> to indicate the end of the header. Each complete HTML document begins with <html> and ends with </html>.

Tools used to design Web pages for viewing by a particular Web browser often support extensions that enhance the appearance of HTML pages when viewed by that Web browser. These extensions, however, are not part of the official HTML standard. Web page designers who take advantage of extensions for one browser may actually do

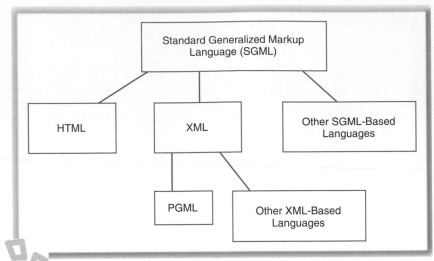

Figure 4-15   Document Description Languages Derived from SGML

a disservice to users who attempt to view the page using a different version. This is because a browser, unlike most programming languages, will simply ignore tags it does not understand instead of treating them as program command errors. Both Netscape Composer and Microsoft Front Page support extensions that their target browsers (*Netscape Navigator* and *Internet Explorer,* respectively) understand but competing browsers will ignore.

In order to exploit the capabilities of competing browsers, many e-commerce Web sites contain multiple sets of Web pages with each set optimized for the latest version of a particular browser. HTTP servers at these sites identify the browser being used to request a particular page and respond with the appropriate browser-specific version of the page.

One of the most important enhancements to HTML is the <object> tag. This allows all categories of programming language objects—including Java or ActiveX applets, images, embedded HTML documents, or JavaScript objects—to be processed with one tag rather than requiring specific tags for each object type.

Another recent enhancement is support for *cascading style sheets (CSSs),* which enable Web page designers to specify a consistent structure and layout (a common "look") for multiple HTML documents at the same Web site. Because a CSS style sheet can be stored in an external file that can be referenced by multiple HTML documents, when the style sheet is changed, all the HTML documents that reference the style sheet are automatically changed. This means that each of the Web pages does not have to be individually changed when the business decides to change the overall look of its Web site.

Dynamic HTML

Dynamic HTML (DHTML) gives Web page designers greater control over how an HTML page appears in an Internet user's browser window. For example, with DHTML, the designer can specify the exact position where a graphic object, such as the business's logo, should appear. Also, because DHTML is a combination of CSS style sheets, scripts, and HTML, Web pages can be updated in response to user actions without requiring the browser to reconnect to the Web site and download a new version of the page. For example, a visual special-effect element such as a "mouseover" pop-up text box could appear when the user positions the mouse pointer over a particular point on the Web page. DHTML would also enable the data on a page to be re-sorted at the request of the user.

Needless to say, the actions supported by DHTML can only be carried out by a DHTML–enabled browser that is capable of taking advantage of the processing power of the user's computer. Not only does DHTML enable the addition of interesting visual effects within a browser window, but it also helps to minimize the workloads of HTTP servers while maximizing the actions that users can take advantage of on a Web page without having to reconnect to the HTTP server and download an updated version of the page. This is especially good for e-commerce sites because it helps to minimize frustrating slow downloads that often cause potential customers to abort transactions before completing them.

Extensible Markup Language (XML)

Extensible Markup Language (XML) is a standard language for describing data. It is used to describe data so that it can be interpreted or manipulated by Java or other applications resident on user computers. Through the use of Extensible Stylesheet Language (XSL), XML can be converted to HTML for display by a Web browser. In the future, industry experts predict that XML data may be requested, processed, and displayed by browsers in a wide range of devices, including Internet-ready PDAs and cellular telephones, and interactive televisions.

An XML document looks very much like an HTML document. However, it includes new tags to describe the meaning of data elements. Examples of important XML tags are summarized in Table 4-17. The tags DOCTYPE and ELEMENT (see Table 4-17) are known as document type definition (DTD) tags; DTD tags can be used by XML processors to validate the XML document against its own definitions. XML tags are interpreted by XML processors, which may be included in browsers as plug-ins or helper programs. Most XML processors are written in Java, and future versions of Web browsers are likely to incorporate XML processors as XML becomes more widely used to describe data. An example of an XML document is found in Figure 4-16.

Extensible Markup Language (XML) A standard language for describing data. It is used for defining data elements on a Web page and business-to-business documents. It uses a similar tag structure as HTML, but unlike HTML, XML defines what data elements contain rather than how they are displayed.

Other Important Markup Languages

Other markup languages have been developed to enable special effects and file types to be rapidly downloaded for display in browser windows. Some of the common file formats are summarized in Table 4-18. Important markup languages that network

Table 4-17   Key XML Tags

XML Tag	Description
DOCTYPE	Defines the type of XML document
ELEMENT	Defines the data fields included in the XML document
ATTLIST	Defines the allowable attributes for the data elements in the XML document
PCDATA	Defines an element as a string of characters

```
<XML>
<!DOCTYPE purchases [
<!ELEMENT main (purchase)*>
<!ELEMENT purchase (date, account?, item+)>
<!ELEMENT date (#PCDATA)>
<!ELEMENT account (#PCDATA)>
<!ELEMENT item ((itemnumber itemdescription, quantity)|#PCDATA)*>
<!ELEMENT itemnumber (#PCDATA)>
<!ELEMENT itemdescription (#PCDATA)>
<!ELEMENT quantity (#PCDATA)>
<P>]></P>
<main>
<purchase>
<date> 11/31/2000 </date>
<account> Stamper </account>
<item>
<itemnumber> 12345 </itemnumber>
<itemdescription> 10/100 8-port Ethernet Hub </itemdescription>
<quantity> 2 </quantity>
</item>
<item>
</itemnumber> 98765 </itemnumber>
<itemdescription> 10/100 Ethernet Adapter </itemdescription>
<quantity> 16 </quantity>
</item>
</purchase>
</main>
</XML>
```

Figure 4-16   An Example of an XML Document

Table 4-18   Examples of Web Page Graphics Files

Acronym	Meaning	Description
GIF	Graphics exchange format	GIF files are relatively compact, thereby enabling images to be downloaded quickly. Because of this, they are widely used on Web pages.
JPEG	Joint photographic experts group	JPEG is a common graphics format for compressing still images that can be rendered on different displays and at different resolutions. It supports a wider range of colors than GIF files and is especially well suited for storing and rendering photographs and images.
PNG	Portable network graphics	PNG is a file format for compressed graphic images that is expected to eventually replace GIF because the same image can be compressed by an additional 10 percent to 30 percent (relative to GIF).

professionals and Web page designers should be familiar with include Vector Markup Language (VML) and Precision Graphics Markup Language (PGML).

VML   Traditionally, Web page graphic images such as GIF and JPEG have been raster images, a format that converts an image into a set of pixels and is best suited for photographs and complex illustrations. Vector Markup Language (VML) uses vector graphics and treats images as a set of lines and curves. As a result, vector graphics is particularly well suited for graphs, charts, and line art illustrations. VML images (of the same graph or chart) are smaller than GIF or JPEG format files and enable Web page designers to cut and paste graphics from different applications without quality loss. Because VML is based on XML, images that are embedded into HTML documents can interact with other elements in the document.

PGML   Precision Graphics Markup Language (PGML), like VML, is vector-graphics based. It is used by Web page designers who require precision control over Web page elements such as font, layout, color, and composition. It also enables designers to produce complex animations.

VRML   Virtual Reality Markup Language (VRML) is used to display 3-dimensional graphics in VRML–capable Web browsers. Users with VRML–capable browsers are able to interactively manipulate the 3-D graphics and to move them around a virtual environment in a near real-time mode. VRML is an open standard that has been leveraged to support graphically intensive Web applications such as computer-aided design (CAD), computer-aided engineering (CAE), and architectural design. More information on VRML and VRML–capable browsers is available at www.vrml.org.

SERVER CONFIGURATIONS

As businesses and other organizations become increasingly dependent on their Web sites, they face a number of challenges. As noted earlier, organizations must keep up with the evolution of markup languages and browsers in order to ensure that they are capable of delivering interest-provoking Web page content. Additionally, organizations must take steps to ensure that users can access their Web sites 24/7. As a result, many businesses have implemented server configurations that enhance fault tolerance and reliability. Some of the approaches being used include server farms, load balancing, and server clustering.

Server Farms

When Internet users access Web pages at large commercial Web sites, they typically are gaining access to a group of servers that share a common URL rather than a single host. This collective "host" is typically referred to as a **server farm**. They are created because even extremely large servers are unable to handle the Web site's Internet user traffic and processing requirements. Server farms are also common at large Web sites because they help to ensure reliable access and fault tolerance. If one of the servers in the Web farm is inoperable, others are likely to still be accessible. Although they do not guarantee 24/7 Internet user access to the Web site, server farms are capable of adding redundancy. (Even server farms are vulnerable to denial of service attacks; also, in some instances, software glitches have caused all servers in a server farm to

server farm A group of network servers that are housed in one location. A server farm provides bulk computing for specific applications such as Web site hosting. The group of servers that make up a server farm typically shares a common URL. Server farms are created because even extremely large servers are unable to handle all the Internet user traffic and processing requirements at some Web sites.

crash at the same time.) Server farms are also scalable. As traffic at the Web site increases, more servers can be added to handle the additional traffic. When implemented properly, server farms are able to handle large volumes of user requests quickly, thereby reducing the chance for slow response and user frustration.

Load Balancing

load balancing Fine tuning a computer system, network, or disk storage system to more evenly distribute the data and/or processing across available resources. In server clusters, load balancing is used to distribute incoming transactions evenly to all servers, or to redirect them from busy to less busy servers.

Load balancing involves the use of a router or switch to transfer individual Internet user Web page requests to particular servers in the server farm. Typically, the switch or router determines which server to send a request to on the basis of its processing speed, its current workload, or the type of Web page content that it stores. For example, if a particular server in the Web farm already has a long queue of user requests, the router or switch will send a new request to one of the other servers in the Web farm. As noted earlier, at many commercial Web sites, multiple versions of the same Web page (each of which has been optimized for a particular browser version) are available. In this case, a particular user's request for a Web page will be transferred to the server in the server farm that stores the version of the page that will have the best appearance in the user's browser window. Load-balancing routers and switches can also be used to route requests to servers designated to handle particular TCP/IP applications such as FTP or SMTP. Figure 4-17 illustrates load balancing at a server farm.

Figure 4-17   Load Balancing at a Server Farm

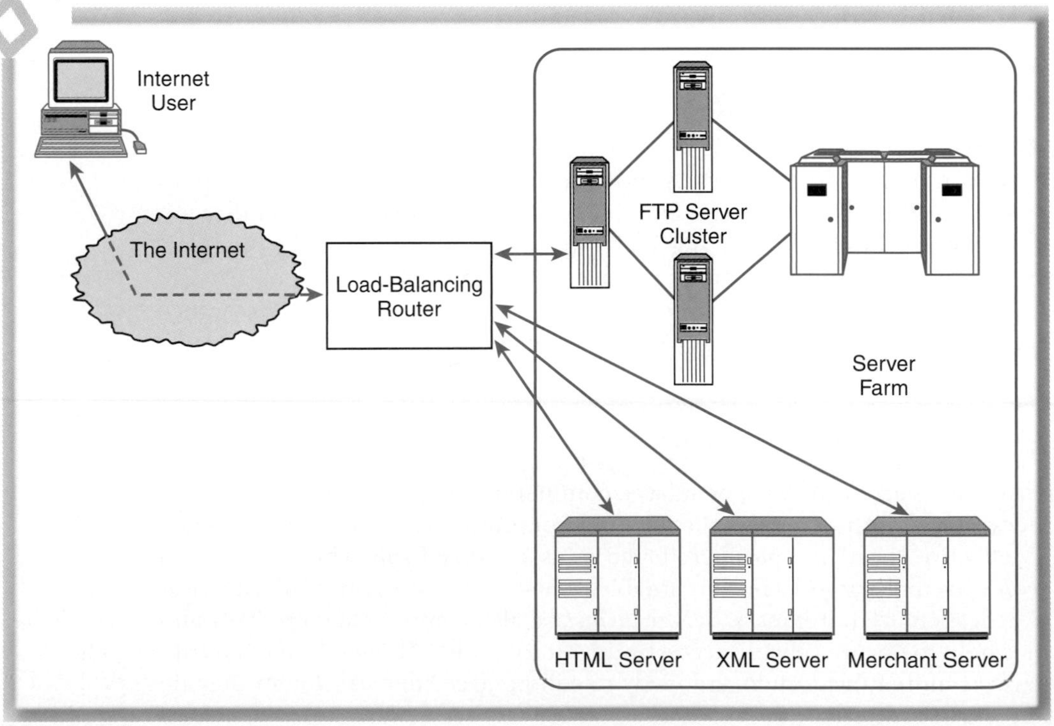

Server Clusters

When organizations implement **server clusters**, a group of servers acts as a single "team" and is responsible for allocating the total workload that they are responsible for handling. Server clusters can be an attractive option when there are so many requests for a particular application (such as FTP) that a single server cannot process them in a timely manner. When this happens, the overworked server will automatically transfer the request to another server in the cluster that is capable of processing it more rapidly. Some organizations have implemented server clusters in place of load balancing. Others are using a combination of load balancing and clustering, where high-speed switches or routers send requests for particular applications to the appropriate cluster that, in turn, allocates them among the servers on the basis of their current workload.

Fault tolerance can be enhanced in server clusters via a process called *automatic failover*. With automatic failover, other servers in the cluster will automatically take over the workload of a server that has failed. This is often accomplished by sending a single user request to two servers in the same cluster. Although one of the two servers (which is typically referred to as the *primary server*) is responsible for processing the request, should it fail before processing is complete, the second server (called the *backup* or *duplexed server*) will automatically take over and finish processing the request.

The software and hardware needed to implement and support server clusters are available from vendors such as Compaq, Hewlett-Packard, Intel, Microsoft, and Novell. In some instances, several hundred servers can be included in the same cluster. Server clusters are emerging rapidly, especially in organizations with large commercial Web sites.

server cluster When a group of servers acts as a single "team" and is responsible for allocating the total workload that they are responsible for handling.

TCP/IP AND SECURITY

As noted in Chapter 3, conducting business on the Internet requires a variety of new security measures in order to ensure the integrity of online transactions. Securing transaction and payment information transmitted over the Internet is an important aspect of electronic commerce. Companies with Web sites that are not yet engaging in Internet-based business transactions still need to protect their networks by implementing firewalls and other safeguards to prevent unauthorized access by outsiders.

When a company connects its network to the Internet, its systems are susceptible to unauthorized access by outsiders. Most companies want Internet access without exposing all of their systems to public access. As we noted in Chapter 2, this is usually accomplished by implementing firewalls. A firewall is software (or a combination of hardware or software) that sits between the Internet and the protected enterprise network. A firewall's role is to control and monitor traffic between them.

Proxy Servers

A **proxy server** is a device that functions as a proxy for a network's hosts/nodes that want Internet access. As illustrated in Figure 4-18, a proxy server separates a network from the Internet. All incoming and outgoing TCP/IP packets are passed through the proxy server. To outsiders, it appears that all Internet traffic is coming from the proxy

proxy server A device that functions as a proxy for a network's hosts/nodes that Internet users want to access. Proxy servers stand between a private network and the Internet and help prevent outsiders from accessing internal addresses and other details about the network.

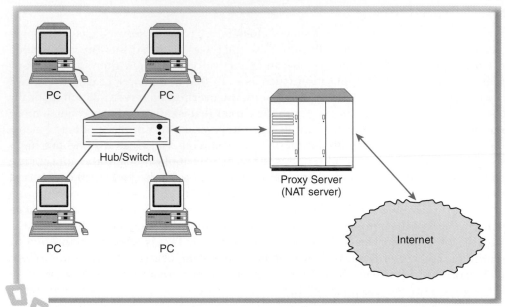

Figure 4-18   A Proxy Server Stands Between the Internet and a Private Network

server rather than from the individual hosts/nodes on the network. In other words, outside hosts/nodes see the entire network as only a single host (the proxy server); the IP addresses of individual hosts/nodes in the network are hidden behind the proxy server, thereby increasing network security.

A proxy server can also enhance network security by examining traffic coming into a network and rejecting communication that it determines to be a security risk. When used in this way to filter traffic, the proxy server functions as a *firewall*. As noted in Chapter 2, a firewall limits traffic between the Internet and a network in order to protect the security of the network. Hence, a proxy server can be a firewall when it is configured to filter the messages that pass through it.

Organizations that access the Internet through an ISP often use proxy servers. In such instances, the ISP needs only to assign a static or dynamic IP address to the proxy server. Firms with private IP networks (internets) are other common users of proxy servers because the reserved IP addresses that they use are not allowed on the Internet.

Network Address Translation (NAT)
An important proxy server capability. NAT enables all the hosts/nodes in a network to access the Internet through a single public IP address (such as that for a proxy server or router).

Network Address Translation (NAT) is an important proxy server capability. NAT enables all the hosts/nodes in the network to access the Internet through a single public IP address (such as that for a proxy server or router). When a host/node on the network tries to access the Internet, it must go through a server, router, or other device that substitutes its own IP address for that of the computer requesting Internet access. When NAT is used, it appears that all Internet traffic from the network originates from the NAT server instead of from the individual hosts/nodes on the network. Responses to Internet requests from a client are first returned to the NAT server; the NAT server then relays the responses back to the original client. Only the packets that are responses to a specific request are accepted, and the server is often configured to scan the data in the packets for viruses or other dangerous content.

Proxy and NAT servers also assist network managers in monitoring network users' Internet activities. They are capable of keeping logs of all outgoing and incoming traffic, can restrict user access to certain sites, or can restrict user access to the Internet to certain times of the day. Proxy servers can also be used to cache frequently accessed sites in order to expedite repeated user requests for the same information.

Virtual Private Networks

An outgrowth of firewalls, proxy servers, and business use of the Internet is **virtual private networks (VPNs)**. A VPN is a private network operated over a public network such as the Internet. A VPN does not need to be implemented over the Internet; VPNs can also be implemented in other public networks such as the Concert Virtual Network Service, Worldsource VNS, and Fonselect VPN. However, in this text, we will consider the Internet-based VPNs.

Tunneling protocols are typically used to provide virtual private networking capabilities over the Internet. These provide a private, secure communication channel over the Internet backbone. Examples include point-to-point tunneling protocol (PPTP), layer two forwarding (L2F), and layer two tunneling protocol (L2TP). The set of standards used to ensure the security of virtual private networks in TCP/IP networks is called *IPSEC*.

IPSEC

The **Internet Protocol Security Architecture** (**IPSEC**) is a result of the work of the Security Working Group of the IETF, which realized that IP needed stronger security to support evolving Internet applications and uses. IPSEC was proposed in 1995 as an option that could be implemented with IPv4 (Internet Protocol version 4) and as an extension header in IPv6.

IPSEC supports authentication, integrity, and confidentiality in IP packets. Authentication and integrity can be provided by appending an optional *authentication header (AH)* to the original IP packet. Data confidentiality can be provided within IP packets because of IPSEC's compliance with IP *encapsulating security payload (ESP)*. ESP encrypts the data within the IP packet as well as its original IP header and attaches another unencrypted IP header to the encrypted packet so that it can be used to set up virtual private networks within the Internet between IPSEC–compliant servers. In essence, IPSEC adds a new "security" layer to the TCP/IP protocol stack. This layer is created by encapsulating an original IP packet in a new IP packet. The encapsulation process usually takes place in IPSEC–compliant border routers or IPSEC servers. The encapsulated packet is then passed from one network's Internet border router across the TCP/IP (or Internet) backbone to the border router of the destination network by using the "IP within IP" mechanism (which is known as *IP encapsulation*). The border router (or an IPSEC server) at the destination de-encapsulates the packet and sends the original packet to the destination host. In this way, secure data is transferred from one site to another across the TCP/IP backbone. The general process is illustrated in Figure 4-19.

Tunneling protocols are typically associated with VPNs. **Tunneling** occurs when a message is encapsulated within another message at the same layer of the TCP/IP protocol stack. With most VPNs, tunneling occurs at the IP layer. Because IPSEC adds encryption and authentication to IP encapsulation, the exchange of packets between IPSEC–compliant servers or routers offers much greater security than is possible with usual (non–IPSEC) packets across TCP/IP networks.

virtual private network (VPN) Using shared communication systems such as the public Internet to establish private links for a corporate network. VPN software typically uses tunneling protocols, strong encryption, and authentication algorithms to ensure the privacy of the company's data.

tunneling protocols Protocols that are capable of encapsulating data structured in other data communication protocol formats. Tunneling protocols are widely used to provide virtual private networking capabilities over the Internet.

Internet Protocol Security Architecture (IPSEC) A security protocol from the IETF that provides authentication and encryption over the Internet. IPSEC is implemented at the network layer in order to secure data transmissions across the network.

tunneling Transmitting data structured in one protocol format within the format of another protocol. An example of tunneling is when a message is encapsulated within another message at the same layer of the TCP/IP protocol stack.

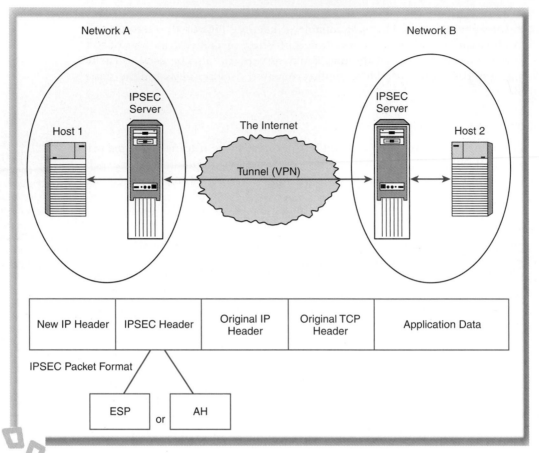

Figure 4-19   An Example of IPSEC Implementation and Encapsulation

Because IPSEC enables secure communications across public TCP/IP networks such as the Internet, it is being used to (1) build secure VPNs among branch offices within a single company; (2) implement secure remote access to corporate networks over the Internet for telecommuters and mobile workers; (3) establish secure extranet connections with business partners; (4) enhance the security of B2B e-commerce over the Internet; and (5) provide security for a variety of other distributed applications including e-mail, file transfer, and remote logon. This is possible because IPSEC enables all IP layer traffic to be encrypted and authenticated.

In the past, businesses typically implemented wide area networks by leasing transmission facilities from a common carrier. The transmission facilities were owned by the common carrier but dedicated to the leaseholder. The transmission media leasing expense was large for companies with big WANs. If a company connects the networks at its various operating locations via the Internet, its data transmission costs can be dramatically reduced. The problems inherent in this approach are security and availability. Availability is an important issue, especially when sufficient bandwidth must be reliable and available to support an organization's e-commerce and e-business applications.

Because the Internet is a shared resource, the bandwidth available to a single user or company can vary. When Internet traffic is high, the total bandwidth available to a single user or business decreases. This can cause slower Web page download speeds and frustrate potential online buyers. Companies that need guaranteed bandwidth for business-to-business applications may choose to use other public networks, such as those mentioned previously, for intracompany or intercompany connections. Because of the obvious cost benefit, the trend, however, is toward using the Internet as the foundation for e-commerce and e-business applications.

SUMMARY

All hosts on the Internet must have a unique address. Currently, with IPv4, host addresses are 32-bit entities; however, the next version of the IP protocol, IPv6, will use 128-bit addresses. An Internet address has several representations: the 32-bit number, a dotted quad, a fully qualified domain name, and a Uniform Resource Locator (URL). The first portion of the 32-bit address represents a network number, and the remaining bits represent host numbers within that subnet. Addresses fall into several classes: A, B, C, D, and E. However, only class A, B, and C networks are in common use. The difference between the classes is the number of bits used to denote the network and host portions of the addresses.

A network host or node may have its Internet address assigned statically or dynamically. Users who gain access to the Internet through an Internet service provider (ISP) are typically allocated a dynamic IP address. Dynamic Host Configuration Protocol (DHCP) is the most widely used dynamic addressing scheme. ISPs with DHCP servers have a range of IP addresses that can be used by their subscribers. When a user connects to the ISP's DHCP server, an available (currently unused) address will be assigned.

For Internet hosts on LANs, the address resolution protocol (ARP) is used to convert an IP address into a media access layer (MAC) address. This translation is necessary because message delivery within a LAN occurs at the data link layer of the OSI reference model; an IP address is maintained at the network layer.

Routing between hosts and networks on the Internet is done by the IP protocol, which operates at the network layer of the OSI reference model. Routers are devices responsible for moving messages between networks. Each router maintains a routing table that contains information about paths to other networks. Through the information contained in the routing table, a router can move a message through the Internet (or internet) toward its destination network.

Network managers use a number of tools to monitor and manage network traffic. Important Internet tools for network managers include Finger, Ping, Tracert, and WHOIS.

The growing importance of the Web for electronic business has made it important for network managers to have a working knowledge of Web page design tools, such as hypertext markup language (HTML), Dynamic HTML (DHTML), and Extensible Markup Language (XML). In order to enhance the fault tolerance of commercial Web sites, many organizations have implemented server farms that use load balancing or server clusters to expedite the processing of user requests.

The security of TCP/IP networks can be enhanced through the use of firewalls and proxy servers. Proxy servers stand between a network and the Internet. When a proxy server is used, all Internet traffic to and from the network flows through the proxy server; outsiders view the network as a single host (the proxy server) because the IP addresses of the other hosts/nodes in the network are hidden behind the proxy server.

Traffic between networks over TCP/IP backbone networks such as the Internet can be made more secure through the use of virtual private networks (VPNs) and IPSEC technologies. VPNs use tunneling protocols in order to establish secure communication across TCP/IP backbones. IPSEC enables encrypted TCP/IP packets to be transmitted across the Internet backbone over virtual private networks between IPSEC–compliant servers, which are similar to proxy servers.

KEY TERMS

- address resolution protocol (ARP)
- class A address
- class B address
- class C address
- class D address
- class E address
- domain name
- Domain Name System (DNS)
- domain name system (DNS) server
- dotted-quad notation
- Dynamic Host Configuration Protocol (DHCP)
- dynamic IP address
- dynamic IP addressing
- Extensible Markup Language (XML)
- Finger
- Internet Protocol Security Architecture (IPSEC)
- Internet Protocol version 6 (IPv6)
- load balancing

- Network Address Translation (NAT)
- ping
- proxy server
- Request for Comment 760 (RFC 760)
- reverse address resolution protocol (RARP)
- router
- routing table
- server cluster
- server farm
- socket
- static IP address
- subnet
- subnet mask
- Tracert
- tunneling
- tunneling protocols
- Uniform Resource Locator (URL)
- virtual private network (VPN)
- WHOIS database

REVIEW QUESTIONS

1. Describe the distinctions among class A, B, C, D, and E IPv4 addresses.
2. Define and give an example of a
   a. dotted-quad notation
   b. URL
   c. domain name
3. What are reserved IP addresses? Why do these exist?
4. What is the hierarchy of an Internet domain address?
5. List five root-level domain names that do not represent countries. List what each represents.
6. List five of the newly approved domain names, and briefly describe what each represents.
7. What does ICANN do?
8. What is a subnet? How are subnets identified in extended network addresses?
9. What is a subnet mask? What role do subnet masks play in data communication?

10. Compare static and dynamic IP addresses.
11. Describe the operation of the Dynamic Host Configuration Protocol (DHCP).
12. Describe the operation of address resolution protocol (ARP). When is ARP used, and when is it necessary?
13. What is the Domain Name System (DNS)? What role does the DNS play in Internet operations?
14. What kinds of information are contained in an IP routing table?
15. What are well-known ports? Provide examples of well-known ports. What is a socket?
16. Briefly describe the capabilities of
    a. Finger
    b. Ping
    c. Tracert
    d. WHOIS
17. Describe the distinctions among the following Web page design tools:
    a. HTML
    b. DHTML
    c. XML
    d. VML, PGML, and VRML
18. Describe the distinctions among the following:
    a. server farm
    b. load balancing
    c. server clusters
19. Describe how server farms, load balancing, and server clusters enhance a Web site's reliability, scalability, and fault tolerance.
20. What is a proxy server? How can proxy servers be used to enhance network security?
21. What are the capabilities of Network Address Translation (NAT) servers?
22. What is a virtual private network (VPN)? What is the role of tunneling protocols in VPNs?
23. How does IPSEC help to ensure the integrity of packets transmitted across the Internet backbone?

PROBLEMS AND EXERCISES

1. A company has a class B address space and wants to define 8 subnets using this address space. The dotted quad for the address is 131.10.0.0. What is the subnet mask for this? List the dotted-quad representation for each subnet.
2. A network node has an IP address of 203.149.55.79. The network's subnet mask is 255.255.255.192. What IPv4 network class is the node's network? What is the node's subnet value? What is the node's host address within the subnet?
3. Use the Internet to find out more about IPv6 and why it is being adopted. Summarize your findings in a paper or PowerPoint presentation.
4. If you have Finger and Ping available, use each to see what information they provide.
5. What is the dotted-quad representation of your Internet provider's URL?
6. Use the Internet to find information on the latest versions of HTML, DHTML, and XML. What new features/capabilities are being built into Web browsers to take advantage of the new developments in the evolution of these markup languages?
7. Use the Internet to identify major cluster hardware/software vendors, their major products, and the major features/capabilities of their products.

8. Use the Internet to learn more about the tunneling protocols used to implement virtual private networks. Summarize your findings in a paper or PowerPoint presentation.

9. Use the Internet to learn more about proxy servers and NAT. Summarize your findings in a paper or PowerPoint presentation.

10. Use the Internet to find information that you can use to describe recent developments in IPSEC.

Chapter Cases
Internet2 and NGI

Did you know that there are two U.S. networks where users are receiving connections over 800 times faster than a regular 33.6-kbps dial-up connection and over 200 times faster than a DSL connection? One of these networks, called Internet2, consists of high-speed data links among universities and research laboratories, similar to the ARPAnet network from which today's Internet emerged. Internet2 has an infrastructure that supports IPv6, quality of service, and multicasting. The other network, called Next Generation Internet (NGI), is a federally funded project to develop Internet2 applications to support federal agencies.

In October 1996, a group of academics and scientists met to establish a new Internet where researchers could work on advanced network technologies. This group formed the University Corporation for Advanced Internet Development (UCAID) to oversee what came to be called the Internet2 project. Internet2 brings together institutions and resources from academia, industry, and government to develop new technologies and capabilities that can then be deployed in the global Internet. UCAID is a not-for-profit consortium led by over 190 U.S. universities working in partnership with the government and leading companies such as IBM, Cisco, and Qwest.

Will Internet2 replace the Internet in the future? (*Hint:* No.) Internet2 is not a separate physical network and will not replace the Internet. Internet2 uses the connectivity existing in the Internet from telecommunication network operators, but it also leverages advanced backbone networks, such as the Abilene network and the very-high performance Backbone Network Service (vBNS), to support the development and deployment of new high-speed, high-bandwidth applications. Moreover, Internet2 will only be used for research purposes; the Internet will be more oriented to commercial and general use purposes.

vBNS is a network provided under a cooperative agreement between the National Science Foundation (NSF) and MCI to NSF–approved research institutes and universities. Abilene provides a complementary option to the vBNS and uses high-speed SONET facilities and IP-over-SONET routers. Abilene is operating initially over OC-48 (2.4 giga-

bits per second) backbone links; however, Abilene is currently being upgraded to leverage new links running at OC-192 (9.6 gigabits per second) and beyond.

But, in spite of the different purposes behind the Internet2 and NGI projects, their researchers are already working together in many areas. For example, Internet2 universities are participating in NSF NGI programs, and over 150 universities have already received grants to support developing connections to their advanced backbone networks. Working together will help ensure an interoperable and highly developed network infrastructure for research and the development of technologies and applications that are likely to lead to continuous improvement of the global Internet.

Internet2 and NGI will make it possible to develop applications that require higher performance not available on the current Internet, such as digital libraries, teleconferencing, telemedicine, and teleimmersion. Some of the recently developed teleconferencing applications are being used in Oklahoma and Boston. At the University of Oklahoma, music students connected through an advanced network are accessing teleconferenced classes at transmission rates of 15 mbps. At MIT, students are engaged in joint classes with students at the University of Singapore. Classrooms are equipped with special devices that let the MIT professor lecture half of the class and the professor at Singapore lecture the other half.

Telemedicine applications are being tested at The Ohio State University. These experiments are showing the huge promise in combining Internet2 capabilities, two-way real-time video, robotic devices, and remote instrumentation. Medical students, who are hundreds of miles away from their traditional classroom, can see a detailed video of laparoscopic surgery or other medical procedures at the surgical site. Telemedicine will also make it possible to get immediately needed care to people wherever they are located and will help aging people or people with physical limitations to keep their independence.

Teleimmersion will allow people anyplace in the world to feel as if they are sharing the same physical space through the development of "telecubicles" and "haptics." Haptics instruments will allow people to feel objects that are physically thousands of miles away from them. McDonald's has already started running experiments over Internet2. The fast-food chain is planning to set telecubicles in its restaurants so customers can meet with friends or family, who can be in other places of the world, to enjoy eating together.

CASE QUESTIONS

1. Use the Internet to find out more about teleimmersion applications and their potential applications. Summarize your findings in a table or paper.
2. Use the Internet to identify other types of applications being developed by Internet2 and NGI researchers. Summarize your findings in a paper or PowerPoint presentation.
3. Networks that rival Internet2 and NGI are being developed in other countries. Use the Internet to find out more about these networks, why they are being developed, and how they are likely to be used in the future.
4. Use the Internet to get information about GEANT. Compare and contrast GEANT and Internet2.
5. What future benefits are businesses likely to experience as the result of the Internet2 and NGI projects?

SOURCES

Lipschultz, David. "Internet2 Puts Broadband to the Test." *InternetWeek* (July 18, 2001). Retrieved August 3, 2002 from www.internetweek.com/indepth01/indepth071801.htm.

Mears, Jennier. "Internet2 Gaining (Sponsored) Users." *Network World* (July 22, 2002, p. 29).

Whiting, Rick. "Videoconferencing's Virtual Room." *InternetWeek* (April 1, 2002). Retrieved August 3, 2002 from www.informationweek.com/story/IWK20020329S0008.

Note: For more information on Internet addressing and operation, see an additional case on the Web site, www.prenhall.com/stamper, "IP Network Services."

Voice-Oriented Networks

**Part II
Understanding
Internet Access
Technologies: Voice
Networks, Modems,
and LANs**

After studying this chapter, you should be able to:

- Describe the history of the telephone industry in the United States.
- Describe the characteristics of telephone end offices.
- Discuss the implications of the Telecommunications Reform Act of 1996.
- Identify and briefly describe the characteristics of competitive local exchange carriers.
- Describe the differences between analog and digital voice signals.
- Identify and briefly describe local loop Internet access options.
- Compare the transmission services provided by common carriers.
- Identify and briefly describe the major types of wireless voice communication systems.
- Describe the common carrier services available for mobile computing.
- Describe the characteristics of private branch exchanges and Centrex systems.
- Identify and briefly describe important business applications of voice networks.

This chapter discusses one of the major categories of networks serving as an underlying foundation of the Internet, voice-oriented telecommunications networks. Most businesses and consumers gain access to the Internet via ISPs, and telephone lines remain the most common link between the business or consumer and the ISP. Prior to the Internet, businesses typically used telephone carrier circuits to build wide area networks (WANs) to interconnect the networks at their geographically dispersed operating locations. Businesses and other organizations continue to rely on telecommunications from telephone carriers to satisfy their voice and data communication needs and to implement applications that enable them to be more competitive. Hence, there are many reasons why it is important for data communication students to have a basic understanding of voice-oriented networks.

As a result of the emergence of new technologies and telephone company services, setting up and managing today's communication networks are more complex than ever. More vendors are providing communication services over a wider variety of speeds. Different forms of communication also are increasingly being integrated onto one transmission medium. As a result, the sphere of responsibility for the modern data communication manager is expanding. In addition to selecting communication facilities for data transmission, the communication manager may also be responsible for selecting hardware and software that can meet the corporate needs for data, voice, video, facsimile, and other forms of electronic communication.

TELEPHONE NETWORKS AND THE INTERNET

One of the primary goals of the designers of ARPAnet was to be able to provide reliable and secure file transfers over telephone circuits. As noted in Chapter 2, packet-switching technologies, which had been pioneered by the Rand Corporation, were chosen as one of the foundations of ARPAnet because of their ability to continue to function even if major parts of the network were disrupted or destroyed by warfare or natural disaster. Both businesses and value-added networks (VANs) have traditionally created packet-switching networks by utilizing telephone lines leased from telephone carriers. Frame relay service providers have also leased telephone circuits to create their networks.

Although Internet designers envisioned a data communication network built largely on telephone circuits, the evolution of the Internet has inspired Internet telephony and voice-over-IP (VoIP) services and applications. Users of applications such as Net2Phone and dialpad.com are able to use their computers to initiate no-cost long-distance telephone calls over the Internet. These applications divide digitized voice messages into IP packets and route them over the Internet. End-office Internet connections convert the packets into the form needed to transmit them over local telephone circuits and deliver them to the appropriate telephone. This process is illustrated in Figure 5-1.

Wireless telephone networks, such as cellular phone networks, are also evolving. In addition to supporting the voice communication needs of mobile workers, these

Figure 5-1   Using Internet Telephony Software to Make Calls over the Internet

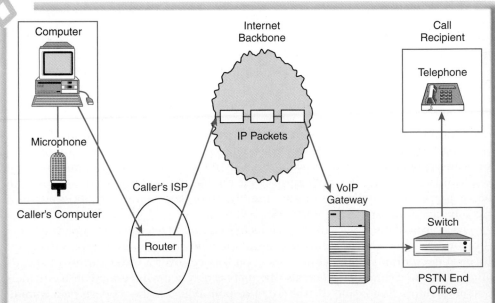

now also provide individuals with another means of gaining access to the Internet. Industry experts predict that *mobile commerce (m-commerce)*—the ability to make Internet-based purchases using a digital wireless telephone or personal digital assistant (PDA)—will grow dramatically between now and 2005. Some expect that most e-commerce transactions will involve wireless communication devices by 2010.

The evolution of the Internet and wireless telephone networks is having a major impact on the telephone industry. Telephone industry experts expect that the majority of long-distance telephone calls will eventually be routed, at least in part, over the Internet. Many telephone carriers are already leveraging the Internet to lower their long-distance voice-communication costs and are able to pass along their cost savings to consumers in the form of lower per-minute connection rates.

THE U.S. TELEPHONE INDUSTRY

Each country has one or more entities responsible for providing telephone and telecommunication systems. Some countries have federal or quasi-federal agencies responsible for this. For example, several countries have a postal, telephone, and telegraph (PTT) agency that operates under the auspices of the government and is a protected, regulated monopoly responsible for providing such services. In some instances, these regulated agencies have been deregulated and operate as nongovernment companies with competitors. Because of wide variation in how they are set up and their services, it is unrealistic to discuss the telecommunication industries of all countries; therefore, we will concentrate on the telecommunication industry in the United States. First, we look at the organization of the common carrier communication network. We consider how the network was organized in the United States both before and after the **AT&T divestiture** and the consequences of deregulation.

Predivestiture Organization

Before divestiture, AT&T dominated the telephone service industry. Figure 5-2 illustrates the organization of the predivestiture AT&T network. Note that there is a hierarchy of switching stations through which a call can be forwarded. A telephone subscriber is connected to a local switching office called a *class 5 office*. Class 5 offices are also called **end offices** because they are at the extremities of the telephone-switching network. An end office is often referred to as a *central office (CO)*. The circuit between a business or home and the end office is called the **local loop**. If the subscriber calls another subscriber who is also attached to the same local office, the call is switched through that single end office. This is illustrated in Figure 5-2 by subscriber A's connection to subscriber B. It is also possible for subscriber C to call subscriber D, whose telephone is connected to another class 5 office in the same general area. C's call goes directly from C's end office to D's end office and then to D's local line. Both calls are local calls and will incur no long-distance fee.

If the call is not local, like subscriber E's connection to subscriber F, the call is routed from the class 5 station to a class 4 station, called a **toll center**. This initiates the billing process for the call. From the class 4 station, the call goes to a class 3 station, called a **primary center**. At this point, if the call is destined for a regional high-use area, the class 3 station might route the call directly to the recipient's class 5 local switch. Alternatively, the call is routed up through the class 2 station, termed a **sectional center**, to a class 1 station, called a **regional center**. The class 1 station then passes the call to another class 1 station. A class 1 station might then send the call to another class 1 center. Class 1 centers form a backbone transmission network. When the call reaches the class 1 station closest to the call's recipient, the connection is switched down through the hierarchy until it reaches the recipient's class 5 end office. At the end office, the call is switched to the recipient's local line.

AT&T divestiture In 1984, AT&T was broken up into independent RBOCs and a separate AT&T company. The divestiture ended the regulated monopoly of AT&T as well as freeing AT&T and the RBOCs to enter into business areas previously denied to them.

end office A telephone company office to which a subscriber is directly connected. Also called a class 5 office.

local loop The circuits between a customer and the telephone company's end office. The local loop is sometimes called the *last mile*.

toll center In a telephone network, a toll center is a class 4 switching office. Also called a class 4 station or tandem office. Unlike a class 5 office (end office), a tandem office does not connect directly to the customer. Instead, it provides connections between end offices or between networks, and always deals with trunk lines rather than customer lines.

primary center A telephone company class 3 station. A primary center is one station higher than a toll center.

sectional center In the telephone network, a class 2 station.

regional center A class 1 telephone station.

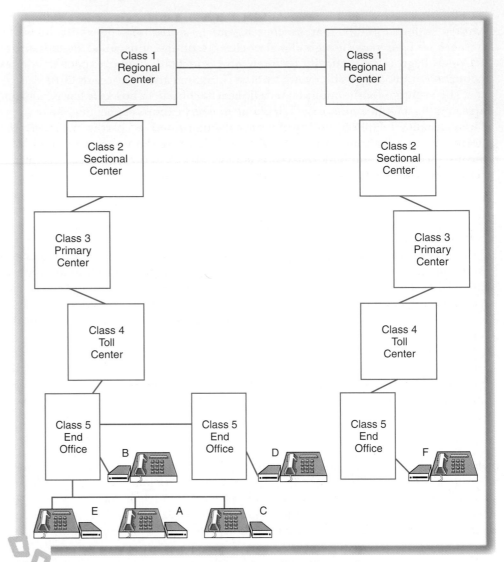

Figure 5-2   Predivestiture Telephone Switching Network

Postdivestiture Network

The divestiture in 1984 broke up AT&T into independent **regional Bell operating companies (RBOCs)** and a separate AT&T company. The divestiture not only ended the regulated monopoly AT&T had enjoyed but also freed AT&T and the RBOCs to enter into business areas formerly denied them, such as the computer industry. RBOCs are responsible for handling subscriber services within their area; one of the functions of AT&T is to provide long-distance services. The divestiture resulted in a revamping of how long-distance calls are handled.

Local calls are handled in much the same way as in the predivestiture era. However, the regions served by RBOCs were divided into **local access and transport**

regional Bell operating company (RBOC) The AT&T divestiture resulted in the formation of RBOCs and a separate AT&T company. An RBOC is responsible for subscriber telephone services within its region of the United States.

areas **(LATAs)**. A LATA corresponds to a common calling area. In areas of high population density, such as the San Francisco Bay area, several area codes may fall within the same LATA. All calls originating and terminating within a LATA are handled exclusively by the RBOC. Any call that crosses a LATA boundary becomes the responsibility of a long-distance carrier, such as AT&T, MCI, or Sprint.

Each telephone subscriber is free to choose a long-distance carrier, and long-distance carriers are required to have equal access to subscribers. To provide equal access, each LATA has a designated interchange **point of presence (POP)**. An inter–LATA call is routed to the POP, where it is accepted by the designated long-distance carrier. The long-distance carrier routes the call to the POP in the recipient's LATA, and the call is switched to the recipient's end office and telephone. This is illustrated in Figure 5-3.

THE TELECOMMUNICATIONS REFORM ACT OF 1996

The basic telecommunications act under which the United States operated before 1996 was passed in 1934, before computers, television, and cellular telephones. A change was long overdue. The AT&T divestiture had a significant impact on telephone and data communication services, but it did not address the broad scope of

local access and transport area (LATA) A geographic region set up to differentiate local and long distance telephone calls. Telephone calls between parties within a LATA (intraLATA) are handled by the local telephone companies. IntraLATA telephone services are under the jurisdiction of state public utility commissions. Calls between LATAs (long distance calls) are handled by interexchange carriers (IXCs). IXC services are governed by the FCC.

point of presence (POP) In the U.S. public telephone network, a point at which a transfer is made from a local telephone company to the long-distance carrier. A POP is the point at which a line from an interexchange carrier (IXC) connects to the line of the local telephone company.

Figure 5-3   Postdivestiture Long-Distance Switching

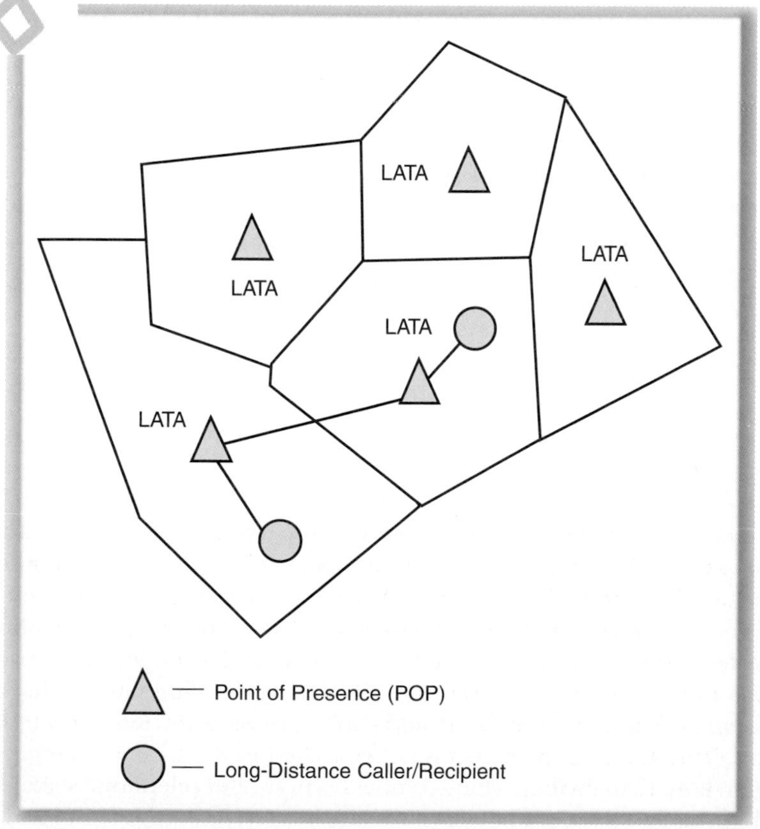

telecommunication. After the divestiture, the RBOCs provided local telephone service, and AT&T, MCI, Sprint, and other companies provided long-distance services. Other companies were involved in cable television and other broadcast services. The **Telecommunications Reform Act of 1996** is a broad reform of the spectrum of telecommunication that reduces government regulation and widens competition. We will focus only on the areas that significantly affect data communication.

Before the Telecommunications Reform Act of 1996, long-distance carriers could not provide local service, and cable TV companies could not provide services typically assigned to the telephone carriers, such as data transmission. The Telecommunications Reform Act of 1996 changed the rules for service providers and extended competition for local and long-distance services. Long-distance carriers can compete on the local level, and the RBOCs can enter the long-distance market. The Telecommunications Reform Act of 1996 does not require companies to build the cable infrastructure to provide local or long-distance services. Two capabilities, interconnect and wholesaling, are stipulated in the act to give companies access to the existing telephone networks.

Wholesaling means that the owners of a telephone network must allow any organization to acquire and resell their existing services. Thus, if you wanted to go into the telephone business, you could lease lines from an existing carrier and resell services over those lines at a profit under these provisions. Thus, a long-distance carrier can provide the entire communication package, local and long-distance, to its customers; similarly, local carriers can do the same by acquiring long-distance lines.

The interconnect provision prohibits a common carrier from charging unreasonable rates for services terminating in their cable network. Without this provision, a local carrier could charge high termination rates and essentially prohibit competition.

The Telecommunications Reform Act of 1996 encourages competition in all aspects and markets of telecommunications services and carriers. The legislation opened the door for companies to provide local access service in competition with regional Bell operating companies (RBOCs); such companies are known as **competitive access providers (CAPs)** or **competitive local exchange carriers (CLECs)**. This enabled cable television companies to compete with local telephone companies for telephone service. It also enabled telephone companies to compete with cable television companies in providing television service to local subscribers.

COMPETITIVE LOCAL EXCHANGE CARRIERS (CLECS)

Companies that seek to offer local access service in competition with RBOCs or local telephone companies are known as competitive local exchange carriers (CLECs). As a result of the Telecommunications Reform Act of 1996, thousands of CLECs are expected to emerge in the next few years. Among the new competitors are cable, electric, and wireless firms that partner with other companies that have greater telecommunications expertise. For example, in 1997 Potomac Electric Power partnered with RCN in Washington, DC, to create a CLEC providing local and long-distance telephone service, cable television service, and Internet access. Rural electrical cooperatives have also been able to expand their services and revenue streams by entering partnerships that allow them to compete with local telephone and cable television carriers for telecommunication services. This follows a trend that is not restricted to the United States. In Germany, for example, more than 60 local utility companies now offer telephone services.

Cable firms in the United States have also started to compete in local telephone markets. Cox Cable, for example, offers telephone service in Nebraska and California.

Telecommunications Reform Act of 1996 U.S. legislation that increased competition among intrastate and interstate communication companies and deregulated the cable television industry.

competitive access provider (CAP) An organization that competes with the established telecommunications provider in an area.

competitive local exchange carrier (CLEC) An organization offering local telephone service that is not a traditional telephone company.

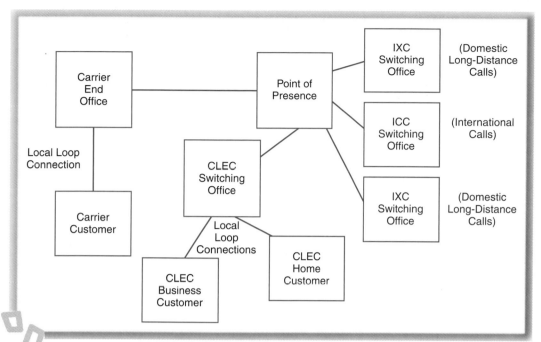

Figure 5-4   Relationship of CLECs to Local Carriers, Interexchange Carriers (IXCs), and International Common Carrier (ICC) Switching Offices

MediaOne is another cable firm that offers telephone service in California and Florida. Currently, most cable companies are able to offer telephone service by connecting to the traditional telephone system; however, in the future, they may connect directly to the Internet itself. Figure 5-4 illustrates that most CLECs are able to gain access to long-distance services and traditional local telephone networks at the local point of presence.

VOICE TRANSMISSION: BASIC CONCEPTS

Audio signals, including the human voice, are analog signals. This means that they can be represented as a continuous analog wave that vary in frequency and amplitude. Figure 5-5 illustrates an analog wave.

As noted in Chapter 1, the telephone networks envisioned by Alexander Graham Bell were designed to transmit voice signals from source to destination. To do so, traditional telephone handsets included technologies to convert sound waves into analog electrical signals that were transmitted over telephone circuits and subsequently converted back to sound waves at the receiving telephone handset.

Transmitting Voice Signals over Analog Telephone Circuits

A traditional telephone handset contains both a transmitter and a receiver. The transmitter, found in the handset's mouthpiece (the part you speak into), contains a moveable diaphragm that reacts to changes in the frequency and amplitude of the caller's voice. Carbon granules on the diaphragm strike electrical contacts in the mouthpiece at varying locations in response to changes in the caller's voice signals. As a result, the

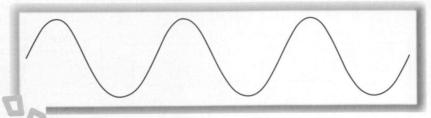

Figure 5-5   An Analog Wave

transmitter sends out an analog electrical signal that, like the caller's voice, varies in wavelength and amplitude. This analog electrical wave is transmitted over telephone circuits to the receiving telephone handset, where a receiver in the earpiece (the part of the handset you listen to) converts the electrical signal back into sound waves using a process that is essentially the reverse of that used by the mouthpiece to convert sound waves to electrical waves. Like the mouthpiece, the earpiece contains a movable diaphragm that acts like the speakers attached to your computer or home entertainment system. The main components of a traditional analog telephone are illustrated in Figure 5-6.

Figure 5-6   Major Components of a Traditional Telephone Handset

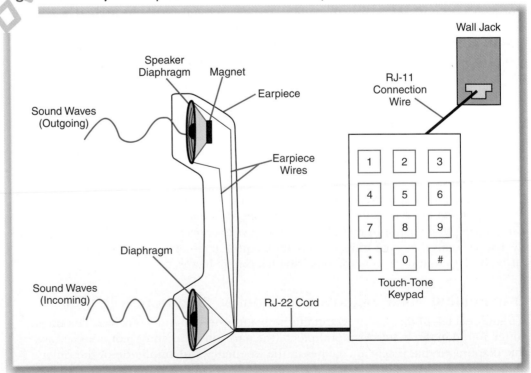

Although some signal quality is lost when the sound wave is transformed into an electrical signal and subsequently converted back to a sound wave, the sound that is reproduced in the receiver's handset sufficiently resembles the original signal to enable the receiver to clearly recognize what the person on the other end of the line is saying. In fact, telephone network designers made decisions early on about what constituted reasonable representations of human voice signals. They made decisions about the bandwidth of voice-grade circuits that are still implemented today.

The usable bandwidth allocated to each voice-grade telephone circuit is 3,000 Hz (see Figure 5-7). This bandwidth was selected because it is sufficient to provide a reasonable reproduction of human voice sound waves. Unlike a digital circuit, the bandwidth of an analog circuit is measured by the range of frequencies it can carry.

Although the total bandwidth per voice-grade circuit is 4,000 Hz, the two *guardbands* consume 1,000 Hz of the total, leaving only 3,000 Hz for the actual transmission of the electrical analog signal that represents the caller's voice signals. The guardbands are included to separate adjacent voice-grade circuits in "stacked" channels and to prevent the signals carried by stacked circuits from interfering with one another.

The important thing to remember is that the usable bandwidth on a local loop circuit between a business or residence and the telephone company's end office has a usable bandwidth of 3,000 Hz. The bandwidth is the same whether you are carrying on a telephone conversation or using the circuit to establish a modem connection with your ISP.

Touch-Tone Telephones

Touch-tone telephones enable telephone users to use their telephone equipment as a data communication terminal. A variety of touch-tone telephone business applications have been developed. For example, some banks allow customers to pay bills and transfer money between accounts using touch-tone telephones. Many credit card issuers have implemented interactive voice response systems that enable cardholders to check current balances or obtain a list of their most recent transactions. Many colleges and universities allow students to register for classes using touch-tone telephones.

Figure 5-7   Analog Dial-Up Telephone Circuit

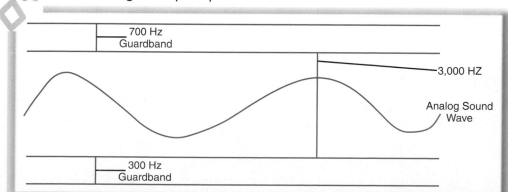

Touch-tone telephones have 12 keys, so 12 different codes can be transmitted. Each key on the telephone keypad transmits a high frequency and a low frequency. The combination of the two frequencies uniquely defines which key has been pressed. Figure 5-8 shows the relationship between the telephone keypad and the frequencies each transmits. For example, if a user presses the 9 key, the frequencies 852 Hz and 1,447 Hz are transmitted. Because only 12 key codes are available, the telephone is limited in its use as a data communication input device. In spite of this limitation, the number of business data communication applications of touch-tone telephones is increasing.

Digitizing Voice Signals

As the telephone network evolves, analog circuits and switching technologies are giving way to digital circuits. Today, digital telephone circuits connect most end offices to class 4 toll centers. Similarly, digital circuits typically provide interconnections among class 4, class 3, class 2, and class 1 centers within the public switched telephone network (PSTN). This means that long-distance telephone conversations that originate and end with voice-grade analog circuits are digitized for transmission between end offices over long-distance circuits. The process used by telephone companies to convert signals from analog to digital form (and vice versa) is transparent to telephone users. Eventually, the vast majority of local loop connections in the United States and other developed nations will also be digital.

Digital local loop connections have been implemented in most urban areas in the United States. In these areas, analog voice signals are converted into discrete electric pulses (see Figure 5-9). The telephone handsets used in digital networks contain a **codec,** which is short for coder/decoder. Its job is to sample analog voice signals and to transform them into a stream of binary digits suitable for transmission over a digital circuit. The sampling and transformation process performed by the codec in a digital telephone handset is call *voice digitization*.

The voice digitization process is relatively straightforward. As a caller speaks into the mouthpiece of the digital telephone handset, the analog voice signal is sampled by

codec A codec is hardware or software that converts analog sound, speech, or video to digital code and vice versa. In a digital telephone network, its job is to sample analog voice signals and to transform them into a stream of binary digits suitable for transmission over a digital circuit.

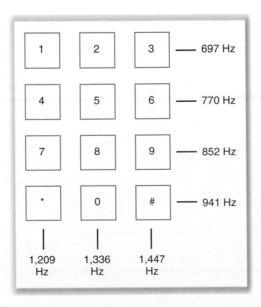

Figure 5-8 Touch-Tone Telephone Code

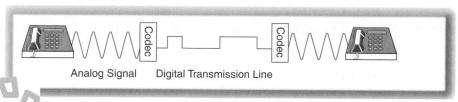

Analog Signal   Digital Transmission Line

Figure 5-9   Codec Converting Analog and Digital Signals

the codec, typically at the rate of 8,000 samples per second. The sampling process is illustrated in Figure 5-10. This sampling rate produces a digitized version of the voice signal that reasonably resembles the caller's spoken words when it is converted back to an analog signal by the codec in the receiver's telephone handset.

An 8-bit binary number (or 1 byte) is used to represent each analog signal sample. Because an 8-bit code allows 2^8 (256) possible values, each analog signal sample is assigned a value that ranges from 0 to 255 depending on its location or amplitude when the sample is taken. In Figure 5-10, for example, the amplitude of the voice signal when sampled is equivalent to a value of 135 (on a scale of 0 to 256). The 8-bit binary number representing amplitude position 135 is 10000111. This binary number would be transmitted over the digital circuit to the codec in the receiver's handset, which, in turn, produces an analog signal with an amplitude level of 135 in the handset's earpiece.

By taking 8,000 samples per second and converting each sample into an 8-bit binary number, a data stream of 64,000 bits per second is produced. Hence, it should

Figure 5-10   Sampling and Digitizing Analog Signals

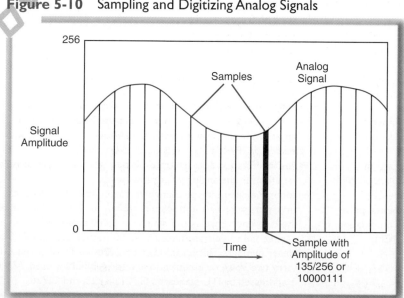

not be surprising to learn that a digital circuit for voice communications typically has a bandwidth of 64,000 bits per second. In the Digital Service Hierarchy, a 64,000 bps circuit is called a DS-0 circuit.

Voice Digitization Codes

pulse code modulation (PCM) A technique for converting analog signals into digital form that is widely used by the telephone companies. PCM samples the analog waves 8,000 times per second and converts each sample into an 8-bit code, resulting in a 64 kbps data stream.

adaptive differential pulse code modulation (ADPCM) An advanced form of pulse code modulation (PCM) used to convert analog sound into digital data and vice versa. Instead of coding an absolute measurement at each analog sound sample, it codes the difference between consecutive samples.

The most widely used voice digitization technique is **pulse code modulation (PCM)**. Illustrated in Figure 5-10, this approach samples the amplitude of the analog signal and transmits an 8-bit binary number representing each amplitude sample to the receiver.

Other voice digitization techniques include pulse amplitude modulation (PAM), pulse duration modulation (PDM), pulse position modulation (PPM), and adaptive differential pulse code modulation (ADPCM). These are briefly summarized in Table 5-1.

Voice Compression

Voice compression involves the transmission of information about sampled voice signals between digital telephone handsets in place of an 8-bit binary number for each sample. By substituting information about the voice signal samples for actual samples, less bandwidth (than the usual 64,000 bps) is needed to transmit a caller's spoken words. As a result, voice compression typically enables multiple conversations to be simultaneously carried on a single DS-0 circuit.

Adaptive differential pulse code modulation (ADPCM), whose major characteristics are summarized in Table 5-1, is an example of a voice compression technique. Rather than transmitting an 8-bit binary number representing the amplitude of each voice signal sample, ADPCM transmits a 4-bit code that represents the approximate amplitude difference (change) between consecutive samples. The receiver uses the 4-bit code to "reconstruct" the original analog voice signal.

Because ADPCM uses a 4-bit code to represent changes in the amplitudes of consecutive samples in place of an 8-bit code for each sample, it enables two conversations to be simultaneously transmitted on a single DS-0 circuit. Other voice compression

Table 5-1   Voice Digitization Techniques

Voice Digitization Technique	Characteristics
Pulse amplitude modulation (PAM)	Varies the amplitude or voltage of transmitted electrical pulses in relation to variations in the speaker's analog voice signals. Used in early private branch exchange (PBX) systems.
Pulse duration modulation (PDM)	Varies the duration of transmitted electrical pulses to reflect variations in the analog voice signal. Also known as *pulse width modulation (PWM)*.
Pulse position modulation (PPM)	Varies the duration *between* transmitted electrical pulses to reflect variations in the analog voice signal samples.
Adaptive differential pulse code modulation (ADPCM)	Encodes the difference or change in amplitude of consecutive amplitude samples and transmits an 8-bit binary number reflecting the difference. Enables the data from 8,000 analog voice samples per second to be transmitted in 4,000 (rather than 8,000) 8-bit binary numbers. This means that a 64,000 bps DS-0 circuit can carry two voice communications when ADPCM is used. ADPCM is addressed by ITU standards G.721, G.723, and G.726.

approaches enable a telephone conversation to consume as little as 4,800 bps of bandwidth. These highly efficient approaches involve the application of microprocessors called **digital signal processors (DSPs)**. These microprocessors are programmed to accept, manipulate, and compress PCM code. DSPs at the receiver are capable of decompressing and reconstructing the PCM code to enable the subsequent conversion to the original voice signal.

Although there are obvious business benefits to voice compression because it enables multiple conversations to be carried simultaneously over the same DS-0 circuit, it also has its drawbacks. The quality of compressed voice transmission is typically inferior to a 64,000 bps PCM digital transmission and transmissions over analog voice-grade circuits. Lost voice quality is particularly apparent in highly compressed voice signals.

Signal quality loss is not unique to voice compression. As we will discuss later in the chapter, it also occurs when video signals are digitized and compressed by a sender and decompressed and converted back to analog form by the receiver. Technically, it can be a problem whenever analog signals are digitized, compressed, and then subsequently decompressed and reconstructed. The one exception to this is the digitization and compression of music, because more than 40,000 samples per second are used to digitize musical recordings.

> **digital signal processor (DSP)**
> A special-purpose microprocessor used for digital signal processing.

LOCAL LOOP OPTIONS

As noted previously, the circuit between a business or home and the local telephone company's end office is called the local loop. When a subscriber calls another subscriber who is also attached to the same local office, the call is switched through that single end office. Several local loop connection options are available from carriers. These include dial-up circuits, ISDN, and digital subscriber lines (DSLs). Although all of these options can be used for voice communications, DSL is most likely to be reserved for high-speed Internet access. Additional high-speed Internet access options include cable modems and DirectPC. These are available from competitive local exchange carriers (CLECs). Although the Telecommunications Act of 1996 enables CLECs to also offer voice-communication services, to date these are available only in a small number of areas.

Internet service providers (ISPs) may support a limited range of Internet access options. Some support only dial-up connections or the local loop options available from the telephone company end office (such as ISDN and DSL). Other ISPs, especially those in large urban areas, support a wide range of connection options found in the local area from both carriers and CLECs, including dial-up, DSL, ISDN, cable modem, T-1 and T-3 connections (discussed later in the chapter), and wireless connection options.

Dial-Up Circuits

In addition to being the most common medium for terrestrial wire-line voice communications, dial-up circuits are the most common means of accessing the Internet. According to Statistical Research Incorporated (SRI), dial-up telephone connections continue to be the most common means of establishing Internet connections within the United States (see cyberatlas.internet.com/markets/broadband/article/0,,10099_481071,00.html#table). This is illustrated in Table 5-2. Although the percentage of Internet users taking advantage of high-speed broadband services is increasing, more than 80 percent of users in the United States access the Internet via dial-up telephone lines. SRI's research also indicates that more than 20 percent of U.S. households with Internet access have installed a second telephone line for Internet access.

According to Nielsen/NetRatings, as of November 1999, only 5.9 percent of Internet users in the United States were accessing the Internet via a high-speed

Table 5-2   Internet Access Connections in the United States

Internet Access Connections		
Connection Type	Spring 2000 (%)	Fall 2000 (%)
Broadband Total	5	11
Cable modem	4	7
DSL	1	3
Other	<1	1
Telephone Connection Total	94	89
Shared line (both voice and data)	75	68
Dedicated line for Internet access	19	21

SOURCE: Adapted from SRI (cyberatlas.internet.com/markets/broadband/article/0,,10099_481071,00.html#table)

connection (ISDN, T-1, satellite, cable modem, or some type of digital subscriber line [DSL]). This is illustrated in Table 5-3, along with the fact that Internet users are often connecting to their ISPs with older, slower modems. By the end of 2001, the percentage of ISP subscribers connecting to ISP via broadband services (such as ISDN, DSL, or cable modems) had risen to 14 percent of the U.S. homes with Internet access; 86 percent of the households still relied on dial-up modems for Internet access (see cyberatlas.internet.com/markets/broadband/article/0,,10099_957511,00.html).

ISDN

Integrated Services Digital Network (ISDN) is available in most local subscriber areas within the United States. Its attraction to business and individual subscribers lies in its ability to simultaneously support voice and data communications over the same connection. It also supports desktop-to-desktop videoconferencing. ISDN is described in more detail later in the chapter.

Digital Subscriber Lines

Digital subscriber lines (DSLs) are an emerging service that provides much faster transmission rates than analog modems and ISDN. DSL refers to a variety of telephone services being used for high-seed Internet access. DSL services include asymmetric DSL (ADSL), rate adaptive DSL (RADSL), high data rate DSL (HDSL), symmetric

Integrated Services Digital Network (ISDN) An international telecommunications standard for providing a digital service from the customer's premises to the dial-up telephone network that enables the integration of voice and data transmission (and other formats such as video and graphic images) over a digital transmission network. ISDN is offered by numerous common carriers.

Table 5-3   Internet Access Speeds in November 1999

Internet Connection Speed	Percent of Internet Users
14.4 kbps	8.3
28.8/33.6 kbps	45.2
56 kbps	40.7
High speed*	5.9

Includes ISDN, cable modems, satellite, and xDSL
SOURCE: Nielsen/Net Ratings

DSL (SDSL), and very high data rate DSL (VDSL or BDSL). The major characteristics of each are summarized in Table 5-4.

ADSL

Asymmetric DSL (ADSL) is the most widely used type of DSL. Unlike ISDN, which requires a special connection in place of a traditional telephone connection, ADSL employs the same copper wires used to carry voice services. ADSL works at higher frequencies than those used for telephone services. This enables ADSL users to have a high-speed Internet connect and still make/receive telephone calls.

ADSL connections are dedicated (rather than dial-up) connections. Once installed and operating, ADSL subscribers are always connected to the Internet. This has the advantage of not having to establish a connection each and every time that one wants to access the Internet, which is necessary when connecting via a dial-up circuit. ADSL's "always on" connection, however, makes it easier for unauthorized users to hack into the subscriber's computer.

The *asymmetric* in ADSL refers to the difference in data rates between upstream and downstream transmissions. In typical Internet access, the number of bits transmitted upstream from a user's computer to the Internet is much smaller than the number of bits the user's computer receives. Consequently, asymmetric transmissions (like those used in the high-speed switched analog modems) provide faster service to a user. The upstream rates for ADSL will vary from 16 kbps to 640 kbps, and the downstream rates will vary from 1.5 mbps to 9 mbps. The speeds depend on the gauge of the wires being used and the distance between the subscriber's location and the telephone company end office. To date, carriers have been conservative in the data rates offered in their ADSL deployments. The maximum distance between the subscriber's equipment and the telephone end office for ADSL is approximately 5.5 km (18,000 feet); currently T-1 speeds (1.5 mbps) can be attained at this distance over traditional 24-gauge telephone wires. Higher speed transmissions are available when the distance is lower. ADSL has been standardized by ANSI and the European Telecommunications Standards Institute.

RADSL

A rate adaptive digital subscriber line (RADSL) adapts the transmission speed depending on the length of the loop and the quality of the lines being used. Otherwise, it is similar in distance and speeds to ADSL. Both ADSL and RADSL are well suited to applications in which more data flows in one direction than in the other, as in Internet access.

digital subscriber line (DSL) DSL refers to a range of switched telephones services being used for high-speed Internet access. Some of the more popular DSL services are *asynchronous DSL, rate adaptive DSL, high-data-rate DSL, single-line DSL,* and *very-high-speed DSL.*

asymmetric digital subscriber line (ADSL) A digital switched technology that provides very high data transmission speeds over telephone wires. The speed of the transmission is asynchronous, meaning that the transmission speeds for uploading and downloading data are different. Downstream rates are faster than upsteam rates in ADSL.

Table 5-4   Major Characteristics of xDSL Services Offered by Carriers

Name	Acronym	Maximum Upstream Data Rate	Maximum Downstream Data Rate	Maximum Distance from End Office to User Site
ADSL	Asymmetric digital subscriber line	16 to 640 kbps	1.544 mbps*	18,000 feet
HDSL	High data rate DSL	1.544 mbps	1.544 mbps	12,000 feet
RADSL	Rate adaptive DSL	1 mbps	7 mbps	18,000 feet
SDSL	Symmetric DSL	1.544 mbps	1.544 mbps*	10,000 feet
VDSL	Very high data rate DSL	51.84 mbps	2.3 mbps*	1,000 feet

Slower rates are available for user sites that are further from the end office.

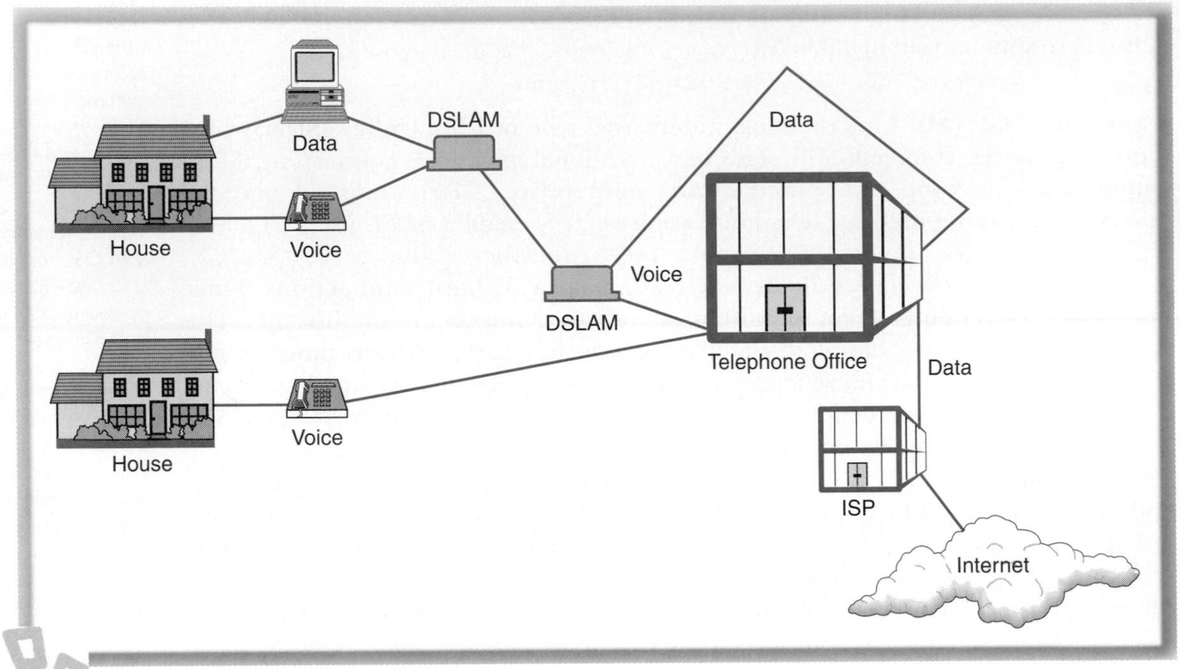

Figure 5-11　DSLAM Voice and Data Switching

HDSL

HDSL will provide speeds equivalent to T-1 (1.5 mbps) or E-1 (2 mbps) lines. E-1 is the European equivalent of T-1. The T-1 speed will require a user to have two telephone lines, and three lines are required for E-1 speeds. As technology improves, the number of lines required may decrease or the speed will increase. The transmission is symmetric, meaning that the upstream and downstream data rates are the same. Symmetric transmission is useful for applications in which the upstream and downstream data rates are approximately the same, such as computer-to-computer transfers and video-conferencing. The maximum distance between the user's premises and the telephone exchange is approximately 3.7 km (12,000 feet) over 24-gauge UTP (unshielded twisted pair).

SDSL

SDSL was developed by a company, not a standards group. The benefit of SDSL is that it operates on a single telephone line and has symmetric download and upload speed. This kind of service is well suited for individual users who need upload speeds beyond that for ADSL. SDSL speeds are T-1 or E-1, with a maximum distance between the subscriber and telephone end office of approximately 3 km (10,000 feet) over 24-gauge UTP.

VDSL

VDSL provides very high data rates of 12.9 to 51.8 mbps downstream and 1.5 to 2.3 mbps upstream. The transmission is therefore asymmetric. With the higher speeds, the distance is much shorter, approximately 1.35 km (4,500 feet) over 24-gauge UTP.

All of the DSL technologies require an xDSL modem/voice splitter at the subscriber end and compatible equipment at the common carrier end. The common carrier will terminate the DSL lines with DSL access multiplexors (DSLAMs). A DSLAM splits the traffic on the DSL line into a data switch or a voice switch, depending on the type of data being transmitted. This is illustrated in Figure 5-11.

Cable Modems

Historically, the coaxial cable used by cable television supported only one-way signal transmission. The evolution of cable television systems, however, has resulted in the increasing prevalence of two-way transmission. As a result, cable television providers are moving into the data communication business, primarily to provide Internet access. With a **cable modem** attached to a cable TV line, a user can realize downstream speeds of 10 mbps. A maximum upstream rate of 2 mbps is most common. Other advantages of cable access include availability and interoperability with television programming. For many households, the cable is already in place, and using the cable for Internet access does not tie up a telephone line. Cable modem technology allows simultaneous transmission of television and Internet data, so one person could be surfing the Internet while others are using the same medium for television programming. Figure 5-12 illustrates a typical cable modem implementation.

cable modem A modem that provides an interface between a user's computer system and a cable TV service that provides Internet access.

Most cable modems connect to personal computers via a standard 10BaseT network adapter card (these are discussed more fully in Chapter 11). Because users must share available bandwidth with other active users on the same cable segment (which may include up to 500 households), each user's data throughput decreases as the number of simultaneous users increases.

In 1998, the ITU adopted the *Data Over Cable Service Interface Specification (DOCSIS)* as an international standard for data transmission over cable systems. DOCSIS defines modulation methods and protocols for bidirectional data transmissions up to 30 mbps over cable systems.

Figure 5-12   A Typical Cable Modem Configuration

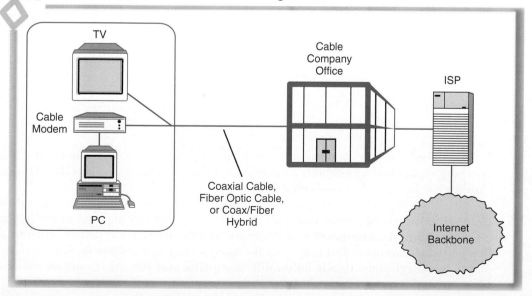

It is important to note that many cable television providers have been replacing coaxial cable with fiber optic cable in their backbone systems. Using more fiber in their networks enables carriers to increase bandwidth and thereby offer a greater number of television, data, or voice channels. Service reliability is typically increased through the use of more fiber. In addition, cable provider operating and repair costs are typically decreased.

Security remains an issue for cable modem users because the PC is connected to the Internet whenever the PC is turned on. This "always on" connection makes it easier for hackers and other unauthorized individuals to access the cable modem customer's computer. Personal firewalls are being used by an increasing number of broadband services customers to address such security concerns.

Wireless Local Loop

wireless local loop (WLL) A local loop (last mile) option that provides communications to the home or office via wireless transmission.

Wireless local loop (WLL) systems, like cellular telephone networks, carry voice and data over radio frequencies between local users and telephone company end offices. Several kinds of wireless technology systems are being tested and deployed by carriers as WLL solutions.

One WLL approach, pioneered by AT&T, involves placing an antenna on a utility pole (or another structure) in a neighborhood. Each antenna is capable of serving up to 2,000 homes. Subscribers must have an 18-inch antenna installed on their homes. Through the use of high-performance digital signal processing (DSP) technology, this system is able to provide each subscriber with two telephone lines and 128 kbps Internet access.

Another emerging WLL solution is *local multipoint distribution service (LMDS);* LMDS offers services that are comparable to those available from cable television providers. LMDS can be used to provide local voice services along with high-speed data services with maximum downstream data rates of 2 gbps and maximum upstream rates of 200 mbps.

COMMON CARRIER SERVICES

Common carriers provide a broad range of services. The major services are discussed in the following sections.

Switched Lines

circuit-switched connection Calls that take place over dial-up lines through end-office switches. Circuit switching provides a temporary, but dedicated, connection between two stations; it is widely used in the analog-based telephone system in order to guarantee steady, consistent service for two people engaged in a phone conversation.

The kind of line typically installed in a home or business is a switched (or dial-up) line. When placing a call, a caller picks up the handset, waits for a dial tone, and dials the number of the location he or she wants to call. This traditional kind of telephone service is what is meant by *plain old telephone service (POTS).* The telephone network that handles such everyday telephone service is called the *public switched telephone network (PSTN).*

Switched lines simply make use of the existing telephone circuits and end-office switching equipment to establish a connection between sender and receiver. This facility is available wherever telephone wires exist.

The calls that take place over dial-up lines through end-office switches are called **circuit-switched connections**. When a call is placed, the switching equipment in the end office finds the best possible path (circuit) to the destination that is available at that particular moment. Two calls from the same sender to the same receiver that are placed just seconds apart may follow different paths, and the quality of one may be superior that of the other. Hence, it makes sense to hang up and redial when you experience a noisy or "bad connection."

For data communications, the speed of the lines depends on the quality of telephone equipment and the modem used. Plain old telephone service (POTS) using the standard analog format currently supports up to 56 kbps. Digital switched services provide much higher data rates.

Because they are more expensive for dedicated use than leased lines, switched lines are used when the amount of transmitted data is small or when many locations must be contacted for short periods. Two examples are a team of salespeople entering information on their portable terminals, and a central host computer for a retail organization that contacts each retail outlet at the close of the business day to collect sales and inventory data. In both of these situations, the amount of data to be transferred is small, and the number of locations may be large or variable. Switched lines become more expensive as the connection time increases (especially for long-distance and international connections), and their cost-effectiveness may depend on their location, the time of transmission, and the number of required connections

Leased Telegraph-Grade Lines

Leased telegraph-grade lines provide lower transmission rates than the voice-grade lines described here. They are used for very low transmission rates and are seldom used for data communication. These are, however, still leveraged for communications among physically challenged (physically handicapped) individuals and handicap service providers.

Leased Voice-Grade Lines

Leased lines are used if the connection time between locations is long enough to cover the cost of leasing or if speeds higher than those available with switched lines must be attained. An analog voice-grade leased line, which is also called a *dedicated* or *private line,* bypasses the carrier's switching equipment to directly connect two or more locations. Once installed, the leased line is available to the user 24 hours a day. Needless to say, businesses gain the most value from leased lines when they are used to (close to) capacity, 24/7/365.

Leased-line charges include installation charges (which can be hefty) and flat monthly charges that, unlike dial-up circuits, do not vary by usage. The monthly cost of a leased line is a function of the distance covered, the transmission speed of the line, and the line's susceptibility to error. Common carriers provide a wide variety of options to satisfy diverse needs. For example, a leased line would enable users in a sales office in Seattle to communicate with a transaction-processing server in San Francisco. For this application, the data volume is low and a low transmission speed is sufficient, but the connection is maintained throughout the business day, which makes the leased line cost-effective. An application in which a leased line would be used for both economy and speed is when two distant computers—in Chicago and Los Angeles, for example—must exchange high volumes of information in a timely manner and for interregional traffic on the Internet.

Telephone companies can provide **conditioning** for leased telephone lines to reduce error rates and increase transmission speeds. One example of conditioning is the use of special equipment that equalizes the signal delay for all frequencies. The five levels of conditioning are C1 through C5, with level C3 not commercially available. Conditioned leased lines typically operate at speeds up to 64 kbps. Digital data transmission may be considerably faster.

leased line A private communications channel leased from a common carrier. Lines are leased when the connection time between locations is long enough to cover the cost of leasing or if speeds higher than those available with switched lines must be attained.

conditioning A service provided by telephone companies for leased lines. It amplifies weak signals and reduces the amount of noise on a line, providing lower error rates and increased speed.

Digital Services

Like analog services, common carrier digital transmission services can either be dial-up or leased. Both dial-up and leased services can be used for either voice or data communications. It is important to note, however, that modems are not used to interface with carrier digital services. Modems are only needed for analog voice-grade circuits. Instead of modems, a **channel service unit/data service unit (CSU/DSU)** is used. Although CSU/DSUs can be purchased from data communication equipment vendors, most users lease or purchase them from carriers. CSU/DSU transmission speeds range from 56 kbps to 45 mbps (or more) depending on the digital service that is being subscribed.

channel service unit/data service unit (CSU/DSU) A pair of communications devices that connect a customer's in-house line to an external digital circuit (T1, DDS, etc.). It is similar to a modem, but connects a digital circuit instead of an analog circuit. The CSU terminates the external line at the customer's premises; the DSU does the actual transmission and receiving of the signal and provides buffering and flow control.

Dial-Up Digital Services

Dial-up digital services include switched 56K (switched 56 kbps) and ISDN. Interest in both of these services has been fueled by the Internet and business/consumer interest in Internet access speeds that are higher than those supported by modems over POTS. ISDN, for example, typically offers Internet access speeds of 128 kbps. Subscribers interface their computers with the ISDN network using a device that is alternatively called a *digital modem, network termination unit (NTU),* or *terminal adapter.* This device has equivalent functionality to a CSU/DSU. A switched 56K CSU/DSU is used to interface with switched 56K services.

Costs for these services (beyond installation costs) usually include a flat monthly network access fee in addition to usage fees. Additional fees may include a monthly CSU/DSU (or ISDN digital modem) lease/rental charge.

Narrowband Digital Services

Narrowband digital services are leased digital lines with speeds less than those for T-n services. *Digital data services (DDS)* with speeds of 2,400; 4,800; 9,600; 19,200; or 56,000 kbps can be leased. DDS lines of 9,600 kbps or more are most common in the United States. DS-0 lines, the standard digital telephone line, can also be leased.

Narrowband digital circuit speeds are controlled by the end office. CSU/DSUs at customer locations are set to the speed of the circuit.

Broadband Digital Services

Broadband digital services allow very high data transmission rates and are the most popular and widely used kinds of digital services that are available. Broadband digital services include xDSL services, cable modem services, and T-n services. Costs for T-n services are typically flat monthly fees that vary by distance. T-1 (1.544 mbps) services typically cost upwards of $1,000 per month, although lower monthly rates are available in some urban areas. T-3 (45 mbps) services typically cost upwards of $10,000 per month.

T-n Services

T-n is a general term for several classes of high-speed services, such as T-1, T-3, and T-4. T-1 service, also called *DS-1 signaling,* provides digital transmission rates of 1.544 mbps. A T-1 communication link is created by multiplexing (combining) a number of lower speed lines. Although the implementation may vary, generally a T-1 circuit is created by multiplexing twenty-four 64-kbps (DS-0) services. The product of 24 and 64,000 is 1.536 million. The additional 8,000 bps are control bits.

Higher speeds are available with T-3 and T-4 services, also called *DS-3* and *DS-4 signaling,* respectively. T-3 service provides a data rate of 45 mbps and is derived from multiplexing six hundred seventy-two 64-kbps services. T-4 service provides transmission at 274 mbps and is derived from multiplexing four thousand thirty-two 64-kbps services. DS-3 and DS-4 signaling are part of a hierarchy of standards known as the digital service hierarchy (which is summarized in Table 5-5). T-1 is the most common option used today, and T-1 subscribers interface with T-1 transmission services via a T-1 CSU/DSU. As the need for speed increases and the rates for T-3 and T-4 services decline, higher speed services such as T-3 are likely to become more common.

Many ISPs connect to network service providers (NSPs) or the Internet backbone via T-1 lines. Larger ISPs, especially in urban areas, take advantage of T-3 lines for Internet access. The Internet itself makes extensive use of T-3 fiber optic lines for high-speed backbone links.

Full-motion video and audio applications are likely to become more common as high-speed data services become more prevalent and affordable. Video compression, which is accomplished using algorithms similar to those used for voice compression, is necessary for video transmissions over T-1 and T-3 lines; although rarely used, uncompressed video transmission requires a bandwidth of 90 mbps.

Fractional T-n Services

A T-1 service that began to appear in the late 1980s is known as fractional T-1 service. Before fractional T-1, high-speed digital transmission options were limited to 56 or 64 kbps or 1.544 mbps, with few options in between. Fractional T-1 is intended to fill this void by providing a portion of a T-1 line to customers. Organizations needing data rates higher than 64 kbps but less than the 1.544 mbps of a T-1 line can subscribe to fractional T-1 service. For speeds between T-1 and T-3, fractional T-3 services are available. **Fractional T-n service** allows a user to share a T-n line with another subscriber by using a prespecified subset of the total number of 64 kbps lines that are multiplexed together to form the T-n circuit. A fractional T-1 subscriber could subscribe to 64, 128, 192, or 256 kbps and up. Some common carriers limit the available increments by allowing multiples of 1, 2, 4, 6, 8, and 12 channels for speeds of 64, 128, 256, 384, 512, and 768 kbps. Fractional T-n services allow the subscriber to optimize the line speed and the cost of the service.

fractional T-n service A service that provides less than full T-n (such as T-1 or T-3) capacity in specified increments; FT-1 service uses 64 kbps increments.

Switched Multimegabit Data Service

Switched multimegabit data service (SMDS) is a high-speed connectionless digital transmission service. "Connectionless" means that the sender and receiver do not need to be connected via a dedicated link. In SMDS, the common carrier provides the user with access points for both sender and receiver. With SMDS, data is broken

switched multimegabit data service (SMDS) A high-speed, switched data communications service offered by the local telephone companies that is used by most subscribers for interconnecting LANs in different locations.

Table 5-5   Digital Signal (DS) Service Hierarchy

Digital Service Level	Transmission Service	Transmission Rate	Number of Voice Channels
DS-0	DS-0; switched 64K	64 kbps	1
DS-1	T-1	1.544 mbps	24
DS-1C	T-1C	3.152 mbps	48
DS-2	T-2	6.312 mbps	96
DS-3	T-3	44.736 mbps	672
DS-4	T-4	274.136 mbps	4,032

Table 5-6 The CCITT Digital Service Hierarchy

Digital Service Level	Transmission Service	Transmission Rate	Number of Voice Channels
1	E-1	2.048 mbps	30
2	E-2	8.448 mbps	120
3	E-3	34.368 mbps	480
4	E-4	139.264 mbps	1,920
5	E-5	565.148 mbps	7,680

down into transmission packets. The common carrier provides high-speed switching equipment that routes these packets to their destination address. SMDS speeds are 1.54 mbps (T-1) and 44 mbps (T-3); 155 mbps services are available in some areas. SMDS can be used for high-speed data transmissions such as the long-distance interconnection of LANs.

E-n Services

The digital service hierarchy standards and T-n services are used to define high-speed digital data services in North America. Internationally, CCITT standards and E-n services prevail. The CCITT digital service hierarchy is summarized in Table 5-6.

SONET Services

synchronous optical network (SONET)
A fiber-optic transmission system employed by telephone companies and common carriers for high-speed digital traffic. SONET is specified in the Broadband ISDN (B-ISDN) standard.

Synchronous optical network (SONET) is a very high speed optical transmission service available in large metropolitan areas with an appropriate fiber optic cable infrastructure. Like the digital service hierarchy, SONET has its own hierarchy of service levels. Because SONET provides optical transmission services, the digital service levels in SONET's hierarchy of services are called *optical carrier (OC) levels*. These are summarized in Table 5-7.

Integrated Services Digital Network

Increased use of common carrier equipment for data communication has prompted carriers to reevaluate their networks and services. Many have reached the conclusion that subscribers are interested in solutions that involve using the same network for

Table 5-7 SONET Optical Carrier (OC) Standards

Digital Service Level	Transmission Rate
OC-1	51.84 mbps
OC-3	155.52 mbps
OC-12	622.08 mbps
OC-24	1.244 gbps
OC-48	2.488 gbps
OC-192	9.953 gbps
OC-768	38.813 gbps

transmitting data in all its various forms. These forms could include digital data, voice, facsimile, graphics, and video. The benefits to the user community of this kind of network are higher transmission speed and potential cost reductions for communication services resulting from the ability to combine multiple data forms onto one network.

One objective of the carrier service known as *integrated services digital network (ISDN)* is to allow international data exchange. This requires interfaces between a number of national and regional providers of ISDN services. In 1984, the ITU produced the first of what is likely to become several standards for ISDN implementations. This standard provides for the several different kinds of service described here.

The ISDN system specifies three basic kinds of channels, designated as B, D, and H types. Within the type H channel, several options are available. These options are summarized in Table 5-8. ISDN provides two interface structures designated as basic service and primary service. The basic service is designated as $2B_{64} + D_{16}$ (or 2B+D), which indicates that it consists of two type B channels and one 16-kbps type D channel, for an aggregate speed of 144 kbps. The primary service has a different configuration for North America and Japan than for Europe. The North American and Japanese specification is designated as $23B_{64} + D_{64}$ (23B+D), for an aggregate speed of 1.544 mbps. This is the same speed as the T-1 service. In Europe, the primary service is designated as $30B_{64} + D_{64}$, for an aggregate speed of 2.048 mbps, equivalent to E-1, the European version of T-1 transmission.

ISDN was one of the first high-speed alternatives to switched analog connections for Internet access. ISDN used for Internet access usually provides speeds of 128 kbps. Furthermore, with the right interfaces, the ISDN line can provide voice telephone service while also providing data transmission; however, in this mode the data transfer rate is typically reduced to 64 kbps. As noted previously, ISDN line interfaces are called *network termination (NT) devices, digital modems,* or *terminal adapters.* Beyond Internet access, ISDN has other uses, some of which are digital voice transmission; providing interconnections among geographically dispersed LANs; office automation (routing and access to documents); security via transmission of graphic images, such as signatures for check-cashing verification or freeze-frame images to security guards; video telephone service; and concurrent transfer of voice and data. (For example, two users can be engaged in a telephone conversation while simultaneously transmitting data between their workstations.)

Table 5-8   ISDN Channel Types and Options

ISDN Channel Types
    B: 64 kbps
    H0: 384 kbps (=6B)
    H11: 1.544 mbps (=23B + $1D_{64}$), North America and Japan
    H12: 2.048 mbps (=30B + $1D_{64}$), Europe
Control Data
    D: Both 16 and 64 kbps
Basic Service Options
    $2B_{64} + D_{16}$ = 144 kbps
Primary Service
    $23B_{64} + D_{64}$ = 1.544 mbps, North America and Japan
    $30B_{64} + D_{64}$ = 2.048 mbps, Europe

Value-Added Networks

Beyond switched, leased, or other digital services and ISDN, carriers also offer packet-switching services.

packet switching
The transmission of a message by dividing the message into fixed-length packets and then routing the packets to the recipient. Packets may be sent over different paths and arrive out of order. At the receiving end, the packets are reordered. Routing is determined during transmission of the packet. Packet-switching networks are also known as packet distribution networks, public data networks, and X.25 networks, or value-added networks.

Packet switching is the technology of transmitting a message in one or more fixed-length data packets. A packet-switching network is also sometimes called a *packet distribution network (PDN), public data network* (also *PDN), X.25 network* (*X.25* is a standard designation), or *value-added network (VAN)*. Henceforth, the abbreviation *PDN* is used. A PDN generally connects a user and the nearest node in the PDN. The PDN routes the data packets to their final destination by finding the best route for each packet (packet switching).

Subscribers to packet-switching services are usually charged a monthly network access charge and usage fees. Usage fees are assessed on how much data is transmitted rather than connection time or distance between sender and receiver. Often, subscriber total cost is less than what would be incurred by using either dial-up or leased lines.

Packet-switching services were initially designed to support data communications, and most are limited to still doing same. Packet-switching services that support both voice and data are available in some areas.

Some carriers provide value-added applications such as electronic data interchange (EDI) over PDNs. Frame relay and asynchronous transfer mode (ATM) services are also available from carriers. Packet switching, PDNs, frame relay, and ATM are discussed more fully in Chapter 8.

WATS

Wide area telecommunications (or telephone) service (WATS) includes both inbound and outbound services. The inbound WATS service includes the familiar toll-free 800- and 888-prefix numbers. A customer may subscribe to an inbound service, an outbound service, or both. Numerous businesses use inbound services to facilitate customer contact, telephone-based ordering, and customer service. The common carrier charges a flat monthly fee for the service, which covers a specific number of hours of connect time to designated regions. The cost of the service is based on both the number of hours of connect time and the distance to be covered by the service. When WATS service is used for data transmission, the effect is the same as using switched lines, but the cost of the call differs. The number of WATS prefixes has increased in response to increased business demand for WATS services.

Satellite Service

Satellite radio transmission transmits data via very-high-frequency (VHF) radio waves and requires line-of-sight transmission between stations. As may be observed in Table 5-9, VHF signals fall about midway in the range of frequencies for radiated media used for data and voice communications. Both land-based stations and orbiting stations are used.

geosynchronous orbit A satellite orbit in which the satellite orbits at the same rate as earth's rotation. Satellites in geosynchronous orbit at the height of 22,282 miles and within 4 degrees of the equator are *geostationary* with respect to earth; they are always positioned over the same location.

Commercial communication satellites are typically placed in an equatorial, geosynchronous orbit at an altitude of 22,300 miles. A **geosynchronous orbit** means that the satellite remains stationary relative to a given position on the earth, as illustrated in Figure 5-13. At this altitude, only three satellites are required to cover all points on the earth, as shown in Figure 5-14. Because there is limited room for geosynchronous orbiting satellites, a variation called *inclined-orbit satellites* is being used more often. Inclined-orbit satellites are positioned 22,282 miles above the equator; however, inclined-orbit satellites move slightly north and south of the equator, as illustrated in Figure 5-15. This movement requires that the earth stations track the movement of the

Table 5-9   Frequency Spectrum Classification

Frequency (Hz)	Wavelength
10^{16}	X rays, gamma rays
10^{15}	Ultraviolet light
10^{14}	Visible light
10^{13}	Infrared light
10^{12}	Millimeter waves
10^{11}	Microwaves
10^{10}	UHF television
10^{9}	VHF television
10^{8}	VHF TV (high band) FM radio
10^{7}	VHF TV (low band) Shortwave radio
10^{6}	AM radio
10^{5}	Very low frequency
10^{4}	Very low frequency
10^{3}	Very low frequency
10^{2}	Very low frequency
10^{1}	Very low frequency

satellites. Typically, tracking antennas are smaller (1.2 to 2.5 m in diameter) than the more traditional earth stations (which may be 7 m in diameter or larger). These smaller antennas are called *very-small-aperture terminals (VSATs)*. The added expense of having a tracking antenna is typically offset by lower transmission costs.

Low-orbit satellites (also called **low-earth-orbit [LEO] satellites**) are also beginning to be used more extensively. Several companies are implementing networks of low-earth-orbit satellites (approximately 400 to 1,000 miles high). Other satellite-based networks designed to support Internet access use **medium-earth-orbit (MEO) satellites**, whose orbits range from 6,250 to 10,000 miles (10,000 to 16,000 km) above the

low earth orbit (LEO) satellites Communication satellites that orbit approximately 400 to 1,600 miles high and that can be used as orbiting routers.

medium-earth-orbit (MEO) satellites Communication satellites whose orbits range from 6,250 to 10,000 miles (10,000 to 16,000 km) above earth. Both LEO and MEO satellite networks can be used to provide voice and data services.

Figure 5-13   Geosynchronous Satellite Orbit

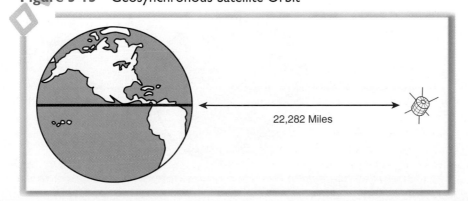

22,282 Miles

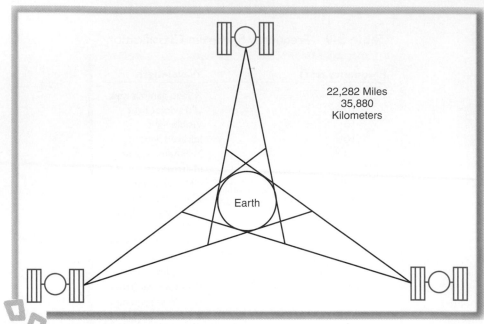

Figure 5-14   Geosynchronous Satellite Positioning

earth. Teledesic, for example, is building a network of 30 MEO satellites that will support up to 100 mbps uplink and 720 mbps download speeds (see Chapter 2 case). Both LEO and MEO satellite networks can be used to provide voice and data services. Business uses of these networks include paging, mobile telephones, personal communications services, communication with vending machines (the machine can report low stock levels), and videoconferencing. Some of these networks, such as the Teledesic network, will eventually have enough satellites in place to provide worldwide

Figure 5-15   Inclined-Orbit Satellite

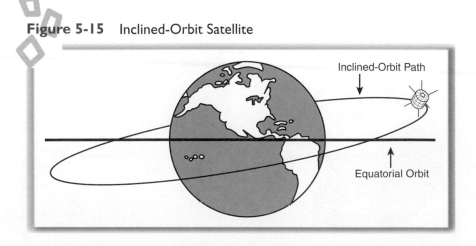

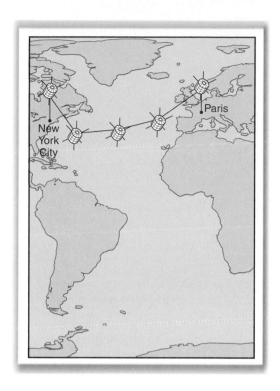

Figure 5-16   Transmission with Low-Orbit Satellites

coverage. An example of how a message would be routed from New York to Paris by such a system is shown in Figure 5-16.

Technology

The basic components of satellite transmission are the earth stations and the satellite component called a **transponder**. The transponder receives the transmission from earth (*uplink*), amplifies the signal, changes the frequency, and transmits the data to a receiving earth station (*downlink*). The uplink frequency differs from the downlink frequency so that the weaker incoming signals are not interfered with by the stronger outgoing signals. Satellite frequencies are spoken of in pairs, such as 12/14 GHz. The first number represents the downlink frequency and the second the uplink frequency. Thus, 12/14 GHz means a downlink transmission frequency of 12 GHz and an uplink transmission frequency of 14 GHz. To avoid interference, geosynchronous communication satellites must be separated by an arc of at least 4 degrees, as depicted in Figure 5-17. (This has led to concern, especially among countries currently incapable of launching satellites, that only a limited amount of space is available for these satellites and that the space will be allocated without their obtaining a slot. Low-orbit and inclined-orbit satellites provide alternatives to geosynchronous satellites, but there are still space limitations.) Each transponder has a transmission rate of approximately 50 mbps, which can be divided into sixteen 1.5-mbps channels, four hundred 64-kbps channels, or six hundred 40-kbps channels. This means that each transponder could handle 400 simultaneous digital telephone calls or 600 simultaneous analog voice transmissions. Although this transmission rate is high, there still is a significant delay because the signals must travel a long distance from source to destination.

Because satellites, transponders, and noninterfering frequency bands are limited resources, a single transponder is typically shared by several terrestrial stations, signal

transponder In satellite communication, a transponder receives the transmission from earth (uplink), amplifies the signal, changes frequency, and retransmits the data to a receiving earth station (downlink).

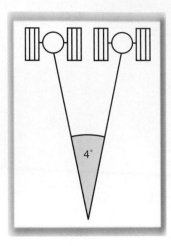

Figure 5-17   Satellite Separation

sources, or carriers. In addition, multiplexing is typically used to ensure that the transponder is being used to its full capacity. The most widely used multiplexing techniques for satellite transmissions are

➤ *Frequency division multiple access (FDMA)*. In this approach each ground station (uplink) is assigned a specific frequency slot and bandwidth with a specific transponder.

➤ *Time division multiple access (TDMA)*. This involves a time-sharing approach for dividing total transponder capacity. Each ground station (sharing the same transponder) is given access to the satellite for a brief period of time, based on the amount of data it has to transmit. Digital transmission is used, but through TDMA, the data from each ground station is transmitted in bursts.

➤ *Code division multiple access (CDMA)*. CDMA involves the use of digital signal processors to spread digital signals from multiple ground stations across the frequency bandwidth allocated to a particular transponder.

Propagation Delay

propagation delay
The amount of time it takes for a signal to travel from its source to its destination.

The amount of time it takes for a signal to travel from its source to its destination is called **propagation delay** (or *latency*). Because most data communication signals travel at nearly the speed of light, propagation delay on earth is insignificant (about 5 milliseconds for a 1,000-mile journey). Actual terrestrial transmission speeds are somewhat slower due to characteristics of the medium and the characteristics of transmission equipment; however, the propagation delay is barely noticeable in response times. Across the extremely long distances of space, however, propagation delay can be noticeable. The delay includes travel time as well as the time required to accept, enhance, and retransmit the signal. Propagation delay, which is sometimes called *latency*, becomes significant for applications that have sending times of less than a quarter-second or response times of a half-second or less. Propagation delay is ordinarily ignored for terrestrial links, but satellite transmission system designers must be aware of this factor. Table 5-10 gives an example of how propagation delay is computed for a transaction in which a remote terminal sends a message to a host computer and receives a reply from it.

Satellite Providers

The several providers of transponders for satellite communication include Hughes Network Systems, Comsat, AT&T Tridom, GTE Spacenet, and Scientific Atlanta, as well as broadcast agencies in Canada, Japan, Europe, and Russia. The number of

Table 5-10   Satellite Propagation Delay

Remote-satellite input uplink	22,300 mi
Satellite-host input downlink	22,300
Host-satellite response uplink	22,300
Satellite-remote response downlink	22,300
Total distance	89,200 mi

Travel time = 89,200 mi/186,000
    mi/s = 0.48 s

transponders per satellite is typically between 12 and 24. Providers of satellite time usually lease a whole transponder, but it is also possible to sublease transponder subchannels from another user. Satellites make expansion of a data communication network easy. All that is required is to add earth stations (except when the area being served is outside the area served by the satellites being used). Satellite networks can present security problems, however, because transmission can be intercepted by anyone with proper receiving equipment.

MOBILE VOICE/DATA COMMUNICATION SERVICES

Mobile services unleash a user from telephone lines. Mobile services are used for telephone services, pagers, facsimile transmissions, and data transmissions. Traditionally, mobile services have been associated with low data transmission rates, generally 28,800 bps or lower; however, these technologies are evolving rapidly, and much higher speeds will be supported in the future. Available mobile services include cellular telephony, cellular digital packet data (CDPD), mobile radio data, and personal communication services (PCS). Use of these services requires the proper interfaces, such as radio-frequency modems. Furthermore, there is no guarantee that the interface for one service will work with that for other services. Users planning to use two or more of these services should be looking for solutions that integrate them.

Cellular Telephony

Cellular telephony has demonstrated explosive growth over the last decade, and the emergence of new technologies and services is likely to fuel continued growth for some time to come. Most terrestrial wireless transmissions are typically cellular. Transmissions originate in geographically delimited cells, each of which is serviced by a single base station transceiver (see Figure 5-18). Each of the base stations is connected to a *mobile telephone switching office (MTSO),* which tracks the location of local users and provides an interface to other MTSOs and the public switched telephone network. As mobile users move from cell to cell, a handoff operation between base stations is executed by the MTSO. The capacity of a given cellular telephony service is a function of the number of calls that can be handled in each cell, the size of the cells, and the number of the nearest neighbor cells. Cells are typically larger in rural areas than in urban areas. *Microcells,* which may be as small as 100 feet, are found in some highly congested urban areas. Traditional cellular systems require a minimum cell size of 100 feet.

Both analog and digital cellular telephone/data networks exist, but newer systems use digital rather than analog technologies. Voice compression is common in

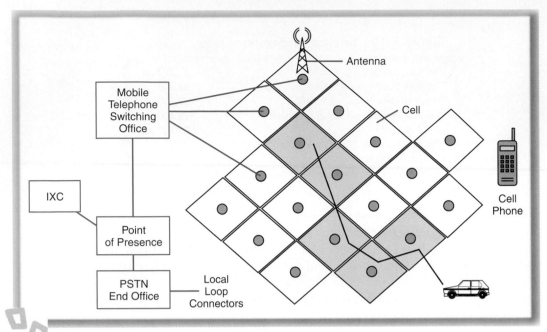

Figure 5-18   Cellular Telephony System

digital systems, thereby increasing the number of voice transmissions that can be carried simultaneously within a given cell. Digital systems enable mobile telephone handsets to be smaller (due to fewer electronics) and have lower power requirements and better battery life. Digital systems also support superior error-correction/detection and security schemes. Three generations of wireless telephone technologies have been identified.

First-Generation Systems

In first-generation cellular systems, cells are generally large, as were the channels used to support voice communications. This limits the number of simultaneous users. These are typically analog cellular systems using frequency modulation (FM) as the transmission mode (the analog signals carried over first-generation networks fall in the FM frequency range; see Table 5-9).

In the United States, the *Advanced Mobile Phone System (AMPS)* serves as the standard for first-generation cellular telephony. The standard enables users to "roam" outside their cellular service providers' "local" calling area by specifying standard interfaces and call handoffs between MTSOs. Cellular digital packet data (CDPD) is a first-generation digital standard used in the United States, but it is much less common than AMPS.

In Europe, the *Global System for Mobile Communications (GSM)* emerged as the first-generation cellular telephony standard in order to address nine different incompatible standards used during the early 1980s. Once adopted, it quickly became the norm in Europe and spread to many other countries. GSM is found in most countries outside the United States. GSM systems are digital and often employ TDMA.

Second-Generation Systems

Second-generation cellular telephony networks emerged during the 1990s. These support microcells, are assigned bandwidth that is approximately three times larger than that of first-generation cellular networks, and, because they use digital transmission, take advantage of voice compression and digital signal processing (by placing a microprocessor in each cell phone) to support a range of services beyond voice communications, such as personal communication services (PCS), paging, e-mail, and Internet access.

In Europe, *distributed communication service (DCS),* a modification of GSM, is the second-generation cellular telephony standard. In the United States, no clear second-generation standard has emerged. Although a modified version of DCS and alternative TDMA standards are leading contenders, user ability to "roam" will be limited until a common standard is adopted.

Third-Generation Cellular Telephony

Third-generation cellular telephony represents an important step toward universal personal telecommunications and global communications access. An important objective of third-generation technologies is the ability to support voice, data, multimedia, and video services over higher speed wireless communications networks.

Third-generation cellular telephony devices are already being marketed, and the International Telecommunications Union (ITU) is advocating the adoption of *International Mobile Telecommunications (IMT)* standards to ensure international roaming capabilities and advanced services (such as call waiting) that are currently available only to wire-line telephone subscribers. Other capabilities outlined in the ITU's IMT-2000 initiative include support for both packet- and circuit-switched data services, data rates up to 384 kbps for individual users, and data rates equivalent to E-1 services (2.048 mbps) for business offices. An example of a third-generation cellular system is UMTS (Universal Mobile Telecommunications Systems). The commercial rollout of UMTS began in 2002.

Third-generation (3G) cell phones (which are also called *smart phones*) will allow more data-intensive services to be sent to and from cell phones and other handheld devices such as wireless personal digital assistants (PDAs). 3G devices can transmit pictures, video, and music along with voice, making them wireless videophone technologies. Internet access and the ability to send/receive e-mail and facsimiles (faxes) are common functions supported by 3G cellular telephony technologies.

Mobile Radio Services

Mobile radio services include voice-oriented mobile dispatch systems as well as mobile data transmission services. Mobile radio services for data transmission are also available. Two examples of mobile radio services for data transmission are RAM Mobile Data from Bell South Mobility and RAM Broadcasting, and Ardis from Motorola and IBM. Both of these services are available in most metropolitan areas in the United States.

mobile radio services Include voice-oriented mobile dispatch systems as well as mobile data transmission services.

Personal Communication Services

Personal communication service (PCS) was originally used to provide paging devices with enhanced paging services, including two-way paging, text messaging (which allows short text messages to be displayed on the pager monitor), and voice paging (which enables voice mail to be forwarded to a pager). The PCS market has expanded to include digital transmission for telephone and portable computers. Today, PCS is

personal communication service (PCS) A mobile communication service providing cellular telephone, paging, and other mobile voice and data communication services.

best described as an integrated set of services that leverages the capabilities of traditional landline telephone networks, second- and third-generation cellular telephone networks, paging networks, and mobile satellite transmission networks.

Currently, an individual may have many numbers in order to take advantage of communication services. These often include an office telephone number, a home phone number, a cell-phone number, a fax number, and a pager number. With PCS, a single *personal phone number (PPN)* is the ideal. All the services listed here (voice communications, pages, and fax) could be delivered to the same "follow me everywhere" PPN.

Needless to say, the portable devices users need to take advantage of PCS must be able to handle telephone calls/services, pages, and facsimile transmissions. Some second-generation and most third-generation cellular telephony devices have such capabilities.

Like cellular telephony, PCS technology uses multiple fixed stations to communicate with users in a local area or cell. As a user moves from one cell to another, communication control is transferred to the new cell. Currently, transmission speeds are equivalent to those of cellular telephone speeds. Because several competing transmission technologies are being used for PCS services, communication devices may not interoperate among service providers.

PRIVATE BRANCH EXCHANGES AND CENTREX SERVICES

Private Branch Exchanges

private branch exchange (PBX) An inhouse telephone switching system that interconnects telephone extensions to each other as well as to the public switched telephone network (PSTN). PBXs often support least cost routing for outside calls, call forwarding, conference calling, and call accounting. Modern PBXs typically support digital transmission and switching among inhouse telephone extensions, but may support interfaces to both analog and digital PSTN lines.

A **private branch exchange (PBX)** is a private, on-premises telephone switch that is owned or leased by an organization. Having a PBX within a company is similar to having a private end-office switch—it interconnects all the telephones within the business facility and provides access to the public telephone network. In essence, a PBX is a smaller, privately owned version of the switches found in telephone company end offices that are used to establish circuit-switched connections for telephone calls. Most of the PBXs found in today's organizations are digital and utilize PCM.

In the past, prior to the AT&T divestiture, U.S. telephone companies provided and retained ownership of all telephone equipment on company premises, including all telephone handsets and wiring. Now, U.S. businesses have the option of leasing telephone equipment from a telephone company or purchasing and operating their own telephone equipment. Most large organizations and many smaller ones have chosen to install PBXs and, in essence, establish their own internal telephone company. This is the case in most countries around the world.

Within a company, some of the telephone calls are between employees in the same building complex. Rather than routing these calls through the telephone company's end-office switch, a PBX switches the calls internally while routing external calls through the telephone company's system. Depending on the size of the organization, internal calls may only require callers to use a 3- or 4-digit "extension" number; external calls, however, require callers to enter the recipient's 7- (or 10-) digit telephone number. In addition, most PBXs require callers to enter a prespecified number (often "9") to access an "outside" line before entering the numbers needed to establish an external connection.

Internal switching with access to telephone company end offices for external calls is illustrated in Figure 5-19. An organization can also interconnect PBXs at multiple operating locations via leased lines to form larger private telephone networks. This is illustrated in Figure 5-20. ISO standards have been developed to help ensure interoperability among PBXs from different vendors. ISO's *Q.Sig* standard has been

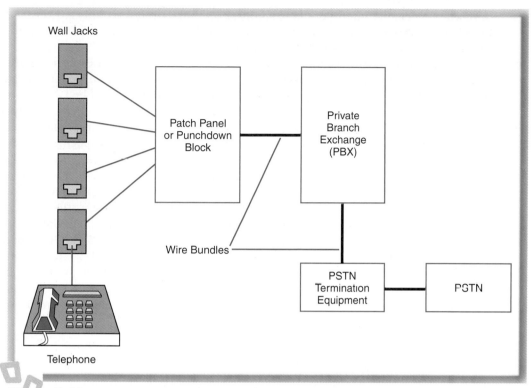

Figure 5-19   Example of a PBX Implementation

Figure 5-20   A PBX Network for a Company with Offices in Three Major Cities. Interoffice Calls Are Routed over Leased Lines. Other Outgoing Calls Are Handled by the Public Telephone Network

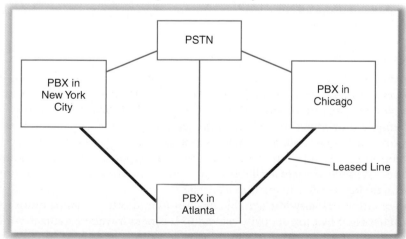

developed to enable interoperability among PBXs that are interconnected via ISDN. Q.931 is an ISDN standard that allows interoperability between PBX and public switched telephone network features/services.

In the past, private branch exchange (PBX) telephone switches were separate from data communication networks. More recently, PBXs have been integrated into networks, primarily to provide capabilities similar to those supported by LANs. Using the PBX system as a LAN medium can be efficient because the wiring is already in place. The disadvantage of using PBX systems for LANs is lower transmission speed and competition between data and voice for available transmission capacity.

PBXs enable businesses to take advantage of a wide range of services (see Table 5-11). Although the availability of these varies by PBX model and vendor, Table 5-11 assists us in understanding why PBXs are attractive to businesses and other organizations. Many PBXs also support data transmission and the interconnection of an organization's computing technologies. *Voice-over-data,* the ability to transmit voice and data simultaneously over the same PBX connection, is supported by many PBXs. Other data-oriented PBX features and services include fax transmission, file and printer sharing, ISDN interfaces, LAN/PBX interfaces, PBX-to-host interfaces (PBX interfaces for mainframes and minicomputers), and T-1/E-1 interfaces. Although these are not supported on all PBXs, they illustrate that PBXs can play a key data communications role within organizations.

Centrex Services

Centrex service A local telephone company service that provides PBX capabilities to a company. With the Centrex service, the PBX equipment is located on the telephone company's premises.

Centrex service is essentially a PBX service provided by a common carrier. Instead of the switching equipment being located on the customer's premises, the common carrier provides the switching equipment on the common carrier's site (see Figure 5-21). This allows several locations in a city to share the same switch and use the same calling prefix, and allows extension dialing as though the telephones were located in one building and served by an on-site PBX. Like a PBX, Centrex service can be used to transmit data as well as voice.

BUSINESS APPLICATIONS OF VOICE NETWORKS

Businesses are leveraging voice networks in numerous ways to reduce expenses, enhance worker productivity, and improve customer service. Among the major kinds of business-oriented voice network applications are videoconferencing, support for telecommuters and mobile workers, computer-integrated telephony, and interactive voice response systems.

Videoconferencing

videoconferencing An electronic meeting between two or more geographically separated individuals who use a network or the Internet to transmit/receive voice/audio, video, and other data signals.

Videoconferencing is best described as an electronic meeting between two or more geographically separated individuals who use a network or the Internet to transmit/receive voice/audio, video, and other data signals. Videoconferencing systems, in essence, enable individuals to participate in "face-to-face" meetings even though they are geographically separated. Such systems enable meeting participants to verbally exchange their thoughts and views as well as a variety of supporting data. Traditionally, businesses have leveraged services available from common carriers and third-party vendors to implement videoconferencing applications.

Videoconferencing systems enable businesses and other organizations to reduce travel expenses and lost productivity related to business travel. Organizations can also use such systems to deliver training and instruction to remote locations, to interview and screen job candidates, and to make important corporate announcements to

Table 5-11 Examples of PBX Features/Services

PBX Feature/Service	Description
Automated attendant	Recorded messages for incoming callers that provide instructions for connecting to specific extensions and the operator
Automatic call distribution	Enables incoming calls to be routed directly to certain PBX extensions without going through the central switchboard
Automatic number identification	Displays the originating telephone number for an incoming call
Call accounting	Enables managers to obtain detailed reports on all calls (local and long distance) placed from any phone attached to the PBX
Call forwarding	Enables recipients to forward incoming calls to other PBX users
Call holding	Enables a call recipient to put an incoming caller on hold
Call pickup	Enables a user to pick up another PBX user's incoming calls
Call restriction	Enables managers to prevent specific phones from placing outgoing or long-distance calls
Call waiting	Informs PBX users of incoming calls while they are currently engaged in a phone conversation with someone else
Camp on	Button used when a call results in a busy signal; intended recipient called automatically when he/she hangs up
Conference calling	Allows three or more people to converse simultaneously
Interactive voice response	Delivers menu options for incoming callers, some of which enable the callers to engage in customer service activities such as account inquiries
Last number redial	Enables users to use a redial button to dial the last number dialed
Least cost routing	Automatically selects the least expensive routing for an outgoing long-distance call
Message center	Allows incoming callers to leave a message for a PBX user with a live operator
Music/ads on hold	Incoming callers on hold hear music or prerecorded ads while they wait to be connected to a PBX user
Paging	Enables switchboard operators to page specific PBX users when they are out of their offices
Speed dialing	Enables users to use a 1- or 2-digit code to dial frequently called numbers
Voice mail	Enables incoming callers to leave digitized voice messages for specific PBX users
Wireless telephone support/integration	Allows wireless phone users to take advantage of PBX features such as conference calls, call forwarding, camp on, last number redial, and speed dialing

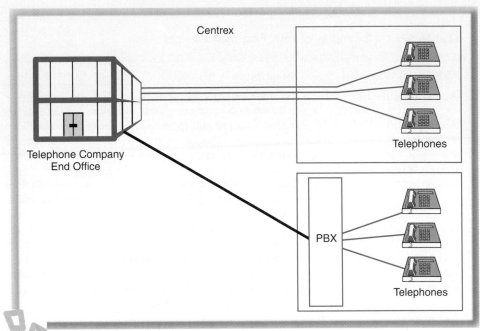

Figure 5-21   A Comparison of Centrex PBX Implementations

employees at geographically dispersed operating sites. Such systems vary in cost and sophistication, but the trend is toward increased use of videoconferencing.

Videoconferencing System Components

The basic components of a videoconferencing system are illustrated in Figure 5-22. The codec is the most important component of the videoconferencing system and is responsible for digitizing analog video and voice signals in a manner that is similar to PCM. The codec is also responsible for compressing outgoing video and audio signals as well as decompressing incoming signals. Digital signal processors (DSPs) and compression algorithms similar to ADPCM play an important role in video compression. Compression is necessary to transmit video signals over carriers' digital services, such as T-n services. As noted in Table 5-12, uncompressed videoconference transmissions require a bandwidth of approximately 90 mbps—the equivalent of two T-3 lines. Because of the expense associated with transmitting uncompressed video, the vast majority of videoconferencing systems in today's organizations employ some level of video compression.

Other components that may be included in videoconferencing systems include the following:

> *Document cameras.* These enable images of documents and 3-dimensional objects to be sent from one videoconferencing site to the other(s).

> *Electronic blackboards/whiteboards.* Participants at one site can "write" on these and electronically transmit the written images to the other site(s).

> *Facsimile transmission devices.* These enable participants at one site to "fax" document images to the other site(s).

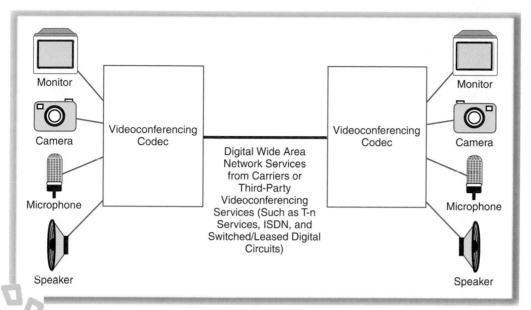

Figure 5-22   Basic Components of Videoconferencing Systems

➤ *Computer-generated graphics.* Presenters can transmit presentation graphics images (such as PowerPoint slides) to the other site(s).

➤ *Telemedicine data image transmission.* This involves the transmission of medical imaging data such as X rays, CAT scans, and MRIs from one videoconferencing site to the other(s).

Voice Network Services Used for Videoconferencing

Videoconferencing systems interface with a variety of services available from common carriers and third-party vendors. These are summarized in Table 5-13. As noted previously, ISDN networks were designed to support the simultaneous transmission of voice, image, data, and video—the essential signal ingredients for videoconferencing. Table 5-13 indicates that some PBXs also support videoconferencing applications.

Table 5-12   Bandwidth Requirements for Video and Audio Transmissions

Signal Type	Bandwidth Requirements
Uncompressed video	90 mbps
High-resolution compressed video	6 to 24 mbps
Compressed video	384 kbps to 1.544 mbps
Still image video	128 kbps
Digitized audio	64 kbps
Compressed audio	4.8 to 32 kbps
Analog audio	3 kbps

Table 5-13   Voice Network Services and Interface Technologies Used for Videoconferencing

Voice Network Service	Interface Device/Technology
Leased digital services (56K, 64K, T-n)	CSU/DSU or PBX
Switched digital services (56K, 128K, 348K)	Switched services CSU/DSU or PBX
Leased T-1	T-1 multiplexor
Multiple switched digital lines (56K or 64K)	Inverse multiplexor
ISDN	ISDN basic rate interface (BRI)
Satellite transmission services	Satellite dish, uplink/downlink, and other ground station technologies

Inverse multiplexors are able to aggregate a sufficient number of switched digital circuits for the duration of a videoconference and enable organizations to avoid the monthly charges associated with leased digital services. The ability of an inverse multiplexor to "grab" sufficient bandwidth to support a videoconference has earned it the title of a *"bandwidth on demand"* interface device.

Videoconferencing System Categories

Videoconferencing systems come in various shapes and sizes. These include the following:

- ➤ *Videoconferencing rooms.* These are permanently installed systems that include all the basic components of a videoconferencing system (codec, cameras, microphones, monitors) as well as other special-purpose equipment and interfaces such as those for personal computers, document cameras, electronic whiteboards, and telemedicine image transmission. Installation costs for such solutions typically range from $10,000 to $100,000.

- ➤ *Tabletop systems.* These are usually less sophisticated and less expensive than room-based solutions. They are often used to support small-group videoconferencing.

- ➤ *Rollabout systems.* These put the basic components of a videoconferencing system on a cart that can be moved to any room with the appropriate voice digital network service/interface.

- ➤ *Desktop system.* These are PC–based systems that enable videoconference images to be displayed on a computer monitor. Outgoing video images originate with a small camera, typically mounted on the user's monitor, as well as the user's computer. Software such as Microsoft's Net Meeting may be used to support desktop-to-desktop videoconferencing over the Internet, ISDN, or dial-up connections.

- ➤ *LAN–based systems.* LAN–based systems enable multiple videoconferencing desktop systems attached the same LAN to participate in the same videoconference. Such systems enable desktop-to-desktop videoconferencing among users attached to the same LAN and also provide support for videoconferencing among geographically dispersed locations.

- ➤ *Cellular-based systems.* As noted previously in our discussion of cellular telephony technologies, some third-generation cellular devices will support wireless, mobile videoconferencing.

Reduced travel expenses is a common cost justification for implementing video-conferencing technologies within organizations. Some industry experts predict that increased use of videoconferencing will result in significant business trip reductions (ranging from 25 percent to 33 percent) over the next 2 decades. Evidence is also mounting that videoconferencing can contribute to increased productivity and customer service.

Increases in business use of videoconferencing are also being fueled by the adoption of international interoperability standards. In the past, videoconferencing products were often incompatible because different vendors used different formats. For most organizations, the best solution for ensuring interoperability was to use a single vendor's hardware and software. Today, because most vendors manufacture their products to conform to international standards, interoperability problems have lessened. For example, *H.320* enables equipment manufactured by different vendors to work together over ISDN connections, and *H.323* provides similar interoperability over IP networks including the Internet. MPEG-2 is used in LAN–based videoconferencing systems and in some private WANs. Such standards have bolstered the growth of videoconferencing systems of services to double-digit annual percentages. Further advances in video and audio compression technologies as well as increased availability of broadband services are likely to contribute to increased business use of videoconferencing in the years ahead.

Webcasting

Webcasting is also becoming more common. **Webcasting** may be described as one-way videoconferencing in which all transmitted content is sent from an Internet server to a user's Web browser plug-in. Today's plug-ins typically support streaming video and audio. Unlike the kinds of videoconferencing discussed earlier, with webcasting there is limited interaction between the user and server beyond establishing the connection and beginning the webcast download. Webcasts of live concerts have increased in popularity, and Victoria's Secret fashion show webcasts continue to attract millions of viewers. To date, no international standards for webcasts have been developed; however, RealNetworks.com products are generally considered to be de facto standards for both video and audio webcasting.

Telecommuting and Mobile Computing

Telecommuting

Businesses often leverage voice networks to support telecommuting and mobile computing. **Telecommuting** enables employees to access an organization's shared computing resources from their homes or at other locations, such as telecommuting centers, that are geographically separated from the organization's major operating locations. Traditionally, businesses have preferred to locate their major offices in urban settings, often in expensive downtown locations. Telecommuting allows employees to connect to and use the information resources located at the major business offices from their homes or from telecommuting centers located near their homes in suburban locations. Through telecommuting, organizations can help to minimize the size and operating expense of urban business centers while still ensuring that they have sufficient employees to fulfill work requirements. Today, organizations may have some employees who only telecommute; however, the employee who commutes to the urban office most of the time and telecommutes part of the time is most common.

To support telecommuting, the remote work locations must be appropriately equipped. The typical minimum requirements include a personal computer with a modem, a second telephone line and telephone for business use, and appropriate

webcasting To send live audio or video programming over the Web. Webcasting is the Internet counterpart to traditional radio and TV broadcasting. Webcasting may also be described as a one-way videoconference in which all transmitted content is sent from an Internet server to a user's Web browser plug-in.

telecommuting Working at home and communicating with the office by electronic means. Telecommuting enables employees to access an organization's shared computing resources from their homes or other locations, such as telecommuting centers, that are geographically separated from the organization's major operating locations.

communications and applications software. Employees may use PSTN dial-in circuits to establish connections with LAN modems, communication servers, or the modem in the computer in their personal office at the urban location (LAN modems and communication servers are discussed more fully in Chapter 13). Fax machines are also commonly used by telecommuters. Desktop-to-desktop videoconferencing is increasingly used to provide additional support for telecommuters, especially for providing valuable "face time" with managers and work team members.

Many organizations take advantage of switched or leased digital circuits and CSU/DSUs to provide higher speed connections between *telework* locations and urban offices. ISDN and xDSL lines are being increasingly used to support telecommuting, and T-n connections may be employed to support the remote work of Web designers, engineers, and other power users. Some organizations have chosen to bypass the services available from telephone carriers and use cable modems and other services from CLECs to support their telecommuters.

The results of many research investigations suggest that telecommuting is often associated with increased employee productivity. Some of the factors that contribute to productivity increases include the following:

➤ Being able to work in a quieter, less distracting work environment facilitates concentration.

➤ Telecommuting often enables organizations to move technical support and help-desk operations that involve remote diagnosis and troubleshooting from downtown locations to telework centers. Doing this contributes to reductions in the size and overhead expense of downtown business offices.

➤ The ability to have access to the organization's computing resources both during and outside normal office hours contributes to the ability to meet project deadlines.

➤ Telecommuting enables workers to be productive even when it is necessary for them to stay at home with a sick loved one.

➤ Telecommuting often contributes to increased job satisfaction, decreased worker turnover, and increased employee retention. Over time, these boost overall productivity and profitability through decreased recruiting, training, and turnover costs.

➤ The ability to expand the organization's workforce through full-time, day-shift teleworkers and after-hours workers contributes to increased sales, improved customer service, and improved customer retention.

mobile computing
Using a computing device and wireless transmission services to communicate with home offices while in transit. Mobile computing has expanded the role of broadcast radio in business data communications. It requires a wireless medium such as cellular radio, radio nets, and low-orbit satellites to enable mobile workers to transmit data and messages to home offices from remote locations.

Mobile Computing

Mobile computing involves the provision of remote data communication support for salespeople, field representatives, and customer service representatives while they are "on the road" and away from urban business offices or telework centers. Such workers are often equipped with laptop or notebook computers and portable printers. Many are outfitted with pagers, personal digital assistants (PDAs), and second- or third-generation cellular telephony devices such as "smart phones." Mobile workers may connect to corporate networks from customer locations via dial-up PSTN or cellular connections or through PCS. Such workers may also use the data ports and Internet-access services that are increasingly available at hotels and motels to access the information resources at corporate offices.

Cost justification for mobile computing is provided by the impact that improved communications has on customer service and sales. For example,

➤ Mobile workers are able to maximize "face time" with existing and potential customers. This usually contributes to improved customer service and increased sales.

➤ Customer inquiries can typically be addressed more rapidly.

➤ Mobile computing technologies enable mobile workers to have better communications with coworkers and customer support staff at corporate offices. This enables them to address customer problems more effectively and in a more coordinated manner.

➤ The technologies often enable mobile workers to make better use of their time and to complete more sales calls through the ability to verify customer availability for scheduled contacts and to adjust appointment schedules on the fly.

➤ When appropriately outfitted, mobile workers can stay on the road and in contact with customers for extended periods of time. In addition to enhancing customer service and retention, it minimizes the need for extensive mobile worker office space in business offices. Rather than having large, rarely used home offices for mobile workers, organizations increasingly have a small number of cubicles with network docking stations for mobile workers to use when they are not on the road.

The evolution of cellular telephony networks and services will help to fuel business use of mobile computing technologies in the years ahead. Business use of mobile computing is also facilitated by PBX interfaces for mobile/wireless phones.

Computer-Integrated Telephony

As the name implies, **computer-integrated telephony** (also known as *computer telephone integration—CTI*) integrates telephone and computer technologies for business purposes. The term refers to an increasingly wide range of applications that increase worker productivity and enhance customer service. A common example of CTI involves the use of caller ID (automatic call identification) to trigger the retrieval of a customer's account information from organizational databases. This eliminates the need to ask for the caller's name and account number and expedites addressing the caller's request or problem. By integrating telephone and database technologies in this way, both worker productivity and customer service can be enhanced.

An example of Web-based computer-integrated telephony is the use of standby human attendants to help customers complete online orders. An increasing number of e-commerce Web sites now include "call" buttons. When a customer encounters a problem or has a question when placing an order online, they can click on the "call" button; within a matter of seconds or minutes, a company representative will call the customer. Typically, the company representative's computer screen shows where the customer is in the online order placement process or the problem that they have encountered. Through the use of this form of CTI, organizations have been able to reduce the incidence of aborted online order attempts.

Other examples of computer-integrated telephony applications include the following:

➤ *Audiotext.* Audiotext applications deliver audio information to callers that is based on touch-tone keypad responses to prerecorded prompts and questions.

➤ *Automated call distribution.* This is widely used in call centers that employ a large number of customer service agents/representatives. Callers use a single number (often an 800 number) to contact the organization; incoming calls are automatically distributed to the first available representative. Music/messages on hold applications are often used in conjunction with automatic call distribution; some of these specify the caller's place in the service queue and the estimated time to being served.

➤ *Interactive voice response.* Interactive voice response (IVR) systems are similar to audiotext applications in that callers respond to prompts and questions by using the touch-tone keypads on their phones. IVR applications, however, go beyond audiotext by enabling customers to conduct business transactions. Banking IVR applications, for

computer-integrated telephony Integrates telephone and computer technologies for business purposes. Computer integrated telephony is also called computer telephone integration (CTI) and involves combining data with voice systems in order to enhance telephone services.

example, often enable customers to transfer money from one account (such as savings) to another (such as checking) or to request a banking document to be faxed to them.

➤ *Outbound dialing.* This CTI application is often used by telemarketing centers. It involves the utilization of a telephone number database. The application accesses an uncalled number from the database, automatically dials the number, and quickly passes answered calls to available agents. Although it facilitates the productivity of telemarketers, outbound dialing is not always viewed positively by consumers.

CTI applications development tools are commercially available. Most provide a visual programming environment that facilitates the development of CTI applications using C++ or Visual Basic.

Traditionally, PBXs have played an important role in computer-integrated telephony, especially those that support PBX-to-host interfaces. Today, however, personal computers can be equipped with telephony boards to enable the development of computer-integrated telephony applications that do not directly involve a PBX. In large organizations, client/server CTI is often used. A CTI server that is interfaced with the PBX is used to distribute calls to client PCs. In this way, CTI applications can be implemented on a common shared network.

IP Telephony

Like computer-integrated telephony, IP telephony is an example of the convergence of telephone and computer technologies. Because of the cost savings and cost avoidance potential of utilizing the Internet for voice communications, **IP telephony** (or *voice-over-IP [VoIP]*) is another important voice-oriented business application. Today, VoIP can be implemented as extranets, intranets, within LANs, or through dial-in modem connections. PBXs that support VoIP (those with IP interfaces) can route outgoing calls over the Internet instead of over switched or leased carrier lines. This is illustrated in Figure 5-23.

Packet-switched networks (such as TCP/IP, PDN, frame relay, and cell relay networks) are capable of carrying voice calls very efficiently. Some are capable of providing telephone-quality voice communications by using as little as 8 kbps of bandwidth compared to the 64 kbps that is reserved for each call in standard circuit-switched digital circuits available from common carriers. Because the infrastructure costs associated with building packet-switched networks are lower than traditional alternatives, new providers of voice telephony services increasingly are using packet-switching network architectures.

Organizations have several options for implementing VoIP. They may

➤ Use carrier-provided facilities and carrier-operated network backbones to create private IP–based networks. This is often accomplished by adding a VoIP gateway that is interfaced to the company's PBX at each of its major operating locations and routing interoffice voice traffic through the gateway.

➤ Take advantage of shared (public rather than private) PSTN VoIP gateways available from local exchange carriers (LECs).

➤ Take advantage of VoIP services available from competitive local exchange carriers (CLECs). For example, some cable television service providers also support cable modem and VoIP services for both residential and business customers.

Like VoIP, frame relay networks and services have evolved to the point that they can now be leveraged by organizations to support both voice and data communications. Frame relay networks/services, like packet-switching networks and services, are available from common carriers and third-party vendors. Cell relay networks/

IP telephony The two-way transmission of audio over a packet-switched TCP/IP network. IP telephony is often called *voice-over IP* or *VoIP* when it is implemented in a private intranet or WAN. When used on the public Internet, it is generally called *IP telephony* or *Internet telephony.*

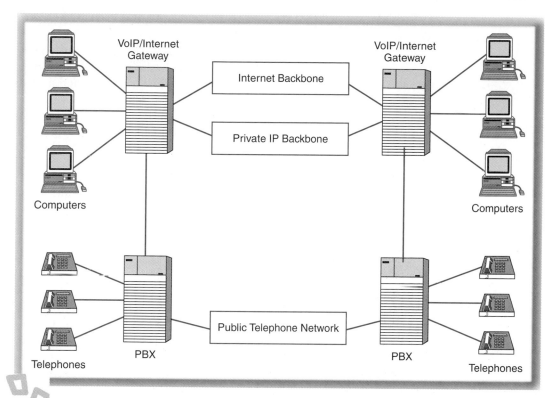

Figure 5-23   Using VoIP to Bypass the PSTN

services (notably ATM—asynchronous transfer mode) are available from these same sources and are capable of supporting voice, data, image, multimedia, and video-conferencing applications. Both frame and cell relay networks are discussed more fully in Chapter 12.

Today, VoIP is one of the hottest networking applications. Organizations that have had large international or domestic long-distance calling expenses are likely to benefit from the maturation of VoIP technologies.

SUMMARY

Common carriers provide the communication infrastructure for local and long-distance data communication. A wide variety of services is available. These services cover switched, leased, and public packet-switching technologies operating at a variety of speeds. The trend has been for faster transmission capabilities and the integration of voice, video, and data.

Historically, national and local governments have regulated telecommunication companies. The regulations typically provide protection for both the consumer and the telecommunication company. Today, this is changing. In many countries, telecommunication providers are evolving to meet the changing demands of international communication. Often, this evolution involves deregulating the communication providers. An example of such deregulation is the U.S. Telecommunications Act of 1996, which enhances competition for local and long-distance services by facilitating the ability of competitive access providers (CAPs) and competitive local exchange carriers (CLECs) to provide voice and data services in local markets.

Today, a company or individual needing communication services can typically choose from several vendors and classes of services. Switched services range from traditional analog services up to 56 kbps to multimegabit digital services such as xDSL and SMDS. Dedicated services such as T-1, T-3, and T-4 and fractional T-n services provide various combinations of speed and cost in North America; E-n services are most common in the rest of the world. Other high-speed services, such as those listed in the Digital Service Hierarchy, the CCITT Digital Hierarchy, and SONET's Optical Carrier (OC) standards, are also available. Today, ISDN services are available from carriers in most areas in the United States.

Packet distribution networks give users the ability to interconnect communication equipment in a variety of locations. PDNs (which are sometimes called VANs—value-added networks) have the benefit of charging only for the packets transferred. For users needing to connect equipment in many locations with a moderate amount of data to be transferred on a regular basis, a PDN can be a compromise between switched and leased services. For some applications, the cost can be lower than those of switched or leased connections.

Mobile communication is a rapidly expanding sector in data communication. Common carriers are increasing the options and speeds of wireless technology. Cellular telephony networks and services are maturing rapidly, and digital personal communication services are growing in popularity. Third-generation cellular services include wireless Internet access and a variety of wireless applications including wireless videophone services. Emerging satellite services will further expand both the availability and speed of mobile communication.

Digital private branch exchanges (PBXs) are widely used by business organizations to support internal voice and data communications as well as access to public telephone network services. Centrex services are widely available from common carriers and provide businesses with PBX–like functionality without the requirement of installing and maintaining their own telephone switch.

Organizations are leveraging voice-oriented networks and services for a variety of business applications such as videoconferencing, telecommuting, mobile computing, computer-integrated telephony, and IP telephony. Organizations now have a variety of videoconferencing options ranging from room-based systems capable of accommodating large geographically dispersed groups to desktop-to-desktop systems that can be used for person-to-person internal and external videoconferences. Telecommuters and mobile workers are able to access and take advantage of corporate computing resources from remote locations such as their residences, customer premises, and hotel rooms. Computer-integrated telephony applications are enhancing the productivity of call center workers and telemarketers. IP telephony is helping organizations to minimize their long-distance voice communication costs by routing voice calls over the Internet or private IP networks.

KEY TERMS

- adaptive differential pulse code modulation (ADPCM)
- asymmetric digital subscriber line (ADSL)
- AT&T divestiture
- cable modem
- Centrex service
- channel service unit/data service unit (CSU/DSU)
- circuit-switched connection
- codec
- competitive access provider (CAP)
- competitive local exchange carrier (CLEC)

- computer-integrated telephony
- conditioning
- digital signal processor (DSP)
- digital subscriber line (DSL)
- end office
- fractional T-n service
- geosynchronous orbit
- Integrated Services Digital Network (ISDN)
- Internet telephony
- leased line
- local access and transport area (LATA)
- local loop
- low-earth-orbit (LEO) satellites
- medium-earth-orbit (MEO) satellites
- mobile computing
- mobile radio services
- packet switching
- personal communication service (PCS)

- point of presence (POP)
- primary center
- private branch exchange (PBX)
- propagation delay
- pulse code modulation (PCM)
- regional Bell operating company (RBOC)
- regional center
- sectional center
- switched multimegabit data service (SMDS)
- synchronous optical network (SONET)
- Telecommunications Reform Act of 1996
- telecommuting
- toll center
- transponder
- videoconferencing
- webcasting
- wireless local loop (WLL)

REVIEW QUESTIONS

1. Describe how the Internet has contributed to the convergence of voice and data communications.
2. Describe the pre–AT&T divestiture telephone system in the United States.
3. What effect did the AT&T divestiture have on the U.S. telephone industry?
4. Describe the characteristics and differences among the following:
   a. end offices
   b. local loops
   c. class 4, class 3, class 2, and class 1 centers
   d. regional Bell operating companies (RBOCs)
   e. local access and transport areas (LATAs)
   f. point of presence (POP)
5. Describe the impacts of the Telecommunications Reform Act of 1996 on the telephone industry.
6. What are CAPS? What are CLECs? Provide examples of CLECs.
7. What is the bandwidth of a voice-grade communication circuit? What are guardbands, and what role do they play in stacked voice-grade circuits?
8. What is the role of touch-tone phones in data communications?
9. Describe the voice digitization process.
10. Describe the differences between PCM and ADPCM.
11. What is meant by voice compression? What is the role of digital signal processors in voice compression?
12. Identify each of the major local loop options available from carriers and CLECs.
13. Describe the differences among each of the following:
    a. ADSL
    b. RADSL
    c. HDSL
    d. VDSL
    e. SDSL
14. Describe the characteristics of cable modems.
15. Describe the characteristics of wireless local loop (WLL) options.
16. Describe the characteristics of PSTN circuit-switched connections.
17. What are the differences between switched connections and leased lines?

18. What is conditioning?
19. Describe the characteristics of a channel service unit/data service unit (CSU/DSU).
20. Describe the differences among dial-up, narrowband, and broadband digital services. Provide examples of each.
21. Describe the characteristics of T-n and fractional T-n services.
22. What is SMDS?
23. Describe each of the following:
    a. the Digital Service Hierarchy
    b. the CCITT Digital Hierarchy
    c. SONET's hierarchy of optical carrier (OC) services.
24. What are the characteristics of ISDN? Describe the differences between BRI and PRI.
25. What are value-added networks (VANs)?
26. What is WATS?
27. What are the characteristics of satellite radio transmission? Describe the differences among the following:
    a. geosynchronous orbits
    b. low earth orbit (LEO)
    c. medium earth orbit (MEO)
28. Describe the role of each of the following in satellite radio transmission:
    a. VSATs
    b. transponders
    c. uplinks and downlinks
    d. FMDA, TMDA, and CMDA
    e. propagation delay
29. Describe the characteristics of cellular telephony networks. What role do MTSOs play in cellular telephony networks?
30. Describe the differences among the three generations of cellular telephone.
31. Describe the characteristics of personal communication services (PCS).
32. What is a PBX? Describe the functions/features supported by PBXs.
33. What are the characteristics of Centrex systems?
34. Identify and briefly describe several major business applications that leverage voice networks.
35. What is the business rationale for videoconferencing?
36. What are the major components of videoconferencing systems? How may videoconferencing systems be categorized?
37. What is webcasting?
38. Compare and contrast telecommuting and mobile computing. What is the business rationale for each? What technologies are associated with each?
39. What is computer-integrated telephony? Identify and briefly describe several computer-integrated telephony applications.
40. What is IP telephony? Why is it growing in popularity among business organizations?

PROBLEMS AND EXERCISES

1. Much has been written about the Telecommunications Reform Act of 1996 and whether it has facilitated/enhanced competition in local telephone markets. Research the literature and summarize what industry experts are saying on this topic.
2. Dialpad.com and Net2phone enable computer users to initiate telephone calls from their computers. Use the Internet to find out more about these products, their costs, configuration requirements, capabilities, and limitations. Summarize your results.

3. Identify competitive access providers (CAPs) and competitive local exchange carriers (CLECs) operating in your area. What services do they provide? What do these services cost, and how do they compare to the services provided by carriers in your area?

4. Research the costs associated with ISDN in your local area. What are the installation and monthly charges?

5. Research the costs associated with subscribing to a PDN. What are the monthly charges, and what are the packet charges?

6. Research the costs for T-n services in your local area.

7. Identify second- and third-generation cellular telephony services available in your area. What are the costs for PCS services?

8. Research the wireless local loop (WLL) available in your local area. Identify typical monthly costs for residential subscribers.

9. Research the xDSL services that are available in your local area. Identify typical installation costs and monthly charges.

10. Use the Internet to identify three major PBX vendors. Describe the characteristics, functionality, and cost ranges for their best selling products.

11. Use the Internet to identify new standards being considered by standard-setting organizations for cellular telephony, PBXs, and videoconferencing.

12. Use the Internet to identify computer-integrated telephony applications beyond those identified in the chapter.

13. Use the Internet to identify several major vendors of desktop-to-desktop videoconferencing products. Describe the characteristics, functionality, and costs of their best-selling products.

14. Use the Internet to research mobile computing and sales force automation technologies. Describe the patterns and trends that may be observed.

15. If an analog line has a bandwidth of 360,000 Hz, how many simultaneous voice or data transmissions can the line carry (that is, how many individual voice-grade dial-up circuits can the line be subdivided into)?

16. It costs approximately $100,000 to equip an upscale videoconferencing room and approximately $1,500 in communication charges for a multipoint 1-day videoconference. Identify the travel costs associated with flying four executives (two each from Denver and Phoenix) to Atlanta for an all-day face-to-face conference; costs should include round-trip airfare (using current business class airfares), $50 for round-trip ground transportation, hotel costs for overnight lodging (at $150 per room per person), and per diems (at $50 day). What is the travel total cost for a face-to-face meeting? How many videoconferences must be held for an organization to recoup its initial investment in the videoconferencing equipment through the elimination of travel costs? How many more videoconferences must be held before the organization will recover its cumulative communication charges from the travel expenses videoconferencing would eliminate?

Chapter Cases
Municipal Networks versus Carriers

We are living in the Information Age, where high-speed networks enable an increasing number of people to access virtually any kind of data and information. However, municipal leaders in many areas, especially those in rural areas, worry that this information revolution will not get to their communities anytime soon. Poor service and slow movement toward broadband Internet-access services from telephone carriers, Internet service providers, and cable companies have encouraged some municipal governments to go on the offensive and build their own fiber optic networks that compete with those provided by private industry. For many communities, the construction and operation of municipal network infrastructures may be the fastest (and in some cases the only) way to deliver advanced telecommunication services to their citizens. Although the creation of municipal networks has some carriers crying "foul," the business reality is that without them, high-speed Internet access would not be available to local citizens. Distant from large markets, small communities in less populous areas (which carriers view as less profitable markets) might otherwise have to wait a long time before private industry provides advanced services.

In Tacoma, Washington, for example, the cable service was so inefficient that the municipal government implemented a fiber optic network to satisfy the community needs. The new network provided residents with high-quality cable images and high-speed Internet connections, and prompted many citizens to change their cable service. To avoid losing its customers, the local cable company had to upgrade its network to compete with the municipal services. Many other cities around the United States have implemented their own fiber optic networks, including LaGrange (Georgia), Gainesville (Florida), and Ashland (Oregon). Other cities, like Glasgow (Kentucky), have extended the technological capabilities of their existing municipal cable systems to allow high-speed Internet connections.

Municipal networks are funded by special municipal bonds or cash generated by local utilities, and according to some city officials, these networks are the Information Age equivalent of improved roads and sewers. For the telecommunications industry, the new competition has not been well received. Regional phone and cable companies

have invested billions to improve their connections to homes and businesses, but the returns have not been as desired. Small communities are the most affected because it is very expensive to extend high-capacity lines to them and to the homes within them. This is part of the reason why only 9 percent of U.S. households had high-speed cable and Internet service by the end of 2001.

Because local governments are less concerned about turning profits, municipalities are more willing to incur the large expenses required to extend high-capacity lines to remote locations. Some municipalities in rural areas started building their own telecommunication networks in the 1960s, but with the passage of the Telecommunications Act of 1996, an explosion of activity has taken place. The act encouraged competition in the provision of cable, Internet, and telephone service, and it also stated that communities could build and operate their own communications infrastructure.

Local governments often have economic reasons for building high-speed networks. High-tech businesses usually require advanced telecommunication systems and services; as a result, a city's telecommunication infrastructure can be an important factor in attracting high-tech firms. Rural towns, as well as large cities, know that an advanced telecommunications network can be a factor in attracting new businesses. For example, the Glasgow, Kentucky, fiber optic network encouraged Franchino Mold & Engineering Co. to open a new facility, in part because the city's network allowed the new facility to easily exchange data with its headquarters in Michigan.

Big phone and cable companies like AT&T complain that government-built systems often receive unfair advantages (such as bond financing and tax exemptions) and are, therefore, less expensive to implement and operate. Municipalities may also have an easier time gaining access to rights-of-way and licensing (because of imminent domain laws and control of licensing boards). Private carriers have pressured some states (like Arkansas, Florida, Texas, and Missouri) to restrict or ban municipal networks from providing telecommunication services. Telecom companies are also trying to stop proposed municipal networks with aggressive local public relations campaigns directed to persuade voters that municipal systems would lose money and be a tax drain. For example, the local cable company in Tacoma asserted in local newspapers that the fiber optic network had lost $15.7 million in 3 years and, therefore, taxpayers would have had to pay that amount.

However, according to a Federal Communications Commission report, competition from cities generally has stimulated private telecom providers to add new services, cut prices, and become more responsive to customers. In Tacoma, the local cable company responded to the municipal networks by putting in new fiber optic lines, lowering cable prices, and introducing an interactive service that combined television and the Internet. Tacoma was the second place in the country where AT&T broadband, which acquired the local cable company in 1999, offered that service.

In order to avoid an "us versus them" mentality, Charlottesville, Virginia, partnered with nTelos, Inc., to implement a fiber optic network. The city saved hundred of thousands of dollars by not having to install the cables needed for the network and granted nTelos right-of-way access to cable trenches and utility poles in exchange for eight strands of "dark" fiber (unused, "unlit" fiber strands) for future expansion. The city now has a 4-node 8.5 mile Ethernet and TCP/IP network running at 622 mbps; it can be upgraded to 2.5 gbps as the city's communication needs grow. The network replaces a 45-mbps ATM network, and it supports H.323 videoconferencing. Support for videoconferencing means that accused criminals can be arraigned without being moved from jail to the courtroom. It also means that prisoners can be examined by University of Virginia doctors without having to leave the jail via telemedicine applications. The city also plans to leverage the network to provide distance learning and video training to schools and fire stations. E-governance applications that will enable citizens to conduct city business without having to set foot in city hall are also planned.

CASE QUESTIONS

1. Outline the arguments for and against allowing municipalities to compete with carriers in the provision of high-speed Internet access. Take a stand for or against such competition and justify your choice.
2. Some private carriers say municipal network initiatives prevent them from providing their services. Do you agree with that statement? Why or why not?
3. Some cities (such as Glasgow, Kentucky) claim that the creation of a high-speed municipal network helps them attract high-tech industries. Use the Internet to find out if this has been the case for any of the other cities mentioned in the case.
4. Some cities (such as Charlottesville, Virginia) have installed networks for cost savings or cost avoidance reasons. Use the Internet to find out if any of the other cities in the case are leveraging the municipal network via applications that reduce or avoid costs.

SOURCES

Armstrong, D., and D. Berman. "Municipal Networks Become Rivals for Fiber Optic Telecom Companies." *Wall Street Journal Online* (August 17, 2001, p. R17).

McCombs, H. "How the Telecommunications Act Affects You." *The American City & County* (August 1997, Issue 112, pp. 30–46).

Rendleman, John. "Virtual Government in Virginia City." *InformationWeek* (February 25, 2001, p. 72).

Strover, S., and L. Berquist. "Telecommunications Infrastructure Development: The State and Local Role." Rural Policy Research Institute–University of Missouri, Iowa State University, and University of Nebraska. Retrieved February 10, 2002, from www.rupri.org/pubs/archive/reports/1999/P99-12/P99-12.PDF.

Note: For more information on voice-oriented networks, see an additional case on the Web site, www.prenhall.com/stamper, "Small Business PBX/Messaging Services."

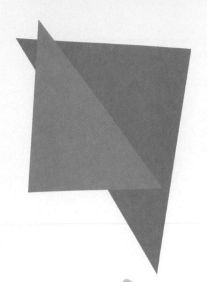

Chapter 6

Modem
Fundamentals

After studying this chapter, you should be able to:

■ Explain the role of modems in Internet connections.

■ Identify and briefly describe the major data encoding schemes used in data communications.

■ Briefly describe the difference between half-duplex and full-duplex transmission.

■ Briefly describe the difference between serial and parallel transmission.

■ Describe the advantages of digital transmission in comparison to analog transmission.

■ Describe the differences among amplitude, frequency, and phase modulation.

■ Identify modem-level data compression approaches.

■ Identify key ITU and MNP modem standards.

■ Briefly describe modem-level security options.

■ Identify and briefly describe data communication error sources and error prevention approaches.

■ Identify and briefly describe data communication error-detection and correction approaches.

■ Briefly explain modem-level flow control processes.

■ Briefly describe the role of communication software in managing modem-level operations.

Despite the growing popularity of broadband Internet-access technologies such as DSL, most consumers still use dial-up modems to establish Internet connections via an Internet Service Provider (ISP). Many businesses also use dial-up modems to gain Internet access or to establish connections between geographically separate operating locations. Because of the prevalence of modem use, it is important for data communication professionals and users to understand modem operations and capabilities. It is also important to study modems because they help to illustrate a variety of fundamental data communication transmission concepts, including signal modulation, half-duplex transmission, serial transmission, flow control, and error detection and correction. In this chapter, attention is focused on how modems work and their roles in data communication. This chapter also focuses on fundamental error-detection and correction processes used by modems and many other kinds of data communications equipment.

DIAL-UP INTERNET ACCESS VIA ISPs

An individual or a business typically gains access to the Internet via an Internet service provider (ISP). In the United States, ISPs provide access to the Internet at three basic levels: national, regional, and local. National providers are commercial entities that sell access to the Internet in various cities. On a national scale, you can access Internet services through providers such as America Online (AOL), EarthLink, and regional or long-distance telephone providers. Regional providers sell access in a region. In the United States, a region might consist of several contiguous states or just a major section of a state. Local and regional telephone providers and regional network companies may serve as regional ISPs. Local providers are proprietors of networks attached to the Internet and provide individual access to the network. An example of a local ISP is Hometown Computing (www.htcomp.net); this firm provides Internet connections in several small towns in Central Texas. Most countries with large numbers of Internet users also have multiple ISPs competing for individual and business subscriptions.

Most ISPs have adopted flat rate subscription plans for individuals and businesses, providing unlimited Internet access for a fixed monthly fee. Business subscriptions to ISPs are typically more costly than individual subscriptions, especially for businesses that enable Internet users to place online orders. Customers need 24/7 access to business commerce servers and, therefore, must always be connected to the ISP or a Web-hosting service. ISPs charge more to business subscribers who require "always on" connections. Some ISPs provide other subscription plans whose cost is tied to the amount of connect time (for example, 100 hours per month for $6 versus unlimited access for $15 a month).

All ISP subscriptions provide Internet access, and most subscriptions also include one or more electronic mailboxes on the ISP's POP e-mail server. Some ISPs provide individual subscribers with disk space on the ISP's Web server for a personal homepage. Web-hosting services ranging from Web page design and content maintenance to full-service e-commerce applications may be available for business subscribers.

Many ISPs provide a variety of connection interfaces, ranging from dial-up connections, ISDN, xDSL, and cable modems. Some ISPs even support T-n services such as T-1 and T-3 connections. **Wireless service providers (WSPs)** are also becoming more prevalent. WSPs are companies that provide wireless Internet access to users with wireless modems, smart phones, or Web-enabled PDAs or handheld computers. The basic and most widely used connection, however, is a dial-up modem connection.

As discussed in Chapter 2, ISPs install a bank of modems for the subscribers and a high-speed connection to another ISP or to a network service provider (NSP) for its own Internet connection. T-1 and T-3 lines are commonly used for ISP-to-ISP and ISP-to-NSP connections. ISPs typically have more subscribers than modems and are able to minimize their communication costs by counting on the fact that not all subscribers will be online at once. Some ISPs may have a user-to-modem ratio of 10 to 1 or more; others have a smaller ratio of 4 or 5 to 1. The user-to-modem ratio affects your ability to access the ISP's network.

The two protocols most commonly used by individual subscribers using dial-up connections to connect to their ISP are the **Serial Line Internet Protocol (SLIP)** and the **point-to-point protocol (PPP)**. The SLIP protocol is older and less desirable than the PPP protocol; today, SLIP is rarely used in the United States. The AppleTalk Remote Access (ARA) protocol enables Macintosh computer users to gain access to the Internet via an ISP over dial-up connections. With each of these protocols, the subscriber's computer is issued an Internet address (IP address) that enables it to send

wireless service provider (WSP) A company that provides wireless Internet access to users with wireless modems, smart phones, or Web-enabled PDAs or handheld computers. Examples of WSPs include GoAmerica Communications, OmniSky, and SprintPCS.

Serial Line Internet Protocol (SLIP) A protocol used for Internet access over serial lines, such as dial-up telephone access. SLIP has been generally replaced by the newer point-to-point (PPP) protocol.

point-to-point protocol (PPP) A protocol used to provide serial transmission to the Internet over serial point-to-point links such as switched telephone connections. Also, a protocol that allows routers to establish data link connections and to exchange configuration information.

and receive packets across the Internet backbone. Although both SLIP and PPP allow the use of the IP protocol over serial lines, PPP is more robust than SLIP because it was expressly developed by the Internet Engineering Task Force (IETF) to provide high-quality connections to the Internet via switched dial-up lines. PPP is widely supported by communication and remote access servers (discussed in Chapter 13); this protocol enables teleworkers and other remote users using dial-up connections to log into LANs to access shared computing resources as they would from a LAN–attached microcomputer.

Because ISPs have more subscribers than modems, they are typically unable to allow all subscribers to simultaneously access the Internet. Subscribers to ISPs with lower subscriber-to-modem ratios (such as 5-to-1) are likely to establish Internet connections more reliably than subscribers to ISPs with higher ratios (such as 15-to-1). Business subscribers should pay particular attention to subscriber-to-modem ratios when selecting an ISP. The quantity and quality of technical support provided by competing ISPs should also be considered when selecting an ISP.

To better understand the role of modems in Internet connections and other kinds of data communications, let us quickly review the basic aspects of the data communication process (see Figure 6-1).

Communication of any kind requires a message, a sender, a receiver, and a medium. In addition, the message should be understandable, and there should be some means of error detection.

When dial-up circuits are used, the sender is typically a microcomputer or terminal equipped with a modem. The sending side of the communication link is responsible for encoding and transmitting a message in a form that receivers at the other end of the communication medium can decode and understand. Senders are also typically responsible for appending error-check information to the messages that they transmit; this information is used by receivers to verify that the messages transmitted to them are complete and correct.

Messages are carried from sender to receiver through some medium of communication. In data communications, a variety of media may be used to carry messages from senders to receivers, including wires, radio waves, and light pulses.

A message and a sender can exist without a receiver; however, without a receiver, no communication takes place. For example, signals have been beamed into space in

Figure 6-1   Essential Features of Data Communications

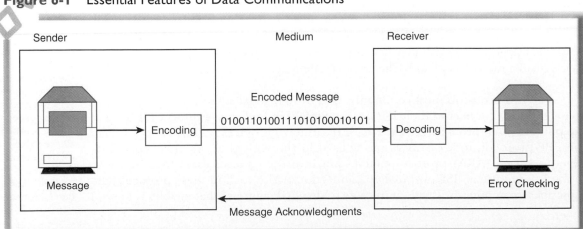

an attempt to contact other intelligent life-forms, but until these signals are received, no communication has occurred. When dial-up circuits are used to transmit messages from senders to receivers, receivers are typically equipped with modems. Modems are always used in pairs; if the sender employs a modem to transmit a message, the receiver must also be equipped with a modem.

If a sender's message is not understood correctly by the receiver, accurate communication does not take place. In human communication, language differences can inhibit a listener from correctly understanding what a speaker is trying to communicate; a translator or interpreter may be necessary to overcome language differences between senders and receivers. Computer systems have similar obstacles to communication. For instance, data can be represented by any of several different codes; the two most common are the American Standard Code for Information Interchange (ASCII) and the Extended Binary-Coded Decimal Interchange Code (EBCDIC). If a message is encoded and transmitted in ASCII, but the receiver only understands EBCDIC, the message will not be understood (or will be incorrectly understood) unless it is translated from ASCII to EBCDIC.

Data communications also involves error detection and correction. This involves the use of special schemes for determining whether an original message has been distorted during transmission. All such schemes involve transmitting additional information along with the data, which increases the chances of detecting errors. Receivers use the additional information to determine whether it contains errors or is error free. When receivers detect errors, they typically ask the sender to retransmit the message. Some error-detection and correction schemes, however, enable receivers to correct errors at their end of the communication medium and reduce the need for message retransmission.

DATA CODES

As Figure 6-1 illustrates, encoding is one of the first requirements of a communication system. Senders must transform the message into a form that is suitable for transmission over the communication medium and understandable (decodable) by the receiver. In data communication, the encoding process involves transforming human readable data (words, numbers, images, and sounds) into a form suitable for transmission over an electronic link. At the other end of the communication medium, the decoding process involves transforming electronic signals back into a human readable form.

In microcomputers and other digital computers, data is stored as sequences of binary digits (bits), each with a value of either 0 or 1. Bits are used because they represent two discrete states (such as "on" and "off") that can be represented by discrete voltage levels, radio signal frequencies, or light frequencies/levels. Because bits can be represented as discrete signals, they can be easily transmitted and received by data communication equipment over both cable-based and wireless communication media. When bits are represented as discrete signals, such as different electric voltage levels, they are considered to be in a **digital format**.

To provide meaning to a sequence of bits, you must set up the number of bits that will be grouped to represent each individual data character. The series of bits that represents an individual character (such as the lowercase letter *h*) is called a **byte**. The number of bits that make up the characters also determines the number of distinct characters that can be represented. Once the number of bits per byte is decided, it becomes possible to create an encoding scheme, or translation table, by which the system translates each character into a unique group of bits. Table 6-1 lists several data encoding schemes as well as the number of bits per character and the number of characters that can be represented by those codes.

digital format When bits are represented as discrete signals, such as different electric voltage levels, they are considered to be in a digital format.

byte A fixed-length series of bits that represents an individual character (such as the lowercase letter *h*). Traditionally, a byte is made up of eight binary digits (bits).

Table 6-1 Common Data Codes

Coding Scheme	Number of Bits	Characters Representable
Standard ASCII	7	128
Extended ASCII	8	256
EBCDIC	8	256
Unicode (ISO 10646)	16	65,536

Some encoding schemes used in communication systems are not well suited for data communications because the number of bits representing individual characters is variable rather than fixed. For example, in the encoding scheme of telegraphy, Morse code, each character is represented as a combination of dots and dashes. Although these could be also interpreted as "bits," Morse code is not suitable for data communication because individual characters are represented by a different number of bits (for example, the letter *A* is represented by dot-dash and the letter *S* by dot-dot-dot). Telegraphers distinguish one letter grouping from another by the time delay between characters. Such a scheme is not practical for computer-based systems. As a result, virtually all computer codes use a fixed number of bits per character.

ASCII

American Standard Code for Information Interchange (ASCII) A code that uses 7 or 8 bits to represent characters. ASCII is one of the most widely used character encoding schemes.

American Standard Code for Information Interchange (ASCII) and EBCDIC (see next section) are the most commonly used data encoding schemes. ASCII (also known as *USASCII* and *IRA—International Reference Alphabet*) is the most widely used data code. It was once implemented primarily as a 7-bit code, but today, the extended 8-bit version is also widely used. With 7 bits, 128 (2^7) characters can be represented; with 8 bits, 256 (2^8) characters are available. As an alternative to the 8-bit code, the 7-bit form can be extended by using reserved control characters to shift from one character set to another. Extending the number of characters provides additional character sets for graphics and for foreign languages such as Katakana. The 7-bit ASCII code is presented in Table 6-2.

EBCDIC

Extended Binary-Coded Decimal Interchange Code (EBCDIC) A character encoding scheme that uses 8 bits to represent each character. This data code was first used in the 1960s on the IBM System/360 and is still used in IBM mainframes and most IBM midrange computers.

Extended Binary-Coded Decimal Interchange Code (EBCDIC) uses 8 bits to form a character; 256 characters can be represented. The EBCDIC code is presented in Table 6-3. As Tables 6-2 and 6-3 show, both ASCII and EBCDIC have some codes (such as ASCII 0000000 and 0000011) with mnemonic names such as NUL and ETX. These special characters are used to provide control information to nodes on the network as well as to delineate data bits and overhead information in packets.

The EBCDIC tables show gaps following the letters *i, r, z, I, R,* and *Z.* The gaps represent unassigned bit values. This is a disadvantage because the unassigned bit values fall within the letter sequence; the ASCII tables have no such gaps. If these values are ever assigned, it may interrupt the collating sequence of the letters. The gaps also make arithmetic operations on the characters more difficult. In ASCII, we can obtain the numeric value of an ASCII character and manipulate it arithmetically, such as by adding 15 to the numeric representation of the letter *A* to obtain the letter 15 characters down the alphabet from A; this may be used by a data encryption algorithm.

Table 6-2 The USACSII 7-Bit Code

Low-Order Bias	High-Order Bits							
	000	001	010	011	100	101	110	111
0000	NUL	DLE	SPACE	0	@	P	`	p
0001	SOH	DC1	!	1	A	Q	a	q
0010	STX	DC2	"	2	B	R	b	r
0011	ETX	DC3	#	3	C	S	c	s
0100	EOT	DC4	$	4	D	T	d	t
0101	ENQ	NAK	%	5	E	U	e	u
0110	ACK	SYN	&	6	F	V	f	v
0111	BEL	ETB	'	7	G	W	g	w
1000	BS	CAN	(	8	H	X	h	x
1001	HT	EM	)	9	I	Y	i	y
1010	LF	SUB	*	:	J	Z	j	z
1011	VT	ESC	+	;	K	[	k	{
1100	FF	FS	,	<	L	\	l	|
1101	CR	GS	-	=	M	]	m	}
1110	SO	RS	.	>	N	^	n	~
1111	SI	US	/	?	O	—	o	DEL

Table 6-3(a) The EBCDIC 8-Bit Code

Low-Order Bias	High-Order Bits							
	0000	0001	0010	0011	0100	0101	0110	0111
0000	NUL	DLE	DS		SPACE	@	-	
0001	SOH	DC1	SOS					
0010	STX	DC2	FS	SYN				
0011	ETX	DC3						
0100	PF	RES	BYP	PN				
0101	HT	NL	LF	RS				
0110	LC	BS	ETB	UC				
0111	DEL	IL	ESC	EOT				
1000		CAN						
1001	RLF	EM						\
1010	SMN	CC	SM		¢	!	|	:
1011					.	$	'	#
1100	FF	IFS		DC4	<	*	%	@
1101	CR	IGS	ENQ	NAK	(	)	-	'
1110	SO	IRS	ACK		+	;	>	=
1111	SI	IUS	BEL	SUB	|		?	"

Table 6-3(b)   The EBCDIC 8-Bit Code

			High-Order Bits						
		1000	1001	1010	1011	1100	1101	1110	1111
	0000					{	}	\	0
	0001	a	j	~		A	J		1
	0010	b	k	s		B	K	S	2
	0011	c	l	t		C	L	T	3
	0100	d	m	u		D	M	U	4
Low-Order Bias	0101	e	n	v		E	N	V	5
	0110	f	o	w		F	O	W	6
	0111	g	p	x		G	P	X	7
	1000	h	q	y		H	Q	Y	8
	1001	i	r	z		I	R	Z	9
	1010								
	1011								
	1100								
	1101								
	1110								
	1111								

Another disadvantage of EBCDIC is that some characters—such as [and]—have not been defined. Omission of these characters raises problems in programming languages such as Pascal and C, which use these symbols.

Unicode

In the early days of computing, 5-bit and 6-bit data codes were employed in data communications. The transition from 5-bit and 6-bit codes to the 7-bit and 8-bit codes used today was necessary to increase the number of unique characters that could be represented. Today, the two most common data communication codes (ASCII and EBCDIC) are 7-bit and 8-bit codes, which are able to represent 128 and 256 unique symbols, respectively. For more than a decade, data communication experts have been debating whether this is a sufficient number of symbols. An 8-bit code can represent the 26-letter Roman alphabet (both uppercase and lowercase), the 10 Arabic numerals (0 through 9), and punctuation, totaling approximately 100 characters and symbols. Additional bit patterns may be required for line control, so perhaps up to 128 characters can be used. What are the rest of the bit combinations used for in an 8-bit code?

For one thing, there may be a need to accommodate other alphabets, such as Greek and Cyrillic (Russian), and their accompanying diacritical marks, such as the tilde, umlaut, and accents. Still, 256 bits can accommodate the Roman alphabet and one other alphabet, with characters left over—until we look at Asian and Middle Eastern languages. The Kanji character set used for written communication in Japan and China, however, contains more than 30,000 ideograms and symbols. Clearly, 256 unique symbols do not go very far toward accommodating the needs of these Asian languages. In addition to accommodating various alphabets, a data code may need to transmit, store, manipulate, and display graphic information, thus requiring additional characters. Line drawing characters can easily exceed 100 different symbols.

Several microcomputers use an extended ASCII code to permit use of business graphics symbols. Traditional data communication data codes are, however, inadequate for meeting the communication demands among different cultures and languages. To address the limitations of 8-bit codes, a 16-bit international data code has been created. This data encoding scheme is alternatively known as *ISO 10646* and Unicode.

Unicode is capable of representing 65,536 (2^{16}) characters. Because it is backward compatible with ASCII, Unicode includes the Roman alphabet, Arabic numerals, and the punctuation and special symbols found in the ASCII table. It also includes the Greek, Hebrew, Russian, and Sanskrit alphabets as well as more than 2,000 Han characters for Asian languages such as Chinese, Japanese, and Korean. A large number of mathematical and technical symbols, punctuation marks, and publishing symbols are also supported by Unicode. Unicode is supported by an increasing number of microcomputer operating systems, including Windows NT, Windows 2000, and Windows XP.

Unicode A data-encoding scheme capable of representing 65,536 (2^{16}) characters. A superset of the ASCII character set that uses two bytes for each character rather than one. Because it is able to handle more than 65,000 character combinations, it can represent the alphabets of most of the world's languages. Alternatively known as *ISO 10646*.

Touch-Tone Telephone Code

As discussed in Chapter 5, touch-tone telephone code turns a touch-tone telephone into a data communication terminal. Some banks allow customers to pay bills and transfer money between accounts using touch-tone telephones, and many colleges and universities allow students to register for classes using touch-tone telephones. Telephones have 12 keys, so 12 different codes can be transmitted. Each key on the telephone keypad transmits a high frequency and a low frequency. The combination of the two frequencies uniquely defines which key has been pressed. Because only 12 key codes are available, the telephone is limited in its use as a data communication input device.

TRANSMITTING ENCODED DATA

Serial Versus Parallel Transmission

The bits that represent an encoded character can be transmitted either simultaneously or one at a time. When the bits are transmitted simultaneously, it is called **parallel transmission**. When parallel transmission is used for data communications, multiple wires connect the sender and receiver, and the bits that make up a single encoded character are transmitted simultaneously over different wires. When the bits are transmitted in sequence, one at a time, over the same wire, it is called **serial transmission**. Both parallel and serial transmission are depicted in Figure 6-2.

Parallel transmission is used internally within digital computers to send data between components. It is also widely used to transmit/receive data via a microcomputer's parallel port. Although a printer is commonly connected to a microcomputer via its parallel port, some input devices, such as scanners, may interface with the microcomputer via the parallel port. Some printers are capable of interfacing with microcomputers via the serial port. USB (universal serial bus) ports have emerged as popular alternatives to parallel and serial ports because they support higher input and output transmission speeds. FireWire ports support higher transmission speeds than USB ports and are widely used to attach digital cameras and other video devices to the computer.

Serial transmission is more widely used than parallel transmission for data communication; both USB and FireWire use serial transmission. Although parallel transmission is faster than serial transmission because it is capable of transmitting multiple bits per clock cycle rather than one bit per clock cycle, it is limited to short distance transmissions (such as those between a computer and an attached printer). The wires in a parallel cable are likely to have slightly different transmission speeds, and after traveling for more than a few meters, it is quite possible for bits transmitted during

parallel transmission When the bits that make up a byte are transmitted simultaneously. Parallel transmission involves transmitting one or more bytes at a time using a cable with multiple lines dedicated to data (8, 16, 32 lines, etc.).

serial transmission When the bits that make up a byte are transmitted in sequence, one at a time, over the same wire.

```
Message to Be Transmitted: LINE
Representation: ASCII
L    1001100
I    1001001
N    1001110
E    1000101
1001100  1001001  1001110  1000101
L        I        N        E
(a) Bit Serial Transmission
        1 1 1 1
        0 0 0 0
        0 0 0 0
        1 1 1 0
        1 1 0 1
        0 0 1 0
        0 1 0 1
        L I N E
(b) Bit Parallel Transmission
```

Figure 6-2   Serial Versus Parallel Transmission

different clock cycles to reach the receiver at the same time. If this happens, the decoding process in the receiver will interpret characters that are different from what the sender transmitted, and communication errors will occur.

Asynchronous Versus Synchronous Transmission

Electronic communication systems use electric currents to encode/represent bits. As Figure 6-3 illustrates, negative voltage might be used to represent a 1 bit and positive voltage used to represent a 0 bit on a wire connecting sender and receiver. In such a scheme, receivers interpret positive voltage signals as 0 bits and negative voltage signals as 1 bits.

asynchronous transmission (async) The oldest and one of the most common data link protocols. Each character is transmitted individually with its own error detection scheme, usually a parity bit. The sender and receiver are not synchronized with each other. Also known as start-stop protocol.

Asynchronous Transmission   **Asynchronous transmission (async)** is the oldest and one of the most common data link protocols. Like many of the techniques used in data communication, it is derived from the telegraph and telephone industries. In asynchronous transmission, data is transmitted one character at a time, and sender and receiver are not synchronized with each other. The sender is thus able to transmit a character at any time, and there may be lengthy delays between transmissions. The receiver must be prepared to recognize that information is arriving, accept the data, possibly check for errors, and print, display, or store the data in memory. Individual characters also can be separated over different time intervals, meaning that no synchronization exists between individual transmitted characters.

Modems for dumb terminals typically support asynchronous transmission, and those for smart and intelligent terminals can also typically communicate asynchronously. Modems for personal computers may use async transmission via their serial port for microcomputer-to-host connections; however, most of the modems used with today's microcomputers are capable of both asynchronous and synchronous transmission.

Asynchronous transmission is also called a *start–stop protocol*. This term and the terms *mark* (1 bit) and *space* (0 bit) are holdovers from telegraphy. It is called

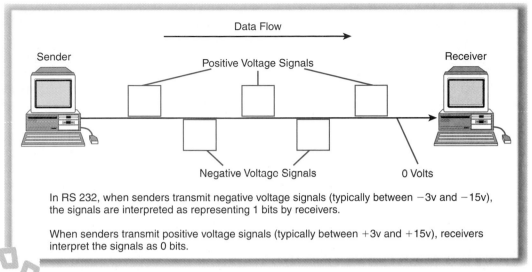

In RS 232, when senders transmit negative voltage signals (typically between −3v and −15v), the signals are interpreted as representing 1 bits by receivers.

When senders transmit positive voltage signals (typically between +3v and +15v), receivers interpret the signals as 0 bits.

Figure 6-3   Using Positive and Negative Voltage Levels to Represent 0 and 1 Bits

start–stop because each character is framed by at least one start bit and at least one stop bit, as illustrated in Figure 6-4. Before establishing a communication session, the sending and receiving modems must agree on the number of bits that will be used to represent each data character (typically 7 or 8). This is one of the negotiations that occurs between modems during the **handshaking** process. The two modems must also agree on the use of parity for error detection. If parity checking is to be used, both modems must agree on either even or odd parity and on the number of parity bits that will be used. Typically, only 1 parity bit is transmitted per character, but it is possible to include more than 1 parity bit per transmitted character. When 2 parity bits are used, one can be used to check the character's higher order bits, and the other can be used to check the character's lower order bits. The two modems must also agree on a transmission speed, because this determines how often the receiver will sample the line for

handshaking Signals are transmitted back and forth over a communication network that establishes a valid connection between two stations.

Figure 6-4   Asynchronous Transmission of the ASCII-7 Letter *F*

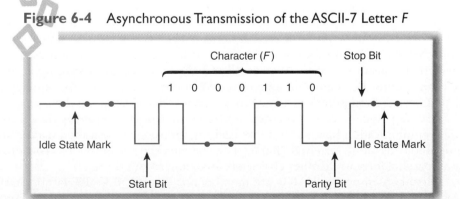

incoming characters. Finally, there must be agreement as to what will terminate the communication session between modems. A session terminator may be defined as a set of characters called *interrupt characters,* a count of a specific number of characters, or a timeout interval. For the following discussion, we will assume that sending and receiving modems have completed the handshaking process and have agreed on the number of bits per character (7), parity (1 parity bit, odd parity), session termination, and maximum transmission speed.

An asynchronous communication link between sender and receiver is either idling or transmitting data. In the idle state, the async line is held in the mark condition, which is a continuous stream of 1 bits. To transmit a character, the sending modem first transmits a start bit (a 0 bit) and then the bits representing the character; this is followed by the parity bit (based on the number of 1 bits for the encoded character) and a stop bit. A character's arrival at the receiver is signaled by a start bit, which is a change in the state of the line from a mark (1) to a space, or a 0 bit. The start bit is followed by 7 data bits, 1 parity bit, and a stop bit, which is a return to a 1 bit or mark condition. The ASCII representation for the character *F* is 1000110; the async representation for transmitting this character is given in Figure 6-4. After a character is transmitted, the line goes back to the idle state until the next start bit is encountered.

The UART   At the heart of asynchronous transmission is a processing chip called the **universal asynchronous receiver/transmitter (UART)**. The UART accepts characters via parallel transmission from the terminal or computer and places them on the circuit serially. (Recall that parallel transmission is used to transmit data between components within the computer.) It also accepts bit serial transmissions from the communication line and passes the characters to the data terminal equipment in bit parallel fashion. The UART is the interface between the parallel transmission within the computer and the serial port. It is responsible for parallel to serial conversion and vice versa.

To detect an incoming character, the UART typically samples the state of the communication circuit at a rate 16 times the expected bit rate. On a 1,200-bps line, 1 bit passes every $1/1,200 = 0.000833 = 0.833$ ms, so a sampling of the line is taken every 52 microseconds. (Today, much higher line speeds are common; the 1,200 bps is only used because of its easier mathematical calculations.) Figure 6-4 illustrates this situation. The line is sampled so often to identify immediately when the state of the line has changed from the mark condition to the space condition.

Having detected the start bit, the UART then assembles the next 7 bits that should make up the character. The ninth bit, the parity bit, follows the start bit and the 7 data bits. The parity bit is received and checked against the 7 data bits already received. If parity does not check, then a parity error message is sent to the transmitter so the character can be retransmitted. If parity checks, the next bit is examined to see whether it is a stop bit or a mark condition. If a stop bit or mark condition is not detected, a transmission error is assumed to have occurred. If everything is correct, the UART sends the character, now converted to the form needed for parallel transmission over the computer's internal buses, and returns to sampling the line.

A UART usually has two registers (buffers) available for receiving data from the serial communication line and two for receiving internally transmitted data from the computer. This allows received characters to be checked for parity and converted to serial/parallel form while other characters are being received.

Most contemporary UARTs are members of the 16550 UART family. A 16550 UART has 16-byte buffers (previous UART generations had 1-byte buffers) and are

universal asynchronous receiver/transmitter (UART)
Accepts characters via parallel transmission from the terminal or computer and places them on the circuit serially.

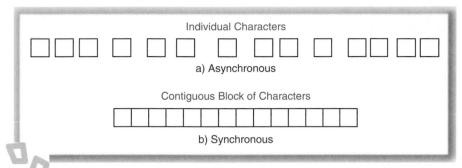

Figure 6-5   Asynchronous Versus Synchronous Transmission

capable of transmission speeds up to 115.2 kbps. Microcomputers are equipped with a UART for each serial port. A UART is also included on internal modem cards; when a modem card is used, parallel/serial conversion is performed by the UART on the card itself because the UARTs for the serial ports are bypassed.

Synchronous Transmission   **Synchronous transmission** allows sender and receiver to be synchronized with each other. Modems that support synchronous transmission have internal clocks that are set in time with the modem at the other end of the communication line by a bit pattern, or sync pattern, transmitted at the beginning of a message. For long messages, these sync patterns are periodically inserted within the text to ensure that the modem clocks remain synchronized. Synchronized clocks are one feature that separates asynchronous transmission by modems from synchronous transmission; although there is a clocking function in async transmission, the two modem clocks are not synchronized. In synchronous transmission, the failure to remain synchronized results in communication errors and possible data loss.

Another difference between asynchronous and synchronous transmission is that instead of serially transmitting character by character, synchronous transmission involves sending a block of characters at a time. Figure 6–5 illustrates the differences between asynchronous and synchronous transmission. The modems used in today's data communication networks typically support synchronous as well as asynchronous communication sessions.

Synchronous transmission is typically more efficient than asynchronous communications because the percentage of data bits to overhead bits is significantly less. Hence, the number of data bits transmitted in a given time interval (data throughput) is typically higher for synchronous than for asynchronous transmission. For example, asynchronous transmission using 1 start bit, 7 bits per character, 1 parity bit, and 1 stop bit is only 70 percent efficient; the packets used in synchronous transmission, however, are typically more than 90 percent efficient.

synchronous transmission The transmission of data in which both stations are synchronized. Codes are sent from the transmitting station to the receiving station to establish the synchronization, and data is then transmitted in continuous streams. Modems that support synchronous transmission have internal clocks that are set in time with the modem at the other end of the communication line by a bit pattern, or sync pattern, transmitted at the beginning of a message.

DATA FLOW

Every data communication network must have some mechanism for control over the flow of data between senders and receivers. This is accomplished at two levels. The first level provides for contention control, which determines which sender(s) may transmit at a given point in time, the conditions under which transmission of data is allowed, and the pacing of data transmission. The more basic level of data flow relates to the transmission equipment used: lines, modems, and computing devices. The three elementary kinds of data flow are simplex, half duplex, and full duplex.

Simplex Transmission

In simplex transmission, data may flow in only one direction, like traffic on a one-way street. Radio and television transmissions, illustrated in Figure 6-6(a), are examples. In simplex transmission, one station assumes the role of transmitter, and the other station is the receiver; these roles may not be reversed. Although this may appear rather limiting, simplex transmission has numerous applications. Devices such as keyboards, microcomputer monitors, and optical character recognition (OCR) scanners involve simplex communication. Communication with printers that are capable of transmitting status information back to the host is not classified as simplex, but data collection devices that serve as input devices only do use simplex communication. In solar energy research installations, heat sensors, solar monitors, and flow meters are used to monitor the environment and transmit samples of data via a simplex line. A building environmental monitoring system also operates in this mode, sending temperature and humidity readings to a computer that controls the heating and cooling of the building. Simplex lines are less common in business applications than half-duplex or full-duplex lines. Simplex lines are used for some printers, for monitoring devices in environment and process control applications, for transmitting stock exchange data (stock tickers), and for most radio and cable television data transmissions.

Figure 6-6   Examples of Data Flow

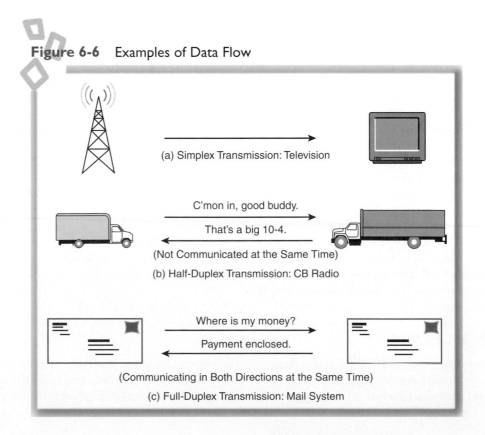

(a) Simplex Transmission: Television

C'mon in, good buddy.

That's a big 10-4.

(Not Communicated at the Same Time)

(b) Half-Duplex Transmission: CB Radio

Where is my money?

Payment enclosed.

(Communicating in Both Directions at the Same Time)

(c) Full-Duplex Transmission: Mail System

Half-Duplex Transmission

In half-duplex transmission, data may travel in both directions, although only in one direction at a time, like traffic on a one-lane bridge. Figure 6-6(b) shows the example of citizens' band (CB) radio, where radio operators on the same frequency may be either sender or receiver but not both at the same time. Half-duplex transmission is a common method of flow control in local area networks (LANs). Modem-to-modem communications may also be half duplex.

Full-Duplex Transmission

In full-duplex mode, data can be transmitted in both directions simultaneously, like traffic on a two-way street. An example of data transmission using full-duplex capabilities is the postal service: Letters can be transmitted in both directions simultaneously, as illustrated in Figure 6-6(c). Figure 6-7 shows that with full-duplex communication a network node functions simultaneously as a sender and receiver; this is not the case with half-duplex or simplex transmission. Full-duplex operations are effected in radio-wave transmissions by using two different frequencies, one for each direction. With coaxial cable, full-duplex operations require broadband transmission, the ability to take the cable's total bandwidth and divide it into subchannels to enable bidirectional transmission over different subchannels. Switched telephone connections commonly use full-duplex flow control, and because the majority of modem-to-modem communication sessions occur over switched dial-up connections, most of the modems used with today's microcomputers are capable of full-duplex transmission.

INTERFACES AND INTERFACE STANDARDS

Interfaces between computer equipment and communications media are largely determined by the nature of the communication medium itself. We have already noted that data communication networks can be classified as cable-based or wireless. Twisted-pair wires, coaxial cable, and fiber optic cables are the most widely used kinds of cabling in LANs and other data communication networks. Different interfaces/connectors are used for each of these different kinds of cabling, and wireless interfaces are different from those for cable-based networks.

Figure 6-7   Data Flow Alternatives

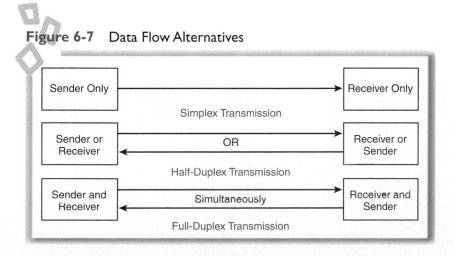

No discussion of interfaces and interface standards is complete without differentiating between the two major classes of data communication equipment. The two classes of equipment in data communication are **data communications equipment (DCE)** (modems, media, and media support facilities such as telephone switching equipment, packet/frame relay access devices and switches, routers, microwave relay stations, and satellite transponders) and **data terminating equipment (DTE)** (including terminals, servers, and workstations). The physical interface is the manner in which these two classes of equipment are joined together. Figure 6-8 depicts a data communication linkage, with the DCE and DTE components identified.

The interface between DCE and DTE can be divided into four aspects: mechanical, electrical, functional, and procedural. The mechanical portion includes the kind of connectors to be used, the number of pin connections in the connectors, and the maximum allowable cable lengths. The electrical characteristics include the allowable line voltages and the representations for the various voltage levels. The functional interface specifies which signals—timing, control, data, or ground leads—are to be carried by each pin in the connector. Table 6-4 lists the signals assigned to each of the 25 pins in an RS-232-C interface.

Procedural characteristics define how signals are exchanged and delineate the environment necessary to transmit and receive data. One pin or conducting wire in the connector might represent the ability of a DTE device to accept a transmission; when the DTE device is ready to receive data, a signal is raised on that lead. When no signal is raised on that circuit, transmission to the terminal is not valid. Table 6-5 shows a procedural interface to transmit from a host to a terminal.

Interface Standards

Numerous standards are adhered to in establishing an interface between DCE and DTE. The following brief descriptions familiarize you with the major standards and what they generally cover.

data communications equipment (DCE) One class of equipment in data communication, including modems, media, and media support facilities. Also called data circuit-terminating equipment.

data terminating equipment (DTE) A computer or terminal that is the source or destination of signals on a network.

Figure 6-8   DTE and DCE Components

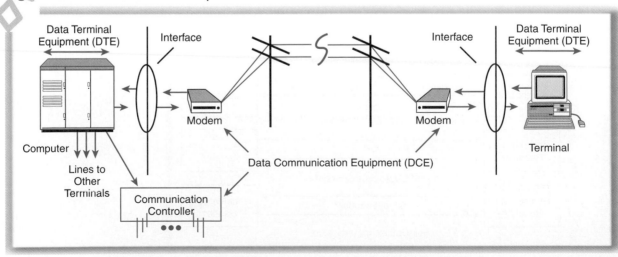

Table 6-4   Interface Connector Pin Assignments

Pin Number	Circuit	Description
1	AA	Protective ground
2	BA	Transmitted data
3	BB	Received data
4	CA	Request to send
5	CB	Clear to send
6	CC	Data set ready
7	AB	Signal ground (common return)
8	CF	Received line signal detector
9	—	(Reserved for modem testing)
10	—	(Reserved for modem testing)
11		Unassigned
12	SCF	Secondary for pin 8
13	SCB	Secondary clear to send
14	SBA	Secondary transmitted data
15	DB	Transmission signal timing
16	SBB	Secondary received data
17	DD	Receiver signal timing
18		Unassigned
19	SCA	Secondary request to send
20	CD	Data terminal ready
21	CG	Signal quality detector
22	CE	Ring indicator
23	CH/CI	Data signal rate selector
24	DA	Transmit signal element timing
25		Unassigned

Table 6-5   Procedural Interface Between Processor and Terminal

1. Processor and terminal raise data terminal ready signal to modem.
2. Modems raise data set ready signal.
3. Processor raises RTS (request to send) signal.
4. Processor's modem sends a carrier signal.
5. Terminal's modem detects carrier and raises CD (carrier detect) signal to processor's modem.
6. Processor sends data on transmit data.
7. Processor's modem modulates data onto the carrier wave.
8. Terminal's modem demodulates data onto received data.
9. Processor lowers RTS signal.
10. Processor's modem drops CTS and carrier wave.
11. Terminal's modem drops CD.
12. Transmission is complete.

RS-232-C   Currently in the United States, the predominant interface standard is the Electronic Industries Association (EIA) RS-232-C standard; for microcomputers, it has become synonymous with the term *serial port*. RS-232-C is the most widely acceptable standard for transferring encoded characters across copper wires between a computer or terminal and a modem. This standard defines serial, asynchronous communication.

The RS-232-C standard was established in October 1969 and reaffirmed in June 1981. RS-232-C encompasses serial binary data interchange at rates up to 20,000 bps and a recommended distance of up to 50 feet; longer distances are possible for shielded wires. (Shielded wire is certified by the manufacturer as capable of spanning 500 feet at 9,600 bps.) When used in conjunction with members of the 16550 family of UARTs, speeds up to 115.2 kbps are possible. RS-232-C has its greatest application in interfacing to wire media, where this bit transmission rate is most common. It covers private, switched, and leased connections, with provisions for autoanswer switched connections. In serial binary transmission (or bit serial transmission), bits are transmitted in single file on the wire. RS-232-C addresses character transmission with 7 data bits per character. Voltage levels used to transmit data range from –15 volts to +15 volts (see Figure 6-9). Negative voltages are used to represent 1 bits, and positive voltages are used to represent 0 bits.

The RS-232-C standard does not specify size or kind of connectors to be used in the interface. It does define 25 signal leads, 3 of them unassigned, 2 reserved for testing, and the remaining 20 used for grounding, data, control, and timing (see Table 6-4). In the absence of a standard, one connector—a 25-pin connector—has become common in implementing RS-232-C connections. Actual transmissions typically use fewer than 25 signal leads. A simple modem interface can require that only 7 pins be active, yet on occasion connectors supporting 15, 9, and 7 pins are used to interface with these devices. The RS-232-C standard covers all four aspects of the interface: mechanical, electrical, functional, and procedural. This is significant because other interface specifications treat them separately, which means two or three standards may be cited that together form the equivalent of what is specified by RS-232-C.

Figure 6-9   RS-232-C Signaling Conventions

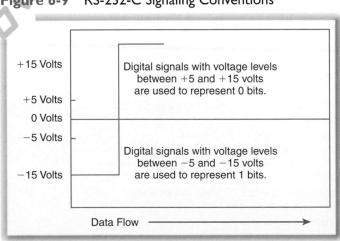

RS-422   The RS-422 standard addresses speeds up to 10 mbps over distances up to 1,200 feet. Usually associated with a 37-pin connector (that can also be implemented on a 25-pin or 9-pin connector), this EIA electrical specification mandates a balanced ground line for each signal pin rather than a shared common ground.

RS-423   The RS-423 standard addresses speeds up to 10 mbps over distances up to 1,200 feet. Like RS-422, RS-423 is usually associated with a 37-pin connector (but may also be implemented on a 25-pin or 9-pin connector). This EIA electrical specification mandates a shared common ground wire for the signal pins in the connector.

RS-449   Because of the speed and distance constraints of the RS-232-C standard, the EIA RS-449 standard was adopted. It provides for a 37-pin connection, cable lengths up to 200 feet, and data transmission rates up to 2 mbps. RS-449 equates with the functional and procedural portions of RS-232-C. (The electrical and mechanical specifications are covered by RS-422 and RS-423.)

ISO and ITU Standards   The International Standards Organization (ISO) and the Consultative Committee on International Telegraph and Telephony (CCITT), a sub-committee of the International Telecommunications Union (ITU), also have adopted standards that are widely used. The most significant of these international standards for interfaces are briefly described here.

- ➤ ISO-2110: A functional interface standard similar to the functional portion of RS-232-C, describing which signals will be carried on specific pins
- ➤ ITU V.10 and V.11: Electrical interfaces similar to those specified by RS-422 and RS-423
- ➤ ITU V.24: Covers both the functional and the procedural aspects of a 25-pin interface similar to that specified by RS-232-C
- ➤ ITU V.25: Covers the procedural aspects of establishing and terminating automatic calling unit connections over switched lines
- ➤ ITU V.28: Covers the electrical interface in a manner similar to that of RS-232-C
- ➤ ITU V.35: Defines a 34-pin connection for interfaces with speeds of 48,000 bps
- ➤ ITU V.50: Addresses serial transmission up to 48 kbps using an M-block connector; V.35 widely used on DCE that interfaces with high-speed carrier services
- ➤ ITU X.20 and X.21: Cover the interface between DCE and DTE for packet distribution networks (PDNs) (PDNs are discussed in detail in Chapter 12.)
- ➤ ITU X.24: Covers the functional aspects of interface for PDNs

USB and FireWire

USB (Universal Serial Bus) is a hardware interface for connecting peripheral devices such as a keyboard, mouse, joystick, scanner, printer, or camera to a computer. Since first appearing in 1997, USB has rapidly become a popular interface largely because it has a maximum bandwidth of 12 mbits/second, which is much faster than the speeds supported by traditional serial and parallel ports. USB enables peripherals to be daisy-chained through and enables up to 127 devices to be attached to a computer via a single USB port. External multiport USB hubs are available that enable multiple peripheral devices to share a single USB port on the computer. Fast peripheral devices can use the full bandwidth; lower speed ones can transfer data using a 1.5 mbits/second subchannel. USB also supports MPEG-1 and MPEG-2 digital video.

USB also supports *hot swapping;* hot swap capability allows peripheral devices to be plugged in and unplugged without turning the system off and rebooting. Full support

Universal Serial Bus (USB) A hardware interface for peripherals such as the keyboard, mouse, joystick, scanner, printer, and telephony devices that also supports MPEG-1 and MPEG-2 digital video. USB has a transmission speed of 12 mbps and supports up to 127 attached devices.

for USB, including hot swapping, began with Windows 98. The most recent version of USB, USB 2.0, supports a maximum bandwidth of 480 mbits/second. This solidifies USB's chances of being the serial interface of the future against challengers such FireWire.

FireWire is a high-speed serial bus that allows for the connection of up to 63 peripheral devices through a single FireWire port. Originally developed by Apple and Texas Instruments, FireWire is also known as the *IEEE 1394 standard,* the *i.Link connector,* and the *high-performance serial bus (HPSB).* The original IEEE 1394 standard addressed transfer rates of 100, 200, and 400 mbits/second. The most recent FireWire standard, IEEE 1394b, provides 800; 1,600; and 3,200 mbits/second speeds.

Like USB, FireWire supports hot swapping and multiple speeds on the same bus. It supports *isochronous* (time sensitive/dependent) data transfer in order to guarantee bandwidth for multimedia data transfers such as real-time videoconferencing. FireWire is frequently used for attaching digital cameras and other video devices to the computer.

Other Standards   The U.S. government and U.S. military have their own interface standards. Specifically, MIL-STD-188-114 and U.S. government standards 1020 and 1030 provide for electrical interfaces similar to those of RS-422 and RS-423.

SIGNAL REPRESENTATION AND MODULATION

In a data communications system, the communication medium serves as a conduit for data. The two basic classes of data representation on any communication medium are analog and digital.

Digital Data Transmission

As noted previously, when characters and symbols are encoded as unique, fixed-length sequences of bits that can be represented by discrete signals, they are said to be in digital form. All data communication media are capable of transmitting information in either digital or analog form; however, in early data communication networks, computer data was transmitted mostly in analog form. The primary reason for this is that the providers of communication transmission facilities had established analog facilities for voice transmission. However, advances in digital technology and lower prices for digital transmission electronics are bringing about a change to digital transmission. Most major metropolitan areas in the United States and around the world are well along in their analog-to-digital transition, but digital transmission services for nonurban areas are less prevalent. If telephone companies were to begin today, it is likely that their transmission facilities would be digital rather than analog. There are four primary reasons for this.

Advantages of Digital Transmission

The advantages of digital transmission for data communication are lower error rates, higher transmission rates, elimination of the need to convert from digital format to analog and back to digital, and better security.

Lower Error Rates   Most telephone networks transmit signals over wires or via radio frequencies, continually amplifying the signals to overcome attenuation. Long-distance transmission demands that the signals be amplified multiple times to overcome attenuation. Because it is difficult to filter out introduced noise or distortion that corrupts analog signals, both are amplified and propagated along with the original signals.

Like analog signals, digital signals also attenuate. Figure 6-10(a) shows a digital signal as it is originated. Figure 6-10(b) illustrates a possible effect of attenuation on

---

FireWire A high-speed serial bus that allows for the connection of up to 63 peripheral devices through a single FireWire port. Also known as the IEEE 1394 standard, the original specification addressed data transfer rates of 100, 200, and 400 mbps. FireWire supports hot swapping, multiple speeds on the same bus, and isochronous data transfer.

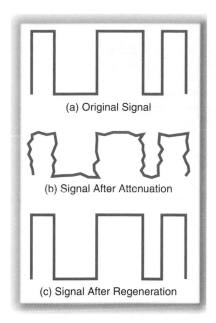

(a) Original Signal

(b) Signal After Attenuation

(c) Signal After Regeneration

Figure 6-10   Digital Signal Regeneration

that signal. A digital signal represents only two discrete values, so it is possible to completely regenerate the signal. Restored to its original state and strength, the data can be forwarded to the next regeneration point or to the final destination without any associated noise. This is accomplished by a digital regenerator or repeater. Figure 6-10(c) shows a regenerated signal.

Higher Transmission Rates   Another benefit of digital transmission is increased transmission speed. With digital transmission, switched connections commonly operate at speeds of 128 kbps, and with digital subscriber line technology, speeds of 6 mbps and higher are possible. The current limit is 56 kbps for switched analog circuits and approximately 64 kbps for leased analog telephone lines.

No Digital–Analog Conversion   Digital transmission theoretically avoids the need for conversion between formats. Unfortunately, not all locations are served by digital carrier services, In addition, the connection from a given business or residence to the digital transmission and switching equipment is often an analog dial-up circuit. This makes it necessary to convert a signal from digital to analog and back to digital for transmission to the message's destination. The device that converts the analog signal to digital for transmission over digital circuits is known as a *codec,* an acronym for coder–decoder. Codecs are discussed in Chapter 5; Figure 6-11 illustrates the role of a codec in the digital transmission of voice signals.

Security   Companies are becoming increasingly concerned about security of data and voice transmissions. One method for protecting these transmissions is encryption. Although encryption algorithms exist for both analog and digital formats, digital encryption algorithms are more advanced and hence more secure and difficult to crack. Therefore, digital transmissions have the potential for greater security.

Pulse Code Modulation

As discussed in Chapter 5, in order to transmit voice signals over digital transmission lines, it is necessary to transform a sender's analog voice signals into digital representation and then convert the digital patterns back to analog format for the call recipient.

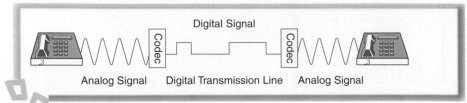

Figure 6-11　Codec Converting Analog and Digital Signals

digital transmission
A transmission mode in which data are represented by binary digits (bits) rather than by an analog signal. Discrete signal elements are used to distinguish between 0 and 1 bits.

analog transmission
Refers to the transmission of data over telephone lines in which the data is represented by a continuously varying electrical signal. Data are represented in analog form by varying the amplitude, frequency, or phase of a wave.

This is illustrated in Figure 6-11. A variety of conversion techniques exist, but the most commonly used is known as pulse code modulation (PCM). On a communication wire, PCM represents the bits of encoded voice signals as pulses of current. For example, a pulse of 3 volts could represent a 1 bit, and 0 voltage could represent a 0 bit. In some schemes a 1 bit would be represented by a voltage of $+1.5$, and the 0 bit by a voltage of -1.5. The first technique is called unipolar signaling; the latter is bipolar signaling. These techniques are illustrated in Figure 6-12.

As discussed in Chapter 5, sampling is used to convert analog signals to digital formats. Chapter 5 discusses PCM and other analog signal digitization approaches more extensively.

Analog Transmission

Today's computers store data in digital form and transmit digital data via their parallel or serial ports. As noted previously in our discussion of the RS-232-C standard, in **digital transmission**, the 0 and 1 bits that make up ASCII–encoded characters are represented by discrete voltage levels when transmitted over wires. **Analog transmission** refers to measurable physical quantities, which in data communications take the form of voltages and variations in the properties of waves. Data is represented in analog form by varying the amplitude (height), frequency (period), or phase (relative starting point)

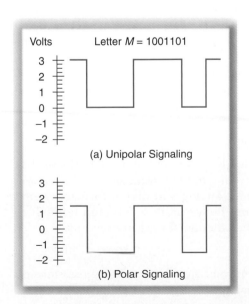

Figure 6-12　Unipolar and Bipolar Signaling

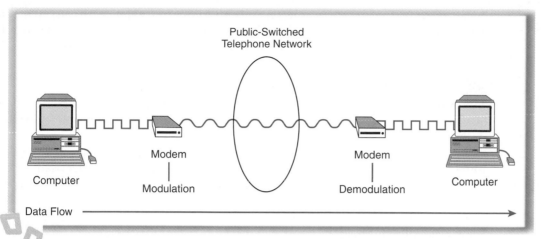

Figure 6-13   The Role of Modems in Modulation and Demodulation

of a wave. Translation from digital format to analog format and back to digital format is accomplished by a device known as a **modem** (an acronym for modulator–demodulator). A modem accepts digital signals (discrete voltage levels), transforms the digital signal into a corresponding analog signal, and passes the analog signal along the communication medium to another modem. The receiving modem translates the analog signal back into digital form. This process is illustrated in Figure 6-13.

To better understand this process and how a modem converts a digital signal into a corresponding analog signal that can be transmitted over dial-up circuits, it is useful to review the characteristics of dial-up circuits (see Figure 6-14). As noted in Chapter 5, the telephone network was originally designed to carry voice conversations with a reasonable sound quality. Telephone network designers deemed that a frequency bandwidth of 3,100 Hz (ranging from 300 Hz to 3,400 Hz) was sufficient for reasonable sound quality. Guardbands ensure separation of dial-up circuits when they are "stacked"

modem Short for *modulator-demodulator*. A device that changes digital pulses to analog signals (typically audio frequencies) for transmitting data over analog telephone circuits. Also used for some fiber optic transmission and any transmission mode requiring a change from one form of signal to another.

Figure 6-14   Characteristics of an Analog Dial-Up Circuit

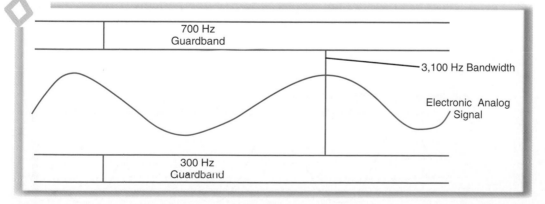

on carrier trunk lines used for interoffice connections and satellite circuits. When a dial-up circuit is used for modem-to-modem connections, the circuit's 3,100-Hz bandwidth is used to carry analog signals from sender to receiver.

Carrier Signals

carrier signal A wave that continues without change. The carrier signal can be modulated by a modem so a receiver can interpret the information being transmitted.

One of the trigonometric relationships between angles in a right triangle is called the *sine* of the angle. The values for the sine of an angle vary from 1 to −1, and a continuous curve of this function can be plotted. Figure 6-15 depicts a simple sine wave. A wave of this form has the potential for carrying information. If the wave continues without change, as depicted, no information can be discerned. Such an unmodulated signal is called a **carrier signal**. The purpose of a modem is to change, or modulate, the characteristics of the carrier wave so a receiver can interpret information. The simple sine wave has several properties that can be altered to represent data: amplitude (height), frequency (period), and phase (relative starting point). Modems alter one or more of these characteristics to represent digital signals representing bits.

During the handshaking process (that series of high-pitched screeches and "dings" that you hear when you use a dial-up circuit to connect to an ISP), the two modems raise a carrier signal and agree on how it will be manipulated to represent 0 and 1 bits. Manipulation can involve the alteration of the carrier wave's amplitude, frequency, or phase. In some modulation schemes, more than one of these wave characteristics is simultaneously modulated.

Amplitude Modulation

amplitude modulation (AM) A data transmission technique that represents data by varying (modulating) the amplitude of the carrier wave.

The simplest characteristic to visualize is **amplitude modulation (AM)**. Figure 6-16 represents two sine waves superimposed on one another. One curve represents sin *x* and the other represents 2 sin *x*. Note that the 2 sin *x* curve has twice the amplitude of the sin *x* curve. (Varying the amplitude of a curve is similar to changing the voltage on a line.) How is this variation used to convey information? Suppose the bit pattern 1001001 is to be transmitted. If a 1 bit is represented by the curve of 2 sin *x* and an 0 bit by the curve traced by sin *x*, the bit pattern would be represented by the modulated sine curve depicted in Figure 6-17.

Frequency Modulation

The period, or frequency, of a sine curve is the interval required for the curve to complete one entire cycle. In the simple sine curve, the period is 2 p (pi), where pi is approximately 3.14159. In data transmission, such intervals are only seconds, so the

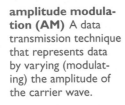

Figure 6-15   Simple Sine Wave

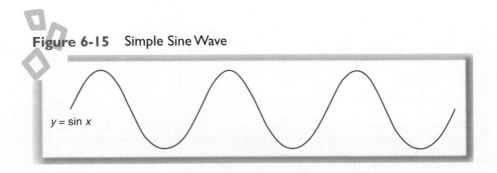

y = sin *x*

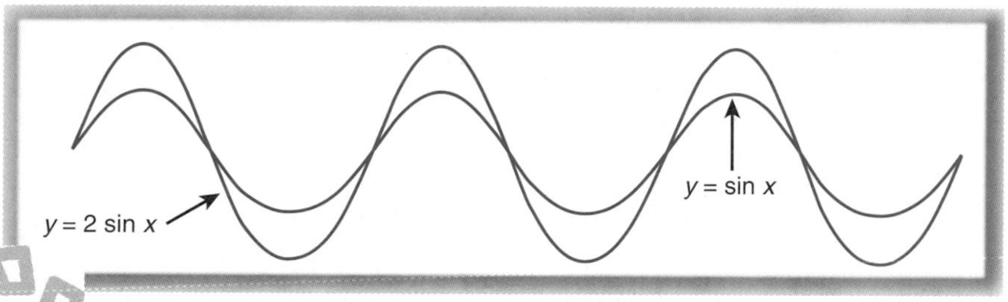

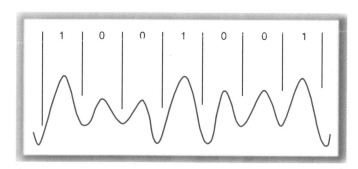

$y = 2 \sin x$

$y = \sin x$

Figure 6-16   Superimposed Sine Waves, Example 1

period is the number of seconds required for the wave to complete one cycle. The mathematical function that alters the period is sin nx. Figure 6-18 shows the curve of sin $2x$. When the horizontal axis represents time, the period is frequency (oscillations) per unit of time. Hertz (Hz) is the term used to denote frequency; 1 Hz is 1 cycle per second. Although the human ear can detect a wider range of frequencies, dial-up circuits in telephone networks use the frequency range between 300 and 3,400 Hz, which is satisfactory for carrying electrical representations of voice signals. Figure 6-19 shows an example of frequency modulation for our selected bit pattern 1001001.

To convey analog versions of digital signals by **frequency modulation (FM)**, or *frequency shift keying (FSK)*, is to vary the frequency of the carrier wave. For example,

frequency modulation (FM) A data transmission technique that represents data by varying (modulating) the frequency of the carrier wave.

1   0   0   1   0   0   1

Figure 6-17
Amplitude
Modulation

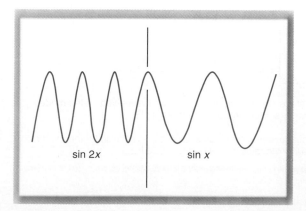

sin $2x$ sin x

Figure 6-18   Curve of
Sin $2x$

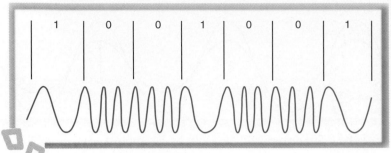

Figure 6-19   Frequency Modulation

to transmit the binary pattern 1001001 by frequency modulation on a dial-up circuit, a frequency of 1,300 Hz can represent the 1 bit, and a frequency of 2,100 Hz can represent the 0 bit. This process is illustrated in Figure 6-20. When the modem at the other end of the dial-up circuit receives a 1,300-Hz analog signal via the communication medium, it converts it back into a −15 volt digital signal, which the DTE will recognize as a 1 bit. When the receiving modem detects a 2,100-Hz signal, it converts it to a +15 volt digital signal that the DTE will recognize as a 0 bit. The signal received must typically be within 10 Hz of these values to be acceptable, which means the range for a 1 bit is 1,290–1,310 Hz. These frequency values used to represent 0s and 1s must be dif-

Figure 6-20   Modulating the Frequency of a Carrier Signal to Represent Bits

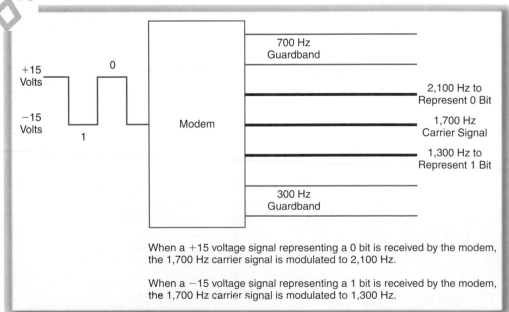

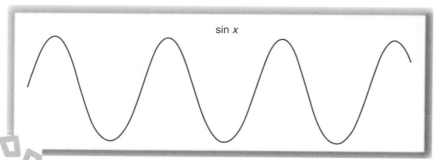

Figure 6-21   Curve of Sin *x*

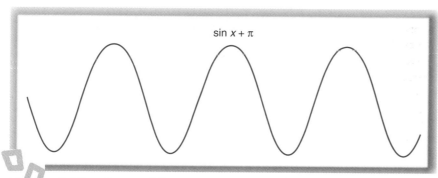

Figure 6-22   Curve of Sin *x* + π

ferent enough from one another to minimize the possibility of signal distortion altering the values transmitted and causing the receiving modem to misinterpret the sender's transmission. Thus, if the 1 bit were represented by 1,500 Hz and the 0 bit by 1,510 Hz, a decrease of only 10 Hz would change a 0 bit into a 1 bit.

Phase Modulation

A third modulation technique is **phase modulation** (phase shifting). If the simple sine curve is represented by sin *x*, then a change of phase is represented by sin $(x + n)$. Figure 6-21 shows the curve of sin *x*, Figure 6-22 shows the curve of sin $(x + \pi)$, and Figure 6-23 shows the two curves superimposed on one another. Transmitting the bit pattern of 1001001 using phase modulation, where a 1 bit is represented by no phase change and an 0 bit by a change in phase of π radians, yields the curve in Figure 6-24.

Bit Rates, Baud Rates, and Bandwidth

Up to this point, we have only considered the transmission of analog signals that represent individual bits. Many of the modems used with today's computers are capable of transmitting analog signals that represent combinations of two or more bits. In this

phase modulation
A change in the phase of a carrier signal. Commonly used alone or in conjunction with amplitude modulation to provide high-speed transmission (4,800 bps and higher).

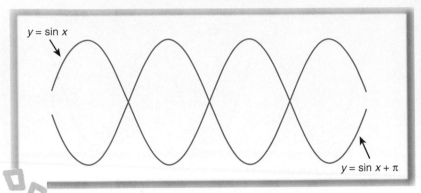

$y = \sin x$

$y = \sin x + \pi$

Figure 6-23   Superimposed Sine Waves, Example 2

section, we will discuss how this is accomplished. Prior to beginning this discussion, however, it is important for you to have a clear understanding of two other relevant terms: bandwidth and baud rate.

Bandwidth   The bandwidth of an analog communication channel is the difference between the minimum and maximum frequencies it can carry. A voice-grade dial-up channel that can transmit frequencies between 300 and 3,400 Hz has a bandwidth of 3,100 Hz. For digital circuits, bandwidth is measured in bits per second instead of a frequency range. For both analog and digital circuits, bandwidth is a measure of the amount of data that can be transmitted per unit of time and is directly proportional to the maximum data transmission speed of a medium. The higher the bandwidth is, the greater the data-carrying capacity.

Baud Rate   The baud rate is a measure of the number of discrete signals that can be observed (transmitted or received) per unit of time. For modems, the baud rate measures the number of signals it is capable of transmitting or receiving per second. Although baud rate and bit rate (or transmission rate measured in bits per second) are often used interchangeably, they are not identical. A modem's baud rate and trans-

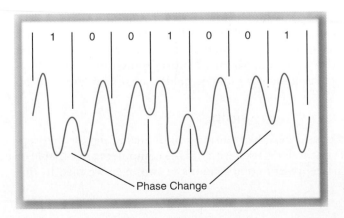

| 1 | 0 | 0 | 1 | 0 | 0 | 1 |

Phase Change

Figure 6-24
Phase Modulation

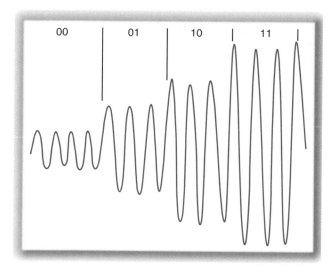

Figure 6-25   Dibits Using
Amplitude Modulation

mission rate are the same only when the modem is only limited to modulating the carrier signal to represent a single bit. For example, if the modem is capable of modulating the carrier signal 3,200 times per second, but can only represent a 0 or a 1 each time it alters the carrier signal, both its baud rate and bit (transmission) rate are 3,200. A modem's bit rate is higher than its baud rate when it is capable of transmitting/ receiving signals that each represent a combination of two or more bits. For example, if the modem is capable of modulating the amplitude of the carrier wave in four different ways (see Figure 6-25) each amplitude can represent a 2-bit combination (00, 01, 10, or 11). This technique is called **dibits**.

dibits A transmission mode in which each signal conveys 2 bits of data.

Now suppose the modem's signaling rate of 3,200 changes per second is maintained. The baud rate remains at 3,200, but the bit rate doubles to 6,400 bps because

Figure 6-26   Using Dibits and Amplitude Modulation to
Represent the Bit Pattern 1001001

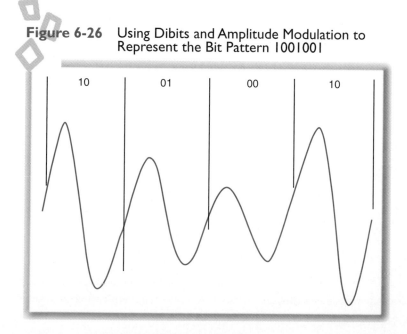

each modulated signal represents two bits. Figure 6-26 shows the amplitude-modulated transmission of the bit pattern 1001001 using dibits (with 1 bit added to make the number of bits even).

Similarly, eight signal levels (amplitude levels, frequencies, or phase shifts) can be used to represent 3 bits per signal, a technique called **tribits**. A 3,200-baud modem that is capable of representing 3-bit combinations (tribits) each time it modulates the carrier wave is capable of transmitting 9,600 bps. If 16 different signaling levels are used, 4 bits per signal could be represented, a technique called **quadbits**. Modems used with today's microcomputers typically are able to represent more than 1 bit per signaling event; for most, the bit rate is, therefore, a multiple of the baud rate (such as 2, 3, 4, 6, or 12 times the baud rate).

Phase modulation is often used on today's modems because it lends itself well to the implementation of dibits, tribits, and quadbits. Dibit transmission can be accomplished with four phase shifts through a technique called *quadrature phase shift keying (QPSK)*. Eight phase shifts are needed to support tribit transmission. Figure 6-27(a) shows eight different angles in a full circle. Suppose each angle is used as a phase shift in phase modulation. Thus, with eight different signals we can represent 3 bits of information per signal, or tribits. In Figure 6-27(b) the eight angles are combined with two levels (amplitudes) of signal, providing 16 different signals, each of which can represent 4 bits. This combination provides a quadbit capability known as **quadrature amplitude modulation (QAM)**. When QAM is used with a 3,200-baud modem, a transmission rate of 12,800 bps can be achieved.

The baud rates supported by today's modems are typically lower than their bit per second transmission rates. Modems that support ITU's V.34 standard, for example, achieve speeds of 28,800 bps by representing 12 bits/baud at a baud rate of 2,800 and speeds of 33,600 bps by representing 9 bits/baud at a baud rate of 3,200. The standards that a given modem supports are the keys for determining the modem's capabilities. This will become clear in the following section on modem capabilities.

tribits A method of modulation that allows 3 bits to be represented by each signal.

quadbits A technique in which each signal carries 4 bits of data. Requires 16 different signals.

quadrature amplitude modulation (QAM) A modulation technique using both phase and amplitude modulation.

Figure 6-27   Phase Modulation Angles and Amplitudes

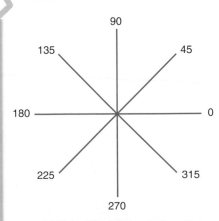

(a) Eight different phase changes suitable for tribits.

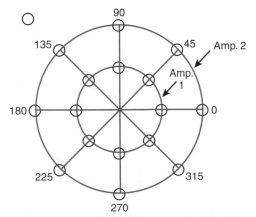

(b) Eight phase changes plus 2 amplitudes yield 16 different signals for quadbits. The 16 different signals are represented by circles.

MODEM CAPABILITIES

Modems fall into three basic categories: copper-based, radio frequency, and fiber optic. Copper-based modems are used to interface to twisted-pair wires or other kinds of copper cabling such as coaxial cable; radio-frequency modems are used for wireless communication; and fiber optic modems are used with fiber optic cable. The principle of each kind of modem is essentially the same: changing signals from one format to another and then back again. Copper-based modems change a device's digital signals to analog or digital electrical signals; radio-frequency modems change digital signals to radio frequencies; and fiber optic modems change a device's digital signals to optical digital signals.

Copper-based modems for establishing connections over dial-up circuits are the most widely used. As noted earlier in the chapter, these may be an external device equipped with one port for connecting with the computer's serial port and a second for connecting to standard twisted-pair telephone cabling (RJ-11), or a modem card with an RJ-11 connection interface that plugs into one of the computer's expansion slots. As noted in Chapter 5, cable modems that support coaxial cable interfaces rather than RJ-11 connections are growing in popularity, because they enable cable service subscribers to enjoy higher speed Internet access than is possible over dial-up telephone lines. "Modems" for IDSN and DSL connections are often classified as additional examples of copper-based modems; however, it is important to note that these function more like codecs (the coder–decoders found in digital telephones—see Chapter 5) than traditional dial-up modems because they interface with digital, not analog, carrier services.

As we consider modem standards and capabilities, it is important to remember that modems are always used in pairs (see Figure 6-28) and that the maximum data throughput that can be achieved between a given pair of modems is dependent on the

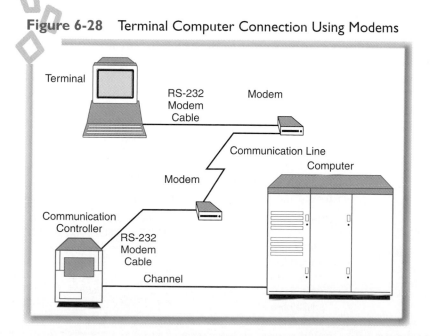

Figure 6-28   Terminal Computer Connection Using Modems

Terminal

RS-232 Modem Cable

Modem

Communication Line

Computer

Modem

Communication Controller

RS-232 Modem Cable

Channel

least sophisticated modem in the pair. For example, if one of the modems is capable of transmitting 53,000 bps, while the other is capable of transmitting/receiving a maximum of 33,600 bps, the maximum communication speed between the pairs will be 33,600 bps. During the handshaking process, the two modems exchange information with one another about their capabilities. The information they exchange is used to determine transmission speed, the error-detection and correction approach that will be used, and whether they have a commonly supported data compression approach that may be used to enhance throughput. As you read this section, it will become clear that modems may have a wide range of capabilities by virtue of conforming to widely accepted standards.

Speed

All modems are designed to operate at a specific speed or range of discrete speeds. Most of the modems used with today's computers are variable-speed modems. Speed changes can be accomplished by setting via switches on the modem, via program control, or by automatic adjustment of the transmission speed.

Several standards relate directly to the maximum bit rate over dial-up circuits. As Table 6-6 illustrates, most of these are ITU V.xx standards, although some are older and slower standards like the Bell standards. In the United States, the modems used by the largest segment of users that have Internet access are V.90 and V.34 modems. These are backward compatible with older modem standards and are therefore capable of communicating with older modems at slower transmission speeds, if this is necessary.

You may have noticed in Table 6-6 that V.90 modems are examples of *asymmetrical transmission* technologies, because they are capable of receiving data at higher speeds than they are able to transmit. This matches the network traffic patterns of most Internet users whose server requests are typically short (such as Web page URLs) and whose server responses are much larger (often Web page text and graphics). It also takes advantage of the fact that most ISPs have high-speed digital connections to the Internet (such as a T-1), while most of their subscribers access their services at much lower speeds. V.90 downstream links use pulse code modulation (PCM); as noted in Chapter 5, PCM is a form of digital transmission, not analog. In practice, V.90 downstream links rarely exceed 45 kbps and carrier limitations restrict speeds over dial-up circuits to a maximum of 53 kbps.

In order to keep transmission speeds as high as possible during a communication session, both V.90 and V.34 modems have adaptive line probing and fallback/fallforward capabilities. **Adaptive line probing** monitors the characteristics of the dial-

adaptive line probing Monitors the characteristics of the dial-up connection throughout the communication session between the modems.

Table 6-6   Maximum Transmission Speeds Specified by Modem Standards

Modem Standard	Maximum Transmission Rate	Baud Rate(s)
V.90	56,000 bps (downstream)	3,000, 3,200 for downstream
	33,600 bps (upstream)	2,400, 2,743, 3,429, 3,800 for upstream
V.34	28,000 bps/33,600 bps	3,000, 3,200 for 28.8 kbps
		2,400, 2,743, 2,800, 3,429 for 33.6 kbps
V.32ter	19,200 bps	2,400
V.32bis	14,400 bps	2,400
V.32	9,600 bps	2,400
V.22bis	2,400 bps	600
Bell 212A	1,200 bps	600
Bell 103	300 bps	300

up connection between the modems throughout the communication session. In order to optimize the transmission rate, baud rates, carrier wave frequency, modulation method, and other transmission parameters can be changed during the session. **Fallback** capabilities enable these modems to begin speed negotiations during the handshaking process at the highest possible rate and to systematically adjust the rate downward until a common rate can be identified. For example, a V.90 modem would first attempt to negotiate the highest possible V.90 speed before dropping back to lower V.90 speeds, V.34 speeds, or V.32 speeds; the goal is to establish the highest possible initial transmission rate between the pair of modems. If line conditions degrade during the communication session, fallback capabilities also enable the modems to drop back to lower speeds. **Fallforward** capabilities enable an increase in transmission speeds in response to improved line conditions.

Modems that support the *MNP (Microcom Networking Protocol) Class 10* standard also support dynamic speed shifts in response to changes in the condition of the connection during the communication session. **Dynamic speed shifts** enable the transmission speed and modulation approach to be either increased or decreased in response to varying line conditions. *MNP Class 10* support is especially desirable for wireless modems for notebook computers that are used to establish connections over cellular telephone networks.

V.92 is one of the newest modem standards approved by the International Telecommunications Union (ITU). Like other modem standards, V.92 is backward compatible with V.90 and earlier modem standards. Like V.90, V.92 modems use PCM for downstream links; unlike V.90, V.92 modems are capable of upstream data rates of 48,000 bps. The increased upstream rate is likely to be beneficial to remote workers, especially those who need to share larger files across dial-up links. Additional V.92 capabilities are identified in subsequent sections of this chapter.

Connection Options

Autoanswer, autodial, automatic redialing, and keyboard dialing features are supported by many modems, especially those used with switched telephone lines. Most newer modems can react to the ring indicator on the line and automatically answer an incoming call. Autodialing means that the modem can dial a number itself. Many modems have the capability of storing frequently called numbers. Automatic redialing modems automatically redial a call that resulted in a busy signal or no connection. Finally, keyboard or programmable dialing means that the number can be dialed using the keyboard of a terminal or via program control. The V.92 standard also supports call waiting. When a call-waiting signal is received, the V.92 modem can pause the online connection for up to 2 minutes to enable the user to answer the phone. When the user hangs up, the V.92 modem resumes its data communications session.

Pocket modems are often used to support mobile computing. For example, Personal Computer Memory Card International Association (PCMCIA) modem cards are widely used in notebook computers. PCMCIA modem cards for dial-up connections provide RJ-11 interfaces; those for establishing connections over cellular networks are equipped with wireless transmitters/receivers.

Voice-Over-Data

Voice-over-data capability allows voice communications and data transmission to take place simultaneously over the same circuit. Both DSL and ISDN modems commonly support voice-over-data. This arrangement is also beneficial when a business data transmission application requires a dedicated circuit to a remote location.

fallback A modem feature that enables systematic downward adjustments in transmission rates in response to changes in the transmission line.

fallforward Enables an increase in transmission speeds in response to improved line conditions.

dynamic speed shifts Enable the transmission speed to be either increased or decreased in response to varying line conditions.

V.92 One of the newest modem standards approved by the International Telecommunications Union (ITU). Like other modem standards, V.92 is backward compatible with V.90 and earlier modem standards and uses PCM for downstream links; V.92 modems are capable of upstream data rates of 48,000 bps. V.92 reduces connection time (handshaking) by remembering the previous settings negotiated when dialing the same telephone number. It also supports call waiting by allowing the data session to be paused while a voice call is taken.

Data Compression

data compression
Enables modems to have data throughput across a communication link that is greater than the transmission speed that they use to communicate. This is accomplished by substituting large strings of repeating characters or bits with shorter codes. The extent to which a file can be compressed depends on the type of data in the file and the data compression algorithm used. V.42bis, MNP 5, and V.44 are widely supported data compression standards.

V.42bis An ITU standard for modem data compression. It uses the Lempel Ziv algorithm to achieve up to a 4:1 compression ratio.

Data compression enables modems to have data throughput across a communication link that is greater than the transmission speed that they use to communicate. This is accomplished by substituting large strings of repeating characters or bits with shorter codes. Modems that support data compression maintain code "libraries" that enable receivers to look up shorter codes transmitted by senders and translate them into the longer strings of characters or bits that they represent.

The data compression process is illustrated in Figure 6-29. This figure shows how a pair of 28,800-bps V.34 modems that each support V.42bis (a data compression standard that supports a 4:1 data compression ratio) are able to achieve throughputs up to 115,200 bps. Such speeds are only possible when both modems support the same data compression standard; support for data compression standards is determined during the handshaking process.

Several widely accepted standards exist for data compression. These include V.42bis, MNP class 5, MNP class 7, and V.44. Of these, V.42bis and MNP class 5 are found most commonly in today's modems.

V.42bis uses the Lempel Ziv data compression algorithm that is capable of compressing files and increasing throughput by a ratio of 4:1. Before transmitting signals over the dial-up circuits, V.42bis data compression software/firmware in the send modem examines incoming digital signals from the computer. The sender creates and stores an 11-bit code (key) for each repeating pattern of characters (up to 32 characters in length) that it identifies. This code is also sent to the receiver for storage in its library. The code/key creation and sharing process occurs throughout the communication session between the modems to enable their libraries to be constantly updated. Each time the sender subsequently encounters a repetitive pattern of characters, it transmits the 11-bit code instead of the 32 bytes normally required to represent the characters. When the code is received, the receiving modem consults its library to identify the 32-character pattern that it should send to the computer to which it is attached.

Figure 6-29   An Example of Data Compression Between V.34 Modems That Support V.42bis Data Compression

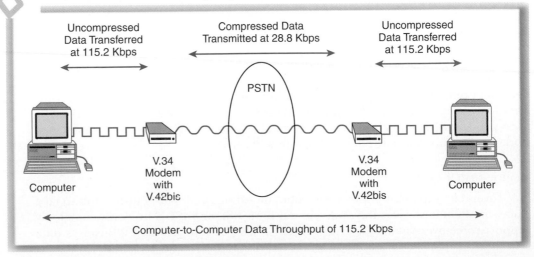

Although a data compression ratio of up to 4:1 is possible when identical V.42bis modems are used, compression ratios in the neighborhood of 2.5:1 are most common. This results from the fact that some data streams contain more repeating characters (and thus are more compressible) than others.

MNP Class 5 supports two different data compression algorithms: Huffman encoding and run-length encoding. Compression ratios of 1.3:1 to 2:1 are possible when a pair of modems supports MNP Class 5 data compression.

> *Huffman encoding* involves the re-encoding of ASCII characters. Frequently used characters, such as *a, e, i,* and *s,* are represented by 4 bits; rarely used characters such as *z* and *x* are represented by as many as 11 bits. On the balance, Huffman encoding enables the characters found in files and other messages to be transmitted using fewer bits.

> *Run-length encoding* looks for repeating characters. When a particular character repeats more than three times, this algorithm sends three repetitions of the character along with a field indicating the total number of times the character is actually repeated.

MNP Class 7 employs a data compression algorithm that is capable of increasing throughput by up to 300 percent. ITU's **V.44** data compression standard is capable of increasing the throughput levels possible with V.42bis from 20 percent to 100 percent. V.44 is supported by V.92 modems. Table 6-7 summarizes the kinds of data compression standards supported by today's dial-up modems.

Security

Business organizations often require modems used for dial-in access, such as LAN modems (which enable remote users to have dial-in access to LAN resources) and modems connected to communication servers, to include features that inhibit unauthorized users from gaining access to corporate computing resources. Such modems are likely to require remote users to enter a password before allowing them to use the internal network. The modem answers the incoming call and prompts the caller for a user ID and password. If the caller fails to respond with a valid user ID or password in a predetermined time interval, the dial-up connection is terminated by the answering modem.

Some dial-in modems also include **callback** features. These modems terminate the connection after the caller has supplied a valid user ID or password and subsequently

MNP Class 5
Supports two different data compression algorithms: Huffman encoding and run-length encoding. Compression ratios of 1.3:1 to 2:1 are possible when a pair of modems supports MNP Class 5 data compression.

MNP Class 7
Employs a data compression algorithm that is capable of increasing data throughput by up to 300 percent.

V.44 A data compression standard that is capable of increasing the throughput levels possible with V.42bis from 20 percent to 100 percent. V.44 is supported by V.92 modems.

callback A security feature supported by some modems. This enables the modem to terminate the connection after the caller has supplied a valid user ID and/or password and subsequently dials in to the user's modem after identifying his/her phone number in its authorized user database.

Table 6-7   Data Compression Standards Supported in Popular Modems

Modem Standard	Data Compression Standards Supported
V.92	V.44, V.42bis, MNP5
V.90	V.42bis, MNP 5
V.34	V.42bis, MNP 5
V.32ter	V.42bis, MNP 5
V.32bis	V.42bis, MNP 5
V.32	V.42bis, MNP 5

dials into the user's modem after identifying their phone number in its valid user database. Such modems may be used to restrict user access to particular time periods, such as specific times of the day or days of the week; some also capture usage information such as user ID, log-in time/date, applications accessed, and session duration. Although most callback modems only use a designated phone number stored in the valid user database, some include *variable callback* capabilities to better address the needs of mobile users.

Password and callback features can go a long way toward ensuring that only authorized users are able to dial into an organization's networks. To protect the integrity of data transmitted across dial-up connections, some modems support *encryption*. Modem-level encryption processes usually take place prior to data compression and signal modulation; receiving modems typically decode the modulated signal and uncompress the data before decrypting the message. Encryption processes are discussed more fully in Chapter 16.

ERROR DETECTION AND RECOVERY

In order to ensure that data is not changed or lost during transmission, error-detection and error-recovery processes are standard aspects of modem operations. As Figure 6-30 illustrates, both the sending and receiving modems are involved in the error-detection process. During the handshaking process, the pair of modems agrees on the error-checking process that will be used during their communication session. Once agreement is reached, the sending modem will transmit the agreed-upon error check along with the data. The receiver will subsequently calculate its own error check based on the data that it receives and compare its calculated error check to that transmitted by the sender. If the two values match, the receiver accepts the data and relays it to the computer to which it is attached. If the values are different, the receiver concludes that a transmission error has occurred. Transmission errors trigger an error-recovery process. The recovery process often involves the retransmission of the data by the sender; however, if the sender has transmitted sufficient overhead information in

Figure 6-30   The Overall Modem-to-Modem Error-Detection Process

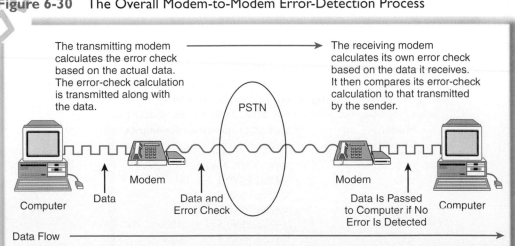

addition to the data, the receiver may be able to restore the transmitted data to its correct form without asking the sender to retransmit it.

Analogous error-detection and recovery processes are used in virtually all other data communication networks, including packet switching, frame relay, and ATM networks (see Chapter 12). Error-check fields are included in most packet formats; their content is calculated by senders and used by receivers to determine whether transmission errors have occurred. In packet-switching networks, error checks are performed at each network node, including all the packet switches that process a packet along its route from sender to receiver. Point-to-point error checking is also used in frame relay and cell relay (ATM) networks. However, although point-to-point error recovery is used in packet-switching networks, end-to-end error recovery is used in frame relay and ATM networks. This enables intermediate switches to simply discard frames/cells detected as containing errors and requires recipients to request senders to transmit the missing data.

Error Sources

There are many sources of transmission errors over dial-up connections. The most common are attenuation, impulse noise, crosstalk, echo, phase jitter, envelope delay distortion, and white noise.

Attenuation   Attenuation, the weakening of a signal as a result of distance and characteristics of the medium, can produce a significant number of data errors. For a given gauge of wire and bit rate, a signal can be carried for a certain distance without enhancement. Beyond that distance, a repeater or amplifier must be included to ensure that the receiving station can properly recognize the data.

Impulse Noise   **Impulse noise** is characterized by signal spikes. In telephone circuits, it can be caused by switching equipment or lightning strikes; in other situations, it can be caused by transient electrical impulses, such as those occurring on the floor of a factory whose manufacturing equipment requires large amounts of electricity. As the equipment cycles up and down, there can be sudden changes in the amount of power that it draws. Setting an electrical charge in motion generates a magnetic field, and magnetic fields can affect signals transmitted through unshielded data communication wires.

Impulse noise, the primary cause of data errors in telephone circuits, is heard as a clicking or crackling sound. It usually is short (several milliseconds), with varying levels of magnitude. Figure 6-31 illustrates the impact of noise on an analog data communication signal such as that transmitted between modems over dial-up circuits. As you can see, when the noise is superimposed on the original signal, the resulting signal may cause the receiver to misinterpret the original signal.

So, what's the big deal about a few bits being transformed during transmission? Consider the situation in Figure 6-32. In this case, the noise results in just one bit being changed during transmission. However, the bit in this instance is part of the binary representation of a customer's bank balance. The correct balance, stored in the host, is $100, but as the result of a 1-bit transmission error, the balance displayed on the teller's screen is $228. Unless appropriate error-detection and correction processes are in place to minimize the impacts of noise on transmitted signals, transmission errors could cause significant customer service and operation problems in this bank.

Crosstalk   **Crosstalk** occurs when signals from one channel distort or interfere with the signals of a different channel. In telephone connections, crosstalk sometimes appears in the form of another party's conversation being heard in the background. Crosstalk is also present in radio-frequency and multiplexed transmissions when the

impulse noise A noise characterized by signal spikes. In telephone circuits it can be caused by switching equipment or by lightning strikes and in other situations by transient electrical impulses such as those occurring on a shop floor. A common cause of transmission errors.

crosstalk When the signals from one channel distort or interfere with the signals of a different channel.

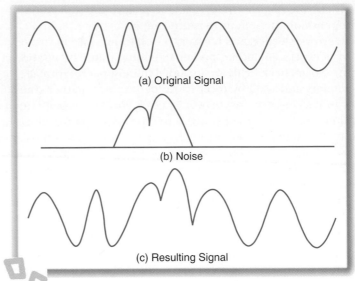

Figure 6-31   Impact of Noise on a Data Signal

frequency ranges are too close together. Crosstalk in twisted-pair wire connections occurs when wire pairs interfere with each other as a result of strong signals, improper shielding, or both. Another common cause of crosstalk is interference between receivers and transmitters when a strong outgoing signal interferes with a weaker incoming signal. Crosstalk is directly proportional to distance, bandwidth, signal strength, and proximity to other transmission channels; it is inversely proportional to shielding or channel separation. Crosstalk is not usually a significant factor in data communication errors.

One special form of crosstalk is *intermodulation noise,* which is the result of two or more signals combining to produce a signal outside the limits of the communication channel. Suppose one mode of frequency shift keying (FSK) modulation represents

Figure 6-32   Transmission Error

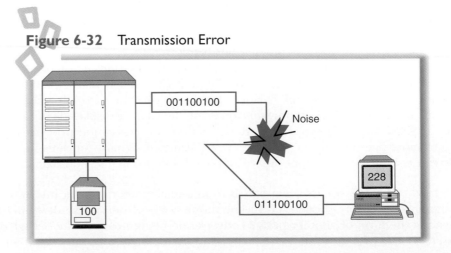

a 1 bit as a frequency of 1,300 Hz and an 0 bit as a frequency of 2,100 Hz, with a variation of 10 Hz. Intermodulation noise might result in two acceptable signals, such as 1,305 Hz and 2,105 Hz, combining to form a signal of 3,410 Hz (1,305 + 2,105 = 3,410). This signal is out of the accepted frequency range of voice communication over telephone lines (300–3,400 Hz).

Echo   **Echo** is essentially the reflection or reversal of the signal being transmitted. This is most likely to occur at junctions where wires are interconnected or at the end of a line in a LAN. Telephone companies have installed echo suppressors on their networks to minimize this echo effect. The echo suppressor works by allowing the signal to pass in one direction only. In voice transmission, the suppressor continually reverses itself to match the direction of conversation. Obviously, this would impede data transmission in full-duplex mode, so echo suppressors are disengaged when full-duplex transmission is required.

> **echo** The reflection or reversal of the signal being transmitted. Also, a transmission convention in which the receiver of data sends the data back to the sender to assist in error detection.

Phase Jitter   **Phase jitter** is a variation in the phase of a continuous signal from cycle to cycle; it is especially significant when the modulation mode involves phase shifting, as is typically the case for today's high-speed modems.

> **phase jitter** A variation in the phase of a continued signal from cycle to cycle.

Envelope Delay Distortion   **Envelope delay distortion** occurs when signals that have been weakened or subjected to outside interference by transmission over long distances are enhanced by being passed through filters. Passing the signals through a filter delays them a certain amount, depending on the frequency of the signal.

> **envelope delay distortion** Occurs when signals that have been weakened or subjected to outside interference by transmission over long distances are enhanced by being passed through filters. Passing the signals through a filter delays them a certain amount, depending on the frequency of the signal.

White Noise   **White noise**, also called *thermal noise* or *Gaussian noise*, results from the normal movements of electrons and is present in all transmission media at temperatures above absolute zero. The amount of white noise is directly proportional to the temperature of the medium (hence, the term *thermal noise*). White noise also is distributed randomly throughout a medium (hence, the term *Gaussian noise*). White noise in telephone circuits is sometimes heard as static or hissing on the line. The magnitude of white noise usually is not sufficient to create data loss in wire circuits, but it can become significant in radio-frequency links such as microwave and satellite. Because white noise is proportional to bandwidth as well as temperature, improperly focused antennas (such as those directed toward the sun) can create enough disturbance to produce errors.

> **white noise** One source of data communication errors. It results from the normal movements of electrons and is present in all transmission media at temperatures above absolute zero. Also known as thermal noise or Gaussian noise.

Electromagnetic Interference (EMI)   Wireless communications involving radio signals transmit electromagnetic waves between nodes. Electromagnetic waves are produced by the oscillation of electrons. Electromagnetic waves are also by-products of fluorescent lights and some kinds of electricity-hungry manufacturing equipment. **Electromagnetic interference (EMI)** occurs when electromagnetic waves from an extraneous source produce noise on a communication channel. Although primarily a problem for wireless communications, EMI can also be the source of communication errors on unshielded or improperly shielded communication cabling in "noisy" manufacturing environments.

> **electromagnetic interference (EMI)** Occurs when electromagnetic waves from an extraneous source produce noise on a communication channel.

Impact of Data Errors

Table 6-8 shows the possible effects of impulse noise of various durations for different transmission speeds. It is significant that fewer bits are subject to error when transmission is at lower rather than higher speeds. Although the figure applies to any kind of

Table 6-8   Potential Number of Corrupted Data Bits

Line Speed (bps)	Impulse Noise Duration (ms)				
	0.2	0.4	0.6	0.8	1.0
300	0.06	0.12	0.18	0.24	0.30
1,200	0.24	0.48	0.72	0.96	1.20
2,400	0.48	0.96	1.44	1.92	2.40
4,800	0.96	1.92	2.88	3.84	4.80
9,600	1.92	3.84	5.76	7.68	9.60
19,200	3.84	7.68	11.52	15.36	19.20

noise for the same durations, impulse noise was chosen because it is one of the most common types of noise affecting telephone wires. The most significant thing shown by Table 6-8 is that the potential number of bit errors increases with both duration of the noise and line speed. Although the table stops short of depicting the transmission speeds supported in today's modems, it illustrates the impacts of noise on transmitted signals quite well: The longer the duration of the noise is, the greater the number of bits that will be impacted. The ideal is to eliminate all errors, but a rate below one error per 100,000 bits is usually considered to be satisfactory. (Most copper-based media and wireless transmission systems are designed for less than one error per 1 million bits transmitted.)

Error Prevention

The best way to guard against transmission errors is to correct their source. Eliminating all noise is impossible, but error-prevention techniques can reduce the probability of data corruption from error sources. Such techniques include telephone line conditioning, reducing transmission speed, shielding, using repeaters and amplifiers, and using better equipment. Flow control approaches can also prevent data loss caused by buffer overflows when data is transmitted between DCE or between DCE and DTE.

Telephone Line Conditioning   When a dedicated line is leased from a telephone company, *conditioning*, sometimes called *equalization,* can be included for an additional charge. The two classes of conditioning are class C and class D, with four commercial levels of class C conditioning: C1, C2, C4, and C5. Each level of class C conditioning provides increasingly stringent constraints on the amplitude and phase distortion permitted on the line. A line with C5 conditioning should be less prone to errors than a line with C1 conditioning. One useful aspect of class D conditioning is that the telephone company will inspect the circuits available between the desired communication points to select the one with the least amount of noise. Users can also obtain equipment, such as certain modems, that aids in the conditioning of lines. Although line conditioning is not really an option for dial-up connections, it can be a valuable prevention approach for modem-to-modem connections over leased lines.

Lower Transmission Speed   As illustrated in Table 6-8, noise is less likely to cause bits to be changed at lower transmission speeds. Previously in the chapter, it was noted that many of the modems used today support adaptive line probing and possess fallback/fallforward capabilities. A pair of 56-kbps V.90 modems, for example, may fall back to 33.6 kbps or 28.8 kbps downstream transmission rates if adaptive line probes reveal eroding line conditions during their communication session. Modems that support MNP class 10 will increase or reduce their transmission speed in response to changing line conditions.

Modems that support MNP class 4 and MNP class 10 assist in minimizing errors and the need for error-recovery processes by increasing or decreasing the amount of data included in each packet in response to improving or eroding line conditions via a process called **adaptive size packet assembly**. When line conditions are good, lines can be used most efficiently, and data throughput can be optimized by sending large packets. When line conditions erode and errors are detected, modems that support MNP class 4 and MNP class 10 will reduce the packet size. When no errors are detected over an extended period of time, pairs of modems that support these standards will increase the size of the packets they transmit.

Shielding Although additional shielding of leased telephone circuits is not a user option, shielding can be provided for private lines to reduce the amount of crosstalk, impulse noise, and electromagnetic interference from the environment. Media shielding for coaxial cable or shielded twisted-pair wires is often used for LANs in noisy manufacturing settings.

Repeaters and Amplifiers Signal regenerators, such as repeaters, can be placed at intervals along a communication line to strengthen and forward the signal. Digital signal noise can usually be eliminated as the signal is regenerated. For analog signals, however, it is difficult to separate most noise from the signal; as a result, noise that affects an analog signal during transmission is amplified during the signal regeneration process. The primary function of repeaters and generators is to restore signals to their full strength and overcome signal loss due to attenuation (see Chapter 13). Repeaters, however, do a better job than amplifiers in cleansing the signals that they regenerate.

Better Equipment Because some older switching or mechanical equipment and some older transformers and power supplies are more likely to produce noise than newer equipment (such as electronic switches), replacing older components with better equipment can reduce the amount of noise. In some instances, replacing cable connectors and cabling can also help to reduce data transmission errors.

Flow Control **Flow control** mechanisms control the flow of data to and from buffer memory in order to avoid data loss from buffer overflows. Flow control software in DCE monitors the amount of free space in its buffer memory and signals senders to stop transmitting data when there is insufficient free space. RS-232 specifies one flow control approach. In this approach, the transmitting device only continues to transmit when there is a sufficiently strong current on pin #5—the clear-to-send pin. If the receiver's buffer is too full to receive additional data, it will "drop" the voltage level on pin #5, which signifies that the sender should stop transmitting data. Flow control can also be implemented by requiring a receiver to transmit an XOFF control character to a sender when its buffer is full, and it cannot receive any more data; the receiver would subsequently transmit an XON character to the sender when it is once again capable of receiving data.

Error Detection

Unfortunately, the remedies just cited to minimize the number of errors may be impractical from either a cost or a feasibility standpoint. Because total error elimination is impossible, it is also necessary to determine whether a transmission error has occurred and, if errors have occurred, to return the data to its proper form. Error-detection

adaptive size packet assembly Modems that support MNP Class 4 and MNP Class 10 and assist in minimizing errors and the need for error-recovery processes by increasing or decreasing the amount of data included in each packet in response to improving or eroding line conditions via this process.

flow control A mechanism used by network protocols to provide message pacing so the sender does not send data faster than the receiver is able to accept it.

algorithms in data communication networks are based on the transmission of additional overhead information (sometimes called *redundant information*) along with the data itself. In the early days of telegraphy, one way to ensure correctness of data was to transmit each character twice.

It is important to note that transmitting overhead information in addition to data over a circuit with limited bandwidth reduces data throughput from its highest potential level; this is a trade-off that should not be overlooked by network designers and administrators. Although the transmission of overhead data can increase the reliability of the transmission by facilitating error detection and recovery, doing so reduces potential data throughput. As the error rate approaches zero, so may the effective use of the medium. In general, middle-ground approaches that can detect almost all errors without significantly reducing the data-carrying capacity of the medium are desirable.

Several error-detection techniques have been developed for data communications; these vary in complexity. The following discussion begins with less sophisticated approaches before addressing the more complex ones.

parity check The same as parity error checking. For each character transmitted, an additional bit, the parity bit, is attached to help detect errors. The bit is chosen so that the number of 1 bits is even (even parity) or odd (odd parity).

Parity Checking   One of the simplest and most widely used forms of error detection is known as a **parity check** or *vertical redundancy check (VRC)*. It is the most commonly used error-detection and recovery approach for asynchronous transmission. A parity check involves adding a bit, known as the *parity bit,* to each character during transmission. The parity bit is selected so the total number of 1 bits in the code representation of each character adds up to either an even number (even parity) or an odd number (odd parity); this selection occurs during the handshaking process. Each character is checked upon receipt to see whether the number of 1 bits is even or odd. Consider the string of characters *DATA COMM,* as coded in 7-bit ASCII with odd parity. The representations of these characters plus the parity bit for odd parity are given in Table 6-9. It can be seen that the number of 1 bits in each 8-bit sequence (octet) is always odd (either 1, 3, 5, or 7); the parity bit ensures this. If even parity were chosen, the parity bit would be selected so the number of 1 bits would always be an even number.

Besides even and odd parity, you can have no parity, a parity bit with no parity checking, mark parity, or space parity. If there is no parity bit or if the parity bit is not checked (called *no parity check*), the ability to detect errors using this method is lost (although other methods, described later, could be used). Mark parity means that the parity bit is always transmitted as a 1 bit, and space parity means the parity bit is always transmitted as a 0 bit. Clearly, mark and space parity are ineffective as error-detection

Table 6-9   Parity Bit Generation

Letter	ASCII	Parity Bit	Transmitted Bits
D	1000100	1	10001001
A	1000001	1	10000011
T	1010100	0	10101000
A	1000001	1	10000011
Space	0100000	0	01000000
C	1000011	0	10000110
O	1001111	0	10011110
M	1001101	1	10011011
M	1001101	1	10011011

schemes. If two stations attempting to communicate disagree on the parity scheme, all messages will be seen as being in error and will be rejected.

In the odd parity example in Table 6-9, each character transmitted consists of 8 bits: 7 for data and 1 for parity. Parity enables the user to detect whether 1, 3, 5, or 7 bits have been altered in transmission, but it will not catch whether an even number (2, 4, 6, or 8 bits) has been altered. One common error situation involves burst errors, or a grouping of errors (recall the possible effect of impulse noise during high transmission rates). The likelihood of detecting errors of this nature with a parity check is approximately 50 percent. At higher transmission speeds, this limitation becomes significant. (A burst error for the duration of 2 bits does not necessarily result in 2 bit errors. Zero, 1, or 2 bits could be affected.)

Longitudinal Redundancy Check (LRC)   We can increase the probability of error detection beyond that provided by parity by making, in addition, a **longitudinal redundancy check (LRC)**. With LRC, which is similar to VRC, an additional, redundant character called the *block check character (BCC)* is appended to a block of transmitted characters, typically at the end of the block. The first bit of the BCC serves as a parity check for all of the first bits of the characters in the block; the second bit of the BCC serves as parity for all of the second bits in the block; and so on. Table 6-10 is an example of LRC. An odd parity scheme has been chosen to perform the redundancy check, so each column has an odd number of 1 bits.

LRC combined with VRC is still not sufficient to detect all errors (no scheme is completely dependable). Table 6-11 presents the same DATA COMM message transmission, with errors introduced in rows and columns marked by an asterisk. Although both LRC and VRC appear correct, the data received is not the same as that transmitted. Adding LRC to VRC brings a greater probability of detecting errors in transmission.

Checksums   Similar to LRC, **checksums** are the results of error check algorithms calculated on blocks of data bytes rather than single characters. Checksums, moreover, are calculated by adding the decimal values of each of the characters in a block of data characters. The decimal value of a character is calculated from the decimal equivalents of each of the bits in the encoded character. For example the decimal value for the letter D in Table 6-11 is 68. [Going from right to left, there is a 0 in the 0's (2^0) place; a 0 in the 2's place (2^1); a 1 in the 4's (2^2) place; 0s in the 8's (2^3), 16's (2^4), and 32's (2^5)

longitudinal redundancy check (LRC) An error-checking technique in which a block check character is appended to a block of transmitted characters, typically at the end of the block. The block check character checks parity on a row of bits (the bits in a particular bit position for each character in the block). LRC is often used in combination with vertical redundancy checking (VRC) which appends a parity bit to each character.

checksum A technique used to check for errors in blocks of data. The sending application generates the checksum from the data being transmitted. The receiving application computes the checksum and compares it to the value computed and sent by the sending station.

Table 6-10   LRC Generation

Letter	ASCII	Parity Bit	Transmitted Bits
D	1000100	1	10001001
A	1000001	1	10000011
T	1010100	0	10101000
A	1000001	1	10000011
Space	0100000	0	01000000
C	1000011	0	10000110
O	1001111	0	10011110
M	1001101	1	10011011
M	1001101	1	10011011
BBC	1000001 1	0	10000110

Table 6-11   LRC Transmission Errors

Letter	ASCII	Parity Bit	Transmitted Bits
	**		
D	1000100	1	10001001
A	1000001	1	10000011
T	*1100100	0	10101000
A	*1110001	1	10000011
Space	0100000	0	01000000
C	1000011	0	10000110
O	1001111	0	10011110
M	1001101	1	10011011
M	1001101	1	10011011
BBC	1000011	0	10000110

places; and a 1 in the 64's (2^6) place. By adding the decimal values for the 1 bits in the character, a sum of 68 is obtained.] The decimal values of all characters in the data block are summed, yielding a checksum; the binary equivalent of the checksum is placed in a checksum field by the sender and transmitted along with the data block.

The receiver calculates its own checksum for the data block as it is received. It then compares its calculated checksum to that transmitted by the sender. If the values are the same, the receiver concludes that no transmission errors occurred. If the values differ, the receiver decides that the data block contains errors and initiates error-recovery procedures.

cyclical redundancy check (CRC) An error detection algorithm that uses a polynomial function to generate the block check characters. CRC is a very efficient error-detection method.

Cyclical Redundancy Check (CRC)   A **cyclical redundancy check (CRC)** can detect bit errors better than VRC, LRC, or both. Similar to a checksum, a CRC is computed for a block of transmitted data. The transmitting station generates the CRC and transmits it with the data. The receiving station computes the CRC for the data received and compares it to the CRC transmitted by the sender. If the two are equal, then the block is assumed to be error free. The mathematics behind CRC requires the use of a generating polynomial and is beyond the scope of this book.

If the CRC generator polynomial is chosen with care and is of sufficient degree, more than 99 percent of multiple-bit errors can be detected. Several standards—CRC-12, CRC-16, and CRC-32—define both the degree of the generating polynomial and the generating polynomial itself. Of these, CRC-16 and CRC-32 are used most widely. CRC-12 specifies a polynomial of degree 12, and the last two standards specify a polynomial of degree 16 and 32, respectively. As a result, the BCC (error check) field will include 12, 16, or 32 bits. CRC-16 can detect all single-bit and double-bit errors, all errors in cases in which an odd number of bits is erroneous, two pairs of adjacent errors, all burst errors of 16 bits or fewer, and more than 99.998 percent of all burst errors greater than 16 bits.

When CRC-32 is used, all burst errors of 32 bits or less can be detected, and burst errors larger than 32 bits can be detected 99.9999847 percent of the time.

Because of its reliability, CRC has become the predominant method of error detection for synchronous transmission. Packet formats are illustrated at many points in this book. Those with 16-bit error-check fields usually employ CRC-16 as their error-detection scheme; those with 32-bit error check fields typically use CRC-32.

Sequence Checks   If sending and receiving nodes are connected directly, the receiving station receives all transmissions without the intercession of other nodes. However, in large communication networks such as the Internet, packet-switching networks, and frame relay networks, multiple intermediate nodes may be involved in routing a message to its final destination. As noted in Chapter 12, packetizing is commonly used in such networks, and large files and messages are divided into a number of packets prior to their transmission. In connectionless networks, the individual packets of multi-packet files/messages may be routed along different paths across the network and may be received out of order. In such a case, it is important to assign sequence numbers to the packets so the ultimate receiver can determine that all sender packets have indeed arrived and can put them back into their proper sequence. If a data packet arrives and an error is detected, or if some of the packets in a sequence have not been received, the recovery method is to ask the sender to retransmit the erroneous or lost data. An acknowledgment usually is transmitted by the receiver back to the sender for all blocks received correctly; if a packet is not positively acknowledged by the receiver, the sender is typically responsible for resending it. This obligates the transmitting node to retain all transmitted packets until they have been acknowledged. Being able to request that a message be retransmitted implies that the flow control is either half duplex or full duplex. If an error is detected on a simplex line, the recipient cannot send a request for retransmission. The only recourse in this case is to ignore the message or to use the message as received.

Transmitting devices store packet sequence numbers in buffer memory until the packets they transmit are positively acknowledged. This means that flow control mechanisms are also involved in error-detection and recovery processes. Flow control mechanisms are discussed in the previous section on error prevention.

Miscellaneous Error-Detection Techniques   Several other methods increase the probability of detecting data errors.

➤ *Check digits.* Check digits or check numbers are one or more characters (often simply the sum of fields being checked) that are appended to the data being transmitted. They are usually generated by the sending application or device and checked by the receiving application or device.

➤ *Hash totals.* One technique that validates operator input and augments an error-detection scheme involves appending a hash total, which is the sum of a group of items. For a batch of credit card authorizations, the sum of all charges can be computed separately or by the input device. Computing separately before operator input provides an accuracy check of data entry as well as transmission. The receiving computer sums the number of fields transmitted and compares its total with the transmitted hash total. If the totals agree, it is assumed that there are no errors; if the hash totals do not agree, the data must be retransmitted.

➤ *Byte counts.* A byte count field can be added to a message. When an entire block of data is sent at one time (synchronous transmission), the loss of a character would ordinarily be detected either by LRC with VRC or by CRC. When every character is transmitted individually with its own error-detection scheme (asynchronous transmission using parity checking), a lost character can go undetected. Transmitting one or more characters that indicate the total number of characters in the message helps detect transmission errors in which entire characters may be lost.

➤ *Character echoing.* In some systems, especially with asynchronous transmission, the characters transmitted are echoed to the user as a check. Because of the additional line time required, this technique is less often used in synchronous transmissions. Consider an operator at an asynchronous terminal: When a key is struck, the character is transmitted to the host computer, which echoes (resends) the received character to the terminal. If the character displayed at the originating terminal is incorrect, the operator backs up the cursor to the character position and enters the correct character. With a high-speed communication line, it appears to the operator as though the character is locally displayed as well as being transmitted to the host; with low-speed communication links, or when communicating with a busy processor, the echoing may become somewhat apparent. Echoing has the disadvantage of doubling the chances of obtaining an error, as the message must be transmitted twice. The original message may be received correctly, but if the echoed message has been corrupted, the original sender will detect an error.

Error Recovery

No matter what error-detection approach is used, the detection of data transmission errors by receivers normally triggers error-recovery processes. Error recovery is also known as *error correction*. Two major error-correction processes exist. The first involves the retransmission of the data by the sender, and the second involves the receiver's use of redundant overhead information to correct an error without retransmission. The most common error-correction mechanism is to retransmit the data. In asynchronous transmission, individual characters are retransmitted, whereas in synchronous transmissions, one or more blocks may need to be retransmitted. This kind of correction is known as *automatic repeat request (ARQ)*. If an error-correcting code is used, the transmitted data can be corrected by the receiver. This approach, however, is seldom the case in data communication.

Automatic Repeat Request (ARQ) A method of handling data communication errors in which the receiving station requests retransmission if an error occurs.

Automatic Repeat Request (ARQ)   **Automatic Repeat Request (ARQ)** is the most widely used error-recovery approach in data communications. In this approach, message acknowledgements are employed by receivers to let senders know whether or not to retransmit data. The mechanism used to effect retransmission is the positive or negative acknowledgment, often called *ACK* and *NAK,* respectively. ACK and NAK characters are two of the special codes included in the ASCII and EBCDIC data encoding schemes. With discrete ARQ, as the receiving modem receives data from the sender, it uses the error-detection approach (such as VRC, LRC, or CRC) that was agreed upon during the handshaking process, performs its own error-check calculation, and compares the result with the error-check value transmitted by the sender. If the two values are equal, the data is assumed to be error free, and the receiver returns a positive acknowledgment (ACK) to the sender; if the two are unequal, a negative acknowledgment (NAK) is returned, and the sender retransmits the data. Of course, the sender must retain all messages until they have been positively acknowledged. Flow control mechanisms (mentioned previously in the chapter) that manage buffer memory in senders and receivers are involved in ARQ error-recovery processes.

In some instances, the retransmitted data is also detected as containing one or more errors. This may be due to an error-prone communication link or faulty hardware or software. To cut down on continual retransmission of messages, a *retry limit—* typically between 3 and 100—can be set. A retry limit of 5 means that if the same data is received in error more than once, the sender will attempt to retransmit it a maximum of five times; if the message is not successfully received by the fifth try, the receiver either terminates the dial-up connection or disables the sender. The objective of a retry limit is to avoid the unproductive work of continually processing corrupted messages. Once the cause of the problem has been corrected, the communication path is reinstated.

There are three major kinds of ARQ. These are discrete ARQ, continuous ARQ, and selective ARQ.

➤ *Discrete ARQ* is also known as *stop-and-wait* ARQ. In this approach, the sender transmits a character or packet and waits for a positive (ACK) or negative (NAK) before transmitting another character or packet. If an ACK is returned by the receiver, the sender transmits the next character or packet (depending on whether asynchronous or synchronous transmission is being used). If a NAK is returned, the sender transmits the original character or packet. This transmit-wait-transmit/retransmit process continues throughout the communication session. Because of the significant amount of time consumed by senders waiting to know what to do next, discrete ARQ is the least efficient ARQ error-recovery scheme.

➤ *Continuous ARQ* is also known as a *go-back-N ARQ*. It is also called a *sliding window protocol*. It eliminates the need for senders to wait before sending each subsequent packet by appending a *sequence number* to each packet. The sequence number enables the sender to keep transmitting packets, up to a fixed limit (such as four or eight) without waiting for an acknowledgement (ACK or NAK) from the receiver. The receiver performs the agreed-upon error check and acknowledges each packet. In contrast to discrete ARQ, however, acknowledgements in continuous ARQ include the packet sequence number as well as an ACK or NAK. When the receiver detects an error, it transmits a NAK along with the packet's sequence number. When the sender receives the NAK, it transmits the original packet and all the other packets following the one detected as containing one or more errors in sequence.

➤ *Selective ARQ*, like continuous ARQ, is a sliding window protocol that is more efficient than discrete ARQ. It is implemented in the same way as continuous ARQ except that it only requires the retransmission of packets received with errors. Because only select packets are retransmitted, rather than the original packet and all subsequent packets in the sequence, it is more efficient than continuous ARQ and typically has the highest data throughput rates of the various ARQ error-recovery mechanisms.

Forward Error-Correction Codes   Some error-detecting schemes allow the receiver not only to detect errors but also to correct some of them. Such codes are called **forward error-correcting codes**, the most common being *Hamming* codes and *Trellis Coded Modulation (TCM)*. As with all error-detection codes, additional, redundant information is transmitted with the data. However, because the volume of redundant information is greater when forward error correction is used, total data throughput can be less than that for other error-detection and recovery approaches. Error-correcting codes are convenient for situations in which single-bit errors occur, but for multiple-bit errors, the amount of redundant information that must be sent is cumbersome. The effectiveness of forward error-correcting codes is reduced by transmission noise that often creates bursts of errors, so these codes are not used as commonly as are error-detection schemes. Error-correcting codes have good applications in other areas, such as memory error-detection and correction, where the probability of single-bit errors is higher. *Error correcting control (ECC)* memory *(ECC RAM)*, for example, is often used in servers to facilitate the correction of data transmission errors between the internal components of a server. Some systems use a 6-bit Hamming code for each 16 bits of data to allow for single-bit error correction and double-bit error detection.

Error-Control/Recovery Standards

The two most widely supported error-detection and control standards used with today's modems are MNP class 4 and V.42. **MNP Class 4** uses adaptive size packet assembly to avoid errors when full-duplex transmission is used over dial-up circuits. It supersedes *MNP Class 2* (byte-oriented full-duplex asynchronous transmission) and *MNP Class 3* (full-duplex synchronous/asynchronous bit-oriented transmission) and increases asynchronous throughput by removing start and stop bits. **V.42** supports two

forward error-correcting codes Error-detecting schemes that allow the receiver not only to detect errors but also to correct some of them.

MNP Class 4 Uses adaptive size packet assembly to avoid errors when full duplex transmission is used over dial-up circuits. It supersedes MNP Class 2 (byte-oriented full-duplex asynchronous transmission) and MNP Class 3 (full-duplex synchronous/asynchronous bit-oriented transmission) and increases asynchronous throughput by removing start and stop bits.

V.42 An ITU standard for error checking that supports two error control/recovery processes: MNP Class 4 and Link Access Protocol for Modems (LAP-M). LAP-M is the primary protocol and MNP Class 4 is provided as an alternative protocol for compatibility.

link access protocol for modems (LAP-M) Builds on MNP Class 4 error control by adding selective ARQ.

error-control/recovery processes: MNP Class 4 and **link access protocol for modems (LAP-M)**. LAP-M builds on MNP Class 4 error control by adding selective ARQ. A pair of modems that supports V.42 negotiate the use of MNP Class 4 or LAP-M during the handshaking process. Modems manufactured by Microcom may also support *MNP Class 9* error control, which uses a proprietary "piggy-back" selective ARQ acknowledgment scheme to optimize throughput. Table 6-12 summarizes the error-control/recovery standards supported by the modems used with today's computers.

MODEM/COMPUTER COMMUNICATIONS

One of the roles of communication software is to enable microcomputer users to view and modify modem settings. Figure 6-33 illustrates some of the modem settings options that can be accessed via the Control Panel in Windows. If needed, error control, transmission speed, flow control, data compression, and UART settings can be altered via the communication software modules bundled with Windows. "Hyper Terminal" is another Windows communication software module (accessible via the Accessories menu) that enables users to set/modify terminal emulation settings used for microcomputer-to-host connections.

Hayes AT command set Most of the communication software used with today's computers issues Hayes AT command set instructions to modems, and modems that understand these instructions are said to be *Hayes compatible*. Such instructions activate modem features. Most modem manufacturers fully or partially support the AT command set for modem control.

Most of the communication software used with today's computers issues **Hayes AT command set** instructions to modems, and modems that understand these instructions are said to be *Hayes compatible*. When a microcomputer user wants to establish a data communication session over a dial-up connection, their communication software sends a *setup string* to the modem. The setup string specifies what settings are to be used for communication sessions with other modems and how the modem and computer will interact with one another. The sending and receipt of the setup string is similar to the handshaking process that occurs between a pair of modems at the beginning of a communication session.

SPECIAL PURPOSE MODEMS

Besides traditional modems used for connections over dial-up circuits, a variety of special purpose modems are found in data communication networks. Several of these are alternatives to dial-up modems.

Multiport Modems Multiport modems enable multiple terminals/microcomputers to share a single dial-up or dedicated connection. These operate in a manner similar to multiplexors (see Chapter 10).

Table 6-12 Error-Control Standards Supported in Popular Modems

Modem Standard	Error-Control/Recovery Standards Supported	Transmission Types Supported
V.92	MNP classes 1–4, V.42, TCM	Full duplex; half duplex
V.90	MNP classes 1–4, V.42, TCM	Full duplex; half duplex
V.34	MNP classes 1–4, V.42, TCM	Full duplex; half duplex
V.32ter	MNP classes 1–4, V.42, TCM	Full duplex; half duplex
V.32bis	MNP classes 1–4, V.42, TCM	Full duplex; half duplex
V.32	MNP classes 1–4, V.42, TCM	Full duplex; half duplex

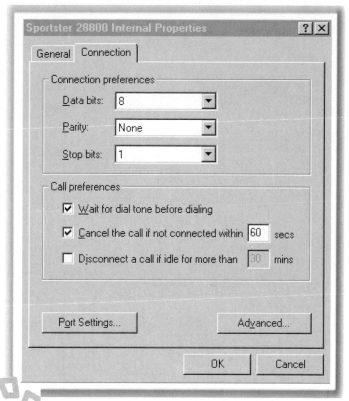

Figure 6-33a   Modem Settings Accessible via Control Panel in Windows

Short-Haul Modems   For short distances, short-haul modems can be used. These typically allow for transmission distances up to several miles, at varying speeds. As distance increases, speed decreases. Table 6-13 presents the relationship between distance and speed with short-haul modems. Strictly speaking, distance is a function of the resistance of wires in the communication medium, and speed is a function of the capacitance and resistance of the conductor. For practical purposes, distance and speed are functions of the thickness or gauge of the conductor. Table 6-13 holds for 24-gauge wire; greater speeds or distances are possible with 19-gauge wire, and lower speeds or distances would result from the use of 26-gauge wire.

Modem Eliminators   For very short distances, modem eliminators provide additional savings and very high data transmission rates. Modem eliminators, also called *line drivers* or *null modems,* can connect two devices that are in close proximity. A modem eliminator provides clocking and interface functions between two devices. One modem eliminator can replace two modems, as illustrated in Figure 6-34. The distances to be spanned are covered by interface specifications such as the RS-232-C standard, which recommends a distance of 50 feet for standard wires, or the RS-449 standard, which specifies 200 feet. Although manufacturers usually certify their modem eliminators at these standard distances, longer distances are possible. One use of

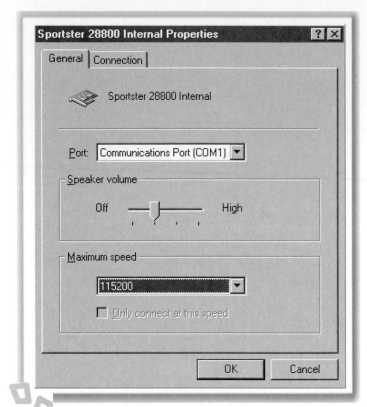

Figure 6-33b   Speed and Port Settings Accessible via Control Panel in Windows

modem eliminators is high-speed, computer-to-computer communication links. Data transmission rates up to 2 mbps can be supported by modem eliminators.

CSU/DSUs   Modems are not needed when computers interface with switched or leased carrier digital circuits. CSU/DSUs are used in place of modems in these situations. When connected to switched digital services, CSU/DSUs include dialing capabilities. The CSU connects to a digital line and terminates the digital signal. The DSU transmits digital signals onto the digital line. A CSU/DSU may be separate units, or their functions may be integrated into a single unit. CSU/DSUs provide a variety of interface options, such as T-1, fractional T-1, and frame relay interfaces. Some have integrated modems to allow network support staff to dial in and remotely operate the unit.

Fiber Optic Modems   Modems are also used for fiber optic transmission at speeds ranging from 1,200 bps up to 50 mbps, with popular intermediate speeds of 56 kbps, 100 kbps, 250 kbps, 1.544 mbps, 5 mbps, and 10 mbps.

Cable Modems   As noted in Chapter 5, cable modems have emerged as one of the most popular local loop options for broadband Internet access. There are two major international standards for cable modem products. The Data Over Cable Service

Figure 6-33c   Error and Flow Control Settings
Accessible via Control Panel in Windows

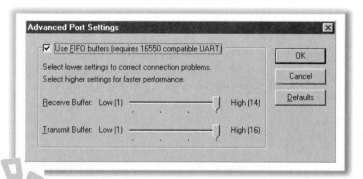

Figure 6-33d   UART Settings Accessible via Control
Panels in Windows

Table 6-13   Short-Haul Modems: Speed vs. Distance

Distance (Miles)	Maximum Speed Using AWG 24 Wires
3.0	128 kbps
4.6	64 kbps
4.8	56 kbps
5.0	48 kbps
5.5	32 kbps

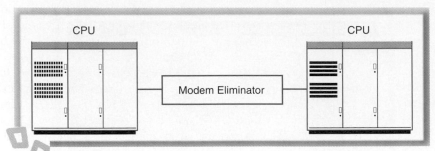

Figure 6-34   Modem Eliminator

Interface Specification (DOCSIS) is widely accepted in the United States. The DOCSIS specification is recognized by the ITU as ITU J.112. In Europe, the DVB/DAVIC (Digital Video Broadcast/Digital Audio Visual Council) EuroModem standard is widely accepted.

The DOCSIS standard specifies the frequency ranges to be used for upstream and downstream channels to subscriber computers. Cable modem termination system (CMTS) equipment at cable service provider offices communicates with the cable modems at subscriber locations. Most cable modems are external devices that connect to a personal computer through a standard 10BaseT Ethernet card or universal serial bus (USB) interface, although internal PCI modem cards are also available.

ISDN Modems   ISDN modems are sometimes called *terminal adapters, NT-1 units,* or *digital modems.* Like dial-up modems for analog telephone lines, ISDN modems can be implemented as external units or expansion cards. Voice-over-data is supported by ISDN modems, and some ISDN modems are cable V.90/IDSN hybrids that are capable of being connected to either ISDN or traditional dial-up circuits. ITU's V.110 and V.120 are the most widely accepted standards for ISDN modems.

DSL Modems   DSL modems are used to connect to DSL services. As noted in Chapter 5, DSL modems in subscriber computers communicate with DSL access multiplexors (DSLAMs) at local telephone company central offices. Voice-over-data is typically supported by DSL modems. As a result, DSL subscribers are often able to avoid the cost of a second dial-up telephone line for Internet access. The *ITU's G.lite* standard specifies a maximum download of 1.5 mbps. This was adopted in 1999. ITU's G.992.1 standard specifies higher connection speeds (up to 8 mbps downstream and 1 mbps upstream).

SUMMARY

Although broadband Internet access via cable modems and DSL is increasing in popularity, dial-up modems are used most frequently to connect to ISPs and gain access to the Internet. Modem-to-modem communications illustrate a variety of fundamental data communication processes, including character encoding, parallel versus serial transmission, asynchronous versus synchronous transmission, half-duplex versus full-duplex transmission, carrier wave modulation and demodulation, data compression, and error detection and recovery.

Several different communication codes are used in data communication to transform human-readable characters into digital formats—fixed length strings of bits. ASCII and EBCDIC are the most widely used data communication codes. Unicode (ISO 10646) is emerging as another important character-encoding scheme.

Both parallel and serial transmission may be used to transmit encoded characters. Parallel transmission is used for internal data transmissions between computer components and is also widely used to send files to attached printers. Serial transmission is used most widely for data communications. UART (Universal Asynchronous Receiver/Transmitter) chips convert incoming serial signals to the parallel signal format used for internal communications.

Encoded characters can be transmitted via asynchronous or synchronous transmission. Asynchronous transmission involves the transmission of one character/byte at a time, whereas multiple data characters are transmitted in blocks/packets when synchronous transmission is used. Today's modems commonly support both asynchronous and synchronous transmission.

The basic kinds of data flow found in data communications are simplex, half duplex, and full duplex. Most modems used with today's computers support both half and full duplex.

A wide variety of interfaces and interface standards exist for connecting data communication equipment (DCE) and data terminal equipment (DTE). RS-232-C, however, is the most widely supported standard for DCE/DTE interfaces.

Digital circuits are becoming more prevalent among carriers. The advantages of digital transmission for data communication are lower error rates, higher transmission rates, elimination of the need to convert from digital format to analog and back to digital, and better security. Traditional dial-up connections, however, require the digital signals emerging from computer ports to be converted to analog form. Modems use amplitude, frequency, and phase modulation to represent bits on analog circuits; phase modulation is used most commonly. Most of the modems used today are capable of representing multiple bits (such as dibits, tribits, or quadbits) rather than single bits each time that they modulate the carrier wave.

Today's modems are capable of operating at various speeds and support data compression. V.34 modems are capable of a maximum of 33.6 kbps. V.92 modems have 56-kbps download speeds and 48-kbps upload speeds. Data compression makes it possible to have data throughput rates that exceed modem transmission speeds. V.42bis and MNP Class 5 are the most widely supported data compression standards. Password systems, callback capabilities, and encryption can be used to enhance the security of modem-to-modem communications.

All data communication systems, including modem-to-modem communications, must be able to address data transmission errors. Detecting errors requires that redundant information be transmitted with the data. The three most common error-detection schemes in data communication are vertical redundancy check (VRC), longitudinal redundancy check (LRC), and cyclic redundancy check (CRC). The most effective is CRC. In some protocols, sequence checking is also used to improve the reliability of transmission. MNP class 4 and V.42 are the most common error-control standards supported by today's modems. These typically support both continuous and selective automatic request for transmission (ARQ), which are more efficient than discrete ARQ. Forward error-correction codes are sometimes used to enable the receiver not only to detect errors but also to correct some of them.

Communication software enables users to modify modem settings. The Hayes AT command set is used most commonly to modify modem configurations. A variety of special purpose modems exists, including multiport modems, short-haul modems, modem eliminators, fiber optic modems, cable modems, ISDN modems, and DSL modems.

KEY TERMS

- adaptive line probing
- adaptive size packet assembly
- American Standard Code for Information Interchange (ASCII)
- amplitude modulation (AM)
- analog transmission
- asynchronous transmission (async)
- Automatic Repeat Request (ARQ)
- byte
- callback
- carrier signal
- checksum
- crosstalk
- cyclic redundancy check (CRC)
- data communications equipment (DCE)
- data compression
- data terminating equipment (DTE)
- dibits
- digital format
- digital transmission
- dynamic speed shifts
- echo
- electromagnetic interference (EMI)
- envelope delay distortion
- Extended Binary-Coded Decimal Interchange Code (EBCDIC)
- fallback
- fallforward
- FireWire
- flow control
- forward error-correcting codes
- frequency modulation (FM)
- handshaking
- Hayes AT command set
- impulse noise
- link access protocol for modems (LAP-M)
- longitudinal redundancy check (LRC)
- MNP Class 4
- MNP Class 5
- MNP Class 7
- modem
- parallel transmission
- parity check
- phase jitter
- phase modulation
- point-to-point protocol (PPP)
- quadbits
- quadrature amplitude modulation (QAM)
- Serial Line Internet Protocol (SLIP)
- serial transmission
- synchronous transmission
- tribits
- Unicode
- universal asynchronous receiver/transmitter (UART)
- Universal Serial Bus (USB)
- V.42
- V.42bis
- V.44
- V.92
- white noise
- wireless service provider (WSP)

REVIEW QUESTIONS

1. What is PPP? What role does it play in data communications?
2. What is meant by "digital format"?
3. Compare ASCII and EBCDIC.
4. What are the limitations of a 6-bit data code?
5. What are the limitations of an 8-bit data code?
6. What is Unicode (ISO 10646)? Why is Unicode emerging as an important character-encoding scheme?
7. Compare parallel and serial transmission.
8. Compare asynchronous and synchronous transmission.
9. What is the role of UART chips in data communications?
10. Define
    a. simplex transmission
    b. half-duplex transmission
    c. full-duplex transmission
11. Compare DCE and DTE.

12. What is RS-232-C? What is specified by this standard?
13. Compare digital and analog signal transmission.
14. Identify and briefly describe the advantages of digital transmission.
15. What is a modem?
16. What is a carrier signal?
17. Compare amplitude, frequency, and phase modulation.
18. What is meant by "baud rate"? Why is a modem's baud rate typically less than its bit rate?
19. Compare dibits, tribits, and quadbits.
20. Compare the transmission speeds of V.34, V.90, and V.92 modems.
21. Describe
    a. adaptive line probing
    b. fallback
    c. dynamic speed shifts
22. Compare MNP Class 5 and V.42bis.
23. What are the characteristics of callback modems?
24. Briefly describe each of the following:
    a. white noise
    b. impulse noise
    c. echo
    d. attenuation
    e. electromagnetic interference
25. Describe the major ways to prevent data transmission errors.
26. What is flow control? Why is flow control needed in data communications?
27. Describe how parity checking works.
28. What are checksums? Briefly describe the use of checksums in error detection.
29. Explain why CRC is a better error-detection scheme than parity or longitudinal redundancy checks.
30. Explain the role of sequence checks in error detection and recovery.
31. What is ARQ?
32. Compare stop-and-wait, go-back-N, and selective ARQ.
33. Describe the characteristics of forward error-correction codes.
34. Compare MNP Class 4 and V.42.
35. Explain how communications software is used to change modem settings.
36. What is the Hayes AT command set? What is a setup string?
37. Compare short-haul modems and modem eliminators.
38. Identify the major standards for each of the following:
    a. cable modems
    b. ISDN modems
    c. DSL modems

PROBLEMS AND EXERCISES

1. Use the Internet to identify the national, regional, and local ISPs in your area. (*Hint:* You may want to consult www.thelist.com.) Summarize your results in a table.
2. Use the Internet to find out more about PPP. Develop a paper or PowerPoint presentation that describes how PPP works.
3. Use the Internet to find out additional information about UARTs. Summarize the features and capabilities of UARTs being installed in today's computers in a paper or PowerPoint presentation.
4. Label each of the following items as simplex, half duplex, or full duplex:
    a. commercial radio
    b. CB radio

    c. television

    d. smoke signals

    e. classroom discussion

    f. family arguments

    g. ocean tides

    h. short-wave radio communication

5. Calculate the line time required for the following transaction. Assume a line speed of 28,800 bps, and 10 bits per character.

    a. The operator enters a 10-character employee ID.

    b. The system returns a 500-character employee record.

    c. The operator changes the zip code and retransmits only the 5-character zip code back to the system.

    d. The system acknowledges receipt and positive action by sending the operator a 20-character message.

6. Use the Internet to learn more about parallel interface connections (such as Centronics connectors) and standards (such as EPP). Summarize what you find in a paper or PowerPoint presentation.

7. Use the Internet to find out more about USB and FireWire ports. Compare/ contrast these with traditional serial and parallel ports, and explain why they are increasingly popular interface alternatives to traditional ports.

8. Explain how a modem would convert digital electric signals into analog form using frequency modulation.

9. Why is Morse code not a viable alternative for data communications?

10. Use the Internet to find out more about V.92 modems, their baud rates, and how they compare to V.90 modems in terms of features/capabilities. Summarize your findings in a paper or PowerPoint presentation.

11. The handshaking process is mentioned frequently throughout the chapter. Make a list of the aspects of modem-to-modem communications that are negotiated and agreed upon during the handshaking process. Summarize your list in a table.

12. You use your V.92 modem to connect to a V.90 modem at your ISP. What is the highest data compression ratio that can be negotiated during handshaking? Why? If this ratio cannot be used, what others could be agreed upon by this pair of modems?

13. If the speed of transmission on a line is 33,600 bps and that line is hit by lightning that causes an impulse distortion of 3.5 ms, what is the maximum number of bits that could be in error?

14. Describe how parity checking works. If even parity is used, what will the parity bit be for the ASCII characters *P, A, R, I, T,* and *Y*? What would be the LRC BBC for these characters?

15. What would be the checksum for the ASCII characters identified in problem 14?

16. Use the Internet to find out more about Trellis Coded Modulation (TCM). Explain how TCM helps to prevent data transmission errors and the need for senders to transmit packets.

17. Use the Internet to find out more about forward error-correction codes such as Hamming code. Identify and compare several forward error-correction codes in a paper or PowerPoint presentation.

18. Use the Internet to find out more about cable modems and DSL modems. Compare their features, capabilities, and standards in a paper or PowerPoint presentation.

Chapter Cases
PDAs in the Military

Would you think of a handheld computer as a military weapon? In fact, handhelds' benefits are already being seen in the military. In Afghanistan, almost half of all U.S. Navy sailors have a Palm V to track enemy movements, conduct ship inspections, access military and personal e-mails, and perform other tasks. The *USS McFaul's* sailors, for example, can reply to personal e-mails in their leisure time by establishing a connection between the Palm and infrared ports installed in the ship. When the sailors are on duty, these pocket-sized devices are being used as logistical and tactical weapons of modern warfare.

The most popular brands in sailors' hands are Palm Pilot and HandSpring Inc; Palm sold between 30,000 and 50,000 Palms to the Navy and 25,000 to 30,000 units to the Army in 2000 and 2001. In addition to the Palm V's standard features, the handheld computers issued to *USS McFaul* sailors include a new security software package called "Restrictor," which requires a "log-on" ID and authentication password to protect business sensitive notes and contact information stored on the computers in case they are lost or misplaced. The devices are primarily used for data collection and information distribution. The cost of Palm and Handspring devices can be as low as $150 per unit.

PDA vendors tout handheld devices as the next major advancement in the Internet-based technologies. They claim that handhelds represent the third evolution of the Internet after e-mail and the World Wide Web and are the key to the future evolution of the Internet. Although military leaders do not disagree with this assessment, they recognize that these handheld devices also have tremendous potential as strategic weapons for the U.S. Army, U.S. Air Force, and U.S. Navy.

Several PDA vendors, such as Symbol Technologies Inc. and Paravant Computer Systems Inc., have already committed to supply the military with foolproof handhelds. Some of their models are waterproof, resistant to extreme temperatures, sealed against dust, and designed to resist 4-foot drops onto concrete.

In 1999, Symbol Technologies executives signed a $248 million contract to supply industrialized handheld devices to the U.S. Department of Defense. Symbol Technologies' models include the Symbol PPT 2700 and the Symbol PDT 7200. The Symbol PPT 2700 combines strong mobility, bar code scanning, and wireless LAN connectivity with the new Microsoft Pocket PC platform. It has been ergonomically designed to enable convenient one-handed data capture operation, while providing a secure and comfortable fit in the hand. It is sealed to IP54 standards for protection against windblown rain and dust, and withstands multiple drops onto concrete up to 4 feet (1.2 meters). It also comes with 16 MB of RAM and 12 MB of flash ROM for data or program storage. It measures 7 inches long by 3.625 inches wide by 1 inch high and weighs 11.8 ounces. Its list price in early 2002 was $1,250.

The Symbol PDT 7200 has been designed for extreme environments and features a powerful 32-bit 486-based processor, voice paging, touch screen control, and one-and-two bar code scanning. It comes with 4 MB, expandable to 16 MB, of RAM and runs industry-standard Microsoft MS-DOS or Microsoft Windows CE. This device assures excellent performance running data-intensive applications such as tracking inventory, ordering merchandise, or managing equipment. It measures 7.8 inches long by 5.9 inches wide by 3.7 inches high and weighs 21 ounces.

Paravant Computer Systems Inc., a defense electronics company, has already developed three handhelds for military purposes and has others in mind. The case for Paravant's pocket storable RHC-500 device is made of high-impact plastic that has been reinforced to endure electromagnetic interference and fungus; as a result, it can easily track troop movements in extreme environments. The RHC-2000 features encryption keys and provides a number of other security mechanisms to ensure the safe storage of mission-critical data and information. A third Paravant pocket storable device, called the *Leopard,* includes applications that can find targets by interacting with laser binoculars. Paravant's PDA models for the military are priced between $600 and $7,500.

The key in this information era is to provide soldiers with all information needed to perform their duties and enhance their quality of service. The Space and Naval Warfare Systems Center and

Warrior Solutions Inc. are developing PDA software that promises to map enemy locations, track personnel, and conduct heat-stress surveys. The Space and Naval Warfare Systems Center has a team of software programmers dedicated to developing handheld software. Moreover, the U.S. Navy has begun outfitting its ships (including the *USS McFaul*) so that they can serve as platforms for testing handheld devices.

Defense contractors such as Warrior Solutions Inc. are also helping to transform PDAs into key elements of the modern warfare arsenal. Warrior Solutions Inc. has developed two handheld software programs called *Platoon Personnel* and *Platoon*

Leaders' Guide. Platoon Personnel provides assistance with daily administrative tasks for the U.S. Army. Platoon Leaders' Guide provides instructions for fighting, based on current doctrine.

Although PDAs are unlikely to be perceived as devices to be feared by the general public, it is apparent that the military recognizes their potential to provide tactical and operational support for personnel in the field. With initiatives under way to develop and enhance military application software for handhelds, PDAs may soon be feared by foes on future battlefields.

CASE QUESTIONS

1. How can PDAs be used to enhance the leisure-time activities of military personnel?
2. Why is PDA security an important issue for military applications?
3. Use the Internet to update and extend the range of PDA applications in the military. What are the major characteristics of these new applications?
4. What can businesses learn from military applications of PDAs? What kinds of applications being used in the military could be adapted for use by business organizations?
5. Use the Internet to identify medical applications of PDAs in the military. How are these similar to and distinct from PDA medical applications outside the military?

SOURCES

Pui-Wing, Tam. "U.S. Forces Pack Pocket Computers in Afghanistan." *Wall Street Journal* (October 23, 2001, pp. B1, B4).

Symbol Technologies Inc. Retrieved February 6, 2002, from www.symbol.com.

"*USS McFaul* Gets Technology into Sailor's Palms." *AllHands* (2000). Retrieved February 7, 2002, from www.mediacen.navy.mil/pubs/allhands/nov00/pg6g.htm.

Warrior Solutions Inc. Retrieved February 7, 2002, from www.warriorsolutions.com.

Note: For more information on modem fundamentals, see an additional case on the Web site, www.prenhall.com/stamper, "DSL vs. Cable Modems: What's the Best Choice?"

Introduction to Local Area Networks

After studying this chapter, you should be able to:

■ Describe the characteristics of local area networks (LANs).

■ Identify and briefly describe the major reasons why businesses implement LANs.

■ Identify several alternatives to full-fledged LANs.

■ Identify and briefly describe criteria used to select among LAN alternatives.

■ Briefly describe the major hardware components of LANs.

■ Identify and briefly describe the kinds of communication media found in LANs.

■ Describe LAN-to-Internet interfaces.

In the early days of networking, local area networks (LANs) were created by businesses to connect minicomputers, mainframes, and supercomputers. During the 1980s, soon after the proliferation of microcomputers in business organizations, LANs were installed to link microcomputers. Today, the microcomputers used by most employees in business organizations are attached to local area networks, and it is via these connections that users are able to access other computing resources such as mainframes, supercomputers, and the Internet. In this chapter, we focus on the reasons why LANs have become fundamental building blocks in the development of corporate, enterprise-wide networks. We will also discuss the different kinds of hardware found in business LANs.

WHAT IS A LOCAL AREA NETWORK?

A **local area network (LAN)** is designed to serve the needs of business users in a limited geographical area. A LAN may be limited to a single room, a building, or a campus. Some may serve broader geographical areas, but even the most geographically expansive LANs rarely cover more than a few kilometers. Communication speeds in LANs typically exceed those of dial-up modems and broadband Internet-access technologies

local area network (LAN) A data communication network that servers use in a confined geographic area and that uses high transmission speeds, generally 1 mbps or higher. Major LAN components include servers, workstations, network operating systems, communication links, and wiring center technologies.

273

such as digital subscriber lines (DSLs) and cable modems. LAN communication speeds are generally also faster than those found in wide area networks (WANs); only a few WAN services, such as SONET (synchronous optical network) services, are capable of providing communication speeds that exceed those found in LANs. Typical LAN speeds today range from 10 mbps to 1 gbps. Because a wide variety of computing devices can be attached to LANs, LANs are capable of providing rapid, transparent access to diverse applications needed by business users in the limited geographic areas that they serve.

LANs have become fundamental building blocks for enterprise-wide networks. LANs are found in both large and small organizations. In small organizations, a LAN may be the only network that exists. In large organizations, there are likely to be multiple LANs interconnected by bridges, routers, switches, and other internetworking technologies. Such internetworking technologies also enable LAN users to access WAN services or computing resources at other geographically dispersed business locations. LANs also bring Internet resources to the desktops of business users; they are a primary means for workers and employers to access and leverage the Internet.

BUSINESS RATIONALE FOR LANs

Businesses became interested in microcomputer LANs during the 1980s, not long after desktop systems began to proliferate in the offices of most business professionals. Business organizations recognized the resource-sharing potential of LANs as well as their ability to enhance communication among employees. Cost-effectiveness, support for work groups, ability to share large files, management control, and modular expansion are other reasons for the popularity of LANs among business organizations.

Cost-Effectiveness

LANs enable organizations to attach and share a variety of computing resources including microcomputers, printers, scanners, fax machines, and modems. Expensive peripherals that businesses would consider cost prohibitive to attach to each user's microcomputer, such as color laser printers, can be justified, because LANs provide the mechanism for sharing them among all (or select) LAN users. Data and software can also be shared by LAN users. The ability to share resources has a direct impact on an organization's expenses. If users can share hardware, less hardware is needed. Less obviously, cost-effectiveness may derive from the ability of users to be more productive as a result of better communication with coworkers. Although some kinds of LANs can be expensive to implement and maintain, the ability to share computing resources is one of the primary reasons why LANs are common in businesses.

Support for Work Groups

Just as microcomputers have expanded the potential for individuals to be productive, LANs make it possible for work groups to be more productive. Work-group productivity tools, collectively known as *groupware*, allow members of a work group to communicate and coordinate activities. A variety of groupware applications exist, such as group calendaring systems, work-flow systems, and electronic meeting systems. These and several other kinds of group productivity tools are discussed more fully in Chapter 1.

Large Data Transfers

The high speeds found in LANs enable users to share large files. Today, many graphical and multimedia files are justifiably called *BLOBs (binary large objects)* because they consume many megabytes of storage space. Although such files may take an enormous amount of time to transmit between modems across standard dial-up circuits, they can be sent between users of the same LAN in seconds or even fractions of a second.

Management Control

Businesses are also attracted to LANs because they have the potential to provide better management control over computing resources. A LAN can help a company standardize its microcomputer environment. Application standards are often more easily enforced in LAN environments. For example, if a business wanted to limit its support to a single word processing program, such as Word 2000, it could require users to access the word processing program from a LAN file server rather than from the hard drive of LAN–attached workstations. This would force LAN users to access the same version of the word processing program and would avoid file sharing and file conversion/reformatting challenges associated with network environments that allow users to use a variety of word processing programs.

When employed in LANs, *metering software* can help network managers ensure compliance with software license agreements. (Software license agreements are discussed more fully in Chapter 9.) If, for example, the organization has a license that limits the number of concurrent users of a wireless application development tool, metering software will ensure that the maximum number of users specified by the license agreement is not exceeded. If the maximum number was 10, and 10 copies of the application development tool are in use, additional users requesting the tool will receive a message from the metering software indicating that their request cannot be satisfied at that point in time. In practice, it is rare for all users to need the same application at the same point in time. Metering software can help an organization keep up with the demand for its software applications. In many instances, they find that fewer licenses are needed than would be required to install a copy of each application on each computer in the network; this has the potential to reduce expenses.

LANs also help networking professionals combat one of the most unsettling problems facing today's computer users: computer viruses. Virus detection software installed on LAN servers can be updated daily and used to scan (and disinfect) LAN–attached workstations at specified intervals. Diskless workstations, including some thin clients (microcomputers with scaled-down capabilities), can provide additional protection against virus infections by reducing the possibility of users unleashing a virus on infected disks.

Modular Expansion

LANs also enable organizations to grow their networks incrementally and in a modular fashion. As noted in Chapter 13, segments can be added to existing LANs via repeaters or bridges. In addition, it is relatively easy to add new workstations, servers, printers, or peripherals to a LAN or LAN segment in order to keep up with an expanding user base or the need for new computing equipment and resources.

Additional Sources of Business Interest in LANs

There are a variety of other reasons for organizations to be interested in LANs. Several of these are summarized here.

➤ Uptime/reliability of LANs is high when they are properly administered.
➤ LAN network operating systems continue to mature, thereby facilitating LAN administration.
➤ LANs provide the ability to share data.
➤ LANs provide the ability to adapt to changing hardware and software requirements.

➤ Software upgrades can be rapidly distributed to LAN users.

➤ LANs may be linked to other LANs, WANs, and carrier services such as frame relay and ATM (asynchronous transfer mode).

➤ LANs provide the ability to leverage interconnection technologies to access Internet resources.

➤ LAN-to-host interfaces enable LAN users to access minicomputer and mainframe applications.

➤ Businesses have the option of private ownership and control of LAN equipment or leasing.

➤ There is widespread availability of LAN administration training and certification programs.

➤ Price/product competition among LAN equipment and software vendors helps to ensure the cost effectiveness of LANs.

➤ LAN administration and technical support may be outsourced if in-house costs become excessive.

➤ LANs help organizations move from centralized to distributed or client/server computing environments.

➤ Wireless LANs and wireless segments to cable-based LANs increase the variety of LAN options available to business organizations.

➤ LAN options exist for businesses of all sizes, from the very small to the very large.

➤ Software vendors are creating LAN versions of business software that formerly were only available for minicomputer or mainframe platforms; this enables organizations to migrate (downsize) applications from larger, more expensive host-based systems to LANs.

Added Responsibilities of LANs

It is quite clear that LANs have a number of features that businesses find attractive. However, implementing a LAN brings additional responsibilities and the need for network management. Effectively managing a LAN involves much more than providing technical support for attached microcomputers. Depending on the number of users and applications, LAN management ranges in scope from a part-time responsibility to a full-time job for one or more employees. Many organizations employ a full-time networking professional for every 35 users; other organizations have higher user/networking professional ratios such as 50:1 or higher. The number of networking professionals needed to support a LAN adds to the LAN's total cost of ownership. The cost to support and administer a LAN should not be overlooked when selecting among LAN alternatives.

LAN ALTERNATIVES

We can look at LAN alternatives from two perspectives: different kinds of LAN implementations or hardware and software alternatives to LANs. In this section, we discuss both. We start by looking at the ways LANs can be implemented.

LAN Implementation Alternatives

A LAN can be implemented by using dedicated servers, using nondedicated servers, and as a peer-to-peer implementation.

dedicated server
One or more computers that operate only as a file, database, or other type of server in a computer network.

Dedicated Servers   In a **dedicated server** LAN, one or more computers are designated as servers; servers provide users with access to shared computing resources in the network, and dedicated servers serve only in that capacity. They do not double as user computers. The majority of today's LANs are classified as client/server LANs because they include dedicated servers. This is certainly true of most large LANs. However, the average number of nodes in microcomputer LANs is relatively small, and many LANs have fewer than 20 nodes. For these small LANs, a dedicated server (which is likely to be underused) may reduce the cost-effectiveness of the network. In such cases, nondedicated servers may be more cost-effective solutions.

Nondedicated Servers   Some of the operating systems used to support smaller LANs do not require dedicated servers; one or more nondedicated servers is sufficient. A **nondedicated server** can be used as both a server and a workstation. Because it is capable of providing other LAN users with access to computing resources under its control, it functions as a server. However, a nondedicated server can also be used as a user workstation. For example, it is hard to imagine four users in a typical office keeping a dedicated server busy most of the time. If the server is allowed to also function as a workstation, it is likely to be used more effectively in a small office environment.

> **nondedicated server** A computer that can operate as both a server and a workstation in a computer network.

The advantage of nondedicated servers is more effective use of computing resources. There are also some disadvantages. A nondedicated server must divide its workload between its application work and its server work. Sometimes, it might be very busy in both roles. In these instances, both those using the nondedicated server as a server and those using it as a workstation will experience service degradation. If these conflicts occur too often, the LAN administrator should consider transforming the computer into a dedicated server. Another disadvantage of nondedicated servers is the increased likelihood of server failures. Simply running both user applications and the software needed to enable the workstation to function as a server increases the possibility of failures (freeze-ups and crashes) because the machine is required to function in two capacities: server and workstation. However, the most probable source of a nondedicated server failure is the user application or the users themselves. If the application gets locked, the server may be unable to attend to its server duties. If the user powers the server down or unintentionally formats the server disk, the server function will also be disrupted.

Peer-to-Peer LANs   Nondedicated servers are common in peer-to-peer LANs. In a peer-to-peer LAN, any or all nodes can operate as servers. If five microcomputers are networked in a peer-to-peer LAN, the network administrator can designate which computer resources are shareable and which are not. One of the five computers, for example, may have a high-speed laser printer attached to it as well as a slower color ink-jet printer. In a peer-to-peer network, the laser printer could be shared with other LAN users while the ink-jet printer remains private to the microcomputer's regular user. Similarly, specific directories stored on the hard drive of one of the computers in a peer-to-peer network can be designated as shareable while the others are not.

All of the widely used microcomputer operating systems support peer-to-peer networking, including Windows 95, Windows 98, Windows Me, Windows NT Workstation, Windows 2000, Windows XP, Linux, OS/2, and the various System/Mac OS versions found on Macintosh computers from Apple. When equipped with network adapter cards, microcomputers running these popular desktop operating systems can be configured for printer and file sharing. In addition, when needed, access to specific files or printers can be controlled via passwords. Before Windows became the dominant platform for peer-to-peer networks, products such as LANtastic and Personal NetWare were used to create peer-to-peer LANs.

Peer-to-peer LANs are an option for many small LANs. As the number of users increases, however, full-fledged LANs with client/server network operating systems such as NetWare or Windows 2000 Server become increasingly desirable because of their superior ability to support dedicated servers. The main business benefits of a peer-to-peer network in comparison to a full-fledged LAN are low cost per node and lower total cost of ownership. A major disadvantage of peer-to-peer LANs is a limited number of capabilities relative to those found in full-fledged LANs.

Other Implementations

Alternative implementations to a LAN include centralized computer systems; service bureaus; sub–LANs; and zero-slot LANs.

Centralized Computer Systems   In the early days of computing, the traditional approach to networking was host-centric (see Figure 7-1). Large, central computers are still a mainstay in the computing environments of many business organizations and serve as the primary means for processing large volumes of data, producing big reports, supporting special-purpose hardware devices such as check reader/sorters, and so on. For example, banks often process their daily closing work on midrange systems or mainframes rather than microcomputers or networks of microcomputers. Networks built around midrange systems are still widely used in business organizations, and because of this, centralized computer networks remain as viable options to LANs for many firms.

Figure 7-1   A Central Host Computer Network

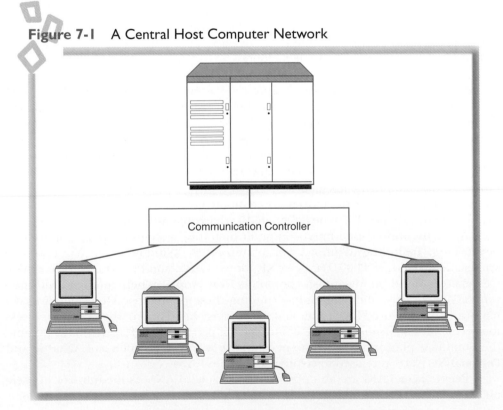

Communication Controller

Service Bureaus Another alternative available to some organizations is a computer **service bureau**. This alternative provides the same computing and connectivity capabilities as the large, central host alternative but without the high initial costs. The subscriber pays for the amount of computing resources (disk storage, processing time, and printed output) used. Subscribers also pay for custom software modifications and possibly a monthly subscription fee. This pricing structure is similar to that offered by telephone systems, with a monthly connection charge regardless of usage and a second charge based on the amount of use. If usage is high, costs can be significant.

Service bureaus are still popular among smaller credit unions and financial services firms. FiTech, for example, is a service bureau with headquarters in Atlanta, Georgia, that provides transaction processing, accounting, and reporting applications for more than 50 credit unions in the southeastern United States. Most subscribers connect to FiTech hosts via leased circuits. Although most service bureau subscribers also have LANs to support general-purpose applications such as word processing and spreadsheets, internal file and data sharing related to their core processes is accomplished via the service bureau.

Today, many service bureaus are called **application service providers (ASPs)**. ASPs, sometimes called *commercial service providers*, are organizations that host software applications on their own servers within their own facilities. Customers rent the use of the application(s) and access the ASP over a private line connection (leased line) or via the Internet.

Zero-Slot LANs Some low-speed LANs use "standard" microcomputer components such as a serial, parallel, or USB port for connecting one node to another. These LAN implementations are sometimes called **zero-slot LANs** because they do not require an additional slot on the microcomputer's expansion board for a LAN adapter card. Because LAN adapter cards are not needed in zero-slot LANs, these kinds of LANs are typically less expensive to implement than full-fledged LANs. Typically, installation costs are limited to cables, LAN software, and perhaps server hardware.

Sub–LANs **Sub–LANs** provide a subset of full-fledged LAN capabilities, primarily peripheral sharing and file transfer. They differ from a LAN in two ways: A sub–LAN's data transfer rates and costs are lower than those of a LAN, and file transfer capabilities are typically less transparent than on a LAN. On most sub–LANs, if a user needs to transfer a file to another workstation, the sender must first call the person operating the receiving workstation to manually establish the setting for data transfer.

Sub–LANs are implemented with data switches. **Data switches** provide connections between microcomputers in much the same way that a telephone company provides connections between callers. A switch configuration is shown in Figure 7-2. If device A must connect with device B, the switch establishes the connection, as illustrated in Figure 7-3. Many data switches are designed specifically for sharing peripheral devices, such as printers and plotters, and use manual switching. This means that a user must turn a switch selector knob on the switch box to make the proper connection. With software controlled switching, a user can enter the address of a desired device. If the device is not already in use, the connection is made; otherwise, the user must wait until the device is available. The connection remains active until one of the two stations requests a disconnect; alternatively, a disconnect may occur after a specified time of inactivity. Software-controlled switching does not solve the file transfer problem described earlier. Operators at the sending and receiving computers still must coordinate file transfer by starting the file transfer software at each end of the connection.

service bureau An organization that provides data processing and online services for other companies. A service bureau may offer a variety of software packages, batch processing services, or custom programming. Subscriber charges are typically based on the volume of data stored on the system and processing time used and usually connect to the service bureau through dial-up connections, private lines, the Internet, frame relay, or other WAN services.

application service provider (ASP) Organization that hosts software applications on its own servers within its own facilities. Customers rent the use of the application(s) and access the ASP over a private line connection (leased line) or via the Internet.

zero-slot LAN A low-speed LAN using standard microcomputer components that do not require the use of an additional slot on the computer's expansion board for a LAN adapter.

sub–LANs Networks that provide a subset of LAN capabilities, primarily peripheral sharing and file transfer, but that have lower data transfer rates and transparency than a full-fledged LAN.

data switch A switch box implemented on sub-LANs to provide connections between two network-attached devices.

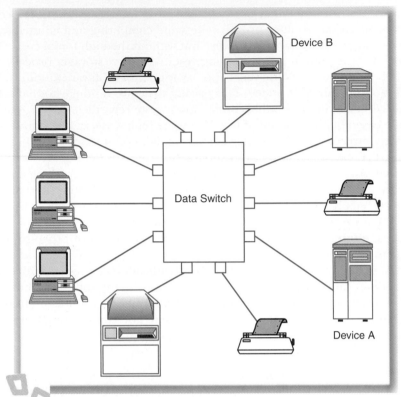

Figure 7-2   Switch Configuration

Sub–LANs are inexpensive. A serial or parallel interface is typically used between the microcomputers and the switch. Because serial and parallel ports are either standard or low-cost options, the cost for the microcomputer components is limited to those ports and a cable.

The disadvantages of a data switch are the low speed of the communication link; lack of user transparency, expandability, and ability to interface to other networks; and contention. The line speeds supported may be 19.2 kbps or slower. Such speeds may be adequate for small file transfers and retrieving individual database records but not for large data transfers such as downloading program files, large documents, or large portions of a database. The ability to connect sub–LANs to other networks is generally poor.

Contention can also occur when using a data switch. If two users want to connect to a device such as a printer at the same time, only one of the connections can be made. The first request received is granted, and the second user must wait until the first connection is severed. Some data switches have onboard random access memory (RAM) to alleviate this contention problem. If multiple outputs for the same printer are received, one can be held in the switch's RAM until the printer becomes available. In the earlier situation, both users would perceive that their connection request was honored. Data switches are an effective, low-cost way to share peripherals and accomplish infrequent transfers of small files. They are not well suited for downloading software programs or large data files or for frequent file exchanges.

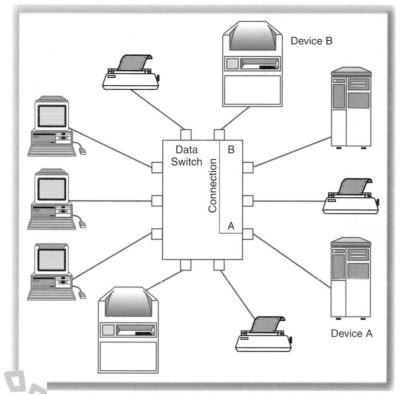

Figure 7-3 Connecting Hardware with a Switch

Comparison of Alternatives

Table 7-1 compares the LAN alternatives just discussed. The evaluation rates several criteria on a scale of 1 to 5, with 1 being best. As an example of how to interpret Table 7-1, consider the first line, which rates the number of workstations. A large, conventional LAN and a mainframe or minicomputer will allow hundreds or thousands of work-stations or terminals; therefore, these two alternatives receive the highest rating. A service bureau will also provide access to a large number of terminals but generally at a higher cost, so this alternative is rated below the mainframe and large, conventional LAN alternatives. Sub–LANs, zero-slot LANs, and other low-cost LAN alternatives are usually quite restrictive regarding the number of workstations allowed and thus tie for the lowest rating in this category.

Emerging Alternatives to Full-Fledged LANs

Over the last few years, additional alternatives to full-fledged LANs have emerged. These include home networks and personal area networks (PANs). Although the topic of home networks may seem out of place in a business data communications book, it is not. Many small office/home offices (SOHOs) leverage home network technologies for their shared computing needs.

Table 7-1   Rating of LAN Alternatives and a Conventional LAN

	A	B	C	D	E
Number of workstations	1	2	3	3	1
Initial cost	5	4	1	1	3
Personnel costs	5	1	1	1	2
Operations/maintenance costs	5	4	1	3	3
Expandability	1	2	3	3	1
Microcomputer workstation support	4	3	2	1	1
User transparency	3	3	4	1	1
Accommodation for multiple users	1	1	4	3	2
Ease of use	3	4	4	2	1
Ease of management	3	1	2	4	3
Interface to other networks	1	5	5	4	1

*A = large, centralized computer systems; B = use of a service bureau; C = sub–LANs; D = zero-slot and low-cost
LANs; E = conventional LAN, such as Ethernet or token ring; 1 is the highest (best) rating*

CEBus (Consumer Electric Bus) An EIA standard for networks in homes that are implemented using various media including AC power lines, telephone lines, coaxial cable, and wireless.

home network A communications network for computers in the home. The term includes the implementation of full-fledged LANs, such as Ethernet LANs, in homes or the creation of specialized networks that use existing phone or power lines or wireless media.

NAT (Network Address Translation) Converts the address of each LAN node into one IP address for the Internet and vice versa. NAT is often used in conjunction with proxy servers to enhance the security of the LAN.

Home Networks   The technology literature includes competing definitions of the term *home network*. In some instances, home networks are defined as networks within homes that are used to synchronize clocks and to control devices such as lights and appliances. When used in this context, a home network is part of a *smart* or *digital home*—a fully automated residence with network sockets in every room, whose computing devices and appliances conform to a common internetworking standard. **CEBus (Consumer Electric Bus)** is one of the most widely supported standards for digital homes. It is an EIA standard for networks in homes that are implemented using various media, including AC power lines, telephone lines, coaxial cable, and wireless. *Common Application Language (CAL)* is used to communicate commands over the media; CEBus supports the Home Plug & Play standard to provide uniform communication among household objects via CAL. More information on CEBus can be found at www.cebus.org.

The second definition of home network found in the technology literature is most relevant to this book. A **home network** is a communications network for computers in the home. The term includes the implementation of full-fledged LANs, such as Ethernet LANs, in homes or the creation of specialized networks that use existing phone or power lines or wireless media. Industry estimates suggest that more than 6 million homes in the United States have some kind of home network; by 2004, the number is expected to exceed 15 million. The increasing availability of DSL, cable modems, and other kinds of broadband Internet access has fueled consumer interest in home networks. Many home network options enable multiple users to share a single DSL or cable connection. Inexpensive gateways and broadband routers for home networks with firewall software and other security features have also contributed to the increasing popularity of home networks. Such gateways and routers transfer data to microcomputers and other devices through the use of NAT and similar protocols. As noted in Chapter 4, **NAT (Network Address Translation)** converts the address of each LAN node into one IP address for the Internet, and vice versa. NAT is often used in conjunction with proxy servers to enhance the security of the LAN.

Cable-Based Home Networks   Cable-based home networks typically enable computers to communicate over existing power or telephone lines. Although some full-fledged cable-based LANs have been created in homes using standard LAN cable options such as Category 5 twisted pair, these are relatively rare. To date, most power-line–based home networks have supported the X10 protocol or the CEBus specification and have offered limited data channel bandwidth. Competing power-line technologies from Intellon Corp. (www.intellon.com) offer communication speeds from 1 to 10 mbps.

Many home owners have opted for telephone-line–based home networks over power-line–based networks. These allow computers to communicate over the telephone lines installed in the residence by plugging into phone jacks. Both voice and data communications can be supported, because voice uses only a small portion of the bandwidth available on telephone lines, even low-grade phone wires. *HomePNA (Home PhoneLine Networking Alliance—www.homepna.org)* is one of the popular specifications for telephone-line–based home networks and essentially enables the home owner to create a 10-mbps Ethernet network using existing phone lines. HomePNA allows devices to be up to 1,000 feet apart and can support a household area up to 10,000 square feet.

Wireless Home Networks   Wireless home networks are also popular. These largely eliminate the need to piggyback the home network on existing cabling. Essentially, these enable home owners to create small, wireless LANs. (Wireless LAN architectures are discussed more fully in Chapter 8.) Many of the wireless home network options are classified as *wireless personal area networks (WPANs);* these are discussed in the following section.

Personal Area Networks   Like home network, the term *personal area network* has more than one meaning in the technology literature. Usually, a **personal area network (PAN)** refers to short-range wireless networks that provide very inexpensive communications among intelligent devices. *Wireless personal area networks (WPANs)* serve individuals or small work groups over limited ranges. WPANs may be used to transfer data between laptop or PDA and desktop computers, servers, and printers in a manner that is analogous to how a cordless phone communicates with its base station. The term *personal area network* is also used to refer to a transmission technology developed by IBM that lets people transfer information by touch. In many instances, the body's own conductivity is used as a communications medium. For example, by holding a pager in one hand, you could transfer the calling telephone number to a cell phone held in the other hand. By shaking hands, electronic business cards could be exchanged by executives. PAN devices worn on the wrist or as jewelry could be used to transmit IDs to ATMs, security checkpoints, and to other check-in, checkout devices. As you can see, wireless communications is common to both definitions of personal area network.

Bluetooth (www.bluetooth.com) and HomeRF (www.homerf.org) are the two most widely adopted specifications for wireless PANs. **Bluetooth**, named for the tenth-century Danish King (King Harald Blatan—"Bluetooth") who began to Christianize the country, is an open standard for short-range transmission of digital voice and data between mobile devices (phones, PDAs, and laptops) and desktop devices. Because Bluetooth uses omnidirectional radio waves, it is capable of transmitting data through walls and other nonmetal barriers. It transmits in the unlicensed 2.4-GHz band and uses a frequency-hopping spread-spectrum technique that changes its signal 1,600 times per second. Data transfer rates up to 720 kbps are provided within a range of 10 meters. If a data transmission encounters interference from other devices, the transmission speed is automatically reduced.

HomeRF (Home Radio Frequency) also provides WPAN capabilities. HomeRF operates in the same 2.4-GHz frequency band as Bluetooth and enables up to 127 devices within 150 feet to be addressed at a data rate between 1 mbps and 2 mbps. HomeRF uses the *shared wireless access protocol (SWAP)* to enable communication among mobile and desktop devices. It employs a frequency-hopping technique that changes

---

personal area network (PAN) A short-range wireless network that provides inexpensive communications among intelligent devices.

Bluetooth An open standard for short-range transmission of digital voice and data between mobile devices (phones, PDAs, and laptops) and desktop devices. Bluetooth, which supports both point-to-point and multipoint applications, transmits in the unlicensed 2.4 GHz frequency band using a frequency-hopping spread-spectrum technique that changes its signal 1,600 times per second. Because Bluetooth uses omni-directional radio waves, it is capable of transmitting data through walls and other nonmetal barriers.

HomeRF (Home Radio Frequency) Provides wireless personal area network (WPAN) capabilities. HomeRF operates in the same 2.4 GHz frequency band as Bluetooth and enables up to 127 devices within 150 feet to be addressed at a data rate between 1 mbps and 2 mbps.

its signal 50 times per second. It transmits frames (20 milliseconds in length), and each frame contains both data and voice slots.

WPAN capabilities may also be supported via infrared light transmissions. Laptops or PDAs with **IrDA (Infrared Data Association) ports** can exchange data with similarly equipped desktop systems and printers. Line-of-sight transmission is required by IrDA. IrDA provides a half-duplex connection at the physical layer with speeds up to 115.2 kbps and thus can be used with a standard UART chip. At the data link layer, IrDA uses an adaptation of HDLC called the *Infrared Link Access Protocol (IrLAP)*. The Infrared Link Management Protocol (IrLMP) is used for handshaking between two IrDA devices as well as the multiplexing of two or more simultaneous data streams.

Bluetooth and HomeRF are well positioned to proliferate home and small office networks in the years ahead. These small, wireless LANs, however, are more limited than full-fledged wireless LANs in that they have a more limited transmission range and do not support roaming. Because of these limitations, they are classified in this text as LAN alternatives.

IrDA (Infrared Data Association) port Computers equipped with IrDA ports can exchange data with similarly equipped desktop systems and printers. Line-of-sight transmission is required by IrDA.

LAN COMPONENTS

Although sub–LANs, home networks, and the emerging LAN alternatives discussed earlier may be appropriate networks for small businesses, most business organizations implement full-fledged LANs. Full-fledged LANs have several major components including servers, client workstations, communication media, wiring center technologies, network interface cards, and LAN software. These are illustrated in Figure 7-4.

Servers

To make an informed decision regarding server hardware, you must understand what the server does. Services provided by servers include file and application services, database access, printer services, and communication services (access to dial-in/dial-out modems, facsimile [fax], and remote access). You may also encounter terminal servers that allow terminals to be attached to a LAN; the terminal server provides the necessary computation capabilities. Modem and fax servers allow users to share modems and fax machines. A remote access server provides LAN services to users who access the LAN via telephone lines or mobile services. File, database, application, and printer servers are the most common server types and are the primary focus of this chapter. Other kinds of servers found in some LANs include

➤ *Terminal servers,* which allow terminals to access the network. However, a terminal attached to a LAN does not have the same functionality as a microcomputer attached to a LAN.

➤ *Communication servers,* which allow users to share one or more dial-out modems or to access WAN services. Communication servers are discussed in Chapter 10.

➤ *Fax servers,* which enable users to share facsimile machines.

➤ *Remote access servers,* which allow remote users dial-in access to LAN resources.

➤ *Citrix™ servers,* which enable Windows applications to be run on older microcomputers whose architectures normally preclude such applications.

➤ *Thin client servers,* which enable network computers (NCs) and other thin clients to access computing resources stored on LAN servers.

Because of their prevalence and importance in business organizations, we begin our discussion of servers by focusing on those that provide LAN users with access to file and database services.

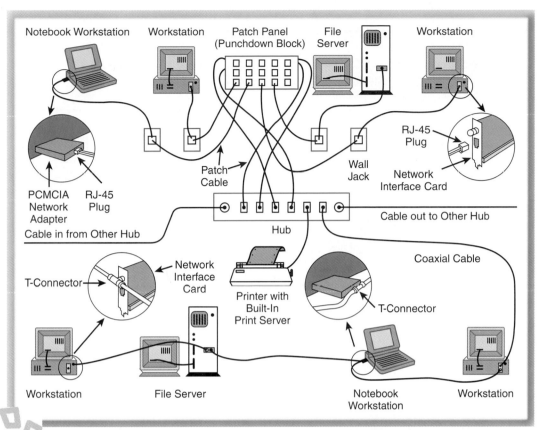

Figure 7-4   Major LAN Components Include Servers, Workstations, Communication Media, Wiring Centers, Network Adaptors, and Connectors

File Services   File service is one of the primary jobs of a server. The purpose of a file server is to provide user access to data, programs, and other files stored on the server's disk drives. It should be transparent to the users that the data or files they are using are located on the server's disk drives rather than on a local disk drive. Over time, several technologies have been developed to provide file services. File and database servers are the most commonly used today.

File Servers   A **file server** allows users to share files. If several LAN users need access to an application such as word processing, only one copy of the application software resides on the file server. Individual users can share this application if the users' company has the appropriate product license agreement with the vendor. In this case, one copy of the program files can satisfy the needs of all application users. When a user enters a command to start an application (often by clicking on a shortcut or selecting from a program menu), that application is downloaded from the server into the user's workstation. Consider the disk space savings in a company having 100 users for a product that requires 250 MB of disk storage. Storage on a file server requires only 250 MB of disk space for all users. Storing the same application on 100 users' local disk drives requires 25 GB of disk space. File server technology is illustrated in Figure 7-5.

file server A high-speed computer in a network that stores and provides access to programs and data files shared by network users. It functions like a remote disk drive.

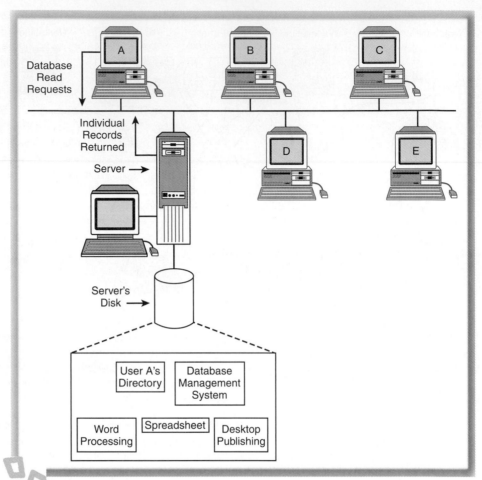

Figure 7-5   File Server Technology

When a user needs data from the file server, that data is transferred to the user's workstation. This is suitable for small files, but consider the impact of such technology when one is accessing a large database. If a user enters a request that requires looking at thousands of records, each record must be transferred over the LAN to the user's workstation.

Suppose that you want to determine the average grade point average (GPA) for all students in your school and that there are 40,000 records in the student file. With file server technology, the database application runs on your workstation; it is downloaded to your workstation when you start the application. When you make your request to find the average GPA, each student record is transferred over the network to your workstation, where the GPA data is extracted and computations are made. This is how the application would operate if the database were stored locally. Transferring all 40,000 database records over the network can place a heavy load on the medium and reduce its performance. In a case like this, it is more efficient to have the server do the calculations and pass only the response over the network. A database server performs this function.

Database Servers   The database server was developed to solve the problem of passing an entire file, several files, or large portions thereof over the medium. The most common example of a database server is the SQL server. **Structured Query Language (SQL)** is a standard database definition, access, and update language for relational databases. An SQL server accepts a database request, accesses all necessary records locally, and then sends only the results back to the requester. In the GPA example, all 40,000 student records still must be read, but the computation is done by the SQL server. Only one record containing the average GPA is sent back over the network to the requester. This reduces the load on the network medium, but it does place an extra load on the server. The server must not only access the records, but it must also perform some database processing. This can affect other users who are also requesting SQL services. The SQL server must be powerful enough to provide services effectively for all users and avoid becoming a performance bottleneck.

An interface also must exist between the application software making the database request and the SQL server. The interface must be capable of translating an application's data needs into an SQL statement. This means that an SQL server cannot work unless the application or an application interface exists that can generate the SQL syntax. SQL server technology is illustrated in Figure 7-6.

Application Servers   In client/server (C/S) computing environments, the processing associated with a particular application may be accomplished on several network nodes. An **application server** is a node that provides application-oriented processing on the server side of C/S computing. Application servers should be able to run standard programs to allow distribution of an application over a network. A standard program is one that can be easily created with standard programming tools such as a C++ compiler, JAVA, and Visual Basic. Although this may sound simple, some network operating systems (the operating systems that control servers) are better suited for providing application services than others. For example, Novell's older NetWare 3.x and 4.x network operating systems require that applications run on the server be network loadable modules (NLMs). NLMs must be written using NetWare application program interfaces, and it is more complicated for the typical programmer to create NLMs than standard executables. Programs that can run under the Windows NT Server, Windows 2000 Server, Windows XP, Linux, or UNIX operating systems do not run under those versions of NetWare unless NLMs are created for them. Thus, NetWare 3.x and 4.x are not as well suited to function as application servers. In contrast, Microsoft's Windows NT Server and the other network operating systems mentioned earlier can run standard Windows applications and are better suited to the role of application server.

Server Disk Drives   File and database servers share the need to access data efficiently. When choosing a file or database server, you should carefully select the server's disk subsystem, which consists of the disk drives and the disk controllers. Two factors are critical when choosing server disk drives: storage capacity and average access time.

Server disk drives are typically high-performance, high-capacity units, which means that they have fast access times and can store large amounts of data. The capacity to store large amounts of data is important, because the server is often called upon to store a large number of data and program files. A file server is essentially an extension to each user's hard disk. Space to store individual user data—together with the shared storage needed for application software, databases, several versions of desktop operating system software, utility programs, print files, and electronic mail messages—can easily require several gigabytes. Some network operating systems cannot be

Structured Query Language (SQL) A relational database language developed by IBM and later standardized by the American National Standards Institute.

application server A server in a network that provides application-oriented processing on the server side of client/server computing. Unlike a file server, which stores shared programs and data, an application server runs the programs and processes the data.

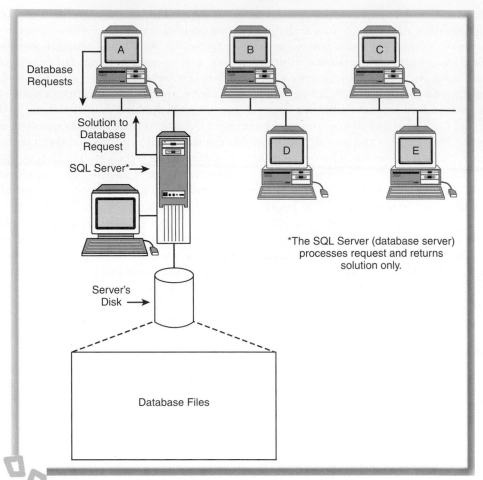

Figure 7-6   SQL Server Technology

installed unless there is at least a gigabyte of disk storage. Although not all of this is needed to store the network operating system itself (most NOSs consume less than 200 MB), some vendors maintain that at least a gigabyte of disk storage is needed to ensure proper performance.

An SQL server must store database files as well as the SQL server software. Organizations adopting SQL server technology usually have large databases and require high-volume storage. The need for large amounts of data storage can be satisfied by one high-capacity drive or several lower capacity drives; both alternatives offer benefits. Having fewer disk drives provides a configuration that is easier to manage. Having several smaller capacity drives is beneficial because several disks can be working simultaneously to satisfy user requests, and the impact of a disk failure can be lessened. Suppose you need 50 GB of storage. You could select one 50-GB drive or three 20-GB drives. With one drive, it is simple to determine file allocation: All files are placed on that drive. With three drives, your objective should be to spread the files over the three drives to provide rapid data access and to ensure equivalent activity.

If an application requires 45 disk accesses per second, a single fast disk drive may have difficulty keeping up with this load. With three drives and a good distribution of files, you may have only 15 requests per drive per second. This configuration may be more expensive, but it provides better performance. Remember, for file or SQL server disk drives, you should select those with sufficient storage capacity and speed to meet your performance objectives. A powerful processor with a slow disk subsystem can cripple your network. This point cannot be overemphasized.

A second factor to consider when choosing a disk drive is the **access time** of the disk itself. The three components of disk access are seek time, latency, and transfer time. The **seek time** is the time required to move the read/write heads to the proper cylinder. Once the heads are positioned, you must wait until the data revolves under the read/write heads; this is called **latency** (or *rotational delay*). The average latency is one-half the time required for the disk to make a complete revolution. **Transfer time** is the time required to move the data from the disk to the computer's memory. Fast disks have average access times of less than 10 ms. In contrast, floppy disk drives may have access times of approximately 200 ms. As a general rule, file servers should have disks with fast average access times.

Finally, you also need to consider the *disk drive interface*, or the *controller*. The disk drive interface sets the standards for connecting the disk drive to the microprocessor and the software commands used to access the drive. There are a variety of disk drive interfaces. Some are well suited to server operations, and some are too slow for most LANs. The two interfaces most commonly used for microcomputer-based servers are the small computer system interface (SCSI, pronounced "scuzzy") and the integrated drive electronics (IDE) or enhanced IDE (EIDE) interface. Both interfaces provide high-speed data transfers and large-capacity disk drives. SCSI generally is more efficient and is currently the interface of choice.

SCSI drives are generally preferred for LAN servers. The maximum capacity of SCSI drives has historically been greater than for EIDE drives. However, capacity is not the most critical factor. SCSI controllers have higher data transfer rates than IDE controllers. Today's Ultra SCSI controllers can transfer from 20 to 320 MB per second. In addition, SCSI interfaces allow more devices to be attached. In the original specification, eight devices could interface with a single SCSI controller, one of which is the host adapter. This allows seven devices such as disks, tapes, and optical drives to be attached to one interface. In contrast, only two drives can be attached to an EIDE interface. More recent SCSI controllers support even more devices; many Ultra SSCI versions (e.g., Ultra2, Ultra3 or Ultra4) support up to16 devices. With an EIDE interface, only one of the disk drives can be working at a time. Thus, if two drive requests are pending, one for each drive, one request is held until the first is completed. In contrast, two SCSI drives can be working simultaneously. This allows for parallelism in the input/output (I/O) process. To attain parallelism with EIDE drives, two controllers would be required, one for each drive. Finally, it is possible for one SCSI device to communicate directly with another device on the same SCSI interface. This feature could be used to back up data from a disk directly to a tape drive. Because servers often have multiple disk drives and the need to optimize I/O, SCSI interfaces are usually preferred.

Server Memory A server is a combination of hardware and software. The software should be designed to take full advantage of the hardware; in Chapter 9, you will learn techniques for ensuring this compatibility. Memory is often a good hardware investment, because many software systems can take advantage of available memory to

---

access time The total time required in accessing data on a disk, including seek time, latency, and transfer time.

seek time The time it takes to move the read/write head from its current location to a particular track on a disk.

latency The amount of time it takes for the disk to rotate until the required location on the disk is under the read/write head. Sometimes called *rotational delay*.

transfer time The time it takes to transmit or move data from one place to another; the time interval between starting the transfer and the completion of the transfer. When retrieving data from a local disk, transfer time is the amount of time required for the data to be sent over the channel to the CPU's memory.

cache memory
High-speed memory that improves a computer's performance. Memory and disk caches are in every computer to speed up instruction execution and data retrieval. A memory cache is a memory bank that serves as a bridge between main memory and the CPU. It is faster than main memory and allows instructions to be executed and data to be read at higher speed.

disk caching A disk cache is a section of main memory or memory on the disk controller board that serves as a bridge between a disk and the CPU. When the disk is read, a larger block of data is copied into the cache than is immediately required. Subsequent "read" operations will first look for the data in the disk cache. If the data is already stored in the cache, there is no need to retrieve it from the disk, which is slower to access.

provide better performance. High-speed **cache memory** can significantly improve a computer's performance. Today, most dynamic microcomputer memories, such as SDRAM, operate at speeds of 30–50 nanosecond. High-speed cache memory operates at speeds that are approximately four to five times faster than RAM. Obviously, it is faster for a processor to fetch instructions from cache memory than from RAM. The processor first looks for the instruction in cache memory. If it is found in cache, the fetch is very efficient. If the instruction is not in cache, it and a block of the following instructions are transferred from lower speed RAM into cache. This increases the chances that the next instruction will be found efficiently in cache memory.

Another form of caching is called **disk caching**. Disk caching is similar in function to cache memory, except that main memory serves as a high-speed buffer for slower disk drives. In both kinds of cache, memory is used as a buffer for lower speed hardware. When choosing a LAN operating system that provides disk caching, you need to configure the server with sufficient memory to make caching effective. The fundamental premise of disk caching is that a memory access is faster than a disk access (nanoseconds versus milliseconds). A disk cache, therefore, attempts to keep frequently accessed data in memory. Caching works as follows: If a user's request for data is received, cache memory is searched before the data is physically read from the disk. If the data is found in cache memory—a process known as a *logical read*—then the data is made available almost instantly. If the data is not found in cache memory, then it is read from the disk, which is called a *physical access*. As data is read from the disk, it is also placed into cache memory so that any subsequent read for that data might be a logical read.

Disk caching taken to the fullest extent results in all data residing in memory and all reads being logical reads. This is rarely the case. However, it should be clear that effective use of cache memory can improve performance. Because disk caching requires memory, sufficient memory must be available to provide a large percentage of cache hits, in which the data being read is found in cache memory. Consider the following example, which illustrates the effects of having too little memory.

Suppose that LAN data requests cycle through four records, A, B, C, and D, and that you have only enough cache memory for three records. When additional space is needed, the cache management scheme typically replaces the record that has been dormant the longest with a new record. Records A, B, and C have been read in that order and are in cache memory, as illustrated in Figure 7-7(a). A request is issued for record D, but it is not in cache memory, so a physical read is required. Record D is read and must be inserted into cache memory. Because record A is the least recently used, record D replaces record A, as illustrated in Figure 7-7(b). Next, a request is received for record A. Because it is not in cache memory, a physical read is issued, and record A replaces the least recently used record, record B. Cache memory now looks like Figure 7-7(c). Next, a request is made for record B, which is also not in cache memory, as illustrated in Figure 7-7(d). Record B is read and replaces record C. Unfortunately, record C is the next record to be read and again requires a physical read. It is read into cache memory, replacing record D. Then, the cycle repeats again. In this simple example, the cache is one record too small and is totally ineffective. In fact, it is counterproductive, as the processor must search cache memory for records that are not cache resident, incurring extra overhead.

The problem of insufficient cache memory can be corrected by expanding the cache memory. In the example, just one more record slot results in 100 percent cache hits after the four initial reads. Of course, this example is contrived, and 100 percent cache hit rates are rarely attainable. The example demonstrates that there is a critical threshold for cache memory. If the available memory is under this threshold, cache can be ineffective.

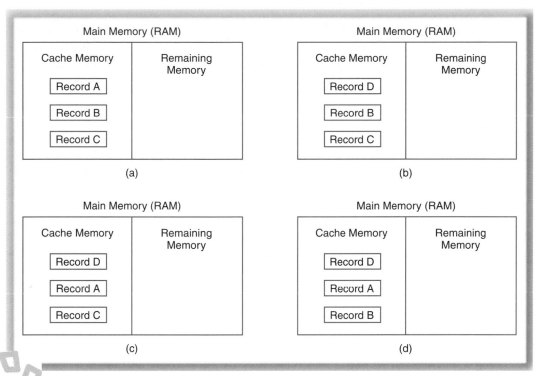

(a)

(b)

(c)

(d)

Figure 7-7   Example of Disk Cache Memory

When the available cache memory is over this threshold, cache can be very effective. Some users have experienced cache hits as high as 80 percent to 90 percent. The hit rate depends on the access patterns, so this figure does not hold true for all systems.

An ample amount of memory is important for reasons other than disk caching. You also should have sufficient memory to avoid disk swapping. Most of today's memory management schemes are based on **virtual memory management**, which uses the disk as an extension of memory so each program has virtually all the memory it needs. Virtual memory management allows the real memory of a system to be less than the aggregate memory required by all the applications. To do this, application code and data are swapped back and forth between the disk and memory. Virtual memory breaks up each program into small segments, called "pages," and only brings as many pages into memory as fit into a reserved area for that program. When additional pages are required, it makes room for them by swapping them to disk. It keeps track of pages that have been modified, so that they can be retrieved when needed again. The swap rate goes up if the available memory is too small. When the swap rate increases, the operating system is spending extra time managing memory, and less time is available for doing application work. The amount of application work done per unit of time decreases as the swap rate increases.

Today, server memories typically begin at 128 MB, with many servers configured at 156 MB or higher. Servers are often equipped with *ECC (error-correcting code) memory* that tests for and corrects errors on the fly. ECC memory uses circuitry that generates checksums. (Checksums are discussed in Chapter 6.) With ECC memory, a checksum

virtual memory management
A memory management technique that uses disk as an extension of memory, thereby allowing virtually unlimited memory capacity for applications and data. With virtual memory, one can run programs that do not reside entirely in memory.

is typically added to each 32-bit word. In other words, 7 bits of correcting code are added to each 32 bits of data placed in memory. When data is retrieved from memory, the checksum is recomputed to determine if any of the data bits have been corrupted. ECC memory can detect and automatically correct 1-bit errors within words and can detect, but not correct, multiple bit errors.

Processors and Processor Speed   The processing power of the server is also a critical factor. It seldom makes sense to select a server that has fast disks and sufficient memory but a slow CPU. In general, the server ought to be one of the fastest (if not the fastest) computers on the network. One exception to this generalization is a server providing small amounts of data to graphics workstations. Most graphics applications require high-speed processors to create and print graphic images. In these networks, the workstation computing power may equal or exceed that of the server.

For additional processing power in one server, multiple–CPU systems are available. Multiple–CPU systems can be **symmetrical multiprocessing (SMP)** or asymmetrical multiprocessing systems. An SMP system has CPUs that are alike and that share memory, processing responsibility, and I/O paths. In asymmetrical systems, the processors may be of different kinds, and one processor may be dedicated to I/O operations while another is dedicated to application processing. SMP systems allow for load balancing, whereas asymmetric systems do not. Thus, in an asymmetrical multiprocessing system, one processor can be extremely busy while another has little to do. Most multiprocessor servers are SMP servers. SMP hardware must be supported by the network operating system to take advantage of the additional processors.

> **symmetrical multi-processing (SMP)**
> An SMP system has multiple CPUs that are alike and that share memory, processing responsibility, and I/O paths.

Although some servers are equipped with processors that have been designed for use in servers, many rely on the same processors found in LAN workstations. In 2002, many servers were sold with Pentium 4 processors with clock speeds ranging from 1 to 2.5 gigahertz. Pentium 3 processors with clock speeds of 1 gigahertz or less were also available on numerous server products during 2002. Most major business-oriented microcomputer vendors have families of server products. Compaq, for example, markets its Proliant servers. Hewlett-Packard, IBM, Dell, Gateway, Micron, and Sun are other major sources of servers for business clients.

Expansion and Power   A server should have sufficient expansion capability and the power to use the expansion slots effectively. Server capabilities and capacity can be expanded by adding hardware to the existing server or by adding servers. Expanding the capabilities of an existing server is often less expensive than adding a new server, so it is typically wise to choose a server with adequate expansion options. Expansion options include the ability to add more memory, disks, printers, or other hardware devices that users can share, such as modems, fax machines, tape drives, optical disk drives, and scanners.

System Bus   A computer's bus provides the connection among system components such as the CPU, memory, and device controllers. The size, speed, and kind of bus affect the computer's performance. The bus size determines how many data bits can be transferred among system components at one time. A server with a 32-bit bus takes twice as many transfers for 1,000 bytes of data as a system with a 64-bit bus, and the operation takes approximately twice as long to perform; a 96-bit or 128-bit bus provides better performance than a 64-bit bus. The speed of the bus determines how fast data is transferred along the bus. A faster bus provides better performance than a slower one. Bus speed, like clock speed, is measured in megahertz (MHz). The system buses in most servers and workstations operate at a maximum of 533 MHz; many have system buses with 166 MHz, 133 MHz, or 100 MHz. Older machines may be equipped with 66-MHz system buses.

Expansion Bus   A microcomputer's expansion bus interfaces with its system bus. Microcomputers use three main expansion bus architectures: industry standard architecture (ISA), extended industry standard architecture (EISA), and peripheral component interconnect (PCI). The ISA bus is the one on which the original IBM PC was based, and it is still widely used. Today's microcomputers have 16-bit ISA expansion slots. The EISA bus is an improvement over the original ISA bus by extending the bus to 32-bits and providing bus mastering. In order to accommodate older ISA expansion cards, EISA runs at the traditional ISA 8 to 10 MHz speed. The expansion boards of most of today's microcomputers include a mix of PCI and ISA or PCI and EISA slots. PCI runs at 33 MHz. PCI Version 2.1 runs at 66 MHz and thus provides more rapid data transfer rates than an ISA or EISA bus. PCI supports 32-bit and 64-bit data paths, and bus mastering up to 264 million bytes per second transfer rates. PCI allows IRQs to be shared; because there is a limited number of assignable IRQs, the ability for devices plugged into PCI slots to share a single IRQ can be an important feature. In a PCI–only machine, there can never be an insufficient number of IRQs because all can be shared.

Some systems have additional buses, such as a separate bus for the monitor and for disk drives. Having multiple buses and multiple data paths between devices can further improve performance in both servers and workstations.

Many industry experts expect to replace the PCI bus in high-end servers. *Infiniband* is an input/output architecture that uses a point-to-point switching architecture similar to mainframe channels rather than the shared bus technology used with PCI and a data path with a maximum speed of 6 gbps. InfiniBand is a combination of Intel's NGIO (Next Generation I/O) and Future I/O from IBM, HP, and Compaq; more information on infiniband is available at www.infinibandta.org.

Workstations

Some LANs are homogeneous, which means that all the workstations are from the same vendor, have the same basic hardware configuration, run the same version of the same operating system, and use essentially the same applications. It is easier to configure this kind of network than one that is heterogeneous, but homogeneous networks are less common. Often, a network is assembled from workstations acquired over time. These workstations usually represent different levels of technology and perhaps use different versions of operating systems. Consider a network with the following workstations:

- ➤ IBM or compatible with an ISA or EISA bus
- ➤ IBM or compatible with an ISA and PCI bus
- ➤ Apple Macintosh or compatible
- ➤ Sun SPARC workstations

For some components of a heterogeneous network, hardware and software options can be limited. There may, for example, be limited options for LAN adapter cards for some of your machines. You will find numerous options for a LAN with only IBM–compatible workstations and several for LANs with only Apple workstations, but some of these options do not support both kinds of microcomputers within the same LAN. Fortunately, interoperability of different hardware platforms on a single LAN is becoming more common.

Diskless Workstations   When configuring a LAN, you may want to consider **diskless workstations**. As the name implies, a diskless workstation has no local disk drives. Instead, a diskless workstation has its boot logic in a read-only memory (ROM) chip. This chip contains the logic to connect to the network and download the operating

diskless workstation
A workstation that has no local disk drives. The programs and data used by diskless workstations are retrieved from network servers. *Network computers (NCs)* and *thin clients* are typically diskless workstations.

system from the server. Thus, a diskless workstation cannot be used in a stand-alone mode; it is fully dependent on the server for all of its software, and it cannot function if the network or server is not operating. This is the disadvantage of a diskless system. Its advantages are cost, security, and control.

Because diskless workstations have no disk drives, they are less expensive than those with disks. Moreover, the maintenance costs for diskless systems are less than for systems with disk drives. Diskless systems provide extra security because users are unable to copy the organization's data onto local hard or floppy disk drives. This is important, because an organization's primary security risk is its employees. Diskless systems also provide a greater measure of control, because employees cannot introduce their own software into the system. This not only ensures that standard software and data are used but also reduces the chances of computer viruses being introduced into the network.

Thin clients may be diskless. Server disks may instead be used to store individual files and programs. Although thin clients may be equipped with fast processors, they often share more in common with terminals than with traditionally configured microcomputers.

Workstation Memory and Speed   Like servers, workstation memory configurations are important. You need to ensure that LAN workstations have sufficient memory to run applications, its desktop operating system, and client modules of the LAN network operating system. Today's LAN workstations typically have a minimum of 128 MB of RAM, and many are equipped with 256 MB or more. Dynamic RAM, such as RDRAM, is most common in LAN workstations, but static RAM may be employed in some LANs, especially "noisy" environments that include electricity-hungry manufacturing equipment. ECC memory is not usually included in LAN workstations; however, as noted earlier, it is often desirable to have ECC memory in LAN servers.

The speed of the workstation's processor must be compatible with the kind of work for which it is being used. If you use the workstation for word processing, a low-speed processor probably is satisfactory. However, a workstation used for graphics work requires a high-speed processor. Basically, it is the application, not the LAN architecture, that determines the configuration requirements of the workstations. In 2002, most of the workstations being added to LANs (as new machines or replacements) were equipped with system buses with speeds ranging from 100 to 400 MHz and Pentium 3 or Pentium 4 processors operating from 1 GHz to 2.5 GHz. Vendors of business LAN workstations include Compaq, Dell, Gateway, Hewlett-Packard, and Micron.

LAN workstations are often equipped with a mix of PCI and ISA expansion slots. Although network adapter cards may be available for each, PCI network adapters are typically preferred. This preference stems from the higher PCI bus speed and data transfer rates.

Communication Media

conducted media
Media that use a conductor such as a wire or fiber optic cable to move a signal from sender to receiver.

radiated media
Media that use radio waves of different frequencies or infrared light to broadcast through air or space and accordingly do not need a wire or cable conductor.

Like the transmission media commonly used in today's data communication networks, the communication media found in LANs can be broken down into two major classes: conducted and radiated. **Conducted media** use a conductor such as a wire or a fiber optic cable to move the signal from sender to receiver. Conducted media for LANs include twisted-pair wires, coaxial cables, and fiber optic cables. **Radiated media** in wireless LANs include radio waves of different frequencies and infrared light. Both conducted and radiated LAN media are discussed in the following section. The discussion focuses on the characteristics that make each medium desirable or undesirable as LAN media, including speed, security, distance, susceptibility to error, and cost. These attributes form the basis of the selection criteria discussed later in the chapter.

Conducted Media

Wires   Wires are the earliest and currently the most commonly used data transmission medium in LANs. The advantages of wires are their availability and low cost. In comparison to fiber optic cable, however, wires are more susceptible to signal distortion and transmission errors; fiber optic cable has greater bandwidth than wires and, therefore, greater potential to be able to grow as the need for high-speed, high-performance LANs increases among business organizations. Despite these limitations, LAN implementations run at speeds up to 1 gbps over copper wires; this enables businesses to use low-cost wires for very-high-speed LANs.

Wire/Cable Cost, Gauge, and Types   LAN cabling ranges in cost from approximately 2 cents per foot to more than $1 per foot, depending on the shielding, gauge, and number of conducting wires in the cable. The wires most commonly used in LANs and other data communication networks are made of copper. In the United States, wire gauges 19, 22, 24, 26, and 28 are most common. Figure 7-8(a) shows a single-conductor wire. Wires in data communication networks are usually bundled, providing multiple conductors inside one insulating sheath. The number of conducting strands in such a cable varies, with 4, 7, 8, 10, 12, 15, and 25 conductors being the most common. Figure 7-8(b) shows a wire bundle with multiple conductors. In 2002, a 500-foot (120-m) trunk cable including 25 unshielded twisted pairs could be purchased for approximately $800 ($1.60 per foot).

Twisted-Pair Wires   Ordinary telephone wire consists of a twisted pair of wires. Bundles of these wire pairs from telephones in a given area are sheathed together. Each pair of wires is twisted together to minimize signal distortion from adjacent wire pairs in the sheath. Figure 7-8(c) depicts an individual twisted-pair wire. Twisted-pair wires are currently the most common media in LANs, but those used in LANs are not the same as those used with telephones. The two basic kinds of twisted-pair wires found in LANs are unshielded (UTP) and shielded (STP). STP wires have an extra foil cladding that protects the wires from external interference and are well suited for LANs in "noisy" working environments. UTP is less expensive than STP and is much more common than STP in LANs. When used in LANs, twisted-pair wires commonly operate at speeds ranging from 10 mbps to 1,000 mbps; however, some LANs operate at speeds less than 10 mbps.

Figure 7-8   Kinds of Wires

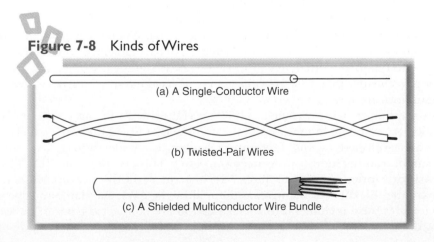

(a) A Single-Conductor Wire

(b) Twisted-Pair Wires

(c) A Shielded Multiconductor Wire Bundle

LAN twisted-pair wiring consists of a bundle of color-coded wires, usually four or eight wires. Two of these wires with matching color codes form a pair; these are twisted about each other. One such color scheme uses a solid color and a solid color with a white stripe as a pair; for example, a solid blue wire and a blue-and-white-striped wire form one pair, and an orange and orange-and-white-striped wire form another pair. One pair may be used to transmit data, and the other is used to receive data. Twisted-pair wires are classified in several of the following ways: (1) by American wire gauge (AWG) rating, (2) by shielding (either UTP or STP), or (3) by categories that define the wire's rated acceptable speed and error characteristics.

AWG Rating   The AWG rating is a measure of the thickness of the copper conductor in the cable. The higher the AWG rating, the smaller the diameter of the wire; that is, a wire with an AWG rating of 12 is thicker than one with an AWG rating of 24. In general, faster maximum transmission rates and higher prices are associated with lower AWG ratings. This is because the wider a wire is, the less its resistance, and the higher its bandwidth rating. Twisted-pair wires used in LANs typically have an AWG rating of 22 to 26. Standard telephone wires may be smaller, with an AWG rating of 28. When selecting LAN wiring, you ordinarily do not need to consider the AWG rating of the wires, because it is included in the specifications used to define wire categories (such as Category 1, Category 3, and Category 5).

UTP and STP   You might have been wondering about the significance of twisted wires as opposed to straight wires. When electrical signals are transmitted over wires, an electromagnetic field is created along the axis of the wire. This electromagnetic field may affect the signals being transmitted along adjacent wires. When the wires are twisted about each other with at least two twists per foot, the effect of the electromagnetic field is minimized. This kind of interference, called *crosstalk*, is measured in decibels and is discussed in Chapter 6 in the section on error sources. Straight wires are more susceptible to crosstalk than are twisted-pair wires.

Even though twisting pairs of wires together minimizes crosstalk, it does not eliminate it, and there are other sources of transmission errors. Some of these errors can be reduced by shielding the wires. Shield twisted-pair (STP) wires have a metal foil or wire mesh wrapped around individual wire pairs, with a metal braided shield around the twisted-pair wire bundle itself; the entire bundle is enclosed in a polyvinyl chloride (PVC) jacket. Twisting pairs of wires helps eliminate interference from neighboring wires; the metal shielding helps prevent ambient distortion from heavy-duty motors, electrical or magnetic fields, and fluorescent lights. UTP wires, as the name implies, have no protective metal covering. Consequently, UTP wires are more susceptible to environmental noise that can disrupt the signal. When the signal is disrupted, transmission errors are likely to occur. When errors are detected, the data must be retransmitted, and the efficiency of the network is reduced. Companies use UTP because it is cheaper than STP. UTP may safely be used in environments where external disruptions are rare.

In addition to being classified as UTP or STP, twisted-pair wires are classified by categories. Several different rating classifications exist. One of the principal classifications was developed by the Electronics Industries Association (EIA) and the Telecommunications Industries Association (TIA). This classification, EIA/TIA-568, defines six categories of wires (see Table 7-2). In general, the distinctions between categories are the thickness of the wire, as defined by the AWG standard, and the error characteristics. Also included in the specification are connector types to be used in making the connection of the wires to wiring hubs and wiring closet punchdown blocks

Table 7-2   EIA/TIA Twisted-Pair Wire Categories

Category 1 Wire Category 1 wire is the traditional telephone wire. It uses thin copper conductors and is not rated for LAN speeds.

Category 2 Wire Category 2 wire is certified for speeds up to 4 mbps. This kind of wiring has been used in older networks that operated at or below this speed. Because most of today's LAN implementations operate at 10 mbps or higher, category 2 wires are rarely found in today's LANs.

Category 3 Wire The specifications for category 3 wire are more stringent than those for categories 1 and 2. Category 3 wire must have at least three twists per every foot of wire, and no two pairs should have the same number of twists per foot. This configuration provides better protection from cross-talk and provides more error-free transmissions than categories 1 and 2. Category 3 wire is common in LANs operating at 10 mbps, and some 100-mbps implementations allow category 3 wires over short distances.

Category 4 Wire Category 4 wire is used in some 16 mbps LANs. It must meet higher standards for attenuation, cross-talk, and capacitance than lower categories. Capacitance is a measure of the energy stored by the cable. If the stored energy is high, transmission errors are more likely than if the energy level is low.

Category 5 Wire Category 5 wire (commonly called *CAT-5*) is the most prevalent UTP cable found in data communication networks. To be classified as CAT-5, the cable must be able to support data or voice at 100 MHz over 22 or 24 AWG wires. The attenuation and cross-talk characteristics of category 5 wires are better than those of category 4 wires. It is used for high-speed twisted-pair LANs such as 100BASETX and X3T9.5 (FDDI over UTP).

Enhanced Category 5 Wire EIA/TIA expanded the CAT-5 standard to include enhanced category 5 (Category 5e) in 1999. Relative to CAT-5, enhanced category 5 cable has better cross-talk and attenuation characteristics; it is capable of supporting voice and data transmissions over 100 MHz over 22 or 24 AWG. It is becoming an increasingly popular option for LANs with speeds from 100 mbps to 1 gbps.

Category 6 Wire This recently ratified EIA/TIA standard covers twisted-pair cabling capable of supporting networks with speeds of 250 mbps or higher. Cross-talk, system noise, and attenuation characteristics of category 6 wire are superior to those for enhanced category 5. Category 6 wire is being positioned to support very-high-speed LANS such as Gigabit Ethernet.

or patch panels. A *punchdown block* is a communications device used to interconnect communication wires. A *patch panel* consists of a group of sockets for communication wires that function as a manual switching center for incoming and outgoing line.

Connectors   Two connectors for twisted-pair wires are defined by the EIA/TIA-568 standard. An eight-pin modular connector, typically a telephone-like connector called an *RJ-45 jack,* is used to connect to a LAN network adapter and to a wiring hub or wall outlet as well as to punchdown blocks. The use of RJ-45 connectors in LANs is illustrated in Figure 7-21.

Table 7-3 summarizes the characteristics of the EIA/TIA wire categories, and Figure 7-9 illustrates a generic twisted-pair wiring layout. Other wire classifications other than those just described exist. For example, IBM Corporation established a wiring classification and cable layout plan using four wire classification types: type 1, type 2, type 6, and type 9. Like the EIA/TIA classification, these classifications specify different AWG specifications and error characteristics. Pricing for the different wire

Table 7-3   Twisted-Pair Wire Category Characteristics

Category	Maximum Data Rate	Typical Use
1	1 mbps	Telephones, low-speed LANs
2	4 mbps	Token ring LANs
3	10 mbps	Ethernet LANs
4	16 mbps	Token ring LANs
5	100 mbps and 1 gbps	Ethernet and Fast Ethernet LANs, FDDI LANs, CDDI LANs, and asynchronous transfer mode (ATM) LANS
5e	Enhanced 100 mbps to 1 bps	Fast Ethernet, ATM, and Gigabit Ethernet LANs
6	100 mbps to 1 gbps	ATM and Gigabit Ethernet LANs

classifications tends to increase in relation to the category's maximum bandwidth. Prices within the same category are also found. For example, cable costs can vary by as much as 15 to 20 cents per foot for enhanced category 5 cable. As of this writing (2002), category 3 cable costs begin at about 5 cents per foot; category 4 cable costs begin at about 9 cents per foot; category 5 cable costs begin at about 11 cents per foot; enhanced category 5 cable costs begin at about 13 cents per foot; and category 6 cable costs begin at about 18 cents per foot.

An additional configuration for twisted-pair wires is plenum cables. Normal cables are insulated with *polyvinyl chloride (PVC)*. In the case of fire, PVC cables may

Figure 7-9   Generic Twisted-Pair Wiring Layout

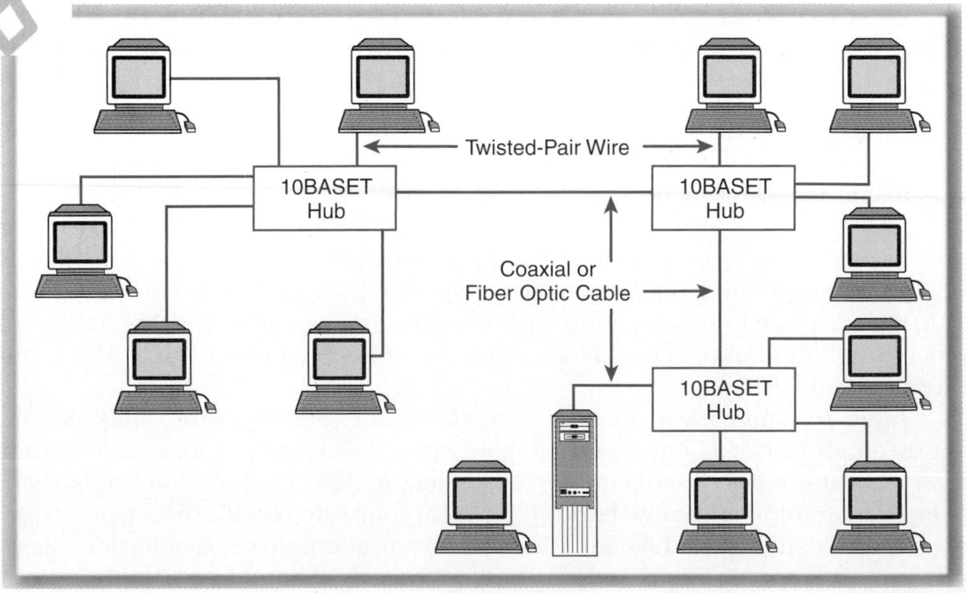

emit a hazardous gas, and building codes may prohibit the use of such cable in certain areas. Plenum space is defined as the air space between the ceiling and the next floor, and ordinances may require that cables in plenum areas be enclosed by metal conduits or be plenum rated. *Plenum* cables are coated with a coating such as Teflon, which does not emit noxious gases during fires. Plenum cables are two to three times more costly per foot than PVC cables. For example, if a 1,000-foot spool of PVC UTP has a price of 11 cents per foot, a 1,000-foot spool of Plenum UTP will have a price of 22 cents to 33 cents per foot.

Because twisted-pair wires are capable of supporting high data transmission speeds at a low cost, they are currently the most widely implemented LAN media. In early LANs, coaxial cable was the most common medium, and in the future, fiber optic cable may become the most widely used conducted communication medium in LANs.

Coaxial Cable   During the 1980s, coaxial cable was the most widely used communication medium in LANs. Coaxial cable was also used to connect terminals with terminal controller units in centralized, host-based networks. It is still used in some networks, including those that include midrange systems such as the IBM AS/400. Data transmission rates of up to 100 mbps can be supported over coaxial cable, and the theoretical bit rate is more than 400 mbps.

broadband transmission A form of data transmission in which data are carried on high-frequency carrier waves; the carrying capacity of the medium is divided into a number of subchannels, such as video, low-speed data, high-speed data, and voice, allowing the medium to satisfy several communication needs.

Technology   Coaxial cable comes packaged in a variety of ways, but essentially it consists of one or two central data transmission wires surrounded by an insulating layer, a shielding layer, and an outer jacket, as depicted in Figure 7-10. Data transmission over coaxial cable involves two basic techniques: baseband and broadband. In **broadband transmission**, the data is carried on high-frequency carrier waves; thus, several channels may be transmitted over a single cable. Frequency separation, using guardbands, helps keep one signal from interfering with another. Broadband technology allows one medium to be used for a variety of transmission needs, so that voice, video, and multiple data channels of varying transmission speeds can all exist on one cable. A subchannel with frequencies between 200 and 250 million hertz (MHz) might be used to carry video data; a subchannel operating between 175 and 200 MHz could be used for a LAN; voice data could be carried on a subchannel operating between 50 and 75 MHz; and so on.

Baseband transmission, on the other hand, does not use a carrier wave but sends the data along the channel by voltage fluctuations. Baseband technology cannot transmit multiple channels on one cable, but it is less expensive than broadband because it can use

baseband transmission Sends the data along the channel by means of voltage fluctuations. The entire bandwidth of the transmission line is used to carry data.

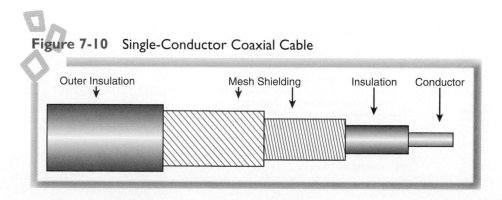

Figure 7-10   Single-Conductor Coaxial Cable

Outer Insulation   Mesh Shielding   Insulation   Conductor

less expensive cable and connectors. Some coaxial cable can be used for either baseband or broadband. Baseband and broadband transmission are illustrated in Figure 7-11.

Advantages and Disadvantages The television industry has helped develop coaxial cable technology, including the ability to add stations or tap into a line without interrupting existing service. In an environment where workstations are regularly added, moved, or deleted, the ability to alter the equipment configuration without disruption to existing users is significant. However, the ability to tap into the cable without disrupting service is a disadvantage if a high degree of security is required. Coaxial cable shielding provides a high degree of immunity to externally caused signal distortion. In LANs of less than a half-mile range (the distance varies with specific implementations), signal loss or attenuation is not a concern; for longer distances, repeaters that enhance the signals are necessary.

Security may be considered both an advantage and a disadvantage of coaxial cable. If a very secure medium is required, with taps being difficult to make and easy to detect, coaxial cable presents a serious problem. Whenever distances are great, attenuation becomes a problem, as does the cost of the greater amount of cable and the repeaters that must be installed to enhance the signals over long distances. The advantages of coaxial cable include its high data transmission rates, its immunity to noise or signal distortion (compared with twisted-pair wires), its capability for adding stations, and its reasonable cost over short distances.

Coaxial cable was once the primary LAN medium. It is used less often in today's LANs for several reasons: high speeds over cheaper twisted-pair wires, reduced costs for fiber optic cables, and ease of maintenance for fiber optic cables. Coaxial cable is heavy, bulky, and harder to deploy than twisted-pair wires and fiber optic cable.

The two most common kinds of coaxial cable found in data communication networks are RG58 and RG62. RG58 cable, sometimes called *thinnet* or *cheapernet cable,* is used to support 10Base2 Ethernet LANs (see Chapter 8). RG62 is used for terminal-

Figure 7-11 Baseband and Broadband Transmission

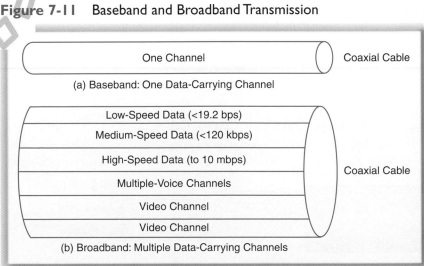

host connections in centralized host–based networks, especially those built around IBM mainframes. RG58 is priced at about 30 cents per foot, and RG62 is priced at about 20 cents per foot. Twinax cables (coaxial cable with two core communication wires instead of one) are used for connections with IBM's popular line of AS/400 minicomputers. RG59 cable is used for cable TV connections. Like twisted-pair cable, both PVC and plenum coaxial cable are available; plenum costs approximately twice as much per foot as PVC coaxial cable.

High-speed, broadband Internet access via cable modems is fueling renewed interest in coaxial cable as a data communication medium. Although it no longer is a major player in LANs, it has the potential to become another media option for homes and small businesses whose Internet access is accomplished through cable service providers.

Connectors   The most common connector found in LANs that use coaxial cable as communication media is called a *T-connector*. A T-connector provides an interface between the coaxial cable interface on a LAN adapter card or PCMCIA card and the coaxial cable itself. Older LANs using thick coaxial cable used *attachment-unit interface (AUI) connectors*.

Fiber Optic Cable   Fiber optic cable is used by telephone companies in place of long-distance wires and increasingly by private companies in implementing local data communication networks.

Technology   Fiber optic cables come in three varieties, each with a different way of guiding the light pulses from source to destination. All three have the same basic form and characteristics. One or more glass or plastic fibers are woven together to form the core of the cable. This core is surrounded by a glass or plastic layer called the *cladding*. The cladding is covered with plastic or some other material for protection. Figure 7-12 shows a side view and a cross section of a fiber optic cable. All three cable varieties require a light source; laser and light-emitting diodes (LEDs) are most commonly used.

The oldest of the three fiber optic technologies is **multimode step-index fiber**. The conduction core of this cable is the largest of the three, approximately 100 microns (100 millionths of an inch) for the core and 140 microns for the

multimode step-index fiber The oldest fiber optic technology, in which the reflective walls of the fiber move the light pulses to the receiver.

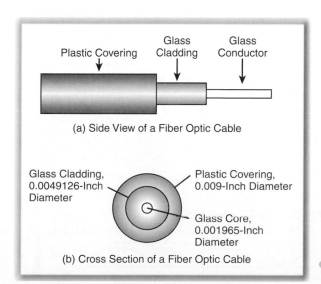

(a) Side View of a Fiber Optic Cable

Plastic Covering   Glass Cladding   Glass Conductor

Glass Cladding, 0.0049126-Inch Diameter

Plastic Covering, 0.009-Inch Diameter

Glass Core, 0.001965-Inch Diameter

(b) Cross Section of a Fiber Optic Cable

Figure 7-12   Views of a Fiber Optic Cable

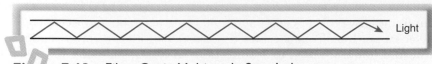

Figure 7-13   Fiber Optic Multimode Step Index

multimode graded-index fiber Refracts the light toward the center of the fiber by variations in the density of the core.

single-mode transmission The fastest fiber optic technique, in which the light is guided down the center of an extremely narrow core.

cladding. With multimode step index, the reflective walls of the fiber move the light pulses to the receiver, as illustrated in Figure 7-13. The light pulses traveling straight through the core arrive at the end of the fiber slightly ahead of those being reflected off the walls. This limits the transmission speed, and this form of fiber is the slowest of the three with a maximum speed of 200 mbps. In **multimode graded-index fiber**, light is refracted toward the center of the fiber by variations in the density of the core (see Figure 7-14). The diameters of the core and cladding for multimode graded index are generally 62.5 and 125 microns, respectively. (50/125 is also available.) Multimode graded-index fiber is commonly used in LANs and is capable of supporting transmission speeds of more than 3 gbps. The third and fastest fiber optic technique is **single-mode transmission**. With single-mode transmission, the core is very small, typically 8.3 or 9 microns (with 100 to 125 micron cladding), and the light is guided down the center of this extremely narrow core (see Figure 7-15). Single-mode fiber is commonly used for longer distance communication links and very-high-speed LANs. Single-mode fiber typically support speeds up to 100 gbps; however, when used in LANs, the maximum speed is typically 1 gbps. A comparison of the diameters of the three kinds of fiber optic cable is given in Figure 7-16.

Benefits and Cost   One shortcoming of fiber optics is the inability to add new nodes while other nodes are active. Although it is now relatively easy to splice the fiber optic cable and add new stations, the network or a portion of the network must be down while the splice is being prepared. Fiber optic links for very short distances cost more than wires (prices start at about 40 cents per foot for bulk multimode cable and about 30 cents per foot for single mode), but as distance or the required transmission rate increases, fiber optics becomes cost-effective. The break-even point generally occurs when the distance is so great that twisted-pair wires or coaxial would require expensive signal-enhancing equipment. A significant advantage of fiber optic cable over copper wire is its lower size and weight; it is about one-twentieth as heavy and one-fifth as thick as equivalent copper wire (either coaxial or twisted pair). Very low error rates, security, and immunity to environmental interference are additional benefits.

Figure 7-14   Fiber Optic Multimode Graded Index

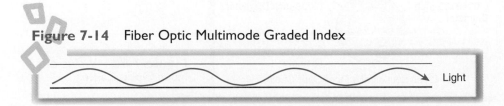

Light

Figure 7-15   Fiber Optic Single Mode

Connectors   The most common connectors used with fiber optic cable are ST and SC connectors (see Figure 7-17). The most common connectors for LANs that use twisted-pair or coaxial cables are illustrated in Figure 7-18. Of the fiber optic connectors, the ST connector is most common; it uses a bayonet locking system to ensure a constant connection. SC connectors have a molded body and use a push-pull locking system. FDDI connectors are used in FDDI LANs (see Chapter 8), and MTRJ connectors (see Figure 7-18) are found in some fiber optic–based networks.

Radiated Media

The two most common kinds of radiated communication media used in wireless LANs are spread-spectrum radio and infrared light. Of these, spread-spectrum radio is the most widely used.

The frequencies of these and other kinds of radiated media are provided in Table 7-4.

Spread-Spectrum Radio   The primary application of **spread-spectrum radio (SSR)** for data communication is wireless LANs. SSR has long been used by the military to provide reliable radio communication in battlefield environments where signal jamming can be expected. One characteristic of SSR is reliability in environments where signal interference is likely.

Two methods, frequency hopping and direct sequencing, are used to provide SSR signals. With **frequency hopping**, data is transmitted at one frequency; then, the

spread-spectrum radio (SSR) The primary application of SSR in data communication is for use with wireless LANs. It has a characteristic reliability in environments where signal interference is likely. It works by continuously changing the carrier frequency according to a unique pattern in both sending and receiving devices.

frequency hopping A spread-spectrum radio (SSR) transmission technique in which the transmission frequency is changed at regular intervals over a fixed spectrum. Data are transmitted at one frequency, the frequency changes, and the data are transmitted at the new frequency. Each piece of data is transmitted over several frequencies to increase the probability that the data will be successfully received.

Figure 7-16   Diameter Comparison of Fiber Optic Cable

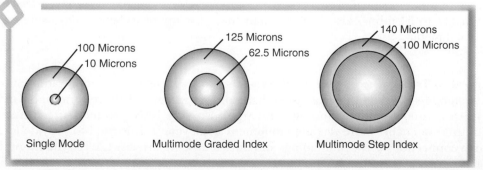

100 Microns
10 Microns

125 Microns
62.5 Microns

140 Microns
100 Microns

Single Mode   Multimode Graded Index   Multimode Step Index

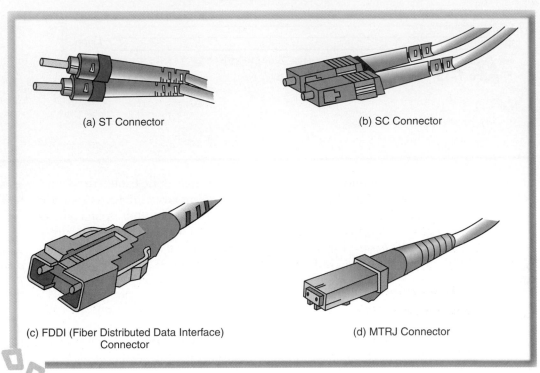

(a) ST Connector

(b) SC Connector

(c) FDDI (Fiber Distributed Data Interface) Connector

(d) MTRJ Connector

Figure 7-17   Fiber Optic Cable Connectors

direct sequencing
A spread-spectrum radio (SSR) transmission technique that sends the same data out over several different frequencies simultaneously to increase the probability of success.

infrared transmission Uses electromagnetic radiation of wavelengths between visible light and radio waves. As a line-of-sight technology, it may be used to provide local area connections between buildings. It is also the medium used in some wireless LANs; diffused infrared light transmissions may be used in place of line-of-sight connections in wireless LANs.

frequency is changed, and data is transmitted at the new frequency, and so on. Each piece of data is transmitted over several frequencies to increase the probability that it will be successfully received. As mentioned earlier, two widely accepted standards for wireless networks, Bluetooth and HomeRF, both rely on frequency hopping. **Direct sequencing** sends data over several different frequencies simultaneously. When used in wireless LANs, SSR distances are limited to approximately 1,000 feet, making it useful for small LANs or as the medium for small wireless segments of larger cable-based LANs. Examples of SSR being used in a large LAN include the use of portable computers and LAN connections in an area in which it is difficult or expensive to install conducted media. SSR signals can penetrate normal office walls, but signal strength is reduced considerably by concrete and metal walls. Like most radiated media, SSR is susceptible to signal interference and interception. The speed of data transmission (11 to 54 mbps) also is lower than that of many of today's LANs using conducted media.

Infrared Transmission   **Infrared transmission** uses electromagnetic radiation of wavelengths between those of visible light and radio waves. Infrared transmission is typically line-of-sight technology, but some wireless LAN products use diffused infrared to enable more flexible equipment deployment. It is used to provide local area connections between buildings and is used in some wireless LANs. Data transmission rates are in wireless LAN range from 1 mbps to 10 mbps.

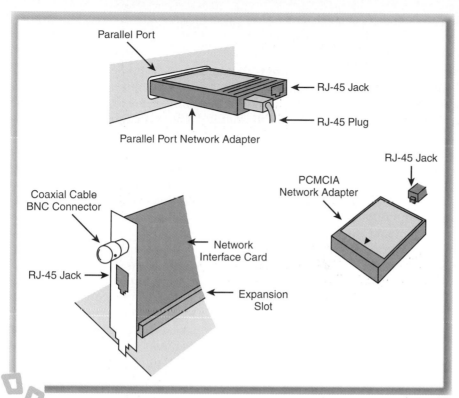

Figure 7-18 Connectors Used in Cable-Based LANs with Twisted-Pair Wires or Coaxial Cable

Table 7-4 Frequency Spectrum Classification

Frequency (Hz)	Wavelength
10^{16}	X rays, gamma rays
10^{15}	Ultraviolet light
10^{14}	Visible light
10^{13}	Infrared light
10^{12}	Millimeter waves
10^{11}	Microwaves
10^{10}	UHF television
10^9	VHF television
10^8	VHF TV (high band)
	FM radio
10^7	VHF TV (low band)
	Shortwave radio
10^6	AM radio
10^5	Very low frequency
10^4	Very low frequency
10^3	Very low frequency
10^2	Very low frequency
10^1	Very low frequency

Wiring Center Options

wiring hub A central interconnection point for workstations, servers, and other network equipment that is used in numerous LAN implementations to provide node-to-node connections.

Hubs   Most LAN architectures use **wiring hubs** to provide device interconnection. A wiring hub is a concentrator that serves as a central interconnection point for workstations, servers, and other LAN equipment. Most workstations and servers connect to hubs via twisted-pair wires. Hubs in Ethernet LANs are sometimes called *concentrators;* a hub in a token-ring LAN is often called a *multistation access unit (MAU)*. Hubs designed for use with particular LAN architectures and a hub designed for a particular architecture, such as a 100BaseTX Ethernet, will not work in another architecture; hence, it is essential to choose a wiring hub of the proper architecture.

Hubs vary in the number of ports available. For smaller LANs, 4- and 8-port hubs are common. Common configurations for larger LANs are 12-, 16-, and 24-port hubs. Hubs may be stand-alone or stackable. A stand-alone hub is usually enclosed in a chassis and has two or more ports that allow wire-based connections to other hubs. *Stackable hubs* are modular hubs that can be stacked on top of each other or mounted in a wiring rack. Stackable hubs share a backplane, so multiple hubs can be treated as a single hub. (A *backplane* is a board that holds the bus interface in modular devices, allowing new modules to be added easily when needed. The modules plug into the backplane, which contains a bus over which signals are transmitted. A backplane is similar to the buses found in a computer.) The common backplane provides a high-speed interconnection between the hubs. By concentrating the hub connections into a stackable unit, the network administrator creates one central location for resolving wiring problems.

Some hubs have reliability and maintenance features that help minimize the possibility of failure and streamline the repair process. Dual power supplies with shared power enhance reliability. During normal operation, the hub draws power from both power supplies; if one power supply fails, the remaining one can provide power for the entire hub. Hot-swappable components simplify maintenance; *hot-swappable* means that the hub can be repaired while it is functioning, which minimizes or eliminates downtime. For example, a failed power supply can be replaced while the hub is operating, without interrupting network operations.

It is important to have the ability to manage wiring hubs. Some hubs collect data about network traffic and make this data available through one of several available network management standards. The principal network management standards are the Simple Network Management Protocol (SNMP) and the Common Management Information Protocol (CMIP). SNMP is part of the Transmission Control Protocol/Internet Protocol (TCP/IP) suite, and CMIP is an ISO OSI standard. More information on these two network management protocols is provided in Chapter 15. Managed hubs support one or more of these network management standards; unmanaged hubs do not. Although unmanaged hubs are less expensive than managed hubs, their utility is limited in today's business LANs.

LAN switch A wiring hub with integrated media access control (MAC) layer switching or bridging capability. Most LAN switches provide switched connections among LAN nodes at the data link layer (Layer 2) of the OSI reference model.

LAN Switches   **LAN switches** physically resemble wiring hubs, but their function is quite different. For example, consider an Ethernet hub like the 8-port hub shown in Figure 7-19. When a node transmits a packet, the hub sends the packet out on all other ports, so each node receives the packet. In contrast, a switch examines the packet and finds the address of the recipient. A connection between the sender and recipient is established, and the packet is sent directly to the recipient through a single outgoing port. While that connection is being used, two other nodes can also be communicating over a different connection. Switches therefore increase the aggregated data rate (throughput) on the network.

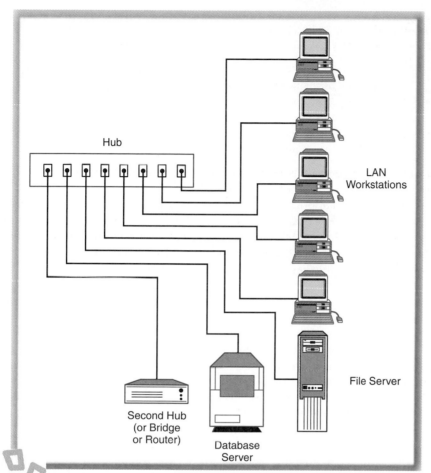

Figure 7-19   A Hub's Role in a LAN

Virtual LANs   Some switches provide LAN administrators an additional configuration alternative: that of creating **virtual LANs (VLANs)**. In a nonvirtual LAN, all nodes connected together via hubs, switches, or a common medium are on the same physical LAN. Switches allow the network administrator to group a set of workstations connected to a switch into one virtual LAN and another group of workstations into a different virtual LAN. The virtual LANs thus created function as though they were separate physical LANs. The switch provides the ability to provide these logical groupings.

LAN switches that support virtual LANs differ from those that do not in how they handle broadcast and multicast messages. Broadcast and multicast messages are only sent to virtual LAN members by hubs that support virtual LANs; such messages are sent to all connected devices by hubs that do not support virtual LANs. Layer 2 switches are used to implement most virtual LANs; however, in some instances layer 3 switches are used. Layer 3 switches are able to process OSI layer 3 addresses. Layer 3 switches are often called *routing switches*, because their filtering/forwarding processes are based on network layer addresses and protocols. Layer 3

virtual LAN (VLAN) A logical group of workstations interconnected to one or more LAN switches that function as a self-contained LAN or workgroup. Switching software enables network managers to create virtual LANs. Workstations in a virtual LAN do not have to be physically connected to the same switch or LAN but function as though they are all attached to the same physical LAN.

switches enable network managers to create virtual LANs for users that are physically connected to different networks that use different network layer protocols.

There are several advantages of virtual LANs. These include the following:

> A user on a virtual LAN can move physically to a different switch connection or node and still be included on the same virtual LAN.

> The administrator can easily change a user from one work group to another by assigning the user's workstation to a different virtual LAN.

> Virtual LANs reduce the costs associated with physically adding, moving, and changing a node from one physical LAN to another.

The disadvantage of virtual LANs is that currently there are only proprietary standards for transmitting/sharing virtual LAN information among switches. Hence, a business interested in supporting virtual LANs is often limited to purchasing switches from a single vendor. For example, one vendor may allow the network administrator to group nodes by their network addresses, whereas another may allow grouping by an identifier such as a node name. Because of these differences, one vendor's switch may not interoperate with another vendor's switch in setting up virtual LANs.

Wireless LAN Hubs   Wiring center options for wireless LANs depend on the kind of communication medium that is used. When infrared light serves as the communication medium, a ceiling-mounted hub such as that depicted in Figure 7-20(a) may be used to provide node-to-node connectivity; these also serve as the access to backbone cables and enterprise computing resources. When spread-spectrum radio is the communication medium, wireless hubs (called *access points*) such as the ones depicted in Figure 7-20(b) provide node-to-node connectivity and access to computing resources on the organization's cable-based networks. IEEE 802.11-compliant wireless hubs help ensure interoperability among hubs manufactured by different vendors. Some of the newer IEEE 802.11 wireless hubs enable the colocation of two or more hubs. Colocation can enhance wireless LAN performance by enabling workstations in overlapping coverage areas to connect to the hub with the lowest load (traffic) level at that point in time. IEEE 802.11-compliant hubs also typically support roaming; mobile devices can move between hub coverage areas (cells) without interruption in network services.

LAN Adapters

network interface card (NIC) An expansion card that allows a computer to communicate via a network. A NIC provides the connection between the medium and the bus of the workstation or server. Also known as LAN (or network) adapters.

LAN adapters, which are also known as **network interface cards (NICs)**, provide the connection between the medium and the bus of the workstation or server. LAN adapters are designed to support a specific LAN architecture (such as Ethernet, token ring, or FDDI) using a specific medium, although a few can support multiple medium types. For example, some Ethernet NICs have an RJ-45 interface for twisted-pair wires and a BNC (Bayonet-Neill-Corcelman) interface for coaxial cable (see Figure 7-21). After you match medium and architecture, there are additional choices to make: vendor, workstation/server expansion bus architecture, and adapter architecture.

The choice of a LAN adapter vendor determines the support, quality, and price of the LAN adapter. Just as you should be careful when selecting vendors for other LAN hardware and software, you should also be careful in choosing the vendor of individual components such as LAN adapters. The LAN adapter that is initially the least expensive may prove to be more costly in the long run if it is of inferior quality, if it does not have a good vendor support policy, or if the vendor goes out of business, making replacement LAN adapters difficult to obtain.

LAN adapters are installed in each workstation and server. The LAN adapter must be compatible with the bus architecture of each computer into which it is

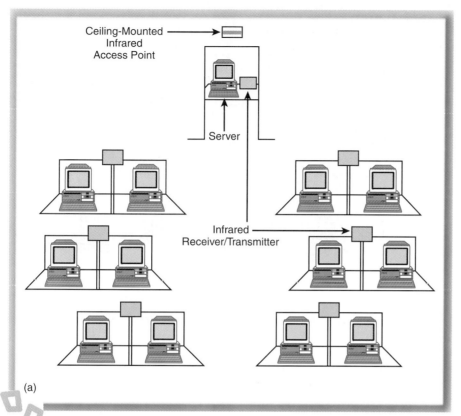

(a)

Figure 7-20a   Wireless LAN Hubs

installed. Although adapters for both ISA and PCI expansion bus architectures are available for IBM–compatible machines, PCI adapters are generally preferred by LAN administrators. If there is a mixture of workstation types, such as IBM–compatible and Macintosh computers, LAN adapters for both kinds of machines should be available. Older Macintosh computers have a NuBus expansion bus architecture, and LAN adapters for these machines must be selected accordingly. If interfaces for laptop computers are to be supported, Personal Computer Memory Card International Association (PCMCIA) network adapters should be available. PCMCIA cards are also known as *PC cards*.

LAN adapters also have their own onboard architectures. LAN adapters for IBM or compatible systems often come in 8-bit, 16-bit, 32-bit, and 64-bit architectures. The 32-bit and 64-bit adapters are most common today, and these are almost always more expensive and faster than the corresponding 16-bit and 8-bit adapters. By faster, we mean that a 32-bit or 64-bit adapter can transfer data between the computer and the medium faster than a 16-bit adapter, which is faster than an 8-bit adapter. The onboard architecture does not affect the speed at which data is transferred over the network medium. A 32-bit adapter is faster than a 16-bit adapter; it transfers data between the adapter and memory 32 bits at a time, whereas the 16-bit adapter transfers data in 16-bit groups.

Network adapter cards carry out several important LAN functions. These include monitoring activity on the communication medium, providing each workstation/server

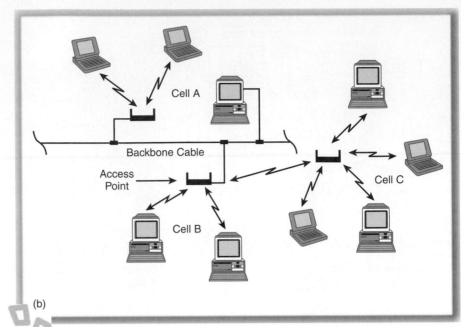

(b)

Figure 7-20b   Wireless LAN Cells Interconnected to a Cable-Based LAN

communication interface unit (CIU) In a LAN, the CIU provides the physical connection to the transmission medium.

bus interface unit (BIU) In a LAN, the BIU provides the physical connection to the computer's I/O bus.

transceiver A device that receives and sends signals. A transceiver helps form the interface between a network node and the medium.

connector Establishes the physical connection between the computer and the medium. In general, a connector is any plug, socket, or wire that links two devices.

with a unique identification address, recognizing and receiving data destined for the workstation, creating the frames/packets in which data to be transmitted over the medium is placed (frame building), removing overhead information from incoming data frames/packets (unpacking received frames), and controlling LAN speed. (NICs are responsible for transmission speeds in the LAN; 100-mbps NICs must be used if 100 mbps are desired.)

As noted earlier, the LAN adapter cards installed in servers and workstations must be compatible with the LAN communication medium you choose. It is the medium that primarily influences the way in which physical connections are made within a LAN.

From a generic perspective, the objective of network connection—connecting a computer to the LAN medium—is to provide a data path between the medium and the computer's memory. To accomplish this, there must be a connection to the communication medium and a connection to the computer's bus or channel. The interface or connection to the medium is called the **communication interface unit (CIU)**, and the interface or connection to the computer's bus is called the **bus interface unit (BIU)**. These functions, illustrated in Figure 7-22, are provided by the LAN adapter.

A key component of the network connection is a **transceiver**, which establishes the connection to the medium and implements the transmit and receive portion of the LAN's communication protocol. In a few Ethernet LANs, the transceiver is connected directly to the medium. Most of today's Ethernet implementations have a transceiver that is located on the LAN adapter, as illustrated in Figure 7-23.

The physical connection between the computer and the medium is established through **connectors**. Many different kinds of connectors are used, but the principal ones include RJ-45 connectors for twisted-pair wires; BNC-, TNC- (T-connectors), or N-type connectors for coaxial cable; and ST and SC connectors for fiber optic cable.

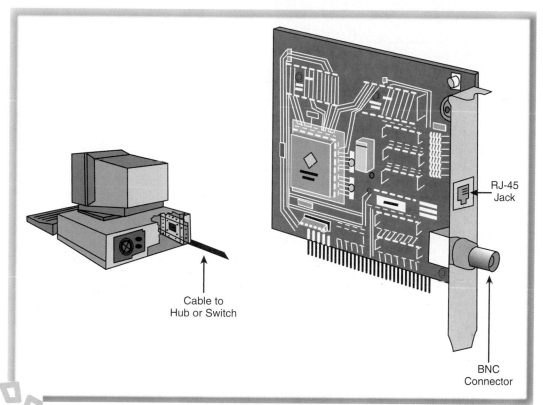

Figure 7-21   A Network Interface Card (NIC)

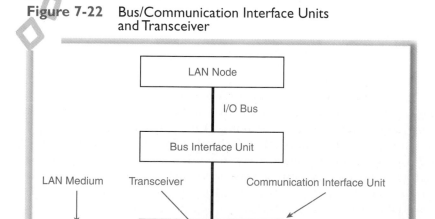

Figure 7-22   Bus/Communication Interface Units and Transceiver

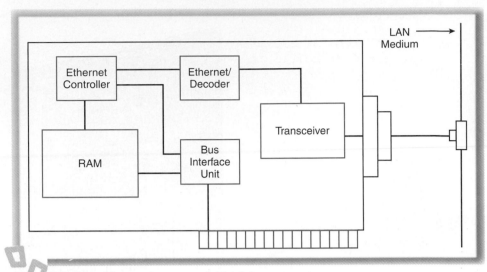

Figure 7-23   Transceiver on a LAN Adapter

LAN adapters for wireless LANs use an antenna to connect to the communication medium. There are several kinds of wireless LAN adapters.

➤ *PCMCIA cards for notebook computers.* Most of these have omnidirectional antennae.

➤ *Station adapters for desktop computers.* As of 2002, many are PCI cards that include a PCMCIA wireless LAN card. Similarly constructed ISA cards are available from some vendors.

➤ *External adapters that plug into workstation USB ports.*

A wide variety of connector adapters allow you to change connector types. One adapter for coaxial cable–based Ethernet LANs can change a BNC to a TNC-type connector. **Baluns** are adapters that change coaxial cable connectors to twisted-pair wire connectors. These adapters allow you to transfer from one medium to another or from a connector for one medium to a different medium.

In some LANs, connecting a computer to the medium is sufficient for making that computer active on the network. Most full-fledged LAN implementations, however, use wiring hubs to provide node-to-node connection. As noted earlier, several kinds of connection hubs are commonly used, including managed/unmanaged shared-media hubs, token-ring multistation access units (MAUs), and LAN switches.

A variety of other hardware components are sometimes needed to make the network function. On bus networks that enable workstations to connect directly to the communication medium, **terminators** are often needed to prevent signal loss. Terminators are used at the ends of a coaxial cable bus to prevent echo.

LAN Software

LAN software is the other major component of a LAN. Two major categories of LAN software exist: LAN system software (such as the LAN network operating system) and LAN application software (such as groupware and other applications supported on the LAN). LAN software is discussed more fully in Chapter 9.

baluns Adapters that change coaxial cable connectors into twisted-pair wire connectors, allowing transfer from one medium to another or from a connector for one medium to a different medium.

terminators Resistors at a cable end that absorb the signal and prevent echo or other signal noise.

ADDITIONAL LAN HARDWARE

File, data, and print sharing are three of the major drivers of LAN implementation among business organizations. Hence, it is not surprising that printers are among the other major hardware components of LANs. In addition to printers, backup devices and uninterruptible power supplies (UPSs) are other important hardware components in LANs.

Printers and Print Servers

One major factor that affects the success of a LAN is printer support. Although a printer is technically not LAN hardware, printers are an integral part of a LAN. Some LAN network operating systems have restrictions regarding the distribution of printers and the number of printers that can be supported by one server. Suppose that network printers must be attached to a server and that each server can support a maximum of 16 printers. An organization that needs 50 printers, therefore, must have at least four servers.

You must be concerned not only with the number of printers but also with the kind of printers supported and the way in which they are supported. A **printer driver** is a software module that determines how to format data for proper printing on a specific kind of printer. The printers you intend to use must be supported by the software drivers provided by the LAN network operating system vendor. You may find that a laser printer you attach to the LAN can operate in text mode but is restricted in its graphic mode operation or in its ability to download fonts. Be sure to consider interoperability of hardware and software components to ensure that they meet your needs. Some LAN network operating systems provide a utility program that allows you to tailor a generic printer driver to work with a specific printer you want to use. This utility allows you to define printer functions and the command sequences essential to invoking those functions. Because new printer technologies are constantly appearing, this utility is quite useful.

printer driver A software module that determines how to format data for proper printing on a specific type of printer. It converts an application program's printing request into the language the printer understands.

Print servers manage shared printers and print queues. A LAN file server can be used as a print server. This is an acceptable solution for smaller LANs, but as the size of a LAN increases, dedicated print servers (either stand-alone devices or a computer) are common. Print servers may also be a preferred solution in environments (such as libraries) where printing is a primary LAN function. Typically, a single print server can serve a fixed number of printers. The two main functions performed by a print server are print job distribution and print job sequencing. *Job distribution* involves routing print jobs to the printers controlled by the print server. A common job distribution approach is to route a particular user's print jobs to the printer(s) located closest to the user's workstation. Other distribution management options can be used to ensure that

print server A computer that allows several users to direct their printed output to the same printer. A print server may control the distribution of network user print jobs to multiple printers.

➤ Print jobs that include color graphics are routed to printers with color graphic capabilities (such as color ink-jet or laser printers).

➤ Print jobs that require many pages of printed output are routed to printers with high page-per-minute (ppm) printing rates.

➤ Print jobs are not routed to printers that are off-line.

➤ Print jobs that could be routed to two or more printers are sent to the printer with the smallest print queue.

Job sequencing involves the management of print queues for the individual printers controlled by the print server. Because printing is one of the slowest operations that occur in any computing system, including LANs, print jobs often arrive at a printer faster than they can be printed. Most print queues use a "first in, first out" job sequencing as a default, but it is often desirable to be able to change the order of print jobs, purge duplicate print jobs, and so forth. In some businesses, users are assigned different print priorities. Executives, for example, may have their print jobs placed at the beginning of a print queue no matter how many jobs are waiting to be printed. Very large print jobs may be assigned priorities that require them to be printed out during nonpeak work hours (such as the wee hours of the morning) when they are least likely to delay the printing of smaller jobs.

Backup Devices

fault tolerance The ability to continue, nonstop, when component failure occurs. In networks fault tolerance is often achieved by a combination of hardware and software techniques that improve the reliability of a system.

No business LAN is complete without backup devices. Backup devices help ensure network **fault tolerance** (resistance to network failures or crashes). Fault tolerance may include the use of **server duplexing** (running two or more servers in tandem, with each functioning as a backup to at least one other server). Duplexing servers involves connecting them electronically so that one trails the other by a few milliseconds and can take over for the lead server should it malfunction. Duplexing servers is common in server clusters, especially when load balancing is used to spread out the workload among clustered servers. This is a common practice among high-volume e-commerce sites where reliable 24/7 access is critical. Server clusters support server duplexing. Load balancing is commonly used in server clusters to reduce the probably of crashes as the result of lead servers becoming overwhelmed by network traffic. Both server clusters and load balancing are discussed more fully in Chapter 4.

server duplexing Running two or more servers in tandem with each functioning as a backup to at least one other server.

One of the LAN administrator's most important duties in regard to LAN fault tolerance is to make periodic file backups. A **backup** is a copy of files made at a specific time; it is used to restore the system to a workable state following a system failure or an event that damages the data, or to restore data that is needed only on a periodic basis. For example, research data that is needed only once or twice a month and year-end payroll data that is needed temporarily to file workers' tax notices can be backed up and then replaced on disk on an as-needed basis.

backup A duplicate resource that can be substituted for a network component should failure occur. Network managers are often responsible for file backups.

The most common backup device found in LANs is a magnetic tape drive, and a variety of these are available. Removable disk drives and optical disk drives are alternatives. The primary backup technologies are described here and listed in Table 7-5.

Floppy Diskette Drives   Although floppy diskettes may be used as the backup medium, they are likely to be suitable options only for small LANs. The diskette drives used to make backups may be server or workstation drives. The major disadvantage of

Table 7-5   Primary File Backup Technologies

Backup Technology	Capacity
Diskette backup	1.44 MB, 2.88 MB, 20 MB
Hard drive, fixed	Multiple capacities
Removable cartridge disks	40 MB to over 1 GB
Tape backup, 4 mm or 1/4 inch	To 15 GB, 60 MB, 150 MB, 160 MB, 500 MB, 1.2 GB, 2.2 GB, 15 GB, 30 GB (compressed)
Tape backup, 8 mm or VCR	To 2.2 GB
Tape backup, 9-track	To 100 MB
Optical drives, WORM	To 4 GB
Optical drives, rewritable	To 4 GB
Digital versatile disks	10–14 GB

this backup method is the low capacity and speed. Typical diskette capacities of IBM–compatible systems are 720 KB, 1.44 MB, and 2.88 MB. Diskettes with capacities of up to 20 MB are also available. Often, however, the capacity of server hard disks is 80 GB or more. A large LAN may have hundreds of billions of bytes of disk storage. Backing up this amount of data to 1.44-MB (or even 20-MB) diskettes is cumbersome. The advantages of diskette backup are high availability on workstations and servers and low cost. Diskette backup for LANs with small disk requirements or for backing up a few small files can be practical, but for large-disk systems, the number of diskettes needed to store all the data is high. This process is slow and subject to errors, and requires handling many diskettes.

High-Capacity Removable Disks   High-capacity removable disk drives have become quite common on servers and workstations; Zip drives are one example. Disks used in such drives range in capacities from 100 MB to multiple gigabytes. Although these may be valuable for backups for particular files, they are cumbersome for full backups of high-capacity server disks.

Hard Disk Drives   A hard disk drive on a server or a workstation may also be used for backup. The arguments for and against this alternative are much the same as those for diskettes. The major difference is that the capacity of hard disk drives is greater than that of diskettes. If the hard disk is not removable, it is difficult to keep multiple generations of backups, a procedure that is important for a comprehensive backup plan. For example, many widely accepted backup schemes involve at least three generations of backups, which means that if you make a backup weekly, 3 weeks' worth of backups are always available. Some hard drives have removable disk cartridges, which are an excellent backup alternative because they provide high capacity (typically ranging from 800 MB to 20 GB) and rapid access.

Many LAN file servers include multiple hard drives or support RAID capabilities in order to increase the LAN's fault tolerance. A junior version of server duplexing (mentioned earlier) is the duplexing of disk drives within the same server. This often involves the use of two separate disk controllers (IDE or SCSI) so that if one controller fails, the other will take over. The primary vulnerability of this approach is that if the server processor fails, both controllers are useless unless the second controller is controlled by a separate processor. This is why server duplexing is widely viewed as a superior approach to duplexed controllers. *Disk mirroring* enables data to be duplicated on two disks controlled by a single controller. This can be an acceptable backup approach as long as the controller for the mirrored disks does not fail.

Disk mirroring is one of the kinds of data duplication supported by servers with RAID capabilities. **RAID (redundant arrays of independent disks)** enables data to be stored on two or more disks by combining multiple disks, disk drives, and disk controllers in an array. Often, one of the disks in the array is assigned the task of storing error-correction codes derived from the data stored on the other disks; this information can be used to reconstruct damaged or missing data in the event of disk or disk drive failure. The drives in most of today's RAID systems are hot-swappable—they can be removed or replaced without having to power down the server. Most RAID systems also support *data striping;* this enables data to be distributed between disk drives at the block (packet), byte, and bit levels.

Optical Disk Drives   Optical disk drives are gaining popularity as backup devices. The reasons for this are their decreasing costs and large storage capacity, and the recently introduced ability to erase and rewrite to optical disks. There are two classes of optical disk drives: WORM (write once, read many) and erasable drives. As the name

RAID (redundant arrays of independent disks) A method of storing data on multiple hard disk drives for faster access, greater reliability, or both. RAID is a fault tolerant disk storage technique that spreads one file plus the file's checksum information over several disk drives. If any single disk drive fails, the data stored thereon can be reconstructed from data stored on the remaining drives.

implies, WORM technology allows you to write to the medium only once. Because you cannot erase a WORM disk, it can only be used once to make a backup. However, this means that the data stored on a WORM disk cannot be changed. CD-R (compact disk–recordable) disks are examples of WORM technologies. Erasable optical drives have generally replaced WORM drives as the preferred optical technology. The costs of erasable drives and CD media have become very affordable, and the typical rewritable CD (CD-RW) has a storage capacity of 650 MB. Emerging CD standards promise to provide several gigabytes of storage per CD. Although the digital versatile disk (DVD) format provides double-side/double-density recording and may have a storage capacity exceeding 14 GB per diskette, it is not widely used for LAN backups. Rewritable DVD disks used in LANs typically have capacities ranging from 2.6 to 9.4 GB.

Virtual Disk Systems   Virtual disk systems provide continuous real-time backup services for LANs. These are among the most sophisticated and expensive backup systems for LANs. Virtual disk systems eliminate the need for periodic backups (daily, weekly, or monthly) by virtue of backing up LAN data automatically and transparently. Although such systems require enormous storage capabilities, in the event of a network crash, the network manager can turn back the clock to a few nanoseconds prior to the failure and re-create all data that existed at that time.

Magnetic Tape Drives   As mentioned earlier, magnetic tape systems are the most common backup device found in LANs. Magnetic tapes are less expensive than the other options. They hold large volumes of data, are easy to use and store, and generally provide good performance. A variety of tape backup devices is available. The drives themselves are relatively inexpensive, and you can choose from a wide range of data capacities. Some of the tapes being used today have capacities ranging from 10 to 100 GB. Tape drives vary in the size of the tape and recording method. If more than one tape drive is to be used in one organization, it is best to establish a standard tape configuration so the tapes can be exchanged among the different drives. The main magnetic tape options are summarized in Table 7-6.

Table 7-6   Magnetic Tape Backup Functions

Back up all files
Back up all files modified since a particular date
Back up by directory
Back up by list of files
Back up all but a list of files to be excluded
Back up by index
Back up by interface to a database
Back up using wildcard characters in file names
Create new index on tape and disk
Maintain cross-reference of tape serial numbers and backup
Back up manually
Back up automatically by time or calendar
Start backup from workstation or server
Compress data
Back up many volumes
Generate reports

Like other hardware discussed in this chapter, the tape drive must be compatible with the server or workstation on which it is installed. A drive usually has a controller that must be installed in the computer, so you must select a drive that has a controller compatible with your equipment. Also, you need backup software and procedures to make backups. The most common server tape drive controller interface is SCSI because of its high data transfer rates.

Uninterruptible Power Supplies (UPSs)

Backup power supplies are also common features in today's LANs. Like duplexed servers and hot-swappable components, backup power supplies are designed to improve network reliability and fault tolerance. However, RAID systems, duplexed controllers, and duplexed servers will only enhance network fault tolerance if power is available.

An **uninterruptible power supply (UPS)** is a hardware device that provides power to devices in the event of a power outage. Every server and other key LAN components should be protected by a UPS, because the cost of a UPS is small relative to the cost of servers crashing because of power loss. An unexpected server crash can result in a time-consuming network recovery. A server crash can cause data to be lost. Should the crash occur in the midst of a transaction involving multiple file/database updates or during a backup process, the result can be inconsistent file/database data. For example, a related set of updates for index tables for a database access method may be in progress at the time of failure. If an entry is made in one index table, and the corresponding update in another index is nullified by a server failure, data pointed out by the index tables may be unable to be located.

A UPS uses batteries as a source of power when a power outage occurs. During normal operation, power is available from the main power supply. This power is passed through the UPS and maintains the charge on the batteries. If the main power source fails, the UPS battery takes over and continues to supply power to the connected devices. The duration of UPS power varies depending on the power load drawn from the equipment and the capacity of the UPS itself. The power load drawn relies on the total ratings of the equipment being sustained by the UPS, so different configurations consume different amounts of power. UPSs come in different sizes, and the size is usually measured in volt-amps (VA), but wattage is another measure sometimes used to describe the power rating. The higher the VA rating is, the more power is available. Generally, LAN administrators configure the power of the UPS to sustain the equipment it powers for approximately 30 minutes to an hour. UPS sizes run the gamut from the ability to provide power for a small microcomputer for a few minutes to supplying power for large mainframe systems for several hours. Other capabilities of a UPS include surge protection, power smoothing, battery-level indicators, and brownout protection.

Some UPS systems are combined with software to provide management capabilities. The UPS typically communicates with the computer via a serial connection. Software in the computer can interrogate statistics maintained by the UPS and report on those statistics. Information that might be reported includes high and low power levels supplied by the main power source, battery condition, power consumption over time, and temperature. Software features also include some management capabilities, such as automatically shutting the system down and starting the system at certain times and initiating alarms for out-of-tolerance situations such as low battery or overload situations.

uninterruptible power supply (UPS)
A backup power unit that continues to provide power to a computer system during the failure of the normal power supply. A UPS is often used to protect LAN servers from power failures.

STORAGE AREA NETWORKS (SANs)

Data storage needs are burgeoning in many business organizations. Steadily increasing storage requirements are being driven by the general trend toward Internet applications, including rich Web site content, business multimedia, graphically intensive applications, and online transactions. Increasing storage needs are also fueled by the development of intranets and knowledge management systems, data warehouses, document management systems, and extranets, as well as enterprise-wide applications such as customer relationship management (CRM), enterprise resources planning (ERP), supply chain management (SCM), and electronic procurement applications.

storage area network (SAN) Enables storage to be physically separated from an organization's servers and managed as a central resource while still logically controlled by each server's application software.

Storage area networks (SANs) are increasingly popular scalable, server-independent storage solutions among business organizations. A SAN enables storage to be physically separated from an organization's servers and managed as a central resource while still logically controlled by each server's application software. The SAN is a logical extension of the server's local storage. Servers have transparent access to SAN storage devices, and the amount of disk space mapped to each server can be increased or reassigned to other servers on-the-fly without having to power down the SAN. Tape backup devices can be connected to the SAN to back up (and, when necessary, restore) data without affecting servers or their applications. All in all, SANs have the promise of emerging as robust, fault-tolerant storage systems.

There are two main ways of implementing SANs: centralized and decentralized. As illustrated in Figure 7-24(a), a centralized SAN ties multiple application servers to a single storage system. The central storage system consists of a large RAID device with large amounts of cache and redundant (uninterruptible) power supplies. A decentralized SAN, illustrated in Figure 7-24(b), can connect dispersed file/application servers with multiple, distributed-storage devices via one or more SCSI or Fiber Channel switches.

network attached storage system (NAS) Connects to a LAN like a file server and uses a client-like network operating system module that specializes in handling I/O (input/output) requests. A NAS can be added or removed from a LAN in the same way that any other LAN node is added or removed.

Network attached storage systems (NASs), illustrated in Figure 7-24(c), are similar to centralized SANs. A NAS, however, connects to a LAN just like a file server and uses a client-like network operating system module specialized for handling I/O (input/output) requests. A NAS can be added or removed from a LAN in the same way that any other LAN node is added or removed. Unlike a SAN, a NAS must be rebooted in order to reconfigure it. Another difference between a NAS and a SAN is the connection. In a SAN, application servers interface with storage devices via a SCSI or fiber channel connection or switch; in contrast, application servers interface with a NAS via an Ethernet hub or switch.

LAN-TO-HOST INTERFACES

Many organizations already had centralized, host-based data communication networks in place when microcomputers and microcomputer-based LANs began to proliferate in business computing during the 1980s. The emergence of LANs led to the distributed and client/server network architectures that dominate today's business computing landscape.

As LANs became more prevalent, organizations faced the challenge of integrating them with existing host-based networks. A number of LAN-to-host interfaces have emerged, including some that have had to address major differences between LAN and WAN data link protocols. Today's LAN-to-host interfaces include

➤ *Installing a NIC in the host and establishing node-to-host connections via LAN hubs or switches.* As is the case for other LAN-to-host interfaces, terminal emulation software or cards are often installed in LAN nodes to enable them to interface with specific mainframes or minicomputers.

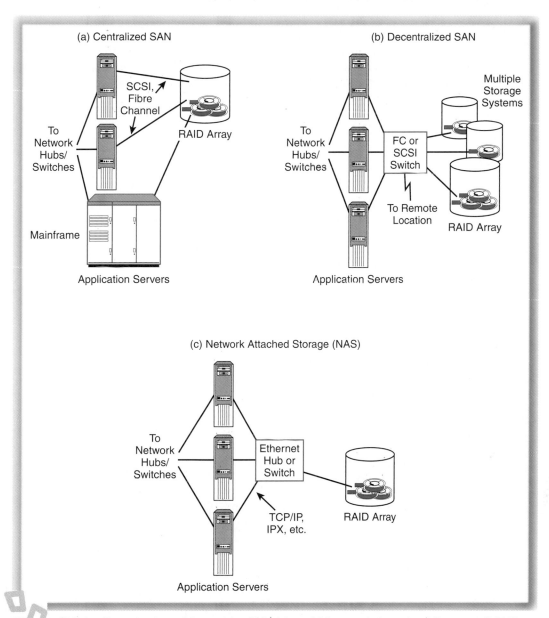

Figure 7-24 Storage Area Networks (SANs) and Network Attached Storage (NAS)

➤ *Dedicated connections between LAN nodes and the host.* In this case, LAN–attached workstations also have a dedicated point-to-point connection to the host.

➤ *Switched or dedicated connections between LAN nodes and the host via modems.* Modems in LAN–attached workstations establish communication sessions with modems at the host-end over switched or dedicated lines.

➤ *Shared/multiplexed connections between LAN nodes and the host.* LAN–attached nodes may have a point-to-point connection to a multiplexor, which, in turn, is connected to a multiplexor at the host-end via a single shared communications line.

➤ *Shared connections to the host via a LAN communication server.* As noted in Chapter 9, communication servers enable LAN nodes to interface with remote hosts over various communication lines, including dial-up, packet switching, frame relay, and T-n.

➤ *Connections via distributed or collapsed backbone networks using internal routers or level 3 switches.*

➤ *Gateways used to establish connections between LANs and SAN hosts.*

Most of these LAN-to-host interconnection options are discussed more fully in Chapter 10. The others are addressed in Chapter 13.

SUMMARY

LANs have been fundamental building blocks in enterprise networks since the 1980s. LANs are designed to serve the computing needs of users in a limited geographic area and have transmission speeds up to 1 gbps. Business organizations implement LANs because they are cost-effective, provide support for work groups, enable the rapid transfer of large data files among users, facilitate management control of network resources, enable modular or incremental network expansion, and because they make business sense for a variety of other reasons.

LANs may include dedicated and nondedicated servers. LAN alternatives range from small peer-to-peer LANs, zero-slot LANs, and sub–LANs to full-fledged LANs. Home networks and personal area networks are growing in popularity and represent an emerging alternative to full-fledged LANs.

The major hardware components of LANs include servers, workstations, communication media, wiring centers (hubs and switches), and network adapter cards. LAN network operating systems and application software represent the major software components of LANs. A variety of servers may be found in LANs. File servers are the most common. Print servers and database servers are also quite common. Communication servers, terminal servers, and facsimile servers are communication-oriented servers found in some LANs. Workstations running a variety of desktop operating systems may be attached to the same LAN. Twisted-pair wires are the most common communication media found in LANs. Fiber optic cable and coaxial cable are other wire-based LAN communication media; spread-spectrum radio and infrared light are the most common wireless media used in LANs.

LAN wiring center options include hubs and switches. Shared media hubs have been widely used in the past, but these are giving way to LAN switches in many business organizations. Network adapters are installed in servers and workstations to enable them to share the LAN's communication medium. For desktop workstations, network interface cards (NICs) that plug into expansion slots typically serve as network adapters. PCMCIA network adapters enable notebook computers to attach to LANs. Network adapters control LAN speed and implement a LAN's communication protocol.

Other common LAN hardware components include connectors, printers, backup devices, and uninterruptible power supplies. Storage area networks are becoming more widely used by organizations to address the increasing business data storage requirements. LAN workstations interface with centralized hosts in a variety of ways.

KEY TERMS

- access time
- application server
- application service provider (ASP)
- backup
- baluns
- baseband transmission
- Bluetooth
- broadband transmission
- bus interface unit (BIU)
- cache memory

- CEBus (consumer electric bus)
- communication interface unit (CIU)
- conducted media
- connector
- data switch
- dedicated server
- direct sequencing
- disk caching
- diskless workstation
- fault tolerance
- file server
- frequency hopping
- home network
- HomeRF (Home Radio Frequency)
- infrared transmission
- IrDA (Infrared Data Association) port
- LAN switch
- latency
- local area network (LAN)
- multimode graded-index fiber
- multimode step-index fiber
- NAT (Network Address Translation)
- network attached storage system (NAS)
- network interface card (NIC)
- nondedicated server
- personal area network (PAN)
- print server
- printer driver
- radiated media
- RAID (redundant arrays of independent disks)
- seek time
- server duplexing
- service bureau
- single-mode transmission
- spread-spectrum radio (SSR)
- storage area network (SAN)
- Structured Query Language (SQL)
- sub–LANs
- symmetrical multiprocessing (SMP)
- terminators
- transceiver
- transfer time
- uninterruptible power supply (UPS)
- virtual LAN (VLAN)
- virtual memory management
- wiring hub
- zero-slot LAN

REVIEW QUESTIONS

1. What are the characteristics of local area networks?
2. Identify and briefly describe the major reasons why LANs are popular among business organizations.
3. In what ways may LANs contribute to better management control over computing resources?
4. What added responsibilities are associated with the implementation of LANs?
5. Briefly discuss the advantages and disadvantages of nondedicated servers.
6. Briefly describe the characteristics of each of the following: peer-to-peer LANs, service bureaus, zero-slot LANs, and sub–LANs.
7. What are the alternative meanings of the term *home network?*
8. Compare CEBus, HomePNA, and personal area networks.
9. Compare Bluetooth, HomeRF, and IrDA.
10. Identify and briefly describe the major criteria that should be considered when selecting alternatives to full-fledged LANs.
11. Identify and briefly describe the major kinds of servers found in LANs.
12. Compare file servers, database servers, and application servers.
13. What is access time? Identify and briefly describe the following components of access time: seek time, latency, and transfer time.
14. What is a disk drive interface/controller? Compare IDE, EIDE, and SCSI controllers.
15. How do cache memory and disk caching contribute to server performance?
16. What are the characteristics of ECC memory?
17. What are the characteristics of symmetrical multiprocessing (SMP) systems?
18. Compare ISA, EISA, and PCI buses.
19. What are the characteristics of diskless workstations?
20. Compare conducted and radiated media.

21. What wire gauges (AWG ratings) are common in LANs?
22. Compare unshielded and shielded twisted-pair wires. When should shielded twisted pair be used?
23. What are the characteristics of punchdown blocks and patch panels?
24. Compare PVC and plenum cables.
25. What are the characteristics of coaxial cable?
26. Compare broadband and baseband transmission.
27. Compare RG58, RG59, and RG62 coaxial cable.
28. What are the characteristics of fiber optic cable?
29. Compare multimode step-index, multimode graded-index, and single-mode fiber optic cable.
30. Compare the costs of twisted-pair, coaxial, and fiber optic cable.
31. Compare twisted-pair, coaxial, and fiber optic connectors.
32. Compare frequency-hopping SSR and direct-sequencing SSR.
33. What are the characteristics of wiring hubs?
34. What are hot-swappable components?
35. How do LAN switches differ from shared media hubs?
36. What are the characteristics of virtual LANs?
37. What are the characteristics of IEEE 802.11 access points?
38. What factors must be considered when selecting NICs for LAN servers and workstations?
39. What functions are performed by LAN adapters?
40. Compare CUIs, BUIs, transceivers, baluns, and terminators.
41. Compare printer drivers, print servers, and print queues.
42. Compare print server job distribution and job sequencing activities.
43. What is fault tolerance? Describe the role of each of the following in LAN fault tolerance: server duplexing, disk mirroring, disk duplexing, RAID, virtual disk systems, and UPS.
44. Compare the advantages and disadvantages of each of the following as backup storage media: floppy diskettes, high-capacity removable disks, hard disk drives, optical disk drives, and magnetic tape drives.
45. Compare SAN and NAS.
46. Identify and briefly describe the various kinds of LAN-to-host interfaces.

PROBLEMS AND EXERCISES

1. Use the Internet to identify the distinctions among peer-to-peer communications, peer-to-peer networks, and peer-to-peer communications. Summarize your findings in a paper or table.
2. Use the Internet to find out more about Network Address Translation (NAT). Summarize your findings in a paper or PowerPoint presentation that describes how NAT works and where it is used in today's networks.
3. Assume that you have four computers (two desktop IBM–compatibles, one PowerMac, and one IBM–compatible notebook—all lack network adapters) in your residence and that you want to create a home network. Use online sources to identify the components that you will need to implement a HomePNA network. Identify specific product vendors and prices for components. Also find vendors, products, and prices for a HomeRF network. Summarize your findings in a paper or PowerPoint presentation.

4. Use the Internet to find out more about personal area networks (PANs) and summarize your findings in a paper or PowerPoint presentation. Your summary should describe the differences in how Bluetooth and HomeRF work.

5. You want to connect five microcomputers, all of which are located in one 20-by-30-foot room of your company's office complex. Users must share printers extensively and do a limited amount of file sharing. Cost is a critical LAN alternative selection consideration. What LAN alternative would you use? Explain how you reached your decision.

6. Use the Internet to investigate wireless Ethernet adapters that use spread-spectrum and infrared transmission. Prepare a set of graphs comparing these adapters on maximum transmission speed, maximum coverage area (transmission distance), and cost per workstation. Include the information for cable-based 10BaseT Ethernet adapters in each graph.

7. A small insurance company wants to connect its 10 microcomputers in a LAN. The company is located in an old house that has been renovated. Estimates of network traffic indicate that LAN transmission speeds must be at least 2 mbps but that speeds over 15 mbps are unlikely to be needed. There are no devices in the house that have the potential for disrupting signals on either radiated or conducted media. What medium would you recommend? Justify your answer.

8. A corporate office needs to connect several departmental LANs. Layer 2 switches will be used to interconnect the LANs, and the medium used to connect the switches must operate at 100 mbps or more. The medium will be run through elevator shafts and a machine room, so signal distortion is a concern. What medium would you recommend? Justify your answer.

9. Use the Internet to find out more about Citrix servers and their capabilities. Summarize your findings in a paper or PowerPoint presentation that outlines the business benefits and costs of such servers.

10. Use online sources to identify the characteristics and capabilities of IDE, EIDE, SCSI, and Ultra SCSI controllers. Develop a graph comparing the data transfer rates of these controllers.

11. Suppose you need to establish a small network with one server and 15 workstations. Describe the hardware configuration (memory, disk controllers, cache memory size, expansion and bus architecture) that you would recommend for the server and workstations. Assume that all workstations will have the same configuration. Consult online sources such as Black Box Network Services (www.blackbox.com) and Data Comm Warehouse (www.warehouse.com) to identify the hardware costs for your LAN. Include the server, workstations, network adapters, a tape backup device, three laser printers, and three ink-jet printers in your cost estimates. The server must have at least 60 GB of disk storage, 128 MB of memory, and a UPS.

12. Assume that you need 6,000 feet of cabling to create a LAN with a minimum transmission speed of 100 mbps that will be used to create a 40-node LAN. Consult online (or print) sources such as Black Box Network Services and Data Comm Warehouse to identify current cabling and connector costs for each of the following medium options: category 5 UTP, category 5 STP, category 5 enhanced, category 6, multimode fiber optic cable, and single-mode fiber optic cable. Both PVC and Plenum options should be identified. Summarize your findings in a table.

13. Use the Internet to find out more about frequency-hopping SSR and direct-sequencing SSR. Identify two or more specific LAN products that use one of these two wireless transmission approaches. Compare the products on maximum data

throughput rates and maximum transmission distances. Summarize your comparative information in a table.

14. Security is an important concern with wireless LANs. Use the Internet to outline wireless LAN security concerns and the approaches being used to address them.

15. Consult online sources to compare the costs of the following Ethernet wiring center options. Identify several products in each category and their current prices. Summarize your findings in a table.
    a. 24-port 10/100 stackable, unmanaged shared media hub
    b. 24-port 10/100 stackable, managed shared media hub
    c. 24-port 10/100 stackable Ethernet switch

16. Use the Internet to find out more about storage area networks (SANs), network attached storage systems (NASs), and Fiber Channel. Cite specific examples illustrating business use of these technologies. Summarize your findings in a paper or PowerPoint presentation.

Chapter Cases
Telework Takes Off

Telework is making it possible for people to work at a distance from their main offices. Thanks to the proliferation of electronic and mobile communications devices, specialized telework software, and, in some cases, special hardware, more companies are realizing the benefits of telework. Telework is also commonly known as *telecommuting*. Today, telework may also include aspects of mobile computing.

But why telecommute? Government and technology companies were the forerunners in the research and adoption of telework by their organizations. Some of the reasons for implementing telecommuting include reductions in operating costs, avoiding traffic congestion, and protecting the environment. Another driver is the recognition that telework is an effective backup option against natural disasters or other calamities—it provides a way to keep employees working even when it is impossible for them to commute to the office.

Companies such as IBM and Cisco Systems have been leaders in implementing these new practices. Because they are among the major suppliers of telework products, it is important for them to serve as role models for how telework can be implemented. These companies employ thousands of people who work part-time or full-time from home.

After the September 11, 2001, terrorist attacks, the popularity of teleworking has increased. In the New York City metropolitan area, telework provided a recovery mechanism for many companies that lost physical space at the World Trade Center. It also became instantly popular among employees who were concerned about the security of their families and wanted to be close to them in case of additional attacks. As a result, an increasing number of companies are now starting to think about teleworking as a contingency plan.

Although the number of teleworkers has never been higher in the United States (today there are approximately 30 million people who telework at least one day a week), the growth rate for telework has not lived up to previous predictions. The slower increases that have been witnessed are typically attributed to management reluctance, adopt telework options and employee fears. A main concern among managers is privacy, especially the potential for sensitive information to be leaked outside of the

company. Moreover, traditional managers often believe that if they cannot see their people working, it is because they are not really working. Trusting workers to be self-disciplined and productive outside the confines of the office has been difficult for some managers. Employees' fears include the famous phrase "out of sight, out of mind." Many employees are afraid of not getting face-to-face communication with their bosses and fear that this might result in being passed over for promotions in the future.

So, what can organizations do to get rid of these fears among managers and employees and start implementing a beneficial teleworking program? Prudential Financial provides a good example for illustrating how this might be done. The company won the 2001 User Excellence Award for an IP VPN project, which cut annual remote charges by 50 percent. The $1.5 million project is providing the company annual savings of $7 million and is also reinforcing a new virtual enterprise concept among employees. The company has been successful in attracting high-quality employees who want to work at home to avoid commuting to the workplace. Through the high-speed VPN that has been created to support telecommuters, employees can access the same information remotely (and securely) that is available to workers at the office.

At Prudential Financial, managers have remained open-minded about the potential of telework and strongly believe that telecommuting is giving the company a way to be successful in the new economy. The "out of sight, out of mind" phrase is not part of the managers' and employees' mindsets. Employees can receive performance reviews by phone in order to ensure that they are performing up to expectations and not endangering their promotion potential. Approximately 90 percent of Prudential's teleworkers are using the new virtual private network to support their remote work activities.

Once a major concern, security issues are no longer a major issue at Prudential Financial. They have moved from a 30-day static password to a 60-second dynamic password. This means users log into the VPN through RSA's SecurID tokens; users enter their SecurID token, and it generates automatically a personal identification number and a dynamic password, which is displayed on the token. The PIN and dynamic password enable teleworkers to remotely access all the computing resources that are available to workers at the office.

But, does this mean that all companies and jobs are conducive to teleworking? Can any employee perform well as a teleworker? Unfortunately, the answer to both questions is "no." Jobs that require a lot of personal interaction with colleagues and customers are not the best candidates for telework. Managers should evaluate the job and figure out if it could be performed with the same (or better!) efficiency at home, before investing in setting up home offices. In addition, not all employees are good candidates to be teleworkers.

Research suggests that, initially, managers should pick the best performers at the office and give them the option to work at home. Managers must also be prepared to monitor/measure the performance of teleworkers on a regular basis. Before

being allowed to telecommute, potential teleworkers should be able to make a strong case to their managers that their performance will be the same or better while teleworking. They also need to show that they are capable of working well independently, and that telecommuting will not undermine their ability to maintain high levels of customer satisfaction. Teleworkers should be reminded that constant feedback and strong networking skills are especially important while working at home. Personal and home-office telephone numbers can be invaluable for keeping people in communication.

Many teleworkers admit that at the beginning, lack of physical face-to-face interaction seems awkward. However, thanks to modern technology tools such as videoconferencing and voice mail, it is easy to adapt quickly to this new way of working.

CASE QUESTIONS

1. Why is it important for telework product vendors such as IBM and Cisco Systems to be early adopters and users of telework technologies?
2. Why are DSL connections, cable modems, and ISDN popular in the home offices of telecommuters? What telework advantages do these connections provide over dial-up modems?
3. People issues, rather than technological issues, are typically cited as the main reasons why telecommuting has not grown as rapidly as industry experts predicted several years ago. Use the Internet to identify additional people issues (beyond those in the case) that are responsible for slower-than-expected growth of telework.
4. How has the federal government fueled business interest in telecommuting in the United States? What laws and regulations have

spurred increased levels of telework in the United States?
5. What data communication technologies have the greatest potential for providing "electronic face time" between teleworkers and their bosses?
6. What data communication technologies have the greatest potential for monitoring/measuring the ongoing performance of teleworkers?
7. Use the Internet to update the data on the volume of U.S. workers who are teleworkers. Identify the kinds of jobs/occupations in which telework is increasing most rapidly.
8. Use the Internet to identify companies not mentioned in the case that have initiated successful telework programs. What patterns may be observed in the characteristics of the telework programs that they have initiated?

SOURCES

Hawkins, C. "Ready, Set, Go Home." *Black Enterprise* (August 2001). Retrieved June 22, 2002 from www.blackenterprise.com/PageOpen.asp?Source=ArchiveTab/2001/08/0801-47.htm.

Lublin, J. "Managing Your Career: Telecommuters Learn to Put Bosses at Ease and Get Promoted, Too." *Wall Street Journal* (November 23, 2001, p. B1).

Martin, M. "A Grand Telework Plan." *Network World* (November 12, 2001). Retrieved June 22, 2002 from www.nwfusion.com/best2001/userex_pru/userex_pru.html.

Zbar, J. "Ten Tips to Telework." *Network World* (November 12, 2001). Retrieved June 22, 2002 from www.nwfusion.com/nct.worker/research/2001/1112networkerfeatside2.html.

Note: For more information on local area networks, see an additional case on the Web site, www.prenhall.com/stamper, "Home Networks."

LAN Architectures

After studying this chapter, you should be able to:

- Identify and describe the components of LAN architectures.
- Compare the major LAN topologies.
- Describe the major LAN media access control protocols.
- Recognize the advantages and disadvantages of each LAN media access control protocol.
- Compare the major LAN architectures.

When called upon to build a LAN, you will probably investigate the capabilities of products provided by a variety of vendors. You will discover several ways in which to build a LAN, and you also might hear conflicting statements about the merits of each. In this chapter, you will learn about the network layouts that vendors most commonly propose. You will also read about LAN topologies, media access control protocols, common ways in which topologies and media access control protocols are combined, and the strengths and weaknesses of several LAN configurations. The LAN components covered in this chapter exist at the OSI physical and data link layers.

WHAT IS MEANT BY LAN ARCHITECTURE?

If you evaluate vendor proposals during the LAN selection process, you are likely to read opening statements intended to give you a general idea of the kind of solution proposed. Some examples include:

> "We are happy to propose a NetWare IEEE 802.3 network for your consideration."
>
> "We believe that a FDDI LAN will best suit your purposes."
>
> "Our solution uses Microsoft's Windows 2000 Server and Ethernet."

media access control (MAC) protocol A protocol found at the media access control (MAC) sublayer of the OSI reference model's data link layer. The MAC protocol defines how a station gains access to the media for data transmission. Common MAC protocols are Carrier Sense Multiple Access and Collision Detection (CSMA/CD) and token passing.

network topology The logical or physical arrangement of network nodes; a model for the way in which network nodes are connected. Logical topologies include broadcast or sequential (ring). Physical topologies include bus, ring, and star.

LAN architecture The overall design of a LAN. A LAN architecture includes its hardware, software, topology, and media access control (MAC) protocol.

bus topology A physical network topology in which all network attached devices connect to a common communication pathway or channel. In LANs the communication medium in a bus topology often consists of a single wire or cable to which nodes are attached via connectors and/or transceivers.

Ethernet A LAN implementation using the CSMA/CD protocol on a bus. The IEEE 802.3 standard is based on Ethernet. A popular LAN implementation.

These statements encapsulate three major components of LANs: the LAN network operating system software, the topology, and the **media access control (MAC) protocol**. A **network topology** is the model used to lay out the LAN medium and connect computers to the medium. A MAC protocol operates at the OSI data link layer and describes the way in which a network node gains access to the medium and transmits data. The combination of these three components is what we call the **LAN architecture** and provides much of the uniqueness of a LAN. In general, when designing a LAN, you will be considering three basic topologies—ring, bus, and star—and two basic MAC protocols—contention and token passing. The major distinctions between two proposed LAN alternatives with the same overall architecture (such as two Ethernet LANs) are most likely to lie in the proposed network operating system, the hardware, and the medium. A number of vendors, such as Apple, Microsoft, Novell, Red Hat, and Solaris, provide networking operating system software.

When you are selecting a LAN, one idea is paramount: You are selecting a system. The system has many components, and the overall success of the LAN is determined by how well these components can be integrated to form a complete system. Interoperability among components is the key, not the efficiency of a single component. For example, you must be able to attach workstations to the LAN and support each workstation's operating systems. The LAN might have IBM or IBM–compatible workstations together with Apple Macintosh systems, all with a variety of operating systems and printers. The system you choose must support the full range of components that you intend to include.

LAN TOPOLOGIES

What do we mean when we talk about a LAN topology? First, the term *topology* derives from a mathematics field that deals with points and surfaces in space—that is, with the layout of objects in space. Thus, LAN topology is the physical layout of the network. Another way you can look at a topology is as a model for the way in which you configure the medium and attach the nodes to that medium. In general, LAN topologies correspond to the OSI physical layer because the major focus is on physical connections among LAN hardware components. However, it is also important to understand logical topologies.

LANs have three basic topologies: bus, ring, and star. Each configuration is illustrated in Figure 8-1. Let's take a closer look at each topology.

Bus Topology

In a **bus topology**, illustrated in Figure 8-1(b), the medium consists of a single wire or cable to which nodes are attached via connectors or transceivers (see Chapter 7). The ends of the bus are not connected. Instead, they are terminated by a hardware device called a *terminator*, as discussed in Chapter 7. The downside of the linear bus topology illustrated in Figure 8-1(b) is that a loose connection or break at any point along the bus can disrupt communications for the entire network. A variation of a bus topology has spurs to the primary bus formed by interconnected minibuses (see Figure 8-2). This variation of the bus topology is quite common.

Several LAN standards refer to bus implementations. The most common of these is an implementation originally known as **Ethernet**. Ethernet LAN specifications were originally proposed by Xerox Corporation in 1972. Soon thereafter, Xerox was joined in establishing the Ethernet standard by Digital Equipment Corporation (DEC) and

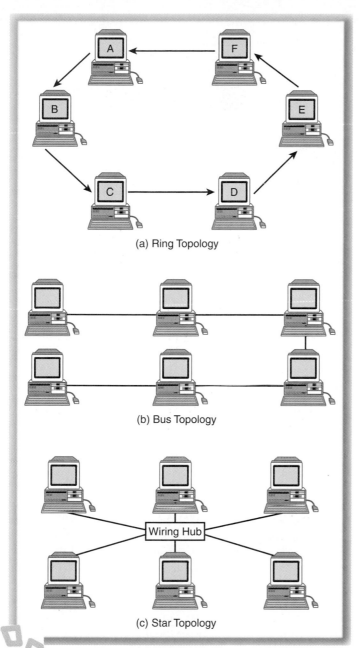

(a) Ring Topology

(b) Bus Topology

(c) Star Topology

Figure 8-1   Basic LAN Topologies

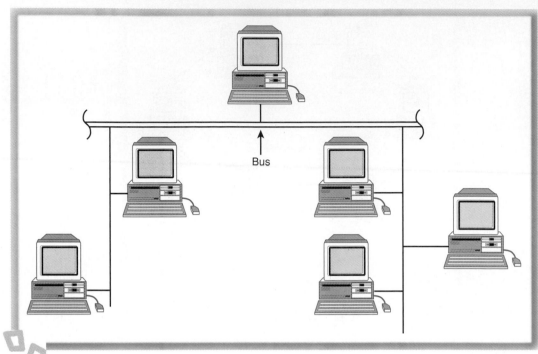

Figure 8-2   Bus Topology with Spurs

Institute of Electrical and Electronics Engineers (IEEE)
A professional society that establishes and publishes documents and standards for data communication. IEEE has established several standards for both cable-based and wireless LANs, including IEEE 802.3, IEEE 802.5, and IEEE 802.11.

IEEE 802.3 standard The IEEE standard that addresses Ethernet LANs. It covers a variety of physical implementations of Ethernet all of which use CSMA/CD as the MAC protocol.

Intel Corporation. The **Institute of Electrical and Electronics Engineers (IEEE)** 802 Committee then developed the **IEEE 802.3 standard**, which encompasses most of the premises of the original Ethernet specification. Thus, the IEEE 802.3 standard is sometimes called an *Ethernet implementation* standard. The IEEE 802.4 standard also proposes a bus technology. The primary difference between the two is the MAC protocol. The IEEE 802.3 standard specifies a contention protocol, and the 802.4 standard uses a token-passing protocol. These protocols are covered later in this chapter.

The most common speeds of today's bus-oriented LANs are 10, 100, and 1,000 mbps. Versions of the IEEE 802.3 and 802.4 standards specify each of these speeds. Currently, 100-mbps LANs are in fairly common use, and 1-gbps LANs began emerging in 1997. IEEE 802.3 and 802.4 media include twisted-pair wires, fiber optic cables, or coaxial cables. Very-high-speed bus architectures typically use twisted-pair wires or fiber optic cables as media. Ethernet LANs have also been implemented using spread-spectrum radio (SSR) as the medium.

Ring Topology

In a **ring topology,** the medium forms a closed loop, and all stations are connected to the loop or ring. Like a linear bus, a weakness of this physical topology is that communications for the entire network may be disrupted if one of the microcomputers or network adapters malfunctions. We first look at the basics of a ring and then at some specifics of two implementations.

On a ring, data is transmitted from node to node in one direction. Thus if node A in Figure 8-3 wants to send a message to node F, the message is sent from A to B,

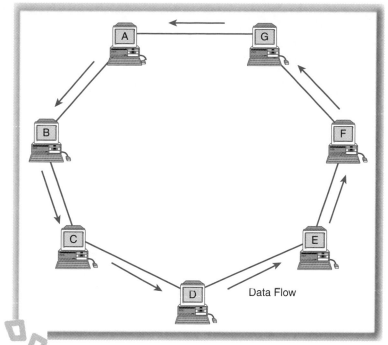

Figure 8-3   Token Passing Within a Ring Topology

from B to C, from C to D, and so on, until it reaches node F. Usually, node F then sends an acknowledgment that the message was successfully received back to node A, the originator of the message. The acknowledgment is sent from node F to G, and then from G to A, completing one journey around the loop.

Nodes attached to the ring may be active or inactive. An **active node** is capable of sending or receiving network messages. An **inactive node** is incapable of sending or receiving network messages; for example, an inactive node may be powered down. Naturally, nodes may go from inactive to active and from active to inactive. For example, when a worker leaves at night, she might turn her workstation off, placing the workstation in an inactive state. In the morning, she powers up her system and brings it into the active state. A failed or inactive network node must not cause the network to fail; an overview of how such a network failure can be prevented is included later in this chapter.

The most commonly used microcomputer ring network is a token-passing ring. IBM's LAN approach has been widely adopted and conforms to the **IEEE 802.5 standard**, so we describe it here. Realize, however, that we are discussing only the MAC protocol used in IEEE 802.5-compliant LANs; the physical topology in IBM's token ring network is a star. FDDI (fiber distributed data interface) LANs also employ token passing and have a physical ring topology. The token-passing rings we are describing can be implemented using a variety of different network operating systems, including Linux, Microsoft's Windows NT Server, Novell NetWare, and Windows 2000 Server.

As pointed out in Chapter 7, in IBM's token-passing ring network, stations (nodes) are connected to a *multistation access unit (MAU)*. This is illustrated in Figure 8-4. You

ring topology A LAN topology in which stations are attached to one another in a logical or physical circle. In a physical ring the medium forms a loop to which workstations are attached. In both physical and logical rings, access to the medium is passed from one station to the next; also, data are transmitted from one station to the next around the ring. Generally, the access protocol used in a ring topology is token passing.

active node A node capable of sending or receiving network messages.

inactive node A node that may be powered down and is incapable of sending or receiving messages.

IEEE 802.5 standard An IEEE standard for token-passing networks including token ring LANs.

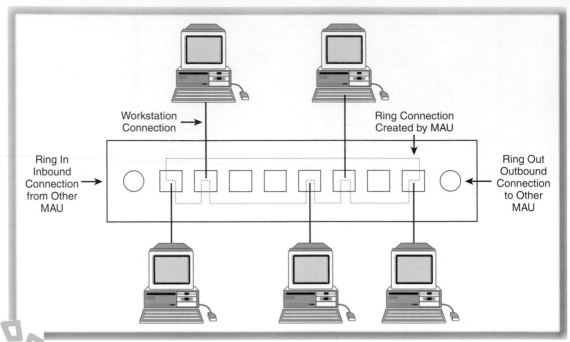

Figure 8-4 Multistation Access Unit (MAU)

can see that this configuration looks like the star configuration of Figure 8-1(c): The physical ring is implemented within the MAU (see Figure 8-5). Figure 8-6 shows the connection of two MAUs. When connected in this fashion, the physical rings within each MAU are connected to form a larger ring. IBM token-passing ring speeds are 4, 16, and 100 mbps using twisted-pair wires or fiber optic cable as the medium.

Another network that uses a ring topology is a high-speed MAN, which is designed to cover a wider geographical area than a typical LAN. The American National Standards Institute (ANSI) standard for this kind of network is called the *Fiber Distributed DataInterface (FDDI) standard* and is discussed later. The IEEE 802.6 specification, also discussed later in the chapter, addresses an alternative MAN architecture to FDDI.

Star Topology

star topology
A physical network topology using a central station (typically a hub or switch) to which all other nodes have point-to-point connections. All communication among nodes occurs through the central station. Today, this is the most widely implemented LAN topology.

Figure 8-7 shows a **star topology**. In LANs with star topologies, all nodes are connected to some kind of wiring center such as a hub, concentrator, MAU, or switch. This is the most common kind of topology for microcomputer LANs.

By isolating each node on its own network segment, star topologies minimize the possibility of network disruption caused by a single malfunctioning connection, network adapter, or workstation. If such a failure occurs, it is limited to a particular segment while the rest of the network continues to function. In addition to the ability to establish a segment for each LAN–attached device, the central connection points in

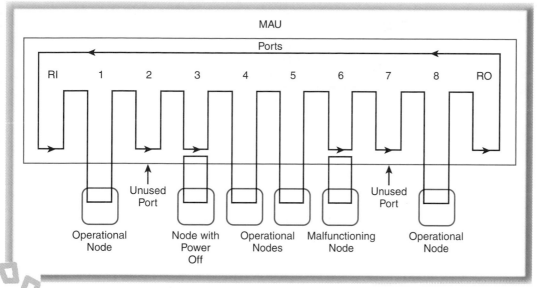

Figure 8-5   Physical Ring Implementation Within a MAU

star topologies are logical locations for installing data traffic monitoring, network security, and other network management capabilities. All network data traffic flows through these wiring centers, and they are natural points for monitoring and capturing data on network usage and performance.

The downside of having all network data pass through central wiring centers resides in the fact that hub/switch failure brings down the entire network. The potential for the LAN hub or switch to be a single point of failure provides a strong argument in favor of "managed" hubs. Managed hubs enable network administrators to monitor data traffic and network performance; unmanaged hubs do not.

Ethernet 10BaseT and 100BaseTX LANs are examples of star-wired LAN topologies. ARCnet is another example of a star topology. Each of these is briefly discussed here.

ARCnet (Attached Resource Computer Network) technology was developed in the 1970s by Datapoint Corporation to form networks of their minicomputers. The technology was well developed when microcomputer LANs were evolving, and the technology was readily adopted. Because it was so widely used, ARCnet became a de facto microcomputer LAN standard. An ARCnet configuration, such as that illustrated in Figure 8-8b, is a token-passing bus but does not conform to the IEEE 802.4 standard. ARCnet uses both active and passive hubs to connect network nodes. An *active hub* provides signal regeneration and allows nodes to be located at distances up to 2,000 feet from the hub. A *passive hub* does not provide signal regeneration, and nodes cannot be located more than 100 feet from the hub. ARCnet speeds are 2.5 mbps, 20 mbps, and 100 mbps, and two or more speeds can be used in the same network. ARCnet media are usually either twisted-pair wires or coaxial cables. Fiber optic cables are also used for ARCnet LANs, primarily in higher speed implementations. ARCnet was a common LAN implementation during the early days of

ARCnet (Attached Resource Computer Network) Among the first LAN implementations capable of connecting up to 255 nodes in a star topology over twisted-pair wires or coaxial cable.

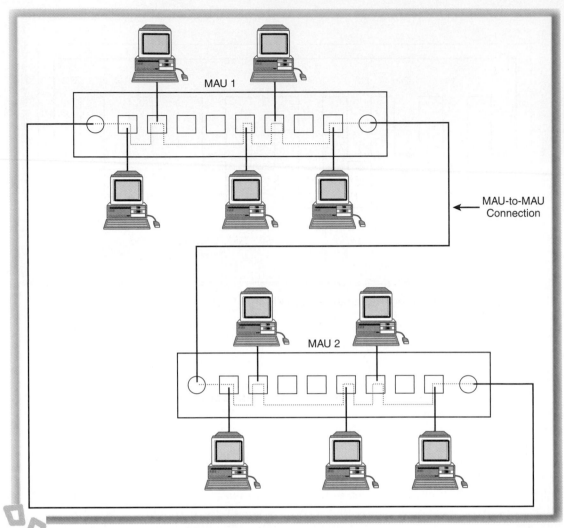

Figure 8-6   MAU-to-MAU Connection

microcomputer LANs because it provided proven technology at a low price. Few new LANs, however, are being implemented using this architecture.

An Ethernet star-wired LAN configuration is similar to the basic star topology [Figure 8-1(c)] in that each workstation is connected to a wiring hub. This is now the most common physical Ethernet LAN topology, and it is an excellent example of the distinction between physical and logical network topologies.

Logical Topologies

Every LAN has both a physical and a logical topology. A LAN's **logical topology** is more concerned with how messages are passed from node to node within the network than with the manner in which nodes are physically connected to form a network. Two logical LAN topologies exist: sequential and broadcast.

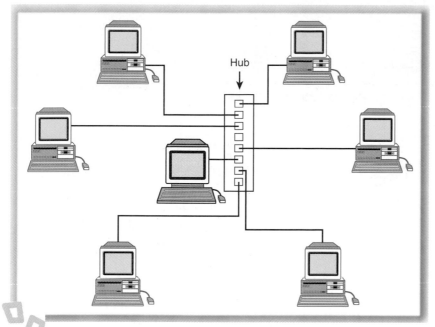

Figure 8-7   Star Topology

Sequential (Ring)   The *sequential* logical topology is also called a *ring* logical topology because data is passed from one node to another in a ring-like sequence. Each node in the ring examines the destination address field of each data packet it receives in order to determine if it is the intended recipient. If another node is the intended recipient of the data packet, the node passes the packet to the next node in the ring/sequence. The node only extracts the data from the packet if its address is in the packet's address field.

Although token ring and ARCnet LANs typically have physical star topologies, their logical topology is sequential. In both these kinds of LANs, data packets are

Figure 8-8a   ARCnet Bus Configuration

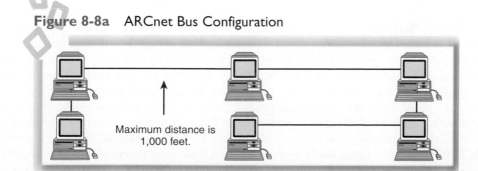

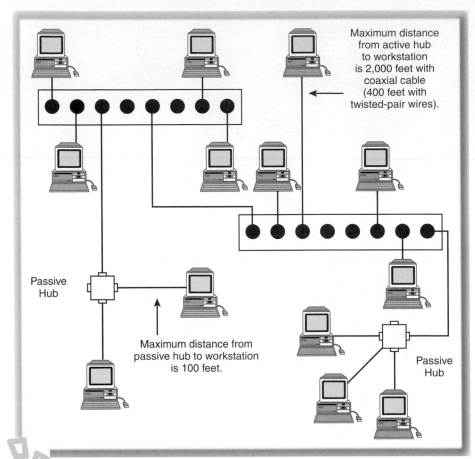

Figure 8-8b   ARCnet with Active and Passive Hubs

passed node to node in a preestablished sequence. This underscores an important point: There is no necessary correspondence between a LAN's physical topology and its logical topology. A LAN that is physically wired as a star topology (as is usually the case for token ring LANs) may possess a ring logical topology. The name "token ring" derives from its logical topology rather than its physical topology.

Broadcast   Nodes in LANs that have a *broadcast* logical topology transmit each packet to all the other nodes in the network. Each node receives all the packets transmitted by all other nodes and examines each packet that it receives to determine if it is the intended recipient. If it is not the intended recipient, the node simply ignores the packet. It only extracts data from the packets that are addressed to it.

Ethernet LANs have a logical broadcast topology. As noted previously, Ethernet LANs are typically implemented as physical star or bus topologies. This, too, illustrates that there is no necessary correspondence between a LAN's physical and logical topology. Today, you are most likely to encounter LANs with physical star topologies. However, because the physical star may have either a sequential or a broadcast logical topology, it is important to know what data link and MAC protocol are used in the LAN in order to determine which of the two logical topologies it has.

DATA LINK AND MEDIA ACCESS CONTROL PROTOCOLS

The physical layer of the OSI reference model describes the medium, the connectors required to attach workstations and servers to the medium, and the representation of signals using the medium, such as voltage levels for baseband transmission or frequencies for broadband transmission.

Once connected to the medium, a network node must have the ability to send and receive network messages. This function is described by the data link layer of the OSI reference mode. A convention, or protocol, must exist to define how this function is accomplished. The method by which a LAN workstation is able to gain control of the medium and transmit a message is a MAC (media access control) protocol. The MAC protocol is implemented in LANs as one of two sublayers of the OSI reference model's data link layer. The other sublayer is the LLC (logical link control) sublayer. We first look more closely at the functions provided by a data link protocol.

Data Link Protocols

In general, a data link layer protocol establishes the rules for gaining access to the medium and for exchanging messages. To do this, the protocol describes several aspects of the message exchange process. Six of the most important aspects are in delineation of data, error control, addressing, transparency, code independence, and media access.

Delineation of Data   A data link layer protocol must define or delineate where the data portion of the transmitted message begins and ends. You may recall from the discussion of the OSI reference model in other chapters that each layer may add data to the message it receives from the layers above it. The data link layer is no exception. Some of the characters or bits it adds to the message may include line control information, error detection data, and so on. When these fields are added, a data link protocol must provide a way to distinguish among the various pieces of data. This can be accomplished in two basic ways: by framing the data with certain control characters or by using a standard message format wherein a data segment is identified by its position within the message.

The framing technique is used in two kinds of data link protocols: asynchronous transmission and binary synchronous transmission. These protocols are common in WANs (see Chapter 10) and are also discussed in Chapter 6. Most of today's LANs use a standard message format for sending data. For example, an Ethernet message has several distinct parts, as illustrated in Figure 8-9. (Note: There are several different formats for Ethernet frames in Figure 8-9.) The message frame begins with a 64-bit synchronization pattern. The synchronization bits give the receiving node an opportunity to sense the incoming message and establish time or synchronization with the sending node. The message is received as a stream of continuous bits, so it is important that the receiving node be able to clock the bits in as they arrive. The IEEE 802.3 Ethernet standard uses a 64-bit synchronization pattern; however, the standard divides this into a 56-bit group and an 8-bit group. The first 56 bits are for synchronization, and the 8 bits that follow signal the start of the frame and thus indicate where the first bit of the remaining frame can be found. The next two fields are the addresses of the destination node and the sending node. Each address is 48 bits long.

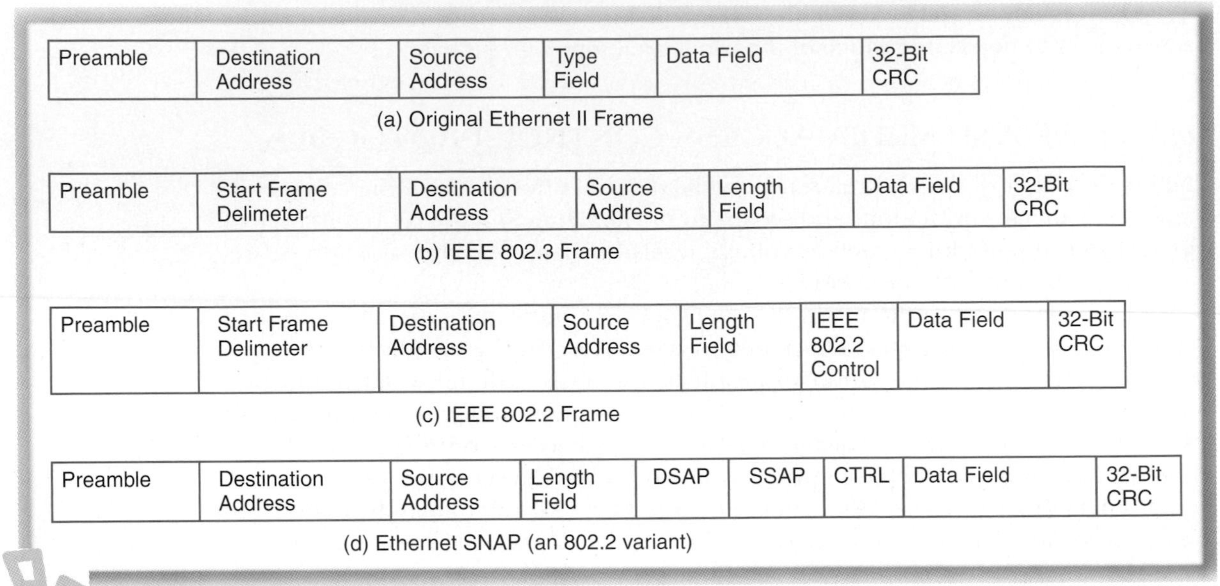

Preamble	Destination Address	Source Address	Type Field	Data Field	32-Bit CRC

(a) Original Ethernet II Frame

Preamble	Start Frame Delimeter	Destination Address	Source Address	Length Field	Data Field	32-Bit CRC

(b) IEEE 802.3 Frame

Preamble	Start Frame Delimeter	Destination Address	Source Address	Length Field	IEEE 802.2 Control	Data Field	32-Bit CRC

(c) IEEE 802.2 Frame

Preamble	Destination Address	Source Address	Length Field	DSAP	SSAP	CTRL	Data Field	32-Bit CRC

(d) Ethernet SNAP (an 802.2 variant)

Figure 8-9   Ethernet Message Formats

octet A group of 8 bits used in data communication protocol frame formats.

The 16-bit field type is a control field. In the IEEE 802.3 Ethernet standard, this represents the length of the data field that follows. The length is expressed as the number of 8-bit groups, or **octets**. If the message is short, extra bits may be added to make the entire message long enough to allow the message to clear the length of the network before the sending node stops transmitting. This is essential to ensure correct transmission. The frame check sequence, a 32-bit cyclic redundancy check (CRC) field, as illustrated in Figure 8-9, provides for error detection.

Error Control   Error control is used to detect transmission errors. Common error-detection techniques are parity and cyclic redundancy checks. These techniques are discussed in Chapter 6.

Addressing   Communication between two network nodes is accomplished through an addressing scheme. Network addressing is similar to addressing used for postal mail. A postal address is a hierarchical addressing scheme, with the hierarchy being individual recipient, street address, city, state, country, and zip code. Networks also use a hierarchical addressing scheme, with the hierarchy being application, network node, and network. Like postal addresses, network addresses must be unique; otherwise, ambiguity arises as to which node is the recipient. At this point, we are concerned only with network node addressing, not network or application addressing.

Each network has a specific way in which it forms station addresses. In Ethernet and the IBM token ring, each address is 48 bits long. Each Ethernet or IBM token ring LAN adapter card has its address set by the manufacturer. This ensures that all nodes, regardless of location, have a unique address. (*Note:* Many Ethernet adapters store their addresses in an updateable chip. Because these addresses may be changed by software utilities, they are not guaranteed to be unique once changes have been made.) In

ARCnet, a node address is an 8-bit entity, and the LAN administrator typically sets the node address through switches on the LAN adapter. In other LANs, node source and destination addresses are included in the MAC headers of messages being transmitted.

Transparency   In data link protocols, *transparency* is the ability of the data link to transmit any bit combination. We want protocols to be transparent, because they can be used to transfer binary data such as object programs, as well as text or multimedia data. The Ethernet message illustrated in Figure 8-9 provides transparency: No bit patterns in the data field can cause confusion in the message.

Code Independence   **Code independence** means that any data code, such as ASCII, EBCDIC, or Unicode, can be transmitted. These codes use different bit patterns to represent many of the characters. Code independence is important, because often you must communicate with or through computers having a data code different from that of your computer. In the Ethernet protocol, this is accomplished by sending data in octets. The octets are not tied to any particular code, so any code can be used. If your computer uses a 7-bit code, such as one of the two ASCII codes, the only requirement is that the total number of bits transmitted be divisible by 8. Thus, if you are sending one hundred 7-bit characters, the total number of bits in the data portion must be 704. The last 4 bits are added to pad out to an integral number of octets $(700/8 = 87.5;$ 704 bits are necessary because 704 is a multiple of 8).

Media Access   **Media access** is the way in which a device gains access to the medium—that is, the protocol by which a device gains the right to transmit data on the medium. This convention is covered next.

MAC Protocols

LAN technology adheres to two primary data link protocols: token passing and contention. In the IEEE 802 standards, the data link layer is divided into the two sublayers: LLC and MAC (see Figure 8-10). The LLC (logical link control) provides the functions of flow control, message sequencing, message acknowledgment, and error checking. The MAC (media access control) layer describes token passing and contention.

Contention   In a true **contention** MAC protocol, each network node has equal access to the medium. Although variations of this protocol exist, essentially each node monitors the medium to see whether a message is being transmitted and if no message is detected, any node can begin a transmission.

The act of listening to the medium for a message is called *carrier sensing*, because when a message is being transmitted, a carrier signal is present. Several nodes can have messages to send. Each of them may detect a quiet medium, and each may begin to transmit at one time. The ability of several nodes to access a medium that is not carrying a message is called *multiple access*.

If two or more nodes begin to transmit at the same time, a **collision** is said to occur. Multiple simultaneous transmissions cause the messages to interfere with each other and become garbled. It is imperative that collisions be detected and that recovery from collisions be effected. When a collision occurs, the messages are not transmitted successfully. On detecting a collision, the sending nodes must resend their messages. If both nodes immediately attempt to retransmit their messages, another collision might occur. Therefore, each node waits a small, randomly selected interval before attempting to retransmit. This reduces the probability of another collision.

code independence The ability to transmit data regardless of the data code, such as ASCII or EBCDIC.

media access The way in which a network device gains access to the communication medium. This is usually governed by a media access control (MAC) protocol specifying how the device gains the right to transmit data on the medium.

contention A media access control convention governing how devices obtain control of a communication link. In contention mode, devices compete for control of the line either by transmitting directly on an idle line or by issuing a request for line control. It typically follows a first-come, first-served methodology except when two devices contend for the communication link at the same point in time.

collision In the CSMA/CD media access control protocol and other contention-based communication protocols, a collision occurs when two stations attempt to send a message at the same time. The messages interfere with each other, so correct communication is not possible.

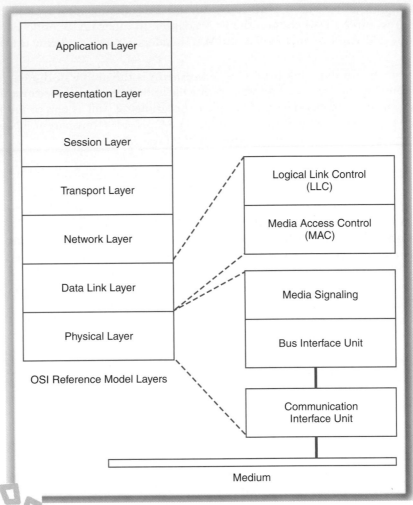

Figure 8-10   LLC and MAC Sublayers of the OSI Reference Model's Data Link Layer

There is only a small time interval during which a collision can occur. For example, suppose that two nodes at the extremities of a 1,000-meter bus network have a message to send and that the medium is not being used. The collision interval is the time it takes for a signal to travel the length of the cable. Because the signal travels at nearly the speed of light, the collision window is the time it takes for the signal to travel 1,000 meters, the signal's propagation delay. The propagation delay is approximately 5 nanoseconds per meter. For a 1,000-meter segment, the maximum propagation delay is therefore approximately 5 microseconds (5 millionths of a second). Although this interval is small, collisions can still occur.

The media access control technique just described is known as **Carrier Sense Multiple Access and Collision Detection (CSMA/CD)**. It is the most common of the access strategies for LANs with physical bus topologies and logical broadcast topologies. CSMA/CD is the MAC protocol used in Ethernet LANs. Because most conducted media LANs found in today's organizations are Ethernet LANs, CSMA/CD is the most widely used MAC protocol.

The CSMA/CD MAC protocol, sometimes called *listen-before-talk*, is summarized in Table 8-1. You should note that the CSMA/CD protocol is a broadcast protocol. All workstations on the network listen to the medium and accept the message. Each message has a destination address. Only a workstation having an address equal to the destination address can use the message. Using a broadcast technique makes it easy for new workstations to be added to and removed from the network.

CSMA/CD is known as a *fair protocol*, meaning that each node has equal access to the medium. In a pure CSMA/CD scheme, no one node has priority over another. Variations of this protocol exist that give one workstation priority over another and minimize the likelihood of collisions. One of these protocol variations divides time into transmission slots. The length of a slot is the time it takes a message to travel the length of the medium. Nodes on the network are synchronized, and each node can begin a transmission only at the beginning of its allocated time slot. This protocol has proven to be more efficient for networks with lots of message traffic.

A variation of CSMA/CD is **Carrier Sense Multiple Access and Collision Avoidance (CSMA/CA)**. This is widely used in wireless LANs because collisions cannot be detected in wireless networks as they can in wire-based LANs. This protocol attempts to avoid collisions that are possible with the CSMA/CD protocol. Collisions are avoided because each node is given a wait time before it can begin transmitting. For example, suppose there are 100 nodes on the network, and the propagation delay time for the network is 1 ms. Node 1 can transmit after the medium has been idle for 1 ms. Node 2 must wait 2 ms before attempting to transmit, node 3 must wait 3 ms, and so on. Each node, therefore, has a specific time slot during which it can transmit, and no collisions will occur. However, the node with the lowest priority time slot may experience long delays in getting access to the medium.

Token Passing

The second major MAC protocol is token passing. It is used on both bus and ring topologies. **Token passing** is a round-robin protocol in which each node gets an equal opportunity to transmit. An overview of the token-passing protocol is given in Table 8-2. With token passing, the right to transmit is granted by a token that is passed from one node to the next. A token is a predefined bit pattern that is recognized by each node. The token is a packet (usually a 24-bit packet) that is generated by a designated computer attached to the network, called the **active monitor**. The token is passed among the network-attached computers until one of the computers wants to use the communication medium to transmit a message. When the token reaches this computer, the computer captures the token and changes its status from "free" to "busy," transmits its data, and holds onto the token until it receives an acknowledgment that the data was

Carrier Sense Multiple Access and Collision Detection (CSMA/CD) A media access control technique that resolves contention between two or more stations by collision detection. It is used in Ethernet LANs and is often referred to as the "Ethernet protocol."

Carrier Sense Multiple Access and Collision Avoidance (CSMA/CA) A LAN media access control method that attempts to avoid contention among stations and message collisions. It is widely used in wireless LANs.

token passing A media access control protocol in which a string of bits called the token is passed from network node to network node in a logical ring. A computer that receives the token is allowed to transmit data onto the network and after transmitting its data, the computer passes the token to the next computer in the ring.

active monitor In a token ring network, the active monitor is the station that controls the token. It maintains clock synchronization, detects and corrects errors in the token frame format, and generates a new token in the case of token loss.

Table 8-1   CSMA/CD Media Access Control Protocol

1. Listen to the medium to see whether a message is being transmitted.
2. If the medium is quiet, transmit message. If the medium is busy, wait for the signal to clear and then transmit.
3. If a collision occurs, wait for the signal to clear, wait a random interval, and then retransmit.

Table 8-2   Token-Passing Media Access Control Protocol

1. Wait for transmit token.
2. If transmit token is received and there is no message to send, send the token to the next mode.
3. If transmit token is received and there is a message to send, then
   a. Transmit message.
   b. Wait for acknowledgment.
   c. When acknowledgment is received, pass token to the next node.

successfully delivered to the intended recipient. Data recipients confirm successful delivery by setting status flags in the data frame to indicate that they have copied the data contained in the frame that they received. Data recipients then begin the process of forwarding the acknowledgment to the sender by passing the data frame with the reset frame status flags to the next node in the network so that it can make its way back to the sender. When the sender receives the acknowledgment, it changes the token status from "busy" to "free" and passes it along to the next node in the network.

In a physical ring topology, the token is passed from one node to the adjacent node. On a token-passing bus, the order of token passing is determined by the address of each node; the physical topology is a bus, but the logical topology is a ring. The token is passed in either ascending or descending address order. If it is passed in descending order, the station with the lowest address passes the token to the node with the highest address. The routing of a token from high to low addresses in a token-passing bus is illustrated in Figure 8-11. In LANs with a physical star topology, token passing from node to node takes place in the hub or MAU (see Figure 8-12).

Some LANs employ slightly modified variations on the general process just described in order to enhance network performance. For example, some token-passing LANs require the sender to change the token's status from "busy" to "free" and to pass it to the next node immediately after transmitting its data. This eliminates the need for the sender to wait for an acknowledgment from the recipient before releasing the token. Other token-passing LANs circulate more than one token. The token-passing protocol does not allow a node to monopolize the token and the network. Note that, unlike the CSMA/CD protocol, the token-passing protocol does not allow collisions to occur.

Token-Passing Ring   In a token-passing LAN with a physical or logical ring topology, the token can become lost if a node holding the token fails or if transmission errors occur. Recovery from such problems involves the active monitor. Other nodes are designated as standby monitors. The active monitor periodically issues a message indicating that it is active. The standby monitors accept this status and remain in standby mode. If the active monitor message fails to appear on time, a standby monitor assumes the active monitor role. A major function of the active monitor is to ensure that the token is circulating. If the token does not arrive within a certain amount of time, the active monitor generates a new token. This technique is guaranteed to work because the token circulation time is very predictable.

Active monitors are also responsible for regenerating damaged tokens and for removing data frames from the ring that have not been removed by senders after being acknowledged. Software located in chips on token ring network adapter cards handles token regeneration and token passing.

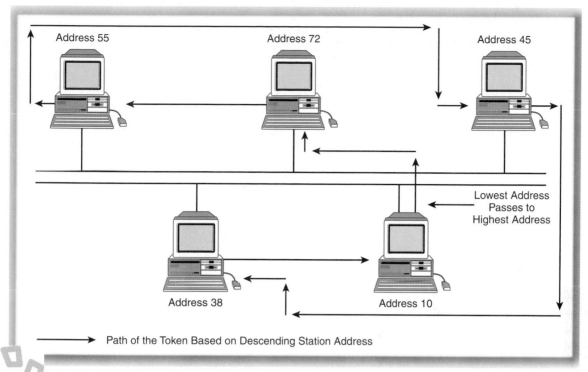

Address 55   Address 72   Address 45

Lowest Address
Passes to
Highest Address

Address 38   Address 10

Path of the Token Based on Descending Station Address

Figure 8-11   Token-Passing Bus

Token-Passing Bus   Token passing is slightly different on a token-passing bus. On a bus, the token is passed from one workstation to another based on station addresses. As mentioned earlier, the token can be passed in ascending or descending address order. Let us assume that the token is passed in descending address order, so the station with the lowest address forwards the token to the station with the highest address. This token-passing scheme is illustrated in Figure 8-11. Such a protocol must allow for new workstations to be inserted and active ones to be deactivated.

Suppose a station attempts to send the token to the next station, and the next station has been shut down. Recovery must be possible when a station goes from active to inactive status. For example, when a sending station does not receive the token back in a prescribed interval, the sending station transmits the token to its neighbor again. If a second failure occurs, the sending station assumes that the neighboring station is inactive and issues a message, asking for the address of the next station. The "who is next" message contains the address of the unresponsive station. The successor of the failed station recognizes the address in the "who is next" message as its predecessor station and responds. If the successor node has also failed, another "who is next" message is then sent out with the entire address range of the LAN. If any other stations are active, they respond.

Allowance also is made in the token-passing bus protocol for new stations to enter the LAN. Periodically, stations issue a "solicit successor" message. This message contains the sending station's address and the address of that station's current successor node. Stations receiving this message inspect the addresses of the sender and the

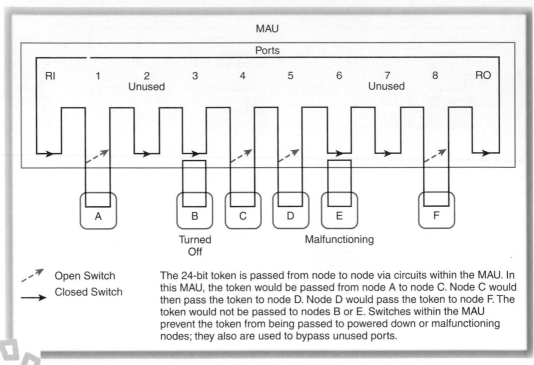

Figure 8-12 Token Passing Within a Token Ring MAU

successor. If a station has an address that falls between these two addresses, it responds to the message. Two stations can respond at the same time, in which case a collision occurs as in CSMA/CD, and collision resolution is triggered. This allows an orderly process for insertion of new stations.

Token Passing and CSMA/CD Compared

The pros and cons of the token passing and CSMA/CD protocols are summarized in Table 8-3. Note that each protocol has advantages and disadvantages. In practice, both have been noted to have good performance.

PHYSICAL LAYER DATA ENCODING

Ethernet uses baseband transmission. When a workstation with data to transmit senses that the communication medium is not in use, its Ethernet network adapter card transmits digital signals (representing the binary numbers that comprise Ethernet data link layer frames) directly onto the communication medium. *Manchester encoding* has traditionally been used with Ethernet. When Manchester encoding is used, each transmitted bit includes a transition. As illustrated in Figure 8-13, a 1 bit has a transition from up to down within the time interval used to represent a bit; a 0 bit has a transition from down to up. The use of such transitions compensates for the fact that the clocks in the sending and receiving Ethernet adapter cards are not perfectly synchro-

Table 8-3   MAC Protocol Comparison

Token Passing	CSMA/CD
Access is equal for all nodes.	Access is equal for all nodes.
Access window is predictable.	Access window can be unpredictable.
Maximum wait time to transmit is token circulation time.	Maximum wait time to transmit is unpredictable and depends on collisions.
Average wait time to transmit is predictable: half the maximum circulation time.	Average wait time to transmit is unpredictable.
Network congestion does not adversely affect network efficiency.	Network congestion may result in collisions and reduce network efficiency.
A node must wait for the token before being able to transmit.	A node may be able to transmit immediately.
One node cannot monopolize the network.	One node may be able to monopolize the network.
Large rings can result in long delays before a node obtains a token.	A node can transmit when the network is quiet.
Performance is consistent for large, busy networks.	Performance is unpredictable for large, busy networks because of possibility of collisions.

nized. By including a transition in the middle of the time interval for each bit, the receiving adapter can synchronize its clock to that of the sending adapter. Once the clock is synchronized, the receiver is able to delineate each bit and determine whether it is a 0 or a 1.

With the increase from 10 mbps to 100 mbps or 1,000 mbps speeds, new encoding schemes are being used. 100BaseT Ethernet, for example, uses 4B5B, which is more efficient than Manchester encoding. In this encoding scheme, every group of clock periods is used to send 4 bits in order to provide sufficient transitions to ensure clock synchronization between the sending and receiving adapter cards. 10/100 adapter cards, however, still employ Manchester encoding for 10-mbps transmissions.

Other physical layer encoding schemes are used in token ring and FDDI LANs. As noted in Figure 8-13, Differential Manchester encoding is used in token ring networks and NRZI (Non-Return to Zero with Invert on Ones) encoding is used in FDDI networks. How each of these differs from Manchester encoding is summarized in Figure 8-13.

LAN ARCHITECTURES

As indicated in the foregoing discussion, there are multiple aspects of LAN architecture. These include the LAN's physical topology, the LAN's logical topology, and the LAN's MAC protocol. In most instances, the physical layer data encoding scheme is also considered to be an aspect of a LAN's architecture. The LAN's network operating system may also be included as part of a LAN's architecture. Next we discuss the major LAN architectures found in today's business networks. We will focus most of our attention on the most widely used LAN architectures: Ethernet and token ring. In addition, we will discuss FDDI and ATM LAN architectures, as well as wireless LAN architectures.

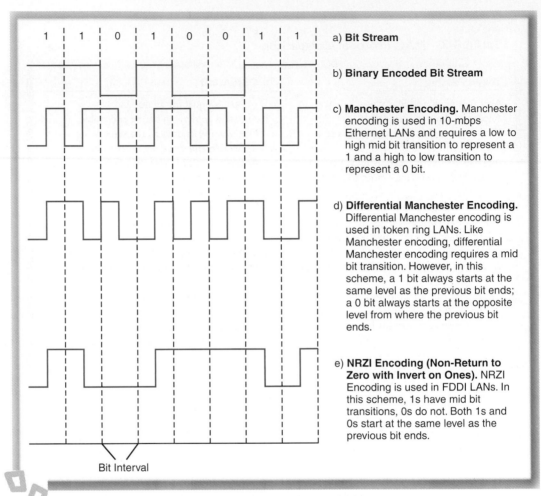

a) **Bit Stream**

b) **Binary Encoded Bit Stream**

c) **Manchester Encoding.** Manchester encoding is used in 10-mbps Ethernet LANs and requires a low to high mid bit transition to represent a 1 and a high to low transition to represent a 0 bit.

d) **Differential Manchester Encoding.** Differential Manchester encoding is used in token ring LANs. Like Manchester encoding, differential Manchester encoding requires a mid bit transition. However, in this scheme, a 1 bit always starts at the same level as the previous bit ends; a 0 bit always starts at the opposite level from where the previous bit ends.

e) **NRZI Encoding (Non-Return to Zero with Invert on Ones).** NRZI Encoding is used in FDDI LANs. In this scheme, 1s have mid bit transitions, 0s do not. Both 1s and 0s start at the same level as the previous bit ends.

Bit Interval

Figure 8-13 Physical Layer Data Encoding Used in LANs

Ethernet

As noted previously, Ethernet LAN specifications were originally outlined by the Xerox Corporation in 1972. The IEEE 802.3 standard encompasses most of the premises of the original Ethernet specification; today, IEEE 802.3-compliant LANs are commonly referred to as Ethernet LANs.

There are a wide variety of IEEE 802.3-compliant networks. These are summarized in Table 8-4. Today, most Ethernet LANs are implemented as a physical star, but some have a physical bus topology. Ethernet LANs have a broadcast logical topology and use CSMAS/CD as the MAC protocol. Of the alternatives described in Table 8-4, 10BaseT, 100BaseTX, 100BaseFX, and 1000BaseSX are the most common Ethernet implementations.

Table 8-4   IEEE 802.3 Alternatives

1Base5	1-mbps baseband medium with a maximum segment length of 500 m. (A baseband medium is one that carries only one signal at a time, as opposed to a broadband medium that can carry multiple signals simultaneously.) The segment length is the length of cable that can be used without repeaters to amplify the signal. This standard encompasses implementations commonly known as *StarLAN*.
10Base5	10-mbps baseband medium with a maximum segment length of 500 m.
10Base2	10-mbps baseband medium with a maximum segment length of 185 m. The cable used in this implementation is commonly called *Thinnet* or *Cheapernet*.
10BaseT	10-mbps baseband medium with twisted-pair wires as the medium.
10Broad36	10-mbps broadband medium with a 3,600-m segment length.
100BaseTX	100-mbps baseband medium with twisted-pair wires as the medium.
100BaseFX	100-mbps baseband medium using fiber optic cable.
100VG-AnyLAN	A specification of the IEEE 802.12 subcommittee. This specification competes with 100BaseT for the 100-mbps Ethernet market. The specification calls for twisted-pair wires and can support either CSMA/CD or token-passing technologies.
1000BaseSx	1,000-mbps baseband medium using fiber optic cable.

You may infer from this nomenclature that, in general, the initial number represents the speed of the medium in millions of bits per second. The "base" or "broad" designator represents baseband or broadband, respectively. With five exceptions, 10BaseT, 100BaseTX, 100BaseFX, 100VG-AnyLAN, and 1000BaseSx, the last number represents the segment length of the medium in hundreds of meters.

Ethernet Frame Formats

The most widely used Ethernet/IEEE 802.3 frame formats are illustrated in Figure 8-9. The data fields in the Ethernet II and IEEE 802.3 formats hold from 46 to 1,500 bytes. The data fields are capable of containing frames used by other protocols such as TCP/IP or IPX/SPX. In Ethernet II frames, the type field is used to identify the specific kind of protocol found in the data field. In IEEE 802.3 frames, this information is indicated in the length field, which specifies the length of the variable-length 802.2 or Ethernet SNAP frame found in the data field. CRC-32 is the error-detection algorithm used by all Ethernet frame formats.

IEEE 802.2 and Ethernet SNAP frame formats found in the data fields of IEEE 802.3 frames enable IEEE 802.3 frames to carry the complete TCP/IP, IPX/SPX frames or frames used by other upper layer protocols. Recall, for example, that TCP/IP adds TCP and IP headers to user data. When TCP/IP packets are passed from the network layer to an Ethernet LAN's data link layer, the TCP and IP headers must remain intact. This is accomplished by placing them along with the data to be transmitted in the IEEE 802.2 control fields of IEEE 802.2 frames; subsequently, the IEEE 802.2 frames are embedded within IEEE 802.3 frames. When Ethernet SNAP frame formats are used, the kinds of protocols (e.g., TCP/IP or IPX/SPX) embedded in the data field are identified in the destination service access point (DSAP) and source service access point (SSAP) fields.

Fast Ethernet
Refers to 100BaseT Ethernet implementations that comply with the IEEE 802.3u standard. 100BaseT transmits at 100 mbps. Like regular Ethernet, Fast Ethernet is a shared media LAN that uses CSMA/CD as the media access control protocol.

Fibre Channel
Gigabit Ethernet evolved ANSI's X3T11 Fibre Channel standard. The X3T11 specifications for Fibre Channel include a medium speed of 1 GHz and a data rate of 800 mbps. Fibre Channel is often used to build storage area networks (SANs), and implementations that support speeds over 2 gbps. In the future, transmission speeds are expected to exceed 4 gbps.

Isochronous Ethernet Enables 10BaseT Ethernet LANs located at different geographic locations to be connected via ISDN. The IEEE 802.9a specification addresses Isochronous Ethernet; also called Iso-Ethernet. This enhancement enables Ethernet to handle real-time voice and video by providing a total bandwidth of more than 6 mbps that can be used for video-conferencing. Isochronous Ethernet can be integrated into an existing network through the addition of Isochronous Ethernet hubs and replacement of standard Ethernet NICs with Isochronous Ethernet adapters.

Ethernet frames are generated/built by chips on Ethernet network adapter cards. The destination and source addresses are MAC layer addresses. These consist of the ROM addresses etched into Ethernet adapters when they are manufactured. Transceivers found on Ethernet network interface cards (NICs) control transmission speed. Collision detection and recovery are also implemented on Ethernet NICs.

Fast Ethernet   Ethernet implementations with 100-mbps transmission speeds are called **Fast Ethernet** LANs. Several versions of 100-mbps Fast Ethernet LANs exist, including 100BaseTX (usually called *100BaseT*), 100BaseT4 (100-mbps transmission over Category 3, 4, or 5 unshielded twisted-pair wires), and 100BaseFX (see Table 8-4). The "Base" in each of these names stands for "baseband transmission." Like other Ethernet LANs, Fast Ethernet LANs have a broadcast logical topology and are typically implemented in physical star topologies. The *IEEE 802.3u* specification covers Fast Ethernet LANs.

Many of the Ethernet network adapters in use today are 10/100 cards. This means that their transceivers are capable of transmitting at 10 mbps or 100 mbps. Such NICs enable a 10-mbps Ethernet LAN to be upgraded to a Fast Ethernet LAN. Numerous vendors also have Ethernet 10/100 mbps shared media hubs or switches to facilitate the migration from 10 to 100 mbps.

100BaseT LANs typically use category 5 UTP cabling, although Cat-5 Enhanced and Cat-6 cabling may be used instead of Cat-5. 100BaseFX LANs typically use multimode fiber cabling, although single-mode fiber may be used to extend the maximum range of cable runs. SC connectors have eclipsed ST connectors in popularity in 100BaseFX LANs.

Gigabit Ethernet   Gigabit Ethernet evolved from ANSI's X3T11 **Fibre Channel** standard. The X3T11 specification for Fibre Channel includes a medium speed of 1 GHz and a data rate of 800 mbps. Gigabit Ethernet increases the communication medium speed to 1.25 GHz and increases the data transfer rate to 1 gbps. The IEEE 802.3z specification addresses Gigabit Ethernet LANs.

Three major versions of Gigabit Ethernet LANs exist: 1000BaseSX, 1000BaseLX, and 1000BaseT. The "SX" means short wavelength, the "LX" means long wavelength, and the "T" means twisted pair. 1000BaseSX uses multimode fiber and enables LAN nodes to be separated as much as 550 meters. 1000BaseLX is more expensive than 1000BaseSX, uses either multimode or single-mode fiber, and is capable of extending the maximum distance between LAN nodes up to 5 kilometers. Although most 1000BaseT implementations use Cat-6 or Cat-5 Enhanced UTP, some employ Cat-5 cabling.

Iso-Ethernet   Iso-Ethernet, which is also called **Isochronous Ethernet**, enables 10BaseT Ethernet LANs located at different geographic locations to be connected via ISDN (see Figure 8-14). The IEEE 802.9a specification addresses Isochronous Ethernet.

Iso-Ethernet is best suited to organizations that need to transport time-sensitive data (including voice, video, and streaming multimedia data) among geographically dispersed operating locations. Multimedia traffic can be transferred between locations at a rate up to 6.144 mbps. Iso-Ethernet enables more traditional data to be transferred among locations at rates up to 10 mbps.

Iso-Ethernet hubs are typically called *attachment units* and have per-port costs that range from $350 to $500. Attachment units enable node-to-node communications at each operating location and also provide the interface to the ISDN network. Iso-Ethernet nodes can be a maximum of 100 meters from an attachment unit. Special network adapter cards are used for Iso-Ethernet, and these typically range in cost from $150 to $300 per NIC.

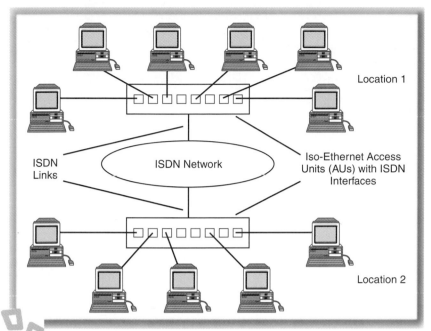

Figure 8-14   Using Iso-Ethernet to Connect Ethernet LANs at Two Locations via ISDN

Token Ring

Token ring networks use a token-passing MAC protocol over a logical ring (sequential) topology. Physically, token ring networks look like a star. When data travels from one node to another, it must first go through a hub called a **multistation access unit (MAU)**. Twisted-pair wire is typically used to connect token ring nodes and MAUs. Transceivers on the token ring NICs usually operate at 16 mbps, although 4-mbps and 100-mbps token ring network adapters also exist. Cat-3 cabling is typically used for 16-mbps (and 4-mbps) token ring LANs; Cat-5 or multimode fiber is most common for 100-mbps token ring implementations.

A MAU typically provides connections for eight workstations (see Figure 8-4). As illustrated in Figure 8-6, token ring LANs expand in size by connecting multiple MAUs in a ring of their own via their Ring In (RI) and Ring Out (RO) ports. The interconnected MAUs can be placed in one rack or be distributed among different wiring closets.

MAUs serve as active monitors within token ring LANs. If a node is turned off or is malfunctioning, the MAU to which it is attached can exclude it from the ring by closing a switch, which prevents the token from being passed to the node (see Figure 8-12).

Because the NICs in each node in a token ring network have repeater capabilities, each node can be located up to 300 meters from the MAU to which it is attached when UTP is used. If fiber is used, the distance can be extended to a maximum of 3,000 meters.

Token Ring Frame Formats

The IEEE 802.5 standard addresses token ring networks. As mentioned previously, the token that is passed among token ring nodes is a 24-bit data packet [see Figure 8-15(a)]. As illustrated in Figure 8-15(a), the 3-octet token consists of a *starting delimiter*, an *access*

multistation access unit (MAU) A central hub in a token-ring LAN.

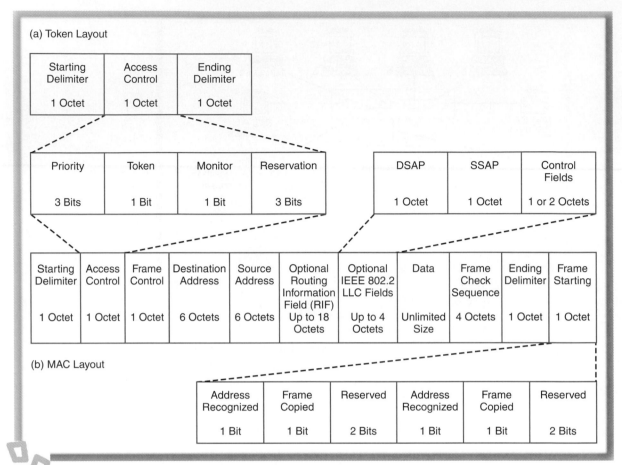

Figure 8-15   IEEE 802.5 Token and MAC Frame Layouts

control field, and an *ending delimiter.* When the *token bit* in the access control field is set to 0, the receiving node interprets this as a free token. If the node has no data to send, it passes the 3-octet token to the next node in the ring. If, however, the node has data to send, it changes the token bit from 0 to 1 to indicate a busy token and builds the rest of the IEEE 802.5 MAC frame by appending address information, data, and the other fields [illustrated in Figure 8-15(b)] before passing the frame to the next node in the ring.

The next field in a busy token (an IEEE 802.5 MAC frame with a token bit set to 1 in the access control field) is the *frame control field.* This indicates whether the frame is a network management frame or whether it contains data. Network management frames are usually generated by active monitors and are read by each receiving node. Frames carrying data are only read/processed by intended recipients.

As illustrated in Figure 8-15(b), *destination and source address fields* follow the frame control field in IEEE 802.5 MAC frames. The NIC in a receiving node reads the destination address to determine if it is the frame's intended recipient. If it is not, it passes the frame to the next node in the ring. If it is the intended recipient, it transfers the rest of the frame's contents into memory and sets the *address recognized* and *frame copied* bits to 0 in the *frame status* octet (the last octet in the IEEE 802.5 MAC frame). Note that there are two sets of address recognized and frame copied bits in the frame status field; this redundancy helps eliminate communication errors.

The *routing information field* plays an important role when source routing bridges (discussed in Chapter 13) are used to interconnect two or more token ring LANs. This is an optional field in IEEE 802.5 MAC frames and is included only when source routing bridges are used. If needed, optional *IEEE 802.2 LLC fields* follow the optional routing information field. These serve the same purpose in 802.5 frames as they do in 802.3 (Ethernet) frames. When needed, IEEE 802.2 SNAP is supported in LLC control fields that follow the DSAP and SSAP octets.

The *data field* contains upper-level overhead fields (such as TCP and IP headers) and the sender's data. If the 802.5 frame is designated as a network management frame (in the frame control field), the network management information is carried in the data field. Although there is not a fixed length to the amount of data that the data field contains, there is a limit on how long a node can hold onto a token before releasing it to the network. The time limit is typically 10 msec, and this translates into a data field maximum of 16,000 to 18,000 bytes.

The *frame check sequence* field is used for error detection. Like Ethernet LANs, IEEE 802.5 token ring LANs use 32-bit CRC for error detection.

The *ending delimiter* serves several purposes. It lets the receiving node know that it has reached the end of the frame and also indicates whether there is more related data to follow in another frame. It is also used to indicate whether the frame should be ignored because it contains an error. Frames detected as containing errors are returned (node to node) to the sender who is responsible for removing them from the network.

The *frame status field* enables receivers to tell senders whether or not the frame was successfully delivered. Upon recognition of its address, the receiver changes the address recognition bits to 1; upon successful copying of the frame's data, the frame copied bits are changed to 1. There are two sets of address recognition and frame copied bits within the frame status field to ensure redundancy. If these bits are identical in both locations, the sender is assured that the frame was successfully delivered.

Token Ring Operations   The 24-bit (3 octet) token illustrated in Figure 8-15(a) must be passed continuously among network nodes even if none have data to transmit. The network cannot function properly unless the token is circulating continuously. One of the main responsibilities of the active monitor is to ensure that the token is continuously being passed.

Ethernet and Token Ring: What Network Is Best for Your Organization?

Ethernet and token ring LANs are both more common than the other LAN architectures discussed in this chapter. In most business organizations, LAN selection processes often boil down to a comparison of the relative merits of these competing architectures. Although the total number of Ethernet LANs far exceeds the number of token ring LANs, this does not necessarily mean that Ethernet architectures are superior.

Ethernet's significantly larger market share is largely driven by the fact that it is less expensive to implement an Ethernet LAN to serve the needs of a fixed number of users. Ethernet NICs are significantly less expensive than token ring NICs. Ethernet hubs/switches are significantly less expensive than comparable MAUs. If an organization has a limited amount of money to invest in a network, it will be able to address the needs of more users by choosing Ethernet over token ring.

If performance, not cost, is considered, Ethernet does not have a competitive advantage over token ring. Because Ethernet uses CSMA/CD, its performance degrades when a high percentage of potential network users actually generate network traffic. As the number of users and the number of messages being sent increases, so does the probability of collisions. If the collision rate is high, the effectiveness of the LAN decreases. When the LAN is busy, network efficiency may drop, and effectiveness may drop when it is most needed. LAN vendors and researchers often run numerous tests to gauge the effect of high collision rates. Although such tests may suggest no appreciable drops in performance under heavy loads, the true test of LAN performance comes from actual use. Under light load conditions, access to the medium and the ability to transmit are good; there is little waiting time to transmit. Performance under heavy loads, however, can be unpredictable. In addition, although vendors claim that 10BaseT Ethernet LANs have data throughput rates close to 10 mbps, most organizations experience throughput rates of 6 mbps under normal traffic levels. When switches are used instead of shared media hubs, Ethernet speeds run closer to 90 percent of capacity.

Token passing eliminates the possibility of collisions. As a result, token ring LANs typically show less performance degradation under heavy traffic loads than Ethernet LANs. Because the medium is accessed through the possession of a token, and because each station is assured of receiving the token, it is possible to predict the maximum and average times needed for a station to transmit its message. When network traffic is light, a token ring node may need to wait longer than an Ethernet node to transmit its data. When network traffic is heavy, however, the token ring workstation may wait less time than a counterpart in an Ethernet LAN to transmit its data. Regardless of the wait time, a token ring workstation is assured that it can transmit in a predictable amount of time. The maximum time a token ring station must wait is given by

$$T_{Max} = (\text{Number of Nodes} - 1) \times (\text{Message Transmit Time} + \text{Token - Passing Time})$$

Thus, a station that has just passed the token to its neighbor may become ready to send a message. That station must wait until the token comes back around. The worst-case scenario would be that every other station has a message to transmit. Thus, the station must wait on all other stations in the ring to transmit their messages and pass the token. On average, a station ready to transmit must wait for only half the other stations. The enhanced predictability of token ring LANs translates into an effective data throughput rate that is just shy of the 16-mbps rate marketed by vendors.

In summary, choosing between Ethernet and token ring architectures often amounts to weighing Ethernet cost advantages against token ring's performance advantages. In terms of market share, installed base, and dollars and cents, Ethernet seems to be winning over performance consistency. There are other reasons why Ethernet is winning the battle for market share. First, there are no gigahertz versions of token ring; as a result, upgrade possibilities are limited. Second, only a handful of vendors still manufacture token ring hardware, so supply risks also exist. Without the competition that exists among Ethernet equipment vendors, organizations that choose token ring networks may face high equipment replacement costs.

ARCnet

As noted previously in the chapter, ARCnet (attached resources computer network) LANs were among the first local area networks. ARCnet LANs are typically implemented as physical stars (see Figure 8-8), but have logical broadcast topologies. Although it uses a token-passing bus MAC protocol, it does not conform to the IEEE 802.4 standard. ARCnet LAN speeds are 2.5 mbps, 20 mbps and 100 mbps, and two or more speeds can be used in the same network. Traditionally, RG-62 coaxial cable was used as the communication medium; today, either twisted-pair wires or fiber optic cable is more common.

FDDI

The American National Standards Institute (ANSI) first recognized **Fiber Distributed Data Interface** (**FDDI**, pronounced "fiddy") in 1984 in its X3T9.5 specification. Although it provides transparent interoperability to IEEE–compliant upper layer protocols such as TCP/IP by supporting IEEE 802.2 LLC protocols, FDDI has never been officially addressed in an IEEE standard. The only IEEE standard that is related to FDDI is the IEEE 802.6 standard for metropolitan area networks (MANs); the IEEE 802.6 specification is summarized later in the chapter.

ANSI originally established FDDI as a 100-mbps network architecture based on fiber optic cable. FDDI's physical topology consists of two fiber optic cable rings. FDDI is one of the few LAN architectures with a true physical ring topology. Data traffic is transported on both rings in opposite directions. One of the rings is designated as the *primary data ring;* the second is a secondary/backup data ring that can be used when the primary ring or an attached workstation fails (see Figure 8-16). A variation of FDDI called **Copper Distributed Data Interface (CDDI)** has also been recognized in the TP-PMD (twisted pair–physical media dependent) standard based on UTP.

Fiber Distributed Data Interface (FDDI) An ANSI standard token passing network that uses optical fiber cabling and transmits at 100 mbps up to 2 kilometers. Its heyday as a LAN and MAN access method was the mid-1990s.

Copper Distributed Data Interface (CDDI) A version of FDDI that uses UTP (unshielded twisted pair) wires rather than optical fiber as the communication medium.

Figure 8-16   FDDI Network Configuration and Key Technologies

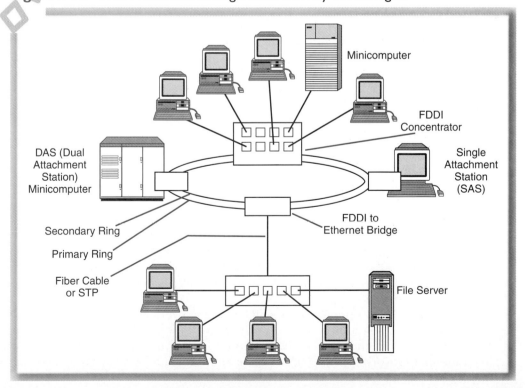

single attached station (SAS) Some FDDI NICs enable a workstation to be attached only to the primary data ring, often via a concentrator; workstations that connect to a FDDI network in this fashion are called single attached stations (SASs).

dual attached station (DAS) Workstations in FDDI networks that attach to both FDDI rings.

Workstations attach to FDDI rings via FDDI NICs or external controllers. Some NICs enable a workstation to be attached only to the primary data ring; workstations that connect to a FDDI network in this fashion are called **single attached stations (SASs)**. Workstations with NICs that attach to both FDDI rings are called **dual attached stations (DASs)**. FDDI network adapter cards are very expensive. SAS cards typically cost at least $1,500, and DAS cards may cost as much as $7,500.

Servers and workstations may also connect to FDDI rings via FDDI concentrators or hubs (see Figure 8-16). Like enterprise/collapsed backbone switches (discussed in Chapter 13), FDDI hubs typically have a modular chassis designed to support various media and connectors. FDDI-to-Ethernet bridges facilitate FDDI/Ethernet interoperability and enable Ethernet LANs to connect to FDDI backbone networks.

FDDI networks are capable of maintaining a speed of 100 mbps over distances up to 200 km. The maximum cable segment allowed without repeaters is 2 km. The 200-km distance can be attained by connecting 100 such segments. Up to 1,000 nodes can be connected to the ring.

FDDI's logical topology is sequential/ring. It uses a modified token-passing MAC protocol. It uses 11-octet tokens and a unique data frame format. With a LAN spanning distances up to 200 km, it is not efficient to have only one message on the ring at one time. FDDI allows multiple messages to be circulating at a given time. The protocol for doing this is as follows: Only one token circulates around the line. When a station receives the token, such as node A in Figure 8-17(a), it removes the token from the ring and transmits its message. At the end of its message, A appends the token, as illustrated in Figure 8-17(b). The next node, node B, sees the token and can piggyback a message onto the existing message. Node B then appends the token onto the message, as illustrated in Figure 8-17(c). A's message continues to circulate around the ring until it gets to the recipient, node X. X returns the message to A as an acknowledgment, and A removes its message from the ring, as illustrated in Figure 8-17(d). The specification also allows a node to transmit multiple messages (frames) in succession without having to wait for the receipt of an acknowledgment frame from the recipient. Hence, multiple frames can be circulating at any given time in FDDI LANs. A transmit time limit is established during which a node is allowed to send multiple messages while it holds the token. If the node has few frames to transmit, it will release the token before the time limit expires, even if it has not received acknowledgments from the receiver. However, if the node has not finished transmitting all of its data frames when the transmit time limit is reached, it must stop transmitting and release the token.

Unlike IEEE 802.5 token ring LANs, active monitor responsibilities are distributed to all nodes in FDDI LANs. This is one of the reasons why FDDI LANs are able to *self-heal* after link or node failure. When such failures occur, network traffic can be rerouted by adjacent nodes in the ring (see Figure 8-18). This enhances the fault tolerance of FDDI LANs.

Two addressing modes are allowed in a FDDI network. One mode uses a 16-bit address, and the other uses a 48-bit address. However, the standard does not stipulate the exact format of addresses. The FDDI ring can be used as a backbone network to connect multiple LANs (see Figure 8-19), as a high-speed LAN connecting large computing systems, and as a high-speed document delivery system for office automation and graphics applications.

Over time, FDDI's popularity as a high-speed network architecture has declined. Numerous competing alternatives, including Fast Ethernet, Gigabit Ethernet, and 100VG-AnyLAN, can match or exceed FDDI on ease of use and performance. For a fixed number of workstations, each of these alternatives is typically less expensive to implement than FDDI.

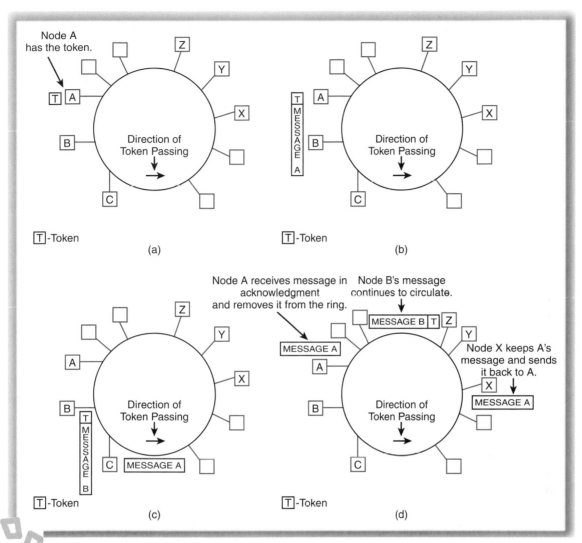

Figure 8-17   Message Passing in a FDDI LAN

100VG-AnyLAN

100VG-AnyLAN is derived from a 100-mbps version of Ethernet developed by Hewlett-Packard that is capable of transporting both IEEE 802.3 and IEEE 802.5 (token ring) frames. It is sometimes called *100BaseVG*. Like Ethernet, 100VG-AnyLAN was initially developed as a shared media LAN, but it employs *demand priority access (DPA)* rather than CSMA/CD as the MAC protocol in order to enable real-time video and voice frames to be given high priority. Although both Ethernet and token ring frames can be delivered, they cannot be delivered simultaneously within the same 100VG-AnyLAN network. 100VG-AnyLAN is covered by the proposed IEEE 802.12 specification.

As illustrated in Figure 8-20, 100VG-AnyLAN provides a mechanism for inter-connecting 100BaseT and 100-mbps token ring LANs via specialized hubs and

100VG-AnyLAN
An IEEE specification for twisted-pair wire or fiber optic cable Ethernet LANs with a speed of 100 mbps.

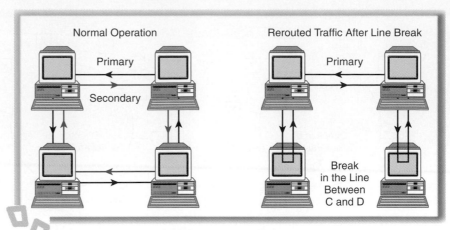

Figure 8-18   FDDI's Self-Healing Capability

Figure 8-19   FDDI Backbone Network Connecting LANs

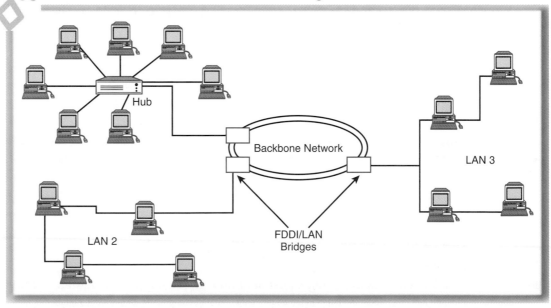

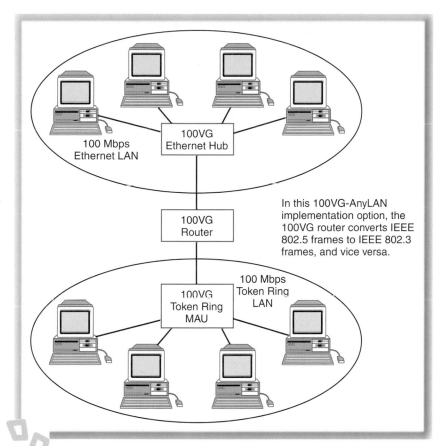

In this 100VG-AnyLAN implementation option, the 100VG router converts IEEE 802.5 frames to IEEE 802.3 frames, and vice versa.

Figure 8-20 An Example of a 100VG-AnyLAN Network

routers. Nodes may be up to 2,500 meters apart, and there may be up to four hubs or repeaters between any pair of end nodes. Category 3, 4, or 5 UTP is most common in 100VG-AnyLAN networks, but type 1 STP, multimode fiber, or single-mode fiber can also be used.

100VG-AnyLAN hubs control network access. These hubs poll (scan) each port in a round-robin sequence to determine if attached nodes have data to transmit. Particular ports, such as those involved in the delivery of time-sensitive voice or video frames, can be assigned a high-priority status. This enables 100VG-AnyLAN networks to handle multimedia traffic quite well. In addition to ports, particular applications can be designated as high or low priority. Through the use of round-robin polling and priority assignments, the demand priority access protocol used in 100VG-AnyLAN networks is able to eliminate the collisions inherent in Ethernet LANs as well as the token delays that can impact the performance of token ring networks.

As you might expect, 100VG-AnyLAN–compliant network adapter cards are needed for network nodes. The NICs installed in token ring nodes must be both 100-mbps token ring– and 100VG-AnyLAN–compliant. Ethernet nodes require NICs that are compliant with both 100VG-AnyLAN and Fast Ethernet. In general, the prices for 100VG-AnyLAN–compliant network adapters tend to fall in line with those for token ring LANs. 100VG-AnyLAN compliant hubs have price ranges from $200 to $300 per port.

ATM LANs

Another LAN architecture that does a good job of supporting multimedia traffic is ATM (asynchronous transfer mode). ATM is a switched network architecture that employs 53-octet cells to transmit data. ATM is also used in WANs (see Chapter 12). Two data link sublayers are defined: ATM adaptation layer (AAL) and asynchronous transfer mode (ATM)—from which this kind of network gets its name. The use of consistent cell lengths and predictable cell delivery times from the ATM protocol enable time-sensitive data such as voice and video to be delivered effectively over ATM networks.

ATM LAN emulation When ATM LAN emulation is employed, LAN MAC addresses are converted to ATM network addresses. ATM LAN emulation enables virtual LANs to be created across an ATM backbone by using ATM switches to handle messages exchanged among logical work-group members.

ATM physical topologies are stars. Nodes with ATM NICs connect to an ATM LAN switch. Most ATM LAN switches are capable of interfacing with higher speed enterprise ATM switches or SONET services. ATM NICs with speeds of 25, 100, or 155 mbps are available. As the speed increases, so does the price.

As illustrated in Figure 8-21, Ethernet and token ring nodes can interface with an organization's ATM backbone network via *ATM access/gateway switches*. Virtual LANs can be created across an ATM backbone through **ATM LAN emulation**. When ATM LAN emulation is employed, LAN MAC addresses are converted to ATM network

Figure 8-21   Interconnecting LANs via an ATM Backbone

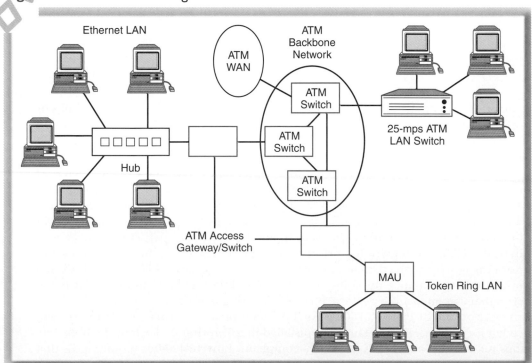

addresses; messages among logical work-group members can thus be forwarded via the organization's ATM switches to intended recipients.

Three-Tier Architectures and Virtual LANs

Traditionally, LANs have been classified as having 2-tiered client/server architecture with clients located on one tier and servers on the second. Over time, 3-tiered C/S architectures, such as the one illustrated in Figure 8-22, have also become quite common. In a 3-tier C/S architecture, application software is distributed among three kinds of computers: the user's client computer, a middle-tier server, and one or more backend servers. The client computer may be a microcomputer, a network computer (thin client), or even a terminal. Middle-tier servers essentially function as gateways between clients and backend servers. When used in a distributed database environment employing diverse database management systems (DBMSs), middle-tier servers incorporate the middleware needed to convert protocols and convert client requests for data into the syntax needed by the DBMS of the backend data server that can satisfy the client's request. In other networks, middle-tier servers function as gateways between client applications and backend legacy applications. Because the interaction between middle-tier servers and backend severs follows general C/S models (which are discussed more fully in Chapter 11) in any given interaction between clients and backend servers, the middle-tier server functions both as a client (by mapping client requests to the appropriate backend server) and as a server (by forwarding backend server responses to client requests to the appropriate client).

As discussed in Chapter 7, data link layer switches are also becoming more common in LANs. LAN switches function like bridges by sending packets to their destinations based on the recipient's hardware (physical) address. Most LAN switches are called **Layer 2 switches,** because the switched connection is based on the MAC layer destination address included in data link layer frames transmitted between

Layer 2 switch
A network device that forwards traffic based on MAC layer (Ethernet or Token Ring) addresses. Most LAN switches are called Layer 2 switches because the switched connection is based on the MAC layer destination address included in data link layer frames transmitted between LAN–attached devices.

Figure 8-22   Three-Tier Client/Server Computing Architecture

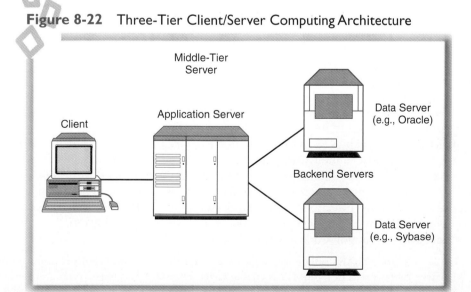

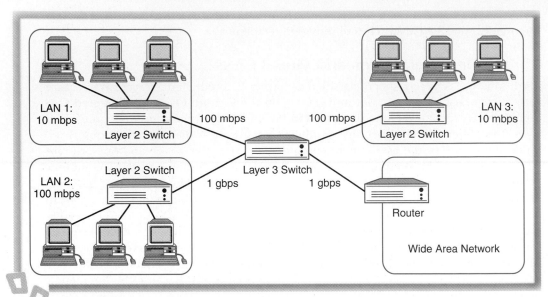

Figure 8-23   Layer 2 and Layer 3 Switches in LANs

Layer 3 switch
A network device that
forwards traffic based
on Layer 3 informa-
tion. Layer 3 is the net-
work layer of the OSI
reference model.
When network layer
destination addresses
(such as IP addresses)
are used to establish
switched connections
instead of MAC layer
addresses, the switch
is called a Layer 3
switch.

LAN–attached devices. When network layer destination addresses (such as IP addresses) are used to establish switched connections instead of MAC layer addresses, the switch is called a **Layer 3 switch.** Both Layer 2 and Layer 3 switches are illustrated in Figure 8-23.

Both Layer 2 and Layer 3 switches can be used to create 3-tier C/S LANs. These switches also enable organizations to implement virtual LANs.

Virtual LANs

Virtual LANs are logical network designs that are dependent upon LAN switches to provide functionality. Special virtual LAN software, supported in Layer 2 and Layer 3 LAN switches, enables virtual LANs to be created and maintained. In essence, a virtual LAN is a logical grouping of work-group members that does not require each member of the group to be physically attached to the same switch. In Figure 8-23, for example, a virtual LAN could be created by designating two users in LAN 1 and two users in LAN 2 as members of the same work group. A second virtual LAN could be created by designating one user in each of the three LANs as a member of a second work group. The use of virtual LANs enables users to be assigned to more than one work group, if necessary, regardless of where their workstations are physically attached. In Figure 8-23, all Layer 2 switches and the Layer 3 switch would have to be equipped with the same virtual LAN software in order to create and support virtual LANs within the organization. Because there are no interoperability standards for virtual LANs, a single vendor's equipment and software are needed to support multiswitch virtual LANs.

There are two major kinds of virtual LANs:

1. Layer 2 virtual LANs only employ Layer 2 switches. Direct interconnections among Layer 2 switches in different LANs enable Layer 2 virtual LANs to be created. All switching in these virtual LANs is based on the MAC addresses of the attached workstations.

2. Layer 3 virtual LANs employ at least one Layer 3 switch, such as the one depicted in Figure 8-23. Switching/routing among virtual work-group members is based on network layer addresses (for example, IP addresses) rather than MAC addresses.

The ability to facilitate work-group-related communication among users whose workstations are physically attached to different LANs is one of the main reasons why businesses are attracted to virtual LANs. Lack of interoperability standards and the evolution of routing and switching technologies that offer similar functionality without the burden of being shackled by proprietary vendor solutions have made the future of virtual LANs questionable.

WIRELESS LAN ARCHITECTURES

In comparison to the LAN architectures discussed previously in the chapter, wireless LANs are relatively new. Their popularity, however, is growing rapidly for a variety of reasons. For example, they can be implemented quickly and, in some instances, enable networks to be created in locations that would otherwise be difficult or impossible to network (such as buildings on the Historic Register, whose integrity would be threatened by the installation of network cabling). In addition, portable/notebook computers equipped with wireless LAN adapters can instantly establish a LAN connection via the nearest access point (wireless hub), and many of today's wireless LAN alternatives enable users to "roam." In campus settings (business or university), users with wireless adapters can access network resources as long as they are within the coverage area of a wireless hub. Access points that interface with cable-based LANs or backbone networks essentially create wireless extensions to existing networks.

As noted in Chapter 7, technologies such as Bluetooth enable users to instantly establish wireless *personal area networks (PANs)*. Although these and most other wireless data communication options cannot match the speed and performance of today's high-speed LAN architectures, they can, nonetheless, play an important role in meeting the computing needs of today's increasingly mobile workforce.

In Chapter 7, it is noted that the two most widely used wireless communication media are infrared light and spread-spectrum radio (SSR) signals. LANs that use infrared technologies are much less common than those that use SSR technologies.

Infrared LANs

LANs that rely on infrared light as the communication medium transmit signals whose wavelengths fall between those of visible light and radio waves (see Table 8-5). Although some infrared LAN products use *line-of-sight* transmission technologies, others use *diffused infrared transmission* to enable more flexible deployment of nodes. Line-of-sight infrared LANs are capable of transmission speeds up to 10 mbps over a maximum distance of 90 feet. LANs with diffused infrared transmission can range in speed from 1 mbps to 10 mbps over a maximum distance of 30 feet. Needless to say, these distance limitations are very constraining. As a result, infrared LANs tend to be restricted to single-room networks.

Spread-Spectrum Radio (SSR) LANs

The primary application of SSR for data communications is wireless LANs. SSR has a long history of military use because of its ability to provide reliable communication in battlefield environments where signal jamming and other kinds of signal interference are likely.

Two transmission methods, frequency-hopping spread spectrum (FHSS) and direct sequence spread spectrum (DSSS), are used in SSR networks. With **frequency-hopping spread spectrum (FHSS)**, data is transmitted at one frequency; then the

frequency-hopping spread spectrum (FHSS) FHSS continuously changes the center frequency of a conventional carrier several times per second according to a pseudo-random pattern and set of channels. Data are transmitted at one frequency, then the frequency is changed and data are transmitted at the new frequency, and so on. This makes it very difficult to illegally monitor the spread spectrum signals and increases the probability that transmitted data will be successfully received.

Table 8-5 Frequency Spectrum Classification

Frequency (Hz)	Wavelength
10^{16}	X rays, gamma rays
10^{15}	Ultraviolet light
10^{14}	Visible light
10^{13}	Infrared light
10^{12}	Millimeter waves
10^{11}	Microwaves
10^{10}	UHF television
10^{9}	VHF television
10^{8}	VHF TV (high band) FM radio
10^{7}	VHF TV (low band) Shortwave radio
10^{6}	AM radio
10^{5}	Very low frequency
10^{4}	Very low frequency
10^{3}	Very low frequency
10^{2}	Very low frequency
10^{1}	Very low frequency

direct sequence spread spectrum (DSSS) Sends data over several different spread spectrum radio frequencies simultaneously using the full bandwidth of the communication channel.

frequency is changed, and data is transmitted at the new frequency, and so on. Each piece of data is transmitted over several frequencies to increase the probability that it will be successfully received. **Direct sequence spread spectrum (DSSS)** sends data over several different frequencies simultaneously. Both kinds of SSR signals can penetrate office walls, but concrete and metal walls can cause significant reductions in signal strength. Today, DSSS is used more frequently in wireless LANs than FHSS.

The Federal Communications Commission (FCC) limits SSR transmission in wireless LANs to the following frequency ranges: 902 to 928 MHz; 5,150 to 5,350 MHz; 5,725 to 5,825 MHz; and 2.4 to 2.4835 GHz. Several electronic devices, including cordless phones and wireless scanners, are also licensed for operations in the 902- to 928 MHz range and thus can be a source of interference and errors for wireless LANs that operate in this range. Microwave ovens can interfere with SSR signals for LANs that operate in the 2.4- to 2.4835 GHz range. The two ranges between these extremes were approved by the FCC in 1997 in response to the increasing popularity of wireless LANs.

Transmission speeds for SSR wireless LANs range from less than 1 mbps to 54 mbps over distances ranging from 100 to 1,000 feet. In the past, larger coverage areas were associated with lower transmission speeds. For many of the products on the market today, this is no longer the case.

Wireless LAN Topologies

Wireless LANs are typically implemented as physical stars. Nodes connect to wireless hubs that are typically called *access points*. Access points can be stand-alone devices or can interface with cable-based networks in order to provide wireless segments for an otherwise wire-based LAN. Access points are often deployed within an organization to provide some overlap in coverage area. A wireless node located within overlapping coverage areas will use the access point with the strongest signal.

A broadcast logical topology is most common. Most wireless LANs use a modified version of the CSMA/CD as the MAC protocol. Some wireless LAN products, however, have a logical sequential/ring topology and use a wireless variation of token passing as the MAC protocol.

The IEEE 802.11 specification addresses wireless LANs. It addresses FHSS, DSSS, and diffuse infrared transmission, as well as user roaming capabilities. The original specification addressed transmission speeds up to 2 mbps; the IEEE 802.11b specification increased the maximum transmission speed to 11 mbps, and the 802.11a specification further increased the maximum speed to 54 mbps. A 54-mbps wireless LAN standard has been proposed by the European Telecommunications Standards Institute (ETSI); it would use the 5-GHz frequency range.

The IEEE 802.11 standard also identifies *CSMA/CA (Carrier Sense Multiple Access with Collision Avoidance)* as the MAC protocol for IEEE 802.11–compliant LANs. Like CSMA/CD, IEEE 802.11 LANs attempt to avoid collisions by requiring nodes to listen to the communication medium before transmission and not transmitting if other nodes are using the medium. Collision avoidance is also supported by requiring all nodes in the network to wait a random amount of time before transmitting after the medium is clear. The amount of time that each node must wait after the medium is clear is called *slot time;* slot time is measured in microseconds. In addition, a node with data to transmit first sends out a data packet similar to a token; this data packet is sent to the destination node. The packet contains data link layer header and information fields and is used to establish a wireless point-to-point circuit between the sender and recipient. Once established, the point-to-point circuit remains in place until the transmitting node receives an acknowledgment from the destination node that the message was received and that no errors were detected.

Important Wireless LAN Standards

As noted earlier, IEEE 802.11x standards are the most important wireless LAN (WLAN) specifications that exist today. As noted in Table 8-6, the IEEE 802.11b standard is currently the dominant WLAN standard. However, the IEEE 802.11a standard promises to usher in a new generation of high-speed wireless LANs. Because security remains a critical issue with WLANs, products that comply with the IEEE 802.11x standard are likely to have an edge in the marketplace.

Interoperability among WLAN networks and technologies has been the focus of several standards summarized in Table 8-6, including IEEE 802.11e, IEEE 802.11f, and the WISPR standard. The Wireless Ethernet Compatibility Alliance has developed a *Wireless Fidelity (WiFi)* certification to promote interoperability among WLAN products. WiFi certification for wireless adapters means that most WLAN adapter cards will work with most access points, even those manufactured by different vendors. The Wireless Ethernet Compatibility Alliance has also been promoting standards that support effective inter-access-point communication (such as the IEEE 802.11f standard). This alliance also supports the WISPR standard that will enable users to roam across public WLAN networks. Public WLAN networks are being implemented in both private sector and public sector organizations. In Starbucks coffee shops, for example, patrons with WiFi-certified cards are able to access the Internet via their laptops. A variety of libraries, hotels, and universities are also leveraging WiFi to enable clients and visitors to access the Internet via their wireless networks. The *WISPR standard* will enable users to roam from one publicly accessible WLAN to another.

Table 8-6   Important Wireless LAN Standards

Standard	Description
IEEE 802.11	Original WLAN standard; supports 1- to 2-mbps transmission speeds
IEEE 802.11b	Currently the dominant WLAN standard; supports transmission speeds of 11 mbps
IEEE 802.11a	High-speed WLAN standard for 5- to 6-GHz band; supports 54 mbps
HiperLAN2	Competing high-speed WLAN standard for 5- to 6-GHz band; supports 54 mbps
IEEE 802.11g	High-speed WLAN standard for 2.4-GHz band; supports 20+ mbps transmission speeds
IEEE 802.1x	Comprehensive security framework for all IEEE networks including WLANs and Ethernet
IEEE 802.11i	Wireless-specific WLAN security standard that complies with IEEE 802.1x
IEEE 802.11e	Quality of service (QoS) mechanisms that support all IEEE WLAN radio interfaces
IEEE 802.11f	Defines communication between WLAN access points
IEEE 802.11h	Defines spectrum management techniques for IEEE 802.11a WLANs
WISPR	Wireless ISP roaming standard recommended by the Wireless Ethernet Compatibility Alliance to enable roaming among multiple public WLAN networks

MAKING THE DECISIONS

Without even considering the network operating system software alternatives (which are discussed in Chapter 13), the number of alternatives available in choosing a LAN can be overwhelming. You have three basic conducted media choices or two choices in wireless medium technology; three major topology choices; two primary media access control choices; and a wide variety of vendor choices. The issue then becomes which is the best configuration for your company and applications. If one clear option were superior for all applications and for all users, the choice would be easy. However, applications vary significantly with respect to the number of nodes, number of concurrent users, data access needs, distance spanned, and budget. Some of the other major factors influencing LAN selection are summarized in Table 8-7. Of these factors, cost, number of concurrent users, speed, vendor support, manageability, scalability, and security are among the most important.

Cost

If cost were not a consideration, LAN selection would be easier. You could buy the fastest, biggest workstations and servers available and use the most comprehensive LAN network operating system and application software available. Deciding the specific hardware and software modules to fit this description might not be simple, but lack of price constraints would make selection much easier. However, cost often is an overriding constraint to LAN selection in business organizations, and network administrations are often forced to choose the best LAN option that fits a prespecified budget. No matter the budget maximum, network managers should always strive to identify the most cost-effective LAN solution for each situation.

For a fixed number of nodes, Ethernet architectures are among the least costly to implement no matter which speed level is needed (10 mbps, 100 mbps, or 1,000 mbps). There are numerous manufacturers of Ethernet network adapters, hubs, and switches.

Table 8-7   Major Factors Influencing LAN Selection

Cost	Number of workstations	Type of workstations
Number of concurrent users	Type of use	Number of printers
Medium and distance	Speed	Applications
Expandability	Device connectivity	Connectivity with other networks
LAN software and hardware	Vendor	Adherence to established standards
Vendor support	Manageability	Security

This contributes to price competition and ensures that the hardware components needed to implement Ethernet LANs are readily available. Network adapters, hubs, and switches for token ring LANs are more costly than those for Ethernet LANs; in order to serve the same number of users, a token ring LAN costs approximately twice that of an Ethernet LAN. ATM adapters and switches are more costly than those for token ring. FDDI adapters and concentrators are among the most expensive, and because there are fewer FDDI component vendors today than there were during the 1990s, there is less price competition and more limited availability of FDDI components.

Hardware and software are not the only costs associated with LAN implementation. Other costs that should be considered during LAN selection include immediate and recurring costs, such as those shown in Table 8-8. Immediate costs are those incurred when installing a LAN. Recurring costs are the costs of operating and updating the LAN and training LAN users and administrators. When both immediate and recurring costs of LAN options are identified, organizations take important steps toward identifying **total cost of ownership**. Today, the total cost of ownership of LANs and other IT projects is often evaluated and used as a basis for determining which LAN options/IT projects to implement. Total cost of ownership includes all cost aspects of a LAN option/IT project, including ongoing costs for support, management, and maintenance over the entire expected life span of the network/system.

total cost of ownership Includes all cost aspects of a LAN/IT project including on-going costs for support, management, and maintenance over the entire expected life span of the network/system.

Number of Concurrent Users and Type of Use

The number of concurrent users expected during normal and peak network usage periods is often an important factor in selecting among LAN alternatives. Some networks have restrictions regarding the number of active users. For example, the license

Table 8-8   Immediate and Recurring LAN Costs

Immediate Costs	
Equipment upgrades	Training (users, operators, administrators)
Documentation	Installation of cabling
Site preparation	System software installation
Hardware installation	Creative user environments
Installing applications	Space required for new equipment
Testing	Supplies and spares
Recurring Costs	
LAN management: personnel costs	Hardware and software maintenance
Consumable supplies	Training (new users, administrators)

for a network operating system may limit the number of concurrent users to five, but more than five workstations can be attached to the network. The license for a second network operating system may require the number of concurrent users to equal the number of workstations attached to the network, that is, one license per attached machine, no matter how many concurrent users there are.

In general, an increase in the number of concurrent users also increases LAN traffic and workload. In LANs that employ contention-based data link protocols (such as Ethernet), network responsiveness may decrease as the number of concurrent users increases. Network responsiveness is more stable in LANs that employ token-passing protocols, but the major kinds of token-passing LANs (token ring and FDDI) are typically significantly more costly to implement than Ethernet LANs. Other ways to improve LAN responsiveness when the number of concurrent users is high include upgrading to a faster LAN (one with higher transmission speeds), using additional or more powerful servers (which means more expensive computers), or using more efficient (and typically more costly) LAN software.

The number of concurrent users of a LAN application also has an impact on the cost of the application. Software vendors vary in their user license provisions; in general, application costs are directly proportional to the number of concurrent users. As the number of concurrent users goes up, so do software costs. To better understand the effect of concurrent users on LAN performance, let's look at two very different ways of using a LAN.

Suppose that the primary LAN application is word processing, and the normal operating mode is as follows: LAN users access the word processing software on a file server at the beginning of their work shifts; they save their documents on a local disk drive; and they periodically print documents. What demands are placed on the LAN? The demand is heavy when a user starts the word processing program. The program must be downloaded, or transferred from the server to the workstation. The user does not need LAN services again until he prints a document or, in some cases, requires an **overlay module** for the word processor. An example of an overlay module is a spelling checker. Current microcomputer software is so rich in capabilities that all the functions cannot always be included in one memory-resident module. An overlay module overcomes this constraint by sharing memory with other overlay modules. When overlay modules are used, LAN requests are, therefore, infrequent, but the amount of data transferred is large. Adding users may not significantly increase the LAN workload if there is a considerable amount of idle time between user requests for LAN resources. If you have used a LAN in a classroom situation, you probably have experienced this kind of usage. At the beginning of the class, LAN response is slow: Many students are starting an application at nearly the same time, and the demand for LAN resources is high. After that, however, LAN responsiveness improves because LAN usage becomes intermittent.

Suppose instead that the primary LAN activity is database access, with users continually accessing and updating a database. In this case, the LAN is constantly busy transferring large and small amounts of data. Adding new users in this instance can have a noticeable impact on LAN performance.

Communication Speed

LAN speeds can be somewhat deceptive. A LAN speed quoted by the vendor is the speed at which data is transmitted over the medium. You cannot expect the LAN to maintain this speed at all times. Time is required to place data onto the medium and to clear data from the medium. It is important to select a LAN capable of meeting the

overlay module A memory management technique wherein the program is divided into two distinct segment types: the resident or main segment and the overlay segments. Overlay segments share the same memory area. Typically, only one of the overlays is in memory at any given time. When a different overlay segment is required, it replaces the memory resident overlay segment.

organization's performance goals. If network managers want users to access data from LAN servers at transfer rates comparable to that of a local hard disk, lower speed LANs are less likely to be viable options. LAN speeds range from 1mbps to 1gbps, and the trend is toward higher speeds because of greater LAN use and the kinds of data now being used in LAN applications. Wireless LAN architectures are currently bunched at the low end of the communication speed spectrum. Applications using graphics, audio, and full-motion video are becoming more common. These applications require the transfer of large amounts of data and place a heavy load on the media and servers.

Vendor and Support

When you select a LAN, you are selecting much more than hardware and software. You also are selecting a vendor or vendors with whom you expect to have a long-term relationship. Your vendors ought to be available to help you with problems; provide you with maintenance and support; and supply you with spare parts, hardware and software upgrades, and new equipment. You can be more successful with a good vendor and a less capable LAN than with a poor vendor and a superior LAN, especially if your vendor can quickly resolve problems, obtain needed equipment, and so on. Evaluate prospective vendors and their support policies as carefully as you evaluate the equipment itself.

Manageability

Never underestimate the time and effort required to operate and manage a LAN. Even a small, static LAN requires some management once it has been installed and set up. Occasionally, a user might be added or deleted, applications may be added or updated, and so on. The major ongoing activities will be backing up files, taking care of printer problems, and solving occasional user problems. In a large LAN, management is a full-time job that often involves more than one person. Network management is discussed more fully in Chapters 14 and 15. During the selection process, you must ensure that your LAN will have the necessary management tools or that third-party tools are available. Third-party tools are those written by someone other than the LAN vendor. The tools you need depend on the size of the LAN and complexity of the users and applications involved. As a minimum, you should be able to easily accomplish the tasks listed in Table 8-9.

Security

With stand-alone microcomputers, security generally is not an issue. Stand-alone microcomputer systems are usually single-user systems, and system security features, such as password-controlled screen savers, are rarely used. As a result, access to the system is tantamount to access to all data stored on that system. By contrast, data in a LAN is shared. This does not imply that all users have unlimited access to all data. LAN network operating system and database software typically includes mechanisms for controlling the ability of individual LAN users to access data. Most allow network managers to establish/withhold, read, write, create, and purge rights for individual users for each file. Special security challenges, however, exist for wireless LANs, and the manner in which these are addressed may be especially relevant when choosing among wireless LAN products. More comprehensive coverage of network security is provided in Chapter 16.

Table 8-9   LAN Management Tasks

User/Group Oriented	
Add, delete users and groups	Set user/group security
Set user environment	Solve user problems
Printer Oriented	
Install/remove printers	Set up user/printer environment
Maintain printers	
Hardware/Software Oriented	
Add/change/delete software	Add/change/delete hardware
Diagnose problems	Establish connections with other networks
Plan and implement changes	
General	
Make backups	Maintain operating procedures
Carry out recovery as necessary	Educate users
Plan capacity needs	Monitor the network
Serve as liaison with other network	
administrators	

Other LAN Selection Criteria

As noted in Table 8-7, there are a number of other criteria that may be important in the selection of a particular LAN. Additional issues to consider when selecting among LAN alternatives include the number of user workstations to be supported; the type and variety of desktop operating systems found on user workstations; anticipated LAN applications; the distance between LAN nodes; the communication medium; required type and nature of printing support; the expandability/scalability of the LAN; connectivity with other networks; and adherence to widely supported standards. These are briefly discussed in Table 8-10.

IEEE LAN STANDARDS

As noted in Table 8-10, adherence to widely supported standards is an important factor when selecting a LAN architecture. Throughout this chapter, you have encountered a number of LAN standards, most of which are IEEE standards. You may have noticed that these invariably start with "IEEE 802"; this is because these were created by IEEE Project 802 Subcommittees.

    The IEEE established a standards group called the *802 Committee* during the 1970s. This group is divided into subcommittees, each of which addresses specific LAN issues and architectures. The subcommittees and their objectives are summarized here.

802.1: High-Level Interface   The high-level interface subcommittee addresses matters relating to network architecture, network management, network interconnection, and all other issues related to the OSI layers above the data link layer, which are the network, transport, session, presentation, and application layers.

802.2: Logical Link Control   IEEE has divided the OSI data link layer into two sublayers: logical link control (LLC) and MAC. The MAC sublayer implements protocols such as token passing or CSMA/CD. Figure 8-10 illustrates the relationship between

Table 8-10   Additional LAN Selection Factors

Number of Workstations The number of workstations is often a key factor in network configuration. LAN architectures differ in the maximum number of workstations that can be supported. If you exceed that maximum, you must make some provisions for extending the maximum number. A variety of techniques exist for doing this, and each increases the total cost of the LAN. Other workstation costs can be incurred as well. If you intend to use existing microcomputers on the LAN, they may need to be upgraded. For example, because LAN software is resident in each workstation, the amount of RAM may have to be increased.

Type/Variety of Workstation Operating System When selecting a LAN network operating system, it is important to ensure that it will interoperate effectively with the type and variety of desktop operating systems found on user workstations. If you need to mix the types of workstation operating systems on the LAN to support your user base, increases in installation and maintenance costs are likely.

Applications Many major application software packages once only available on mainframes and minicomputers are now available in LAN–compatible versions. Applications communicate with the network through interfaces called *application program interfaces (APIs),* and a variety of APIs are in use. If the application uses an interface not supported by a particular LAN network operating system, the application is unlikely to work on that network. Some software simply is not LAN compatible. It either cannot run on a LAN at all or it does not support sharing on a LAN but can be used by one user at a time. Custom-written applications also may not be LAN compatible. It is important to determine whether software you intend to use on the network will work on the LAN configuration you are considering.

Distance and Medium LANs can serve a limited geographical area at high speeds, but each LAN architecture has a maximum distance it can cover. In general, as the distance your LAN needs to cover increases, your LAN options decrease. Distances for popular microcomputer LANs range from a few hundred meters to several thousand meters. The type of communication medium to be used should also influence the selection process. If your facility already has wiring installed, you may want to select a LAN that can use that type of wiring. Each medium has speed and error characteristics. Wireless LANs have some of the most restrictive distance and speed limitations. If your LAN wiring must pass through areas that can induce transmission errors (such as areas that produce electrical or magnetic interference), you may need to select a LAN option that is capable of supporting shielded twisted-pair or fiber optic cable. One company came to this realization the hard way. In wiring the building with unshielded twisted-pair wires, the company ran the wiring through the shaft of a freight elevator. The freight elevator was seldom used; however, every time it was operated, the motor interfered with the data being transmitted on the LAN, causing numerous transmission errors. Replacing the cabling in the elevator shaft with more error-resistant wiring eliminated the periodic failures.

Number and Type of Printers The number and distribution of printers can affect your LAN decision as well. Some LAN network operating systems have maximum limits on the number of printers they can support. With such systems, if you need a large number of printers, you may need to break the LAN into smaller sections interconnected by bridges in order to provide printing services beyond the maximum number of printers per LAN. You also must ensure that the LAN you select is capable of supporting the types of printers you will be using. Each printer requires printer driver software to direct its operation. The driver software knows how to activate the special printer features needed to print special typefaces, underlining, graphics, and so on. Spooler software is responsible for writing printed output to shared printers. It follows that there must be an interface between the spooler and the printer drivers. When selecting a LAN, you must ensure that the printers you plan to use are supported and that they are supported in the manner in which you plan to use them.

Expandability After installing a LAN, you probably will need to add workstations to it in the future or to move workstations from one location to another. The ease of doing this varies among LAN implementations. The ease may depend on the medium used and on the way in which the medium was installed. Adding new nodes to some systems using twisted-pair wires or coaxial cable is quite easy. Adding a new node to a fiber optic cable may require cable splicing, which means that you must cut the cable, add the connectors, and rejoin the cable so the light pulses can continue along the cable. Fiber optic cable splicing technology has improved and is not difficult; however, adding a new node is still more difficult than for twisted-pair wires or coaxial cable.

Connectivity to Other Networks A LAN is often only one part of an organization's computing resources. Other facets may include WANs, large stand-alone computers, or other LANs. If there are other LANs, they may have different architectures. Although most LANs provide a variety of connection capabilities, immediate and anticipated connectivity needs should be considered when selecting a particular LAN configuration.

Table 8-10   (cont.)

Compatibility with Existing LAN Software and Hardware If your company already has microcomputers and associated software and hardware, it probably wants to preserve its investment in them. If investment preservation is important, new LAN software and hardware should be selected that is compatible with the existing equipment.

Adherence to Established Standards Some LANs conform well to widely recognized standards for LAN implementation, whereas others do not. A LAN's adherence to a standard does not necessarily mean that it is superior to nonstandard LANs. However, there are benefits to choosing a LAN that conforms to a standard. Because standards are published, any company can design components that work on the LAN. This creates competition, gives users alternative sources of equipment, and usually drives down the cost of components. Adopting a standardized LAN also is often regarded as a safe decision because the community of users is often large. This generates a body of expertise that new users can tap for information or personnel. On the other hand, a nonstandard LAN may provide innovative features that are not yet covered by standards. Adopting such a LAN can place an organization ahead of competition that is using a more conventional system.

the LLC and the MAC sublayers. The objective of the LLC is to provide a consistent, transparent interface to the MAC layer, so the network layers above the data link layer are able to function correctly regardless of the MAC protocol.

802.3: CSMA/CD   The IEEE 802.3 standard covers a variety of CSMA/CD architectures that are generally based on Ethernet. Several alternatives are available under this standard. As previously noted, many of these are summarized in Table 8-4.

802.4: Token Bus   The IEEE 802.4 standard subcommittee sets standards for token bus networks. The standard describes how the network is initialized, how new stations can insert themselves into the set of nodes receiving the token, how to recover if the token is lost, and how node priority can be established. The standard also describes the format of the message frames.

802.5: Token Ring   The IEEE 802.5 standard subcommittee sets standards for token ring networks. The standard describes essentially the same functions as those described by the token bus network.

802.6: Metropolitan Area Networks (MANs)   As noted previously, the FDDI family of technologies was proposed as a standard for metropolitan area networks. The IEEE 802 LAN standards committee, however, chose a competing set of specifications, IEEE 802.6, for a MAN. The standard is also called the *distributed queue dual bus (DQDB)* standard.

As the name DQDB indicates, the architecture uses two buses. Each bus is unidirectional, meaning that data is transmitted in one direction on one bus and in the other direction on the second bus, as illustrated in Figure 8-24. Each node must, therefore, be attached to both buses. The specification also allows for a variation called a *looped bus*. The looped bus still uses two one-direction buses; however, each bus forms a closed loop, as illustrated in Figure 8-25. Several speeds are defined in the standard. Speeds depend on the medium used. With coaxial cable, the speed is 45 mbps; the speed is 156 mbps over fiber optic cable. Distances up to 200 miles are supported. This subcommittee sets standards for networks that can cover a wide area and operate at

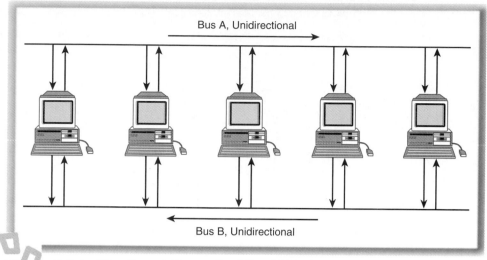

Figure 8-24   Distributed Queue Dual Bus MAN Architecture

high speed. Distances of up to 200 miles and speeds on the order of 100 mbps are being considered for MANs. A MAN could transmit voice and video in addition to data.

802.7: Broadband Technical Advisory Group   This group provides guidance and technical expertise to other groups that are establishing broadband LAN standards, such as the 802.3 subcommittee for 10Broad36.

802.8: Fiber Optic Technical Advisory Group   This group provides guidance and technical expertise to other groups that are establishing standards for LANs using fiber optic cable.

802.9: Integrated Data and Voice Networks   This committee sets standards for networks that carry both voice and data. Specifically, it is setting standards for interfaces to ISDN networks.

802.10: LAN Security   This committee addresses the implementation of security capabilities such as encryption, network management, and the transfer of data.

802.11: Wireless LANs   These standards cover multiple transmission methods to include infrared light, as well as a variety of broadcast frequencies to include spread-spectrum radio waves and microwaves. Thus, many of the existing wireless implementations are covered under the standards proposed. A variety of IEEE 802.11x standards have been adopted or recommended. These are summarized in Table 8-6.

802.12: Demand Priority Access Method   This subgroup developed the specifications for the data link layer protocol in 100VG-AnyLAN networks. The protocol specifies 100-mbps speeds over twisted-pair wires.

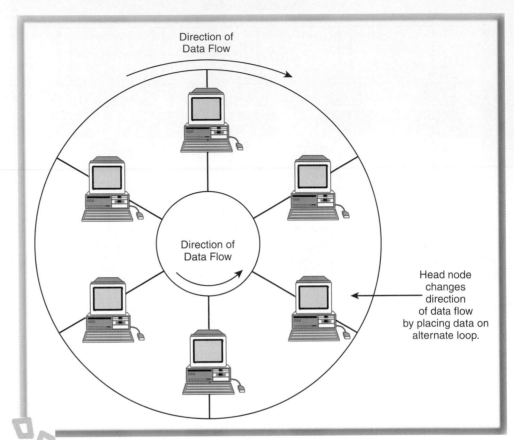

Figure 8-25   Looped Bus MAN

SUMMARY

LAN architectures encompass physical LAN topologies, logical LAN topologies, and media access control (MAC) protocols. Ethernet LANs and token ring LANs, for example, represent two of the most widely implemented LAN architectures. Network operating systems are sometimes also used as LAN architecture identifiers; examples include Linux LANs, NetWare LANs, Solaris LANs, and Windows 2000 Server LANs. In addition, the kind of communication media used in LANs is sometimes used to differentiate among LAN architectures, for example, cable-based versus wireless architectures.

There are three major physical LAN topologies: star, bus, and ring. In star topologies, each LAN node connects to some kind of wiring center, such as a hub, concentrator, multistation access unit (MAU), or switch; these are the most common kind of physical LAN topology. In bus topologies, each node is connected to a single wire or cable. These were the most common topologies in early LAN implementations, but they are less likely to be used today. In a ring topology, the communication medium forms a closed loop, and all nodes are connected to the loop. Physical ring topologies are the least common physical LAN topologies.

There are two major logical LAN topologies: sequential and broadcast. Unlike physical topologies, which focus on how nodes are physically connected to form a network, logical topologies are concerned with how messages are passed node to node within the network. The sequential logical topology is also called a ring logical topology, because messages are passed from one node to another in a ring-like sequence. In contrast, nodes in LANs with a broadcast logical topology transmit each packet to all other nodes in the network. There is no direct connection between a LAN's logical topology and its physical topology. For example, physical stars can have either a broadcast or a sequential logical topology.

MAC protocols are concerned with how nodes take turns using the LAN's communication medium to transmit data. They are also concerned with ensuring that error-free messages reach their intended recipients. The two most common MAC protocols are CSMA/CD (carrier sense with multiple access and collision detection) and token passing. CSMA/CD requires nodes to monitor the communication medium and to wait until the medium is clear before transmitting data. Collisions occur when two nodes transmit at the same time. When collisions occur, each transmitting node is required to wait a random time interval before attempting to transmit again. In token passing, data packets called tokens are passed sequentially from one node to another. Collisions are eliminated in token-passing LANs because nodes can only transmit data when they receive a token.

LANs with Ethernet architectures are most likely to have a physical star topology; some, however, have a bus topology. Ethernet LANs have a logical broadcast topology, and CSMA/CD is the MAC protocol. The IEEE 802.3 specification addresses Ethernet implementations and the format of data frames passed within Ethernet networks. Major categories of Ethernet LANs include 10-mbps LANs (such as 10BaseT), 100-mbps Fast Ethernet LANs (such as 100BaseTX or 100BaseFX), and 1,000-mbps Gigabit Ethernet LANs. Isochronous Ethernet architectures enable Ethernet LANs at geographically dispersed locations to be connected via ISDN.

Token ring architectures are addressed in the IEEE 802.5 specification. IEEE 802.5-compliant LANs typically have a physical star topology, a sequential/ring logical topology, and token-passing MAC protocol. The IEEE 802.5 specification defines the format of the tokens and data frames that are passed from node to node.

100VG-AnyLAN architectures enable Ethernet and token ring LANs to be combined into a single logical LAN. These typically use specialized hubs in a physical star topology as well as a special MAC protocol called the demand priority access (DPA) protocol.

FDDI and ATM are other important cable-based LAN architectures. FDDI architectures have a physical ring topology and a logical sequential/ring topology, and use a modified version of token passing as the MAC. FDDI LANs can cover larger geographic areas than other LAN architectures. ATM LANs are physical stars with ATM switches as the central wiring center where nodes connect. ATM LANs operate at 25 mbps, 100 mbps, or 155 mbps and get their name from the ATM data link layer protocol that is used. Virtual LANs can be created among Ethernet or token ring nodes across an ATM backbone network via a process called ATM LAN emulation.

Wireless LANs are growing in popularity. Spread-spectrum radio (SSR) is the most common communication medium used in wireless LANs, but infrared light is used in some wireless LAN implementations. Wireless LAN hubs are called access points. The IEEE 802.11 specification addresses wireless LANs. IEEE 802.11b-compliant LANs are capable of transmission speeds up to 11 mbps over short distances. IEEE 802.11a LANs are capable of transmission speeds up to 54 mbps. CSMA/CA (carrier sense with multiple access and collision avoidance) is the MAC protocol used in IEEE 802.11-compliant LANs.

Because there are a variety of LAN topologies, media choices, and product vendors, selecting an appropriate architecture for a particular LAN can be challenging. Important selection criteria include the kinds of applications and number of nodes to be supported, the distance to be spanned, the transmission speed, and overall cost. Other important selection factors include vendor support, manageability, security, and compliance with widely accepted standards. IEEE standards have been developed for most of the LAN architectures discussed in this chapter, including Ethernet, token ring, and wireless LANs.

KEY TERMS

- 100VG-AnyLAN
- active monitor
- active node
- ARCnet (Attached Resource Computer Network)
- ATM LAN emulation
- bus topology
- Carrier Sense Multiple Access and Collision Avoidance (CSMA/CA)
- Carrier Sense Multiple Access and Collision Detection (CSMA/CD)
- code independence
- collision
- contention
- Copper Distributed Data Interface (CDDI)
- direct sequence spread spectrum (DSSS)
- dual attached station (DAS)
- Ethernet
- Fast Ethernet
- Fiber Distributed Data Interface (FDDI)
- Fibre Channel
- frequency-hopping spread spectrum (FHSS)

- IEEE 802.3 standard
- IEEE 802.5 standard
- inactive node
- Institute of Electrical and Electronics Engineers (IEEE)
- Isochronous Ethernet
- LAN architecture
- Layer 2 switch
- Layer 3 switch
- logical topology
- media access
- media access control (MAC) protocol
- multistation access unit (MAU)
- network topology
- octet
- overlay module
- ring topology
- single attached station (SAS)
- star topology
- token passing
- total cost of ownership

REVIEW QUESTIONS

1. What is meant by LAN architecture?
2. What is meant by LAN topology?
3. Compare bus, ring, and star topologies.
4. Compare active and inactive nodes.
5. What are the major characteristics of ARCnet LANs?
6. How does a LAN's logical topology differ from its physical topology?
7. Compare broadcast and sequential topologies.
8. Discuss each of the six aspects of data link protocols.
9. What is meant by MAC protocol?
10. What is the role of the IEEE 802.2 logical link control (LLC) sublayer?
11. Describe how CSMA/CD operates.
12. Describe how token passing works.
13. What are active monitors? What functions are performed by active monitors?
14. Compare token-passing ring and token-passing bus.
15. Compare 10BaseT, Fast Ethernet, and Gigabit Ethernet LANs.
16. Briefly describe the characteristics of Iso-Ethernet networks.
17. Briefly describe the characteristics of token ring LANs.

18. Describe the characteristics of FDDI LANs.
19. Compare single-attachment stations and dual-attachment stations.
20. How does token passing in FDDI LANs differ from that in token ring LANs?
21. Describe the characteristics of 100VG-AnyLAN networks.
22. Describe the characteristics of ATM LANs.
23. What is ATM LAN emulation, and how it is related to virtual LANs?
24. Describe the characteristics of infrared LANs.
25. Compare FHSS and DSSS.
26. What are access points?
27. Describe how CSMA/CA operates.
28. Briefly describe the major LAN architecture selection criteria.
29. Compare the following IEEE specifications: 802.2, 802.3, 802.5, 802.6, and 802.11.

PROBLEMS AND EXERCISES

1. Why is it important to distinguish between a LAN's physical and logical topologies? Why are both important components of LAN architecture?
2. Use the Internet to find out more about the IEEE 802.2 LLC sublayer. Develop a table that summarizes each of the major 802.2 LLC functions and how each of these is implemented/accomplished in Ethernet and token ring LANs.
3. Use the Internet to find out more about active monitors in token-passing LANs. Summarize the major responsibilities carried out by active monitors, the major problems that active monitors address, and the events that trigger the transfer of active monitor responsibilities among nodes.
4. Ethernet hubs are sometimes referred to as a "bus in a box." Similarly, token ring MAUs have been referred to as a "ring in a box." Why is this so?
5. Use the Internet to find out more about differences in Ethernet and token ring LAN performance under light and heavy traffic loads. Develop a chart to summarize your findings.
6. Use the Internet to find out more about 1000BaseT Gigabit Ethernet LANs. Describe how 1-gbps transmission speeds are accomplished over twisted-pair wires in this version of Gigabit Ethernet.
7. Use the Internet to find current cost ranges for Ethernet NICs and hubs/switches. Do the same for token ring. Assume that your organization has $30,000 to invest in NICs and hubs. How many user workstations could be networked if Ethernet is selected? How many could be networked if a token ring architecture is selected?
8. Discuss the cost/performance trade-offs associated when selecting Ethernet and token ring LANs.
9. Use the Internet to identify several organizations that have implemented FDDI networks. Summarize how FDDI networks are being applied by these organizations.
10. Use the Internet to identify several vendors who manufacture ATM adapter cards and ATM LAN switches. Develop a table to summarize costs and transmission speeds for the products that you find.
11. Use the Internet to identify at least five wireless LAN products. Develop a table that summarizes the name of each product, its manufacturer, the kind of transmission that is used (line-of-sight infrared, diffused infrared, FHSS, DSSS), the frequency range if SSR is used, transmission speeds, and maximum distance that a node can be from an access point. If speed varies as a function of distance, this should be reflected in the table.
12. Security is a key issue in wireless LANs. Use the Internet to find out more about wireless LAN security and the features being included in wireless LAN products to enhance security.

13. Use the Internet to identify organizations in New York City that implemented wireless networks in the aftermath of the attacks on the World Trade Center on September 11, 2001. Summarize how these organizations applied wireless LANs and the role they played in recovering from the devastation caused by the attacks.

14. Use the Internet to find out more about *total cost of ownership,* especially LAN TOC. Describe how TOC is calculated, the major components included in its calculation, and its role as a LAN selection criterion.

15. Use the Internet to update the activities (such as new standards and recommended standards) of the following IEEE 802 Subcommittees: 802.3, 802.8, 802.10, and 802.11.

Wireless LANs at UPS

Atlanta-based United Parcel Service plans to spend about $100 million in an ambitious project to install advanced wireless LANs, next-generation scanners, and short-range wireless Bluetooth throughout its 2,000 worldwide distribution centers. The project will allow package sorters to move freely with cordless optical scanners to capture data from packages. Then, this data will be sent to the package-tracking system via Bluetooth and retransmitted to the wireless LAN.

Two advanced wireless technologies will be used in the project: Bluetooth and the IEEE 802.11b wireless standard. The 802.11b standard (also known as "WiFi" for "wireless fidelity") defines the rules used by a local area network to transmit data over the air in a 2.4-Ghz frequency. In a typical WiFi network, users connect to wireless access points that are, in turn, connected to an Ethernet hub. Radio signals enable communication over an area of several hundred feet to 1,000 feet. In addition, roaming users can move from one access point to another like cell phone subscribers can move from cell to cell in a cellular phone network. WiFi provides up to 11 mbps, and its signal can penetrate walls and other nonmetal barriers.

Bluetooth is a wireless personal area network technology developed by the Bluetooth Special Interest Group, a consortium of companies led by Ericsson, IBM, Nokia, and Toshiba. It was conceived for short-range transmission of digital data between mobile devices (PDAs and phones) and desktop devices. In a normal configuration, Bluetooth can provide up to 720-kbps data transfer within a range of 10 meters.

The main problem of using both Bluetooth and WiFi is that each operates in the unlicensed 2.4-Ghz frequency band. For this reason, UPS's wireless LAN vendor, Symbol Technologies Inc., had to develop a special system to resolve any potential signal conflict. As a result, Symbol installed intelligent software in the wireless access points that manage the data flow between package-tracking systems and optical scanners.

The UPS advanced network will have three network sections. In the first network, "wearable" computing and communication devices play a key role. A cordless optical scanner mounted on a finger ring will capture tracking numbers from the packages.

Then, the wireless ring scanner, provided by Symbol, will transmit the data to a package-tracking system carried on the hip of the package sorter. Bluetooth will be used for this finger-to-hip communication. The hip-mounted tracking system will run on a Windows CE–based terminal, code-named *Emerald*, developed by Motorola. UPS estimates that 50,000 Emerald terminals will be required when the system is fully rolled out.

In the second section of the network, the Emerald terminal will retransmit the data received from the ring scanner to a wireless access point via WiFi. Symbol will provide as many as 15,000 Spectrum24 High Rate access points to equip 2,000 UPS shipping hubs (distribution centers) around the world.

In the third network section, the Symbol access point will transmit the data to a server-based application running under Windows 2000. Each distribution center has its own server, which sends data via a global frame relay network to UPS's centralized package-tracking application running on an IBM mainframe at New Jersey.

According to UPS officials, the project is expected to pay for itself in 16 months. Some of the benefits of the new wireless network include standardization on single terminals and network systems, improved user efficiency, improved data integrity, and decreased support costs. UPS also expects to reduce equipment and repair costs by 30 percent, improve uptime by 35 percent, and reduce repair times.

Standardizing on Emerald will allow UPS to replace seven package-tracking applications and nine kinds of devices running on different operating systems—improving information flow and decreasing the cost of system ownership. It will also reduce software and hardware support expenses.

The wireless LAN also raises some security concerns. To prevent unauthorized people from accessing the network, UPS will require password-protected logins from all users and will implement encryption technology on its networks. However, because most of the data transmitted over the wireless LAN consists of package-tracking numbers, transmission security is not as big an issue as it could be.

UPS is not the only overnight package delivery service that is leveraging wireless communication technologies. UPS rival FedEx is also in the process of installing wireless LANs inside and outside the company's distribution centers and sorting facilities, and even onboard its aircraft.

CASE QUESTIONS

1. What is the difference between WiFi and WiFi5? Which are the advantages and disadvantages of each one?
2. Use the Internet to find out more about the FedEx wireless project. How is it similar to and how is it different from UPS's wireless initiatives?
3. Security issues for 802.11 LANs have been identified by many industry experts. What are the major issues, and how are they being addressed? UPS maintains that wireless transmission security is not a big deal for them because only tracking numbers are being transmitted. Do you agree? Why or why not?
4. UPS has chosen to use Bluetooth in one key section of its network and WiFi in another. Do you think this is a good idea? What are the advantages and disadvantages of this arrangement?

SOURCES

Boyd J. "Delivering Bluetooth." *InternetWeek* (August 7, 2001). Retrieved February 12, 2002, from www. internetwk.com/story/INW20010807S0002.

Brewin, B. "UPS to Deploy Bluetooth, Wireless LAN Network." *Computerworld* (July 23, 2001, p. 8.)

Brewin, B. "Wireless LAN Gear Offers Fivefold Increase in Speed." *Computerworld* (November 12, 2001, p. 14.)

Note: For more information on LAN architectures, see an additional case on the Web site, www.prenhall. com/stamper, "Southeastern State University."

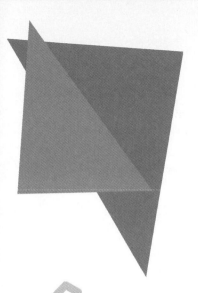

LAN Software

After studying this chapter, you should be able to:

- Differentiate between LAN application and LAN system software.
- Identify and briefly describe several kinds of LAN work-group software.
- Describe the functions of LAN system software.
- Discuss the functions performed by LAN workstation software.
- Explain important characteristics of LAN server software.
- Describe how a spooler works.
- Explain the importance of making backups.
- List backup options and elements of backup procedures.
- Discuss the software requirements for shared data and application use.
- Describe several kinds of software licenses.

In the previous two chapters, you examined the details of the LAN hardware components and architectures. In this chapter, you will learn about LAN application software as well as LAN system software—the software system that drives the hardware. We separate LAN software into two classes: workstation system software and server system software. The success of the LAN depends on how these two software classes and the LAN application software interact in setting up the communication capability.

SYSTEM SOFTWARE VERSUS APPLICATION SOFTWARE

The software found in LANs falls into two main categories: application software and system software. Examples of LAN software included in each category are summarized in Table 9-1.

LAN application software includes the user-oriented programs that enable business users to perform their work activities. Two major categories of application programs exist: general purpose and special purpose. General-purpose LAN applications include software that is widely used by users across the business's divisions or departments—such as word processing, spreadsheet, and database applications. In contrast, special-purpose

Table 9-1   LAN Application and System Software Examples

Application Software	System Software
General-purpose applications (such as word processing, spreadsheets, presentation graphics, and database management)	Server network operating systems (server NOSs)
E-business applications (such as EDI, ERP, CRM, and SCM)	Client network operating systems (client NOSs)
Knowledge management applications	Directory services software
Work-group applications and groupware applications	Media interface software (e.g., NIC drivers)
Transaction processing and e-commerce applications	Print spoolers
Internet browsers	Backup software

LAN applications support the activities of specific divisions/departments or subsets of users. Examples of special-purpose LAN applications include work-group applications (groupware), transaction processing programs, accounting/bookkeeping software, inventory management software, production scheduling software, payroll programs, and project management software.

LAN system software consists of operating systems, utilities, drivers, and other "background" programs that enable application programs to run smoothly on LAN hardware. System software generally serves as the interface between application software and computer hardware, and carries out the vast majority of the essential housekeeping tasks (such as physically storing files on disk, maintaining file management systems, and transferring files to printers for output). The most important kind of system software found in any computer system is the operating system. Utilities, drivers, and several other kinds of system software also play important roles in virtually all computer systems.

A LAN's network operating system (for example, Windows 2000 Server, Linux, Solaris, NetWare) must interoperate with the system software of LAN–attached computers for users to have transparent access to the LAN's shared computing resources. To facilitate transparent access to shared resources, LAN network operating system components are installed in client workstations as well as servers.

LAN system software will be covered in more detail later in the chapter. Before turning to these important aspects of LAN software, we will focus on several major kinds of LAN applications.

WORK-GROUP SOFTWARE

Most LAN implementations have the potential for effectively using **work-group software**, often called *groupware*. In this section, you will learn what a work group is and some of the application tools used to increase work-group productivity.

Before you can fully appreciate the functions of work-group software, you must understand what we mean by a work group and the functions needed by the group. First, a group consists of two or more workers. In doing their jobs, these workers must share information, communicate with each other, and coordinate their activities.

work-group software Software that supports multiple users working on related tasks. Often called *groupware,* this software facilitates the activities of a group of two or more workers by reducing the time and effort needed to perform group tasks. Work-group software includes applications such as messaging, document sharing, group calendaring and scheduling, threaded discussions, videoconferencing, and workflow management.

Specific work tasks that are group activities include meetings, office correspondence, and group decision making. Groupware is designed to make arranging and carrying out these tasks easier and less time-consuming.

The functions performed by groupware are not new. Prior to the development of groupware and the proliferation of LANs within business organizations, these tasks were done manually or with limited degrees of computer support. Networked systems in general and LANs in particular provide the communication link that was needed to computerize many of these tasks. Once LANs and networks became widespread, a variety of groupware applications were created. Some of the more mature categories of groupware applications include e-mail, conferencing, work-flow automation, decision support, and document coauthoring and document management.

E-Mail Administration

Today, awareness of e-mail capabilities spans the globe. At the end of 2002, more than 1 billion e-mail accounts existed worldwide. Because the use of e-mail is so widespread, we will not provide a detailed description of its capabilities here. We will look instead at e-mail administration.

Administering a mail system can be a time-consuming responsibility. User lists and distribution lists must be established and maintained. Periodically, old mail messages may need to be manually removed from the system. There is also the potential for mail to be misused, which may include sending a high volume of broadcast junk mail, hate/love letters, and advertisements for personal gain. One responsibility of mail administration is to set corporate policy for acceptable and unacceptable use of the mail system.

E-mail is a significant communication tool for many companies and has become the fundamental means of communication. In many organizations, increased used of e-mail has contributed to reduced telephone and postage charges. It allows messages to be quickly composed and delivered. Recipients can review their mail at their own convenience, eliminating some of the interruptions of telephone communication.

Some disadvantages also arise from the use of e-mail. Ensuring the security of the organization's e-mail system is an important aspect of e-mail administration. A secure mail system provides options for controlling access to mail messages, such as the ability to encrypt messages. Without such safeguards, one employee may be able to access another's mail file and read their correspondence. One of the corporate e-mail policies should describe penalties for such unauthorized access. On the other hand, in some cases employees have been fired because their e-mail messages fell into the wrong hands. The American Bar Association (ABA) has also been concerned about the use of e-mail. The ABA has studied e-mail usage by attorneys to determine if it violates attorney-client privilege. Like any tool, a mail system can be misused.

It is also important to recognize that e-mail systems can be a primary source of computer virus infections. During 2001, for example, numerous network managers devoted countless hours combating e-mail–spread viruses, including Love Bug, Code Red, Sircam, and Nimda.

E-Mail Interchange Standard X.400

The **X.400 standard** is an important OSI reference model application layer standard related to e-mail administration. It was developed by the ITU, and it provides a framework for the implementation of a worldwide electronic message-handling service. A wide variety of e-mail systems are in use today, ranging from Internet-based systems such as Hotmail and AOL to microcomputer user systems such as Outlook and

X.400 standard
A standard developed by the ITU that provides a platform for the implementation of a worldwide electronic message-handling service.

Eudora to groupware-oriented systems such as Groupwise and Lotus Notes to older host-based systems. Providing a common mechanism to enable message exchange between heterogeneous e-mail systems is the focus of the X.400 standard. In a sense, X.400 is to e-mail systems as the OSI reference model is to the interconnection of different networks.

The implementation of X.400 is based on a hierarchy of entities. The hierarchy is used for implementing worldwide message distribution and for addressing. At the top of the hierarchy is a country, followed by a public administration agency or private regulated operating agency, a company, and a user. Addresses for the senders and recipients of a mail message are generated from this hierarchy. An address consists of a country name, a public utility name, a company name, and a user name.

An X.400 system allows users to exchange electronic messages. The users can be in the same or different companies, can be using the same or different mail systems, and can be in the same or different countries. Mail transfer is accomplished via mail agent processes. Each user has a mail agent called a **user agent (UA)**. A user agent allows a user to compose a message, provides recipient addresses, and receives messages. The interface between UAs is accomplished by **message transfer agents (MTAs)**. An MTA can serve none, one, or several UAs. The network of MTAs is responsible for taking a message from a sender's UA and delivering it to the recipient's UA. This environment is depicted in Figure 9-1, which shows a U.S. user communicating with an Australian user.

The X.400 standard describes two different domains: a private domain, which represents a private e-mail system corresponding to a company in the hierarchy mentioned earlier, and a public domain, which represents a delivery and interconnection network corresponding to the public administration agency in the hierarchy. In some ways, the public domain provides a function similar to that provided by an X.25 network: the ability to provide connections and message routing among systems. The public domain is called an **administrative management domain (ADMD)**, and the private domain is called a **private management domain (PRMD)**. An interdomain interface is defined to establish protocols for passing messages among different domains. Protocols are defined for communicating among ADMDs and between PRMDs and ADMDs, and for the contents of the message itself.

X.400 is significant because it establishes a standard for user communication. It has been implemented in several systems. If the standard is universally followed, computer users anywhere can communicate with each other electronically.

The ITU X.500 Standard

Imagine the complexities of managing a worldwide X.400 e-mail system. Currently, there are more than 1 billion e-mail accounts worldwide, and most e-mail users generate several messages per day. Keeping track of all these users and their mail addresses is a complex task that is addressed by the X.500 standard. The **X.500 standard** specifies how to create a directory system to maintain e-mail user names and their network addresses.

The directory services associated with the major LAN network operating systems in use today have been designed to be compliant with the X.500 standard. For example, Windows 2000 Server's Active Directory (AD) is X.500 compliant. Novell NetWare's Novell Directory Services (NDS), although not technically X.500 compliant, was modeled after the X.500 standard. Workstations attached to LANs that run Windows 2000 Server or any version of Novell NetWare later than NetWare 3.xx are able to exchange e-mail worldwide over the Internet because their directory services conform to X.500. Both AD and NDS are referred to as *global directory services* because they conform to the X.500 directory standard.

---

user agent (UA) A mail agent that allows a user to compose a message, provides recipient addresses, and receives messages.

message transfer agents (MTAs) Interfaces between e-mail user agents.

administrative management domain (ADMD) A public e-mail service defined in the X.400 standard hierarchy that provides a delivery and interconnection network among private e-mail networks.

private management domain (PRMD) A domain that represents a private, in-house e-mail system in the X.400 standard hierarchy.

X.500 standard An OSI protocol for managing online directories and resources. In e-mail administration, it specifies the procedure for creating a directory system to maintain e-mail user names and their network addresses, as well as the names and addresses of other network resources such as printers and servers.

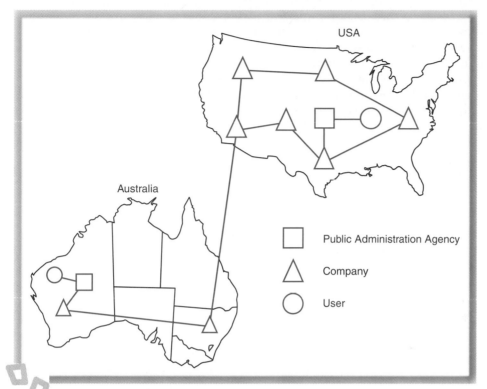

USA

Australia

☐	Public Administration Agency
△	Company
○	User

Figure 9-1   X.400 Connection

Electronic Conferencing Applications

Electronic conferencing applications range from simply arranging meetings to conducting the meetings themselves. Arranging a meeting or conference requires that the participants be notified and that a mutually agreeable meeting date and time be set. Conferencing applications provide assistance with one or more of these tasks. If each attendee maintains an electronic calendar, electronic calendaring groupware can book the meeting at the best time. Given an interval during which the meeting must take place, the groupware application consults the calendars of the attendees. It notes the date and time that all attendees are available and schedules the meeting on their electronic calendars. If scheduling conflicts arise, the application can help resolve them. Some schedulers even double-book participants and allow them to choose which appointment to keep. Others report the conflicts and suggest alternative meeting times with no or reduced conflicts, allowing the person calling the meeting to find the best possible time. Once a meeting is scheduled, the electronic calendar software can issue an RSVP notice to the participants. Like personal calendars, groupware calendars can issue reminders of forthcoming events. The reminder might be a mail message or an audio tone. Today, some even issue reminders to participants' pagers or PDAs. Some groupware allows users to designate recurring meetings, such as weekly, monthly, or biweekly meetings. The scheduler automatically books these meetings for the attendees.

If the meeting is held with participants in different locations, teleconferencing groupware can also assist with communication among the attendees. Some teleconferencing applications allow images displayed on one computer monitor to be displayed on remote monitors. Individuals at all locations can modify the screen image and have the changes immediately reflected on the screens of the other participants. Thus, conference attendees can both view and modify computer-generated data and graphs. Viewing and modifying data coupled with audio transmission and freeze-frame or full-motion video allows geographically distributed conferences to be held, saving both travel costs and personnel time. Another conference or meeting communication aid is the creation and distribution of electronic minutes.

Point-to-point and multipoint desktop-to-desktop videoconferencing over the Internet are among the most recent upgrades to teleconferencing groupware. Packages such as Microsoft's Net Meeting enable users to share screen images, audio, and video images in real time over the Internet.

Work-Flow Automation

Attendees at a meeting may accept action items they must complete, or a work-group manager may assign tasks to work-group members. One responsibility of a work-group manager is monitoring the progress of such tasks. Progress monitoring is not a new concept. For many years, managers have used program evaluation and review technique (PERT) charts or similar methods to track a project's progress and determine its critical path. The critical path of a project is the sequence of events that take the longest to complete. Often, a project can be divided into several tasks. Some tasks can be done in parallel, but other tasks cannot start until one or more tasks have been completed. For example, when you build a house, the roof cannot be put on until the building is framed. Plumbing and electrical wiring can possibly be done concurrently. The project cannot be completed until the path with the longest duration is completed. Thus, project managers pay close attention to the project's critical path to avoid delays. Although some project management work has been computerized for many years, much of the monitoring work was done by people. Groupware has extended the abilities of earlier systems by automating the tracking function.

Figure 9-2 is a PERT chart for selecting a LAN vendor. The critical path for the selection process is indicated by the heavier line. It is the critical path because it has the longest elapsed time between the start and the end points. Groupware helps in monitoring the critical path and keeps the group working together. Through the groupware application, group members can also track the status of other tasks that may affect their work.

With work-flow automation groupware, a manager can assign tasks to individuals or groups (through the group leader). The individual can accept the task, negotiate a change, or refuse the task. Once a task is accepted, a completion date is set. The worker uses the groupware application to record progress and to signal the completion of the task. The manager can then either agree that the task is complete and close it out or reach the decision that the task has not been satisfactorily completed and refuse to accept the work. In the latter case, the worker is notified and must rework the task until the result is acceptable. The groupware work-flow application tracks all tasks and evaluates progress. The group manager can query the system and obtain reports of each task's status. If several tasks are in progress at once and other tasks are awaiting the outcome of those tasks, the groupware monitors the progress of the critical paths and helps the manager keep the project on schedule.

Other functions that may be simplified with work-flow automation software include establishing and monitoring to-do lists; delegating tasks; holding completed

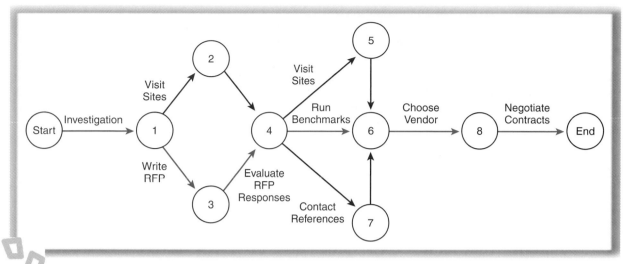

Figure 9-2   PERT Chart for Selecting a LAN Vendor

tasks until released by a manager; deleting tasks; preventing a worker from modifying an accepted task; setting or resetting task start and stop times; adding, deleting, or changing the people responsible for tasks; providing task and group reports; and creating *electronic routing slips* to ensure that group members obtain reports in an appropriate sequence.

Document Coauthoring and Document Management

Word processing, text editors, and document exchange software were among the early document-oriented computer applications. However, most of these systems were designed to allow only one person to manipulate a document at one time. If you have ever worked on a team to write a program, report, or manual, you are probably aware of the limitations inherent in these systems. If you and one of your team members wanted to work on the document at the same time, you found either that it could not be done or that concurrent document updates created version-control problems. In a work group, it is often desirable and sometimes necessary to have several workers actively working on one document simultaneously. Document coauthoring and management applications provide this capability.

A full-function **document coauthoring system** allows two or more workers to work on one document concurrently. Concurrent processing presents some complex problems regarding posting changes to the same pages. Some coauthoring systems do not provide this ability; however, they do provide the management and control abilities that allow a document to be shared without risk of contention or version-control problems. Some document managers help control the flow of documents through the production cycle. Group users are identified as the principal document author, co-authors, or editors. The document manager assists in the production of the document by controlling the flow of the document from one designated user to another.

Document management software can control access to the document by a check-out mechanism. Workers can check out all or portions of the document. Once a portion

document co-authoring system A system that allows two or more workers to work on one document concurrently.

is checked out, update access to that portion of the document by other users is typically restricted because the worker checking it out may change it. If a worker changes the document, the document management software monitors the changes and records the identity of the person making the change. When the document is ready for review, the application can route the document to the proper reviewers and editors. The reviewers and editors then can make notations and suggestions, with or without changing the document itself, and the application will keep track of the person making those remarks.

The trend toward work groups and group-oriented document generation and modification is apparent in the features supported by today's word processing packages. Microsoft Word's *document tracking* features, for example, support most of the document coauthoring capabilities mentioned in the previous paragraph.

Other features of today's document management systems (which are sometimes called *electronic document management systems—EDMSs*) include document organization, archiving, location, and full file searches. Imagine the number of documents generated per year by a large law office. Some law offices generate more than 50,000 documents per year, including wills, contracts, legal briefs, and trial notes. Keeping track of this volume almost necessitates the use of a system that allows documents to be electronically stored, archived to backup media (such as CD-ROMs, microfilm, or microfiche), and retrieved when needed. Today's document management systems allow users to store a single document under a variety of different subjects or indexes. As in a library card catalog, the document can then be found by attorney, client, subject, date created, last date accessed, project, department, author, and a variety of other descriptive categories. Some systems allow users to specify combinations of these attributes as well. Full file searches systematically search files stored on disk or archival directories looking for user-defined text strings.

Document-intensive organizations such as law firms and insurance companies are among the major users of document management systems. These systems are also becoming more common in banks and investment firms as well as among universities and government agencies. Most user organizations report that document management systems improve access to logically related documents, increase worker productivity, and enhance customer service.

Group Decision Support

group decision support software
Facilitates the communication of ideas among the members of a group. Each participant has a workstation from which to make comments and suggestions, which are exchanged among the users in an anonymous way.

LAN–based **group decision support software** facilitates the communication of ideas among the members of a group. Each participant has a workstation from which to make comments and suggestions, which are exchanged among the users in an anonymous way. This allows the lowest member in the organizational hierarchy to feel free to criticize suggestions made by those above them, even those from the person at the top of the hierarchy. The key to making this work is protecting the source of ideas and comments. Included in the software are tools to gather and manipulate data from a variety of sources, such as a database, a spreadsheet, and graphic images. Companies that have invested in group decision support technologies often find that better decisions are reached in a shorter period of time by groups that use the software than by groups that do not.

It is important to emphasize that groupware is not intended to replace person-to-person interactions. Our future should not be one in which we get assignments via computers, where our work is computer graded, and where we are fired or promoted via the computer. Instead, LAN–based groupware applications are designed to complement person-to-person interactions. Groupware provides a tool for assigning tasks to group members and for monitoring the group's progress toward task completion with the objective of making the group more productive.

Time-Staged Delivery Systems

Time-staged delivery systems have some characteristics of a mail system. Time-staged delivery software allows users to identify a transmission package, designate one or more recipients of the package, initiate the delivery of the package, and specify a delivery priority. If we relate time-staged delivery and e-mail to regular mail service, e-mail is like express mail service whereas time-staged delivery is equivalent to parcel post or surface mail. E-mail is usually oriented toward short messages of several pages or less. Time-staged delivery systems may be used for short messages, for transaction routing, or to transmit entire files.

With time-staged delivery, the user specifies a required delivery time. The system then schedules the message transmission to meet the requested goal. Suppose a user needs to send a lengthy report from New York City to each of five manufacturing plants, and that the message must be available at each plant by 9:00 A.M. local time. The report to London must arrive several hours before the one destined for California, so it has a higher priority in transmission than the California-bound package. The delivery system also can use the delivery time to defer transmission until a more convenient time. Rather than sending data in real time, when the system may be quite busy, it can delay transmission until a less busy time, such as the early morning. In distributed processing environments, the ability to designate transmission packages and delivery times can be an important capability. An example of a time-staged delivery system is IBM's SNA delivery system (SNADS).

time-staged delivery systems
Software that allows users to identify a transmission package, designate one or more recipients of the package, and specify delivery priorities, sequences, and times.

GENERIC FUNCTIONS OF LAN SYSTEM SOFTWARE

Application software is designed to solve business problems. It is assisted in this goal by supporting system software such as the operating system (OS), database management systems (DBMSs), and data communication systems. Like all system software, LAN system software is essentially an extension of the OS. It carries out hardware-oriented LAN tasks, such as interfacing to the medium, and input/output (I/O) oriented tasks, such as directing print jobs and disk read/write requests to a server.

System software is designed to insulate applications from hardware details such as I/O and memory management. System software provides an interface through which the applications can request hardware services. The applications make requests for services, and system software contains the logic to carry out those requests for a specific kind of hardware. For example, an application makes disk access requests independent of the kind of disk drive being used. A disk driver is a component of the OS that fulfills the request for a specific kind of disk drive.

LAN system software resides both in the application's workstation and in the server, as illustrated in Figure 9-3. The workstation's LAN system software includes the redirector and the medium interface software. We use the example of a workstation environment to examine the interaction between workstation and server software components.

Consider a client workstation for which the server provides file and printer services. The workstation has local disk drives A (floppy disk), C (hard drive), and D (CD-ROM). The file server's disk drives are known to the workstation as drives F and G. The workstation's local printer ports are LPT1 and LPT2. A local ink-jet printer is attached to LPT1; output to LPT2 is directed to a network laser printer. The key to making this environment work is transparent access to all devices. From the user's perspective, printing to a network printer and accessing a network disk drive are transparent. Thus, the workstation user accesses remote drives F and G in exactly the same way as he accesses local drives A, C, and D. The user also prints to the laser printer as

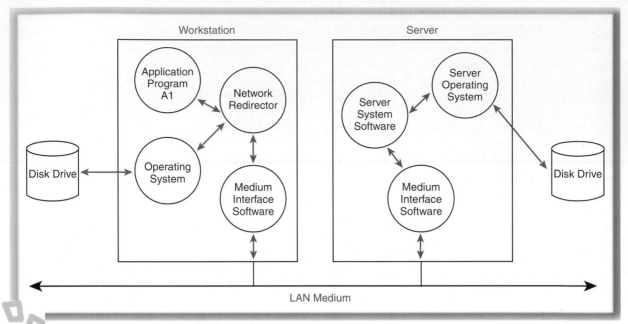

Figure 9-3   LAN System Software in Servers and Workstations

though it were locally attached. Transparent access to network drives is accomplished by the LAN system software. To see how, we consider an application that issues a read for a record located on a file or database server.

System Software Functions

In Chapters 7 and 8, you learned about the key hardware components involved in providing the physical connection between a LAN workstation and a server. LAN system software forms the logical connection by using the hardware to carry on communication sessions between applications on the workstation and applications on the server. The first function of the LAN system software is to set up these logical connections. For now, we assume that this is done when the user issues a server log-on request. If the logon is successful, the user can use the server in accordance with her security controls and access rights.

The OS running in the workstation (which often is Windows 98/2000/XP) is aware only of the devices physically attached to that workstation. In our example, the OS is capable of handling requests to drives A, C, and D and to the ink-jet printer attached to LPT1 on its own. However, it cannot handle I/O requests to drives F and G or direct output to the network printer at LPT2. Ordinarily, when an application on the workstation issues a file or print request, the request is accepted and carried out by the workstation's OS. If a request is made to access a device not attached to the workstation, the OS returns the error message "device not found." To prevent this error message from being returned when the workstation is attached to a LAN, the requests for drives F and G must be intercepted before they get to the OS. The software that reroutes I/O requests is generically called a **redirector**.

The redirector is a software module that intercepts all application I/O requests before they get to the workstation's OS. If the request is for a local device, the redirector

redirector LAN software that routes workstation (client) requests for data to the appropriate network server. In Windows-based peer-to-peer networks, the redirector program intercepts requests for files and printers and directs them to the appropriate remote device if the request is for non-local resources.

passes the request to the computer's OS. Thus, local device access requests are carried out as usual. If the redirector gets a request to access an application on a LAN server, it sends the request over the network to the server. This is illustrated in Figure 9-4.

The server receives a request for file or print service, or in this case, a request for a database record. Many workstations are attached to the network, and any of them can make server requests at any time. The server may receive several requests simultaneously, and efficiency requires that the server be able to work on multiple requests at once. This capability is known as **multithreading** because the server can have multiple transactions in progress at the same time. The server software must keep track of the progress of each transaction.

Suppose the server simultaneously receives two requests for a database record, three requests to write to a network printer, and one request to download an application program. These requests arrive in single file, as illustrated in Figure 9-5. The server accepts the first request, a database record read, and searches disk cache memory. If the record is not in cache memory, the server issues a disk read to satisfy the request. It also remembers the address of the workstation that requested the read. While the disk is working to find the requested record, the server takes the next request, a printer write request, and issues a write to the print queue file. The server then accepts the next request, one for downloading an application program, and issues a read request for the first segment of the program.

At this point, the server is notified that its read for the first database record has been completed. The server recalls the address of the workstation making the request and sends the record back to that workstation. Then the server takes the next request, a database read, and issues the read that satisfies the request. Thus, the server software spends most of its time changing between accepting requests, issuing reads or writes to

multithreading The capacity of a processor to work on multiple requests for the same program at once. Multithreading is an example of multitasking within a single program; it allows multiple streams of execution to take place concurrently within the same program with each stream processing a different transaction or message.

Figure 9-4   Redirector Software

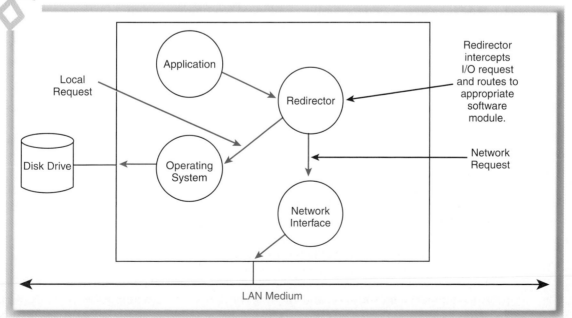

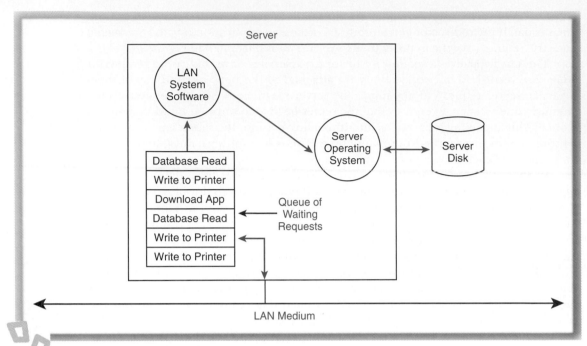

Figure 9-5   Server Request Queue

satisfy them, reacting to completions of those reads and writes, and sending the results back to the requester.

**client/server proto-
col** A communica-
tions protocol that
provides the structure
for server responses
to client requests in a
network.

The application/server protocol just described is an example of a **client/server protocol**. To understand the importance of the multithreading capability of the server, consider the following example of single-threading versus multithreading. Suppose you went to a restaurant, and your waitperson could wait on you only when all tables ahead of you were done. You would end up waiting a long time before getting service, but the service would be great when you finally got it: You would have your waitperson's full attention from placing your order to receiving and paying the check at the end of your meal. However, the waitperson would have large amounts of idle time waiting for the food to be cooked. In a fast-food restaurant, single-threading would mean waiting for the person ahead of you in line to be served before placing your order. Although a single-threading service protocol might be acceptable in a small LAN, in a larger LAN where the server(s) are likely to have multiple concurrent requests, the use of multithreading becomes essential.

We now look at the LAN system software in more detail. We discuss the software components and explore how each component becomes involved in handling a request for shared resources stored on a server.

LAN WORKSTATION SOFTWARE

LAN workstation software can also be divided into three classes: application software, workstation system software, and client network operating system software. LAN workstation system software consists of the workstation's operating system, utilities, drivers, and related software that manage I/O operations and the workstation's other hardware resources. Client network operating system (client NOS) software, which is sometimes called *client software*, makes it possible for workstations to interact with LAN servers and to gain access to the shared computing resources stored on LAN servers.

Workstation Software Interfaces

We use computers as tools to solve problems. Application software has the logic necessary for solving specific problems, but it does not do all the work essential to the problem solution; instead, it relies on system software to perform hardware-oriented tasks such as interfacing with disk drives and printers. Applications make requests to system software (typically operating systems), which then assists the applications in carrying out their work. System software support may come from workstation system software or client NOS software, depending on the application's needs. Workstation system software assists with local requests, and client NOS software assists with requests needing LAN services.

If you have experience with a programming language, you may be familiar with procedures that contain the logic to perform a certain kind of processing. You pass input to a procedure, and it carries out the necessary processing on the input and returns output. For example, a procedure called FINDMAXIMUM accepts a list of numbers as input and returns the largest value in the list. When you invoke the procedure, you are making a request. The procedure acts on your request and returns the results. It is not important that you know how the procedure arrived at its conclusion, only that the conclusion is correct. Similarly, when you make a read or write request to a local disk drive, you do not write directly to the disk. Instead, you pass data to your computer's OS, which carries out this activity on your behalf.

When an application requests a service from the OS, it does so by issuing a signal called an **interrupt**. A computer's OS recognizes many interrupts, some generated by application software and some generated by the hardware. Each interrupt reflects a different class of service. The client NOS software reacts to the interrupt and decides whether it is a server request or a local request. Thus, the *interrupt requests* (called *IRQs*) generated by the application must match those that are expected by the LAN software.

Today, most widely used software packages can run on a LAN; however, some applications operate correctly on one LAN implementation but not on a different one. This can happen because some application software is written specifically for one kind of LAN and generates the proper interrupts only for that LAN's software. For example, most widely used general-purpose application programs (such as those included in Microsoft Office) run correctly in LANs that use Windows 2000 Server, Windows NT, or Novell NetWare. These applications, however, may not run correctly in LANs that use Linux as the network operating system. Hence, when selecting software that is compatible with your hardware and LAN software, you also must determine whether the software will run correctly on the LAN network operating system that you will be using.

The compatibility of an application with a particular network operating system depends on whether or not the application issues interrupts and commands/requests for server-based resources in the predetermined format required by the network operating system's **application program interface (API)**. An API is a language and message format used by an application program to communicate with the operating system or some other control program, such as a communications protocol or database management system (DBMS). APIs are implemented by writing function calls in the program that provide the linkage to the required subroutine (such as "save" or "print" for execution). An API implies that some other program module is available in the

interrupt A signal issued by hardware or an application requesting a service from the operating system. The signal is designed to get the attention of the CPU and is usually generated when I/O is required. Hardware interrupts are generated when a key is pressed or when the mouse is moved. Software (application) interrupts are generated when the program requires disk input or output.

application program interface (API) A language and message format used by an application program to communicate with an operating system or another system control program such as a DBMS or communications protocol.

computer to perform the operation or that it must be linked into the existing program to perform the tasks.

Programmers in today's businesses must be able to understand APIs. Other than writing the business logic that performs the actual number crunching for business applications, the rest of programming consists of writing the code needed by the application to communicate with the operating system and other software programs. The APIs for operating systems can be intimidating, especially calls to print or display. Operating systems such as Windows, Macintosh OS, and UNIX each contain more than 1,000 API calls.

The ability of an application to work correctly with a workstation's operating system is also dependent on whether the application can issue interrupts and commands/requests for local services in the format required by the operating system's API. This is why you may find different versions of the same application for Windows XP and Macintosh OS. Today, network operating systems often support multiple APIs as well as multiple different client operating systems. This is what makes it possible for IBM–compatibles and Apple Macintosh microcomputers to be attached to the same LAN and to run the same applications.

Workstation System Software

The LAN system software installed in workstations basically consists of two parts: One part interfaces with the applications and the workstation's OS, and one part interfaces with the network hardware.

The portion of the software that interfaces with the applications, the redirector, is responsible for handling the application's interrupts. The application generally is not aware that the device it is reading from or writing to is a local device or another LAN–attached device such as a server. This means that any interrupt has the potential to be a LAN service request that must be acted on. The redirector, therefore, accepts all interrupts, whether they are for local or remote requests. Local requests are sent to the workstation's OS, and network requests are passed to the client NOS software installed in the workstation so that they can be sent to the appropriate LAN–attached device via the LAN's communication medium.

Different workstations connected to the same LAN may use different OSs. In a single LAN, some workstations may use a version of Microsoft Windows (XP, 2000, ME, 98, 95, or NT), some may use a version of Apple Macintosh OS, and some may use a version of Linux or UNIX. The client NOS software for LANs that supports heterogeneous client operating systems must be able to accommodate each of these versions and the interrupts they expect.

The medium-interface portion of the client NOS software installed in workstations has two basic functions: placing data onto the network's communication medium and receiving data from the network. This portion of the software is responsible for formatting a message block for transmission over the network. It is closely tied to the LAN system software installed on servers (server NOS software) because it must format message blocks so they are compatible with what is expected by the server; the client NOS software must be able to recognize the format of messages received from the server. This portion of the workstation's client NOS software also interfaces directly to the LAN adapter card.

Just as there may be multiple client operating systems within a single LAN, there may be more than one network operating system in use. For example, one server in a (single) LAN may run Windows 2000, a second server may run NetWare, and a third may run Linux. In order for a workstation to access the resources stored on each of these servers, its client NOS software must be able to appropriately format message blocks for each server as well as be able to recognize the formats of messages received from each server. The ability of a client workstation to transparently interact with multiple servers that run different network operating systems is called **universal client** capability.

Universal client capability requires support for

➤ *Multiple network redirectors.* These capture client interrupts and direct them to the appropriate local or network-attached device.

➤ *Multiple file systems.* Different network operating systems support different file management systems. For example, both Windows 2000 Server and Windows NT support either FAT (file allocation table) or NTFS (NT file system). It is possible for FAT to be supported on some servers and NTFS to be supported on other servers in the same LAN.

➤ *Multiple network transport protocols.* These are found at the network and transport layers of the OSI reference model and are responsible for packaging and transporting messages between clients and servers.

➤ *Multiple MAC–level clients and network drivers.* These enable the workstation to communicate with multiple servers that run different network operating systems.

Table 9-2 provides a summary of the network redirectors, file systems, network transport protocols, and MAC–level clients and network drivers that would have to be supported in a LAN with Windows NT, Windows 2000, and NetWare servers for workstations to have universal client capabilities. Table 9-2 assumes that there would be a mixture of workstation OSs within the LAN, including Windows 95, Windows 98, Windows ME, Windows NT/2000 Workstation, and Macintosh OS.

Supporting Remote Clients

The increasing popularity of mobile computing and telecommuting has increased the need to enable remote users to access shared computing resources stored on LAN servers. This need is usually addressed by installing a **remote access client** on the remote user's computer. The remote access client enables the user to connect to *remote access servers*, which are responsible for controlling access to shared resources within

universal client
A client workstation that is able to transparently interact with multiple servers that run different network operating systems or applications. Web browsers often enable workstations to be universal clients because they are platform-independent.

remote access client Software that enables a computer to connect to a server or other network device at another location or site.

Table 9-2   Supporting Universal Clients in Heterogeneous Platform LANs

Requirements for Supporting Universal Client Capability in a LAN with Multiple Network Operating Systems and Workstation Operating Systems		
Application redirectors	SMB (server message block)	NCP (NetWare core protocol)
File systems	FAT (file allocation table)	NTFS (NT file system)
Network transport protocols	NETBEUI (NetBIOS extended user interface—Microsoft)	TCP/IP, IPX/SPX, AppleTalk
MAC clients/drivers	NDIS (network data link interface—Microsoft)	ODI (open data link interface—Novell)

[1]*Windows 2000 Server, Windows NT, and Netware*
[2]*Windows XP, Windows NT Workstation, Windows 98/95, and Macintosh OS*

the LAN. Remote access servers typically include password systems or more sophisticated mechanisms for authenticating the identities of remote users. They are often also responsible for encrypting and decrypting messages exchanged between remote clients and servers. Remote access servers can be implemented as dedicated machines or as software installed in a LAN file server; access via the Internet may be supported in addition to dial-in access.

Peer-to-Peer Networking Functions

Most of the client operating systems in use today support peer-to-peer networking capabilities, including file and print sharing. For example, Microsoft's peer-to-peer networking support began with Windows 3.11—Windows for Workgroups—and has been included in all subsequently released versions of Windows, including Windows 95, Windows 98, Windows NT/2000 Workstation, Windows ME, and Windows XP.

File and print sharing are the most widely supported peer-to-peer networking capabilities in client operating systems. *File sharing* enables users to create shared directories on their workstations that other LAN users can access. For Windows users, access is gained via Network Neighborhood on the Windows desktop. Password protection is typically used for shared directories to ensure that files in the directories are only accessed by users who know the password. Peer-to-peer networking in operating systems that only support a FAT (file allocation table) system such as Windows 98 and Windows ME only enables two kinds of passwords to be assigned to shared folders: read only and full access. Network users who only know the read-only password for a shared directory (folder) can open the files in the directory but cannot modify/change the files; such users can save copies of the files they access to disk drives on their own workstation. Users with a full-access password can access files in the shared directory, modify the files, and even store new files to the directory. More extensive access rights can be assigned when an NTFS file system is used; NTFS is supported by Windows NT/2000 Workstation.

Password-controlled access to printers attached to a user's workstation is also supported by most of today's client operating systems. Users who know the password to a shared printer attached to another user's workstation are able to route print jobs to that printer. When file or printer sharing is enabled on a user's workstation, the workstation becomes a *nondedicated server* within the network. The distinction between dedicated and nondedicated servers is discussed in Chapter 7.

For LANs in small offices or homes, file and print sharing capabilities may be all the networking support that users require. These peer-to-peer networking functions can be implemented when user workstations running compatible operating systems are attached to a LAN via network adapter cards. It is important to note that file and print sharing capabilities are accomplished by networking capabilities within the client operating systems.The LAN's network operating system (NOS), if one is present, is not involved. In other words, if all the workstations in the LAN are running Windows 95, Windows 98, Windows Millennium Edition, or Windows NT/2000 Workstation, it is possible for them to share files and printers without having to install server NOS software. Only Microsoft client software is needed for file and printer sharing.

Plug-n-Play Capabilities

Another important feature of today's client operating systems is plug-n-play support. Plug-n-play (PnP) support enables the operating system to automatically detect the addition or removal of PnP devices (including network adapter cards); initiate adjustments in IRQ settings, communication channels, COM ports, memory addressing, and the start-up configuration files to avoid conflicts with other devices; and load any new drivers needed to support new PnP devices. The dynamic reconfiguration capabilities associated with PnP support in today's client operating systems has made it easier for networking professionals to install or replace network adapter cards and shared printers.

SERVER SOFTWARE

LAN system software installed on servers is more complex than that installed on client workstations. This is because the server software is usually multithreaded and because the software must work well with the server hardware to provide efficient service in response to client requests. In addition to multithreading, a number of other important functions are supported by the LAN system software installed in servers.

Server Operating Systems

Table 9-3 provides a summary of the leading network operating systems used in today's LANs. Each of these will be briefly described later in the chapter after we look at the functions that LAN network operating systems perform.

LAN NOS Functions

A LAN network operating system (NOS) provides a variety of special capabilities. Among these are I/O optimization, fault tolerance, directory services, application services, file services, networking services, network management services, and security services.

Optimized I/O   A primary service provided by a server is file access. Optimizing this task, or **I/O optimization**, increases the performance of the server. Some optimization methods are hardware oriented and some are software oriented. One commonly used technique is called *disk caching*, which we discussed in Chapter 7.

> **I/O optimization**
> A variety of ways employed to optimize the task of file access on servers. I/O optimization is designed to increase the performance of the server.

Table 9-3   Major LAN Network Operating Systems

LAN NOS	Vendor	Topologies	MAC Protocols
Windows 2000 Server	Microsoft	Star, bus, ring	CSMA/CD, token passing
Windows NT Server	Microsoft	Star, bus, ring	CSMA/CD, token passing
NetWare	Novell	Star, bus, ring	CSMA/CD, token passing
Linux	Red Hat, Caldera, and others (including freeware versions)	Star, bus, ring	CSMA/CD, token passing
Solaris	Sun	Star, bus, ring	CSMA/CD, token passing
AppleTalk	Apple	Star, bus	CSMA/CA, CSMA/CD, token passing

Table 9-4   Disk Seek Enhancement

(a)	Disk read requests (cylinder or track) in order of arrival	Number of cylinders moved (assume a starting position of cylinder 0)
	50, 250, 25, 300, 250, 50, 300	50 + 200 + 225 + 275 + 50 + 200 + 250 = 1,250
(b)	Disk read requests (cylinder or track) in optimal order	
	25, 50, 50, 250, 250, 300, 300	25 + 25 + 0 + 200 + 0 + 50 + 0 = 300
	Savings = 950 cylinders	

disk seek enhancement An I/O optimization technique that reduces the head movement during seeks and improves performance.

read-after-write A fault tolerance capability wherein data are read from disk immediately after being written for verification purposes. This allows immediate detection and correction of write errors due to system problems or bad disk sectors.

mirrored disks A fault tolerance technique in which two disks (or partitions) containing the same data are provided so that if one fails, the other is available, allowing processing to continue. Disk mirroring can be accomplished by writing the same data to two partitions of the same disk or to two separate disks within the same system.

redundant arrays of independent disks (RAID) A method of storing data on multiple hard-disk drives that increases fault tolerance, allows faster access, or both.

parity data In RAID technology, additional data that provide the ability to reconstruct data that have been corrupted. In a RAID system, parity data may be stored on a *parity drive*, a separate disk drive that holds parity bits for the disk array.

Another I/O optimization technique is **disk seek enhancement**. A disk read requires that the read/write heads be positioned to the proper disk location. The act of moving the read/write heads is called a *seek*. The place to which the heads are moved is called a *cylinder* or *track*. Disk requests typically arrive in random order. Disk seek enhancement arranges the requests in order so the read/write heads move methodically over the disk, reading data from the nearest location, as illustrated in Table 9-4. In Table 9-4(a), you can see the order in which several disk requests are received. Table 9-4(b) shows the optimum way to access those records and the savings in number of cylinders when processing the requests in the optimum order. Reducing the number of seeks improves performance.

Fault Tolerance   Some network operating systems (NOSs) provide increased reliability through a feature called *fault tolerance*. If you have only one server and it fails, the network is down. A LAN with fault tolerance allows the server to survive some failures that ordinarily would be disabling. Fault tolerance is usually provided by a combination of backup hardware components and software capable of using the backup hardware.

The lowest level of fault tolerance is the ability to recover quickly from a failure. This means that a failure that shuts the server down may occur, but the system can quickly be recovered to an operational state. One technique that makes this possible involves writing backup copies of critical disk information—disk directories, file allocation tables, and so on—to an alternative disk drive. Another helpful technique is called **read-after-write**. After writing data to a disk, the system reads the data again to ensure that no disk write errors occurred. If the data cannot be read again, the area of the disk containing that data is removed from future use, and the data is written to a good area of the disk.

Fault tolerance can also be provided by **mirrored disks**, which are two disks that contain the same data. Whenever a disk write occurs, the data is written to both disk drives. If one disk fails, the other is available and processing continues. Mirrored disks have an additional benefit: Two disk drives are available, so both disks can work simultaneously on behalf of two different requests. To add an additional level of fault tolerance, some LAN servers support duplexed disk controllers. In this configuration, mirrored disks are controlled by separate controllers rather than a single controller; if a controller fails, another is available to continue working. Thus, you can survive a controller failure and a disk failure.

Mirrored disk reliability can be extended by using **redundant arrays of independent disks (RAID)**. RAID technology spreads data over three or more disk drives. The stored data consists of the actual data plus **parity data** (additional data that provides the ability to reconstruct data that has been corrupted). If one drive fails, the data stored on that drive can be reconstructed from data stored on the remaining drives. Parity data can be reconstructed because the remaining parts of the file are still available. If a section of the file is lost, it can be reconstructed from the parity data and the remaining parts of the file. The advantage of RAID over mirroring is that fewer disk drives are required for redundancy. With mirroring, two drives of data require four disk drives; with RAID, the same information can be stored on three drives with the same level of reliability. Disk mirroring and RAID technology, illustrated in Figure 9-6, can provide more efficient data access because multiple disk drives are available for reading and writing.

The best fault tolerance is provided by **duplexed servers**. With this configuration, one server can fail and another is available to continue working. Even though it appears that this fault tolerance capability is primarily hardware oriented, the software must be able to take advantage of the duplexed hardware. A duplexed server is illustrated in Figure 9-7.

duplexed servers
A fault-tolerance technique in which one server can fail and another is available to continue working. Duplexed servers may both perform the same functions, or one may be a standby, ready to take over should the other fail.

Figure 9-6   Mirrored Disk Drives and RAID Technology

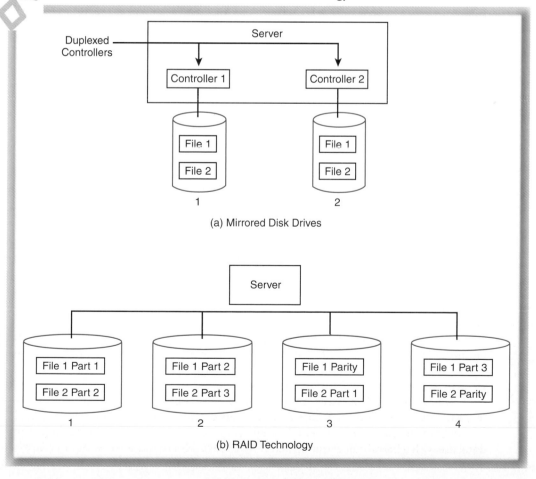

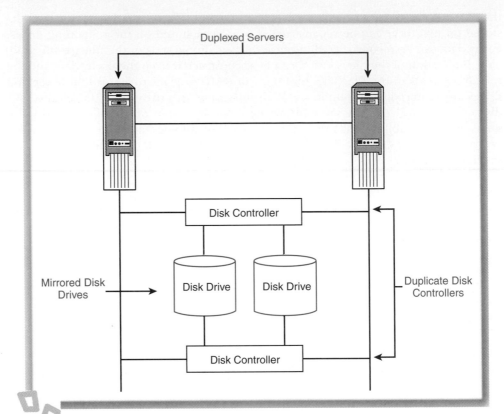

Figure 9-7   Duplexed Servers

clustering A fault-tolerance and perfor-mance enhancement capability whereby multiple servers are housed in the same location. Load balanc-ing is often used to distribute the work-load among clustered servers. If one server in a cluster of servers fails, the remaining servers assume the workload of the failed server.

hot swap Removing a component and re-placing it while the sys-tem is still operating.

global directory services A directory of names, profile infor-mation, and machine addresses of every user and resource on all networks that col-lectively comprise an enterprise-wide net-work. It is used to manage user accounts and network permis-sions across multiple servers and networks. Novell's NDS and Microsoft's Active Directory are ex-amples of global directory services.

A new fault-tolerant capability is **clustering**. Fault-tolerant clustering is supported by most LAN NOSs in use today. If one server in a cluster of servers fails, the remain-ing servers assume the workload of the failed server. The ultimate goal of server clus-tering is to provide load balancing and *failover* capability. Failover is the ability of remaining cluster servers to assume the workload of a failed server in the cluster.

Hot-swappable components also enhance server fault tolerance. A **hot swap** involves pulling out a component and replacing it while the system is still operating. Redundant systems within servers enable virtually any duplexed component to be hot swappable; among these components are drives, circuit boards, and power supplies. A hot swap is sometimes called a *hot fix*.

Directory Services   LAN NOSs have to include a file or database that stores infor-mation about users and system resources, such as servers, printers, and applications. There are two major kinds of directory services used in today's LANs: global directory services and domain directory services.

Global directory services store the information about network users and resources in a single database. This database provides network managers with a single, comprehen-sive view of the network as well as a single point of resource and user management. A database with a hierarchical tree structure (whose levels are modeled after or comply with the X.500 standard discussed previously in the chapter) is commonly used. Figure 9-8

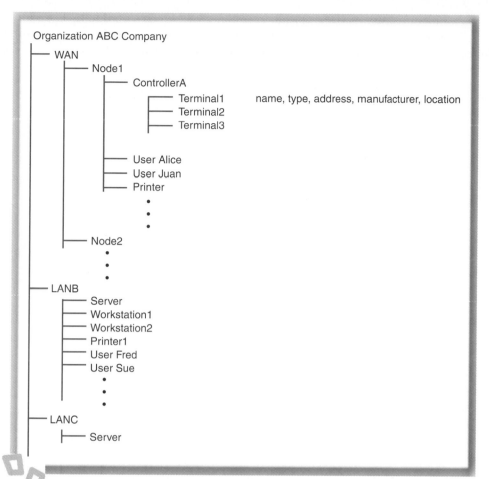

Figure 9-8   Sample Directory Tree

provides an example of the hierarchical tree structure within a global directory service database. It is important to note that all servers within the network can "see" all other servers as well as all other parts of the network. This facilitates the job of making it possible for a user whose workstation is attached to the same LAN as one server in the network to be provided with access to resources stored on servers in other LANs in the network.

A global directory services database can be centralized or distributed. The database is centralized when it is stored on a single server within the network; it is distributed when multiple servers are involved in storing the database. Two kinds of database distribution are possible: physical distribution and replication. With physical distribution, portions of the database are physically stored on multiple servers distributed across the network—no server stores the complete database. When the global directory services database is replicated, identical copies of the database are stored on multiple servers. As you might guess, replication enhances fault tolerance by ensuring redundancy. Regardless of whether the database is centralized or distributed, global directory services provide network managers with a single, comprehensive view of the entire network.

Global directory services typically consider users, servers, and network resources as *network objects*. As illustrated in Figure 9-8, some objects are subordinate to other objects in the hierarchical tree. Objects that can have subordinate items are called *container objects*. Examples of the container objects defined in NDS (Novell Directory Services) include country, organization, and organizational unit (see Table 9-5). Objects that cannot have subordinate objects are called *leaf objects*. Some of the leaf objects available in NDS are computer, group, server, print queue, print server, printer, user, and volume. Each global service directory's hierarchical tree has a unique top-level object called the *root* object or the *top*. Distributed portions of the directory are called *partitions*. Global directory services use a hierarchical naming convention, with the naming hierarchy up to 15 levels deep. A generic four-level object name in the directory might be *company-name.region-name.department-name.user-name*.

Three examples of global directory services are as follows:

1. NDS (Novell Directory Services) is a global, hierarchical directory capable of spanning an entire enterprise network that allows replication and distribution. The ITU X.500 standard served as a model for the implementation of NDS; however, NDS is not X.500 compliant. Defining the NDS directory tree is accomplished via Nwadmin, which is a Windows application. The template for the definition of NDS network objects is called the *schema*. The schema contains the definitions of the objects that can be included in the directory and the properties of those objects. Developers are able to extend the schema by adding new objects or new properties to existing objects. This is accomplished via application program interface (API) procedures available in a developers' toolkit.

2. Active Directory is an advanced hierarchical directory service that supports Windows 2000 Server. Its naming system is built on the Internet's Domain Name System (DNS). Work groups within the network are given domain names just like Web sites. Active Directory can be used in heterogeneous networks (networks whose servers run two or more network operating systems) that include other global directory services such as NDS and NIS.

3. NIS (Network Information Services) is a naming service developed by SunSoft that was once known as *Yellow Pages*. It enables network managers to easily add, delete, or relocate network resources. NIS has become a de facto UNIX standard.

domain directory services A type of directory service that includes the names and profiles of users and network resources located on primary (or secondary) domain controllers within Windows NT domains. It is used to manage user accounts and permissions within and across domains.

Domain directory services subdivide networks into sets of linked subdivisions called *domains*. Within each domain there is a primary server called the *primary domain controller (PDC)* that maintains the directory of users and network resources within the domain. Redundant backups to the PDC as well as other servers in a domain are called *secondary* or *backup* domain controllers. Each domain's directory is established and maintained individually. An individual user account is associated with a single domain; however, the user is able to access network resources (such as servers) in other domains through the creation of *interdomain trusts*. Domain directory services only exist in Windows NOSs, including Windows NT/2000 Server; Novell and UNIX do not use them

LDAP (lightweight directory access protocol) A protocol used to define access to directory services based on the X.500 directory.

Because enterprise networks are often heterogeneous and consist of servers using multiple network operating systems that support different directory services, it has become increasingly important for different directory services to be able to share information with one another. The primary protocol that has emerged to ensure interoperability among different directory services is **LDAP (lightweight directory access protocol)**. LDAP is a simplified version of DAP (directory access protocol), which is used to access information in X.500 directories. LDAP is not a directory service; it is a protocol for exchanging information among different directory services. Network managers can use LDAP to manage global directory services via the Internet using TCP/IP as the transport protocol. LDAP is a sibling protocol to HTTP and FTP. Network managers can gain access to Microsoft's Active Directory via LDAP–compliant

Table 9-5   Sample NDS Objects and Properties

Object	Some Properties	
Computer	Network address	Server
	Serial number	Status
	Operator	Owner
Country (container)	Name	Description
Group	Common name	Full name
	Description	Members
	E-mail address	
NetWare server	Network address	Status
	Operator	Version
Organization	Name	Postal code
	Description	State/province
	Postal address	Telephone number
Print server	Network address	Status
	Operator	
Printer	Default queue	Operator
	Host device	Status
	Network address	
Queue	Device	Server
	Network address	Volume
	Operator	
User	Account balance	Language
	Address	Last log-in time
	E-mail address	Log-in script
	Fax number	Password expiration
	Groups	time, change allowed,
	Home directory	unique required,
	Telephone number	required, minimum
		length
		User ID
Volume	Host server	Status

clients as well as through *ADSI (Active Directory Services Interface)*. ADSI can also be used to access the information in other vendors' directory services. *ODSI (Open Directory Services Interface),* like ADSI, is a programming interface from Microsoft that can be used to access network naming services and directory services.

Application Services

The emergence of client/server computing as a predominant computing environment has made it more important for network operating systems to provide high-quality application services. As discussed in Chapter 8, today's client/server computing environments in LANs are often multitiered with distributed applications. Both 2-tier and 3-tier client/server computing may be implemented within a single LAN. Even in 2-tiered systems, there are distinct client and server portions of applications that must interact to complete processing tasks. In 2-tiered client/server architectures, this means that server network operating systems must be able to efficiently accept/process client requests for application services, execute the back-end portion of applications required to satisfy client requests, and transmit the results of requested application services back to distributed clients. In 3- or n-tiered client/server architectures, server NOS must be able to efficiently carry out all application services tasks found in 2-tiered C/S architectures as well as to efficiently process requests for application services from other servers.

In today's networks, the ability of a server NOS to function as a high-performance application server boils down to how well it supports **symmetrical multiprocessing (SMP)**. An SMP system has multiple CPUs that share memory, processing responsibility, and I/O paths. Load balancing is supported in SMP servers to ensure that processing tasks are distributed across CPUs in a manner that expedites their completion. Server NOSs that support SMP vary in the maximum number of CPUs within the server that can be used; however, all server network operating systems that support SMP provide multithreading and preemptive multitasking. They also avoid conflicts among applications by running different application programs in separate, protected memory locations.

Historically, Windows NT developed a reputation for providing stronger support for application services than Novell NetWare; NetWare developed a reputation for providing stronger support than Windows NT in the areas of file and print services. Over time, however, both NT (which morphed into Windows 2000 Server) and NetWare have made progress in overcoming their weaknesses and building on their strengths.

symmetrical multi-processing (SMP)
An SMP system has multiple CPUs that are alike and that share memory, processing responsibility, and I/O paths.

File Services

Like other files stored on computers, a server's application programs are stored using a particular file system. Server network operating systems vary in the kinds and number of file systems that they support. Some server network operating systems support multiple file systems on a single server through the creation of multiple partitions on the server's disk drive. A Windows NT Server, for example, may support NTFS (NT file system) in one disk partition and FAT (file allocation table) in a second partition. Multiple partitions can also be created to enable more than one operating system to be installed on the same computer. For example, Windows NT could be installed in one partition and Windows 98 in another. Computers with different operating systems installed in two different partitions are called *dual-boot* machines. When a dual-boot machine is turned on, users are able to select which one they want to use. Many server NOS products make it possible to partition disks during the installation process. Third-party products like PartitionMagic make it relatively easy to create and manage disk partitions. Most third-party products support NTFS, FAT, FAT32, and Linuxext2/Swap file systems.

NFS (network-aware file system) is another file system that is widely supported by server network operating systems. NFS is the native file system on UNIX servers. Because UNIX is widely used by Internet hosts, it is important for other server NOSs to support NFS.

In today's client/server network architectures, it is very important for a server NOS to support multiple file systems. As client/server applications execute on an application server, they often need request application services from other servers that employ a different file system. This is especially critical in n-tiered C/S architectures.

Networking Services

Just as it is important for client network operating systems to be able to interface with multiple server network operating systems in today's client/server networks, it is equally important for a server's NOS to be able to interface with a variety of client operating systems. Server network operating systems vary in the number of client operating systems that they support, but all are capable of interfacing with some combination of the following: Windows XP, Windows Millennium Edition (ME), Windows

98/95, Windows NT/2000 Workstation, Macintosh OS, UNIX, Linux, and DOS. Some server network operating systems are capable of interoperating with older versions of Windows (such as Windows 3.11). Increasingly, support is also being provided for the operating systems used in wireless devices, including Palm OS and Windows CE.

Other networking services provided by a server's network operating system may include support for multiple network protocols, multiple network adapter cards, multiprotocol routing, remote access services, and gateway services. Each of these is briefly described here.

➤ Support for multiple network protocols means that the server network operating system is able to simultaneously accept packets from multiple network-layer protocols. Although virtually all of today's server network operating systems support TCP/IP, many also support IPX/SPX or Apple Talk.

➤ Each server connects to a LAN via at least one network adapter card (network interface card). However, if a server's NOS is capable of simultaneously communicating with multiple network adapters, it is capable of supporting multiple network connections. The ability for a server NOS to support multiple simultaneous network connections is especially valuable in networks that use LAN switches.

➤ Support for **multiprotocol routing** means that the server NOS is capable of simultaneously processing multiple network protocols. This goes beyond support for multiple protocols, because the server NOS is able to translate messages received from a client or server in one format into the format required by another client or server. For example, the server NOS may receive a client request for application services in IPX/SPX and can only satisfy the client's request with the help of another server whose NOS does not support IPX/SPX. In order to get the other server's help, the server must convert the client's request from IPX/SPX to TCP/IP format before passing it along to the second server. When the response is received from the second server in the TCP/IP format, the server can repackage the response in the IPX/SPX format for delivery to the client.

➤ Remote access support means that the server NOS is capable of providing remote users (such as telecommuters and mobile users) with reliable access to the full range of network services available to local users.

➤ Gateway services enable LAN clients or servers to access network resources in networks that cannot be interfaced via network layer protocols. In today's n-tiered client/server networks, it makes more sense for a server NOS to provide gateway services than to distribute these capabilities among multiple clients.

multiprotocol routing Providing routing capabilities for two or more communication protocols. This enables the server to provide users in two or more different networks with access to shared computing resources.

Network Management Services

Server network operating systems have a number of built-in network management services. These include directory management tools (such as NetWare's NWADMIN utility), user account creation and management, tools for simultaneously managing multiple servers, tools for monitoring server performance and CPU utilization, tools for analyzing network traffic, tools for managing network file systems (including compressing/archiving infrequently used files), tools for managing backups, and tools for recovering from server failures. These capabilities are addressed more fully in Chapter 15. At this point, however, it is important for you to note that numerous network management capabilities are bundled with server network operating systems.

Security Services

Today's network operating systems include a number of mechanisms for ensuring network security. These include authentication services, authorization services, data encryption, and auditing services.

authentication services Server security processes concerned with verifying the identity of users that log onto a network.

Authentication Services   Server security processes concerned with determining which users are attempting to access the network are called **authentication services**. Most server security processes require users to provide *authentication credentials* to log onto the network and access network resources. *User identification* and *proof of identity* are the two major kinds of authentication credentials that users are required to provide. A user name or log-in name is the major form of user identification required to log on; a password is the most common form of proof of identity. The authentication credentials provided by users who attempt to log onto the network are compared to those in the directory service database. When these match, the user is allowed to log onto the network.

Most server NOSs enable network administrators to create temporary or guest accounts that enable users to log onto the network and access a restricted set of network resources. In many instances, these are authenticated, but sometimes they are not. For example, users who provide a valid user name or log-in name but an expired password may be allowed one or more "grace" logons; they are authenticated but are prompted to change their expired password before accessing the network resources that they normally have rights to access. In some instances, guest users are not authenticated. This is common when users from outside an organization wish to view Web pages on the organization's Web server.

authorization services Control user access to network resources. The set of authorized users of a particular network resource is often maintained in an access control list.

Authorization Services   **Authorization services** control user access to network resources. Few network users have access to all network resources; most are only allowed access to a subset of the network's resources. *Access control lists* are maintained in the directory services databases used with most of today's server NOSs that specify which network resources a user can access as well as the user's permitted access level. Examples of access levels (rights) that users can have in NetWare LANs are provided in Table 9-6.

When a user tries to access a network resource, his authentication credentials are compared to the access control list to determine the user's access level to the resource.

Table 9-6   Examples of Access Rights That Can Be Granted to Users in NetWare LANs

NDS Object Right	Description
Browse	This is the right to see an object in the NDS hierarchical tree. This is essentially "read only" access.
Create	The user is allowed to create new subordinate objects to the current object. This implies that the current object is a container object.
Delete	A user must have this right to delete an object in the NDS tree. In some instances, the user may be able to delete subordinate objects but not the object itself.
Rename	This enables the user to change the name of an object within the NDS tree. Typically, a very restricted number of users are granted the privilege to rename a particular object.
Supervisor	Users with supervisor privileges are granted all rights to an object; they may create, delete, or rename the NDS object and grant other users the right to browse and create/delete/rename subordinate objects.

If, for example, a user in a NetWare LAN attempts to view the NDS root directory, his authorization credentials would be compared to the access control list in the NDS directory service database. If the comparison indicates that the user has the right to browse the root directory (see Table 9-6), the root directory would appear on the user's screen. If the comparison indicates that the user does not have the right to browse the root directory, the server NOS would return an error message, indicating that the user does not have sufficient rights to access this network resource.

Access restrictions can also extend to when, where, and how the user can log onto the network (see Table 9-7). For example, users can be restricted to logging onto the network from particular workstations during specified times of the day and

Table 9-7   Examples of Network Access Controls Supported by NetWare and Windows NT

Access Control	Description	NetWare Support	Windows NT Support
Password expiration	A user's password will expire after a specified time period (e.g., 60 days) or date.	X	X
Minimum password length	Users must select passwords that have or exceed a specified number of characters.	X	X
Password uniqueness	Users cannot use the same password when they change passwords.	X	X
Account lockout	Users cannot log onto the network for a specified time period after a specified number of unsuccessful log-on attempts.	X	X
Workstation restrictions	A user is allowed to log onto the network from a single or specified set of workstations.	X	X
Time restrictions	A user is allowed to log onto the network only during specified hours or on specified days.	X	X
Require passwords	This control requires users to provide passwords when they log onto the network.	X	X
Password changes	This control allows users to change passwords so long as they meet the minimum length restriction and are changed prior to expiration.	X	X
Concurrent log-in restrictions	This control limits the number of concurrent network logins a user may have.	X	No
Grace logins	This control enables users whose passwords have expired to log onto the network using their old password a specified number of times; when the specified limit is exceeded, users will be prompted to change their passwords or to contact the network administrator for a new one.	X	No

days of the week. For added security, users can be required to change their passwords at regular intervals and to use unique passwords with a minimum length (e.g., five characters) to thwart password theft and the use of valid user accounts by unauthorized users.

Today, the authorization services incorporated in server NOSs enable access rights to be assigned to users when user accounts are created. *User templates* can be created to facilitate the process of granting access rights to users when new accounts are created. User templates specify rights that all new users have to network resources. For example, the user template may specify that all new users are allowed to log onto the network between 6 A.M. and 7 P.M. Monday through Friday; that their passwords must be a minimum of five characters long; and that they can access all Office XP applications stored on network servers.

Today's authorization services also typically support *group templates*. Group templates enable members of the same group to be assigned a consistent set of rights to network resources beyond those specified by user templates. By indicating that a particular user is a member of a group, she is automatically granted the rights to access the network resources specified in the group template. When group or user templates are modified, the rights of all group members or network users are automatically updated.

Data Encryption   *Encryption* is the process of converting data into a difficult-to-decipher form before it is transmitted over a network from one computer to another; *decryption* is the process of converting an encrypted message back to its original, unencrypted form. The goal of encryption is to thwart efforts to intercept authentication credentials or important data during its transmission across the network.

Most of today's server NOSs encrypt the authentication credentials that users provide when logging onto the network. Many support the capability of encrypting all messages exchanged between clients and servers. Two popular protocols for encrypting authentication credentials are *PAP (password authentication protocol)* and *CHAP (challenge/handshake authentication protocol)*.

Auditing Services   Auditing services are another important aspect of security services found in today's server NOSs. Auditing services keep track of all network log-on attempts, valid and invalid, successful and unsuccessful. They also monitor all user attempts to access network resources, including user attempts to access resources they do not have rights to access (see Table 9-8). Through auditing services, network managers are able to keep a running log of the resources used by individual users and groups. Running logs of attempts to access the network or specific network resources by unauthorized users are also maintained. Such services can play a key role in network management beyond maintaining network security.

Table 9-8   Sample Audit Events

Create/delete directory	File open/close/create/delete	File read/write
File rename/move	User logon/logoff	User creation/deletion
Print queue create/delete	Server down/restart	Volume mount/demount

Other Important NOS Functions

LAN NOSs provide several other functions beyond those discussed in the previous section. These include print services, backup services, and shared services.

Print Services

LAN users typically share LAN printers. Although only one LAN user can be using a printer to physically print at any given moment, several users may need to logically be allowed to send print jobs to the same printer at the same time. Logical access to a printer by multiple users typically means that printed output is first written to a disk file and subsequently printed when the printer is physically available. The software subsystem that allows several users to logically write to one printer at the same time is called a **spooler.** The operation of a spooler is shown in Figure 9-9. Let us trace the activity of a print job through the spooler.

A user at one workstation is using a word processing program to create a report, and a user at another workstation is using a spreadsheet program to prepare a budget. At nearly the same time, each user selects "Print" from the application program's File menu. The output is directed to LPT2 on each system. On each system, LPT2 is mapped by the network's print services software to a laser printer attached to the LAN's file server. Before sending the print job to the printer, each application first "opens" the printer. The redirector at each workstation directs the "open" request to the server. When the server receives the open request, it is passed to the spooler software. The spooler software prepares to receive each workstation's printed output into a disk file. When each application receives an acknowledgment that the printer has been successfully opened, it begins to send output to the printer.

The spooler receives the output from each workstation and stores the output in that workstation's print file on disk. This process continues until each workstation is finished sending the output to be printed. When the application closes the printer file, the print job is ready to be physically printed by the printer.

When a print job has been saved to disk, the spooler schedules the job for printing. Spoolers have a priority scheme by which they decide which job prints next. Some spoolers print the jobs in the order in which they became ready to print (first in, first out); some print the smallest available job; others print jobs according to user-assigned priorities. When the job has been printed, it may be removed from the disk to make room for other print jobs. Alternatively, the job may be held on disk for printing at a later time, for printing to a different device, or for perusal from a workstation. Spooler systems provide a variety of options regarding the association of logical print devices with physical printers and the treatment of jobs captured in the spooler files. Some of these options are listed in Table 9-9.

spooler A software system that collects printer output (typically on disk) and schedules the data for printing. *SPOOL* is an acronym for *simultaneous peripheral operations online.*

Backup Services

In Chapter 7, we discussed backup hardware and media used in LANs. The software used to perform the backups is as important as the hardware. Backup software is responsible for reading the files being backed up and writing them to the backup device. During recovery, a restoration module reads the backup medium and writes the data back to disk. Several backup software options are available. They all provide the basic functions of backing up and restoring data. However, they differ with respect to backup and restoration procedure, including the options they provide, the devices they support, and their ease of use. Backup devices often come with a backup/restore program (both capabilities are contained on one program), and most LAN system software includes a backup/restore module. Some LAN administrators choose to

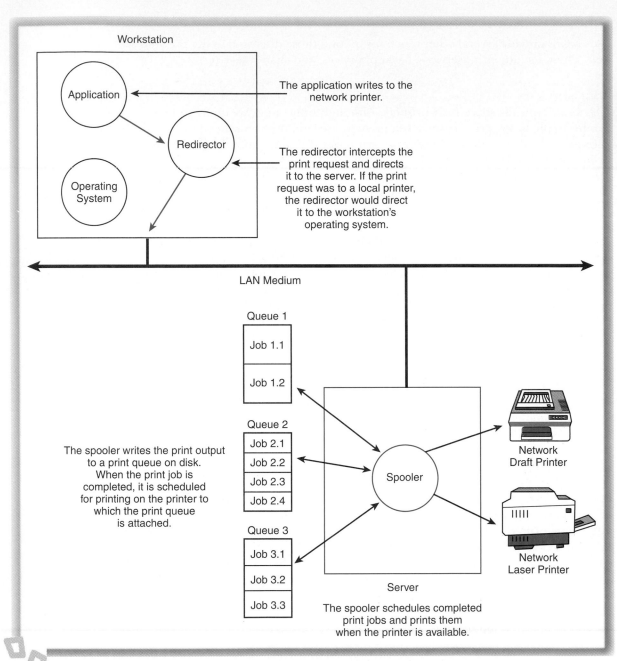

The application writes to the network printer.

The redirector intercepts the print request and directs it to the server. If the print request was to a local printer, the redirector would direct it to the workstation's operating system.

The spooler writes the print output to a print queue on disk. When the print job is completed, it is scheduled for printing on the printer to which the print queue is attached.

The spooler schedules completed print jobs and prints them when the printer is available.

Figure 9-9 Spooler Operation

Table 9-9   Spooler Options

Collect printed output	Attach/detach printers from print queue
Direct print jobs to designated printers	Set/change job priorities
Hold jobs in disk queue after printing	Add/delete printers
Hold jobs in disk queue before printing	Start/stop printers
View jobs on hold in print queue	Start/stop spooler process
Set number of print copies	Print banners
Set print job priorities	Close print jobs based on time-out interval
Delete jobs from print queue	Print statistical reports

purchase a separate, more functional backup system than the LAN or backup device version. Table 9-10 lists some features supported by backup software.

Shared Services

The ability to share network resources in a cost-effective manner is one of the major business motives for installing LANs. Server NOSs play an important role in managing the sharing of network resources by LAN users. In some cases, network application software works along with the server NOS to ensure resource sharing. Four major aspects of network resource sharing are hardware configuration management, application setting management, contention management, and data access security.

Hardware Configuration Management   Software written for stand-alone computers that are not attached to networks need not be concerned with problems of multiple computer configurations. In networks, however, there can be a great deal of variation in workstation memory, disk configuration, printer configuration, and monitor support. In a stand-alone system, the application software is set up to match the configuration of that system. However, a LAN might have many different workstation configurations, and application software stored on network servers should support each configuration as much as possible.

Some applications support only one configuration. The hardware settings of such applications are stored in a single file. One way to use this kind of application in a LAN

Table 9-10   Backup Software Capabilities

Back up all files	Create new index on tape and disk
Back up all files modified since a particular date	Maintain cross-reference of serial numbers and backup
Back up by directory	Manual backup
Back up by list of files	Automatic backup by time or calendar
Back up all but a list of files to be excluded	Start backup from workstation or server
Back up by index	Data compression
Back up by interface to a database	Multivolume backup
Back up using wildcard characters in filenames	Generate reports

is to configure the application for the lowest common denominator of hardware and have each user get essentially the same configuration. Users with high-resolution color graphics monitors might have images displayed in monochrome at low resolution, or a user CD-rewritable drive might have to use a hard disk drive rather than the CD-RW drive for some files. Usually, LAN administrators can avoid the least common denominator approach by storing multiple versions of the application in different disk directories. Users can then use the configuration that most closely matches their computer's hardware configuration profile.

Some applications allow several configuration files and decide which to use by a run-time parameter or by making a default choice if the start-up parameter is not specified. LAN administrators can provide each user with a tailored environment by using a batch start-up file that is executed when the user logs onto the network.

Applications designed for LAN use usually have a user-oriented configuration file. Each LAN user has their personal configuration that is custom-tailored for the specific user and the specific hardware. This provides users with the most flexibility and requires little or no customization by the LAN administrator. Examples of user configuration options are listed in Table 9-11.

Application Setting Management   The software equivalent of hardware configuration management is application setting management. Ideally, users tailor application settings to meet personal preferences. One user may prefer the word processor application to display green characters on a black background with tabs at every five character positions. Another user might prefer white characters on a blue background with tabs at every four character positions. Each user should receive these settings as the default. Application settings can be defined in a way similar to setting hardware options.

Contention Management   You learned a little about contention within LANs in Chapters 7 and 8. Remember that whenever two Ethernet LAN clients use the communication medium to transmit data at the same time, collisions can occur. The media access control protocol used in Ethernet LANs, CSMA/CD, is an example of a contention-based communications protocol. Collisions and collision recovery reduce the throughput of cable-based LANs that use CSMA/CD. Contention for shared network resources can also occur when multiple requests for the same file or database record are simultaneously received by a server.

A classic contention problem is illustrated by two users working on one document or data record at the same time. The same kind of problem can occur when two users access and update the same database record. A primitive way to handle contention is simply to avoid it by scheduling user activities so they do not interfere with each other. On small LANs, this may be possible, but as the number of concurrent users increases, this method becomes clumsy. Rather than avoiding contention, an application or LAN software should prevent contention problems by exerting controls over files or records.

Table 9-11   User Configuration Options

Default disk drive	Disk drive/directory search paths
Default disk directory	Printer mappings
Disk drive mappings	Initial program/menu

One prevention mechanism is activated when an application opens a file. The three basic file open modes are exclusive, protected, and shared. In **exclusive open mode**, an open request is granted only if no other user already has the file open. File open requests from other users also are denied until the application having an exclusive open closes the file.

Exclusive opens may be too restrictive for some applications. Suppose two users, Alice and Tom, are both working on the same word processing document. Alice needs to update the document, and Tom only needs to read it. In this case, Tom will not interfere with Alice's work. A **protected open mode** can satisfy both users' needs. Protected open mode is granted only if no other user has already been granted exclusive or protected mode. Once a file is open in protected mode, only the application with protected open can update the document. **Shared open mode** allows several users to have the file open concurrently. In shared update mode, all users can update the file. In shared read-only mode, all users can read the file but cannot write to it. If Alice opens the document in protected mode and Tom opens the document in shared read-only mode, Alice can read and update the document, but Tom can only read it. Furthermore, Tom cannot open the document in exclusive, protected, or shared update mode while a protected open exists.

Sometimes a read-only application must be protected against file updates. An application that is doing a trial balance of an accounting file must prohibit updates during the reading and calculations. If another application makes changes while the file is being read, the figures may not balance. The trial-balance application can protect against this by opening the accounts file in protected read-only mode. This prevents other processes from opening the file in update mode while allowing them to open the file in shared read-only mode. Table 9-12 shows the combinations of exclusive, protected, and shared open modes.

Exclusive and protected open modes are sufficient for meeting some contention problems, such as our word processing example. However, they are overly restrictive for other applications, such as database processing. One objective of database applications is to help several users share data. Exclusive opens allow only one user at a time to use the data. The problem with file open contention resolution is overcome by exerting controls at a lower level, the record level. Record-level controls are called **locks**.

Suppose Alice and Tom want to update a database. As long as they are using different records, they will not interfere with each other. However, suppose that at some time both Alice and Tom need to access and update the same record, leading to contention problems. If Alice locks the record when accessing it, Tom's read request will be denied until Alice unlocks the record. This process is illustrated in Figure 9-10. Note that Tom must wait until the record has been unlocked before being allowed to proceed.

exclusive open mode A file open mode in which an open request is granted only if no other user has the file opened already.

protected open mode A file open mode that is granted only if no other user has already been granted exclusive or protected mode.

shared open mode A file open mode that allows several users to have a file open concurrently.

locks Record- or file-level control that overcomes the problem with file open contention.

Table 9-12   Comparison of Open Modes

Open Mode Requested	Currently Opened As			
	Exclusive	**Protected**	**Shared Update**	**Shared Read-Only**
Exclusive	Denied	Denied	Denied	Denied
Protected	Denied	Denied	Denied	Granted
Shared update	Denied	Denied	Granted	Granted
Shared read-only	Denied	Granted	Granted	Granted

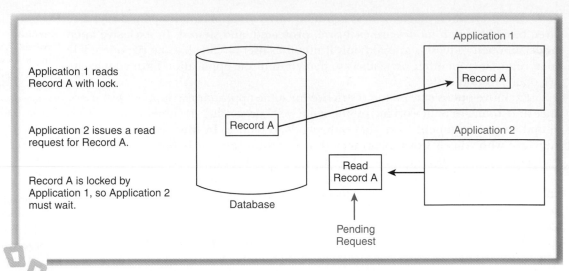

Application 1 reads
Record A with lock.

Application 2 issues a read
request for Record A.

Record A is locked by
Application 1, so Application 2
must wait.

Figure 9-10   Record Locking and Accessibility

Record locking can cause another problem: deadlock, or deadly embrace. Suppose that Alice and Tom are accessing the database. Alice's application reads and locks record A and, at nearly the same time, Tom's application reads and locks record B. After reading record A, Alice attempts to read record B and, of course, waits because the record is locked. If Tom then attempts to read record A, deadlock occurs: Alice and Tom are waiting for each other, and neither can continue until the record they are waiting for is unlocked, which can never happen because there is a circular chain of users waiting on each other. Three or more users can also be involved in this circular chain of events. The deadlock problem is illustrated in Figure 9-11. Deadlock avoidance or resolution methods exist but are beyond the scope of this text. You can read about these methods in many database texts.

Some database systems take care of contention for users. These systems recognize when contention is occurring and prevent the problems associated with it. One convention used to do this is outlined as follows:

➤ User A reads record X.
➤ User B reads record X (and the read is allowed).
➤ User A updates record X (and the update is allowed).
➤ User B attempts to update record X.
➤ The DBMS recognizes that the record has been changed since user B read it.
➤ The DBMS sends the revised copy of record X to user B and notifies the user that the update was rejected because the record was changed by another user.
➤ User B reissues the update or takes another course of action.

In selecting LAN software, it is critical that you understand the problems of configuration and contention. If these issues are not resolved, the effectiveness of the system is reduced or, worse yet, the data becomes corrupted. Sharing data has another side effect that must be addressed: security.

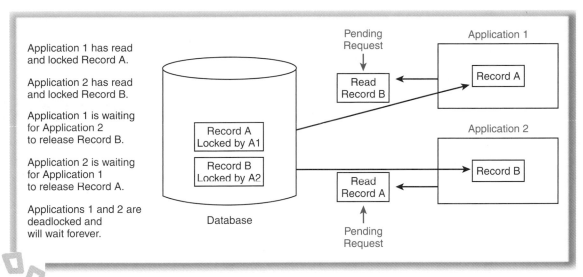

Figure 9-11   Deadlock

Data Access Security   The operating systems used with today's microcomputers are capable of providing file security, but only when they are capable of file sharing. File sharing is discussed previously in the chapter in the section on peer-to-peer networking. In some network environments, multiple users may use the same workstation at different times of the day. For example, two employees who work different shifts within the same organization may be assigned to the same cubicle and workstation. Even though only one employee uses the microcomputer at any point in time, mechanisms need to be in place to ensure that each does not interfere with the other's work. Without data access security mechanisms in place, these users not only have access to another user's sensitive data, but also might accidentally (or intentionally) remove the other user's files. Without data access security mechanisms, access to the computer essentially provides access to all data stored on that computer.

When two or more users share a stand-alone microcomputer, they are limited with respect to their ability to protect that data from unauthorized reading, changes, or destruction. To protect work, a user could store data on a removable disk and store it in a secure place when it is not being used. Another alternative is using applications that provide password security or allow hiding or encrypting data to protect it from misuse.

Today's server NOSs can manage data access security for users who share the same workstation. An individual user's work files can be stored in *user directories* on server disks instead of in files/directories on workstation disks. Like other network resources, files and directories stored on network servers can be restricted or shared through the assignment of access rights. Table 9-13 summarizes the file and directory rights that can be assigned to authorized users in LANs running Novell NetWare.

The LAN system software used in today's networks must also be capable of protecting against software piracy and assisting in preventing the introduction of computer viruses. These and other kinds of network security are discussed in more detail in Chapter 16.

Table 9-13   File and Directory Rights in Novell NetWare

File/Directory Right	Abbreviation	Description
Supervisory	[S]	All rights to the directory, its subdirectories, and their contents
Read	[R]	The right to read (view) an open directory/file
Write	[W]	The right to write to an open file or directory
Create	[C]	The right to create a new file in the directory
Erase	[E]	The right to delete an existing file
File scan	[F]	The right to list the names of files or subdirectories within a directory
Modify	[M]	The right to change file attributes, rename files, and rename directories
Access control	[A]	The right to assign or pass rights to a directory or file to another user

NETWORK OPERATING SYSTEMS

Now that you have a better picture of the capabilities and major functions performed by LAN network operating systems, it is time to take a closer look at some of the major network operating systems themselves. In this section, our focus is limited to client/server network operating systems. The ability of workstation OSs such as Windows XP, 2000, 98, and 95 to carry out peer-to-peer network functions were addressed previously in the chapter.

Novell Operating Systems

Over time, Novell has offered several versions of NOSs. Today, Novell offers two basic systems that support a variety of configuration options. For high-end networks, Novell offers NetWare 5.x and NetWare 6.x. For small networks, such as those to support smaller offices or businesses, Novell offers IntranetWare (NetWare 4.11), a predecessor to NetWare 5.x. Novell Directory Services (NDS) is supported by each of these different versions. These versions are capable of interoperating with older versions of NetWare, such as NetWare 3.x, as well as with Windows NT and Windows 2000 Server. NDS for NT, for example, enables network administrators to use NDS to manage the resources in LANs that use Windows NT. It is quite common to find multiple NOSs in use within the same network, even within the same LAN.

NetWare 4.x

IntraNetWare 4.11 is the version of NetWare marketed to smaller businesses. NDS was first released with NetWare versions 4.0 and 4.1 under the name "NetWare Directory Services." With the release of NetWare 4.11 (IntraNetWare), NDS was reflagged "Novell Directory Services." Because Novell has made NDS available for NOSs other than NetWare, the name change was appropriate. By making NDS available to other NOSs, Novell can position its product at the heart of the network, the repository of information on the enterprise network.

A design objective of 4.x was to support LANs of up to 1,000 users; NetWare 3.x supported up to 250 users. The user interface in 4.x is predominantly GUI (graphical user interface), but some menuing and command line utilities supported in NetWare 3.x are still supported along with the GUI interfaces. NetWare 4.x was the first version of NetWare that provided disk compression utilities that enable infrequently used files/directories to be compressed in order to free disk space for files and directories with high demand rates among LAN users. NetWare 4.x was also the first version of NetWare to support symmetric multiprocessing (SMP) architectures. As noted previously in the chapter, SMP servers have two or more CPUs that allow parallel processing and greater throughput.

NetWare 4.x allows for disk mirroring, disk duplexing, and RAID drives. It also provides read-after-write capabilities and the ability to move data stored in bad areas of the disk to another part of the disk. Disk mirroring and duplexed disks are supported. In addition, NetWare 4.x supports a transaction tracking system (TTS) that is able to restore the integrity of data files by reversing work done on transactions that do not complete successfully. Using TTS helps avoid inconsistent data following a server failure. Support for server duplexing is also available.

I/O optimization features include disk caching and elevator seeking. With elevator seeking, disk access requests are ordered according to their location on the disk. Elevator seeking allows the read/write heads to move systematically over the disk from the inner tracks to the outer tracks and back again. This prevents excessive disk seeking. Faster access to files on disk is provided via directory hashing. Hashing allows a file's location to be determined more quickly than is possible with a sequential search.

Support of network printing has always been one of NetWare's strengths, and with NetWare 4.0, up to 256 printers can be supported by a single server. NetWare 4.x also includes Novell's message handling services (MHS), which provides delivery of messages among servers; part of MHS is a basic e-mail system.

NetWare 4.x was the first version of NetWare to support the encryption of authentication credentials and network auditing capabilities. A wide range of events can be selected to audit, including those summarized in Table 9-8. Enhanced security of NDS objects was also included in NetWare 4.x.

NetWare 4.x includes utilities for remote management that let administrators control a server from any network node. The remote management facility (RMF) allows an administrator to execute console commands, load and unload NetWare loadable modules (NLMs) that support particular applications, and reboot a file server. Novell and Intel combined resources to create a network management package called *ManageWise*. ManageWise allows administrators to monitor server operations by recording information such as memory, CPU, and disk usage. It also provides information on the printing environment. Network troubleshooting software is also supported by NetWare LANalyzer. LANalyzer is a NLM that monitors packets sent to and transmitted by a server. With LANalyzer, a network administrator can identify the kind and source of protocol problems.

Because the NDS is fundamental to the operation of 4.x, it is essential that tools be available for managing, maintaining, and recovering the NDS system. NDS tools are available that allow administrators to manipulate the NDS tree. Branches of the tree (partitions) can be replicated and distributed among servers to ensure redundancy and fault tolerance; distributed branches can also be merged. An example of an NDS tree is provided in Figure 9-12.

NetWare 4.x, like NetWare 5.x and NetWare 6.x, provides support for and interfaces to a variety of other networks and protocols. Included among these are IBM system network architecture (SNA) via a SNA gateway, X.25 networks via a X.25 gateway, LAN-to-LAN interconnections via X.25 packet-switching networks or T-1 lines, connections to structured query language (SQL) servers, support for TCP/IP in addition

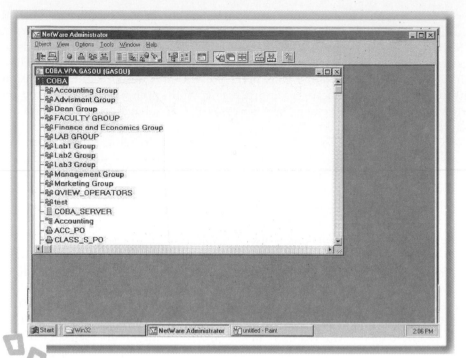

Figure 9-12   An Example of an NDS Tree

to IPX/SPX, remote access services (both dial-in and dial-out), and support for HTTP and World Wide Web servers.

IntraNetWare 4.11 expands on the capabilities of NetWare 4.0 by providing Internet protocols and capabilities. The Internet has become an important business forum, and Internet tools such as browsers, hypertext documents, and the World Wide Web provide users with a wide array of information and services. Because of their ease of use, many companies have begun using Internet tools and protocols on private networks; such private networks are called *intranets*. With IntraNetWare 4.11, a company can use Novell servers to provide services to both the Internet and an intranet. IntraNetWare expands Novell server capabilities to include Web server functions. This extra function is integrated with the NDS, allowing users to access the directory to locate network information or resources.

NetWare 5.x

NetWare 5.x was built upon NetWare 4.x capabilities and World Wide Web orientation. It was designed to create a pure IP environment by making TCP/IP the native communication protocol. By doing so, Novell sought to position NetWare 5.x as a reliable e-business application environment. Integrated support for IBM's WebSphere Application Server illustrates Novell's commitment to e-business architectures. Another example of NetWare 5.x's e-business orientation is eDirectory, which enables organizations to create directory-enabled applications that include customized interorganizational relationships between an organization's networks and those of its customers and suppliers. eDirectory extends NDS's global directory services beyond the enterprise to enable the management of multienterprise networks.

NetWare 5.x also enables network administrators to manage servers from any remote location via a Web browser and the NetWare Management Portal. The NetWare Management Portal is one of three administrative options for network managers; ConsoleOne and ZENworks are the others.

Additional features of NetWare 5.x include the following:

➤ Improved support for Microsoft Office 2000 over that available in previous versions of NetWare

➤ Support for a variety of Internet/Web servers, including FTP servers, news servers, and Web search servers

➤ Enhanced tools for Web application development using NetWare's Enterprise Web Server

➤ Support for scripting languages, including ActiveX, JavaScript, and NetBasic

➤ Enhanced authentication/authorization services, including the ability to create digital certificates with the Novell Certificate Server

➤ eDirectory support for DNS and DCHP services

➤ The ability to monitor and manage WAN traffic using WAN Traffic Manager

➤ The ability to hot swap network interface cards

➤ Enhanced support for mixed client environments, including networks that include both Windows and Macintosh workstations

➤ Increased interoperability with other data communication technologies via support for open Internet standards including LDAP, XML, ODBC, SSL, and SQL

NetWare 6

NetWare 6.0 was released by Novell during the fourth quarter of 2001. As of this writing, relatively few details of this new NOS are available; however, some of the major enhancements beyond NetWare 5.x include

➤ *Elimination of the need to install NetWare clients on workstations.* Authorized users are able to access an organization's NetWare network via a single URL using a Web browser from a workstation running virtually any operating system.

➤ *Support for WAP.* Authorized users with wireless devices can remotely access an organization's NetWare network resources.

➤ *Enhanced support for standard Internet protocols and programming languages.* These Internet protocols and programming languages include HTTP, XML, and Java.

➤ *Support for up to 32 clustered servers as well as SMP servers with up to 32 processors.*

➤ *Enhanced support for remote and mobile users via iFolder.* iFolder ensures that file/data stored on remote/mobile user machines are synchronized with those stored on enterprise servers.

➤ *The ability to enable users to access and print to network printers via the Internet.*

Although it is too early to tell, NetWare 6 appears to be consistent with Novell's goal of creating a network operating system that is capable of integrating multiple corporate networks and public networks (especially the Internet) into a common, manageable, computing environment. Its enhanced support for remote users, including those using wireless devices, is also notable.

Microsoft's Network Operating Systems

Microsoft products have become the 800-pound gorillas in both peer-to-peer and server-based networks. Microsoft became the most significant player in the peer-to-peer arena with the release of Windows 95. Because Windows 95's LAN capabilities are bundled with the operating system, unlike other peer-to-peer network products such as LANtastic, Windows 95 added no additional software cost to businesses who wanted to set up a simple network. Starting with Windows 95 and continuing through later Windows releases including Windows 98 and Windows 2000, a Network Neighborhood icon is established on the desktop to assist users in identifying the available servers and printers. Windows 95 and its successors also allow users to connect to server-based networks, including those running NetWare and Windows NT Server, in addition to enabling connections to other computers in a peer-to-peer mode.

Windows NT Server

Windows NT Server (NTS) has enjoyed considerable success as a LAN NOS. It should not be confused with Windows NT Workstation, which, like Windows 95/98/2000, is essentially an operating system for LAN workstations that can be used for peer-to-peer networking. Like NetWare, Windows NT Server is a client/server network operating system. As noted previously, NTS's widespread acceptance by the marketplace has been driven in part by its reputation as a reliable application server. In contrast to a file server, application servers are active participants along with clients in the processing of data. NTS has gained popularity as an application server because the NT operating system is a 32-bit OS that can directly access up to 4 GB of main memory (RAM). The NT operating system also supports preemptive multitasking and multithreading, which means that it can run several tasks concurrently and switch between them efficiently. Preemption multitasking means that a running process can be suspended by the OS to allow another process access to the CPU. NTS also has good support for SMP servers with multiple processors.

NTS does not have a global, distributed network directory. Instead, NTS uses domain directory services. Domain directory services are discussed in an earlier section of the chapter. In a single-server network there is a single domain; a user logs onto the server, and the user's capabilities are limited to resources available on that server. In a network with multiple servers, there may be single or multiple domains. If all of the servers are included in one domain, a user can log onto the domain server (where the domain directory and access control lists are stored). Depending on the rights assigned to the user, she may be allowed to gain access to the resources on the other servers within that domain after logging on. Domain servers can be primary or secondary. A secondary domain server has a backup copy of the domain directory in case the primary server is not available. When a network is made up of multiple domains, users in one domain are able to gain access to server resources in other domains through a process called *interdomain sharing*. Interdomain sharing is possible via a mechanism known as *trust relationships*. A trust relationship may be established between two domains, and as long as this relationship is maintained, users in one domain can access resources in the other trusted domain.

Domains generally are oriented around networks in a limited geographical area. For controlling access in department or campus environments, domain service is as effective as a global directory. However, because domain directories are not replicated across multiple domains, the network access options of remote users may be limited to the single domain. Such restrictions are avoided by organizations that use global directory services. Companies that have geographically distributed operating locations or have completely separate networks are likely to have several distinct domains. The domain directory of each domain must be administered individually. In trusted domain situations, updates to trust relationships must be made in each domain database before they can take effect. With a global directory, only one update is needed.

In the fault tolerance area, NTS supports disk mirroring and RAID disk arrays. NTS can be installed in FAT format partitions or Windows NT file systems (NTFS) partitions on server disks. With FAT formats, installations lose some of the file security capabilities because this file allocation table does not support as many file attributes as NTFS. The benefit of this format is that NTS can be installed on disks that are currently in use and those disks can be used for Windows applications as well as for the NT server operating system. This may be of benefit in small installations, in which the server may also be needed as a desktop system. The NTFS is preferred because it provides all the benefits of NTS security and performance. The management utilities on Windows NT Server are Windows based, making the network management tasks easier to perform than they are on some competing NOSs.

Windows 2000 Server

Windows 2000 Server is part of Microsoft's Windows 2000 family of operating systems (see Table 9-14). As noted in Table 9-14, Windows 2000 Server is essentially a replacement for Windows NT that offers enhanced scalability and Web server capabilities. Other differences between Windows NT and Windows 2000 Server include:

➤ *Active Directory.* Windows 2000 Server supports Active Directory, a global directory service. It represents a departure from Windows NT's domain directory service. Active Directory is LDAP–compliant.

➤ *Active Directory Service Interface (ADSI).* ADSI is essentially an application programming interface (API) available to programmers so that they can leverage Active Directory objects.

➤ *Encrypted File System (EFS).* When the NTFS format is used, EFS enables the storage of encrypted files. This adds a level of security beyond access control lists and object right assignments within Active Directory.

Table 9-14   Microsoft's Windows 2000 NOS Family

Operating System	Description
Windows 2000 Professional	This replaces Windows NT Workstation in Microsoft's line of desktop operating systems. Like NT Workstation, Windows 2000 Professional is a stable, high-performance, and manageable workstation OS. Unlike NT, it is capable of running Windows 9.x applications. This OS is also compatible with Active Directory.
Windows 2000 Server	This is a replacement for Windows NT Server. It is designed for use by small to medium-sized organizations. It supports file and print sharing, terminal services, and application services. Windows 2000 Server can be used as a Web server via its support for Microsoft's Internet Information Server.
Windows 2000 Advanced Server	This is a more scalable version of Windows 2000 Server. Like Windows 2000 Server, Advanced Server can operate as a file, print, terminal, application, and Web server. It is better suited than Windows 2000 server for use in server clusters because of its support for load balancing. Advanced Server also supports larger memory and more advanced SMP capabilities than Windows 2000 Server.
Windows 2000 Datacenter Server	This is the high-end NOS in Microsoft's family of operating systems. It has the greatest scalability and the largest levels of memory and SMP management. It is designed for use with data warehouses.

➤ *Group policies.* Windows 2000 Server enables policies to be created and enforced for multiple groups within the network. This enables central management of IP subnets and specific groups. Auditing and security analysis to ensure compliance with group policies are also supported.

➤ *Internet connection sharing.* This feature allows users in small networks running Windows 2000 Server to share dial-up or xDSL connections for Internet access.

➤ *Support for Microsoft's Internet Information Server.* This feature enables the creation of intranets and group support systems using Microsoft's Exchange 2000. It also enables network users to run Active Server Pages applications and to share documents over the Internet.

➤ *Lightweight Directory Access Protocol (LDAP) compliance.* As noted previously in this chapter, LDAP enables the integration and interoperability of Active Directory global services with other LDAP–compliant directory services. This facilitates the central management of enterprise-wide networks that utilize a variety of directory services.

➤ *Plug and play.* This facilitates the installation of new workstation and server peripherals such as video cards and network interface cards.

➤ *Windows Scripting Host (WSH).* Windows 2000 Server supports a scripting language that can be used to facilitate dynamic updates affecting major segments of the network or the entire network. Scripts can be written in a variety of scripting languages, including JavaScript or VBscript.

It should be apparent from this list of features that support for global directory services in the form of Active Directory is one of the major differences between Windows NT and Windows 2000 Server. As may be observed in Figure 9-13, Active Directory is structured in a manner that is similar to NDS. Over 16 million objects can

Figure 9-13   An Example of an Active Directory Tree

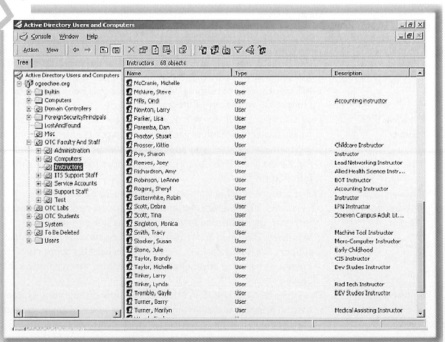

be defined in an Active Directory database. The Windows 2000 Server operating system can support up to 15,000 user connections.

Windows 2000 Server supports a range of Internet and open standards, including the Internet's Domain Name System (DNS), LDAP, and HTTP. Windows 2000 Server security includes file and folder password and access control protection; file, folder, and account auditing; account and network access passwords; server access protection; and server management controls.

Some of Windows 2000 Server's fault tolerance features include recovery from hard disk failures; recovery from lost data in a file; recovery from system configuration features; support for disk mirroring, disk duplexing, and RAID levels 0, 1, and 5; and a variety of potential backup media, including tapes, Zip/Jaz disks, and CD-ROMs. Windows 2000 Server also supports a wide variety of network management services. Some of these are illustrated in Figure 9-14.

open source software Software that is made available for free to the programming development community. The rationale behind making a program's source code available for free is that by having a broader group of programmers reviewing the code, a more useful and more bug-free product for everyone will ultimately be produced.

Linux

Linux (which has several pronunciations, including "line-us," "line-ucks," or "lin-ucks") is a version of UNIX that runs on a wide variety of processors, including Intel's family of Pentium processors (as well as its earlier x86 processors), Alpha, and PowerPC. Linux was released in 1990 by Linus Torvolds, a University of Helsinki (Finland) computer science graduate student. Torvolds transformed Minix, a popular classroom OS teaching tool, into an OS kernal much closer to UNIX.

Since the beginning, Linux has been **open source software**. Open source software is made available for free to the programming development community. Doing

Figure 9-14   Network Management Services Included with Windows 2000

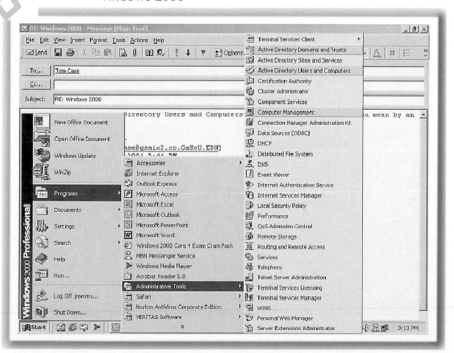

so is based on the assumption that free availability of a program's source code will ultimately result in a more bug-free and useful version of the program because more people, not just programmers employed by vendors, will review the code and identify ways to improve it. The business benefits of open source software include the ability of the organization to modify/customize the product for its own use without having to rely on vendors of proprietary products to do so. Although Linux is freely available, businesses can enter contracts with vendors such as Red Hat Software (www.redhat.com) and Caldera (www.Caldera.com) for technical support and training. However, in order to keep their Linux products open source software, their distribution CD-ROMs include complete source code in addition to tools, applets, and utilities. Many of the applications and utilities that support Linux have been developed by the **GNU project**, which is sponsored by the Free Software Foundation. The GNU (Gnu's Not Unix) project has produced more than 150 software projects, including Linux utilities, editors, compilers, and debuggers. Apache Web server software and sendmail mail server software are other examples of open source software.

GNU project The GNU project has produced more than 150 software projects including Linux utilities, editors, compilers, and debuggers. It is sponsored by the Free Software Foundation.

Linux was originally developed with a command-line interface similar to that available in standard UNIX. Over time, however, a number of graphical user interfaces have been developed, including *GNOME (GNU Network Object Modeling Environment)* and *KDE (K Desktop Environment)*. KDE is also used on UNIX workstations. An example of a GNOME interface is provided in Figure 9-15.

Linux has developed the reputation for being a very stable operating system. Like UNIX, Linux can function as both a workstation OS and a network operating system. Because of its stability, Linux is popular among ISPs as an OS for Web servers. IBM supports Linux on all of its hardware platforms, including its Netfinity servers.

Figure 9-15   Example of a GNOME Interface

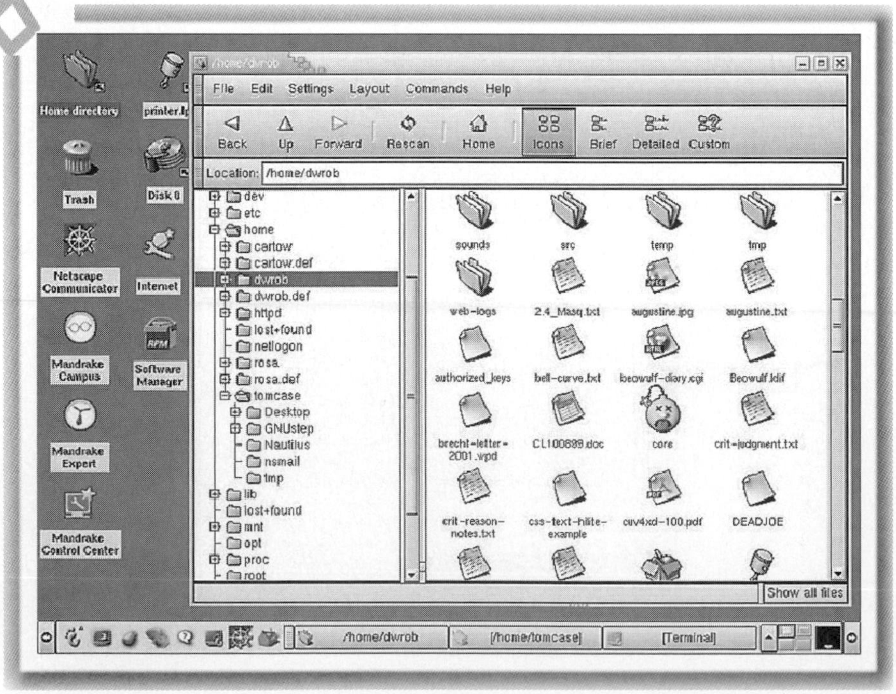

Software vendors, including database vendors such as Oracle, are also supporting Linux. Because of its versatility as both a workstation and network operating system, industry experts anticipate that Linux will become more popular as a LAN OS in the years ahead. An example of Linux's use as a network operating system is provided in Figure 9-16.

UNIX

UNIX is best described as a family of multiuser, multitasking operating systems that is widely used as a master control program on both servers and workstations. (Linux is modeled on the UNIX operating system.) UNIX is extremely popular as the operating system for Internet hosts because of its native support for TCP/IP. Most Web sites run under UNIX. UNIX's popularity is also fueled by the large number of commercial applications available for UNIX servers. Applications written for UNIX are typically scalable and portable. In this context, scalability means that programs written for one UNIX platform (say a minicomputer) can be run on larger (or smaller) systems with minimal modifications. Portability means that programs written using standard UNIX commands in one version of UNIX can be run on other UNIX versions with minimal modifications.

UNIX was developed in 1969 by Ken Thompson and Dennis Ritchie at AT&T's Bell Laboratories (now Lucent Technologies). UNIX is written in C, which was also developed by AT&T. Because both UNIX and C were freely distributed to the government and universities, a considerable number of UNIX enhancements have come from universities, including the University of California at Berkeley. Its free distribution and portability to a wide variety of hardware platforms made UNIX synonymous with the term *open system.*

Figure 9-16(a)   Examples of Linux NOS Capabilities

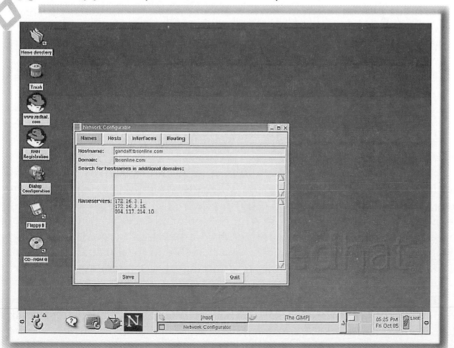

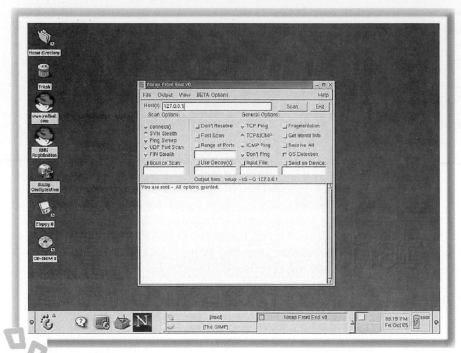

Figure 9-16(b)

NFS (Network File System) A distributed file system developed by Sun Microsystems that is also compatible with DOS- and UNIX-based systems. It allows distributed data to be shared across a network. NFS is the de facto file sharing protocol in a UNIX network.

UNIX consists of a kernal, a file system, and a shell. The file system is a hierarchical, multilevel, tree file system. Today, the most widely used UNIX file system is **NFS (Network File System)**. NFS allows file sharing across computer platforms. Users whose operating systems support NFS have transparent access to files stored on remote systems; remote files appear as locally accessible files. NFS also enables users to redirect print jobs to NFS servers.

The UNIX shell is the operating system's user interface. Initially, UNIX shells were command-line interfaces. The original shell was called the *Bourne shell;* other major command-line shells include the C shell and the Korn shell. GUI interfaces for UNIX include Motif and KDE. More than 600 commands are available to UNIX users to manipulate text and data; on the command line, many of these have a cryptic format (see Table 9-15).

UNIX is widely used for core business applications such as client/server systems and transaction processing systems. Because TCP/IP is its native communications protocol, UNIX supports the full range of TCP/IP application layer protocols, including SMTP and FTP. X Windows enables users to run applications on remote UNIX servers and to view the results on their local screens. As noted earlier, NFS allows files on remote systems to be accessible to local users. In combination, these features have made UNIX the most popular server operating system for Internet hosts.

There are many versions of UNIX in use. Some of the most popular versions are listed in Table 9-16. Of those listed, Sun's Solaris, Digital's UNIX, Hewlett-Packard HP-UX, IBM's AIX, and SCO's UnixWare are the most popular. Linux, which we discussed previously, is another UNIX variant whose popularity is growing rapidly.

Table 9-15   Examples of UNIX Commands

UNIX Command	Specified Action
cd	Change directory
ls	List directory
cp	Copy a file
mv	Rename a file
lpr	Print a file
cat	Display contents
rm	Delete a file
df	Check disk space

SOFTWARE LICENSE AGREEMENTS

From the foregoing discussion in this chapter, it is apparent that network managers have many network operating system, client operating system, and application software options. Often these choices are driven by the kind(s) of application software that the organization needs to support its business processes and objectives. Once the application software is selected, choices can be made about operating systems and network operating systems. In some instances, the range of OS and NOS possibilities may narrow quickly because the selected application software is only available for some, but not all, operating systems. An additional consideration is how well the application software actually runs on the OSs and NOSs for which it is available in networks of similar size. Once the OS(s) and NOS(s) are selected, the appropriate hardware can be identified. For example, the application software that the organization desires to use may only be available for UNIX servers and workstations. As a result, the organization may rule out NetWare and Windows 2000 Server as NOS options. Furthermore, the network manager may learn that the application performs best when used in LANs that use Solaris on Sun SPARCservers and SPARCstations. If the organization is truly committed to using the desired application software, the NOS and hardware choices it should make to ensure its optimal performance are obvious.

There are several other important issues when it comes to selecting and managing the software used in LANs. One of the most important things to know about any

Table 9-16   Some of the Versions of UNIX Found in Today's Networks

UNIX Version	Hardware Platform(s)
Solaris	Sun servers and SPARCstations
AIX	IBM RS/6000 servers/workstations
HP/UX	Hewlett-Packard RISC servers/workstations
Digital UNIX	Compaq Alpha servers/workstations and Encore Alpha servers
Ultrix	DEC VAX servers/workstations
SCO UnixWare	Servers/workstations with Intel processors
MAC A/UX	Macintosh servers/workstations with Motorola processors
MAC AIX	Macintosh servers/workstations with PowerPC processors
IRIX	Silicon Graphics workstations/servers with MIPS processors

license agreement
A legal agreement between the manufacturer and purchaser; it stipulates the rules under which the purchaser is allowed to use a product.

software package used in your network is its **license agreement.** Virtually all software is covered by a license agreement. This is true for both system and application software. The license agreement covers the rules under which you are allowed to use the product. It is a way of protecting both the manufacturer and the user of the product.

To better understand the need for license agreements, we first look at an analogy. Consider the books you purchased for school, which probably were rather expensive. Of course, the publisher does not pay nearly that much to print the book. Part of your book price goes to profit, but the publisher also incurs other expenses. One or more authors worked many hours to write the material; editors worked many hours along with the authors to develop the format and content; designers laid out the style (graphics and page formats); marketing analysts determined a marketing strategy and created advertising brochures; and the sales force was told about the book, its target markets, and key selling points. All of this activity required a considerable investment. Some books never become popular, and the publishing company loses money on them. Others become very popular, and the publishing company makes a profit. Some of that profit is used to offset losses on other projects. Now, suppose someone decides to illegally reprint a text and sell the successful books. With today's technology, it does not cost much just to print these copies. This person can sell the copies for much less than the publisher can, because he has not had to make the investment of developing the work, paying the salaries of editors and production workers, paying royalties to the developers, and so on.

Patent and copyright laws are intended to protect the investment of designers, artists, filmmakers, authors, publishing companies, and so on. Software companies also make a sizable investment in creating application or system software. System analysts design the product, programmers write and debug the code, marketing analysts create a marketing plan, advertising campaigns are developed and implemented, manuals are created, a support organization is staffed and trained, and the product is brought to market.

Several years probably elapsed from the time the product was conceived to the point at which it was ready to sell and make a profit. Thousands of dollars were probably spent before there was any opportunity to sell the software. In addition, once a software product is released, expenses continue. Support staff must be paid, and new enhancements must be designed. As with illegal book printing, the gain from all this effort can be eroded by illegal copying. To give you an idea of the magnitude of this problem, at the end of the 1980s several software piracy shops in Hong Kong were raided. Some estimated the annual loss of revenues to software companies resulting from software piracy in one building alone to be hundreds of millions of dollars.

Software vendors must therefore take steps to protect their investment. Like books, pictures, films, and fashion designs, software can be illegally copied and sold. Software is protected in six basic ways: (1) the code is kept secret so other software houses cannot use special algorithms developed by the company to write a competing system; (2) the code is copyrighted to prevent another company from copying the code and writing a competing system; (3) the software is copy protected to deter the making of illegal copies; (4) the software requires a special hardware device to run; (5) license agreements are used to establish the terms of ownership and use; and (6) legislation penalizing those who do not adhere to the copyright and license restrictions is enacted.

The first two of these measures protect the source code from being used by someone else. During development, it is common to keep the source code of software secret. However, after the product has been released, it is always possible to derive the source code, even if the software is released only in object code format. Deriving the source code from object code is done through reverse engineering. To protect themselves from reverse engineering, software manufacturers usually copyright their software. Copyright laws, originally intended to cover writing, films, and works of art, have been extended to include software. New legislation also has been enacted to further define the restrictions and penalties for unauthorized software copying.

Each of these measures is rather clear; most people understand and observe the rules. However, the remaining two issues—copy protection and license agreements—are less standard and directly involve how the software is used. Software piracy has always been a problem, even before the introduction of microcomputers. With mini-computers and mainframe systems, software piracy is easier to detect, and its incidence is negligible compared to its occurrence on microcomputers. There are two good reasons for easier detection of large system software piracy. First, large computers are used by large organizations with professional data processing departments. Software piracy is difficult to hide in such organizations, and ordinarily anyone found using pirated software is subject to dismissal and the company is subject to lawsuits. Second, large computer sites typically work closely with the software vendor's personnel. The vendor's employees are aware of the software its customers are authorized to use, and it is easy to detect the presence of unauthorized software. Easy piracy detection is not the case with microcomputer software.

A few software companies protect their software by requiring the use of a special hardware device that attaches to a serial or parallel port. Such devices may be called *terminal blocks* or *server blocks,* depending on whether they are attached to network clients or servers, respectively. This device and the software itself work together to provide application security. When started, the application attempts to read data encoded in the device. If the device is not attached, the application terminates. One disadvantage to this approach is that a user may have several applications, each of which needs a different device. Because the number of serial or parallel ports is limited, changing from one application to another may require changing the device. Other companies have accomplished somewhat the same effect by requiring a key disk. The key disk is usually a floppy disk that must be in a disk drive when the application is run. The application uses the key disk only to verify the disk's presence. This technique is seldom used today and, of course, cannot be used with diskless systems.

Originally many microcomputer software vendors used copy protection to deter software piracy. The software diskette was encoded to prevent copying using standard OS copy facilities such as DOS's COPY or DISKCOPY commands. In general, copy protection only gave rise to a new software industry: software to allow copying of copy-protected software. Of course, vendors of such software were careful to point out that the sole purpose of their software was to make a backup copy and not to make illegal duplicate copies. Many companies that once used copy protection have abandoned that means because it proved ineffective. Instead of or in addition to copy protection, software vendors now rely on copyright protection together with software license agreements.

When you buy software, both application software and LAN system software, often the CD-ROM(s) on which the software is stored is sealed in an envelope. Written on or attached to the envelope is text regarding the license agreement and a message that opening and using the software is a commitment to adhere to the stipulations of that license agreement. The license agreement states the conditions under which you are allowed to use the product. In some instances, the license agreement is on a piece of paper that can be read through shrink-wrap packaging. Similar to those printed on envelopes, these state that the user agrees to abide by the license agreement by breaking the shrink-wrap and opening the software packaging.

In essence, when you buy software, you do not get ownership of that product; you are simply given the right to use the product. An attorney might quibble with this statement, but the basic premise is correct. Some license agreements explicitly state that you own the CD-ROM or diskette(s) but not the contents of the CD-ROM or diskette(s). This means that you cannot make copies of the software to give to your friends; you may not be able to run it on several workstations at the same time; you may not reverse engineer it to produce source code for modification or resale; and so on. Your rights to the software are limited to using the software in the intended manner. If you like, you can destroy the software, cease to use it, or give it as a gift. In some instances, you may be allowed to sell it to someone else. In the last two cases, you also transfer the license agreement to the recipient. Some software vendors go so far as to state that transferring the software must be approved by the software vendor. In some cases, the software license covers the use of the accompanying documentation as well.

One of the problems with license agreements is that there are no standards. If you buy two different applications, you may find two different license agreements. To protect yourself and your organization from civil and criminal suits, you must understand the provisions of each agreement. Companies and universities have been investigated for illegally copying software, have been found guilty of the offense, and have been heavily fined. It is important that users respect license agreements.

There are several ways to categorize license agreements. In this book, however, we will only consider some general licensing provisions, namely single user, single workstation; restricted number of concurrent users; site license; single user, multiple workstation; server license; and corporate license.

Single-User, Single-Workstation License Agreements

Single-user, single-workstation license agreements are the most restrictive. They specify that the software is to be used on one workstation only and by only one person at a time. If you have a microcomputer that is shared by multiple users across the workday, only one user can run the software at any time. In most instances, restricting the software to only one machine also implies a single user.

This license agreement also means that if an office has two or more computers, a separate copy of the software must be purchased for each machine on which the software is to be used. If you have two employees, one on a day shift and one on a night shift, using the same software but on different workstations, each needs a licensed copy of the software. In this situation, the software is never used concurrently, but two copies are required. One of the ways in which software vendors enforce this policy is through the software installation procedure. The install process counts the number of installations. When you install the product, the counter is decremented to zero, and you are not able to install the program on another system. To move the software to another system, you must uninstall the software. The uninstall process removes the application from the computer's disks and increments the installation count. Another method used to enforce a single-user, single-workstation license is the requirement for a key disk described earlier.

Single-User, Multiple-Workstation License Agreements

This kind of license agreement relaxes the constraints of the single-user, single-workstation agreement. It usually also relies on the honor system for enforcement. Software vendors that use this agreement recognize that different people may want to use the software and at different workstations, such as in the office and on a portable computer. The purchase of a single copy of the software allows the owner to install it on several systems. However, the license restricts use of the software to one user at a time per software copy. Suppose an office with 10 workstations must do word processing. With this license agreement, the company can buy five copies of the software and install them on 10 different systems. Each of the 10 employees can use the word processor, but only five employees can use the product concurrently. As long as five or fewer employees use the word processing application at any one time, the company has lived up to the license provisions. Note that it is possible for six users to inadvertently use the application at the same time, in violation of the license agreement.

Restricted Number of Concurrent Users

On a LAN, it is common for several users to run an application concurrently. Three employees may be doing word processing, 10 may be using the spreadsheet software, and 25 may be using the database software. With file or database server technology, only one copy of each application is on the server's disks. Most LAN–compatible software is inherently designed for multiple users; however, some software vendors place restrictions on the number of concurrent users. The main idea behind this strategy is to charge by the number of users.

Consider the database needs of the company just mentioned, where the maximum number of concurrent database users is 25. The database vendor has a license agreement that allows 10 concurrent users for a certain fee. The company also has an expansion policy that allows additional concurrent users to be added in groups of 10, with an additional fee for each such group. The company must purchase three modules to satisfy its need for 25 concurrent users. This kind of license is typically enforced by a metering program that controls the concurrent use of the application. When a user starts the application, the meter program increments a counter by 1. When a user exits the application, the counter is decremented by 1. If the license agreement is for 30 users, a user can run the application as long as the counter is 29 or fewer. If the counter is 30, a user requesting the application receives an error message indicating that the application is not available. Metering software is available to monitor and manage compliance with software licenses for all software access through a network's server(s).

Server License

A server license allows an application to be installed on one server. All users attached to that server may use the application. If a company has three servers and wants to use the application on each of them, the company must purchase three licenses or three copies of the software.

Site License

A site license gives the user unlimited rights to use the software at a given site. The site may be a single LAN or multiple LANs at one location.

Corporate License

A corporate license gives a corporation unlimited use of the software at all locations. In order to accommodate telecommuters and mobile workers, some corporate license agreements allow employees to install a copy of the software on a home computer or a portable notebook computer. Some software vendors restrict a corporate license to all locations within one country. Sometimes, the right to reproduce documentation is also granted to the corporation.

The license agreement is intended primarily to protect the rights of the manufacturer. However, the holder of a license agreement also has certain rights, which may include the following:

➤ The owner can transfer or assign the license to another user.
➤ The owner can get a refund if the product is defective or does not work as stated.
➤ Legal rights may be granted by certain states or countries regarding the exclusion of liability for losses or damage resulting from the use of the software.
➤ The user can terminate the license by destroying the software and documentation.

When selecting application and system software for your organization's networks, you must take care to understand fully all the conditions of the license agreements. Each user should have access to the software services that they need to effectively perform their jobs, but this does not mean that each employee should have or needs to have access to all the software available within the company. Different license and pricing policies among competing products can result in substantial differences in availability or cost to your company.

INTEROPERABILITY OF SERVER SOFTWARE

It has become commonplace for large LANs to have multiple servers. It is also increasingly common to have servers within the same network that run different server network operating systems. As a result, the interoperability of server software is an important issue in today's LANs.

Many large LANs have a mixture of servers running NetWare, Windows NT, or Windows 2000 Server in order to capitalize on NetWare's traditional strengths in the areas of file and print services and Windows NT's strengths for application services. In addition to NetWare and Windows 2000 Server, many LANs also include Linux servers. When multiple servers running different NOSs are required or desirable, network managers face the challenge of ensuring that they interoperate correctly. Interoperability is less of a challenge when a network's multiple servers all have the same hardware and software platforms.

interoperability
The ability of network components to connect to the network and communicate with shared network resources. In general use, interoperability refers to the capability of two or more hardware devices or two or more software routines to work together.

Interoperability is the ability of all network components to connect to the network and to communicate with shared network resources. From a global view, this means the ability to interconnect different networks so that nodes on one network are able to communicate with nodes on the same network or on another network. On a single network, it means that any node can access resources to which it has appropriate security. Interoperability is usually easy in a homogeneous network, in which only one NOS version is used and the workstations are all the same kind and use the same OS. Networks using a mixture of NOSs and workstation OS platforms make interoperability more complex.

Part of the interoperability complexity of LANs with mixed server and workstation platforms stems from the need to support multiple application systems, file systems, network transport protocols, and MAC specifications (see Table 9-2.). Additional complexity is added when network users need to have access to resources stored on the LAN's multiple servers that use different directory services and access control lists. Table 9-17 lists complications that may exist as a result. How well the server NOSs handle these issues affects the interoperability of the network.

Table 9-17   Possible Complications of Having Two Network Operating Systems in One LAN

Compatibility of user identifiers and passwords
Synchronization of user identifiers and passwords across servers
Ability to simultaneously access data on two servers
Ability to access data on one server and print to spooler on another
Applications that can run from both servers
Support for common application program interfaces
Support for common protocols at the OSI network and transport layers
Ability to use/have two redirector processes

SUMMARY

LAN software can be separated into application software and system software. LAN application software includes the user-oriented programs that enable business users to perform their work activities. This includes general-purpose applications that are used by most LAN users as well as special-purpose applications (such as accounting and inventory management software) that are only used by specific subsets of network users. Work-group software is also classified as application software; work-group software includes e-mail, electronic conferencing, work-flow automation, document coauthoring/management, group decision support, and time-staged delivery software.

LAN system software consists of operating systems, utilities, drivers, and other "background" programs that enable application programs to run smoothly on LAN hardware. LAN system software is found on both workstations and servers.

The LAN system software installed on workstations, which is called client NOS software, is responsible for intercepting application I/O requests and deciding whether the request is local or network. If the request is local, the client NOS software passes it along to the workstation OS. If the request is for a network resource, the client NOS software formats a network message and sends the request over the network for processing.

The operating systems used on LAN workstations can be used as peer-to-peer network operating systems. Both file sharing and printer sharing can be accomplished through today's client operating systems without the involvement of a client/server network operating system. Windows 98, Windows 2000, Windows XP, and Macintosh OS are some examples of client operating systems with peer-to-peer networking capabilities.

LAN server software is more complex than LAN workstation software. Some of the major functions performed by a server NOS include I/O optimization, fault tolerance, directory services, application services, file services, networking services, network management services, and security services. Other important LAN NOS functions include print services, backup services, and shared services. Collectively, these functions help to make performance better, to improve reliability, or to protect data from accidental or intentional damage.

A number of network operating systems are used in today's LANs. These include NetWare 5.x/6.x, Windows NT Server, Windows 2000 Server, Linux, and UNIX. The software used in today's LANs is typically covered by a license agreement that describes the manner in which the software may be used. In using the software, an organization agrees to abide by the licensing provisions, which typically limit the number of concurrent users and the hardware platforms on which the software may be installed. License agreements protect the software vendor's investment in manufacturing and distributing the software and give the user rights to use and upgrade a product. System administrators must ensure that the licensing provisions are followed.

When choosing LAN software, it is important to consider how that software will interoperate with other software, other networks, and your hardware. Poor interoperability increases the complexity of using a LAN and decreases its usability.

KEY TERMS

- administrative management domain (ADMD)
- application program interface (API)
- authentication services
- authorization services
- client/server protocol
- clustering
- disk seek enhancement
- document coauthoring system
- domain directory services

- duplexed servers
- exclusive open mode
- global directory services
- GNU project
- group decision support software
- hot swap
- I/O optimization
- interoperability
- interrupt
- LDAP (lightweight directory access protocol)
- license agreement
- locks
- message transfer agents (MTAs)
- mirrored disks
- multiprotocol routing
- multithreading
- NFS (Network File System)

- open source software
- parity data
- private management domain (PRMD)
- protected open mode
- read-after-write
- redirector
- redundant arrays of independent disks (RAID)
- remote access client
- shared open mode
- spooler
- symmetrical multiprocessing (SMP)
- time-staged delivery systems
- universal client
- user agent (UA)
- work-group software
- X.400 standard
- X.500 standard

REVIEW QUESTIONS

1. Briefly describe the difference between general-purpose LAN application software and special-purpose LAN application software. Provide examples of each.
2. What is work-group software? Identify several of the more mature work-group software applications.
3. Compare the X.400 and X.500 standards.
4. Describe the capabilities of work-flow automation software.
5. Identify the capabilities of document coauthoring and document management software.
6. Identify the features of group decision support software.
7. Explain the functions of workstation redirector software.
8. Explain how an application's request for network services is processed by both the workstation and the server.
9. What is an application program interface?
10. What functions are performed by the medium-interface portion of LAN system software?
11. What are the characteristics of universal clients?
12. What are the characteristics of remote access clients and remote access servers?
13. Identify and briefly describe the peer-to-peer networking capabilities supported in client operating systems.
14. What is meant by plug-and-play capabilities?
15. Identify the major categories of server NOS capabilities.
16. What is the purpose of I/O optimization? Give two examples of how this is supported in servers.
17. What is the benefit of fault-tolerant servers? Provide examples of how fault tolerance is supported in servers.
18. What is failover capability?
19. Compare global directory services and domain directory services. Provide examples of each.
20. What is LDAP? Why is it important in today's networks?
21. What are application services?
22. Identify several different file systems supported by server NOSs.

23. Identify and briefly describe several kinds of network services supported by server NOSs.
24. Identify network management services supported by server NOSs.
25. Compare authentication services, authorization services, encryption, and auditing services.
26. How do user and group templates facilitate user account creation and management processes?
27. Explain how a print spooler works.
28. Explain two ways application software can be tailored to individual users.
29. What is contention management and why is it important?
30. What is data access security? Why is it important?
31. Briefly describe the evolution of NetWare from NetWare 4.x to NetWare 6.x.
32. Briefly compare Windows NT Server and Windows 2000 Server.
33. What is Linux? Why is it growing in popularity?
34. What are the major features of UNIX?
35. What is a software license? Why are software licenses necessary? Identify several kinds of software licenses.

PROBLEMS AND EXERCISES

1. Use the Internet to research the capabilities of electronic document management systems. Identify the kinds of organizations that use electronic document management systems and how they apply the software. Also identify several electronic document management software vendors and their products. Summarize your findings in a paper or PowerPoint presentation.
2. Use the Internet to learn more about how Windows NT Server and Windows 2000 Server support remote clients. Compare the approaches used by these server NOSs to that used by NetWare 6.
3. Use the Internet to research the peer-to-peer networking capabilities included in Windows XP. Summarize what you learn in a paper or PowerPoint presentation.
4. Use the Internet to find out more about the plug-and-play and hot-swapping capabilities supported by Windows 2000 Server and NetWare 5.x and 6.
5. Use the Internet to find out more about RAID. Summarize the distinctions between RAID levels 0, 1, and 5.
6. Use the Internet to find out more about Novell's NDS and Windows 2000 Server's Active Directory. Summarize how they are similar and how they are different.
7. Use the Internet to find out more about LDAP and how it works. Summarize how the protocol works in a paper or PowerPoint presentation.
8. Use the Internet to find out more about PAP and CHAP. How are they similar? How are they different? Which server NOS supports them?
9. Use the Internet to find out more about how data access security is supported in NetWare 6 and Windows 2000 Server.
10. Use the Internet to find out more about the Free Software Foundation, open source software, and the GNU Project. Summarize what you learn in a paper or PowerPoint presentation.
11. Use the Internet to research the differences between server, site, and corporate software licenses. Summarize how these differ, and use specific products from several vendors to illustrate variations in what these cover.
12. Use the Internet to find out more about software piracy, the Software and Information Industry Association's SPA Anti-Piracy Division, and the NET Act. Summarize what you learn in a paper or PowerPoint presentation.

13. You have been asked to configure the hardware for a LAN to provide office automation capabilities for a small office. The office manager wants you to provide a LAN that will make use of four IBM compatibles with 32 MB of memory, two IBM compatibles with 16 MB of memory, two IBM compatibles with 64 MB of memory, one laser printer, and two ink-jet printers that the office currently owns. Using a physical star topology, draw a network diagram of your proposed LAN. Label all hardware components in your diagram. Prepare a report to accompany your diagram that gives the following details:
    a. equipment, software, and cabling that will be needed to connect each device to the LAN
    b. necessary upgrades to any of the existing hardware to make it possible to run Windows XP on the LAN's microcomputers

14. Consider the office LAN described in problem 13. Some employees want to access the LAN from their homes to transfer files and do remote printing. Configure the hardware, software, and communication capabilities required at the LAN and user ends of the connection.

15. The office described in problem 13 wants to add fax capabilities to the network. The capabilities needed include the ability to send and receive fax transmissions and to store fax images on disk. Images sent and received may be in either hard copy or disk image format. Describe the hardware, software, and communication equipment necessary to create this capability.

Novell's One Net Strategy

Because of the rapid expansion of the Internet, companies are changing the way they do business. Today, success is often dependent on an organization's ability to aggressively transform its business practices to meet the challenges of a rapidly changing competitive environment.

From a technology viewpoint, companies are faced with an increasingly complex and highly uneven network environment with multiple platforms, legacy systems, and internal and external networks. These must be able to work together for companies to be positioned to address continual technology changes that add complexity and threats. For business purposes, every aspect of an organization—its employees, processes, and systems—must be improved to serve new and expanding communities of users that today include the organization's partners and customers.

Information technology is no longer used only to support some processes in the organization, but instead it is becoming the central piece of the organization's success in this very dynamic marketplace. The network has become the new strategic platform for IT and business by providing connectivity and information sharing.

In this new network role, Novell sees a company's network as a global network, which integrates intranets, extranets, and the Internet. Novell's One Net strategy simplifies the way companies transform their processes to support e-business by creating an integrated network to support both internal and external business processes. As noted on the Novell Web site, "In [a] One Net environment, intranets, the Internet, extranets, corporate and public networks, wired and wireless networks all work together across the leading operating environments to give companies the power and flexibility they need to succeed in the Net economy" (www.novell.com).

Customers are embracing Novell's new One Net strategy, because it is focused on business solutions instead of just selling products. By acquiring management consulting vendor Cambridge Technology Partners (CTP), Novell has reaffirmed its new focus on bringing integrated solutions and consulting services to senior IT and business managers. Novell's strategy has shifted toward an emphasis on products for collaboration, security, directory services and network management that collectively have an enormous potential for e-business.

Because of intense competition, especially from Microsoft, Novell is developing products that support open standards, such as XML, and that are independent from its NetWare operating system. It has also begun the process of "unbundling" its product line. For example, products such as ZENworks and GroupWise have been decoupled from NetWare. They now require eDirectory, which can run under different (non-NetWare) platforms such as Windows NT/2000 or Sun's Solaris. Novell claims that via eDirectory, the central piece of its One Net strategy, it will be able to provide companies with a single, comprehensive view of their computing and communications resources without having to worry if the resources are on public or private networks, intranets, extranets, or the Internet.

At Eastern Bank in Lynn, Massachusetts, Novell has integrated Microsoft servers with Novell Directory Services (NDS). Any external authentication is done through Novell, providing just one account to every user, which enables them to access any of the platforms and computing environments within the bank. These platforms and environments include its UNIX or NT servers, its virtual private network, and its Web services.

Despite Novell's new strategy, many companies are migrating to Microsoft Windows 2000 or NT. Novell has lost market share; however, it is not likely to go under because its eDirectory provides businesses with the ability to become more platform independent and to offer business solutions that require an integrated network. eDirectory-based applications are giving Novell a new opportunity to compete and survive in the marketplace. In addition, Novell is promoting portal services into NetWare to bring users on-demand access to network applications through eDirectory.

CASE QUESTIONS

1. Use the Internet to find out more about Novell's eDirectory. How does it differ from NDS? What are the advantages/benefits of eDirectory?
2. Both Microsoft and Sun have competing Net strategies. Use the Internet to find out more about each. Describe the similarities and differences among the Net strategies being pursued by Novell, Microsoft, and Sun. Which do you think is best? Justify your choice.
3. Use the Internet to identify several more companies (in addition to Eastern Bank) that have

adopted eDirectory or Novell's One Net strategy. What patterns can be observed in their reasons for embracing this approach? What patterns may be observed in the payoffs being derived by these companies?
4. Use the Internet to find out more about Novell's corporate financial performance. Has the company's One Net strategy helped Novell remain financially viable?

SOURCES

Anthes, G. "Inside Novell's One Net Strategy." *Computerworld* (November 12, 2001, p. 54.)

Moore, C. "Novell Touts One Net Plan." *InfoWorld* (March 19, 2001, p. 8.)

"Novell: It's One Net." Retrieved March 10, 2002, from www.novell.com.

Note: For more information on LAN software, see an additional case on the Web site, www.prenhall.com/stamper, "Syncrasy Corporation."

Wide Area Networks

After studying this chapter, you should be able to:

■ Define the characteristics of wide area networks (WANs).

■ Compare WANs to metropolitan area networks (MANs) and local area networks (LANs).

■ Discuss the business rationale for WANs.

■ Identify major WAN applications.

■ Describe the major hardware and software components of WANs.

■ Describe WAN topologies and protocols.

As noted in the discussion of data communication and Internet history in Chapters 1 and 2, the 1970s brought a significant growth in wide area network (WAN) technology. One of the biggest growth segments of the communication industry during the 1980s was local area network (LAN) technology. The largest of all WANs, the Internet, was also evolving during these decades, but its most significant growth spurt occurred during the 1990s and continues today. The next few years are likely to be characterized by the continued growth of the Internet and World Wide Web; the widespread interconnection of networks of all kinds; the emergence of wireless (mobile) networks and applications; expansion of the use of multimedia over networks; expanded business use of the Internet; integration of telecommunication networks such as telephone, computer, radio, and television networks; and a significant increase in network speeds and broadband Internet access channels. In the years ahead, differences between WANs and LANs, as well as those between wireless and wire-based networks, may be slight, and we will be able to talk just about networks. Until that time, we need to recognize the existence of different network types and where each fits in the world of data communication.

In this chapter, we first define WANs and compare them to LANs and metropolitan area networks (MANs). We will then turn our attention to why businesses are interested in and leveraging WANs. The rest of this chapter provides an overview of WAN hardware and software components, topologies, and protocols.

WHAT IS A WAN?

wide area network (WAN) A network implementation that consists of multiple networks at geographically distributed locations that are interconnected. Relative to LANs, WANs typically cover a wider geographical area and operate at lower speeds.

A **wide area network (WAN)** is one of the oldest kinds of data communication networks. A WAN is essentially a distributed network that covers a broad geographic area. Typically, a WAN spans a wide geographical area, interconnects networks located at geographically distributed sites, uses transmission media supplied by a common carrier, operates at transmission speeds lower than those for LANs and MANs, and uses data link protocols different from those of LANs and MANs. It is important to note, however, that it is possible for a network to be classified as a WAN even though it is confined to a local area and uses private transmission media rather than those provided by common carriers.

Mainframes and minicomputers often play a prominent role in WANs. Although servers and microcomputers now share the limelight with larger processors in WANs, the larger systems continue to play pivotal roles and are frequently the focal points for network interconnections. Because of this, they are often called *nodes*.

WANs may cover a significant region of a state, an entire state, several states, the entire country, or even the entire world. An example of a WAN is illustrated in Figure 10-1. As a rule of thumb, a network is considered a WAN if a user at one site would normally have to use long-distance services to telephone users at one or more of the other network locations. Although this guideline does not apply in cities with large local calling areas, it is still useful for distinguishing WANs from more geographically limited MANs and LANs.

Because WANs can cover very broad areas, the communication links used to interconnect different locations are often slower than those used in MANs and LANs. However, in some instances, some of the fastest services available from carriers are used in WANs, especially when high-volume data transfers between large computers are required.

Figure 10-1   A Wide Area Network (WAN)

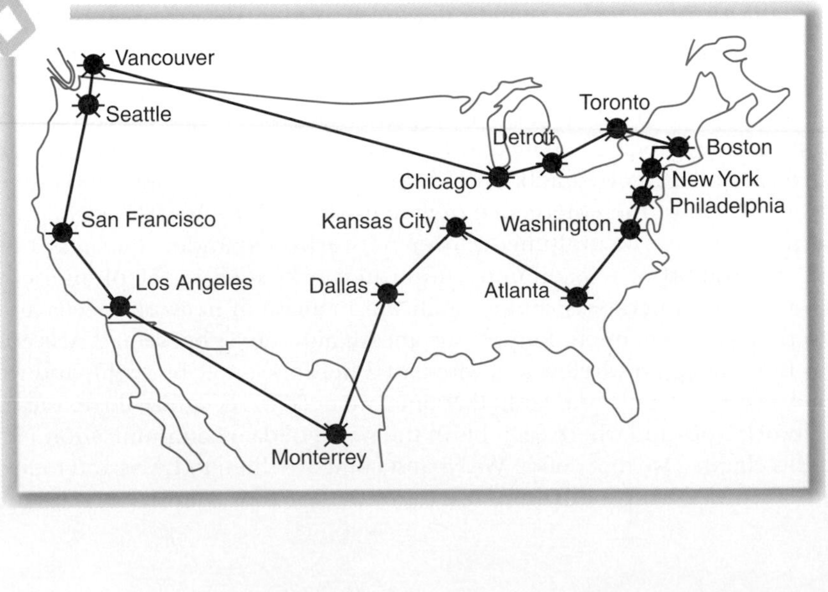

Because it is often easier to grasp what is meant by a WAN by comparing WANs to MANs and LANs, the major characteristics of MANs and LANs are briefly described here.

A **metropolitan area network (MAN)** is a distributed network that spans a metropolitan area (a city and its major suburbs). In terms of geographic scope, a MAN is considered to fall between a WAN and a LAN. Figure 10-2 depicts an example of a MAN.

MANs are addressed in IEEE 802.6 standards. These define media distance limitations between interconnected computers on the order of 200 kilometers (125 miles) and communication speeds of 100 mbps. The standards also recognize that MANs may transmit data, voice, image, and video signals.

MAN media may be private, but they are most frequently obtained from common carriers. One example of a MAN backbone, the fiber distributed data interface (FDDI), operates at 100 mbps. Another example is the *distributed queue dual bus (DQDB)* architecture and access control method addressed in the IEEE 802.6 standard. Carrier services, such as switched megabit data services (SMDS), which are described in Chapter 5, may also provide services to the geographic areas covered by MANs. If these services are available, they may be used by organizations to interconnect the networks found at their different operating locations within the metropolitan area. The transmission speeds supported by SMDS are typically less than that possible on IEEE 802.6 MANs but may be sufficient to meet the inter-site communication needs of the organization.

The data link protocols used by MANs that conform to the IEEE 802.6 standard are similar to those used in LANs. Modified forms of token passing are most common. The major difference between MANs and LANs is the distance spanned.

A *local area network (LAN)* serves the smallest geographic area. A LAN may be restricted to a single room (such as a computer lab at a university), a set of rooms or offices in the same building, or the set of buildings that make up a single business or school campus. Limitations mentioned in IEEE 802.x standards for LANs address the maximum distance between nodes and the communication media that are used. The media limitations for LANs may be as much as several kilometers, but these limitations are commonly less than a few hundred meters. Usually, the LAN medium is privately owned; LANs rarely involve common carrier services other than to provide dial-in or dial-out capabilities. As noted in Chapters 7 and 8, LAN speeds typically range between 10 mbps and 1 gbps.

Today, LANs are among the basic building blocks for enterprise-wide networks and WANs that interconnect multiple operating locations. Most business users gain

metropolitan area network (MAN)
A high-speed communication network that services an area larger than a LAN but smaller than a WAN. A MAN typically covers a geographic area of a city or major suburb.

Figure 10-2   A Metropolitan Area Network (MAN)

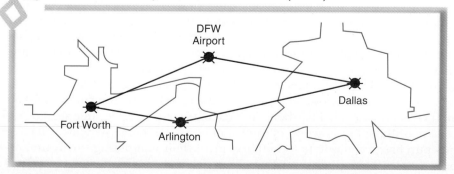

access to WAN computing resources via the local LANs that connect their personal computers. The internetworking technologies that are used to interconnect LANs and WANs are discussed in Chapter 13.

WANS AND THE INTERNET

The Internet is the largest WAN that has been created. It provides a means for interconnecting WANs, MANs, and LANs worldwide. The inception of ARPAnet in 1969 as a 4-node, geographically dispersed network was the first step toward what is now the undisputed largest WAN. The Internet continues to expand with each new household or business that gains access to the Internet via an ISP (Internet service provider).

Carriers continue to provide and upgrade the high-speed fiber optic lines that make up the Internet backbone. Wireless voice and data network companies are contributing to the expansion of the Internet by enabling their subscribers to surf the Net via second- and third-generation cell phones and personal digital assistants (PDAs). In the years ahead, Teledesic's "Internet in the Sky™" promises to bring wireless broadband Internet access to 95 percent of the Earth's surface.

Although Internet backbone speeds may exceed those found in LANs and MANs, Internet access speeds for most users are slower than the transmission speeds supported in LANs and MANs. Internet backbone speeds may exceed a billion bits per second because they leverage high-bandwidth fiber optic connections. Most users, however, interface with the Internet via dial-up circuits, DSL lines, or cable modems. All of these are much slower than the transmission speeds found on many sections of the Internet backbone. Until broadband Internet-access technologies such as digital subscriber lines (DSL) and cable modems are used by a majority of households and businesses, Internet-access speeds will continue to follow the pattern of speed differences that have traditionally been observed among WANs, MANs, and LANs. These access technologies will help to narrow the gap, but not eliminate it.

It is the data link protocol dimension where the Internet least fits our (traditional) definition of a WAN. As noted in Chapters 2 and 4, the TCP/IP protocol stack enables a wide variety of data link protocols to be used locally, including those commonly found in MANs and LANs. Virtually any routable protocol can be used. Although there are some WAN data link protocols whose packets cannot be routed over the Internet without modification, most WAN data link protocols have evolved to interoperate with TCP/IP.

BUSINESS RATIONALE FOR WANS

WANs were the first major category of data communication networks to be used by businesses. The major business motivations for developing WANs were to overcome distance, to overcome the computational limitations of a single computer, and to provide support for localized, departmental computing. Companies that are national or international often have multiple computing sites. Wide area networks are used to connect these geographically dispersed sites and enable the exchange of data and software. In some instances, computing needs at one location exceeded the capacity of a single computer. In these instances, multiple computers were installed at one location and then networked to provide resource sharing as well as greater computing capacity. Shared resources included hardware and data. As computers became smaller and less expensive with the introduction of minicomputers (midrange systems), some departments purchased computers to better control their computing environment. The department-level computers usually were networked with corporate computers and other department-level computers. The last two motivations for WAN networking often resulted in several computers being located in a small geographical area. The mode of interconnection, however, was basically the same as that being used to connect computers over long distances. LAN and MAN technology developed to overcome the speed limitations of traditional WAN interconnections.

Today there are several additional reasons for creating WANs and other data communication networks. These include providing the networking infrastructure required to support groupware, communication among workers, management control, cost-effective resource sharing, and downsizing (the replacement of large computer systems with LANs). Each of the major business reasons for creating WANs is discussed in the following sections.

Large Data Transfers

In a large data processing installation with a variety of host computers, moving data from one system to another once was accomplished by magnetic tape or low-speed communication links (defined as speeds less than 100 kbps). Magnetic tapes provide high data transfer rates but have two disadvantages. First, manual intervention is required to effect data transfers. Operators are required to mount and dismount tapes. This not only tends to slow down the transfer but also often means that the transfer must be scheduled, reducing the potential for instantaneous as-needed transfers. Second, incompatibilities between tape formats on different systems must be accommodated when tapes are used as a transfer medium. There are also constraints when using communication links slower than 100 kbps, because large file transfers may be very time-consuming. For example, consider how long it would take to transfer a moderate-size file over a 56-kbps digital circuit. If the file consists of 1 million records and if each record is 100 bytes, it will take just under 4 hours to complete the transfer. This can be calculated in the following manner:

$$(1,000,000 \text{ records}) (100 \text{ bytes per record}) (8 \text{ bits per byte}) / 56,000 \text{ bps}$$
$$= 14,286 \text{ s} = 238 \text{ min} = 3.97 \text{ hr}$$

These figures assume that the line is operating at 100 percent capacity and that there is no protocol overhead (such as the need to resend packets as the result of error checking). Both of these are unrealistic assumptions. As we will see later in the chapter, overhead is associated with all WAN protocols. In addition, error checking, correction, and recovery are ongoing processes in WAN systems. Like the error-checking processes discussed in Chapter 6, WAN error-checking processes can vary considerably in efficiency and in the amount of network traffic that they create. Furthermore, WANs are typically shared by multiple devices in each of several interconnected locations. This means that a single device rarely has dedicated access to the communication circuit's full bandwidth for an extended period of time (such as the 3.97 hours needed to transmit the file in our example). When these realities are factored in, the actual transfer time for our 1-million-record file could exceed 6 hours.

As shown in the following calculation, the same file could be sent across a 100-mbps LAN in 8 seconds.

$$(1,000,000 \text{ records}) (100 \text{ bytes per record}) (8 \text{ bits per byte}) / 100,000,000 \text{ bps}$$
$$= 8 \text{ seconds}$$

A caveat is required at this point: Although the LAN medium is capable of supporting a transmission rate of 100 mbps, the actual data transfer between the two systems is often considerably slower because of the CPU and memory transfer time necessary to send and receive the message. Still, this example illustrates the file transfer differences between WANs and LANs. It also serves as a reminder of the reasons why businesses are interested in high-speed Internet access capabilities.

Resource Sharing

Resource sharing has always been a business motivation for implementing WANs and other data communication networks. This motivation is best exemplified by microcomputer LANs. Early microcomputer LAN systems were oriented primarily toward printer and file sharing (print server and file server technology). Printer sharing allows several users to direct their printed output to the same network-attached printer. With file sharing, two or more users can share a single file. The file can be an application program, a database file, or a work file such as a spreadsheet or word processing document. LANs now are used to share more than printers, disks, and data; interconnecting LANs via WANs enables users to share computing resources across geographically dispersed locations.

Groupware

Work-group productivity tools, collectively called *groupware,* have their roots in WANs. As noted in Chapter 1, groupware allows a group of users to communicate and coordinate activities. Basic groupware capabilities such as e-mail and project management systems were common WAN applications before the introduction of microcomputers. Today, WAN–oriented groupware also includes enhanced e-mail systems, group calendaring systems, computer conferencing and electronic meeting systems, distributed group decision support systems, distributed work-flow systems, instant messaging, videoconferencing systems, and Web-based collaborative computing systems. Lotus Notes and GroupWise (from Novell) are examples of groupware.

Communication

Most of us view telephone networks as a way to allow people to communicate. We use data communication networks for the same reason. However, in a data communication network, the entities that communicate with each other are not necessarily people. The network depicted in Figure 10-3 represents communication among a variety of users and applications: a person-to-person communication, a person-to-application communication, and an application-to-application communication.

The messages being exchanged can also differ. The person-to-person communication may be an electronic conversation, with the two parties exchanging messages in real time, as illustrated in Figure 10-3. User A types a message on the terminal and presses the enter key, and the message is immediately displayed on user B's workstation. The person-to-application communication may be a user making an inquiry into the corporate database. In Figure 10-3, the user communicating with the application might be checking on a shipment for a customer. The application-to-application communication may be the transfer of a file from one node to another.

Communication among business users can also be enhanced through the use of *electronic bulletin board systems (BBSs),* threaded discussions, real-time chats, instant messaging, and videoconferencing. BBSs enable workers to post new information or questions as well as to review what others have posted. The approach is conceptually similar to that used by USENET newsgroups and Web-based technical service sites. Voice mail systems and personal communication services (PCS) are examples of other wide area networking applications that facilitate communication among business users.

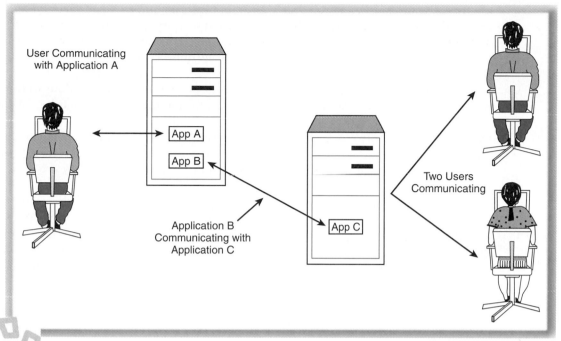

Figure 10-3   Applications and Users Communicating in a Network

Cost-Effectiveness

Cost-effectiveness is one of the major business drivers for WANs. Cost-effectiveness derives from several sources, including resource sharing, the ability to facilitate the coordinated work of work teams, and enhanced communications. For examples, if users can share hardware, less hardware is needed. Less obviously, cost-effectiveness may derive from the ability of users to communicate and thus improve their productivity. One direct benefit is the reduction of paperwork and the expense associated with paper-based processing. *Electronic data exchange (EDI),* for example, reduces the need for paper-based processing and also facilitates communication between organizations. Internet banking and Web-based transaction processing are gaining favor among financial organizations and businesses because they translate into more cost-effective transaction processing than the paper-oriented systems they are replacing.

Competitive Advantage

WANs are also helping organizations to operate more efficiently, enhance decision making, and be more innovative. Through WAN links, data can be instantly transmitted among an organization's geographically dispersed operating locations. Both productivity and decision-making effectiveness can be enhanced. For example, because of WANs, stockbrokers can execute more trades in the same time period than they could through voice networks. WANs can also be beneficial by reducing *information float,* the time it takes to get information from the source to the decision makers. For example, e-mail and fax technologies enable documents to be transmitted around the world almost instantaneously, and the timely receipt of information facilitates decision making. WANs enable publishers such as the Gannett Corporation (which publishes *USA Today*) to distribute page images to its widely dispersed printing plants. WANs also contribute to the competitiveness of overnight package delivery companies such as United Parcel Service and Federal Express.

WANs enable a company's geographically dispersed operating locations to function as if they were all located at a single site. As a result, the company may be able to realize the economies of scale enjoyed by larger single-site firms. For example, by using a WAN to link inventory databases among sites, a firm is likely to be able to maintain less aggregate inventory. Also, through WANs, organizations can often exert better managerial control over their dispersed subunits, ensuring that they are consistently adhering to the organization's operating procedures.

WANs have allowed some organizations to create an "electronic presence" in geographical areas where they lack a physical presence. For example, through WANs, a financial services organization can provide its full range of products to remote field offices staffed by skeleton crews. In some instances, the electronic presence has the effect of extending business hours across time zones. Business Web sites have also enabled organizations to establish a 24/7 electronic presence.

WAN COMMON CARRIER SERVICES

As noted in our definition of WANs, the communication media used to connect geographically dispersed network sites are usually supplied by common carriers. Today, WANs employ the full range of common carrier services and mobile/voice communication services described in the previous chapter. PBX and Centrex services are also important facets of many WANs, as are Internet applications such as voice-over-IP (VoIP), IPsec, and virtual private networks (VPNs).

Table 10-1 summarizes the major switched and leased common carrier services utilized in WANs in the United States. Many of these services are discussed more fully in Chapter 5. Packet switching, frame relay, and ATM are discussed in Chapter 12.

WAN HARDWARE

Virtually all of the data communication hardware discussed in this book is utilized in today's WANs. This includes LAN hardware (discussed in Chapters 7 and 8), internetworking hardware (Chapter 13), Web servers (Chapter 4), firewalls (Chapters 3, 4, and 16), and the wide range of hardware found in voice-oriented networks (Chapters 5 and 6). In the following sections, we will focus on other computing and communications hardware used to support data transfer among WAN nodes, some of which has been in use since the creation of the first data communication networks. This includes hosts, terminals, front-end processors, concentrators, multiplexors, and controllers. Figure 10-4 provides an illustration of how this WAN hardware might be configured.

Hosts

In WANs, hosts have traditionally been mainframes or minicomputers (midrange systems). Today, however, microcomputer servers may also function as WAN hosts. In large WANs, several mainframes or midrange computers may be used as hosts; when these are interconnected by WAN communication links, they are often called network *nodes*. Like servers in local area networks, WAN hosts typically enable network users to access application programs and database management systems. Because WAN hosts are interconnected, users at one location are typically able to access network resources at other WAN locations.

Table 10-1   Switched and Leased (Nonswitched) Carrier Services
Commonly Used in WANs

Service	Type	Characteristics
Dial-up	Switched	This service is relatively inexpensive and has low-speed data transfer rates.
ISDN	Switched	This service operates at higher speeds than dial-up connections. Costs include a fixed monthly charge plus usage time based on the duration of the network connection; long-distance charges also apply.
SMDS	Switched	This is most frequently used in MANs and supports data transmission rates between 1.54 mbps and 44.736 mbps. Monthly charges are based on the bandwidth of the access link and the volume of traffic over the access link.
X.25 packet switching	Switched	This service is widely used to provide switched data transfer among geographically distributed locations. Subscriber charges are based on the volume of data transferred between locations.
Frame relay	Switched	This service is frequently used to provide high-speed data transfer rates among geographically dispersed LANs. Data transfer rates are comparable to those for T-n services.
ATM	Switched	Asynchronous transfer mode (ATM) supports speeds between 25 mbps and 155 mbps. ATM is widely viewed as technically superior to many of the other switched services listed in this table.
Dedicated analog	Leased	This is traditionally the least expensive lease option, although it is slower than many of the other leased options with a maximum data transfer rate of 56 kbps. A fixed monthly charge is based on data transfer rate.
Digital data services	Leased	These high-quality digital lines require CSU/DSU interfaces. Like dedicated analog lines, a fixed monthly charge is based on link speed/bandwidth.
Digital subscriber line	Leased	This service provides a high-speed, "always on" Internet connection that supports voice-over data. Monthly charges are fixed. Usage is growing rapidly among both residential and business customers.
T-n services	Leased	These are traditionally the most widely used digital leased lines for high-traffic data and voice. Fixed monthly charges vary across locations and are most competitive in large urban areas.
SONET	Leased	The highest-speed leased lines that are available use SONET. Costs are a function of the bandwidth of the leased link.

Terminals

A **terminal** is defined as an input or output device that may be connected to a local or remote host. The terminal is (at least at certain times) dependent on the host for computation, data access, or both. The phrase *may be connected* allows for switched connections and terminal devices that have some degree of processing power of their own, such as a microcomputer; such devices may only be connected to a host on a periodic basis.

terminal An input/output device that can be connected to a local or remote computer, called a host computer.

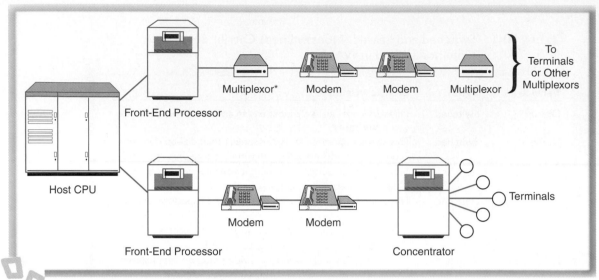

Figure 10-4   Hardware Configuration
Modems are not required for some multiplexors.

Terminal Types

A wide variety of terminals are found in WANs. The characteristics of some of the major kinds are described here.

uploading The transfer of files or programs from a terminal (local device) to a host (remote device).

downloading The act of transferring programs or data from a host (or remote device) to a terminal (or local device).

terminal emulation A software program and/or a hardware interface that allows a microcomputer to function as if it were a specific type of terminal. Terminal emulation software for today's microcomputers often supports a variety of terminal types.

➤ *Microcomputers.* Microcomputers are an integral component of computer networks because they can augment the host by doing a portion of the processing. They may be grouped together in a LAN, connected as terminal devices to a host computer, or both. Microcomputers are used in WANs in a variety of ways, including uploading processed data to the host, downloading host data for processing, and terminal emulation. **Uploading** happens when the terminal transfers files or programs to the host. **Downloading** is the act of transferring programs or data from a host to a terminal. With **terminal emulation**, a software program and a hardware interface allow the microcomputer to function as if it is one of the host's typical terminals.

➤ *Network computers (NCs).* Network computers are essentially scaled down microcomputers. Although they are usually equipped with the same processors as those found in microcomputers, some NCs are *diskless workstations* and rely on network servers for storage and access to application programs and data. Because they lack components typically included in microcomputer systems, NCs are sometimes called *thin clients.* NCs with processing capabilities that are equivalent to microcomputers are sometimes called *fat clients.*

➤ *Data entry and display.* A video display unit (VDU) or a hard-copy device such as a teletypewriter (TTY) can serve for data entry, data display, or both. Such devices can carry on a dialogue with the host(s) and get data from and provide data to the business's applications. A VDU is also sometimes called a *video display terminal (VDT).*

➤ *Display-only devices.* A display-only device often serves as a receiver of data. The monitors displaying arriving and departing flights in airports are examples of display-only devices. Some kinds of remote printers also fit in this class, although some also have the ability to transmit control information such as "out of paper" or "not ready to receive" to the host.

➤ *Point-of-sale terminals.* Point-of-sale (POS) terminals are commonly found at the checkout counters in grocery and retail stores. They may play a key role in several business applications, including those used to help maintain inventory, record gross receipts, and transfer money from a buyer's account to a merchant's account. The capabilities of POS terminals vary significantly.

➤ *Portable terminals.* One application for portable terminals or microcomputers is in direct sales. Some marketing agencies provide their salespeople with portable terminals capable of storing information in memory. The salesperson records customer orders during the day and can use a telephone link to transmit the orders to the home office for processing. Handheld or wearable portable terminals are used in some retail and wholesale locations as wireless POS terminals.

➤ *Touch-tone telephones.* Touch-tone telephones can be used in bill paying, account inquiry or transfer applications, and student registration. Although not used extensively because of their limited input and output capabilities, they work well for certain applications.

➤ *Automated teller machines.* Most banks now have networks of automated teller machines (ATMs) that enable the customer to personally handle simple banking transactions such as deposits, withdrawals, and account balance inquiries. ATMs have had a significant impact on the way people use banking services. Through the ATM, bank customers can get cash or make deposits 24 hours a day and without the assistance of a teller. The ATM provides convenience to the bank customer and reduces the personnel a bank needs to provide services. The customer and the computer combine to accomplish services that formerly required the assistance of a bank teller.

➤ *Sensor devices.* Sensor devices are used in laboratory, hospital, or data collection applications, often for input only. For example, many newer, large office buildings have computer-controlled environmental monitoring systems. Sensors located throughout the building alert the system to areas in which temperature is outside the comfort zone. The host responds by sending a message to an output-only terminal device that switches on heating or cooling.

Terminal Capabilities

As indicated earlier, there is a wide variety of terminal types. There is also a wide range of terminal capabilities. Traditionally, terminals have been classified as dumb, smart, or intelligent, although no distinct lines separate these classes.

A **dumb terminal** passively serves for input or output and does no additional processing. Because dumb terminals usually have no memory to store data, each character entered must be transmitted immediately to the host, unsolicited; the host must always be ready to accept data from the terminal. A dumb terminal generally operates in conversational mode, in which the terminal user and the host exchange messages in response to each other via asynchronous transmissions.

Smart terminals can do anything a dumb terminal can; however, smart terminals have memory. Data entered by the operator can be saved in the terminal's memory until an entire record or several screens of data have been entered. The terminal can then transmit all the entered data in one or more blocks, a capability called *block mode.* Often the screen can be divided into multiple windows, with each window representing a different object set. One window might represent text being written, one might contain notes about the text, another might contain a graphic image of an item being described in the text, and a fourth might contain a menu of tasks or commands that are valid in the current window. Most smart terminals are also addressable, which means that they can be given a name that both they and the host recognize. Thus, the host can transmit data addressed to that terminal, and the terminal will recognize that the data is intended for it and store the data in its memory. Smart terminals are subject

dumb terminal A terminal that passively serves for input or output but performs no local processing. It typically consists of a keyboard and CRT (cathode ray tube) monitor.

smart terminal A terminal with some local processing or memory capabilities. Unlike a dumb terminal, a smart terminal can save data entered by the operator into memory. This enables one or more entire screens of data to be transferred to the host; this eliminates the need to transfer data character-by-character as is typically the case with dumb terminals.

to host control, which means that the host can specify when the terminal is allowed to send or receive data; position the cursor on the display; designate that certain fields, such as an employee's salary, are protected from alteration; control the keyboard and disallow any data entry; specify the display attributes of fields such as *blink* and *half intensity*; and read from or write to selected portions of the display.

Addressing, memory, and host control capabilities enable several terminals to share the same medium and thereby reduce transmission costs.

Smart terminals may also support auxiliary data entry devices such as light pens, mice, and touch screens. Many can have a printer attached for printing a displayed page and for automatic logging of data received by the terminal. Many smart terminals have additional keys known as *function keys*, or *program attention keys*, that transmit specific character sequences to the host. Function keys allow the operator to indicate to the application what function is to be performed on the data provided. The number of function keys per terminal typically ranges from 4 to 32; some special-purpose terminals have 50 or more function keys.

An **intelligent terminal**, such as a microcomputer or network computer (NC), has all or most of the capabilities of a smart terminal, but it can also participate in the data processing requirements of the system. In some situations, the intelligent terminal is completely independent of the host; however, to satisfy our definition of terminal, at some point the intelligent terminal must be connected to a host processor for processing or data access. Because this terminal is programmable, it is also possible for an intelligent terminal to act as host for another terminal. Intelligent terminals may have secondary storage in the form of disk or tape, and an attached printer is a common option. If no auxiliary storage is available, programs can be downloaded to the terminal from the host computer. Like smart terminals, intelligent terminals can be controlled from the host and can operate in both conversational and block modes. Processing functions available on intelligent terminals include storage and display of screen formats, data editing, data formatting, compression/decompression, and possibly some local database access and validation.

intelligent terminal
A terminal that has both memory and local data processing capabilities. Intelligent terminals are sometimes called *programmable terminals*. Some intelligent terminals have local disk or tape storage, but most do not.

Advantages of Smart and Intelligent Terminals

The advantage of smart terminals over dumb terminals is a certain amount of independence between the terminal operator and host. Once a data entry screen is displayed, the operator is free to enter data at her own pace, unrestricted by the transmission speed of the line. Any errors made by the operator can be corrected without the host's involvement. The operator can move the cursor to any field in the record and can correct any data before transmission to the host. The host then controls the terminal and solicits inputs and outputs according to its priorities rather than being periodically interrupted by unsolicited inputs, as is the case with dumb terminals. The advantages of intelligent terminals over smart terminals stem from the fact that control and processing are local. Some data, such as customer data, can be maintained locally where it is used frequently, and line time is not required for obtaining customer information, transmitting screen templates, or correcting edit errors.

Input and Output

Terminal output can be hard copy and soft copy. Hard-copy output leaves a permanent record of the data sent to the terminals; soft-copy output leaves no record of the inputs or outputs. Hard copy uses some kind of printed output; soft copy uses a display monitor such as a CRT (cathode ray tube). The most common input mechanism is the keyboard, which can be configured in a variety of ways. Some configurations support foreign languages, whereas others have preprogrammed keys that support specific applications, such as specimen description keys for medical laboratories. Other input devices include various kinds of readers—badge readers and OCR (optical character recognition) readers—and light pens, mice, trackballs, joysticks, touch screens, sensors, voice recognition and generation equipment, and digital image processing devices that scan graphic images and create digital images of them.

Cost

The cost of terminals varies dramatically, from several hundred dollars for a dumb terminal to tens of thousands of dollars for special terminals such as very-high-resolution graphics terminals with imaging devices. Cost analysis is difficult because cost factors such as line use, operator acceptance, efficiency, and local processing ability are not always easy to quantify.

Speed

The speed at which a terminal accepts and transmits data depends on the terminal hardware, the kind of line to which it is attached, and the kinds of modems used (if any). Any given terminal can receive and transmit information at a discrete set of rates. An unbuffered hard-copy terminal may have a maximum receive speed of 1,200 bps because its print capacity is 120 characters per second. A VDU device, on the other hand, may be capable of receiving data at 56 kbps or more. In addition to the maximum available speed, the intermediate speeds available should be considered. Some terminals only have one or two speed settings, whereas others support a range of speeds, such as 300, 600, 1,200, 2,400, 4,800, 9,600, 19,200, 38,400, and 56,000 bps.

Display Attributes

Hard-copy devices have very few display attributes to select, with the possible exception of colored pens for plotters, graphics, italics, underline, type fonts, or overprint. Video display units have several display attributes to consider, including multiple colors, shading or intensity, reverse video, and highlighting such as blinking fields. Screen size and character size also should be taken into consideration because the number of characters per line and the number of lines per screen can vary significantly.

Terminal Configurations and Line Disciplines

On any communication channel, the two options for attaching terminals are point to point and multipoint. **Point-to-point connections** use a communication line to connect one terminal to the host computer. Point-to-point connections are common in computer-to-computer communication, local connections between a host and a terminal where the cost of the line is negligible, and remote connections with only one remote terminal. The method for controlling which station is allowed to use the communication link is sometimes called a *line discipline*. Today, the term "communication protocol" is more likely to be used than line discipline. Data flow in a point-to-point configuration is usually determined by contention.

In the **contention mode**, the host and the terminal contend for control of the medium. The terminal and the host are considered to have an equal right to transmit to the other. To transmit, one station issues a bid for the channel, asking the other party for control. If the other is ready to receive data, control is granted to the requester. Upon completion of the transfer, control is relinquished, and the link goes into an idle state, awaiting the next bid for control. A collision can occur when both stations simultaneously bid for the line. If this occurs, either one station is granted the request based on some predetermined priority scheme or each station waits awhile

point-to-point connection A connection using a communication line that provides a direct communication path from one machine to another. Point-to-point connections may be used to connect a terminal or computer to a host computer.

contention mode A type of communication line discipline in which the host and the terminal contend for control of the medium by issuing a bid for the channel. Bids are typically handled on a first-come, first-served basis.

and then reattempts the bid. With the latter approach, the time-out intervals must not be the same, or another collision occurs. Conflicts for the use of the channel in a point-to-point configuration typically are few, because only the host and the terminal are candidates for transmission.

For communication among several terminals over a long distance, true point-to-point connections would be quite expensive, because each terminal would require a separate line with a pair of modems. Several techniques have been developed to allow several terminals to share one communication link. One approach is called a **multipoint connection**. The number of terminals allowed to share the medium depends on the speed of the medium and the aggregate transmission rate of the terminals. As the number of terminals on the line increases, the average time each terminal has access to the link decreases. With terminals, the most common approaches to multipoint connections are polling and multiplexing.

Polling   The process of asking terminals whether they have data to transmit is called **polling**. In polling, one station is designated as the *supervisor* or *primary station*; this role is almost always assumed by the host computer, although other pieces of equipment such as controllers or concentrators may be used instead. There is only one primary station per multipoint link; all other stations are called *secondary stations*. In the discussion that follows, we assume that the host computer is the primary. The primary station is in complete control of the link. Secondary stations may transmit data only when given permission by the primary station. Each secondary station is given a unique address, and each terminal must be able to recognize its own address. Although there are several distinct methods of polling, essentially the process works as follows. The primary is provided a list of addresses for terminals on a particular link. Several multipoint lines may be controlled by one primary, although addresses on a given line are unique. The primary picks an address from the list and, using that address, sends a poll message across the link. The poll message is very short, consisting of the poll address and a string of characters that has been designated as a poll message. All secondary stations receive the poll message, but only the addressee responds. The poll message is an inquiry to the secondary station as to whether it has any data to transmit to the primary. If it has data to transmit, the secondary responds either with the data or with a positive acknowledgment and then the data. If the secondary station has no data to send, it responds with a negative acknowledgment. Upon receipt of either the data or the negative acknowledgment, the primary selects another station's polling address and repeats the process. The two basic kinds of polling are roll call and hub polling.

➤ In *roll-call polling*, the primary obtains a list of addresses for terminals on the line and then proceeds sequentially down the list, polling each terminal in turn. If one or more stations on the link are of higher priority or are more likely to have data to send, their address could be included in the list several times so they can be polled more often. Roll-call polling is illustrated in Figure 10-5.

➤ *Hub polling* requires the terminals to become involved in the polling process. The primary sends a poll message to one station on the link. If that station has data to transmit, it does so. After transmitting its data or if it has no data to transmit, the secondary terminal passes the poll to an adjacent terminal. This process is repeated until all terminals have had the opportunity to transmit. The primary then starts the process again. Hub polling is illustrated in Figure 10-6. In the diagram, if T2 were not operational, T3 would pass the poll to T1.

Selection   When the primary has data to send to one or more secondary stations, it selects the station in much the same manner as with polling. Some terminals have two addresses, one for polling and one for selecting. In the selection process, the primary

multipoint connection A connection in which several terminals share one communication link. A multipoint line may be used to interconnect terminals and a host at a single location or to interconnect terminals and hosts at multiple remote sites.

polling A type of line discipline in which a central computer or host systematically asks its attached terminals whether they have data to transmit. Round-robin interrogation is typically used to determine when a terminal is ready to send data.

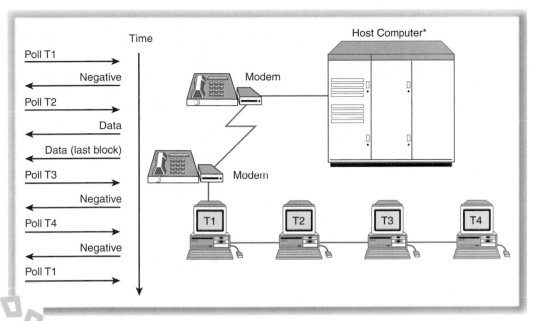

Figure 10-5   Roll-Call Polling

May be a cluster controller, communication controller, front-end processor, or other equipment.

Figure 10-6   Hub Polling

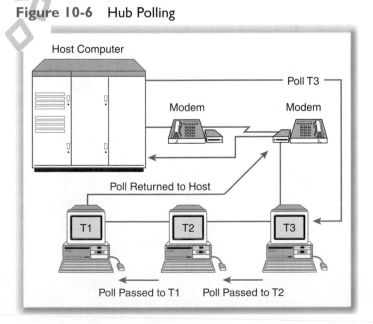

sends a selection message to the terminal. A selection message consists of the terminal's selection address and an inquiry to determine whether the terminal is ready to accept data. The terminal may respond positively or negatively. If the terminal's buffer is full, it cannot accept additional data and responds negatively. After a positive acknowledgment to the selection message, the primary transmits the data to the terminal. In some multipoint networks, the primary can send a message to all stations simultaneously via a broadcast address, which is one address that all terminals recognize as their own.

Advantage of Multipoint Connections   The advantage of multipoint lines is economic. First, only one communication link is required for a host to communicate with several terminals; second, if modems are required on the link, fewer modems are necessary. In a true point-to-point link, a pair of modems is often required for each terminal, one at the host end and one at the terminal end. For multipoint links, at most one modem per terminal and one at the host are required. In some instances, a terminal cluster controller may be used at the terminal end, and if the terminals are sufficiently close to the controller, individual terminal modems are not necessary; only a host and cluster controller modem are required. If plans call for 10 terminals to be located remotely, 10 point-to-point lines would require 20 modems. For a multipoint line, at most 11 modems would be required, and possibly 2 would be sufficient. Figure 10-7 presents multipoint configurations, together with their required modems.

Disadvantages of Multipoint Connections   There are also disadvantages to the multipoint configuration. First, terminals used in this environment must have some intelligence, making them more expensive than terminals in the point-to-point connection. This higher cost is usually negligible, however, when compared to the savings in medium and modems. Because the medium is shared among several terminals, a

Figure 10-7   Multipoint Configurations

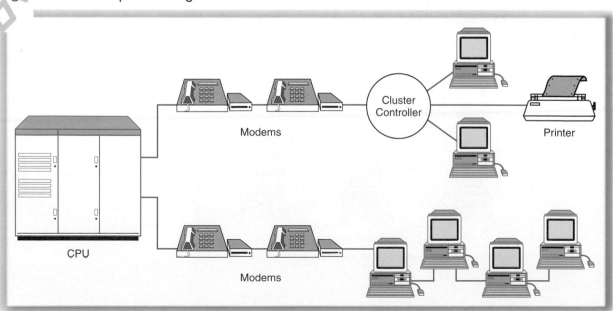

terminal may have to wait to transmit its information. If messages are short, the wait time should not be long; on the other hand, if messages are lengthy, as when a micro-computer transfers a file, the other terminals may have to wait an inordinate amount of time. Delays also have an impact on response times, and this delay should be factored into the response time calculations for a multipoint line.

Multiplexors

Polling requires the use of smart terminals that are addressable and have memory. Another line-sharing technique, *multiplexing*, does not generally require the use of smart terminals. Multiplexing technology allows multiple signals to be transmitted over a single link. Multiplexing has been used by telephone companies for many years to combine multiple voice-grade circuits into a single high-speed circuit for long-distance communication. In data communication networks, *multiplexors*, or muxes, allow several devices to share a common circuit.

How Multiplexors Work

Remote locations often have multiple devices that must communicate with a host. Multiplexing provides an alternative to a point-to-point connection and polling. Figure 10-8 presents a general mux configuration. Several communication lines enter the mux from

Figure 10-8   General Multiplexor Configuration

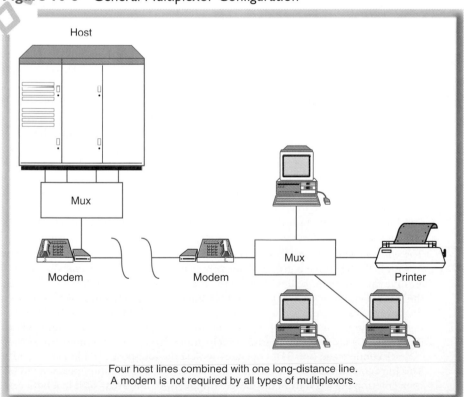

Four host lines combined with one long-distance line.
A modem is not required by all types of multiplexors.

the host side. The mux combines the data from all incoming lines and transmits it via one line to a mux at the receiving end. This receiving mux separates the data and distributes it among the outgoing terminal lines. The number of lines going into the mux on the host side is the same as the number going out to terminals (or other muxes) on the remote side.

To the user, the multiplexor appears to function as though there were several physical lines rather than just one. The configuration of one high-speed link and a pair of multiplexors, however, costs less than that of several lower speed links with a pair of modems for each. Applications written for a point-to-point terminal connection also can be used without change. The multiplexor makes the line sharing transparent to the user because the application essentially sees a point-to-point line.

Kinds of Multiplexors

A communication link is divided among several users in two basic ways. The first technique, known as *frequency division multiplexing (FDM)*, separates the link by frequencies. The second technique, known as *time division multiplexing (TDM)*, separates the link into time slots.

➤ *Frequency division multiplexing (FDM).* In FDM, the available bandwidth of the circuit is broken into subchannels, each of which has smaller bandwidths. Consider an analog telephone circuit (such as those described and illustrated in Chapter 5) with a bandwidth of 3,100 Hz, a frequency range of 300 to 3,400 Hz, and a line-carrying capacity of 38,400 bps. On this line, we could have one terminal operating at 38,400 bps; however, instead of one terminal running at 33,600 bps, we want to have three terminals operating at 9,600 bps. In order to keep the signals from interfering with one another, the three 9,600-bps lines must be separated by guardbands. If the recommended separation for a 9,600-bps circuit is 480 Hz, two guardbands of 480 Hz each will be needed. Each of the three 9,600 subchannels, therefore, has a bandwidth of 713 Hz, derived as follows:

$$3,100 \text{ Hz (total bandwidth of circuit)} - 960 \text{ Hz (two guardbands at 480 Hz each)}$$
$$= 2,140 \text{ Hz } / 3 \text{ channels} = 713 \text{ Hz per channel}$$

Similarly, a 56,000-bps channel might be divided into four 13,400-bps channels. The higher the speed of individual channels, the larger the guardbands must be. Figure 10-9 illustrates an FDM configuration and the division of the channel into several subchannels. There is no need for modems in this configuration because the FDM functions as a modem by accepting the signal from the data terminal equipment (DTE) and transforming it into a signal within a given frequency range. Thus, the modem is integrated into the FDM. Each line in the FDM is mapped onto one of the subchannels. The first line's signal is passed along the first subchannel, the second line is passed along the second subchannel, and so on. If terminals on that line are not busy, that portion of the carrying capacity goes unused.

➤ *Time division multiplexing (TDM).* TDM is roughly equivalent to time-sharing systems. As with FDM, TDM has a group of lines entering the mux, one circuit shared by all, and the same number of lines leaving the mux at the other end. Instead of splitting the frequency, however, TDM shares time: Each line is given a time slot for transmitting, which is accomplished by interleaving bits or characters (bytes). Bit interleaving is more common for synchronous (block at a time) transmissions, and character interleaving is more common with asynchronous (character at a time) transmissions.

To understand how TDM operates, look at the four-port TDM in Figure 10-10(a). This mux combines signals from the four lines onto a single communication circuit. Data entering the TDM from the devices on the input line are placed in a buffer or register. With character interleaving, first a character from line 1 is transmitted, then a

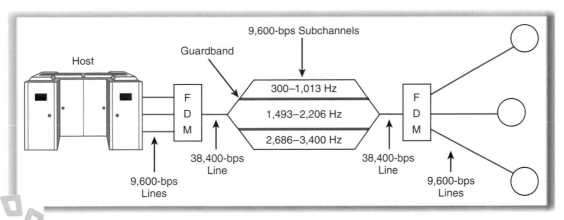

Figure 10-9   Frequency Division Multiplexor Configuration

Figure 10-10(a)   Time Division Multiplexor

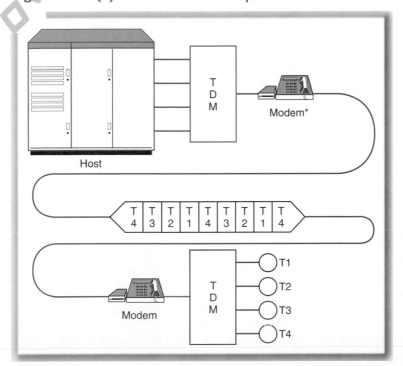

A modem is not required for all TDMs; for example, an in-house digital TDM may not require modems.

character from line 2, one from line 3, one from line 4, and back again to line 1 to repeat the process. Bit interleaving works in the same manner except that a bit instead of a character is taken from each line in turn to form a transmission block. The mux at the other end breaks the data back out and places it on the appropriate line.

As with FDM, each line gets a portion of the available transfer time. However, TDM requires no guardbands, so there is no loss of carrying capacity. Each line is given a portion of the circuit's carrying capacity even though there are no data to be transmitted. Still, the improvement is significant: For example, instead of only three 9,600-bps sublines on a 38,400-bps line, there can be four lines, each capable of 9,600-bps transmission, as illustrated in Figure 10-11, or eight 4,800 bps lines.

A major shortcoming of a time division multiplexor is revealed when attached lines do not have data to transmit. In this circumstance, time slots allocated to idle lines go unused. This is illustrated in Figure 10-10(b). In this figure, both terminals 2 and 3 are idle; they are either not in use or do not have data to transmit to the host at that point in time. The time slots allocated to these terminals by the TDM go unused when the terminals are idle. Hence, the communication circuit is not being used to its fullest capacity.

➤ *Statistical time division multiplexing.* A *statistical time division multiplexor (STDM or stat mux)* improves on the efficiency of TDM by transmitting data only for lines with data to send, so idle lines take up none of the carrying capacity of the communication circuit. The reallocation of time slots from idle to busy terminals is illustrated in Figure 10-10(c). Figure 10-12 illustrates an STDM. Because neither time slot nor frequency is allocated to a specific terminal, an STDM must also transmit a terminal identification along with the data block. When all lines have data to transmit, an

Figure 10-10(b) Time Division Multiplexor with Idle Terminals

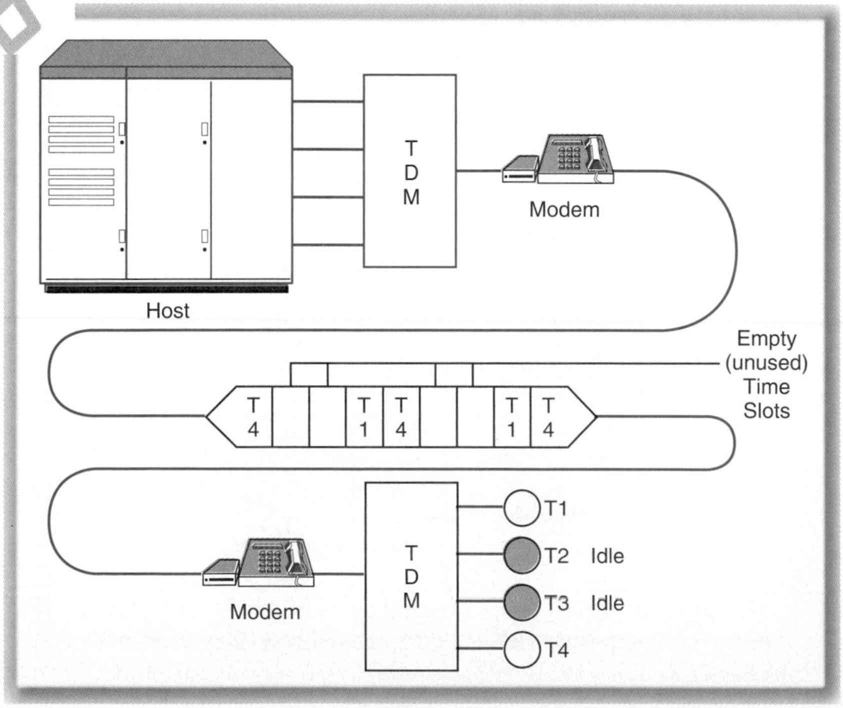

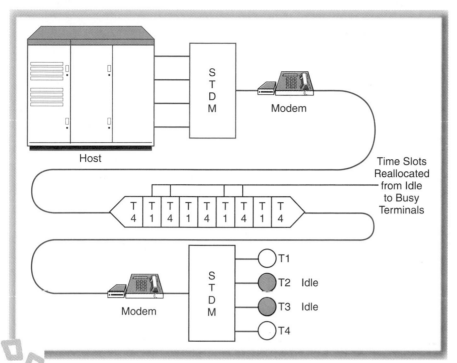

Figure 10-10(c)   Time Slot Reallocation by Statistical Time Division Multiplexor

STDM looks just like a TDM; when only one line has data to send, however, the entire line capacity is devoted to that line by the STDM.

Under good conditions, an STDM on a 56,000-bps line can support up to eight 9,600-bps sublines, or up to 16 4,800-bps sublines. The reason for this apparent increase in carrying capacity stems from the probability that none of the incoming lines will be 100 percent busy. If each line is only 50 percent busy, then 16 4,800-bps lines could be placed on one 56,000-bps link. STDMs also have internal buffers for holding data from a line in case all lines try to transmit at once. Newer stat muxes provide additional capabilities, including data compression, digital data support, line priorities, mixed-speed lines, integrated modems, network control ports for monitoring the multiplexed line, host port sharing (Two or more lines at the terminal end are mapped onto one line at the host end.), port switching (wherein a terminal can be switched from one port to another), accumulation and reporting of performance statistics, automatic speed detection, memory expansion, and internal diagnostics.

All of these features are not likely to be found in one mux. Different manufacturers offer one or more of these capabilities as standard or optional functions. A few of these features can also be found in TDMs. Most of the development and enhancements in the past several years have been devoted to stat muxes because of their higher performance capabilities.

➤ *Wavelength division multiplexing* (*WDM*). WDM is a relatively new multiplexing technique used for optical transmissions over fiber optic cables. Traditionally, a single laser operating at a single wavelength was used to transmit signals over a fiber optic cable. Today, wavelength division multiplexors leverage multiple lasers operating at multiple wavelengths to transmit several signals simultaneously. Multiple data streams represented by

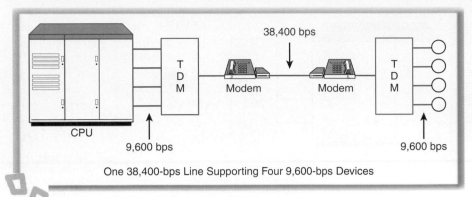

Figure 10-11   Time Division Multiplexing

different wavelengths of light can be transmitted simultaneously over a single optical fiber with WDM. WDM technologies are primarily used by telecommunications carriers over long-distance fiber optic trunks such as those that support SONET (synchronous optical network) services. WDM enables carriers to increase the transmission capacity of their fiber optical networks without having to install more fiber optic cables. Dense WDM (DWDM) combines WDM and TDM in order to further increase the amount of data that can be transmitted over a single fiber. Today, up to 10 gps can be transmitted over each DWDM circuit, and 40 or more simultaneous circuits may be created on each fiber. Industry experts expect DWDM technologies to achieve128 simultaneous circuits within a few years; at 10 gbps per circuit, this means that a single fiber will have a capacity of 1.28 terabits per second (tbps). Industry experts also predict that DWDM transmission speeds will reach 25 tbps in the not too distant future and that DWDM advances will one day enable a petabit (one million billion bits per second) to be carried over a single optical fiber.

Figure 10-12   Statistical Time Division Multiplexing

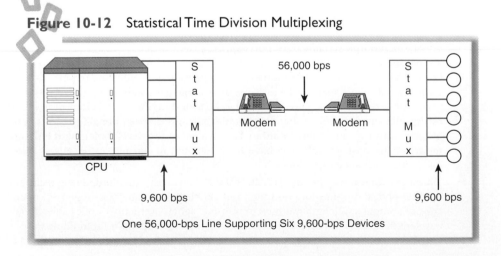

Multiplexor Configurations

In addition to attaching terminals to muxes, other muxes can be added in daisy-chain fashion, a configuration illustrated in Figure 10-13. A *daisy chain*, also called *cascading*, allows some circuits to be extended to another remote point, which is useful in a situation with two areas for data entry. With eight terminals in each area, a 16-port stat mux could provide linkage between the host and area A, and eight lines from area A could travel via an 8-port mux to area B. The number of ports on a mux can vary, but commonly there are 4, 8, 16, 32, 48, or 64 ports. Multiplexor prices vary according to the number of ports and features provided. For a plain 4-port or 8-port stat mux, prices start at about $1,000.

A less common mux known as an *inverse multiplexor* provides a high-speed data path between two devices, usually computers. An inverse mux accepts one line from a host and separates it into multiple lower speed communication circuits. The multiple low-speed circuits are recombined at the other end into a high-speed link, as illustrated in Figure 10-14. A 56-kbps link from a computer to an inverse mux can be split into six 9,600-bps lines and then converted back to a 56-kbps line at the remote end. Inverse multiplexors are often used to support high-end videoconferencing applications.

A variety of other multiplexors are found in today's wide area networks. These include

➤ *Data/voice multiplexors.* These enable both voice and data transmissions to be carried simultaneously over a dial-up or leased digital circuit.

➤ *T-1, fractional T-1, and T-3 multiplexors.* These enable multiple data or voice transmissions to be carried simultaneously over T1, FT1, or T3 lines, respectively.

➤ *Frame relay multiplexors.* These enable a variety of devices including hosts, file servers, PCs, fax machines, and phones to share a connection to a frame relay network; frame relay networks are discussed more fully in Chapter 12.

Figure 10-13   Cascading Multiplexors

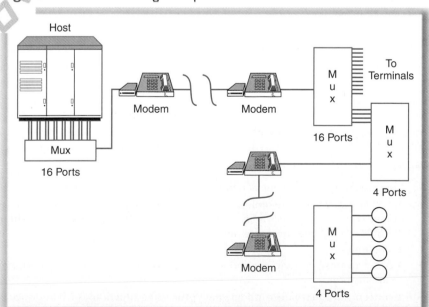

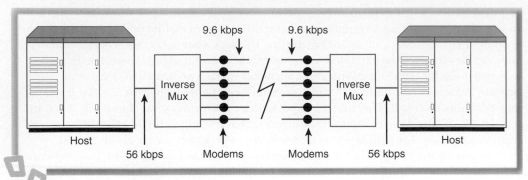

9.6 kbps   9.6 kbps

Inverse   Inverse
Mux   Mux

Host   Host

56 kbps   Modems   Modems   56 kbps

Figure 10-14   Inverse Multiplexor

➤ *ISDN multiplexors.* These enable multiple asynchronous devices to share a single ISDN link to a remote host.

➤ *Fiber optic multiplexors.* These enable multiple devices (typically asynchronous devices) to share a single fiber optic link (up to 10,000 feet in length) to a host. These are often found in small- to medium-size campus environments and are examples of *local* or *short-distance multiplexing.*

➤ *RS-232 multiplexors.* These enable multiple devices to connect to the multiplexor via RS-232 cable and to share a single communications link to a remote host.

➤ *DSL routers.* These enable multiple devices (phones and computers) to share a single DSL line. These rely on FDM to create three logical circuits: a standard voice circuit to support telephone calls, an upstream data circuit from the modem to the DSL multiplexor (DSLAM) at the carrier's central office, and a downstream data circuit from the DSLAM at the central office to the modem. TDM is often used within the upstream and downstream data circuits to enable the creation of multiple channels within each circuit. This enables multiple users to simultaneously share the DSL line.

Concentrators

concentrator A device that joins several communication lines together for transmission onto one transmission line. A concentrator often provides capabilities beyond line sharing such as data editing, polling, error handling, code conversion, compression, and encryption.

A **concentrator** is also a line-sharing device. It functions similar to a mux, allowing multiple devices to share communication circuits. Because a concentrator also has processing capabilities, it can participate more actively than a mux in many applications. In the early 1970s, there was a marked distinction between a concentrator and a multiplexor. As multiplexors took on the additional functions just described, the differences between the two devices narrowed. Currently, the principal differences between a mux and a concentrator are as follows:

➤ Concentrators are used one at a time; multiplexors are used in pairs.

➤ A concentrator may have multiple incoming and outgoing lines, with a different number of incoming lines than outgoing lines; a multiplexor takes a certain number of incoming lines onto one line and converts back to the same number of outgoing lines.

➤ A concentrator is a computer and may have auxiliary storage for use in support of an application.

➤ A concentrator may perform some data processing functions, such as device polling and data validation.

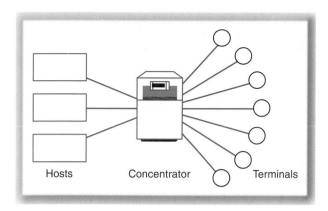

Figure 10-15
Concentrator Configuration

One possible concentrator configuration is illustrated in Figure 10-15.

Concentrators can further aid an application by providing data editing, polling, error handling, code conversion, compression, and encryption. Concentrators can also switch messages between terminals and hosts. In a banking ATM environment where three regional processing centers are responsible for authorizing transactions, each city with multiple ATMs could use a concentrator to handle ATM traffic. The concentrator would have three lines, one each for the three hosts in the three regional processing centers. There would also be one line for each ATM or cluster of ATMs. Based on the customer's ATM card number, the concentrator would switch each transaction to the processing center closest to the customer's home branch.

Front-End Processors

A **front-end processor (FEP)**, sometimes called a *communication controller* or *message switch*, is used at the host end of the communication circuit, just as a concentrator is used at the remote end. The FEP takes over much of the line management work from the host; in many respects, FEPs and concentrators serve the same function. An FEP configuration is shown in Figure 10-16.

An FEP interface with a host system uses one or more high-speed links. The FEP is responsible for controlling the more numerous low-speed circuits. All functions of a

front-end processor (FEP) A communication component placed at the host end of a circuit to take over a portion of the line management work from the host. It is typically a computer that handles communications processing for the host. Also called a communication controller or message switch.

Figure 10-16   Front-End Processor Configuration

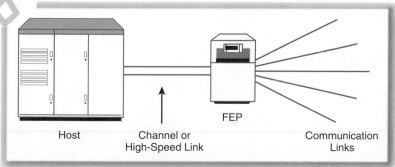

Host   Channel or   FEP   Communication
              High-Speed Link   Links

concentrator can also be performed by an FEP, except, of course, concentrating message traffic for multiple remote terminals onto one communication line. FEPs may be either special purpose or general purpose. Special-purpose FEPs, such as IBM's communication controllers, are designed specifically for data communication. Their operating system and software are solely communication oriented. General-purpose computers, such as minicomputers, are also used as FEPs. When general-purpose computers are used in this way, their role is generally restricted to providing data communication functions.

Port Concentrators

Multiplexors allow multiple terminals to share one communication link. However, for each terminal attached to a multiplexor there must be one communication port at the host end to receive the signal, which makes the multiplexor appear to be a point-to-point connection for both terminal and host. All systems have an upper limit to the number of communication ports that may be configured, and, of course, there is a cost to providing ports. A *port concentrator*, illustrated in Figure 10-17, allows multiple input streams from a multiplexor to be passed to the host through a single communication port. This is beneficial not only in reducing the hardware cost of the host but also in allowing for expansion beyond the port limitations of a particular processor. Port concentration requires that a software module be available in the host to receive the multiple terminal messages and then route them to the appropriate applications.

Port Selector or Data Switch

A *port selector* helps determine which users are granted access to applications for which the number of potential terminal users far exceeds the number of available lines, as in reservation and library systems. If a particular system allows a total of 1,000 terminals to communicate with a host at one time and there are 8,000 potential users, obviously not all of these users can have access to the system at once. A port selector helps to determine which users are granted access. For switched lines, the port selec-

Figure 10-17   Port Concentrator

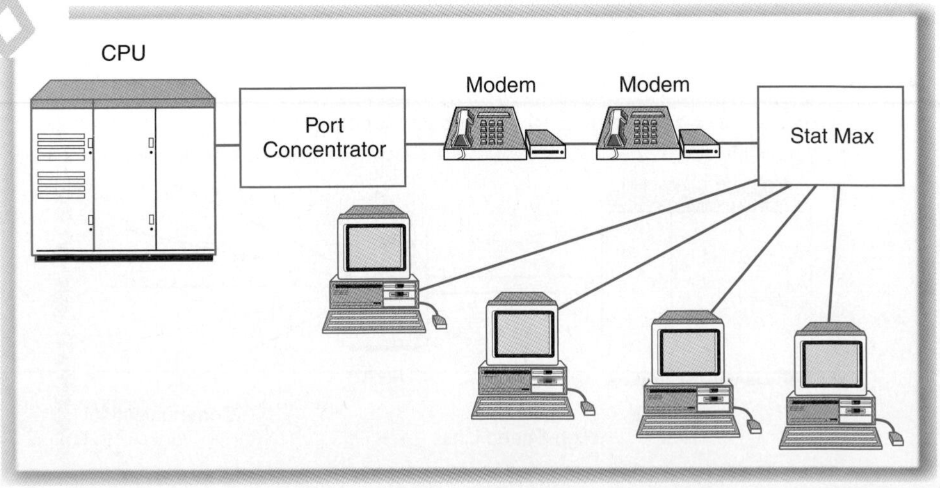

tor can act as a rotary, allowing users to dial one number and connecting the incoming calls to any available switched port. It can also enable switched users to connect to an unused dedicated port. Port selectors can sometimes make connections to several hosts. Some port selectors give the user considerable control over how many ports will be used for switched calls, how many can be shared between dedicated and switched users, and how many can be routed to another host. Thus, the ports and the class of users who may select them can be configured to meet specific needs.

Cluster Controllers

A *cluster controller*, depicted in Figure 10-18, is designed to support several terminals. It manages the terminals, buffers data being transmitted to or from the terminals, performs error detection and correction, and polls. Because of the role that these technologies play in terminal-to-host communication, they are often called *terminal controllers*. The controller may be attached to the host either locally or remotely. Although every terminal attached to a cluster controller usually uses the same communication protocol, the devices themselves may differ. The remote cluster controller in Figure 10-18 has microcomputers and a network printer attached.

WAN TOPOLOGIES

Network topologies define how network nodes are connected. There is considerable variability among WAN topologies; however, the major forms include star, hierarchical, interconnected, ring, bus, or combinations of these.

Star Network

In a **star network,** the central or hub node serves as a message switch by accepting a message from the originating node and forwarding it to the destination node, as illustrated in Figure 10-19. A star configuration has several advantages. First, it provides a short path between any two nodes with a maximum of two links, or hops, to traverse. The time needed for the message to go from the central node to a peripheral node or vice versa is even shorter, because only one hop is required to get from source to destination. On the other hand, having the central node involved in the transmission of

star network A network topology using a central system or station to which all other nodes are connected, often by point-to-point connections. All data are transmitted to or through the central system.

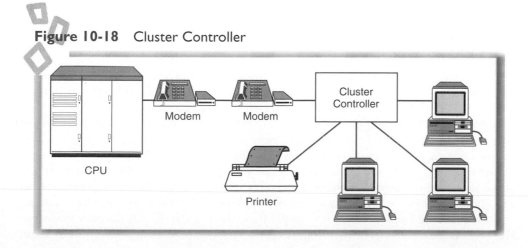

Figure 10-18   Cluster Controller

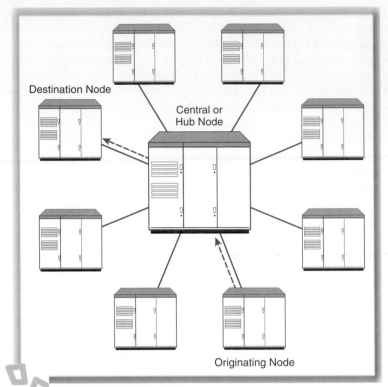

Figure 10-19   Star Configuration

every message can lead to congestion at the central site. This causes consequent message delays, and such congestion is exacerbated when the central node is functioning for more than just message switching. If the central node is also the central processing system, as is often the case, higher priority processing requirements could make the processor temporarily unable to attend to communication functions. This problem is more likely to occur in a uniprocessor system than in a multiple-processor system.

A star configuration also provides for a high degree of network control. Because the central node is in direct contact with every other node and all messages flow through it, a centralized location exists for message logging, gathering of network statistics, and error diagnostics and recovery. However, this centralized control and dependence on a centralized system sometimes are considered a disadvantage rather than an advantage. In a corporate network, having a centralized system may be consistent with a centralized management control philosophy. Close control of all other data processing centers by a main data processing center may be consistent with corporate management objectives. In a network of peer organizations, having one organization act as a point of centralized control may be undesirable. Consider a network of major universities, where it may be difficult to reach agreement as to which university will serve as the centralized controller. Even after the decision is made, dependence on one data center for communication services may be undesirable for the other nodes.

Expanding a star network is a simple procedure because only the new node and the central node need to be involved. It simply requires obtaining the communication link, connecting the two, and updating the network tables in the other nodes. Some instances also require that a new system generation be performed for the other nodes. A new system generation is usually required if adding a new node exceeds the limits of memory allocated to the network routing tables. For dynamic networks, it is common to allocate space for potential nodes to reduce the number of system generations that must be performed.

Star systems can be troubled by low reliability. The loss of the central node is equivalent to loss of the network. Failure of a peripheral node has little impact on the network as a whole, however, because only messages bound for that node are undeliverable. The best candidate for the central node is a fault-tolerant system that is almost immune to failure.

Star systems can have the disadvantage in a long-distance network of higher circuit costs. This is particularly true when the centralized node is not in the geographic center of the network. Other topologies are better able to configure the links between nodes, so the distance spanned by the media is minimized.

Hierarchical Network

A **hierarchical topology**, shown in Figure 10-20, is also called a *tree structure*. Directly connected to the single root node (node A) are several nodes at the second level. Each of these can have several cascaded nodes attached. This kind of network, often found in corporate computer networks, closely resembles corporate organization charts. With the corporate computer center as root node, division systems are attached directly to the root, regional systems to divisional systems, districts to regions, and so on. Corporate reports from a lower level are easily consolidated at the next higher

hierarchical topology A network topology in which the nodes are arranged hierarchically. Also known as a tree structure.

Figure 10-20   Hierarchical Topology

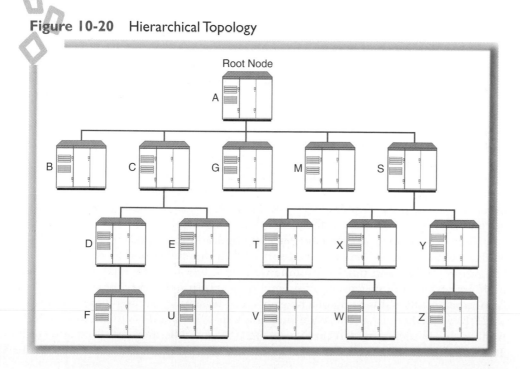

level, and the network generally mirrors the information flow pattern in the corporation. Information flowing from a district in one division to a district in a different division would need to go through the root or corporate node. As with a star system, this allows for a great deal of network control.

Media costs for a hierarchical topology are likely to be lower than for a star topology, assuming that the lower level nodes are closer to the next higher level than they are to the root. It is possible, of course, to devise configurations in which media costs are higher than for a centralized system. A hierarchical network can require quite a few hops for a message to reach its destination. If node F in Figure 10-20 needed to send a message to node Z, the message would have to pass through five intermediate nodes (F—>D—>C—>A—>S—>Y—>Z). In the hierarchical topology, nodes tend to communicate with neighboring nodes, so the need for a leaf node on one side of the hierarchy to communicate with a leaf node on the other side of the hierarchy is presumably small.

Expansion and reconfiguration of a hierarchical network can pose problems. In the configuration of Figure 10-20, splitting node C into nodes C and K, with D and F under C and E under K, would require more work than in the star configuration. Node K would have to be linked to node A, and node E would have to be unlinked from C and relinked to K. Although this may not sound difficult, it costs time and money to change circuits from one location to another, especially with circuits provided by a common carrier. As with most configuration changes, network routing tables must be updated, and system or network regeneration may be needed. Failure of the root node in a hierarchical configuration is less costly than in a star configuration, but it does present a serious reliability problem. In fact, the failure of any node other than those at the extremities makes it impossible to reach that node or any of its subordinate nodes. Congestion at the root and high-level nodes is also a potential problem.

Interconnected (Plex) Network

interconnected (plex or mesh) network A network topology in which any node can be directly connected to any other node. There are at least two communication paths to each node in this net-like communications network topology.

Two forms of an **interconnected (plex or mesh) network** are shown in Figure 10-21. In the fully interconnected network, Figure 10-21(a), every node is connected to every other node with which it must communicate. In the past, fully interconnected topology was required because the available network software was not sophisticated enough to perform the routing and forwarding functions. Current network software allows for but does not require fully interconnected nodes. Message traffic patterns are used to determine where links should be installed. As might be expected, the links in a fully interconnected network are quite costly. The number of links required for a fully interconnected network of n nodes is $n(n - 1)/2$. The performance of an interconnected system is generally good, as direct links can be established between nodes with high amounts of data to exchange. Costs can also be controlled because interconnected topology is capable of the shortest or least expensive configuration. Any of the other topology types can be mimicked by an interconnected topology, although routing and control mechanisms would probably be different.

The expandability of interconnected configurations depends on the kind of network and how the new node is to be connected. In the fully interconnected network, expansion is costly and time-consuming because a link must be established to every node with which the new node must communicate. In networks that do not require full interconnection, insertion of a new node can be simple. Adding node H in Figure 10-21(b) would be very simple, requiring only a link from node G to the new node H. Adding a node such as node C in Figure 10-21(b) would be more involved and costly. The impact of node failure depends on the specific configuration. Alternative paths

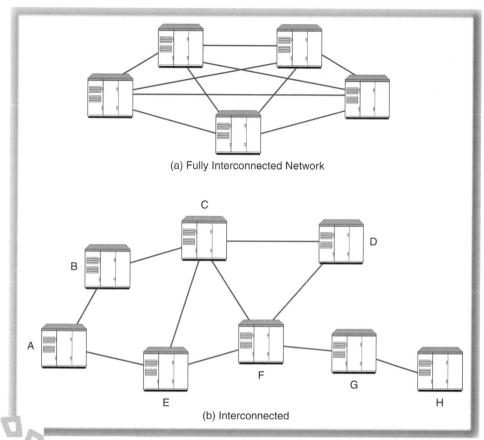

(a) Fully Interconnected Network

(b) Interconnected

Figure 10-21   Interconnected Configurations

around a failed node are sometimes available. If node C in Figure 10-21(b) fails, all other nodes are still able to communicate. The loss of node F, however, would isolate nodes G and H. Because all nodes in an interconnected topology are equal, control is distributed rather than centralized.

Hybrid Networks

Combinations of the topologies previously discussed are sometimes integrated into one network. One such combination is a backbone network—such as a ring—with spurs attached. The backbone nodes can be dedicated to message transfer and data communication while the other nodes are used for both data processing and data communication. In widely distributed systems with many nodes, this helps reduce the number of hops, the length of the links, and congestion problems. If the backbone is implemented as a ring or with multiple paths available, reliability is also high. The cost of hybrid networks can be quite low because different topologies can be used for network segments. Table 10-2 summarizes the different kinds of topology with respect to cost, control, number of hops (speed), reliability, and expandability.

Table 10-2   Network Topology Characteristics

Topology Type	Cost	Control	Number of Hops	Reliability	Expandability
Star	Can be high	Very good	Maximum of two	Poor	Good
Hierarchical	Can be high	Good	Can be many	Fair	Fair to good
Interconnected, full	Highest	Distributed	One only	Good	Very poor
Interconnected, other	Can be lowest	Distributed	Can be many	Good	Good
Ring	Good	Distributed	Can be many	Good	Good
Bus	Good	Distributed	N/A	Good	Good

WAN DATA LINK PROTOCOLS

As noted previously, polling and contention are used in some WANs to determine or control the order in which network devices are allowed to transmit data. Two fundamental categories of WAN data link protocols underlie polling and contention. These are typically asynchronous and synchronous protocols. Asynchronous is often used to connect hosts with POS terminals and in other transaction processing environments. Synchronous protocols are used for high-volume data transfers between hosts and for downloading and uploading entire files between hosts and terminals. We begin the discussion with asynchronous, the first WAN data link protocol.

Asynchronous Transmission

asynchronous transmission (async) The oldest and one of the most common data link protocols used for communication between terminals and hosts. Each character is transmitted individually with its own error detection scheme, usually a parity bit. The sender and receiver are not synchronized with each other. Also known as start-stop protocol.

Asynchronous transmission (async) is the oldest and one of the most common data link protocols. Like many of the techniques used in data communication, it is derived from the telegraph and telephone industries. In asynchronous transmission, data is transmitted one character at a time, and sender and receiver are not synchronized with each other. The sender is thus able to transmit a character at any time. The receiver must be prepared to recognize that information is arriving, accept the data, possibly check for errors, and print, display, or store the data in memory. Individual characters also can be separated over different time intervals, meaning that no synchronization exists between individual transmitted characters.

Most dumb terminals are async devices, and many smart and intelligent terminals can also communicate asynchronously. Personal computers running terminal emulation software often use async transmission to communicate with host systems. Async transmission is also called a *start-stop* protocol. This term and the terms *mark* (1 bit) and *space* (0 bit) are holdovers from telegraphy. It is called start-stop because each character is framed by a start bit and a stop bit, as illustrated in Figure 10-22.

Compatibility of Sending and Receiving Stations   A communication link is either idling or transmitting data. In the idle state, an async line is held in the mark condition, which is a continuous stream of 1 bits (111111111111. . . .). The sending and receiving stations must agree on the number of bits per character before establishing the communication link. If parity is to be transmitted for error detection, both stations must agree on either even or odd parity and on whether the parity bit is to be checked. (The parity bit could be transmitted but not checked by the data link software or hardware.) The stations also must agree on a transmission speed because this determines the interval at which the line is sampled. Finally, there must be agreement as to what will terminate the message. A message terminator is usually a defined set of characters

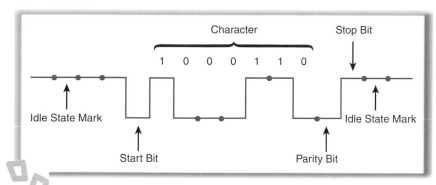

Figure 10-22   Asynchronous Transmission of the ASCII-7 Letter *F*

called **interrupt characters,** a count of a specific number of characters, or a time-out interval. For the following discussion, we will assume that sending and receiving stations are the same with respect to the number of bits sent per character, parity, message termination, and maximum speed of the link (as detected by the receiving modem). The line is in the idle state, meaning that a continuous stream of 1 bits is being transmitted. There are 7 data bits (using an encoding scheme such as the 7-bit version of ASCII) and 1 parity bit, and odd parity will be checked.

interrupt characters A set of characters that terminate a message or cause an interruption in transmission to perform a special action, such as a backspace.

Transmitting a Character   A character's arrival is signaled by a start bit, which is a change in the state of the line from a mark to a space, or a 0 bit. The start bit is followed by 7 data bits, 1 parity bit, and a stop bit, which is a return to a 1 bit or mark condition. If parity does not check or if the tenth bit is not a 1, it is assumed that an error has occurred. Appendix A describes how checking for start, stop, data, and parity bits is physically accomplished. The ASCII representation for the character F is 1000110; the async representation for transmitting this character is given in Figure 10-22. After a character is transmitted, the line goes back to the idle state until the next start bit is encountered.

Interrupt Character Transmission Termination   If interrupt characters are being used to end a transmission, each character received must be examined to determine whether it matches one of the interrupt characters. If they match, the message is considered complete and is delivered to the intended application. This is the usual way async communications are completed. On terminals, the character that is transmitted when the operator presses the return key—usually a carriage-return character—is often one of these termination characters. Other interrupt characters can also be specified.

Character Count Termination   *Character-count termination* is used when the number of characters transmitted is large or when data are received from a device that transmits continuously without sending termination characters. Some news wire services send large amounts of text for a story without including message termination characters. The receiving computer must be capable of accepting the entire story regardless of its length. Because the message is received by a buffer whose capacity may be too small to store the entire message, a character-count termination allows the computer to save the data in blocks and avoid buffer overflow.

Time-Out Interval Termination   Another termination mechanism is the time-out interval. This method is effective with a character count or when data is received from sensor-based or laboratory equipment. In conjunction with character count, the time-out interval is beneficial when the size of a message can vary. Suppose the termination character count is 100, and the message is 350 characters. If only character-count termination is used, the first 300 characters would be received routinely in three data groups, but the last 50 characters would be held in the buffer until it was filled, which would occur only when the next message is sent. A time-out termination prevents unnecessary delays in completing such a message. In the laboratory situation, a long interval between data arrivals means that the entire data stream has arrived or the equipment is out of order. The time-out interval is not a good terminator for data being input by an operator, because if the operator should take a break in the midst of input, a time-out interval would prematurely terminate the message.

Why Is Asynchronous Transmission Popular?

Although the oldest WAN protocol, asynchronous transmission remains one of the most common data link protocols for several reasons. First, for several years it was the only way to transmit data. Many terminals and controller boards were designed for async operation. Thus, async technology is well developed, and a wide variety of hardware options are available at low prices. Async also is very well suited to many types of applications. People performing data entry in a conversational mode or even in block mode operate at speeds compatible with async protocol. The primary drawback of async is its inefficient use of the circuit.

Synchronous Transmission

Synchronous protocols can be divided into three groups: character oriented, byte count oriented, and bit oriented. The last is the newest technology and the basis for many current data communication systems. **Synchronous transmission** allows sender and receiver to be synchronized with each other. Synchronous modems have internal clocks that are set in time with each other by a bit pattern, or sync pattern, transmitted at the beginning of a message. For long messages, these sync patterns are periodically inserted within the text to ensure that the modem clocks remain synchronized. Synchronized clocks are one feature that separates asynchronous modems from synchronous ones; although there is a clocking function in async transmission, the clocks are not synchronized. The clocks on asynchronous modems are used to pace the bits on the line on the sending side and to sample the line when awaiting data on the receiving side. Once data starts arriving, the sampling rate is adjusted to the pace of the arriving characters so the characters can be recognized (see Appendix B).

> **synchronous transmission** Allows the sender and receiver to be synchronized with each other. Synchronous modems have internal clocks that are set in time with each other by a bit pattern, or sync pattern, transmitted at the beginning of a message.

Another difference between asynchronous and synchronous transmission is that instead of transmitting character by character, synchronous transmission involves sending a block of characters at a time. Failure to remain synchronized results in lost data. Figure 10-23 illustrates the differences between asynchronous and synchronous transmission.

Character Synchronous Protocols

Data Delineation in Synchronous Protocols   One of the functions of a data link protocol is data delineation. With synchronous protocols, three methods are used to affect this. Some synchronous protocols are positional, some use a framing technique, and others use a byte count to delineate data. Positional protocols delineate fields by the use of fixed-length fields on the message (except perhaps on the data field), by indicating the size of the message with a character count embedded in the message, or

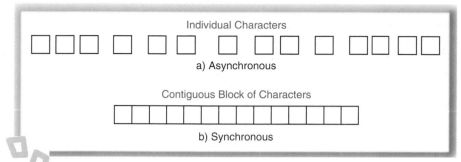

Figure 10-23   Asynchronous Versus Synchronous Transmission

both. Framing protocols use reserved characters or bit patterns to delineate data and control fields within the message. Byte count protocols delineate data by including the number of characters being transmitted within the message.

Positional Protocols   An example of a positional protocol is the frame format used in CSMA/CD (Ethernet) LANs; this is illustrated in Figure 10-24. All fields, except the data field, are a specific number of bits in length, and each field (including the data field) is always at the same specific location within each frame. When the sender has finished transmitting its data, the end of the transmission is indicated by dropping the carrier signal on the medium, signifying to all attached devices that the communication medium is idle (not in use). Manchester encoding, which is used in 10BaseT Ethernet implementations, transmits frames in a manner that allows the receiver to synchronize its clock with the sender's.

Neither framing characters nor character counts are used in positional protocols to define where address fields and data begin. When CSMA/CD frame formats are used, the first 64 bits are always the preamble field, the next 48 are the destination address, and so on. All frames transmitted in Ethernet networks adhere to this fixed format.

Framing Protocols   A message may have several parts: a header, an address, data, and a block check character. If a message contains both a header and data fields, a framing protocol would use a special control character to indicate the start of the

Figure 10-24   CSMA/CD Message Format

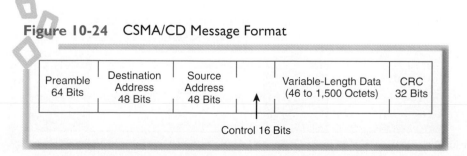

header, another control character to indicate the start of the data field, and a third control character to designate the end of the data field. This is illustrated in Figure 10-25. Other framed messages between the same sender and receiver could have different parts; for example, the header field could be omitted.

Byte Count Protocols   A byte count protocol includes the number of characters being transmitted in the message header. The recipient of the message reads the header and uses the message length stored there to determine the size of the message. Because the header is a fixed length, the remainder of the message can be delineated from the message size.

Standards for Character Synchronous Protocols   A number of widely accepted standards have been developed to specify how character synchronous protocols are to be implemented. Examples of standards that address character synchronous protocols include American National Standards Institute (ANSI) standards X3.1, X3.24, X3.28, and X3.36. IBM's Binary Synchronous Communications (BISYNC or BSC) protocol has become a de facto industry standard communication protocol supported by many manufacturers. Because it is so common, BISYNC is used as a model of character synchronous protocols in the following discussion.

BISYNC was introduced by IBM in 1967 as the data link protocol for remote job entry, using the 2780 workstation. Since that time, its use has expanded to many other applications and with several other devices. Only two data codes are commonly used by BISYNC: ASCII and EBCDIC. One or more synchronization characters are transmitted at the beginning of each transmission block to synchronize sending and receiving modems. The receiving modem uses this bit pattern to establish timing and get in step with the sender. To maintain timing for long transmission blocks, additional sync characters are inserted at regular intervals. The number of sync characters required depends on the equipment being used, although two or three is the usual number. Figure 10-26 shows a message with BISYNC control characters for synchronization (SYN), the start of text (STX), and the end of text (ETX). BISYNC supports both point-to-point and multipoint configurations.

Message Control   Each transmitted block can have an optional header field for message control that designates such items as routing information, priority, and message type. The beginning and end of text are identified by framing the data with control characters. An STX character signals that the data portion of the text is starting. One of several characters—such as ETX, ETB, or EOT—can be used to identify the end of a block of data, depending on whether an intermediate or final block is being transmitted. The

Figure 10-25   Framing for a Character Synchronous Message

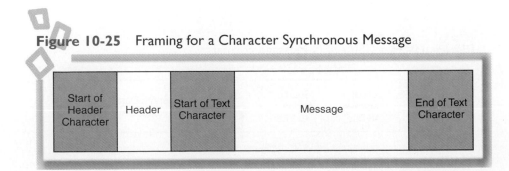

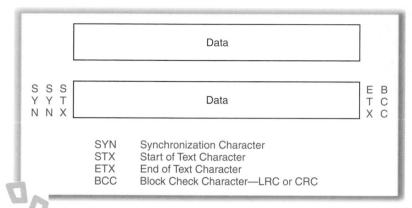

Figure 10-26   BISYNC Control Characters

ETB control character designates the end of the transmission block, ETX signals the end of the text, and EOT means end of transmission. Lengthy messages are ordinarily broken down into segments or blocks. If a message were broken into four different transmission blocks, the first three blocks would terminate with the ETB control character and the last would terminate with the EOT character. Error-control procedures involve either parity checking or VRC and LRC (vertical redundancy checking and longitudinal redundancy checking), both of which are discussed more fully in Chapter 6.

One limitation of BISYNC is that it is essentially a half-duplex protocol, so each message transmitted must be acknowledged by the receiver before the next message can be sent. This is not a major concern for many applications, especially those involving terminal data entry, for which the amount of time required to acknowledge is short compared with the speed of data submission. For host-to-host communication, on the other hand, half duplex can be quite restrictive.

Byte Count Synchronous Protocols

The difference between byte count synchronous protocols and BISYNC lies in how they signal the beginning and end of messages. They are called *byte count protocols* because the number of characters in the message is given in a required message header, as illustrated in Figure 10-27. The header is a fixed length, and the data field is of variable length. One advantage of byte count protocols is their transparency. With the byte count provided, it is clear where the message begins and ends: The header is always x characters long. Therefore, the beginning of the data is x characters from the beginning of the message, the data span the byte count number of characters, and following that may be a block check character (BCC) or CRC (cyclical redundancy checking) characters. Because there is no need to scan the input stream for termination characters, any bit pattern can be represented within the data stream.

Message Sequence Numbers   Some implementations of byte count protocols also include message sequence numbers. Each transmitted message is given a sequential number, allowing multiple messages to be transmitted without any acknowledgment. If three bits are used for sequencing messages, eight different sequence numbers (0 through 7) can be generated. When the count reaches 7, the next number assigned

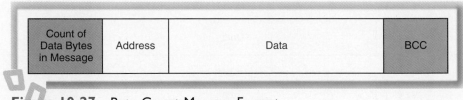

Figure 10-27   Byte Count Message Format

is 0. This allows up to eight messages to be transmitted before being acknowledged. The ability to send multiple messages without an acknowledgment can save a significant amount of time, especially on slower links or links with a high modem turnaround time. An example of a byte count synchronous protocol is Digital Equipment Corporation's Digital Data Communication Message Protocol (DDCMP). Its message sequencing allows 256 message numbers.

Bit Synchronous Protocols

Bit-oriented synchronous data link protocols use bits rather than bytes to delineate data and provide message control. The first bit-oriented synchronous data link protocol, Synchronous Data Link Control (SDLC), was introduced by IBM in 1972. Since then, numerous other bit-oriented data link controls have surfaced. The major bit synchronous protocols are as follows:

➤ *Synchronous Data Link Control (SDLC).* SDLC is from IBM.

➤ *Advanced Data Communications Control Procedure (ADCCP).* ADCCP is an ANSI standard data link protocol. (ADCCP is often pronounced "addcap.")

➤ *High-Level Data Link Control (HDLC).* HDLC is a standard of the International Standards Organization (ISO).

➤ *Link Access Procedure, Balanced (LAPB).* LAPB is designated as the data link protocol for the X.25 packet distribution networks discussed in Chapter 12; LAPB is an adaptation of HDLC.

All of these bit synchronous protocols operate similarly. Although there are both national and international standards for bit synchronous protocols, SDLC is used in the following discussion as the model for bit-oriented data link protocols because it is used in many IBM installations and represents many bit synchronous implementations. Many vendors also support SDLC as a connection to IBM networks and devices. More detailed information regarding SDLC may be found in Appendix C (www.prenhall.com/stamper).

Synchronous Data Link Control   SDLC operates in full-duplex or half-duplex mode on nonswitched (leased, dedicated) lines in both point-to-point and multipoint configurations. In half-duplex mode, it also allows switched, point-to-point configurations. Under SDLC, it is possible to configure stations in a loop, as depicted in Figure 10-28. Data are transmitted in one direction around the loop, as with hub polling. In all configurations, including point to point, one station is designated as the primary station, and the others are secondary stations. The primary controls the link and determines which station is allowed to transmit.

At the application level, a given application transmits a message. At the transport layer, the message may be broken down into packets. At the data link layer, a packet may be broken down into frames. Thus, the basic unit of transmission in SDLC is the

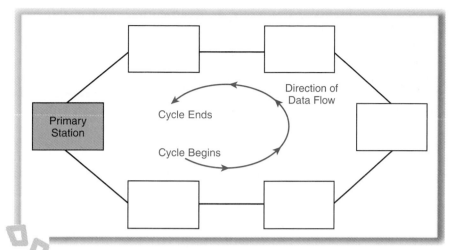

Figure 10-28   SDLC Loop Configuration

frame, presented in Figure 10-29. The flag field is used to indicate the beginning and end of the frame. The bit pattern for the flag, 01111110, is the only bit pattern in the protocol that is specifically reserved; all other bit patterns are acceptable. (This is discussed further in the SDLC section on transparency.) The second field within the frame, the address field, is 8 bits. A maximum of 256 unique addresses is possible. Other data link protocols, such as ADCCP and HDLC, allow the address field to be expanded in multiples of 8 bits, significantly increasing the number of addressable stations per link. The control field, also 8 bits, identifies the frame type as unnumbered, informational, or supervisory. Only the first two of these three types are used to transmit data, with the primary data transport frame being the information frame.

The data field, always omitted for supervisory frames, is optional on unnumbered frames and is usually present on information frames. The only restriction on the data field is that the number of bits must be a multiple of eight, or an octet. This restriction does not mean an 8-bit code must be used; in fact, any code is acceptable. But if necessary, the data being transmitted must be padded with additional bits to maintain an integral number of octets (no partial octets). If the data being transmitted consists of 5 Baudot characters, at 5 bits each, only 25 bits would be required for

frame A term used to describe a transmission packet in bit-oriented WAN protocols. The term is also used to describe a data link layer transmission packet transmitted by a LAN node.

Figure 10-29   SDLC Frame Format

8 Bits	8 Bits	8 Bits	Variable	16 Bits	8 Bits
Flag 01111110	Address	Control	Data (Optional Octets)	Frame Check Sequence	Flag 01111110

the data, and an additional 7 bits would be required to complete the last octet. Following the optional data field is a frame check sequence for error detection, which is 16 bits. The final field of the frame is the flag that signals the end of the message. The bit pattern for the ending flag is the same as that for the beginning flag. Thus, the ending flag for one frame may serve as the beginning flag for the next.

SDLC is a positional protocol, which means that each field except the data field has a specific length and location relative to adjacent fields. No special control characters (except for the flag characters) are used to delimit the data or headings in the message. For control frames, which are either unnumbered or supervisory, the control function is encoded in the control field. Unnumbered frames have 5 bits available to identify the control function, so 32 different function types are possible. The supervisory frame has only 2 bits available, so a maximum of four functions can be defined.

Number Sent (Ns) and Number Received (Nr) Subfields   In information frames, the control field contains two 3-bit fields known as the *number sent (Ns)* and *number received (Nr)* subfields. The Ns and Nr counts are used to sequence messages. Three bits allow for eight numbers, 0 through 7. When transmitting an information frame, the sender increments the Ns field value. The Ns or Nr number following 7 is 0; thus, the number sequence cycles through those eight values. The Nr field is used to acknowledge receipt of messages. Every time a message is received, the receiver increments the Nr count, which represents the number of the frame expected next. An Nr count of 5 means message number 5 should arrive next. The Ns and Nr counts are compared every time a frame is received to make sure no messages have been lost. This scheme allows seven messages to be sent before an acknowledgment is required. The ability to receive up to seven frames without acknowledgment improves performance; however, it also places a burden on the sender, which must be ready to retransmit any unacknowledged frames. This requires that messages be saved in the sender's buffers until acknowledged, which can create problems for systems with small buffers or memory. Examples of how the Ns and Nr fields are used are found in Appendix C (www.prenhall.com/stamper).

Both ADCCP and HDLC allow the control field to be expanded to provide for larger Ns and Nr counts, as illustrated in Figure 10-30. When the control field is

Figure 10-30   Control Fields for Information Frames

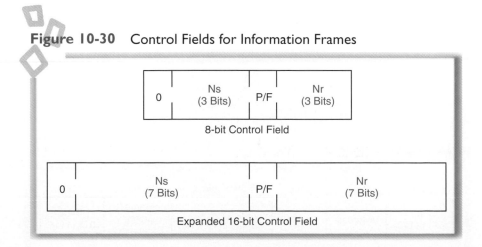

expanded to 16 bits, the Ns and Nr fields can each be 7 bits, which allows 128 sequence numbers, and up to 127 messages can be transmitted before being acknowledged. This arrangement is especially beneficial with satellite links because of the propagation delay for response, which can cause a small number of unacknowledged frames to create undesirable delays. Recall from Chapter 5 that satellite signals incur a one-way propagation delay of approximately a quarter of a second. If 10,000-bit blocks are being transmitted on a 1-mbps satellite link, then 25 blocks theoretically could be transmitted every quarter of a second. With 3-bit Ns and Nr fields, only 7 blocks could be sent before waiting for an acknowledgment. In this case, transmission time for 18 blocks would be lost, limiting the available capacity.

Choosing a Data Link Protocol

Although several other data link protocols exist, those described in this chapter are the most common. The question is: Which one is appropriate for which application? Table 10-3 compares synchronous and asynchronous protocols. When selecting the proper protocol, the network designer must first choose a protocol supported by the hardware vendor. Most vendors support some version of asynchronous, character synchronous, and bit synchronous protocols. Second, the kind of hardware used in an application partly dictates the data link protocol. Most terminals support one or possibly two protocols; the exception is intelligent terminals, which can support a wide variety of protocols. Third, the network support provided by the vendor affects the choice of data link protocol. Many newer network systems have been designed around a bit-oriented synchronous protocol. Because not all users have compatible terminals, accommodations are often made to support other protocols, such as BISYNC.

In practice, do not select a protocol and then gather the equipment to support it. Instead, select a network design, a hardware vendor, and associated hardware, each of which dictates a particular protocol. Most current data link technology and development for WANs are based on bit-oriented synchronous protocols. There are several bit-oriented implementations, and several standards exist. The industry trend is toward higher speed transmission and efficient use of the data link, which definitely favor synchronous transmission protocols.

Table 10-3   Comparison of Asynchronous and Synchronous Protocols

Asynchronous	Synchronous
Character-at-a-time transmission	Block transmission
Modems not synchronized	Modems synchronized
Error detection commonly parity	Error detection commonly CRC or parity plus LRC
Fixed overhead per character	Fixed overhead per block (may be less efficient for small messages but more efficient for large ones)
Less efficient use of communication link	More efficient use of communication link
Lower cost devices	Higher cost devices

WAN SOFTWARE

Application Software

A generic software configuration within a WAN host is depicted in Figure 10-31. At the heart of the system is the application software. The goal of WAN *application software* is to solve a business or scientific problem, not to solve computer system problems. An example of a system problem is the details of how to display data on a terminal. In the early days of computer programming, an application program needed to contain logic to communicate with specific hardware devices. If a new terminal was introduced into the system, application programs had to be changed to support the differences between the new terminal and terminals the program already supported. If all currently supported terminals had monochrome screens and the new terminal had a color screen, the application program had to be modified to be able to display colors. When application software is responsible for device handling, the application programs take longer to create, test, and modify. The application programmer must have device interface skills as well as application design skills.

System Software

Most current systems provide system-level software that eliminates the need for hardware-dependent logic in application software. This allows programmers to focus their attention on business problems. To support this objective, software such as database management systems and teleprocessing monitors were developed to control and manage data and terminal devices, and access methods were added to provide easier access to data and terminals. These software capabilities provide functions common to most application programs and remove the details of file and device access from application software. This follows a trend of system-level software: making the system easier to program and use. Programs interface to devices via well-defined user interfaces. Just as the adjacent levels of the OSI reference model have interfaces that allow data to flow between layers, messages and data flowing between application programs and the database or data communication system pass through interfaces to reach their destination. Perhaps the most important piece of software in effecting this is the operating system.

Operating System

The *operating system (OS)* helps applications by performing interface, process management, and file management functions, as listed in Table 10-4. The OS performs all of these functions in a manner largely transparent to the application program and the programmer. The OS also performs many functions for an executing program, but these functions are carried out without the programmer explicitly requesting them. The OS, the overall manager of the computing system, is loaded when the system is started, and portions of the OS remain memory resident so they are always available to provide management and interface functions. One of the functions provided by the OS is managing the input/output (I/O) subsystem. The parts of the operating system that perform this task are called *I/O drivers*.

I/O Drivers

I/O driver System software that manages the operating system's input/output subsystem by providing low-level access to I/O devices.

The **I/O drivers** in Figure 10-31 provide the low-level access to devices. On the database side, the devices are tapes and disks; on the data communication side, they are communication lines. In data communication, low-level access involves implementing the data link protocols, such as asynchronous or HDLC, error detection, and buffer management. For disk drives, the I/O driver issues seek, read, and write commands. The specifics of I/O drivers are system and device dependent.

Table 10-4   Operating System Functions

Interface Functions—Provide Interface To
    Users   I/O system
    File system
Process Functions
    Schedule processes for execution   Start/stop processes
    Establish process environment   Enforce process priorities
    Prevent processes from interfering with each other   Allow multiprocessing/multitasking
Management Functions
    Manage memory   Manage I/O system and devices
    Manage access to CPU   Manage user access through security
                                           provisions

File Management Functions
    Allocate disk space   Maintain disk directories
    Manage file attributes (owner, date and time   Provide file security
       updated, and so on)

Figure 10-31   Generic Software Configuration for WAN Hosts

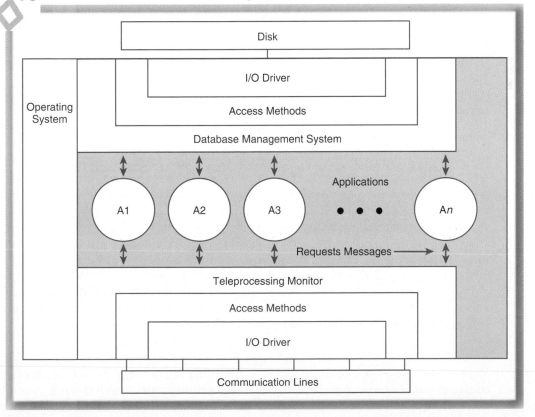

Access Methods

access methods A network control or operating system subsystem that provides input and output services as an interface between an application and its associated devices. It translates I/O requests into low-level requests tailored to the file or device being accessed and performs the storage, retrieval, and data transmission functions associated with I/O requests.

Access methods exist for both database and data communication systems. Access methods generally separate the application from physical characteristics of the data or devices the application is accessing. An access method essentially functions as a black box to translate user read and write requests into lower level requests tailored to the file or device being accessed. Database access methods allow users to retrieve data. Applications often need several data retrieval methods. With personnel files, for instance, an employee record might need to be accessed via employee name, employee number, and Social Security number. Access methods provide the ability to select a specific record from the database with a small number of disk accesses. Some access methods also allow records to be retrieved in order on a key, which provides a logical ordering to the records. Thus, one access method might be used to retrieve personnel records in employee name order, and another access method might be used to retrieve personnel records in department order.

Data communication access methods allow users to display data on a terminal and to retrieve data that has been entered on the terminal. How data is displayed on terminals may vary from one terminal to another. Access methods are covered in more detail later in this chapter.

Database and File Management Systems

database management system (DBMS) A system that organizes data into records, organizes records into files, provides access to the data based on one or more access keys, and provides the mechanism for relating one file to another. DBMS software controls the organization, storage, retrieval, security, and integrity of data in a database.

A **database management system (DBMS)** organizes data into records, organizes records into files, and provides access to the data based on one or more access keys. A DBMS also provides a mechanism for relating one file to another. In a university database, records are maintained on students, classes, and teachers. File relationships allow users to answer requests such as "Which students are enrolled in section 4 of tapeworm taxonomy?" and "List the advisors for all students majoring in mathematics." Both requests require that data be extracted from at least two files via relationships that exist between the files (such as a teacher-advises-student relationship). A **file management system (FMS)** provides a subset of the capabilities found in a DBMS. An FMS is oriented toward one file and hence does not provide file relationships. Database and file management systems provide data services to application processes. Applications issue database requests to store, modify, retrieve, or delete data, and the DBMS carries out these requests.

file management system (FMS) An FMS provides functions such as storage allocation and file access methods for individual files.

Teleprocessing Monitor

Whereas the DBMS provides an application with access to data, application access to terminals or other nodes is provided by a *teleprocessing monitor (TM), transaction control process,* or *message control system (MCS).* A data communication access method can partially fulfill this function. Similar to the way in which a DBMS allows applications to share data, insulates the applications from the physical details of data storage, and provides data independence, the TM enables different terminals to interface with multiple applications and removes an application from details such as the physical differences among terminals and among network nodes. Whereas the DBMS uses different data access methods to provide multiple paths to data, the TM uses different terminal access methods to give access to multiple terminal types. A more detailed description of the TM and its associated access methods can be found later in this chapter.

Transaction Flow

With this brief overview of the application software environment, we now see how the software components cooperate in processing a transaction. The following example assumes that our system is configured to allow recovery from most system failures and that the transaction will be entered by a user at a terminal. For specifics, this discussion assumes a single-system environment; with only minor changes, this discussion could fit a client/server environment in which the client and server are in separate computers.

Preparation for a transaction begins before the user enters the information. The first step in a system start-up, of course, is loading the operating system. Following that, the system and application software, such as DBMS, TM, spooler, and e-mail systems, are started.

The application programs in Figure 10-31 receive their inputs from the TM or transaction control process. Once the applications start, they must establish a session with the TM. In some TM systems, applications run directly under the control of the TM. In other systems, applications are more independent of the TM. In the first case, the applications are tightly coupled to a single TM; in the second case, applications can receive messages from one or more TMs as well as from other sources.

Regardless of the implementation, a data path always exists or can be established between applications and a TM. Once this path exists, the application issues a read request on its message file or otherwise indicates its readiness to accept a message for processing. The TM displays an opening screen on each terminal under its control and then initiates a read for each terminal. Typical opening displays are a menu of available transactions or a user log-on screen.

Multiple TMs may be in operation concurrently, and each TM exclusively controls several terminals. Terminals may be moved from one TM to another, but they may be attached only to a single TM at any one time. However, not all terminals in the system need to connect to a TM. Some terminals may be used outside the TM for applications such as program development. Terminals may also alternate between use for transaction processing under TM control and use for other applications outside TM control.

The TM examines the transaction and determines which application(s) should process it. Some transactions require the services of more than one application process. The TM may send each participating application its work at the same time, or the TM may wait until one application finishes before sending the second application its portion of the work.

Access Methods

As noted previously, data communication access methods give system users easier access to terminal devices. They provide connection, disconnection, and data transfer services to the applications.

Application–Terminal Connection

Several approaches have been used to provide access methods, but we discuss only the most practical implementation. One function of an access method is to provide terminal–application connections. This may be accomplished by having a pool of applications and a pool of terminals available, as illustrated in Figure 10-32. The access method serves as a switch to connect terminal requests with the proper applications.

Accessing a Terminal

Because an access method separates the application program from the terminal access logic, access methods can be used with or without a TM, depending on the environment. Figure 10-33 illustrates two situations: TM present and TM absent. The access method performs fewer functions when the TM is present, because some functions, such as message routing and data editing, are performed by the TM.

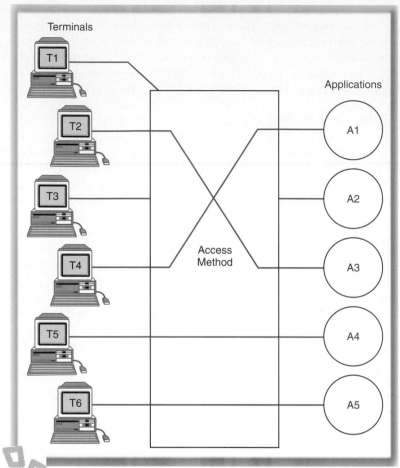

Figure 10-32   Access Method and Pooled
Application–Terminal Connections

The first requirement of accessing a terminal from a program is to connect the two. The access method serves as an intermediary in this case. Either the application initiates a connection by issuing an open or connect request to the access method or the terminal initiates the action by issuing an application log-on request through the access method. Once the connection is established, a communication path exists, and the terminal and application can exchange data. Connection requests can be denied for security reasons or because the application or device is already occupied.

Without a TM, the access method makes the connection between an application program and a terminal. In some implementations, the connection is static: The application and terminal are attached to each other, and the terminal can run only the transactions provided by that particular application. For the terminal user to access another application process, the terminal must first be disconnected from its current access application and then reconnected to the new one. Other systems provide more flexibility in making the connection between a terminal and an application. For ex-

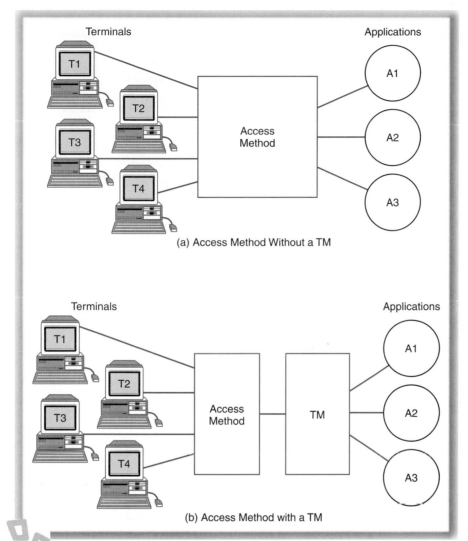

Terminals   Applications

(a) Access Method Without a TM

(b) Access Method with a TM

Figure 10-33   Access Method with and without a Teleprocessing Monitor (TM)

ample, IBM's *Virtual Telecommunications Access Method (VTAM)* provides several methods for terminal–application connections.

Transaction Control Processes in Teleprocessing Monitors

TM Configuration

The configuration of the TM is depicted in Figure 10-34. Because the TM serves as a switch between applications and terminals, it must be aware of the terminals attached to it, the transactions that can be submitted, and the applications responsible for processing those transactions. In this environment, any terminal can access any application

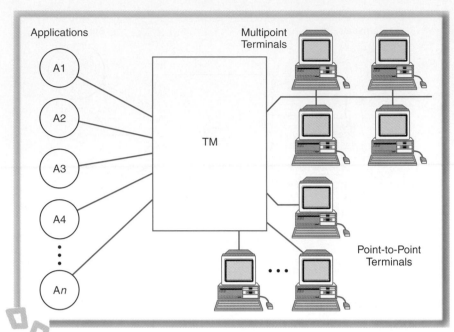

Figure 10-34   Generic TM Configuration

known to the TM. Implementation can be as a monolithic process, as in Figure 10-35(a) or as multiple processes, as in Figure 10-35(b).

Single Threading Versus Multithreading

multithreading The capacity of a single program or process to work on multiple requests at once. This enables multiple streams of execution to take place concurrently within the same program with each stream representing a different message or transaction.

single threading The capacity of a single program or process to work on one request at a time; a message or transaction currently being processed must be completed before the next can begin.

The efficiency of the application environment depends on how quickly transactions can be processed. If multiple transactions can arrive at once, good performance requires that parallelism in transaction processing be provided. This means that the TM may need to process several transactions concurrently, a concept known as **multithreading**. With **single threading**, a process accepts an input, processes the input to completion, produces an output, and then is ready to accept another input for processing. A TM operating in this manner would accept an input from one terminal, send the transaction to an application process, wait for the response, and send the result back to the terminal. Then, the TM would accept another transaction and process it. Meanwhile, other terminals may be waiting for service. This processing method results in long delays for terminals with queued requests.

The difference between single threading and multithreading can be likened to what happens in a grocery store when people queue up at the checkout counter. The checkout clerk represents the TM process, and the customers represent the terminals. The clerk ordinarily operates in a single-threaded manner, processing one customer and one customer only until the total order has been tabulated and the money collected before turning to the next customer. If an object does not scan correctly, everyone waits while an assistant checks the price. Looking up the price is analogous to accessing a disk, with the assistant as the DBMS. Everyone waits while the clerk scans each item, missing prices are checked, coupons are deducted, and the check is written

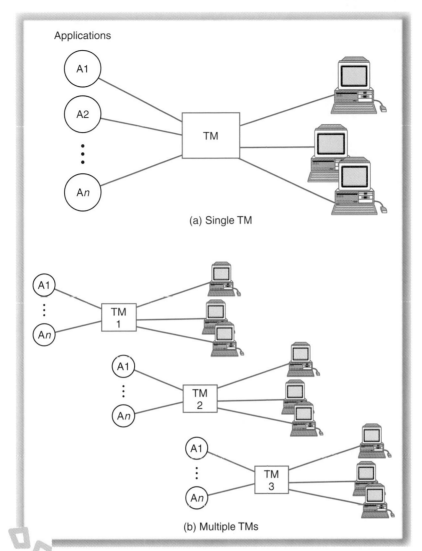

Figure 10-35   TM Configurations

and verified. To improve efficiency, the clerks could be multithreaded: Everyone in the line would get attention as time allows. The clerks would maintain separate totals for each customer. While a missing price was being checked, the clerk could move on to the next customer's order. While a check is being written, another customer could be served. Of course, the multithreaded clerk must be much more flexible than the single-threaded clerk. Multiple totals are accumulated, items are taken from the correct basket and placed in the proper bag, and the totals are delivered to and collected from the proper customers. Multiple application threads are active simultaneously within a multithreaded process. A comparison of single-threaded and multithreaded processes is presented in Figure 10-36.

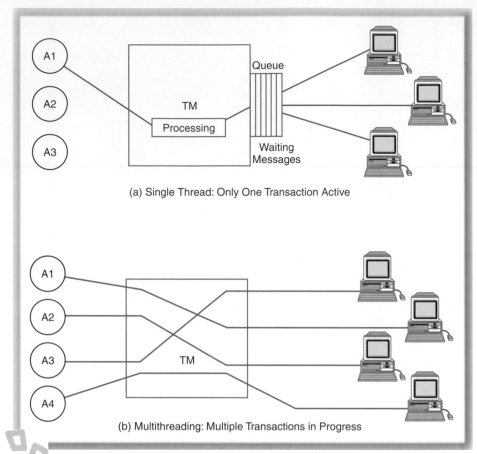

(a) Single Thread: Only One Transaction Active

(b) Multithreading: Multiple Transactions in Progress

Figure 10-36   Single Threading Versus Multithreading

Maintaining Context

context data
A requirement of multithreaded processes that entails unifying the work by keeping track of the completed parts as well as the parts yet to be worked on, and ensuring that an interrupted transaction is restarted at the correct point.

An additional requirement of multithreaded processes is maintaining **context data**. Each single-threaded transaction is completely self-contained. In a multithreaded process, a transaction might be separated into several parts, and each part might be acted on by a different program. To unify this work, one program must keep track of the completed parts and the parts yet to be worked on and ensure that an interrupted transaction is restarted at the correct point. The action to be performed also may be contingent on a previous activity. For instance, in searching a database for an employee named "Smith," an application might select and display the first 10 Smiths plus additional identifying information. If none of the 10 names is correct, the next 10 are displayed, and so on until the proper Smith is found. The search for the next 10 names is contingent on where the previous search stopped.

Like the multithreaded grocery clerk, the TM must handle multiple customers at once. Suppose a TM controls four terminals (T1, T2, T3, and T4) and three applications (A1, A2, and A3). At the start of the system, all three applications request to open, or connect, to the TM. The TM records this information and issues a command to open and display the first screen, and posts a read on each of the four terminals. At this point, the TM is awaiting input from the terminals or a process. This kind of interleaved processing continues throughout the workday.

Maintaining context can also be done outside the TM. It could also have been maintained within the application or the terminal. However, the application is not as logical a place as the TM for maintaining context; multiple copies of one application may be used to increase efficiency, in which case the TM would have to send the second part of a transaction to the same process that worked on the first part. Saving context in application programs also makes those application programs more complex. Some designers prefer to remove this kind of complexity from the application. Because many TM processes are supplied by software or computer vendors rather than being written by the end user, it benefits the user to have the multiuser complexity in the TMs and not in the applications.

Memory Management

To manage context information and accept data from both terminals and applications, the TM must provide **memory management** functions. At any time, the TM can receive a message from either terminals or applications, and multiple messages may be queued up simultaneously. The way in which TMs manage memory varies. Essentially, the TM must have sufficient memory available to provide storage for terminal and application messages as well as for context data. Sometimes this requires virtual memory algorithms similar to those used by some operating systems: The disk is treated as an extension of memory, and data is swapped back and forth between real memory and disk.

Transaction Routing

The TM also must provide **transaction routing**, which means routing the transaction received from a terminal to one or more application programs. Several techniques are used to determine how to route a transaction. One method uses a transaction code embedded within the data message itself. The terminal operator enters the transaction code in the text of the message, as illustrated in Figure 10-37. The TM must recognize this code and route the transaction accordingly. Another method is based on context and a signal from the terminal. The signal is usually either a transaction code or the operator pressing a designated function key. Other signals may be indicated by using a light pen, mouse, or touch screen.

Transaction routing requires that the TM know which application handles a given transaction and the path or connection that leads to that application. Transaction routing could be table driven, in which case the TM would look up the transaction ID in a table that provides directions to the proper application process. Alternatively, a procedural interface with a case statement or similar construct would result in a program call or a message being sent to that process.

Transaction Log

The TM is a logical place to implement transaction logging. A **transaction log** captures the transaction inputs, usually on tape or disk. Once inputs are captured, the system can assure the user that the transaction will be processed. This does not necessarily mean that the transaction will be successfully completed (errors could prevent that); it does mean that the transaction will not be lost should a system failure occur. In addition to its use in recovery, transaction logging is sometimes required by auditors, especially in financial transactions. Electronic data processing (EDP) auditors periodically check transaction sources and trace them through the system to determine whether they were correctly processed. If transaction logging is implemented, as soon as a

memory management Functions provided by an operating system or program, such as a teleprocessing monitor or transaction control process, that manage the system or program's memory area.

transaction routing The routing of a transaction received from a terminal to one or more application programs.

transaction log Records all transaction inputs and is used in recovering from failures and in system auditing.

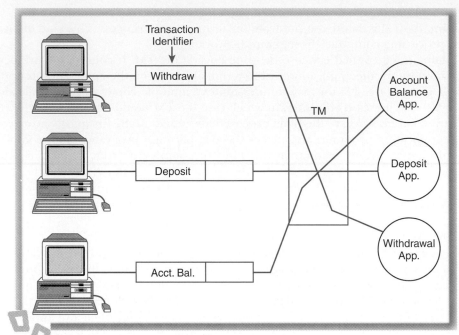

Figure 10-37   Transaction Routing in a TM

transaction is received by the TM or transaction control process, the transaction is written on the log file. Usually, the TM appends additional information to the message, such as a date/time stamp, transaction ID, or similar identifying information. Sometimes, the completion of a transaction is also logged. In recovery situations, this prevents a transaction from being processed twice.

In some systems, the transaction log is synchronized with the database logging function to ensure that a message received by the system will be processed and that no duplicate transactions will be processed if a failure occurs. One system even guarantees that transactions requiring reprocessing in the event of a failure will be processed in the original order. This last is an important feature in banking applications. For instance, an account with an initial $100 balance receives a $500 deposit and then a $200 withdrawal. In the time-compressed recovery situation, the transaction could possibly be processed in reverse order, meaning that the withdrawal would be rejected for insufficient funds or the account would be overdrawn.

Security and Statistics

A TM can be a focal point for online transactions entering the system, so it is a logical place to collect statistics and provide for security. Several statistics that are necessary to effectively manage a network system can be collected in the TM, including the total number of transactions from all terminals, kinds of transactions, number of characters transmitted to and from a terminal, application processing time per transaction, and number of transactions per terminal. Security at the terminal and transaction levels could be enforced at the TM. All online transactions for terminals managed by a TM must be routed through the TM, making the TM a logical place to implement security.

Table 10-5   TM Activities

Provides a user interface with the TM subsystem	Formats data for terminals and applications
Manages memory	Routes messages to server processes
Provides an interface between applications and terminals	Gathers statistics
Manages applications	Provides testing and debugging facilities
Logs messages	Assists in providing security
Participates in recovery	Assists in implementing a priority system
Provides transaction definition	
Edits data fields	

Message Priorities

The TM is also in an ideal position to assist with implementing message priorities within the online system. Every message received could be examined for priority, or priorities could be assigned by the TM. Priorities could be established according to the source and kind of message. Priority messages could then be given service first and routed to special server applications to expedite message processing.

Operation Interface

An **operation interface** gives a network administrator the ability to monitor and control the TM environment. Monitoring the TM environment includes looking at statistics such as buffer use, number of transactions waiting in various queues for service, and busy rates for lines, devices, and the TM. Controlling the TM includes activities such as adding terminals and applications, starting or stopping devices, and reconfiguring the system. This may be accomplished through an operation interface program.

Other TM Functions

Additional functions that a TM might carry out include the following:

➤ If an application fails, the TM should be able to automatically restart it. If a transaction arrives for a process that is not currently running, the TM should be able to activate the process.

➤ If one application receives so many requests that response times become degraded, the TM should be able to initiate additional copies of that process to enhance performance.

➤ If a process has been inactive for a long time, the TM should be able to optionally delete that process to free the resources the process is holding. Table 10-5 summarizes the activities of a TM.

operation interface
An interface that enables a user to use, monitor, and control a system. In systems that employ teleprocessing monitors, the operation interface enables network administrators to monitor and control the TM environment.

SUMMARY

Although WANs are the oldest form of data communication network, they have been significantly affected by the Internet. Relative to MANs and LANs, WANs span a wider geographic area, often have lower transmission rates, and have different data link protocols. Like other data communication networks, WANs facilitate resource sharing and communication across dispersed operating locations, support groupware applications, and contribute to organizational efficiency and cost effectiveness.

Common carrier communication media and services are typically used to interconnect WAN nodes. Although WANs include the hardware found in LANs and MANs, mainframes and minicomputer hosts continue to play a prominent role. Dumb, smart, and special-purpose terminals are key elements of the WANs of business organizations. Other WAN hardware includes muliplexors, concentrators, cluster controllers, and front-end processors. WAN hardware is deployed in a variety of topologies, with star, hierarchical, interconnected (plex), and hybrid being the most common.

Two main categories of WAN protocols exist: asynchronous and synchronous. Asynchronous protocols transmit one character at a time; synchronous protocols transmit blocks of multiple characters. Asynchronous transmission continues to be widely used for online transaction processing applications. Synchronous protocols, however, are better suited than asynchronous protocols for high-volume data transfers. The three major categories of synchronous protocols are character synchronous, byte synchronous, and bit synchronous.

Several kinds of WAN system software are involved in online transaction processing applications, involving the real-time exchange of data and messages between terminals and hosts. These include the host's operating system, I/O drivers, access methods, database and file management systems, and teleprocessing monitors. The primary responsibilities of teleprocessing monitors include transaction routing (establishing connections between terminals and applications), maintaining context, and maintaining transaction logs.

KEY TERMS

- access methods
- asynchronous transmission (async)
- concentrator
- contention mode
- context data
- database management system (DBMS)
- downloading
- dumb terminal
- file management system (FMS)
- frame
- front-end processor (FEP)
- hierarchical topology
- intelligent terminal
- interconnected (plex or mesh) network
- interrupt characters
- I/O driver
- memory management
- metropolitan area network (MAN)
- multipoint connection
- multithreading
- operation interface
- point-to-point connection
- polling
- single threading
- smart terminal
- star network
- synchronous transmission
- terminal
- terminal emulation
- transaction log
- transaction routing
- uploading
- wide area network (WAN)

REVIEW QUESTIONS

1. How are WANs different from MANs and LANs?
2. How has the Internet affected WANs?
3. Identify and briefly describe the major reasons why businesses implement WANs.
4. Identify and briefly describe each of the major kinds of terminals found in WANs.
5. Compare dumb, smart, and intelligent devices.
6. Describe several terminal input devices and several terminal output devices.
7. Compare point-to-point and multipoint connections. What are the advantages and disadvantages of multipoint connections?

8. Describe the differences among contention, polling, and selection.
9. What are multiplexors? How do multiplexors work?
10. Compare frequency division, time division, and statistical time division multiplexors.
11. Compare inverse multiplexors, concentrators, cluster controllers, and front-end processors.
12. Compare star, hierarchical, and interconnected (plex) networks. Describe the advantages and disadvantages of each topology.
13. Describe the characteristics of asynchronous transmission.
14. Distinguish between positional and framing synchronous protocols.
15. How does a byte synchronous protocol work?
16. Summarize the similarities and differences between asynchronous and synchronous protocols.
17. Identify and briefly describe the characteristics of each of the major kinds of WAN system software.
18. What functions are performed by a host's operating system in a WAN?
19. Describe the functions performed by a data communication access method.
20. Describe the functions performed by a teleprocessing monitor (TM).
21. Compare single threading and multithreading.
22. Why is multithreading an attractive TM feature?
23. Why are transaction logs important?

PROBLEMS AND EXERCISES

1. Use the Internet to research the characteristics of network computers. Identify several major vendors and their major products. What is a typical cost range for a network computer?
2. Use the Internet to research the characteristics and business applications of wireless terminals.
3. Use the Internet to research the characteristics and business applications of wearable microcomputers, especially those used in transaction processing.
4. Use the Internet to identify trends in ATM terminals. What new features/functions are popular?
5. Use the Internet to identify major multiplexor vendors and their products. What is a typical cost range for a statistical time division multiplexor?
6. Calculate how long it would take (in seconds) to transfer a file that contains 2 million 150-byte records that have been encoded in ASCII-8 (an 8-bit encoding scheme) between two WAN hosts using each of the following WAN services. (Assume that the transmission link operates continuously at 100 percent capacity and that there is no protocol overhead.)
   a. a 56,000-bps leased circuit
   b. ISDN
   c. T-1
   d. T-3
   e. 155-mbps ATM
   f. OC-48
7. Assume that you have a 1 million, 100-byte file encoded in ASCII-8 that must be transmitted from one WAN host to another in less than 2 minutes (120 seconds). What minimum transmission speed would be required? What WAN services have sufficient capacity/bandwidth to accomplish this? (Assume that the transmission link operates continuously at 100 percent capacity and that there is no protocol overhead.)

8. Communication efficiency is calculated using the following formula:

efficiency = number of data bits / (number of data bits + number of overhead bits)

If ASCII-8 is used to encode data, calculate the communication efficiency of each of the following:
   a. asynchronous transmission with one start, one stop, and one parity bit.
   b. asynchronous transmission with one start, two stop, and one parity bit.
   c. a BISYNC frame with two SYN characters, one STX, one ETX, a 16-bit BCC, and a 1,000-byte data field (see Figure 6-26).
   d. an SDLC frame (see Figure 10-29) with a 1,000-byte data field.

9. A financial services network requires a total of 400,000 10-bit characters to be transmitted from Tampa, Florida, to Seattle, Washington, during an 8-hour workday. If the average data entry clerk can type 20 words per minute (assume six characters per word), how many multiplexed terminals and data entry clerks are needed to enter the data that must be transmitted?

10. Your employer has determined that it needs a WAN topology providing low cost, good reliability, and expandability. In order to minimize response times, there should be a limited number of hops between hosts. Which topology would you recommend? Why?

11. Diagram a sequence of message exchanges between a terminal and a host using SDLC that illustrates the changing of Ns and Nr subfields.

12. Is maintaining context necessary for multithreading TMs? Why or why not?

13. Popular host operating systems in WANs are UNIX, MVS, VMS, and OS/400. Use the Internet to research each of these operating systems and provide an overview of the major characteristics and advantages of each.

14. Use the Internet or other online sources (such as Lexis/Nexis) to identify the leading DBMS vendors and their major DBMS products.

Videoconferencing and Web Conferencing

Conferencing is a way for people in different places to get in touch through electronic devices. There are three different kinds of conferencing: teleconferencing (or audio conferencing), videoconferencing, and Web conferencing. Although teleconferencing (via conference calls) represents 80 percent of the current conferencing market—mainly because it has been on the market longer and phone lines are easy to use—this case will focus on videoconferencing and Web conferencing. Videoconferencing and Web conferencing are giving a big boost to the conferencing industry. By 2005, Web conferencing is expected to have 55 percent of the conferencing market.

Until 2001, the biggest barriers to videoconferencing were the less-than-ideal experiences users had and the high costs of videoconferencing equipment. Users found videoconferencing hardware difficult to use, and even when they learned how to use it, the quality of the images was often not good enough to have a satisfactory videoconferencing meeting. Moreover, just a few years ago, a basic videoconferencing room was a luxury that costs between $40,000 and $50,000; for many businesses, videoconferencing technology and operating cost were equal to or more expensive than traveling.

However, since 2001, video and Web conferencing are attracting more executives' attention. The economic slowdown and the September 11, 2001, terrorist attacks boosted the videoconferencing market because of increased traveling costs and safety issues. After September 11, many employees were reluctant to fly, and videoconferencing gave companies the possibility of continuing their normal activities without having to travel. In fact, according to market research, videoconferencing companies experienced increased sales and services volumes of 30 percent to 50 percent immediately after the terrorist attacks.

However, the big question is whether videoconferencing companies will be able to retain their newly acquired customers. Will companies maintain an interest in videoconferencing as a mechanism to replace face-to-face meetings? Videoconferencing vendors believe that they will be able to hold onto their new customers because their networks and technologies are now available at lower prices and have higher performance levels. This means that users are benefiting from improved videoconferencing experiences.

How has technology improved in recent years? The videoconferencing technology standard in use is the H.320, which defines the communications protocol and compression algorithm to reduce digital video into small data packets. Those packets can be transmitted over LANs or WANs and even over the plain old telephone system (POTS). The H.323 standard defines protocols for LAN–based videoconferencing; the H.324 standard makes possible POTS–based conferencing. In addition, systems based in the H.323 and H.324 standards can interoperate with one another.

Videoconferencing also requires high-speed lines. Analog TV–quality images require a constant bandwidth of 768 kbps to transmit 24 frames per second. With lesser bandwidth, fewer frames can be sent, which in turn decreases the performance and videoconferencing experience for users. At 384 kbps (12 frames per second), images are more than usable, but they often lack the quality required for "serious" videoconferencing applications.

The Internet has also impacted videoconferencing systems. Although the public, global Internet cannot guarantee the quality of service (QoS) required for voice and real-time video, IP–based intranets can. Businesses can implement the videoconferencing QoS standards in their 100-mbps Fast Ethernet networks to ensure high-quality videoconferencing experiences for users.

Additionally, data conferencing is enhancing the uses of videoconferencing. The T.120 standard allows sharing data and documents among multiple participants; it is the standard for whiteboards, application sharing, and application viewing. Although data conferencing does not require the use of video, when used in conjunction with videoconferencing, it allows more active participation for each conference member. Thus, participants have the ability to discuss topics face to face, exchange documents, make written suggestions, and use any data collaboration tool that could enhance the videoconferencing experience.

Videoconferencing is expected to keep growing in the coming years. Currently, the National Tele-immersion Initiative (NTII), one of the Internet2 working groups, is experimenting with teleimmersion technology that will combine videoconferencing with virtual reality systems. The "office of the future" project consists of a set of video cameras providing 3-D videoconferencing on big flat screens. Participants could also engage in collaborative work, manipulating 3-D objects by using laser pointers.

CASE QUESTIONS

1. Use the Internet to find out more about the H.323, H.324, and T.120 standards. What characteristics/specifications are associated with each? Why are these standards needed?

2. Use the Internet to identify current cost ranges for each of the following: high-end videoconferencing rooms, roll-about systems, and desktop videoconferencing systems. Summarize the major components included in each and representative cost ranges.

3. Elimination/reduction of travel costs is one of the major cost justification factors for investing in videoconferencing systems. Use the Internet to find information on several companies that have invested in videoconferencing technologies. Identify other reasons (beyond travel expense reductions) why they have done so.

4. Use the Internet to find out more about the NTII. Identify and summarize the major applications being tested. Describe how this is likely to affect videoconferencing in the future.

SOURCES

DeZoysa, S. "A New Image for Videoconferencing." *Telecommunications* (December 2001, Issue 35, pp. 28–31).

Meyers, K. "Meeting by Remote: Teleconferencing Takes Flight." *Coloradobiz* (January 2002, Issue 29, pp. 38–40).

Roberti, M. "Meet Me on the Web." *Fortune* (Winter 2002, Issue 144, p. 37).

Note: For more information on wide area networks, see an additional case on the Web site, www.prenhall.com/stamper, "New WAN Hardware for Syncrasy?"

Wide Area Network Architectures

After studying this chapter, you should be able to:

■ Describe the characteristics of wide area network architectures.

■ Describe the characteristics, advantages, and disadvantages of centralized architectures.

■ Describe the characteristics, advantages, and disadvantages of distributed systems.

■ Explain the fundamental concepts of client/server computing.

■ Discuss the role of middleware in client/server networks.

■ Describe the challenges that business organizations must address when implementing international networks.

The previous chapter provides an overview of the major technologies (hardware, software, and data link protocols) found in wide area networks (WANs). This chapter considers the deployment and configuration of WAN technologies to form network architectures. It also takes a closer look at three major kinds of WAN architectures found in today's business organizations: centralized, distributed, and client/server architectures. This chapter also provides insights into the major issues that must be addressed by multinational businesses in developing international architectures to support their operations. We begin our discussion of these important concepts by defining the term *network architecture*.

network architecture The overall design of a data communications system that includes the network's hardware, software, access methods, and communication protocols; the way in which media, hardware, and software are integrated to form a network.

WHAT IS NETWORK ARCHITECTURE?

A **network architecture** is essentially a blueprint (plan) for how the hardware and software in a network should be deployed or configured. WAN architectures subsume the concepts introduced in Chapter 10, including WAN topologies, the WAN services employed to interconnect hosts (nodes), and the software and protocols used within

WANs to facilitate resource sharing among hosts and communication between nodes and terminals. WAN architectures also subsume WAN switching and transmission architectures (such as circuit switching, packet switching, frame relay, and cell relay) that are discussed more fully in Chapter 12.

Two basic hardware configurations supported by network architectures are *point-to-point* and *multipoint* connections. As noted in Chapter 10, a point-to-point connection is essentially a simple dedicated connection between two computers; multipoint connections enable two or more networked devices to share the same communications medium.

Over time, three major kinds of network architectures have emerged as predominant WAN architectures. These are centralized architectures, distributed architectures, and client/server computing architectures. The bulk of the discussion in the rest of this chapter is devoted to describing the characteristics, advantages, and disadvantages of each of these.

CENTRALIZED NETWORK ARCHITECTURES

Prior to the development of microcomputers during the 1970s, most computer networks in organizations were centralized, host-based systems such as that depicted in Figure 11-1. Within such systems, the processing power for the entire company was concentrated in a single large processor (the host) or a limited number of large processors. Because most of the hosts in such networks were mainframe computers, they are often referred to as being *mainframe-centric* architectures.

During the 1950s and 1960s, batch processing was common in centralized networks. In addition, punched cards and tapes were commonly used for data input and storage. With *batch processing*, data were collected for predefined time periods and

Figure 11-1   Centralized Host-Based Network

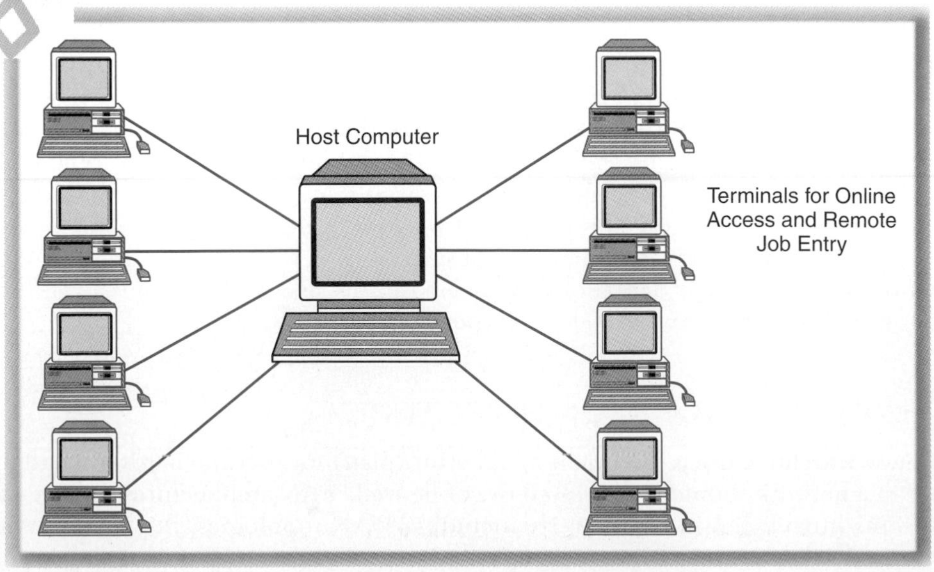

then processed all at once. Batch processing stands in contrast to *immediate processing* or processing data as it is entered via terminals. Immediate processing is also called *online processing* or *real-time processing.*

Online access to a host is one of the key characteristics of immediate processing systems. The evolution of operating systems for host computers during the 1960s saw the addition of *multitasking* capabilities that made it possible for the host to concurrently work on multiple tasks for multiple users. Multitasking operating systems also facilitated remote job entry—the ability for users to perform processing tasks on a host from geographically dispersed terminals. As a result, users from all parts of the organization were able to harness the power of the host processor. Online access, remote job entry systems, and online processing helped to solidify business interest in computing networks and paved the way for the development of distributed processing systems and client/server computing architectures.

The first terminals used in centralized systems were dumb terminals (which are described in the previous chapter). Over time, centralized systems and their support equipment have grown more efficient and sophisticated. In many of today's business organizations, smart terminals, intelligent terminals, microcomputers, or network computers (NCs) have replaced dumb terminals. Collectively, these have enabled centralized processing architectures to become more efficient by relieving hosts of some of their processing responsibilities.

Because centralized, host-based networks permit multiple users to simultaneously share large central computers, they are still widely found in business organizations. Such architectures are especially likely to be employed by organizations that rely on large central databases for order processing, inventory management, and other transaction processing operations. Although the Internet has emerged as an important e-business network, mainframe-centric backbone networks continue to be the locus of mission-critical applications for many business organizations.

Centralized architectures, however, also have shortcomings. For example, relying exclusively on a centralized, host-based computing arrangement is like putting all one's eggs in one basket. The organization is dependent on the host and the communication lines between it and terminals. If either is damaged or malfunctions, users are unable to access the applications that they rely on to perform their jobs. In addition, hosts may bog down during peak business periods when too many users need to simultaneously use the network. Overall network performance and response times may degrade significantly during peak business periods. As a result of these shortcomings, many organizations have chosen to supplement or replace centralized computing architectures with distributed or client/server computing architectures.

IBM's Systems Network Architecture (SNA)

Vendor offerings play a major role in wide area network implementation and configuration. Almost every major computer vendor outlines enterprise-wide network architectures, including WAN architectures, which illustrate how its equipment can be deployed to support an organization's computing and data communications needs.

The following section is devoted to IBM's SNA, which is widely recognized as a de facto industry standard for mainframe-centric computer networks. Most networks that have been designed around IBM mainframe systems use SNA. Because a wide range of computers manufactured by different vendors is typically found in business organizations, the evolution of enterprise networks has involved developing SNA or TCP/IP interfaces for non–IBM equipment and networks. Because of SNA's sizable installed base, many other computer manufacturers have developed the ability to attach their mainframes to SNA networks as a type of SNA node.

Systems Network Architecture (SNA)
IBM's architecture for building a computer network. Encompasses hardware and software components, establishment of sessions between nodes, and capabilities such as office and message/file distribution services. It describes the logical structure, formats, protocols, and operational sequences for transmitting data between IBM software and hardware devices.

Systems Network Architecture (SNA), announced by IBM in 1974, provides the framework for implementing data communication networks using IBM or IBM—compatible equipment. SNA is not a product per se but a blueprint for how hardware, software, and users interact in exchanging data on IBM systems. A network based on SNA consists of a variety of hardware and software components in a well-defined configuration.

Why SNA?

Since the 1960s, IBM has been the leader in computer sales and installations. The move to SNA was prompted not so much by competition from the outside but by competition from within IBM itself. Before 1974, the implementation of communication systems had been somewhat random: If a new terminal was developed, a new or modified access method and data link protocol were likely to accompany it. By 1974, IBM was offering more than 200 different models of communication hardware, 35 different device access methods, and more than a dozen data link protocols. Continuing this product proliferation would have created an enormous burden for IBM's support and maintenance. SNA was the offshoot of attempts to integrate all these functions into a single, cohesive network architecture.

The objective of any network is to enable users to communicate with one another. Users in SNA are either people working at a terminal or operator's console or applications that provide services for other programs or terminal users. Thus, a user is an entity with some degree of intelligence. A terminal is not a user, although the terms *terminal operator* and *terminal* are often used synonymously. SNA was developed to provide communication paths and dialogue rules between users. A layered network architecture similar to the OSI reference model was developed to facilitate such communication.

SNA Layers

The early releases of SNA referenced either 6 or 4 functional layers. The discrepancy between a 6-layer and a 4-layer definition is explained by the fact that layers 3 through 5 are sometimes called a *single layer*, known as the *half-session layer*. The lowest OSI reference model layer, the physical layer, is not usually specified in SNA, nor is the application layer included. However, both layers obviously must exist. The 4-layer definition is given in Table 11-1. The 6 layers are identified in parentheses, where applicable. In the current version of SNA, the layering has been redefined. The presentation service layer is omitted, and the service manager is now called the *function management layer*. Although the layering carries different names, the functions each performs are similar to those for the OSI reference model.

Table 11-1   SNA Layers

Layer 1	Data link control
Layer 2	Path control
Layer 3	Half-session layer, consisting of
	Transmission control (layer 3)
	Flow control (layer 4)
	Presentation service (layer 5)
Layer 4	Service manager (layer 6)

SNA also defines four distinct hardware groupings called *physical units (PUs)*. The four **physical units (PUs)** are numbered 1, 2, 4, and 5, with no PU currently assigned to number 3. These device types are listed in Table 11-2. The hardware configuration consists of IBM or IBM–compatible CPUs, communication controllers, terminal cluster controllers, and terminals, printers, or workstations. These are typically interconnected via traditional wire-based data communication media (such as twisted pair, coaxial cable, or fiber optic cable). Other vendors' equipment may also be included in the network if that equipment conforms to the SNA protocols. The preferred data link protocol is SDLC, but accommodations have been made for other protocols, including asynchronous transmission.

Logical Units and Sessions

Users of SNA are represented in the system by entities known as **logical units (LUs)**. An LU is usually implemented as a software function in a device with some intelligence, such as a CPU or controller. The dialogue between two system users is known as a *session*. Because a logical unit is the agent of a user, when one user wants to establish a session with another user, the LUs are involved in establishing the communication path between the two. A session involves two different LUs; the activities and resources used by one LU in a session are called a *half-session*. In the SNA layering in Table 11-1, the half-session layers represent the functions that would be performed by an LU for its user.

Session Types   Many different kinds of sessions can be requested, such as program to terminal, program to program, or terminal to terminal. Each category can be further stratified as to terminal type (interactive, batch, or printer) and application type (batch, interactive, word processing, or the like). One LU also can represent several different users, and a user can have multiple sessions in progress concurrently. If a terminal (operator) wants to retrieve a record from a database, the terminal must use the services of an application program to obtain the record. Each user—the terminal and the database application—is represented by an LU. The terminal LU issues a request to enter into a session with the database application LU. The application LU can either accept or reject the session request. The LU typically rejects transactions for security reasons (the requesting LU lacks authority to establish a session with the application LU) or because of congestion (the application LU has already entered into the maximum number of sessions it can support). If the session request is granted, a communication path is established between the terminal and the application. The two users continue to communicate until one of them terminates the session. Figure 11-2 shows several sessions between users communicating through their respective LUs.

physical unit (PU)
In SNA, a hardware unit. Four physical units have been defined: type 5, host processor; type 4, communication controller; type 2, cluster or programmable controller; and type 1, a terminal or controller that is not programmable.

logical unit (LU)
In IBM's SNA, a unit that represents a system user. Sessions exist between LUs or between an LU and the SSCP. Several types of LUs have been defined for SNA.

Table 11-2   SNA Physical Units

Physical Unit	Hardware Component
Type 1	A terminal device (e.g., an IBM 3278 terminal)
Type 2	A cluster controller (e.g., an IBM 3274 cluster controller)
Type 4	A communications controller (e.g., an IBM 3725 or 3745 communications controller)
Type 5	A host processor (e.g., an IBM 4381 or 3094 computer)

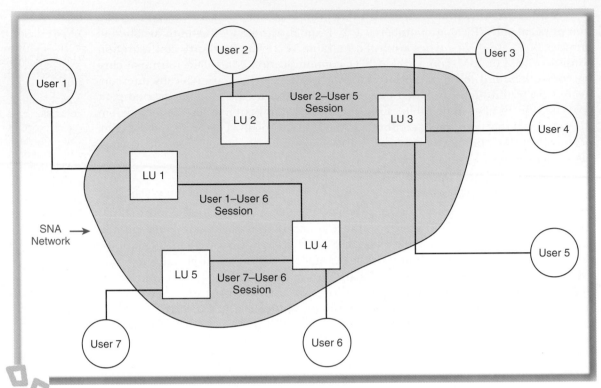

Figure 11-2   SNA Sessions and Logical Units

LU Types   Seven LU types have been defined within SNA. These are numbered from 0 to 7, with the definition for LU type 5 omitted. It is important to note that the LU types refer to session types, not to a specific LU. Thus, a specific LU can participate in a type 1 LU session with one LU and a type 4 LU session with another. For two LUs to communicate, they must both support and use the same LU session type. Of the seven LU types, all but types 0 and 6 address sessions with hardware devices such as printers and terminals. LU type 6 is defined for program-to-program communication. It has evolved through two definitions, LU 6.0 and LU 6.1, to its current definition, LU 6.2. LU 6.2 is a key SNA capability.

> **LU 6.2** An SNA logical unit type representing a program-to-program session. It is a peer-to-peer SNA protocol that establishes a communication session between two programs.

There are several significant aspects of LU 6.2. First, **LU 6.2** defines a protocol for program-to-program communication. Most of the other LU types are somewhat hardware oriented, involving sessions between IBM 3270 terminal devices, cluster controllers, printers, and so on. A program-to-program communication interface is more general and can have wider uses than hardware-oriented interfaces. Second, program-to-program sessions provide a communication path for applications distributed over multiple nodes. Two applications communicating with each other are not required to be in the same node. This capability supports transaction-processing systems with multiple processing nodes. For example, an inventory inquiry can start on a network node in a sales office and communicate with a warehouse node application to determine whether stock exists to cover a pending order. Finally, and perhaps most significantly, a program-to-program interface is more generic than a session type involving specific hardware devices. This means that other vendors' equipment can enter into SNA sessions with an application process running in an IBM processor as long as the communicating program in the vendor's processor adheres to the session rules. This allows an application on vendor A's hardware to enter into a transaction with a database application running on an IBM node.

Many vendors have implemented an LU 6.2 capability for their SNA interface because such an interface can be made device independent. Given the configuration illustrated in Figure 11-3, a program in vendor X's system can interface to its terminal device on one side and to an IBM application on the other. This logically provides the ability for a non–IBM terminal to interface to an IBM application system. Without LU 6.2, vendor X would need to appear to the IBM application as one of the supported hardware types, such as an IBM 3270 terminal or cluster controller. The International Standards Organization (ISO) also has agreed on a transaction interface that is compatible with IBM's LU 6.2 session.

Systems Services Control Point

As mentioned earlier, a dialogue between two users within the SNA environment is called a *session*. A supervisor or intermediary is involved in establishing a session. In SNA, this extremely important entity is known as the **Systems Services Control Point (SSCP)**; it resides in a host processor, which is a physical unit type 5. Not all PU type 5 devices house an SSCP. The SSCP is the software controlling its host's portion of the network. The devices controlled by the host and its SSCP represent a **domain**.

Networks implemented under early versions of SNA had only one SSCP and thus only one host computer. The host controlled the entire network. In 1979, SNA was enhanced to allow multiple-host systems and, hence, multiple domains. This became necessary because large SNA networks were being implemented. Multiple SSCPs were better able to manage many devices and sessions. A two-domain SNA configuration is shown in Figure 11-4.

Systems Services Control Point (SSCP) In IBM's SNA, the process in a host that controls a domain. It is responsible for initializing network components, establishing sessions, and maintaining unit status.

domain In IBM's SNA, a domain consists of the collective set of network components managed by a Systems Services Control Point. In the Internet, domains refer to the type of organization. Top-level domains include *gov, mil, org, com, net,* and *edu.* In Windows NT, a domain is a collection of network resources that are grouped together for ease of access and administration.

Figure 11-3   Non–IBM Vendor in an LU 6.2 Session

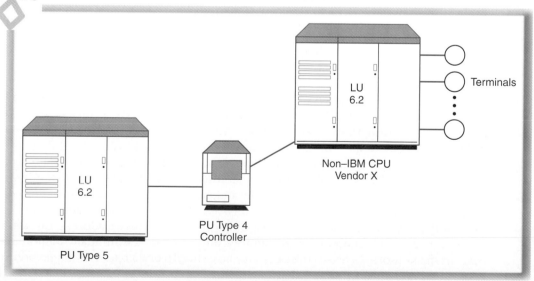

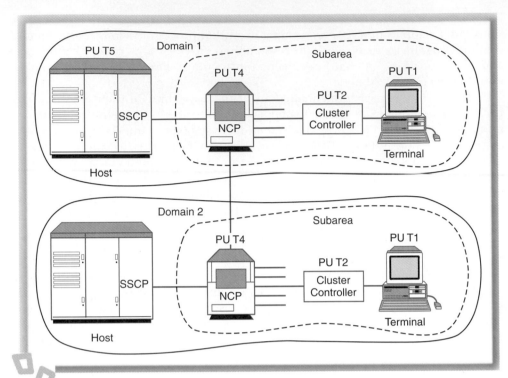

Figure 11-4   IBM SNA Network

Physical Unit Control Point (PUCP) In IBM's Systems Network Architecture, a PUCP resides in nodes that do not contain a Systems Services Control Point. The PUCP is responsible for connecting the node to and disconnecting the node from the network.

Network Addressable Unit (NAU) In IBM's SNA, any device that has a network address, such as logical units and physical units.

subarea A portion of an SNA network consisting of a subarea node (a host node or communication controller—PU types 5 and 4, respectively) together with all network resources supported by the subarea node.

Within a given domain the SSCP is the controlling entity. It is responsible for the physical and logical units within its domain. In fulfilling this obligation, the SSCP manages its units, including unit initialization, maintaining the status of individual units, placing units online and off-line as necessary, and serving as mediator in the establishment of sessions. Physical units subordinate to an SSCP must be able to carry on a dialogue with the SSCP. To accomplish this, a subset of the SSCP functionality, called a **Physical Unit Control Point (PUCP)**, resides in SNA nodes that do not contain an SSCP. A PUCP is responsible for connecting the node to and disconnecting the node from the SNA network.

Addressing

For one user to communicate with another, an address is required, because messages are sent to a specific unit using its address. Addressable components in SNA are called **Network Addressable Units (NAUs)**. An NAU can be an SSCP, an LU, or a PU. Network addresses are hierarchical in nature. You have already learned that an SNA network consists of domains. Domains consist of subareas. A **subarea** consists of a communication controller (such as an IBM 3745 communication controller) and all its NAUs or of a host/SSCP together with all of the locally attached NAUs. Figure 11-5 shows two subareas. Each subarea has a unique address. NAUs within one subarea are known by a local address. An SNA address consists of two parts, a subarea address and a unit address. The combination of subarea address and unit address uniquely identifies an NAU in the network. In SNA, addresses may be either 16 or 23 bits. The longer address is known as *extended addressing*, which allows for a larger number of NAUs in a network.

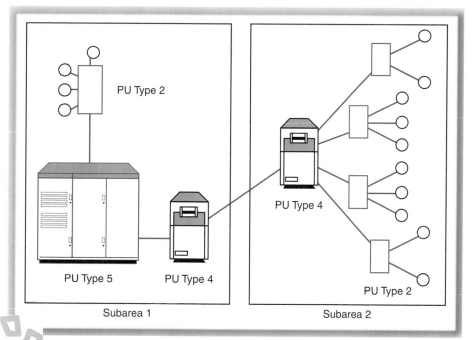

Figure 11-5   SNA Network with Two Subareas

In extended addressing mode, the first 8 bits represent the subarea, and the last 15 bits represent the device within the subarea. The 16-bit address can be decomposed into a subarea and device address on a network-by-network basis; two networks can decompose the address in different ways. One network could have an 8-bit address for both subareas and devices, whereas another could adopt a split of 7 bits for subareas and 9 bits for devices.

Communication Between Users

If users A and B are in the same domain, communication between them is established as follows. The LU representing user A sends a message to the SSCP, requesting a session with user B. On behalf of user A, the SSCP contacts the user B LU to request a session and also to provide information about user A, including user A's access profile and type. User B either accepts or rejects the session request. If the session is rejected, user A is so notified. If user B accepts the invitation to enter into a session with A, a communication path must be established. Communication between users in different domains is established in a way similar to that for a single domain, except that the SSCPs in both domains are involved: The request goes from an LU to its SSCP to the SSCP in the other domain and then to its LU.

Path establishment was easy in early SNA implementations because only one path existed between LUs. Currently, two routing methods are supported: end-to-end routing and virtual routing. In *end-to-end routing*, for which at least one of the nodes must be a type 5 PU or terminal, the path is determined and maintained through the entire session (unless the path is broken). In *virtual routing*, no permanently established path exists; instead, each node consults its routing table to determine to which node the message should be forwarded. The path control half-session layer is responsible for path allocation. Each available path is given a weighting that assists in route determination. A route might be selected based on best use according to such factors as security, speed, and propagation delay (as for satellite links). Up to five different paths between any two LUs can be described.

Additional SNA Elements and Capabilities

Network Control Program   The **Network Control Program (NCP)**, which resides in a communication controller such as the IBM 3745, controls communication lines and the devices attached to them. It works with the Virtual Terminal Access Method (VTAM)—a kind of teleprocessing monitoring and control process that resides in the host. VTAM serves as the interface between application programs and the network. Teleprocessing monitor and control programs are discussed in the previous chapter.

Advanced Communications Facility   The *Advanced Communications Facility (ACF)* was introduced in 1979. It provides such features as interdomain communication, improved error and testing capabilities, and dynamic device configuration.

Network Performance Analyzer   The *Network Performance Analyzer (NPA)* provides performance information for the system, including information on lines, buffers, errors, queue lengths, and data transmission rates.

Network Problem Determination Aid   The *Network Problem Determination Aid (NPDA)* collects, maintains, and reports information on error conditions within the network. It also allows for testing of the system concurrent with production operations.

NetView, NetView/PC, and NetView/6000   In 1986, IBM announced two network management packages for use in SNA systems. NetView runs on IBM hosts, and NetView/PC on microcomputers. With NetView, IBM has consolidated several previous network management facilities (including NPDA) and enhanced them to provide more comprehensive management capabilities. NetView/6000 was introduced in 1992 and is designed to provide network management functions for open systems, specifically non–SNA networks. Today, Tivoli, an IBM partner, oversees the ongoing evolution of NetView.

SNA Distribution Services   *SNA Distribution Services (SNADS)* allow users to exchange documents using the SNA network. Document interchange differs from the typical SNA session. In a typical SNA session, the sender and receiver are synchronized regarding information exchange. By *synchronized*, we mean that the users communicate (through their LUs) and agree to carry on a conversation. In contrast, with document exchanges the users may not be synchronized. A sender may dispatch a document without first coordinating the transmission with the recipient. The recipient can then request access to the document at its convenience. SNADS provides the ability to distribute documents in such a manner. This is particularly helpful for office automation applications such as network mail and document distribution.

Other SNA Capabilities   SNA is being continually upgraded to meet changing communication needs. It has evolved from an IBM–only network architecture to include internetworking with other networks. Accommodations made in this regard include support for the TCP/IP protocol suite; accommodations for LAN interfaces; alterations that reduce the hierarchical nature of the network and provide support for peer-to-peer communication via advanced peer-to-peer networking; support for distributed databases; and internetworking.

Advanced Peer-to-Peer Networking (APPN)

As we noted earlier, SNA is a proprietary network implementation. Proprietary networks were common in the 1960s and 1970s, but today open architectures are the norm. In a traditional SNA network, sessions are established when two entities need to communicate, and the session setup is mediated by the SSCP; this works well when all components and protocols are SNA compatible. However, this is a problem on open networks with a variety of components and protocols that are not SNA compatible. For example, today's networks typically consist of several LANs connected to a WAN, with computers ranging from desktop systems to mainframes. With the advent of open systems, it became necessary for IBM to extend SNA to enable communication between such objects in a peer-to-peer fashion. Advanced peer-to-peer networking (APPN) is a major part of this capability. It allows SNA users to retain their investment in SNA hardware, software, and personnel while opening the network to a multitude of devices.

APPN allows independent LUs to enter into sessions without the cooperation of the SSCP. APPN reduces the dependence on a host node and allows applications to specify session characteristics such as the type of path and security required. Non–IBM vendors have implemented APPN interfaces on their systems. This capability provides an easy way for programs to independently enter into a session and provides a way for applications that run on non–IBM computers to communicate via the services of SNA.

With APPN, LUs and a session are still required. What changes is the way the session is established. In the original version of SNA, LUs were given a network address, as described earlier, and hence were NAUs. APPN networks do not use the same type of addressing. A client may request to establish a session with a server somewhere in the network. APPN maintains directories of resources and establishes a route between the client and the server. A session between the two is established, and communication between the client and server is established. APPN allows any end user on the network to directly establish a connection with any other end user.

APPN provides several services in addition to peer-to-peer networking. Message traffic priorities can be set via a class-of-service capability. This reduces congestion delays for high-priority messages. High-performance routing provides the ability to route traffic around link failures and reconfigure routes to avoid congestion.

LAN-to-Host Connections

APPN is IBM's response to the evolution of distributed and client/server architectures and enterprise-wide networks that leverage local area networks as fundamental building blocks. As we will see in our discussion of LANs, later in the text, there are often major differences between LAN and WAN architectures, especially when it comes to communication protocols. SDLC is SNA's data link protocol, and its use has created challenges to interconnecting SNA and LANs.

Figure 10-29 in the previous chapter illustrates a layout of an SDLC frame. Because it contains only one address field, SDLC does not contain the addressing information required by routers; routers need both sender and recipient addresses to carry out their routing processes. The nonroutability of SDLC frames is one of the main challenges to SNA/LAN integration. This challenge has been addressed in various ways, including the following:

> ➤ *Adding LAN adapters to SNA cluster controllers to overcome frame format and other protocol differences between SNA and LANs.* This essentially makes the cluster controller another LAN–attached device. Messages received by the cluster controller for the host utilize the LAN data link protocol to ensure delivery to the appropriate microcomputer.

➤ *Encapsulating SDLC frames in TCP/IP packets.* This is a form of tunneling, which is described more fully in Chapters 2 and 4. IBM has developed its own form of TCP/IP encapsulation, known as *data link switching (DLSw)*. Cisco Systems has also developed software called *SNA switching services (SNASw)* to address this problem.

➤ *Utilizing LAN/WAN gateway technologies (protocol converters).* An example of this is illustrated in Figure 11-6.

The need for companies to address LAN/WAN interface challenges stems from the fact that many companies entered the microcomputer age with a large computer already installed. As these companies increased their use of microcomputers and installed one or more LANs, the large computer continued to play an important role in meeting their computing needs. For example, the large host computer might be used for payroll or large database applications. Even companies that replaced or are in the process of replacing hosts with LAN technology go through a period when both computing environments exist. Companies that use hosts and LANs usually need to exchange data between the two environments. Although this might be accomplished via storage media exchange (where data on the host is copied onto a disk or tape and transferred to the LAN and vice versa), often a LAN–host direct connection is the most efficient way to exchange data between these computer systems.

Figure 11-7 illustrates one potential way to connect a LAN to a host computer. It also illustrates how a remote user can gain access to computing resources stored on

Figure 11-6   Gateway Connecting a LAN and a WAN

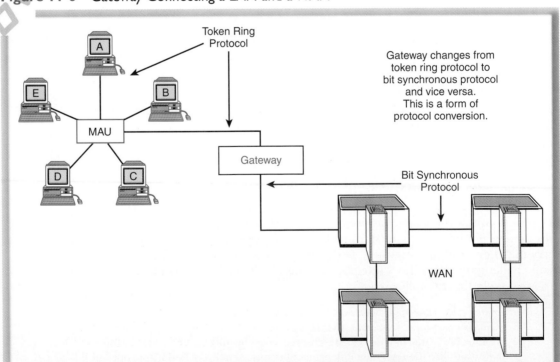

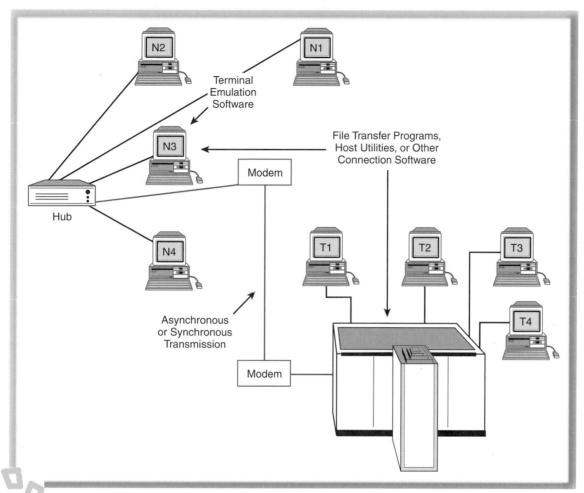

Figure 11-7 LAN-to-Host Connection

hosts. Before discussing the ways in which the LAN–host connection can be made, we look at several alternative ways in which a LAN user can interact with a host.

In Figure 11-7, a user at node N1 might need to view, update, or evaluate data that is stored in the host's database. This user can do the work on the host or he can do the work on his LAN workstation. A user at node N2 might need to send an e-mail message to a user at terminal T1. A user at node N3 might need to run an application that exists only on the host. The application may be available only on the host for a variety of reasons: It has not yet been implemented on the LAN, it needs special hardware available only on the host (such as a typesetting machine), or it requires computing power beyond that available on the LAN. One way to enable users at nodes N1, N2, N3, and N4 is via a LAN modem (a modem with a network interface card) that is capable of establishing a connection with a modem attached to the host. This connection alternative is illustrated in Figure 11-7. LAN modems are discussed more fully in Chapter 13.

The three preceding examples cover most of the general host computer connection needs of LAN users. These needs can be summarized as using host data and applications, transferring data from host to LAN or LAN to host, using host hardware or software resources, and communicating with other users attached to the host. A host user will probably have the same basic needs for accessing computer resources available on LANs.

The Host as a LAN Node

Some hosts have the ability to connect to the LAN as a node. This is accomplished by installing a LAN network adapter card in the host and is arguably the most effective way of establishing the connection. The host can thus operate as a server, responding to all of the previously discussed needs.

Asynchronous Connections

In Chapters 2 and 10 (and Appendix B www.prenhall.com/stamper) we discuss the asynchronous data transmission. Virtually every kind of data terminating equipment (DTE)—such as hosts, terminals, microcomputers, and network computers—has the ability to send and receive asynchronously. The serial port(s) on a microcomputer is an asynchronous communication port. Because most computers support this protocol, it is sometimes used to link a microcomputer to a host. Usually, a microcomputer attached to a host asynchronously operates in one of two modes: file transfer or terminal emulation.

Terminal Emulation   Terminal emulation software allows a microcomputer to imitate one or more types of terminals. This capability is commonly used when connecting to a host computer. When installed and used on a microcomputer, terminal emulation software enables the PC to become a *virtual terminal*. For example, a user may connect to a mainframe and establish an IBM 3270 terminal session with an application or a user may connect to an electronic bulletin board for information by emulating a standard teletypewriter (TTY) terminal or a VT100 terminal. Although in some instances the role of terminal emulation (and bulletin board systems) has been replaced by Internet connections wherein the microcomputer communicates with other computers using Internet protocols and software, terminal emulation remains a fundamental (and widely used) connection alternative. Through terminal emulation software, a microcomputer is able to access host-based applications and computing resources. However, when not online to the host, the microcomputer can be used as a regular PC to run the wide range of applications (such as word processing or spreadsheets) that have been developed for microcomputers.

Terminal emulation programs generally provide the ability to imitate a variety of terminal types. For example, HyperTerminal emulation software in Windows allows users to emulate the terminal types listed in Table 11-3; a cross section of terminals emulated by a variety of other emulators is given in Table 11-4. Furthermore, terminal

Table 11-3   HyperTerminal Emulation

ANSI Standard	TTY	Minitel (France)
VT100	VT52	Viewdata (United Kingdom)

Table 11-4   Terminals Emulated by a Variety of Emulators

VT52 or VT 100, 200, 300, 600 series	AT&T 600 and 700 series
Tektronix 4000, 4100, 4200 series	Hewlett-Packard 700 series
ANSI	Wyse 50, 60
TTY	Televideo 900 series
IBM 3100, 3270, 5200 series	

emulation packages usually provide capabilities beyond simple emulation. Some common functions include the following:

➤ File transfer protocols allow for uploading and downloading files. Common transfer protocols supported include XMODEM, YMODEM, ZMODEM, Kermit, BLAST, ASCII, IND$FILE, and CompuServe.

➤ Scripting allows command sequences to be placed in an executable script. Scripts can be used to provide unattended operation and to automate frequently used command sequences.

➤ Buffer control allows the user to scroll the buffer to view forwards and backwards.

➤ Network support allows operation over networks such as LANs, SNA, and the Internet.

A summary of terminal emulation capabilities is given in Table 11-5.

Dedicated Connection per Microcomputer   Host computers can usually accommodate many asynchronous connections. Small minicomputers usually support 32 or more, and large mainframes may accommodate hundreds. One way to connect a LAN node to a host is to provide a direct connection between a port on the host and each microcomputer needing a host connection. This is illustrated in Figure 11-8. In the figure, nodes N1, N2, N4, and N5 each have a dedicated connection to the host. Nodes N3 and N6 are not directly connected to the host but are able to communicate with the other nodes, because all nodes are connected to the same hub.

A **dedicated connection** provides direct host access, and the microcomputer does not use LAN resources for communicating with the host. In the typical connection, the microcomputer appears to the host as though the microcomputer were a host terminal. In addition to the serial port, the microcomputer needs terminal emulation software to establish the connection and carry on a host session. Terminal emulation software is available from many sources and can emulate a wide variety of terminals. With dedicated connections, the LAN administrator and data processing department can easily control which LAN nodes have access to the host. Nodes without a direct connection cannot make a host connection.

dedicated connection A connection providing direct access to the host using non-LAN resources for communication between the host and the microcomputer.

Table 11-5   Terminal Emulation Software Capabilities

Scripts	Mouse support	File transfer
Terminals emulated	Network support	E-mail
Phone directory	Text editor	Password entry
Capture of data to a disk		

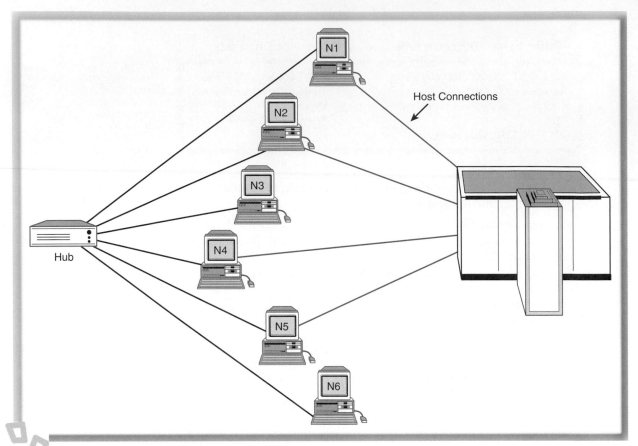

Figure 11-8   Multiple LAN-to-Host Connections

A dedicated connection has several disadvantages. First, as with all asynchronous connections, the speed of the link is slow. Asynchronous speeds can be faster than 100,000 bps, but typically for microcomputer connections the speed is 56 kbps or less. If many LAN nodes must communicate with the host, many host ports are required. This not only reduces the number of ports available to the host's terminal users but also is somewhat costly. The cost for host ports can be significant and is burdensome if microcomputer users only need occasional access to the host. Finally, when operating in terminal emulation mode, the microcomputer loses some of its processing capabilities. It can essentially do only what a terminal can do. Specifically, the microcomputer can send and receive data but (usually) cannot use this interface to have a local application, such as a database management system, directly access data on the host.

Multiplexing   As noted in Chapter 10, a *multiplexor* is a hardware device that allows several devices to share one communication channel. Multiplexing typically is used to consolidate the message traffic between a computer and several remotely located terminals, as illustrated in Figure 11-9. This technique can also be used to allow several microcomputers to share a communication link to a host processor.

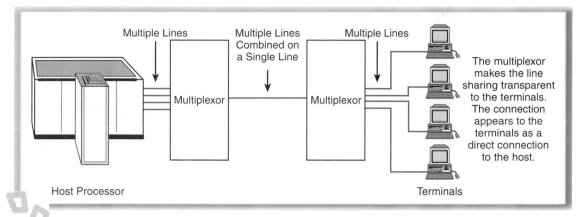

Figure 11-9   Multiplexor Connection

Shared Asynchronous Connections   In some applications, each LAN node needs occasional access to the host, but the number of concurrent connections is far fewer than the number of LAN nodes. A dedicated line per node is excessive in such situations. A better solution is to share asynchronous connections. The most common way to share connections is via a *communication server* or front-end processor (FEP), as illustrated in Figure 11-10.

In Figure 11-10, the communication server has four connections to the host. A microcomputer needing host services requests a connection through the communication server. If all four ports are in use, the request is denied. If a host port is free, the request is honored, and the microcomputer is connected to a vacant host port. You might note that the communication server functions much like a telephone switch.

Communication servers also may provide connections for remote hosts. The usual way a connection is made to a remote host is via a modem connection. The line to the remote host may be dedicated or switched. A dedicated line is continuously available; a switched line connection is established on an as-needed basis. The typical example of a switched line is a dial-up telephone line. The link between two devices is made via a telephone call, remains active during the length of the session, and is broken when the session is completed. Rather than providing each LAN node with a dedicated modem, the communication server can provide modem sharing. The technique for doing this is much like the sharing technique described in the previous paragraph.

Other Types of Host Connections

Asynchronous connections are common because they are easily implemented and are supported by most host systems. On the microcomputer side, all that is necessary is a serial port and terminal emulation or file transfer software. The only host-specific characteristic is the type of terminal being emulated or the file transfer software. Other types of vendor-specific connections exist.

Because of the dominant role played by IBM systems, many of these connections are based on IBM software and hardware technologies. These connections might also work on non–IBM equipment because many large-computer companies support one or more IBM communication protocols. Two of the most common IBM interfaces are described here.

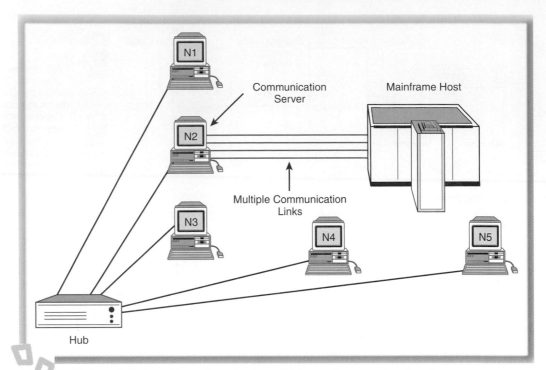

Figure 11-10 LAN-to-Host Connections Using a Communication Server

IBM-3270 Emulation A mainstay of IBM's communication networks is the family of 3270 terminals. The family consists of a variety of terminals, printers, and cluster controllers. The communication protocol used for 3270 devices is a synchronous protocol, either binary synchronous (BISYNC) or synchronous data link control (SDLC), both of which were discussed in Chapter 10.

IBM-3270 emulation can be effected through a communication server or through individual LAN nodes. When emulation is implemented at individual LAN nodes, a synchronous communication controller must be installed in the microcomputer. The controller provides the necessary line interface. If a communication server is used, the server must have a synchronous communication port. Aside from the protocol interface, the connection works much like the asynchronous connection described earlier.

LU 6.2 Connection For many years, IBM networks have been designed around IBM's Systems Network Architecture (SNA). As noted earlier in this chapter, SNA users communicate through sessions and a variety of session types are defined. Logical units (LUs) represent users in establishing, using, and ending a session. One type of session allows programs to communicate with other programs. This type of session is called an *LU 6.2* session. Support for LU 6.2 sessions is available for microcomputers and is being increasingly used to establish host connections. The advantage of an LU 6.2 interface is that a microcomputer application can communicate directly with a host application or with an application on another network node (as opposed to the microcomputer simply acting as though it were a terminal).

Interconnection Utilities

Having the ability to establish network connections is one part of communicating among networks. Another part is having utilities that help you use those connections. Many such utilities are available. Some are commercial products, and others are available in the public domain for no or little cost. Some utilities used to enable remote or LAN users to access host computer applications and data are briefly described here.

File Transfer Utilities   **File transfer utilities** allow you to move files between network nodes. File transfer capabilities are an intrinsic part of many routers. FTP, for example, enables files transfers to take place between computers in TCP/IP networks. Kermit is another file transfer utility that runs on a wide variety of computer platforms. It uses asynchronous communication links to transfer files whose data is in ASCII form. Two common microcomputer file transfer utilities are XMODEM and YMODEM. Kermit, XMODEM, and YMODEM are often included in terminal emulation programs.

> **file transfer utilities** Programs that enable files to be transmitted from one computer in a network to another.

Remote Logon   **Remote log-on facilities** allow users to log on to a remote system. A remote logon essentially establishes a remote user as a local user on the remote node. Once a user has successfully logged on to the remote node, commands issued by that user are processed and acted on by the remote node rather than by the local node. When the user logs off from the remote node, his session is reestablished on the local node.

> **remote log-on facilities** Network utilities that allow users to log on to a remote system, thereby establishing the user as a local user on the remote node.

DISTRIBUTED PROCESSING SYSTEMS

Implementing interfaces among LANs and WANs is one path to creating distributed processing systems. In this section, we will take a closer look at distributed processing systems as well as distributed databases.

Distributed System Definitions

Systems can be distributed in a variety of ways. As we noted in Chapter 6, a variety of topologies are found in WANs to enable users to access computing resources located at geographically dispersed hosts. In Chapters 7 through 9, distributing processing activities among LAN servers and workstations is discussed. Data also can be distributed over two or more LAN nodes, such as file servers, SQL servers, and client workstations.

The ultimate goal of distributed processing and databases is essentially to make the network the computer. As we have already noted, in early computing systems, all data and processing were confined to one computer. In early networks, we were only able to distribute the computing load among several computers by replicating what was done on individual computers. If a network had three nodes, processing was taking place simultaneously on all three computers, but most of the processing entailed a single program on one system accessing and processing data on the same system. The network was used primarily to transport completed reports, for data input on terminals attached to a remote host, and so on. Ideally, we would like to have the aggregate resources of a network applied as appropriate to cooperatively work on problems. In this ideal processing environment, a single transaction might use the processing resources of several computers, access and update data in a database distributed over multiple disk drives on multiple geographically dispersed computer nodes, and perhaps even enable processed data to be output in several distributed locations. Such distributed collaboration of hardware and software naturally is transparent to users of this ideal processing environment.

Before we introduce the technology of distributed processing and distributed databases, we first define more precisely the various aspects of distributed systems. First, there is a distinction between distributed processing and distributed databases. From the preceding paragraph, you may have an intuitive idea about these distinctions. **Distributed processing** refers to the geographic distribution of hardware, software, processing, data, and control. The data communication system is the glue that holds the distributed system together and makes it workable. Geographic distribution does not mean great distances. As stated earlier, a LAN is a distributed processing system and, by definition, serves a limited area. A company also can have a distributed system contained in a single computer room. The key factor in having a distributed processing system is networking two or more independent computing systems so that there is an interdependence among the nodes. The dependence can be for processing power, data, application software, or use of peripherals. This arrangement enables two or more separate CPUs to share work on the same application program.

Often, distributed systems also are characterized by distribution of control. If the nodes are placed in different locations, there is local responsibility for each node. For example, a manufacturing organization may have processing nodes in the headquarters offices, regional offices, and warehouses. In each of these locations, there will be an operations staff responsible for running the systems. There may also be a local support and development organization responsible for developing, installing, and maintaining applications and databases.

Data is often one of the objects distributed in a network. People often refer to data distribution as a **distributed database**. However, simple data distribution is not sufficient for a distributed database. To have a true distributed database, there must be a comprehensive, coordinated system that manages the data. Later in this chapter, you will learn about the requirements of a distributed DBMS and how it differs from distributed file systems. Because distributed data and databases are an important aspect of distributed systems, a large portion of this chapter addresses the issues surrounding this topic.

One objective of distributed processing is to move data and processing functions closer to the users who need those services and thereby to improve the system's responsiveness and reliability. A second objective is to make remote access transparent to the system user, so the user has little or nothing special to do when accessing the other nodes of the system. How these objectives are met is explained later. First, however, we will briefly review how distributed systems evolved.

Evolution of Distributed Systems

At the dawn of the computer age, computers were big and expensive, and operating systems were either nonexistent or incapable of supporting multiple job streams. As a result, for the organizations that could afford it, computer systems were acquired for every department needing computational power. In a manufacturing organization, one computer would be dedicated to inventory, one to accounting, and one to manufacturing control. These were decentralized processing systems, but they were very different from the current concept of distributed systems in one important respect: the sharing of resources.

Duplicated Databases and Inconsistent Data

Processors in early systems usually were not connected via communication links. As a result, each maintained its own database, often with duplicated data. Both the warehouse database and the accounting department database contained the same customer information, the former for shipping and the latter for invoicing. When a cus-

---

distributed processing The geographic distribution of hardware, software, processing, data, and control.

distributed database A database wherein data are located on two or more computing systems connected via a data communication network. The fact that data are distributed should be transparent to database users.

tomer moved, the address change was probably not reflected in both databases at once, and in some instances not before a considerable amount of time had elapsed. Such redundant storage of data, with the attendant update problems, created data inconsistencies. Data inconsistencies often are manifested by conflicts in reports. As a consequence, shipments or invoices could be sent to the incorrect address and perhaps be lost. Because each department was essentially the proprietor of its own system, there was little sharing of computer resources. This meant that one system might be inundated with work while another was idle. One possible early decentralized processing system is depicted in Figure 11-11.

Centralization

Early decentralized systems were far from ideal. In addition to data inconsistencies, there were extra costs for hardware, operations, maintenance, and programming. As systems grew larger and operating systems became more comprehensive, there was a movement to large, *centralized systems*, as illustrated in Figure 11-12. At that time, large, centralized systems had the benefits of a single operation center, control, and (according to some) economies of scale, as a single large system was likely to cost less than several smaller decentralized systems. In many organizations with centralized systems, a single programming department was established for all application development and

Figure 11-11   Early Distributed Processing System

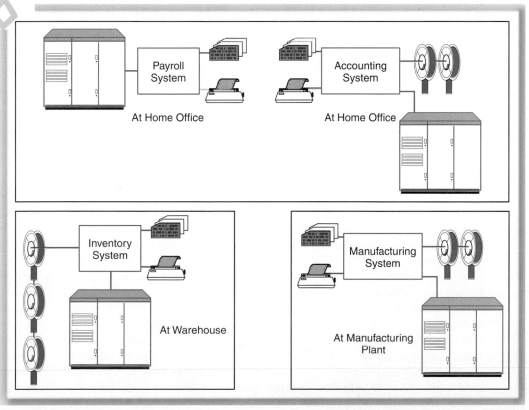

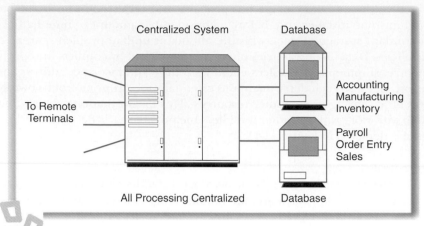

Figure 11-12   Centralized System

maintenance. To reduce data redundancy and promote data sharing among users, centralized databases also were established.

Disadvantages of Centralization

It was later found that large, centralized systems also have inherent problems. First, if the large central system fails, the entire system fails; if a component fails, all or part of the application system may be unavailable. In the decentralized approach, failure of a single host results in part of the overall system being lost, but many processing functions can be continued. In this respect, decentralized systems are more reliable than a single centralized system.

Many end users—the accounting department, warehouse staff, and so forth—found that their needs were not met by a centralized system. Because the system was shared, users often found it unresponsive; there was often difficulty running jobs and getting resources for new development. With a departmental system in a distributed or decentralized environment, a user contends only with other users in the department, so it was easy to establish priorities. However, setting interdepartment priorities was not easy sometimes. The same held true for programming. In the centralized environment, a programming team may have been assigned to develop an application or a new report for a department. Because developers were not under the direct control of the department, it was sometimes difficult for the department to change priorities and directions.

Expansion and growth of the large, centralized system posed another problem for some companies: controlling system growth. Too often, growth was not in small, manageable increments but in giant steps, such as conversion to a larger processor with a different operating system. This conversion meant downtime while the new system was being installed. Sometimes, programs had to be revised, and new program bugs were encountered. The change was usually disruptive to all users. In contrast, when upgrading a distributed system, growth was generally in smaller, more manageable increments. In addition, if a new processor became necessary, only those using that node were affected, not the entire user community.

Networked Systems

Networking provides some of the benefits of both centralized and distributed environments: more localized processing and control with shared data, processing power, and equipment. We again use a LAN as an example, however, these comments also generally apply to WANs. In a LAN, end users have a workstation capable of performing a variety of application functions such as word processing and spreadsheets. Each workstation is also able to call on the processing power and database capabilities of a larger system—a server or host processor—to accomplish more complex and time-consuming processing tasks. Some of the data required frequently by a user at a workstation may reside on the workstation's local disk drives. This may include documents in process and budget data for spreadsheets. Data that either is infrequently used or is too big for the workstation's local disks can be maintained at a larger host. Although this data is maintained by another node, the workstation can access that data as though it were stored locally. Workstations are also able to share other network resources such as printers and magnetic tape drives. The key to a distributed system is making resource distribution transparent to the users. When the resources being distributed are data, sophisticated network software is necessary. The software responsible for doing this is called a **distributed file system (DFS)**.

Distributed File Systems

In distributed systems, users must have the ability to locate and use remote files as though those files were locally resident. The objectives of a DFS are given in Table 11-6 and are described below. Again, do not confuse a DFS with a distributed DBMS. Although there are similarities between the two, distributed database systems significantly extend the capabilities of a DFS.

Transparent Access   **Transparent access** means that a user at one node must be able to access distributed files as though they were located on the user's local node. This means a user should be able to use the file system commands of the local system to access remote files, even if the remote file is located on a node with a different operating and file system.

Operating System Independence   In building a distributed system, a user should be able to configure heterogeneous systems. This may mean that different operating systems and file systems are involved. Not only should designers be able to build a system composed of different hardware and software, but also they must make these differences transparent to users.

File System Independence   With file system independence, different file systems, such as DOS, UNIX, and VMS, may be used in one network. Just as important, the differences among the file systems should be transparent to users. For example, the local

distributed file system (DFS) Network software responsible for making network resources available to multiple users regardless of their location in the network. NFS (Network File System) is an example of a distributed file system.

transparent access The ability of a user to access distributed files as though they were located on the user's local node. Transparent access is a characteristic of well-designed distributed file systems.

Table 11-6   Distributed File System Objectives

Provide transparent access to distributed files	Provide contention resolution
Provide operating system independence	Provide security
Provide file system independence	Provide file directory information
Provide architecture independence	Provide location independence

file system commands should be functional when a user accesses a file on a remote node with a different file system.

Architecture Independence   The DFS should allow any network configuration (star, bus, ring, interconnected, and so on). Neither the architecture nor the network software should limit the ability to distribute files.

Contention Resolution   The DFS ought to provide a mechanism that prevents data corruption due to contention. Such corruption can result when two or more users try to access and update the same file or record.

Security   A DFS must provide the requisite level of security. Files should be able to be secured for local access only or for remote access. When remote access to a file is allowed, the DFS must be able to grant or deny requests based on the requester's ID. Inherent in this requirement is the ability to provide user identities for users on a node that does not support user IDs (such as a single-user microcomputer) and to reconcile network differences among user IDs.

File Directory Information   The DFS is responsible for transparently satisfying user requests. This means it must maintain a directory of remote files and their locations. When a user requests access to a file, the directory is consulted to find the node that houses the file.

Location Independence   Location independence means that a file can be located at any node in the network. A file also must be able to be moved from one node to another without disrupting applications or user access to that file.

Several DFS implementations exist. The one most often used for networks with equipment from a variety of vendors is the *Network File System (NFS)*, developed by Sun Microsystems. It is implemented not only on Sun systems but also on a variety of UNIX–, VMS–, and DOS–based systems. Sun Microsystems has placed the NFS protocol specifications in the public domain to allow other vendors to implement it. The objective of publishing the protocol was to spread its use and establish NFS as a standard.

A UNIX operating system DFS, *Remote File Sharing (RFS)*, was initially restricted to UNIX–based systems. This protocol is supported by AT&T, the originator of the UNIX operating system. With RFS, files that physically exist on one node can appear as though they reside on other nodes. Thus, a user can access the remote file as though it were a local file.

Advantages and Disadvantages of Distributed Systems

Advantages

Each distributed system just described has several advantages. For one, storing data close to the location that uses it most minimizes the amount of data that must be transmitted across the network between nodes and provides better response times. Because data ownership and maintenance are typically local responsibilities, there is more of a vested interest in keeping the data current. Third, nonlocal transactions are still possible, as are transactions that must span several nodes, the only penalty being slower response times due to slow transmission speeds on the communication links. Distributed systems also give local users more control over their data processing system. This provides users with the flexibility to tailor changes to their own needs without disrupting other network nodes. Reliability also is higher than with a centralized system, for the failure of one node does not mean the entire system is down. Each node has most of the data it needs to continue local processing, so applications can continue with only a slight degradation in service.

Disadvantages

There are also disadvantages to the distributed approach.

Slower Multiple-Node Transactions   Whenever a transaction must span more than one node, response time is longer than if the transaction ran on one node only. Suppose a salesperson for a computer vendor enters an order for a new system consisting of minicomputers, CD-ROM storage silos, and microcomputer terminals. The response time for placing the order will be faster if all the equipment is available in the local warehouse than if each component must come from a different location. In the latter case, a message might have to be sent to the other warehouses in sequence until the order was filled.

Maintaining Transaction Integrity   A transaction is an unitary piece of work—a group of updates that must all be completed for database consistency. In a centralized database, this unitary property is guaranteed by the DBMS's recovery system. However, when a transaction updates files on several nodes, several independent DBMSs are involved. Each may be capable of guaranteeing the integrity of the portion of the transaction processed on its system, but there is no coordination among the various DBMSs. In fact, it may be difficult to establish a consistent, unique transaction identifier for node-spanning transactions.

Contention and Deadlock   Update transactions on multiple nodes increase the risk of contention and deadlock. For most host-based DBMSs, a record being updated is locked until the end of the transaction to avoid the problems of concurrent updates. Because a transaction that spans several nodes is likely to be slower than one on a single node (because of data communication transmission time), affected records remain locked longer. Thus, the probability increases that the records will be needed by another transaction, and hence the amount of contention and the potential for deadlock increases.

Potential for Failure   The longer response time for transactions that span multiple nodes also increases the probability of a failure that will produce an unsuccessful transaction.

Determining Participating Nodes

Most DBMSs available today were not originally designed for distributing data over several nodes/hosts. With a transaction that accesses and updates records on multiple nodes, the system must determine which other nodes must be involved. It is unthinkable to require the user to do this, because one of the objectives is to make the distributed nature of the system transparent. It is also desirable to reserve the ability to redistribute data and processes without disrupting users.

One approach to identifying the location of resources is to programmatically define the nodes that are to participate by coding the locations into the programs. This requires that the programming staff know the location of data their programs are using. As nodes are added or data is relocated, it is likely that program changes also will be required. Although this approach is preferable to relying on the user to determine the location of files, it creates considerable problems with respect to maintaining the system, extending the system through the addition of nodes, and redistributing data and other system resources.

Network Dictionary of Locations   A better way to identify resource locations is to have a network dictionary of locations that describes the locations of all distributed data and processing entities referenced in the system. The application or transaction control process can access the dictionary to learn where the required resources are located. Redistribution of files requires a simple update to the dictionary, and programs are not affected by such changes.

Central Versus Distributed Data Dictionary   The data dictionary can be either centrally located and maintained or replicated at all nodes. The centralized approach, with several weaknesses, is the less desirable. First, when the central node becomes unavailable, the distributed system is inoperable. Local operations could continue, but finding remote resources would be impossible. The centralized dictionary approach can be augmented by establishing one or more alternative nodes with backup dictionary capability. The backup nodes are used if the primary fails.

A second problem with a centralized dictionary is that additional access time is required to obtain the information, and the possibility exists that the central node will become a performance bottleneck. In a LAN with high-speed links, communication time might not be significant. But in a WAN, accessing data via a slow communication link that also requires several hops through intermediate nodes can significantly slow the application response time, especially if the dictionary must be consulted several times for each transaction.

A *distributed data dictionary* resides on all nodes or strategically located nodes. This provides faster access to the dictionary than in the centralized approach. The disadvantage of distributed dictionaries is the need to keep all dictionaries properly updated, particularly if the contents change often. Such updating adds traffic across the network and may contribute to increased response times and decreased network performance, especially during peak business periods. Despite this shortcoming, a distributed dictionary usually gives better performance than a centralized one.

Routing, Transmission, and Processing

Once the locations of the distributed resources have been determined, a strategy must be developed for accessing and processing the data. Designers of distributed systems have several options in determining how the remote processing and accesses will be handled. In general, the strategy selected depends on the type of transaction.

Remote Access and Local Processing   One method for processing with distributed data is remote access and local processing. This type of transaction is used effectively when most of the data being accessed is needed at the local node. Consider a system for a state's highway patrol force. If a state trooper stops a car and inquires regarding the driver's record, the application on the local node in the state trooper's vehicle issues a read request for the driver's files on a remote, centralized host. The set of records for the driver is transmitted from the remote host to local node and is displayed on the display device in the trooper's car. If the driver is cited for a violation as a consequence of the trooper's work, the driver's record might be modified locally, and then a local request for updating the record in the remote file at the centralized host is made. The revised record is transmitted over the network, and the database is updated as a consequence of the remote update request. The characteristics of the police transaction are that every record accessed was transmitted over the network to the local node, all processing was done locally, and all updates were brought about via local requests.

Partial Remote Processing   A second method for handling distributed processing requires that the remote node perform some amount of application processing. Consider a user request to list all employees with more than 10 years of service and a salary below $20,000. For a company with 100,000 employees, all 100,000 records must be accessed to satisfy the query. Passing each of the 100,000 records to the user's node for selection would create a lot of traffic on the communication medium and take considerable extra time. A much better alternative is to have a server process on each remote node access the records, select the ones that meet the specified conditions, and then transmit only the results to the user's node, where the list will be consolidated and displayed.

Total Remote Processing   Consider a transaction that updates records at a remote node. When the record is required locally, the remote record is transmitted to the local node, an update is made, and the record is sent back to the remote node for updating in the database. In some instances, the entire update can be performed remotely, as in giving an across-the-board pay raise to employees.

Suppose a company decides to distribute the personnel and payroll applications and maintains that data in each of five regional processing centers. A manager in the corporate headquarters may have the responsibility for administering a 4 percent pay raise for all 100,000 employees. If the first strategy is used, each of the 100,000 records must be read remotely, transmitted over the network, updated, sent back over the network, and updated in the database. For this transaction, however, there is no need to transmit any data to the local node. A better alternative is to send the request to a server process on the remote node and have all the work done there.

Many other examples of the division of activity among nodes could be cited. In essence, there are only the three basic methods just discussed: access remote records, pass them to the local node, process the records locally, and then return them to the remote nodes for updating as necessary; send messages to remote application servers that accept and process data and then return only the required information to the requesting nodes; or a combination of the two approaches, which is sometimes the best alternative. The design objective is always to make the transaction as efficient as possible, which means minimizing the transmission of many records between nodes.

Database Management in Distributed Systems

Having discussed how data can be manipulated with remote file systems, we now look at the more complex problem of distributed databases. Most current DBMSs were originally designed to operate on only one node. There was no need to keep track of files or databases on another node or to manage transactions that span multiple nodes. In some instances, the problem of distributed transactions is compounded by having two different database management systems involved. One example is when one node uses one vendor's hardware and software and another node uses a different vendor's hardware and DBMS. The DBMSs will cooperate with each other only through user-written programs or routines (middleware) or because they both comply with widely accepted standards such as ODBC (Open Data Base Connectivity).

Rules for a Distributed Database

You have already read about the objectives of distributed file systems. A similar set of objectives or rules has been established for distributed databases. These rules, given in Table 11-7, are explained here. Note that in some instances the rules are comparable to those for distributed file systems and that the rules extend the capabilities of remote file systems.

Rule 1   Local autonomy means that users at a given node are responsible for data management and system operation at that node. A local node has a certain amount of independence regarding these local operations. This independence is not

Table 11-7   Date's 12 Rules for Distributed Databases

Local autonomy	Distributed query processing
No reliance on a central site	Distributed transaction management
Continuous operation	Hardware independence
Location independence	Operating system independence
Fragmentation independence	Network independence
Replication independence	DBMS independence

unrestrained, however. As with individuals in a free society who have individual independence, the independence extends only where it does not adversely affect another member of the society. Thus, a local node does not typically have the independence to arbitrarily remove its node from the network if that action is detrimental to operation of the distributed system. Another implication of local autonomy is that users at a node accessing only data local to that node should neither experience performance degradations nor need to interact with the system differently as a result of being part of a distributed system.

Rule 2   No reliance on a central site means that all nodes in the distributed system shall be considered as peer nodes, with no node identified as a supervisor. Furthermore, there shall not be one node on which other nodes must rely, such as a single node that contains a centralized data dictionary or directory.

Rule 3   Continuous operation means that adding nodes to the network, removing network nodes, or having one node fail will not affect availability of other nodes. Naturally, a single node failure will probably disrupt access for the users local to that node; however, users at other nodes can continue to use the distributed database, and their disruption is limited to an inability to access data stored only at the failed node.

Rule 4   Location independence means that data can be placed anywhere in the network and that its location is transparent to those needing access to it. Data can be moved from one node to another, and users or programs needing access to that data are not disrupted.

Rule 5   Fragmentation independence means that data that appears to users as one logical file can be transparently partitioned over multiple nodes. The distributed DBMS is responsible for making the various fragments appear as a single file.

Rule 6   Storing the same file in multiple locations is called *replication*. Replication independence means that any file can be replicated on two or more nodes and that such replication is transparent to both users and applications. Replication is desirable for files that must be accessed by several nodes, such as a network directory. Replication can enhance performance and availability. The distributed DBMS is responsible for managing updates to replicated data and keeping the replicated data consistent.

Rule 7   When we discussed access strategies for distributed files, three alternatives were given: remote access and local processing, partial remote processing, and total remote processing. The alternative used depended on the application program's logic. *Distributed query processing* means that a user at one node can start a query involving data on other nodes. Access and processing strategies such as those discussed earlier must be supported. The location of the data must be transparent to the user and the application. The query also must be completed in an optimum way. This might mean that database servers on several nodes cooperatively work on a portion of the query. In this way, the minimum amount of data is transmitted over the network to the requesting node. The DBMS is responsible for determining the access strategy and carrying it out.

Rule 8   *Distributed transaction management* means that node-spanning transactions must be allowed. Moreover, transactions that update data on several nodes must be recoverable. This requires that a transaction started on one node can update records on other nodes and that the DBMSs on those other nodes coordinate their activities regarding locking records and effecting transaction backout and recovery.

Rule 9   Hardware independence means that the distributed network can consist of hardware from a variety of vendors. Nodes in the distributed system can come from a variety of vendors, such as IBM, Hewlett-Packard, or Compaq.

Rule 10   When different hardware vendors supply network nodes, it is likely that different operating systems will be used. This capability is known as *operating system independence*.

Rule 11   Another consequence of rule 9, hardware independence, might be that different network architectures, software, and protocols are used. If the vendors design their network systems according to the OSI reference model and related standards, such interconnection is easier. Network independence means that multiple kinds of network software may be used in connecting the nodes together. Some network nodes may be part of an SNA network; others may be members of a DECNET architecture (a WAN architecture from Digital Equipment that competes with SNA), and still others may be nodes on an Ethernet LAN. Using disparate network systems must not adversely affect distributed database capabilities.

Rule 12   DBMS independence means that a variety of DBMSs may be used in the distributed database. One node might use a nonrelational database such as IMS, another might use DB2, and a third might use Oracle. Each DBMS has a different data access and manipulation language, has different recovery mechanisms, and stores data in different formats. The distributed DBMS must make these differences transparent to both users and applications. A user also should be able to access data managed by such a variety of DBMSs without learning a variety of data access languages. Specifically, users should be able to access distributed data using the same interface they use to access data stored locally. This rule implies that database recovery systems be coordinated and database language differences accommodated. Implementation of this rule is very complex.

Currently, there is no system that fully adheres to all of these rules. Creating a distributed environment that truly encompasses all 12 rules will require a considerable investment. Until then, those who want to implement distributed databases must settle for less than the capabilities implied by these rules. The best way to implement distributed databases today is to use hardware and software from one vendor only and to choose database systems that support distributed capabilities and comply with open database standards such as ODBC and DCE (Distributed Computing Environment).

CLIENT/SERVER COMPUTING SYSTEMS

It should be quite apparent from the foregoing discussion of centralized and distributed processing systems that networks are changing the way we view computing and how we design application systems. Data processing has evolved from batch-oriented systems on stand-alone computers to online transaction processing with terminals and a host computer to distributed application processing using several computers that may be widely geographically dispersed. One upshot of the emergence of microcomputers and distributed processing systems has been the creation of distributed software and distributed data architectures. The primary distributed data and software architecture is called **client/server (CS) computing**. C/S computing divides the work an application performs among several computers. In C/S computing one application, called the *client,* requests processing services from another application, called the *server.* In LANs, the client and the server processes typically run in different computers. Some of the more common server functions in client/server computing networks are database services, in which a database server processes database requests. E-mail services that leverage servers to route and store mail messages for clients are other examples of client/server computing. In today's complex network environments, a client application may use the services of several different geographically dispersed server applications in carrying out its work.

The concept of C/S computing was not initially developed for networking; however, networks in general and LANs specifically have created an environment amenable to C/S technology. Perhaps looking at the precursors of today's C/S environment will make it easier to understand today's C/S implementations. Figure 11-13 depicts a large host computer to which many terminals are connected. Terminal users each have a set of applications and transactions they are allowed to run, and different users may have different sets of capabilities. A person's job needs determine which applications and transactions may be used. Figure 11-13 shows the classes of software components in the host processor: a teleprocessing monitor (TM) and transaction control process, applications, and a database management system (DBMS).

Consider the needs of Kim, a specific terminal user. Kim works in the personnel department. Some of the functions she can do are adding employees, updating employee records, and deleting the records of employees who left the company more than 3 years ago. The add-employee transaction requires the services of three different applications, one each for employee, insurance, and payroll updates. When Kim requests that a certain transaction, such as adding an employee, be run, the request is received by the transaction control process within the TM. This TM process is responsible for routing the transaction to the appropriate applications. In this case, three applications must work on the transaction, a capability called *cooperative computing.* In this scenario, the transaction control process requests each application to perform a service. In some systems, the transaction control process is called a *requester,* and the applications are called *servers.* In today's terminology, the transaction control process could be called a *client.* The client makes requests that are carried out in whole or in part by other processes, called *servers.* In this example, the applications in turn make requests of the DBMS and the operating system for services they perform. Thus, a server can also become a client.

In WANs, some companies have extended this type of C/S technology by allowing the server processes to be on nodes different from the one on which the client is running. This provides a distributed processing environment in which the hardware, software, and data resources of several computers combine to solve a problem. In essence, with C/S computing the network becomes the computer. We can also talk about server classes. A server class is represented by one or more applications, all of

client/server (CS) computing An application processing framework in which the processing load is divided among several processes called clients and servers. Clients issue requests to servers, which provide specialized services such as database processing and mail distribution. When clients and servers are located in different computers, application processing is distributed over multiple computers and, in effect, the network becomes the computer.

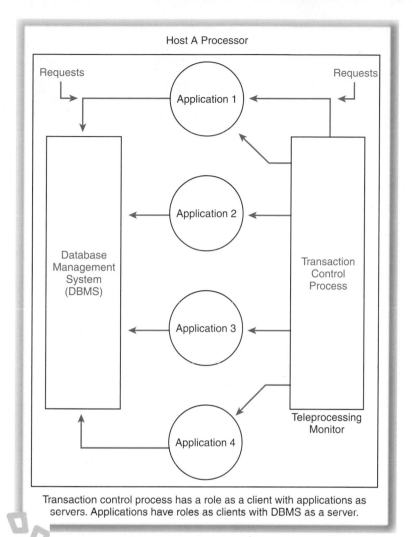

Transaction control process has a role as a client with applications as servers. Applications have roles as clients with DBMS as a server.

Figure 11-13   C/S Computing in a Mainframe Computer

which can carry out certain tasks. With server classes, a client does not need the services of a particular server process because any process in the class can perform the requested service.

A LAN C/S configuration is illustrated in Figure 11-14. This figure shows two instances of C/S computing: a database or SQL server and an e-mail server. (SQL is an abbreviation for "structured query language," a standard database language.) Earlier, we described how a database server works. An e-mail server operates like a post office for its clients. An e-mail server performs functions such as supplying mail addresses given a user's name, distributing mail, and providing mail agent functions. There are several types of mail agents, one of which is a vacation agent. An e-mail vacation agent can provide services such as collecting incoming mail in an electronic folder or rerouting mail to another designated user while the original recipient is away.

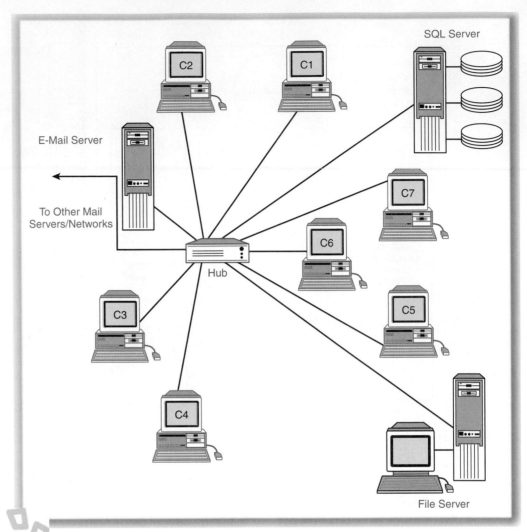

Figure 11-14   LAN C/S Computing Environment

In LAN C/S technology, clients typically run in workstations and request services from microcomputer, minicomputer, or mainframe nodes that operate exclusively as servers. Alternatively, C/S computing can be implemented in a peer-to-peer LAN. In a peer-to-peer C/S environment, server and client processes can be running in the same node. In Figure 11-15, both client A and server 1 are running in node 1.

Advantages of C/S Computing

System Expansion   Growth is one objective of many companies, and it is often accompanied by the need for additional computing power. With C/S computing, the computing power is distributed over multiple processors. Because the computer is the network, in C/S computing we can expand the computer by adding hardware and software components to the network. Adding to the network can be done in small,

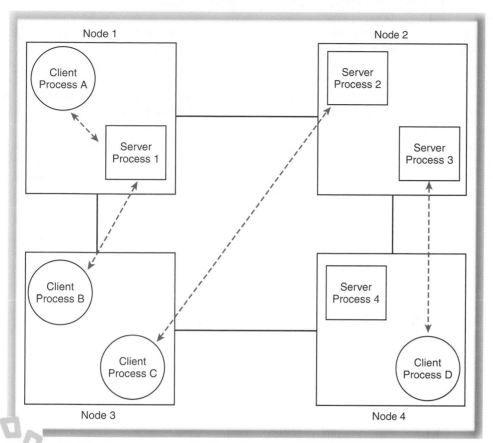

Figure 11-15   Peer-to-Peer C/S Environment

manageable increments. This means that the computer can be scaled up (or down) without incurring large expenses and major hardware upgrades. Applications also can be easily expanded. Once the C/S environment is set up, new applications can be quickly installed and can immediately take advantage of the services available. This growth is made easier because the application functions provided by the server processes are already in place, and the work of application programmers is reduced.

Modular Applications   C/S applications are generally improved because applications are modular. Modularity can reduce the memory required for client applications and optimize server processes. Part of the application logic is contained in the servers and, therefore, does not need to be replicated in the client portion of the code. An analogy may be helpful here. If you are building a house, you would probably not do all of the jobs yourself because it would be difficult for you to learn all of the necessary carpentry, plumbing, electrical, and landscaping skills. However, if you become a client and use the services of those who already know how to do these things, you will probably get the job done faster and better. This analogy applies directly to the concept of C/S computing. Server modules are optimized to perform their function on behalf of their clients, and the clients do not need to be burdened with the logic essential to performing those tasks.

Portability Some computer systems are better able to perform certain jobs than others. For example, some platforms are noted for their ability to do high-resolution graphics applications, such as computer-aided design and drafting (CAD); other hardware and software combinations are well suited for office automation applications. The combination of hardware and software of an SQL server also makes the server able to manage data more effectively than a general-purpose computer and operating system. As new technologies emerge, the C/S environment provides an easy way to integrate such technologies into the network. A company can switch among hardware and software vendors to find its ideal computing system. Ordinarily, these changes will not affect the remaining components. Using an SQL server as an example, if a new, more powerful server engine becomes available, it should be easy to install the new engine in place of existing SQL servers or to simply add the new server to augment existing servers.

Standards The emergence of client/server computing has led to the creation of new standards for the way in which clients and servers communicate. The availability of these standards has enabled software and hardware from a variety of vendors to be integrated to create modular, flexible, extendable enterprise-wide computing environments. As mentioned previously, using networking technologies that comply with ODBC (open database connectivity) helps ensure connectivity among geographically dispersed DBMSs from different vendors. Other major C/S computing architectures are discussed later in this chapter.

Disadvantages of C/S Computing

One disadvantage of C/S technology in WANs is reduced performance because of the slowness of the communication links. In LANs, the high-speed communication link does not become an obstacle to C/S performance. Another disadvantage of C/S computing on networks is the complexity of creating the optimum C/S environment. This disadvantage is common to C/S implementations in both WANs and LANs. Once these problems are overcome, several advantages are afforded by C/S computing.

C/S Technologies

In this section, we look at some of the key technologies that underlie C/S computing. We will examine the interfaces that exist between clients and servers as well as standards that are being developed.

Clients and servers must have a way to communicate with each other. There are two basic ways in which this is done: *remote procedure calls* and *messages*. You may be familiar with programming languages that support local procedure calls. With local procedure calls, one segment of a program invokes logic in another program segment called a *procedure*. The procedure does its work, and then the results and processing control are passed back to the point in the program from which the procedure was called. You can think of the procedure as performing a service for the program. Remote procedure calls extend this concept to allow an application on one computer to call on the services of another process. The process being called could be running in the same computer or, as is typically the case in C/S computing, the process being called could be running in another computer. Moreover, the process being called may not be running at the time of the call. The remote procedure call in this instance initiates the server process on the other computer. This process is illustrated in Figure 11-16.

Relative to remote procedure calls, message exchange is a more flexible method of communication. The client and the server enter into a communication session and exchange information. The client sends a request, and the server responds with the answer to the request (see Figure 11-17).

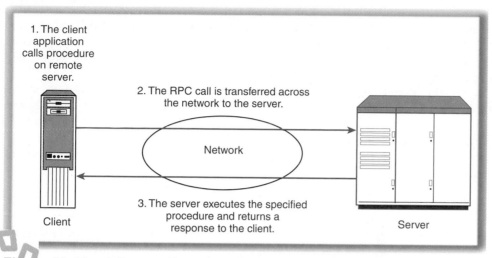

Figure 11-16   A Remote Procedure Call in a C/S Network

Figure 11-17   C/S Message Exchange

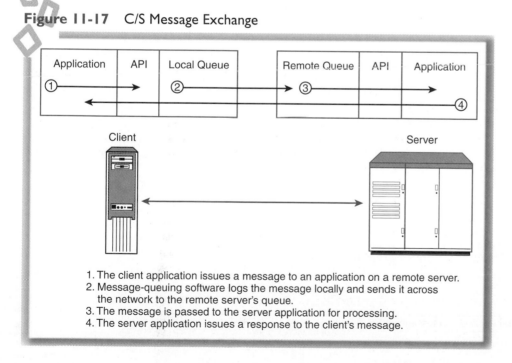

Clients communicate with servers through an *application program interface (API)*, as illustrated in Figure 11-18. Although standards are being developed that will facilitate C/S interfaces across multivendor hardware and platforms, to date, interoperability problems among client/server products has inhibited many businesses from realizing the true potential of C/S computing architectures.

In the ideal C/S computing environment, programmers are provided with the tools needed to access computing resources across platforms and geographic locations. These tools enable system developers to implement applications that look and act the same on various clients (such as microcomputers, dumb terminals, workstations, and network computers) and that utilize the same method to access data regardless of its physical location and local DBMS.

Middleware

middleware A software interface that functions as an intermediary between clients and servers. Middleware enables one application to communicate with another that runs on a different platform, comes from a different vendor, or both. Examples of middleware include transaction processing monitors, distributed object systems (such as CORBA), and distributed database middleware that provides a common interface between a query and multiple, distributed databases.

The most common way to meet this programming challenge involves the use of standard programming interfaces and protocols that have come to be called **middleware**. Standard programming interfaces enable system developers to implement the same application on a variety of servers and clients. Standardized protocols enable various servers to interface with a wide range of clients that need to access them. In sum, one of the main objectives of middleware is to serve as an intermediary between clients and servers. This means that the middleware is responsible for making the connection between clients and servers even though they have different operating systems and may use a variety of communication protocols to interface with one another. Middleware enables the entire distributed system to be viewed as a single set of applications and resources available to users. Physical locations of data or applications can remain transparent to users. Middleware cuts across the variety of client and server platforms in the network and is responsible for routing client requests to the appropriate server.

Table 11-8 provides some insight into the variety of client and server OSs that may be found in C/S computing environments. Table 11-9 summarizes some of the different client and server DBMSs that may be found in a C/S network. In many businesses, the range of client and server operating systems and database management systems is much greater than that illustrated in Tables 11-8 and 11-9.

Table 11-10 identifies some of the major network transport APIs found in client/server networks. Each network transport protocol offers an API to enable com-

Figure 11-18   C/S Application Program Interface

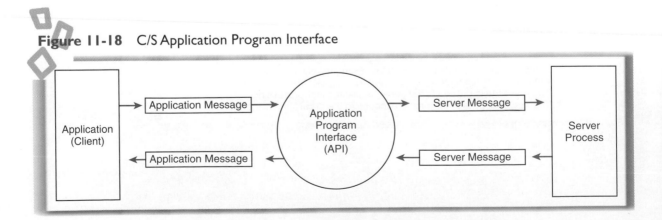

Table 11-8   Examples of Server, Client, and Network Operating Systems Found in C/S Networks

Server Operating Systems	Client Operating Systems	Network Operating Systems
MVS	Windows 95/98/2000 ME	Novell 4x/5x/6
O/S 400	Windows NT/2000 Professional	Windows NT/2000 Server
VMS	Macintosh OS	Windows XP Server
UNIX (and variants such as AIX)	X-Windows	UNIX
Linux	Linux	Linux

Table 11-9   Examples of Server and Client DBMSs Found in C/S Networks

Server DBMSs	Client DBMSs
Oracle	Access
Sybase	Foxpro
DB/2	Approach
Informix	Paradox

Table 11-10   Examples of Network Transport APIs in C/S Networks

Network Transport API	Description
LU 6.2	Supports application-to-application communication in IBM's SNA and APPN architectures
Sockets	Supports communication among UNIX servers and clients
TCP/IP	Primary C/S network transport API in Novell and Windows NT/2000 networks
Appletalk	Network API in Macintosh LANs
Mobile middleware	Used to enable mobile computing and communication technologies to interface with an organization's C/S network

mands to be passed among application programs on servers and clients. For a server request initiated by a client, a network transport API includes information indicating the location and path to the destination server, the client's authorization to access the destination server, and information to establish a session between the client and the server.

Because there is often a wide range of operating systems, DBMSs, and network transport APIs needed to ensure connectivity among the various multivendor hardware platforms (such as microcomputers, minicomputers, and mainframes) found in today's C/S networks, the importance of middleware cannot be overlooked. In many ways, middleware is the "glue" that holds complex C/S architectures together and provides interconnectivity among diverse, geographically distributed computers and applications.

As illustrated in Figure 11-19, middleware provides distributed system services among application programs on clients and servers regardless of the platform differences that exist among them. For this to work, middleware modules are installed on both clients and servers in C/S computing networks. As C/S architectures have continued to evolve, the need for middleware standards has emerged.

One example of middleware and its standardization efforts is the Distributed Computing Environment (DCE) specifications established by the Open Software Foundation. DCE addresses the use of remote procedure calls, security, name services, and messages for C/S computing. Another example is the Object Request Broker (ORB) established by the Object Management Group. A client communicates with a server through the services of the ORB. The ORB receives a client's request, finds a server capable of satisfying that request, sends the message to that server, and returns the response to the client. The ORB thus provides client and server independence. Any client that can communicate with the ORB is then able to communicate with any server that can communicate with the ORB. This provides both hardware and software independence. CORBA (Common Object Request Broker Architecture) defines a standard API through which clients and servers can access ORBs. The fundamental process, illustrated in Figure 11-20, represents a cross between remote procedure calls and messaging.

Figure 11-19   Middleware's Role as a Distributed Systems Services Provider

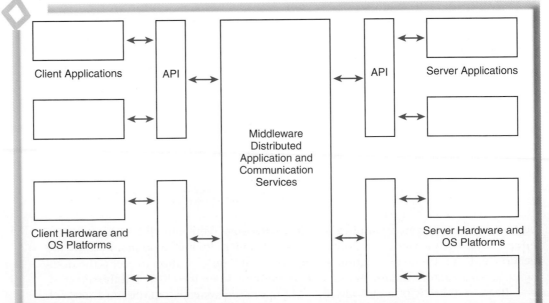

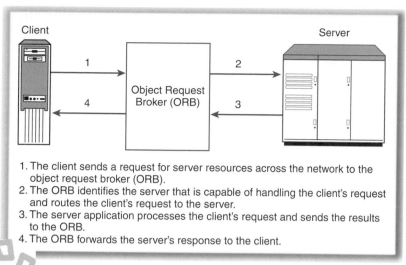

1. The client sends a request for server resources across the network to the object request broker (ORB).
2. The ORB identifies the server that is capable of handling the client's request and routes the client's request to the server.
3. The server application processes the client's request and sends the results to the ORB.
4. The ORB forwards the server's response to the client.

Figure 11-20   The Role of Object Request Brokers (ORBs) in C/S Networks

The CORBA standard was developed by the Object Management Group (OMG) to enable communication among distributed objects. It provides a mechanism for executing programs (objects) written in different programming languages running on different platforms no matter where they are located in the network. CORBA is suited for 3-tier (or *n*-tier) client/server applications, where processes running in one computer require processing to be performed by another computer in the network. (Three-tier C/S architectures are discussed later in this chapter.) CORBA is sometimes described as an "object bus" or "software bus," because it addresses a software-based communications interface through which distributed objects are located and accessed.

An interface definition language (IDL) is used to define CORBA objects. This describes the processing (methods) the object performs and the format of the data sent and returned. IDL compilers for each major programming language such as C, C++, Java, Smalltalk, and COBOL let programmers use familiar constructs. CORBA enables both client and server applications to talk to each other in their respective programming languages. IDL definitions are stored in an interface repository, which can be queried by a client application to determine what objects are available.

When an application is running in a computer, a CORBA client requests the remote CORBA objects it needs via an object request broker (ORB). The ORB provides a proxy object to the client using a process that creates the illusion that the remote object is a local one. The client and server communicate by exchanging messages whose formats are defined by the General Inter-ORB Protocol (GIOP). GIOP is independent of any specific network transport protocol. However, when GIOP is sent over TCP/IP, it is called *IIOP (Internet Inter–ORB protocol).*

We can use three models to represent the distribution of functions in a C/S environment. First, the majority of the application logic can reside in the client system, with only the specialized server logic residing in the server system, as illustrated in Figure 11-21(a). In this model, the server is less burdened and can be more responsive to volumes of client requests. This is usually the model used for database servers. In a

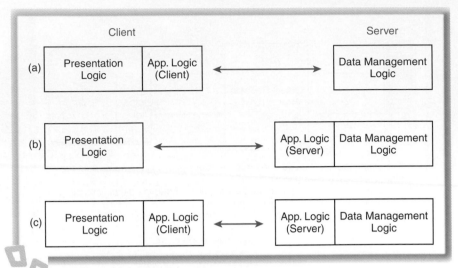

Figure 11-21 C/S Application Models

database server, the server responds to a client's request for data, and data meeting the constraints of the request are returned to the client for processing. This model is sometimes called the *data management model.*

A second model uses the client primarily to display or print data, and the data management and application logic are resident on the server, as illustrated in Figure 11-21(b). This approach could be used for graphics applications wherein a high-speed server processor is used to generate the drawing details, and the workstation is responsible for displaying the details on the monitor. This model can be called the *presentation model.*

The third possibility embeds application logic in both the client and the server, as illustrated in Figure 11-21(c). This model might be used in a transaction processing system in which the application contains logic about customers, and the server contains the application logic for banking accounts.

Figure 11-21 illustrates that there can be considerable variation in the level of interaction between clients and servers when solving a problem or processing an application. Table 11-11 provides additional insight into how the level of interaction can vary. C/S network planners and developers need to consider these options when determining the optimal interaction level for particular C/S applications in their networks.

Table 11-11 also illustrates that today's concept of client/server computing is broad enough to subsume both of the WAN architectures discussed earlier in the chapter: centralized host-based processing systems and networks characterized by distributed processing and distributed databases. Although the evolution of C/S architectures is toward cooperative, peer-to-peer C/S computing that optimally utilizes the processing capabilities of diverse, geographically dispersed platforms and applications, it is important to bear in mind that it is possible for a C/S architecture to also include traditional centralized and distributed processing systems when there is a clear business rationale for doing so.

Table 11-11   Client/Server Computing Categories

Name	Description
Host-driven terminal emulation	This occurs when the client connects to the server in the same manner that a terminal connects to a host. Because the server does virtually all the processing, this form of host-based processing is not true client/server computing as the term is generally used because microcomputer clients are generally limited to terminal emulation.
Host-driven front-ending	This occurs when the client converts messages transmitted by the server/host into a more user friendly interface than the standard interface provided by the server. All important processing is done at the server; the only real work done by the client is the provision of user friendly interfaces. This is sometimes called *server-based processing*.
Host-driven C/S computing	This form of C/S computing occurs when the client carries out application processing actions for the server/host. For example, the server may cause the client to display a window, dialog box, or menu. One or more of the displayed options can be carried out by the user's client computer under the direction of the server. After the option is executed, the result is returned to the server to complete the processing activity.
Client-driven C/S computing	This occurs when virtually all of the application processing is done on the client with limited involvement of the server. The server, for example, may carry out client requests for data and return requested data to the client to complete the processing task. This is among the most common forms of C/S computing used today because it enables user applications to be tailored to local needs. This approach is also called *client-based processing*.
Peer-to-peer C/S computing	This is also called *cooperative processing* because the client and server cooperate in performing processing operations. This is the most sophisticated form of C/S computing as well as the most difficult to maintain. However, it allows microcomputers and server platforms to be leveraged in an optimal fashion to enhance user productivity and network efficiency.

Three-Tier C/S Architecture

Traditionally, client/server architecture involved two tiers (levels). Clients were located on one tier, and servers were located on the second. Over time, 3-tier C/S architecture, such as the one illustrated in Figure 11-22, has become commonplace. In a 3-tier C/S architecture, application software is distributed among three types of computers: the user's client computer, a middle-tier server, and one or more back-end servers. The client computer may be a microcomputer, a network computer (a thin or fat client), or even a terminal. The distinctions among these different types of terminals are discussed in Chapter 10. Middle-tier servers are essentially gateways between clients and back-end server. When used in a distributed database environment employing diverse DBMSs, middle-tier servers incorporate the middleware needed to convert protocols and convert client requests for data into the syntax needed by the DBMS of the back-end data server that can satisfy the client's request. In other networks,

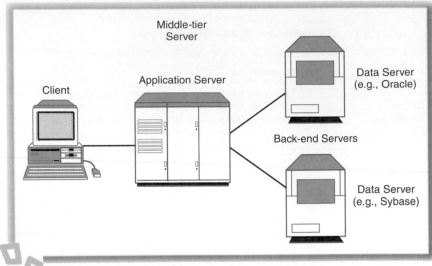

Figure 11-22   Three-Tier Client/Server Computing Architecture

middle-tier servers function as gateways between client applications and back-end legacy applications. Because the interaction between middle-tier servers and back-end servers follows C/S models, in any given interaction between clients and back-end servers, it functions both as a client (by mapping client requests to the appropriate back-end server) and as a server (by forwarding back-end server responses to client requests to the appropriate client).

Many network designers view 3-tiered C/S architectures as the fundamental building blocks of *n-tiered C/S architectures* with several middle tiers between clients and back-end servers. Such architecture holds the promise to revolutionize client access to data and information as well as C/S computing.

INTERNATIONAL NETWORKS

Data communication networks are not confined to national boundaries, and today, the operations and WAN architectures of many companies are international in scope. International computer networks help many of these companies manage their data and provide communication among employees. International networks are used by banks for money transfer and financial planning applications. Manufacturing companies leverage international networks to schedule production of parts in multiple locations for assembly at a central location. Virtually all multinational companies (companies with operating locations in two or more nations) have the opportunity to use international networks and e-mail for immediate, timely communication. E-mail also helps eliminate the problems of time-zone differences. For example, working hours may not overlap between offices in England and Australia, but e-mail provides quick communication during an employee's normal working hours.

Groupware and videoconferencing applications enable work and project teams whose members are scattered across several nations to coordinate their efforts. Such applications have enabled some organizations to form and manage *virtual teams* of programmers capable of cooperatively working on the same program 24/7. For example, programmers in Singapore may work on the program for 8 hours before passing it along to programmers in Helsinki to complete an 8-hour shift before sending it to programmers in Denver. When the programmers in Denver complete their workday, the program is passed back to the programmers in Singapore to begin the cycle again. Needless to say, when managed appropriately, globally scattered programming teams can help organizations complete and implement new programs more rapidly than is typically possible by one team in the same geographic location.

Despite the business advantages of implementing WAN architectures to support multinational operations, designing and implementing international networks is more difficult than building a national network. The problems that may be encountered include politics, security, regulations, hardware, and language.

Politics

On occasion, the problems to be resolved with international networks are political rather than technical. One company reported that it was given permission to install a microwave link in a particular country. However, that country's government suggested that the company double the capacity of the network. Upon completion, the microwave system was nationalized by the government, and the company that built it was "given" half of the carrying capacity of the network. Political instability within a nation can make it difficult for a company to implement and maintain its ideal WAN architecture.

Security

As messages pass from node to node in a network, it is possible for them to be captured and for someone to read or even change the contents of the message. Furthermore, if a company is using public networks such as the Internet, the possibility of message tampering is greater because the message flows through systems outside the control of the company. Consequently, for secure transmissions, messages should be encrypted with a strong encryption algorithm. In the name of national security, some countries (including the United States) want to have the right to decrypt intercompany messages that cross their borders. Hence, even if encryption is used, government officials in some countries may have the ability to access and read messages passed between a company's multinational locations.

Regulations

Networks require communication links. In many countries, the communication networks are controlled by an agency we shall call the postal, telephone, and telegraph (PTT) authority. The PTT often is a government agency or government-regulated agency with exclusive rights to provide communication facilities. The regulations under which the PTTs operate generally were designed for their nation's original mission of postal, telephone, and telegraph communication. These regulations sometimes impede the establishment of international data communication systems.

Sometimes regulations are established to protect or subsidize certain interests. In some countries, restrictions exist regarding which equipment can be connected to a network. A few countries require that hardware used in a network be manufactured in whole or in part within the country. Pricing regulations in some countries are structured so data communication services help subsidize individual telephone services. Regulations often prohibit competition in providing communication facilities. Thus, it is often difficult to set up a network using services provided by a single communication carrier, especially if it is headquartered outside the country. Many PTTs recognize that regulations must be changed to meet the needs of international networks; therefore, some countries have begun to deregulate their communication industries. Deregulation typically means opening competition regarding equipment that can be attached to the network and the cost and provision of communication facilities.

International networks sometimes conflict with other national interests. Some countries impose an import duty on software. Sometimes the duty is on the value of the carrying medium, such as a magnetic tape; other countries tax the value of the imported software. International networks provide the ability to import software over the network, making the collection of tariffs more difficult. Some countries view international networks as potential threats to national economic security. Data regarding national resources, the economy, and people can be more easily collected and transmitted to another country through international networks. Several nations are attempting to legislate solutions to these concerns.

Hardware

As mentioned earlier, in some countries restrictions exist regarding the source or type of equipment that can be attached to the communication facilities of a PTT. Several countries require that all or part of the equipment used within the country be locally manufactured. Some do not require the equipment to be manufactured in-country but still restrict the equipment that can be used to that manufactured by a selected group of companies. Most countries require that equipment attached to communication networks meet minimum technical specifications. Specifications also differ among countries. A communication controller that is certified for operation in the United States may not meet the tighter specifications for grounding that exist in Australia.

Another technical difference that must be accommodated is variations in power supplies among countries. When ordering equipment for a specific node, one must be sure that the equipment's power supply needs are consistent with the power available in that location. Many times, new hardware also must be certified by a host country before it can be attached to the communication network. For example, a company that wants to connect a fax controller to the host country's carrier network may be required to first allow the controller to be tested and evaluated. It is not unusual for certification to take several months and require that equipment and circuit schematics be provided for the evaluation process. Thus, introduction of new equipment into a network can incur substantial delays.

Language

Another problem needing resolution in international networks is language. Network managers at different locations must be able to communicate to resolve differences. Several different countries and, therefore, several different languages may be involved in solving one problem. This makes it necessary to have not only technical expertise but also linguistic expertise in the network management organization. Data generated in one location may need to be translated when used in another country. Such translation may be manual or through language translation programs. Accompanying the need to translate from one language to another is the need to have hardware and software capable of displaying local character sets, such as Kanji in China and Japan, Hongul in Korea, and Farsi in Arab countries. Accommodations also must be made when the number of characters in a national character set exceeds the capacity of a particular code. For example, 7-bit ASCII codes can accommodate 128 distinct characters, but there are more than 30,000 Kanji characters.

Other Issues

An international network typically involves the coordination of several communication providers. One of the easier methods of creating an international network is to use the services of existing X.25 networks. The ease derives from the fact that most public X.25 network providers have established interconnections, and the network implementer need not be concerned about PTT interfaces. If a company decides to procure exclusive links such as leased lines, creating the network may be more difficult. Responsibility for determining the correct interfaces and resolving problems must be assumed by the company. Problem resolution can be somewhat difficult in an international network. Consider a link from Australia to France. The end-to-end connection may use links from Australia to the United States, to England, and then to France. Thus, four PTTs, several protocols, a variety of vendor equipment, and several time zones may be involved. If a problem arises in transmitting data between the French and Australian nodes, the sheer number of vendors involved can cause delays. On more than one occasion, a problem has been allowed to continue while two PTTs debated over which one was responsible for the problem.

Pricing an international network can present several difficulties. First, collecting tariff information can be time-consuming. When multiple nodes exist within a country, we typically must deal with both local tariffs and international tariffs. In some cases, there may be multiple circuit providers, a variety of available rates, and variations between local and long-distance rates. In addition to tariffs for the use of lines, in some countries we also must determine the costs of taxes applied to the movement of data over a country's borders and taxes on imported software.

The International Telecommunications Union (ITU) and other international communication organizations realize the existing limitations and problems in implementing international connections and are addressing the issues. Standards such as OSI, X.25, and the X.400 e-mail interface ease the burden of establishing international networks. Deregulation of the communication industries in some countries has allowed the introduction of new equipment and competition among providers of communication links. Issues such as the rights of communication facilities provided from a foreign country, such as a Canadian PTT operating circuits in the United States, are being discussed. All these efforts should make establishing international networks easier; however, the problems inherent in international networks will always be greater than those for domestic networks. Another international body has proposed a treaty, the *General Agreement on Tariffs and Trade (GATT)*, that will ease the problems of international networks. Among the treaty provisions are stipulations regarding the use and cost of private lines.

We are, of course, just scratching the surface of the challenges that organizations face in their efforts to implement and maintain international networks. The emergence of the global marketplace and the Internet as a commerce media continues to put pressure on nations to facilitate the development of international data communication networks that meet the needs of multinational organizations.

THE INTERNET'S IMPACT ON WAN ARCHITECTURES

The Internet is the world's largest and most comprehensive wide area network. As a network of networks, it enables WAN-to-WAN, LAN-to-LAN, and LAN-to-WAN interconnectivity, regardless of the architecture or geographic location of the WAN or LAN. In spite of global reach and interconnection potential, it is important to be mindful of the fact that there are several entire countries that have limited Internet access or lack it altogether. Worldwide, high-tech infrastructure is still patchy. Although some governments (such as Malaysia, South Korea, and Taiwan) have invested millions of dollars in their telecommunications and electrical infrastructures, there is virtually no Internet penetration in areas such as Africa, Indonesia, Laos, and Vietnam. High-tech infrastructure is also spotty in South America, where, like China, the cost of high-speed leased lines is 8 to 10 times that in the United States.

Although the number of households with Internet access continues to increase, most of the growth has occurred in developed countries in North America and Europe. Hence, the Internet's potential to open truly global markets is yet to be realized.

In spite of this limitation, the Internet is having a significant impact on WAN architectures. For example, the Internet has facilitated the emergence of 3-tiered C/S architectures that are now evolving into even more complex and sophisticated *n*-tiered architectures. On the other hand, it has also led to increased server-based processing that is reminiscent of centralized, host-based processing systems. Whereas network designers were once wrestling with the pros and cons of "fat" versus "thin" clients (microcomputers versus network computers), they are now examining the advantages and disadvantages of distributed "fat" servers with processing capabilities that match those of minicomputers and mainframes. Fat servers can do virtually all the processing work for superthin, diskless clients that have the look and feel of dumb terminals.

The ability of network designers to leverage the Internet and World Wide Web to build extranets, electronic marketplaces, and multilocation intranets has resulted in making the Internet an important component of many WAN architectures. For example, when organizations move EDI traffic to the Internet, they are altering the mix of carrier and VAN services that have traditionally served as key aspects of their network infrastructures. In a growing number of instances, the Internet is becoming the backbone (network) in business WAN architectures.

In the future, the Internet seems destined to assume a greater role in WAN architectures. The Internet fits nicely with the evolution of C/S computing through its ability to provide users with access to geographically distributed data and applications. The emergence of Internet-accessible storage area networks (SANs) capable of safekeeping the contents of data warehouses as well as personal data may alter traditional data storage strategies. The evolution of Internet-based application service providers (ASPs) that do specialized processing for business subscribers via the Internet also has the potential to establish the Internet as the centerpiece of WAN architectures for businesses.

SUMMARY

A WAN architecture is a blueprint of how the hardware, software, and data in a network are deployed. WAN topologies, WAN services, and WAN protocols are aspects of WAN architectures. Over time, three major WAN architectures have emerged: centralized architectures, distributed architectures, and client/server computing architectures.

IBM's Systems Network Architecture (SNA) is a prime example of the evolution from host-based, mainframe-centric computing to distributed and C/S architectures. Over time, it has matured as a network product by overcoming the challenges associated with integrating local area networks into the network architecture and adding application-to-application processing capabilities via the LU 6.2 protocol.

Distributed processing systems have emerged as viable WAN architectures. These often incorporate the distribution of processing activities as well as the distribution of data. Although there are a number of challenges associated with distributed processing systems, these are largely offset by the potential benefits associated with distributing data to where it is used most often and from the cost savings that can accrue from sharing data resources and processing activities across geographically dispersed locations.

The client/server (C/S) model has become a widely used architecture for distributing applications within WANs. In C/S computing, clients are able to take advantage of servers' shared computing resources (such as applications and data). C/S computing provides an environment for controlled, incremental growth, modular applications, and application portability. Middleware is used in C/S architectures to overcome hardware and software platform differences across network nodes and to ensure that users have transparent access to geographically dispersed applications and data. Over time, 2-tiered C/S architectures have given way to more sophisticated and robust 3-tiered and *n*-tiered C/S architectures.

International WANs are required by multinational organizations to ensure coordination of their global operations through electronic communication. Such companies, however, face numerous challenges in developing and maintaining international data communication networks, including politics, security, regulations, hardware, language, tariffs, and standards. Although still falling short of complete global reach, the Internet is emerging as a key component of international WANs.

The Internet is having a significant impact on the evolution of WAN architectures. Its fundamental configuration promotes 3-tiered as well as *n*-tiered C/S architectures. However, high-powered "fat" servers have led to a resurgence of server-based processing similar to the mainframe-centric host-based processing that characterized the very first data communication networks. The Internet is also altering the mix of WAN services to which businesses can subscribe.

KEY TERMS

- client/server (CS) computing
- dedicated connection
- distributed database
- distributed file system (DFS)
- distributed processing
- domain
- file transfer utilities
- logical unit (LU)
- LU 6.2
- middleware

- Network Addressable Unit (NAU)
- network architecture
- Network Control Program (NCP)
- physical unit (PU)
- Physical Unit Control Point (PUCP)
- remote log-on facilities
- subarea
- Systems Network Architecture (SNA)
- Systems Services Control Point (SSCP)
- transparent access

REVIEW QUESTIONS

1. What does network architecture mean?
2. What are the characteristics of centralized network architectures?
3. Contrast batch and real-time processing.
4. What are the advantages and disadvantages of centralized architectures?
5. What is SNA? Why was it created?
6. What are the four types of physical units in SNA? What is the role of each in the network?
7. What are the characteristics of the logical units found in SNA?
8. Explain how a session is established in SNA.
9. What is LU 6.2? Why is it important?
10. Contrast SNA domains and subareas.

11. What is APPN? Why is it important?
12. Why is SDLC considered to be a nonroutable protocol? What approaches are used to address this limitation of SDLC?
13. What is terminal emulation? What role does terminal emulation play in micro-to-mainframe connections?
14. Describe a dedicated connection.
15. Describe the role of communication servers in LAN-to-host connections.
16. Contrast file transfer and remote log-on utilities.
17. What is distributed processing? What are the main objectives of distributed processing systems?
18. What is a distributed database?
19. What are the characteristics and objectives of a distributed file system (DFS)?
20. What are the advantages and disadvantages of distributed processing systems?
21. Contrast remote and local processing in distributed systems.
22. Identify and briefly describe the 12 rules for distributed databases.
23. What is client/server computing?
24. Describe the advantages and disadvantages of client/server computing.
25. Contrast remote procedure calls and messages as forms of communication between clients and servers.
26. What are application program interfaces (APIs)? Why are they important?
27. What is middleware? What role does middleware play in C/S architectures?
28. Contrast 2-tier and 3-tier client/server architectures.
29. Identify and briefly describe the challenges that organizations face when implementing international networks.
30. What impact is the Internet having on WAN architectures?

PROBLEMS AND EXERCISES

1. Use the Internet to research the differences between "fat" and "thin" clients. Identify and briefly describe the advantages and disadvantages of each.
2. Use the Internet to identify the most widely used types of terminal emulation in today's data communication networks. Describe why these are so widely used.
3. Use the Internet to research the literature on distributed DBMSs. Identify major distributed DBMS vendors. Compare two distributed DBMS products on the extent to which they conform to Date's 12 rules for a distributed database.
4. Your employer has asked you to design the placement of files for a personnel database. Your company has four regions, each of which has a personnel office; there is also a personnel office in a separate world headquarters complex. The files in the system are employee, benefits, job history, payroll, department, skills, insurance, and insurance claims. Devise a plan for placing each of these files, assuming each location has computer facilities. Would you recommend a distributed database solution? If so, would you replicate any files? Would you partition any files? Document/justify your decisions.
5. Use the Internet to research the characteristics of "fat" servers. Identify and briefly describe the advantages and disadvantages of fat servers in C/S architectures.
6. Use the Internet to identify the characteristics and functionality of Citrix servers. Describe how Citrix servers can assist organizations in prolonging the useful life of microcomputers.
7. Use the Internet to research the literature on application service providers (ASPs). Identify several ASPs, their services, and fee structures. What role are ASPs likely to play in business network architectures in the years ahead?

Chapter Cases
Boeing's Network Infrastructure

In 2001, Boeing developed an aggressive 90-day relocation plan to get IT systems running into its new headquarters in Chicago by September 4. The plan consisted of the configuration of a sophisticated telecommunications system and computing infrastructure for approximately 400 employees located on 12 floors. More than 225 miles of data, communications, and security cable were installed to support more than 300 computers and 500 telephones. The offices were also equipped to support wireless connectivity for future applications.

This ambitious plan was implemented on time because of an appropriate network design, the company's previous experience with installing similar networks at other Boeing locations, and the appointment of in-house people with the right skills. Robert Paul, executive director of shared services, was designated the manager in charge of the IT relocation project. His team was completed with Paul Kraus, one of Boeing's top network gurus; Roland Pfaff, an expert in office operations support; and Harry Williams, an expert in applications and systems integration.

The computing infrastructure at Boeing's Chicago office consists of 400 Dell C600 laptop and L400 notebook computers with docking stations, and four hundred 18-inch flat-panel monitors. These computers are connected over 100M bit/sec Fast Ethernet to a Cisco Catalyst 6500 network switch on each of the 12 floors. About 4,800,000 feet of category 5 copper cables were used to install the floor networks.

The Catalyst 6500 switches are linked to a Gigabit Ethernet connection running over optical-fiber cable. About 690,000 feet of optical-fiber cable were used to connect all 12 switches to a bank of two Cisco 7605 routers, one primary and one backup. The routers are connected to application servers at St. Louis and Seattle data centers through the

Sprint network. The Chicago LAN is linked to the Sprint network via 45M bit/sec DS3 lines, and dual 155M bit/sec OC-3 lines are used to connect the Sprint network to the data centers.

The Chicago headquarters host only a few special-purpose servers; the St. Louis and Seattle data centers host the company's main application servers, including its servers for Microsoft Office and PeopleSoft applications. In addition, the phone system at the Chicago office consists of a Lucent G3 PBX switch and 650 Avaya telephones.

The Chicago offices are also equipped to support wireless technology, which will help the company to save money in the future. At Boeing, tens of thousands of employees move from office to office each year. To address this problem, a long-term IT plan considers the installation of wireless LAN cards on the laptops, so Boeing employees will move freely and connect from anywhere in the major locations.

In the e-business arena, Boeing is leveraging its network infrastructure as well as the Internet to facilitate information exchange among its geographically dispersed business units. XML and portal technology, for example, is being used within the company's space and communications division (which accounts for more than 15 percent of Boeing's annual revenues) to provide uniform Web access to a wide range of applications. Over 7,000 employees are using the portal, and as a result, redundant engineering and design processes are being eliminated, and the maintenance costs for some systems have been cut in half. The portal is helping Boeing to reengineer the work flow and processes, reduce costs, and increase efficiency within this important division. Future consolidation of databases and programs should result in additional cost savings and efficiency gains.

CASE QUESTIONS

1. Use the Internet to find out more about the characteristics of docking stations and notebook computers. Describe the advantages and disadvantages of docking stations and how they enable laptop computers to interface with LANs.

2. Using the information provided in the case, create a diagram illustrating the interconnections among Boeing's switches, routers, WAN services, and data centers. Label the communication link speeds for these interconnections.

3. What types of wireless adapters should Boeing consider using in its notebook computers to enable its employees to move freely among its major operating locations? Justify your recommendation(s). (*Hint:* Review the textbook's sections on wireless LANs to identify appropriate adapters.)

4. If you had been in charge of implementing the network infrastructure at Boeing's Chicago office, would you have installed category 5 cables? Why or why not?

5. Critique the overall network infrastructure that Boeing has put in place in Chicago and its other major data centers. What would you do differently? Why?

6. Use the Internet to identify several different ways that Boeing is using data communications infrastructure and applications to be competitive. Develop a summary table of the applications that you find that is rank ordered in terms of importance. Your table should include a column for justifying the rank you assign to each application. One of the rows in the table should be the portal and XML technology being used within its space and communications division.

SOURCES

Boeing News. "Boeing Begins World Headquarters Operations in Chicago." Boeing news release. Retrieved March 16, 2002, from www.boeing.com/news/releases/2001/q3/nr_010904z.htm.

Boyd, J. "Boeing Links Apps via XML." *InternetWeek* (November 12, 2001). Retrieved March 28, 2002, from www.internetweek.com/enterprise/enterprise111201.htm.

Cope, J. "IT Plan Speeds Boeing Relocation." *Computerworld* (July 30, 2001, Volume 35, Issue 31, p. 15).

Note: For more information on wide area network architectures, see an additional case on the Web site, www.prenhall.com/stamper, "Telemedicine."

Wide Area Network Services

After studying this chapter, you should be able to:

- Describe the differences between circuit-switched and packet-switched networks.
- Describe the differences between connection-oriented and connectionless networks.
- Describe the characteristics, advantages, and disadvantages of packet distribution networks.
- Describe the characteristics, advantages, and disadvantages of frame relay networks.
- Describe the characteristics, advantages, and disadvantages of cell relay networks.
- Describe the characteristics of broadband WAN services.
- Discuss the Internet's impact on WAN services.

As we have noted in previous chapters, one of the most significant differences between wide area networks and local area networks found in business organizations is ownership of the communication medium. Although the media found in LANs are typically owned, most business organization WANs rely on communications media and technologies provided by third-party carriers.

This chapter focuses on some of the major specialized data transmission services available from common and third-party carriers that businesses leverage to provide cost-effective communication among geographically dispersed nodes. Most of our attention is devoted to packet distribution, frame relay, and cell relay networks and how they differ from circuit-switched networks. Broadband network services and the Internet's impacts on WAN services are also addressed. Our discussion begins by describing some of the fundamental differences among circuit-switched and packet-switched networks and the characteristics of value-added networks (VANs).

WAN SERVICES FUNDAMENTALS

There are two major categories of wide area network connections: *circuit-switched networks* and *packet-switched networks*. Switching is fundamental to both approaches. Without switching technologies, which establish paths across networks from senders to receivers, every possible source of data worldwide would have to be directly connected to every possible data recipient. The addition of each new device to the network would demand establishing point-to-point connections between it and all the existing network devices.

Circuit-Switched Networks

Switching allows temporary connections to be established and maintained between senders and receivers so that they can exchange messages and information. At the conclusion of the communication session between a given sender and a given receiver, the temporary connection can be terminated, thereby freeing up the resources needed to support the session so that they can be used to create temporary connections between other senders and receivers. As discussed in Chapter 5, telephone calls are routed through central office switches. These switches are used to establish a temporary circuit between the caller's phone and the party to whom the caller wishes to talk. This connection lasts only for the duration of the call. PBXs function in a manner that is similar to central office switches.

There are three phases to circuit-switched communications:

➤ *Creation of the temporary circuit*. Before voice or data transmissions between sender and receiver begin, an end-to-end circuit must be established. Switches must have the capabilities and capacity to establish requested connections. A sender (caller) specifies the intended recipient by dialing the recipient's telephone number. The switching equipment determines whether the circuit to the recipient is in use (busy) and establishes a direct link between the caller and call recipient through the switching equipment if it is not.

➤ *Information transmission*. Once the end-to-end circuit is created, information (voice or data) can be transmitted between sender and recipient. Typically, the transmission is full duplex, meaning that signals can be transmitted simultaneously in both directions. As noted in Chapter 5, the signals transmitted may be analog or digital, depending on the nature of the circuit-switching network.

➤ *Circuit termination*. After information is transferred between senders and receivers, the end-to-end connection between them is terminated. This is usually triggered when one of the two nodes involved in the information exchange "hangs up." When this happens, the switching resources that had been allocated to the temporary circuit are released for reallocation to other network users.

circuit-switched network A network that provides a temporary, but dedicated, communication connection between two network nodes no matter how many switching devices the data is routed through. Circuit switching was originally developed for the analog-based telephone system in order to guarantee steady, consistent service for two people engaged in a phone conversation.

Using central office switches to establish a temporary connection between two telephone users is an example of circuit switching. In **circuit-switched networks**, a switched dedicated circuit is created to connect two (or more) parties. To telephone users, the temporary circuits that are created appear to be dedicated point-to-point connections between the parties involved in the telephone call. It is as if a direct physical path is established between the parties involved in the communication session. The physical resources needed to create the temporary connection are dedicated to the circuit between sender and receiver for the duration of their call.

Multiple switches may be involved when callers use the public telephone network to establish long-distance circuits. As may be observed in Figure 12-1, long-distance connections typically involve switching equipment in two end offices and one or more intermediate exchanges.

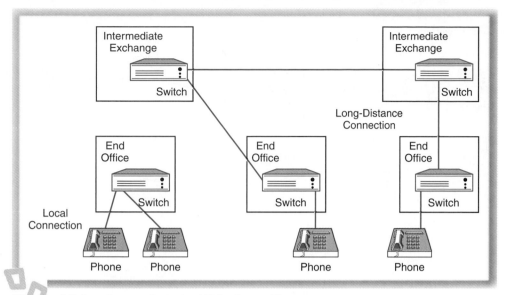

Figure 12-1   Circuit-Switched Telephone Connections

Because there is a limit to the number of switched connections that can be established at a particular point in time, it is possible for users of circuit-switched networks to be unable to place a call or initiate a data communication session during peak usage time. Callers typically encounter messages such as "I'm sorry, but all circuits are busy. Please try again later" when central office switches are oversubscribed. Such messages indicate that insufficient resources are available to create additional connections.

In many locations, the proliferation of additional residential telephone lines used to establish connections to Internet service providers (ISPs) has required central offices to install additional circuit-switching capacity. ISPs that offer unlimited Internet access for a fixed monthly charge unwittingly encourage their subscribers to establish switched connections that may last for hours and thereby tie up circuits for extended periods of time.

The potential for circuit-switched networks to be overburdened during peak traffic periods can be problematic for business organizations that require reliable availability of connections among network nodes. This often drives businesses to leased (dedicated) circuits that bypass central office dial-up switches or to third-party firms that offer packet-switching services. Figure 12-2 summarizes the fundamental differences between circuit-switched and packet-switched networks.

Packet-Switched Networks

Packet-switching networks provide an alternative to circuit-switched networks. In packet-switched networks, data is *packetized*. **Packetizing** involves the segmenting of data transmitted between networked devices into structured blocks, frames, or packets that contain a sufficient amount of overhead information, beyond the data itself, to ensure delivery to intended recipients.

A **packet** is essentially a group of bits that are organized in a predetermined structure. Each packet contains data bits as well as additional overhead information/data

packetizing Involves the segmenting of data into blocks for transmission in packet switched networks. In packet switched networks, data transmitted between networked devices is sent in structured blocks, frames, or packets that contain a sufficient amount of overhead information, beyond the data itself, to ensure delivery to intended recipients.

packet A unit of data transmission. The packet consists of the data to be transmitted together with the headers and trailers affixed by the various layers in the OSI reference model. The terms packet, frame, and datagram are often used interchangeably in packet switched networks.

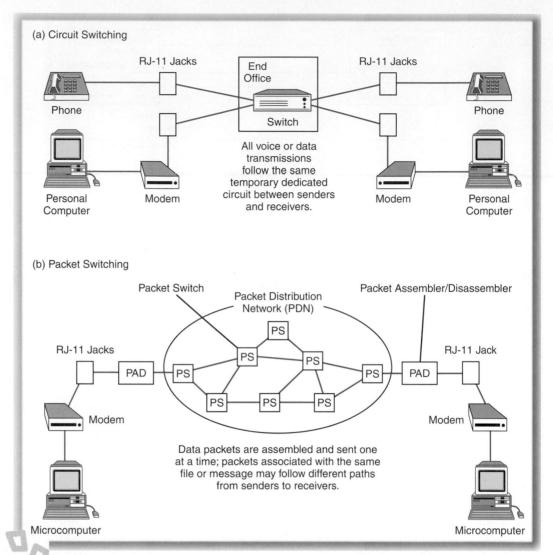

Figure 12-2 A Comparison of Circuit Switching and Packet Switching

used to ensure error-free transmission to intended recipients. Depending on the transmission service that is employed, the packets that flow between senders and receivers may be called *blocks, cells, datagrams, data units, frames,* or several other names.

Figure 12-3 illustrates the layout of high-level data link control (HDLC) packets found in X.25 packet-switching networks. During the packetizing process, data is placed in the information field, and each of the other overhead information fields is created. The contents of the overhead information fields are briefly summarized here.

➤ *Flag.* This 8-bit field is used to specify the beginning and end of an individual packet. It assists receiving communication devices in differentiating one packet queued from another.

8 Bits	8 Bits	8 Bits	Variable	16 Bits	8 Bits
Flag	Address	Control	Data (Optional Octets)	Frame Check Sequence	Flag

Figure 12-3 HDLC Frame Format

- *Address field.* The address field specifies the address of the intended recipient of the packet.
- *Control field.* The control field transports packet sequence numbers and retransmission requests. Packet sequence numbers are important when lengthy messages/files must be segmented into multiple packets prior to transmission.
- *Frame check sequence.* This 16-bit field is used for error checking. It allows recipients to determine whether the data in the information field has been altered during transmission. The same generalized error-checking process used in modem-to-modem connections (discussed in Chapter 6) is employed in WANs. The 16-bit frame check sequence field for HDLC suggests that a 16-bit checksum or CRC-16 is used for HDLC frames.

Because each packet contains nothing but 1s and 0s (bits) to represent both data and overhead information, the communication devices used in packet-switching networks depend on the packet's predetermined structure. These devices must know exactly where the data is located within each packet as well as the exact location of each piece of overhead information.

Packetizing provides network designers with an alternative or complement to multiplexing (which is discussed in Chapter 10) as a means for enabling multiple communication sessions over a common communications link. In packet-switched networks, **packet assemblers/disassemblers (PADs)** can be used in place of multiplexors. In many instances, however, PADs are integrated into special modems or multiplexors that interface with packet distribution networks. PADs are responsible for assembling packets (adding destination address and other overhead information to their predefined locations in the packet) prior to their transmission over the packet-switching network and for dissembling packets (removing the overhead information) so that the data can be delivered to its intended destination. At a minimum, the overhead information must include the information required to route the packet through the network and deliver it to its intended destination.

packet assembler/disassembler (PAD) PADs are responsible for assembling packets (adding destination address and other overhead information to their predefined locations in the packet) prior to their transmission over the packet-switching network and for dissembling packets (removing the overhead information) so that the data can be delivered to its intended destination.

Packet-switching networks are designed to enable packet switches to process any packet of data regardless of the sender or receiver. For this to happen, each packet must include recipient address information. Including packet recipient address information in each packet enables each packet switch to make routing and forwarding decisions based on the packet's address and current network conditions.

When compared to circuit switching, packet switching has a number of advantages and disadvantages. Advantages include the following:

- A single link between packet-switching nodes can be simultaneously shared by multiple senders and receivers. Senders are not denied access during peak traffic periods (as they might be on circuit-switched connections). Instead, their packets are queued and transmitted as rapidly as possible over the packet-switching network.

> Packet priority systems can be implemented. This can be especially useful during peak data communications traffic periods. High-priority packets can be transmitted before lower-priority packets.

> Subscribers to packet-switching services are often charged on the volume of data (number of packets) transmitted rather than how long they are connected to the network.

Disadvantages include the following:

> Variable transmission delays caused by packet processing and packet queues at packet-switching nodes (switches) in the network can occur. Because each packet-switching node "reads" each packet to determine how it should be routed to its destination, data transmission time can be greater. Additional transmission time is required when queues at nodes get large. Once a circuit is established in circuit-switched networks, no transmission delays are encountered.

> In some packet-switching networks, packet size is variable. This may cause longer packets to be sent along different routes through the network than shorter packets. Variable packet sizes can also contribute to longer packet processing times at intermediate network nodes.

> Because overhead data must be included in packets, transmission efficiency and network throughput may be lower in packet-switched networks than in circuit-switched networks. In a circuit-switched network, once the circuit is established, overhead data related to source and destination addresses are not needed.

datagram The basic unit of data (packet) transmitted in packet-switched networks, including TCP/IP networks. Each datagram contains source and destination addresses as well as data.

connectionless A communications network architecture that does not require the establishment of a session between two nodes before the start of data transmission. The transmission of frames within most LANs is connectionless. The use of UDP packets within TCP/IP networks is also connectionless. Because a dedicated connection is not established between two nodes in a connectionless network, the packets of multipacket files/messages may not follow the same physical path from sender to receiver.

Switching Alternatives in Packet-Switched Networks

Because lengthy files/messages are segmented into multiple packets prior to being transmitted one at a time over a packet-switched network, the network must be able to route the packets associated with a particular file/message through to the network and deliver them to the intended recipient. Two fundamental approaches are used to accomplish this in today's packet-switched networks: the datagram approach and the virtual circuit approach.

Datagram Approach A **datagram** is the basic unit of data (packet) transmitted in packet-switched networks, including TCP/IP networks. Each datagram contains source and destination addresses as well as data. In the datagram approach, each packet is routed independently without consideration of packet sequence numbers of multipacket messages or files. When a packet arrives at a switch, the intended recipient's address and information from other packet-switching nodes about network traffic conditions is used to determine how it will be routed. Because each packet is processed independently, it is likely that each of the packets that make up a multipacket message or file will follow a different path through the network to the intended recipient and may arrive out of sequence. The PAD closest to the recipient puts the packets into their appropriate sequence before delivering the message/file to the recipient.

Because a temporary path is established for each datagram, two datagrams from the same source can have two different circuits established to the same recipient. This type of circuit allocation is called **connectionless,** because a dedicated connection is not established and because the packets of multipacket files/messages do not follow each other in sequence over an actual or virtual circuit or connection.

Datagram service has the potential of fast service for short, unrelated messages, and they have lower overhead because they do not require a virtual circuit. Certain features of datagrams, however, make them undesirable for many applications. First, the arrival order of datagrams is not guaranteed; each datagram sent by a particular node may take a different route. Second, and more important, arrival itself is not guaranteed because the PDN establishes datagram arrival queue depths; a datagram is discarded if the queue is full when the datagram arrives. This problem is compounded by the fact that recovery of lost datagrams is the responsibility of the user, not the PDN, making datagrams best suited to messages of low importance and messages where speed is more critical than the possibility of lost data (such as in process control environments and certain military situations). These characteristics are the reason why connectionless packet networks are sometimes called *unreliable* packet networks.

It is primarily because of datagram services that packet-switching networks have traditionally been depicted as "clouds." After data is packetized at PADs, packets enter a cloud of packet switches. Packet-switching equipment within the cloud takes care of routing packets until they emerge from the cloud for delivery to intended recipients. Packet paths within the cloud are transparent to senders or receivers; when datagram services are used, there is no guarantee that a packet that enters the cloud will emerge and be delivered to intended recipients.

Virtual Circuit Approach   The **virtual circuit** approach is similar to establishing a circuit in a circuit-switched network before exchanging information between senders and receivers. In this case, the route of the packets that comprise a multipacket file or message is preplanned before any of the packets are transmitted. Once the route is established, all the packets follow the same route through the network for delivery to the intended recipient. Unlike circuit-switched connections, an end-to-end dedicated circuit is not established; segments of the preestablished route (or the entire route) are shared with other senders and receivers.

Packet-switching networks that establish virtual circuits are often called **connection-oriented** packet networks. Once a virtual circuit is established, multipacket messages/file packets follow one another in sequence over the same path to the intended recipient. **Call setup packets** are used to establish the source-to-destination circuit. These special packets are used to identify the best path to the destination through the network. The details of the virtual circuit that is established via the call setup packets are stored in a **virtual circuit table**. When message packets arrive at a packet switch in the network, the switch consults the virtual circuit table to identify which outgoing link they should be routed over.

The paths followed by packets in connection-oriented packet networks are known as *logical channels*. Because the virtual circuit is established prior to data transfer, each packet's overhead information includes a *logical channel number* when it is created by the sender's PAD. As they are created, logical channels are incorporated in the network's virtual circuit tables. This facilitates packet routing because packet switches along the path only need to compare each packet's logical channel number to the logical circuits in virtual circuit tables to determine how the packet should be routed.

Because virtual circuits are established in connection-oriented packet networks, checksum error detection and ACK/NAK retransmission control can be implemented. These (which are discussed in Chapter 6) help ensure error-free delivery of all the packets in multipacket messages/files. The inclusion of such error-control features enables connection-oriented packet networks to be called *reliable* packet switching networks.

There are two types of virtual circuits found in connection-oriented packet networks. These are switched virtual circuits and permanent virtual circuits. Each is briefly described here.

virtual circuit A temporary communications path created between devices in a switched communications network. Once established, all messages sent between the devices follow the same path for the duration of the communication session.

connection oriented A communications network architecture that requires the establishment of the session between two nodes before transmission can begin. Circuit-switched networks (including the PSTN) are connection oriented because they require a dedicated channel for the duration of a communication session between two nodes. Packet-switched X.25, frame relay, and ATM networks that require receiving nodes to acknowledge their ability to accept data prior to the start of data transmission are also considered connection oriented.

call setup packet Used to establish the source-to-destination virtual circuit. These special packets are used to identify the best path to the destination through the network.

virtual circuit table Tables located within switches in packet-switched networks that store virtual circuit details. When data packets transmitted over virtual circuits arrive at a switch, the virtual circuit table is consulted to identify which outgoing link they should be routed over.

switched virtual circuit (SVC) One of the types of virtual circuits in packet distribution and other connection-oriented communication networks. When a session is established between two users, an end-to-end virtual circuit is determined and allocated for the duration of the session. Similar to a switched connection, the end-to-end connection is terminated when the communication session ends.

permanent virtual circuit (PVC) A point-to-point virtual circuit that is established prior to data transmission. A PVC is one of the types of virtual circuits in packet-switched networks. It provides a permanent link (like a leased line) between two nodes. It is usually established when two nodes require continuous or frequent transmission. Virtual private networks (VPNs) rely on PVCs.

Switched Virtual Circuit   A **switched virtual circuit (SVC)** is similar to a switched communication link in that both are established when needed by a session and dissolved when the session ends. When an SVC session is established between two users, an end-to-end circuit is allocated for the duration of the session. This is accomplished via a call setup request that is initiated by the user. On receiving a call setup request, the packet-switching network establishes a transmission link for the session. The switched virtual circuit is dissolved at the end of the session, a process known as *call clearing*. *Clear request packets* are used to delete the logical channel from virtual circuit tables once data transfer between sender and receiver has been completed.

Permanent Virtual Circuit   A **permanent virtual circuit (PVC)** is usually selected when two nodes require almost continuous connection. A PVC is similar to a circuit-switched leased communication link. Once a PVC circuit is permanently allocated between two nodes, no call setup or call clearing is required. The logical circuit between sender and receiver is permanently stored in the virtual circuit table.

Routing and Congestion Control in Packet-Switching Networks

Because multiple paths can be established through switching points in packet-switching networks, packet routing and congestion control are important to maintaining adequate network performance. To promote effective packet routing decisions at network switches, the switches are constantly exchanging information about the state of the network and its traffic. Of particular import is information about *failed switches or links*. If a switch is not functioning or if the usual links to it are not available, it obviously should not be included in a packet's route to its destination. Packets should also be routed around *congested* switches in order to ensure adequate network performance. As a result, switches also exchange information with one another about their queue lengths (the number of packets that have been queued but not processed).

Congestion control is focused on keeping the number of packets within a portion of the network at levels that minimize transmission delays caused by lengthy packet queues. If packets arrive at switches faster than they can be processed and transmitted, packet queue lengths will grow in size, and network throughput will be reduced. The exchange of queue length status information among switches in the network is the primary means of avoiding network performance degradation due to congestion.

ITU-T X.25 standards for packet distribution networks do not discuss the internal workings, such as routing and congestion control, within packet-switching networks. However, it is important to recognize that how routing and congestion control are handled is an important determinant of packet-switching network performance.

PACKET DISTRIBUTION NETWORKS (PDNs)

The concept of a packet distribution network (PDN) was first introduced in 1964 by Paul Baran of the Rand Corporation. It was presented as a process of segmenting a message into specific-size packets, routing the packets to their destination, and reassembling the packets to re-create the message. In 1966, Donald Davies of the National Physics Laboratory in Great Britain published details of a store-and-forward packet distribution network. In 1967, plans were formulated for what is believed to be the first packet distribution network, ARPA, which became operational in 1969. ARPAnet soon expanded from 4 nodes to more than 125 nodes, became an important component of the NSFNet, and later evolved into the Internet.

A PDN is sometimes called an *X.25 network*, a *packet-switching network*, or a *public data network*. *Packet distribution* and *packet switching* both refer to how data is transmitted: as one or more packets with a fixed length. The "X.25" designation stems from ITU's recommendation X.25; this defines the interface between data terminal equipment (DTE) and data circuit–terminating equipment (DCE) for terminals operating in the packet mode on public data networks. The term *public data network,* which derives from the X.25 recommendation, is somewhat of a misnomer because packet-switching networks also have been implemented in the private sector and do not have public access. When the network is public, however, users subscribe to the network services much as they subscribe to telephone services.

The term *value-added network (VAN)* is often used in conjunction with PDNs because PDN network proprietors provide not only a communication link but also include value-added services such as message routing, packet control, store-and-forward capability, network management, compatibility among devices, and error recovery.

Packet distribution networks specify a selection of different packet sizes, with sizes of 128, 256, 512, and 1,024 bytes being most common. All packets transmitted must conform to one of the available packet lengths; individual users subscribe to a service providing one of the available packet sizes. Limiting the number of variations in packet size makes managing message buffers easier and helps to even out message traffic patterns.

PDN Equipment

Two types of machines have been defined for use within a PDN: packet-switching equipment (PSE), which accepts and forwards messages, and signaling terminal equipment (STE), which is used to interface two different PDNs according to ITU standard X.75. The standards for a packet-switching network specify interfaces and functions of the PSEs and STEs, but not the nature of the equipment itself. Figure 12-4 illustrates the connections between users' equipment and the PSE.

PDNs and the OSI Layers

Only three OSI layers have been described for PDNs because a PDN is only responsible for message delivery. The three layers of the OSI reference model responsible for message delivery are the physical, data link, and network layers. This is illustrated in Figure 12-5. From the PDN user's perspective, all seven OSI layers exist; the application, presentation, session, and transport layer functions are implemented in the user's segment of the network. However, the X.25 standard is designed to assure transparent access to OSI layers 4 through 7 by serving as a delivery service between computers.

The physical level of an X.25 packet-switching network addresses the physical interface between the data terminal equipment (DTE) and the link that attaches the equipment to packet-switching nodes. The ITU-T physical layer standard for X.25 networks is known as *X.21.* In most implementations, however, EIA's RS-232 standard (discussed in Chapter 6) serves as the physical layer protocol between terminals and packet-switching nodes.

The link level of an X.25 packet-switching network corresponds to OSI's data link level. It is responsible for providing reliable data transfer across the physical link by transmitting data as a sequence of packets. An X.25 network's link level standard is **LAPB (Link Access Procedure—Balanced)**. LAPB is a subset of **HDLC (high-level data link control)** that defines a packet structure that is very similar to SDLC frames in SNA networks. The layout of an HDLC packet is illustrated in Figure 12-3. Like other data link layer protocols, HDLC is responsible for appropriately packetizing the data to be transferred, assuring reliable and error-free end-to-end data delivery, and providing point-to-point packet delivery between adjacent packet-switching nodes.

Packet layer protocol (PLP) is the packet (network) layer protocol in the X.25 protocol stack. PLP's main responsibility is to establish, maintain, and terminate

Link Access Procedure—Balanced (LAPB) A bit synchronous protocol similar to and derived from high-level data link control (HDLC). LAPB is the protocol specified for X.25 networks and plays an important role in error correction and recovery.

high-level data link control (HDLC) An ISO communications protocol used in X.25 packet-switching networks. HDLC is found at the data link layer of the OSI reference model.

packet layer protocol (PLP) The packet (network) layer protocol in the X.25 protocol stack. PLP's main responsibility is to establish, maintain, and terminate virtual circuits within connection-oriented packet networks.

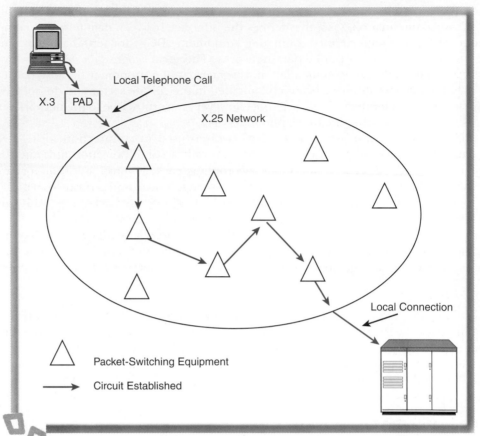

Figure 12-4 Connections in an X.25 Network

virtual circuits within connection-oriented packet networks. As noted previously, call setup packets, call acceptance packets, clear request packets, and clear confirmation packets are used in the establishment, maintenance, and termination of end-to-end connections in X.25 networks.

The total effect of the 3-layer X.25 protocol stack is to produce packets in a standard format that are acceptable to public packet-switched networks. By taking care of packetizing and data transfer processes, X.25 offers network transparency to the upper layers of the OSI protocol stack (layers 4-7).

Example of a Packet-Switching Data Transfer Session

To illustrate how a packet-switching network functions, we follow a message as it proceeds from the starting terminal to its destination address, using a switched virtual circuit connection.

Establishing the Virtual Circuit The communication process begins when a user connects to the PDN by dialing the nearest PDN access port. (This is a local telephone call in most large cities.) After a log-on procedure, the address of the other node (the

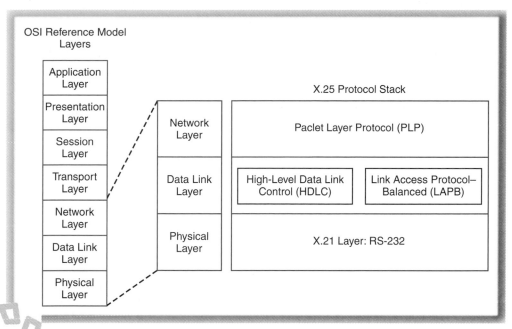

Figure 12-5 X.25 and the OSI Reference Model

intended recipient) is supplied. The PDN then goes through the process of establishing the virtual circuit. The call sequence is as follows:

1. A call request (call setup) packet is sent from the sending node to the receiver. The call request is delivered to the receiver as an incoming call packet (see Figure 12-6). The receiver may accept or reject the call.

2. If the receiver wishes to accept the connection, it transmits a *call-accepted packet* that is presented to the sender as a call-connected message. This establishes the connection, and data exchange may begin.

3. To terminate the connection, either node can transmit a clear request packet to the other. The recipient of the clear request acknowledges the disconnection with a *clear confirmation control packet.*

Data Exchange   Data exchange can begin once the virtual circuit has been established. The data portion of the HDLC frame is restricted to a specific maximum length (128 octets recommended, with 16, 32, 64, 256, 512, and 1,024 specified as options). The Ns and Nr subfields (the number sent and number received subfields, whose roles are discussed in Chapters 6 and 10) are defaulted to 3 bits each, but they also may be expanded to 7 bits. In the defaulted situation, up to seven frames can go unacknowledged, although the X.25 specification recommends that no more than three frames be sent before acknowledgment. This acknowledgment limit can be altered at the discretion of the implementer and would almost always be increased when the Ns and Nr subfields are expanded to 7 bits. The PDN uses a portion of the data field for control information: circuit addressing, packet sequence numbers, and packet confirmation. Three or four octets are used in information packets for this purpose, four when the sequence numbers are 7-bit entities.

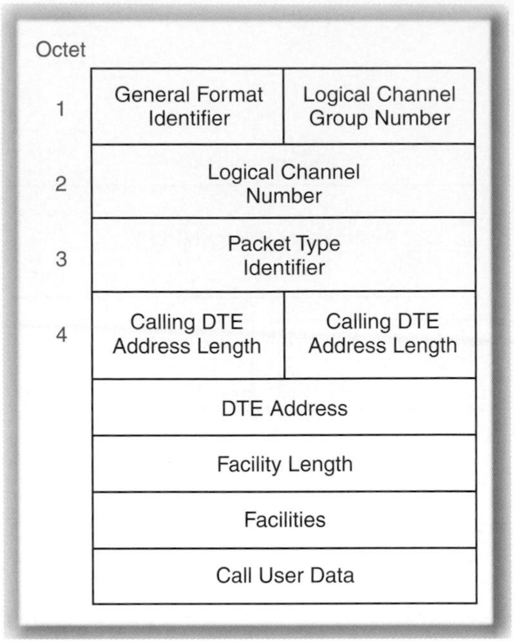

Figure 12-6 Call Request and Incoming Call Packet Format

Packet Assembly/Disassembly   The first step in sending the data is to assemble the packets, a function performed by a packet assembly/disassembly (PAD) module. The PAD function is not considered a part of the PDN; rather, it is the responsibility of the data terminal equipment. However, because many terminals used in PDNs lack the intelligence to perform this function, most PDNs still provide this capability. PAD functions are specified in the ITU X.3 standard. The PAD acts on one end to transform a message into one or more packets of the required length and then reassembles the message at the other end. The PAD is also responsible for generating and monitoring control signals such as call setup and clearing.

Once the message has been transformed into packets, the packets are passed to the PDN in accordance with the X.25 interface. The PDN then moves the data through the network for delivery to the destination. The receiving PAD takes the information from the data portion of the packet and reassembles the message.

Important PDN Standards

A number of important standards are associated with X.25 packet distribution networks. Like the X.25 standard, these have been developed by the ITU-T. As noted previously, the X.21 standard specifies the interface between user terminal equipment and PDN packet-switching nodes; the X.3 standard applies to the packet assembly/disassembly process. Other important standards include the following:

➤ *X.28*. This governs dial-up asynchronous access to PDNs.

➤ *X.32*. This governs dial-up synchronous access to PDNs.

➤ *X.75*. This defines the interface between different public packet-switching networks, both national and international. It is commonly viewed as a PDN gateway protocol.

➤ *X.121*. This is a global addressing scheme for PDNs, which includes a 4-bit code for specifying global zones, country codes, and PDN codes within countries. It also includes a 10-bit address for the destination node.

Several of these are illustrated in Figure 12-7.

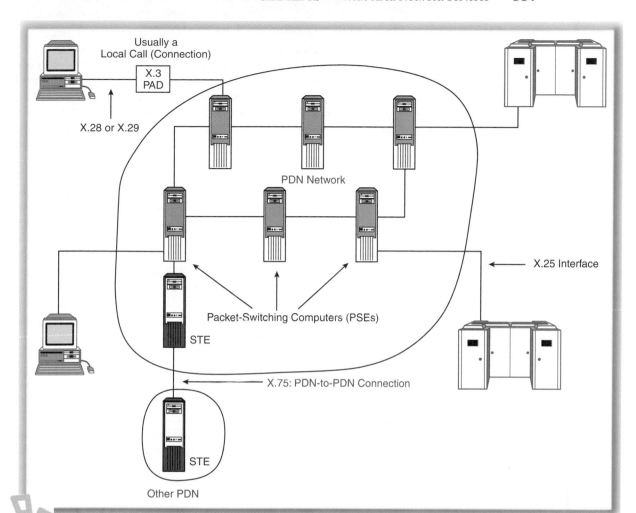

Figure 12-7   PDN General Configuration

PDN Implementations

The use of PDNs has increased significantly since the first PDN was established, and most developed countries currently have access to at least one. In addition to the privately implemented NSFNet, public networks in the United States include those offered by AT&T, CompuServe, GE Information Services, Infonet Services, MCI Communications, and the Sprint Corporation, to name a few. Implementations outside the United States include Datapac in Canada, Transpac in France, EuroNet in Europe (essentially an extension of Transpac), Britain's Packet Switching Service (PSS), Germany's DATEX-P, and Japan's Nippon Telephone and Telegraph (NTT) DDX-2 system. Interconnections exist among these networks, providing international networking capabilities at a reasonable cost.

Advantages and Disadvantages of PDNs

PDNs have several advantages. First, the user is charged for the amount of data transmitted rather than for connect time. Organizations that send low volumes of data over a long period of time will find the charges for a PDN lower than the fixed monthly charges for leased lines or switched lines because subscribers are billed on the volume of data sent. The PDN also gives access to many different locations without the cost of switched connections, which usually involve a charge for the initial connection plus a per minute use fee. Access to the PDN is most often via a local (or toll free) telephone call, which also reduces costs. Maintenance of the network and error recovery are the responsibilities of the PDN, not the subscriber.

There are also disadvantages to using a PDN. Because the PDN is usually shared, users must compete with each other for circuits. Thus, it is possible for message traffic from other users to impede the delivery of a message. In the extreme case, a switched virtual circuit to the intended destination may be unobtainable. This is also true for a switched connection from a common carrier. If the number of data packets to be transferred is great, the cost of using a PDN can exceed that of using leased facilities; in these instances, the organization is better off with a common carrier leased line. Because the PDN is controlled by its proprietor, the individual user is unable to make changes that might benefit an individual application, such as longer messages or larger packets, longer message acknowledgment intervals, and higher transmission speeds, all of which are set by the PDN administrators.

The error-detection and correction processes used in X.25 networks are also disadvantages. PDNs employ *node-to-node (hop-to-hop; point-to-point)* error detection and correction (see Figure 12-8). Each packet received by an X.25 packet switch is checked for errors before being forwarded to the next hop on the way to its intended destination. If no errors are detected, a positive acknowledgment (ACK) is sent to the previous node, signaling that it is okay to forward the next packet. If errors are detected, however, a negative acknowledgment (NAK) is sent to the previous node, signaling the need to retransmit the packet. In this scheme, it is incumbent on each node to refrain from transmitting a packet until it receives a positive acknowledgment for the packet that preceded it. It is also necessary for each node to buffer each transmitted packet until it receives a positive acknowledgment from the next hop along its path. Hence, X.25 PDNs are examples of *store-and-forward* networks; packets are stored at packet-switching nodes until a positive acknowledgment is received, indicating that it is okay to clear the packet from its buffer.

Such an error-control scheme was appropriate when the long-distance circuits connecting X.25 switches were more error-prone and less reliable than they are today. X.25 was first introduced over 2 decades ago, when the quality of telecommunication lines was much worse than today and communication errors were more common. To compensate for these shortcomings, extensive error checking was implemented in X.25. However, the highly reliable digital circuits now available to connect PDN nodes make point-to-point error-detection and correction schemes and the additional network traffic and packet processing that they require unnecessary.

As discussed previously, call control packets are used in X.25 networks to set up and clear virtual circuits. Virtual circuits must be established before a PAD can complete its routing calculations for multipacket messages/files. This slows down the packetizing process and delays the transmission of packets to the next packet-switching node on their path to their intended destination. Each packet must be "processed" at each packet-switching node before being transmitted to the next node. This processing requires performing an error-detection check on each packet and the transmission of either a positive acknowledgment to the previous node if no errors are detected or the transmission of a

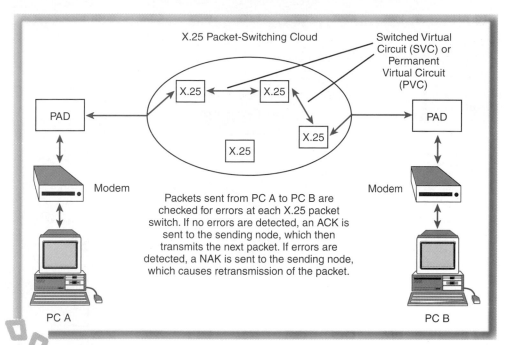

Figure 12-8   X.25's Point-to-Point Error Detection and Correction

request to retransmit the packet if the error-detection check reveals errors. These acknowledgments increase the number of packets that must be transferred between packet-switching nodes and reduce the network's data throughput, especially during peak traffic periods. X.25 also demands additional processing overhead because each packet-switching node must store each transmitted packet in a buffer until it receives a positive acknowledgment from the next node along the packet's path to its destination.

The upshot of X.25's node-to-node error-detection and correction process is diminished network speed and performance. Most X.25 PDNs support a maximum bandwidth of 64 kbps. As a result, they are not as well suited for providing WAN links between geographically dispersed networks (such as 100-mbps Ethernet LANs) as other packet-switching options. In response to these limitations, two newer packet-switching methods have emerged that provide higher bandwidth and superior network throughput (the amount of data transmitted across the network in a given time period). These two options are frame relay and cell relay.

FRAME RELAY NETWORKS

Frame relay is an outgrowth of X.25 networks and is designed to eliminate much of the overhead associated with X.25 networks in order to take advantage of the higher speed, less error-prone, and more reliable digital circuits that are available to connect switching nodes. Although companies can build their own private frame relay networks, most leverage frame relay services available from common carriers. An example of a frame relay network is provided in Figure 12-9.

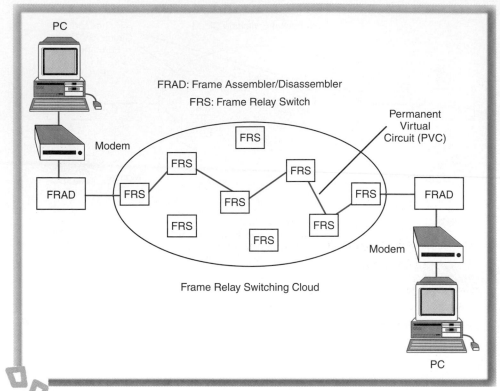

Figure 12-9 Frame Relay Network Components

Frame relay and cell relay networks have higher throughput than X.25 networks because they use higher bandwidth digital circuits to connect switching nodes and because they use *point-to-point error detection* and *end-to-end error correction* in place of X.25's point-to-point error-detection and correction scheme. Frame (and cell) relay's higher transmission speeds make these WAN services more attractive than X.25 networks for interconnecting high-speed, geographically dispersed networks.

Frame relay's point-to-point error-detection and end-to-end error-correction scheme requires much less error-control traffic than that found in X.25 networks. This process is illustrated in Figure 12-10. Similar to X.25 networks, each frame in a frame relay network is examined for errors at each frame relay switch. However, there is no need to send an acknowledgment to the previous frame relay switching node. Instead, error-free frames are forwarded to the next hop, and frames with errors are *discarded*. Because the error-detection process results in frame forwarding or discarding, there is no store-and-forward requirement in frame relay networks.

The discarding of bad frames by intermediate nodes automatically triggers a "missing frame" retransmission request by recipients. Although recipients still check for errors, they only have to do so for frames that emerge from the cloud of frame relay switches after having been checked and certified as being error free at each of their hops through the network. Although errors may occur as frames emerge from the frame relay network cloud and make their way through **FRADs** (**frame assembler/dissembler**

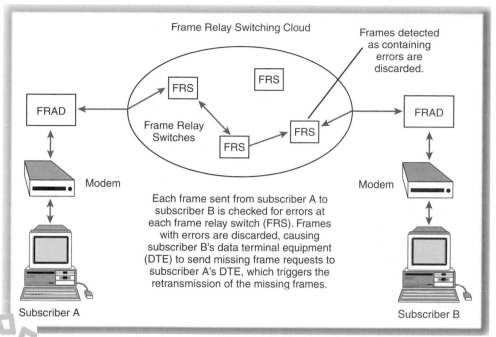

Figure 12-10   Frame Relay's Point-to-Point Error Detection and End-to-End
Error Correction

devices or *frame relay access devices*) to recipients, missing frames are most likely to be
responsible for triggering frame retransmission requests sent by recipients to senders.

It is important to note that frame relay networks only demand frame buffering at
senders and receivers. There is no store-and-forward requirement for frame relay
switches within the network cloud because they are only responsible for error detection, not error correction. Store-and-forward capabilities are only needed at end
nodes in frame relay networks. Unlike X.25 packet switches, frame relay switches only
have to perform an error check in order to make a forward or discard decision as well
as a routing decision for the error-free frames to be forwarded. By not having to transmit acknowledgments to sending nodes or process acknowledgment/retransmission
requests from receiving nodes, frame relay switching is able to achieve higher throughput than X.25 networks with less delay.

Frame Formats

Frame relay frames are formatted with FRAD devices or in computers with frame relay
protocol software that gives them the capability to build or dissemble frames directly.
Frames are variable in length, with some frames carrying up to 8,000 bytes (characters). Figure 12-11 illustrates the generic layout of a frame. The frame format illustrated in Figure 12-11 is a subset of the *LAP-D (link access procedure-D channel)* protocol.
(The D channel is the same 16-kbps data channel used in ISDN's basic rate interface
[BRI]; this channel is responsible for transporting network control information for
ISDN communication sessions. Like ISDN, frame relay networks use a separate channel for transmitting network control information, such as virtual circuit table updates

Flag (1 Octet)	Address (2–4 Octets)	Information (Variable)	Frame Check Sequence (FCS) (2 Octets)	Flag (1 Octet)

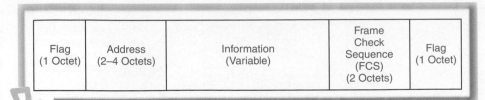

Figure 12-11 Frame Relay Frame Format

and retransmission requests. In X.25 networks, network control information is transferred over the same channels as those used to transmit data packets. The use of separate channels for data transmission and network control is another reason why throughput is higher in frame relay networks than in X.25 networks.)

The flag field is a unique pattern of bits that delimits the start and end of the frame. The frame check sequence (FCS) field is used for error detection. The content of the FCS field is typically a checksum derived from the characters stored in the information field. (Checksums are discussed in Chapter 6.) This is calculated by the FRAD as the frame is being built. Each frame relay switch calculates its own checksum as it processes the frame and compares it to what is stored in the FCS. If they are the same, the frame is determined to be error free; if there is a mismatch, the frame is determined to contain errors and is discarded.

As Figure 12-11 illustrates, the address field in frame relay frames may be as small as 2 bytes or as large as 4 bytes. The default 2-byte address field layout is illustrated in Figure 12-12. Regardless of its length, the address field carries a *data link connection identifier (DLCI)* that serves the same function as a virtual circuit in X.25 networks. The EA (extended address) fields contain address extension bits, and the C/R (command or response) field is application specific and not used by standard frame relay protocols.

Three bits in frame relay frames are related to congestion control in frame relay networks. Collectively, they enable frame relay devices to dynamically alter the flow of network traffic when network congestion occurs. The *BECN (backward explicit congestion notification)* bit indicates that congestion avoidance procedures should be initiated if network congestion is encountered, even if this demands sending the frame backward

EA 0	C/R	Upper DLCI (6 Bits)	EA 1	DE	BECN	FECN	Lower DLCI (4 Bits)

EA: Address Field Extension Bit
C/R: Command/Response Bit
DLCI: Data Link Connection Identifier
DE: Discard Eligibility (1 Bit)
BECN: Backward Explicit Congestion Notification (1 Bit)
FECN: Forward Explicit Congestion Notification (1 Bit)

Figure 12-12 Frame Relay Address Field

in the network to enable routing around congested nodes. The *FECN (forward explicit congestion notification)* indicates that congestion avoidance procedures should be initiated to ensure that it is not forwarded to nodes ahead that are heavily congested. The *DE (discard eligibility)* bit—when set—indicates that the frame is a candidate for being discarded when network congestion can only be relieved by discarding frames.

Frame Relay Circuits

Most frame relay networks only support permanent virtual circuits (PVCs) for routing frames from senders to receivers through the frame relay network cloud. These establish permanent, point-to-point connections across the frame relay network. Although switched virtual circuits (SVCs) have been defined by the Frame Relay Forum (FRF)—an organization of more than 300 frame relay equipment vendors, carriers, end users, and consultants that has assumed responsibility for developing frame relay standards—they have not been widely implemented. Unlike a PVC, an SVC is established on a call-by-call basis, and the circuit that is established is determined by the end points (sender and receiver) and the level of network congestion. Relative to PVCs, SVCs can find alternate routes when some links are overloaded or fail. In 1998, MCI became the first telecommunications carrier to provide SVCs through a service called HyperStream SVC. It offers speeds between 16 kbps and 6 mbps and enables subscribers to mix SVCs and PVCs on the same access port.

The use of PVCs enables frame relay networks to be used to create virtual private networks (VPNs)—a service that enables a private network to be configured within a public frame relay network. As noted in previous chapters, VPNs are increasingly popular on the Internet because the Internet has created a lower cost alternative to carrier-provided VPNs. However, the first VPNs were implemented over frame relay or switched megabit data services (SMDS) networks.

Advantages and Disadvantages of Frame Relay Networks

Frame relay services are provided by all the major telecommunications carriers in the world as well as by third-party VANs. As a result, many organizations rely on frame relay services in their international data communication networks. Frame relay speeds are typically between 56 kbps and 1.54 mbps. The high speeds that are now supported by frame relay make it an attractive (and usually lower cost) substitute to leased T-1 connections and significantly expand the number of applications that can take advantage of the service. For example, at the higher speeds, frame relay services can provide a high-speed connection between geographically distributed LANs or high-speed Internet access through the frame relay service provider's connection. Frame relay services can also be used to transmit voice as well as data. Frame relay service providers have been experiencing increased demand for their services over the last decade and have been increasing their capacity in response to the increasing demand. Further growth in the demand for frame relay services in the years ahead is anticipated.

Like X.25, frame relay is a delivery service. Because it encapsulates rather than processes user data, it is protocol independent and can forward frames/packets used in a variety of different networks, including SNA, Ethernet, and TCP/IP. Such protocol independence is facilitated by the variable length information fields in frame relay frames; this enables a frame relay network to accommodate data packets of various sizes associated with virtually any native data communications protocol. Because protocol conversion is unnecessary, frame relay offers faster and less expensive switching than alternative WAN services that require protocol conversion.

Frame relay speeds are increasing. Although the original maximum speed was 1.54 mbps, frame relay now offers speeds up to 45 mbps. Such speeds mean that frame relay is especially attractive for connecting larger business sites to Internet service providers (ISPs). Many ISPs, especially those in urban areas, support frame relay–based Internet access. The higher speeds also make frame relay services attractive to organizations that desire relatively high-speed WAN links between geographically dispersed LANs.

Although not developed as a protocol for transporting digitized voice, since 1996 an increasing number of frame relay vendors have introduced FRADs that are capable of digitizing voice signals and delivering voice frames to recipients at the same rates that they were originally transmitted. Voice-over-frame relay capabilities along with cost-effective data transmission have been fueling the growth of frame relay services.

Variable length frames and the need for better coordination among frame relay network service providers continue to be among the major limitations of frame relay networks. Variable frame lengths make it virtually impossible to guarantee how long it will take to deliver a message via a frame relay network. Longer frames demand greater processing time, and a mix of long and short frames within the frame relay cloud at any point in time is beyond the control of frame relay network proprietors. Unpredictable frame delivery time is especially problematic for subscribers that want to transmit time-sensitive information such as video or voice over the frame relay network. For such applications to work well, video and voice frames must be delivered in a predictable, timed fashion.

Lack of transparent access across different frame relay networks continues to be another limitation of frame relay networks. The Frame Relay Forum has developed interconnection standards to ensure interoperability across the networks provided by different carriers; these have not been widely adopted.

ASYNCHRONOUS TRANSFER MODE (ATM)

Asynchronous transfer mode (ATM) is a high-bandwidth, low-delay, packet-switching and multiplexing technology that can handle many types of network traffic and WAN services. It is versatile enough to be implemented across network backbones, LANs, and WANs and can even be used for micromainframe connections. ATM's low delay means that it supports voice and videoconferencing applications in addition to data traffic.

ATM represents another step in the evolution of frame relay by using frames that do not vary in size. Fixed length packets (such as those used in ATM) can be switched more easily and thus enable faster transmission rates than is possible with either X.25 or frame relay networks. Over the last decade, maximum ATM transfer rates have been doubling annually. By 1998, ATM data transfer rates of 2.488 gbps (OC-48) had been achieved. By 2000, OC-192 rates were achieved (9.953 gbps).

ATM is a **cell relay** system. Conceptually, cell relay is similar to frame relay. Both employ point-to-point error detection and end-to-end error correction. Like frame relay systems, cell relay takes advantage of the reliability of high bandwidth digital circuits that are used to interconnect data communications equipment (DCE) in order to provide faster packet switching than X.25. Like X.25 and frame relay, ATM enables the multiplexing of multiple logical connections over a single physical interface. The key physical difference between cell relay and frame relay is the use of fixed-size packets, called **cells**, that are 53 octets in length (1 octet = 8 bits). Each cell contains 48 bytes of user data packets and 5 bytes of control data.

Cell relay's constant cell sizes enable more processing instructions to be incorporated into cell relay switch hardware and firmware. The result is predictable cell processing, forwarding, and delivery rates. Predictable delivery times make cell relay systems a better choice than X.25 or frame relay for time-sensitive data such as voice and video transmissions.

asynchronous transfer mode (ATM) A high-speed transmission cell-switching network that supports real-time voice and video as well as data. ATM is defined in the Broadband ISDN (B-ISDN) standard. Logical channels are used to establish end-to-end connections to ensure quality of service (QoS). ATM is widely used in carrier and large enterprise backbone networks. It is highly scalable and supports transmission speeds from 1.5 mbps to 9.953 gbps.

cell relay Similar to frame relay except for the use of small fixed-size packets (cells). Both frame relay and cell relay systems employ point-to-point error detection and end-to-end error correction. Like frame relay systems, cell relay employs high bandwidth digital circuits to interconnect data communications equipment (DCE) in order to provide higher data transmission rates than X.25.

cell In ATM networks, cells are small fixed-size packets that are 53 octets in length (1 octet = 8 bits). Each cell contains 48 bytes of user data packets and 5 bytes of control data.

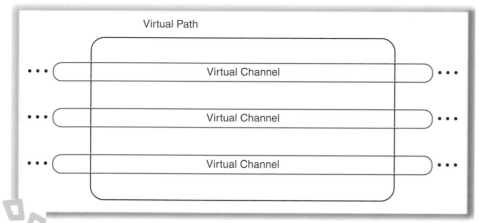

Virtual Path

Virtual Channel

Virtual Channel

Virtual Channel

Figure 12-13   ATM Virtual Channels in ATM Virtual Paths

Virtual channels are used in ATM to establish logical connections between senders and receivers. These are similar to the X.25 and frame relay virtual circuits and serve as the basic unit of switching in an ATM network. Virtual channels between two end users are set up through the network; once established, a full-duplex, variable-rate flow of cells is exchanged over the connections. Virtual channels are also used to exchange network control information.

Virtual paths are also supported in ATM. Virtual paths are best described as a bundle of virtual channels that have the same end points (see Figure 12-13). When a virtual path is established between two end users, all the cells flowing over virtual channels connecting senders and receivers are switched together. In videoconferencing applications, establishing a virtual path might mean that video data is sent over one virtual channel, audio data is sent over a second, and data is sent over a third virtual circuit within the virtual path.

ATM Cell Formats

The ATM Forum, which is made up of more than 900 member companies, has assumed a major role in the development of ATM specifications. It works closely with the International Telecommunications Union (ITU) and the American National Standards Institute (ANSI), North America's representative on the ITU, to develop internationally recognized ATM standards. Two cell formats have been specified by the ATM forum. One is called the **user-network interface (UNI)**; UNI cells carry data between the user and the ATM network. The other is called the **network-network interface (NNI)** and is used to carry network control information between ATM switches. NNI also enables network control information to be exchanged between *different* ATM networks and thus plays the same role as the X.75 internetwork standard for X.25 PDNs. Both UNI and NNI formats are illustrated in Figure 12-14.

The fields in UNI and NNI cells are similar. These are briefly described here.

➤ The *generic flow control (GFC)* field in UNI cells provides a mechanism to alleviate address network access congestion caused by different flow control signaling required by different devices (voice, video, or data) sharing the same network access circuit. It can be used as a multiple-priority-level indicator to control service-dependent information flow.

virtual channel
Used in ATM to establish logical connections between senders and receivers. These are similar to the X.25 and frame relay virtual circuits and serve as the basic unit of switching in an ATM network. Once established, a full-duplex, variable-rate flow of cells can be exchanged by the devices.

virtual path A bundle of virtual channels that have the same endpoints. When a virtual path is established between two end users, all the cells flowing over virtual channels connecting senders and receivers are switched together.

user-network interface (UNI) The interface between the end user and the network; the term is used in both ATM and frame relay networks. In ATM, UNI refers to one of two cell formats specified by the ATM forum; UNI cells carry data between the user and the ATM network.

network-network interface (NNI) In ATM networks, NNI refers to the interface between two ATM devices (typically ATM switches). It also refers to one of two cell formats specified by the ATM forum. NNI is used to carry network control information between ATM switches. NNI also enables network control information to be exchanged between different ATM networks.

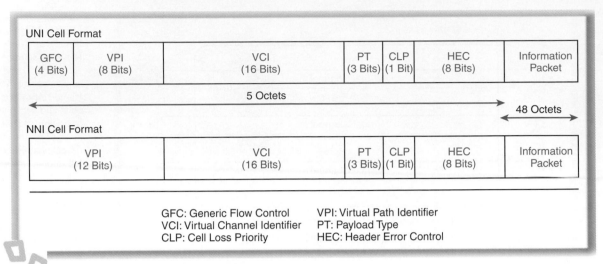

Figure 12-14   ATM Cell Formats

➤ The *virtual path identifier (VPI)* field is an 8-bit field in UNI cells and a 12-bit field in NNI cells. It serves as a routing field for the ATM network. It uniquely identifies the connection between two network end points. A VPI consists of several virtual channel identifiers (VCIs).

➤ The *virtual channel identifier (VCI)* field uniquely identifies a channel within the virtual path that a particular type of information (voice, video, or data) should follow. It provides service-dependent routing between two network end points.

➤ The *payload type (PT)* field indicates whether the type of information carried in the information field is user data or network control information.

➤ The *cell loss priority (CLP)* field is used to provide cell discard eligibility in the event of network congestion. If the CLP bit is turned on, it becomes a candidate for discarding if cell relay switch queues become congested. It serves an equivalent role to the discard eligibility field in frame relay frames.

➤ The *header error control (HEC)* field is an 8-bit code that can be used to correct single-bit errors in the cell header (the GFC, VPI, VCI, PT, and CLP fields) and to detect double-bit errors. Double-bit errors that are detected at a cell relay switch will cause the switch to discard the frame. The ability to correct single-bit errors (especially those in the VPI and VCI fields) helps to ensure cell delivery to intended receivers.

ATM Protocol Stack

Like other packet-switching networks, ATM is essentially a protocol-independent and protocol-transparent delivery service. As Figure 12-15 illustrates, the ATM protocol stack maps most directly to the data link and physical layers of the OSI reference model.

User inputs (such as voice, data, and video) are processed into 53-byte cells at the *ATM adaptation layer (AAL)* before being forwarded to ATM switches for delivery to intended recipients. There are multiple sublayers to both the AAL and physical layers in the ATM protocol stack. These are responsible for segmenting and reassembling different types of user inputs (such as voice, data, and video), address assignment and translation, cell delineation, multiplexing, and the physical transport of cells across

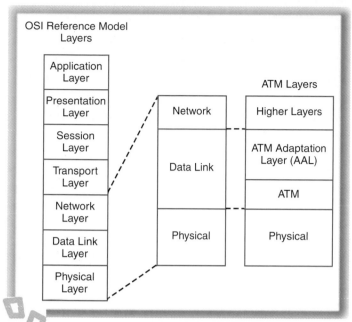

Figure 12-15   ATM and the OSI Reference Model

the network. To accommodate different types of ATM traffic—whether time sensitive or not—five different levels of service, called *quality of service levels,* were specified. Only four are typically implemented because two of the levels were not sufficiently distinct. The levels of service are called *ATM adaptation layer (AAL) protocols;* the basic provisions for each are specified in Table 12-1.

Advantages and Disadvantages of ATM

Relative to X.25 and frame relay networks, ATM offers several advantages. These are summarized here.

➤ Higher scalability and maximum supported bandwidth (for example, OC-48 to OC-192)

➤ Low latency (low delivery delay)

Table 12-1   ATM Adaptation Layers

Adaptation Layer	Type of Service	Applications
AAL-1	Constant bit rate	Voice and video
AAL-2	Time sensitive but variable bit rate	Packetized voice
AAL-3/4	Bursty, connection-oriented service needing extra error checking	Applications where delays can be tolerated (e.g., file transfer)
AAL-5	Similar to AAL-3/4	Applications desiring less overhead for error checking

➤ Support for multiple types of user data (voice, data, or video) over the same shared communication lines

➤ Ability to be used in LANs as an alternative to Ethernet, token ring, and FDDI

➤ Provides a migration path to high-speed transmission rates

➤ Provides a high-speed WAN link for geographically dispersed LANs

In spite of these advantages, companies typically are only deploying ATM to the desktop to support bandwidth-hungry applications such as imaging, computer-aided design/computer-aided manufacturing (CAD/CAM), videoconferencing, animation, and complex graphics.

The drawbacks to ATM include the following

➤ New adapter cards must be installed in LAN servers and workstations.

➤ New LAN hubs and network management software must be installed.

➤ The high overhead of ATM cells (5 of 53 bytes) is considered to be excessive for lower-speed lines and too inefficient for high-speed circuits.

➤ Performance improvements over Fast and Gigabit Ethernet to the desktop are undetectable for many user applications.

➤ Packet over SONET (POS) is emerging to challenge ATM as a high-speed network backbone and WAN service.

ATM: A Universal Networking Technology

The maximum bandwidths, efficiency, and flexibility of ATM make it appealing as a universal networking technology. Because it can provide predictable delivery of a wide range of user data, a variety of business telecommunications needs can be satisfied by ATM. Public ATM network providers maintain a core network of high-performance cell relay switches that are interconnected with high-bandwidth digital circuits such as SONET. Both public ATM network providers and third-party firms provide ATM service switches (edge nodes) at the edge of ATM networks that are capable of providing protocol conversion interfaces to other networks such as frame relay and SMDS (see Figure 12-16).

Although the composition of an ATM network is not unlike X.25 or frame relay networks, the nature of the cells entering the ATM "switching cloud" translates into greater functionality than what is possible with these alternative packet-switching approaches. As a result, ATM has a superior chance of serving as a multipurpose WAN service for business organizations.

OTHER WAN SERVICES

Several other network services often found in the WAN implemented by business organizations include T-1 services, SONET, and ISDN. Each of these is briefly described here.

T-1 Services

framing A control procedure used with multiplexed digital channels, such as T-1, that inserts bits so that the receiver can identify the time slots allocated to each subchannel.

As noted in Chapter 5, T-1 lines are some of the most widely used leased digital circuits in North America; E-1 lines, which have a bandwidth of 2.048 mbps, are used in most other parts of the world. Each T-1 line has a bandwidth of 1.544 mbps, which is subdivided into twenty-four 64-kbps channels. Some of these channels can be used to transmit voice; others are used to transmit data. Channels are differentiated via an adaptation of time division multiplexing (TDM) that is called **framing.** Pulse code modulation (which is discussed in Chapter 5) is used to digitize voice signals for transfer over designated voice channels in the T-1 frame.

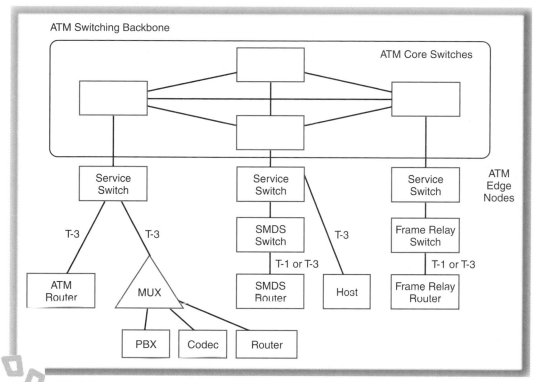

Figure 12-16   ATM Network

A technique called *periodic framing* is employed to build T-1 frames. In this process, each of the 24 channels is allocated 8 bits. Each set of 8 bits represents one voice or data sample and is called a *time slot*. Each T-1 frame (which is sometimes called a *D-4* frame) consists of 192 bits (8 bits per channel × 24 channels) as well as a terminating *framing bit* for a total of 193 bits. Figure 12-17 depicts a D-4 frame. The 24 channels in a T-1 frame can be reallocated to users when there are fewer than 24 simultaneous users. If only two users are sharing the T-1 line at a given point in time, each can be allocated a group of 12 channels. If there is no competition, a single user may be allocated all 24 channels. Similarly, two or more businesses may share a single T-1 line via a similar channel reallocation process known as *fractional T-1 (FT-1)*.

Businesses use a variety of equipment to access T-1 services, including T-1 CSU/DSUs, T-1 multiplexors, T-1 channel banks, and T-1 switches (see Figure 12-18). Each of these is briefly discussed here.

➤ *T-1 CSU/DSUs.* T-1 CSU/DSUs (channel service unit/data service units) are the most widely used T-1 service interfaces found on business customer premises. These are capable of providing 1.544-mbps WAN links for routers, PBXs, and other data communications equipment used by businesses.

➤ *T-1 multiplexors.* T-1 multiplexors enable several lower bandwidth digital channels (data or voice) to share a single T-1 line. CSU/DSU capabilities are typically incorporated in T-1 multiplexors. Cost-conscious businesses that are unable to take full advantage of the full T-1 bandwidth may choose to implement *fractional T-1 (FT-1)*

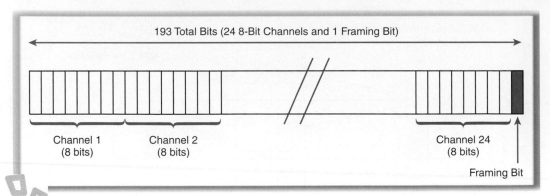

Figure 12-17   T-1 Frame Format

Figure 12-18   T-1 Service Access Technologies

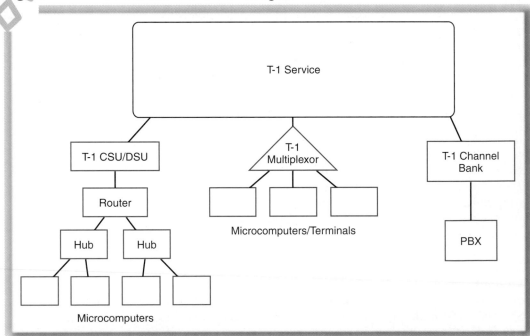

multiplexors; organizations desiring to leverage T-1 services to support videoconferencing or LAN-to-LAN communications over WAN links may employ *T-1 inverse multiplexors (T-1 IMUXs).*

➤ *T-1 channel banks.* Like a T-1 multiplexor, a T-1 channel bank has built-in CSU/DSU capabilities. In contrast to T-1 multiplexors, T-1 channel banks are capable of interfacing with a wider variety of different speed, different transmission protocol input data channels. For example, both asynchronous and synchronous data input channels are supported by T-1 channel banks; analog voice input may also be accepted. Although a T-1 multiplexor requires digitized voice input, T-1 channel banks accept analog input and digitize it prior to transmission over the T-1 link.

➤ *T-1 switches.* T-1 switches are available for organizations that want to interconnect geographically dispersed locations via T-1 links and thereby create private WANs capable of delivering data and voice to different operating locations.

SONET Services

Synchronous optical network (SONET) is an optical transmission interface/specification for high-speed digital transmission over optical fiber. SONET standards have been established by ANSI (e.g., ANSI's T1.105 and T1.106 standards), and compatible specifications have been established by the International Telecommunications Union (e.g., ITU-T recommendations G.707, G.708, and G.709).

SONET specifications define a hierarchy of standardized digital data transfer rates over optical media. An abbreviated set of SONET specifications and their ITU-T equivalents is provided in Table 12-2. As Table 12-2 illustrates, the lowest data transfer level (51.84 mbps) is referred to as *STS-1 (Synchronous Transport Signal Level 1)* or *OC-1 (Optical Carrier level 1).* The lowest data transfer level (155.52 mbps) in the ITU-T Synchronous Digital Hierarchy is STM-1.

An STS-1 channel is capable of carrying multiple lower-speed signals such as multiple DS-1 (1.544 mbps) or E-1 (2.048 mbps) signals or a single higher-speed signal such as DS-3 (45 mbps). An STS-3 channel is capable of handling three DS-3 circuits or up to nearly 100 DS-1 channels. The Digital Service (DS) Hierarchy is discussed in Chapter 5.

STS-1 frames are the fundamental data transmission format in SONET. These consist of 810 octets and can be logically depicted as a matrix that consists of nine rows with 90 octets in each row (see Figure 12-19). The first three octets in each row (or a total of 27 octets) carry overhead information; the remaining 87 octets in each row carry user data (or *payload* in SONET terminology). The payload area of each STS-1 frame can be flexibly allocated to lower bandwidth digital channels such as DS-0 (64 kbps), DS-1, and DS-2. The channels that are defined within the payload areas of STS-1 frames are called *virtual tributaries.* Virtual tributaries (VTs) are equivalent to circuit-switched

Table 12-2   Examples of SONET Optical Carrier (Levels)

SONET Designations	ITU Designation	Data Rate
STS-1/OC-1		51.84 mbps
STS-3/OC-3	STM-1	155.52 mbps
STS-12/OC-12	STM-4	622.08 mbps
STS-48/OC-48	STM-16	2.48832 gbps
STS-192/OC-192	STM-64	9.95328 gbps

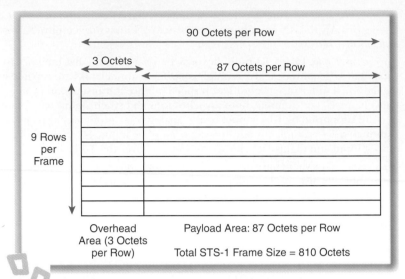

Figure 12-19   SONET Frame Format

connections between two network end nodes. These are also similar to virtual circuits in packet-switched networks.

SONET services are available in most large metropolitan areas in North America. Businesses must have special fiber optic termination interfaces installed on their premises in order to access SONET services. Organizations with steadily increasing high-bandwidth telecommunication requirements are likely to find SONET services to be an attractive option because they provide a migration path to higher bandwidth channels, as these are required.

SONET service access technologies found on subscriber premises go by several names including *broadband bandwidth managers, cross-connect switches,* and *add-drop multiplexors.* These devices are capable of combining several digital T-1 or T-3 signals into a single SONET signal. Some ATM switches have SONET interfaces to enable organizations to take advantage of carrier or third-party SONET services.

The introduction of **wavelength division multiplexing (WDM)** has made it easy for SONET service providers to add capacity to their networks without the need to add more fiber optic links. As noted in Chapter 11, WDM enables multiple light wavelengths (colors) to be simultaneously transmitted over a single optical fiber. Some *dense wavelength division multiplexing (DWDM)* systems can support more than 150 wavelengths per fiber with each wavelength carrying up to 10 gbps. Such systems enable a signal fiber to carry more than 1 trillion bits per second (1,000 gpbs). WDM and DWDM enable the transmission capacity of existing carrier fiber infrastructures to be dramatically increased without having to install additional fiber optic cables.

ISDN

Integrated Services Digital Network (ISDN) is widely used by businesses to provide digital WAN services among geographically dispersed operating locations. ISDN is attractive to many organizations, especially small to medium-size companies; it is widely

wavelength division multiplexing (WDM) Enables multiple light wavelengths (colors) to be simultaneously transmitted over a single optical fiber; this enables a different signal to be transmitted within each unique color band. Some *dense wavelength division multiplexing (DWDM)* systems can support more than 150 wavelengths with each wavelength carrying up to 10 gbps. Such systems enable a signal fiber to carry more than 1 trillion bits per second (1,000 gpbs).

available in both urban and rural areas, and it is capable of simultaneously transporting digitized data, voice, and video. In spite of its widespread availability within the United States, business and residential subscribers must be within 18,000 feet (about 3.4 miles) of an ISDN switch to take advantage of this digital network service. Recall that DSL subscribers have an identical distance requirement.

ISDN switches are the core of the ISDN network (see Figure 12-20). These switches enable both local and long-distance connections to be established among ISDN subscribers who typically pay a flat monthly fee plus per minute usage charges to use the network. Long-distance per minute charges are higher than local per minute charges. The two major categories of ISDN are narrowband ISDN and broadband ISDN.

Narrowband ISDN

Narrowband ISDN is essentially a circuit-switched digital network service that allows temporary connections to be dynamically created and terminated among ISDN subscribers. Once a connection is established, it can be used to simultaneously transport voice, data, and video.

Two different narrowband ISDN service levels are available. Each of these is briefly described here.

➤ *Basic rate interface (BRI).* The basic rate interface is a 144-kbps interface that is often called *2B+D* because it consists of two 64-kbps *bearer (B)* channels and one 16-kbps *data (D)* channel. User data (voice, data, and video) are carried on the B channels;

Figure 12-20   An ISDN Network

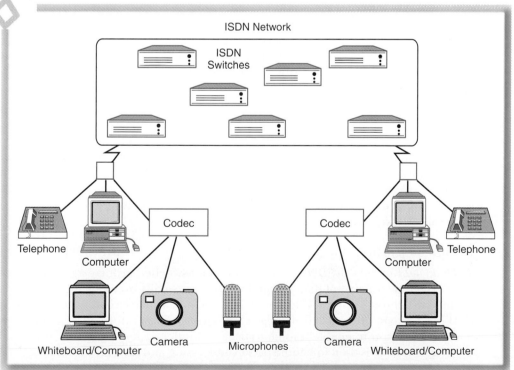

network control and management data (e.g., call setup, call termination, and caller ID) are carried on the D channel. As mentioned previously in this chapter, the ISDN D channel may also play an important role in ISDN–X.25 interfaces.

➤ *Primary rate interface (PRI)*. ISDN's primary rate interface is also called *23B+D* because it is composed of twenty-three 64-kbps bearer channels and one 64-kbps data channel. The combined bandwidth of these channels (1.536 kbps) means that PRI can be mapped nicely into a T-1 circuit.

In order to use ISDN's digital circuits, analog devices such as fax machines have to be equipped with *ISDN terminal adapters*. ISDN terminal adapters essentially function as modems that convert analog signals into digital form for transmission over the network. ISDN terminal adapter cards are available to enable microcomputers to interface with the ISDN network; ISDN terminal adapters also are available as stand-alone units.

Broadband ISDN

Broadband ISDN (B-ISDN) provides much higher bandwidth connections between ISDN end nodes than narrowband ISDN. Broadband ISDN is best described as *ATM over SONET* because it employs SONET OC circuits to interconnect ATM cell relay switches. The combination of ATM switching and SONET optical transmission services enables predictable, low-latency delivery of voice, video, image, and data between broadband ISDN end nodes.

Broadband ISDN is able to interface with a variety of existing services (e.g., T-1, frame relay, SMDS, and narrowband ISDN). It also has the potential to support bandwidth-hungry applications such as telemedicine and video on demand.

WIRELESS WAN SERVICES

An increasing number of organizations are turning to wireless WAN services to satisfy some of their telecommunications needs. Wireless WAN services are used to support a variety of applications, including Internet access for mobile computers, package tracking, database access, remote monitoring, and credit card verification. Many service providers have emerged to help organizations satisfy their need for wireless WAN services. Several of the major types of wireless WAN services are discussed in this section.

Circuit-Switched Cellular Services

A cellular telephone subscriber can send data over analog cellular networks using a modem and a properly equipped cellular telephone (see Figure 12-21). Data is transmitted over a dedicated cellular channel at a rate between 9,600 bps and 14,400 bps, depending on the telephone, modem, and service provider's equipment. The subscriber is charged for the data transmission, as they would also be for the other cell phone calls that they initiate/receive.

Cellular Digital Packet Data (CDPD)

Cellular digital packet data (CDPD) is similar to circuit-switched cellular services in that it involves the transmission of data (including fax and e-mail) over existing cellular network infrastructures using a wireless modem. However, unlike circuit-switched cellular, CDPD divides data into packets that each contain sufficient information about its origin and destination to enable it to be transmitted independently of other packets. IP (Internet protocol) is used to handle packet addressing and formatting. Hence, CDPD is a wireless form of packet switching.

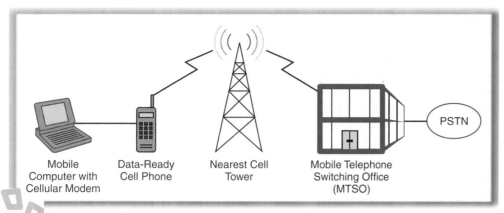

Figure 12-21   Circuit-Switched Cellular Service

CDPD is much slower than wire-based packet-switching services, operating at a maximum rate of 19,200 bps. In addition, it is only capable of routing traffic between two CDPD wireless modems or from one CDPD modem to the Internet. Because CDPD is IP–based, CDPD modems function as IP nodes on the network. No connection to the public switched telephone network exists.

CDPD is a multivendor standard that can be deployed with minimum additional equipment. Because more vendors are providing CDPD services, its coverage area is approximately equivalent to that for current cellular analog networks.

CDPD is leveraged to support *two-way messaging* (enhanced paging) applications. Two-way messaging enables short text messages to be transmitted between wireless transmission devices such as pagers and personal digital assistants (PDAs). Because CDPD includes store-and-forward capabilities, two-way messaging service providers are able to guarantee message delivery to mobile users even if their communication devices are not in service at the time the message is initially sent. Message receipt acknowledgments are also common in CDPD two-way messaging services.

Advanced Radio Data Information Service (ARDIS)

Advanced Radio Data Information Service (ARDIS) is a wireless packet-switched service that was cooperatively developed by IBM and Motorola and is now owned and operated by the American Mobile Satellite Corporation (AMSC). Unlike CDPD, ARDIS is a data-only wireless WAN service.

ARDIS is available in approximately 400 metropolitan areas in Canada, Puerto Rico, the United States, and the Virgin Islands. ARDIS service automatically switches between satellites and terrestrial-based towers, depending on whether subscribers are in rural or metropolitan environments.

Mobitex

The Mobitex network was initially launched by Ericsson in Sweden in 1984. It is now available in the majority of EU (European Union) countries, Australia, Chile, Korea, Nigeria, Singapore, and the United States. Although introduced as a voice and data standard, most Mobitex networks are data only.

Mobitex, like CDPD, is a wireless packet-switched network. Each packet contains sufficient source and destination information to be routed independently, and packet sizes range up to 512 bytes.

Mobitex users are assigned network access numbers that function similarly to telephone numbers on a cellular telephone system. Messages are routed first through the sender's home area, then to a regional exchange (if the receiving device is outside the home area, but in the regional coverage areas), and then to a network control center (if the receiver is outside the regional area).

Metricom

Metricom services are currently limited to the San Francisco Bay area, Seattle, and Washington, DC. It also provides services to more than 100 K–12 schools, 10 universities, and the Sun Microsystems' corporate campus. The Metricom system supports gateways to the Internet and IP–based corporate intranets, X.25 networks, public telephone networks, and LANs. Subscribers typically experience data transfer rates of 28,800 bps.

Metricom may be described as a *microcell spread-spectrum* radio network. It uses frequency-hopping spread spectrum over 162 different frequency channels within the 902- to 928-MHz ISM (industrial, scientific, medical) band.

Metricom services leverage a mesh network containing numerous radio nodes. In metropolitan areas, these are usually attached to utility poles or building rooftops. These nodes communicate with each other as well as with subscriber wireless modems. Subscriber data is sent in packets that have a maximum length of 1,183 bytes. Each packet first travels to the nearest mesh radio node and then is passed to one or more other mesh radio nodes until it reaches a network interconnection center (see Figure 12-22). The network interconnection center is responsible for ensuring that the packet is routed to its intended destination. The packet may be routed over the Internet, through radio mesh nodes to mobile recipients, or through the telephone

Figure 12-22   A Metricom Network

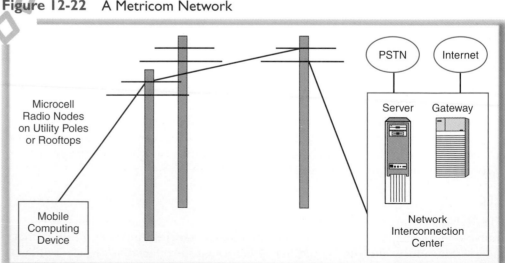

network to a recipient's modem. Packets are typically routed around busy nodes and, as a result, the packets that make up multipacket messages/files may follow different paths from senders to receivers through the Metricom network.

Personal Communication Services (PCS)

Personal communications services (PCS) are discussed in Chapter 5 as a way for second- and third-generation wireless transmission services to deliver transparently a variety of telecommunication services to mobile subscribers at any time, regardless of their geographical location, over digital cellular networks. Voice, two-way messaging, fax, e-mail, file transfer, transaction processing, and database queries may be supported on wireless devices (such as PDAs) by PCS service providers. The convergence of such services via PCS could lead to personal telephone numbers, a single number that would replace the separate home, office, cell phone, pager, and fax numbers that many business professionals must use. Wireless *short message services (SMS)* to PCS units are expected to show explosive growth over the next decade.

Broadband Wireless Services

As noted in Chapter 5, broadband wireless services are emerging that are capable of supporting multiple simultaneous transmissions at speeds ranging from 128 kbps to 155 mbps. Wireless T-1 services are most commonly used and are available from a variety of vendors. Satellite broadband wireless services are also available. (Satellite-based communications are discussed in Chapter 5.)

CHOOSING AMONG WAN SERVICES: BUSINESS CONSIDERATIONS

Businesses have many issues to consider when choosing WAN services. Major issues include availability, data transmission rates, and costs. Other business issues include the ability to transmit a variety of user data (voice, data, and video) via the WAN service, network reliability, security, expandability, and support for mobile users.

Availability

The WAN services discussed in this chapter are not universally available. Many services, especially wireless WAN services, are only available to organizations with operating locations in large urban areas. For some services, only a few geographical areas are served. Organizations that need to interconnect operating locations in both urban and rural areas are likely to have fewer options than those whose offices are only found in large urban centers.

Organizations that rely on WAN services for international networking may have to rely on X.25 PDNs, frame relay services, ISDN, and circuit-switched and leased circuits from common carriers. The creation of wireless international networks poses special challenges for business organizations due to incompatible communication protocols and the current lack of worldwide wireless service providers. Although pure play international wireless WAN may not be feasible to create, wireless segments of otherwise wire-line international networks are viable options.

Data Transmission Rates

There are significant differences in data transmission rates among the WAN services that are available to business subscribers. X.25 networks are among the most pervasive in terms of availability, but they are the slowest of the packet-switching networks.

Frame relay offers higher speeds, but although some organizations may consider frame relay speeds sufficient for interconnecting geographically dispersed LANs, other businesses may find ATM, SONET, and B-ISDN to be more attractive options.

With the exception of broadband wireless WAN services, most wireless WAN service options operate at speeds that are significantly lower than wire-line WAN service options. In fact, many wireless WAN services such as CDPD and ARSDIS operate at speeds that are lower than those that can be achieved via dial-up modem connections.

Cost Considerations

Organizations must carefully evaluate the fixed and variable costs when choosing among WAN services. X.25 and frame relay services are often attractive; additional equipment and installation costs are often quite low, and subscriber charges are based on the volume of data transferred rather than the length of time they are connected to the network. Flat monthly charges are typically assessed for T-1 services, and because of competition, the rates in urban areas may be half of those in rural areas.

Business costs associated with equipping themselves to take advantage of ATM services are often sizable, as are the one-time charges associated with installing SONET access technologies. ISDN installation charges are typically more reasonable, and because of the slower transmission speeds that are supported, ISDN monthly charges are also typically lower.

The cost for wireless WAN services is often greater than their wireless alternatives. For example, wireless T-1 services may cost five to 10 times that of wire-based T-1 services. Also, despite lower transmission speeds, wireless packet-switched networks (such as CDPD) are more expensive on a per packet basis than wire-based packet switching services.

THE INTERNET'S EFFECT ON WAN SERVICES

The Internet is having a significant impact on the evolution of WAN services. An increasing number of organizations are leveraging ISDN, frame relay, and T-1 services to connect to the Internet via ISPs. Other businesses are seeking ways to bypass WAN services to enable them to route voice, data, and video over the Internet.

Like X.25, frame relay, and cell relay networks, TCP/IP—the Internet protocol—is based on packet-switching techniques. Like its packet-switching cousins, the Internet is capable of both connectionless and connection-oriented (e.g., virtual private networks) data transmission. Also, because TCP/IP is indifferent to local connections from the network layer of the OSI model and below, packet-switching networks can function effectively as delivery services for TCP/IP traffic.

Most WAN services, including many wireless WAN services (especially those that are packet oriented) provide interfaces to the Internet and other IP networks. Gateway technologies enable many WAN service providers to leverage the Internet as a multipurpose data transmission mechanism between geographically dispersed subscribers. As mobile commerce (m-commerce) becomes more pervasive, most wireless services will require Internet interfaces.

SUMMARY

Switching is needed to establish connections between senders and receivers across networks. The two major types of wide area network connections are circuit-switched connections and packet-switched connections. Circuit-switched connections are provided by telephone companies to support local and long-distance voice and data services. These involve the creation of a temporary circuit between sender and receiver, information transmission, and circuit termination. When circuit-switched networks are overloaded, subscribers are temporarily unable to access them.

Packet-switching networks provide an alternative to circuit-switched networks. In packet-switched networks, packet assembler/disassembler (PAD) devices are used to packetize data—segment it into structured blocks, frames, or packets that contain a sufficient amount of overhead information to ensure delivery to intended recipients. Both connectionless and connection-oriented packet-switching networks are available. In connectionless packet networks, the packets that make up multipacket messages or files may follow different paths through the network to receivers. In connection-oriented packet networks, the packets that make up multipacket messages or files follow one another in sequence through the network from sender to receiver over temporary or permanent virtual circuits. Virtual circuits are similar to the switched connections found in circuit-switched networks.

X.25, frame relay, and ATM are the three most common types of packet-switching networks. X.25 is the oldest and slowest of the three. X.25 network throughput is limited by its use of point-to-point error detection and correction. Both frame relay and ATM leverage reliable digital circuits to connect their switching nodes and use point-to-point error detection with end-to-end error correction to enable higher levels of network throughput than X.25. ATM achieves faster transmission speeds than frame relay through the use of fixed-length cells rather than variable-length frames and because ATM switching nodes are connected by very high-speed optical circuits.

Other wire-line WAN services include T-1 services, synchronous optical network (SONET) services, and both narrowband and broadband ISDN. Wireless WAN services are also available. These include wireless T-1 services, circuit-switched wireless services, cellular digital packet data (CDPD), Advanced Radio Data Information Service (ARDIS), Mobitex, Metricom, and personal communication services (PCS).

Businesses have many issues to consider when choosing WAN services. Major issues include availability, data transmission rates, and costs. Other business issues include the ability to transmit a variety of user data (voice, data, and video) via the WAN service, network reliability, security, expandability, and support for mobile users.

The Internet is affecting the evolution of WAN services. An increasing number of businesses require seamless interfaces between the Internet and frame relay, cell relay, and T-1 services. Wireless WAN services also require Internet gateways to support mobile workers and mobile commerce applications.

KEY TERMS

- asynchronous transfer mode (ATM)
- call setup packet
- cell
- cell relay
- circuit-switched network
- connectionless
- connection-oriented
- datagram
- frame assembler/dissembler (FRAD)
- framing
- high-level data link control (HDLC)
- Link Access Procedure–Balanced (LAPB)
- network-network interface (NNI)
- packet
- packet assembler/disassembler (PAD)
- packet layer protocol (PLP)
- packetizing
- permanent virtual circuit (PVC)
- switched virtual circuit (SVC)
- user-network interface (UNI)
- virtual channel
- virtual circuit
- virtual circuit table
- virtual path
- wavelength division multiplexing (WDM)

REVIEW QUESTIONS

1. Describe the three phases of circuit-switched communications.
2. What are the characteristics and limitations of circuit-switched networks?
3. What are packets? What is packetizing? Why are frame check fields included in packets?
4. Compared to circuit-switched networks, what are the relative advantages and disadvantages of packet-switching networks?
5. What is a packet assembler/disassembler (PAD)? What is a packet switch?
6. What are the positive and negative aspects of datagram services in packet-switching networks?
7. What is a virtual circuit? What is the role of virtual circuit tables in a packet-switching network?
8. What are the differences between connectionless and connection-oriented packet networks?
9. Describe the roles of call setup packets and logical channel numbers in packet-switching networks.
10. Compare switched virtual circuits (SVCs) and permanent virtual circuits (PVCs).
11. How is congestion control handled in packet-switching networks?
12. What is a packet distribution network (PDN)? Why are PDNs often called X.25 networks or value-added networks (VANs)? What does the X.25 standard define?
13. What is LAPB? What is PLP?
14. Identify and briefly describe the importance of each of the following ITU standards: X.3, X.21, X.28, X.32, X.75, and X.121.
15. What are the advantages and disadvantages of PDNs?
16. What is point-to-point error detection and correction?
17. Compared to X.25, what are the relative advantages and disadvantages of frame relay?
18. What is point-to-point error detection? What is end-to-end error correction?
19. What is LAP-D?
20. How is congestion control addressed in frame relay networks?
21. What are the advantages and disadvantages of frame relay networks?
22. What are the differences between ATM and frame relay?
23. What is the difference between a virtual channel and a virtual path?
24. What is the difference between UNI and NNI?
25. What functions are performed at the ATM adaptation layer (AAL) of the ATM protocol stack?
26. What are the advantages and disadvantages of ATM?
27. What are T-1 services? What interface equipment is used by businesses to access T-1 services?
28. What are SONET services?
29. What is wavelength division multiplexing (WDM)?
30. What is ISDN? What is the difference between basic rate interface (BRI) and primary rate interface (PRI)?
31. What is Broadband ISDN (B-ISDN)?
32. Briefly describe each of the following wireless WAN services.
    a. circuit-switched cellular services
    b. cellular digital packet data (CDPD)
    c. Advanced Radio Data Information Service (ARDIS)
    d. Mobitex
    e. Metricom

 f. personal communication services (PCS)

 g. broadband wireless

33. Identify and briefly discuss the major issues that businesses consider when choosing WAN services.

34. How has the Internet affected WAN services?

PROBLEMS AND EXERCISES

1. The following formula is used to calculate transmission efficiency (TE):

$$TE = D \ / \ O + D \qquad \text{where: } D = \text{number of data bytes}$$
$$O = \text{number of overhead bytes}$$

 Using the information provided in this chapter, calculate the transmission efficiency of X.25, frame relay, and ATM.

2. How are customers charged for ISDN services in your region? What are the charges for basic rate interface (BRI) and primary rate interface (PRI) services in your region?

3. Use the Internet to research ISDN terminal adapters and other major types of ISDN access equipment (e.g., ISDN modems). Identify major vendors, products, and product costs. Summarize your findings in an executive summary or PowerPoint presentation.

4. Research the availability and costs of T-1 services in your region. Use the Internet to research T-1 services access equipment (such as T-1 multiplexors, T-1 channel banks, and T-1 switches). Identify major vendors, products, and costs. Summarize your findings in an executive summary or PowerPoint presentation.

5. Research the availability of X.25 and frame relay services in your region. How are subscribers charged for X.25 and frame relay services by service providers in your region?

6. Use the Internet to research frame relay standards. Identify and briefly describe newly adopted frame relay standards as well as proposed standards that are being considered for adoption. Summarize your findings in an executive summary or PowerPoint presentation.

7. Research the availability of ATM and SONET services in your region. Use the Internet to research ATM and SONET services access equipment. Identify major vendors, products, and costs. Summarize your findings in an executive summary or PowerPoint presentation.

8. Use the Internet to research ATM standards. Identify and briefly describe recently adopted ATM standards as well as proposed standards that are being considered for adoption. Summarize your findings in an executive summary or PowerPoint presentation.

9. Develop a table that compares the following services in the areas of availability, error detection and correction, and transmission speed: X.25, frame relay, and ATM.

10. Research the availability of personal communication services (PCS) in your region. Identify the applications that are supported by PCS carriers in your region (e.g., Internet access or two-way messaging). What are the charges for PCS services in your region?

11. Use the Internet to research mobile commerce (m-commerce) applications. Identify the wireless services and communications devices that are needed to support m-commerce. What type of growth is expected for m-commerce during the

next 5 years? What are the implications of m-commerce for wireless WAN services and service providers?

12. Use the Internet to research ARDIS services and their associated costs. What are the advantages and limitations of ARDIS for business subscribers?

13. Use the Internet to identify cost ranges for ATM network adapters and ATM LAN switches. Develop an equipment cost estimate for a 25-node ATM LAN for an engineering firm that requires videoconferencing support and the exchange of complex CAD/CAM and engineering drawings.

14. Use the Internet to research the cost differences between traditional and wireless T-1 services. Summarize your findings in an executive summary or PowerPoint presentation.

15. Research the availability of broadband wireless services in your region. Summarize your findings in an executive summary or PowerPoint presentation.

Telematics

Telematics (also called *infomobility*) refers to the merger of GPS receivers, GIS mapping, wireless communications, and the Internet with automobiles and other vehicular systems. Car manufacturers such as General Motors, BMW, Ford, Mercedes-Benz, and Fiat, already offer telematics systems in some of their models, especially in their luxury cars.

Magneti Marelli, a subsidiary of Italian manufacturer Fiat has designed a navigation system called *Route Planner,* which integrates functions such as navigator, points of interest, and traffic information to assist the driver. It also provides entertainment functions such as satellite radio, CD–based telematics applications, voice recognition, emergency assistance, and medical assistance. Route Planner can be extremely valuable to tourists and first-time travelers to an area by providing in-vehicle information about how to get from the rental car agency to their travel destination or hotel.

The first factory-installed Magneti Marelli system is called *Connect,* an option for both the Alfa Romeo 147 and the Fiat Doblo. This system provides roadside and medical assistance, route information, and legal assistance in case of an accident. It even enables drivers and passengers to make hotel reservations en route.

Magneti Marelli has also developed a prototype "Internet car" system, which provides a JavaOSGI framework to allow remote software management, Internet access to car portal Web pages, and Internet-based services that include map on demand and traffic Webcams. It is also integrating wireless connectivity and wired optical connectivity. Viasat, a joint venture between Magneti Marelli and Telecom Italia, has also developed an Internet car prototype, which includes an in-vehicle PC, a GPS–based navigator, a radio, a cell phone, and a touch-screen monitor/control center.

The United Kingdom has also been busy developing telematics applications for their road system. The developer, SBD, has been working with Toyota since 2000 on the system. The system combines the functions of route planning and congestion avoidance warning in the new Toyota Avensis and Corolla models for 2002. The system has 1,500 different event codes to provide drivers with as much information as possible about traffic and alternative routes.

In April 2000, the American Automobile Association (AAA) launched a wholly owned subsidiary called *Response Services Center* that is capable of delivering wireless mobile emergency assistance to AAA members. It supports the delivery of mapping applications to mobile client smart phones, wireless PDAs, in-vehicle telematics units, and other mapping devices. Microsoft Corporation provides support for the Response Service Center's Car.NET Framework, the software that enables AAA to provide telematics applications for its members. Microsoft also provides its Automotive Mobile Information Server (MIS) and will develop a version of WindowsCE for automotive platforms.

In June 2001, BMW launched the first "intelligent" car in Asia, which has a GPS receiver and a digital map on CD-ROM that can help the driver to find/follow a desired route through synthesized voice directions. It also allows drivers to preprogram a target destination and then just follow the car's movements by viewing a color map on an in-vehicle monitor; it can provide alternative routes to the destination in case the driver gets lost or misses a turn.

General Motors (GM) was the first company to bring in-car navigation systems to U.S. drivers when it introduced its OnStar system in 1996. GM's OnStar system integrates GPS and wireless technology to bring personalized service 24 hours daily, 365 days a year. Its service includes automatic notification of air bag deployment, stolen vehicle tracking, emergency and roadside assistance, and remote diagnostics. OnStar is now available on 32 of GM's 54 models, including its Cadillac models, and its future looks bright. Industry experts predict that more than 10 million American motorists will subscribe to telematics services by the end of 2004 and that this number will climb to more than 40 million by 2010. Worldwide estimates call for more than 100 million telematics services subscribers by 2010.

Telematics systems have been lurking around the automobile market for some time. However, their adoption has been slow primarily because the benefits telematics systems offered did not justify the high prices of them. In fact, there is the lingering question about whether customers are willing to pay for in-vehicle information that they can get on the radio or find in their laptop, PDA, or PC before getting into the car. Making telematics systems affordable is one of the key points to success in the marketplace. This is a difficult task because they require an intensive development effort to adapt the system to the vehicle environment. The vehicle environment is often much harsher than most computing environments because of vibration, humidity, dust, and abrupt changes of temperature.

Rental car agencies have also contributed to the telematics debate by using these applications to track how their vehicles are actually used (or abused) by the individuals who rent them. Telematics has been used by some rental car agencies to track driving speed and off-road use of their vehicles. This has drawn the ire of some renters facing high surcharges for driving at excessive speeds or driving in rough terrains in violation of their rental contracts. The

GPS–based systems being used enable rental car agencies to know the exact location of each telematics-equipped vehicle in its fleet at any point in time. These systems can also be used to continually monitor a vehicle's speed and transmit the information back to a central computer. This enables the company to flag the records of renters who promised to abide by posted speed limits on their rental contracts and to add contract-stipulated surcharges to customer invoices when the vehicle is returned to the travel agency. Some renters feel that the rental companies that use telematics in this fashion are violating the privacy of renters or are engaging in a form of price gouging. Rental car agencies maintain that they are just taking advantage of these technologies to protect their investment and to reduce the wear and tear of their fleet of vehicles caused by renter abuse.

CASE QUESTIONS

1. Telematics applications have traditionally been offered in luxury vehicles as an interesting high-tech option. Some automobile industry critics argue that they should be standard features in all new vehicles because they have the potential to reduce accidents and save lives. Other industry experts counter that in-vehicle telematics may contribute to higher accident rates by distracting drivers from paying full attention to their primary duty behind the wheel: driving. Identify the arguments on both sides of the "telematics and safety" issue. Which side do you feel has the stronger arguments? Why?

2. Use the Internet to identify trends in telematics service features and subscription rates.

Summarize your findings in a paper or PowerPoint presentation.

3. Use the Internet to find out how telematics is being used by trucking and logistics companies. What competitive advantages are being realized by trucking and logistics companies through the telematics applications they are using?

4. Use the Internet to find out more about the controversial use of telematics applications by rental car agencies. Are such uses an invasion of privacy or a means to extract higher fees from customers? Are rental car agencies just protecting their investments? Outline the arguments on both sides. Which side do you feel has the stronger set of arguments? Why?

SOURCES

Anonymous. "Telematics Device Steers Drivers away from Traffic Holdups." *Professional Engineering* (January 16, 2002, Issue 15, Volume 1, p. 61).

Lenatti, C. "The Telematics Challenge." *Information-Week* (April 1, 2002). Retrieved July 6, 2002 from www.informationweek.com/story/IWK20020328S0017.

Luccio, M. "Telematics Today: Smart Cars, Informed Drivers." *GPS World* (August 2001, Volume 12, Issue 8, pp. 28–89).

Neely, L. "Driving the Future." *Electronics* (February 18, 2002, Volume 48, Issue 8, pp. 4–5).

Note: For more information on WAN services, see an additional case on the Web site, www.prenhall.com/stamper, "Service Level Agreements."

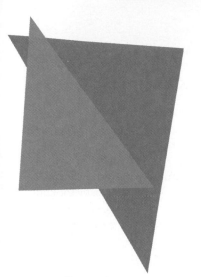

Internetworking Technologies

After studying this chapter, you should be able to:

■ Identify and briefly describe different ways networks can be interconnected.

■ Describe the characteristics and functionality of each of the following internetworking technologies: repeaters, bridges, routers, and gateways.

■ Identify and briefly describe several major routing algorithms and routing protocols.

■ Describe the characteristics of backbone networks.

■ Identify and briefly describe the functionality of switching technologies.

■ Identify and briefly describe remote access technologies for LANs.

INTRODUCTION

By this point in the book, it should be quite apparent that computing environments for most business organizations are complex. The computing resources found in larger organizations are typically diverse, and business computer networks can range from a small LAN comprised of a handful of microcomputers to multiple LANs and WANs connecting hundreds or thousands of different computers: microcomputers, minicomputers, mainframes, and supercomputers. Today, it is common for a large organization to have many LANs, a WAN, and connections to public data networks (e.g., X.25, frame relay or ATM) and the Internet. Multiple network architectures (centralized, distributed, and client/server) may be used by organizations with geographically dispersed operating locations. To support such complex data communication environments, business organizations leverage a variety of internetworking technologies. These enable businesses to make better use of their hardware and software resources and allow users to communicate more easily.

    Internetworking technologies make it possible to connect one LAN to another LAN, to establish LAN–host connections, to create intranets and extranets, to take advantage of frame relay or cell relay services from carriers, or to connect two or more different WANs. Several of the data communication technologies discussed in the previous chapter have important roles in establishing connections among multiple networks. These include PADs (packet assembler/disassemblers) and packet switches, FRADs (frame relay access devices) and frame relay switches, ATM switches, and middle-tier servers in n-tiered client/server networks.

You have also been previously introduced to the important role played by routers in the operation of the Internet (in Chapter 4). In this chapter, we take a closer look at routers and other major internetworking technologies leveraged by business organizations to create enterprise-wide networks, including repeaters, bridges, gateways, and switches. We will also discuss the remote access technologies that enable teleworkers and mobile workers to access corporate networks and computing resources.

As you read this chapter, it will become increasingly apparent that network managers in business organizations are concerned with internetworking technologies because of their potential to maximize network performance. Large LANs, for example, may be broken into smaller segments interconnected by bridges, routers, or switches. This improves communication within each segment because fewer devices compete for the bandwidth of the shared communication medium. When servers are isolated on a single segment, response times to user requests for the shared computing resources they manage can be minimized, and overall network throughput can be increased. Network performance may also be enhanced by connecting servers to very high-speed backbone networks that can be accessed by user workstations via routers. Bridges, routers, and switches—three key internetworking technologies that enable segmentation and the isolation of network resources—also help to control network congestion by only forwarding frames/packets that should be forwarded from one network segment to another. In larger networks, routers help to address network traffic congestion in similar fashion to packet and frame relay switches (discussed in Chapter 12) by determining the "best" route for an individual packet to its destination based on prevailing network conditions.

INTERNETWORKING TECHNOLOGIES AND THE OSI REFERENCE MODEL

Throughout this text, we have frequently referred to the OSI reference model. We will continue to do so in this chapter because most network interconnections are established at the physical, data link, and network layers of the OSI reference model.

What do we mean when we say the connection interface is made at the physical, data link, or network layers? An interface that operates at the physical layer must be sensitive to signals on the medium. One that operates at the data link layer must be aware of data link protocol formats (e.g., packet, frame, or cell layouts). One that operates at the network layer must use a common network layer protocol (such as IP) and be able to route messages to the next node along the path to its destination. The interconnection at a specific layer must know the implementation details of that layer. We begin by looking at physical layer interconnections.

Physical Layer Connections

As signals are transmitted through a medium, the signals weaken. This is called **attenuation**. Signals may also become distorted during transmission from sender to receiver by noise and other error sources identified in Chapter 6. Both attenuation and distortion can contribute to a signal becoming unintelligible to a receiver unless it (the sig-

attenuation A weakening of a signal (decrease of signal strength) as it travels through a communication medium. The extent to which a signal attenuates is a function of distance traveled and characteristics of the medium.

nal) can be amplified or regenerated. In digital data communication systems, signal regenerators that are generically called **repeaters** are placed at regular intervals to amplify or regenerate the signals that they carry. In analog transmission systems, signals may be amplified but not regenerated. In most instances, amplification simply strengthens the signal and also amplifies any noise (errors) that has crept into the transmission. This is illustrated in Figure 13-1(a). When digital transmission is used, it is typically possible to regenerate the original signal and restore its original strength and values. Because a digital signal has only two states, a 0 or a 1, a regenerator can examine an incoming signal, decide which of the two states the signal represents, and restore the signal to its original value and strength, as illustrated in Figure 13-1(b). In sum, both distortion and attenuation may be addressed by the signal regenerators used in digital transmissions; however, those used for analog transmissions are typically limited to only overcoming attenuation.

A hardware device that amplifies or regenerates an attenuated signal at the physical layer is called a *repeater*. The function of a repeater is similar to that of some non-electronic data transmission techniques. You may be familiar with communication techniques such as semaphore flags. Semaphores are line-of-sight transmissions. If the message must be transmitted over long distances, relay stations are necessary. If station A in Figure 13-2 needs to transmit a message to station D, the signaler at station B reads the signal sent from station A and resends the message to station C, where the message is repeated and sent to station D. At each relay station, the signal is essentially amplified. If an error in transcribing or transmitting the message is made at any point, the error is propagated to subsequent stations.

In a similar manner, repeaters can be used to extend the length of the communication medium on a LAN. As Figure 13-3 illustrates, repeaters are found at the physical layer of the OSI model. As a physical layer device, a repeater must know and obey all the physical layer conventions regarding signaling and connections (such as those

repeater A communications device that amplifies analog signals or regenerates digital signals in order to extend the transmission distance. Repeaters work at the physical layer of the OSI reference model and can be used to tie two similar LANs together. Repeaters are available for both electronic and optical signals.

Figure 13-1   Signal Amplification and Regeneration

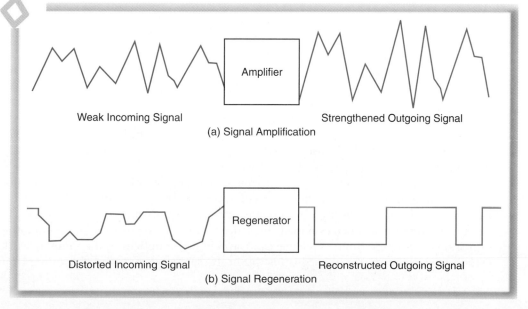

Weak Incoming Signal   Strengthened Outgoing Signal

Amplifier

(a) Signal Amplification

Regenerator

Distorted Incoming Signal   Reconstructed Outgoing Signal

(b) Signal Regeneration

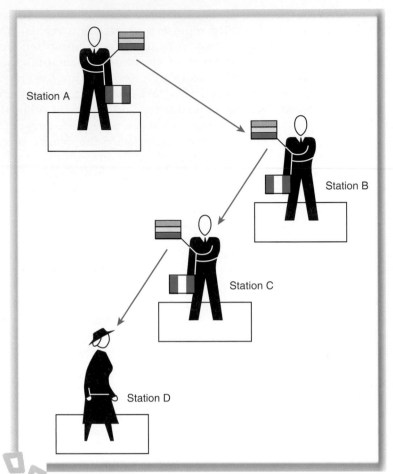

Figure 13-2   Signal Relay Stations

specified by the RS-232 standard). Repeaters are commonly used in LANs to extend the distance the signal can travel over the medium and still maintain signal strength. LAN standards limit the number of repeaters that can be used for a single LAN and, therefore, limit the maximum length of the LAN medium.

Amplifiers and shared media hubs are other physical layer connectivity technologies. Amplifiers are used to strengthen analog signals. Like repeaters, amplifiers can be used to address signal attenuation. Shared media hubs, patch panels, and powered punchdown blocks used in LANs typically include repeater capabilities and thus may also be categorized as physical layer connection devices.

It must be noted that some industry experts argue that physical layer connection devices should be omitted from discussions of internetworking technologies because they lack the intelligence to distinguish one network segment or subnet from another. The absence of such intelligence essentially relegates them to being devices for regenerating signals; extending the distance signals can travel between devices in the same network; creating two or more physical segments within the same network; and converting from

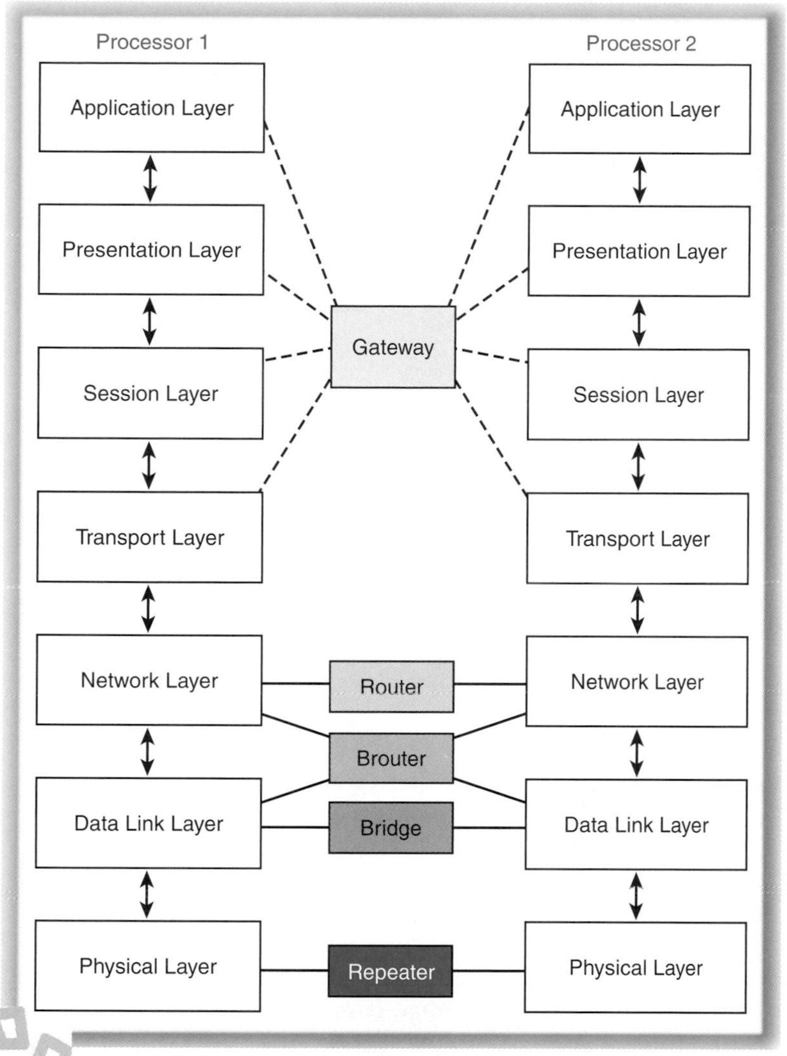

Figure 13-3   Internetworking Technologies and the OSI Reference Model

the signal/media type used in one network segment to a different signal/media type used in a second network segment (for example, from fiber optic cable to unshielded twisted pair). Although there is considerable merit in these arguments, the use of repeaters and other physical layer connection devices to interconnect network segments provides the underlying rationale for discussing them alongside other more intelligent and sophisticated internetworking devices such as bridges, routers, and gateways.

Data Link Layer Connections

Three functions of the data link layer of the OSI reference model are delineation of data, error detection, and address formatting. A data link protocol is concerned with getting data from the current node to the next node. A message may pass through several data

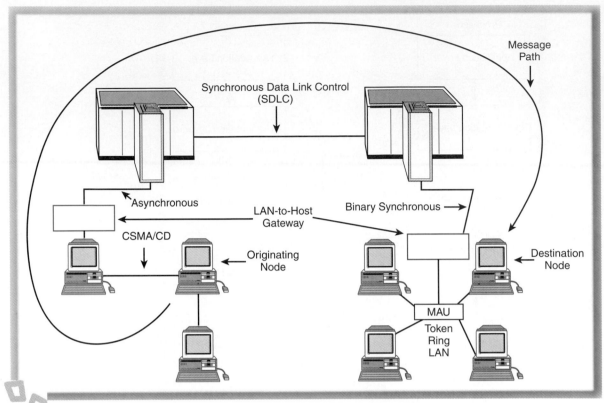

Figure 13-4   Message Passing Through Several Different Data Link Protocols

link protocols on its path from the source node to the destination node, as illustrated in Figure 13-4. In this example, a message passes from a LAN data link protocol to a WAN data link protocol and back to another (in this case different) LAN data link protocol.

A key internetworking technology that operates at the data link layer is called a **bridge**. Bridges are found at the data link layer of the OSI model (see Figure 13-3). Bridges are most commonly used in LANs to overcome limitations in distance or in number of workstations per LAN. A bridge is seldom necessary in WANs because they do not have distance limitations; however, remote bridges may be used to interconnect geographically dispersed LANs. Routers and other network layer technologies are most frequently used to interconnect two or more WANs.

Bridges possess more intelligence than physical layer connection technologies. A bridge examines each of the data link layer frames transmitted by devices attached to each of the two LANs that it interconnects. This examination, called *filtering*, involves the determination of each frame's intended recipient and which of the two LANs the recipient is physically attached to. For some frames, the intended recipient is physically attached to the same LAN as the frame's sender; in this case, the bridge may have little or nothing more to do with them. If the intended recipient is not physically attached to the same LAN as the sender, the bridge initiates a *forwarding* process that culminates in the transmission of the frame onto the other network. In some cases, forwarding requires the bridge to reformat the sender's frame before transmitting it onto the other LAN.

bridge An internetworking technology that connects two LAN segments at the data link layer of the OSI reference. A bridge may be used to connect LAN segments that use similar or dissimilar data link protocols. A bridge may be inserted into a network to segment it, contain traffic within segments, and improve performance.

Bridges originally connected LANs of the same type, such as two token ring LANs or two Ethernet LANs. (Both token ring and Ethernet LANs are discussed more fully in Chapter 8.) These early bridges indiscriminately forwarded all message traffic (all frames) from one LAN onto the other LAN and thus were usually employed to overcome the maximum number of workstations that could be included in a single LAN. Today's bridge technology is more sophisticated and can connect LANs using different data link protocols, such as bridging a token ring LAN to an Ethernet LAN. In addition, bridges now selectively forward frames. Frames transmitted between two nodes physically attached to the same LAN are ignored by the bridge; only frames that originate in one LAN but are addressed to a computing device in the other LAN are forwarded by a bridge, as illustrated in Figure 13-5.

Note that although a bridge is found at the data link layer of the OSI model, the bridging process requires data in either LAN to be sent from the data link layer down to the physical layer, over the communication medium to a physical layer, and back up to the data link layer. Technically, a bridge is connected to each LAN at the physical layer and receives each frame transmitted by each computer in both LANs. When the bridge receives a frame, the frame passes from the bridge's physical layer to its data link layer. The bridge then examines the destination address in the frame header to determine whether the intended recipient is located in the same LAN as the sender or in the other LAN. After determining the frame recipient's LAN, the bridge passes the message to the proper LAN using the services of the physical layer connection.

Many organizations have chosen to replace bridges with layer 2 switches, which enable multiple simultaneous transmissions to take place within and across the LANs they connect. This capability enables more data throughput (the volume of data transmitted among networked devices in a given time period) across the data communication medium than is possible with traditional bridges. Like bridges, layer 2 switches perform bridging functions based on the physical addresses of the

Figure 13-5   Bridge Packet Forwarding

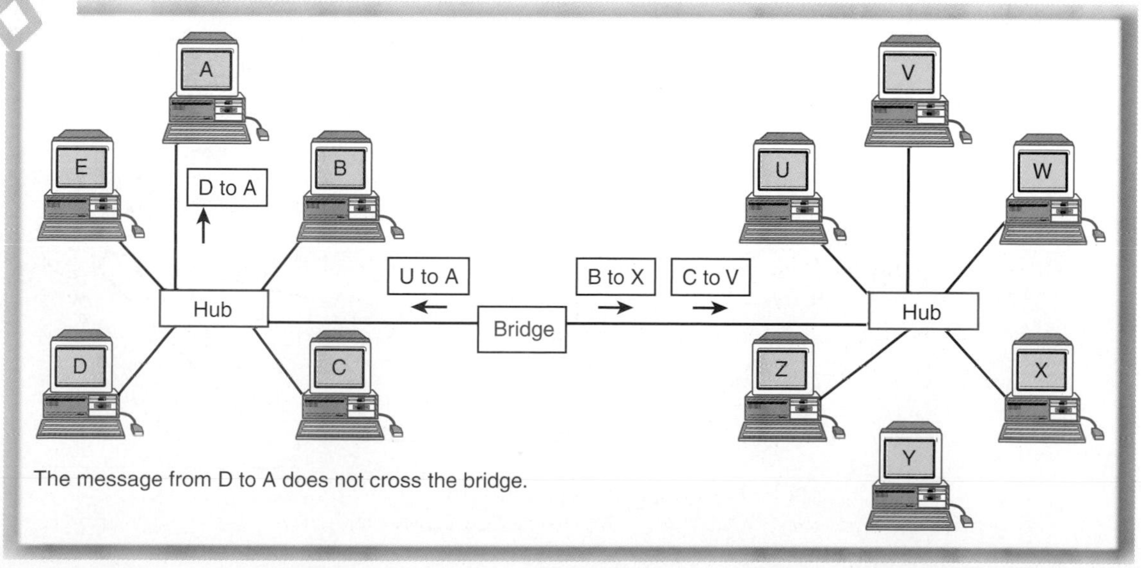

The message from D to A does not cross the bridge.

router An internetworking device that uses network addresses to forward data packets from one local area network (LAN) or wide area network (WAN) to another. Based on routing tables and routing protocols, routers read the network address in each transmitted frame and make a decision on how to send it based on the "best" (most expedient) route by considering traffic load, line costs, speed, bad lines, etc. Routers work at the network layer of the OSI reference model. Routers can be used to segment LANs in order to balance data traffic and to filter traffic for security purposes. Routers are also used at the edge of the network to interconnect remote offices.

sender and the intended recipient. Layer 2 switches are discussed more fully later in the chapter.

Network Layer Connections

The network layer of the OSI reference model is responsible for packet routing and the collection of accounting information. Internetworking technologies at the network layer are responsible for routing an incoming message for another node onto an appropriate outbound path. Networks use a variety of routing algorithms (discussed later in the chapter), and multiple routing paths may be available in some networks, as illustrated in Figure 13-6. Thus, a message for node X that arrives at node B in Figure 13-6 will arrive at the physical layer and be moved up through the data link layer to the network layer. If the packet is not intended for an application that is directly attached to node B, the network layer routing process determines the outbound path for the message and sends it down to the data link layer, which formats the packet with the proper data link control data (perhaps a data link protocol different from that of the arriving message). The data link layer then passes the frame (packets are called *frames* at the data link layer) down to the physical layer for transmission to the next node along the path to the final destination.

A key interconnection technology that operates at the network layer of the OSI model is called a **router** (see Figure 13-3). A router is not sensitive to the details of the data link and physical layers. Thus, a router can be used to connect different types of networks, such as a token ring LAN to an Ethernet LAN or a LAN to a WAN service such as a frame relay network. A router examines the destination address in the packet header, determines the route the packet should follow to reach that address, and pro-

Figure 13-6   Several Routing Paths in a Network

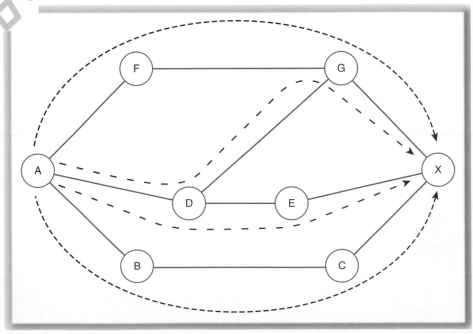

vides the addressing required by the network and data link layers for delivery. For two nodes to exchange data using a router, they must share a common network layer protocol. Today, most network architectures support IP (Internet Protocol), the network layer protocol of the TCP/IP protocol stack, in addition to network layer protocols that are unique to particular network architectures (such as packet layer protocol [PLP] in X.25 networks). This enables most network architectures to interface with the Internet.

Switches with routing capabilities have been implemented by some organizations. Such switches, known as *layer 3 switches*, are described more fully later in the chapter.

Connections Above the Network Layer

Network connections that operate at the transport layer or above are generically called **gateways** (see Figure 13-3). A gateway is used to connect dissimilar networks by providing conversion from one network protocol to another. In making this interconnection, the gateway must accept packets from the LAN, extract the data from the packets, and format the data in a packet according to the WAN protocol, or vice versa. As noted in Chapter 11, gateway technologies are often required to connect LANs to IBM SNA networks because of limited routing capabilities of SDLC (synchronous data link control) packet formats used in SNA. Similar measures must be taken for other

gateway A computer or internetworking device that performs protocol conversion between different types of networks or applications. Gateways function at the transport layer (and above) in the OSI reference model.

Figure 13-7(a)   Gateway Connecting a Token Ring LAN and a SNA Network

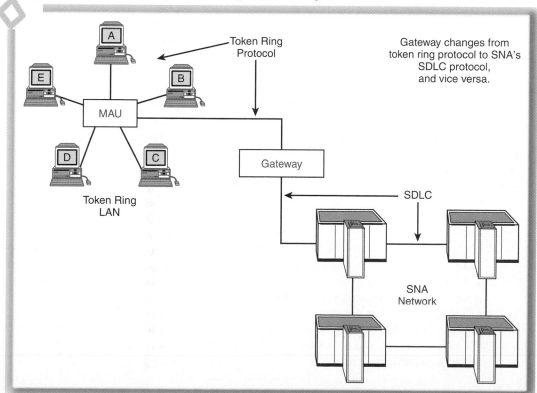

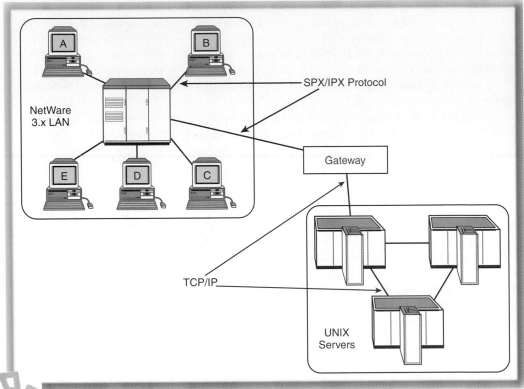

Figure 13-7(b) Gateway Connecting a NetWare LAN and a UNIX Network

nonroutable protocols. The use of a gateway to connect a token ring LAN to a SNA network is illustrated in Figure 13-7.

Which Interface Is Right for You?

We have introduced four network interconnection capabilities: repeaters, bridges, routers, and gateways. How do you choose the right one? In general, you should choose the connection at the lowest OSI level possible. Thus, a repeater is usually preferable to a bridge, and a bridge is usually preferable to a router. As you move up the OSI layers, your connection must be more intelligent and do more work, and it is likely to have a lower packet exchange rate. These are not the only deciding factors, however.

A bridge can replace a repeater, and a router can replace a repeater or a bridge; however, the opposite is not always true. A repeater cannot always substitute for a bridge, and a bridge cannot always substitute for a router. If you have the option of using a repeater, you might instead choose to use a bridge. This decision makes sense if the bridge can handle the message traffic and if you already have the bridge components. A bridge also allows some LAN isolation capability that a repeater does not provide. Thus, you might choose a bridge over a repeater to provide an extra level of network security.

BUSINESS RATIONALE FOR INTERNETWORKING TECHNOLOGIES

As noted in Chapters 7 through 9, LANs are fundamental building blocks in today's enterprise-wide networks. By definition, a LAN serves a limited geographic area, and most LAN specifications place a limit on the maximum distance between devices connected to the same LAN. Companies that have LANs in geographically separated locations, or LANs that cover distances longer than the maximum allowed, often have a need for inter–LAN exchanges. Users on one LAN may want to exchange e-mail messages with users on the other LAN, or a user on one LAN may want to use resources located on another LAN. Internetworking technologies enable businesses to overcome distance limitations outlined in LAN specifications.

Distance limitations or geographic separation is not the only reason for having multiple LANs within the same organization. Differences in departmental computing requirements are often another powerful rationale for having a multi–LAN environment. A company that is interested in department-level computing might implement a LAN for each department or for specific groups of departments. For example, a computer software manufacturer may go to great lengths to protect the integrity of new products that are being developed. Often, details of new developments are not shared with employees unless they are directly involved with developing a new product. Having separate LANs allows the company to separate functions and provides additional security of information. Among the software company's departments, there might be a LAN shared by new software development and documentation employees, another for employees who provide technical support for the company's existing software products, one for accounting, one for personnel, and one for marketing. This separation/segmentation reduces the likelihood that new software being developed will inadvertently or intentionally be released prematurely to customers by technical support or marketing employees. Likewise, personnel information can be more easily protected if it is isolated on a separate LAN. Separating/segmenting LANs can help ensure that employees in different departments have access to resources that they need to perform their jobs and ensure that they cannot readily access data or information in other LANs that are not directly related to their job functions. Internetworking technologies, however, will enable employees whose computers are physically connected to one LAN to access resources located in other LANs that they have a legitimate right to use.

A third reason for inter–LAN connections is to consolidate independent LANs that were formed in an ad hoc manner in order to establish enterprise-wide networks or to enable resources located in one LAN to be accessed by users in other LANs. Over the past decade, many colleges and universities have interconnected LANs that were initially implemented independently by the departments or colleges of computer science, business, engineering, and nursing to serve the needs of their students and faculty. Internetworking technologies have allowed universities to share resources initially purchased and installed by one department/college with appropriate students and faculty in other areas.

Another reason for forming several small LANs rather than one large one is limitations on medium capacity. LANs supporting graphically intensive applications, such as CAE (computer-aided engineering), videoconferencing, and multimedia applications, need to send high volumes of full-motion video and sound data in short amounts of time. Such applications can best be supported on slower LANs operating at 10 or 16 mbps when these are segmented in a manner that limits the number of workstations competing for the shared bandwidth of the communication medium. Despite the motivation to create several LANs, the need for inter–LAN message exchanges demands appropriate internetworking technologies.

A fifth reason for having multiple LANs is the number of users per LAN. A LAN with hundreds of users might provide worse performance than the same LAN with dozens of users. Ideally, LAN administrators seek to maintain the responsiveness of a LAN (as measured by response times and network throughput) even when more users are added. Responsiveness may be maintained by adding more resources to an existing LAN—more memory, more disks, or another server—or by splitting the LAN into two or more smaller LANs. When splitting a LAN, the administrator strives for a proper balance of users and resources; however, a perfect balance is not always attainable because of distance, physical location, or differences in work-group sizes. Because inter–LAN communication involves more overhead than intra–LAN communication, an administrator must consider grouping users and resources so the number of inter–LAN messages is reduced. Members of a department or work group often communicate with each other more than with members of other departments or work groups. Thus, splitting an oversize LAN often results in a configuration split along departmental or work-group lines.

Companies may also have several WANs. Multiple WANs often arise from corporate mergers and acquisitions. When two companies combine, each may have a WAN already in place. These WANs sometimes use different vendors' network architectures. After the merger, it is usually desirable to create a single WAN; however, preexisting incompatibilities may make it necessary to retain separate WANs that are interconnected via routers or gateways. Sometimes, independent networks are started in regional areas and later need to be connected to form national and international networks. A company may also want to connect its network to external networks such as the Internet.

Different WANs also can arise from the need to support different work tasks. A bank might use one vendor's hardware and network architecture to set up a network of automated teller machines and a different network to support its back office, platform, and administrative applications. Similarly, a manufacturing company may use one type of hardware and network to support research and development operations and another for sales and administrative purposes.

There are many good reasons for having several different networks in an organization. At some point, however, the value of integrating these separate networks into one enterprise network is recognized. As a generic model for connecting separate networks, we use LANs as an example of both LAN-to-LAN and WAN-to-WAN connections. This is appropriate because the first two types of connections, repeaters and bridges, are most common in LANs. Routers are common to both LANs and WANs. Now that we have introduced the basic types of network interconnections and have outlined the business rationale for their use, we examine some of the major internetworking technologies in greater detail.

REPEATERS: CONNECTING LAN SEGMENTS

As noted in Chapter 12, there are several major LAN architectures, and the specifications for each include a distance restriction. The distance limitation for a particular LAN architecture essentially specifies how far apart two LAN–attached devices can be before signal attenuation is likely to be a problem. For example, one of the IEEE 802.3 standards for Ethernet LANs, 10Base5, specifies a maximum medium distance of

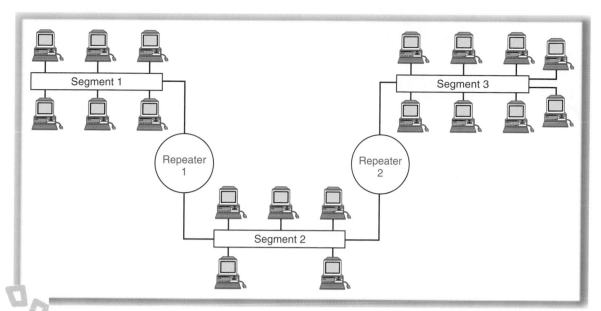

Figure 13-8   Repeaters Connecting Three LAN Segments

500 meters per LAN segment. To span longer distances, a repeater can be used to connect two segments. The standard allows for a maximum of four repeaters, for a total distance of 2,500 meters per LAN. Two repeaters connecting three segments in an IEEE 802.3 10Base5 network is illustrated in Figure 13-8. The use of repeaters to connect LAN segments located on different floors of the same building is illustrated in Figure 13-9.

The primary function of a repeater is to overcome signal attenuation. It may, however, also compensate for signal distortion. Weak signals can result in transmission errors. A received signal must be sufficiently strong for the receiver's electrical circuitry to

Figure 13-9   Using Repeaters to Connect Four LAN Segments on Two Floors of a Building

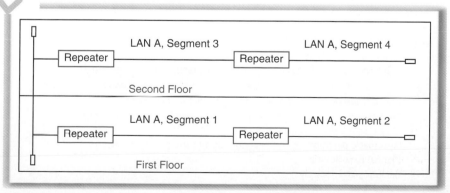

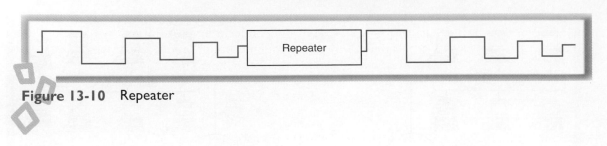

Figure 13-10   Repeater

detect and correctly interpret the signal. If the signal is too weak, it may not be detected or correctly interpreted. *Signal loss* occurs when the signal attenuates so much that the receiver is unable to detect the signal. Incorrect interpretation of attenuated signals is a form of transmission error. Both signal loss and transmission errors contribute to decreased network performance.

Repeater Capabilities and Limitations

A repeater is a simple hardware device that accepts a signal, regenerates or amplifies it, and passes it along at full strength. This is illustrated in Figure 13-10. Because a repeater regenerates all signals between two network segments, a computer in one segment can communicate with a computer in the other segment. In fact, when repeaters are used to connect LAN segments, sending and receiving computers cannot distinguish whether they are attached to the same or different segments. A repeater does not buffer messages passed between segments and does not read or process complete frames or data packets; a repeater does not distinguish between the signals that correspond to valid frames and other electrical signals. When interference (such as a lightning strike) generates unwanted electrical noise on one segment, a copy of the electrical noise is passed to the other segment if it cannot be filtered out during the signal regeneration process. Similarly, if a station in segment 1 and a station in segment 3 of the network in Figure 13-8 try to transmit at the same time, a collision will occur, and copies of the overlapping signals that result from the collision will be re-created in all three LAN segments.

Table 13-1 summarizes important repeater capabilities and characteristics. Note that one capability of some repeaters is media transfer. Although it is not commonly needed, this capability allows a network manager to change media from twisted-pair wires on one LAN segment to fiber optic cable on another segment at a repeater junction. Also note that repeaters can be used to isolate network resources (such as servers) on specific segments in order to enhance adequate access to sharing computing technologies. A final point to keep in mind as we discuss other internetworking

Table 13-1   Repeater Characteristics and Capabilities

Media transfer, such as coaxial cable to twisted-pair wires
Multiple ports allowing one repeater to connect three or more segments
Diagnostic and status indicators
Automatic partitioning and reconnection in the event of a segment failure
Manual partitioning
Backup power supply

technologies is that repeating capabilities are built into most network connections including bridges, routers, gateways, and switches. All connection points present the opportunity to regenerate signals that travel across communication media. In LANs, hubs and network interface cards (NICs) may regenerate the signals that they receive to ensure sufficient signal strength within the network.

Regenerating Wireless Signals

Signal attenuation is a factor in the performance of both cable-based and wireless LANs. Wireless LAN specifications indicate the maximum distance between worksta-tions and wireless hubs, and most wireless LAN administrators will attest that it is important to stick to the specified limits.

   Attenuation is also a factor in wireless WANs (such as satellite-based, terrestrial microwave, or cellular data). Atmospheric absorption caused by oxygen and water vapor (suspended water droplets associated with rain and fog) can cause signal attenua-tion in wireless WANs. Signal loss caused by oxygen is especially problematic for signals in the 50- to 70-GHz frequency range, and water vapor is likely to cause the scattering of radio signals transmitted in the 20- to 25-GHz frequency range. *Rainfade* (attenuation or signal loss caused by heavy downpours) can be a problem for wireless communica-tions in areas of the world that have very high levels of annual rainfall. Minimizing the distance between transmitters and avoiding the use of frequency ranges that are most prone to atmospheric absorption are two ways to address these problems.

   Other causes of attenuation in wireless networks include the general tendency for wireless signals to disperse as they travel greater distances *(free space loss)*; *refraction* (bending) of radio signals as they travel through the atmosphere; and *thermal (white) noise* created by the activity of devices and media used in the wireless network. Each of these sources of wireless signal attenuation contributes to the need to regenerate wire-less signals as they travel between senders and receivers.

Repeater Costs

Most repeaters for Ethernet, token ring, or ATM LANs range in price from less than $300 to $1,500. Repeaters for Ethernet LANs may cost less than $30, and most cost less than $1,000. As noted previously, repeater capabilities are included in LAN hubs, patch panels, and switches. Typically, Ethernet shared media hubs are less expensive than Ethernet switches on a price-per-port basis. In addition, unmanaged shared media hubs are usually less expensive (price-per-port) than managed hubs.

   The communication medium can also make a difference in repeater costs. Repeaters for LANs using twisted-pair wire are typically less expensive than using fiber optic cable; some fiber optic repeaters may cost more than $2,500.

BRIDGES: CONNECTING TWO LANs

Like a repeater, a bridge can be used to connect two LAN segments. However, because they do more than simply regenerate signals, bridges are not necessarily an appro-priate substitute for repeaters, especially if cost is a factor within an organization. Because bridges possess more intelligence than physical layer connection devices, they are more costly to implement. Bridges typically range in cost between $1,500 and $5,000, with the majority of bridges falling in the $1,500 to $3,000 price range. Wireless bridges are usually more expensive than cable-based bridges; these typically cost between $3,000 and $5,000, and some cost more than $10,000.

Unlike repeaters, bridges only handle complete frames. This means that bridges can isolate problems to a LAN or LAN segment and reduce the likelihood of transferring noise/interference from one network segment to the other. Noise resulting from a collision or electrical interference originating on one of the LANs connected to the bridge will result in the bridge's reception of an incorrectly formed frame. If the frame is not complete and correct, the bridge discards it. Thus, the bridge inhibits problems on one LAN or LAN segment from affecting the other. Because of filtering, bridges also reduce the probability of collision by reducing the amount of traffic that each LAN would have if the two LANs were interconnected by a repeater.

Bridges "listen" to traffic on each LAN segment or LAN and, because of this they are often called *promiscuous* internetworking technologies. They receive all frames generated by both network segments. When a bridge receives a frame from one segment, the bridge verifies that it is complete and correctly formatted and, if necessary, forwards the frame to the other segment. When a bridge is used to connect two LANs or two LAN segments, a computer attached to one segment can send a frame to computers in the other segment as well as to computers in its own segment. Thus, two LANs or LAN segments connected by a bridge behave like a single LAN.

Bridges are often stand-alone devices; however, a conventional microcomputer may be converted to a bridge by installing an appropriate network interface card for each LAN (or LAN segment) into two of the PC's expansion slots and installing bridging software. PCs that are converted into bridges are dedicated to the bridging process; they do not run application software.

Frame filtering is one of the most important functions performed by a bridge. Unlike a repeater, a bridge does not forward a frame from one network segment to the other indiscriminately. A bridge uses the physical address found in the frame's header to determine whether to forward the frame. The bridge knows the computers attached to each network segment. When the bridge receives a frame from one segment, it checks the destination address in the frame header and decides that the frame should be forwarded to the other segment; this process is called **filtering**. Filtering rates for bridges are measured in frames or packets per second and typically vary from 7,000 to 50,000 frames per second. Some bridges, however, have filtering rates that surpass 55,000 frames per second.

When a bridge receives a frame from a computer in one segment and the intended recipient is in the same segment, the bridge will handle the frame in one of two ways, depending on the data link protocol used in the LAN segment. In an Ethernet LAN, the bridge will discard the frame because each transmitted frame is received by all LAN–attached devices, including the intended recipient. In a token ring LAN, however, the bridge may have to forward the frame to the next computer in the ring, depending on the location of the sender, recipient, and bridge in the ring. The data link protocols for both Ethernet and token ring LANs are discussed more fully in Chapter 8.

A bridge only forwards a frame when the destination computer is not part of the sender's network segment. When a bridge determines that the destination computer is in the other segment, it sends a copy of the frame to the other segment. This is called **forwarding**. Like filtering, forwarding is measured in packets or frames per second. Forwarding rates are typically slower than filtering rates; forwarding rates for bridges typically vary from 700 to 20,000 frames per second, but some high-performance bridges are capable of forwarding more than 25,000 frames per second. Forwarding rates are typically higher for bridges that connect similar LANs (or LAN segments)—e.g., Ethernet-to-Ethernet or token ring–to–token ring LANs—than for bridges that connect dissimilar LANs (e.g., Ethernet-to-token ring). This is because **format conversion** (the reformatting

---

filtering In a bridge, filtering is a process employed to examine the data link layer frames transmitted by devices attached to each of the LANs that it interconnects. This examination involves the determination of each frame's intended recipient and which of the LANs the recipient is physically attached to.

forwarding The process used by a bridge to send a frame from one LAN segment to another.

format conversion The reformatting of data from the frame format used in one network segment to that used in the other segment.

of data from the frame format used in one network segment to that used in the other segment) is often necessary for bridges connecting dissimilar LANs.

Early bridges were used to connect two network segments that used the same data link protocol. Today, we also have bridges with format conversion capabilities that connect LANs that use different data link protocols. An upshot of this evolution is the need to be aware that the use of the term *bridge* can vary. Sometimes, a bridge is defined in the original sense: a device connecting two identical networks. Others use the broader definition of a device used to connect two networks at the data link layer. For example, you may encounter bridges that connect a token ring to an Ethernet LAN. You may even encounter devices called **brouters** that are capable of providing this functionality; brouters typically support both bridging and routing capabilities. Figure 13-11 illustrates two LANs, LAN A and LAN B, using a token ring protocol. Figure 13-12 depicts the use

brouter An internetworking device that provides the functions of a bridge and router.

Figure 13-11   Token Rings Connected by a Bridge

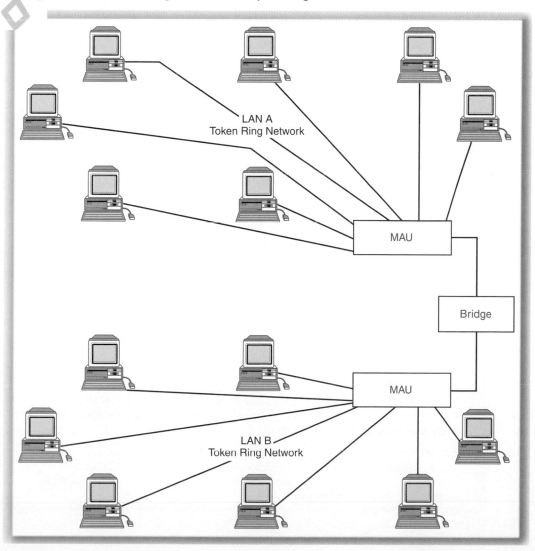

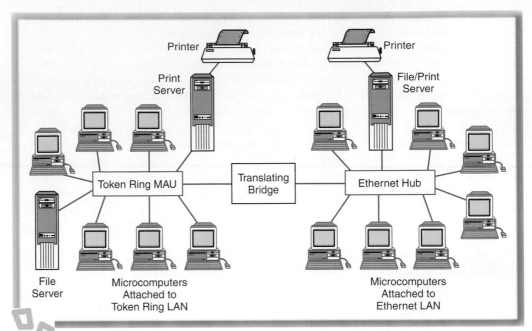

Figure 13-12   Using a Bridge to Connect a Token Ring LAN and an Ethernet LAN

of a bridge to connect a token ring LAN to an Ethernet LAN. Some of the major functions performed by bridges are summarized in Table 13-2.

A bridge must know the addresses of the computers attached to each of the network segments it connects. Because the bridge knows the format of the frames used by the data link protocol in each network segment, the bridge can find the source and destination addresses in the frame and use those addresses in its filtering and forwarding processing. The only additional information the bridge must know is the LAN to

Table 13-2   Basic Bridge Functions

Packet Routing Function
  1. Accept frame from LAN A.
  2. Examine address of frame.
  3. If frame address is a LAN A address, allow the frame to continue to LAN A.
  4. If frame address is a LAN B address, transmit the frame onto the LAN B medium.
  5. Do the equivalent for LAN B frames.

Additional Functions

Media conversion	Remote connection	Speed connection
Learning	Signal conversion	Frame statistics
Token ring to Ethernet conversion		

which the destination node is connected; however, when first installed, the bridge does not know which of the two LANs a sender is physically attached to. This was not an issue in many early bridges that indiscriminately transferred each frame onto both LANs, thus eliminating the need to know which segment the destination computer was attached to. Other early bridges required network managers to provide a network *routing table*. A bridge's **routing table** contains node addresses and the LAN identifier for the LAN to which the node is connected. The routing tables for these older bridges were static; if a new node was added to one of the network segments, the routing tables in all bridges had to be manually updated. Until that happened, the new node did not receive messages from computers attached to other network segments. As shown in Figure 13-13, network interconnections using bridges can also be more complex than a single bridge connecting two networks. A network routing table for bridge B1 in Figure 13-13 is shown in Table 13-3.

Most bridges being sold today are called **learning bridges** or *adaptive bridges*. Learning bridges build their routing tables from messages they receive from network-attached devices. They get their name from the fact that they "learn" the locations of computers automatically and do not need to be manually loaded with a predefined routing table. They do this by listening to each of the segments to which they are

routing table An information source containing node or network addresses and the identification of the path to be used in transmitting data to those nodes or networks. This may be a database in a router.

learning bridge A bridge that builds its own routing table from the messages it receives, rather than having a predefined routing table.

Figure 13-13   Network Interconnections Using Bridges

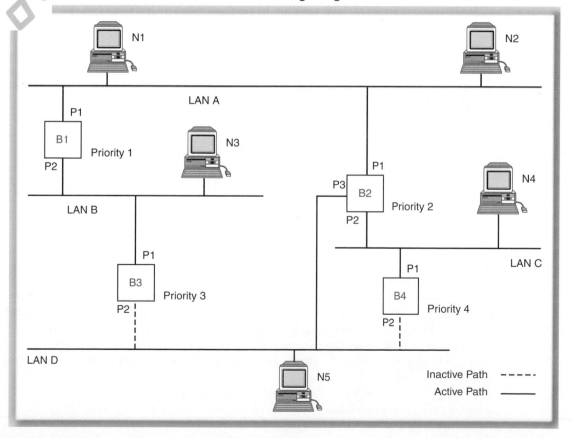

Table 13-3 Bridge B1's Network Routing Table

Node	Port	Comments
N1	P1	
N2	P1	
N3	P2	
N4	P1	Bridge B2 routes
N5	P1	Bridge B2 routes

attached and forming a list of computers located on each segment. When the learning bridge receives a frame, it extracts the sender's physical address from the frame header and adds the address to the list of computers attached to the segment. It also extracts the destination address from the frame and forwards the frame to the other network segment if the destination address is not in the list of addresses for the sender's network segment. Essentially, the network administrator needs only to connect a learning bridge to both LANs, and the bridge is immediately operational. Two methods are commonly used for bridges to learn and build their routing tables: spanning tree and source routing. (Both are described later.)

To better understand how learning bridges work, we start with a sample bridge configuration, as illustrated in Figure 13-13. Figure 13-13 shows four LANs (A, B, C, and D), four bridges (B1, B2, B3, and B4), and five nodes (N1, N2, N3, N4, and N5). In this figure, each bridge has two ports labeled P1 and P2. Bridge B2 has a third port, P3. Note that in this configuration, at least two paths exist between each pair of LANs. LAN A can get to LAN D via bridges B1 and B3 or directly via bridge B2; LAN D can get to LAN C directly through bridge B4 or bridge B2 or indirectly through bridges B3, B1, and B2.

In this example, we assume that each bridge has a fully developed routing table like the one shown for bridge B1 in Table 13-3. Note also that the routing table includes only one route for each node. If a route changes for some reason, the bridge will update its routing table to show the new route. Some networks use routing algorithms that allow multiple active paths between two nodes, but this is atypical for bridges.

B1 can learn its routing information in two ways. Suppose bridge B1 receives a frame from N1 destined for N2 (see Figure 13-13). Because each LAN frame contains the address of the sender, or source, and the recipient, or destination, the bridge can examine its routing table for the destination address. In this case, the address is local because both the source and the destination addresses are on LAN A. Because the destination address is local, no further action is required; the bridge essentially does nothing because no further processing of the frame is needed. In a token-passing LAN, the bridge may need to forward the frame to the next node on the LAN. In a CSMA/CD LAN, the bridge will do nothing, because all frames are broadcast to all nodes in the LAN segment. The intended recipient will be processing the frame at the same time that the bridge is filtering the frame and determining that it does not have to be forwarded to the other LAN segment.

Suppose bridge B1 receives a frame on port P2 from LAN B, with a source address of N3 and a destination address of N2 (which is located in LAN A). The bridge again consults its routing table for the destination address and finds the address to be a nonlocal node (that is, an address for a node that is not in the same segment as the sender). The routing table specifies the outbound port on which to send the frame, P1 in this instance. The bridge takes the frame as received and transmits through port P1 onto LAN A. If the LANs have different data link protocols, the bridge will also reformat the frame to make it compatible with the frame format used by the data link protocol in the recipient's network. Similarly, if bridge B3 receives a frame from node N5 with a destination of N2, B3 will consult its routing table, find that the path to N2 is port P1, and transmit the frame on LAN B. Bridge B1 on LAN B will receive this frame, consult its routing table, and forward the frame to LAN A through port P1. You may be wondering why bridge B4 did not also transmit the frame onto LAN C, or why bridge B2 did not also transmit the frame, creating a duplicate frame. The answer lies in how bridges operate and learn.

The Spanning Tree Algorithm

Spanning tree algorithms, which enable bridges to exchange routing information with each other, can be used on any type of LAN. The IEEE 802.1 Media Access Control Bridge Standards Committee selected the spanning tree algorithm as the standard for all IEEE 802.x LAN standards.

In developing the algorithm for spanning trees, let us first look at a simple case. You may wish to refer to Figure 13-13 during this discussion. Recall that each LAN frame contains the source address and the destination address. If bridge B1 receives a frame on port P1, the bridge assumes that the source address is a node local to LAN A. Because a bridge receives all network traffic on a LAN to which the bridge is connected (bridge B1 gets all message traffic on LANs A and B), a bridge soon learns all of the local node addresses from the source addresses in these messages. If a source address is not found in the bridge's routing table, the address is added to the table.

Suppose node N3 in Figure 13-13 sends a message to node N2. If the destination address of N2 is already in B1's routing table, the bridge forwards the frame accordingly. If the destination address is not already in the bridge's routing table, the bridge needs to locate the address. The bridge does this by sending the frame out on all ports other than the one on which it was received, which is called **flooding**. (The frame will also be sent to all nodes on the LAN on which it was received.) In this instance, the frame will be transmitted on port P1. Flooding ensures that a frame will arrive at its destination by sending it along all possible paths. The bridge will eventually receive an acknowledgment that the frame was received or a message from the receiving node. The acknowledgment contains the address of the original recipient, N2 in this case. From this acknowledgment, the bridge can determine the direction in which the node lies (by which port the bridge received the message), and it adds this information to its routing table.

Sometimes, a path may become unavailable, or new bridges or paths may become operational, which may cause routing information to change. To keep routing as efficient as possible, each bridge sends status messages periodically to let other bridges know of its current state. Also, status messages are sent immediately if the topology changes so that bridge routing tables can be appropriately updated.

Let's consider a more complex situation, in which multiple bridges are connected to the same network, and there may be multiple paths between LANs and perhaps multiple ports per bridge, as illustrated in Figure 13-13. If node N5 sends a message to node N2, does the frame get sent via bridge B2 or via bridges B3 and B1 or even via bridge B4 and then bridge B2? To reconcile such decisions, each bridge is given a priority. If two or more bridges are available, the bridge with the highest priority is chosen. If the path along that route becomes disrupted, the path can change, and the highest priority alternative path is activated. We will now consider in more detail how this occurs.

A bridge has at least two ports. An *active port* accepts frames from the LAN end of the port; an *inactive port* blocks or does not accept frames from the LAN end of the

spanning tree algorithm An IEEE standard algorithm that enables alternative data paths between network segments to be identified. The algorithm dynamically determines the best path from source to destination. The algorithm creates a hierarchical tree that "spans" the entire network; it determines all redundant paths between network segments and allows only one of them to be active at any given time.

flooding A technique used by a bridge to locate a destination address not present in the bridge's routing table by sending a packet out on all possible paths. An acknowledgment from the receiving station contains the destination address of the packet, which can then be added to the bridge's routing table.

port. An inactive port still can be used to transmit frames. However, these frames must originate from the bridge end of the port. Each bridge is assigned a priority by the administrator or via a process called the *distributed spanning tree algorithm (DST)*, which leads to the specification of forwarding priorities among bridges.

The bridge with the highest priority is designated as the *root bridge*. Each bridge has an active port in the direction of the root bridge. Other ports are active or inactive depending on the priority of the bridge and the configuration. Figure 13-13 also shows the priority of each bridge (with 1 representing the highest priority) and the active and inactive paths. A port is active if its path is active; otherwise, it is inactive. All bridges have their port in the direction of the root bridge active. Therefore, frames from the root direction can be forwarded and received. For all other cases, the active port from a LAN is toward the bridge with the highest priority. Ports on the root bridge are always active. Thus, in Figure 13-13, LANs A and B will choose bridge B1's ports as the active ports. LAN C is connected to two bridges, B2 and B4. B2 will be chosen because it has the higher priority, and B2's port P2 will be active. B4's port P1 is also active because P1 is in the direction of the root bridge. LAN D is connected to three bridges, B2, B3, and B4. Because B2 has the highest priority, it will be chosen as the active bridge. Port P2 on bridges B3 and B4 will be inactive and will not accept frames from LAN D.

The advantages of the spanning tree algorithm are that it is data link protocol independent, bridges can learn the topology of the network without manual intervention, and paths can change if an existing path becomes inoperable or if a better path is introduced. The algorithm's overhead includes the size of the routing table for networks with many communicating nodes, and the extra network traffic resulting from status messages between bridges and flooding. *Fast spanning tree (IEEE 802.1w)* has been proposed to reduce the amount of time required to update a network's bridges when link changes occur.

Source Routing

source routing
A learning bridge algorithm in which the sending node is responsible for determining the route to the destination node. The routing information is appended to the message, and the bridges along the route use the routing information to move the message from the source to the destination.

In practice, spanning tree algorithms have been more commonly used for Ethernet LANs, and **source routing** is more common for token-passing LANs. Source routing relies on the sending node to designate the path for a packet. Suppose node N5 in Figure 13-13 wants to send a packet to node N2. If N2 is in N5's routing table, the packet is sent along that route; otherwise, N5 must determine the best route to N2. N5 does this by sending an *explorer* or *discovery packet* on all routes available. In this case, the discovery packet is sent on port P2 of bridge B4, port P3 of bridge B2, and port P2 of bridge B3. Each bridge, in turn, transmits the packet on each port except the one on which the packet was received. Moreover, each bridge appends its information to the packet. Thus, node N2 receives several packets, each containing the identity of each bridge through which the packet traveled. All of these packets are returned to node N5. N5 selects the path from all the alternatives returned. In our example, node N5 will probably receive four discovery packets with paths B4–B2, B2, B3–B1, and B4–B2–B3–B1. Upon receiving the four responses from its discovery packets, node N5 will choose one. B2 would probably be the best route because there is only one bridge through which the message must pass. Realize, however, that path B3–B1 might be faster if B2's connections on ports P1 or P3 are slower than the connections for bridges B3 and B1.

After N5 discovers the path to node N2, whenever node N5 needs to transmit to node N2, it appends the selected routing information to its packet. Each bridge along the way investigates this information to determine by which route to send the packet.

You might have already noticed that the algorithm just explained has one possible fault. The discovery packet sent from bridge B4 will reach bridge B2, and B2 will send the packet out on all ports except the ones on which it was received (ports P3 and P1). The packet on port P3 will be directed back to LAN D and will again reach bridges B4 and B3. A mechanism must be in place to prevent discovery packets from looping through the network. This is accomplished in one of two ways. First, a maximum number of hops is specified. If the maximum is set to 10, then a packet that has not reached its destination after traversing 10 bridges is discarded. The second way to prevent a loop is to discard a packet that recirculates through the same bridge. For example, one of N5's discovery packets will go from B4 to B2 and then back to B4. When B4 finds that it has already handled that packet, it will discard the packet.

The advantage of the source routing algorithm is that bridges are not responsible for maintaining large routing tables for extensive networks. Each node is responsible for maintaining routing information only for the nodes with which it communicates. The disadvantages are the overhead of sending numerous explorer packets during the discovery process and the extra routing data that must be appended to each message.

Other Bridge Capabilities

In the preceding discussion, we did not consider the interconnected LANs' locations and media. Bridges are available that will accommodate media differences. Suppose LAN A in Figure 13-13 uses fiber optic cable and LAN B uses twisted-pair wires as the medium. You could, therefore, select a bridge (B1 in Figure 13-13) to connect LANs A and B with a fiber interface for one port (port 1) and an interface for twisted-pair wires on the other port (port 2).

Remote Bridges

There are also several bridging options for connecting geographically distributed LANs. Two bridges, called *remote bridges,* are typically needed to connect geographically separated LANs (see Figure 13-14). Some of the connection options available for remote bridges are summarized in Table 13-4. *Speed conversion* is often supported by remote bridges because the speed of a WAN connection between remote LANs usually is much slower than the speed within either LAN. This speed difference can cause the bridge to become saturated with messages if there are many inter–LAN packets. Bridges with speed conversion capabilities have memory that allows some messages to be buffered, which helps reconcile the differences in transmission speed. If too many messages arrive in a short period, however, the buffer may become full, and newly arriving packets may be lost. Note that this condition can also occur when two local LANs that operate at different speeds are connected (such as a bridge between a 10-mbps Ethernet LAN and a 100-mbps Ethernet LAN). A bridge also must do some processing to determine where a packet must be routed. Except for very slow LANs, the processing time may exceed the arrival rate. Thus, bridges connecting LANs with high packet arrival rates can also become saturated.

As illustrated in Figure 13-14, **remote bridges** are employed to interconnect LANs via WAN services. Remote bridges are used in pairs, with one on either side of the WAN connection. Most remote bridges contain one network interface card supporting a LAN data link protocol (e.g., an Ethernet or token ring card) and another card to provide the serial interface required by the WAN service (e.g., RS-232 or V.35). WAN services used to interconnect LANs include leased 56-kbps digital lines, ISDN, T-1, and frame relay. Remote bridges often connect to such services via modems or CSUs/DSUs. Data compression is often supported by remote bridges in order to enhance throughput across WAN links.

remote bridge
An internetworking device that connects two LAN segments at geographically dispersed locations via WAN links or services. Remote bridges are used in pairs with one on either side of the WAN connection.

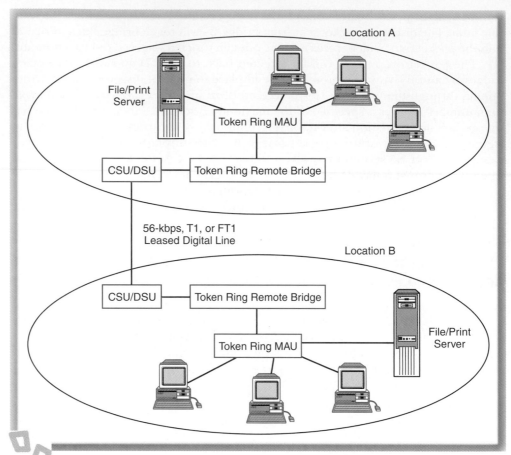

Figure 13-14   Using Remote Bridges to Connect Two Geographically
Dispersed LANs

Table 13-4   Remote Bridge Connection Alternatives

xDSL connections
T-1 line
Fractional T-1
X.25 or frame relay networks
Integrated services digital network (ISDN)
Wireless connections using spread-spectrum radio

Wireless Bridges

Wireless bridges are available for bridging remote LANs that are located within a few miles of each other. These typically employ spread-spectrum radio transmission and enable businesses to eliminate the monthly costs of leased lines or other network usage charges associated with the WAN services available from carriers. Most support the spanning tree algorithm and use encryption to ensure the security of messages exchanged wirelessly between the LANs.

ROUTERS: NETWORK LAYER CONNECTIONS

Four major functions are carried out by communication technologies that operate at the network layer of the OSI reference model: routing, network control, congestion control, and collection of accounting data. Whereas the data link layer is primarily concerned with moving data between two nodes within the same network segment, the network layer is concerned with end-to-end routing, or getting data from an originating node in one network segment to its ultimate destination in another network segment. As illustrated in Figure 13-3, routers are the key network layer internetworking technology. Packet, frame relay, and cell relay switches (discussed in Chapter 12) are other examples of network layer technologies.

Because there may be a variety of paths from the originating node to the destination node across an internet or the Internet, network layer technologies must be aware of alternative paths in the network and be capable of choosing the best one. Selection of the best path depends on several factors, including congestion, number of intervening routers, and speed of links connecting intervening routers.

Network control involves sending node status information to other routers and receiving status information from other routers needed to determine the best routing of individual packets to their intended destinations. Network layer technologies must enforce any priority schemes associated with the packets traveling across the network. They must also play an active role in congestion control. **Congestion control** involves reducing transmission delays that might result from overuse of some circuits or because a particular router in the network is busy and unable to process messages in a timely fashion. Network layer technologies should adapt to these transient conditions and attempt to route messages around such points of congestion. Not all systems can adapt to the changing characteristics of the communication links. In networks that rely on protocols that broadcast packets, there may be very little that can be done to overcome network congestion problems.

network control
Involves the sending and receiving of node status information to other nodes to determine the best routing for messages.

congestion control
The reduction of transmission delays by sharing information about network traffic and message queue length among routers or network switches.

Message Routing

One function of the network layer, **routing**, is achievable through several algorithms used to direct messages from the point of origination to final destination. Message routing processes can be either centralized or distributed. Routing itself can be static, adaptive, or broadcast and is governed by a network routing table resident at the router. The network routing table lists the addresses of other nodes in the network along with the link or path to each node. Subnet masks (discussed in Chapter 4) are often used in IP network routing tables to summarize the complete range of nodes that can be accessed via a particular link. Link/path information in network routing tables typically specifies a *next-hop router*, the next router in the network that the packet should be sent to on its way to the destination node. For example, if a packet destined for node X arrives at router K, the network routing table is consulted to identify the next-hop router on the path from K to X. Once the next-hop router is identified,

routing Forwarding data to its destination. Routers employ routing algorithms to determine the "best" route to a message's destination. Multiple routing algorithms exist.

router K will transmit the packet via the communication port that serves as the interface between K and the next-hop router. Network routing tables can also contain more information than just the next link, such as network congestion statistics. The following discussion provides a summary of some of the major routing techniques.

Centralized Routing Determination: The Network Routing Manager

In networks that centrally determine packet routing, one router is designated as the **network routing manager** to which all other routers periodically forward such status information as queue lengths on outgoing and incoming links and the number of messages processed within the most recent time interval. The network routing manager is thereby provided with an overview of network functioning, the location of any bottlenecks, and the location of underused facilities. The routing manager periodically recalculates the optimal paths between nodes, and constructs and distributes new routing tables to all routers in the network.

Centralized routing determination has many disadvantages. The routing manager's ability to receive many messages from the other routers increases the probability of congestion, a problem that can be exacerbated if the routing manager is itself used to accept and forward data packets. Networks are sometimes subject to transient conditions, such as when the transfer of a large file between nodes saturates a link (or set of links) for a short period of time. By the time information about the congestion caused by the file transfer is relayed to the routing manager and a new routing is calculated, the activity may have already ceased, making the newly calculated paths less than optimal and inconsistent with the true level of congestion within the network. Routers that are physically closer to the routing manager may receive the newly calculated routing tables before those that are more remote, leading to transient inconsistencies in how packets are routed. Figure 13-15 shows a change in the message path. Under the old routing mechanism, the route was A→B→D→X, whereas the new path is A→C→D→X. Also, the new path from router B to node X is B→A→C→D→X. If B receives a new routing table from the network routing manager node while router A is still using the old routing table, then for a message destined from A to X, A will route it to B and B will route it back to A, continuing until A receives the new routing

network routing manager A designated node used for centralized routing determination that has an overview of network functioning, location of any bottlenecks, and location of used facilities.

Figure 13-15 Change in the Message Path

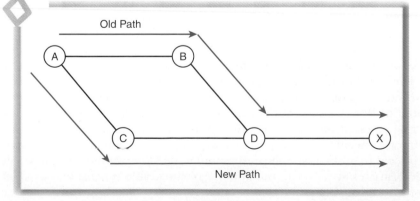

table. Transmission of the routing tables themselves also may bias the statistics being gathered to compute the next routing algorithm because this creates additional network traffic.

An additional problem with centralized route calculations is the amount of CPU processing power needed, because network performance hinges on the reliability of the routing manager. If the routing manager fails, either the routing remains unchanged until it recovers and is operational or another routing manager must be selected. The best situation is to have alternative routing managers available in case the primary routing manager fails. This is implemented most efficiently by having the routing manager send "I'm alive" messages at predefined intervals; if the backup routing manager fails to receive this message within the prescribed interval, it assumes that the manager has failed and takes over routing manager duties for the network. The backup manager's first responsibility is to broadcast that network status messages should now be routed to it.

Distributed Routing Determination

Distributed routing determination relies on each router to calculate its own routing table listing the best routes from it to nodes in the network. This requires each router to periodically transmit its status to its neighbors. As this information ripples through the network, each router updates its table accordingly. This technique avoids the potential bottleneck at a centralized route manager, although the time required for changes to flow through all the routers in the network may be quite long.

distributed routing determination
A routing algorithm in which each node calculates its own routing table based on status information periodically received from other nodes.

Static Routing

The purest form of **static routing** involves always using one particular path between a router and particular network nodes; if the link to the next-hop router is down, communication from the router to particular nodes becomes impossible. Fully interconnected networks (such as that depicted in Figure 10-21) sometimes rely on static routing; the only path between any two nodes is the link between them. If that link is down, the available network software is incapable of using any alternative paths. Because fully interconnected networks have become rare, static routing has largely disappeared. Today, static routing refers to the situation in which a selected path is used until some drastic condition makes that path unavailable. An alternative path is then selected and used until the route is switched manually, a failure occurs on the alternative path, or the original path is restored.

static routing
A form of routing in which one particular path between two nodes is always used.

When multiple paths exist across a network to a particular node, some routing algorithms weight each path according to perceived use, which is called **weighted routing**. The path is then randomly selected from the weighted alternatives. Figure 13-16 shows three paths from router A to node X, via routers B, C, and D. Suppose the network designers had determined that the path through router B would be best 50 percent of the time; the path through router C would be best 30 percent of the time; and the path through router D would be best 20 percent of the time. When a packet arrives at router A that is destined for X, router A generates a random number between 0 and 1. If the random number is 0.50 or less, the packet is transmitted to router B; if the random number is greater than 0.50 and less than or equal to 0.80, the path to router C is selected; otherwise, the path through router D is selected. The path that particular packets follow from router A to node X will vary, but each path's likelihood of being selected remains constant. This type of routing can be changed only by altering the route weighting for particular paths to destination nodes in the routing tables.

weighted routing
When multiple paths exist, each is given a weight according to perceived use. A random number is generated to determine which of the available paths to use, based on their weights.

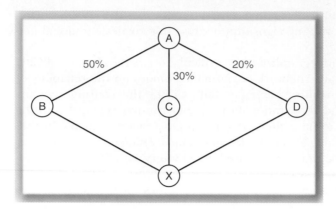

Figure 13-16   Weighted Routing

Adaptive Routing

Adaptive routing, sometimes called *dynamic routing,* attempts to select the best current route for the message or session. The best route may be determined by several different parameters, such as queue lengths at next-hop routers and link speed.

Quickest Link   The simplest adaptive routing algorithm is to have the router pass along the message as quickly as possible, with the only restriction being not to pass it back to the sending node/router. When a packet arrives at a router, the router looks at all potential outbound links, selects the one with the least amount of activity, and sends the message out on that line. The router makes no attempt to determine whether the selected path will bring the packet closer to its destination. As a result, this type of algorithm is not very efficient and often causes a message to be shuffled to more routers than necessary to get it to its destination; such shuffling adds to network congestion. Conceivably, a packet could be shifted among routers in the network for hours before arriving at its destination.

Best Route   More intelligent adaptive routing techniques attempt to select the best route for a packet from the router to the destination node, as determined by one or more of the following parameters: the number of required hops, the speed of the links, the type of link, and congestion. Link congestion occurs when message traffic on a link is heavy, similar to freeway congestion during rush hours.

Best route routing relies on current information on the status of the network. If a node is added to the network or if one is taken off the network, that information must be reflected in routing tables in order to facilitate best route calculations. Knowing the speed of the links between hops and the number of hops between a router and a particular node is also important. Paths between routers connected by high-speed fiber optic links may be preferable to those that require packets to be transmitted across 56-kbps lines. Because routers make best path determinations for each packet that they receive, a packet is temporarily delayed at each router it encounters on its path from sender to destination. Hence, many best route algorithms attempt to minimize the number of hops (routers) that a packet must go through before arriving at its destination; by minimizing the number of hops, the packet is often able to cross the network in the shortest amount of time. Incoming and outgoing packet queues at alternative next-hop routers may also be taken into account when making best path determinations because lengthy queues can also delay the delivery of the packet to its destination. In Figure 13-17, if router A receives a packet destined to node C, the route from A to node C through B is the shortest but probably

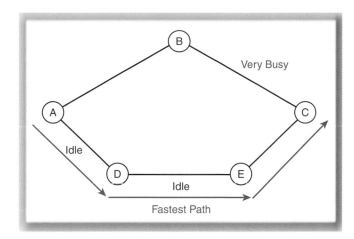

Figure 13-17   Routing Around Congestion

not the quickest at that time. The route from A to C through routers D and E would be more efficient because the link from B to C is congested.

Broadcast Routing

Broadcast routing is exemplified by multicasting, an IP addressing technique discussed in Chapter 4. *Multicasting* is an addressing technique that enables a source to send a single copy of a packet to a specific set of recipients through the use of multicast addresses using class D addressing. When class D addressing is used, a host can send the same packet to all hosts/nodes in a multicast group. Only the hosts/nodes in the multicast group will read the packet; other nodes need only read the first four bits of the destination IP address, determine that it is intended for a class D multicast group, and ignore the rest of the information in the packet. When a host begins the destination IP address with 1110, the packet will be sent to all the hosts in the specified class D multicast group. (This is called *broadcasting*.)

broadcast routing
Routing in which the message is broadcast to all stations on a network or network segment. Only the stations to which the message is addressed accept it.

IP Routing

As noted in Chapter 4, when an Internet node sends a message to another Internet node across the Internet backbone, it must know the destination node's IP address. The address may be resolved from a URL supplied by the user or obtained from a hypertext link or similar mechanism. As is the case for other networks, Internet routers rely on routing tables that contain network information essential to making intelligent routing decisions. In discussing how IP routing works, let us consider the network illustrated in Figure 13-18. In the figure, the clouds represent networks, and the network addresses are shown within the clouds. Each router is connected to two (or more) networks (some routers have more than two ports), and each router port has an address on the attached network. Therefore, router A is connected to subnet 1 and has the address of 10.0.0.4 on network 1 and address 20.0.0.6 for the attachment to network 2.

At least three types of routers can be identified by organizations whose networks are attached to the Internet: internal routers, border routers, and external routers. *Internal routers* are used to route packets between the networks included within a particular subnet or between subnets. *Border routers* route messages between an organization's network and the Internet. *External routers* route packets between border routers across the Internet backbone. The various types of routers are depicted in Figure 13-19.

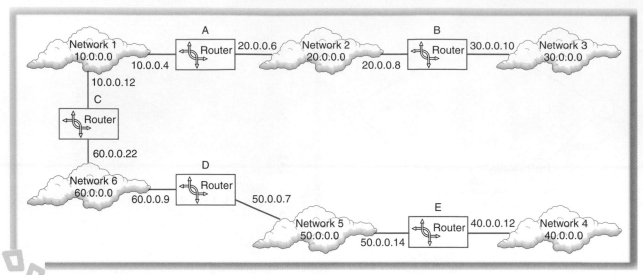

Figure 13-18   Routing in an IP Network

Figure 13-19   Internal, Border, and External Routers

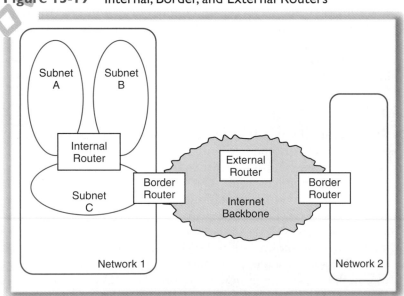

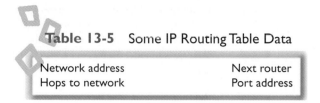

Table 13-5 Some IP Routing Table Data

| Network address | Next router |
| Hops to network | Port address |

Each router maintains a router table. Some of the information contained in those tables is given in Table 13-5, and the routing table for router A (based on the data in Table 13-5 and Figure 13-18) is given in Table 13-6. The network address in the routing table is the destination address part of a network or subnet mask (discussed in Chapter 4). The next router is the address of the next-hop router that should receive a packet intended for a device within the destination network/subnet. The number of hops to the network is a measure of the distance across the network from the current router and the destination network; the hop count specifies the number of routers or gateways through which the packet must travel to reach the destination network. The hop count does not consider the speed of the links connecting the routers on the path to the destination. Other routing table implementations use an additional distance measure called *ticks*, which represent the speed of transmission over a route. The port address is the address onto which the router will transmit the message to get it to the next router or to the network/subnet.

IP Routing Algorithm

The algorithm that the IP uses to route a message from source node to destination node is essentially as follows:

1. The source node obtains the destination node's IP address.
2. The IP protocol builds the IP header and affixes it to the packet.
3. The source node sends the packet to the router.
4. The router determines the network address of the destination node.
5. If the network address is this network, the router uses a local delivery method and skips the remaining steps. For example, it may use the ARP (address resolution protocol—discussed in Chapter 4) if the intended recipient is in a LAN in the network and transmit the packet to the recipient's media access control (MAC) address.
6. If the destination network is another network, the router consults the routing table for the network address.
7. The router sends the message to the next router along the path to the destination network.

Table 13-6 Router A's Routing Table (See Figure 13-18)

Net Address	Next Router	Hops	Port
10	None	Directly connected	10.0.0.4
20	None	Directly connected	20.0.0.6
30	B	1	20.0.0.6
40	C	3	10.0.0.4
50	C	2	10.0.0.4
60	C	1	10.0.0.4

8. The receiving router decrements the time-to-live field. The time-to-live field is a field in the IP header that indicates how long a packet will last before being discarded. The value of the time-to-live field is the number of hops remaining. The time-to-live field is decremented by each router, and the router setting the field to zero discards the packet.

9. If the time-to-live field is 0, the packet is discarded.

10. Return to step 4.

Note that in step 9, a packet may be discarded. The sending node sets the time-to-live counter to its initial value, and each time the packet passes through a router, the counter is decremented. The router that sets the counter to 0 will not attempt to forward the packet. This keeps packets from circulating endlessly through the network, an event that could occur if routing tables were not consistent. If a packet is discarded, it is the responsibility of the TCP process on the destination node to recognize the problem and request that the packet be resent. A flow chart of the IP routing process is shown in Figure 13-20.

Routers

Routers are used to connect LANs to LANs, WANs to WANs, and LANs to WANs at the network layer of the OSI reference model. As in any form of communication, a common language or protocol is needed. In a bridge, the common protocol is the data link protocol. Because the data link protocol may not be common for all links on networks connected with a router, a common internetwork protocol is needed at the network layer to interconnect networks with different data link protocols. Although the network interconnection is established at the network layer, data link and physical layer services are also involved in the transmission of packets between networks.

A variety of network protocols are used for network interconnection. For example networks that use older versions of the Novell NetWare operating system (versions 3.xx and below) employ IPX/SPX to interconnect LANs. IPX/SPX can be used to establish the common basis of communication between token ring LANs and Ethernet LANs running older versions of Novell NetWare as the LAN operating system. However, IPX/SPX is not supported by some WAN protocols and by some LAN products provided by other network vendors. As a result, IPX/SPX cannot be used as the routing protocol for these multivendor networks. This forces network administrators to find other network layer protocols commonly supported by the networks to be interconnected. Several internetwork protocols have been developed, but the most common of these is TCP/IP. TCP/IP is supported by most network product vendors, including Microsoft and Novell. As a result, it is an appropriate protocol to use to illustrate network layer routing.

TCP/IP Routers

As noted in Chapter 2, TCP/IP was developed by the Advanced Research Projects Agency (ARPA) of the U.S. Department of Defense (DOD). It originated as an internetwork protocol and has evolved over time into a suite of protocols addressing a variety of network communication needs, one of which is the routing of packets across backbone networks. Note that TCP/IP is not just a microcomputer protocol. On the contrary, it was developed on large systems and was later transported to microcomputers. Because TCP/IP runs on a wide variety of platforms, it is an ideal choice for a routing protocol on the Internet. Other functions provided by the TCP/IP protocol suite include file transfer, e-mail, and logons to remote nodes.

Using TCP/IP's routing capabilities, users may be on either the same or different networks, networks that are directly connected by a bridge or router, or

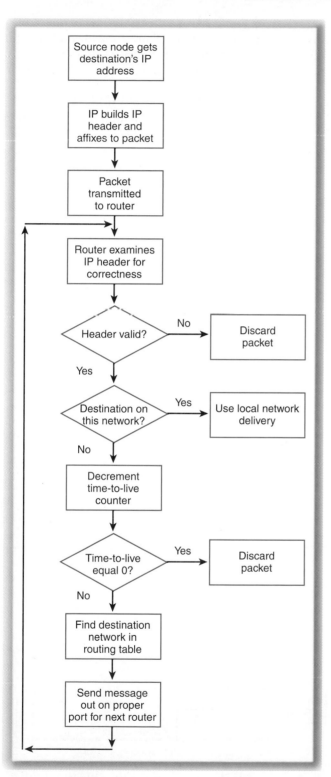

Figure 13-20   Routing Process

networks with one or more intermediate networks, as illustrated in Figure 13-21. In addition to providing network interconnection, TCP/IP also provides services for file transfers, e-mail, and provisions for a user on one network to log on to a host in another network attached to the Internet. These capabilities are discussed in Chapters 2 and 4.

Figure 13-21 illustrates how networks might be connected using TCP/IP. The networks depicted in Figure 13-21 can be either LANs or WANs, and the routers used to interconnect the networks must be able to support each network's data link protocol and to interface with the physical links used to connect the networks. Although routing tasks are performed at the network level, the messages transmitted and received by each node must pass through the data link and physical layers. The key is that the information needed to determine how to forward the message is understood by the router's network layer logic.

Figure 13-21   TCP/IP Routing in a Network

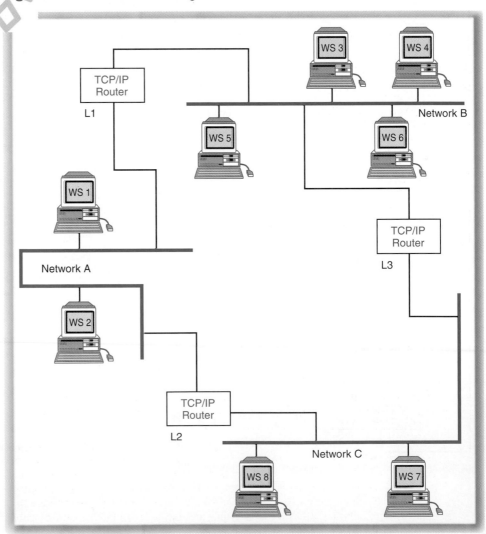

CHAPTER 13 Internetworking Technologies **619**

In Figure 13-21, assume that network A is an Ethernet LAN, network B is a token ring LAN, and network C is a WAN. Nodes in networks A and B will be able to exchange messages over L1 if they share a common network layer protocol. Nodes in networks A and C will be able to exchange messages over L2 if they share a common network layer protocol. The data link protocols used in networks A, B, and C may be different, but the nodes in them will be able to exchange messages so long as each pair of networks shares a common network layer protocol. A key point to remember is that routers may support multiple data link protocols.

TCP/IP consists of two distinct protocols, the Transmission Control Protocol (TCP) and the Internet Protocol (IP). The TCP operates at the transport layer, and the IP operates at the network layer. Before tracing the flow of a message transfer using TCP/IP, let us first review the major functions of each protocol.

IP provides two basic services: breaking the message up into transmission packets and addressing. Many data link protocols have a maximum size for transmission packets. For example, an Ethernet LAN packet may contain up to 1,500 characters. Some networks, however, have a maximum packet size of 128 characters. To carry out its role at the network layer, IP must be aware of data link layer frame size differences. On occasion, this requires that the IP break a message into smaller packets of the appropriate size. IP is also responsible for packet routing. To do this, the IP must determine the address of the next router on the path to the message's destination.

There are several functions an IP does not perform. IP is not responsible for guaranteeing end-to-end message delivery. TCP protocol is held accountable for message delivery. If a packet is lost during transmission, the TCP, not the IP, is responsible for ensuring that the packet is retransmitted. Also, IP does not guarantee that the individual packets included in a multipacket message will arrive in the correct order. TCP is responsible for packet sequencing and ensuring the delivery of packets to applications on destination hosts. Thus, the primary functions of the TCP are to provide message integrity, to provide acknowledgment of the reception of the complete message by a destination node, to regulate the flow of messages between source and destination nodes, and to ensure that messages are delivered to appropriate applications located on destination nodes. Like IP, TCP also may divide the message into smaller transmission segments. These segments usually correspond to an IP transmission packet.

As illustrated in the following example, TCP and IP cooperate in sending a message from one node to another. This example also helps to clarify the functions of a router. For this example, we assume that node WS1 on network A in Figure 13-21 needs to send a message to WS3 on network B. TCP/IP uses the following procedure to carry out this transmission.

1. To start the process, the TCP module in node WS1 receives a message from one of the applications that it is currently running. The TCP attaches a header to the message and passes it down to the IP module in node WS1. The message header contains the destination address for the intended recipient; the packet also contains an error-detection field and a message sequence number. These are used to ensure that the message is received without errors and to ensure that messages are received in the proper sequence or can be reordered into the proper sequence by TCP in the receiving node.

2. Node WS1's IP determines whether the destination is an internetwork address. If the address is on the local network, such as node WS2, then the IP passes the message to the data link layer so that the message can be appropriately formatted for transmission over the network's shared communication medium. If the destination is a node on another network, the IP finds the best path to the destination and forwards the message to the next IP node along that path. In this case, the IP module in node WS1 would probably send the message to the TCP/IP router connecting network A and network B.

3. The IP module at the router receives the message, examines the address, and determines that the destination address is in network B. If network A and network B use different data link protocols, the IP may break the message up into packets of the appropriate size for transmission over network B. IP adds a header to each packet and passes it down to the data link layer. The data link layer appends its transmission information and transmits the packets over link L1 to network B.

4. WS3 receives a packet, strips off the data link layer control data, and passes the message to the IP layer, then to the TCP layer. TCP then decodes the header attached by the sender's TCP module. TCP checks the packet for errors, such as message sequence errors or CRC errors. If no errors are detected, the TCP determines the appropriate destination application within WS3 and sends the message to it. The packet's application destination is identified as a port number included in the packet's TCP header. For example, if the packet contains a request for a Web page, the TCP header would include port 80, designating HTTP as the application destination. Other *well-known port numbers* included in TCP packet headers are discussed in Chapter 4.

On the path from source to destination, the message may pass through several IP routers and traverse links with several different data link protocols. TCP/IP routers are responsible for generating the destination address and intermediate addresses along the way, and for ensuring the correct delivery of the message.

Xpress Transfer Protocol (XTP) An extension of TCP/IP that enhances performance by reducing the amount of processing and allowing some functions to be worked on simultaneously.

TCP/IP is continually being extended to meet new communication needs. One extension, **Xpress Transfer Protocol (XTP)**, enhances TCP/IP performance by reducing the amount of processing and allowing some functions to be worked on in parallel. One example of parallelism is the ability to transmit data while the CRC error check field for the packet is being computed.

From the preceding discussion, you should realize that a node in one network that must communicate with a node on another network must both have TCP/IP installed. Most of today's LAN operating systems install TCP/IP software modules on servers and clients.

ISO Routing Standards

The International Standards Organization (ISO) has also developed standards for functions similar to those provided by TCP/IP. The counterpart to IP is the **Connectionless Network Protocol (CLNP)**. In addition to forwarding messages, CLNP can provide message services such as message priorities, route selection parameters, and security parameters. The ISO has defined five classes of transport protocols: abbreviated TP0, TP1, TP2, TP3, and TP4. The classes are based on the error characteristics of the network. The lower classes assume better network error performance and, hence, provide less end-to-end support. TP4 makes no assumptions about the error characteristics of the network and provides the highest level of error detection and recovery. Combining the transport protocols with CLNP yields a service similar to that of TCP/IP. The ISO services are abbreviated TPn/CLNP, where n represents a number between 0 and 4.

Connectionless Network Protocol (CLNP) The ISO counterpart to the Internet Protocol, this protocol provides message services such as message priorities, route selection parameters, and security parameters.

Router Functionality

Like bridges, the speed of routers is often measured specified in their maximum filtering rates and forwarding rates. Both of these are measured in packets per second. Filtering is necessary because the router must determine whether the packet received is intended for a recipient in the same network as the recipient or a different network. Forwarding processes in routers are more complex than those of bridges. Before forwarding the packet, the router must determine the recipient's network, the best path to the recipient's network, and the recipient's availability. (Routers closest to an unavailable recipient may be required to store messages for later delivery.) The additional processing done by routers and their store-and-forward capabilities means that they are more complex and more costly than bridges.

Unlike bridges, routers do not promiscuously receive all packets transmitted by the devices in each of the networks that they interconnect. They only receive and process (filter/forward) packets destined for nodes in networks other than the sender's. As a result, when network segments are joined together by a router, each of the segments maintains its separate identity even though it is now part of an internetwork. (Recall that bridges make separate segments operate as one signal composite network.)

Because routers maintain the integrity of individual network segments, they can be used to limit access to a network. As noted in Chapter 4, firewall software may be implemented in routers to filter/check incoming or outgoing messages in order to bolster network security. In some instances, application-specific filtering may be performed by a router. For example, the router may forward incoming e-mail messages, but strip off all e-mail attachments to minimize the likelihood of virus infections.

Unlike bridges, routers use network layer addresses rather than hardware addresses to forward the packets they receive. In addition, routers discriminate among data packets according to network protocol types (e.g., TCP/IP, IPX/SPX, and SNA). For example, a router may open the packets addressed to it by nodes in an Ethernet LAN and forward the IPX/SPX traffic they carry to one network and all TCP/IP traffic to another network. (Ethernet frames may encapsulate multiple network layer protocols.) Routers that are capable of forwarding messages using more than one network layer protocol are known as **multiprotocol routers**. Such routers know that different network layer protocols have different packet structures and lengths, and are capable of interpreting, processing, and forwarding data packets for two or more protocols.

Nonroutable protocols, such as SDLC (synchronous data link control) used in SNA networks, are handled either by having the router act like a **translating bridge** (a bridge that reformats the packets received from one network into the data link format required by the other network) or by *encapsulation* (taking the entire packet including overhead fields and placing it in the information/data field of routable network layer protocol). Encapsulation is commonly supported by TCP/IP routers.

Routers that are only required to route packets associated with a single network layer protocol often have filtering and forwarding rates that are higher than those of multiprotocol routers. This derives from the fact that these routers know the exact location and length of the recipient's destination address in each packet and do not need to reformat packets prior to forwarding them.

Dial-Up Routers

Dial-up routers enable geographically dispersed LANs to be connected by ISDN or another dial-up digital WAN service. These make business sense when the volume of inter–LAN traffic is insufficient to justify the monthly charges for connecting the two LANs via a leased line. As illustrated in Figure 13-22, dial-up routers are used in pairs. When the router receives a packet destined for the LAN at the other site, the dial-up router establishes the dial-up connection to the router at the other end and transmits the packet to the router at the other end. At the conclusion of the data transmission, the dial-up connection is terminated. By only establishing the dial-up connection on demand, network connection charges can be minimized. In order to further minimize connection charges, router table updates are performed at predetermined times or are piggybacked on inter–LAN data exchange sessions.

multiprotocol routers Routers that are capable of forwarding messages using more than one network layer protocol.

translating bridge A bridge that reformats the frames received from one network into the data link frame format required by the other network.

dial-up router Enables geographically dispersed LANs to be connected by ISDN or another dial-up digital WAN service.

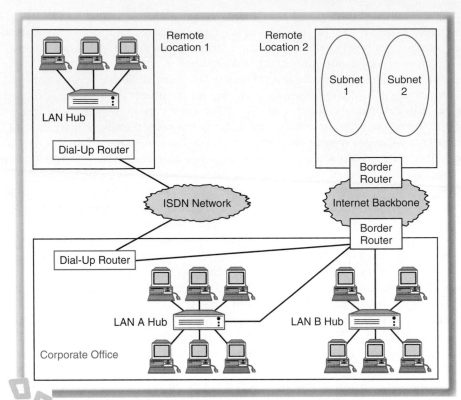

Figure 13-22   Using Dial-Up Routers to Connect Remote Business Locations with Corporate Headquarters

High-Speed Routers

edge router A high-speed internetworking device that enables network traffic to be routed over high-speed ATM networks and SONET services.

In order to meet the demands of increasing internet and Internet traffic, high-speed routers have been developed and implemented. **Edge routers**, for example, have been developed to enable network traffic to be routed over high-speed ATM networks and SONET services. By incorporating routing functionality within LAN switches at the "edge" of an ATM backbone, inter–LAN traffic can be switched with minimal delay across the ATM backbone and eliminate the need for packets to take an extra hop to a border router.

Other router advancements include the creation of routers that only inspect the first packet in multipacket messages and routers that use application-specific integrated circuits (ASICs) that assist in the routing process. In the first type of high-speed router, the first packet of a multipacket message is analyzed at the network layer, and the best route to the destination is determined. After the route is calculated, the rest of the packets that make up the complete message are forwarded at the data link layer, using the route established for the first packet. ASICs are at the heart of the other major type of high-speed routers. Up to 1 million packets per second can be handled by a single ASIC chip. By incorporating multiple ASICs within the same router, routers with speeds in excess of 200 million packets per second have been developed. Some router vendors are working toward *terabit routers* that will be capable of handling trillions of packets per second.

Routing Protocols

Routing protocols enable routers to adapt to changes in network conditions and topologies. Best path decisions are only likely to be optimal when routers have up-to-date information about network traffic and status. Routers within a network exchange information with one another to ensure that the information in their router tables is current. Recall that the exchange of router table updates is especially important in networks that rely on dynamic routing algorithms. Standards for routing protocols have emerged to ensure that routers manufactured by different vendors are able to exchange router table updates.

Many early routing protocols were designed for smaller networks. Over time, they have become unsuitable for large-scale enterprise networks, especially those connected to the Internet. For example, routing information protocol (RIP) was at one time the most popular routing protocol. Other routing protocols that have been largely supplanted by new routing protocols designed for today's complex networks include Gateway-to-Gateway protocol (GGP), Interior Gateway Routing Protocol (IGRP), Exterior Gateway Protocol (EGP), and Inter-Domain Routing Protocol (IDRP).

There are three major categories of routing protocols: distance vector, link state, and path vector. Each category uses different methods to determine the best route for a packet to its destination. Distance vector and link state protocols are best suited for interior routing (e.g., routing among an organization's subnets). Path vector protocols are best suited for border routing (e.g., establishing routes across the Internet backbone to another network).

Distance Vector Protocols   When distance vector protocols are used, each router's router table indicates the distance to every other router. This information is periodically broadcast to all other routers in the network so that they can update their routing tables and adapt to changes in the network topology. When the router receives a packet, it usually selects the path with the shortest distance to the destination. RIP and EIGRP (Enhanced Interior Gateway Routing Protocol) are examples of distance vector protocols:

➤ *Routing information protocol (RIP)* is still popular for small networks with few routers, but most organizations have outgrown RIP. It works by counting the number of hops between any two points in the network and usually selects the route with the fewest hops. With RIP routers, broadcast router tables update one another every 30 seconds.

➤ *Enhanced Interior Gateway Routing Protocol (EIGRP)* is an enhanced version of IGRP that enables "distance" to a destination to be calculated through the use of multiple factors in addition to the number of hops, such as bandwidth between hops, current traffic volume on available links, and router queue lengths.

Link State Protocols   Instead of basing routing decisions on tables listing the distance to every other router in the network, routers that support link state routing protocols compute best routes by consulting a complete copy of the map of the network topology. This map is stored as a database where each record corresponds to a link in the network. Link state protocols include Open Shortest Path First (OSPF), NetWare Link Services Protocol (NLSP), and the IS-IS (Intermediate System-to-Intermediate System) protocol.

➤ *Open Shortest Path First (OSPF)* has been recognized by the Internet Engineering Task Force (IETF) and the Internet Architecture Board (IAB) as the routing protocol of choice for the Internet.

➤ *NetWare Link Services Protocol (NLSP)* was designed by Novell to improve the performance of IPX traffic in larger internetworks. NLSP only transmits router table update information every 2 hours unless a change in the network topology occurs.

➤ *Intermediate System-to-Intermediate System (IS-IS)* is an OSI reference model link state routing protocol that enables routers that use different routing protocols to exchange routing table update information in a common format. This enables routers in the network to send only one set of router table updates even though other routers in the network may employ different routing protocols.

Path Vector Protocols   Routers that support vector protocols maintain comprehensive lists of routes and networks, making them well suited for use as border routers. In these protocols, each router broadcasts the complete list of networks and routes that it knows to lie between the sender and recipient. This information enables router tables to be updated without the need to maintain a complete map of the network topology; because the topology of the Internet is constantly changing, path vector protocols are ideal for border routers.

Border Gateway Protocol (BGP) is the most widely used path vector protocol, especially by organizations with multiple Internet connections and organizations that receive traffic via multiple ISPs. BGP enables a business's interior routing protocols to use the most cost-effective Internet link; if one Internet link fails, BGP automatically redistributes traffic among the remaining functioning links. BGP is expected to become more popular as business needs for reliable and redundant Internet links increase.

GATEWAYS: CONNECTING NETWORKS ABOVE THE NETWORK LAYER

The interface between two dissimilar networks is called a *gateway,* which is basically a protocol converter. A gateway reconciles the differences between the networks it connects. With a repeater, a bridge, or a router, the communicating nodes share a common protocol at the physical, the data link, or the network layer, respectively. If it is necessary to connect two nodes that do not share a common protocol, a gateway or protocol converter can be used to make the connection. Naturally, the gateway must be able to understand the protocol of the two networks being connected and also must be able to translate from one protocol to the other. If two networks to be connected do not share a common network layer protocol, a gateway can be used to connect them above the network layer. The location of gateways in the OSI reference model is illustrated in Figure 13-3.

The components of a gateway are the network interfaces and the logic that carries out the conversion necessary when moving messages between networks. The conversion must change the header and trailer of the packet to make it consistent with the protocol of the network to which the message is being transferred. This may include accommodating differences in speed, packet sizes, and packet formats.

As noted in Chapter 11, gateways may be used to connect a LAN to a SNA network. Because SNA frames lack fields needed for routing at the network layer, SNAs and LANs may have to rely on gateways to establish a connection between them above the network layer. A gateway between an Ethernet LAN and SNA, for example, would be capable of accepting packets transmitted by Ethernet nodes and reformatting them for transmission to SNA nodes (and vice versa).

In some instances, a complete network or WAN service may serve as a gateway between two other networks. For example, if both a LAN and a WAN interface to a frame relay network, the frame relay network can serve as a gateway that allows nodes on the LAN and the WAN to communicate. In this case, there are two gateways, one

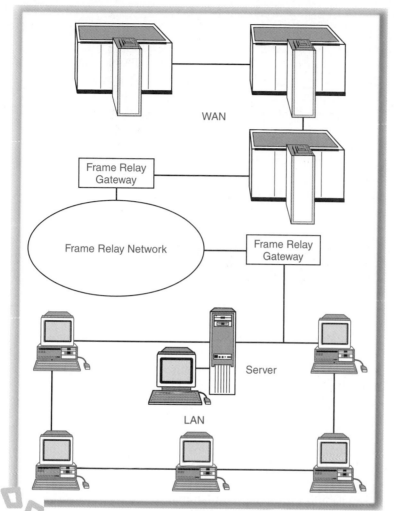

Figure 13-23   WAN-to-LAN Connections over a Frame Relay Network

from the LAN to the frame relay network and one from the frame relay network to the WAN. This is illustrated in Figure 13-23.

SWITCHES

Packet-switching technologies (including frame relay and ATM switches, which are discussed in Chapter 12) are used by many businesses to interconnect geographically dispersed networks. Recall that these carry out congestion and network control functions (such as routing packets around congested links and network switches) similar to routers and that the trend is toward connecting switches with high-speed digital links. Higher speed WAN links have also increased the demand for high-speed routers and other high-performance internetworking technologies. One response to this has been the incorporation of switching technology into routers.

Layer 2 and Layer 3 Switches

As discussed in Chapter 7, data link layer switches have also become common in LANs. Unlike shared media hubs, LAN switches support multiple simultaneous communication sessions among network-attached devices. This dramatically increases the LAN's data throughput—the amount of data transmitted across the network's communication medium in a given time interval. Over time, the cost of LAN switches has decreased to the point where they are comparable in price to manageable shared media hubs. As a result, many organizations are building new LANs around LAN switches instead of shared media hubs or are replacing shared media hubs with LAN switches in order to improve network performance.

As an interconnection technology, most LAN switches function like bridges by sending packets to their destinations based on the recipient's hardware (physical) address. Such LAN switches are often called **layer 2 switches**, because the switched connection is based on the destination address in data link layer packets. When network layer destination addresses are used to establish switched connections, as they are when switching capabilities are incorporated into routers, the internetworking technology is called a **layer 3 switch**. As noted in Chapter 7, both layer 2 and layer 3 switches can be used to create virtual LANs.

A *virtual LAN (VLAN)* is a logical subgroup within a local area network that is created via software rather than the physical grouping of cables in wiring closets. VLANs enable user workstations and other network devices to be combined into a single unit regardless of the physical LAN segment where they are attached. It also allows traffic to flow more efficiently within the logical group.

Most VLANs function at layer 2 of the OSI reference model. Because the purpose of creating a VLAN is to isolate traffic within the logical group, a router is typically required to "bridge" two or more VLANs. The router, of course, works at layer 3, and VLAN bridging via routers requires the identification and coordination of the VLAN network segment, which can be a complicated job. The data communication industry is working towards "virtual routing" solutions (such as the IEEE 802.1q standard addressing the virtual routing of Ethernet frames) in order to facilitate the evolution of intranets and knowledge management applications within organizations. However, until such solutions become widespread, most organizations must be content with layer 2 virtual LANs. LANs that are built around switching architectures, such as ATM LANs, are also capable of supporting virtual LANs.

There are two major categories of layer 3 switches: packet-by-packet and flow-based. *Packet-by-packet* layer 3 switches operate identically to routers except that the forwarding is carried by hardware (ASICs) rather than software; this dramatically increases the router's forwarding rate. *Flow-rate* layer 3 switches only have to determine the best route for the first packet in a multipacket message, thereby eliminating the need to perform packet-by-packet routing for multipacket messages.

Layer 4 Switches

Layer 4 switches have also been developed. These can route/forward TCP/IP messages based on the information in the TCP header in addition to layer 2 and layer 3 addresses. Layer 4 switches can be used, for example, to deliver a packet directly to a TCP/IP application (such as HTTP or SMTP) based on the application's TCP port number. They can also be programmed to ignore specific types of packets and thus can be programmed to function as a firewall.

The locations of layer 2, layer 3, and layer 4 switches are illustrated in Figure 13-24. An example of a network using both layer 2 and layer 3 switches is depicted Figure 13-25.

---

layer 2 switch
An internetworking device that, like a bridge, forwards traffic based on MAC layer (Ethernet or token ring) addresses. Some layer 2 switches support virtual LANs.

layer 3 switch
An internetworking device that forwards traffic based on layer 3 (the network layer in the OSI reference model), typically at very high speeds. A router with incorporated switching capabilities is called a layer 3 switch. Layer 3 switches may be used to create virtual LANs.

layer 4 switch
An internetworking device that integrates routing and switching by using layer 4 and layer 3 information. When used in TCP/IP networks, well-known port numbers can be identified to expedite the delivery packets to applications. Layer 4 switches can also be programmed to ignore specific types of packets and thus can be programmed to function as a firewall.

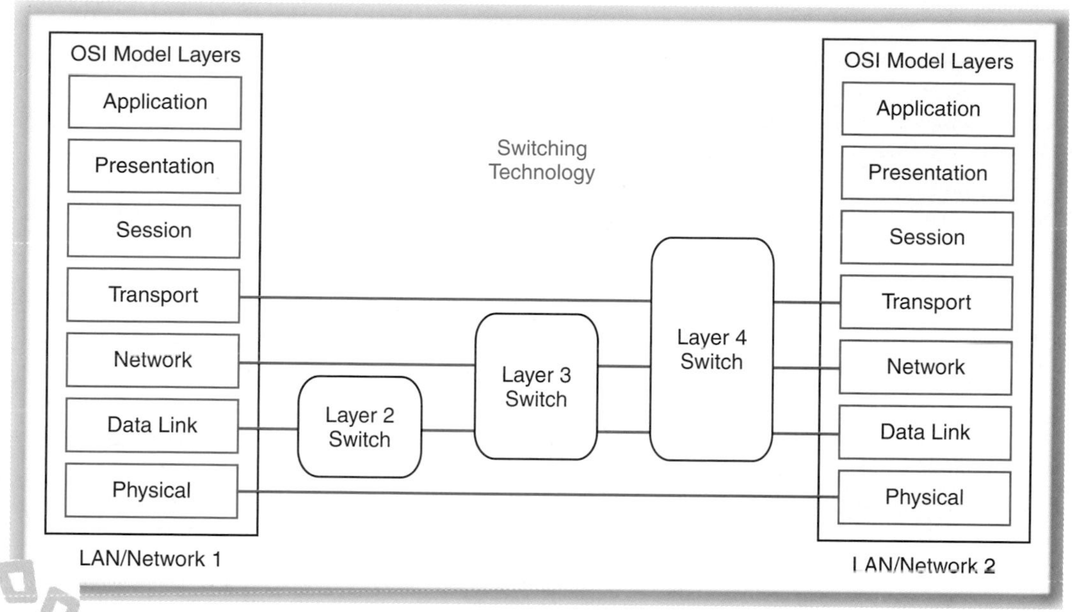

Figure 13-24   Relationship Between Switching Technologies and the OSI Reference Model

Backbone Switches

Switches are also used to interface LANs with backbone networks. The two types of switches that may be used for this are as follows:

➤ *Backbone-attached LAN switches.* These enable switched connections between devices attached to the same LAN as well as switched access to a high-speed backbone network or a backbone router. These may be used to connect LANs to *distributed backbone networks,* such as that depicted in Figure 13-26.

➤ *Backbone switches.* Backbone switches are more sophisticated than backbone-attached LAN switches; in some instances, they function as self-contained backbone networks or **collapsed backbone networks**. These may be used to establish switched interconnections among various types of LANs (such as Ethernet, token ring, or ATM) within the same building as well as switched access between LANs and a distributed corporate backbone network (see Figure 13-27). Such switches enable a variety of modules to be installed in a single chassis equipped with a high-performance switching backplane or matrix. An Ethernet module installed in the chassis would, for example, enable an Ethernet LAN to have switched connections to the other LANs attached to the backbone switch as well as switched access to the corporate backbone network. Modules for WAN services such as frame relay, ISDN, and ATM can be installed in the chassis to enable messages destined for other networks to be sent via a WAN service. Backbone switches include internal or border router capabilities and firewall functionality.

collapsed backbone network A network configuration that provides a backbone in a centralized location, to which all subnetworks are attached. A collapsed backbone can be implemented in a router or switch that uses a high-speed backplane to establish interconnections among various types of LANs (Ethernet, token ring, ATM, etc.) within the same building as well as switched access between LANs and a distributed corporate backbone network.

PROVIDING REMOTE ACCESS TO LANs AND WANs

Businesses and other organizations use a variety of remote access approaches to support teleworkers and mobile users. The remote access technologies that they employ essentially interconnect users in remote locations to shared LAN or WAN resources.

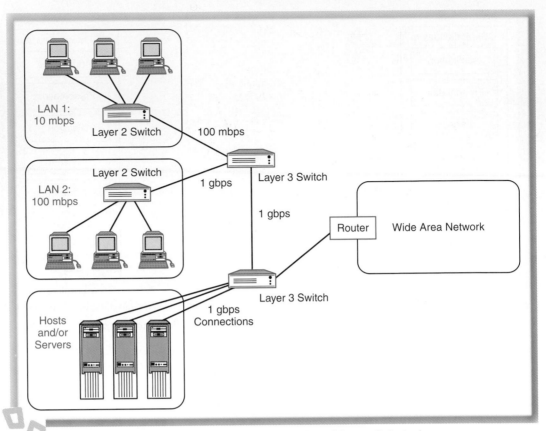

Figure 13-25 An Example of the Use of Layer 2 and Layer 3 Switches at a Single Location Within a Business Organization

Although remote users may be required to access these resources at much slower rates (e.g., via V.90 56-kbps modems or ISDN), they nonetheless have access to the same resources as colleagues whose machines are directly attached to the LAN or WAN.

Such access is called *remote client* or *remote node* computing when client applications are run on remote users' machines that communicate with LAN (or WAN) server applications via dial-up links. In this instance, a modified client version of the network operating system used in the LAN or WAN is installed on the remote machine that enables it to communicate with LAN/WAN servers over dial-up connections. Other than this, the remote client operates in the same manner as a local (LAN–attached) client.

Another type of remote access is called *remote control*. In this instance, applications are run on the server rather than on the remote client. Because only keystrokes and screen images are exchanged between the remote machine and the server, the remote PC functions as a terminal or thin client rather than as a full-fledged client. The differences between remote node and remote control are illustrated in Figure 13-28.

Several approaches are used to address remote access security concerns. These include the following:

➤ *User ID and password controls.* Remote users are typically required to supply valid user ID codes and passwords in order to log into LANs and WANs. *Dial-back systems* may also be used; after the user has supplied a valid ID and password, the LAN or

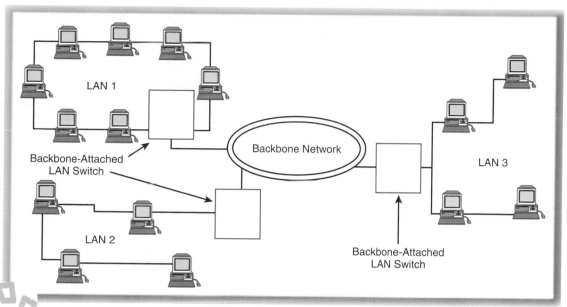

Figure 13-26   Backbone Network Connecting LANs

WAN may terminate the connection and then call the user back using a prespecified number.

➤ *Encryption.* Encryption is often used to mask user IDs and passwords sent across the dial-in connection. All subsequent transmissions between the remote user and the LAN/WAN server may also be encrypted.

➤ *Remote client authentication.* Smart card technologies, biometric devices (including retina scan or handprints), or other remote client authentication devices can be used to verify the identity of the remote user. Remote client authentication protocols such as PAP (password authentication protocol) and CHAP (challenge handshake authentication protocol) have been developed to address remote client authentication concerns.

Remote Access Technologies

There are several ways for remote users to access resources stored on LAN servers. These are depicted in Figure 13-29 and briefly described here.

➤ *Dial-in connection to a microcomputer attached to a LAN.* A user whose office computer is attached to a LAN may be able to gain remote access to LAN resources by dialing into a modem installed in the LAN–attached PC. Using products such as AT&T's VNC—Virtual Network Computing (www.uk.research.att.com/vnc)—remote users can run applications on the LAN–attached PC from a PC at their residence.

➤ *Dial-in connection to a LAN modem.* Remote users may also be able to access LAN resources by dialing into a LAN modem. A **LAN modem** is essentially a modem that is equipped with a network interface card that enables it to be directly attached to the LAN. LAN modems are sometimes called *dial-in servers.*

➤ *Dial-in connection to a communication server.* In this approach, remote users gain access to network resources by dialing into a **communication server**. As illustrated in

LAN modem
A modem that is equipped with a network interface card that enables it to be directly attached to the LAN; a LAN modem is sometimes called a dial-in server because it enables remote users to access LAN resources via dial-in connections.

communication server A server that provides access to remote users, typically via analog modem or ISDN connections. A communication server typically supports dial-up protocols and access controls (authentication); it may be a dedicated server or a regular file server with remote access software.

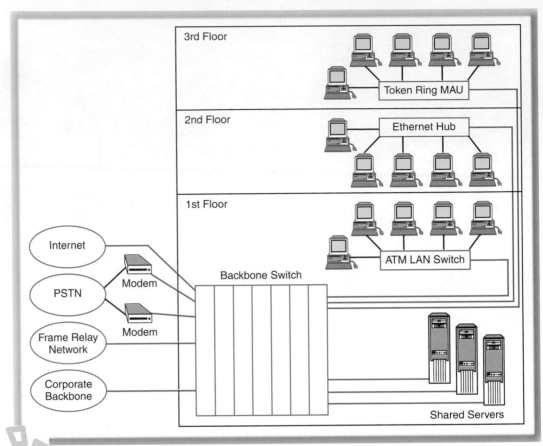

Figure 13-27   Using a Backbone Switch As a Collapsed Backbone Network Within an Office Building with Connections to a Distributed Corporate Backbone Network and Various WAN Services

Figure 13-30, a communication server can typically support multiple remote users simultaneously because it has several modem connections as well as multiple network interface cards. Communication servers may support both dial-in connections for remote users and dial-out connections for local users. In addition, communication servers may support DSL, ISDN, frame relay, and other WAN service connections. Communication servers go by many names, including *access servers*, *remote access servers*, *remote node servers*, and *telecommuting servers*. Communication server modules are available for backbone switches in order to enable remote access capabilities. Large-scale remote access servers capable of supporting more than 1,000 telecommuters or mobile users are also available.

WIRELESS ACCESS TO CORPORATE NETWORKS

Just as the increasing popularity of telecommuting and mobile work has increased business use of remote access technologies, the explosion in wireless communications and applications is fueling interest in wireless internetworking technologies. Two important wireless interconnection technologies are wireless bridges and mobile IP. Each of these is briefly discussed here.

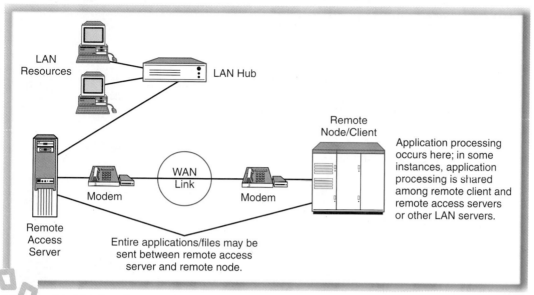

Figure 13-28(a)   Remote Node Computing

Figure 13-28(b)   Remote Control

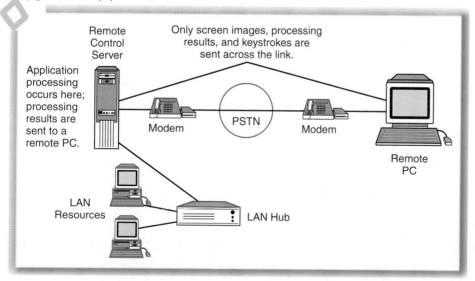

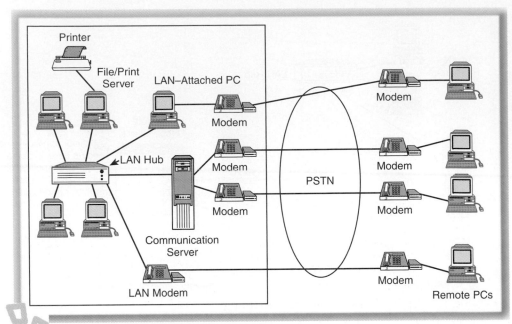

Figure 13-29   Remote Access to LAN Resources via LAN–Attached PC, Communication Server, or LAN Modem

➤ As noted previously in our discussion of bridges, *wireless bridges* enable organizations to link LANs that are located within a few miles of each other. Because they employ spread-spectrum radio transmission instead of dial-up or leased lines to connect the LANs, wireless bridges enable businesses to avoid WAN service charges. Most use encryption to ensure the security of inter–LAN message exchanges.

mobile IP An IP enhancement that allows packets to be forwarded to moving users. It enables users to "roam" among wireless LANs.

➤ **Mobile IP** enables users to "roam" among wireless LANs. This proposed standard enables users to maintain a constant network connection even when they move out of the transmission range of one wireless LAN and into that for another. Essentially, the user is always connected to the network via the nearest wireless LAN. Mobile IP is limited to the TCP/IP network and requires the installation of a mobile IP client on each mobile wireless device to enable it to communicate with the mobile IP server or router in the user's "home" network. As the user "roams," the mobile IP client updates the home network server/router on the user's location; the server will route packets to the user based on their last reported location.

INTRANETS AND EXTRANETS: INTERCONNECTIONS VIA WEB TECHNOLOGIES

Organizations are increasingly leveraging TCP/IP applications and internetworking technologies to create intranets and extranets. As noted in Chapter 3, intranets leverage Web technologies to facilitate internal communication and information sharing among an organization's employees, even if they are spread across geographically dis-

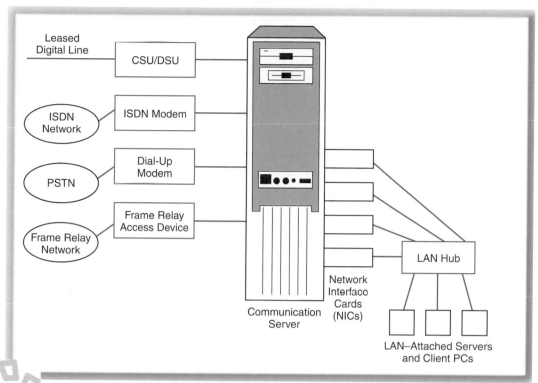

Figure 13-30   Depending on Business Needs, Communication Servers Can Provide Users at Remote Locations with Access to LAN Resources via a Variety of WAN Services/Networks

persed sites. Intranets play a key role in the knowledge management systems found in today's organizations.

Most intranets are TCP/IP based and use a range of TCP/IP applications (including HTTP, SMTP, and FTP) to facilitate information and knowledge sharing among employees. Internal routers are often used to interconnect subnets, and border routers may be used to ensure that employees are able to access shared resources in geographically remote networks. Layer 2 and layer 3 switches may also be employed to facilitate communication among intranet users. Border routers used to establish internetwork connections across the Internet backbone may use encryption to ensure message integrity; they may also serve as firewalls. IPsec and virtual private networks (VPNs) may also be used to protect the security of intranet messages that are exchanged via the Internet.

Extranets are interorganizational systems that leverage Web technologies to link computer networks of two or more business partners. Most message exchanges occur across the Internet via border routers or over point-to-point dial-up or leased circuits. When business partners exchange information across the Internet backbone, their border routers are also likely to include firewall capabilities and may support VPNs. Extensible markup language (XML) has emerged as an important business-to-business data sharing language; *ebXML* has been proposed to facilitate the development of business-to-business extranet applications.

SUMMARY

Stand-alone networks (self-contained networks that are not connected to other networks) are rare in today's business organizations. Often, there is a business need to connect several LAN segments, connect separate LANs, connect LANs to WANs, or to connect one WAN to another WAN. A variety of internetworking technologies are used to network interconnections.

Repeaters are used to connect LAN segments. Repeaters operate at the physical level of the OSI model. Their main job is to regenerate attenuated signals. Repeaters accept a signal from one network segment, amplify or regenerate the signal, and forward it to the next network segment. Repeaters enable network designers to create LANs whose communication medium is longer than maximum specified lengths.

Bridges connect LANs at the data link layer of the OSI model. A bridge receives a packet, looks at its destination address, and, if the address is a node on a LAN other than the one from which the packet was received, the bridge transmits the packet to the other LAN. Most of today's bridges are learning bridges. Learning bridges use spanning tree or source routing algorithms to learn the location of network nodes and can adapt to changes in network paths. Wireless bridges are available to connect LANs that are no more than a few miles apart.

Routers operate at the network layer of the OSI reference model. A router receives a packet, determines the address of the destination, and chooses the best route for the packet to take across the network to its destination. A packet may be processed by numerous routers as it travels to its destination. Routers rely on routing tables and routing protocols to make best path decisions. Smaller internets may use static routing algorithms to ensure that packets with particular network addresses always follow the same path through the network. Dynamic routing algorithms that base routing decisions on prevailing network traffic conditions are common in larger internets and the Internet. Routing technologies are evolving rapidly. Dial-up routers are available to enable LANs to exchange packets across dial-up connections. High-speed routers have also been developed that are capable of handling millions of packets per second.

A gateway is a name applied to network connections between heterogeneous networks. Because heterogeneous networks do not share a common network layer communication protocol, network interconnections are made above the OSI reference model's network layer. A gateway must be able to reformat packets received from one network into the format used in the other network. Gateways may also be required to perform speed conversion and error-checking functions.

Switches are being increasingly used to interconnect networks. Layer 2 switches function like bridges and can connect two or more LANs at the data link layer. Layer 3 switches combine switching and routing capabilities. LANs can be connected to high-speed corporate backbone networks via backbone-attached LAN switches or more sophisticated backbone switches.

Several remote access technologies are available to enable telecommuters and mobile workers to access shared computing resources stored in LANs and WANs. Options include allowing remote users to establish dial-in connections to LAN–attached microcomputers, LAN modems, or communication servers. Mobile IP allows users to "roam" among wireless LANs without losing a network connection.

Web technologies are playing an increasing role in network interconnections. Many organizations are leveraging these and TCP/IP applications to create intranets and extranets.

KEY TERMS

- adaptive routing
- attenuation
- bridge
- broadcast routing
- brouter
- collapsed backbone network
- communication server
- congestion control
- Connectionless Network Protocol (CLNP)
- dial-up router
- distributed routing determination
- edge router
- filtering
- flooding
- format conversion
- forwarding
- gateway
- LAN modem
- layer 2 switch

- layer 3 switch
- layer 4 switch
- learning bridge
- mobile IP
- multiprotocol routers
- network control
- network routing manager
- remote bridge
- repeater
- router
- routing
- routing table
- source routing
- spanning tree algorithm
- static routing
- translating bridge
- weighted routing
- Xpress Transfer Protocol (XTP)

REVIEW QUESTIONS

1. Provide at least two reasons why network managers may choose to subdivide a large LAN into two or more smaller segments.
2. What is attenuation? What data communication problems may be caused by attenuation?
3. Identify the OSI level at which each of the following operates.
   a. bridge
   b. repeater
   c. router
   d. gateway
4. Identify and briefly discuss the reasons why businesses may choose to have multiple LANs and multiple WANs.
5. Compare the capabilities of repeaters, bridges, and routers.
6. Identify and briefly describe the major causes of wireless signal attenuation.
7. Describe the differences between filtering and forwarding processes in bridges and routers.
8. What information is included in a bridge routing table?
9. What is a learning bridge? How are the spanning tree algorithm and source routing used by bridges to identify the LAN locations of computing devices?
10. What are the characteristics of remote bridges? What are the characteristics of wireless bridges?
11. What is the difference between network control and congestion control?
12. What are the characteristics of centralized routing determination? What are the disadvantages of centralized routing determination?
13. What are the characteristics of distributed routing determination?
14. What are the differences among static, weighted, and adaptive routing?
15. Compare quickest link routing and best route routing.
16. What are the differences among internal, border, and external routers?
17. Describe how TCP/IP sends a message from a node on one network to a node on another network.

18. What are the characteristics of multiprotocol routers? What are the characteristics of dial-up routers?
19. What are the characteristics of high-speed routers? What approaches are being used to increase the speed of routers?
20. What is the role of routing protocols in today's networks?
21. What are the differences among distance vector, link state, and path vector protocols? Identify examples of each.
22. What are the characteristics of gateways?
23. Compare layer 2, layer 3, and layer 4 switches.
24. What are the characteristics of backbone switches?
25. How does remote node computing differ from remote control?
26. What are the differences between LAN modems and communication servers?
27. Briefly describe the characteristics of mobile IP.
28. Identify and briefly describe the internetworking technologies used in intranets and extranets.

PROBLEMS AND EXERCISES

1. Evaluate the following LAN situations. State whether the LANs can be consolidated with a repeater, bridge, or router. Give all possible types of connection. State which connection alternative you would choose, and state why you chose it.
   a. Two Ethernet LANs. One LAN has a maximum length of 1,000 meters, and the other has a maximum length of 2,500 meters.
   b. Three LANs running Novell NetWare as the network operating system. One LAN is ARCnet, one is a token ring, and one is Ethernet 100BaseT (see Chapter 12).
   c. Three Ethernet LANs located at three different locations within the same small city. The farthest distance between any pair of LANs is 4 kilometers.
2. Your company has two Ethernet LANs, one in your eastern office and one in your western office (the distance between them is several hundred miles). The company wants to connect these LANs so users can more easily exchange data. The data being exchanged is primarily small messages, such as e-mail messages and small data files. Occasionally, a file several megabytes in size must be exchanged, but in these situations, the exchange is not time critical (for example, it could occur overnight). Devise a way to connect these LANs. Describe the type and speed of communication channel you would use to make the connection. Explain/justify your decision.
3. Suppose the two LANs described in problem 2 were different, such as a token ring and a CSMA/CD bus. Would your decision be different? Explain any differences and the reason for your decision.
4. Suppose the situation in problem 2 were different in that the large files (2 MB or less) had to be exchanged within 2 minutes or less. Would your solution be different? Explain any differences and the reason for your decision.
5. A company has two large computers connected by a synchronous communication line having a speed of 56 kbps. These computers are geographically separated, one in an eastern office and one in a western office. Each location also has a LAN. The company wants to allow all computer users, those connected to the LANs as well as those connected to the large computers, to be able to communicate. Is the current connection sufficient for the proposed configuration? Why or why not? Explain your answer.

6. Assuming that the existing communication link described in problem 5 is used for the long-distance connection, answer each of the following:
   a. What is best way to connect the LANs to the large computers? Justify your recommendation.
   b. Describe the changes a LAN packet will undergo as it moves from a LAN to a large system, to the other large system, and then to the other LAN. Assume the LANs at both locations are homogeneous (e.g., that both are Ethernet or token ring LANs).

7. Assume that your employer just assigned you the task of identifying vendors, products, and prices for a repeater to connect two Ethernet LANs, one using twisted-pair cabling and the other using fiber optic cable. Use the Internet to identify repeater vendors, specific products, and prices. (*Hint:* www.blackbox.com and www.datacommwarehouse.com may be good places to start your search.) Summarize the results of your search in a table.

8. Use the Internet to identify bridge vendors, specific products, capabilities (filtering rates, forwarding rates, and other functionality), and prices. Identify at least two product alternatives for each of the following networking requirements:
   a. a transparent bridge to connect two Ethernet (IEEE 802.3) LANs
   b. a transparent bridge to connect two token ring (IEEE 802.5) LANs
   c. a translating bridge to connect an Ethernet LAN and a token ring LAN
   d. a wireless bridge to connect two Ethernet LANs
   e. a remote bridge to connect two geographically dispersed Ethernet LANs
   Summarize the product alternatives for each networking requirement in a table.

9. Use the Internet to identify router vendors, specific products, capabilities (forwarding rates, routing protocols support, and other functionality—such as firewall and VPN capabilities), and prices. Identify at least two product alternatives for each of the following networking requirements:
   a. an internal router to connect two 10-mbps Ethernet LANs and a 100-mbps Ethernet LAN
   b. a dial-up router to connect two geographically dispersed Ethernet LANs
   c. a border router to connect three geographically dispersed networks, each of which contains at least one Ethernet LAN
   Summarize the product alternatives for each networking requirement in a table.

10. Use the Internet to identify edge router vendors, specific products, capabilities (forwarding rates, routing protocols support, and other functionality—such as firewall and VPN capabilities), and prices. Summarize the product alternatives for each networking requirement in a table.

11. Use the Internet to identify high-speed router vendors, specific products, capabilities (forwarding rates, routing protocols support, and other functionality), and prices. Summarize the product alternatives for each networking requirement in a table.

12. Use the Internet to identify layer 2 and layer 3 switching product vendors, specific products, product capabilities (such as speed or media conversion and network layer routing protocols supported by layer 3 switches), and prices. Summarize the product alternatives for each networking requirement in a table.

13. Use the Internet to identify backbone switch vendors, products, capabilities, and prices. Identify component and total costs for a backbone switch with the following modules:
   a. 10-mbps (10BaseT) Ethernet
   b. 100-mbps (100BaseT) Ethernet
   c. 16-mbps token ring

    d. ISDN connections

    e. frame relay connections

14. Use the Internet to identify LAN modem and communication server vendors, products, capabilities, and prices. Identify at least two LAN modem product alternatives and at least two communication server alternatives. (Each communication server must be able to simultaneously support a minimum of four dial-in/dial-out connections.) Summarize the product alternatives for LAN modems in one table and those for communication servers in a second table.

15. Use the Internet to identity at least two mobile IP vendors, products, product capabilities, and prices. Summarize product alternatives in a table.

Remote Control Software

Have you considered implementing remote control software to enable you to access files stored on your office or home PC from remote locations? This has become an important question for many workers, and there are a variety of ways to accomplish remote access and remote control. As a result, there are several issues that should be considered and addressed before choosing a remote control alternative.

Essentially, remote control software enables a remote user to access and take control of another computer, which is usually called the "host." This can be accomplished by installing remote control software on both the host and a remote computer. After the installation of the remote control software, a "remote" data communication session can be established between the host and remote computer. The remote control software enables the host computer to be controlled by the remote PC. These two computers can be connected over the Internet through TCP/IP, via LAN protocols, and even over dial-up modem connections.

Remote control has many potential advantages for business organizations. The most obvious advantage is that it enables technical support people or employees to gain access to corporate networks from home, hotels, and other remote locations by establishing remote sessions to their office PC. Remote control also enables remote workers to access files on their office PCs when they need to work from home, or when they forget to access or update a file before leaving work at the end of a busy day. Moreover, employees who are not in the same place can collaborate with each other by viewing the same documents and making suggestions. Hence, remote control software can play a key role in providing support for telecommuters and mobile workers.

Another significant advantage of remote control software lies in its ability to be used by networking and technical support professionals to check users' PC configurations remotely without having to go to the users' officers to check out and diagnose problems that they are experiencing with their PCs. This can lead to quicker troubleshooting of problems and superior PC support.

There are many remote control applications on the market. Four of the most used applications are pcAnywhere (Symantec), Carbon Copy (Altiris), Control IT (Computer Associates), and Virtual Network Computing (AT&T Research Labs UK). The most important feature of remote control software is flexibility. All these products are very flexible and work across TCP/IP networks, LANs, and dial-up connections. PcAnywhere, Control IT, and Carbon Copy work in Windows platform. Virtual Network Computing (VNC) also offers a cross-platform feature that allows a Windows host computer to be controlled by a Mac or UNIX machine.

Virtual Network Computing is free software, but it offers limited capabilities compared to the other three products, which provide file transfer and the ability to record and play back remote control sessions. According to many industry analysts, pcAnywhere and Carbon Copy are considered to be the two best products because they support multiple connection options, have superior logging and security features, and are very customizable to meet specific remote control needs. Today, however, both network administrators and users desire the flexibility of being able to establish remote sessions over the Internet to gain more flexibility. Carbon Copy and pcAnywhere do not work very well over the Web, especially when they have to cut through corporate firewalls and security. New products such as uRoam's FirePass and GoToMyPC can solve these problems, pass most firewalls, and offer remote control features that are comparable to those found in Carbon Copy and pcAnywhere.

uRoam's FirePass is an Internet application that installs in an hour and immediately gives users very secure and convenient remote access to network resources and their own office computers. Users can gain secure access from any Internet browser, including those in customers' offices, home offices, or virtually any other location in the world. They can have access to their host computer even from a PDA or WAP phone because there is no client setup or software needed on the remote access device.

GoToMyPC is a product of Expercity Inc, a Californian-based company. It is a Web-based service that allows users to remotely control any of their computers from any other PC in the world with Internet access through a secure, private connection. Similar to FirePass, GoToMyPC's users can control their PCs without having to install any special software in the host computer and, therefore, avoid complicated setups. Users only have to set up the target machine (host) in advance. To do this, users have to register at GoToMyPC.com and download the software to the target/host machine. Setting up preferences is facilitated by a setup wizard included in the download. In the remote machine, a self-launching Java plug-in from the GoToMyPC Web site allows users to have access to the host PC at any time from anyplace in the world. Once installed, the user can transfer files and access e-mail, applications, documents, and other network resources.

According to Expercity Inc., GoToMyPC also offers a cross-platform feature to access the host computer from a UNIX or Mac box. Some network administrators have expressed concern that GoToMyPC opens up a host computer to potential hacking problems, but security is very tight through an AES (Advanced Encryption Standard) encryption using 128-bit keys. Two passwords are required, one to log on to the service and another to have access to the host PC. Because of these features GoToMyPC has won several reviews and awards from many of the most influential business presses, including *Fortune, PC Magazine, CNET, ZDNet, eWeek,* and *Yahoo! Internet Life.*

CASE QUESTIONS

1. Use the Internet to find examples of companies that are leveraging remote control software to support telecommuters or mobile workers. Develop a table that identifies each company, the remote control software product(s) they are using, and reported benefits from using the software. Identify the patterns that may be observed across the entries in the table.

2. Use the Internet to find examples of companies that are leveraging remote control software to provide remote PC or networking support. Develop a table that identifies each company,

the remote control software product(s) they are using, the types of remote support being provided, and reported benefits from using the software. Identify the patterns that may be observed across the entries in the table.

3. Use the Internet to find out more about the security risks associated with remote control software and its use. Summarize the risks in a table or PowerPoint presentation.

4. Why is there is a trend toward remote control software that supports remote sessions over the Internet?

SOURCES

Mossberg, W. "Personal Technology. Here's How to Run Your PCs Remotely by Using the Internet." *The Wall Street Journal* (September 6, 2001, p. B1).

Ohlhorst, F. "Symantec Proves Fittest in Remote-Control Apps." *Crn: The Newsweekly for Builders*

of Technology Solutions (November 19, 2001, p. 18).

Strom, D. "Control Everything." *Network World* (August 20, 2001, pp. 39–41).

Note: For more information on internetworking technologies, see an additional case on the Web site, www.prenhall.com/stamper, "Routers and Denial of Service Attacks."

Network Management Objectives

Part IV
Network
Management

After studying this chapter, you should be able to:

■ Present a brief history of network management.

■ List the objectives of network management.

■ Describe ways of meeting network management objectives.

■ Explain what ergonomics means and the importance of ergonomically designed terminals.

■ Describe the network management organization.

■ Distinguish between managing a WAN and managing a LAN.

Once a network is installed and operational, it must be managed. Proper management keeps the network components functioning in an optimal way. In this chapter, we look at some techniques and tools for network management. This chapter begins with an overview of network management and its history. This chapter next identifies some of the major objectives and functions of network management, and how those objectives can be met. You then learn about generic and specific network management systems and some of the key issues associated with WAN and LAN management.

WHAT IS NETWORK MANAGEMENT?

Network management encompasses a wide range of strategic, tactical, and operational management activities related to the network infrastructures in today's organizations. Five major categories of network management activities have been addressed in the

ISO Management Framework Five major categories of network management activities have been addressed in the ISO 7498-4 document that has come to be known as the ISO Management Framework. These are: accounting management, configuration management, fault management, performance management, and security management.

ISO 7498-4 document that has come to be known as the **ISO Management Framework.** These are as follows:

Accounting management. Important activities in this category include

➤ Monitoring, recording, storing, and reporting network usage statistics

➤ Maintaining a usage accounting system for charge-back purposes

➤ Allocating network resources in accord with network usage quotas

Configuration management. Important activities in this category include

➤ Compiling and maintaining a database containing up-to-date descriptions of all network components

➤ Configuration control, including configuration updates and remote configuration control

➤ Network version control support/facilitation

Fault management. Activities in this category include

➤ Network monitoring for abnormal performance or faults

➤ Handling/processing network alarms/alerts

➤ Diagnosing/troubleshooting the causes of network faults and propagation of errors

➤ Initiating and maintaining error-recovery measures

➤ Implementing a trouble ticket system to facilitate the rapid correction of network problems

➤ Implementing a help desk for network users

Performance management. Activities in this category include

➤ Monitoring the network for traffic bottlenecks and other sources of less-than-optimal network performance

➤ Measuring, processing, storing, and reporting network performance statistics

➤ Establishing quality of service (QoS) parameters

➤ Capacity planning and the development of proactive performance plans

Security management. Important activities in this category include

➤ Intrusion detection

➤ User authentication and access control

➤ Implementation of an appropriate encryption mechanism to ensure message privacy

➤ Development and implementation of network security policies

Telecommunications Management Network (TMN) framework A set of international standards for network management from the ITU. This framework has four functional layers: business management, service management, network management, and element management.

strategic network management Addresses the role of networks and networking in an organization's computing infrastructure over the long term. Strategic network management addresses the alignment of networking resources, organizational resources, and the organization's strategic initiatives.

The International Telecommunications Union's Telecommunications Standards Sector (ITU-T) has also developed a network management framework called the **Telecommunications Management Network (TMN) framework.** Four functional layers are identified in this framework. These are

Business management. This considers the business aspects of network management, including providing support for strategic business initiatives and financial planning.

Service management. This focuses on identifying, implementing, supporting, and managing telecommunications services needed to meet the business management layer's business and financial goals. Quality of service agreements and assurances are handled at this layer.

Network management. This layer addresses the management of the network infrastructure used to deliver the services specified at the service management layer.

Element management. This layer involves the management of the individual network elements (components) that make up the network infrastructure specified at the network management layer.

In addition to viewing network management via frameworks for categorizing activities that networking professionals carry out, the various aspects of network management can also be classified as being strategically, tactically, or operationally oriented. **Strategic network management** addresses the role of networks and networking in an organization's computing infrastructure over the long term. It is focused on ensuring that the organization has the network infrastructure that it needs to achieve its long-range goals and objectives. An important aspect of strategic network management is the creation of network plans that specify how the organization's network infrastructure (including its LANs, WANs, communication services, and interfaces with the network's business partners via extranets, EDI, online markets, and other interorganizational systems) and network applications (such as its intranets, extranets, and e-business applications) will change in both the near and long term. An organization's long-range network plans should also address how the following will be accomplished:

➤ New and emerging communication technologies and applications (such as wireless applications) will be incorporated into the organization's networking infrastructure.

➤ Data will be distributed among nodes in the enterprise-wide network.

➤ Network security will be enhanced.

➤ System availability will be improved.

➤ Current network problems/shortcomings will be proactively addressed.

➤ The personnel needed to develop, operate, and maintain the network infrastructure and applications will be acquired and developed.

Capacity management, risk management, and contingency planning are other strategically oriented network management activities. Today, these strategic network plans typically range from 3 to 5 years; some, however, may have a time horizon of 10 years or more. Usually, an organization's highest ranking network managers are responsible for developing network plans and for carrying out other strategic network management functions.

An organization's midlevel network managers are typically responsible for **tactical network management**. Tactical network management includes the translation of strategic network plans into more detailed actions. For example, tactical network management involves the development of implementation plans and schedules for changes to be made in the organization's LANs and WANs that are specified in the organization's strategic network plans. Tactical network management also involves the development of plans and timetables for adding or changing network interconnections, incorporating new technologies, redistributing data among network nodes, and implementing new security technologies. Asset management (monitoring and managing the technologies that make up the network infrastructure), service level management (ensuring compliance with service level agreements), and change management (managing the implementation and documentation of changes to the network infrastructure) are other aspects of tactical network management.

The development of plans for installing LANs in new facilities is an aspect of tactical network management. Such plans often specify the following:

➤ The process and timetable to be used to select the application and system software (server NOS and client NOS) to be used in the new LAN

➤ The process and timetable to be used to identify/select the LAN hardware to be installed in the new LAN (such as servers, workstations, communication media, and wiring centers [hubs])

➤ The locations of computer cabling, electrical cabling, and lighting cabling (including the specification of locations for conduit, electric sockets, and computer jacks throughout the facilities)

➤ The installation timetable for network cabling

➤ The installation timetable for network hardware

➤ The timetable for installing and testing LAN software

tactical network management Tactical network management includes the translation of strategic network plans into more detailed actions.

Other important tactical management functions associated with the implementation of new LANs include selecting vendors, negotiating purchase/leasing contracts, negotiating installation contracts, hiring and training LAN administrators, training LAN users, and developing follow-up evaluation and maintenance plans. The vendor selection process often involves the following four steps once LAN software and hardware components have been identified:

➤ Identification and initial screening of potential vendors
➤ Giving vendors that survive the prescreening process an opportunity and timetable for responding to an RFP (request for proposal), RFQ (request for quotation), or RFB (request for bid)
➤ Evaluation of vendor responses to the RFP, RFQ, or RFB
➤ Development, negotiation, and signing of purchase/lease contracts and license agreements

operational network management Concerns the activities associated with managing the day-to-day operations of installed networks. This typically involves troubleshooting and incident management, managing users, adding/replacing network hardware, installing/upgrading software, performing network backups, and maintaining network security.

If LAN component vendors are to be directly involved in the installation of LAN components, it may also be necessary to negotiate an installation contract with them to ensure that the components are implemented in accord with a timetable that is acceptable to the organization.

Operational network management concerns the activities associated with managing the day-to-day operations of installed networks. This typically involves troubleshooting and incident management (identifying and correcting problems experienced by network users); managing users (adding new users, deleting user accounts, and modifying access control lists that specify which network resources users are able to access and use); adding/replacing workstations, servers, or peripheral devices; installing new software; performing network backups; and maintaining network security. Table 14-1 summarizes some of the additional tasks associated with operational network management. In most organizations, lower ranking network managers/administrators are responsible for operational network management activities.

Table 14-1   Examples of Operational Network Management Tasks

➤ Designing and implementing directory services structures
➤ Creating, maintaining, and deleting user accounts
➤ Establishing and changing user and work-group access privileges
➤ Establishing and changing security for server directories, files, and resources
➤ Creating log-in scripts for work groups and individual users
➤ Adding/removing workstations, servers, printers, and other devices from the network
➤ Installing, updating, and testing software applications
➤ Establishing and changing shared usage configurations for workstations
➤ Creating and modifying network drive mappings
➤ Monitoring server operations
➤ Establishing and changing print server configurations
➤ Performing network backups
➤ Troubleshooting network access problems
➤ Performing preventive and corrective maintenance
➤ Providing user training, support, and documentation
➤ Creating and maintaining network documentation
➤ Implementing server, workstation, and printer upgrades
➤ Developing RFQs and RFBs for new LAN components

HISTORY OF NETWORK MANAGEMENT

An organization's network management team has historically been responsible for the selection, implementation, testing, expansion, operation, and maintenance of the data communication portion of the organization's computing environment and IT infrastructure. Over time, their responsibilities have evolved and become more complex. Early networks were concerned with the transmission of character-oriented data. Currently, data being transmitted by high-speed networks also includes graphics, voice clips, and video. Some companies are also combining telephone services with computer data on the same medium. With the integration of voice, data, and video transmissions on a common medium, the role of network management is expanding to include management of all of the telecommunication needs of an organization. In the past, voice, video, and data communication were usually separate and were managed by different groups. In today's communication environment, integrating and sharing media and hardware components can produce significant savings for a company. Covering all facets of telecommunication management is beyond the scope of this text. In this chapter, we confine the discussion to management of a data communication network.

The role of network manager, like that of database administrator, is a relatively new position within the data processing industry. Both positions were created by the technological expansion of the 1970s and the recognition of the increasing importance of these technologies to the storage, retrieval, and maintenance of business data. These positions are similar in several respects. Both have high visibility among system users. The database administrator is called when required data is unavailable. If network workstations do not work or network response time is unsatisfactory, the network manager is notified. Both roles are responsible for configurations, planning, tuning, and establishing standards and procedures in their respective areas. Both positions require personnel with a strong technical background, good leadership qualities, and an ability to work well with people who have wide ranges of technical expertise. These positions and the importance of an organization's processing and communication resources have been validated by new executive positions such as chief information officer (CIO), chief technology officer (CTO), and chief knowledge officer (CKO), which have been appearing in many companies.

In the remainder of this chapter, the terms **network manager**, *network administrator*, and *LAN administrator* refer to the function of network management and, therefore, to a team of people rather than to a single person.

NETWORK MANAGEMENT OBJECTIVES

Network Requirements

Business organizations are using networks for a diverse set of data communication applications. No matter how complex these applications are, or how the network is being used by a business, several requirements must be met for the network to be viewed positively by managers and users. These include performance, consistency, flexibility, availability, reliability, recovery, and security.

Performance

The performance of a network can be measured in several ways. Two very common measures are response time and throughput. **Response time** is the interval between entering a message and getting a response from the destination node. Response time has two major components: the time required for data transmission and the time

network manager
A person or management team responsible for configuring, planning, monitoring, tuning, and establishing standards and procedures for a network. Many titles exist for network managers across organizations including *LAN administrator, network administrator, system administrator,* and *WAN administrator.*

response time The amount of time it takes a computer system to comply with a user's request. Usually the time elapsed between the user pressing a key (or clicking a mouse button) to send the request and the return of the first character of the computer system's response.

required for processing the message. Data transmission time is often a function of the speed of the communication circuit(s) between the sender and receiver. For example, the time it takes to transfer a file from an Internet host to a PC is likely to be much faster if they are linked by a digital subscriber line (DSL) supporting download speeds of 640 kbps or more than if sender and receiver have to use 56-kbps modems to communicate over dial-up telephone circuits.

The time it takes a node to process and respond to a message it has received is typically a function of the complexity of the message. This is especially true when the message is a business transaction. Some transactions can only be completed through large numbers of input-output (I/O) operations (such as database accesses and updates). These more complex transactions take longer to process than simple, straightforward transactions.

throughput The amount of work performed by a system per unit of time. The total useful information communicated or processed during a specific time period.

Throughput is the amount of work performed by the network in a specified unit of time. Like response time, throughput is influenced by the speed of the communication circuits and the complexity of transactions, especially when transactions can only be processed through the collaboration of multiple nodes. Network throughput, however, is also affected by the amount of overhead data that must be transmitted to ensure that messages are correctly and securely routed to their destinations. As you will learn later in the book, routing processes and network management systems often involve the exchange of large numbers of messages among network nodes containing data about the status of the network (such as which links or circuits are overloaded or which servers are unavailable). These exchanges add a significant amount of traffic on the network and take up space on links and circuits that could otherwise be used to transmit business data. When this happens, network throughput is reduced, and response times are likely to be adversely affected.

In successful networks, both response time and throughput are adequate to meet business needs. This usually means that response times are low and throughput is high. When response times and throughput are not acceptable, network managers often engage in "network tuning" to bring them back in line.

There are other measures of network performance, such as turnaround time and transaction rate; however, for business data communication applications, response times and throughput are generally considered to be the key measures.

Consistency

consistency A consistent system is one that works predictably with respect to the people who use the system, response times, and throughput.

Consistency is used to describe a data communication system that works predictably both with respect to response times and throughput by network users. Inconsistent response times can be extremely annoying to network users and may be less desirable than a slow but consistent response time. Complete consistency, of course, is difficult to achieve because of occasional periods of heavy ("peak") processing demands and network traffic. One common network design objective is for the response time for most transactions of a given type to be lower than a certain threshold, such as 3 seconds. Needless to say, users are likely to be frustrated when the same transaction takes 3 seconds 50 percent of the time, 10 to 30 seconds 35 percent of the time, and more than 30 seconds 15 percent of the time. Such inconsistency not only is frustrating, but it also limits the network's ability to assist users in being productive workers.

Flexibility

flexibility The ability to have growth and change with minimal impact on existing applications and users.

One constant in today's business data communications networks is change. Over time, there are alterations in both the number and types of transactions, data, and applications supported on the network. In network environments, **flexibility** means that both growth and change must be accommodated with minimal impact on existing applications and users. The ability to increase processing power, the number of computers attached to the network, the capacity of communication circuits, and the size and number of databases are critical to the long-term effectiveness and success of a network. Many businesses have learned that one of the best ways to ensure flexibility is to use industry-standard network architectures and protocols. This approach makes it easier to add or upgrade nodes and ensures connectivity among network components.

Availability

Availability requires the network, and the applications that it supports, to be continuously available to users during the workday. In an increasing number of businesses, this means 24/7/365 user access; that is, the network is available to users 24 hours a day, 7 days a week, 365 days a year. For some business applications, significant financial losses can result from the network not being available when users need it. For example, an airline might be unable to sell seats on a flight if its reservation system is down, or it may over-book a flight and cause extra work for airline employees and penalty payments to travelers for their inconvenience.

Reliability

A network's availability is often a function of the reliability of its components. **Reliability** is a measure of the frequency of network failure (or lack thereof). In the minds of users, a network is typically perceived to be reliable if it performs consistently across time and is available whenever they need it. A network failure is any event that prohibits users from using the network as they usually do during the workday. This includes any hardware breakdown, such as a processor failure in a server that is not fault tolerant, as well as an application or system software failure or the failure of the medium (such as a faulty data communication link or circuit). **Mean time between failure (MTBF)** is a measure of the average time until a given component may be expected to fail after it has been first put in use, and **mean time to repair (MTTR)** is the average time required to fix a failed component. Both figures are important in determining the frequency of failure and the time required to return the network to successful operation.

One way to improve the reliability of data communication systems is to increase **fault tolerance,** the ability to continue processing despite component failure. There are levels of fault tolerance. In a fully fault-tolerant system, single points of failure do not cause system failure, because every key component in the network has a backup component that takes over if a failure occurs. Fault-tolerant networks are created using both fault-tolerant hardware and fault-tolerant software.

Recovery

Recovery addresses the fact that all computer systems and networks, even those built for continuous operation, can fail. In some cases, it may not be the network that fails, but either the source of power or the people who are responsible for network operations and maintenance. Regardless of the cause, the system must be able to recover to a consistent point. For business transactions, recovery means that when the network is brought back up, databases have no partially updated transactions, no transactions that have been processed twice, and no transactions that have been lost. When network recovery works the way that it should, users are advised of the state of all work they had in progress at the time of failure in order to keep them from submitting duplicate transactions or failing to reenter a transaction not received by the database server before the failure.

reliability The probability that the system will continue to function over a given time period.

mean time between failure (MTBF) A measure of the average amount of time a given component can be expected to operate before failing.

mean time to repair (MTTR) The average amount of time between the failure of a device or service and its repair.

fault tolerance The ability to continue to operate, without stopping, when a network component fails. Fault-tolerant networks often use a combination of hardware and software techniques that improve the reliability of a system. Redundant components are widely used to increase fault tolerance. Many systems monitor component operations and immediately switch to a redundant component when a component failure is detected.

Security

Security has become increasingly important as the microcomputer and the Internet have made many computer networks accessible to almost everyone. As more businesses use the Internet for electronic commerce and as the number of computer systems accessible to Internet users continues to grow, organizations face greater challenges in ensuring the privacy and security of sensitive information in their databases, including financial data and classified military information. Unfortunately, security has not always received a high priority in system and network design, so making up for these deficiencies is necessary in the development of future systems and the enhancement of existing ones. Network security is discussed in more detail in Chapter 16.

Three overriding objectives of network management are to support system users, keep the network operating efficiently, and provide cost-effective solutions to an organization's telecommunication requirements. If these three objectives are met, the network management team will be successful.

Supporting System Users

Supporting system users means empowering them with the hardware and software tools to do their jobs effectively. Essentially, it means keeping the network users satisfied. User satisfaction can also be enhanced by providing proper user training, warning users of periods when the network will be taken out of operation, fixing problems that limit user access to required network resources, and keeping users informed of system changes and their consequences.

Keeping the user community informed is one of the easiest and most overlooked ways to achieve user satisfaction. Users should be informed of scheduled downtime, imminent downtime, periods when other processing requirements are likely to increase response times, certain changes in hardware or software, and changes in personnel with whom users will be interacting. This information can be disseminated in several ways, the most direct being general e-mail distributions to all network users. Users are generally understanding when downtime is unanticipated and no prior warning is possible. On the other hand, users may be less understanding if they arrive on Saturday afternoon to catch up on some work and find the system down for a scheduled but unannounced reason. Many NOSs include modules that can be used to send notices to users when they log on to the system and that send notices to online users of system status for short-term, emergency network interruptions.

Another useful communication medium is newsletters, which can alert users to downtimes scheduled for preventive maintenance and reconfigurations, announce new capabilities, serve as a training aid, answer frequently asked questions, solicit comments and suggestions, and generally help people feel they are an integral part of the network team. Newsletters are able to reach all users of a system and thus are a valuable communication resource.

Meetings between users and the network management team should be held periodically to promote communication. In many organizations, this is done at least quarterly. Mature systems not undergoing change may require less frequent meetings than those that are new, changing, or experiencing problems. Such forums allow people to air grievances, disseminate information, propose new ideas, educate users and network managers, resolve problems, plan for future changes, and establish new goals. For more hands-on communication, formal and informal training can be helpful. Some companies find informal seminars at lunchtime or after hours a very effective way to exchange information. Formal training classes serve not only to educate users but also to establish contacts within the organization. New users, in particular, will find it easier to call on an expert should a problem arise if they have been given an opportunity to work with that person during a noncrisis situation.

Measures of System Effectiveness

One of the priorities of network managers is to ensure that users have access to the network and its resources when they need it. In most businesses and in many other organizations, workers depend on computers and networks to perform their jobs. Frustration is sure to arise when workers are unable to access the computing resources they need to be productive. Network downtime or malfunctions can be major causes of worker stress and productivity declines. As a result, network managers strive to ensure that the network provides good performance, is available when needed, and is reliable when being used.

Good Performance   In many organizations, good network performance means a predictable transaction response time. Response time depends on the nature of the transaction. Transactions differ in the amount of work to be accomplished by network servers and the volume of messages/data that must be transmitted across the network in order to complete them. For every transaction performed over the network system, a realistic response time objective should be established. Predictable response times require that most transactions be completed within a small range around the established response time goal. For example, for an expected transaction response time of 10 seconds, it is realistic to expect 95 percent of all transactions of that type to be completed within the 9 to 11 second range, and 100 percent of such transactions to be completed within 20 seconds. Erratic response times are more likely to be negatively perceived by users than slow but predictable responses. Of the two major response time components—processing time and communication time—the network manager ordinarily has little or no control over the application processing and database access components unless the manager is directly involved in choosing the application software and configuring the server(s) on which the application is run. The network manager does, however, have control over network configuration and the speed of the communication medium. The configuration aspects include the number of workstations on a given network segment; communication hardware used (such as hubs, switches, routers, multiplexors, front-end processors, and concentrators); the configuration of network workstations used; the number of intermediate nodes through which transaction messages must travel (hops); networking software; and error prevention/correction mechanisms. Each of these contributes to the overall performance of the network and its ability to predictably process transactions.

Availability   **Availability** means that all necessary components are operable and accessible when a user requires them; for a LAN user, these include the workstation, network adapters, hubs or switches, servers, printers, and LAN software. Accessibility means the user can use the network resources when needed. In a network that has a license agreement for an application program that limits the application's use to 10 concurrent users, the application will not be available to an eleventh authorized user if it is already being used by 10 coworkers. No authorized users, however, will be able to access the application software if the network itself is unavailable. If the network is out of service, no users are able to access the computing resources they need to be productive. Because of this, network managers strive to maximize network uptime and user access to network resources. Three factors influence network uptime/availability: operational considerations, mean time between failures (MTBF), and mean time to repair (MTTR).

Operational considerations may require that portions of the network or network resources be temporarily taken out of service. In some instances, this can be scheduled

availability All necessary components of a network are operable and accessible when a user requires them. Availability implies reliability. Fault-tolerant systems are typically "high availability" systems.

to minimize the disruption of user work activities. For example, some areas of an online transaction processing system may be available only during standard working hours. If payroll transactions typically take place during standard work hours, the payroll system may be unavailable at night. In some installations, the entire online transaction processing system may be shut down at night to ensure that transactions only take place during specified work hours. Other operational requirements such as preventive maintenance and installation of new hardware or software can temporarily remove all or parts of the system from use. Generally, operational considerations can be planned around work schedules to enable online users to work without being disrupted.

Mean time between failures (MTBF) is the average period that a network component can be expected to operate before failing. A switch with MTBF of 2,000 hours that operates an average of 8 hours a day, 23 days a month, would be expected to fail once every 10.87 months. (2,000 hours/[8 hours a day × 23 days a month]) = 10.87 months.) MTBF figures are typically provided by manufacturers of data communication hardware components in order to indicate the reliability of their products. Although the figures provided should not be assumed to be exact, they do provide network managers some idea about how long a given component can be expected to operate before having to be repaired or replaced.

Mean time to repair (MTTR) is the average amount of time required to place a failed network component back into service. For certain components, repair time is fairly constant, such as replacing a failed disk drive in a server with a spare. For some network components, however, there may be considerable variations in repair time. Some components require a specially trained repairperson to travel to the location of the failed component, and run various diagnostic routines and testing procedures before fixing the component and getting it back in service.

The availability of a network component can be defined by the probability function[1]

$$A(t) = a \;/\; (a + b) + b \;/\; (a + b) \times e^{-(a+b)t}$$

where $a = 1/\text{MTTR}$, $b = 1/\text{MTBF}$, e is the natural logarithm, and t is a time interval. The equation gives the probability that a component will be available when required by a user. For a router with an MTBF of 2,000 hours and an MTTR of 0.5 hours (typical of replacement with an on-site spare),

$$a = 1 \;/\; 0.5 = 2 \text{ and } b = 1 \;/\; 2,000 = 0.0005$$

The router's availability for an 8-hour period, then, is

$$A(8) = 2 \;/\; (2 + 0.0005) + 0.0005 \;/\; (2 + 0.0005) \times e^{-2+0.0005)8}$$
$$= 0.99975 + 2.8 \times 10^{-11}$$
$$= 0.9997$$

On average, network managers and users can expect the router to be unavailable three times in every 10,000 tries. Because the exponential term approaches zero and becomes insignificant as the time interval increases, availability in such cases becomes

$$A = \text{MTBF} \;/\; (\text{MTBF} + \text{MTTR})$$

Table 14-2 shows availability given different values for MTBF and MTTR.

---

[1]Nickel, Wallace E. "Determining Network Effectiveness." *Mini-Micro Systems* (November 1978).

Table 14-2   Availability for Several MTBF and MTTR Values

	MTBF				
	10	100	1,000	10,000	100,000
MTTR					
1	0.90909091	0.99009901	0.99900100	0.99990001	0.99999000
2	0.83333333	0.98039216	0.99800399	0.99980004	0.99998000
5	0.66666667	0.95238095	0.99502488	0.99950025	0.99995000
10	0.50000000	0.90909091	0.99009901	0.99900100	0.99990001
20	0.33333333	0.83333333	0.98039216	0.99800399	0.99980004

Availability with Multiple Components   If several components—such as workstation, hub, medium, and router—must be linked together to make the system available to the user, then system availability is given by the product of the availabilities of the component parts (Nickel, 1978):

$$A_s = A_w \times A_h \times A_l \times A_r$$

where A represents availability, and the subscripts w, h, l, and r represent the system, workstation, link, and router, respectively. If each component has an availability of 0.999, the user will see a system availability of

$$A_s = 0.996006 = 0.996$$

In this situation, statistically the user would find the system unavailable 4 times out of every 1,000 attempts, or once every 250 attempts. The availability factor is important in determining how many spare components to stock and how much productive time might be lost when the system is unavailable. Figure 14-1 illustrates system availability as a function of MTBF and MTTR.

It is important to note that the availability formula presented here applies when the following two conditions are met:

1. The network components are linked together in a series.
2. The availability of each component is independent of the availabilities of other components.

Availability formulas for parallel components also exist and provide a mathematical basis for using redundant components/systems to improve availability.

Reliability   As noted earlier in the chapter, *reliability* is the probability that the network will function consistently across time. In the minds of network users, the network may be perceived to be unreliable if it is down too often or for extended periods of time during standard work hours. In other words, user perceptions of the network's reliability are often correlated with the network's availability. Users will also have negative perceptions of the network's reliability if response times for specific transactions are inconsistent or if the system returns different responses to the same user command.

Nickel's assessment of reliability focuses on the consistency of response times and how this is related to the likelihood of network component failure. According to Nickel, if a transaction requires 3 seconds for a response to be received, then the reliability of the system is the probability that the system will not fail during that 3 seconds.

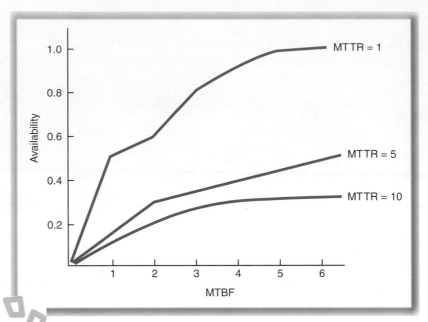

Figure 14-1 Availability, MTBF, and MTTR

Reliability of the network includes error characteristics of the medium and stability of the hardware and software components. More specifically, network reliability is a function of the MTBF. In some cases, the user will see circuit errors in the form of slow response times. Data received in error will cause retransmissions, slower response times, and congestion of the medium. If the errors are persistent, the retry threshold for the link might be exceeded and the link consequently removed from service. If modems are a part of the connection between users and network resources, a large number of errors may cause the modems to change to a lower speed to minimize the impact of the errors (see Chapter 6).

Hardware or software component failure is usually experienced by the user as network downtime. With fault-tolerant systems, the effect is either negligible or somewhat slower response times, depending on network traffic and processing demands. Even though the workstation and all components of the network except one are functioning properly, the user, who is unable to continue working because of that one failed component, views the network as being down.

The reliability function, which is the probability that the system will not fail during a given period, is given by

$$R(t) = e^{-bt}$$

where b is the inverse of the MTBF, as described earlier. The time units used for MTBF and t must be the same. If the MTBF for a server is 2,000 hours, and a transaction requires 1 minute to complete, then the reliability is

$$R(1 / 60) = e^{-(1/2,000 \times 1/60)} = e^{-(1/120,000)} = 0.999992$$

All times are expressed in hours. This equation shows that if the server is available at the beginning of the transaction, the probability is high that it will remain available throughout a 1-minute transaction.

Reliability with Multiple Components   Like availability, network reliability is the product of the reliability of its components. If a system consists of a workstation, a medium, two hubs, and a server, the reliability of the system from the user's perspective is

$$R_s = R_w \times R_h \times R_l \times R_h \times R_c$$

where *s, w, h, l, h,* and *c* represent the reliability of the system, workstation, hub, medium link, hub, and server, respectively. Figure 14-2 shows reliability as a function of the MTBF.

Overall Effectiveness   The overall **effectiveness** of a network is a measure of how well it serves users' needs. Mathematically, effectiveness is given by the following formula:

$$E = A \times R$$

where *E* is the effectiveness of the network, *A* is the network's availability, and *R* is the network's reliability. From the user's point of view, the network is likely to be perceived as being effective when its availability is high and when the network performs consistently across time. Because both availability and reliability are related to MTBF and MTTR, the formula also suggests that network managers should strive to use network components with high MTBF and low MTTR. Network components will fail, but if they can be repaired/replaced quickly, network availability and effectiveness can remain high. The trade-offs between network availability and reliability are illustrated in Figure 14-3.

effectiveness A measure of how well a system serves users' needs. Effectiveness of a system is a function of its availability and reliability. Fault tolerance and consistency are likely to positively influence user perceptions of the system's effectiveness.

Figure 14-2   Reliability and MTBF

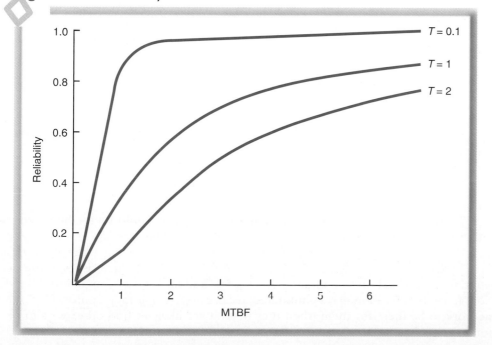

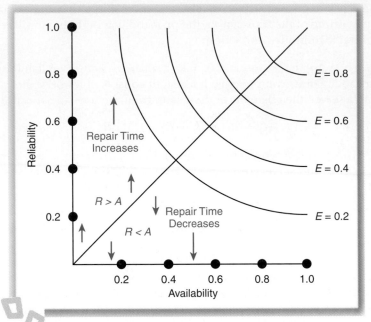

Figure 14-3   Reliability, Availability, and Effectiveness

Reliability of Backup Components   In many networks, alternative or replacement components are available should one component fail. Communication paths often have alternative links available, and fault-tolerant systems often have available backup servers, disk drives, hubs/switches, network adapters, or other components. Such network backup/replacement components increase the MTBF of the network, which increases the network's reliability, availability, and effectiveness. With backup components available (such as duplexed servers or disk drives) that operate in parallel with primary network components in a standby mode should the primary components fail, the reliability of the components is given by (Nickel, 1978):

$$R_p = 1 - (1 - R_s)^2$$

where R represents reliability, p represents the components operating in parallel, and s represents a single component. If the reliability of a communication link is 0.995, the reliability of the link with a backup is

$$R = 1 - (1 - 0.995)^2 = 0.999975$$

This means that the probability that a network user would be unable to access either the primary or the backup link is less than 1 in 10,000.

Network managers should strive to ensure that users perceive the network as being effective, useful, and usable. If users fail to see these characteristics in the network, there are likely to be high levels of user frustration and user complaints. In addition, network utilization may be inhibited; users who feel that they cannot rely on the network to be there for them when they need it are likely to find other ways to perform their job tasks that do not involve the use of the network.

Network managers can enhance network availability and reliability in a number of ways. These include the following:

➤ Building fault tolerance into the system

➤ Incorporating plug-and-play capabilities wherever possible within the network

➤ Having spare components on hand so that failed components can be replaced quickly

➤ Regularly backing up critical files and applications

➤ Ensuring that the network support staff are well-trained and have ready access to diagnostic and troubleshooting tools

➤ Using network monitoring and management tools to alert the organization's network professionals of impending component failures (such tools are discussed in Chapter 15)

Cost-Effectiveness

Another objective of network management is the provision of cost-effective solutions to the data communication needs of the organization and its users. As discussed throughout this text, there are typically multiple solutions available to address the data communication needs of network users. Network management is responsible for selecting solutions that are feasible and cost-effective. This requires network managers to select wisely among the many options that are available and to choose options that will help the organization reduce or avoid costs over the long term. If the network cannot contribute to the financial position of a company, it probably should not be implemented.

Planning   Effective network planning can play a significant role in ensuring cost-effective computing and networking solutions. When configuring a network, there are two basic alternatives: installing equipment to meet immediate needs and paying the price of upgrading when the time comes (which sometimes leads to lower immediate costs but a higher cost of expansion) or immediately buying equipment in anticipation of future needs (which creates higher immediate costs with low-cost, easy expansion). Buying immediately for future needs is sometimes risky because technology changes so quickly. Usually, the best alternative is to purchase modular equipment, which can be upgraded in small increments so overpurchasing is seldom necessary and expansion is easy. A variation of this approach is the planned movement (migration) of equipment, whereby lower capacity equipment is gradually moved to areas where it can continue to be used productively as newer, higher capacity equipment is acquired. Such planned migration of networking equipment can prolong the useful life of network components and allow the organization to get the most from the money that it invested in them.

Modular Expansion   Modular growth is available for several network components, the most fundamental being the workstations and servers. Many computer vendors offer a broad line of systems that allow growth within the product line. Most vendors have several different product families spanning the distance between workstations to mainframes, and within each family there is also a certain amount of growth potential. The transition from one product family to another, however, is not always easy. This often requires a recompilation of programs and application program rewrites. In addition, when an organization reaches the top of one product family and is ready to upgrade to the next one, the processors, operating systems, and network software often are not the same as those in current use, even if they are produced by the same vendor.

modular expansion
A system that allows
the user to upgrade
from a small system to
a more powerful sys-
tem incrementally by
adding other modules
that are similar or
identical to those that
are already in place.

Over time, a number of vendors have devised approaches for **modular expansion** that enable organizations to expand processing capabilities within a product family rather than having to upgrade from one product family to another. Additional processing capability can be achieved, for example, by adding more of the same types of servers that the organization is already using. There is no need to remove, sell, or return the existing equipment; it is simply augmented to provide the additional processing power. Computer vendors that offer this capability, such as Compaq, Dell, Gateway, Hewlett-Packard, IBM, and Micron, recognize that expansion is very common for their successful customers and that facilitating modular expansion is a good way for them to attract and retain business customers. Modular expansion is also facilitated by most of today's network operating system vendors (such as Microsoft, Novell, and Red Hat) whose products support symmetric multiprocessing (SMP) and server clustering. Most storage area network (SAN) and network attached storage (NAS) vendors also have products that enable modular expansion.

Planned Equipment Moves   Planned equipment moves are an alternative when modular expansion is not possible. For example, the central site could begin with a 4-port multiplexor, with remote sites also having 4-port multiplexors. As the number of applications in a remote site grows, the central-site 4-port mux could be moved there; a new 8-port mux could be added to the central site; and the old 4-port mux could be used in a new location or cascaded off the 8-port mux. This is illustrated in Figure 14-4. Similarly, low-speed hubs/switches can be moved to low-traffic locations as they are replaced by high-speed hubs/switches. If the older equipment is not needed, it may be possible to keep it in inventory to be used as replacements for failed equipment. This

Figure 14-4   Relocation of Components

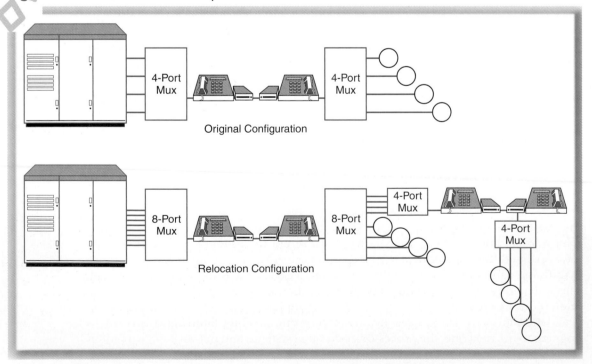

type of *equipment migration* requires longer range planning than the other options; however, the financial rewards may make it preferable to the disposal of old equipment, possibly at a significant loss, every time a new piece is acquired.

ACHIEVING NETWORK MANAGEMENT OBJECTIVES

In most business organizations, the objectives of network management are met by a combination of competent staff, hard work, careful planning, good documentation, implementing standards and procedures, communicating with users, and being able to work with network component vendors and other people to resolve problems. Although some of these elements may be absent in a successful network, the probability of success is often directly proportional to how well these elements are realized.

Competent Staff

Arguably the most important factor in the achievement of network management objectives is ensuring that the organization is able to attract and retain competent networking professionals (such as WAN managers, LAN administrators, and network technicians) Having a competent staff can go a long way toward ensuring that the network is perceived as being effective, available, and reliable by network users. Specific staff qualifications depend on the hardware and software used, but some generalizations can be made. The functions of network management can be grouped into the areas of design and configuration, testing, diagnosis, documentation, repair, and, sometimes, coding. The team must have detailed knowledge of both hardware and software; ideally, every member of the team would know both areas, but often some are experts on hardware, whereas for others, the specialty is software. The staff should be versatile and creative in resolving problems because many solutions are ad hoc, temporary ones that require ingenuity. Finally, and perhaps most important, staff should be able to work well with both technical and nontechnical personnel. Being able to describe the technology to those not "in the know" and to elicit the necessary technical information from nontechnical users is critical to the team's success.

Design and Configuration

The networking staff should be skilled in the use of network diagnostic and planning tools. (Some of these are described later in this chapter.) In design and configuration, they should understand configuration alternatives and the strengths, weaknesses, and ergonomic features of different configurations. They must be willing and able to keep up with changes in hardware and software of the existing network as well as capabilities offered by other vendors. WAN professionals also must be able to make sense of the multitude of different fee/tariff structures for the services offered by competing carriers.

Ergonomics

Ergonomics, also called *human engineering*, is the science of designing equipment to maximize worker productivity by reducing operator fatigue and discomfort while improving safety. Currently, a very important consideration in microcomputer design and selection is the unit's human engineering. Several physical problems have been attributed to poor terminal design, including exposure to radiation emitted by monitors, headaches, eyestrain, carpal tunnel syndrome and other repetitive motion disorders, and arthritic conditions resulting from prolonged workstation use. In the not-too-distant past, a major concern of terminal and workstation use was the emission of

ergonomics The science of people-machine relationships. It involves designing equipment to maximize worker productivity by reducing operator fatigue and discomfort while improving safety.

radiation by VDUs (video display units) and monitors. Terminal and microcomputer monitors emit low-level radiation, and users working near the monitors are exposed to those emissions. Some studies have noted a higher incidence of birth defects among women working at VDUs, and lawsuits have been filed in this regard. According to U.S. law, radiation emitted from a terminal must be less than 0.0005 rems per hour at a distance of 2 inches from the screen. Although most VDUs and monitors comply with these requirements, radiation emission remains an important issue in today's organizations, especially for workers whose jobs require continual use of these network components.

Other important ergonomic factors include monitor position, monitor display, and keyboard position. Among the most common user complaints are head, neck, and eyestrain. Head and neck strain can be caused by the user having to adjust to the fixed position of a monitor. An ergonomically designed monitor can be tilted and swiveled to a position that is comfortable for the user. Finger, hand, and wrist strains result from improper positioning of the keyboard. The keyboard should be detached from the monitor so that it can be moved to a position comfortable for the user; wrist guards and split keyboard designs can also contribute to reduced incidence of carpal tunnel syndrome and keyboarding-related repetitive motion injuries. Computer furniture is also an ergonomic factor to consider. With a chair that can be raised and lowered and a movable keyboard platform, the computer system can be adjusted comfortably to the user. Again, the key is to have a unit capable of adjusting to a user rather than requiring a user to adjust to the equipment.

Eyestrain can be caused by poorly formed characters, flickering screens, and poor foreground/background colors. A good monitor has crisp, well-formed characters and images, and the contrast between foreground and background colors should be visually pleasing. Ergonomic studies show that green or amber foreground characters on a black background are easier on the eyes than other combinations, such as white letters on a black background. Another factor affecting eyestrain is screen flickering. CRT screen images are constantly refreshed by "repainting" the screen image. Low refresh rates cause screen images to fade before being refreshed, creating a flickering effect that can cause headaches and eyestrain.

Ideal Terminal Characteristics   The ideal VDU display should be easy on the eyes, with a nonglare surface. Green phosphor or amber characters on a black background are preferred to white characters on a black background. The display device should tilt and swivel for ease of reading. The screen image should be refreshed at a sufficient rate to avoid flicker, and contrast should be adjustable to ease eyestrain. Display characters should be well formed and easy to read. The keyboard should be detachable and at a convenient height. Keys should be sculpted and arranged for easy access. The keyboard should emit a click to reinforce each keystroke, and the loudness of the click should be controllable, from inaudible to somewhat loud.

Diagnosis

Diagnostic and troubleshooting skills are an important aspect of networking staff competency. The organization's networking staff should be skilled in rapidly diagnosing the causes of communication and network access problems, especially when network uptime of 100 percent is critical to the organization's normal functioning. Network failures are likely to prevent employees from fully performing their job functions and to decrease their productivity. In some situations, direct revenue may be lost, such as when online ordering systems fail.

Planning

Planning is another key to success. Because of the dynamic nature of networks, constant planning and planning revisions are necessary to ensure that network management objectives are met. Too often, network managers are so caught up in day-to-day activities that they ignore long-range planning. This behavior is both common and self-perpetuating. Without good planning, problems occur more often and require a greater amount of time to be solved. There is often truth to the adage "If you fail to plan, you plan to fail." Corporate (long-term) goals and objectives are generally established by upper-level managers as part of the strategic planning process. Planning that defines the actions essential to accomplishing strategic goals and objectives should include short-term and long-term objectives. Short-term planning includes scheduling of personnel, hiring, training, budgeting, and network maintenance and enhancement activities. Long-term planning involves predicting and resolving expansion issues, integrating new technologies, and budgeting. The importance of network planning cannot be overemphasized because so many aspects of network management revolve around these plans, including the development of an appropriate network infrastructure within the organization and the development of a competent staff to support the network infrastructure.

Documentation, Standards, and Procedures

Documentation, standards, and procedures are an outgrowth of good planning. Good documentation includes source code listings of the software, logic diagrams, internal and external specifications for the system, wiring and connection diagrams, hardware specifications, and users' manuals. Table 14-3 includes some of the items included in an organization's network documentation. Documentation is used in all phases of network management, and good, up-to-date documentation can facilitate the jobs of networking managers and support technicians.

Standards and procedures together provide consistency in system management. Standards set minimal acceptable levels of performance and implementation. Procedural guidelines aid in operating and maintaining the system and are especially necessary in resolving problem situations.

In summary, achieving network management objectives requires a group of talented people who

> ➤ Have the right tools in place
> ➤ Have a well-defined but flexible direction for the short term and the long term
> ➤ Are willing to work unusual hours in sometimes difficult or stressful environments
> ➤ Can work effectively with people at all levels of capability

The growth in network management has placed large demands on the supply of qualified people. As a result, network management personnel are currently some of the most difficult IT professionals to find and retain.

ORGANIZING NETWORK MANAGEMENT FUNCTIONS

Once a system has been successfully installed, tested, and made operational, the day-to-day management of the network begins. Operations tasks include monitoring, control, diagnostics, and repair. Just as application developers design a system to solve business problems, network managers should design a system—partially manual, partially automated—that addresses the problems of operations. The manual portion of the system is necessary for restoring a down system, a task that cannot be accomplished with software when the hardware is not running.

Table 14-3   Examples of Network Documentation

> ➤ Network graphs/maps for each WAN, LAN, and backbone network
> ➤ Wiring diagrams for all networks
> ➤ Lists of all internetworking equipment (such as bridges, routers, and switches), their physical addresses, and their network addresses
> ➤ Lists of all network backup, redundancy, and security components and their locations
> ➤ Serial number inventory of all data communication equipment
> ➤ Copies all network component purchase orders
> ➤ Copies of all network software license agreements
> ➤ Preventive maintenance schedules and procedures for network hardware
> ➤ List of all network troubleshooting and diagnostic tools
> ➤ Equipment movement (migration) plans
> ➤ The organization's strategic network plan
> ➤ The organization's tactical network plans
> ➤ Training/development plans for network personnel
> ➤ Disaster, recovery, and contingency plans/procedures
> ➤ Diagnostic/troubleshooting procedures/guidelines for network hardware components
> ➤ Operations manuals for network hardware
> ➤ Copies of all local, state, and federal codes/regulations with which the organization must comply
> ➤ Network software documentation
> ➤ Network hardware maintenance logs
> ➤ Vendor maintenance specifications for network hardware (MTBF and MTTR)
> ➤ Network equipment warranties
> ➤ List of all dial-in connections
> ➤ WAN service contracts with carriers and third-party companies
> ➤ Vendor technical service contact information and contracts
> ➤ Backup procedures and schedules
> ➤ User authentication and authorization policies
> ➤ Current copies of user IDs, passwords, e-mail addresses, and workstation addresses
> ➤ Complete set of IP addresses and NIC addresses

Control

Control functions to be performed include putting failed lines or client workstations back in operation, adding new lines or workstations, and taking failed components out of the system. Control of a geographically separated, multiple-platform network is somewhat more difficult because parts of the control function must also be distributed. The distributed case is discussed here because a subset of it applies to single-site networks.

network control center The central location for network control activities within an organization that is responsible for monitoring the network and taking corrective action when necessary. It can range from a single software application on a network node, to a single workstation with multiple network monitoring tools, to a "war room" that controls a large enterprise or carrier network.

Network Control Center   A **network control center** is responsible for monitoring the network and taking corrective action when necessary. In an organization that has a distributed network spanning geographically dispersed sites, it is not uncommon to have more than one control center. In a network of cooperating, independent users, such as a network of universities, each node can participate in the management and control functions, with each installation being responsible for control of its part of the network. However, the central control site is usually able to resolve internode communication problems.

Network control centers are typically equipped with one or more dedicated computers running network control software. Several companies provide hardware and software designed specifically for network control. A network control system typically consists of special monitors/agents that collect **network statistics** that are periodically transmitted to a network database for storage and analysis. The monitoring systems gather information such as error rates, data transfer rates, and the number of retransmission attempts resulting from errors. Trend analysis of this data can help determine gradual degradation so faults are immediately reported and corrective measures taken.

Network Monitoring   The network control center staff is responsible for analyzing the data collected by network monitors/agents in order to probe network nodes for problems and to identify needed changes in the network's configuration. The network statistics that are gathered and stored in the network database enable network managers to identify necessary or desirable changes to the system. These include

- ➤ Bringing lines and workstations into and out of service
- ➤ Bringing network applications to an orderly halt and starting network applications
- ➤ Altering network parameters, such as firewall packet-filtering parameters
- ➤ Checking for line errors and implementing corrections
- ➤ Initiating and evaluating line traces
- ➤ Running diagnostic routines
- ➤ Adding and deleting users from the system
- ➤ Controlling passwords for local and remote nodes
- ➤ Maintaining the control center database

In addition to network statistics, network databases at the control center contain data about the network configuration, the software versions in use in all network locations, hardware component configurations, names of contact individuals at remote sites, histories of problems and solutions, outside contact points for vendors, and some of the documentation for the network.

Problem-Reporting System   Ideally, an online **problem-reporting system** should also be available for retrieving trouble reports via keywords. This capability is especially helpful in managing a distributed network in which problems can be encountered and resolved in multiple locations simultaneously. An online problem-reporting system can help managers avoid having to repeatedly solve the same problem.

Problem-Reporting Procedure

Another important function of a control center is the recording of problem incidents and their resolution. Some solutions may lie outside the control center; however, the center should remain active as an intermediary in resolving the problem. For example, some vendor hardware contracts and software licensing agreements require the organization to contact the vendor when problems are identified because the vendor is responsible for correcting the problem. In some instances, the contract/agreement is nullified if the organization fails to contact the vendor and attempts to correct the problem on its own. Although such contracts/agreements may mean that the MTTR failed network components may be high, in some instances, this is unavoidable.

This section describes a prototype for a problem reporting and resolution system at a network control center. Please note that although a computerized problem-reporting system is assumed, a manual system with the same functionality could exist.

network statistics Information, such as error rates, data rates, and the number of retransmission attempts resulting from errors, that is collected to analyze network performance trends.

problem-reporting system A system administration feature that records, assigns, and tracks problems.

Network managers often publish and distribute problem-reporting procedures to users. When users are familiar with these procedures, network managers and their support staff are likely to be able to rectify problems faster and more easily. The procedures distributed to users typically specify the information that users should be ready to provide when reporting a problem and to whom the problem should be reported. Users are generally directed to contact their control center about network problems by telephone, but some automated systems also enable users to report problems via e-mail or the Web. When the problem report call is received, the network manager obtains all relevant information, including

- ➤ Date and time of the call
- ➤ Date and time the problem was first observed
- ➤ Name of the caller and how the caller might be reached
- ➤ Names and contact information for any other personnel involved in the problem
- ➤ A brief but detailed description of the problem
- ➤ Whether the problem is reproducible or intermittent
- ➤ Possible contributing external influences, such as installation of a new software release, reconfiguration, power glitches, or the equipment being used

A problem report containing the relevant information is generated, and a copy is generally returned to the individual reporting the problem. As soon as the problem is resolved, the solution is noted in the trouble report, a final copy is sent to the reporting installation, and the trouble report is marked closed. If the solution is not immediately known, the control center begins its evaluation, first searching the problem database to determine whether such a problem was resolved in the past. If not, problem investigation begins. The first objective of such an investigation is to isolate the problem and pinpoint the source of the difficulty, which can involve looking at statistics and system console or log messages, initiating line traces, using line monitors, taking program dumps or traces, debugging, or running hardware diagnostics. If the problem is isolated to an area of vendor responsibility, such as network control programs, the vendor is contacted, and the supporting documentation is passed to the vendor for analysis. The degree of vendor involvement varies among vendors, and even within one vendor company, the support level can vary among individual customers, depending on the expertise available. Some users provide a vendor with a complete analysis and suggested solution, whereas others simply report the existence of a problem and leave the diagnostics to the vendor.

Additional Control Center Responsibilities

The additional responsibilities of the network control center staff include creating and maintaining documentation, implementing security, establishing procedures, performing release control, and training personnel. As noted previously, network documentation, which should be kept current, includes operations manuals, procedures for emergency and routine activities, notification lists, contingency plans, hardware and software inventories, source program listings, and statistics. Security measures include creating and assigning passwords, setting user access levels, monitoring and reacting to unsuccessful log-on attempts, ensuring that passwords are changed periodically, and checking physical security where applicable. Procedures should cover normal operating guidelines as well as those for handling abnormal situations such as network failures. Escalation policies, policies that bring problems to the attention of higher management levels if the problem persists, along with appropriate contact names and contact information are also included. **Release control** includes the instal-

release control
Procedure including the installation, testing, and implementation of new versions of hardware and software to ensure compatibility of new features with existing software and hardware.

lation, testing, and implementation of new versions of hardware and software to ensure compatibility of new features with existing software and hardware, and to uncover any new problems, which are often introduced with new releases. Finally, training involves all levels of personnel who use or maintain the network.

LAN VERSUS WAN MANAGEMENT

Although many aspects of LAN management are similar to those of WAN management, these two major categories of network management differ in many ways. WAN management typically involves geographically distributed nodes; some local autonomy in the management of networks at geographically distributed locations; diverse hardware platforms and network protocols; a variety of media types and speeds; and third-party media vendors.

Historically, WAN management responsibilities typically grew out of the data processing departments in business organizations. As a result, WAN management concerns have traditionally been more technically oriented than those for LAN management, which primarily grew out of stand-alone microcomputer environments. If a business location has interconnected LANs and WANs, responsibility for management of the interconnection interfaces often falls on the WAN management team. This means the WAN management team must be aware of large and small system concepts, whereas the LAN administrator is not usually required to have knowledge of large systems and WANs.

Consider the enterprise network portrayed in Figure 14-5. Each LAN will probably have an administrator who is responsible for keeping the LAN functioning. The WAN managers are responsible for

➤ Keeping all WAN nodes operating properly
➤ Working with common carriers to obtain and maintain links between nodes
➤ Maintaining connections between subnetworks
➤ Coordinating efforts of subnet managers
➤ Managing LAN/WAN interfaces at the different locations
➤ Establishing standards for WAN interfaces and data communication equipment
➤ Administering corporate license agreements for all network and workstation software
➤ Maintaining the network database
➤ Managing the network control center
➤ Developing network contingency plans
➤ Developing budgeting processes for multiple locations that ensure that new enterprise-wide network products can be funded

Having evolved from mainframe management environments, WAN management personnel are typically highly experienced data processing personnel who know the intricacies of data communication subsystems and large system operating systems. In contrast, a LAN administrator may have limited technical background in comparison to his counterparts in WAN management. We have already described the profile of a network management team and the skills they need. Let us now look more closely at one of the entry levels of network management: LAN administration.

In a six-person office in which each person has a stand-alone microcomputer workstation, how do you imagine the management and operations of the workstations are conducted? In most offices,

➤ Each person is responsible for backing up their data (if it is done at all).
➤ Each person is responsible for operating a microcomputer.

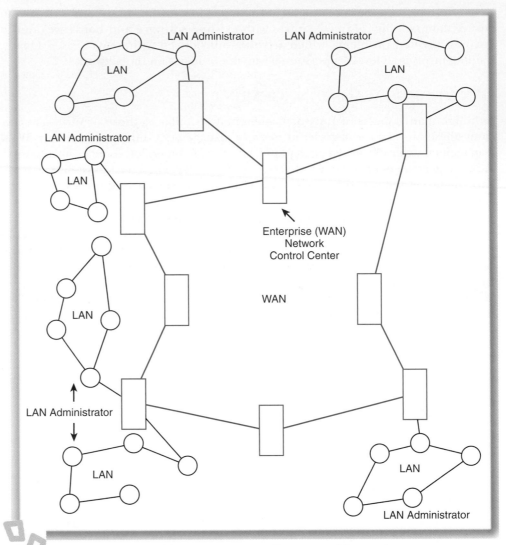

Figure 14-5 Network Management in an Enterprise Network

➤ There is no office data processing manager (although there may be a local "expert" on whom others rely for help).

➤ No provisions are made for security.

➤ If resource sharing exists, it is done via disk exchange (sneaker net) or printer switches.

➤ If someone makes a mistake or if one system fails, it has little impact on the others.

➤ A certain amount of software trading occurs because the office does not have sufficient copies for each user.

➤ Everyone wants the best printer attached to their computer.

Now, suppose the office manager informs everyone that a LAN is about to be installed, and that, after the dust settles, a more effective computing system will be available. The manager probably is correct with respect to the LAN providing a more effective computing platform. However, let us look at another implication of a LAN: LAN management.

In switching from a stand-alone microcomputer environment to a LAN, it is essential to have one or more people designated as LAN managers. If the LAN is large, several people may be actively involved as LAN managers; if the LAN is small, one person may be the principal manager and the second the alternate. (What constitutes a small, medium, or large LAN is difficult to define. For our purposes, small LANs are those with fewer than 50 workstations and only one server; a medium LAN has 50 to 150 nodes and three or fewer servers; all other LANs are considered large. Be aware that some small LANs can be as complex to manage as large ones.) An alternate LAN manager may be designated to assist the primary manager as necessary and to fill in when the primary is absent.

During installation, LAN management is a full-time job. After the LAN is in operation, management tasks are less time-consuming. For a small LAN, management tasks may consume only a few hours a day; for a large LAN, management is typically a full-time position and may even require multiple full-time LAN administrators. The bottom line is that there are costs associated with ongoing LAN management after network installation that should not be overlooked by organizations.

LAN Management Tasks

Before a LAN is installed, LAN managers should be hired or existing personnel in the organization should be trained to be LAN managers. Training may involve courses that prepare networking personnel for the tests associated with certifications such as the MCSE, CNA, or CNP. The amount of training varies according to the complexity of the system. At a minimum, LAN managers should know the fundamentals of data communication and how to

- ➤ Connect and disconnect LAN workstations
- ➤ Diagnose and correct LAN communication medium problems
- ➤ Add and delete LAN users
- ➤ Manage directory services to ensure user access to needed LAN resources
- ➤ Implement LAN security
- ➤ Create, modify, and manage the printing environment
- ➤ Install and modify LAN applications
- ➤ Perform system backups
- ➤ Recover from system failures
- ➤ Monitor and evaluate network performance
- ➤ Add new resources, such as new servers
- ➤ Maintain LAN documentation and procedures
- ➤ Assist in setting up LAN interconnections to other networks
- ➤ Detect and remove viruses

Connecting and Disconnecting Workstations   Many LANs are not static. New workstations must be added and existing ones moved to different segments or removed, particularly during LAN installation and the initial stages of operation. The procedures for installing a new workstation vary from one implementation to another, but usually the following steps are required:

1. Install the LAN adapter in the workstation.
2. Establish a connection on the medium for the new workstation. This may require the use of a new port on a multistation access unit (MAU), shared media hub, or switch. In

some instances, it may mean a direct connection to the LAN medium (such as in a FDDI LAN) or a new BNC connection on a coaxial cable that serves as a linear bus.

3. Connect the workstation to the medium by establishing a connection between the LAN adapter and the medium. For wireless LANs, network managers must ensure that user workstations are able to communicate correctly via access points.

4. Install network software (such as client NOS modules) in the workstation.

5. Boot the new workstation, and test its ability to communicate over the network.

Once the new workstation is working, the network documentation ought to be updated to reflect the new address (both NIC and IP address if static IP addresses are used for workstations) and wiring circumstances.

Diagnosing and Correcting Problems   In some LANs, the most common problems are faulty network adapter cards and medium faults such as wiring breaks or loose connectors. Being able to locate and correct these faults is critical to the success of the LAN. A host of other problems can occur as well, including improperly installed network operating system software, improperly installed application software, user errors, malfunctioning/broken equipment, improper security settings, and incomplete or incorrect access control lists. Solving these problems requires diagnostic skills and the right set of tools; such tools are discussed in Chapter 15.

Adding and Deleting Users   LAN users must identify themselves when logging onto the LAN as part of the authentication process. As noted in Chapter 9, a user's authentication credentials typically include a valid user ID and password. Each user is authorized to run certain applications and perform a set of actions on selected files. These privileges are maintained in the network directory's access control lists. The network manager must assign user IDs for new users and delete or modify users from the network's directory services when a user ceases to be employed by the organization or changes job functions. Users are usually associated with a group (one for personnel administration, one for payroll administration, and so on). Like users, groups are assigned access privileges for specific network resources. Again, it is the responsibility of the LAN manager to define the composition of required groups and their access privileges and to assign individuals to one or more defined groups. Sometimes, the LAN manager will delegate user and group administration functions to unit managers.

For each new user, the LAN administrator typically creates or assists in creating the user's environment. Some of the tasks associated with adding a new user to the network include

➤ Creating a home directory for the user on the file server

➤ Adding the user to the network mail system

user log-on script
A set of actions to be taken when the user logs on, such as setting search paths and initial menus.

➤ Creating a **user log-on script** (a set of actions to be taken when the user logs on, such as setting search paths and initial menus)

➤ Setting default security parameters

➤ Setting limits on resource use, such as the maximum amount of server disk that the user can consume

➤ Setting printer mappings

➤ Specifying the days of the week and time periods during the day that the user can log on to the network

Creating User Environments   The LAN administrator must assist in creating the proper environment for each user. This includes providing access to the proper applications, setting up user menus as called for, setting up the proper printing environment, and providing access to the necessary servers. Much of this can be accomplished via batch files and user log-on scripts. The key to setting up these environments is to make LAN use transparent, so the user has access to the necessary LAN facilities without having to be aware of the details of the LAN itself.

Implementing Security   A primary motivation behind LAN creation is the ability of users to share computing resources. It is important to note, however, that users rarely require universal access to network resources and that network security is likely to be enhanced when users are only able to access the shared computing resources that they need to perform their jobs. Just because a resource is capable of being shared, however, does not mean that any user should be able to read or modify the file, run the application, or use the printer. Instead, the LAN manager must create an access profile for each user, group, file, application, and hardware device. Some attributes thus defined are given in Table 14-4.

There may be more or fewer capabilities depending on the particular implementation. Additional utilities often can be purchased to enhance the capabilities provided with the LAN software. For example, LAN operating systems may not include modules that provide the ability to remotely view what is displayed on a workstation's monitor or to take control of the keyboard, but several utilities can be installed on the LAN that would enable network managers to do this.

Table 14-4   Security Attributes

File Capabilities
    Ability to examine a directory listing
    Ability to read or write a file
    Ability to delete, rename, or create a file
    Ability to execute an application
    Ability for several users to simultaneously use a file
    Ability to restrict a file to one user at a time
    Ability to define file ownership
    Ability to pass privileges on to another user
User and Group Capabilities
    Allow file access according to the capabilities just described by user and group
    Require a password
    Require passwords to have a minimum number of characters
    Require passwords to be changed at certain intervals
    Allow logons only during specified times
    Allow a user to log on only from selected workstations
    Include users in a group
    Specify account expiration date
    Restrict amount of disk space used
    Detect multiple log-on attempts and deactivate workstation or account
Monitoring Capabilities
    Identify users logged on to system
    View information about users
    View information about jobs
    View a user's activity on servers
    View what is displayed on a workstation
    Take control of a workstation's keyboard

dedicated printer
A printer that can be used only by a person at the workstation to which the printer is attached.

shared printer
A printer controlled by a server and available to designated users. Nondedicated servers often control access to shared printers in peer-to-peer networks; print servers typically control access to shared printers in client/server networks.

spooler Software that manages printing in a computer. It collects printer output (typically on disk), schedules the data for printing, and feeds the print images to the printer at slower printing speeds. *SPOOL* is an acronym for *simultaneous peripheral operation online.*

Creating, Modifying, and Managing the Printing Environment   Two types of printers are available to LAN users: dedicated and shared. **Dedicated printers** are attached to workstations and can be used only by a person at that workstation. **Shared printers** are those controlled by a server and available to designated users. The latter type of printer is discussed in this section.

The general layout for a LAN printing system is illustrated in Figure 14-6. Spooling operations associated with shared printers are discussed in Chapter 13. In general, an application on a LAN user's workstation goes through the following steps to print a document on a shared printer:

1. The application opens a printer port, such as LPT1 or LPT2, and begins writing to that device.
2. The LAN printer software intercepts the print stream and routes it over the network to the server.
3. The server print job collector accepts the print stream and stores it in a file.
4. Steps 2–3 continue until the application closes the connection to the printer port or until a time-out limit of no print output is reached. In either case, the workstation software sends an end-of-job designator to the server.
5. The server closes that print job and schedules the job to be printed.
6. The printer driver looks at the scheduled jobs, selects the one with the highest priority, and prints it on the printer.
7. On completion of printing a job, the printer driver selects the next available job and prints it, and so on.

From the LAN user's perspective, the needed printer is always available and dedicated to that user. It is the **spooler** that provides this virtual printer capability. The spooler can also provide other functions, such as printing multiple copies, printing a document on several printers, holding a document on disk after printing or instead of printing, printing selected portions of a document, and printing banners before each print job.

Figure 14-6   Printer Alternatives

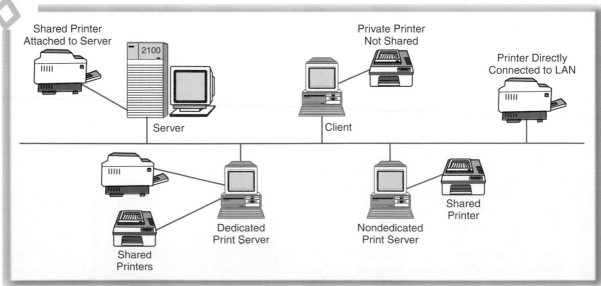

At the more detailed level, there are many factors to consider and parameters to set when installing and controlling a printing subsystem. The factors are too many to cover in detail here, and the ways in which they are established vary from one LAN to another. In essence, the LAN administrator carries out the following tasks:

➤ Mapping printer ports on workstations to a server print queue

➤ Mapping print queues to one or more printers

➤ Associating a printer with one or more print queues

➤ Changing the print queue and printer port configuration

➤ Assigning a printer priority scheme, such as printing small jobs before large jobs

➤ Monitoring the print jobs routed to particular printers

➤ Removing print jobs from print queues

➤ Starting or stopping print jobs or printers

➤ Adding or deleting printers to the network

Being able to obtain printed output is one of the basic needs of LAN users. With all the configuration options typically available, the LAN administrator can provide an environment that meets or exceeds the needs of the LAN users; on the other hand, a poorly designed configuration can hinder printing effectiveness and user productivity.

Installing and Modifying Applications   When installing a new application, the LAN manager must plan how the application will be used, which users will need it, and on which server(s) the application will reside. Applications not designed for shared use must be installed in a way that prohibits concurrent usage. Applications that can be used concurrently must be installed in a manner that maximizes their capabilities for each user. Most important, the LAN administrator must understand and comply with the application vendor's **software license agreements.** License agreements vary considerably. Some software programs are licensed for only one workstation; some are licensed for a specific number of concurrent users, such as four concurrent users; some are licensed to allow access for all users on a specific server; and some are licensed to allow access for all users on all servers.

Obviously, understanding the license agreement is important for application selection and installation.

Each application user ideally is able to match their hardware with the application's features. Accordingly, a user with a color monitor ought to be able to tailor the application and have it display that user's preferred foreground and background colors. A user with a monochrome display monitor will have a different user profile that runs correctly on his workstation. Other features that might be accounted for include the type of graphics adapter, display size, amount of memory available, and so on. Once the application is operational, the LAN administrator is responsible for installing application upgrades. A major application release sometimes provides significant changes in the system operation and the user interface to the system. The LAN manager must plan for the transition from the old system to the new one. In such cases, it is usually prudent to have both application versions available to make the transition to the new application easier.

software license agreement A document provided by the software vendor that specifies the rights and restrictions of software users.

Performing System Backups   LAN administrators must develop backup policies, procedures, and schedules that help to ensure that data files and programs can be recovered in the event of network failures. Ensuring that backup procedures are carried out correctly and on schedule is especially important for mission-critical files and applications (files and applications that must be accessible for the organization to carry out its normal operations). Backup devices and the associated software capabilities are discussed in Chapters 7 and 9.

Recovering from System Failures   A primary purpose of performing backups is to be able to quickly recover from network failures. The LAN administrator must develop procedures to be implemented if the LAN fails. Because some failures do not affect files, the recovery procedures must encompass more than file recovery. For example, a workstation may fail in the middle of performing a client/server application. The LAN administrator should have a procedure for recovering both the application and the lost work should such a failure occur.

Monitoring and Evaluating Performance   LAN usage is likely to change over time. New users might be added; some workstations may be deleted; and applications may be added, upgraded, or deleted. The LAN administrator must monitor LAN usage and plan necessary changes. If usage increases, a new server may be needed or, if multiple servers exist, the usage may need to be better balanced among them through the creation of well-thought-out network segments. Things the LAN administrator may monitor include printing environment, server disk utilization, number of active users, typical data transfer rates, peak data transfer rates, application usage, transmission faults, communication error rates, and server utilization statistics. Based on the performance statistics, the LAN administrator plans corrective action to ensure acceptable levels of network performance.

Adding Resources   LAN administrators must plan the acquisition and integration of new network resources. If a new file server is added (beyond those already in place), the LAN administration must decide which files are to be placed on the new server and which users the file server will primarily serve. After integrating the new server, the administrator will monitor LAN activities to ensure that service is satisfactory and that all components are used effectively.

Maintaining LAN Documentation and Procedures   Much of the success of network administration stems from having good, current documentation and procedures. The LAN administrator is responsible for creating and keeping this documentation up to date.

Assisting in Setting Up LAN Interconnections   In Chapter 9, you read about the ways in which one network can be connected to another network. The LAN administrator is involved in setting up the proper hardware and software interfaces on the LAN side of the connection. If two LANs are being connected via a bridge, router, or brouter, the administrator may be responsible for all of the interconnection details.

Detecting and Removing Viruses   One concern of both LAN and WAN administrators at all levels in the network management hierarchy is the proliferation of computer viruses and similar disruptive programs or code modules. It is estimated that over 100 new viruses are released in general circulation each month; furthermore, recent surveys have estimated that only one-third of the installed virus detection/removal programs are current. Additionally, viruses are taking on new forms. Macro viruses are now imbedded in word processing documents, and new or existing viruses are coded so that their signature can change and thus make them harder to detect. Before macro viruses, a virus was embedded only in executable programs. Because viruses are constantly changing, today's network administrators must have up-to-date virus detection and removal software and procedures as well as employee procedures to prevent the inadvertent introduction of viruses. There are several sources of software for virus detection, and many of them can stay memory resident and provide continuous scanning. All network administrators need to include computer viruses in their planning and procedures.

WAN Management Tasks

The responsibilities of WAN managers differ somewhat from those of a LAN manager. A LAN administrator is an integral part of the network management team; however, in this section the term *WAN management team* refers to the group of network managers whose responsibilities include WAN management. Some LAN management tasks typically *not* carried out by a WAN manager include creating user environments, a task typically carried out by programming personnel; creating, modifying, and managing the printing environment, a task typically carried out by operations personnel; installing and modifying network applications, a task typically carried out by programming and operations personnel; and performing backups, a task typically carried out by operations personnel.

A representative list of WAN management tasks includes the following:

➤ Connecting and disconnecting workstations
➤ Diagnosing and correcting medium problems
➤ Adding and deleting users
➤ Implementing security
➤ Recovering from system failures
➤ Monitoring and evaluating performance
➤ Adding resources, such as a new server
➤ Maintaining network documentation and procedures
➤ Assisting in setting up network interconnections
➤ Detecting and removing viruses
➤ Interfacing with carriers and WAN service providers
➤ Estimating equipment and media costs
➤ Configuring network components to meet transmission and cost requirements
➤ Interfacing with corporate and vendor personnel in devising network solutions
➤ Resolving problems regarding international telecommunication
➤ Developing and maintaining network software
➤ Coordinating and consolidating network management

Tasks in this list up to and including detecting and removing viruses are common to LAN and WAN management and have been discussed earlier. Let us look at the management tasks that are unique to WANs.

Interfacing with Carriers and WAN Service Providers   As discussed in Chapter 8, most business WANs use carriers and WAN service providers to interconnect geographically distributed operating locations. In the United States, businesses typically can choose from among several carriers for the interconnections and WAN services that they need. Each carrier/service provider has characteristics that set it apart from its competitors. Differences among carriers may include rates, types of media and services, locations served, and quality of service and support. The WAN management team must be familiar with the advantages and disadvantages of each common carrier and choose the most cost-effective alternatives.

Network problems in WANs can be caused by a company's equipment, by a carrier's equipment, or by the interface between the two. When problems occur that cannot be isolated to the company's equipment, the network management team must work with carriers in diagnosing and correcting the problems.

Estimating Equipment and Media Costs   A LAN administrator will also carry out this task; however, the number of options and range of prices are much greater in a WAN. In configuring portions of a WAN, the management team is likely to evaluate several carriers, several services per common carrier, and different data communication equipment from a variety of vendors. Often the number of potential WAN solutions is large. If a company considers three carriers, two services per carrier, and five different vendors with similar data communication equipment, each of which has three pieces of equipment to consider, the number of combinations of vendors, services, and equipment is 90. Choosing the best one requires considerable analysis and expertise.

Configuring Network Components   Like estimating equipment and media costs, configuring network components is a process of evaluating a large number of alternatives. A LAN's standard and topology limit the ways in which network components can be added. In a WAN, there are usually fewer restrictions, the configuration task is much more complex, and the cost of solutions is often greater than for LAN configuration solutions. For example, adding a node to a LAN usually means finding the closest wiring hub or cable and attaching the node to it. Adding a node to a WAN often requires obtaining one or more communication lines from a common carrier, deciding which existing nodes the new node is to be linked to, procuring the hardware and software for the new node, preparing the site for installation of the new node, and training personnel to manage the new equipment.

Resolving Problems Regarding International Telecommunication   In Chapter 11, you read about international networks. LAN administrators need not be concerned with international issues. Managers of international WANs must address the issues raised in Chapter 11, including politics, regulations, hardware, language, and tariffs. The WAN management team must consider these issues in estimating network costs, use, and configuration both within and across the nations in which they have business sites.

Developing and Maintaining Network Software   A LAN administrator is responsible for setting up a user's application environment but seldom gets involved in fixing or writing network software. The WAN management team may need to customize some characteristics of the network or install corrections to faulty network programs. If a company has a unique device that must be attached to the network, the WAN management team may need to write the network interface code or modify an existing interface. When errors are detected in network software, the software vendor may distribute patches to the code. The WAN management team is responsible for inserting the patches and testing the system to ensure that it works properly.

Coordinating and Consolidating Network Management   A LAN administrator is usually responsible for one or more LANs in a specific location. The WAN management team is responsible for the coordination and consolidation of all aspects of network management, including the operation and interconnection of subnets. The knowledge and responsibilities of the WAN management team are far beyond those of the LAN manager. Problems that cannot be solved by local operations or LAN management personnel become the responsibility of the WAN management team. WAN managers must remain aware of problems in all segments of the network to avoid duplicating diagnosis and correction of problems that have already been encountered and resolved.

Ensuring WAN Security   A key aspect of the responsibilities of the WAN management team is ensuring the security of the network. Virus management, intrusion detection, and taking steps to prevent or recover from denial of service attacks are some of the important security concerns of WAN managers. Implementing appropriate encryption mechanisms and identifying network vulnerabilities are other important aspects of WAN security management. The importance of network security and the steps that network managers can take to enhance the security of their networks are discussed more fully in Chapter 16.

THE INTERNET'S IMPACT ON NETWORK MANAGEMENT

The Internet and the growing importance of e-business applications have created new challenges and new opportunities for network management. Needless to say, business Web sites have become a competitive requirement, and ensuring reliable access to business Web sites has become an important facet of new management responsibility. Web site traffic and Web server utilization rates must be monitored to ensure that visitors and business partners are able to access the information and applications that they need. Additional Web servers, storage systems (such as SANs and NASs), and communication link bandwidth must be planned for and implemented as needed to sustain growth in e-business applications. E-business applications (such as ERP, CRM, and e-procurement) often must be integrated with legacy systems to provide a network infrastructure capable of supporting traditional back-office functions as well as e-business initiatives.

The implementation and refinement of interorganizational networks with business partners also present new challenges for network managers. EDI, extranets, and online markets used to link an organization with its suppliers and customers mean that network managers are responsible for ensuring reliable and cost-effective ongoing communications between its networks and those in firms with which it does businesses. Like the organization's network infrastructure, these too must be planned for and appropriately implemented. These also mean the expansion of an organization's strategic network planning team to include representatives from key business partners as well as the creation of cross-organization project teams for supply-chain management and other interorganizational e-business applications.

As intranets and knowledge management systems become more common in organizations, internal shifts in the focus of LAN managers are taking place. In addition to traditional LAN management tasks, network administrators are also becoming responsible for ensuring that information workers have access to data warehouses and organization knowledge repositories via Web browsers and other Web-based applications. This means the incorporation of new servers and storage systems for intranet and knowledge management applications in addition to enhanced support for groupware and other collaborative computing tools.

Telework, especially Web-based telework, is also providing new challenges for network managers. An increasing percentage of North American workers telecommute for a portion of each workweek, and some employees perform the majority of the tasks they are responsible for from remote locations. To support mobile workers and other teleworkers, network managers must be able to provide them with secure, reliable access to the computing resources that they need. Remote access servers and communication servers may have to be added to the network infrastructure to accommodate teleworkers. Firewalls must be configured to enable remote workers to gain access to the servers required to perform job tasks. Access control lists for the authorization modules of network operating systems that support Web-based remote access, such as NetWare 6.0, must be appropriately managed and maintained to ensure teleworker access to network resources.

Many organizations are also starting to support wireless Internet applications, including mobile commerce applications. Business Web sites must be able to provide wireless users with pages optimized for wireless Web browsers. In addition, network managers must be able to ensure the security of mobile commerce transactions. Strategic network management in many organizations now includes plans to roll out or build wireless Internet applications. Tactical network management activities and operational network management are being affected by the implementation of these plans.

The Internet has opened new opportunities for hackers and unauthorized users to invade corporate networks. Today's network security must include appropriate security for its business Web site. In some instances, even the content of Web pages must be protected via digital watermarks or embedded digital certification information to ensure that it is not stolen or misused by potential harm doers. As noted previously, the Internet has also meant the addition of firewalls to many business networks. This means that today's network managers must also be familiar with firewall configuration, encryption, virtual private networks (VPNs), and Internet security standards and technologies. Organizations with e-commerce sites also require network managers to be familiar with digital certificate technologies and protocols such as Secure Sockets Layer (SSL) and Secure Electronic Transaction (SET) that are used to ensure to integrity of Web-based transactions.

SUMMARY

As the use of data communication expands, so has the importance of network management. Network management encompasses a wide range of strategic, tactical, and operational management activities related to the network infrastructures in today's organizations. Strategic network management is focused on the role of networks and networking in an organization's computing infrastructure over the long term. Its purpose is to ensure that the organization has the network infrastructure required to achieve its long-range goals and objectives. Tactical network management includes the translation of strategic network plans into more detailed actions. For example, tactical network management involves the development of implementation plans and schedules for changes to the organization's LANs and WANs that are specified in strategic network plans. Operational network management involves managing the day-to-day operations of installed networks. This includes troubleshooting identified problems; managing users; adding/replacing workstations, servers, or peripheral devices; installing new software; performing network backups; and maintaining network security.

Three overriding objectives of network management are to support system users, keep the network operating efficiently, and provide cost-effective solutions to an organization's telecommunication requirements. Users are likely to consider the network to be efficient and effective if the network resources they require to be productive are available when needed and if the network performs consistently and reliably across time. Network planning that includes modular expansion and appropriate equipment migration contributes to the provision of cost-effective telecommunication solutions.

Network management objectives are easier to achieve when the organization is capable of attracting and retaining knowledgeable network management and support personnel who can work well with a broad spectrum of users. Network personnel who are skilled in network planning, problem diagnosis, maintaining network documentation, and the effective use of network management tools are best positioned to contribute to the effective management of today's networks.

The heart of operational network management activities in many organizations is the network control center that is responsible for monitoring the network and taking corrective action when necessary. Network control centers are typically equipped with one or more dedicated computers running network control software that collects and stores a variety of network statistics such as error rates, data transfer rates, and the number of retransmission attempts resulting from errors. Such software enables problems to be identified quickly so that corrective actions can be taken. Trend analysis of network statistics often plays a significant role in network planning.

The Internet and the growing importance of e-business applications have created new challenges and new opportunities for network management. The creation of interorganizational networks with business partners, intranets and knowledge management systems, and systems to support teleworkers and wireless Internet users have added new facets to network management in today's organizations. Network security, in particular, has become a very important aspect of network management as the result of the implementation of business Web sites and Web-based transactions.

KEY TERMS

- availability
- consistency
- dedicated printer
- effectiveness
- ergonomics
- fault tolerance
- flexibility
- ISO Management Framework
- mean time between failure (MTBF)
- mean time to repair (MTTR)
- modular expansion
- network control center
- network manager
- network statistics
- operational network management
- problem-reporting system
- release control
- reliability
- response time
- shared printer
- software license agreement
- spooler
- strategic network management
- tactical network management
- Telecommunications Management Network (TMN) framework
- throughput
- user log-on script

REVIEW QUESTIONS

1. Identify and briefly describe the network management activity categories included in the ISO Management Framework.
2. Identify and briefly describe the network management layers included in the Telecommunications Management Network framework.
3. What is strategic network management?
4. What is included in long-range network plans?
5. What is tactical network management?
6. What is included in LAN installation plans?
7. Briefly describe the vendor selection process.
8. What activities are associated with operational network management?

9. What are the three overriding objectives of network management?
10. Why is user satisfaction an important network management objective?
11. Why are predictable transaction times important?
12. Compare network availability, reliability, and effectiveness.
13. Compare MTBF and MTTR.
14. Identify the steps that network managers can take to enhance network availability and reliability.
15. Describe how planning, modular expansion, and network equipment migration contribute to cost-effective telecommunications solutions.
16. Why is ergonomics important in today's networking environments?
17. Why is maintaining network documentation an important aspect of network management? Identify several examples of network documentation.
18. What is a network control center? What activities are performed by network control center personnel?
19. What types of network statistics are collected by network monitoring systems? How are statistics used in network management?
20. How do network problems get reported and resolved? What documents are generated as a result of the problem-reporting system? Who receives copies of these documents?
21. List 10 LAN management tasks.
22. What must a LAN manager do when installing a new workstation?
23. Briefly describe how WAN management is different from LAN management.
24. Briefly describe how the Internet has changed network management.

PROBLEMS AND EXERCISES

1. Use the Internet to find out more about the ISO Management Framework (ISO 7498-4) and the ITU-T Telecommunications Management Network (TMN framework. Develop a table for each framework that includes a more complete and in-depth list of activities for each category in the framework than that provided in this chapter. After developing the tables, describe the similarities and differences between the two frameworks.
2. Use the Internet and library resources to find out more about the nature and scope of strategic network management. Focus especially on the characteristics and abilities of managers involved in strategic networks. Summarize your findings in a paper or PowerPoint presentation.
3. Use the Internet and library resources to learn more about requests for proposals (RFPs), requests for bids (RFBs), and requests for quotations (RFQs). Compare the contents of RFPs, RFBs, and RFQs. Also compare vendor responses to each of these.
4. Use the Internet and library resources to find out more about the activities carried out by LAN managers. What salaries are earned by LAN managers? What professional certifications are in greatest demand?
5. Response time is often considered a key determinant of network performance. Calculate the response time for a response of 2,000 characters transmitted over a 28,000-bps data communication line. What is the response time if the 2,000 characters were transmitted over a 1 million–bps DSL line?
6. If a network adapter card has a MTBF of 30,000 hours and a MTTR of 2 hours, what is its availability?
7. If network availability is 0.99 and network reliability is 0.87, what is network effectiveness?

8. A company has decided to install a LAN and has collected data from two vendors regarding their equipment reliability. The figures the company obtained are as follows (in hours):

Device	Vendor A		Vendor B	
	MTBF	MTTR	MTBF	MTTR
Workstation	4,000	2.5	3,500	1.5
LAN adapter	8,000	1.0	8,500	1.0
File server	3,500	4.5	3,500	5.0

Which vendor has the better availability? Which vendor has better reliability? Which vendor has better effectiveness?

9. Use the Internet to find the networking occupations and skills that are in most demand today. (*Hint:* Use the search features available at www.computerjobs.com or another online job search site.) Summarize your findings in a paper or PowerPoint presentation.

10. Besides the ergonomic requirements of workstations, what other environmental guidelines should be followed with respect to a network user's work environment? What lighting, noise dampening, and furniture should be available to protect the user? How often should breaks be taken?

11. Design a problem-reporting form. What are the essential elements of a problem-reporting form?

12. A personnel file stored on a network server contains data regarding an employee's name, address, date of birth, date of hire, performance rating, and salary. You have been assigned to set security for this file for all employees and employees in the personnel and payroll departments. Suppose that you can set security attributes on each data item. What attributes would you assign to
    a. all employees?
    b. employees in the personnel department?
    c. employees in the payroll department?
    Explain your decisions.

13. How are backup files used in recovering from a disk crash that destroys both the disk and the data stored thereon?

14. Use the Internet to learn more about how network management has been affected by one of the following:
    a. the creation of interorganizational networks
    b. intranets and knowledge management systems
    c. telework
    d. wireless applications
    Summarize your findings in a paper or PowerPoint presentation.

Self-Service Call Centers

Call centers are an important part of any organization. They are the point of contact between the organization and its customers. Through them, customer questions about products, services, or payments are answered. Call centers are being transformed from call distributors that route calls to appropriate agents to complete solutions that provide automated services. These self-service call centers are much cheaper than human-operated call centers, and studies even indicate that many customers prefer them.

With the widespread acceptance of the Internet, many consumers now expect to find "call centers" within Web sites. Consumers expect advanced online applications where they can find all the information they need, including options to update personal information, check the status of orders, change passwords, and research products or services. Furthermore, Web sites can provide voice-chat applications, so customers can talk to service representatives online.

One of the main problems customers find in the Web is the lack of intelligent search capabilities. Ask Jeeves Inc. has spent several years trying to solve that problem with an advanced search engine that supports natural language questions. The company has integrated this technology in a software solution called "JeevesOne" to help organizations answer customers' questions without human intervention. The software mines data from 255 document types and can be customized to suggest related products or services. JeevesOne can also be integrated with other systems, such as billing, order management, enterprise resource planning, and customer-relationship management applications.

Call centers provide self-service capabilities through interactive voice technology and phone keypads. Interactive voice technology allows organizations to configure voice-based menus to route calls to the appropriate department. This menu-based system can also provide services that do not require human intervention. For example, some banks use self-service call centers to allow customers to check their balances, pay bills, or transfer funds from their accounts. Other companies use special applications to gather the customer identification, so when the customer reaches the appropriate

department, an employee can see all the customer information and start a personalized conversation.

Moreover, speech recognition technologies are being used to replace or enhance the standard touch tone of the voice-based menus. These technologies can recognize simple commands of the human voice, such as numbers or letters. For example, UPS's customers can use touch tones or voice commands to enter their identification number.

Advanced speech technologies include natural language processing to recognize pertinent information from callers speaking normal phrases. Aspect Communications Corp. has developed a self-service application equipped with enhanced voice recognition. Furthermore, the software is able to record customers' voices when they speak at the prompt. Then, it recognizes the customer during subsequent calls, which adds a level of security beyond passwords. This technology is not only faster than touch-tone systems, but also safer. In the future, customers will be able to speak requests and the call center application will provide a customized menu with information relevant to that customer.

Other companies like Empirix Inc. offer applications to test call centers. Empirix's Hammer Call Patrol software ensures that self-service call centers route calls to the appropriate menus or agents. The application regularly makes calls to the self-service telephone lines and makes choices according to predefined programs. Then, the software records all the activity, including busy calls, dropped calls, and incorrect prompts, and notifies a designated person about any errors.

Self-service call center technologies are attractive to networking professionals, but sometimes they fall short of satisfying customer needs. No matter how sophisticated the technology is, customers who use it are humans. Humans fail to read directions, get confused, misunderstand instructions, and at times cannot find answers to their questions. To make things worse, some companies do not use the tools properly. Very often, the menu tree of options is poorly designed because it is based on the company's organization and not on the way customers find information. Thus, if a company calls its human resources department "employee relations," some callers may not understand that and will call the operator to find "human resources."

In addition, some companies have the customer information stored in multiple databases, and sometimes those databases are not integrated with one another. As a result, callers may be required to repeat their account numbers several times to different operators to find out answers to simple inquiries like payment or shipment information.

CASE QUESTIONS

1. What business trade-offs are associated with self-service call centers?
2. Describe the potential use of self-service call centers in network problem-reporting and problem-tracking systems. What limitations can be identified for using self-service call centers to facilitate network management?
3. Use the Internet to find out more about help desks. What are the similarities and differences between call centers and help desks? What technologies used to support help desks are also used to support call centers?
4. Use the Internet to find out more about consolidated service desks. What are the similarities and differences between call centers and consolidated service desks? What are the network management benefits of consolidated service desks?

SOURCES

Maselli, J. "Call Center Self-Service." *Information Week* (October 1, 2001, Issue 857, p. 47).

Maselli, J. "Voice Recognition Aims to Lower Call Center Costs." *Information Week* (October 22, 2001, Issue 860, p. 63).

Tehrani, R. "Taking the Frustration out of Customer Service." *Customer Inter@Ction Solutions* (October 2001, Volume 20, Issue 4, pp. 10–12).

Note: For more information on network management objectives, see an additional case on the Web site, www.prenhall.com/stamper, "Web-Based Project Management."

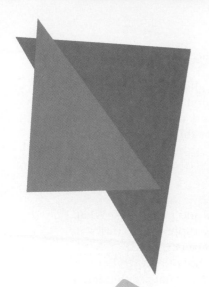

Chapter 15

Network Management Systems

After studying this chapter, you should be able to:

■ Describe the characteristics of network management systems.

■ Identify and briefly describe the major components of network management systems.

■ Identify key network management system standards and protocols.

■ Identify several examples of network management system products.

■ Identify network management modules incorporated in network operating systems.

■ Describe network tuning processes.

■ Describe the role of network simulation software and workload generators in network planning.

■ Identify the diagnostic, monitoring, and troubleshooting tools used by network managers.

This chapter begins with a discussion of a generic network management system (NMS) and NMS protocols, and concludes with an overview of tools used in the management of day-to-day network operations. Between these end points, examples of NMS products are provided along with how network management software is used to ensure acceptable levels of network performance both in the short run and the long term.

WHAT IS A NETWORK MANAGEMENT SYSTEM?

A network should be under continuous scrutiny to ensure that users are satisfied with its performance and that it continues to be a cost-effective telecommunication solution for the organization. Too often, network problems surface through user complaints. Problem-reporting and tracking systems (discussed in Chapter 14) provide network managers with a way to document network problems discovered by users and their resolution. This is usually not the way a network manager wants to learn about problems. A far better way is to have potential problems detected and reported by a network management system, so problems may be corrected before users become aware of them. Correcting problems before they impact users is likely to affect user perceptions of the network's availability, reliability, and effectiveness.

A **network management system (NMS)** is a combination of hardware and software used by network managers to monitor and administer the network. The NMS must be able to determine the status of network components such as modems, lines, workstations, servers, hubs, switches, routers, and multiplexors. If a device's status indicates that malfunctions are occurring, the NMS will either take automatic corrective action or alert a network manager of the condition. The network manager may then use network control functions of the NMS to take corrective action. An NMS also gathers network statistics, such as line use information, together with capabilities for evaluating those statistics. The information produced assists network supervisors in network tuning and capacity planning.

In the past, many network operating system vendors neglected the area of network management. With few exceptions, the network operating system software and network hardware were designed and manufactured with limited built-in support for their management. Although management of small networks is not difficult, the need for more sophisticated network management capabilities changed as the composition of networks changed. This was especially true when businesses made the move to online transaction processing systems and distributed client/server computing platforms and applications. These changes have had a significant impact on the need to manage networks in two ways. First, the number and complexity of network nodes have increased. Early networks often consisted of one central host computer with communication controllers and terminal devices. The host assumed a supervisory role and provided a centralized point of control and network management. Often the communication links in these centralized, host-based networks were point-to-point leased or switched lines. In contrast, many of today's networks have multiple, distributed servers and hundreds or thousands of connected devices. An organization's network may consist of LANs, WAN frame relay services, leased lines, satellite links, switched lines, PBX systems, mobile communication devices, and other communication technologies. Numerous interfaces between different types of equipment and networks are common in today's businesses.

Second, many of today's networks consist of a myriad of network hardware and software components from numerous vendors. Managing a large network with homogeneous hardware components provided by a single vendor can be difficult. When network components are supplied by multiple vendors, however, network management challenges are magnified. In the past, effectively managing a large network with components from multiple vendors approached the impossible. Fortunately, this problem has been recognized by NMS vendors. The NMSs in use today typically accommodate diverse hardware and software platforms. A summary of major NMS features is provided in Table 15-1.

Managing Complex Networks

To understand the challenges associated with managing complex networks, consider a hypothetical network of a large, international manufacturing firm. This company has processing nodes in many locations throughout the world. A small portion of this network, found in one of the company's manufacturing locations, is depicted in Figure 15-1. The backbone network at this manufacturer is an SNA network (see Chapter 11), and there are two domains. The major components of the network at this location come from seven different vendors. The host processors in both domains are from vendor A. The communication controllers were purchased from vendor B, but run IBM NCP (Network Control Program) software. The engineering and development department has an IEEE 802.3–compatible LAN to support its design efforts. The

network management system (NMS) A combination of hardware and software used by network managers to monitor and administer a network. NMSs monitor active communications networks in order to diagnose problems and gather network statistics for administration and network tuning. Examples of network management products are Tivoli's NetView, HP's OpenView, Sun's SunNet Manager, and Novell's NMS.

Table 15-1   Examples of NMS Components/Capabilities

➤ Topological maps of the network and its segments
➤ Server status monitoring
➤ Communication media monitoring
➤ DCE monitoring (such as hubs, switches, routers, and multiplexors)
➤ Hacker/unauthorized intruder detection
➤ User log-on statistics
➤ Software utilization statistics
➤ Server utilization rates
➤ Software metering to ensure compliance with software licenses
➤ Transmission error statistics
➤ Event logging
➤ Network alert and alarm management and logging
➤ Trend analysis tools for analyzing network statistics
➤ Graphical presentation of network statistics and trends
➤ Problem diagnosis and solution recommendations
➤ Account management
➤ Workstation configuration information
➤ Hub/switch monitoring and management
➤ Firewall configuration management
➤ Router monitoring and configuration management
➤ User security and access level management
➤ Tools for managing user log-on scripts

workstations are high-performance, special purpose machines and were provided by two other vendors, C and D. The bridge interconnecting the LAN and the SNA network was manufactured by vendor D. The interface to the SNA network is via LU 6.2. The office automation system uses equipment from vendor E and interfaces to the SNA system in the same way as the engineering bridge. The PBX system obtained from vendor F is also tied into the network. Modems and multiplexors used to connect the manufacturer to other company locations were all obtained from vendor G. Some of the information needed by network managers to keep this network running smoothly is summarized in Table 15-2.

In a large network consisting of multiple, geographically distributed operating locations, the volume of network management data/information can be huge. If all of the data that is gathered is sent to the network managers at one central location, both network managers and the NMS would have a difficult time keeping up with it. Simply receiving the data is not enough; it must be received in a usable format. Hence, a key NMS responsibility is ensuring that the correct data is received and that it is in a usable format. Figure 15-2 shows a network component, a portion of the NMS, and the connection to the network control center. The key components of NMSs include monitors, filters, alerts/alarms, a network database, and a network management console.

Network Management Software Categories

Three types of network management software are used in today's organizations: point management software, application management software, and system management software. Each of these is briefly described here.

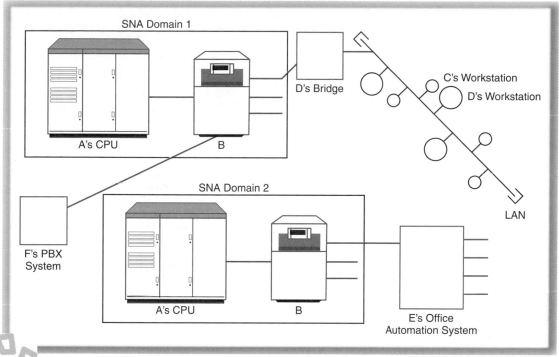

Figure 15-1   Integrated Network

Table 15-2   Network Management Information

Servers	Routers/Switches
Status	Status
CPU busy rates	Processor busy rates
Internal queues, such as on TCP	Buffer use
Transaction turnaround time in the CPU	Queues
Buffer use	Peak activity time
Peak activity times	Performance during peak activity
Performance during peak activity	
Lines	**Workstations**
Status	Status
Number of failures	Number of failures
Number of retries	Failure types
Aggregate data rate	Number of transactions
Peak activity time	Type of transactions
Performance during peak activity	Transaction response time
Active devices on the line	
Line quality	
Changes in line quality	

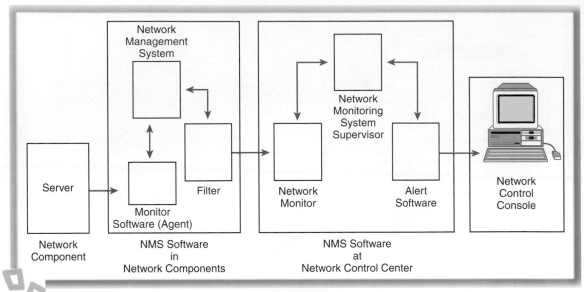

Figure 15-2 Network Management System

Point Management Software

Point management software enables network managers to monitor the performance of specific network devices such as servers, bridges, routers, gateways, and switches. Such software is also known as *device management software*. Utilization/traffic volumes and error conditions are among the key network performance data captured by point management software and delivered to network managers.

Application Management Software

Application management software monitors the performance of important applications used in networks. This enables network managers to ensure that the business's applications are functioning within specified parameters. If not, immediate corrective action may need to be taken. Real-time order-entry systems, online transaction processing systems, and enterprise resources planning (ERP) systems are examples of important applications that business organizations are likely to use application management software to monitor. The network traffic associated with such applications may be given higher priority over other types of network traffic. Significant delays and abnormally slow response times for the programs monitored by application management software trigger alerts and alarms, informing network managers of problems that need their immediate attention or corrective action. Point/device management software is often included in application management software to enable network managers to determine whether problems associated with monitored applications are hardware or software based.

Enterprise Management Software

Enterprise management software includes point/device management capabilities, desktop management/electronic software distribution capabilities, and root cause analysis capabilities. Desktop management/electronic software distribution enables network management to install software or software upgrades on client computers over the network. The ability to "push" software from network servers to clients means that network managers do not have to physically install software or software upgrades on each of the clients attached to the network. Such *electronic software distribution (ESD)* capabilities decrease the costs associated with client configuration management. ESD software also facilitates the maintenance of network documentation by automatically producing and updating a database detailing the software installed on each client attached to the network. *Root cause analysis* capabilities enable network managers to get a handle on the underlying causes of network problems/failures. This is important because a single device failure can result in an alarm storm (multiple problem reports from point/device management software in different network devices) as other monitored communication devices in the network are impacted by a particular device's failure. The ability to quickly identify the failed device means that problems can be addressed more quickly and efficiently. Without this capability, network managers might have to check out each device that generated a problem report in the alarm storm until the failed component was identified.

NMS Components

The monitors found in enterprise NMSs are distributed among network components. The monitors are often called **agents** (or *daemons*) and are frequently located in network servers/hosts as well as in manageable hubs/switches, bridges, routers, and other communication devices. Agents gather status and operational data from the components they are monitoring at regular time intervals. Ordinarily, the data is routine and indicates that the component is functioning within normal operating parameters; such data is either ignored or logged for later evaluation. If the specific component being monitored is a communication line, the information captured by the NMS will include the number of errors encountered since the last status report, current line status, line quality, number of retries on the line, and number of characters transmitted or received.

The NMS modules installed in network components analyze the incoming data for irregularities such as unusually high numbers of errors. When irregularities are detected, these NMS modules send warning information about the abnormalities to the network control center by way of a **filter**. Filters format warning messages pertaining to the abnormalities detected by agents and forward them to the network control center. Filters are used to avoid flooding the control center with repetitious mundane status information indicating that the component is functioning normally and also to avoid flooding the control center with redundant messages about the same problem.

NMS modules at the control center analyze incoming messages from filters for display on network control center console(s). Most NMSs enable the data to be displayed in a variety of formats, including text-based tables, graphs, and network maps. NMS report generator capabilities enable various display options; they also enable network managers to analyze network statistics stored in network management databases for network tuning and planning purposes.

Alerts and Alarms

When monitors detect significant changes in key network statistics, the departures from normalcy are brought to the attention of the network managers via **alerts** or **alarms**. Alerts and alarms inform network personnel of serious irregularities in network component performance. The terms are often used synonymously; however, in some NMSs, alerts are used to inform network managers of important, but less critical, network performance problems than alarms. An alert may indicate a potential or

agent A software component that collects data about a network device, which is then stored in the management information base. In client/server computing, an agent performs information preparation and exchange on behalf of a client or server process. In e-mail systems, agents can act on behalf of users to operate on mail. For example, a vacation agent could automatically generate standard replies and file mail messages or forward them to another user. Agents in network management systems gather operational and status information at regular intervals from the network components they are monitoring. Because they work in the background, NMS agents are often called *daemons*.

filter In NMSs, a filter is a software component used to screen and format data sent to the management center. In data communications, *filtering* refers to discarding packets that do not meet forwarding criteria.

alert A signal (typically audio or visual) issued by the network management system that some predefined event or error condition has occurred. An alert typically indicates that a statistic, such as current line status, line quality, or number of retries on the line, has changed since the last status report. The terms alert and alarm are often used synonymously, but in some NMS systems, alarms are designated as being more serious than alerts.

alarm Used to inform network personnel of very important network performance abnormalities (such as a router failure or server crash) that require immediate attention and correction.

emerging problem situation (for example, a sudden increase in transmission errors). Text messages or changes in the background screen colors of network management console monitors are often used to signify that noteworthy abnormalities in network performance are occurring. Whereas a green background might indicate performance within normal ranges, a change to a yellow could be used to indicate slight departures from normalcy, and changes to a red background may indicate significant abnormalities that may demand immediate attention from network managers. When problems are detected, root cause analysis capabilities in the enterprise NMS are also likely to assist network managers in solving the problem by indicating the potential causes and perhaps even recommending solutions.

Alarms are used to inform network personnel of very important performance abnormalities (such as a router failure or server crash) that require immediate attention and correction. When such conditions are detected, the NMS may issue audio signals via network management consoles, cause the NMS console monitors to flash, or initiate calls to network personnel pagers in order to attract immediate attention to the problem so that it can be corrected as soon as possible.

The essential idea behind alerts and alarms is that network data collected by agents/monitors that is not within accepted tolerance levels must be brought to the attention of the network managers. An alert or alarm is necessary for a data communication line if the line is down, the error rates have exceeded predefined thresholds, the number of retries is excessive, or the communication medium is congested. A change in service level also may be cause for an alert or alarm to be issued for a network component that is being closely monitored. For example, if a line has been operating between 20 percent and 25 percent capacity and suddenly experiences 50 percent load capacity, an alert may signal this change; if the load capacity should suddenly be 75 percent, an alarm may be issued.

When an alert condition has been detected by a monitor/agent, it must be forwarded to the network management center. Steps that may be taken in this process include the following.

1. *Identification of probable causes of the alert condition.*
2. *Formatting the message for the NMS presentation services.* Component addresses, status, and probable causes must be identified. In Figure 15-2, this function is performed by the software component identified as a filter, which is used to screen and format data sent to the management center.
3. *Transmission of the data to the control center for display.*
4. *Passing the message through a formatter at the control center.* This determines where and how the message is to be displayed. As noted earlier, many NMS presentation services use color monitors to present the data. Warnings may be displayed in yellow, outages in red, and major catastrophes in blinking red with an audio signal.
5. *Logging the message in an alert history file in the network database.*
6. *The network management team acting on the alert as necessary.* The network management team will document the event and its solution in the network control center's problem-reporting and tracking system (which may be part of the NMS).

Alerts, alarms, and statistics indicating normal operations are stored in an enterprise NMS database called a *management information base (MIB)*. MIBs include standardized field definitions and indexes that enable network managers to access network data from network management consoles. The data stored in the MIB may be subsequently evaluated for trend analysis and capacity planning.

As mentioned earlier, obtaining the proper information to manage a network is difficult enough in a homogeneous network environment. In a mixed-vendor configuration, additional complexities must be resolved. Suppose, for example, that the NMS modules at the network management control center in Figure 15-2 are installed in a host processor provided by vendor A and use network management software provided by vendor A. Vendor A's network management tools may only be capable of monitoring its own equipment in the network and presenting network management messages in a specific format. In the configuration shown, if the server being monitored is not one of vendor A's servers, it may not be capable of being monitored by vendor A's enterprise NMS.

There are numerous problems that must be resolved when the computing and communications equipment in the network comes from multiple vendors. These include obtaining status information from each vendor's equipment, formatting the alerts in a manner consistent with the enterprise NMS host's requirements, and routing alerts and alarms and their associated data to the host node for display on network consoles.

Once an alert has been raised, network managers must react to it. For example, if a device is malfunctioning and disrupting the network, the device typically must be deactivated until the problem is fixed. A vendor's enterprise NMS usually provides an interface that allows the network managers to deactivate a malfunctioning device and later bring it back online, especially if the device is also manufactured by the vendor. If equipment from several vendors is found on the network, such deactivation may not be possible. This is because vendors may install different peripheral control utilities and use different command languages for formatting network management messages. In vendor A's environment, the command to bring a failed terminal (whose network name is TERMINAL-X) back online may be RESTORE TERMINAL-X; in vendor E's NMS system, the same command may be DEVICE TERMINAL-X UP. Thus, once an alert that TERMINAL-X has failed has been received at the network control center, correcting the problem may not be simple if TERMINAL-X was manufactured by vendor E and vendor A's enterprise NMS is used at the network control center. One cannot expect network managers to know the command languages required to remedy faults on several different vendor systems, especially when each vendor's system has several interfaces for fault correction (e.g., one interface may be used for physical devices and another for logical devices and connections).

To reduce the complexities of dealing with multiple-vendor equipment, and sometimes even a variety of interfaces from one vendor, the NMS may provide a command mapping function. This allows the network managers to work with one command language that has a consistent interface. The command mapping function selects the proper interface programs to receive the message and translate the command into a format acceptable to these programs.

NETWORK MANAGEMENT PROTOCOLS

Network interconnection raises an additional network management problem. The problem is how to monitor nodes on one subnetwork from a node on a different subnetwork, such as monitoring a node on a token ring from a network management console attached to an IBM SNA network. To facilitate the exchange of management data among network nodes, a network management standard or protocol is essential. If such standards exist, network designers can build their networks with the ability to exchange management and control data. Two key standards have evolved: the **Simple Network Management Protocol (SNMP)** and the **Common Management Information Protocol (CMIP)**. Pronounced "C-mip," CMIP is also sometimes called the *Communications Management Information Protocol*.

Simple Network Management Protocol (SNMP) A widely used network monitoring and control protocol. Data is passed from SNMP agents to the network management console used to oversee the network. The agents send information contained in a MIB (Management Information Base) that defines the data obtainable from the device and device properties that can be controlled (turned off, on, etc.). Almost all network management software products support SNMP.

Common Management Information Protocol (CMIP) An ISO network monitoring a control standard. Also known as the *Communications Management Information Protocol*.

Simple Network Management Protocol (SNMP)

The SNMP is a part of the TCP/IP suite described in Chapter 2. Originally, the protocol was implemented on UNIX systems. Since the first SNMP products appeared in 1988, they have rapidly gained acceptance and popularity. The protocol is endorsed by companies such as IBM, Hewlett-Packard, and Sun Microsystems and is implemented on most microcomputer, minicomputer, and mainframe computers under a variety of operating systems. As the protocol has spread, its capabilities also have been expanded to accommodate new needs. Currently, the SNMP standard is *SNMP version 2* (*SNMP2*), also known as *SMP (simple management protocol)*.

SNMP has four key components: the protocol itself, the **Structure of Management Information (SMI)**, the **Management Information Base (MIB)**, and the **Network Management System (NMS)**.

> ➤ The SNMP is an application layer protocol that outlines the formal structure for communication among network devices. Today, SNMP is the de facto standard for transporting data among network management system components.

> ➤ The SMI details how every piece of information regarding managed devices is represented in the MIB.

> ➤ As noted previously, the MIB is a database that defines the hardware and software elements to be monitored. SNMP2 expanded the capabilities of the original MIB, and this new version is called MIB II.

> ➤ The NMS is the control console to which network monitoring and management information are reported.

The components of the SNMP are shown in Figure 15-3.

Each SNMP network device has an agent that collects data for that device. The data is stored in the device's MIB; SMI specifies how information about the device is represented in the MIB. A vendor that manufactures a device adhering to the SNMP standard will include an agent as one of the device components. Thus, there are agents for routers, servers, workstations, bridges, terminal servers, multiplexors, hubs, repeaters, concentrators, and other network devices. An SNMP *management component* interfaces with agents to provide network control. The management component uses three basic commands—GET, SET, and TRAPS—to control a device. The *GET* command allows the management component to retrieve data stored in the device's MIB; and the *SET* command allows data fields stored in the device's MIB to be reset. *TRAPS* allows an SNMP device to trap and forward unsolicited data; for example, a trap would be used to notify the management component of an alert condition. One example of a trap is a cold-start trap that notifies the management component when a device has been powered up.

An MIB contains information that the network administrator needs to monitor and control the network. MIB may be defined as an SNMP structure that describes the particular device being monitored. Hence, each device being monitored has its own individual MIB that contains data about only that device. A device MIB has two parts: a proprietary part in which data defined by the device vendor is saved and the part in which data common to all MIBs is stored. The data stored in device MIBs can be collected in a network management MIB that contains data for multiple network components. Another SNMP standard also provides for a **Remote Monitoring MIB (RMON MIB)**, which describes nine different device groups. A vendor must choose an appropriate group for a device and is required to support all data objects defined for that group. There is also an ability to support devices that do not directly support SNMP.

The original RMON MIB standard was developed in 1991. It only required compatible devices to collect and analyze data link layer and physical layer statistics.

Structure of Management Information (SMI) A component of the SNMP that details how information is represented in the Management Information Base.

Management Information Base (MIB) A database that defines the hardware and software elements to be monitored in SNMP. Each monitored device in SNMP-compliant NMSs has a small MIB containing information about itself. Information from this device database is sent to the network management console (the terminal or workstation used to monitor and control a network) and to an enterprise MIB.

Network Management System (NMS) The SNMP component used to monitor and administer the overall communications network.

Remote Monitoring MIB (RMON MIB) An SNMP standard that describes nine different device groups. A vendor must choose an appropriate group for a device adhering to this standard and is required to support all the data objects defined for that group.

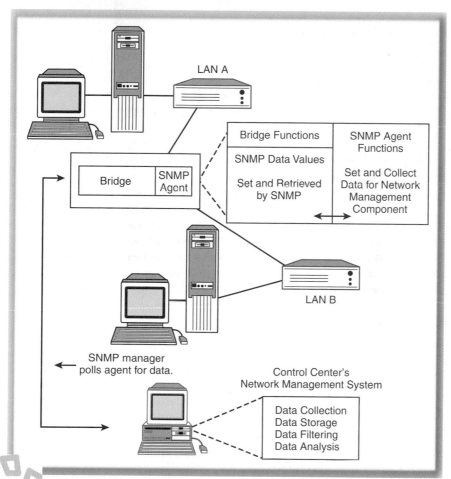

LAN A

Bridge Functions	SNMP Agent Functions
SNMP Data Values	
Set and Retrieved by SNMP	Set and Collect Data for Network Management Component

Bridge | SNMP Agent

LAN B

SNMP manager polls agent for data.

Control Center's Network Management System

Data Collection
Data Storage
Data Filtering
Data Analysis

Figure 15-3 Details of the SNMP Environment

RMON2 requires compatible technologies to collect and analyze network layer statistics in addition to data link and physical layer statistics. RMON2 is designed to help network managers do a better job of pinpointing network traffic sources and line loads within a network. *RMON3* is designed to overcome RMON2's inability to collect and analyze WAN performance statistics; it provides a way for proprietary WAN management tools to share data and interoperate.

Remote Monitoring (RMON) extensions to SNMP enable comprehensive network monitoring capabilities. In standard SNMP, the device has to be queried/polled by the NMS to obtain information. RMON, in contrast, is proactive and can trigger alarms on a variety of traffic conditions beyond the functioning of individual network devices. RMON2 can also monitor the kinds of application traffic that flow through the network.

SNMP allows network managers to get the status of devices and set or initialize devices. If problems occur, an event mechanism generates a message that is displayed on the network management console. As a simple protocol, SNMP has a few shortcomings. Its command set is limited, there are limited provisions for security, and, because it lacks a strict standard, there is some inconsistency among different vendors' implementations.

Remote Monitoring (RMON) Extensions to standard SNMP that provide more comprehensive network monitoring capabilities. Unlike standard SNMP, which requires monitored devices to be queried to obtain information, RMON is proactive and can be configured to trigger alarms on a variety of traffic conditions, including specific types of errors. RMON2 is also capable of monitoring the kinds of application traffic that flow through the network.

Like RMON MIB, SNMP has evolved over time. SNMP2 (or SMP) support goes beyond SMNP by supporting multiple transport protocols (such as IPX and AppleTalk), not just TCP/IP. It also has *bulk retrieval mechanisms* that enable multiple pieces of information to be retrieved at one time from a given agent. (SNMP only allowed one piece of information at a time to be retrieved from a given agent.) This helps to reduce the total amount of network traffic generated by the network management system. SNMP2 enables multiple agents to be installed in a single component and increases the security of network traffic.

Common Management Information Protocol

The International Standards Organization's (ISO) Common Management Information Protocol (CMIP) is another important NMS protocol. CMIP has a more complex protocol for exchanging messages among network components and has the potential for better control and the ability to overcome SNMP limitations. Although there are no provisions for direct interoperability of SNMP and CMIP, some NMS products communicate concurrently with SNMP agents as well as CMIP agents. Although CMIP has been endorsed and supported by AT&T, Digital Equipment Corporation, and other data communication equipment vendors, it has not been successful in dislodging SNMP as the de facto NMS standard.

NMS PRODUCTS

Network management systems should be able to collect information from a variety of network components across the network and to display it in a clear, meaningful way. Today, it is also important for them to monitor and manage distributed network components, including servers, workstations, applications, routers, and switches. Table 15-3 summarizes some of the major NMS products being used today.

Despite compliance with NMS standards such as SNMP, RMON MIB, and CMIP, NMS products fall well short of full interoperability. If more than one NMS product is used within an enterprise, there are likely to be redundant MIBs (even redundant component MIBs), redundant polling of agents/monitors to retrieve component per-

Table 15-3   Examples of NMS Products

Vendor	Product
American Power Conversion	PowerNet
AT&T	Accumaster
Bay Networks	Optivity Enterprise
BMC Software, Inc.	Patrol View
Cabletron	Spectrum
Cisco Systems	Cisco Works
Computer Associates	CA-Unicenter
Hewlett-Packard	HP OpenView
Intel	LANDesk Manager
Legato	Networker
Novell	ManageWise
Tivoli	NetView
3Com	Transcend Enterprise Manager

formance statistics, and the need to have multiple agents on network components to report to different NMS MIBs. Having multiple NMSs also may make it challenging or impossible for topologies or maps to be exchanged among the NMSs or for the NMSs to exchange alert and alarm settings for particular components. Lack of common application program interfaces (APIs) is a primary cause of lack of NMS product interoperability.

Although there is variation in the level of functionality across NMS software products, most do an acceptable job of monitoring network activity levels, detecting abnormal network performance, and issuing alerts and alarms. Some, but not all, NMS products can diagnose and fix detected problems without the direct involvement of network managers. Ideally, future NMS product versions will integrate application management, system administration, and network management and be able to improve the performance of distributed applications in response to network status changes.

With this general overview of network management products in mind, we now look at three specific NMS products: OpenView from Hewlett-Packard, NetView from Tivoli (an IBM partner), and ManageWise, a Novell product.

HP's OpenView

OpenView is network management software from Hewlett-Packard. It is an enterprise-wide network management solution that supports the SNMP and CMIP protocols. Third-party products that run under OpenView support SNA and DECnet protocols. Industry research indicates that OpenView is the most widely used enterprise NMS.

OpenView is a network management platform that supports a wide range of network management applications. Among the major applications that run under OpenView are OperationsCenter, AdminCenter, HP TopTools for Hubs and Switches, and HP OpenView Observer.

OperationsCenter focuses on the monitoring and resolution of server problems (usually UNIX servers). A daemon (agent) installed in the server monitors server operations and processes and sends alerts to OperationsCenter consoles when something goes wrong. In many instances, OperationsCenter modules can instruct the agent to take predefined actions to correct problems as they arise. For example, if a process fails, OperationsCenter might instruct the agent to restart it. If this does not correct the problem, OperationsCenter can alert human operators that additional action is needed. All events of this nature are tracked and logged.

AdminCenter provides the capability to manage a network of UNIX servers en masse. It facilitates the management of disk space, user accounts, groups, and other network objects; all of these can be time-consuming day-to-day tasks associated with operational network management.

HP TopTools for Hubs and Switches has the capability of simultaneously monitoring traffic on up to 1,500 network segments. It is a Web-based tool that oversees the hubs and switches across the network, and it has the potential to improve performance in Ethernet network segments. These modules have been included in HP hubs and switches since 1998.

HP OpenView Observer monitors the performance of e-business–oriented software and business Web sites. It captures information on response time, modem speed, and the user's ISP. It is designed to help network managers identify and isolate bottlenecks that degrade Web site visitors' online experience.

Like most enterprise NMS products, OpenView products work best in networks where the majority of the equipment in use has been manufactured by Hewlett-Packard. To its credit, HP has made the APIs for applications such as OperationsCenter and AdminCenter available to other vendors to enable competitors to provide

OpenView agents in their hardware/software. HP TopTools for Hubs and Switches has also been made available as a plug-in for other vendors' enterprise NMS products.

Tivoli's NetView

Although not as widely used as OpenView, Tivoli's NetView is another leading network management system product. It is targeted for IP networks and is designed to enable centralized management of distributed network resources (applications, workstations, servers, hubs, switches, bridges, and routers) in a single network control center. The original NetView, released by IBM in 1986, consolidated and extended several network management packages that had been used to monitor and control IBM SNA networks; it included control services and diagnostic control capabilities, such as hardware monitoring, session monitoring, and status monitoring. Hardware monitoring collects status information from physical devices, and session monitoring provides information on SNA sessions. Status monitoring provides display information regarding system components and assists in restarting system elements following a failure. The control function provides the ability to activate and deactivate devices.

Today, NetView allows centralized control of a distributed system that consists of IBM, IBM–compatible, and non–IBM equipment. It displays network topologies, correlates and manages network events (transient and extended changes in normal network performance), and gathers performance data useful for network tuning and planning. It includes modules for quickly diagnosing/identifying causes of network problems (root cause analysis) and resolving them. It enables network managers to isolate faulty network equipment so that it can be fixed and brought back into service quickly. Distributed network management is also possible with NetView.

NetView users indicate that the product interfaces well with products from most leading networking product vendors, that it is very scalable, and that it has very good network statistic analysis, trend identification, and reporting capabilities. NetView's databases also maintain a device inventory to facilitate network asset management.

Novell's ManageWise

Like NetView, Novell's ManageWise can be used as an enterprise-wide NMS, but its strength lies in its ability to provide a network management solution in networks that include heterogeneous LAN segments (such as Fast Ethernet, token ring, and FDDI) that include both NetWare and Windows NT/2000 servers. ManageWise makes it possible to manage any SNMP–compliant device in a heterogeneous network from a single network control center console. It also enables network managers to remotely manage LAN segments, thereby helping to minimize the network's total cost of ownership.

Central management of several important network management tasks is facilitated by ManageWise, including directory services monitoring, server management, desktop (workstation) management, software distribution, network performance monitoring, problem diagnosis and resolution, virus detection and eradication, network traffic analysis, and network inventory management. Network planning and optimization are also facilitated via reporting modules for ManageWise MIBs.

Previously, ManageWise was known as Novell's *Network Management System (NMS)*. Like NMS, ManageWise includes network mapping capabilities and a network inventory database that includes details about servers, workstations, LAN adapters, wiring hubs, bridges, and routers.

RMON agents and ManageWise filters provide statistics and alerts to the ManageWise network control console. SNMP devices are polled, and the data retrieved from them are stored in the ManageWise MIB. Other ManageWise features include

➤ APIs (application program interfaces) to enable ManageWise integration with other network management systems, including NetView

➤ Modules for monitoring packets, protocols, and media

➤ Modules to track wiring hub performance

➤ Automatic server fault detection and alert notification

➤ Graphical and text reporting

➤ Modules for setting alarm and alert thresholds for SNMP devices

Intel's LANDesk Manager is one of ManageWise's main competitors. Both of these products are well-suited for organizations whose networks are LAN oriented. HP OpenView and CA-Unicenter are two of NetView's major competitors.

NETWORK MANAGEMENT TOOLS

In addition to network management software, an organization's network management team often requires a variety of tools to carry out their responsibilities. These can be divided according to their function: diagnostic tools, monitoring tools, and management tools.

Diagnostic Tools

Diagnostic tools are used by network administrators to troubleshoot and resolve network problems. As such, they play an important role in operational network management. Depending on the nature and complexity of the network, different types of diagnostic/troubleshooting tools are needed. Examples of widely used diagnostic and troubleshooting tools are briefly discussed here.

LAN Analyzers   A **LAN analyzer** monitors network traffic, captures and displays data sent over the network, generates network traffic to simulate load or error conditions, tests cables for faults, and provides data helpful for system configuration and management. LAN analyzers sometimes include *packet sniffer* software to examine network traffic for routine inspection and for detecting bottlenecks or problems.

Digital Line Monitors   Digital **line monitors**, also known as *protocol analyzers*, are used to diagnose problems on a communication link. Their basic function is to attach to a communication circuit so the bit patterns transmitted over the circuit can be displayed for analysis and problem solving by networking specialists.

Analog Line Monitors   An **analog line monitor** measures and displays the analog signals on the communication circuit or on the data communication side of the modem, enabling the user to check for noise and proper modulation. Analog line monitors are used primarily by common carriers to evaluate their circuits.

Features common on line monitors, both digital and analog, include video display, data capture to disk or tape, trap setting for selected bit patterns, graphics displays, programmability, multiple protocol support, and integrated breakout boxes.

Breakout Boxes   A **breakout box** is a passive, multipurpose device that is patched or temporarily inserted into a circuit or communications interface. Once installed, it is possible to monitor activity on each of the circuits, change circuit connections, isolate a circuit to prevent its signal from passing through to a receiver, and measure voltage levels. Breakout boxes may also be equipped with bit pattern generators and receivers to enable them to transmit and receive selected bit patterns; this enables technicians to determine the effects/behavior of known data patterns on the circuit.

LAN analyzer
A diagnostic tool that monitors network traffic, captures and displays data sent over the network, generates network traffic to simulate load or error conditions, tests cables for faults, and provides data helpful for system configuration and management.

line monitor
A device (or software) used to monitor traffic on a network. Line monitors can read unencrypted data transmitted over the network and are often used to diagnose problems on a communication link. Also known as a *protocol analyzer.*

analog line monitor
A diagnostic tool that monitors and displays the analog signals on the communication circuit or the data communication side of the modem, enabling the user to check for noise and proper modulation.

breakout box A passive, multipurpose diagnostic device that is patched or temporarily inserted into a circuit at an interface. Often used for multiple-line cable testing, a breakout box provides an external connecting point to each wire that allows a small LED to be attached to each line; when a signal is present on the line, the LED glows.

cable tester A diagnostic tool used to detect faults in cables by generating and monitoring a signal along the cable.

emulator A diagnostic tool that enables the user to check for adherence to a specific communication protocol.

protocol analyzer A diagnostic tool for displaying and analyzing communication protocols. Protocol analyzers are capable of capturing and analyzing individual data packets/frames transmitted over network media. They can be used to test whether individual workstations are transmitting appropriate data link layer frame formats or network layer packet formats. A protocol analyzer also can be used to analyze (sniff) the contents of individual packets/frames. Also known as digital line monitors.

remote control software Software that enables a user at a local computer to have control of a remote computer. It allows a network administrator to view a remote user's monitor and to take control of the remote user's keyboard. It can be used to take control of an unattended desktop personal computer from a remote location as well as to provide technical support and instruction to remote users.

Cable Testers   **Cable testers** are used to detect faults in cables by generating and monitoring a signal along the cable. By monitoring the signal, a cable tester not only can detect faults in the medium itself, or in medium connections, but also can identify the location of the fault.

Emulators   An **emulator** is a diagnostic tool that enables the user to check for adherence to a specific protocol. For example, a vendor must have its frame relay software certified by a frame relay network provider before being allowed to connect to the system to avoid disrupting other system users; one way the software can be tested is with an emulator. The emulator acts like a frame relay node, generating both correct and incorrect messages to ensure that the system reacts according to the frame relay specifications. Emulators of this type usually allow the user to specify the types of messages to be transmitted. Emulators also can be used during the development process to ensure that the interfaces between software levels are correct.

Protocol Analyzers   **Protocol analyzers** capture and analyze individual data packets/frames transmitted over network media. They can be used to test whether individual workstations are transmitting appropriate data link layer frame formats or network layer packet formats. They can also be used to analyze the contents of individual packets/frames. By being able to graphically display the contents of the frames transmitted by devices attached to the network, they can help network managers determine the extent to which specific devices contribute to network traffic and errors. Protocol analyzers are sometimes called *sniffers*.

Remote Control Software   **Remote control software** tools allow a network administrator to remotely view a user's monitor and take control of the user's keyboard. This capability is helpful during initial diagnostic work because it allows the network administrator to experience the problem firsthand. Sometimes, the problem can be resolved remotely, thus providing more immediate correction and a reduction in the diagnostic time required by hands-on diagnostics.

Current Documentation   One of the best diagnostic tools is current documentation, including software lists that reflect the correct release and patch levels, logic diagrams, internal documentation, maintenance manuals, and any other supporting documents. Although documentation may seem obvious as a diagnostic tool, its importance cannot be overstated. Key documents that network technicians need to consult are compatibility lists. Each piece of network hardware and software is usually accompanied by a vendor-provided compatibility list. It is important that related products adhere to the same standards because incompatibilities are a major source of network problems.

A variety of other diagnostic/testing/troubleshooting tools are likely to be included in the network management and maintenance toolbox. Some of these are summarized in Table 15-4.

Diagnostic tools help locate problems in the network, whereas monitoring and management tools are used to avoid problems in the network. Monitoring and management functions include capacity planning, general project management, performance, and configuration. Several of these tools have been developed for microcomputers and are affordable by most organizations. Capacity planning is an extremely important function of network managers, who must recognize when resources are approaching full capacity and plan for expansion or reconfiguration to avoid saturation and decreased service. Project management tools allow a manager to plan and

Table 15-4   Additional Network Diagnostic/Troubleshooting Tools

Diagnostic/Testing Tool	Function
Bit error rate tester (BERT)	BERT is used to determine reliable data transmission over a communication link by sending specific bit patterns and data packets over the link.
Pocket adapters	Pocket adapters enable a network technician to establish a network interface through a workstation's or server's parallel or serial port. Through bypassing the computer's existing network adapter, it is possible to determine whether the installed adapter is the source of the computer's communication problem.
Block error rate tester (BKERT)	BKERT calculates the percentage of frames/packets received by a network device that contain at least one error. It can help locate upstream sources transmission errors.
Fiber identifier	A fiber identifier is used to locate nonworking fibers in fiber optic networks.

monitor the progress of projects. System performance and configuration address how well the system is working and the location and types of network components.

Four tools that are very effective in planning for capacity are metering software, performance monitors, simulation models, and workload generators.

Monitoring Tools

Network monitoring tools help network managers to determine if current network configurations are continuing to meet the needs of network users. Data captured by these tools can be analyzed to determine whether changes to current configurations are likely to improve network performance or to better serve users over time. Because of this, they are useful in managing current network operations as well as for network planning. Examples of network management tools in this category include metering software, performance monitors, simulation models, workload generators, log files, and network configuration tools.

Metering Software   **Metering software** is used to enforce adherence to software license agreements. Metering software installed on a LAN server keeps track of the number of copies of a particular application stored on the server that are currently being used. If an organization has a license to concurrently run 25 copies of a word processing program, network managers set the metering count to 25 for that application. Whenever a user starts the application, the counter is incremented by 1, and when a user exits the application, the counter is decremented by 1. If the usage counter is at 25 and a user attempts to start the application, the metering software denies the request.

Performance Monitors   **Performance monitors** provide snapshots of how a system is functioning, typically capturing such information as number of transactions, type of transaction, transaction response times, transaction processing times, queue depths, number of characters per request/response, buffer use, number of I/Os, and

metering software A monitoring tool used on LANs to enforce adherence to software license agreements by keeping track of the number of times an application is executed. Metering software is capable of limiting the number of concurrent users of an application to ensure compliance with the software license agreements.

performance monitor A monitoring tool that provides snapshots of how a system is functioning, which helps network managers identify trends in the use or misuse of the network.

processing time by process or process subprogram. When collected over time, information of this nature enables the management team to identify trends in the use or misuse of the network. These trends include such things as whether the number of a specific type of transaction is steadily increasing and whether the capacity for handling that transaction type is being reached—or whether users are playing games during lunch hour when the peak processing load occurs.

As noted previously in this chapter, network management system (NMS) products incorporate performance monitoring functions. As discussed in Chapter 9, network operating system server software typically includes performance monitoring capabilities.

simulation model
A monitoring tool that allows the user to describe network and system activities and to receive an analysis of how the system can be expected to perform under the described conditions.

Simulation Models   **Simulation models** allow the user to describe network and system activities and to receive an analysis of how the system can be expected to perform under the described conditions. This service is especially useful during network planning and development to predict response times, processor use, and potential bottlenecks. After networks are installed and operational, simulation models help determine what size transaction load is likely to reach or exceed the network's maximum capacity as well as the effect of adding transactions, applications, servers, workstations, and communication equipment (such as bridges, switches, and routers) to the existing network.

The majority of the network simulation software used today enables network managers to change network hardware or software configurations, modify resource utilization and data traffic rates, and run tests to determine how network performance would be affected by these and other changes. Network simulation models enable network managers to estimate server utilization, disk utilization, data traffic over specific links, message queues at routers and switches, print queue lengths, and response times to user requests for specific network resources under varying operating conditions. This helps network managers determine the types of performance demands that can exceed current capacity levels. Network simulation software can also help network managers identify under- or overutilized components in the network's current configuration.

The value of network simulation models is in their ability to anticipate how a new network configuration is likely to perform in advance of its implementation. They also allow network managers to compare likely performance levels of alternative network configurations, thus facilitating the selection of configurations with the greatest probability of satisfying future computing needs.

workload generator
A monitoring tool that generates transaction loads and pseudo-application processes for execution on a proposed configuration to illustrate how a system will actually function.

Workload Generators   Whereas the simulation model predicts system use, a **workload generator** actually generates the transaction loads and pseudoapplication processes for execution on current or proposed network configurations. If the model and the workload generator were perfect, the results would be identical; in actual practice, however, some variation between the two is likely to occur. A workload generator together with a performance monitor can illustrate how the current system will actually function under increasing workloads or how a proposed configuration is likely to perform under normal workloads. It also can be used for stress testing (which involves placing increasingly higher performance demands on the network until the network crashes) and to determine appropriate thresholds for network alerts and alarms. By being able to see how network performance is likely to be affected by increasing network workloads, workload generators help network managers predict when current network capacities will be reached.

As with any model, simulation models and workload generators are only as good as the inputs, the people who use and interpret them, and the closeness of the models to actual use. Their value decreases with the amount of time required to use them and increases with their ability to portray an application accurately. This means they should be used carefully and the results interpreted sensibly.

Log Files   **Log files** are another valuable tool in monitoring a system. Certain logs, such as a system log or network messages, should be maintained continuously, whereas others can be used only when necessary. A line trace, for example, is a log of the activity on a particular line that is normally used only when a problem has been detected. Some software has been designed to log specific network activities on demand; the network manager would enable or disable the logging, depending on what information is required. Log files are used for both diagnostic functions and predictive or management functions.

Network Configuration Tools   **Network configuration tools** are used to plan the optimum network configuration with respect to sources and types of circuits. In the past, these have been expensive to purchase or use, and some were limited to one common carrier's facilities or geographical locations. These systems are now available on microcomputers and at more affordable prices.

Management Tools

Menuing and Inventory Software   **Menuing software** is used in both LANs and WANs to provide network users options (such as log-on options and printer choices) via a menu of choices. On LANs, menu software allows a network administrator to quickly implement a set of choices and the actions associated with those choices. **Inventory software** is capable of interrogating many components of a LAN and collecting information on those components. Examples of the data collected include network addresses, CPU types, operating systems, disk use on servers and workstations, and workstation and server memory configurations. Many of the statistics needed by a network administrator in managing and fixing a network are automatically provided and reported by inventory software.

Project Planning Tools   **Project planning tools** are beneficial in the administration of the network, in planning the activities of the team members, in the installation of new equipment and software, and in numerous other management activities. Many of these tools are now available on microcomputers, bringing them to more users at a low cost.

Database Management Systems and Report Generators   Database management systems and report generators are also useful management tools. The database can be used to store statistical and operational information, which a good query/report writer can select, synthesize, and summarize. These systems can schedule members of the network management team, store and retrieve error and trouble report information, and produce reports on modeling. Database management systems are available on most systems today and can be very useful in storing, modifying, and retrieving data about the network management function. State-of-the-art systems enable users to define a database; enter, modify, and delete information; and generate reports without having to write much code. Many of the microcomputer relational model database systems provide all these features and are oriented toward users with little expertise in programming or systems.

NETWORK TUNING AND CAPACITY PLANNING

Many of the tools discussed in the previous section play a key role in managing the day-to-day operations of an organization's existing networks. The diagnostic and troubleshooting tools are particularly useful in this regard. The value of other tools extends beyond their ability to facilitate operational network management. Monitoring tools, for example, are also very useful for network tuning and network planning.

---

log files A monitoring tool used for both diagnostic functions and predictive or management functions. In networks, log files may be created to store incoming text dialog, error and status messages, and transaction details.

network configuration tool A monitoring tool used to plan the optimum network configuration with respect to sources and types of circuits.

menuing software A management tool used to provide users with options via a menu of application or command choices.

inventory software A management tool used to collect LAN component data, such as network addresses and CPU types, that will help a network administrator document, manage, and fix a network.

project planning tool A tool used by project managers to define, monitor, and modify project events, resources, and schedules. Project management software is an example of a project planning tool; it is used to monitor the time and resources consumed by project-related tasks.

Network Tuning

Network tuning is concerned with ensuring that network performance levels are maintained at acceptable levels. Frequent analysis of network statistics captured and stored in NMS databases is often an important part of ensuring that the network is performing satisfactorily.

Network component configurations and network use typically change over time. Software and hardware changes have the potential to degrade network performance by placing greater demands on servers, and increasing the number and variety of messages carried over communication links. If multiple changes are made within a short time frame, users may experience longer response times. In some instances, changes to the configuration of network hardware and software components may decrease network availability.

Vigilant network managers are able to identify trends toward unacceptable network performance levels through the analysis of NMS statistics in network databases. Steady increases over time in error rates, alerts, alarms, communication link utilization, and server utilization are often indicative of future performance problems if corrective intervention is not taken.

Upgrading data communication equipment and other network components is one network tuning approach. For example, if users are experiencing slower response times after a new version of an application program has been installed on a server, it may be necessary to increase the server's RAM, increase the number of processors in the server (if it supports SMP), increase the number of simultaneous user connections to the server by installing additional network adapter cards, or make duplicate copies of the application available on additional servers. If users are complaining about increasing delays between print job submission and the printing of the hard copies that they need, it may be necessary to increase the number of printers available to service the print queue.

Network **balancing** is a tuning approach that involves the utilization of existing network resources in a different configuration. Bottlenecks slowing server responses to user requests for a particular application might be overcome by moving the application to another server or by moving other applications also stored on that server to other servers in the network.

Network tuning processes are best handled by experienced network managers and network technicians. Such individuals typically have the most comprehensive and detailed knowledge of the interrelationships among network components. They are also likely to be better able to interpret trends in network statistics and to know when network tuning is needed.

The steps in the network tuning process are summarized in Table 15-5. A useful guideline to keep in mind about network tuning is to implement potential solutions to the problem one at a time. If multiple changes are made in response to an identified problem, it may difficult to isolate which changes do the best job of addressing the problem. By making changes one at a time, network managers are better positioned to assess the performance impacts of each.

Capacity Planning

Capacity planning involves forecasting network use and workloads required for the development of network plans that focus on ensuring that the network will be able to support anticipated performance demands. This process typically includes the analysis of the network statistics stored in NMS network databases (e.g., MIBs) in light of the organization's plans for increasing the number of network users, expanding its num-

Table 15-5   The Network Tuning Process

1. Monitor and capture network performance data.
2. Analyze network statistics; identify network performance trends.
3. Identify network performance problems or potential problems.
4. Diagnose the likely causes of the problem.
5. Identify and prioritize alternative ways to address the network performance problem.
6. Implement the "best" solution to the network performance problem (i.e., the one likely to produce the biggest gain per dollar spent; the quickest/easiest solution to implement).
7. Measure the impact of the chosen solution on network performance.
8. Repeat steps 3–6 until acceptable network performance levels are obtained.

ber of operating locations, and establishing interorganizational data communication linkages with business partners.

As mentioned previously, network simulation tools and workload generators can play an important role in capacity planning. Trend analysis of network statistics can assist network managers in assessing changes in network use and performance over time. Some NMSs include forecasting modules that enable trends in historical data to be projected into the future. Such forecasts enable network managers to determine when user requirements for network resources are likely to reach (or exceed) current capacity levels. This information helps network planners determine how much lead time they have in making changes to the network infrastructure as well as the types of changes that need to be made to ensure adequate network capacity in the future.

THE INTERNET'S IMPACT ON NETWORK MANAGEMENT SYSTEMS

The evolution of the Internet and e-business continues to impact network management systems. Web-based network management systems and protocols are emerging that enable network managers to remotely manage network devices and applications via a Web browser. **Hypermedia management protocol (HMMP)** has been proposed to support such browser-based, Web-based network management. A new Web-based network management information storage specification called the **hypermedia management schema (HMMS)** would allow HMMP–compliant browsers to retrieve data captured by distributed SNMP and other agents from network databases by using an object manager (either Microsoft's DCOM [distributed component object model] or CORBA [common object request broker architecture]). An overview of the proposed Web-based network management architecture is provided in Figure 15-4.

The **common information model (CIM)** supports HMMS. CIM allows network management information collected by a variety of network devices to be transported, processed, displayed, and stored by a CIM–compliant Web browser. CIM's network management data is stored in *modified object format (MOF)* rather than the format specification for SNMP's MIB.

Web-based network management holds the promise of providing a common NMS interface regardless of the network devices that need to be managed. It could overcome the interoperability associated with current NMS products. It would also help network managers provide superior management of Internet-spawned technologies such as firewalls, storage area networks (SANs), and server clusters. Enabling network

hypermedia management protocol (HMMP) A proposed protocol to support browser-based, Web-based network management.

hypermedia management schema (HMMS) Allows HMMP–compliant browsers to retrieve data captured by distributed SNMP and other agents from network databases using an object manager such as Microsoft's distributed component object model (DCOM) or common object request broker architecture (CORBA).

common information model (CIM) An implementation independent model for describing network management information. CIM allows network management information collected by a variety of network devices to be transported, processed, displayed, and stored by a CIM-compliant Web browser.

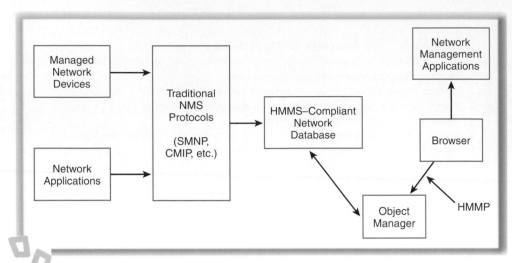

Figure 15-4   A Web-Based NMS

managers to remotely manage network resources from anywhere via a Web browser is also an advantage of this approach.

The Internet is also promoting changes in the network management capabilities bundled with network operating systems. NetWare 6, for example, includes network management modules for interorganizational links between business partners. It also enables users and network managers to remotely access network resources via browsers. Network managers are able to carry out a number of standard network management functions remotely via Web browsers.

SUMMARY

Managing a network can be a complex task, requiring a wide range of information and tools. NMSs and utilities assist the administrator in managing the network and correcting network problems. An NMS collects statistics on network components, provides alerts when proper operation is threatened, and generates standard reports to allow the network manager to monitor performance and take corrective actions before problems develop. Two network management protocols, Simple Network Management Protocol (SNMP) and Common Management Information Protocol (CMIP), have been defined to assist vendors in creating software and hardware that can be monitored. The SNMP is part of the TCP/IP suite and is widely used in a variety of hardware and software platforms. CMIP is an ISO recommendation for collection and reporting of management information. A number of vendors provide NMSs. Tivoli's NetView is a widely used NMS for IP networks. Novell's ManageWise is an enterprise-wide NMS used by organizations with LAN–oriented network infrastructures.

In addition to a comprehensive NMS, a variety of tools and utilities are available to assist network managers in performing their duties. The three major categories of network management tools are diagnostic tools, monitoring tools, and management tools. Diagnostic tools (such as line monitors, cable testers, breakout boxes, protocol analyzers, and remote control software) are used to troubleshoot and resolve network problems; these play a key role in operational network management.

Network monitoring tools (such as simulation models, workload generators, and log files) assist network managers in determining whether current network configurations are continuing to meet the needs of network users over time. Management tools such as network inventory management software, project planning tools, and reporting tools that enable network managers to analyze statistics in network databases are also valuable.

Network monitoring and management tools are useful for network tuning and capacity planning. Network tuning involves making incremental changes to network configurations in order to ensure that network performance remains at acceptable levels. Load balancing is one aspect of network tuning. Capacity planning involves forecasting network use and workloads and the development of network plans that ensure that the network will be able to support anticipated performance demands.

The evolution of the Internet and e-business has spawned Web-based network management systems. HMMP (hypermedia management protocol) is an important new protocol for Web-based NMSs.

KEY TERMS

- agent
- alarm
- alert
- analog line monitor
- balancing
- breakout box
- cable tester
- capacity planning
- common information model (CIM)
- Common Management Information Protocol (CMIP)
- emulator
- filter
- hypermedia management protocol (HMMP)
- hypermedia management schema (HMMS)
- inventory software
- LAN analyzer
- line monitor
- log files

- Management Information Base (MIB)
- menuing software
- metering software
- network configuration tool
- network management system (NMS)
- Network Management System (NMS)
- network tuning
- performance monitor
- project planning tool
- protocol analyzer
- remote control software
- Remote Monitoring (RMON)
- Remote Monitoring MIB (RMON MIB)
- Simple Network Management Protocol (SNMP)
- simulation model
- Structure of Management Information (SMI)
- workload generator

REVIEW QUESTIONS

1. What is a network management system?
2. What functions are performed by network management systems?
3. Identify and briefly describe the major components of a network management system.
4. Compare agents and filters.
5. Compare alerts and alarms.
6. Compare the Simple Network Management Protocol (SNMP) and the Common Management Information Protocol (CMIP).
7. Why are SNMP and CMIP necessary?
8. Compare RMON and RMON2.
9. Compare SNMP and SNMP2.
10. Why is interoperability an issue for NMS products?
11. Compare and contrast OpenView, NetView, and ManageWise.

12. Describe the function and use of
    a. LAN analyzers
    b. line monitors
    c. breakout boxes
    d. emulators
    e. remote control software
    f. current documentation
    g. metering software
    h. simulation models
    i. workload generators
    j. log files
    k. network configuration tools
13. How are project management tools used in network management?
14. What is network tuning? Briefly describe the network tuning process.
15. What is network balancing? Why is it important?
16. What is capacity planning? What NMS components and network management tools assist in the capacity planning process?
17. What is HMMP? Why is it important?
18. What are the major components of a Web-based NMS?
19. What is the common information model (CIM)?

PROBLEMS AND EXERCISES

1. The following table identifies examples of the types of data collected by NMS agents in various network components. Pick two types of data for each component listed in the table and explain how they could be used to manage the network.

Network Component	Types of Data Collected
Server	Status (active/inactive)
	Processor utilization
	Disk utilization
	Cache utilization
	Memory (RAM) utilization
	Application utilization
Print server	Status (active/inactive)
	Print queue status
	Print queue lengths
	Print activity
	Attached printer status
Communication medium	Utilization percentage
	Packet/frame transmission rate
	Packet/frame error rate
	Maximum transfer rate
	Packet type utilization
Internetworking devices (bridges/routers)	Local traffic volumes
	Filtering rates
	Forwarding rate
	Path failures
	Path changes
	Traffic volumes sent per port

2. Use the Internet to research the capabilities of remote diagnostic tools (such as remote control software) used to identify/respond to network problems. Summarize what you learn in a paper or PowerPoint presentation.

3. Use the Internet to identify the network management modules/capabilities bundled with Windows 2000 Server and NetWare. Compare and contrast the network management capabilities of each NOS in a paper or PowerPoint presentation.

4. Use the Internet and other online sources to learn about the features/capabilities and NMS protocol support for two of the NMS products listed in Table 15-3 other than NetView and ManageWise. Summarize what you learn in a paper or PowerPoint presentation.

5. Use the Internet and other online sources to identify proposed changes to SNMP (such as secure SNMP and SNMP3). Summarize what you learn in a paper or PowerPoint presentation.

6. Use the Internet and other online sources to identify proposed changes to RMON (such as RMON3). Summarize what you learn in a paper or PowerPoint presentation.

7. Use the Internet to find out more about DMI (*Hint:* DMI competes with SNMP and CMIP). Compare and contrast DMI and SNMP in a paper or PowerPoint presentation.

8. Use the Internet to learn more about network simulation tools and workload generators. Identify several network simulation software vendors, their major products, and the major features/capabilities of the products. Summarize the information you find in a table.

9. Use the Internet to learn more about the role of help desk management software in network management. Summarize what you learn in a paper or PowerPoint presentation.

10. Load balancing has become an important aspect of network management and performance. Use the Internet and other online sources to learn more about load balancing, load balancing algorithms, and where they are most widely used in today's networks. Summarize what you learn in a paper or PowerPoint presentation.

11. Bandwidth management (traffic shaping) is becoming more important in many business networks. Use the Internet and other online sources to learn more about bandwidth management (traffic shaping) and summarize the information you obtain in a paper of PowerPoint presentation. Identify widely used bandwidth management protocols (e.g., RSVP, COPS, MPLS, and RAP) and summarize their major features/capabilities in a table.

12. Use the Internet to learn more about Web-based network management and CIM. Summarize what you learn in a paper or PowerPoint presentation.

Self-Managing Networks and Network Applications

Self-managing software is one of the promises that several companies have been trying to make come true during the last few years. These applications will be able to troubleshoot and automatically fix errors and change configurations based upon past experience and patterns that the system can detect. This behavior is similar to natural biological behavior of the human being that can respond to a stimulus by instinct or by learning experience.

The high volume of data and computing/communication devices, as well as an increasing number of network users, is driving the growing attraction of today's organizations to self-managing applications. Because of the Internet, networks are becoming both more sophisticated and dynamic. In addition, network administrators are having a hard time trying to optimize corporate networks. Self-managing applications hold the promise of making the network administration task easier and faster.

Vendors such as BMC Software Inc. and Computer Associates are already offering self-managing products. Patrol Perform, BMC Software's product, can monitor servers' processes and identify when there is a slowdown in performance by comparing current processes with previously collected statistical data. Computer Associates' self-managing and predicative software, called Neugents, can identify which router is causing a bottleneck in a network by comparing current performance to performance data captured (and stored) when the network was working optimally.

IBM's eLiza project is believed to be the most ambitious project to develop self-managing applications and self-healing servers; it may eventually work without human intervention. This project involves hundreds of IBM programmers around the world to develop hardware, software, and networks that will distribute computing resources as required, protect business data, and automatically handle a disaster-recovery process. With the eLiza project, IBM is taking proactive steps to help administrators manage future networks that will be more complex than the ones we now have in the market.

IBM is focusing its initial efforts on developing self-managing/self-healing technologies on hardware and operating systems. Since 1994, IBM has been using such technology in the MVS mainframe operating system; now the company wants to apply it to the world of servers and PCs. In the future, IBM intends to turn its attention to self-managing/self-healing storage products and middleware, including MQSeries, CICS, and Tivoli. These applications are not designed to replace human network managers and IT professionals. IBM officials contend that self-managing applications will let IT people focus on major business problems by helping them to automatically solve some of the daily technical problems and configurations.

Sun Microsystems' Jini networking architecture is one of the more mature and established adaptive technologies available in the market. Jini is able to reallocate system resources to components that are up and running by making services that are not working properly inaccessible to users. Jini can handle network errors, remotely update software, and has self-diagnostic capabilities that manage IP changes and network outages without human intervention.

Microsoft has also started developing its first efforts in self-healing features. Microsoft SQL Server 7.0 and SQL Server 2000 have the ability to allocate memory automatically whenever it is necessary to deal with issues such as input/output demands or the volume of a buffer pool. Moreover, Microsoft Windows XP can self-manage software updates by automatically downloading software from the Internet.

At Hewlett-Packard, a team of researchers is developing a self-managing infrastructure, called *Planetary Computing*, and a framework for automatic system configuration, called *SmartFrog (failure recovery of object groups)*. Planetary Computing is designed to handle up to a 50,000-node computing network that can be built, reconfigured, and managed automatically. HP's final goal is to develop intelligent systems that can detect how different devices and processes operate and automatically control their behavior.

These are some of the major companies that are trying to make the dream of self-managing applications come true. Although the perfect system may not yet exist in the market, the work under way by a wide range of companies has network managers eager with anticipation.

CASE QUESTIONS

1. Use the Internet to find out more about IBM's eLiza project. Summarize each of the major initiatives currently under way, and provide several examples of how network technologies are able to adapt to changes or recover from problems without human intervention.

2. Use the Internet to find other companies that are developing self-managing/self-healing applications. Briefly describe several products/initiatives and their potential network management benefits.

3. Why may network managers have mixed (both positive and negative) reactions to self-managing/self-healing applications? How will these applications change the way they perform their jobs?

4. Use the Internet to find information about the capabilities of Novell's ZENworks. Is this another example of the quest to create self-managing applications? Why or why not? Describe ZENwork's policy-based administration feature and relate it to self-managing/self-adapting systems.

5. Explain how self-managing applications and networks are likely to impact a network's total cost of ownership (TOC) and return on investment (ROI) for networking products. Is this likely to promote increased investment in networking technologies? Why or why not?

SOURCES

Garvey, M. "Vendors Deliver on the Promise of Self-Managing Apps." *InformationWeek* (January 14, 2002). Retrieved April 9, 2002, from www.informationweek.com.

Scannell, E. "IBM's Project E-Liza Aims at Self-Managing, Self-Healing Servers." *InfoWorld* (April 27, 2001). Retrieved April 10, 2002, from www.infoworld.com.

Scott, K. "Computer, Heal Thyself." *InformationWeek* (April 1, 2002). Retrieved April 9, 2002, from www.informationweek.com.

Note: For more information on network management systems, see an additional case on the Web site, www.prenhall.com/stamper, "Outsourcing Network Management."

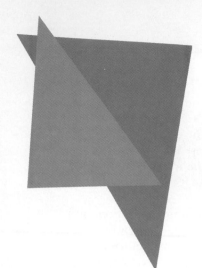

Chapter 16

Managing
Network Security

After studying this chapter, you should be able to:

■ Identify major network security threats.

■ Identify the major elements of network security policies.

■ Compare the three major classes of security: physical, data access, and encryption.

■ Describe how network administrators manage computer viruses and worms.

■ Describe approaches for protecting online transactions.

■ Identify the major trends in network security.

In this chapter, we focus on network security. Business organizations and network planners must consider the security implications of their networks, both the ones that are in place and those to be implemented in the future. The security implications of changes to network infrastructures must also be considered. Security helps protect network resources by limiting access by unauthorized users and preventing authorized users from making mistakes and accessing unauthorized data. The importance of network security has increased as organizations have developed Web sites and the network infrastructure needed to support e-commerce and other e-business processes.

MANAGING NETWORK SECURITY

Network security is concerned with the protection of network resources—such as hardware, software, and data—against alteration, destruction, and unauthorized use. It is also concerned with maintaining network access for users in the face of intentional or unintentional attempts to disrupt normal operations. Security does not prevent unauthorized access to a system, but it makes such access more difficult. Instant

706

access to network resources may facilitate user perceptions of network effectiveness, but security may be compromised if this is provided.

Today, an organization's most important assets, its information assets, are stored on its networks. The "doors" to these assets must be protected even if this causes user delays in accessing them. The delays to access the system should be long enough to make unauthorized access cost prohibitive for potential harm doers or to give the system manager time to detect and apprehend the perpetrator, or both. In the first case, the rewards of unauthorized access would be less than the cost of breaking into the system. In the second, the attempted penetration would be detected and further attempts blocked. From the business manager's perspective, the cost of security should be no more than the potential loss from unauthorized system access.

Note that levels of security may exist. No security means that any user can access and use anything on the system. On a system with no security, users could access human resource management databases to give themselves a raise or a good performance rating. At the other extreme, total security means severe restrictions on the network resources individual users can access and use. Obviously, selecting the proper security level for each user is important. Imposing tighter security makes the network more difficult to use and increases network management costs and the total cost of ownership. Security should protect data and other network resources from intentional or accidental loss or disclosure, without adversely affecting employees' ability to perform their jobs.

Establishing and changing the ability of individual users to access network applications and resources is an important ongoing responsibility of network managers. Most of the tasks associated with this responsibility focus on users working on network-attached workstations. Over time, however, providing access to network resources needed by teleworkers (telecommuters and mobile workers) has also become an important network management task with security implications.

Providing authorized users with remote access to network resources can make the network available to hackers and other individuals who have no business trying to access the organization's computers and data. This can also open the door to viruses and other malicious programs. Danger from without cannot be ignored. Danger from within, however, is often the greater concern. Security experts are quick to point out that most network security breaches are inside jobs. Some security violations are intentional, such as sabotage triggered by employee terminations, disgruntlement, or criminal intent. Other violations are unintentional and result from insufficient user training or inappropriate access controls. Because security breaches may be willful or unintended, network managers must be continually vigilant to ensure that adequate security mechanisms are in place.

Security Threats

At one time, ensuring the security of a network was relatively straightforward. In early host-based, centralized networks (discussed in Chapter 11), security focused on guarding the central host and its resources. Although the security of hosts is still important in many organizations, the emergence of distributed client/server networks and the Internet has compounded the security concerns of network managers. The growing dependence of organizations on their networks and computing systems and increasing numbers of computer-literate network users have also enhanced the importance of network security in today's organizations. Table 16-1 summarizes some of the major security threats in today's network environments.

It is important to recognize that there are both physical and electronic threats to today's networks. *Physical threats* include threats to the network's physical infrastructure

Table 16-1   Examples of Security Threats/Risks in Network Environments

Type/Source of Threat			
Network Users	**Software/Data/Files**	**Physical Threats**	**External**
➤ Fraudulent access or masquerading ➤ Bypass/disable security mechanisms ➤ System software with "backdoors" or known security holes ➤ Applications that are programmed to misbehave ➤ Sabotage ➤ Leakage of confidential or private information ➤ Lack of security accountability ➤ Incompetence, carelessness, and errors ➤ Dishonesty or criminal intent	➤ Viruses, worms, or logic bombs ➤ Unauthorized access ➤ Unauthorized copying or modification ➤ Theft of data or confidential information ➤ Inappropriate/incorrect data access controls ➤ Errors and omissions ➤ Data/files damaged by hardware or software failures ➤ Deliberate corruption or destruction of files by hackers ➤ Inappropriately configured firewalls ➤ Insufficient intruder detection mechanisms	➤ Servers and workstations stored in insecure environments ➤ Natural disasters ➤ Warfare ➤ Terrorism ➤ Inappropriate redundancy and backups ➤ Inadequate safety ➤ Vandalism ➤ Insecure communication links ➤ Destruction/sabotage by disgruntled employees	➤ Hackers ➤ Eavesdropping ➤ Denial-of-service attacks ➤ Fraudulent online transactions ➤ Theft of intellectual property ➤ Espionage ➤ Theft of services ➤ Web site defacing ➤ Use of sniffer program to steal credit card information

caused by natural disasters (such as floods, hurricanes, and earthquakes), warfare, terrorism, riots, vandalism, willful or accidental destruction of equipment, and other events or actions capable of causing major disruptions to normal network operations. *Electronic threats* include those network and business threats posed by hackers (with or without malicious intent), denial-of-service attacks, computer viruses, careless or incompetent users, and disgruntled or frustrated employees.

If unauthorized users (internal or external) can gain access to the network, data and network applications may be vulnerable to potential theft, fraud, or malicious mischief. In some instances, unauthorized access may be part of industrial espionage—the deliberate attempt to rifle through an organization's files and databases to unearth its trade secrets. Today, intruder detection systems are common features in an organization's network security arsenal. At a minimum, these include mechanisms that lock out users after three or more unsuccessful log-on attempts.

Unauthorized access to network resources may result in unauthorized modifications to network applications or data. An employee who gains access to human resource databases that they should not be able to even see may be able to change hourly rates in payroll records, pad hours worked, or create fictitious payroll records. Disgruntled employees may deliberately destroy or corrupt important files/databases. To combat this, numerous organizations now delete an employee's network(s) while they are being informed of their termination. This prevents them from sabotaging the network in response to being terminated.

Serious threats to networks are posed by employees or outsiders with criminal intent to change data or defraud the organization. Some hackers use sniffer programs to intercept e-mail and other network communications in order to identify credit card numbers for future fraudulent use. Other unauthorized users gain access to sensitive data stored on the network for use in extortion attempts.

The introduction of viruses and other malicious software into the network can disrupt network operations and threaten data and application files. As a result, virus detection and eradication have become another major aspect of network security.

Denial-of-service attacks occur when all of a network's resources are taken up by an unauthorized individual, leaving the network unavailable to legitimate users. Typically, this type of attack involves flooding servers with data packets. This increases network traffic, overwhelms servers, and makes it impossible for authorized users to access the information that they need. Some denial-of-service attacks originate from a single source. In *distributed denial-of-service attacks*, the packets that flood the network come from many separate computers that have been previously infected by viruses that enable them to be commandeered by hackers for use in such attacks. Other denial-of-service attacks involve the alteration of routing tables. In such instances, routing tables may be changed to prevent legitimate users from gaining access to the network (by routing network traffic away from the network being attacked). Alternatively, routing tables can be modified to send all packets received by a router to a particular network (thereby flooding the attacked network with packets).

Some denial-of-service attacks involve servers or nodes that are typically considered to be "innocent" by the network that is the target of the attack. They become involved in what are called *syn floods* by forwarding bogus SYN (synchronization request) packets issued by the attacker to the target server. The target server responds with an acknowledgment (ACK)—for which it will receive no response—and holds the session open for a pre-specified time before timing out. When the target server receives a high-volume succession of fake SYN requests, it is prevented from opening legitimate connections.

There is little defense against syn floods because they take advantage of the normal process used to route TCP session requests across the Internet backbone. By not departing from routing protocol, syn floods appear "normal" to the target network.

A nasty new twist on syn flood denial of service attacks is the *distributed reflection denial-of-service (DRDOS)* attack. In this type of attack, innocent servers or nodes receive fake SYN requests from the target server (the SYN requests are *not* transmitted by the target server, but by one or more SYN request generators who are spoofing the target server). This causes the innocent servers to flood the target server with ACK responses to the bogus SYN requests that they received, thereby disrupting normal traffic to or from the target server.

The growth of wireless networks and mobile commerce has confronted network managers with another set of security challenges. These have sometimes been brought into focus by reports issued by network security experts after testing installed and operational wireless networks. It is quite clear that encryption, at a minimum, is needed to protect information transmitted over wireless networks. IEEE 802.11 subcommittees are working on encryption and other security standards for wireless networks in order to address the security deficiencies that have been identified. The current IEEE 802.11 security method is called *WEP (Wired Equivalent Privacy)*. It supports 40-bit or 128-bit

denial-of-service attack An assault on a network that floods it with so many additional requests that regular traffic is significantly slowed or completely interrupted. A distributed denial of service (DDOS) uses multiple computers at different locations to flood the target network with bogus messages. The flood of messages overwhelms network servers or communication equipment and makes it impossible for legitimate users to access network resources.

encryption, but relies on manual encryption key distribution. A new wireless security architecture being developed by IEEE will provide a framework for authentication, encryption, key distribution, and message integrity similar to that employed for wired-based networks. It will also work in conjunction with other major security standards.

Wireless network users have exacerbated wireless security problems by installing "rogue" access points. Industry experts estimate that thousands of unauthorized access points have been added to enterprise networks without the knowledge of corporate IT departments. Users often rationalize that installing additional access points is acceptable, because they are behind enterprise firewalls. Such reasoning, however, is incorrect. Unauthorized access points enable hackers or network snoops using freeware hacking tools to intercept sensitive data via notebook computers equipped with wireless LAN adapter cards from cars parked on the street or in the company parking lot.

Identifying and describing all potential threats to network security is beyond the scope of this book. The remainder of our discussion of network security in this section will focus on some of the major approaches used by organizations to address physical and electronic security threats.

Physical Security Solutions

physical security
Measures, such as door locks, safes, and security guards, taken to control access to restricted areas.

Network security begins with physical security. **Physical security** means using measures such as door locks, safes, and security guards to deny physical access to areas containing key network resources such as servers and mission-critical databases. Because physical security is independent of hardware or software, it can be planned long before the installation of a network and hardware. If access is prevented to important physical components of the network such as network management consoles, communication circuits, servers, and storage area networks, the likelihood of unauthorized access or deliberate equipment destruction or sabotage is significantly decreased. Physical security will not, however, prevent an authorized user from accidentally or intentionally misusing the system. This is significant because studies have shown that the biggest security risk companies face is the accidental or intentional destruction or misuse of data by employees who are able to log on to network resources from workstations outside of the physically secured sites where important network equipment is stored.

Security locks on server room doors and proper staff training regarding computer room access provide a security level adequate for many installations. While the network staff is on duty, they control server room access; during off-shift hours, security guards can take over. Any hard-copy documents that are removed from the computer room can be controlled through corporate policies for dissemination and protection of paperwork.

A common physical security measure is a surveillance system. Security personnel can use this system to screen entry to the premises. The premises may be the property on which the facility is located, individual buildings, rooms within a building, or combinations of these. Additional security can be provided for sensitive areas with closed-circuit television monitors, motion sensors, alarms, and other such intrusion-detection devices. Many installations can justify features such as closed-circuit television and motion sensors because they provide for equipment protection as well as data protection. Use of these devices may result in reduced insurance rates and partially offset their cost.

Other physical security measures that may be used include the following:

➤ Important networking equipment (such as servers, network management consoles, firewalls, routers, switches, and hubs) should be located in secure areas with controlled personnel access.

➤ Access cards, badge readers, *smart cards,* or *biometric verification systems* (such as fingerprint readers, hand/face geometry readers, voice verification systems, retinal scanners, and signature recognition systems) should be used to access physically secured locations.

➤ Nonsecure transmission media should be avoided where possible because the messages transmitted over them are easier to intercept.

➤ Workstation locks or other workstation physical access control equipment such as access cards, smart cards, or biometric verification readers should be used to ensure that network workstations can only be used by authorized individuals.

➤ Switched lines should be avoided, if possible. Recall that switched lines are those that can be accessed through the telephone company's switching equipment. If you have a switched line, anyone with a computer and a modem has the ability to access your system. When they are used, switched lines should be physically disconnected during the hours they are not required, thus limiting the potential for unauthorized use.

➤ Computers used for highly sensitive applications should be disconnected from networks whenever possible, placing an additional barrier to access from other network nodes. For example, some U.S. military computers are connected to a national network, except those that are used for highly classified data.

➤ In most current processing environments, protecting computer rooms from physical access is not sufficient to protect data. Access to data is available via terminals distributed throughout the organization. Many online systems also have the ability to access the system remotely via switched circuits. Because physical security is not enough, other security levels—encryption and access security— must be added.

➤ Fire/smoke detectors, fire extinguishers, sprinkler systems, burglar alarms, surge protectors, and uninterruptible power supplies should be standard aspects of the physical security of network equipment.

➤ Backup equipment and backup procedures are other important aspects of physical security.

➤ A disaster recovery plan should be in place to ensure that the organization can recover from any natural or man-made catastrophe. This plan should include steps to be taken in the event of terrorism, violent takeover, and the willful or accidental destruction of network equipment.

Electronic Security Solutions

In addition to taking steps to ensure the physical security of the network, network managers can take advantage of a variety of electronic mechanisms. Some of the major electronic mechanisms used to protect today's networks are summarized in Table 16-2. Several of these have been identified and discussed in previous chapters.

Encryption

As a general rule, encryption should be used with all media carrying sensitive data. **Encryption** uses mathematical algorithms to disguise information. The encryption algorithm chosen should be capable of deterring unwarranted use of the information by making it too costly or time-consuming to decipher intercepted messages.

Encryption, the process of disguising data, is one aspect of *cryptography*; *decryption*, the process of translating encrypted data back into its original form, is the other major aspect of cryptography. Figure 16-1 illustrates the encryption process. In most instances, encryption algorithms use an encryption key to transform data, called **plaintext** (or *cleartext*), into an encoded form called encrypted text or **ciphertext**; likewise, someone who knows the encryption key can retransform the encrypted data to its original plaintext. Ciphertext looks unintelligible to an intruder or interceptor. Making the transformation from encrypted text to plaintext without the encryption key is a laborious and time-consuming process on the part of intruders.

All encryption algorithms involve substituting one thing for another. For example, in a relatively simple *Ceasar cipher* for English text, each letter in the original

encryption The conversion of data into a secret code in order to protect its integrity during transmission over a network. The original data, or "plaintext," is converted into a coded equivalent called "ciphertext" via an encryption algorithm. The ciphertext is decoded (decrypted) at the receiving end and turned back into plaintext.

plaintext The unencrypted or properly decrypted version of a message or data. Plaintext is comprehensible; it is readable by text editors or word processors. Also known as *cleartext*.

ciphertext Data that has been coded (encrypted, encoded, or enciphered) for security purposes; the encrypted version of a message or data.

Table 16-2   Examples of Electronic Security Mechanisms

➤ Access control lists
➤ Authentication procedures
➤ Automatic logoff
➤ Call-back systems
➤ Call-tracing systems
➤ Digital certificates
➤ Encryption
➤ File and database security controls
➤ Firewalls
➤ Intruder detection systems
➤ Layered IDs
➤ Message logging
➤ Password systems
➤ Pseudo log-on systems
➤ Security audits
➤ SSL, SET, and other security-oriented protocols for online transactions
➤ Terminal profiles
➤ Time and location restrictions
➤ Transaction logs
➤ User profiles
➤ Virus detection and eradication software

plaintext message is substituted with a letter that is k letters later in the alphabet. If $k = 4$, the plaintext letter "a" becomes "e" in ciphertext, the plaintext letter "b" becomes "f" in ciphertext, and so on (see Table 16-3). Please note that there are 25 possible key values for the Ceasar cipher algorithm. Using Ceasar cipher with $k = 4$, the plaintext message "DATA COMM" becomes "HEXE GSQQ."

Figure 16-1   Encryption Process

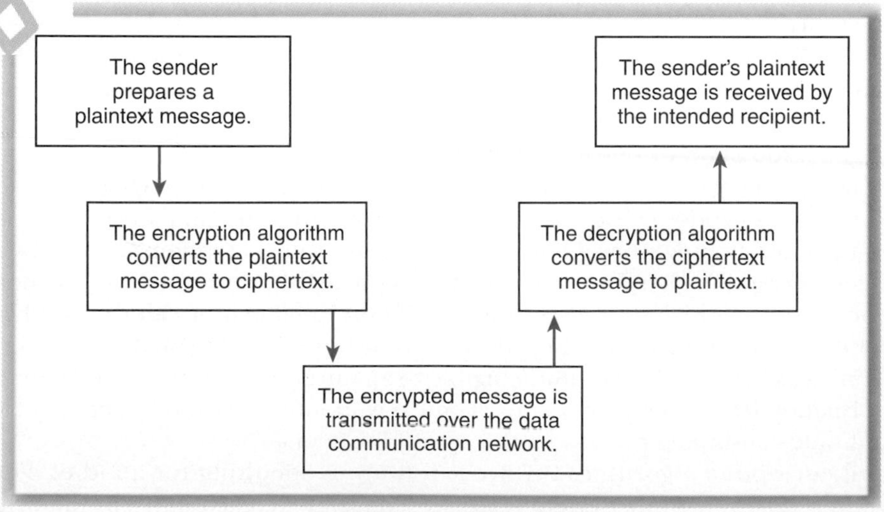

The sender prepares a plaintext message.		The sender's plaintext message is received by the intended recipient.
The encryption algorithm converts the plaintext message to ciphertext.		The decryption algorithm converts the ciphertext message to plaintext.

The encrypted message is transmitted over the data communication network.

Table 16-3   Examples of Ceasar Cipher for English Letters

Plaintext Letter	Ciphertext Letter ($K = 4$)	Ciphertext Letter ($K = 5$)
A	E	F
B	F	G
C	G	H
D	H	I
E	I	J
F	J	K
G	K	L
H	L	M
I	M	N
J	N	O
K	O	P
L	P	Q
M	Q	R
N	R	S
O	S	T
P	T	U
Q	U	V
R	V	W
S	W	X
T	X	Y
U	Y	Z
V	Z	A
W	A	B
X	B	C
Y	C	D
Z	D	E

Like Ceasar ciphers, *monoalphabetic ciphers* substitute one letter in the alphabet with another (see Table 16-4), but without the regular pattern used for Ceasar ciphers. Because any letter can be substituted for any other, there are 26! (on the order of 10^{26}) possible unique pairings of letters with monoalphabetic ciphers. Should monoalphabetic ciphertext be intercepted, the intruder would have a greater challenge breaking the encryption algorithm and decoding the message. Using the monoalphabetic cipher in Table 16-4, the plaintext message "DATA COMM" becomes "QXIX STHH" in ciphertext.

Polyalphabetic encryption algorithms improve upon monoalphabetic algorithms by using multiple monoalphabetic ciphers to encode letters in plaintext messages. The monoalphabetic cipher used for a specific letter depends on its position in the message. Hence, the same plaintext letter appearing in different positions in the message might be encoded differently using different monoalphabetic ciphers. Needless to say, an intruder who intercepts a ciphertext message using polyalphabetic encryption would have an even greater decoding challenge than if a single monoalphabetic cipher were used.

Two major encryption algorithm categories exist: symmetric and asymmetric. With *symmetric algorithms*, the same key (cipher) used to encrypt the message is used to decrypt it. Both the sender and receiver are responsible for keeping the key secret and

Table 16-4   A Monoalphabetic Cipher

Plaintext Letter	Ciphertext Letter
A	X
B	M
C	S
D	Q
E	J
F	O
G	Y
H	A
I	R
J	U
K	D
L	Z
M	H
N	B
O	T
P	E
Q	W
R	V
S	F
T	I
U	K
V	C
W	L
X	G
Y	P
Z	N

Data Encryption Standard (DES)
An NIST–standard symmetric (secret) key cryptography method that uses a 56-bit key. It breaks the text into 64-bit blocks before encrypting them. DES decryption is fast and widely used. Secret keys may be kept secret and reused. Alternatively, DES can be used in combination with public key encryption. In such instances, a secret DES key can be randomly generated for each communication session and transmitted to the recipient using a public key cryptography method such as RSA. Triple DES, an enhanced version of DES, increases security by extending the key to 112 or 168 bits.

because of this, the use of symmetric algorithms is often called *secret key encryption*. When asymmetric algorithms are used, the key used to decrypt the message is different from the one used to encrypt it.

Symmetric Encryption Algorithms

One of the most commonly used yet controversial symmetric encryption algorithms is **Data Encryption Standard (DES)**. The DES standard is maintained by the National Institute of Standards and Technology (NIST). In the past, controversy swirled around this algorithm due to federal government proposals to require its use, with the government holding all DES keys in escrow.

DES encodes plaintext in 64-bit chunks using a 56-bit encryption key. Today, the 56-bit key is considered too insecure for applications such as electronic funds transfers. As a result, many organizations have switched to a stronger variant of DES known as *triple-DES (3DES),* which involves applying the DES algorithm three times instead of once using a different key for each application. Triple DES also provides stronger security by extending the size of the key to 112 or 168 bits.

Other widely used symmetric encryption algorithms include RSA Data Security's *RC4* and NIST's *Advanced Encryption Standard (AES)*. The keys used in RC4 can be up to 256 bits in length, although 40-bit keys are most commonly used. AES has been designed by NIST as a replacement for DES and 3DES. It supports key sizes of 128, 192, and 256 bits. Even with today's most powerful computers using *brute-force* approaches (which attempt to break the code using every possible key), NIST estimates that it would take 150 trillion years to decode an intercepted message encrypted using AES.

The U.S. government views encryption as a potential weapon and regulates its export in the same way that it regulates the export of other weapons that could be turned against it by the receiving party. Currently, exporting encryption algorithms with keys longer than 56 bits is prohibited, but exceptions have been made for some algorithms and for exports to Canada and the European Union. American banks and large U.S. companies with international operations are also allowed to use more powerful encryption approaches for communications with their international offices.

Asymmetric Encryption: Public Key Encryption

Today, asymmetric encryption algorithms are better known as **public key encryption**. Public key encryption uses large prime numbers and two keys; one key is made public, and the other is kept secret by the message recipient. The public key encrypts the data; the private key decrypts the ciphertext. This process is illustrated in Figure 16-2. The keys used in public key encryption are typically 512 or 1,024 bits long.

Public key encryption uses *one-way mathematical functions* to encrypt plaintext messages. Although a public key (one that is known to the sender, receiver, and any potential intruder) is used to encrypt the message, the use of one-way functions ensures that it can only be decrypted with the corresponding private key. Once the message is encrypted with the public key, even the sender is unable to decrypt it without the private key! Only the private key is capable of transforming the ciphertext back to its original form.

public key encryption A type of asymmetric cryptography that uses published public keys to encrypt messages and unpublished private keys to decrypt the messages (or vice versa).

Figure 16-2   Public Key Encryption

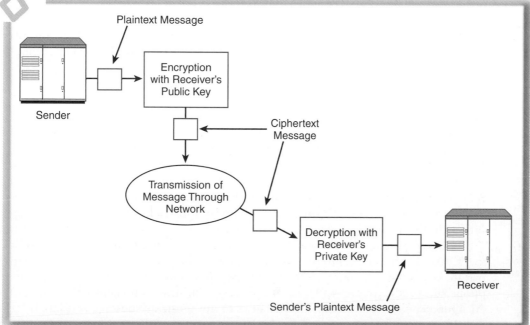

Key administration is an important function in an effective public key encryption program. Administration includes

➤ Key creation
➤ Key distribution
➤ Key storage/safeguarding/restoration
➤ Setting standards for frequent key changes

Standards organizations have recognized the critical nature of key management and have adopted several standards to guide key administrators. Among these are ANSI X9.17, which addresses key management for financial institutions, and U.S. Federal Standard 1027, for security requirements for equipment using the DES standard. An organization that is serious about security and encryption should have one or more people designated as security administrators whose function is to implement security and detect attempts to breach security.

As illustrated in Figure 16-2, asymmetric encryption begins with the sender obtaining the receiver's public key. Public keys are stored in publicly available directories. When a sender wants to transmit an encrypted message to a receiver, the sender looks up the receiver's public key in the directory. The sender then uses the receiver's public key to encrypt the message. The encrypted message is transmitted to the receiver and the receiver uses its private key to decrypt the message.

Today, the Internet is where public key directories are located. **Certification authorities**, such as VeriSign, are part of the Internet's **public key infrastructure (PKI)**. Certification authorities (CAs) are third-party organizations that are trusted to vouch for the authenticity of the individuals that register with them. Certification authorities issue **digital certificates** to registered individuals and organizations that include an individual/organization's public key along with other authentication information. Digital certificates are also called *digital IDs*. When a digital ID is issued to an individual or organization, the certificate is published on the CA's Web site along with the public key associated with the certificate; the corresponding private key is given only to the registered individual or organization. Digital certificates are only issued for pre-specified time periods and it is the responsibility of the registered individuals or organizations to renew them before they expire.

Digital IDs can be attached to encrypted e-mail messages to verify the identity of senders. Digital IDs can also be used to verify a user's (or server's) identity in e-commerce transactions.

RSA is the most popular public key encryption approach. The RSA algorithm is named after its founders, Ron Rivest, Adi Shamir, and Leonard Adelman. *PGP (Pretty Good Privacy)* is another commonly used encryption approach. PGP is a freeware public key encryption approach that is frequently used to encrypt e-mail messages. Public keys are posted on Web pages or publicly accessible PGP servers. Once an intended recipient's public key is obtained, a sender can encrypt messages to the receiver with the knowledge that only the receiver's private key can be used to decrypt the message. Both the SSL (secure sockets layer) and SET (secure electronic transaction) protocols used in e-commerce use asymmetric encryption approaches based on digital certificates. These are discussed later in the chapter.

Digital signatures involve the use of digital IDs to authenticate the senders of messages. In this case, the sender "signs" the message by encrypting the message using a private key. Message recipients use the inverse of the encryption function, the sender's public key, to decrypt the message. This process is illustrated in Figure 16-3. When digital signatures are used, recipients are able to authenticate message senders because they know that only the sender has the key needed to perform the encryption. Time

certification authority (CA) Third-party organizations that are trusted to vouch for the authenticity of the individuals who register with them. Certificate authorities (sometimes called *certification authorities*) issue digital certificates (digital IDs) to registered individuals (or organizations) that include an individual's public key along with other authentication information. A CA also makes the public key associated with a digital certificate available to its intended audience. VeriSign, Inc. is a well-known CA.

public key infrastructure (PKI) A framework for providing secure information exchanges that relies on asymmetric public/private key cryptography for encrypting IDs and data/messages. PKI also involves certification authorities (CAs) that issue digital certificates (digital IDs) that authenticate the identity of people and organizations over public networks such as the Internet.

digital certificate The digital equivalent of an ID card used in public key encryption systems; also called *digital IDs*. Digital certificates are issued by trusted third-party certification authorities (CAs) after verifying that a public key belongs to a certain user (company or individual).

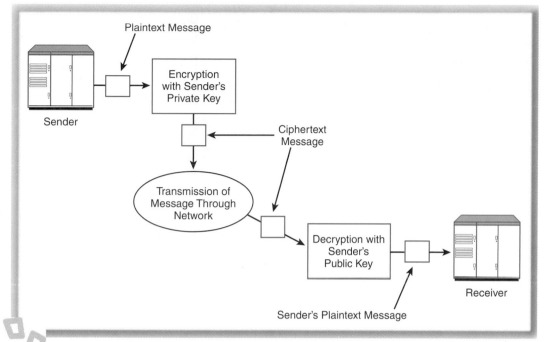

Figure 16-3   Securing Messages with Digital Signatures

and date of message creation can also be included in the digital signature to ensure its originality and that it has not been copied and resent.

Public key infrastructures are used to support digital signatures. A message is signed by an individual when he encrypts the message using his private key and attaches his digital ID. To verify the signature, the recipient looks up the sender's public key in a public key directory. The sender's public key is then used to decrypt the message. The ability of the recipient to use the public key to decrypt the message authenticates the sender as the source of the message. The sender's identity is verified because only the sender knows the private key to encrypt messages that can be decrypted with the public key.

It is important to note that encryption introduces overhead to a network and can slow communication. This is particularly true if the encryption is done with software. Because of this, many organizations that rely on encryption to provide secure message transmission across data communication links choose to use integrated circuits designed for encrypting and decrypting data. The chips may be integrated onto processor or controller boards or used in stand-alone external boxes. The encryption devices can be placed between individual nodes or at the origin and destination of the message. Figure 16-4 illustrates several configuration options. If the encryption devices are placed at each node, the message must be decrypted at each intermediate node, which increases the likelihood of interception. In end-to-end encryption, only the text body can be encrypted, and end-to-end addressing must remain clear so intermediate nodes can perform the routing correctly.

User Identification and Authentication

Encryption is only one electronic security mechanism used in today's data communication networks. Examples of other electronic security measures/policies that might be implemented are given in Table 16-5.

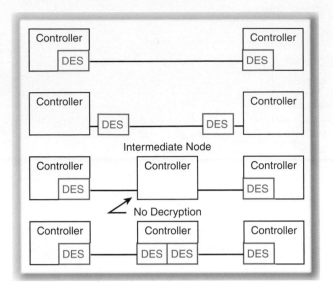

Intermediate Node

No Decryption

Figure 16-4   Encryption Configurations

identification
Information assigned to a specific user of a system for security and control purposes. Identification is used to verify individuals attempting to access network resources as valid users. User identification ranges from simple user names and passwords to possessed objects and biometric security measures such as voice print and fingerprint identification.

authentication
A process in which a system user is required to provide or verify his or her user identification to gain system access. In public key cryptography, digital signatures may be used to authenticate the integrity of transmitted messages.

password   A secret word or code used to serve as a security measure against unauthorized access to networks, data, or applications. A password is typically associated with a user ID to allow access to certain resources. The system, however, can only verify the legitimacy of the password (or password–user ID combination), not the legitimacy of the user.

In most network systems, a two-level system is used to control user access to network resources. The first level of security is user **identification** and authentication. User identification runs the gamut from simply providing a user's name or user ID to biometric measures such as retina scans, voice prints, palm prints, or fingerprint identification. In business applications, identification is generally supplied by user name or electronic badge. After identification comes **authentication**, which requires the user to provide additional information unique to that particular user, such as a password, personal identification number (PIN), or biometric mechanism such as a fingerprint.

Passwords   A **password** is the most common form of authentication. It is maintained in a file of information about network users, which typically includes user ID, password, defaulted security attributes for any files created, and possibly an access profile. Because this file contains the information needed to access any portion of the network, it should be carefully secured and encrypted. Policies should be in place to require frequent password changes, either centrally by the network administrators or in a decentralized manner by the users. Through central management, passwords are changed regularly and assigned randomly. The major flaw of centralized management is the timing of distribution to users: Dissemination of new passwords must be timely and well coordinated. The logistics for centralized password management and distribution in a large, distributed network are considerable. The distribution process also is likely to be the weakest element in the security system. Because passwords are usually distributed in written form via mail or courier, ample opportunity exists for unauthorized users to obtain them.

Personal identification numbers (PINs) function in a manner similar to passwords. A PIN is also an example of a *possessed object* because it is supposed to be used only by an authorized user to gain access to network resources. PINs are widely used to authenticate users of automated terminal/teller machine (ATM) cards. The ATM card distributor usually mails the card to the user and mails the PIN in a separate envelope. This reduces the risk of an unauthorized person obtaining both the card and the password, but it is not a very secure method. Consequently, some banks now allow users to select or change their own PINs, which avoids the need to send the password through the mail.

Decentralized password changes rely on users to change their passwords regularly, either by themselves or through their managers. Individual users can change

Table 16-5   Samples of Network Security Measures

All users must have a password.	Unsuccessful attempts to log on to the system will
Passwords must be at least six characters long.	be recorded. Data recorded will include the
Passwords must be changed at least monthly.	time, terminal from which the attempt is made,
Passwords will be changed immediately if	and the user ID for which the logon is attempted.
there is suspicion that a password has been	Two people will be responsible for encryption key
compromised.	administration.
Passwords will not contain user's initials, month	No single individual can change the encryption key.
abbreviations, or other obvious character strings.	Switched (dial-up) lines will be disconnected when
Passwords must not be written down.	not in use.
Passwords must be created randomly so they	Manual answer and user verification must be used
do not contain sequence numbers or other	for all switched connections, or call-back units
instances of succession.	will be used.
All unsuccessful log-on attempts will be investigated.	Encryption keys will be changed regularly.
All sensitive data will be encrypted.	

their passwords without leaving any written record of the password, and they can make changes as often as they like. The password file can be centrally examined periodically, and if users have not changed their passwords within a specified time, they can be so notified or their access privileges can be revoked until password changes are made. Some network security systems contain provisions for password aging. In this case, the security administrator can specify that users must change passwords at least monthly, and users who have not changed their passwords in the allotted time are warned during their logon. The security administrator may allow the user several such "grace" logons. If the user still fails to make a password change under the established rules, their account is deactivated. The user then needs to contact the security administrator to have the account reactivated.

The biggest problem with user-assigned passwords is that they are typically non-random because users like to select a password that is easy to remember, such as their initials, birth date, or names of family members. Unfortunately, this type of password is also more easily guessed by a potential intruder. Some dos and don'ts regarding password selection are included in Table 16-5.

Biometric Authentication Mechanisms   Biometric authentication devices such as fingerprint readers, hand/face geometry readers, voice verification systems, retinal scanners, and signature recognition systems are being more widely used to authenticate users and control access to network resources. Like PINs, these access controls are examples of possessed objects. These operate by obtaining a scan when the individual requests access to network resources and comparing the scan to a stored image in the database of authorized users. Biometric authentication mechanisms typically provide a much stronger form of access control than relying solely on a combination of user IDs and passwords or PINs. The use of a user ID, password (or PIN), and biometric scan in combination is expected to become a predominant form of user identification and authentication.

Identification and Authentication for Ultrasensitive Applications   Identification and authentication are usually insufficient for sensitive applications because we must also identify what functions a given user may or may not perform. The two most common ways of controlling user access are layers of identification and authentication, or user or application profiles.

Layered IDs   Layers of identification and authentication help to screen access to sensitive transactions. Once users have logged onto the network via the initial identification and authentication procedures, they can be asked to provide additional identification and authentication information every time they attempt to access a new application or a sensitive transaction within an application. In a banking application, an employee might be required to provide another password or authorization code to transfer funds from one account to another. This level of access may allow the employee to check (read) account balances and make changes to data other than account balances. If the employee needs to run a transaction that will change an account balance, she may be required to first provide another password. If the transaction exceeds a certain limit, an additional password may be required.

The advantage of layered IDs is that each application or transaction can have its own level of security, so applications that are not sensitive can be made available to everyone, and those that are very sensitive can be protected with additional levels of security. The disadvantage of layered IDs is that the user must remember several different authentication codes, thus increasing the probability of the codes being written down or stored in an insecure file on the user's workstation and thereby made accessible to others.

user profile
Information that defines the applications and transactions a user is authorized to execute; user profiles can be used as network access controls.

User Profiles   A **user profile** contains all the information needed to define the applications and transactions a user is authorized to access and execute. A user profile, for example, for an employee in the organization's human resource management department might specify that the employee is authorized to add employees, delete employee records, and modify all employee data fields in the employee database except salary. The profiles maintained in a user file can be very detailed, covering each application or transaction, or fairly simple, including only a brief profile. With a brief profile, a user might be assigned an access level to the system for each of four functions: read, write, execute, and purge. Specifically, suppose a user has been given level 8 read access, level 6 write access, level 8 execute access, and level 2 purge access. Each file or transaction is also given an access profile. A user is granted access to the file or transaction only if their access number is equal to or greater than that of the file or transaction. Thus, if the payroll file has access attributes of 8, 8, 10, and 10 for read, write, execute, and purge, respectively, the user just described will be able only to read the information in the file. This is because the user's read access meets or exceeds the file's security profile. A write access of 6 is insufficient to allow the user to write to the file.

The advantage of a brief user profile is its simplicity. Its disadvantage is the difficulty in stratifying all users across all applications and files in this manner. Although this type of profile could be provided for all files or applications, it has the potential to quickly become a complex profile that is difficult to maintain and administer.

In many networks, user profiles are used to specify *log-on restrictions*. These identify specific days and times that the user is allowed to log on and use the network. Thus, most workers can be given a profile restricting their access to the system to normal working days and hours. Attempts to log on or use the network during times outside this profile will be unsuccessful.

Menu Selection and User Profiles   User profiles can be very effective when used in combination with a menu selection system that displays allowable options on the terminal so the user can select the transactions or applications to perform. If a user profile is available, the menu can be tailored to the individual user, and the only transactions the user will see are those to which they have access. In the previous example, the user who could only read the payroll file would see only that option displayed on the menu, whereas the payroll manager would have options to read, add, delete, or modify a much wider range of data elements. The security of the network system is enhanced by denying users knowledge of transactions and files that they are not permitted to access.

Time and Location Restrictions   Time and location restrictions for sensitive network applications can play an important part in network security. In a stock trading application, for instance, buying and selling stock on the exchange is limited to a specific time period, and any attempt to trade stock outside of that time period is rejected. In a personnel application, it would be prudent to restrict transactions that affect employee salary or status to normal working hours. This kind of security can be further enhanced by making sensitive portions of the application system unavailable during nonworking hours.

Transactions can also be restricted by location. A money transfer transaction would be denied to a bank teller's workstation if bank policies dictate that such transactions can only be initiated from bank officer workstations. Also, money transfer transactions can be denied if the workstation is attached to a switched or dial-up communication line rather than to dedicated lines over which such transfers are normally conducted. In a manufacturing plant, a shop floor terminal might be unable to start an accounts receivable or payable transaction because organizational policies mandate that such transactions can only take place at terminals in the accounting department. Location restrictions can be implemented either by attaching applications to specific workstations or by workstation identification coupled with its location and a transaction profile. A terminal profile typically lists the location of the terminal and the transactions valid from that terminal. Such time and location restrictions with user controls (such as the requirement that only certain users are allowed to execute specific transactions from specific workstations during specific time periods) provide a hierarchy of security precautions.

Automatic Logoff   People are often the weakest link in security. All too often, users write their passwords on or near the workstation or they leave the area with their workstation still logged on, allowing anyone to gain access to the network resources and applications that the user has rights to use. This not only jeopardizes the security of the system but also can place the employee's job in jeopardy. Network managers can configure the system to be more secure by logging off any user who has not entered a transaction within a certain amount of time, such as 5 minutes. Users who leave their workstations for more than 5 minutes must go through the identification and authentication procedures again upon returning. Alternatively, the user can be required to go through an authentication procedure for every transaction. Unfortunately, this usually adversely affects user productivity and job performance. The first alternative is simple to implement on most systems, and in most cases user efficiency is not impeded. Screen savers coupled with password controls that blank the screen when the workstation has been idle for a specific time period, say 2 minutes, can also be used to help secure user workstations.

Switched Ports with Dial-In Access

Some of the most vulnerable security points in today's network environments are switched ports that enable dial-in access. Although remote access for telecommuters and mobile workers has numerous business merits, the dangers of this should be evident: It provides an avenue for unauthorized and potentially malicious individuals that have a computer and a modem to gain access to the network. Because of this, extra security precautions should be taken. For example, dial-in access should be operational only during the periods when transactions are allowed. In an order entry application, this would probably be between 8:00 A.M. and 8:00 P.M.; in a university environment, however, this might be 24 hours a day. During the period when transactions are disallowed, the line should be disabled. Callback units, as described in Chapter 6, can be used to ensure that only calls from authorized locations are received.

When switched lines are used, user identification and authentication procedures and restricting transactions are very important to maintain network security. The telephone numbers of the switched lines should be safeguarded as carefully as possible. A manual answer arrangement should be used in high-security installations, thus allowing person-to-person authentication as well as the usual application-based authorization. Another method used to stall unauthorized users of switched lines is to hide the carrier tone until an authentication procedure has been provided, a solution that is most practical when telephones are answered manually. This method is meant to foil hackers who try to gain access to systems by randomly dialing business telephone numbers until a computer installation is reached.

RADIUS (remote authentication dial-in user service) is supported in many remote access technology products. RADIUS enables network managers to manage remote access technology users, log-on restrictions, and access methods. It also enables network managers to track remote access traffic. RADIUS authentication servers support two authentication protocols: *PAP (password authentication protocol)* and *CHAP (challenge handshake authentication protocol).*

Recognizing Unauthorized Access Attempts

All the previously discussed security techniques are simply delaying tactics; their implementation alone may not provide adequate security. A tight security system should recognize that an unauthorized access attempt may be occurring and should provide methods to suppress such attempts. Even low-security systems should discourage brute-force attempts to identify network passwords. A very simple way to counter attempts to identify the password needed to log on from a particular terminal is to temporarily "retire" the affected terminal, meaning that input is not accepted at that terminal for a specified period. Such an algorithm might work as follows: After three unsuccessful access attempts, no input from that terminal would be accepted for 5 minutes. If a 6-character password consisting of only letters and numbers is required to log onto the terminal, there would be more than 2 billion possible passwords. If 1 billion of these were tried, with a 5-minute delay between each three unsuccessful attempts, more than 9,500 years would be needed to gain access. Alternatively, the security system might deactivate the account, disallowing its use to both authorized and unauthorized users. Both workstation timeout and account deactivation are included in network intruder detection systems.

Pseudo Logons   A second algorithm used in some systems simulates a successful logon. After a certain number of unsuccessful log-on attempts, the user receives a successful log-on message. Rather than actually being granted access to the system, however, the user is provided with a fake session. Although this session is being conducted, security personnel can determine the terminal from which access is being made and the types of transactions the user is attempting to run. This type of simulated session can also help keep the intruder busy while security personnel are dispatched to the location for investigation. Again, switched connections make such an activity more difficult, especially with respect to apprehension.

Transaction Logs   Transaction and security logs are important adjuncts to network security. Every log-on attempt should be logged, including date and time, user identification, unsuccessful authentication attempts (with passwords used), terminal identification and location, and all transactions initiated from the terminal by that particular user. If several unsuccessful log-on attempts are made, the information could also be written on the console of the operator or security personnel so other actions, such as investigation, can be initiated. Transaction logs are also beneficial to electronic data processing (EDP) auditors and diagnostic personnel.

Other Intrusion Detection System Features   Three general types of intruder detection systems exist: network-based, host-based, and application-based systems. Network-based systems monitor packets on key network circuits so that network managers can be alerted to the presence of intruders. Host-based systems monitor server activities as well as activity on the server's incoming circuits. Application-based systems monitor the activities of specific applications on network servers, especially database and online transaction processing applications. Two fundamental intrusion detection techniques are employed on each of these three intrusion detection system categories: misuse detection and anomaly detection. Misuse detection involves the comparison of monitored activities with those associated with intrusion patterns; when monitored activities match known intrusion patterns, network managers are alerted to the presence of intruders. Anomaly detection compares monitored activities with normal patterns; when significant departures from normal are detected, the intrusion detection system alerts network managers.

    Honeypots are being used more widely in intrusion detection systems to trick intruders. A honeypot is a server that is configured in a manner that makes intruders think that they have gained access to real network resources. Because they look like the real thing, intruders are led to believe that they have gained access to the production machine rather than a decoy. By allowing intruders to nose around in the honeypot, network managers can learn about the intruder's techniques. This also provides insights into the potential vulnerabilities of production servers.

Virus Detection and Eradication

The need for virus detection and eradication mechanisms to be included in an organization's network security arsenal surfaced in the late 1980s with the introduction of computer viruses, worms, and Trojan horses. Most security countermeasures until that time were oriented toward people actively attempting to breach security for personal gain, revenge, or gratification. During this type of security violation, the perpetrator of the breach or the perpetrator's system was actively connected to the network. In contrast, computer viruses, worms, and Trojan horses operate independently of the person who implanted them. A virus infection can be implanted intentionally or accidentally.

    Numerous categories of computer viruses exist, and although their implementation differs, there is usually a common objective: to bring down a system or disrupt users. A virus is typically a fragment of code that attaches itself to a legitimate program or file. The virus has the ability to duplicate and attach itself to other programs and files. Once attached, the virus may attack a variety of resources. Some destroy or alter disk files, some simply display annoying messages, and others cause system failures.

    Detection and correction of viruses can be time-consuming and expensive. Industry experts estimate that it cost more than $2 billion to address the problems caused by major virus problems in 2001 (which included the Code Red and Nimba viruses) and that the cost of lost productivity caused by viruses in 2001 was more than $4 billion.

Antiviral software is used to eliminate and detect viruses. Viruses can be introduced intentionally or accidentally. An unintentional infection can occur when an employee uses an infected disk or file, unaware that the disk/file carries a virus. Even when introduced unintentionally, within a short time the entire network might be infected. Detection may be made more difficult because some viruses remain dormant for a period of time, propagating themselves before becoming active. New virus strains called **stealth viruses** or **polymorphic viruses** also change their appearance by encrypting themselves or changing their signatures, which makes them quite difficult to identify.

Antidote programs exist for most known viruses, and new ones are developed by Norton, McAffee, and other antiviral software vendors when new viruses are released. Using these antiviral programs can help keep a system healthy, but only if network managers ensure that virus shields are regularly updated, daily if necessary. Network managers should also vigilantly monitor alerts issued by *CERT (Computer Emergency Response Team)* at Carnegie Mellon University. One of CERT's major functions is to alert network managers about newly released viruses that could pose a threat to network security. These alerts enable network managers to take precautionary measures before the new virus infects their networks.

Additional measures also should be taken to prevent virus infections, including procedures to prevent employees from using personal disks in workstations, checking new software on a virus-free system separate from a production system before installing the software for general use, and closely monitoring the source of all new files. Using diskless workstations is another excellent way to limit exposure. Many antiviral software programs can be configured to automatically check disks and e-mail attachments for virus infections before opening files.

A worm is a self-replicating, self-propagating program. Original worm programs were benign. They were designed to replicate themselves on idle network nodes and carry out useful work. However, the most famous worm program was a rogue known as the "Internet Worm." The Internet Worm surfaced in 1988 on the Internet and replicated itself primarily on computers using the UNIX operating system. Once established on such a computer, the worm began replicating itself on other network nodes. Eventually, some of the network nodes became saturated with copies of the worm program, in some instances causing the computers to fail. Although the worm was not released intentionally, the consequences were far-reaching. The Internet Worm illustrated the disruption that could be caused by such programs. CERT was established by the U.S. Department of Defense after the Internet Worm shut down approximately 10 percent of the computers on the Internet.

A Trojan horse program contains code intended to disrupt a system. Trojan horse programs are code segments hidden inside a useful program. Some Trojan horse programs have been created by disgruntled programmers. In one such instance, a programmer inserted code that would periodically activate and erase accounting and personnel records. A Trojan horse program differs from viruses and worms in that it does not attempt to replicate itself. Although the implementation of viruses, worms, and Trojan horses differs, their consequences are often the same: system disruption. A comprehensive security system must guard against each.

Vulnerability Assessment

Comprehensive security measures include the identification of network threats and potential solutions (both physical and electronic). They also include vulnerability assessment. *Network vulnerability* may be described as the manner or path by which a threat is able to gain access to network assets. These are often identified by developing a list of network assets (e.g., hardware, software, and data), identifying each listed asset's poten-

stealth virus A computer virus that is able to keep itself from being detected. A polymorphic virus is an example of a stealth virus.

polymorphic virus A computer virus that has the ability to change its signature or identity each time that it infects a new file, thus making the virus more difficult to detect and eradicate.

tial threats, and then developing the path/manner by which each threat could attack the asset. Vulnerabilities are the weak links in a network security architecture; once identified, steps should be taken to prevent/block threats from attacking network assets.

Risk Assessment

In the context of network security, *risk* is the probability of a particular threat successfully attacking a particular asset via a particular vulnerability. Often, risk assessment is a set of educated guesses. Although risk analysis is a specialized field of study, it is not an exact science. Prioritizing and quantifying network risks is often a combination of objective risk analysis data and subjective judgment. The purpose of risk assessment is to identify the relative importance of threats and vulnerabilities that will enable the organization to systematically prioritize the steps that it will take to prevent threats from attacking assets.

Security Policy

The identification of network threats, vulnerabilities, risks, and solutions is an important step in the development of a comprehensive security architecture for an organization. This identification is also an important input toward the development of a network security policy for an organization. The bottom line is that network security must be planned, carefully implemented, and monitored once it is put in place.

An important element of any network security system is a network security policy. The security policy is a document that sets forth corporate goals and rules. It indicates how those goals and rules are translated into access controls for network applications and data. Some of the topics typically addressed in a network security policy are provided in Table 16-6.

The content of the network policy document varies from company to company because each organization has different security requirements. It is, however, likely to address several key issues, including the following:

➤ *Authentication.* Only authenticated users should be able to access the organization's network resources.

➤ *Access control.* Authenticated users should only be able to access the network resources that they need to perform their jobs; they should not be able to access non–job-related resources.

➤ *Transmission privacy.* Network-based communications should be private and not subject to eavesdropping.

Table 16-6   Security Policy Topics

Password administration	Access to outside networks/nodes
Auditing policy	Control on external access (e.g., switched
Consequences of employees intentionally	and Internet connections)
trying to subvert security	Disaster recovery
Encryption implementation	Designation of personnel for monitoring and
Virus detection procedures	implementing security
Data backup/restore policy	Managing security threats
Introduction of software/data by employees	Security training
(i.e., using media from outside the	Documentation
organization)	Security review procedures

➤ *Confidentiality.* Only authorized users should be able to read data stored on the network; sensitive information/data stored on the network should remain private.

➤ *Data integrity.* Data should be accurate and up to date; data updates (creation, deletion, modification) should only be performed by network users with appropriate security clearance.

➤ *Nonrepudiation.* Network users who attempt to access unauthorized network resources, applications, or data should not be able to deny that they tried to do so.

➤ *Firewalls.* Corporate networks should be protected from intruders who try to gain access to network resources via the Internet.

ISO 7498/2 A network security framework that maps 14 distinct security services to the seven layers of the OSI reference model; the framework is also called the OSI Security Architecture.

Some organizations have addressed these issues by leveraging network security architecture frameworks such as **ISO 7498/2** to develop network security policies and plans. This framework, which is also called the *OSI Security Architecture*, maps 14 distinct security services to the seven layers of the OSI reference model. These are summarized in Table 16-7.

ENSURING THE INTEGRITY OF ONLINE TRANSACTIONS

Ensuring the security and integrity of online transactions has become increasingly important over the last few years with the accelerating growth of e-commerce. Security mechanisms used for Internet-based transactions are extensions of the mechanisms that have been used to ensure the integrity of older online transaction processing systems such as airline reservation systems, electronic funds transfer (EFT) systems, and other financial transaction processing systems. As a general rule, all online transaction processing systems (including e-commerce applications) must include integrity mechanisms as well as mechanisms for recovering from system failures that occur while a transaction is being processed.

Error Detection and Recovery

As noted in Chapter 6, error-detection and recovery mechanisms, specifically redundancy checks and message sequence numbers at the data link and transport layers, are used to ensure the integrity of data against accidental damage during transmission. Recall that these checks provide detection of lost or garbled messages, and the recovery technique is usually to retransmit the message or messages that are in error.

Another level of recovery in data communication systems is the recovery of the system from failure after a message has arrived and before it is processed. This type of recovery ideally is coordinated with the database recovery system. Although individual implementations differ in their approaches, the basic elements of such a recovery system are outlined in this section.

When a message arrives at a network node, a certain amount of processing must be accomplished to satisfy the message requirements. In some instances, the message is forwarded to the next node and stored. After the message has been stored, it can be delivered to a local application or transmitted to the next node on the path to its destination. During this processing cycle, the application(s) processing the message, or the system itself, may fail. This section discusses one option for recovery of a lost message or a failed system.

Transaction Recovery

When a node receives a message and acknowledges receipt to the sender, responsibility for the message is transferred from the sender to the receiver. This means that the receiving node must be able to re-create the message and ensure its correct processing

Table 16-7   Services Included in the ISO 7498/2 OSI Security Architecture

Security Service	OSI Reference Model Layer(s)	Description
Selective field connection integrity	Application	This service provides for the integrity of selected fields transferred over a connection and determines whether field contents have been modified during transfer.
Selective field connectionless integrity	Application	This is the same as above when transmission occurs over a connectionless network.
Nonrepudiation, origin	Application	The data recipient is provided with proof of the data's origin. This prevents the sender from denying transmission of data to the recipient.
Nonrepudiation, recipient	Application	The sender is provided proof that data was received by the recipient. This prevents the recipient from denying receipt of transmitted data.
Connection integrity with recovery	Application, transport	This provides for the integrity of the data transmitted over a specific connection at a given time. Should connection fail//malfunction during transmission, data modification is detected during the recovery attempt.
Connection integrity without recovery	Application, transport, network	This is the same as connection integrity with recovery except that no data recovery is attempted.
Connectionless integrity	Application, transport, network	This service provides data integrity assurances for data as it is passed to higher layers and determines if modifications are made to data as it is passed to higher layers.
Peer entity authentication	Application, transport, network	This service verifies the identity of the peer entity in a data transmission session and provides verification assurance as data is passed to higher levels.
Data origin authentication	Application, transport, network	This service verifies the identity of the data source (sender) and provides verification assurance as data is passed to higher levels.
Access control service	Application, transport, network	This service protects against unauthorized network access, primarily through user authentication.
Connection confidentiality	Application, transport, network, data link	This service provides for the confidentiality of data transmitted between peer entities at a given layer; this is done primarily via encryption.
Connectionless confidentiality	Application, transport, network, data link	This is the same as connection confidentiality for connectionless communication environments.
Selective field confidentiality	Application, transport, network, data link	This service provides for the confidentiality of specific application level data fields (such as personal identification number) transmitted over a specific connection at a given time.
Traffic flow confidentiality	Application, network, physical	This service protects against the unauthorized traffic access/analysis such as wiretapping and eavesdropping and attempts to capture source and destinaton addresses.

in the event of any possible failure. Designers of simple terminal systems sometimes maintain that it is the responsibility of the terminal operator to resubmit any possibly lost messages in the event of a failure. This approach can be justified only on the grounds that it is easier than implementing more sophisticated software that would resolve most of the problems automatically. Although more sophisticated recovery systems slow the system and increase processor use, over the long haul they usually cost less than relying on terminal operators to recover transactions. More sophisticated transaction recovery systems include message logging, mechanisms for ensuring database/system consistency, message processing, and database recovery mechanisms.

Message Logging

message logging
Also called safe storing, this recovery system writes the message to a file before acknowledgment so the message may be reviewed or recovered later if necessary.

Message logging, also called *safe storing*, means writing the message to a file so it can be reviewed or recovered. To ensure that a message can be re-created, the system should log the message before acknowledging it. The object of the recovery process is to close all windows of vulnerability and create a system in which no messages are lost and all are processed only once. If message receipt is acknowledged and then the message is logged to an audit file, there is a small window of time, perhaps 50 milliseconds, during which a system failure could prevent the message from being re-created. If failure occurs after acknowledgment has been returned but before the write to the log file has been completed, the message is lost. Furthermore, it is not enough to initiate the write to the log file and acknowledge the message before the log write is successfully completed. In this case, queues on the log device might delay the write, or a file error could occur that prevents the write from being completed. Thus, the acknowledgment has already been sent, and a failure could again cause the message to be lost. Because it is typically the responsibility of the receiver to re-create a message once it has been acknowledged, it is important to design the system so reception acknowledgment is sent only after the message is logged.

Database–System Consistency

In addition to message logging, a transaction must be started for update transactions. A transaction is a logical collection of processing activities that either will be completely accomplished or will leave the database in the same state as it was before the start of the transaction. Although this may sound complicated, it is actually quite simple, as shown by the following example.

Consider a banking application in which a customer wants to transfer money from a checking account to a savings account. We will call the record in the checking account *record C* and the record in the savings account *record S*. At the beginning of this transaction, record C has a balance of $1,000 and record S has a balance of $3,000.

A transaction is started indicating that $500 is to be deducted from the checking account (record C) and deposited into the savings account (record S). After attempting to process the transaction, the database can be in only two possible states: Records C and S contain either $500 and $3,500 or $1,000 and $3,000. The combination of $500 and $3,000 and the combination of $1,000 and $3,500 are inconsistent states. If a failure occurs when record C has attained the value $500 and record S still has the value $3,000, recovery must be invoked. The recovery process must either roll the value of record C back to $1,000 or roll the value of record S forward to $3,500. This transaction is used in the following discussion. Figure 16-5 illustrates the various states of the database for this transaction.

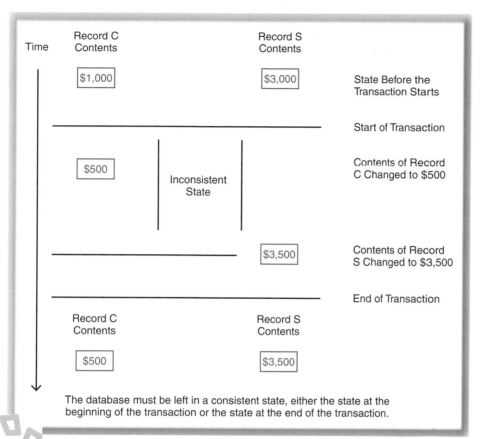

The database must be left in a consistent state, either the state at the beginning of the transaction or the state at the end of the transaction.

Figure 16-5 Database States During Transaction

Message Processing

Once the message has been written to the log file, the acknowledgment returned to the sender, the data edited, and a transaction started, the message can be processed. The transaction is forwarded to a transaction application process. The application process is typically located on a transaction processing server. The unique transaction ID created when the transaction began is passed along with the message.

Database Update   The application accesses the two records to be updated in the database and issues a database write request for both records. Before the updates are posted to the database, the database management system writes the before- and after-images to an audit file. The **before-images** are balances of $1,000 and $3,000 for records C and S, respectively. The **after-images** for those records are $500 and $3,500. After the audit writes have been completed, the writes to the database can be initiated. Just as it was incorrect to acknowledge the message before completing the write to the log file, it is incorrect to write to the database before completing the before- and after-image writes; to do so would create a small time window that would make recovery impossible. If a failure occurs before the audit images are captured on disk or tape, the transaction might be unrecoverable. In some systems, both the database and the

before-image The status of a record before it has been processed.

after-image The status of a record after it has been processed.

audit writes may be deferred until a later time, with the records held in memory for some time to expedite processing. Deferring the writes does not alter the fact that writes to the audit trail must be completed before the writes to the database.

Response Message   Having completed the database updates, the application prepares a response and returns it to the transaction control program. The transaction control program then ends the transaction by writing an end transaction record to the transaction log and ensuring that all audit buffers have been written to the audit file. After both events have occurred, the transaction is completed, and the response message can be sent back to the originating workstation, indicating that the transaction has been processed. Today, most banks in the United States offer Internet banking services; as a result, the originating workstation may be a PC in the bank customer's home or office, and the transfer confirmation will appear on a PC screen in this location.

Recovery After Safe Storing

Recovery following a system failure is a joint effort between database and data communication systems. At any point after the safe storing of the original message, recovery to a consistent state is possible. Suppose a failure occurs after the application has received the message and modified the first but not the second database record. The database system begins the recovery process first. When the system is restored to operational status, the transaction is labeled incomplete. The database management recovery system uses the before-images it captured to restore the database to its state before the beginning of the transaction. The before-image of the updated record is written back to the database, thus erasing the update. Next, the database recovery process sends a message to the transaction control process, advising that the transaction was unsuccessful and the before-images have been posted. The transaction control process retrieves the message associated with that transaction, starts a new transaction, and forwards the message to the application.

Retry Limit   It is possible that the same transaction could fail again, which is often a problem if database files are full, access method tables are full, or unusual data conditions exist, such as division by zero. To protect against an infinite recovery loop, the recovery system should have a retry limit that prevents a transaction from being restarted indefinitely. If the retry limit is exceeded, the failed transaction must be handled differently. One outcome is to display an appropriate error message on the user's screen and to notify the initiator that the transaction cannot be completed. The employee must then follow the necessary preestablished procedures to have the problem corrected. When the cause of the failure has been removed, the transaction can be resubmitted from the transaction log or from the user. In some cases, it is not appropriate to restart from the transaction log. For example, the transaction may have been to book a traveler on a flight. If the system were unable to process the transaction, the traveler may have booked the flight with another carrier.

Audit Trails   Like security systems, recovery systems are not completely reliable. If system failure includes failure of the device (tape or disk) containing the transaction and database audit logs, automatic recovery becomes impossible. In such instances, a database backup version is reloaded, and as many after-images as possible are reposted to the database to bring it forward in time. The images on the medium that failed are not available, of course, so some processing is lost. To limit the exposure due to failure of the audit media, many systems allow the user to have multiple copies of the audit trails. Having audit trails on a disk drive is preferable because of the disk's random access capability; a magnetic tape could be used if no disk is accessible. In addition to the recovery methods just described, recovery can be made easier if good transaction design is used.

Transaction Design

A **transaction** is a user-specified group of processing activities that are either completed or, if not completed, leave the database and processing system in the same state as before the transaction started. Thus, a transaction always leaves the database and the system in a consistent state. A transaction is also a unit of recovery, an entity that the recovery system manages. Recovery and contention have a great influence on transaction design. From the perspective of an application, it makes little difference how or when the transaction begins, ends, or is recovered. From a system design and recovery perspective, good transaction design is very important.

Review of Transaction Activities

Before discussing transaction design, it is useful to discuss the activities needed to start, end, and process a transaction. A generic recovery system is assumed; details vary with implementations. Beginning and ending a transaction require a certain amount of work, and additional work is required when processing a transaction. Starting a transaction demands that a unique transaction identifier be generated. A beginning transaction record is then written to the transaction log. Each record updated by the transaction must be locked to prevent concurrent update problems. Some records that are read but not updated also may have to be locked. All updates must be posted to the before- and after-image audit trail before being written to the database. At the end of the transaction, all audit buffers must be flushed to disk and end-of-transaction markers written to the audit trail.

A simple transaction that updates one record may, therefore, result in five writes: the begin-transaction record, the end-transaction record, the before-image, the after-image, and the record itself, as illustrated in Figure 16-6. This may appear to be a rather high overhead, but it is not. The cost of inconsistent data can be much greater, and many systems use techniques to optimize the capturing of audit images. Audit images are like insurance policies: They cost a small amount over time but pay large dividends when needed.

Grouping Activities into a Single Transaction

Transaction design covers two areas: the grouping of activities into one transaction and the implementation of that transaction within the system. The need for a transaction to leave the system in a consistent state often dictates the transaction's composition. In other cases, the composition is not quite so obvious. In transferring funds from one bank account to another, for instance, it is clear that the deposit and withdrawal must be placed together in one transaction, for to do otherwise would make the database inconsistent. A trial balance would not balance if funds are taken from one place but not deposited in another.

An example of a transaction with less obvious boundaries is adding an employee to a company database. This statement assumes that the transaction activities required are selection and assignment of an employee number, addition of an employee record, and addition of zero to several associated records (employee history, payroll, dependents, and benefits). The employee number is selected so that employee numbers form an increasing numeric sequence with no gaps. This requires reading a control record that contains the next number in the sequence, incrementing the sequence number on the control record, and rewriting the control record.

transaction
A computer-processed task that accomplishes a particular process or result. Transactions typically update one or more master files and serve as an audit trail for future analyses. Transaction volume is an important factor in determining server capacity and network speed needs.

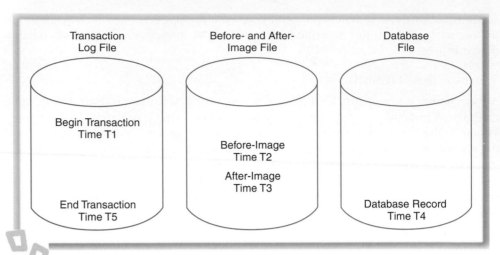

Figure 16-6   Records Written for a Simple Transaction

Although the employee is not fully entered into the system until all these activities have been completed, it may not be necessary to group all activities in a single transaction. The selection and assignment of an employee number and the creation of an employee record are tightly coupled events. Thus, if an employee number has been removed from the control sequence, there should be an employee record with that number, which should be available for reuse if adding the employee to the file fails. However, adding a dependent record, which requires only that an employee record exist, is not so tightly linked with the process of creating the employee record. Indeed, dependent records are often added long after an employee has been hired. The same can be said for payroll records, benefits, and work history. In this example, there might be one or several transactions.

Advantages and Disadvantages of Single Versus Multiple Transactions
What are the advantages and disadvantages of making the employee transaction a single or multiple transaction?

Brief Versus Long Transactions   A single transaction requires only one begin-and-end transaction activity. Although not an overriding consideration, there is an overhead to starting and ending a transaction that a careful designer will attempt to minimize. On the other hand, a long transaction has a greater risk, albeit very slight, of a failure that would involve a recovery. Long transactions also require that records be locked for a longer period, which increases both the likelihood of deadlock and the time the records are unavailable. When record locking is used to resolve the multiple update problems of contention (which arise when two or more users attempt to access the same records), deadlock can occur. As discussed in Chapter 7, deadlock results when two different users (in this case, transactions) have control over records and attempt to access records the other user has already locked, as illustrated in Table 16-8.

Multiple Sessions with One User   The major consideration as to whether to group multiple updates into one transaction is none of these previously discussed ones, however. Because the weakest link in a transaction may be the user, good transaction

Table 16-8   Deadlock Situation

	Transaction 1	Transaction 2
T i m e	Read and lock record A.	
		Read and lock record B.
	Attempt to read record B.	
		Attempt to read record A.
	Wait	Wait

design avoids multiple sessions with the workstation user whenever possible. If it is decided when adding a new employee to treat all activities as one transaction, the following complications could arise. The user begins the transaction by entering the employee data, triggering updates to the employee number assignment file, the employee file, and perhaps a number of access method files. All these updates are accomplished by one interaction with the workstation. Having been updated, the employee number assignment record and the new employee record are locked. The user next enters job history information. If the user takes a lunch break at this point, putting the transaction on hold with its records locked, then, because the employee number assignment record must be used every time an employee is added, no employees can be added during this interval.

The problem with having a transaction span sessions with one user is not just the user's potential absence; it is also the amount of time that a transaction must be held in limbo while the user enters more information. Compared to the milliseconds required to update databases and process transactions, the minutes required to enter the data are rather long. This situation is further complicated when records are locked across sessions with the operator. Fortunately, techniques exist for avoiding such delays.

Avoiding Multiple Sessions   If system design requires all the activities described for adding an employee to be a single transaction, the transaction should be planned to avoid multiple sessions with the user once the transaction begins. Essentially, the solution is to gather all necessary information before beginning the transaction. One way this could be accomplished is described here. The user enters the information for the new employee. The data is edited and, if there are no inconsistencies, the record is safe-stored. The user is then prompted for job history data. Again, edit checks are performed and the record is safe-stored. The same is done for dependent, payroll, and benefits data. If a failure occurs during this process, the data already input is available, so the user does not need to enter it again. Once all of the data has been entered, the transaction is initiated. The database locks are kept for the minimum required time because no additional sessions with the operator are required. Upon completion, the result is returned to the user. Should the user leave the workstation in the middle of the transaction, no records are left locked during the period.

To summarize, transactions should be designed to be as brief as possible and to avoid multiple interactions with a user. The overriding consideration is to design transactions so the database is always left in a consistent state and so recovery can be ensured. The participation of a user in the recovery process should be kept to a minimum. Users should be notified of the last activity completed on their behalf so they can continue from the correct place.

Securing E-Commerce Transactions

A number of protocols have been developed to ensure the integrity of business-to-consumer (B2C) e-commerce transactions. These typically employ a combination of private key, public key, and digital signature encryption. The two protocols that are used most widely are SSL and SET. IPSEC is one of the major approaches used to secure online business-to-business (B2B) transactions.

Secure Sockets Layer (SSL)   SSL is used to secure most B2C electronic commerce transactions. It was developed by Netscape Communications and is supported by most major Web browsers, including Netscape Communicator and Internet Explorer. It operates between the application layer and the transport layer of the TCP/IP protocol stack. It may be described as wrapping an encrypted envelope around HTTP transmissions. It can also be used to disguise other TCP/IP application layer protocol transmissions, such as FTP.

SSL uses public key technologies and digital certificates to authenticate the server in the e-commerce transaction and to protect private information related to the transaction transmitted over the Internet. SSL transactions do not require client authentication, but this is used in some instances. The SSL process is illustrated in Figure 16-7.

The SSL process begins when a client's browser sends a message to a server. Included in the server's response is its digital certificate. The digital certificate enables the client to determine the server's authenticity. Using public key encryption to communicate securely, the client and server negotiate symmetric *session keys* to continue the transaction. Session keys are used only for the duration of the transaction. Once the session keys are negotiated, the transaction is completed using session keys and digital certificates to ensure communication integrity.

Although SSL protects private information related to the transaction as it is passed over the Internet, it does not ensure the protection of private data (such as the buyer's credit card number) once it is decrypted and stored on the business's merchant server. If this data is not encrypted or otherwise secured, it may be vulnerable to

Figure 16-7   Secure Sockets Layer (SSL) Protocol

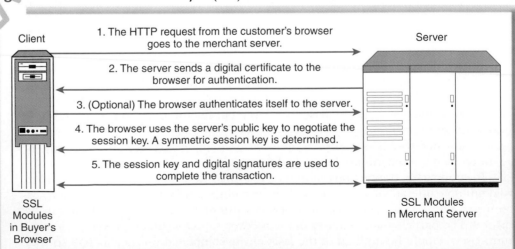

Client

1. The HTTP request from the customer's browser goes to the merchant server.

Server

2. The server sends a digital certificate to the browser for authentication.

3. (Optional) The browser authenticates itself to the server.

4. The browser uses the server's public key to negotiate the session key. A symmetric session key is determined.

5. The session key and digital signatures are used to complete the transaction.

SSL Modules in Buyer's Browser

SSL Modules in Merchant Server

theft by unauthorized individuals. SSL also does not address the integrity of messages transmitted among other entities involved in e-commerce payment transactions: the merchant's bank and the bank that issued the buyer a credit card or digital cash.

Secure Electronic Transaction (SET)   The Secure Electronic Transaction (SET) protocol was developed by Visa International and MasterCard to protect e-commerce credit card payment transactions. It uses digital certificates to authenticate each party involved in the credit card transaction: the buyer, the merchant, and the merchant's bank. SET also uses public key encryption to protect private information related to the transaction that is transmitted over the Internet.

> **digital wallet**
> An electronic equivalent of a wallet that is used for e-commerce transactions. A digital wallet (sometimes called an e-wallet) can hold digital cash that is purchased similar to travelers' checks or to a prepaid account, or it can contain credit card information. The wallet may reside in the user's machine or on a Web payment service's servers. When stored in the user's machine, the wallet may use a digital certificate for identification and authentication purposes. Microsoft's Passport is an example of a digital wallet.

In order to use SET, a merchant must have digital certificate SET software installed on its merchant server. A buyer must have a digital certificate as well as a digital wallet. A **digital wallet** stores credit (or debit) card information as well as a digital certificate verifying the cardholder's identity. Digital wallets (e-wallets) issued by big online shopping portals such as Amazon.com and Yahoo! enable consumers to complete "one-click" transactions. Microsoft's Passport is another example of a digital wallet. E-wallets are also issued by some banks, including MBNA and First USA.

When the customer is ready to place an order online, the merchant server's SET software sends the order information and its digital certificate to the buyer's digital wallet. The buyer selects the credit card to be used for the transaction. The merchant bank's public key is used to encrypt the order information and credit card information. This information is transmitted to the merchant server along with the buyer's digital certificate. This information is sent to the merchant's bank to process the credit card payment. Only the merchant bank can decrypt the information, because its public key was used by the digital wallet software to encrypt the information. The merchant's bank then sends the payment amount to the customer's bank (the bank that issued the credit card) along with its digital certificate. When the charge is approved, the customer's bank sends an authorization back to the merchant's bank. The merchant server is then notified of the authorization approval, and it sends an order confirmation to the customer. This process is illustrated in Figure 16-8.

Because the merchant server never sees the buyer's private information using the SET protocol, the risk of fraud is reduced. However, because SET requires the installation of special software on merchant servers, digital wallets for buyers, and digital certificates for all involved parties, it is more complicated than SSL. As a result, SSL continues to be the most widely used protocol for securing B2C e-commerce transactions.

Internet Protocol Security Architecture (IPSEC)   As noted in Chapter 4, IPSEC was developed by the Security Working Group of the IETF (Internet Engineering Task Force) in order to provide stronger security to support evolving Internet applications.

IPSEC supports authentication, integrity, and confidentiality in IP packets. Authentication and integrity are supported by appending an *authentication header (AH)* to the original IP packet; data confidentiality within IP packets is provided via compliance with the IP *encapsulating security payload (ESP)*. ESP encrypts the data within the IP packet as well as its original IP header and attaches another unencrypted IP header to the packet so that it can be used to set up private virtual networks within the Internet between IPSEC–compliant servers.

IPSEC adds a new "security" layer to the TCP/IP protocol stack through the process of encapsulating the original IP packet in a new IP packet. The encapsulation process usually takes place at IPSEC–compliant border routers or IPSEC servers. The encapsulated packet is then passed from one network's border router across the TCP/IP (or Internet) backbone to the border router of the destination network. The border

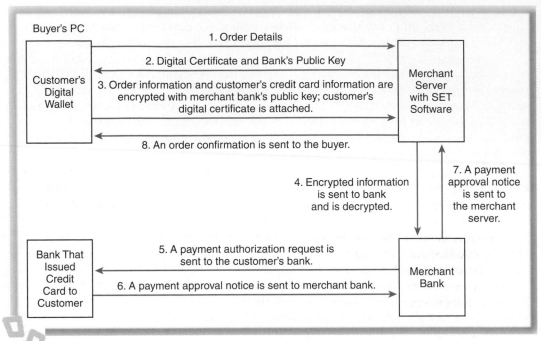

Figure 16-8   Secure Electronic Transaction (SET) Protocol

firewall Software (or a hardware/software combination) that sits between the Internet and the protected enterprise network and controls and monitors traffic between them. A firewall may be a single router that filters out unauthorized packets or may leverage a combination of routers and servers each performing some type of firewall processing. Firewalls are also used to enable authorized remote users access to an organization's internal network as well as to separate a company's public Web server from its internal network. Firewalls may also be used to keep internal network segments secure.

router (or an IPSEC server) at the destination network de-encapsulates the packet and sends the original packet to the destination host. In this way, secure data is transferred from one site to another across the Internet (or TCP/IP backbone). The general process is illustrated in Figure 16-9.

Tunneling protocols and virtual private networks (VPNs) are often used in conjunction with IPSEC. PPTP (point-to-point tunneling protocol), L2TP (layer two tunneling protocol), and L2F (layer two forwarding) are the most widely used protocols for VPNs.

IPSEC is being used in a variety of ways by today's businesses. Major uses include

➤ Establishing secure VPNs among branch offices within a single company
➤ Implementing secure remote access to corporate networks over the Internet for telecommuters and mobile workers
➤ Establishing secure extranet connections with business partners
➤ Enhancing the security of B2B Internet applications such as EDI, supply chain management, and e-procurement
➤ Providing security for a variety of distributed applications, including e-mail and file transfers

Firewalls   Firewalls have emerged as key technologies for ensuring the security of B2B transactions as well as for enhancing the security of corporate networks. Connecting any network to the Internet increases the network's vulnerability to hackers and other unauthorized users who may wish to access the organization's internal computers for malicious purposes.

Most companies want Internet access without exposing all of their systems to public access. Today, this is accomplished by erecting a barrier called a *firewall*. A **firewall** is

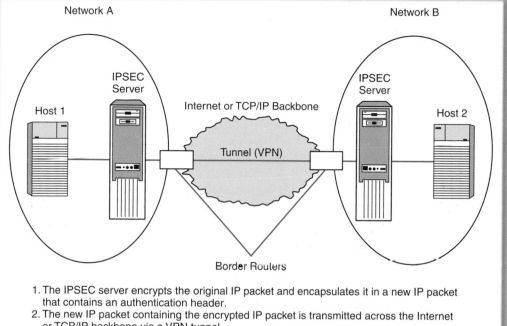

1. The IPSEC server encrypts the original IP packet and encapsulates it in a new IP packet that contains an authentication header.
2. The new IP packet containing the encrypted IP packet is transmitted across the Internet or TCP/IP backbone via a VPN tunnel.
3. The IPSEC server at the destination network uses authentication header information to verify the sender's identity.
4. The IPSEC server at the destination network decrypts the sending host's original IP packet data and transfers it to the intended recipient.

Figure 16-9   Securing TCP/IP Transmissions Using IPSEC

software (or a hardware/software combination) that sits between the Internet and the protected enterprise network and controls and monitors traffic between them. *Personal firewalls* are also available to protect home networks or computers attached to the Internet from unauthorized intrusions. There are several major reasons why organizations implement firewalls. These include the following:

➤ *To prevent or at least inhibit intruders from interfering with the daily operations of the organization's network.* Potential intruders may include malicious hackers intent on disrupting network operations, competitors in search of trade secrets or other key business data, or pranksters who enjoy the challenge of breaking into corporate networks without meaning to do permanent harm.

➤ *To inhibit denial-of-service attacks.*

➤ *To prevent or inhibit intruders from acquiring, deleting, or changing key data stored on the network.* Intruders may attempt to access the network in order to steal customers' credit card numbers or other private data. They may also be intent on modifying or deleting database records or entire files.

➤ *To prevent/inhibit intruders from obtaining business secrets.* Many trade secrets are stored on corporate computers. An organization may also want to protect the secrecy of other information, such as product development plans, research and development initiatives, and merger/acquisition plans. If intruders are able to obtain business secrets, the competitiveness of the organization is jeopardized.

The rationale behind firewall operations is to restrict the data that flows between the Internet and the protected system. This is done in two basic ways: defining the traffic (such as users or addresses) that is allowed to access network resources and disallowing all other communication, or defining what is prohibited and allowing all other transmissions. By defining business partners as authorized users of network resources, secure extranets can be established.

The primary purpose of a firewall is to intercept each packet transmitted over the Internet that is addressed to the network and to decide whether to pass it on to the destination host. Packets originating from unknown or unauthorized IP addresses are carefully scrutinized and, if there are sufficient red flags, are blocked from (not sent to) the destination host. Firewall software can be implemented in routers, dedicated hosts, or both (see Figure 16-10). It is also possible to implement firewalls in other network technologies, including LAN hubs/switches and network adapter cards.

There are several major categories of firewalls. These include the following:

> *Packet filter firewalls.* Packet filter firewalls are the simplest type of firewall. Although these are an acceptable first line of defense, they are the least sophisticated and are the easiest for hackers to get around. More sophisticated firewalls consist of combinations of packet filters and application gateways.

> *Application firewalls/gateways.* Application firewalls/gateways typically include packet filtering capabilities, but they are also capable of filtering out viruses and potentially malicious content such as Java applet and ActiveX controls. However, because of the more thorough checks that these perform, they have the potential to degrade network performance, especially when network traffic is high. An **application gateway** is an application-specific server through which all inbound and outbound data traffic

application gateway
An application-specific server through which all inbound and outbound data traffic must pass. Similar to a proxy server, it is configured to accept requests only from authorized users. Intruders who are successful in breaking into the network may be thwarted from accessing an application by an application gateway.

Figure 16-10   Firewall Options

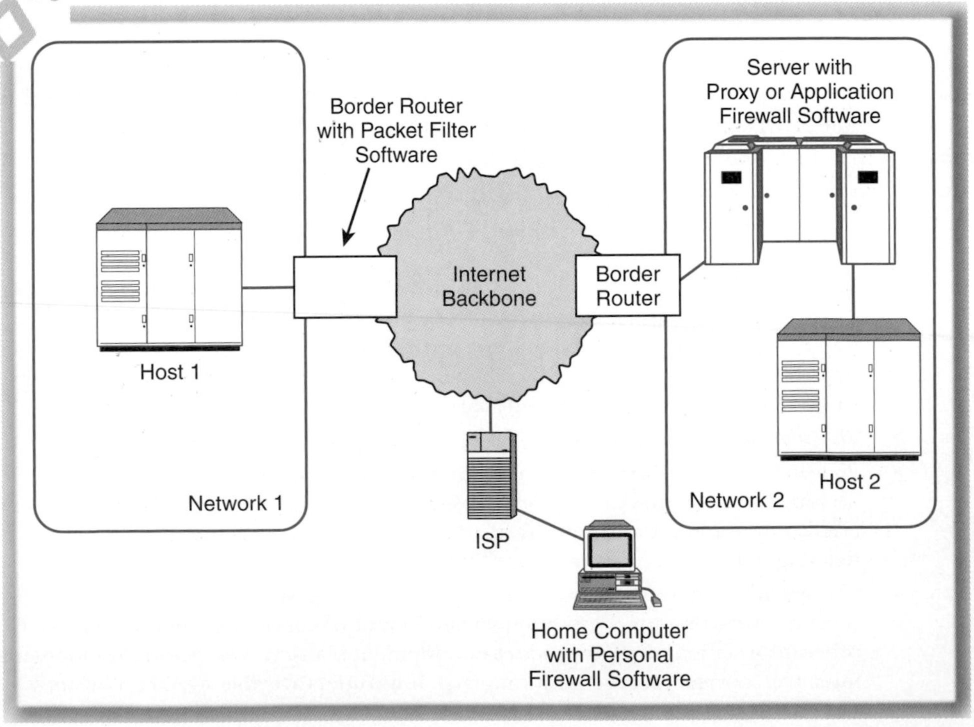

must pass. If configured to only accept requests from authorized users, intruders who are successful in breaking into the network may be thwarted from accessing applications by an application gateway.

➤ *Proxy firewalls.* Proxy firewalls prevent outsiders from seeing the IP addresses of the network's hosts; only the IP address of the firewall is visible to outsiders. These will even thwart hackers' attempts to pick up internal IP addresses by observing Internet traffic originating from the network, because the proxy firewalls substitute their IP addresses for originating hosts' IP addresses in outgoing packets. Any external response to an outgoing packet will come first to the proxy server; the proxy server will then deliver it to the appropriate internal host.

All three types of firewalls require the development of filtering rules. These are essentially if-then-else rules that dictate packet acceptance or rejection.

It is important to note that firewalls are typically used to protect some parts of today's networks, but not all. Web servers and other publicly available resources are not protected by firewalls. Other security mechanisms must be used to ensure that these resources are not violated by unauthorized users. *Internal firewalls* are used by some organizations to provide further assurance that users authorized to penetrate the outer firewall are restricted from accessing network resources that they have no business seeing or using.

TRENDS IN NETWORK SECURITY

Today, as never before, the "network is the computer" in most businesses. Organizations grow increasingly dependent on the availability, reliability, and security of their network infrastructures. For many, when the network is down, it is impossible to conduct business as usual. Business reliance on data communication networks will continue to grow, and it is important for managers to stay abreast of trends in the areas of network security.

Business networks are becoming more accessible to business partners (including suppliers and customers), telecommuters and mobile workers, and consumers who wish to order products or services over the Internet. Although there are compelling business reasons for making business networks more accessible, doing so provides more avenues of attack for hackers and other unauthorized users.

Several key trends in network security can be identified. These include

➤ *Increased vigilance for virus infections.* Virus problems are not going away. In fact, fighting virus attacks continues to consume an inordinate amount of network managers' time. Virus detection and eradication software continues to evolve, but with new viruses appearing daily, the problem is not going away. Network managers are just beginning to combat a new wave of potentially damaging viruses—those that infect wireless data communication devices. There is little doubt that viruses will continue to be a major headache for network managers in the years ahead.

➤ *Continued maturation of firewall technologies.* Firewall technologies are evolving and becoming more sophisticated. They have emerged as mainstream weapons in the battle to secure business networks. Continued improvements in packet filtering algorithms and the ability to safeguard mission-critical applications will make firewalls a standard part of the network security arsenal. The proliferation of intranets is likely to result in increased use of internal firewalls. Compliance with IPSEC and the ability to support virtual private networks are likely to become commonly supported firewall features.

➤ *Increased use of strong encryption algorithms.* The use of encryption to protect data communication transmission is increasing. This is true for internal communications among employees and for communication over the Internet and other WAN services such as frame relay services. The use of public key encryption, digital certificates, digital signatures, and digital wallets is increasing, as is the use of single-session symmetric (private key) encryption. Many organizations are moving toward the use of strong encryption algorithms—those involving keys that are at least 128 bits in length. Look for more business Web sites to require strong encryption for e-commerce transactions.

➤ *Enhanced authentication/authorization controls.* Many businesses are also implementing enhanced authentication and authorization controls. Smart cards and biometric scanners are being increasingly used to verify user identity; in some instances, these are being used in conjunction with user IDs and passwords to add a third requirement to access network resources. Digital certificates, digital signatures, and digital wallets are also being used for authentication/authorization purposes, and their use is likely to increase in the future.

➤ *Nonrepudiation mechanisms.* Authentication/authorization controls also serve an increasingly important role in nonrepudiation. It is becoming more difficult for unauthorized users to deny that they tried to access network resources; network security audit trails provide electronic evidence to the contrary. Even stronger nonrepudiation mechanisms are expected to emerge in the future.

➤ *Denial-of-service attacks.* The increased prevalence of business Web sites and B2C e-commerce increases an organization's vulnerability to denial-of-service attacks. Although denial-of-service attacks were at one time the problem of "pure play" e-businesses (those without bricks-and-mortar outlets), they are now a problem for any business that conducts business over the Internet. B2C e-commerce servers are rarely shielded by firewalls because they are considered to be a publicly available segment of the corporate network. Although border routers are getting better at detecting traffic patterns that are consistent with denial-of-service attacks, they are far from being able to offer bulletproof protection.

➤ *Intellectual property protection.* Protecting Web site content from intellectual property theft is becoming increasingly important for businesses that conduct e-commerce transactions. Hackers have defaced corporate homepages and, in some instances, have stolen business Web site content in order to set up pseudosites used to capture private customer data and conduct fraudulent transactions. An increasing number of businesses are using digital watermarks to protect Web site content. As Web site content becomes more and more important to business competitiveness, the use of such protective measures will increase.

➤ *Protecting the privacy of customer data.* The amount of private data on customers and clients that is stored on business networks is enormous—and growing. Credit card information, investment account information, medical records, and Internet surfing patterns are just the tip of the iceberg. Customers and clients are rightfully concerned about the steps that organizations are taking to protect their sensitive data as well as with how it is being shared with other businesses. Privacy policies must comply with federal and state online privacy laws, and seeking certification from VeriSign and similar organizations with major privacy initiatives is also desirable.

➤ *Increased need for network security specialists.* The increasing complexity of providing adequate business networks has led many organizations to employ network security specialists. These individuals analyze network vulnerabilities, conduct security audits, and address both short- and long-term security problems. As business reliance on networks increases, so does the need for network security specialists. Look for the number of network security specialists to increase over the next decade.

➤ *Development of comprehensive security policies and architectures.* As noted earlier in the chapter, ISO 7498/2 provides a framework for developing an overall security architecture within organizations. Several other standard-setting organizations provide similar guidance to security-conscious network managers. The National Institute of Standards and Technology, for example, publishes a variety of documents related to computer security, access control, encryption, security risk analysis, and contingency planning. Many are accessible online via csrc.ncsl.nist.gov.

➤ Orange Book *certified networking products.* The *Orange Book* is a publication of the National Computer Security Center (NCSC) that provides guidelines for providing confidential protection of sensitive information. These guidelines are used by networking software and product vendors in order to assure their customers that the security features in their products/services will hold up to rigorous scrutiny. In essence, they provide network managers with a benchmark to assess the security features of products that have earned *Orange Book* certification. Although the use of *Orange Book*–certified products in the organization's networking infrastructure does not ensure network security, it can't hurt.

➤ *Increased prevalence of computer incident response teams (CIRTs).* CIRTs are analogous to SWAT teams or firefighting crews; they are composed of individuals trained to respond quickly to specific incidents in order to limit damage and reduce recovery time and costs. CIRTs may be activated by virus, hacker, or denial-of-service attacks. They may also be activated to respond to internal sabotage, successive attempts to gain access to systems or transactions that fall outside of preset boundaries, or cyberterrorism. A CIRT's key mission is to orchestrate a rapid and organized enterprisewide response to computer threats.

The trends identified here are not intended to be an exhaustive list. There are numerous other security issues that can and probably should be added to the list. This set, however, should help you realize that network security is a moving target that is increasing in importance.

THE INTERNET'S IMPACT ON NETWORK SECURITY

It seems appropriate for the final section of the final chapter of this book to focus on the same key topic covered in Chapter 1: the Internet. Establishing interfaces between business networks and the Internet has impacted network security in several ways. It has increased the number of avenues for viruses, worms, and other malicious code to infect business networks. It has spawned new security concerns in the form of denial-of-service attacks, the possibility of Web site content theft or defacement, and the potential for cyberterrorism. Wireless Internet applications are starting to explode and are creating a new realm of network vulnerabilities. Beyond exposing networks and data to new threats, however, the Internet has some very beneficial effects on network security. These include the development of firewalls, virtual private networks (VPNs), and IPSEC technologies. Another benefit is the establishment of CERT, a network security nerve center capable of issuing alerts to network managers before new threats are able to penetrate and disrupt their operations. The Internet has also led to the establishment of the public key infrastructure, digital certificates, digital wallets, and strong encryption algorithms in order to ensure the integrity of data communication transmissions. These can only be considered positives. The evolution of smart card technologies and biometric security mechanisms has picked up momentum because of the Internet.

SUMMARY

Security is a delaying tactic used to deter unauthorized personnel from gaining access to a system and to provide time to catch those who attempt such access. Security of systems and networks is of growing concern to system managers. Security can be implemented at multiple levels within a system. There is an overhead to implementing security precautions, and the cost of the security system should not exceed the potential loss from unauthorized use of the system.

Network security must be planned and monitored. Security policies should be developed that address authentication, access control, transmission privacy, data privacy, nonrepudiation, and other areas of network concern. Appropriate physical and electronic security mechanisms must be implemented to address identified security threats.

Encryption is the primary mechanism used to disguise transmitted data. Encryption algorithms use keys to transform plaintext to unintelligible ciphertext and to decode ciphertext back into its original form. When private key encryption is employed, both the sender and receiver use the same secret key to encrypt and decrypt the messages they exchange. Public key encryption involves using one key to encrypt the data and a different key to decrypt it. Digital certificates are used to support public key encryption. Digital signature encryption is another form of public key encryption. Both private key and public key encryption are used to support the two most widely used e-commerce protocols: SSL (secure sockets layer) and SET (secure electronic transaction).

Authentication mechanisms are used to verify the identity of users attempting to access network resources. User IDs and passwords are the most basic authentication mechanisms. Smart cards, biometric scanners, personal identification numbers (PINs), and digital certificates are other important authentication mechanisms. User profiles and workstation profiles are two of the major types of access control mechanisms used to ensure that network users are only able to gain access to the resources they need to perform their jobs. Intruder detection systems are used to monitor key network technologies such as circuits, servers, and applications for departures from normalcy and potential network misuse.

Virus detection and eradication is an important aspect of network security. Viruses, worms, and other malicious code have the potential to destroy data, crash networks, or disrupt normal network operations in a manner that makes it impossible for network users to perform their jobs. CERT (Computer Emergency Response Team) issues real-time alerts to network managers concerning newly released viruses that could pose a threat to network security.

Data communication and database systems should work together to ensure the integrity of online transactions and to provide a comprehensive recovery that leaves the system in a consistent state, with no transactions lost or processed more than once. The recovery system should also assist with user recovery and establish or help establish users' restart points. Good transaction design is crucial to an effective online application system.

The Internet Protocol Security Architecture (IPSEC) is geared toward providing stronger security for Internet applications. IPSEC technologies support encryption and virtual private networks (VPNs). Firewalls have become standard features in most corporate networks. All firewalls do packet filtering, but some also serve as gateways to important applications on network servers. Personal firewalls are used to secure home computers and home networks with Internet access.

Trends in network security include the maturation of firewall technologies, increased use of strong encryption algorithms, enhanced emphasis on data privacy, and a growing need for network security specialists.

KEY TERMS

- after-image
- application gateway
- authentication
- before-images
- certification authority (CA)
- ciphertext
- Data Encryption Standard (DES)
- denial-of-service attack
- digital certificate
- digital wallet
- encryption
- firewall
- identification
- ISO 7498/2

- message logging
- password
- physical security
- plaintext
- polymorphic virus

- public key encryption
- public key infrastructure (PKI)
- stealth virus
- transaction
- user profile

REVIEW QUESTIONS

1. What are the overall goals of network security?
2. Identify examples of physical and electronic network security threats.
3. What are the greatest security risks a company faces? Why is this so?
4. What are denial-of-service attacks? What are distributed denial-of-service attacks?
5. Describe several physical network security solutions and how they prevent unauthorized access.
6. Describe several electronic network security solutions and how they prevent unauthorized access.
7. What is data encryption? What benefits does it provide?
8. What are the differences between symmetric and asymmetric encryption algorithms? Identify examples of each.
9. What are the characteristics of public key encryption?
10. Why is key administration/management an important part of public key encryption? What is the role of certificate authorities in public key encryption?
11. What are digital signatures? How does digital signature encryption work?
12. What are user identification and authentication? Describe three methods for accomplishing identification and authentication.
13. What are layered IDs? When are organizations likely to use layered IDs?
14. What are user profiles, and what role do they play in network security?
15. What are time and location restrictions? What role do they play in network security?
16. What is RADIUS? Why is RADIUS likely to be an aspect of network security in today's organizations?
17. Describe the role of pseudo logons and transaction logs in intruder detection.
18. What are the differences among network-based, host-based, and application-based intruder detection?
19. How is misuse detection different from anomaly detection?
20. What is a computer virus? How can you protect against computer viruses?
21. How do worms and Trojan horse programs differ from viruses?
22. What is CERT? What role does it play in virus detection?
23. What is a network vulnerability?
24. What is network risk?
25. How are vulnerability and risk assessment used to develop a network security architecture?
26. What are network security policies, and why are they important?
27. What are the characteristics of the OSI security architecture?
28. Describe the role of error detection and recovery in network security.
29. How does message logging help to ensure the integrity of online transactions?
30. What is SSL? How does SSL work?
31. What is a digital wallet? What is the role of digital wallets in e-commerce transactions?
32. What is SET? How does SET work?
33. What is IPSEC? How does it work, and how is it being used?
34. What is a firewall? Why are organizations implementing firewalls?

35. What are the differences among packet filter firewalls, application gateways, proxy firewalls, internal firewalls, and personal firewalls?
36. Briefly describe how the Internet has affected network security.
37. Identify and briefly describe several of the major trends in network security.

PROBLEMS AND EXERCISES

1. How is worker productivity affected by network security? Why must network managers seek to find an appropriate balance between network security and worker productivity?
2. Use the Internet to find out more about ISO 7498/2. Develop a table that includes each of the different network security services addressed by this network security framework, a brief description of each service, and the OSI layer(s) to which each service maps.
3. Use the Internet to find out more about CERT, its evolution, and its role(s) in network security. Summarize the information you obtain in a paper or PowerPoint presentation.
4. Investigate the security features of a network to which you have access. Describe the strong and weak points of the security provided.
5. Research the security capabilities of a current version of Novell Corporation's NetWare or Windows server software (e.g., Windows 2000 Server). Identify the NOS's authentication and authorization controls. What file security attributes are there? What provisions exist for password administration, time and location restrictions, and intruder detection?
6. Use the Internet and other online sources to find information about three recent major incidents of virus infections. What problems were caused, and how were the problems corrected? Were the perpetrators apprehended? If so, what happened to them?
7. Computer crime can result from a lack of network security. Use the Internet to find information about three recent major computer crimes, and describe the nature of each. What network security measures could have prevented these crimes?
8. Use the Internet and other online sources to find information about three recent major denial-of-service attacks. What problems were caused by these attacks, and how were the problems addressed? Were the perpetrators apprehended? If so, what happened to them?
9. Use the Internet and other online sources to find information about five major federal laws related to network security that were passed in the last few years. Describe the provisions of each of the laws and the penalties for violators. Summarize the information you find in a paper or PowerPoint presentation.
10. What is cyberterrorism? What steps should network managers take to combat cyberterrorism?
11. Use the Internet for information about steganography. What are the security implications of steganography?
12. Use online sources to find out more about the public key infrastructure (PKI). Identify the major elements of the PKI, and describe the role of each in key management.
13. The growth of B2C e-commerce has been inhibited by consumer fears about the security of online transactions. Are these fears justified or unfounded? What steps are e-tailers and credit card issuers taking to address consumer fears?
14. Use the Internet to find out more about strong encryption algorithms. What does it take to be classified as a strong encryption algorithm? Identify examples of

strong encryption algorithms. Identify and briefly describe laws regulating the export of strong encryption algorithms.

15. Use the Internet to find out more about PGP, S-MIME, and other approaches for protecting the integrity of e-mail messages during transmission. Summarize how each approach works in a paper or PowerPoint presentation.

16. Protecting the privacy of sensitive customer data (such as medical records and credit card numbers) stored on an organization's servers has become an important security issue. Use the Internet to find out how organizations are using privacy policies and third-party firms such as VeriSign and WebTrust to assure customers that their data is being protected.

17. Find a company that uses e-mail (LAN or WAN based). Interview several mail users to determine how often they use the mail, what they like or dislike about e-mail, and the overall impact of the mail system on how they do business. How would their work be different if e-mail were not available?

18. Use the Internet to find out more about *Orange Book* certification. What does it mean to be *Orange Book* certified? Describe the certification process, and explain why many networking technology vendors do not seek to have their products certified.

Chapter Cases
The Enemy Within

Companies use diverse security tools to protect their networks from unauthorized external attacks; they invest in firewalls, proxy servers, secure gateways, encryption technologies, intrusion detection systems, and network monitoring tools. However, the greatest threats to an organization's network(s) often reside within the company's workforce. These threats range from frustrated employees intent on sabotaging projects or selling confidential information to careless employees who do not store their passwords safely.

In 2000, Internet Trading Technologies Inc. (ITTI), a technology subsidiary of a stock trade regulator, faced threats from two former software developers. The two employees first demanded that the COO (chief operations officer) pay them a substantial amount of money to continue providing contributions to software development projects. Later, after further increasing their demands, both were fired. The next morning, ITTI's applications servers were the targets of denial-of-service attacks. ITTI executives then called the Secret Service. With appropriate monitoring equipment, the federal authorities traced the attacker to a computer at a college in New York, where one of the former employees was a student.

In another case, Robert Philip Hanssen, an FBI agent also known as *Ramon*, was caught selling classified information to the Russians. Ramon was an expert programmer, highly educated, and very introverted. At the beginning, he was loyal to the FBI. Ramon even hacked the computer systems to show his managers some security flaws. But then, something changed. He began to leverage his programming and hacking expertise to obtain the classified information that he sold to the Russians.

Both examples illustrate that today's networks are vulnerable to misuse by knowledgeable insiders. Both examples also raise important questions. How can these threats be detected? What patterns serve as warning signs that trouble may be brewing?

Experts agree that this form of "cybercrime" is often perpetrated by disgruntled or frustrated employees who cannot alleviate their stress. Part of the problem results from not having skilled managers who are capable of mitigating a stressful environment. In fact, a study conducted by psychologists

from Political Psychology Associates Ltd. found that, in most cybercrime cases, attackers were introverted, frustrated with their jobs, incapable of dealing with stress, and extremely computer-dependent. Eugene Shultz, an engineer at the Lawrence Berkeley National Laboratory, also provides compelling evidence that there is a link between job roles and insider activity; this means that very often the offenders are system administrators, network security officers, or even senior executives.

"Honey-pot" servers, or false servers that store fictitious data, can be used to attract and capture hackers, even insiders. For example, when Recourse Technologies was demonstrating its Mantrap honey-pot software, a member of its own network security team tried to hack the "new" server. Apparently, this insider was incapable of distinguishing between the honey pot and the real McCoy. In another instance, a financial firm installed several honey-pot servers after it discovered that it was losing money from its payroll system. The next day, the firm's COO was caught trying to access the information of an executive.

To address threats from within, companies should encrypt sensitive information, publish clear security guidelines, and use network-monitoring tools. In addition, managers should receive special training to handle dissatisfied personnel, especially highly knowledgeable IT staff members. Managers should also be expected to develop leadership skills and to implement managerial practices that help employees feel they are part of the organization. The development of career paths for IT employees and ongoing professional development initiatives, including regular training programs on network security procedures, often prevent a sense of alienation from taking root among IT staff members.

Many of the security breaches involving insiders originate outside of the company and take advantage of indirect help from unsuspecting employees. Industry analysts estimate that around 15 to 20 percent of end users store their passwords on Post-it notes, often attached to their PC's monitor. In addition, many users leave their computers or laptops unattended without password protection. However, the biggest error users make is poorly chosen passwords. Some antihacking experts from NASA recently performed a demonstration in which they identified 60 percent of the engineers' passwords at a manufacturing company in just 30 minutes. In another example, a major bank in the northeastern part of the United States discovered that someone was using information from its customers to per-form unauthorized purchases. The bank then called Internet Security Systems (ISS), an Atlanta-based security firm, to trace the cybercriminal. After ana-lyzing the data for several days, ISS found that the offender was a European contractor who stole the passwords from his mother-in-law, a bank employee.

CASE QUESTIONS

1. Use the Internet to find other examples of cybercrime involving insiders. What are the similarities and differences among these and those reported in the case?
2. Use the Internet to find out more about honey-pot servers. What are their major features/characteristics? Why do hackers, even insiders, have a hard time distinguishing between honey-pot and real servers?
3. What other security technologies identified in the chapter could or should be used to defend an organization's networks from internal threats? Briefly describe how each could or should be used.
4. Some industry analysts suggest that careless users represent the biggest threat to a com-pany's network infrastructure. Provide and describe at least five examples of how user care-lessness can threaten network security.

SOURCES

Verton, D. "The Enemy Within." *Computerworld* (July 9, 2001, pp. 34–35).
Verton, D. "Insider Monitoring Seen as Next Wave in IT Security." *Computerworld* (March 19, 2001, p. 33).
Verton, D. "Top 10 Security Mistakes." *Computer-world* (July 9, 2001, p. 38).

Note: For more information on managing network security and development, see an additional case on the Web site, www.prenhall.com/stamper, "Combating Cyberterrorism."

Index